25th Pacific Asia Conference on Language, Information and Computation 2011

(PACLIC 25)

Singapore
16 – 18 December 2011

Editors:

Helena Hong Gao
Minghui Dong

ISBN: 978-1-62276-507-2

Printed from e-media with permission by:

Curran Associates, Inc.
57 Morehouse Lane
Red Hook, NY 12571

Some format issues inherent in the e-media version may also appear in this print version.

Printed by Curran Associates, Inc. (2012)

For permission requests, please contact the Association for Computational Linguistics at the address below.

Association for Computational Linguistics
209 N. Eighth Street
Stroudsburg, Pennsylvania 18360

Phone: 1-570-476-8006
Fax: 1-570-476-0860

acl@aclweb.org

Additional copies of this publication are available from:

Curran Associates, Inc.
57 Morehouse Lane
Red Hook, NY 12571 USA
Phone: 845-758-0400
Fax: 845-758-2634
Email: curran@proceedings.com
Web: www.proceedings.com

Preface

Welcome to Singapore and welcome to Nanyang Technological University (NTU)! This is the third time that the PACLIC conference comes to Singapore after its two previous visits in 1998 and 2003. This year, the PACLIC 25 is organized by Nanyang Technological University (NTU) and the Chinese and Oriental Languages Information Processing Society (COLIPS).

The PACLIC conference has a long history, dating back to 1982. Over the years, the conference has developed into one of the leading conferences in the research community. Like previous PACLIC conferences, PACLIC 25 has received a wide range of interesting research papers in the fields of theoretical and computational linguistics. The specific research topics that the papers focus on can be classified into the following: cognitive linguistics, corpus linguistics, discourse analysis, formal grammar theory, grammar and parsing, human and machine language processing, information extraction, information retrieval, language acquisition, language resources, language technology and its application, machine translation, morphology, natural language processing, phonology, pragmatics, semantics, speech processing, syntax, and typology.

The paper submissions we received are from 21 countries or regions, including Australia, Canada, China, Czech Republic, Denmark, France, Germany, Hong Kong, India, Indonesia, Italy, Japan, Kingdom of Saudi Arabia, Korea, Malaysia, Myanmar, Philippines, Singapore, Taiwan, Thailand, and the United States of America. To ensure that all papers accepted meet the high quality standard of the PACLIC conference, we had each submission reviewed by three to four experts in the field. As a result, of the 125 valid submitted papers, we accepted 50 (40%) for oral presentations and 25 (20%) for poster sessions.

With such a wide variety of research topics to be presented and participants from all over the world, we believe that this conference will be a truly stimulating scholarly forum. New research findings, new approaches, new ideas for tackling technical challenges and further explorations of a particular research topic, and new information on current research trends will be discussed and shared both within and across disciplines. This scenario is the sign of a most successful conference, which will benefit all the participants as well as the development of the research fields.

A successful conference is the result of many people's efforts and contributions. The quality papers included in the program are the results of our participants' on-going contributions as well as the tremendous efforts made by the program committee members in their paper reviews. Besides the oral and poster paper presentations, the program is enriched by the keynote and invited speakers, Professor Paul Kay from the University of California at Berkeley, Professor Key-Sun Choi from KAIST, and Dr Jian Su, Senior Scientist from the Institute for Infocomm Research. We have also scheduled a panel discussion on multilingualism by several distinguished experts. The panel will be chaired by Prof James German from Nanyang Technology University and the discussion will be led by presentations from Prof Chu-Ren Huang from Hong Kong Polytechnic University, Prof Laurent Prevot from Aix en Provence, and Prof Francis Bond from Nanyang Technology University. Their expertise in their respective fields will provide us with new insights for the current and future research. On behalf of the program committee, we express our heartfelt thanks to them all.

We would like to thank the steering committee for their guidance, and the local organizing committee chaired by Professor Francis Bond at Nanyang Technological University and Dr. Min Zhang at the Institute for Infocomm Research, Singapore, for their dedicated efforts and their excellent coordination with all parties, which has ensured that this conference will be a successful event.

Finally, we wish that you will all enjoy the conference presentations, discussions, and exchanges between old and new friends on the beautiful campus of NTU.

Helena Hong Gao (Nanyang Technological University, Singapore)
Minghui Dong (Institute for Infocomm Research, Singapore)

PACLIC 25 Program Committee Chairs

Organizers

Steering Committee

Jae-Woong Choe, Korea University
Yasunari Harada, Waseda University
Chu-Ren Huang, Hong Kong Polytechnic University
Kim Teng Lua, Chinese and Oriental Languages Information Processing Society
Rachel Edita Roxas, De La Salle University-Manila
Maosong Sun, Tsinghua University
Benjamin T'sou, City University of Hong Kong

Program Committee Chairs

Helena Hong Gao, Nanyang Technological University
Minghui Dong, Institute for Infocomm Research (I^2R)

Co-Chairs

Olivia Kwong, City University of Hong Kong
Shu-Kai Hsieh, National Taiwan Normal University
Donghong Ji, Wuhan University
Seungho Nam, Seoul National University
Rachel Edita Roxas, De La Salle University-Manila

Members

Doug Arnold, University of Essex
Wirote Aroonmanakun, Chulalongkorn University
Timothy Baldwin, University of Melbourne
Francis Bond, Nanyang Technological University
Hee-Rahk Chae, Hankuk University of Foreign Studies
Jason Chang, National Tsing Hua University
Jing-Shin Chang, National Chi-Nan University
Hsin-Hsi Chen, National Taiwan University
Eng Siong Chng, Nanyang Technological University
Siaw-Fong Chung, National Chengchi University
Beatrice Daille, University of Nantes
Danilo Dayag, De La Salle University
Shirley Dita, De La Salle University
Minghui Dong, Institute for Infocomm Research
Alex Fang, City University of Hong Kong
Maria Flouraki, SOAS, University London
Guohong Fu, Heilongjiang University
Helena Hong Gao, Nanyang Technological University
Wei Gao, Chinese University of Hong Kong
Yi Guan, Harbin Institute of Technology
Yasunari Harada, Waseda University
Lin He, Wuhan University
Munpyo Hong, Sungkyunkwan University
Shu-Kai Hsieh, National Taiwan Normal University
Xuanjing Huang, Fudan University
Kentoro Inui, Nara Institute of Science and Technology
Donghong Ji, Wuhan University
Mun-Yen Kan, National University of Singapore
Jong-Bok Kim, Kyung Hee University
Chunyu Kit, City University of Hong Kong
Valia Kordoni, Saarland University
Sadao Kurohashi, Kyoto University
Olivia Kwong, City University of Hong Kong
Tom Lai, City University of Hong Kong

Paul Law, City University of Hong Kong
Hae-yun Lee, Hankuk University of Foreign Studies
Yae-Sheik Lee, Kyungpook National University
Alessandro Lenci, University of Pisa
Gina-Anne Levow, University of Manchester
Haizhou Li, Institute for Infocomm Research
Mu Li, Microsoft
Wenjie Li, The Hong Kong Polytechnic University
Qun Liu, Chinese Academy of Sciences
Qing Ma, Ryukoku University
Yanjun Ma, Baidu
Takafumi Maekawa, Hokusei Gakuen University Junior College
Ruli Manurung, University of Indonesia
Yuji Matsumoto, Nara Institute of Science and Technology
Yoshiki Mori, University of Tokyo
Vincent Ng, University of Texas at Dallas
Jian-Yun Nie, Universit de Montral
Toshiyuki Ogihara, University of Washington
David Y. Oshima, Nagoya University
Ryo Otoguro, Waseda University
Haihua Pan, City University of Hong Kong
Prashant Pardeshi, National Institute for Japanese Language and Linguistics
Ceile Paris, Commonwealth Scientific and Industrial Research Organisation
Jong C. Park, Korea Advanced Institute of Science and Technology
Laurent Prevot, Universite de Provence
Long Qiu, Institute for Infocomm Research
Rachel Edita Roxas, De La Salle University-Manila
Rajeev Sangal, International Institute of Information Technology
Samira Shaikh, State University of New York - University at Albany
Sachiko Shudo, Waseda University
Pornsiri Singhapreecha, Thammasat University
Virach Sornlertlamvanich, Thai Computational Linguistics Laboratory, NICT
Andrew Spencer, University of Essex
I-Wen Su, National Taiwan University
Jian Su, Institute for Infocomm Research
Keh-Yih Su, Behavior Design Corporation
Zhifang Sui, Peking University
Le Sun, Chinese Academy of Sciences
Thanaruk Theeramunkong, Sirindhorn International Institute of Technology
Takenobu Tokunaga, Tokyo Institute of Technology
Shu-Chuan Tseng, Academia Sinica
Josef van Genabith, Dublin City University
Aline Villavicencio, Universidade Federal do Rio Grande do Sul
Haifeng Wang, Baidu
Houfeng Wang, Peking University
Hui Wang, National University of Singapore
Chung-Hsien Wu, National Cheng Kung Univeristy
Dekai Wu, The Hong Kong University of Science and Technology
Jiun-Shiung Wu, National Chiayi University
Deyi Xiong, Institute for Infocomm Research
Jae Il Yeom, Hongik University
Satoru Yokoyama, Tohoku University
Aesun Yoon, Pusan National University
Hao Yu, Fujitsu China Research Center
Min Zhang, Institute for Infocomm Research
Yujie Zhang, Beijing Jiaotong University
Jun Zhao, Chinese Academy of Sciences
Tiejun Zhao, Harbin Institute of Technology
Guodong Zhou, Soochow University
Qiang Zhou, Tsinghua University
Jingbo Zhu, Northeast University, China

Michael Zock, Laboratoire d'Informatique Fondamentale de Marseille, C.N.R.S.
Chengqing Zong, Chinese Academy of Sciences

Local Organizing Committee

Chairs

Francis Bond, Nanyang Technological University
Min Zhang, Institute for Infocomm Research (I^2R)

Members

Ma Bin, COLIPS, I^2R (Sponsorship)
Gao Cong, Nanyang Technological University (Publications)
Chuancong Gao, Nanyang Technological University (Publications)
Petter Haugereid, Nanyang Technological University (Finance)
Jung-Jae Kim, Nanyang Technological University (Workshops)
Tse Min Lua, COLIPS (Committee Member)
Nicole Wong, COLIPS (Committee Member)
Ryo Otoguro, Waseda University (PACLIC 24 Liaison)
Ruli Manurung, University of Indonesia (PACLIC 26 Liaison)

Table of Contents

Invited Talk 1

A Theory of Idioms

Paul Kay, ICSI, UCLA, USA

Abstract

The beginnings of a theory of multi-word expressions (MWEs, AKA idioms) will be sketched. The basic insight on which this approach to MWEs is based holds that many or all MWEs can be analyzed as composed exclusively of special idiom lexemes, frequently homophonous with canonical (non-idiom) lexemes; these interact with the familiar phrasal constructions of the grammar to license idiomatic expressions. The original insight is due to Nunberg et al. (1994). The framework in which the theory is expressed is Sign-Based Construction Grammar (SBCG), which combines some of the insights of Berkeley Construction Grammar (Fillmore et al. 1988, Kay and Fillmore 1999) with recent developments in HPSG (Sag 2010, to appear). Part of the purpose of the talk will be to introduce some of the workings of SBCG via informal exemplification.

Biodata

Paul Kay is Emeritus Professor of Linguistics at the University of California, Berkeley. His research interests, within the broad area of cognitive science, center around language, its structure, and its relation to thought and perception. Much of his research concerns either color naming or grammatical structure.

Invited Talk 2

Linked open data: for NLP or by NLP?

Key-Sun Choi, KAIST, Korea

Abstract

If we call Wikipedia or Wiktionary as "web knowledge resource", the question is about whether they can contribute to NLP itself and furthermore to the knowledge resource for knowledge-leveraged computational thinking. Comparing with the structure inside WordNet from the view of its human-encoded precise classification scheme, such web knowledge resource has category structure based on collectively generated tags and structures like infobox. They are called also as "Collectively Generated Content" and its structuralized content based on collective intelligence. It is heavily based on linking among terms and we also say that it is one member of linked data. The problem is in whether such collectively generated knowledge resource can contribute to NLP and how much it can be effective.

The more clean primitives of linked terms in web knowledge resources will be assumed, based on the essential property of Guarino (2000) or intrinsic property of Mizoguchi (2004). The number of entries in web knowledge resources increases very fast but their inter-relationships are indirectly calculated by their link structure. We can imagine that their entries could be mapped to one of instances under some structure of primitive concepts, like synsets of WordNet. Let's name such primitives to be "intrinsic tokens" that are derived from collectively generated knowledge resource under the principles of intrinsic properties. The procedure could be approximately proven and it will be a kind of statistical logic. We then go to the issues about what area of NLP can be solved by the so-called intrinsic tokens and their relations, a resultant approximately generated primitives.

Can NLP contribute to the user generation process of content? Consider the structure of infobox in Wikipedia more closely. It will be discussed about how NLP can help the population of relevant entries, like the social network mechanism for multi-lingual environment and information extraction purpose.

The traditional NLP starts from words in text but now also works have been undergoing on the web corpus with hyperlinks and html markups. In web knowledge resources, the words and chunks have underlying URIs, a kind of annotation. It signals a new paradigm of NLP.

Biodata

Dr. Key-Sun Choi is a tenured full professor and the head of Computer Science Department, KAIST, Korea. He founded and directed National Language Resource Bank and Korea Terminology Research Center for Language and Knowledge Engineering. He had been a researcher in NEC C&C Lab of Japan, CSLI of Stanford University, and NHK Broadcasting Lab. His areas of expertise are natural language processing, ontology and knowledge engineering, semantic web and linked data, and their infrastructure. He has served as the President (2009-2010) of AFNLP (Asia Federation of Natural Language Processing) and the secretary of ISO/TC37/SC4 for language resource management standards since 2002. His recent works include the creative web such as semantic hierarchy mining from data webs, temporal and spatial entity mining, multilingual information synchronization in Wikipedia context, Korean language processing and Semantic Word Net for CJK called CoreNet. The main issue is about how to gather the human knowledge encoded in the documents, analyze its knowhow, and provide the customized answers depending on the users and their cultural and regional weights.

Invited Talk 3

A Unified Event Coreference Resolution Using Multiple Resolvers

Jian Su, Institute for Infocomm Research, Singapore

Abstract

Event coreference is an important and complicated task in event template extraction and other natural language processing applications. Despite its importance, it was merely discussed in previous studies. In this talk, I present our recent work on a globally optimized coreference resolution system dedicated to various sophisticated event coreference phenomena. Seven resolvers for both event and object coreference cases are utilized, which include 5 event coreference resolvers for event NP-NP, Verb-NP, Verb-Pron, NP-Pron as well as Verb Verb cases with quite some linguistic features different from the object counterparts. Three enhancements are further proposed at both mention pair detection and chain formation levels. First, the object coreference resolvers are used to effectively reduce the false positive cases for event coreference. Second, a revised instance selection scheme is proposed to improve link level mention-pair model performances. Last but not least, an efficient and globally optimized graph partitioning model is employed for coreference chain formation using spectral partitioning which allows the incorporation of pronoun coreference information. The three techniques contribute to a significant improvement of 8.54% in B3 F-score for event coreference resolution on OntoNotes 2.0 corpus.

Biodata

Jian Su is a senior scientist and group leader at the Institute for Infocomm Research, Singapore. Her research interests include information extraction, discourse analysis, text mining, language resources and evaluation, machine translation, segmentation, tagging and chunking, machine learning for natural language.

Web based English-Chinese OOV term translation using Adaptive rules and Recursive feature selection

Jian Qu, Nguyen Le Minh, Akira Shimazu

School of Information Science, JAIST
Ishikawa, Japan 923-1292
qujian@jaist.ac.jp

Abstract. Cross-Language Information Retrieval (CLIR) system uses dictionaries for information retrieval. However, out of vocabulary (OOV) terms cannot be found in dictionaries. Although many researchers in the past have endeavored to solve the OOV term translation problem, but little attention has been paid to hybrid translations "α 1-antitrypsin deficiency (α 1-抗胰蛋白酶缺乏症)". This paper presents a novel OOV term translation mining approach, which proposes a new adaptive rules system for hybrid translations and a new recursive feature selection method for supervised machine learning. We evaluate the propose method with English-Chinese OOV term translation. Our experiments show that adaptive rules system and recursive feature selection with Bayesian Net can significantly outperform existing supervised models.

Keywords: adaptive rules, recursive feature selection.

1 Introduction

CLIR system employs multilingual dictionaries for translating queries from one to another. To ensure a perfect CLIR system, it must use a perfect multilingual dictionary. However, a perfect multilingual dictionary would never be existed due to OOV terms. OOV terms are typically new terms that cannot be found in dictionaries, such as personal names, place names, new technical terms and translated words etc. New OOV terms are emerging every day, this makes it difficult for multilingual dictionaries to cover all translations of OOV terms.

Generally speaking, OOV terms can be translated by three methods, they are: human translation with field of specified knowledge; automatic translation from parallel corpus or comparable corpus (Zhou, Truran et al. 2008); and automatic mining from the Internet (Lu, Chien et al. 2004). Most OOV terms have their correspondent human translation nearby on the Internet (Cheng, Teng et al. 2004; Zhang, Huang et al. 2005; Udupa, K et al. 2009). The quality of the translation is incomparable between human translation and automatic translation. However, automatic translation offers the speed and low cost over human translation. While automatic mining takes the advantage of both human and automatic translation. The translations mined from the Internet are usually high quality and require low man power cost. According to our observation, some translations of the technical OOV term are hybrid translations. Hybrid translations use part target language and part source language, for example, a English OOV term: "DiGeorge's syndrome" and its Chinese translation "DiGeorge's 症候群". "DiGeorge's" are source languages and "症候群" are target languages. Solving Hybrid translations is important because existing approaches would retrieve "症候群" as the translation of "DiGeorge's syndrome". If this translation is applied to CLIR, many disease documents unrelated to "DiGeorge's syndrome" will be retrieved, because many Chinese medical terms end with the term "症候群". In this paper, we propose an OOV term translation method that employs the automatic mining, a novel adaptive rules system for hybrid translations, and a novel recursive feature selection using supervised machine learning by Bayesian net with Adaboost.

2 Related Research Work

Many researchers in the past have endeavored to solve the OOV term translation problem (Cheng, Teng et al. 2004; Lu, Chien et al. 2004; Zhang and Vines 2004; Zhang and Vines 2004; Zhang, Vines et al. 2005; Yuejie, Yang et al. 2009). However, new OOV terms are emerging every day, a perfect method that is able to handle all OOV terms is yet to be discovered. Existing methods for name type OOV terms usually cannot handle technical type OOV terms (Zhang and Vines 2004). Zhang and Vines extract 30 Chinese characters before and after the OOV term when source OOV term is found, then they use lengths and frequencies of translation candidates to select the correct translation. Most researchers approach the OOV term problems with brute force translation candidate extraction (Cheng, Teng et al. 2004; Zhang and Vines 2004), this approach may generate many noises, and it is difficult to handle technical type OOV terms. Especially for hybrid type translations which use part target language and part source language "DiGeorge's syndrome (DiGeorge's 症候群)", "α 1-antitrypsin deficiency (α 1-抗胰蛋白酶缺乏症)". Recently, many researchers started to translate the OOV terms using supervised machine learning (Tiffin, Kelso et al. 2005). Never the less feature selection has always been a problem for supervised machine learning. Traditional feature selections may be time and memory consuming to get high performance. Many supervised machine learning approaches for OOV term translation use support vector machine (SVM) as the classifier for translation selection (Yuejie, Yang et al. 2009), Yuejie, Yang *et al.* use PAT-tree and local maximum algorithm to extract the Chinese translations, then use SVM to select the correct translations. However, SVM works well with OOV terms that have similar properties. Technical OOV terms have very different properties, some can be found in over 100 webpage on the Internet, while others can be found in as little as 3 webpages on the Internet. We propose an OOV term translation method with a novel adaptive rules system for translation candidate extraction to reduce the noise and to handle hybrid translations. We also propose a new recursive feature selection method to gain the advantage of better feature set and high speed with low memory usage. We employee Bayesian Net which can handle diversity of OOV terms together with Meta level-Adaboost that helps with over fitting.

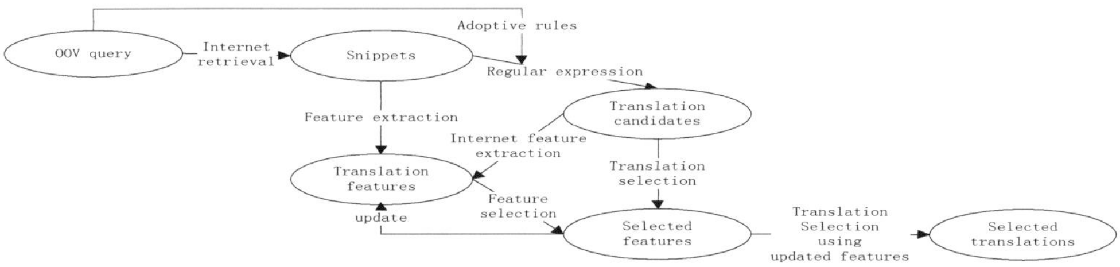

Figure 1: Flow chart of our proposed approach

3 The Proposed Method

Our approach is developed into four parts, they are: firstly, the Internet retrieval; secondly, the translation candidate extraction; thirdly, the feature extraction and finally the translation selection. A flow chart of our approach is shown in Figure 1.

3.1 Internet Retrieval

We feed the complete string of OOV terms to Yahoo API(Yahoo 2009) and limit the result in Chinese language. An example of snippet containing OOV term and its translation is shown in Figure 2.

α 1-抗胰蛋白酶缺乏症|症状|治疗 (Title)
2009年1月10日 ... α 1-抗胰蛋白酶缺乏症(α 1-antitrypsin deficiency)是以婴儿期出现胆汁 ... 的糖蛋白，在化学组成上与正常 α 1-AT 的区别是缺乏唾液酸基和糖基。 ... (Summary)
www.yongyao.net/jbhtml/ α 1-kydbmqfz.htm (URL)

Figure 2: An example of web retrieved snippets of " α 1-antitrypsin deficiency"

Unlike many existing approaches, HTML tags are kept to assist translation candidate extraction.

3.2 Translation Candidate Extraction

The translation candidate extraction is based on the idea that most OOV terms have their correspondent human translation nearby (Cheng, Teng et al. 2004; Zhang, Huang et al. 2005; Udupa, K et al. 2009). According to our observation, we found out some hybrid translations of the OOV terms may not only use the target language alphabets or characters, but also use some alphabets, characters or symbols from the source language. We propose to include the alphabets, characters or symbols of the source language by using an adaptive rules system.

The adaptive rules system uses a set of predefined regular expression matching rules as the base rules. The base rules are modified by each OOV term to form the adapted regular expression matching rules for translation candidate extraction. The base regular expression matching rules are shown in Table 1.

Table 1: Regular expression matching rules

#	Regular expression matching rules
1	Chinese characters
2	Chinese characters/Other characters
3	Chinese characters/Other characters/Chinese characters
4	Chinese characters/Other characters/Chinese characters/Other characters
5	Other characters/Chinese characters
6	Other characters/Chinese characters/Other characters
7	Other characters/Chinese characters/Other characters/Chinese characters
Note: Chinese characters = all Chinese characters Other characters = all non-Chinese language alphabets, characters, symbols.	

The adaptive rules system is developed as follows. Let *Sn* be the snippets retrieved from the Internet, OOV be the source OOV terms, *A* be any alphabets, characters or symbols, *Ac* be any Chinese characters, Re be regular expression matching rules, *Ar* be adopted matching rules, and *Tc* be Chinese translation candidates. For each OOV term, if it is found in the snippets, we add the substring of the OOV term to the regular expression matching rules to create the adopted matching rules. Then we scan for the nearest Chinese character in front of or after the OOV terms. Once we find the Chinese character, we try to match the string around the Chinese character with the adopted matching rules. If there are one or more rules that match the string, we extract the matched parts of the string as the Chinese translation candidates. The detailed algorithm of this method is explained below.

Algorithm Translation candidate extraction

Input: *Snippets retrieved from the Internet Sn, OOV terms OOV, Any alphabets, characters or symbols A, Any Chinese characters Ac, Regular expression matching rules Re,*

Output: *Adopted matching rules Ar, Chinese Translation candidates Tc,*

```
For each OOV found in Sn do
Ar = Re + Substring OOV,
  If (Ac found in front or behind OOV)then
  Continue;
  If(Ar found near Ac+A)then
     Matching Ar with Ac+A;
                    Tc = Ac+A;
     End
  End
End
```

An example of translation candidate extraction is shown in Table 2. As can be seen from this example, the OOV term is α 1-antitrypsin deficiency, we created the adopted matching rules using the substring of the OOV and the base regular expression matching rules in Table 1. The correct translation is extracted as α 1-抗胰蛋白酶缺乏症.

Table 2: Example of translation candidate extraction

OOV	α 1-antitrypsin deficiency	
Snippet	2009 年 1 月 10 日 ... α 1-抗胰蛋白酶缺乏症(α 1-antitrypsin deficiency)是以婴儿期出现胆汁 ... 的糖蛋白，在化学组成上与正常 α 1-AT 的区别是缺乏唾液酸基和糖基。	
Adopted matching rules	1	Chinese characters
	2	Chinese characters/ α /1/-/antitrypsin/deficiency/
	3	Chinese characters/ α /1/-/antitrypsin/deficiency/Chinese characters
	4	Chinese characters/ α /1/-/antitrypsin/deficiency/Chinese characters/ α /1/-/antitrypsin/deficiency
	5	α /1/-/antitrypsin/deficiency/Chinese characters
	6	α /1/-/antitrypsin/deficiency/Chinese characters/ α /1/-/antitrypsin/deficiency/
	7	α /1/-/antitrypsin/deficiency/Chinese characters/ α /1/-/antitrypsin/deficiency/Chinese characters
Matched translations	α 1-抗胰蛋白酶缺乏症 是以婴儿期出现胆汁	

3.3 Feature Extraction

In this subsection, we extracted totally 24 different features from translation candidates. These features include: average distances, co-occurrence distance, term frequencies, symmetric conditional probability (SCP), modified association measures, chi-square, lengths of OOV and translation, and length similarity. We describe the details of these features as follows.

1) Distances between OOV and translation

The closer a translation candidate to its source OOV term the more likely that translation is correct (Cheng, Teng et al. 2004). Some translations occur in front and after the OOV term, but some translations only occur in front or after the OOV term. To present the actual locations between the OOV and translations, we need to consider the average distance $Dist(c_i e_i)$, average front distance $Dist(c_i, e_i)$ and the average back distance $Dist(e_i, c_i)$.

2) Co-occurrence distance

Co-occurrence distance ($CDist$) is the sum of average distance between OOV and translation candidate over the co-occur frequency between OOV and translation candidate. It is computed as follows.

$$CDist = \frac{sum(Dist(c_i e_i))}{tf(c_i e_i)} \quad (1)$$

A modification of this feature ($CwDist$) was proposed by (Yuejie, Yang et al. 2009), they use the web retrieved page count instead of the $tf(c_i e_i)$. It is computed as follows.

$$CwDist = \frac{sum(Dist(c_i e_i))}{S(c_i)} \quad (2)$$

Equation (1) shows the calculation of $CDist$, where $tf(c_i e_i)$ is the co-occur frequency between OOV and translation candidate. Equation (2) shows the calculation of $CwDist$, where $S(c_i)$ is the web retrieved page count of translation candidate.

3) Term frequencies

Term Frequencies are very important statistical features for OOV term translation, the more a translation co-occurs with an OOV term the more likely to be the correct translation. We collect the term frequencies of the translation candidates $tf(c_i)$, OOV $tf(e_i)$, and the co-occur frequencies of translations and OOV $tf(c_i e_i)$. Furthermore, to cope with the average front distance and average back distances, we also collect the front frequency $tf(c_i, e_i)$ and back frequency $tf(e_i, c_i)$ for the translation candidates.

4) Symmetrical Conditional Probability

Symmetrical Conditional Probability (SCP) (Silva, Jos et al. 1999; Cheng, Teng et al. 2004; Lu, Xu et al. 2007) checks each alphabet, character and substring in the possible translation. By calculating the frequency of each substring in the corpus and compare them to the frequency of the translation, it results higher if the substrings of the translation occur less often in the corpus than they occur only within the translation itself. If a translation has higher SCP value, the translation is more likely to be a word phrase and less likely to be a sentence.

$$SCP(c_1 \dots c_n) = \frac{(n-1) f(c_1 \dots c_n)^2}{\sum_{i=1}^{i=n} f(c_1 \dots c_i) f(c_{i+1} \dots c_n)} \tag{3}$$

Equation (3) shows the calculation of SCP, where $(c_1 \dots c_n)$ is any possible translation candidates, n is the number of characters in this translation candidate, $f(c_1 \dots c_n)$ is the frequency of the translation candidate, and $f(c_1 \dots c_i)$ or $f(c_{i+1} \dots c_n)$ is the frequency of any substring of the translation candidate.

5) Modified Association Measures

We propose the modified association measures, which do not require the total number of pages in the Internet. They take the webpage count of OOVs $S(e_i)$, translations $S(c_i)$, the webpage count of OOVs co-occur with translations $S(e_i \wedge c_i)$ and the webpage count of OOVs occur without translations $S(e_i \wedge \neg c_i)$ from the Internet. These features utilize the search engines to remove some possible wrong translation candidates, because search engines use some predefined segmentation tools to eliminate the meaningless Chinese strings.

a) ***Support***

Support is an undirected measure that finds the ratio when e_i and c_i occur together in a same webpage, and it is computed as follow.

$$Supp(e_i \to c_i) = S(e_i \wedge c_i) \tag{4}$$

b) ***Confidence***

Confidence is a directed measure for the ratio that e_i occurs when c_i is occurred, and it is computed as follow.

$$Conf(e_i \to c_i) = \frac{S(e_i \wedge c_i)}{S(e_i)} \tag{5}$$

c) ***Lift or Interestingness***

Lift or interestingness takes the correlation between e_i and c_i, it tests on two hypotheses, first e_i is independent of c_i, so they do not co-occur in the same webpage. Second e_i and c_i are depended and correlated in the same webpage, and it is computed as follow.

$$lift(e_i \to c_i) = \frac{S(e_i \wedge c_i)}{S(e_i) S(c_i)} \tag{6}$$

d) Conviction

Conviction represents the ratio of the expected frequency that e_i occurs without c_i, and it is computed as follow.

$$Conv(e_i \rightarrow c_i) = \frac{S(e_i)(\neg c_i)}{S(e_i \wedge \neg c_i)} \quad (7)$$

Equation (4) is the Support of association measure, equation (5) is the Confidence of the association measure, equation (6) is the Lift of the association measure, and equation (7) is the Conviction of the association measure. e_i is the OOV term, c_i is the translation and $S(e_i)$ is the number of pages returned by the search engine when e_i is submitted as a query. $(\neg c_i)$ is assumed to be 1, because translations of OOV terms have a very small portion when compare to the whole Internet.

6) Chi-square

Chi-square tests a list of possible translation candidates with their source OOV term. A correlation relationship between the OOV term and its translation candidates can be measured by this method.

$$\chi^2(e_i, c_i) = \frac{N \times (a \times d - b \times c)^2}{(a+b) \times (a+c) \times (b+d) \times (c+d)} \quad (8)$$

Equation (8) is the Chi-square tests, where the meaning of each variable is explained as follows

e_i	=	source OOV term	b	=	$S(e_i \wedge \neg c_i)$
c_i	=	translation candidates	c	=	$S(c_i \wedge \neg e_i)$
a	=	$S(e_i \wedge c_i)$	d	=	$S(\neg e_i \neg c_i)$
			S()	=	Is a function that takes a query as the input and returns the number of snippets in the corpus containing that query

7) Length of OOV and translation candidates

The translation of OOV should have similar ratio of length, we collect the lengths of translation candidates ($|c_i|$), lengths of OOV terms ($|e_i|$) and the differences between them $D(|e_i|, |c_i|)$.

8) Length similarity

Other than simple differences between the lengths of OOV and the translations, we also employee the length similarity ratio, it is a normalized length difference $\delta(|e_i|, |c_i|)$. and it is computed as follow (Shi 2010).

$$\delta(|e_i|, |c_i|) = \frac{|c_i| - |e_i| \times c}{\sqrt{(|e_i|+1)\sigma^2}} \quad (9)$$

Equation (9) is the length similarity, where c is a constant indicating the average length ratio between OOV and translations. σ^2 is the variance of $D(|e_i|, |c_i|)$.

3.4 Translation Candidate Selection

In this section, we explain our candidate selection method. It is developed into two parts, the statistical filter, and the Bayesian net candidate selection with recursive feature selections.

One OOV term can retrieve up to few hundreds of translation candidates, most of them are substrings of the correct translation, and some of them are the longer strings of the correct translation. Two features in our feature set can simply filter some wrong candidates, they are co-occur frequency ($tf(c_ie_i)$) and location distance ($Dist(c_ie_i)$). Both features are very important to the candidate selection, if a Chinese translation co-occurs very often with the source English OOV term and this translation is found very close to the source English OOV term, then this translation may less likely be the wrong translation (noise). Our filter takes the top 70% of the co-occur frequency and the shortest location distance between OOV and the translations. A recall test was performed to evaluate the setting of this filter, the result is shown in Figure 3.

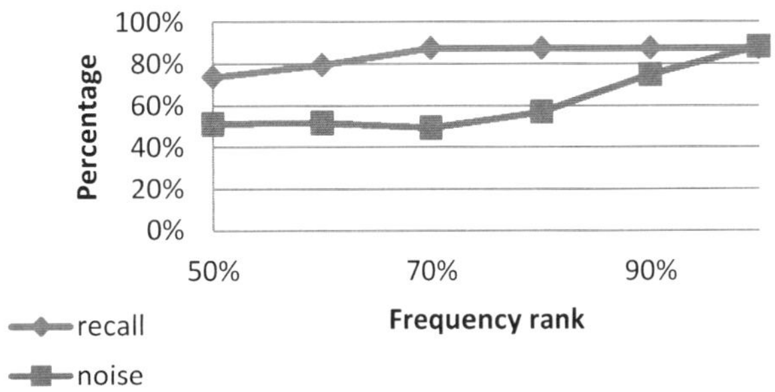

Figure 3: Recalls of frequency rank

To handle the diversity of OOV terms, we employed the Bayesian net which can establish an inference reasoning and causality between OOV terms and the translation candidates. We also employ the Meta level-Adaboost to handle the over fitting problems (Rapidminer 2009).

In order to achieve a low memory usage and high performance feature selection method, we developed a recursive feature selection method. This method loops backward elimination by updating the inputting feature sets with the selected features from the backward elimination. This method is developed as follows. Let *OOV* be OOV terms, *Tc* be translation candidates, *F* be inputting feature sets, *N* be number of iterations, *Ct* be Chinese translations, and *SF* be selected feature sets. We use Bayesian net for candidate selection with *N* times of iterations, backward elimination is employed as the base feature selection method. For each iteration, a set of features will be selected by backward elimination, we then update the inputting feature set for next iteration with the selected features from backward elimination. The detailed algorithm of this approach is shown below.

Algorithm Recursive feature selections

Input: *OOV terms OOV, Translation candidates Tc, Inputting Feature sets F, Number of Iterations N.*

Output: *Chinese Translations Ct, Selected Feature sets SF,*
For i =1 to N do

F = F';
Bayesian net(OOV, Tc) using backward elimination(F),
    F' = SF;
    Ct' = Selected Tc;
End
Ct = Ct';

4 Experiment and Discussion

In this section, we describe our experiments and discuss the results.

4.1 Data Collection

We collected English medical terms from Classification of Diseases, Functioning, and Disability (ICD9 2009). The list is called "International Classification of Diseases, Ninth Revision (ICD-9)". It contains totally 2,741 English Medical terms. We randomly selected 10 percent to reduce the time for human evaluation, because for some OOV terms, the correct translation were not published by Taiwan Center of Disease Controls (Taiwan 2009), and some OOV terms may have few correct translations and not all listed in the Taiwan Center of Disease Controls (Taiwan 2009), so we need to find the correct translation from Internet for evaluation. We extracted any English medical terms that can be found on Chinese webpages according to Yahoo API. These English terms retrieved a total of 12,446 Chinese snippets, and extracted a total of 15,042 possible translation candidates. We also manually queried each English medical term to the web and compare to the published resource of Taiwan Center of Disease Controls (Taiwan 2009) to find the correct Chinese translations for comparison with our experimental results.

4.2 Machine learning setup and error analysis tool

RapidMiner (Rapidminer 2009) is used for machine learning and error analysis since it details out each results on learning process. We used 10-fold Cross Validation to experiment on the data collection.

4.3 Parameters

We used the following setting in our experiments:

Number of Iterations = 2.

Estimate = Simple Estimator.

Searching algorithm = Simulated Annealing.

4.4 SVM method from Yuejie and Length co-occurrence method from Zhang

To compare our method with existing methods, we employ the SVM translation selection method from Yuejie, Yang *et al.* (2009) using their feature set to compare with our translation selection method. We also employ the length co-occurrence method from Zhang & Vines (2004) to compare with our translation extraction method.

4.5 Mining Results and Discussions

We applied our method and length co-occurrence method from Zhang & Vines to the same data collection and the results are presented in Table 3. As can be seen from Table 3, our adaptive rules can extract many translations where Zhang & Vines' method failed to extract, mostly because we considered the existence of the hybrid type OOV translations. Furthermore, to have a fare comparison between translation selection methods, we used our extracted translations to apply with Yuejie's SVM method and our proposed method for translation selection. The Bayesian net with Adaboost outperforms SVM in translation candidate selection with an accuracy of 91.17%. The recursive feature selection improved the performance mainly due to removal of noise features. However, we also observed two iterations of recursive feature selection provided the best results. More number of iterations would diminish the performance. Table 4 shows which features were selected.

Table 3: Comparison of our proposed method with existing methods

Method	Transliteratable OOVs	Correct translations mined	Correct translation mined in OOV terms	Iteration 1			Iteration 2		
				Correct translations selected	wrong translations selected	Correct translations selected in OOV terms	Correct translations selected in OOV terms	wrong translations selected	Correct translations selected in OOV terms
Our method	238	246	228(95.79%)	222	31	213(89.49%)	220	27	217(91.17%)
Yuejie's method using our translations				241	102	161(67.64%)			
Zhang & Vines' method	238	217	159(66.80%)	143(60.08%)					

Table 4: Feature selection of our methods

#	Features	Iteration 1	Iteration 2	#	Features	Iteration 1	Iteration 2
1	$Dist(c_i e_i)$	×		11	$SCP(c_1 \ldots c_n)$	✓	×
2	$Dist(c_i, e_i)$	✓	✓	12	$Supp(e_i \rightarrow c_i)$	✓	×
3	$Dist(e_i, c_i)$	✓	✓	13	$Conf(e_i \rightarrow c_i)$	✓	✓
4	$CDist$	✓	×	14	$lift(e_i \rightarrow c_i)$	✓	✓
5	$CwDist$	✓	×	15	$Conv(e_i \rightarrow c_i)$	✓	✓
6	$tf(c_i)$	✓	✓	16	$\chi^2(e_i, c_i)$	✓	✓
7	$tf(e_i)$	×		17	$\lvert c_i \rvert$	×	
8	$tf(c_i e_i)$	✓	✓	18	$\lvert e_i \rvert$	×	
9	$tf(c_i, e_i)$	✓	✓	19	$D(\lvert e_i \rvert, \lvert c_i \rvert)$	✓	✓
10	$tf(e_i, c_i)$	✓	✓	20	$\delta(\lvert e_i \rvert, \lvert c_i \rvert)$	✓	✓

5 Conclusion and Future work

Cross lingual information retrieval system relays heavily on dictionaries. Many OOV terms cannot be found on these dictionaries. To achieve high performance in CLIR systems, OOV terms need to be consistently updated to these dictionaries. Many researches in the past have endeavored to solve the OOV term translation problem, however they yield low performances with technical OOV term translation, especially hybrid type translations. We proposed a method that uses adaptive rules to handle the translation extraction for hybrid type translations. We also proposed a recursive feature selection for Bayesian net with Ada boost for translation selection. We tested our methods with the ICD9 English medical OOV terms. 12.6% of the experimental data was hybrid translations. Our proposed methods resulted a much higher performance than existing methods with a precision of 91.17%. The findings support the idea that improvements of hybrid translation will improve the overall OOV term translation performance.

We plan to investigate more in adaptive rules for translation candidate extraction, because more improvements on the translation candidate extraction will improve the overall OOV translation performance.

References

Cheng, P.-J., J.-W. Teng, et al. (2004). Translating unknown queries with web corpora for cross-language information retrieval. Proceedings of the 27th annual international ACM SIGIR conference on Research and development in information retrieval. Sheffield, United Kingdom, ACM: 146-153.

ICD9, C. (2009). "International Classification of Diseases,

Ninth Revision (ICD-9)." from http://www.cdc.gov/nchs/icd/icd9.htm.

Lu, C., Y. Xu, et al. (2007). Translation disambiguation in web-based translation extraction for English-Chinese CLIR. Proceedings of the 2007 ACM symposium on Applied computing. Seoul, Korea, ACM: 819-823.

Lu, W.-H., L.-F. Chien, et al. (2004). "Anchor text mining for translation of Web queries: A transitive translation approach." ACM Transactions on Information and System (ACM Trans. Inf. Syst.) **22**(2): 242-269.

Rapidminer (2009). "Rapidminer data mining tool."

Shi, L. (2010). Mining OOV Translations from Mixed-Language Web Pages for Cross Language Information Retrieval. Advances in Information Retrieval. C. Gurrin, Y. He, G. Kazaiet al, Springer Berlin / Heidelberg. **5993:** 471-482.

Silva, J. F. d., S. G. Jos, et al. (1999). Using LocalMaxs Algorithm for the Extraction of Contiguous and Non-contiguous Multiword Lexical Units. Proceedings of the 9th Portuguese Conference on Artificial Intelligence: Progress in Artificial Intelligence, Springer-Verlag: 113-132.

Taiwan, C. o. (2009). "Centers for disease control Taiwan." from http://flu.cdc.gov.tw.

Tiffin, N., J. F. Kelso, et al. (2005). "Integration of text and data-mining using ontologies successfully selects disease gene candidates." Nucleic Acids Res **33**: 1544–1552.

Udupa, R., S. K, et al. (2009). "They Are Out There, If You Know Where to Look": Mining Transliterations of OOV Query Terms for Cross-Language Information Retrieval. Proceedings of the 31th European Conference on IR Research on Advances in Information Retrieval. Toulouse, France, Springer-Verlag: 437-448.

Yahoo. (2009). "Yahoo API." from http://developer.yahoo.com.

Yuejie, Z., W. Yang, et al. (2009). English-Chinese bi-directional OOV translation based on web mining and supervised learning. Proceedings of the ACL-IJCNLP 2009 Conference Short Papers. Suntec, Singapore, Association for Computational Linguistics: 129-132.

Zhang, Y., F. Huang, et al. (2005). Mining translations of OOV terms from the web through cross-lingual query expansion. Proceedings of the 28th annual international ACM SIGIR conference on Research and development in information retrieval. Salvador, Brazil, ACM: 669-670.

Zhang, Y. and P. Vines (2004). Detection and translation of OOV terms prior to query time. Proceedings of the 27th annual international ACM SIGIR conference on Research and development in information retrieval. Sheffield, United Kingdom, ACM: 524-525.

Zhang, Y. and P. Vines (2004). Using the web for automated translation extraction in cross-language information retrieval. Proceedings of the 27th annual international ACM SIGIR conference on Research and development in information retrieval. Sheffield, United Kingdom, ACM: 162-169.

Zhang, Y., P. Vines, et al. (2005). "Chinese OOV translation and post-translation query expansion in chinese-english cross-lingual information retrieval." ACM Transactions on Asian Language Information Processing (TALIP) **4**(2): 57-77.

Zhou, D., M. Truran, et al. (2008). "A Hybrid Technique for English-Chinese Cross Language Information Retrieval." **7**(2): 1-35.

English-Chinese Name Transliteration with Bi-Directional Syllable-Based Maximum Matching *

Oi Yee Kwong

Department of Chinese, Translation and Linguistics, City University of Hong Kong,
Tat Chee Avenue, Kowloon, Hong Kong
Olivia.Kwong@cityu.edu.hk

Abstract. In this paper, we propose a simple and intuitive yet linguistically and practically motivated method for English-Chinese name transliteration generation. Our system is essentially a syllable-based Maximum Matching system. It uses the Onset First Principle to syllabify English names and align them with Chinese names. The bilingual lexicon containing aligned segments of various syllable lengths subsequently allows direct transliteration by chunks. The proposed method was tested on the data from the shared task of the Named Entities Workshop 2009. The results suggest that Forward Maximum Matching performed slightly better than Backward Maximum Matching, but when used together much better results comparable to those of state-of-the-art methods could be attained.

Keywords: Name transliteration, Syllable-based Maximum Matching.

1 Introduction

In this paper, we propose a syllable-based Maximum Matching method for English-Chinese name transliteration generation. Compared to most other popular methods for the purpose, our approach is relatively simple and intuitively appealing, but at the same time it has strong linguistic and practical motivation.

Our system is simply trained on a set of English-Chinese name pairs. Two major principles underlie its design. On the one hand, syllables form the primary units in transliteration. While the rendition of a name in the target language is expected to phonemically resemble its pronunciation in the source language, difference in phonotactics between the two languages would be compromised during transliteration, and incompatible phonological structures might result in extra syllables in the transliterated name. On the other hand, name transliteration tends to be more conventional than innovative, such that the same chunk is often transliterated in the same way even when embedded in different names. Thus, with our proposed method, the Onset First Principle in phonology was used to syllabify English names and align them with the Chinese renditions. A bilingual lexicon containing segment pairs of various syllable lengths was then produced from the aligned names. This lexicon was subsequently used in transliteration, during which a source name was first syllabified and then segmented using Maximum Matching with syllables as the basic units. Target candidates were generated by looking up the bilingual lexicon. Both directions of the Maximum Matching and various ways of ranking the candidates have been tested. Experimental results show that while Forward Maximum Matching performed slightly better than Backward Maximum Matching, their

* The work described in this paper was supported by a grant from City University of Hong Kong (Project No. 7008004).

combined use could lead to much better results comparable to those produced by state-of-the-art methods.

We will briefly review related work in Section 2, and introduce the datasets used in this study in Section 3. The system will be described in Section 4. Experiments and results will be reported in Section 5, followed by future work and conclusion in Section 6.

2 Related Work

The reports of the shared task in NEWS 2009 (Li *et al.*, 2009) and NEWS 2010 (Li *et al.*, 2010) highlighted two particularly popular approaches for transliteration generation among the participating systems. One is phrase-based statistical machine transliteration (e.g. Song *et al.*, 2010; Finch and Sumita, 2010) and the other is Conditional Random Fields which treats the task as one of sequence labelling (e.g. Shishtla *et al.*, 2009). Besides these popular methods, for instance, Huang *et al.* (2011) used a non-parametric Bayesian learning approach in a recent study.

Regarding the basic unit of transliteration, traditional systems are mostly phoneme-based (e.g. Knight and Graehl, 1998). Li *et al.* (2004) suggested a grapheme-based Joint Source-Channel Model within the Direct Orthographic Mapping framework. Models based on characters (e.g. Shishtla *et al.*, 2009), syllables (e.g. Wutiwiwatchai and Thangthai, 2010), as well as hybrid units (e.g. Oh and Choi, 2005), are also seen. In addition to phonetic features, others like temporal, semantic, and tonal features have also been found useful in transliteration (e.g. Tao *et al.*, 2006; Li *et al.*, 2007; Kwong, 2009).

3 Datasets

In the current study, we used the transliteration data provided by the organiser of the transliteration generation shared task (English-to-Chinese track) in the Named Entities Workshop 2009 (NEWS 2009) for testing, which are mostly based on name pairs from Xinhua News Agency (1992). There are 31,961 English-Chinese name pairs in the training set, 2,896 pairs in the development set, and another 2,896 English names in the test set. The Chinese transliterations basically correspond to Mandarin Chinese pronunciations of the English names, as used by the media in Mainland China. The training set and development set were both used for training, and experiments were done on the test set.

All English names were first converted to upper case letters, and all occurrences of "X" were replaced by "KS" before processing to facilitate subsequent syllabification, as a single letter "X" in an English word often corresponds to the consonant cluster /ks/ when pronounced.

4 System Description

Our system is motivated linguistically and for practical reasons. On the one hand, transliteration is to render a source name in a phonemically similar way in a target language, and syllable is an important concept in pronunciation. According to Ladefoged (2006), for alphabetic writing systems, syllables are systematically split into their components. A syllable is composed of an optional onset containing consonants and a mandatory rhyme. The rhyme comprises a mandatory nucleus containing vowels and an optional coda containing consonants. English has complex onsets and codas, whereas Mandarin Chinese has simple onsets and only allows nasal consonants in the coda. According to Dobrovolsky and Katamba (1996), native speakers of any language intuitively know that certain words that come from other languages sound unusual and they often adjust the segment sequences of these words to conform to the pronunciation requirements of their own language. These intuitions are based on a tacit knowledge of the permissible syllable structures of the speaker's own language. Hence, the complex onset in the English syllable "STEIN" (as in Figure 1) violates the onset constraints in

Chinese and is therefore resolved into two Chinese syllables as "斯坦" (*si1 tan3*)[1]. Hence syllable is apparently the proper basic unit for machine transliteration.

On the other hand, during transliteration, people tend not to re-invent the wheel for a similar chunk of syllables in the source name. The examples in Table 1 illustrate this observation. As seen, "JACOB" is consistently rendered as "雅各布" (*ya3 ge4 bu4*) and "STEIN" as "斯坦" (*si1 tan3*) when they appear as part of different names. So based on the concept of translation memory, if a larger chunk can be matched, transliteration becomes easier and less uncertain. In this way, the context embedding a syllable is incorporated, and it might also reduce error propagation in the pipeline during syllabification and phoneme mapping.

With the above linguistic and practical considerations, a syllable-based Maximum Matching approach is thus adopted, and the following subsections explain the steps involved.

Table 1: Examples of Transliteration by Chunks

English	Chinese	Hanyu Pinyin
JACOB	雅各布	*ya3 ge4 bu4*
JACOBS	雅各布斯	*ya3 ge4 bu4 si1*
JACOBSEN	雅各布森	*ya3 ge4 bu4 sen1*
JACOBSTEIN	雅各布斯坦	*ya3 ge4 bu4 si1 tan3*
ARENSTEIN	阿伦斯坦	*a4 lun2 si1 tan3*
BARTENSTEIN	巴滕斯坦	*ba1 teng2 si1 tan3*
DUBERSTEIN	杜伯斯坦	*du4 bo2 si1 tan3*

4.1 Syllabification

The English names in the training data and development data were first syllabified with the Onset First Principle. According to Katamba (1989), the principle suggests that syllable-initial consonants are first maximised to the extent consistent with the syllable structure conditions of the language in question, followed by the maximisation of syllable-final consonants.

In English, written symbols do not necessarily bear a one-to-one relationship with phonological segments. So in practice, with reference to common phonics patterns, we drew up a list of possible onsets containing graphemic units which may correspond to simple phonemes (e.g. "CH", "TH") or complex onsets (e.g. "PL", "STR") to be used in syllabification.

During syllabification, all vowels were first marked as nucleus (N). The longest acceptable consonant sequences on the left of the vowels were then marked as onset (O), and finally all remaining consonants were marked as coda (C). From left to right, syllables are marked for each longest matching chain of ONC, ON, NC, or N. The top half of Figure 1 illustrates these steps with the English name "JACOBSTEIN".

Subsequently, the syllable chain was subject to sub-syllabification considering the difference in phonotactics between English and Chinese. In particular, Chinese syllables have no complex onsets and only allow nasal consonants for codas. So if the syllabification step produces fewer English syllables than Chinese syllables, the sub-syllabification process will try to expand the English syllables, with the number of syllables checked after each expansion. At any point if the English syllables outnumber the Chinese ones, the sub-syllabification process will try to contract the English syllables.

The expansion process will thus follow the order of precedence below:

(1) From left to right, split up complex onsets. For example, "STEIN" is split up into "S/TEIN".

[1] Transcriptions of the Chinese characters in Hanyu Pinyin are given in italics throughout this paper.

(2) From right to left, split up complex codas or separate coda from nucleus if the coda is not available in the target language. For example, "COB" is sub-syllabified as "CO/B".

(3) From right to left, separate liquids and glides ("L", "R", "W") from the nucleus if the Chinese rendition has "尔" (*er3*) or "夫" (*fu1*) in it. For example, with the pair "MINKOWSKI" and "明科夫斯基" (*ming2 ke1 fu1 si1 ji1*), initial syllabification produces three syllables, "MIN/KOW/SKI". During sub-syllabification, "SKI" will be split into "S/KI" with (1) above, but the English side is still one syllable short. So "KOW" will be split into "KO/W" in the next expansion.

(4) From left to right, expand diphthongs as necessary. For example, diphthongs like "IA" will be split up as in "A/ME/LI/A".

The contraction process will follow the order of precedence below:

(1) Contract the name-initial "M/C", if any, with the following syllable.

(2) From right to left, contract nasals, liquids and glides followed by "E" with the previous syllable. For example, "AALLIBONE" for "阿利本" (*a4 li4 ben3*) will be initially syllabified as "AA/LLI/BO/NE", which will then be contracted to "AA/LLI/BONE".

The middle part of Figure 1 illustrates the sub-syllabification process.

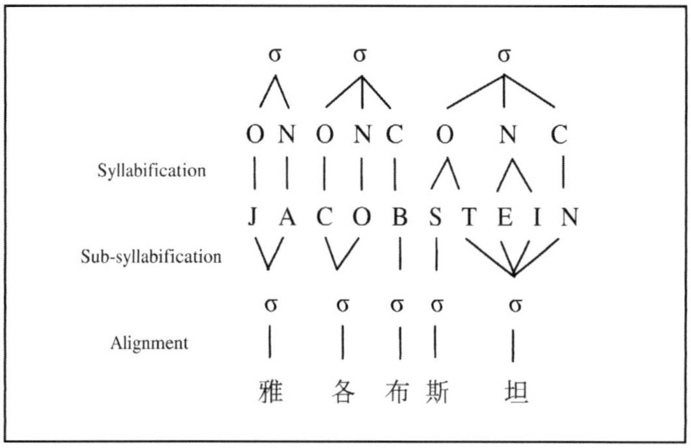

Figure 1: Syllabification and Alignment

4.2 Alignment

Upon syllabification and sub-syllabification, if the number of English syllables equals the number of Chinese syllables, alignment can be done directly in a one-to-one manner. Otherwise the following heuristics would be used to attempt some complex alignments.

(1) As long as Chinese syllables still outnumber English syllables, the next English syllable with four or more letters or starting with two different consonants will absorb two Chinese syllables, assuming such long segments are actually pronounced as two syllables. For example, "A/L/THOU/SE" does not have enough syllables to align with its Chinese rendition "奥尔特豪斯" (*ao4 er3 te4 hao2 si1*), so "THOU" will be forced to take up two Chinese syllables "特豪" (*te4 hao2*).

(2) At any point, if the remaining Chinese syllables fall short of English syllables, the rest will be aligned as a whole without further breaking into syllables. For example, "YON/GE" will simply be aligned with the Chinese name "扬" (*yang2*).

The bottom part of Figure 1 shows the alignment step.

4.3 Lexicon Production

Based on the aligned names, segment pairs of various syllable lengths were extracted to produce a bilingual lexicon as follows:

```
For i = 1 to n (# of aligned segment pairs)
   For j = i to n
      Extract segment-i to segment-j
   Next j
Next i
```

Hence for the aligned name in Figure 1, the following segment pairs will enter into the lexicon:

JA	雅 (*ya3*)
JACO	雅各 (*ya3 ge4*)
JACOB	雅各布 (*ya3 ge4 bu4*)
JACOBS	雅各布斯 (*ya3 ge4 bu4 si1*)
JACOBSTEIN	雅各布斯坦 (*ya3 ge4 bu4 si1 tan3*)
CO	各 (*ge4*)
COB	各布 (*ge4 bu4*)
COBS	各布斯 (*ge4 bu4 si1*)
COBSTEIN	各布斯坦 (*ge4 bu4 si1 tan3*)
B	布 (*bu4*)
BS	布斯 (*bu4 si1*)
BSTEIN	布斯坦 (*bu4 si1 tan3*)
S	斯 (*si1*)
STEIN	斯坦 (*si1 tan3*)
TEIN	坦 (*tan3*)

Note that we use "segment pairs" instead of "syllable pairs" here as the alignment may involve one or more syllables on either side.

4.4 Maximum Matching

During transliteration, an English source name was first syllabified using the syllabification and the first two sub-syllabification steps described above. The name was then segmented using Maximum Matching with the lexicon. It can be done in either direction. The matching was syllable-based, unless even the shortest syllable cannot be matched with the lexicon. In that case the syllable would be matched as a string of characters.

Although the current study focuses on English-to-Chinese transliteration, the same procedures can actually be applied to Chinese-to-English back transliteration as well, since the lexicon contains bilingual segment pairs, and can be looked up bi-directionally. Maximum Matching can be done with the English segments or Chinese segments accordingly. Chinese source names do not need particular syllabification as Chinese characters are syllabic.

4.5 Candidate Generation and Ranking

With the segmented source name, target candidates were generated by looking up the lexicon for each segment and its rendition(s) in the target language. The candidates can subsequently be ranked by different ways. In the current study, we tested ranking with unigram and contextual n-gram probabilities of the segment pairs. Figure 2 shows an example of Maximum Matching and candidate generation for the English name "MARKSTEIN".

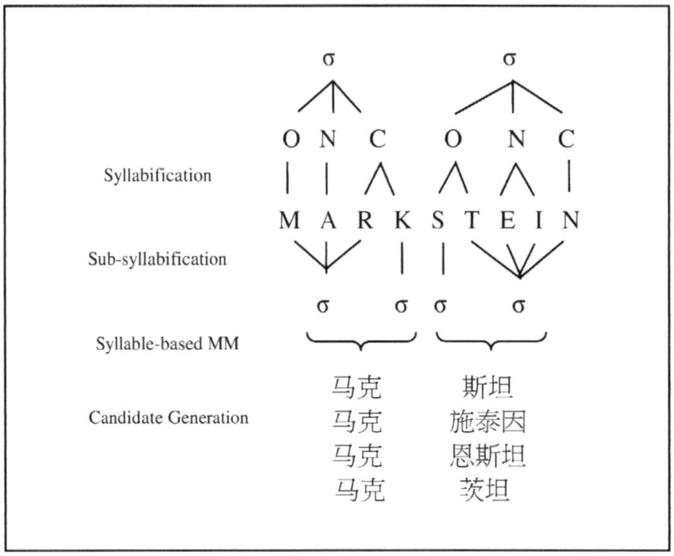

Figure 2: Maximum Matching and Candidate Generation

5 Experiments and Results

The proposed system was run on the test data, with variation on the lexicon containing bilingual segment pairs. One trial used all segment pairs in the lexicon, another used only segment pairs with frequency two or above, and the third trial used only segment pairs with frequency five or above. The lexicon thus contained about 94K entries, 16K entries, and 4K entries respectively. Table 2 and Table 3 show the system performance for Forward Maximum Matching and Backward Maximum Matching respectively, using the different lexicons. The ranking of candidates was by segment pair unigram probabilities. The different trials are indicated by "F" for Forward Maximum Matching and "B" for Backward Maximum Matching, "1/2/5" for the different lexicons, and "U" and "C" for unigram and contextual n-grams respectively. The evaluation metrics follow the definitions in the whitepaper of the most recent NEWS shared task on transliteration generation (Zhang *et al.*, 2011). ACC, Mean F-score, MRR, and MAP_{ref} refer to the Word Accuracy in Top-1, Fuzziness in Top-1, Mean Reciprocal Rank, and precision in the n-best candidates, respectively.

Table 2: Results with Forward Maximum Matching

Metric	F1U	F2U	F5U
ACC	0.6115	0.5974	0.5470
Mean F-score	0.8442	0.8357	0.8144
MRR	0.6887	0.6763	0.6221
MAP_{ref}	0.6115	0.5974	0.5470

Table 3: Results with Backward Maximum Matching

Metric	B1U	B2U	B5U
ACC	0.5967	0.5891	0.5425
Mean F-score	0.8378	0.8301	0.8063
MRR	0.6794	0.6674	0.6167
MAP_{ref}	0.5967	0.5891	0.5425

Table 2 and Table 3 suggest two points of interest. On the one hand, Forward Maximum Matching apparently performs slightly better than Backward Maximum Matching. On the other hand, many of the low frequency segment pairs of various syllable lengths are in fact very useful in transliteration, as is evident from the drop in performance when the lexicon was reduced in the second and third trials.

Studying the results more deeply, it is observed that Forward Maximum Matching and Backward Maximum Matching could be complementary. Many a time matching from both directions might give the same results, but at other times one might produce the favoured segmentation and thus correct transliteration at higher ranks, and vice versa. Take "ABERSFELLER" as an example, Forward Maximum Matching segments it into "ABER/SFE/LLER" and F1U gives "阿伯斯菲勒" (*a4 bo2 si1 fei1 le4*) as the first candidate, while Backward Maximum Matching segments it into "A/BERS/FELLER" and B1U gives "阿伯斯费勒" (*a4 bo2 si1 fei4 le4*) as the first candidate which is the answer in the reference set. So we tried to use both directions of matching in combination, evaluating the unigram rankings of all candidates together. In order to take the context into consideration, instead of segment pair unigrams, we also tested combined Maximum Matching with contextual n-gram probabilities for ranking. Since n-gram probabilities like bigrams for segment pairs directly are expected to suffer from severe data sparseness with larger chunks of syllables, we use the relative position of the segment pair as context, that is, whether the segment pair is at the beginning, middle or end of a name. Table 4 shows the results alongside those reported in other studies using the same datasets. FB1U and FB1C refer to our bi-directional Maximum Matching with unigram ranking and contextual n-gram ranking respectively. SAG refers to the non-parametric Bayesian learning method with Synchronous Adaptor Grammars (with syllable grammars) reported in Huang *et al.* (2011), and JSCM refers to the Joint Source-Channel Model, first used by Li *et al.* (2004) and implemented by Huang *et al.* (2011) on the same datasets as a baseline. Only ACC and Mean F-score were reported. NEWS refers to the best performing system in the NEWS 2009 English-to-Chinese task according to Li *et al.* (2009), and it is a phrase-based statistical machine transliteration system. Our results with bi-directional Maximum Matching are obviously better than Forward or Backward alone, and the results from ranking with simple positional information (that is, FB1C) are comparable to those of SAG and JSCM, though they are not as good as the best performing system in NEWS. Further analysis of the results suggests that while our method has the advantage of being simpler and intuitively appealing, it nevertheless has the following limitations.

Table 4: Results with Bi-directional Maximum Matching Compared with Other Studies

Metric	FB1U	FB1C	SAG	JSCM	NEWS
ACC	0.6119	0.6288	0.666	0.666	0.731
Mean F-score	0.8455	0.8549	0.866	0.857	0.895
MRR	0.7031	0.7176	N/A	N/A	0.812
MAP_{ref}	0.6119	0.6288	N/A	N/A	0.713

The first has to do with the nature of the method. By looking at the largest possible transliterated chunks, we inevitably miss the variations of the smaller units. The test item "ABARBANEL" is a good illustration of this problem. Both directions of Maximum Matching give "A/BARBA/NEL" as the segmentation, and "阿巴巴内尔" (*a4 ba1 ba1 nei4 er3*) is ranked first among other candidates. This is in fact a more than satisfactory transliteration of the name by itself, but the answer in the reference set is "阿巴伯内尔" (*a4 ba1 bo2 nei4 er3*). It happens that "BARBA" had no alignment with "巴伯" (*ba1 bo2*) in the training data, although the simpler syllable "BA" did with "伯" (*bo2*). Transliterating with the longest match has therefore precluded some other possible combinations from being evaluated, and this may account for the relatively lower ACC but similar mean F-score, compared with other systems. Interestingly, however, "巴伯" (*ba1 bo2*) had been aligned with "BARBAR", "BARBE", "BARBER", and "BARBE" in the training data.

The second limitation is related to the origin of the English names. In this study we have based on the phonotactics of English for syllabification, which may not always work well with names from other origins. Take "DESLONGCHAMPS" as an example. As a French name, the "S" in "DES" and "CHAMPS" is usually not pronounced. Although we have the pair "DES/德" (*de2*) in the lexicon, its probability is much lower than the other pair "DES/德斯" (*de2 si1*). On the other hand, "CHAMPS" and "LONGCHAMPS" are not found in the training data, while "LONGCHAMP" is found, with a correspondence to "朗香" (*lang3 xiang1*) but not the expected "朗尚" (*lang3 shang4*). Unseen syllables or segments are thus another major source of errors.

6 Conclusion

We have thus proposed a syllable-based Maximum Matching method for English-Chinese name transliteration generation. Although it may not outperform systems based on phrase-based translation models, it is in fact effective and comparable to many other popular methods and has the advantage of being intuitively simple, linguistically motivated, and easy to implement. Future directions will be along possible improvements of our method, by means of more flexible manipulation of the syllable units, better detection of the origins of English names, as well as incorporation of more re-ranking criteria.

References

Dobrovolsky, M. and F. Katamba. 1996. Phonology: the function and patterning of sounds. In W. O'Grady, M. Dobrovolsky and F. Katamba (Eds.), *Contemporary Linguistics: An Introduction*. Essex: Addison Wesley Longman Limited.

Finch, A. and E. Sumita. 2010. Transliteration using a phrase-based statistical machine translation system to re-score the output of a joint multigram model. In *Proceedings of NEWS 2010*, Uppsala, Sweden.

Huang, Y., M. Zhang and C.L. Tan. 2011. Nonparametric Bayesian Machine Transliteration with Synchronous Adaptor Grammars. In *Proceedings of ACL-HLT 2011: Short Papers*, Portland, Oregon, pp.534-539.

Katamba, F. 1989. *An Introduction to Phonology*. Essex: Longman Group UK Limited.

Knight, K. and J. Graehl. 1998. Machine Transliteration. *Computational Linguistics, 24(4)*:599-612.

Kwong, O.Y. 2009. Homophones and Tonal Patterns in English-Chinese Transliteration. In *Proceedings of the ACL-IJCNLP 2009 Conference Short Papers*, Singapore, pp.21-24.

Ladefoged, P. 2006. *A Course in Phonetics*. Thomson Wadsworth.

Li, H., A. Kumaran, V. Pervouchine and M. Zhang. 2009. Report of NEWS 2009 Machine Transliteration Shared task. In *Proceedings of NEWS 2009*, Singapore.

Li, H., A. Kumaran, M. Zhang and V. Pervouchine. 2010. Report of NEWS 2010 Transliteration Generation Shared Task. In *Proceedings of NEWS 2010*, Uppsala, Sweden.

Li, H., K.C. Sim, J-S. Kuo and M. Dong. 2007. Semantic Transliteration of Personal Names. In *Proceedings of ACL 2007*, Prague, Czech Republic, pp.120-127.

Li, H., M. Zhang and J. Su. 2004. A Joint Source-Channel Model for Machine Transliteration. In *Proceedings of ACL 2004*, Barcelona, Spain, pp.159-166.

Oh, J-H. and K-S. Choi. 2005. An Ensemble of Grapheme and Phoneme for Machine Transliteration. In R. Dale *et al.* (Eds.), *Natural Language Processing – IJCNLP 2005*. Springer, LNAI Vol. 3651, pp.451-461.

Shishtla, P., V.S. Ganesh, S. Sethuramalingam and V. Varma. 2009. A language-independent transliteration schema using character aligned models. In *Proceedings of NEWS 2009*, Singapore.

Song, Y., C. Kit and H. Zhao. 2010. Reranking with multiple features for better transliteration. In *Proceedings of NEWS 2010*, Uppsala, Sweden.

Tao, T., S-Y. Yoon, A. Fister, R. Sproat and C. Zhai. 2006. Unsupervised Named Entity Transliteration Using Temporal and Phonetic Correlation. In *Proceedings of EMNLP 2006*, Sydney, Australia, pp.250-257.

Wutiwiwatchai, C. and A. Thangthai. 2010. Syllable-based Thai-English Machine Transliteration. In *Proceedings of NEWS 2010*, Uppsala, Sweden, pp.66-70.

Xinhua News Agency. 1992. *Chinese Transliteration of Foreign Personal Names*. The Commercial Press.

Zhang, M., A. Kumaran and H. Li. 2011. Whitepaper of NEWS 2011 Shared Task on Machine Transliteration. In *Proceedings of NEWS 2011*, Chiang Mai, Thailand.

Language Model Weight Adaptation Based on Cross-entropy for Statistical Machine Translation

Yinggong Zhao, Yangsheng Ji, Ning Xi, Shujian Huang and Jiajun Chen

State Key Laboratory for Novel Software Technology at Nanjing University, Nanjing 210093, P.R.China
{zhaoyg, jiys, xin, huangsj, chenjj}@nlp.nju.edu.cn

Abstract. In this paper, we investigate the language model (LM) adaptation issue for Statistical Machine Translation (SMT). In order to overcome the weight bias on the LM obtained from the development data, a simple but effective method is proposed to adapt the LM for diverse test datasets by employing the cross entropy of translation hypotheses as a metric to measure the similarity between different datasets. Experimental results show that the cross entropy of a test dataset is closely correlated with the bias in estimating the language models and our adaptation strategy significantly outperforms a strong baseline.

Keywords: Statistical machine translation, Language model, Weight adaptation, Cross-entropy

1 Introduction

Language modeling is applied in many natural language processing (NLP) applications, including automatic speech recognition (ASR) and SMT. In reality, we often encounter the scenario in which the performance of language model learned from given dataset changes drastically among different datasets. Many adaptation techniques have been proposed to tackle this problem in the field of ASR. A similar situation arises with respect to SMT. In SMT we build language model from large amounts of monolingual data but incorporate it in the translation task of the dataset that is not well covered by the model. This inconsistency inevitably affects the SMT training procedure, making adaptation techniques a necessity.

Different from other tasks, language model is incorporated under a log-linear framework in SMT. Specifically, for each source sentence f, we search for the final translation e^* among all possible candidates under the following equation:

$$P(e^*|f) = \arg\max_{e} Pr(e|f) \tag{1}$$

Under log-linear model, the posterior probability $Pr(e|f)$ can be decomposed as:

$$\begin{aligned} Pr(e|f) &= p_\lambda(e|f) \\ &= \frac{\exp(\sum_{m=1}^{M}(\lambda_m \cdot h_m(e,f)))}{\sum_{e'}\exp(\sum_{m=1}^{M}(\lambda_m \cdot h_m(e',f)))} \end{aligned} \tag{2}$$

where $h_m(e,f)$ is a feature function and λ_m is related weight for $m = 1,\ldots,M$.

Under the above framework, we tune the model weight on an independent development dataset, and then we use the obtained weight to translate diverse datasets whose domain or related information might be previously unknown. It is noticeable that the weight obtained from Minimum Error Rate Training (MERT) matches the development dataset well, whereas it would be bias-estimated for others. Although the value of each feature's weight represents its importance in the decoding procedure, such type of importance might vary for different datasets under a specific language model. In this article we concentrate on the bias-estimation of language model weight, i.e., the difference between the oracle and actual LM weight as shown in section 3. We measure the similarity between datasets based on cross-entropy of translation output according to a given language model, adapt the LM weight based on the ratio of the cross-entropy and obtain the final results through a second-pass translation. Our LM weight adaptation method is also related with density ratio estimation, as mentioned in (Tsuboi et al., 2008), in which reweighting approach is proposed to overcome the bias due to the different distribution of test and training data.

The remainder of this paper is organized as follows: Related work of LM adaptation is presented in Section 2. In Section 3 we discuss the problem of LM weight bias-estimation in machine translation. And in Section 4, cross-entropy is proposed as a metric for measuring the similarity between different datasets and we further present our adaptation method. Experimental results are shown in Section 5. We conclude and present several directions for future work in the last section.

2 Related Work

Nowadays LM adaptation in SMT has been paid lots of attentions. There are two main categories for this problem.

The first one is data selection, i.e., when given a test dataset and a large general corpus, which tries to extract sentences from the whole corpus that are relevant to the test dataset under some metric. There are two main approaches for the measurement: One is to apply tf-idf metric (Hildebrand et al., 2005; Lü et al., 2007; Zhao et al., 2004), which arises from information retrieval; while for the other approach cross-entropy (perplexity) is adopted for selection, as reported in (Axelrod et al., 2011; Moore and Lewis, 2010).

The second is model weighting. The main idea is to assign appropriate weight to each model according to the similarity between the model corpus and test dataset. In this approach, the models could be built from domain-specific corpus (Koehn and Schroeder, 2007) when domain of the test dataset is known, or from datasets that belong to different sources (Foster and Kuhn, 2007; Lü et al., 2007) when it is unavailable in advance. Such weighting method even could be apply to either each sentence from the training corpus (Matsoukas et al., 2009) or phrase pair from the phrase-table (Foster et al., 2010). Besides, the work of (Mohit et al., 2009; Mohit et al., 2010) also belongs to such scenario, in which they attempt to build a classifier to predict whether or not a phrase is difficult, then the LM weight is updated for each phrase segment according to its difficulty.

The methods mentioned above try to overcome the difference between the training and the test data. However, the bias between the development and the test data is also an open issue. Not much attention has been paid to the such weight adaptation. In Li et al. (2010), the model weight is tuned on a subset of the development set, which is extracted based on the relevance to the test set.

In this paper, different from (Li et al., 2010), we focus on the adaptation of LM weight only, as LM is one of the key components of SMT and has its own characteristic. In our work, we adopt cross-entropy as a metric, just as (Axelrod et al., 2011; Moore and Lewis, 2010), to measure the similarity between different datasets. However, only LM weight is adjusted during the adaptation, and no extra model needs to be built. Although our method is quite simple and straightforward, the improvements obtained from the adaptation show that the bias-estimation of LM weight due to the difference between development and test dataset is also quite an important issue in SMT.

3 Language Model Weight Mismatch in Statistical Machine Translation

As model weight is tuned on development dataset only but applied to various test datasets, the mismatch between development and test is inevitable. To verify the LM weight bias-estimation for different dataset pairs, we conduct the following experiment in this section: for development dataset pair D(development) and T(test), we firstly learn the weight via MERT on D. Then with all other feature weights fixed, we translate T and record the change of BLEU score compared with baseline during the step-by-step modification of the LM weight by starting from the initial weight with a constant value each time.

Based on the above approach, we use four dataset pairs for comparison under a large scale experiment setting (Section 5.1). Figure 1 shows the relation between the BLEU score of the test datasets and the corresponding LM weight. Specifically speaking, each point $(x,\ y)$ in the figure means that under new LM weight $x * baseline\text{-}LM\text{-}weight$, the BLEU score of test dataset under new weight changes y points compared with baseline. We could observe that for some datasets pair like MT03 as development and MT08 as test, the weight is seriously bias-estimated. The detailed comparison is shown in table 1, in which the oracle performance represents the maximal BLEU score obtained when we manually modify the LM weight. The significant difference between baseline and oracle result (about 3 BLEU points) shows much room for potential improvement. Meanwhile, the weight fits well for dataset pair MT03(development) and MT04(test), since the baseline performance is close to the oracle.

Based on the above observation, we find that the LM weight mismatch is a common phenomenon in SMT. And the bias-estimation is different for various dataset pairs. Thus it is necessary to propose a metric that could measure the similarity between datasets and an adaptation strategy on LM weight, as we will discuss in the next section.

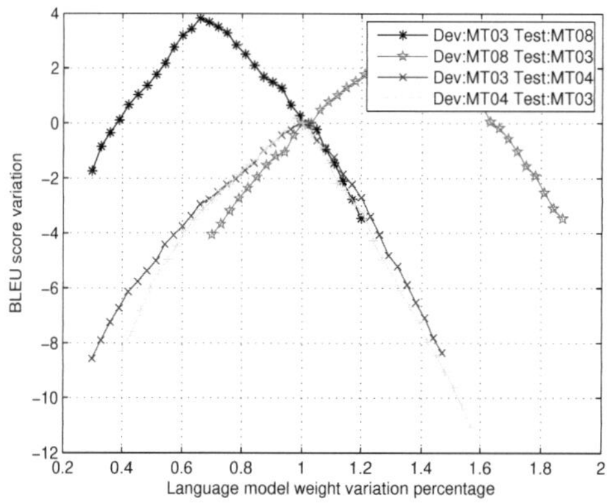

Figure 1: The variation of BLEU score (in value) vs. variation of language model weight (in percentage)

DEV	TEST	Baseline	Oracle
MT03	MT04	37.54	37.55(+0.01)
MT04	MT03	38.76	38.96(+0.20)
MT03	MT08	24.86	28.66(+3.80)
MT08	MT03	35.86	38.77(+2.91)

Table 1: Comparison between baseline and oracle performance under language model weight for different dataset pairs.

4 Dynamic Language Model Weight Adaptation Under Cross Entropy

Entropy is used as a metric to show how much information one dataset contains. Given sentence $X_i = (x_1, x_2, \ldots, x_n)$, the corresponding cross-entropy under specific language model lm could be calculated as:

$$H(X_i) = -\frac{1}{n} \log P_{lm}(x_1, x_2, \ldots, x_n) \tag{3}$$

Given two datasets and one language model, we could use cross-entropy to identify which dataset matches the language model better. As the language model is built on target language in SMT task, we can use the entropy of the translation outputs for each dataset as a measurement of the dataset. Given a language model and two datasets (development and test), the model weights are tuned through MERT on development dataset. Then we compute their cross-entropy after translating both datasets under current weight. Specifically speaking, for a dataset X that contains multiple sentences, we obtain its cross-entropy according to the following equation:

$$H(X) = -\frac{\sum_i \sum_j \log P_{lm}(X_i^j)}{\sum_i \sum_j length(X_i^j)} \tag{4}$$

in which, X_i^j denotes the j_{th} best translation or reference for the i_{th} sentence in the dataset. As the decoder generates translation outputs together with corresponding feature vectors, $\log P_{lm}(X_i^j)$ could be viewed as equivalent to the language model feature.

According to the property of cross-entropy, we can know how the dataset fits the language model. Empirically speaking, a small cross-entropy value indicates a well-matching between the language model and dataset. The language model could thus play a more important role in the translating procedure, which further reveals a large value relatively. Hence, if the test data matches language model better than the development data, the language model weight might be under-estimated; otherwise it would be over-estimated. So we could conclude that cross-entropy difference can be used as a metric for how well the LM weight is estimated.

However, we encounter two problems: Firstly, how can we estimate the degree to which the LM weight is bias-estimated and the second is how we can adjust the weight appropriately. Here we hold the straightforward opinion that the difference of the cross-entropy between test and development data can be a metric for the LM bias-estimation. For the adaptation on the language model weight, we propose an effective method that merely uses cross-entropy. Let D be the development dataset and T be the test dataset. The adaptation approach is shown as follows:

1. Train a log-linear model based on D and obtain feature weight W.
2. Translate D using W and calculate the cross-entropy of D as $H(D)$, similarly translate T and obtain $H(T)$.
3. Modify the LM weight in W_{lm} by:

$$W_{lm} = W_{lm} \frac{H(D)}{H(T)}$$

   and get new weight W'.
4. Translate T again under W' and get the final result.

In the third step, we use the ratio of the entropy of the development and the test dataset for weight adjustment, as it could reflect the variance between these two datasets. It is known that in development dataset each sentence owns references, the reason we use entropy of translation outputs rather than references for development is that in real application we usually translate datasets without references, although it is included for standard SMT evaluation datasets. In fact we could observe that the adaptation result based on the cross-entropy of translation outputs is consistent with that based on cross-entropy of the references, as shown in section 5.2.

5 Experiments

5.1 Experiment Settings

We implement a hierarchical phrase-based decoder according to Chiang (2005). The development data includes NIST 2003 (MT03), NIST 2004 (MT04), NIST 2005 (MT05), NIST 2006 (MT06) and NIST 2008 (MT08). Besides the above four datasets, the test datasets contain all portions of MT06, including newswire (MT06nw), newsgroup (MT06wg) and weblog (MT06wl), and two portions of MT08, including newswire (MT08nw) and webgroup (MT08wg). The statistics are shown in Table 2. All results are measured in case-insensitive BLEU4 (Papineni et al., 2002).

Dataset	MT03	MT04	MT05	MT06	MT08	MT06bc	MT06nw	MT06ng	MT08nw	MT08wg
#Sentence	919	1,788	1,082	1,664	1,357	565	616	483	691	666
#Word	24,900	50,061	30,512	38,984	33,259	11,884	17,971	9,146	18,124	15,145

Table 2: Statistics on development and test datasets.

In the experiments, the training corpus includes LDC2002E18, LDC2003E07, LDC2003E14, LDC2004E12, LDC2004T08, LDC2005E83, LDC2005T06, LDC2005T10, LDC2006E26, LDC2006E34, LDC2006E85, LDC2006E92, and LDC2007T09, which consists of about 8.5M sentence pairs. The word alignment result is trained by GIZA++ in both directions and refined under intersect-diag-grow heuristics. The plain phrases are extracted from the all bilingual training data, while hierarchical rules are only extracted from selected datasets, including LDC2003E14, LDC2003E07, LDC2005T10, LDC2006E34, LDC2006E85, and LDC2006E92, which covers nearly 467K sentence pairs. We further train the 5-gram language model over the English part of training data plus Xinhua portion of the English Gigaword corpus.

5.2 Adaptation on 1-best Translation Result

In this part, we will evaluate the performance of our method introduced in section 4. Under each development dataset, we calculate the cross-entropy of all test datasets, which are displayed in table 3. The results of both baseline and under our adapted method are also presented in table 5.

DEV	MT03		MT04		MT05		MT06		MT08	
TEST	Baseline	Adapted	Baseline	Adapted	Baseline	Adapted	Baseline	Adapted	Baseline	Adapted
MT03	1.8842	1.8842	1.8507	1.8701	1.9953	1.9958	1.8058	1.7992	1.8800	1.8564
MT04	1.7556	1.7353	1.7264	1.7264	1.8720	1.8482	1.6900	1.6679	1.7600	1.7191
MT05	1.8880	1.8884	1.8621	1.8776	2.0022	2.0022	1.8109	1.8091	1.8759	1.8513
MT06	1.9287	1.9361	1.8997	1.9185	2.0459	2.0571	1.8408	1.8408	1.9224	1.9012
MT08	2.1462	2.1787	2.1176	2.1550	2.2890	2.3488	2.0376	2.0587	2.1224	2.1224
MT06bc	1.8324	1.8260	1.8262	1.8150	1.9425	1.9292	1.7657	1.7536	1.8352	1.7995
MT06nw	1.8480	1.8412	1.8175	1.8294	1.9535	1.9469	1.7607	1.7502	1.8378	1.8108
MT06ng	2.2962	2.3440	2.2660	2.3069	2.4436	2.5170	2.1692	2.2047	2.2637	2.2737
MT08nw	2.0602	2.0786	2.0208	2.0556	2.1913	2.2304	1.9548	1.9665	2.0271	2.0166
MT08wg	2.2649	2.3191	2.2544	2.2995	2.4204	2.5120	2.1511	2.1815	2.2527	2.2664

Table 3: .Cross entropy of test datasets on different development datasets, under large scale setting.

From table 5, we may find that the cross-entropy is quite close for some dataset pairs like MT03 and MT05 , which indicates that the adapted score would change little compared with baseline. While for the pair like MT03 and MT08, the remarkable difference means that we can achieve significant improvement (1.60 BLEU points for MT08 test and MT03 development, and 0.99 BLEU points for the reverse). We also obtain similar results on the other dataset pairs, including all separate portions of MT06 and MT08 whose genre information is available. Table 6 displays the oracle test performance in each dataset pair. We can observe that oracle performance for MT05(test) under MT03(development) is 37.54, while the baseline is 37.33, which is consistent with the ratio of cross-entropy between two datasets.

DEV:TEST	Method	1-gram	2-gram	3-gram	4-gram	BP	BLEU	TER
MT03:MT08	Baseline	0.7866	0.4155	0.2276	0.1278	-0.2282	0.2486	0.5904
MT03:MT08	Adapted	0.7708	0.4033	0.2186	0.1222	-0.1318	0.2646	0.5910
MT08:MT03	Baseline	0.7703	0.4611	0.2773	0.1679	0.0000	0.3586	0.5912
MT08:MT03	Adapted	0.7851	0.4733	0.2860	0.1735	0.0000	0.3685	0.5682

Table 4: Detailed analysis of BLEU scores, including n-gram precision and length penalty and TER scores, based on dataset pair of MT03 and MT08.

DEV	MT03		MT04		MT05		MT06		MT08	
TEST	Baseline	Adapted	Baseline	Adapted	Baseline	Adapted	Baseline	Adapted	Baseline	Adapted
MT03	39.14	39.14 (|)	38.77	38.45 (↓)	38.61	38.69 (|)	37.31	37.44 (|)	35.86	36.85 (↑)
MT04	37.52	36.74 (↓)	37.93	37.93 (|)	36.72	36.12 (↓)	35.81	36.84 (↑)	34.66	36.23(↑)
MT05	37.33	37.37 (|)	36.94	37.24(↑)	36.87	36.87 (↑)	35.93	36.07(|)	34.15	35.29 (↑)
MT06	33.58	34.04 (↑)	33.63	35.13 (↑)	33.44	33.49 (|)	36.36	36.36 (↑)	35.04	35.87 (↑)
MT08	24.86	26.46 (↑)	24.18	27.03 (↑)	25.43	26.65 (↑)	27.74	28.86 (↑)	29.29	29.29 (|)
MT06bc	24.22	27.20 (↑)	23.77	27.70 (↑)	24.64	26.26 (↑)	27.37	28.14 (↑)	28.87	28.43 (↓)
MT06nw	40.36	39.91 (↓)	39.97	40.74 (↑)	39.85	39.72 (|)	39.57	40.26 (↑)	37.71	39.72 (↑)
MT06ng	33.81	33.65 (|)	34.23	34.71 (↑)	33.79	33.45 (↓)	36.72	36.53 (|)	35.58	36.61 (↑)
MT08nw	29.40	30.66 (↑)	28.95	31.32 (↑)	29.67	30.31 (↑)	32.47	33.31 (↑)	33.03	33.23 (↑)
MT08wg	18.78	21.09 (↑)	17.81	21.04 (↑)	19.74	20.91 (↑)	21.35	23.06 (↑)	22.72	23.13 (↑)

Table 5: Comparison between baseline and LM weight adaption method using 1-best translation on different dataset pairs, under large scale setting. Symbol(↑) indicates improvement over 0.2 BLEU points, (↑) indicates improvement over 0.2 BLEU points, (↓) means decline over 0.2 BLEU points, (|) shows no noticeable change.

We also calculate the entropy on translations after adaptation of all dataset pairs, which is also listed in table 3. From the results in table 3, we find that the cross entropy usually changes according to the ratio of cross-entropy of development and test datasets. Specifically, the cross entropy of test dataset increases as LM weight decreases, as shown in figure 2, in which we use the same dataset pairs as in section 3. The reason for the phenomenon in figure 2 is that when the LM weight increases, the language model turns to play a more important role in the whole SMT system. As a result, the decoder prefers to select the translations with higher LM scores, which are also with shorter length and smaller cross-entropy.

Furthermore, we want to know what the improvements could be under our adaptation method. Here we take the pair MT03 and MT08 as example, the details of the results are shown in table 4. We may observe that for the pair of MT03 as development and MT08 as test, the length penalty is quite large. Meanwhile our adaptation method could notably reduce such penalty and get significant improvement based on BLEU metric. Although the n-gram precision decrease in some sense,

	MT03	MT04	MT05	MT06	MT08
MT03	39.14	38.92	38.77	38.24	38.44
MT04	37.56	37.93	36.78	37.53	37.48
MT05	37.54	37.55	36.87	36.99	37.21
MT06	36.30	36.42	35.03	36.36	36.43
MT08	28.58	28.55	27.50	29.04	29.29
MT06bc	40.98	41.41	40.18	40.29	40.60
MT06nw	36.74	36.75	35.40	36.74	36.60
MT06ng	28.15	28.31	27.22	28.77	28.77
MT08nw	32.82	33.03	31.79	33.71	33.22
MT08wg	22.83	22.79	21.26	23.24	23.22

Table 6: Oracle performance of different dataset pairs under large scale setting.

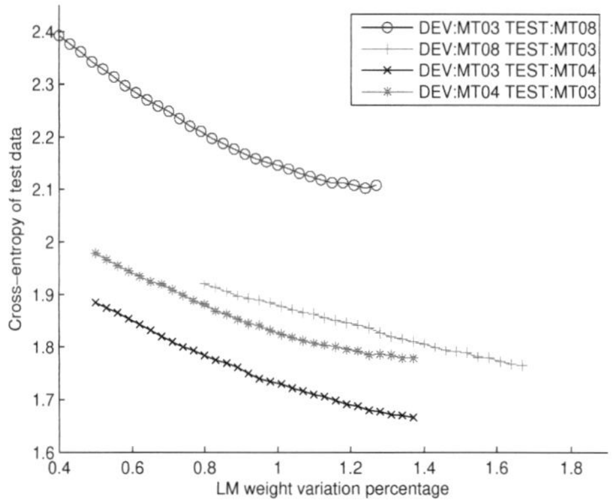

Figure 2: The cross entropy of test vs. LM weight variation in percentage for different dataset pairs

the gain from the length penalty decrease could counteract reduction on the precision. While for the case in which MT08 as development and MT03 as test, the length penalty of both baseline and adapted results are equal, while n-gram precision of adapted method is higher than that of baseline, which leads to improvements on final performance. Meanwhile, we also apply another SMT metric TER (Snover et al., 2006) to evaluate the results of the dataset pair MT03 and MT08, as shown in table 4. When we use MT03 as development and MT08 as test, the TER result shows no improvement. This is consistent with observation from above discussion, as improvement for BLEU mainly comes from length penalty, not n-gram precision. Meanwhile, when we use MT08 as development and MT03 as test, we achieve significant improvement on the TER score. This inconsistency shows some potential difference between the TER metric and the BLEU metric.

However, for some dataset pairs, the adapted result is not so good as the baseline. The reason might be that the closeness of test and development measured through cross-entropy is more significant than the real difference. Taking MT03(development) and MT04(test) for example, from figure 1 we could find that the baseline is almost the same as oracle (0.01 BLEU points difference), while the ratio of the cross-entropy from table 3 is larger than our intuition, making the LM weight over-adapted and the performance decreased. Nevertheless, the results in table 5 show that our method works well for most dataset pairs (33 of 50 groups increase, while only 6 of 50 groups decrease). Although our adaption method is in a sense empirical, we believe it reflects the inherent relations in the LM adaptation.

Furthermore, we want to know the influence of the cross-entropy variation on BLEU score improvements. In figure 3, the X-axis represents the absolute value of relative change between development and test dataset (i.e., $|\frac{H(D)}{H(T)} - 1|$), and the Y-axis displays the improvements of the BLEU score under adaptation. We would observe that all five groups of points are well linear, showing strong correlations between adaptation improvements and cross-entropy difference. Based on above results, we can draw the conclusion that even if cross-entropy may not be the only factor that determines the bias-estimation of LM weight, it is still one of the most important.

5.3 1-best VS. N-best Translation Result Adaptation

In the above part, we utilize mere 1-best translation results for entropy calculation. We wonder what the result would be if more outputs are used. With MT03 as development, MT05 and MT08 as test respectively, we run adaptation under number from 1 to 20 best translations. Results in figure 4 show that the number of translation outputs shows little impact on the adaptation results, since the deviation between maximal and minimal score is quite small(less than 0.2 BLEU score points). And in the following parts, we adopt 1-best translation as default setting.

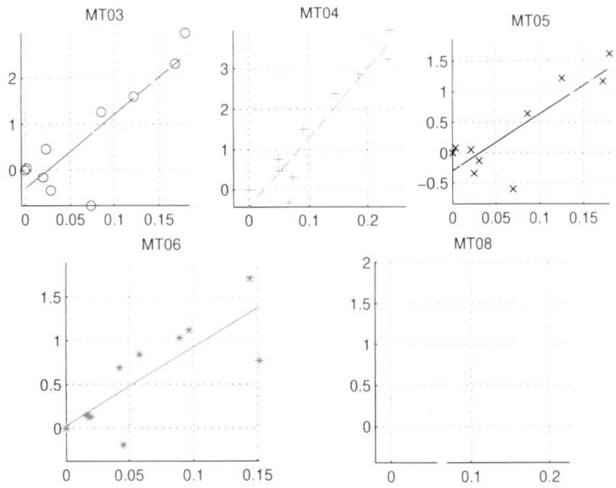

Figure 3: The variation of BLEU score (in value) vs. cross-entropy ratio between development and test dataset under each development datasets

DEV	MT03		MT04		MT05		MT06		MT08	
TEST	Baseline	Adapted	Baseline	Adapted	Baseline	Adapted	Baseline	Adapted	Baseline	Adapted
MT03	39.14	39.14 (|)	38.76	38.82 (|)	38.59	38.49 (|)	37.32	37.47 (|)	35.87	36.70 (↑)
MT04	37.52	37.04 (↓)	37.93	37.93 (|)	36.72	36.50 (↓)	35.80	36.53 (↑)	34.66	35.73 (↑)
MT05	37.33	37.11 (↓)	36.92	37.18 (↑)	36.87	36.87 (|)	35.90	36.22 (↑)	34.15	35.36 (↑)
MT06	33.58	33.85(↑)	33.62	34.51 (↑)	33.41	33.55 (|)	36.36	36.36 (|)	35.04	35.77 (↑)
MT08	24.86	26.23(↑)	24.18	26.30 (↑)	25.43	26.32 (↑)	27.75	28.93 (↑)	29.29	29.29 (|)
MT06bc	24.22	26.06 (↑)	23.77	26.44(↑)	24.64	26.18 (↑)	27.40	28.61 (↑)	28.87	28.48 (↓)
MT06nw	40.36	39.48(↓)	39.97	39.46 (↓)	39.78	39.63 (|)	39.57	40.54 (↑)	37.71	39.75 (↑)
MT06ng	33.81	34.08(↑)	34.23	34.72 (↑)	33.76	33.80(|)	36.73	36.74 (|)	35.59	36.08 (↑)
MT08nw	29.40	30.64 (↑)	28.95	30.85(↑)	29.67	30.32(↑)	32.49	33.10 (↑)	33.05	33.20 (|)
MT08wg	18.78	20.35 (↑)	17.81	20.03(↑)	19.74	20.88(↑)	21.35	22.65 (↑)	22.73	22.99 (↑)

Table 7: Comparison between baseline and LM weight adaption method using references on different dataset pairs, under large scale setting.

5.4 Adaptation on Translation References

In practice, entropy of translation outputs, rather than references, is used for adaptation. Nevertheless, we want to know whether there exists some difference between these two approaches. Table 7 shows the results under adaptation on entropy of references, while the related entropy is shown in Table 8. We could find that adapted results and the cross-entropy are both consistent with those of using 1-best translation, as in SMT the model weight is tuned in the way that tries to make translation outputs as close as possible to the references.

Dataset	MT03	MT04	MT05	MT06	MT08	MT06bc	MT06nw	MT06ng	MT08nw	MT08wg
Entropy	2.3450	2.2456	2.3019	2.3854	2.5778	2.2105	2.3690	2.6281	2.4955	2.6791

Table 8: Cross entropy of each dataset calculated on references.

5.5 Adaptation on Random Test Data

In our experiment, we always use the standard NIST datasets to evaluate the adaptation method. We also want to validate our method under more datasets in this section. Using MT03 as development, we build six extra test datasets by randomly selecting 50, 100, 300, 600, 1200 and 2000 sentences respectively from the collections of MT04, MT05, MT06 and MT08. Related results are shown in Table 9, in which improvements still could be achieved but not so significant as the results in table 5. Based on experimental results, we know that some datasets like MT04 and MT05

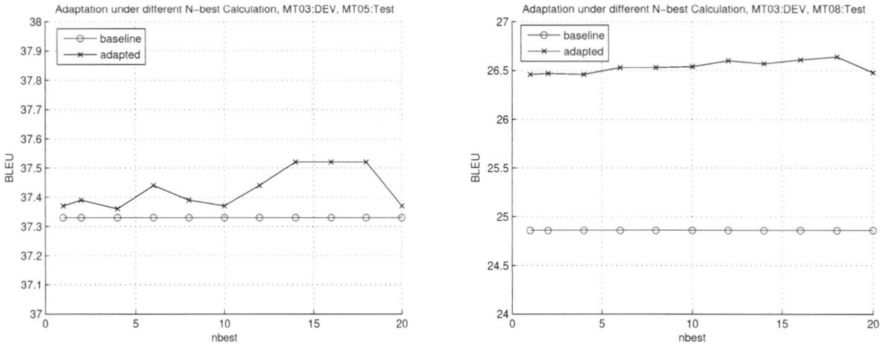

Figure 4: The adaptation results under entropy calculation on different number of translation outputs, with MT03 as Development and MT05 as Test(Left), MT08 as Test(Right)

Random	Baseline	Adapted	Oracle
50	34.52	35.03(+0.51)	35.05
100	34.79	34.33(-0.46)	34.94
300	33.06	33.38(+0.32)	33.82
600	33.48	33.72(+0.24)	34.91
1200	33.64	33.92(+0.28)	35.03
2000	33.72	34.04(+0.32)	35.22

Table 9: Results with MT03 as development and random selected datasets as test, under large scale setting

are close to the development MT03, while some others are different. One basic assumption for our adaptation method is that the dataset is composed of several documents, each belongs to a specific domain. Hence for the random datasets, their distribution is a mixture of multiple sources, making the adaptation performance not so significant as that on normal MT evaluation datasets.

6 Conclusion

In this article, we address the problem of LM weight mismatch between tuning and testing. In particular, cross-entropy on n-best translation hypotheses is adopted as a metric to indicate the bias-estimation in language modeling. Furthermore, an adaptation approach is proposed to adjust the LM weight using the ratio of cross-entropy between different datasets. Experimental results show that our cross-entropy based adaptation strategy significantly alleviates the bias problem of language modeling and significant improvements could be achieved when the test data is quite different from the development.

In this paper, we only tackle the adaptation on corpus level. In future we are going to explore LM adaptation on document and sentence level. Besides, we also intend to apply adaptation to multiple LMs. Although our method works well on most dataset pairs, there still exist some pairs on which our method fails. Therefore, it will be interesting to further investigate the factors that determine the adaptation performance.

Acknowledgments

We thank Shujie Liu for his meaningful suggestions. We would also like to thank the anonymous reviewers for their helpful comments. This work is supported by the National Natural Science Foundation of China (No.61003112) and the National Fundamental Research Program of China (2010CB327903).

References

Amittai Axelrod, Xiaodong He and Jianfeng Gao. 2011. Domain Adaptation via Pseudo In-Domain Data Selection. *In Proceedings of the 2011 Conference on Empirical Methods in Natural Language Processing*, 355-362, Edinburgh, July, 2011.

David Chiang. 2005. A Hierarchical Phrase-based Model for Statistical Machine Translation. *In Proceedings of the 43rd Annual Meeting of the ACL*, 263-270.

Almut Hildebrand, Matthias Eck, Stephan Vogel, and Alex Waibel. 2005. Adaptation of the Translation Model for Statistical Machine translation based on Information Retrieval. *In Proceedings of EAMT*, Budapest, Hungary.

George Foster and Roland Kuhn. 2007. Mixture-Model Adaptation for SMT. *In Proceedings of the Second ACL Workshop on Statistical Machine Translation*, Prague, Czech Republic.

George Foster, Cyril Goutte and Roland Kuhn. 2010. Discriminative Instance Weighting for Domain Adaptation in Statistical Machine Translation. *In Proceedings of the 2010 Conference on Empirical Methods in Natural Language Processing*, 451-459, MIT, Massachusetts, USA, October 2010.

Philipp Koehn and Josh Schroeder. 2007. Experiments in Domain Adaptation for Statistical Machine Translation. *In Proceedings of the Second Workshop on Statistical Machine Translation*, 224-227, Prague, June 2007.

Mu Li, Yinggong Zhao, Dongdong Zhang and Ming Zhou. 2010. Adaptive Development Data Selection for Log-linear Model in Statistical Machine Translation. *In Proceedings of the 23rd International Conference on Computational Linguistics (Coling 2010)*, 662-670.

Yajuan Lü, Jin Huang and Qun Liu. 2007. Improving Statistical Machine Translation Performance by Training Data Selection and Optimization. *In Proceedings of the 2007 Joint Conference on Empirical Methods in Natural Language Processing and Computational Natural Language Learning*, 343-350.

Spyros Matsoukas, Antti-Veikko Rosti and Bing Zhang. 2009. Discriminative Corpus Weight Estimation for Machine Translation. *In Proc. of the Conference on Empirical Methods in Natural Language Processing*, 160-167

Behrang Mohit, Frank Liberato and Rebecca Hwa. 2009. Language Model Adaptation for Difficult To Translate Phrases. *In Proceedings of the 13th Annual Conference of the EAMT*, 160-167.

Behrang Mohit, Rebecca Hwa and Alon Lavie. 2010. Using Variable Decoding Weight for Language Model in Statistical Machine Translation *In The Proceedings of the 9th Conference of the Association for Machine Translation in the Americas*, Colorado

Robert C. Moore and William Lewis. 2010. Intelligent Selection of Language Model Training Data. *In Proceedings of the ACL 2010 Conference Short Papers*, 220-224, Uppsala, Sweden.

Franz Och. 2003. Minimum Error Rate Training in Statistical Machine Translation. *In Proceedings of the 41th Annual Meeting of the Association for Computational Linguistic (ACL)*, Sapporo, Japan.

Kishore Papineni, Salim Roukos, Todd Ward, and Wei-Jing Zhu. 2002. Bleu: a Method for Automatic Evaluation of Machine Translation. *In Proceedings of the 40th Annual Meeting of the Association for Computational Linguistic (ACL)*, 311-318.

Matthew Snover, Bonnie Dorr, Richard Schwartz, Linnea Micciulla and John Makhoul. 2006. A Study of Translation Edit Rate with Targeted Human Annotation. *In Proceedings of Association for Machine Translation in the Americas*

Yuta Tsuboi, Hisashi Kashima, Shohei Hido, Steffen Bickel and Masashi Sugiyama. 2008. Direct Density Ratio Estimation for Large-scale Covariate Shift Adaptation. *In Proceedings of the Eighth SIAM International Conference on Data Mining*, pp. 443–454, 2008.

Bing Zhao, Matthias Eck and Stephan Vogel. 2004. Language Model Adaptation for Statistical Machine Translation with Structured Query Models. *In Proceedings of International Conference on Computational Linguistics(COLING)*, Geneva, August.

A grammar design accommodating packed argument frame information on verbs

Petter Haugereid

Division of Linguistics and Multilingal Studies, Nanyang Technological University,
14 Nanyang Drive, Singapore 637332, Singapore
petterha@ntu.edu.sg

Abstract. This paper presents a comparison of two designs for implementing argument frame information on verbs. In the first design, alternating verbs will be represented with one lexical entry pr. possible argument frame. In the other design, each verb form will be associated with only one lexical entry containing a packed representation of the possible argument frames. The first design represents how valence alternations are treated in lexicalist grammars, while the second shows how valence alternations can be handled in a constructionalist grammar. The comparison is done with an implemented "deep" grammar of Norwegian.

Keywords: HPSG, grammar engineering, lexical representations, under-specification.

1 Introduction

In most "deep" grammar implementations, information about the argument frame of a verb is specified in the lexicon. This can be observed in grammatical frameworks such as Head-driven Phrase Structure Grammar (HPSG) (Pollard and Sag, 1994), Lexical Functional Grammar (LFG) (Bresnan, 2001), and Combinatory Categorial Grammar (CCG) (Steedman, 2000). Deep grammars need to be as precise as possible since they are not only expected to parse grammatical sentences, but also *not* to parse ungrammatical sentences. So, in order to avoid overgeneration, the grammar needs, among numerous other things, to contain information about what syntactic frames a verb is expected to appear in. The most natural place to put this information is in the lexicon.

In this paper I will discuss one problem associated with the way argument frame information is specified in a lexicalist grammar, namely the use of multiple lexical entries for one verb form in cases where the verb may appear in more than one argument frame. Multiple lexical entries for one form leads to an increased processing effort for the parser. A possible solution to this problem is to pack the information from the different entries into one. I will present a constructionalist grammar design, where each verb form is assigned a single lexical entry with a packed representation of the possible argument frames of the verb, using a type hierarchy of argument frame types to account for argument frame alternations. I will show how the grammar design compares to HPSG, which is the framework mostly used for deep grammar implementations, and compare two versions of the implemented grammar, one with an expanded lexicon and one with a packed lexicon, with regard to competence and performance.

2 Valence in HPSG

In HPSG, a transitive verb has the information in Figure 1. The figure illustrates how the valence requirements of a verb is represented by means of lists and also how the linking to the semantics is accounted for.

$$\begin{bmatrix} \text{PHON} \langle \textit{admire} \rangle \\ \text{CAT} \begin{bmatrix} \text{HEAD } \textit{verb} \\ \text{VAL} \begin{bmatrix} \text{SUBJ} \langle \text{NP}_{\boxed{1}} \rangle \\ \text{COMPS} \langle \text{NP}_{\boxed{2}} \rangle \end{bmatrix} \end{bmatrix} \\ \text{CONT}\,|\,\text{RESTR} \left\langle \begin{bmatrix} \text{PRED} & \textbf{\_admire\_v\_rel} \\ \text{ARG1} & \boxed{1} \\ \text{ARG2} & \boxed{2} \end{bmatrix} \right\rangle \end{bmatrix}$$

Figure 1: Lexical entry for the verb *admire*

For each argument realized by the valence rules (Head-Complement Rule and Head-Subject Rule), an element on the valence lists will be unified with it and checked off. A verb projection is accepted as a sentence when both the SUBJ list and the COMPS list are empty.

Implemented HPSG grammars like the English Resource Grammar, ERG (Flickinger, 2000), use a binary Head-Complement Rule to realize the complements (see Figure 2.) This rule realizes one complement at a time (the first) and links the rest of the list in the mother ($\boxed{3}$) (see Sag *et al.* (2003, 97)). If the complement list contains more than one element, the Head-Complement Rule will work repeatedly until the COMPS list is empty.[1]

$$\begin{bmatrix} \textit{phrase} \\ \text{CAT} \begin{bmatrix} \text{HEAD} \boxed{1} \\ \text{VAL}\,|\,\text{COMPS} \boxed{3} \end{bmatrix} \end{bmatrix} \Rightarrow \begin{bmatrix} \text{CAT} \begin{bmatrix} \text{HEAD} \boxed{1} \\ \text{VAL}\,|\,\text{COMPS} \langle \boxed{2} \rangle \oplus \boxed{3} \end{bmatrix} \end{bmatrix}, \boxed{2}$$

Figure 2: Binary Head-Complement Rule

The subject of a clause is realized by the Head-Subject Rule (see Figure 3). This rule has as its head daughter a word or phrase that has an empty COMPS list and an element on the SUBJ list ($\boxed{2}$). The element on the SUBJ list is realized as the non-head daughter, and the SUBJ list of the mother is empty.

$$\begin{bmatrix} \textit{phrase} \\ \text{CAT} \begin{bmatrix} \text{HEAD} \boxed{1} \\ \text{VAL} \begin{bmatrix} \text{SUBJ} \langle\rangle \\ \text{COMPS} \langle\rangle \end{bmatrix} \end{bmatrix} \end{bmatrix} \Rightarrow \boxed{2}, \begin{bmatrix} \text{CAT} \begin{bmatrix} \text{HEAD} \boxed{1} \\ \text{VAL} \begin{bmatrix} \text{SUBJ} \langle \boxed{2} \rangle \\ \text{COMPS} \langle\rangle \end{bmatrix} \end{bmatrix} \end{bmatrix}$$

Figure 3: Head-Subject Rule

The fact that linking is accounted for in the lexicon means that a verb needs to have access to its syntactic arguments in the lexicon. It is therefore difficult to account for verbs with more than one argument frame with only one lexical entry. One approach to this problem is described in Flickinger (2000), which implements a special type of lists in order to account for optional arguments. A list is accepted as empty if all elements on it are marked as OPT +. This approach works well for alternations like the intransitive/transitive alternation, but does not completely eliminate the need for multiple lexical entries (or non-inflectional lexical rules).[2] There are also methods for

[1] By assuming such binary structures, rather than the flat Head-Complement Rule from (Pollard and Sag, 1994, 362–363), the account of adjuncts intervening the complements becomes more straightforward, since a Head-Modifier Rule can be allowed to apply in between two instances of the Head-Complement Rules.

[2] The treatment of ditransitive verbs in combination with passive becomes more challenging, since the passive lexical

making parsing more efficient where local ambiguities are packed while parsing is going on, as shown in Oepen and Carroll (2000), where the packing is done by the parser.

3 Norsyg

Norsyg is a typed feature structure grammar for Norwegian, developed with resources from the open-source repository of the Deep Linguistic Processing with HPSG Initiative (DELPH-IN),[3] in particular the LKB system (Copestake, 2002), which is a software for parsing and grammar development, and the HPSG Grammar Matrix (version 0.8) (Bender *et al.*, 2002), which the grammar Norsyg orignially is based on. Evaluation is done with the [incr tsdb()] system (Oepen and Flickinger, 1998).

Even though much of the feature geometry of the Grammar Matrix has been kept, the design is radically different from that of a standard HPSG grammar. It is now more a constructionalist grammar, rather than lexicalist, inspired by the approach in Borer (2005a,b) and Åfarli (2007).

Norsyg (version 2011-07-28) is a grammar with 4,454 types, 133 features, 144,679 lexical entries (of which 1,436 are hand-built), 52 grammar rules, and 51 lexical rules. In comparison, the ERG (version 2010-10-01) has 7,682 types, 202 features, 35,473 lexical entries, 175 grammar rules, and 73 lexical rules, and JACY (Jacy Japanese Grammar, version 2009-07-05) (Siegel and Bender, 2002) has 2524 types, 183 features, 56,944 lexical items, 51 grammar rules, and 69 lexical rules.

3.1 Linking types

In the approach taken in Norsyg, linking is done in the syntax rather than in the lexical types. Instead of assuming that a lexical entry has detailed information about a certain syntactic frame, which is crucial in an approach that does linking in the lexicon (see Figure 1), it is assumed that a lexical entry by default has little information about its syntactic environment. The syntactic frames are not projections of the lexicon. They are rather constructions made up of *functional signs*, that is inflections, closed class lexical items, and syntactic rules. These signs do the linking of the arguments of the open class lexical items that enter the syntactic frames, realizing what I refer to as subconstructions as they serve as part of a larger, overall construction. In order to avoid overgeneration, the open class lexical items are provided with information that restricts the number of argument frames they can enter.

3.2 Four valence features

In the implementation of a grammar that does linking by means of functional signs realizing subconstructions, I make use of four valence features (ARG1, ARG2, ARG3 and ARG4), corresponding to what in GB is referred to as the "external argument" (ARG1), the "direct object internal argument" (ARG2), the "indirect object internal argument" (ARG3), and "goal/locative oblique" (ARG4). The four features have *synsem* as value.[4] The type *synsem* is given the feature LINK. The value of the LINK feature is the type *link*. In addition, there is a feature ARGFRAME with the value *link*. It is via this feature that a lexeme may put restrictions on what types of constructions it can enter. There is also a feature PART which allows a lexeme to select for particles. The type *valence* now has the definition in Figure 5, rather than the definition with the SUBJ and COMPS lists as presented in Figure 4.

rule looks for the first element on the COMPS list to promote it to subject, and will not be able to find the second element in case the first is not realized.

[3] http://www.delph-in.net.

[4] The type *synsem* is a supertype of *phr-synsem* and *lex-synsem*. This makes it compatible with both words and phrases.

valence	
SUBJ	*list*
SPR	*list*
COMPS	*list*
SPEC	*list*

Figure 4: The type *valence* in the Grammar Matrix

valence	
ARGFRAME	*link*
ARG1	*synsem*[LINK *link*]
ARG2	*synsem*[LINK *link*]
ARG3	*synsem*[LINK *link*]
ARG4	*synsem*[LINK *link*]
PART|SAT	*bool*

Figure 5: The type *valence* in Norsyg

3.3 A hierarchy of linking types

The type *link* has a hierarchy below it. Directly under *link*, there are eight types, one positive and negative type for each of the valence features in Figure 5 (see Figure 6).[5] So there is one *arg1+*, one *arg1–*, one *arg2+*, one *arg2–* and so on.

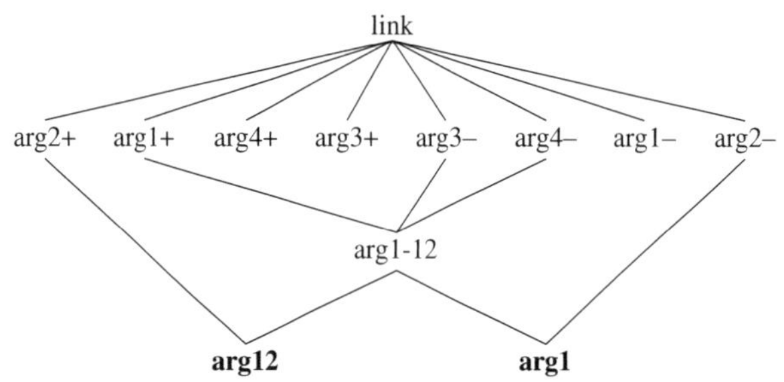

Figure 6: The *link* hierarchy

Each of the types in the bottom of the hierarchy inherits from four of the top types. These types represent different argument frames. For instance, the type *arg12* represents an arg12-construction, which is the frame type for transitive verbs like *devour* in *John devoured the pizza*. The type *arg1* is the type for unergative intransitive verbs like *smile* in *John smiled*. If we study the hierarchy above the bottom types, we see that *arg12* is a subtype of *arg1+*, *arg2+*, *arg3–*, and *arg4–*, and that *arg1* is a subtype of *arg1+*, *arg2–*, *arg3–*, and *arg4–*.

3.4 *Packing* of argument frames

The intermediate types in the hierarchy are inserted in order to allow something that can be thought of as *packing* of argument frames.[6] These types have two or more bottom types as subtypes. So a verb that is specified in the lexicon with an intermediate link type will be compatible with all the frames that correspond to the subtypes of the intermediate link type.

The verb *eat* can occur with two valence frames, as illustrated in (1).[7]

(1) a. John eats.
 b. John eats an apple.

[5] The hierarchy in Figure 6 is very simplified. Most of the intermediate and bottom types are left out in order to keep the illustration as simple as possible.

[6] The term *packing* was suggested to me by Lars Hellan.

[7] Passive and presentational variants of the examples I am using are not assumed to alter the argument frame, so I do not mention them here.

In (1a) *eat* has an arg1-frame, and in (1b) an arg12-frame. In order to allow the verb to enter both frames, it is given the ARGFRAME value *arg1-12* in the lexicon. *arg1-12* inherits from *arg1+*, *arg3-*, and *arg4-*, but is underspecified with regard to arg2. It has two subtypes, namely *arg1* and *arg12*, which means that *eat* can enter the relevant argument frames.

A verb like *break* can enter the frames illustrated in (2).

(2) a. John broke the cup.
    b. John broke the cup to pieces.
    c. The cup broke.
    d. The cup broke to pieces.

(2a) has a transitive frame (arg12-construction), (2b) has a transitive + resultative frame (arg124-construction), (2c) has an unaccusative frame (arg2-construction) and (2d) has an unaccusative + resultative frame (arg24-construction). In order to allow *break* in all these frames, it is specified with the intermediate link-type *arg12-124-2-24*, which has the four subtypes *arg12*, *arg124*, *arg2* and *arg24* (not displayed in Figure 6). In all, the hierarchy below the type *link* consists of 126 types. The most frequent argument frame types with linguistic definitions are given in Table 1. It shows that the most common alternation grouping among the verbs is the transitive/intransitive alternation, with 1815 occurrences. In comparison, the number of verbs alternating between (only) transitive and ditransitive is 56.

Table 1: The 16 most frequent argument frame types in Norsyg

Frequency	Argument frame type	Alternation grouping
3335	arg12	Transitive
1815	arg1-12	Transitive/intransitive
627	arg12-124	Transitive with optional delimiter
513	arg1	Unergative intransitive
341	arg1-14	Intransitive with optional PP complement
338	arg2	Unaccusative intransitive
139	arg12-14	Transitive/intransitive with PP complement (if intransitive)
124	arg1-12-14	Transitive/intransitive with optional delimiter (if intransitive)
114	arg14	Intransitive with PP complement
105	arg12-2	Transitive/unaccusative intransitive (causative/inchoative)
81	arg12-124-14	Intransitive/transitive with optional PP complement
76	arg124	Transitive with PP complement
75	arg1-2	Unergative/unaccusative intransitive
74	arg123	Ditransitive
59	arg12-123-124	Transitive/ditransitive with optional delimiter (if transitive)
56	arg12-123	Transitive/ditransitive

3.5 The composition of subconstructions

Figure 7 gives a simplified illustration of how the information about realized subconstructions in the syntax and argument structure information specified on the main verb is represented.[8] As the figure shows, each valence rule switches a negative LINK value in the mother to a positive

[8] This tree does not reflect the fact that syntactic structures produced by Norsyg actually are left-branching, with the initial constituent at the bottom-left.

LINK value in the daughter. The top node has only negative LINK values. In this way, the LINK values in the bottom of the tree reflect what subconstructions are realized higher up in the tree. The argument structure information specified on the main verb is given as value of the feature ARGFRAME (*arg1-12*). The tree also illustrates how linking is done by subconstructions, rather than in the lexicon. The semantic representation composed in Figure 7 is a decomposed version of the semantic relation in Figure 1. The relations introduced by the subconstructions in Figure 7 can be seen as Parsoninan sub-events.

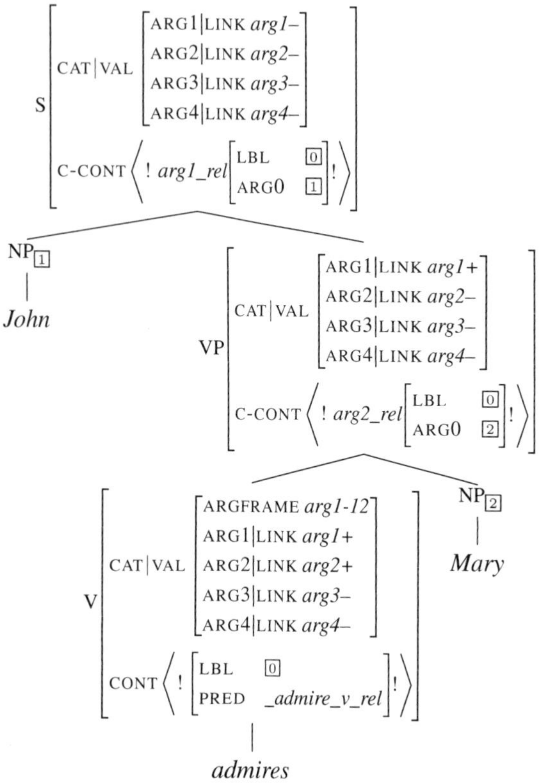

Figure 7: Information about realized subconstructions.

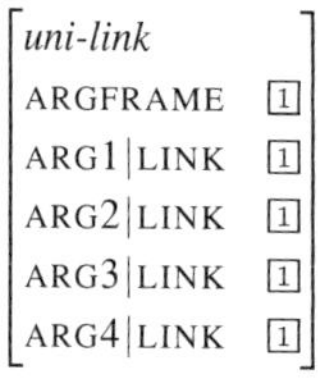

Figure 8: Unification of LINK values and ARGFRAME value.

The type *uni-link* (see Figure 8) unifies the LINK values with the argument structure information specified on the main verb (the value of ARGFRAME). This type applies to constituents at the bottom of the tree where the linking information is available.[9] In the analysis of a transitive sentence like that in Figure 7, the types *arg1+*, *arg2+*, *arg3–*, *arg4–*, and *arg1-12* will be unified. This gives the type *arg12* (see Figure 6).

3.6 Lexical types in Norsyg

There are 100 handwritten and 126 automatically derived lexical entry types for verbs in Norsyg. The lexical type for a transitive verb with an optional NP object, like *eat*, is presented in Figure 9. The feature ARGFRAME is given the value *arg1-12*, which means that the verb is compatible with both the unergative intransitive frame (arg1-construction) and the transitive frame (arg12-construction). The HEAD value of the (optional) ARG2 of the verb is specified to be *nominal*. Since optionality is expressed by means of the argument frame type, there is no need for the

[9] This unification is left out in Figure 7 in order to show how the linking types end up at the bottom of the tree.

feature OPT on syntactic arguments. The PART|SAT value is *plus*, which means that the verb is not a particle verb.

$$\begin{bmatrix} \textit{arg1-12\_np\_le} & \\ \text{CAT|VAL} & \begin{bmatrix} \text{ARGFRAME } \textit{arg1-12} \\ \text{ARG2|CAT|HEAD } \textit{nominal} \\ \text{PART|SAT } + \end{bmatrix} \end{bmatrix}$$

Figure 9: The *arg1-12_np_le* type

The lexical type for verbs like *paint*, which can be both intransitive, transitive and transitive resultative, is given in Figure 10. The ARGFRAME value is specified as *arg1-12-124*, which means that it can enter an unergative frame, a transitive frame, and a transitive frame with a delimiter. The HEAD value of ARG2 is specified to be *nominal*, and the HEAD value of ARG4 is specified to be *adj*. This ensures that the internal argument is an NP, and that the delimiter is an adjective.

$$\begin{bmatrix} \textit{arg1-12-124\_np\_ap\_le} & \\ \text{CAT|VAL} & \begin{bmatrix} \text{ARGFRAME } \textit{arg1-12-124} \\ \text{ARG2|CAT|HEAD } \textit{nominal} \\ \text{ARG4|CAT|HEAD } \textit{adj} \end{bmatrix} \end{bmatrix}$$

Figure 10: The *arg1-12-124_np_ap_le* type

Given the means I have described for restricting the syntactic environment of verbs in Norsyg, the ARGFRAME values, the HEAD values of the ARG2 and ARG4 arguments, the KEY value of the ARG4 argument, and the PRED value of the particles, one is free to give very specific constraints, only allowing one particular argument frame, or one can let the constraints be less specific, so that the verb can enter more frames.

3.7 Adaptation of Norsk Ordbank

Norsyg is adapted to Norsk Ordbank,[10] which is a full-form lexicon for Norwegian with 1,179,549 entries (148,141 different lemmas). The verbs in Norsk Ordbank are annotated with the argument frame information from the NorKompLeks project.[11] A program *convlex* converts the lexicon into a format compatible with the Norsyg grammar (143,263 uninflected lexical entries, of which 8,647 are verbs). It gathers the argument frame information about each verb and creates the corresponding type if this type does not exist already. This is often necessary if a verb can enter many argument frames. The lexical types for verbs have five kinds of information. First, they specify what kind of constructions the verb can enter. If the verb can enter the arg1-construction, the arg12-construction, and the arg124-construction, it is assigned the ARGFRAME value *arg1-12-124*. Second, they specify the HEAD value of the ARG2 argument (if applicable). If the ARG2 is either an NP or a subordinate clause, the new verb lexical entry type inherits from the type *arg2_cp-np*. Third, the ARG3 value is specified to be a reflexive (if applicable). Forth, the new verb lexical types specify the ARG4 value (if applicable). If the ARG4 value is a PP, the type inherits from the type *arg4_pp*. Fifth, the new verb lexical entry type specifies whether the verb is a particle verb. If it is a particle verb, it inherits from the type *part-verb*, and if not, it inherits from *non-part-verb*. Other information, like the PRED values of selected particles and prepositions, is specified on each

[10] http://www.edd.uio.no/prosjekt/ordbanken/

[11] NorKompLeks (NKL) is a Norwegian computational lexicon developed at NTNU, Trondheim, Norway. It contains information about inflectional patterns and phonological representations as well as argument structure frames for verbs. There are 105 different codes for argument structure frames in NKL, and each verb is provided with a list of codes showing the possible argument structure frames.

individual lexical entry. Based on the argument frame information specified on verbs in Norsk Ordbank, the lexicon conversion program builds 126 new types for verb lexical entries in addition to the 100 lexical entry types for verbs that already exist. An example of an automatically created verb lexical type is given in (3).

(3)
```
arg12-124-2_part_np_pp_le := arg2_np & arg4_pp & part-verb &
  [ SYNSEM.LOCAL.CAT.VAL.ARGFRAME arg12-124-2 ].
```

The type in (3) is the type for the verbs *etse* ('corrode'), *helle* ('pour'/'slope'), *hive* ('throw'), *kippe* ('flip up'), and *knalle* ('crack'). What these verbs have in common, is that they can enter the arg12-construction, the arg124-construction, and the arg2-construction, hence the ARGFRAME value *arg12-124-2*. The verbs are particle verbs, so the type inherits from *part-verb*. The verbs require an NP as value of ARG2 and a PP as value of ARG4 (if applicable), so the type inherits from *arg2_np* and *arg4_pp*.

The entry of the infinitival form of *helle* in Norsk Ordbank is given in (4), where the fields in angle brackets show what argument frames the verb can enter, `<intrans2>`, `<adv6>`, and `<part1/ut>`.

(4)
```
27112 helle helle verb inf <intrans2> <adv6> <part1/ut> 021 1
```

These argument frame specifications are translated into the type in (3) according to a table distributed with the Norsyg grammar ('nkl2lkb.txt'). When appearing alone, `<intrans2>` translates into the type *arg2_np_le* (the type for intransitive unaccusative verbs), `<adv6>` translates into the type *arg124_np_pp_le* (the type for transitive verbs with PP complements), and `<part1/ut>` translates into the type *arg12_part_np_le* (the type for transitive particle verbs (the PRED value of the particle *ut* ('out') is specified on the lexical entry)). When these three argument frames appear on the same lexical entry, the type *arg12-124-2_part_np_pp_le* is created, as shown above. It accommodates all the frames just mentioned.The lexical entry of *helle* in the Norsyg grammar is given in (5).

(5)
```
helle-v := arg12-124-2_part_np_pp_le &
  [ STEM <"helle">,
    INFLECTION v1,
    SYNSEM.LKEYS.ALTKEYREL.PRED _ut_p_rel,
    SYNSEM.LKEYS.KEYREL.PRED "_helle_v_rel" ].
```

4 Comparison of 'packed' vs. expanded lexicon

In order to check the impact of a lexicon with packed argument frame representations as described in the previous section, I used the *convlex* program to generate two versions of the lexicon. In the first version, all verbs were given packed representations, and in the other, each argument frame version of a verb was spelled out as a separate lexical entry.

This means that a verb that has the type *arg1-12_np_le* (see Figure 9) in the packed lexicon, in the expanded version is given two lexical entries, one of the type *arg1_le* and one of the type *arg12_np_le* (one for each of the argument structure codes assigned by the original Norsk Ordbank lexicon). 5,329 of the verbs from the Norsk Ordbank lexicon are listed with only one frame, and are therefore given only one lexical entry in the expanded lexicon, while 3,318 verbs are listed with more than one argument frame and are given the corresponding number of lexical entries. This gave me an expanded lexicon with 12,213 lexical entries for verbs, rather than the 8,647 lexical entries for verbs in the packed lexicon, an increase of 3,566.

The data used for the comparison are taken from a 37 million word Norwegian Wikipedia corpus (2,252,972 sentences). I selected 8,271 sentences containing 5-10 words where all the words were covered by the dictionary of the grammar. This set is referred to as *All items* in the next section. The grammar had a coverage of 5,105 sentences with the packed lexicon and 5,078 sentences with the expanded lexicon. Of the sentences that were parsed with both version of the lexicon, 3,446 sentences were given the same number of analyses with both versions. This set is referred to as *Equal coverage* in the next section. I also created a third set of sentences where I excluded the sentences containing the copula verb '*å være*' 'to be' from the *Equal coverage* set, since they are likely to be overrepresented in the data. (Typical short sentences in the Wikipedia data are sentences like *Lesotho er et land i Afrika* 'Leshoto is a country in Africa'.) This set is referred to as *No copula* in the next section and has 1,902 items.

5 Results

I let the grammar loaded with the two different lexicons (*packed* and *expanded*) parse the three sets of sentences described in the previous section (*All items*, *Equal coverage*, and *No copula*) and compared the results. Table 2 shows that the two versions of the grammar, as already noted, have similar coverage on the *All items* set (61.4% and 61.7%), and, as expected, the same coverage (100%) on *Equal coverage*, and *No copula*. The two versions produce slightly more analyses on average with the expanded lexicon (23.69) than the packed lexicon (20.58) for *All items*. For the *Equal coverage*, and *No copula* sets, the two versions (as expected) produce the same number of analyses (14.39 and 13.66, respectively). More importantly, the table also illustrates the difference in lexical ambiguity of the two grammars. The difference in lexical ambiguity of expanded vs. packed is 4.20 vs. 3.41 on *All items*, 3.73 vs. 3.20 on *Equal coverage*, and 3.81 vs. 3.22 on *No copula*. This means that on average more lexical items are entered into the parse chart with the expanded lexicon than with the packed lexicon.

Table 2: Comparison of competence

		Expanded lexicon			'Packed' lexicon		
Data	items	lexical	analyses	coverage (%)	lexical	analyses	coverage (%)
All items	8,271	4.20	23.69	61.4	3.41	20.58	61.7
Equal coverage	3,443	3.73	14.39	100.0	3.20	14.39	100.0
No copula	1,902	3.81	13.66	100.0	3.22	13.66	100.0

Table 3 shows how the use of packed argument frames affects the performance of the parser, compared to the use of the expanded lexicon. When applied to the *Equal coverage* set, the number of tasks is reduced by 10.7%, and the use of space is reduced with 13.3%. Similarly, the number of tasks is reduced by 12.8%, and the use of space is reduced with 13.2%, when applied to *No copula*. The numbers showing reductions for *All data* are less reliable, since the set includes sentences where the two versions of the grammar produce different numbers of analyses.

Table 3: Comparison of performance

		Expanded lexicon		'Packed' lexicon		Reduction (%)	
Data	items	tasks	space	tasks	space	tasks	space
All items	8,271	3,265	208,324	2,480	139,430	24.0	33.1
Equal coverage	3,443	2,022	102,964	1,805	69,540	10.7	13.3
No copula	1,902	1,341	59,080	1,170	51,294	12.8	13.2

One possible objection to this test would be that a grammar without the packing of argument structure information could be implemented in a different way, that would make parsing more efficient. However, this comparison is only done for testing the impact of the packing of argument structure information in a grammar that is implemented similar to Norsyg.

6 Conclusion

I have compared two versions of a lexicon for a grammar implementation. One, where valence alternations are accounted for by means of multiple lexical entries, and one, where valence alternations are accounted for by means of packed type constraints. It has been demonstrated that the packed version of the lexicon introduces fewer lexical items in the parse chart. The use of the packed version of the lexicon also leads to a reduction of tasks performed and space used by the parser.

References

Bender, E. M., Flickinger, D., and Oepen, S. (2002). The grammar matrix: An open-source starter-kit for the rapid development of cross-linguistically consistent broad-coverage precision grammars. In J. Carroll, N. Oostdijk, and R. Sutcliffe, editors, *Proceedings of the Workshop on Grammar Engineering and Evaluation at the 19th International Conference on Computational Linguistics*, pages 8–14, Taipei, Taiwan.

Borer, H. (2005a). *Structuring Sense. An Exo-Skeletal Triology. Volume I. In Name Only.* Oxford University Press.

Borer, H. (2005b). *Structuring Sense. An Exo-Skeletal Triology. Volume II. The Normal Course of Events.* Oxford University Press.

Bresnan, J. (2001). *Lexical-Functional Syntax.* Blackwell Publishers.

Copestake, A. (2002). *Implementing Typed Feature Structure Grammars.* CSLI publications.

Flickinger, D. P. (2000). On building a more efficient grammar by exploiting types. *Natural Language Engineering*, **6**(1), 15–28.

Oepen, S. and Carroll, J. (2000). Ambiguity packing in constraint-based parsing. Practical results. In *Proceedings of the 1st Conference of the North American Chapter of the ACL*, pages 162–169, Seattle, WA.

Oepen, S. and Flickinger, D. (1998). Towards systematic grammar profiling. test suite technology ten years after. *Journal of Computer Speech and Language: Special Issue on Evaluation*, **12 (4)**, 441–437.

Pollard, C. J. and Sag, I. A. (1994). *Head-Driven Phrase Structure Grammar.* University of Chicago Press, Chicago.

Sag, I. A., Wasow, T., and Bender, E. M. (2003). *Syntactic Theory: A Formal Introduction.* CSLI Publications, Stanford, 2 edition.

Siegel, M. and Bender, E. M. (2002). Efficient deep processing of Japanese. In *COLING:02*, pages 1–8, Taipei, Taiwan.

Steedman, M. (2000). *The Syntactic Process.* Cambridge, MA and London: The MIT Press.

Åfarli, T. A. (2007). Do verbs have argument structure? In E. Reuland, T. Bhattacharya, and G. Spathas, editors, *Argument Structure*, pages 1–16. Amsterdam: John Benjamins.

Quantification and the Garden Path Effect Reduction: The Case of Universally Quantified Subject *

Akira Ohtani[a] and Takeo Kurafuji[b]

[a] Faculty of Informatics, Osaka Gakuin University,
2-36-1 Kishibe-minami, Suita 564-8511, Japan
ohtani@ogu.ac.jp

[b] College of Law, Ritsumeikan University,
56-1 Kita-machi, Toji-in, Kita-ku, Kyoto 603-8677, Japan
kurafuji@fc.ritsumei.ac.jp

Abstract. This paper investigates the effect of quantification in sentence processing. The experimental results show that temporarily ambiguous sentences that begin with the universally quantified NPs reduced the garden path effect in contrast to the ones that begin with bare NPs. This fact is accounted for by assuming that discourse representation structures are incrementally constructed, and a tripartite structure introduced by the universal quantifier gives a *room* for temporal ambiguity while a single *box* associated with a bare NP forces one interpretation and to get the correct interpretation, the single box must be rewritten, which results in the garden path effect.

Keywords: temporarily ambiguous sentence, garden path effect, DRT, box merger

1 Introduction

Japanese has several types of *temporarily ambiguous sentences* (TASs) (Inoue, 2006). This paper focuses on the pattern 'NP-NOM [$_{VP}$ NP-ACC V] NP-DAT NP-ACC V' as exemplified in (1).

(1) *Keekan*-ga [$_{VP}$ hanni-o tsukamaeta] otoko-ni ree-o itta.
police.officer-NOM criminal-ACC caught man-DAT thank-ACC said
'A police officer extended his thanks to a/the man who caught a criminal.'

The first NP *keekan-ga* 'police.officer-NOM' tends to be construed as the subject of the following VP, yielding the reading "a police officer caught a criminal" but this interpretation crashes when another NP *otoko-ni* 'man-DAT' shows up after the V *tsukamaeta* 'caught'. To get the correct interpretation, the VP preceding *otoko-ni* 'man-DAT' must be construed as (part of) the relative clause modifying that NP, and the first NP must be construed as the subject of the sentence-final V *itta* 'said'. This reinterpretation process is known as the *garden path* (GP) effect.

However, the GP effect of TAS slightly reduces when only a bare NP *keekan* 'police.officer' in (1) is replaced with a universally quantified NP *subeteno keekan* 'all police officers' as in (2).

(2) *Subeteno keekan*-ga [$_{VP}$ hanni-o tsukamaeta] otoko-ni ree-o itta.
all police.officer-NOM criminal-ACC caught man-DAT thank-ACC said
'All police officers extended their thanks to a/the man who caught a criminal.'

* We are indebted to three anonymous PACLIC reviewers, Masakatsu Inoue and Michinao F. Matsui for their invaluable comments on an earlier version of this paper. All remaining inadequacies are our own. This research is partially supported by Osaka Gakuin University and Grant-in-Aid for Scientific Research (C), 18530578 and 21500152 of the Japan Society for the Promotion of Science (JSPS).

This difference suggests that semantic representations play significant roles since the syntactic structure of (1) and (2) are all the same,[1] and that the quantificational structure introduced by the universal quantifier makes (2) easy to interpret.

In this paper, we claim the relevant semantic representations are built independently of syntactic structures to some extent and then propose algorithms of generating semantic representations which can account for the difference between (1) and (2). The paper is organized as follows. Section 2 shows some basic facts and previous analyses of TASs. Section 3 introduces some theoretical settings. Section 4 and Section 5 provide a formalization and a summary of our analysis presented in this paper.

2 Tripartite Structure Concerning Quantification

Since Bever (1970), TASs like (3) have been discussed from various perspectives and there have been many proposals made in the literature (e.g. syntax-driven model (Frazier, 1979), discourse-based referential-support model (Crain and Steedman, 1985) among others).

(3) *The horse* [$_{\text{VP}}$ raced past the barn] fell.

(3) is well known for the [$_{\text{VP}}$ raced past the barn] can be construed either as the predicate of the subject *the horse* or as the reduced relative clause modifying the subject, and this ambiguity is not resolved until the sentence ends. The general tendency is that the VP is interpreted as the predicate of the subject, and therefore this interpretation crashes when the final verb *fell* shows up.

Menéndez-Benito (2003) reveals that the GP effect slightly reduces when a NP *the horse* in (3) is replaced with a universally quantified NP *every horse* as in (4).

(4) *Every horse* [$_{\text{VP}}$ raced past the barn] fell.

According to her, the GP effect was observed in both (3) and (4), and therefore the VP is initially interpreted as a predicate of the subject, but (4) has less GP effect than (3) in the experiments she conducted. Following Portner (1989), she suggests that perceivers prefer to place as much material as possible in the restrictive clause of a tripartite structure concerning quantification as in (5).

(5)

Quantifier	Restrictive Clause	Nuclear Scope
Every$_x$	*horse(x) & raced-past-the-barn(x)*	*fell(x)*

Kurafuji *et al.* (2007) investigates TASs of the sequence 'NP-NOM [$_{\text{VP}}$ NP-ACC V] NP-DAT V' in Japanese (e.g. (1) and (2)), where the temporal ambiguity is caused by the interpretive indeterminacy of whether the VP functions as the predicate of the subject NP-NOM or the relative clause modifying the NP-DAT. The GP effect takes place when the NP-DAT shows up after the VP. Their experimental results also reveal that sentences with a universally quantified NP subject have less GP effect than those with a bare NP subject do. This result is parallel with Menéndez-Benito's,[2] so that we may also pursue the idea that tripartite structure associated with the universal quantifier is very crucial in sentence processing.

[1] Here we assum the very basic argumentation about syntactic structures; if two nominal expressions bear the same case marker and the same thematic role, they occupy the same syntactic position.

[2] We do not use a sentence with the universally quantified subject *dono keekan-mo* 'every police officer' as in (i).

(i) *Dono keekan*-mo [$_{\text{VP}}$ hanni-o tsukamaeta] otoko-ni ree-o itta.
which police.officer-also criminal-ACC caught man-DAT thank-ACC said
'Every police officer extended his thanks to a/the man who caught a criminal.'

In (i) the subject does not bear the nominative case, so that it might be possible to claim that the syntactic position of such a quantified NP subject is different from the one of a nominative NP. See also footnote 1.

Menéndez-Benito (2003) uses the semantic notion of tripartite structure in her account, but in languages like English, the tripartite structure roughly corresponds to the syntactic structure of the sentences in (3) and (4), as shown in (5), and therefore it is not clear whether the contrast between (3) and (4) is syntactic or semantic. Kurafuji *et al.* (2007), on the other hand, conducted a psycholinguistics experiment in which the sentences like (1) and (2) were displayed on a CRT monitor in a phrase-by-phrase fashion and the reading times for each phrase were recorded. The results of experiment suggest that semantic representations such as (5) can be obtained directly from the sequence of phrases without building syntactic structures.[3]

3 Inter- and Intra-sentential Box Merger of DRT

In a situation like Kurafuji *et al.*'s (2007) experimental setting, the semantic representations of TASs are built in a left-to-right fashion. To account for the GP effect reduction in a TAS which begins with a universally quantified NP, we propose an incremental sentence processing algorithm under the framework of *discourse representation theory* (DRT). The DRT that we follow here is the standard one as proposed in Kamp and Reyle (1993) with one crucial difference. The standard DRT assumes that *discourse representation structure* (DRS) is constructed based on syntactic structure, which means they are built after syntactic parsing. In our model, in contrast, DRSs are constructed phrase-by-phrase, independently of syntactic parsing.

Let us begin with the standard definition of DRS and the operation of *box merger*.

(6) Box Merger

$$<D_1, C_1> \otimes <D_2, C_2> = <D_1 \cup D_2, C_1 \cup C_2>$$

A DRS K is a pair of a set of discourse referents D and a set of conditions C, represented as K $= <D, C>$. This pair is also called a *box*. A box combines with the preceding one by *the inter-sentential merger operator* $\otimes$, which takes the union of the sets of discourse referents and the union of the sets of conditions as given in (6) above (Bos *et al.*, 1994).

With this operation, a discourse representation proceeds, as shown in (7), where u and v are discourse referents and 'u = John', 'u came in', 'v = Mary', and 'v left' are conditions.[4]

(7) John came in. (And) Mary left.

u		v		u v	
u = John	$\otimes$	v = Mary	=	u = John	(Inter-sentential Merging)
u came in		v left		u came in	
				v = Mary	
				v left	

We assume that all lexical items are translated into a box notation. For example, the name *John* is translated into [u : u = John] and the adjective *rich* is translated into [: λx[rich(x)]]. These two boxes are then combined by the intra-sentential merging.

[3] Kurafuji *et al.* (2007) examined the effect of NP types on the degree of GP effect. According to them, the sentence begins with demostrative NP *sono keekan-ga* 'that police.officer-NOM' also has less GP effect than (2), but the status of the sentence with existentially quantified NP *aru keekan-ga* 'a certain police.officer-NOM' is not clear since there was no significant diffrence of reading time between such a sentence and the other types of sentences.

[4] We also use a box notation with brackets as in [u: u = John, u came in] as well as a representation like (7). The treatment of tense and aspect is ignored throughout the paper.

(8) John is rich.

$$\begin{array}{|c|}\hline \text{u} \\ \hline \text{u = John} \\ \hline\end{array} \;\underline{\otimes}\; \begin{array}{|c|}\hline \\ \hline \lambda\text{x[rich(x)]} \\ \hline\end{array} \;=\; \begin{array}{|c|}\hline \text{u} \\ \hline \text{u = John} \\ \lambda\text{x[rich(x)]} \\ \hline\end{array} \qquad \text{(Intra-sentential Merging)}$$

$$\Rightarrow \; \begin{array}{|c|}\hline \text{u} \\ \hline \text{u = John} \\ \lambda\text{x[rich(x)]} \\ \hline\end{array} \qquad (\lambda\text{-Reduction})$$

In addition to the inter-sentential merger operation in (6), we newly introduce *the intra-sentential merger operator* $\underline{\otimes}$, whose definition is the same as the one in (6), but the range of application is different. The inter-sentential merging $\otimes$ applies across a sentence boundary, while the intra-sentential merging $\underline{\otimes}$ applies only in a sentence. The latter applies incrementally from left-to-right.

The λ-formula in conditions is combined with the discourse referent u by λ-reduction.[5]

4 Incremental Building of DRSs

4.1 The GP Effect

The lexical items and their box-translations relevant to our discussion are given in table 1.

Table 1: A Small Fragment of Japanese

Lexical Item	Box-Translation
keekan	[u : police-officer(u)]
hannin	[u : criminal(u)]
otoko	[u : man(u)]
ree	[u : thanks(u)]
tsukamaeta	[e : $\lambda y \lambda x$[catching(e) $\wedge$ agent(x, e) $\wedge$ theme(y, e)]]
itta	[e : $\lambda z \lambda y \lambda x$[saying(e) $\wedge$ agent(x, e) $\wedge$ theme(y, e) $\wedge$ goal(z, e)]]
subeteno	[: [:] $\Rightarrow$ ALL [:]]

Here we assume that verbs introduce an event argument e, and every NP introduces a discourse referent as in [u : P(u)]. The grammatical-role or semantic information indicated by case-markers is important in sentence processing, but we put it aside at this moment.

With these settings, let us firstly consider why the GP effect takes place in sentences as in (1) but not in sentences as in (2). Let us consider the former sentences, repeated as (10).

(9)

Keekan-ga	[$_{VP}$ hanni-o	tsukamaeta]	otoko-ni	ree-o	itta.
police.officer-NOM	criminal-ACC	caught	man-DAT	thank-ACC	said

'A police officer extended his thanks to a/the man who caught a criminal.'

(10) a. [u: police-officer(u)]

b. [v: criminal(v)]

c. [u: police-officer(u)] $\underline{\otimes}$ [v: criminal(v)] = [u, v: police-officer(u), criminal(v)]

d. [u, v: police-officer(u), criminal(v)] $\underline{\otimes}$
[e : $\lambda y \lambda x$ [catching(e) $\wedge$ agent(x, e) $\wedge$ theme(y, e)]] =
[e, u, v: police-officer(u), criminal(v), $\lambda y \lambda x$[catching(e) $\wedge$ agent(x, e) $\wedge$ theme(y, e)]]

[5] It should be noted that in (8) merging of [u : u = John] of type *e* to [: λx[rich(x)]] of type <*e, t*> happens to obey the restriction of types, but the intra-sentential box merging operation we propose here is not type-sensitive (of course λ-abstraction applies type-theoretically).

In the sentence (9), when the first bare NP is given, a discourse referent and its condition are introduced in a single box as in (10a). The second NP also gives another discourse referent and its condition in another box, as in (10b), and then the two boxes intra-sententially merge, as in (10c). The verb *tsukamaeta* 'caught' also introduces another box with an event argument e, and merges to the preceding box as in (10d). Here we propose that the DRS construction algorithm is subject to the following preference rule as a parsing strategy.

(11) The Locality Preference of λ-Reduction
Reduce λ-operators in conditions in box K with
(i) the discourse referents in K, or
(ii) discourse referents in boxes accessible from them, if there is no discourse referent available in the box.

(11) says that the λ-reduction with a discourse referent in the local box is preferred to the same operation with one in a non-local box. It is worth noting that since (11) is a preference rule, it can be violated if a requirement by another principle forces it to be. In (10d), the box has two discourse referents of individual type, u and v, and the rule (11) requires that these discourse referents serve as arguments of *tsukamaeta* 'caught', yielding (12) below.

(12) [e, u, v: police-officer(u), criminal(v), catching(e), agent(u, e), theme(v, e)]

DRS (12) means "a police officer caught a criminal."

Here we assume that the lexical relation between NPs and V and the information of case-markers determine which discourse referent bears the AGENT role and which bears the THEME role. For example, the nominative NP tends to bear the agent role and the accusative NP tends to bear the theme role, and so on. We also assume that after all λ-operators are replaced, the conjunction '$\wedge$' are deleted in representations.

Now what happens when the third NP *otoko-ni* 'man-DAT' shows up? This NP introduces a new discourse referent in a single box, which intra-senentially merges to box (12), as in (13).

(13) [e, u, v: police-officer(u), criminal(v), catching(e), agent(u, e), theme(v, e)] $\underline{\otimes}$ [r: man(r)]
= [e, u, v, r: police-officer(u), criminal(v), catching(e), agent(u, e), theme(v, e), man(r)]

The DRS (13) itself has nothing wrong in principle but it is not favored in processing. One of the possibilities for making (13) intelligible is to yield the reading "a police officer caught a criminal and there is a man." However, to get such an interpretation, man(r) should be associated with an event argument, and the discourse referent r must be linked to a theme role, as in theme(r, e'), where e' is an event argument different from e. In other words, man(r) itself is a well-formed condition, but without an event argument it is not a well-formed event-semantic proposition.

Another possibility is to regard it as an intermediate stage of a DRS of a sequence of sentences as in (14) below, where the dative NP is considered to be the first phrase in the second sentence.

(14) # *Keekan*-ga hanni-o tsukamaeta. Otoko-ni ...
police.officer-NOM criminal-ACC caught man-DAT
'A police officer caught a/the criminal. To a/the man, ...'

However the sequence of sentences in (14) itself sounds quite strange. To improve the sequence, a connective such as *soshite* 'and' should be inserted between the two sentences, maybe for the indication of a sentence boundary to introduce the inter-sentential merging operator $\otimes$. So the possibility of interpreting (13) as a sequence of sentences should also be rejected.

The last possibility is to interpret (13) as part of an incomplete sentence. This is in fact the correct way to go, since the reading that we want is the one in which the dative NP is interpreted as the agent of *tsukamaeta* 'caught'. But here is the problem. In (12) the agent slot of *tsukamaeta* 'caught' has already been filled in by u associated with *keekan-ga* 'police.officer-NOM', so that there is no thematic role for *otoko-ni* 'man-DAT'. In order for *otoko-ni* 'man-DAT' to be part of a sentence, the DRS (12) must be reconstructed, going back to the prior stage (10d). This is the cause of the GP effect.

The important point here is that in (10d), where the box translation of *tsukamaeta* 'caught' is merged, the λ-operators in λyλx[catching(e) ∧ agent(x, e) ∧ theme(y, e)] are replaced with the discourse referents u and v. One might ask what is wrong if λ-reduction does not apply at the stage (10d), and waits for another discourse referent (in this case r associated with *otoko-ni* 'man-DAT'), and after its arrival does the λ-operator bind x with its new discourse referent r, as in (15).

(15) [e, u, v: police-officer(u), criminal(v), λyλx[catching(e) ∧ agent(x, e) ∧ theme(y, e)]]
$\underline{\otimes}$ [r: man(r)]
⇒ [e, u, v, r: police-officer(u), criminal(v), λy[catching(e) ∧ agent(r, e) ∧ theme(y, e)], man(r)]
⇒ [e, u, v, r: police-officer(u), criminal(v), catching(e), agent(r, e), theme(v, e), man(r)]

If this option were taken, the GP effect would not be observed. However, Kurafuji *et al.*'s (2007) experimental result shows that the GP effect actually took place, which means that *keekan-ga*'police. officer-NOM' and *hannin-o* 'criminal-ACC' are interpreted as arguments of *tsukamaeta* 'caught'. In order to account for the GP effect in the present approach, we propose another processing strategy, given in (16).

(16) The Early Completion Strategy
Make a DRS complete as early as possible, where a complete DRS is a DRS which does not contain a λ-operator.

The strategy (16) forces the λ-operators in conditions to be replaced with the discourse referents in the same box as early as possible. The idea behind (16) is that a parser tries to reduce λ-operators as soon as a verb shows up in Japanese. In other words, by (16) the NPs that immediately precede a verb are interpreted as arguments of that verb as long as the NPs' case information is compatible with the verb's argument structure. Given this strategy, the derivation in (15) is not allowed, since the two λ-operators remain not to be replaced in spite of the fact that they should have been replaced with u and v at the prior stage.

Now let us see how the rest of the sentence (9) is processed and the DRS is constructed.

(17) a. [e, u, v: police-officer(u), criminal(v), λyλx[catching(e) ∧ agent(x, e) ∧ theme(y, e)]]
b. (17a) $\underline{\otimes}$ [r: man(r)] ⇒
[e, u, v, r: police-officer(u), criminal(v), catching(e), agent(r, e), theme(v, e), man(r)]
c. (17b) $\underline{\otimes}$ [s: thanks(s)] =
[e, u, v, r, s: police-officer(u), criminal(v), catching(e), agent(r, e), theme(v, e), man(r), thanks(s)]
d. (17c) $\underline{\otimes}$ λzλyλx[saying(e') ∧ agent(x, e') ∧ theme(y, e') ∧ goal(z, e')] ⇒
[e, e', u, v, r, s: police-officer(u), criminal(v), catching(e), agent(r, e), theme(v, e), man(r), thanks(s), saying(e'), agent(u, e'), theme(s, e'), goal(r, e')]

After the GP effect took place at the point of merging of *otoko-ni* 'man-DAT', the parser traces back to (10d), repeated as (17a), where the λ-reduction does not apply yet. Then the discourse referent associated with *otoko-ni* 'man-DAT' is introduced; it bears the agent role of *tsukamaeta* 'caught' as (17b). The boxes associated with *ree-o* 'thanks-ACC' and *itta* 'said' intra-sententially merge to DRSs in (17b) and (17c), respectively, resulting in (17d), the literal translation of which is "a police officer said thanks to the man who caught a criminal."

4.2 The Quantification Effect Case

Next, let us consider the incremental derivation of the sentence (2), repeated as (18).

(18) *Subeteno keekan*-ga [$_{VP}$ hanni-o tsukamaeta] otoko-ni ree-o itta.
all police.officer-NOM criminal-ACC caught man-DAT thank-ACC said
'All police officers extended their thanks to a/the man who caught a criminal.'

The universal quantifier (Q) *subeteno* 'all' is translated into the complex DRS as shown in (19).

(19)

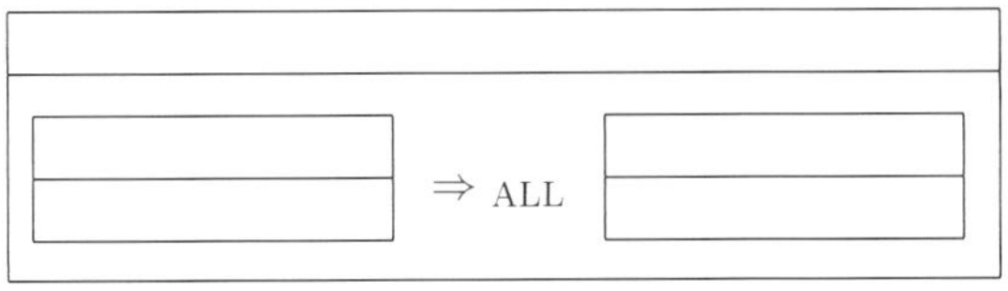

At the next step, the box [u: police-officer(u)] introduced by *keekan-ga* 'police.officer-sc nom' intra-sententially merges to (19), which has three possible merging boxes; the main box, the left sub-box, and the right sub-box. Here we assume that the internal structure of quantified NP gives the information of the merging operation, as shown in (20).

(20) The Tripartite Structure Rule
(i) The box associated with the NP in the sequence 'Q NP-case marker' are merged to the left sub-box introduced by the box associated with Q.
(ii) The boxes associated with the other intra-sentential NPs are merged to the other boxes (i.e. to the main box or to the right sub-box).

According to the rule (20), in the sequence '[$_Q$ *subeteno*] [$_{NP}$ *keekan*]-*ga*,' the box introduced by *keekan* 'police.officer' is merged to the left sub-box, yielding (21).

(21)

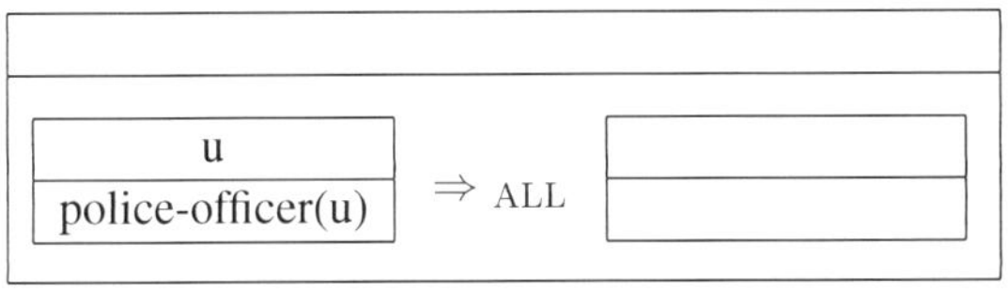

(21) correctly represents the fact that the NP following Q serves as the restrictive clause of that Q. At this point, one might claim that the DRS for the universal quantifier should be something like [: [u : P(u)] $\Rightarrow_{ALL}$ [: Q(u)]], where the both sub-boxes contain the variable u in their conditions. Given the usual translation of a universal quantifier $\lambda Q \lambda P \forall x[P(x) \rightarrow Q(x)]$, in which the antecedent and the consequent clauses share the same variable x, it seems reasonable to assume that the two subordinate boxes in (19) share the same variable in their conditions when a universal quantifier is translated into its box notation.

However, we do not take this position. In our approach such a cooccurrence of u's is underspecified in the lexicon and the desirable result comes from something else such as the requirement of the ban on vacuous quantification, which requires that both the restrictive clause and the nuclear scope contain the same variable bound by the quantifier. We assume that there is a more limited version of this requirement in Japanese semantic processing, as given in (22).

(22) The Ban on Vacuous Quantification (a version of Japanese semantic processing)
A variable introduced in the left sub-box by the tripartite structure rule must also appear in the right sub-box.

In (21) the variable introduced in the left sub-box by the tripartite structure rule (20) is u, and the ban on vacuous quantification (22) requires that u should appear in the right sub-box. This requirement is satisfied if a λ-operator introduced in the right sub-box is replaced with u. A concrete example will be given below.

Let us go back to the derivation of DRS of the sentence (18).

(23) a. [: [u: police-officer(u)] ⇒ $_{ALL}$
[e, v: criminal(v), λyλx[catching(e) ∧ agent(x, e) ∧ theme(y, e)]]]

b. [: [u: police-officer(u)] ⇒ $_{ALL}$
[e, v: criminal(v), λx[catching(e) ∧ agent(x, e) ∧ theme(v, e)]]]

In (23a) *hannin-o* 'criminal-ACC' and *tsukamaeta* 'caught' merge to the right box, following the rule (20), then in (23b) λy is replaced with v, following the locality preference of λ-reduction (11).

At this point, it is important to consider how a sentence like (24) is interpreted.

(24) Subeteno keekan-ga hannin-o tsukamaeta.
all police.officer-NOM criminal-ACC caught
'All police officers caught a criminal.'

In Japanese linguistic literature (e.g. Hoji (1985) among others), it is claimed that in a structure 'Q NP-NOM Q NP-ACC V,' the Q NP-NOM takes wide scope over the Q NP-ACC. In (24), the object is a bare NP and the wide scope reading of the object bare NP is easy to obtain as well as the wide scope reading of the Q NP subject. Likewise, sentences like (18) are ambiguous between the wide scope reading of the Q NP subject and that of the dative bare NP. The question is then what interpretation the participants in Kurafuji *et al.*'s (2007) experiment actually obtained.

In DRT, the scope ambiguity between a universally quantified NP and an existentially quantified NP is unambiguously represented, depending on where the discourse referent associated with the existentially quantified NP is introduced. In a DRT with event semantics like ours, the place of event argument also disambiguates the interpretations. In what follows, just for the sake of presentation, we assume that the participants in their experiment interpreted sentences like (24) is interpreted as "There is a criminal such that all police officers caught her/him together," since this kind of interpretation seems the easiest to obtain.[6]

The interpretation such as "all police officer caught a criminal together" can be represented by assuming that the discourse referent denoting an event of the sub-box is *projected* to the main box, as schematized in (25).[7]

(25) $[_{\text{main box}}\ :\ \ldots [_{\text{sub-box}}\ e : \ldots] \ldots] \ \rightarrow_{\textit{project } e}\ [_{\text{main box}}\ e : \ldots [_{\text{sub-box}}\ : \ldots] \ldots]$

Let us go back to DRS (23b). In (26a), the discourse referent in the sub-box e is projected to the main box following the operation in (25). The DRS (26a) has a variable x bound by the λ-operator, and how to treat this variable is important in derivation. If the sentence ends at this point, this variable is replaced with u in the left box as in (26b).

(26) a. [: [u: police-officer(u)] ⇒ $_{ALL}$
[e, v: criminal(v), λx[catching(e) ∧ agent(x, e) ∧ theme(v, e)]]]
→ $_{\textit{project } e}$ [e : [u: police-officer(u)] ⇒ $_{ALL}$
[v: criminal(v), λx[catching(e) ∧ agent(x, e) ∧ theme(v, e)]]]

b. [e : [u: police-officer(u)] ⇒ $_{ALL}$
[v: criminal(v), catching(e), agent(u, e), theme(v, e)]]

[6] Other interpretations can be captured in our approach, so the choice of this particular interpretation does not have any significance.

[7] This kind of projection is not ad hoc since the treatment of proper nouns requires this type of operation anyway.

This operation does not obey the locality preference of λ-reduction (11). Remember this preference rule is violable if the violation is forced by a principle that must be obeyed. In this case, the ban on vacuous quantification (22) forces the violation of the locality preference of λ-reduction. By replacing of the λ-operator in the right box with u in the left box, the variable introduced in the left sub-box, namely u, appears in the right sub-box, so the ban on vacuous quantification is satisfied. Thus, the resulting DRS (26b) represents "all police officers caught a criminal (together)."

Now let us consider the case where another NP merges to (26a).

(27) a. (26a) $\underline{\otimes}$ [r: man(r)] ⇒
[e: [u: police-officer(u)] $\Rightarrow_{ALL}$
[v, r: criminal(v), catching(e), agent(r, e), theme(v, e), man(r)]]

b. (27a) $\underline{\otimes}$ [s: thanks(s)] =
[e: [u: police-officer(u)] $\Rightarrow_{ALL}$
[v, r, s: criminal(v), catching(e), agent(r, e), theme(v, e), man(r), thanks(s)]]

c. (27b) $\underline{\otimes}$ λzλyλx[saying(e') ∧ agent(x, e') ∧ theme(y, e') ∧ goal(z, e')] $\Rightarrow_{project\ e'}$
[e, e': [u: police-officer(u)] $\Rightarrow_{ALL}$
[v, r, s: criminal(v), catching(e), agent(r, e), theme(v, e), man(r), thank(s),
saying(e'), agent(u, e'), theme(s, e'), goal(r, e')]]

As shown in (27a), the box [r: man(r)] associated with *otoko-ni* 'man-DAT' introduces a new discourse referent r in the right box, and the variable x is replaced with r following the locality preference of λ-reduction (11).

Again, the important point here is the treatment of the agent variable of *tsukamaeta* 'caught'. Unlike the case of the sentence (9) discussed in Section 4.1, the u associated with *keekan* 'police officer' is not in the right box, so that it is not the primary option for the replacement of x. On the other hand, the r introduced by *otoko* 'man' is in the same box as the agent variable is, so the locality preference in (11) chooses r as the agent of the verb.

Then *ree-o* 'thanks-ACC' and *itta* 'said' merge to DRSs in (27a) and (27b), respectively. As discussed above, the λx of *itta* 'said' is replaced with u in the left box to satisfy the ban on vacuous quantification. The final DRS (27c) represents the correct truth conditions of sentence (18).

5 Concluding Remarks

This paper investigated Japanese TASs of the form 'NP-NOM NP-ACC V NP-DAT V.' Such sentences with a bare NP subject and with a universally quantified subject show the difference in reading time based on psycholinguistics experiments (Kurafuji *et al.*, 2007). To account for this fact, we developed the new incremental DRS building algorithm under the framework of DRT (Kamp and Reyle, 1993), in which each lexical item is translated into a box-notation and such a box intra-sententially merges to another box from left to right.

When the subject is a bare NP, a single box is introduced, and boxes introduced by the second NP and the verb are combined with this single box, constituting a new single box. If the argument structure of the verb is saturated in this single box, there is no *room* for a new intra-sententially merged discourse referent. This is the cause of the GP effect. When the subject has a quantifier like *subeteno* 'all', on the other hand, a complex DRS is introduced, which provides a *room* for a new discourse referent, and thus the GP effect does not take place.

We also proposed two parsing strategies; the locality preference of λ-reduction and the early completion strategy. The effects of these strategies are similar to the effect of the minimal attachment (Frazier and Fodor, 1978). However, a syntactic approach with the minimal attachment cannot account for the fact that the universal quantifier reduces the GP effect. So our incremental DRT approach is different from a syntactic approach though they assume the similar strategies.

Our approach can apply to some cases that we did not address in the paper. One is concerned with the interpretation of the Japanese topic marker *wa*. Inoue (1991) reported with a different experimental setting that the GP effect reduces when *wa* is used in the initial NP instead of the nominative case marker *ga*. If our account is on the right track, the fact suggsts that the topic-marked NP introduces a tripartite structure as [u: P(u)] $\Rightarrow_{TOPIC}$ [u: Q(u)], which roughly says "for the topic u, if u has the property P, it also has the property Q." The functional similarity between conditionals and topic expressions has been pointed out in the literature (e.g. Haiman (1978) among others). Our approach thus hacks up such an idea with the experimental results.

We did not go into detail on other quantified NPs with an existantial quantifier like *aru keekan* 'a police officer' and numeral quantifier like *san-nin-no keekan* 'three police officers.' The status of the sentence begins with the former is not clear since there was no significant diffrence of reading time between such a sentence and the sentence with universal quantifier. Regarding the sentence with the latter, we have not conducted any experiments. We will leave the experiments and analyses of these quantifiers for future work.

References

Bever, T. 1970. The Cognitive Basis for Linguistic Structures. *Cognition and the Development of Language*, 279-352. New York: Wiley.

Bos, J., E. Mastenbroek, S. McGlashan, S. Millies and M. Pinkal. 1994. *A Compositional DRS-Based Formalism for NLP Applications. Verbmobil Report*, 59. Universidat des Saarlandes.

Crain, S. and M. Steedman. 1985. On Not Being Led Up the Garden-Path: The Use of Context by the Psychological Processor. *Natural Language Processing*, 163-182. Cambridge: Cambridge University Press.

Frazier, L. 1979. *On Comprehending Sentences: Syntactic Parsing Strategies*. Ph.D. thesis, University of Connecticut.

Frazier, L. and J. D. Fodor. 1978. The Sausage Machine: A New Two-Stage Parsing Model. *Cognition*, 6(4), 291-325.

Haiman, J. 1978. Conditionals Are Topics. *Language*, 54(3), 564-589.

Hoji, H. 1985. *Logical Form Constraints and Configurational Structures in Japanese*. Ph.D. thesis, University of Washington.

Inoue, M. 1991. Bun no Toogoshori ni okeru Jyoshi *Wa* no Kinoo: Gankyuu Undoo Deeta o Shihyoo to shite [The Function of the Particle *Wa* in Sentence Parsing: Evidence from Eye Movements in Reading], *Proceedings of the 33rd Conference of the Japanese Association of Educational Psychology*, 321.

Inoue, M. 2006. Nihongobun no Rikai ni okeru Aimaisee no Kaishoo to Horyuu [Ambiguity Resolution or Retention in Comprehending Japanese Sentence], *Cognitive Studies*, 13(3), 353-368.

Kamp, H. and U. Reyle. 1993. *From Discourse to Logic*. Dordrecht: Kluwer Academic Press.

Kurafuji, T., M. Inoue, M.F. Matsui, T. Miyata and A. Ohtani. 2007. The Effect of Quantification in Japanese Sentence Processing: An Incremental DRT Approach. *Proceedings of the Forth International Workshop on Logic and Engineering of Natural Language Semantics (LENLS2007)*, 179-193.

Menéndez-Benito, P. 2003. Quantification and Syntactic Ambiguity: the case of *Every*. *On Semantic Processing: University of Massachusetts Occasional Paper (UMOP)*, 27, 138-166.

Portner, P. 1989. Processing Indefinite Noun Phrases in Quantified Sentences. *Five College Cognitive Science Paper*, 89-3. University of Massachusetts, Amherst.

A Simple Surface Realizer for Filipino *

Ethel Ong, Stephanie Abella, Lawrence Santos, and Dennis Tiu

Center for Language Technologies, College of Computer Studies
De La Salle University, Manila, Philippines 1004
ethel.ong@delasalle.ph, stephanie.abella@yahoo.com, lawrencesantos@ymail.com, den_tiu@yahoo.com

Abstract. Surface realizers are used at the final phase of natural language text generation to convert abstract or symbolic representations of information to linguistic forms in a particular human language. Rules of grammar for the target language are applied to produce text that is syntactically, morphologically and orthographically correct. In this paper, we present the development of FilSuRe, a simple surface realizer for Filipino. We also present how the Booklat system was produced by revising the realization phase of a prototype automatic story generator system, Picture Books, to use the API library of FilSuRe in order to generate children's stories in Filipino.

Keywords: Surface realization, text generation, story generation, Filipino language.

1 Introduction

Text generation systems are computer applications that use theories of artificial intelligence and computational linguistics to automatically produce documents, reports, explanations, help messages, stories, and other kinds of texts. Such systems typically follow a basic three-stage pipeline presented by Dale and Reiter (2000) comprising of content determination, sentence planning, and surface or linguistic realization.

Surface or linguistic realization is a process whereby abstract or symbolic representations of information are transformed into readable text in a target human language. A number of systems that generate text rely on an external surface realizer during their realization phase to form syntactically and morphologically correct sentence structures. SimpleNLG (Venour and Reiter, 2007) is a popular choice as its library of Java functions provides an interface for applications to build phrases and simple sentences, and to perform inflectional morphological operations and orthography to generate grammatically correct and formatted English sentences. It is a grammar-based realizer engine that accepts canned and non-canned input representations and produces an output string in a deterministic fashion (Gatt and Reiter, 2009).

Various systems have utilized simpleNLG in the latter phase of their generation process. The automatic story generators Picture Books (Hong *et al.*, 2009; Ang *et al.*, 2011) used simpleNLG to transform text specifications in the abstract story tree into story text that can be read by young children. The learning tool for spelling and vocabulary, Pun World (Aban *et al.*, 2010), as well as the learning tool for Filipino heritage learners, SalinLahi (Cheng *et al.*, 2009) utilized simpleNLG to perform formatting on the generated feedback before the surface text is displayed in the user interface. The text generator system, Vigan (Chen *et al.*, 2008), used simpleNLG to transform internal descriptions of museum objects into surface text.

Although the functions provided by simpleNLG to produce a sentence in the target language is flexible enough to accept phrases (i.e., noun phrase, verb phrase, prepositional phrase), the structure of a Filipino sentence necessitates the need for a Filipino text realizer that can support the nuances of Filipino grammar rules, specifically those involving word order, generation of markers for nouns, and morphological rules for generating verbs in various tenses.

In this paper, we present the development of FilSuRe, a simple Filipino surface realizer that was patterned after simpleNLG. It provides a library of Java functions as an interface for applications to generate the correct markers, determiners and inflections of words to build phrases and simple sentences in the Filipino language.

The rest of this paper is organized as follows. Section 2 presents an overview of grammar constructs from the *balarila* or the official grammar of the Filipino language and how this affected the design of FilSuRe. The discussion begins with the types of sentence structures, followed by verbs, nouns, adjectives, and adverbs. Testing of the API through interfacing with an NLG application, the Booklat story generator system, is presented in Section 3. The paper ends with a summary of research findings and further work to improve the library.

2 The Development of FilSuRe

The *Filipino Surface Realizer* (FilSuRe) is a library of Java API functions patterned after simpleNLG to support the generation of simple and grammatically correct Filipino declarative sentences. The library can be utilized by NLP applications that require surface realizers in the last phase of their generation phase to produce surface text in Filipino.

Four main functions are provided in the library, namely *PandiwaSpec* to build verb phrases, *PangngalanSpec* to build noun phrases, *PangukolSpec* to build prepositional phrases, and *PangungusapSpec* to build sentences from the different phrases.

2.1 Structure of Filipino Sentences

A Filipino sentence (*pangungusap*) is comprised of two main parts, the subject (*simuno*) and the predicate (*panaguri*). These two parts gave rise to two forms of sentence structure, the common (*karaniwan*) structure where the predicate precedes the subject, and the uncommon (*di-karaniwan*) structure where the subject appears before the predicate with the structural marker ***ay*** appearing between them (De Vos, 2010).

The two sentences below for "*John ate at home*" exemplify these structures. The free-word order nature of the Filipino grammar is seen in sentences (1) and (2), where in (1) the location (*sa bahay*) precedes the actor (*si John*), while in (2) the actor precedes the location.

Karaniwan:

Kumain sa bahay si John. (1)

Kumain si John sa bahay. (2)

Di-karaniwan:

Si John ay kumain sa bahay. (3)

By default, FilSuRe generates sentences using the *karaniwan* structure. This can be explicitly modified to *di-karaniwan* during the instantiation of a new sentence (*PangungusapSpec*). A set of grammar rules composed of thematic roles dictates the structure of the sentence. During realization, the system parses the rule to identify the order and arrangement of the different parts of a sentence. There are currently 14 grammar rules, shown in Figure 1, that are specified using the notation:

VERB:1;AGTR:1;PATR:1;BENR:0;INSR:0;LOCR:0;TIMR:0;PURR:0;CAUR:0

The thematic roles are verb, agent (*AGTR*), patient (*PATR*), beneficiary (*BENR*), instrument (*INSR*), location (*LOCR*), time (*TIMR*), purpose (*PURR*), and cause (*CAUR*). The 1 or 0 in the thematic rule indicates whether that thematic role is required or optional, respectively. For example, the rule above can be used to generate sentence (4) for "*John ate an apple*". Setting the thematic roles *INSR* and *TIMR* to 1 would generate sentence (5) for "*John ate an apple using a fork last night.*"

Kumain (*VERB*) si John (*AGTR*) ng mansanas (*PATR*). (4)
Kumain (*VERB*) si John (*AGTR*) ng mansanas (*PATR*) gamit ang tinidor (*INSTR*) kagabi (*TIMR*). (5)

ruleid	thematicrule
0	VERB:1;AGTR:1;PATR:1;BENR:0;INSR:0;LOCR:0;TIMR:0;PURR:0;CAUR:0
1	VERB:1;PATR:1;AGTR:1;BENR:0;INSR:0;LOCR:0;TIMR:0;PURR:0;CAUR:0
2	AGTR:1;VERB:1;PATR:1;INSR:0;LOCR:0;TIMR:0;PURR:0;CAUR:0
3	VERB:1;AGTR:1;BENR:1;PATR:1;INSR:0;LOCR:0;TIMR:0;PURR:0;CAUR:0
4	VERB:1;PATR:1;AGTR:1;BENR:1;INSR:0;LOCR:0;TIMR:0;PURR:0;CAUR:0
5	BENR:1;VERB:1;AGTR:1;PATR:1;INSR:0;LOCR:0;TIMR:0;PURR:0;CAUR:0
6	VERB:1;AGTR:1;INSR:1;PATR:1;LOCR:0;TIMR:0;PURR:0;CAUR:0
7	VERB:1;PATR:1;AGTR:1;INSR:1;LOCR:0;TIMR:0;PURR:0;CAUR:0
8	INSR:1;VERB:1;AGTR:1;PATR:1;LOCR:0;TIMR:0;PURR:0;CAUR:0
9	VERB:1;AGTR:1;PATR:0;INSR:0;LOCR:1;TIMR:0;PURR:0;CAUR:0
10	VERB:1;LOCR:1;AGTR:1;PATR:0;INSR:0;TIMR:0;PURR:0;CAUR:0
11	AGTR:1;VERB:1;PATR:0;INSR:0;LOCR:1;TIMR:0;PURR:0;CAUR:0
12	VERB:1;AGTR:1;CAUR:1
13	CAUR:1;VERB:1;AGTR:1

Figure 1: Existing Filipino grammar rules defined in FilSuRe.

2.2 Filipino Verbs

Affixes are used in Filipino verbs (*pandiwa*) to reflect their tenses. Table 1 shows some affixes and the resulting inflected verbs.

Table 1: Examples of Filipino verbs and their inflections.

Past Tense	**-um**	**Um**inom (Drank)	K**um**ain (Ate)
	mag-	**Nag**-ayos (Fixed)	**Nag**luto (Cooked)
	-in	**In**ayos (Fixed)	K**in**ain (Ate)
Present Tense	**-um**	**Umi**inom	**Kuma**kain
	mag-	**Nag-a**ayos	**Naglu**luto
	-in	**Ina**ayos	**Kina**kain
Future Tense		**I**inom	**Ka**kain
	mag-	**Mag-a**ayos	**Maglu**luto
	-in	**A**ayus**in**	**Ka**kain**in**

The affixes are dependent on the focus of the verb that differentiates the grammatical role of the subject of the sentence. These grammatical roles include the actor, object, location, benefactor, instrument and cause. Verbs with the affixes ***um*** and ***mag***, for example, reflect the actor focus or the doer of the action, as exemplified in sentences (6) to (9). In the morphological rules of Filipino, ***mag*** becomes ***nag***, as the case in (8), for present tense. The first syllable of the root word is repeated for present and future tenses, as shown in (8) and (9).

Uminom si Jose ng gatas. (Jose drank milk.) (6)
K**um**ain si Maria ng mangga. (Maria ate a mango.) (7)
Si Juan ay **nag-a**ayos ng kotse. (Juan is fixing a car.) (8)
Magluluto si Linda ng isda. (Linda will cook fish.) (9)

Verbs with the affix ***in*** reflect the object focus or the target of the action, for example, in sentences (10) to (12).

Inayos ni Juan ang kotse. (The car was fixed by Juan.) (10)
Kinakain ni Linda ang isda. (The fish is being eaten by Linda.) (11)
Aayus**in** ni Jose ang pintuan bukas. (The door will be fixed by Jose tomorrow.) (12)

The affix ***in*** is also used to reflect the benefactive focus or the recipient of the action in (13).

B**in**igyan ni Juan ng kendi si Maria. (Maria was given a candy by Juan.) (13)

To be able to generate the correct inflection of a verb, FilSuRe maintains a lexicon of verbs in their root form. Each verb entry is associated with the aspect/tense, focus, corresponding affixes (prefix, infix and suffix), and valid grammar rules to generate sentences in the *karaniwan* and *di-karaniwan* structures. The lexicon currently has 84 unique verbs and 865 total verb inflections. To generate an inflection, the affixes are retrieved and concatenated to the root word based on grammar rules for verbs. Table 2 shows sample entries for the verb *alam* (know).

Table 2: Sample entries in the verb lexicon of FilSuRe.

wordID	rootWord	aspect	focus	prefix	infix	suffix	karaniwanrule	dikaraniwanrule
1	alam	COM	ACTF	naka			0;1;2	3;4
2	alam	COM	BENF	ipina			5;6;7	
5	alam	PRO	ACTF	naka			0;1;2	3;4
6	alam	PRO	BENF	ipina			5;6;7	
9	alam	CON	ACTF	maka			0;1;2	3;4
10	alam	CON	BENF	ipa			5;6;7	

2.3 Filipino Nouns

To create a noun phrase using the *PangngalanSpec* class, the following parameters are needed – the noun itself, its thematic role, classification (i.e., proper or common), grammatical number (singular or plural), and marker type. The classification of the noun must be explicitly specified because FilSuRe does not maintain a database of proper nouns nor does it utilize an external named entity recognizer.

Table 3: ANG, **NG**, and **SA** markers.

	ANG markers	NG markers	SA markers
Singular-Proper	**Si** Jose (Jose)	Aso **ni** Jose (Jose's dog)	Ibinigay **kay** Jose (Gave to Jose)
Singular-Common	**Ang** bata (The child)	Aso **ng** bata (The child's dog)	Ibinigay **sa** bata (Gave to the child)
Plural-Proper	**Sina** Jose at Maria (Jose and Maria)	Pagkain **nina** Jose at Maria (Jose and Maria's food)	Para **kina** Jose at Maria (For Jose and Maria)
Plural-Common	**Ang mga** bata (The children)	Pagkain **ng mga** bata (The children's food)	Para **sa mga** bata (For the children)

There are three groups of markers or determiners (*pantukoy*) in the Filipino language – *ang*, *ng*, and *sa*. They are further classified according to the number and the commonality of the nouns they are describing. ***Ang*** markers (*si/sina, ang/ang mga*) introduce the subject of the sentence. ***Ng*** markers (*ni/nina, ng/ng mga*) show possession of an item by the subject. ***Sa*** markers (*kay/kina, sa/sa mga*) show the target of verbs as well as possession of objects. Table 3 summarizes and provides sample usage of these markers. The marker "***mga***" is the common approach to specifying plural nouns, such as *ang* ***mga*** *bata* (the children).

Markers are generated automatically based on the noun classification, marker type, thematic role, verb focus, and grammatical number, as shown in Table 4.

Table 4: Marker type based on the thematic role and the verb focus.

Thematic Role	Verb Focus	Marker Type
Agent	Actor, Locative	Ang
	Benefactive, Causative, Instrument, Object	Ng
Patient	Actor, Locative, Benefactive	Ng
	Object	Ang
	Instrument	Sa
Beneficiary	Benefactive	Ang
	Actor	Sa

2.4 Filipino Adjectives

An adjective (*pang-uri*) is connected to the word it describes with the use of the connectives (*pang-angkop*) ***na***, ***–g***, or ***ng***. The adjective may precede or succeed the word it describes. The *pang-angkop* ***na*** is used if the first word ends with a consonant other than *n*, such as *mag-aaral na matalino* (student who is smart) and *malinis na paligid* (clean surroundings). The *pang-angkop* ***–g*** is used if the first word ends with *n*, such as *baya**ng** maunlad* (nation that is progressive) and *mayama**ng** kultura* (rich culture). The *pang-angkop* ***–ng*** is used if the first word ends with a vowel, such as *matalino**ng** mag-aaral* (intelligent student) and *mangga**ng** maasim* (mango that is sour).

If a noun phrase has two or more adjectives, FilSuRe adds a comma after every adjective, inserts the connective "***at***" (and) before the last adjective, and applies the rule above on the last adjective that immediately precedes the noun, for example, *masipag, magalang, at masunurin**g** anak* (hardworking, respectful, and obedient child).

If there is an adjective of type *pamilang* (number), then it is placed before all the *panlarawan* (descriptive) adjectives, for example, ***limang*** *magalang na bata* (five respectful kids).

Adverbs (*pang-abay*) are concatenated before the verb they describe using a similar set of rules, except for the pang-angkop ***na*** which is not needed if the adverb ends with a consonant, e.g., *mabilis tumakbo* (ran fast); *mahilig maglaro* (likes to play).

3 Using FilSuRe in an NLG Application

To test the API library of FilSuRe, Booklat, a Filipino version of the Picture Books (Hong *et al.*, 2009) story generator system, was developed. Specifically, the realization phase of Picture Books was revised to use FilSuRe as its surface realizer instead of simpleNLG, in order to generate story text in the Filipino language. All other aspects of Picture Books, namely the picture editor for specifying the story elements, the story planner, and the semantic ontology of commonsense knowledge on storytelling were retained. The story planner generates a story plan in the form of an abstract story tree that is forwarded to the surface realizer.

The abstract story tree contains a collection of character goals representing the sequence of actions and events that occur in the story to be generated (Ong, 2010). A character goal represented below comprises the action (verb), an agent and a patient (some characters in the story), an instrument and a target (some objects used in the story). This representation is easily transformed into a declarative sentence.

CGid(Action:<verb>, Agens:<char>, Patiens:<char>, Target:<obj>, Instrument:<obj>)

The transformation is straightforward. A *PandiwaSpec* object is instantiated for each character goal in the story tree. Inputs to *PandiwaSpec* come from the action attribute of a character goal which provides the root word of the verb. The focus of the verb is taken from the character goal type. All verbs in Picture Books are in past tense; Booklat retains this convention.

The agent and the patient attributes of a character goal are used as inputs to create noun phrases using the *PangngalanSpec* class. This includes pronouns, which were generated by Picture Books' referring expression generator during realization. A mapping of English to Filipino pronouns is used in Booklat.

3.1 Inflection of Verbs

Because Picture Books was designed to specifically use simpleNLG, its character goal is not associated with the focus of the verb. The focus does not affect the inflection of verbs in the English grammar. To compensate for this requirement in Booklat, the default focus was assigned to *actor*, since most sentences in a Picture Books-generated story is declarative in nature where a character performs an action (e.g., "*Rizzy broke the lamp*") or feels an emotion (e.g., "*Rizzy was scared*"). A special case is sentence (14) which was initially generated as sentence (15) to reflect an actor focus. But the more natural way of stating this is in (16) using the benefactive focus.

Mommy Hannah told Roy to brush teeth. (14)
Nagsabi si Nanay Hannah kay Roy na magsipilyo ng ngipin. (15)
Sinabi ni Nanay Hannah kay Roy na magsipilyo ng ngipin. (16)

It was determined that the type of the character goal can be used to dictate the focus. Table 5 shows the assigned focus for each of type of character goals and the sample sentences/verb inflections in Filipino.

Table 5: Types of character goals and the assigned focus.

Character Goal Type	Focus	Sample Filipino Story Text
Character does something	Actor	Kumain si Roy ng matamis (Roy ate sweets)
Character does not do	Actor	Hindi siya nagsipilyo ng ngipin (He did not brush teeth)
Character wants	Actor	Gusto niya na magsipilyo ng ngipin (Roy wanted to brush teeth)
Character continues doing something	Actor (incorrect)	**Tumuloy** si Roy sa pagkain ng matamis (Roy continued to eat sweets)
	Object (correct)	**Tinuloy** ni Roy na kumain ng matamis
Secondary character talks to main character	Actor (incorrect)	**Nagsabi** si Mommy Hannah kay Roy na ...
	Benefactive (correct)	**Sinabi** ni Mommy Hannah kay Roy na ...

3.2 Lexical Choices

The literal translation of parameters in a character goal as inputs to the different phrases of FilSuRe's API resulted in incorrectly sounding sentences. For example, sentence (17) is generated as (18), which, although syntactically and semantically correct, is not the common and natural way of saying this. Sentence (19) is a better way of expressing what a character is feeling. The same is true for other similar sentences shown in (20) and (21).

He felt hurt. (17)

Nakaramdam siya ng sakit. (18)
Nasaktan siya. (19)
Nakaramdam siya ng pagod. ➔ Napagod siya. (He felt tired.) (20)
Nakaramdam siya ng takot. ➔ Natakot siya. (He felt scared.) (21)

3.3 Prepositional Phrases

FilSuRe provides a *PangukolSpec* class that can be used to create prepositional phrases. A prepositional phrase is specified in the *target* attribute of a character goal. However, the *target* attribute is also used to specify the object of the verb, in which case a *PangngalanSpec* is instantiated for the noun phrase. The comparative character goals are shown in Table 6.

Table 6: Character goals with values for the *target* attribute.

Character Goal	Picture Books	Booklat	Picture Books	Booklat
Action	Saw	kita	told	sabi
Agent	she	siya	Mommy Hannah	Nanay Hannah
Patient	null	null	Roy	Roy
Instrument	null	null	null	null
Target	delicious cake	masarap cake	to stay	diyan lang
Target Type	Object	Object	Preposition	Preposition

The prepositions in the *target* attribute of character goals use command verbs. In English, these verbs are set without any inflections. However, in Filipino, infinitive verbs may require inflections. FilSuRe currently only covers verbs that are used in generating declarative sentences. It cannot handle the generation of imperative sentences yet.

3.4 Sentence Structure

Sentences are realized using the *PangungusapSpec* after taking the *PandiwaSpec*, *PangnglanSpec* and *PangukolSpec*. The *di-karaniwan* structure is used if the target sentence is any one of the following – story title, setting (day and place where the story takes place), or statement of the rule (or lesson). Examples of these are shown in Table 7. All other character goal types will be realized following the *karaniwan* structure.

Table 7: Comparative examples of sentences depicting the title, setting and lesson of the story.

Type	Picture Books Sentence	Booklat Sentence
Title	Roy the chicken learns to brush teeth	Si Roy na manok ay natuto na magsipilyo ng ngipin
Setting	The morning was warm.	Ang umaga ay maalinsangan.
	Roy the chicken was in the dining room.	Si Roy na manok ay nasa silid-kainan.
Lesson	Brushing teeth is fun.	Ito ay Masaya.
	Afterwards, Roy always brushed teeth.	Mula sa araw na iyon, siya ay lagi nagsipilyo ng ngipin.

3.5 Other Issues

A Filipino linguist assessed the grammatical correctness of three Booklat stories. These stories were generated from the existing ontology of Picture Books that has been manually populated with 240 relevant concepts and 369 semantic relations, and a lexicon containing 419 words that was populated with corresponding Filipino words. The verb lexicon of FilSuRe has been manually populated with 84 unique verbs that were identified based on the lexicon of Picture Books. The total number of entries in the verb lexicon is 865 by including the different foci, aspects, affixes and sentence grammar rules. The validation of the narrative content is not of primary concern in Booklat since it retained the story planning algorithm of Picture Books.

Booklat uses an extended lexicon from Picture Books (with an added column for Filipino words). This led to the word-per-word translation during the lexicalization process, resulting in incorrect word usage (22) and missing function word (23) to connect the adjective to the noun that it describes.

Mommy Hannah told Roy to take bath. (22)
Incorrect: Sinabi ni Mommy Hannah kay Roy na kuha paliguan.
Correct: Sinabi ni Mommy Hannah kay Roy na maligo siya.

She saw the delicious cake. (23)
Incorrect: Nakita niya ang masarap keyk.
Correct: Nakita niya ang masarap na keyk.

Furthermore, an English word may have multiple counterparts in Filipino. For example, the word "*with*" can precede a person (24) or an object (25). Depending on these two contexts, the corresponding Filipino word would be "*kasama*" or "*gamit*", respectively.

He went with Mommy Hannah to the school. (24)
Pumunta siya kasama ni Mommy Hannah sa paaralan.

He ate the cake with a fork. (25)
Kinain niya ang keyk gamit ang tinidor.

4 Conclusion

We have presented an initial work on the development of a simple surface realizer for use by text generation systems to produce text in the Filipino language. A set of API functions is provided, specifically to create verb phrases, noun phrases, prepositional phrases, and sentences in the *karaniwan* and *di-karaniwan* structure.

Verb phrase generation includes the automatic inflection to produce a verb in the correct tense based on user-specified focus and aspect. This is supported by a manually-populated verb lexicon consisting of the root verb and the set of possible affixes. Grammar rules specifying the structure of Filipino sentences can also be associated to a verb in the lexicon.

Noun phrase generation includes the automatic assignment of a correct marker based on user-specified noun classification and thematic role. Inflecting nouns to reflect their number and inflecting adjectives to reflect the plurality of the nouns they describe are currently not supported and instead rely on user inputs.

The accurate realization of a Filipino sentence depends on the correctness of the data in the lexicon and also from the inputs of the user. All grammar construct rules, such as verb inflection, marker generation for nouns, connective generation for adjectives, are currently programmed into FilSuRe. Future work should explore the use of Finite State Morphology (FSM) to allow for greater flexibility and increased performance.

To test the API, the realization phase of the Picture Books automatic story generation system was modified to make calls to FilSuRe instead of simpleNLG. A major problem encountered in the integration is related to insufficient inputs needed by the different API, which are not available in the abstract story tree provided by the story planner to the realization module. Specifically, these are the parameters needed to generate the correct verb inflection. This was addressed by annotating each character goal type with the correct focus, and fixing the aspect to past tense, the way most children's stories are usually written.

The presence of multiple Filipino lexical choices for a single English word also presented a problem. As in the previous case, this was addressed in the realization phase of Booklat.

A final concern that occurred during the lexicalization process was more of a design decision to extend the lexicon of Picture Books by simply adding a column for the corresponding Filipino word. Future work on Booklat should explore the use of Picture Books' semantic ontology to associate concepts directly with Filipino words.

Because children's stories and other text generation systems may require different kinds of sentences, FilSuRe should be extended to support the generation of imperative, interrogative, and exclamatory sentences.

References

Aban, V.R., T.J. Fernandez, M.C. Pascual and E. Ong. 2010. Exploring Puns for Spelling and Vocabulary Enrichment. *Proceedings of the 7th National Natural Language Processing Research Symposium*, pp. 27-32, Manila, Philippines.

Ang, K., J. Antonio, D. Sanchez, S. Yu and E. Ong. 2011. The Automatic Generation of Children's Stories from a Multi-Scene Input Picture. *Philippine Computing Journal*, 5(2), 30-36, December 2010, Computing Society of the Philippines.

Chen, H.W., M.G. Lim, P.B. Perez, J.P. Reyes and N.R. Lim. 2008. Natural Language Generation of Object Descriptions Based on User Model. *Proceedings of the 22nd Pacific Asia Conference on Language, Information, and Computation*, Cebu, Philippines.

Cheng, C.K., M.R. Antay, M. Jumarang, R.V. Regalado and L.M. Fernandez. 2010. SalinLahi: A Web-Based Interactive Learning Environment for the Filipino Language. *Proceedings of the First International Conference on Heritage / Community languages*. Los Angeles, USA.

De Vos, F. 2010. Essential Tagalog Grammar: A Reference for Learners of Tagalog. https://learningtagalog.com/grammar/index.html.

Dale, R. and E. Reiter. 2000. *Building Natural Language Generation Systems*. UK: Cambridge University Press.

Gatt, A. and E. Reiter. 2009. SimpleNLG: A Realisation Engine for Practical Applications. Morristown, NJ, USA: Association for Computational Linguistics.

Hong, A.J., C.J. Solis, J.T. Siy, E. Tabirao and E. Ong. 2009. Planning Author and Character Goals for Story Generation. *Proceedings of the NAACL Human Language Technology 2009 Workshop on Computational Approaches to Linguistic Creativity*, pp. 63-70, Colorado, USA.

Ong, E. 2010. A Commonsense Knowledge Base for Generating Children's Stories. *Proceedings of the 2010 AAAI Fall Symposium Series on Common Sense Knowledge*, pp. 82-87, Virginia, USA.

Venour, C. and E. Reiter. 2008. Tutorial for SimpleNLG (version 3.7). http://www.csd.abdn.ac.uk/~ereiter/simplenlg/.

Measuring Concept Concreteness from the Lexicographic Perspective *

Oi Yee Kwong

Department of Chinese, Translation and Linguistics, City University of Hong Kong,
Tat Chee Avenue, Kowloon, Hong Kong
Olivia.Kwong@cityu.edu.hk

Abstract. The distinction between concrete and abstract concepts is psychologically valid but so far it can hardly be quantified in any objective way, which prevents it from being further studied in computational linguistics. This paper proposes a systematic way to measure concreteness from the surface structure of dictionary definitions. Comparing the scores from WordNet definitions with human ratings, the method apparently works better for concrete senses than abstract ones, and is not adequate for measuring concreteness on a finer scale beyond the simple dichotomous distinction. Future work thus includes exploring the possibility of deploying a wider range of surface clues from definitions for the purpose and investigating how the method works with definitions from different dictionaries.

Keywords: Concept concreteness, Dictionary definitions, Lexicography, Word senses.

1 Introduction

Most people might find it more than normal that concrete concepts are easier to understand and learn than abstract concepts. Such common sense is supported by ample psychological evidence from lexical decision tasks and children's spoken and reading vocabulary (e.g. Bleasdale, 1987; Kroll and Merves, 1986; Yore and Ollila, 1985). However, few studies have addressed how this apparently trivial observation might imply on the mental storage and organisation of words and their meanings, and whether modelling such distinction between concrete and abstract concepts in computational semantic lexicons might benefit natural language processing tasks like automatic word sense disambiguation. For example, how can concreteness be included in common ontological organisation of semantic lexicons? If concrete concepts are easier for people than abstract ones, should we expect concrete senses to be more easily disambiguated than abstract senses? If this is the case, should we take it into account when evaluating disambiguation performance, perhaps in addition to the similarity among senses (e.g. Resnik and Yarowsky, 1999; Palmer *et al.*, 2006)? Should different information be employed for disambiguating concrete and abstract senses?

One major obstacle to this kind of study is the subjectivity in deciding what is concrete and what is abstract, which is a matter of degree and confounded by many factors. In psychology studies, concreteness (or abstractness) has often been measured by averaging human ratings on a sample of words. Human raters give a score for each word on a scale (e.g. from 1 for highly abstract to 7 for highly concrete), often based on various factors like the familiarity and imageability of the concepts, and frequency of occurrence, but more heavily on their own

* The work described in this paper was supported by grants from the Research Grants Council of the Hong Kong Special Administrative Region, China (Project No. CityU 1508/06H) and the Department of Chinese, Translation and Linguistics of the City University of Hong Kong.

experience and probably private cognition. This way of measuring concreteness is limited in scalability. In addition, ratings on word samples do not say anything on the effect of polysemy. A concrete word may also have some abstract senses, and vice versa, and the raters may not be thinking of the same sense when rating a word.

Only if we can have a way to objectively measure concreteness will it be possible for us to pursue further studies on the role of such intrinsic nature of word senses in lexical resources and natural language processing. In the current study, we investigate the feasibility of obtaining such a measure from dictionary definitions. The surface linguistic structure of a given definition is analysed and mapped to a concreteness score, and the results are compared to human ratings.

In Section 2, we will explain the rationale underlying our approach. The experiment and results will be discussed in Section 3, followed by a conclusion with future directions in Section 4.

2 Our Approach

The way we propose to measure concreteness is based on a simple intuition. Dictionaries constitute an important source of our lexical knowledge. Language learners often form their perception and understanding of words from dictionary definitions. Professional lexicographers are trained to write definitions informatively and consistently, and it is generally assumed in lexicography that concepts corresponding to tangible objects or intangible things are more appropriately defined by different styles. Dictionary definitions thus reflect how lexicographers (who are also human beings) perceive the concepts being defined.

2.1 Definition Styles

The way in which definitions are structured and phrased has undergone considerable evolution in modern lexicography, from "lexicographese" to full-sentence definitions (Atkins and Rundell, 2008). Traditional models tend to explain words through relatively short and concise definitions, in different defining styles, as summarised in Jackson (2002). Examples for various defining styles are shown in Table 1.

Table 1: Examples for Different Defining Styles

Defining Style	Example
Genus + Differentiae	**[bag]** a flexible container (genus) with a single opening (differentiae)
Synonymous Phrase	**[carbon]** carbon paper
Prototype	**[car]** a motor vehicle with four wheels; usually propelled by an internal combustion engine (prototype)
Usage	**[baby]** sometimes used as a term of address for attractive young women
Full-Sentence Definition	**[audience]** The audience at a play, concert, film, or public meeting is the group of people watching or listening to it.

A common way to define a concept is by means of genus (superordinate concept) and differentiae (distinctive features), such as "bag" is defined as a kind of "container" distinguished from other containers by being flexible and having a single opening. For words which are not easy to be defined by a genus term, the definition is often composed with a synonym, a collection of synonyms, or a synonymous phrase. Sometimes it may not be easy to isolate the sufficient and necessary conditions for a sense, and lexicographers will capture the essential constituents in the form of prototype. This is usually combined with genus and differentiae but additionally specifies what is typical of a referent with words like "typically" or "usually". For the rest, where a referent is unlikely to be available, meanings will be explained through their usage in real text. While tangible objects and physical actions are more easily defined with genus, differentiae and prototype, abstract concepts as well as other aspects of meanings like connotation and collocations often need to be defined by other means. Full-sentence definitions, on the other hand, use more natural prose and often embed the word being defined in its typical syntactico-collocational context in the definition (Hanks, 1987). Although this style has been thoroughly used by the COBUILD series of dictionaries, it has not really dominated the dictionary market as anticipated but continues to co-exist with most conventional defining styles in many other dictionaries. In the current study, we focus on the surface structure of the various traditional defining styles for clues on concreteness.

2.2 Scoring Definitions by Surface Structure

Computational linguists have made use of dictionary definitions to semi-automatically acquire simple ontologies for nouns (e.g. Chodorow *et al.*, 1985; Vossen *et al.*, 1989). For instance, apart from real genus, Vossen *et al.* (1989) have also observed other pseudo genus like empty kernels (e.g. a kind of …) and those shifting the definition to some non-NPs (e.g. a manner of speaking …), which they called linkers and shunters respectively in the LINKS Project.

In this study, we also exploit the regularity exhibited in definitions to reveal how concreteness is perceived in the eyes of lexicographers. Based on extensive observation and analysis of dictionary definitions, we started with the definition patterns roughly outlined in Kwong (2008) and fine-tuned them with respect to the outputs given by a dependency parser, and implemented a scoring system which analyses the surface structure of a definition. The basic assumption is that the more concrete a concept, the more conveniently and convincingly it can be explained with reference to its superordinate concept and distinguishing features. Scores are thus assigned according to the presence or absence of various surface structures. Figure 1 roughly maps various patterns to a 7-point scale of concreteness.

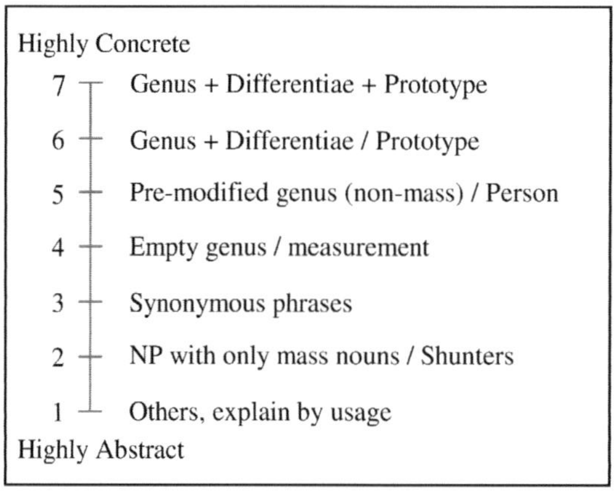

Figure 1: Mapping Definition Patterns to 7-Point Scale

To analyse the structure of the definitions, we make use of the dependency parser from Lund University (Johansson and Nugues, 2008) and detect the various definition patterns by means of the presence or absence of certain dependency relations obtained from the parse results. Only those parses consisting of a root (ROOT) and a predicative complement (PRD) in the form of a noun will be of interest to us. Any of the following dependency relations on the PRD would be considered differentiae: Apposition (APPO), Location (LOC), Modifier of nominal (NMOD), Object complement (OPRD), and Temporal (TMP). If any of such relations has a dependency from words like "usually", "often", "typically", etc., it would be considered a prototype.

The automatic scoring is thus done this way: Given the dependency parse of a definition (such as "car is a motor vehicle ..."), we first look for the ROOT (usually "is") and its dependent PRD. If a PRD as a noun is found, it is treated as the genus and an NP definition is assumed to be identified and further processed. Subsequent analysis of an NP definition includes detecting genitives like "X of Y", checking for differentiae in the form of dependent APPO, LOC, NMOD, OPRD, or TMP to the PRD, and prototypes if such dependencies are marked by words like "usually" or "typically". If no differentiae, prototype, or pre-modifier is present, the definition will be considered a synonymous phrase. The genus is also checked if it is possibly an abstract or mass noun, which is currently approximated by the absence of any indefinite articles and plural markers. The scoring flow is summarised in Figure 2 in the form of pseudocodes with examples.

```
Let Genus X = noun at PRD
Let Score = 4
if (X...of...Y) is found, then
   if X ∈ {kind, type, etc.} and Y is mass, then Score=Score-1          // e.g. a kind of commercial enterprise ...
   else if X ∈ {group, part, etc.} and Y is mass, then Score=Score-1    // e.g. a series of related events ...
   else if Y is –ing verb, then Score=Score -2                          // e.g. the manner of speaking to ...
   else {if X is mass, Score=Score-1; if Y is mass, Score=Score-1}      // e.g. the content of cognition ...
   stop
if X ∈ {person, someone, anyone, etc.}, then Score=Score+1, stop        // e.g. someone who controls resources ...
if X ∈ {something, somewhere, etc.}, then stop                          // e.g. something intended as a guide ...
if ∃ Dependency D ∈ {NMOD, APPO, LOC, TMP, OPRD} ←X at any             // prototype
   word after X and D is preceded by {usually, typically, often,etc.},     e.g. ... usually used for drinking
   then Score=Score+1
if ∃ Dependency D ∈ {NMOD, APPO, LOC, TMP, OPRD} ← X at any            // differentiae
   word after X, then Score=Score+1                                        e.g. [a motor vehicle] with four wheels
if no prototype and no differentiae is found and X is mass,             // synonymous phrase with mass noun,
   then Score = Score -1                                                   e.g. brilliant radiant beauty
else if ∃ Dependency D ∈ {NMOD}← X at any word before X,               // pre-modifiers,
   then Score=Score+1                                                      e.g. a very young mammal
if no prototype and no differentiae and no pre-modifier,                // minimal NP treated as synonym
   then Score=Score-1                                                      e.g. an idea
```

Figure 2: The Scoring Flow

3 Experiment

In the current study, we first used the Lund University dependency parser[1] to parse dictionary definitions, then analysed the parse output according to the above scoring method and compared the results with human ratings.

3.1 Data sources

Kroll and Merves (1986) used 100 abstract and 100 concrete nouns in their lexical study. The words were rated by human subjects for concreteness on a 7-point scale. The abstract and concrete words were matched on the basis of word frequency and word length. The word frequency data were taken from Kucera and Francis (1967). For the current study, a total of 100 word samples (50 concrete and 50 abstract) with frequency greater than 20 were selected from Kroll and Merves' list. The more frequent items were selected so that they would more likely be familiar to our human raters. Sense definitions were collected from WordNet 3.0[2]. WordNet started off as a psycholinguistic project for studying human lexical memory but it turns out to be a large lexical database of English widely used in computational linguistics. It

[1] Downloaded from http://nlp.cs.lth.se/lt_home/

[2] http://wordnet.princeton.edu

contains individual databases for nouns, verbs, adjectives and adverbs. Word senses are grouped as sets of synonyms (i.e., synsets). The synsets are hierarchically organised and linked by relational pointers indicating various kinds of lexical relations such as hyponymy, meronymy, etc. in the noun hierarchy (Fellbaum, 1998). Each synset is associated with a simple gloss like conventional dictionary definitions. For our word samples, the concrete words have 1 to 17 senses and the abstract words have 1 to 9 senses, with 4.36 and 3.44 senses on average respectively.

3.2 Procedures

In addition to the average human ratings available from Kroll and Merves (1986), four human judges were asked to rate the selected samples on a 7-point scale (with 7 for highly concrete and 1 for highly abstract). They were asked to first rate each given word as a whole, and then give a score for individual senses of the words.

The WordNet definitions were first made complete sentences by adding the headword as subject such as "car is a motor vehicle …", and then parsed. The parsing results were analysed by a program implementing the scoring method above, giving a score for each definition and a detailed log for the analysis.

The scores for individual senses were compared to the human ratings we obtained for this study. For the overall concreteness of a word, we tried two ways for estimating it from the individual senses. One is to take the average of the scores from all senses (AvgDef), assuming all component senses of a word contribute equally to its overall concreteness; and the other is to take the score for the first sense (FirstDef), assuming the most frequent or familiar sense dominates one's perception of the word in general. These two measures were compared with the original ratings in Kroll and Merves' study and the ratings of the human raters in this study.

3.3 Results and Discussion

We had assumed the validity of the concrete/abstract distinction from psycholinguistic evidence to start with, and aimed to investigate whether such a distinction would be similarly reflected in dictionary definitions through various defining styles. It is thus important to see if the two groups of words will result in significantly different scores as estimated by different ways (e.g. AvgDef and FirstDef) for the word-level concreteness.

Table 2 shows the mean and standard deviation of the concreteness ratings for the 100 word samples (and for the 50 abstract and 50 concrete samples separately) obtained from human raters and WordNet definitions. The column K&M refers to the original rating from Kroll and Merves (1986). AvgR refers to the average of the four human raters in the current study. AvgDef and FirstDef refer to the scores obtained by the two ways respectively from WordNet definitions.

Table 2: Summary of Concreteness Ratings at Word Level

	K&M	AvgR	AvgDef	FirstDef
All Word Samples (N=100)				
Mean	4.27	4.58	4.34	4.36
SD	1.76	1.79	0.92	1.37
Abstract samples (N=50)				
Mean	2.63	2.96	4.11	3.88
SD	0.58	0.73	1.03	1.47
Concrete samples (N=50)				
Mean	5.92	6.19	4.58	4.84
SD	0.63	0.77	0.74	1.08

The distinction between the two groups of words is particularly clear from the human ratings. With K&M, which is our data source, the abstract samples have a mean rating of 2.63 with standard deviation of 0.58, and the concrete samples have a mean rating of 5.92 with standard deviation of 0.63. A similarly apparent distinction is also seen in AvgR, with mean at 2.96 and standard deviation at 0.73 for the abstract words, and mean at 6.19 and standard deviation at 0.77 for concrete words. Interestingly, the human raters in this study seem to be more lenient in their scores than those in K&M, as shown by the higher mean ratings for AvgR in Table 2 and the distribution of ratings shown in the bar charts in Figure 3. The variation might be related to the small number of human raters in this study and the difference between native and non-native speakers. Nevertheless, the distinction between concrete and abstract words is apparent among human raters.

The difference between the mean scores for abstract words and concrete words is much smaller with the estimation from definition scores. The mean is above 3 for abstract words, and below 5 for concrete words, with both AvgDef and FirstDef. The Mann-Whitney rank test shows that the difference between the means for abstract words and concrete words is statistically significant for both cases. The dispersion of scores for AvgDef and FirstDef is shown in the line charts in Figure 3. There is obviously a mode at 5 for concrete words, and the majority did fall on the high side above 4. The scores estimated from WordNet definitions by FirstDef are roughly bi-modal for the abstract words, while those by AvgDef are somehow averaged out giving a mode at 4. This suggests that words deemed abstract also possess considerable concrete senses, and the first senses of about half of the abstract words are not necessarily abstract or are not defined as if they are abstract in WordNet.

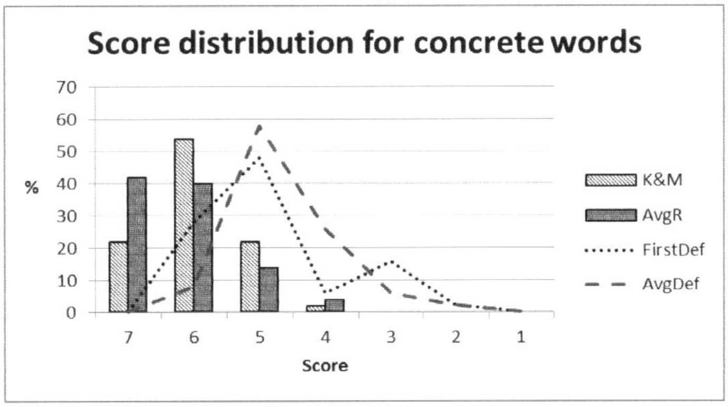

(a)

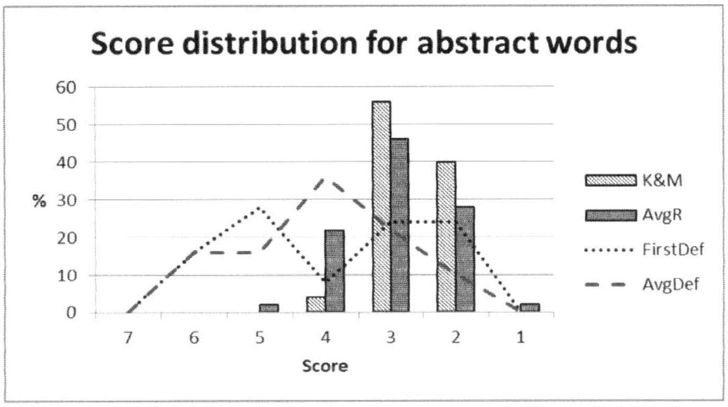

(b)

Figure 3: Score Distribution for (a) Concrete Words and (b) Abstract Words

Table 3 shows the Spearman rank correlation (ρ) and the Kendall's coefficient of concordance (W) between the two sets of human ratings and those between the human ratings and definition scores on all word samples. The former measures the interdependence between two sets of scores and the latter is used for assessing the agreement among raters, or the different rating sources in this study. Values which are statistically significant at least at the 0.05 level are indicated in bold. The human ratings in K&M and those in the current study (AvgR) are quite strongly correlated (ρ=0.848), and the overall ranking is very much similar (W=0.924). The strong agreement among human raters provides evidence that a gradient of concreteness is shared in human cognition.

Comparing with the definition scores, it turns out that the first sense of a word in WordNet is a relatively better indicator of the overall word concreteness than the average of all senses. FirstDef shows better correlation with human ratings (0.301 with K&M and 0.415 with AvgR, both are statistically significant). It suggests that sense frequency might play a very important if not predominant role in one's perception of the concreteness of a word in general, given that the most frequent sense is listed as the first sense in WordNet. However, as seen in Figure 3, FirstDef still has a wider and more even spread of scores across the scale, especially for abstract words. Hence words deemed concrete may more likely have a concrete first sense, while words deemed abstract may also have frequently used concrete senses. Alternatively, many abstract words (and their first senses) might be unexpectedly describable in the lexicographers' minds.

Table 3: Degree of Association between Word Concreteness Ratings from Various Sources

	AvgR	**AvgDef**	**FirstDef**
Spearman Rank Correlation (ρ)			
K&M	**0.848**	0.193	**0.301**
AvgR	--	**0.363**	**0.415**
Kendall's Coefficient of Concordance (W)			
K&M	**0.924**	0.597	**0.650**
AvgR	--	**0.681**	**0.707**

For the sense level ratings, there are 390 senses altogether, 172 are from the abstract word samples, and 218 are from the concrete word samples. Table 4 shows the mean and standard deviation of the concreteness ratings for all senses and separately for senses deemed concrete and abstract respectively by human raters. AvgR is the average rating of the four human raters in this study, and is used as a reference here since no comparable ratings at the sense level are available from previous studies. WN refers to the scores from WordNet definitions.

Table 4: Summary of Concreteness Ratings at Sense Level

	AvgR	**WN**
All Sense Samples (N=390)		
Mean	4.81	4.33
SD	1.31	1.27
Concrete Senses (AvgR≥4, N=270)		
Mean	5.51	4.47
SD	0.89	1.18
Abstract Senses (AvgR<4, N=120)		
Mean	3.24	4.03
SD	0.44	1.49

Similar to word-level concreteness, the mean of human ratings on the concreteness of individual senses is higher than those obtained from definitions. Figure 4 shows the distribution of scores estimated from the definitions, compared with the average human ratings. Apparently our categorisation of the defining styles and surface structures of the definitions has not been able to realistically distinguish concrete concepts on a finer scale (e.g. highly concrete vs mildly concrete) as naturally as human raters.

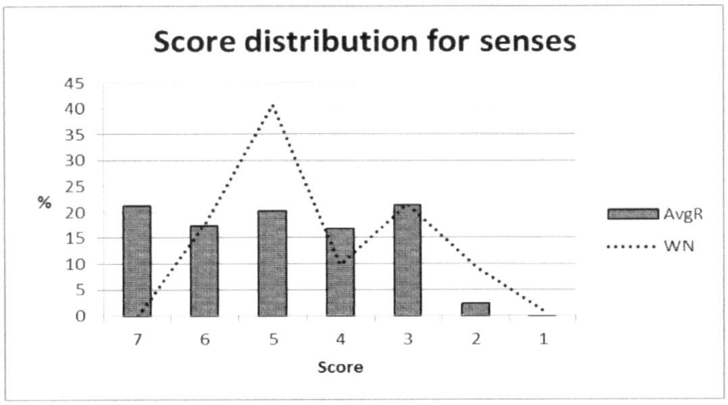

Figure 4: Score Distribution for Senses

Unlike the word level, human ratings for individual senses show less agreement. The variation is particularly apparent for the abstract concepts. For instance, one sense of "devil" is "an evil supernatural being", for which the four raters gave 5, 3, 6, and 2 respectively. The concept is obviously intangible, but individual raters might easily imagine the relevant images as found in fictions and movies. The definition, however, is one of genus and differentiae.

The association between human ratings and definition scores is also weaker at the sense level (ρ=0.257, W=0.628), though still statistically significant. Figure 4 shows a very different distribution of scores obtained from definition structures and human raters. Our categorisation of the definition styles yielded most score 5, which covers only a special kind of genus-and-differentiae definitions. Scores on the two ends of the scale are relatively rare.

Thus our results show that measuring concreteness from dictionary definitions based on the different defining styles apparently works better for concrete senses than abstract ones. Although the two groups of senses can still be told apart in general, the differentiation is not as distinct as is found in human ratings, and definition scores lack the ability to further delineate concepts of different degrees of concreteness on a finer spectrum. There are several factors which might account for this outcome. The range of surface structures we have attended to is quite narrow. On the one hand, the concise conventional defining styles may pose a limit on including further information with differentiae and prototypes. On the other hand, very common concrete concepts may not need so much detailed explanation as others in a dictionary. The assumption that different defining styles are more suitable for concrete concepts and abstract concepts is generally valid. For instance, we do find more definitions involving shunters among the abstract senses. Nevertheless, how a concept is defined may also depend on how describable the concept is, which might just be one dimension amongst others contributing to the concreteness of the concept perceived by humans. As we have observed from the data, apart from parsing errors (e.g. one definition for "dollar" is "a United States coin worth one dollar", but "coin" was tagged as VBP resulting in subsequent parsing error), abstract concepts may also be defined via genus and differentiae, and this might be even more serious with WordNet given its hierarchical organisation of the senses. For instance, the word "concept" is defined as "an abstract or general idea inferred or derived from specific instances" which scored 6 despite the word "abstract" explicitly appears in the definition. However, the

Collins COBUILD Advanced Dictionary[3] defines it as "an idea or abstract principle" which will only score 3 in our system as it is in the form of a synonym. Hence in addition to the dependency structures, there are other surface clues such as lexical choice and length of definition which may suggest on the concreteness of the concept being defined.

Our results do not only echo the subjectivity in human perception of concreteness (and in lexicographers' perception too), but also suggest the multi-dimensionality of concreteness and the importance of finding a systematic measure of this psychologically valid construct so that it can be operationalised and objectively studied in computational linguistics.

4 Conclusion

Hence we have introduced a systematic way of measuring concreteness from how lexicographers understand and explain concepts, by analysing the surface structure of definitions. This is a useful first step to enable further study of a subjective but psychologically valid factor in computational linguistics, especially the construction of semantic lexicons and evaluation for tasks like word sense disambiguation. Current results show that the method works better for concrete senses, and is in many cases able to make a dichotomous distinction between concrete and abstract concepts. However, it is possible that the different defining styles may reveal how describable a concept is, amongst the many factors influencing one's perception of concreteness, and it happens that some abstract senses might be more describable than others. Consequently our method is not adequate for distinguishing concreteness on a finer scale. Our next step is therefore to refine the analysis of definitions in order to deploy a wider range of surface clues, and to investigate how the method works with definitions from other dictionaries.

References

Atkins, B.T.S. and M. Rundell. 2008. *The Oxford Guide to Practical Lexicography.* Oxford University Press.

Bleasdale, F.A. 1987. Concreteness dependent associative priming: Separate lexical organization for concrete and abstract words. *Journal of Experimental Psychology: Learning, Memory, and Cognition, 13*:582-594.

Chodorow, M.S., R.J. Byrd and G.E. Heidorn. 1985. Extracting semantic hierarchies from a large on-line dictionary. In *Proceedings of the 23rd Annual Meeting of the Association for Computational Linguistics,* Chicago, pp.299-304.

Fellbaum, C. 1998. *WordNet: An Electronic Lexical Database.* Cambridge, MA: MIT Press.

Hanks, P. 1987. Definitions and Explanations. In J.M. Sinclair (Ed.), *Looking Up: An account of the COBUILD Project in lexical computing.* London: HarperCollins Publishers.

Jackson, H. 2002. *Lexicography: An Introduction.* London and New York: Routledge.

Johansson, R. and P. Nugues. 2008. Dependency-based Syntactic-Semantic Analysis with PropBank and NomBank. In *Proceedings of the 12th Conference on Computational Natural Language Learning (CoNLL 2008)*, Manchester, pp.183–187.

Kroll, J.F. and J.S. Merves. 1986. Lexical access for concrete and abstract words. *Journal of Experimental Psychology: Learning, Memory, and Cognition, 12*:92-107.

Kucera, H. and W.N. Francis. 1967. *Computational Analysis of Present-day American English.* Providence: Brown University Press.

Kwong, O.Y. 2008. A Preliminary Study on Inducing Lexical Concreteness from Dictionary Definitions. In *Proceedings of the 5th International Workshop on Natural Language Processing and Cognitive Science (NLPCS 2008)*, Barcelona, Spain, pp.84-93.

[3] http://mycobuild.com/homepage.aspx

Palmer, M., H.T. Ng and H.T. Dang. 2006. Evaluation of WSD Systems. In E. Agirre and P. Edmonds (Eds.), *Word Sense Disambiguation: Algorithms and Applications*. Dordrecht: Springer.

Resnik, P. and D. Yarowsky. 1999. Distinguishing systems and distinguishing senses: new evaluation methods for Word Sense Disambiguation. *Natural Language Engineering, 5(2)*:113-133.

Vossen, P., W. Meijs, and M. den Broeder. 1989. Meaning and structure in dictionary definitions. In B. Boguraev and E.J. Briscoe (Eds.), *Computational Lexicography for Natural Language Processing*. London: Longman.

Yore, L.D. and L.O. Ollila. 1985. Cognitive development, sex, and abstractness in grade one word recognition. *Journal of Educational Research, 78*:242-247.

Logical Information Processing of Possibility and Negation: Cases from Taiwanese Hakka *

Chioushing Yeh[a], and Hueiling Lai[b]

[a]Graduate Institute of Linguistics, National Chengchi University,
NO.64, Sec.2, ZhiNan Rd., Wenshan District, Taipei City 11605, Taiwan (R.O.C)
kyoko@nccu.edu.tw
[b]Department of English, National Chengchi University,
NO.64, Sec.2, ZhiNan Rd., Wenshan District, Taipei City 11605, Taiwan (R.O.C)
hllai@nccu.edu.tw

Abstract. This paper attempts to provide a refined description with a quantitative analysis about the deontic modals *zo3-ded4* (做得) and *sii2-ded4* (使得) in Taiwanese Hakka. While the affirmative-negative relationship is symmetrical structurally, it manifests in an asymmetrical manner semantically. The logic notations will be applied to clarify the intriguing interaction of possibility and negation. Under the interaction of semantic meanings and syntactic constructions, the representation of deontic modals in Taiwanese Hakka is therefore clearly elucidated.

Keywords: possibility, necessity, negation, modality, Taiwanese Hakka

1 Introduction

The application of modals reflects the attitude and viewpoint of the speakers toward the conversation. Two types of linguistic forms can be usually found, taking Taiwanese Mandarin for example. The first one is the modal auxiliary verbs such as *neng2* (能), *hui4* (會), or *ke3 yi3* (可以) as in (1) and (2). The other one is the potential construction [Verb-*de*(得)-C-O]. The negative marker *bu* (不) is used to substitute *de* (得) and turns the affirmative potential construction into a negative form [Verb- *bu*(不)-C-O] as exemplified in (3) and (4).

(1) 他能騙過你。
ta1 neng2 pian4 guo4 ni3
he able deceive across you
'He is able to deceive you successfully.'

(2) 他可以騙過你。
ta1 ke3 yi3 pian4 guo4 ni3
he able deceive across you
'He is able to deceive you successfully.'

(3) 他騙得過你。
ta1 pian4 de guo4 ni3
he deceive PM[1] across you

* This study is partly based on the NSC research project *On Hakka genericity-characterizing constructions: Lexical semantics, event frames and information structure* (NSC 100-2410-H-004-185-MY2). Special thanks extend to four anonymous reviewers. We are solely responsible for possible errors.

'He is able to deceive you successfully.'

(4) 他騙不過你。

ta1 pian4 bu guo4 ni3
he deceive NEG across you
'He is unable to deceive you successfully.'

In Taiwanese Hakka (TH), possibility can be expressed by modal verbs and the potential construction [Verb-*de*(得)-C-O] as well. The general form is *zo3-ded4* (做得) while the less frequent one is *sii2-ded4* (使得). Both cases are composed of a verb (that is, *zo3* (做) or *sii2* (使)) and *ded4* (得). The affirmative and the negative types of deontic modals in TH present an asymmetric phenomenon.

Based on the corpus data, the distribution of the linguistic forms of *zo3-ded4* (做得), *sii2- ded4* (使得), *zo3-m5-ded4* (做毋得), *sii2-m5-ded4* (使毋得), and *m5-sii2* (毋使) is presented. Among our data, 229 tokens of *zo3-ded4* (做得), 20 tokens of *sii2- ded4* (使得), 43 tokens of *zo3-m5-ded4* (做毋得), 13 tokens of *sii2-m5-ded4* (使毋得), and 118 tokens of *m5-sii2* (毋使) are collected. The data shows that *zo3-ded4* (做得) is the dominating one to express possibility or permission in deontic modality; the adoption of *zo3-m5-ded4* (做毋得) is preferred than that of *sii2-m5-ded4* (使毋得) in expressing prohibition. However, the role to denote the idea of "not necessarily" falls on *m5-sii2* (毋使) exclusively. The overall distribution is shown in Table 1:

Table 1: The distribution of Taiwanese Hakka deontic modals

	做 type	使 type	TOTAL
example Number/Percentage	做得 229 / 92%	使得 20 / 8%	249 /100%
example Number/Percentage	做毋得 43 / 77%	使毋得 13 / 23%	56 / 100%
example Number/Percentage	*毋做 0 / 0%	毋使 118 / 100%	100 / 100%

This paper therefore attempts to inspect the interaction between semantic manifestation and syntactic structure of TH modality which denotes possibility or necessity. The negation can trigger alternations of the modality or the proposition of modal sentences. In other words, the negator does not necessarily negate the meaning of the modal sentence in a corresponding manner.

The data of potential constructions and related data are mainly based on the *Hoi2liuk7* dialect[2] collected from written materials in Taiwan, including *Hakka dictionary of Taiwan* (臺灣客家話辭典), *Hakka Handbook* (客語實用手冊), various story books such as *Dungshi Hakka Storybooks* (東勢客語故事集), *Miaoli Hakka Storybooks* (苗栗縣客語故事集), *Little Prince* (客家話小王子), *The Story of Touqian River* (頭前溪个故事), *Missing under the Oil Tung Tree* (油桐花下个思念), *Hakka Jokes* (客家笑料), *Hakka magazines* (客家雜誌), and from the oral data extracted from the NCCU Corpus of Spoken Hakka (國立政治大學客語口語語料庫)[3]. The Manual of Taiwanese Hakka Romanization System (臺灣客語拼音使用手冊)

---

[1] The following abbreviations are applied for their corresponding grammatical functions: PM, a potential marker; NEG, a negative marker; PHA, a phase marker; PART, a particle; CL, a classifier; ASP, an aspect marker; and SF, a suffix.

[2] In general, five Hakka dialect varieties can be observed in Taiwan: *Si3yen3* (四縣) Hakka dialect, *Hoi2liuk7* (海陸) Hakka dialect, *Tai3pu1* (大埔) Hakka dialect, *Ngieu5ping5* (饒平) Hakka dialect, and *Seu3on1* (詔安) Hakka dialect.

[3] For more detailed discussion of the NCCU Corpus of Spoken Hakka, please refer to Chu and Lai (2008).

promulgated by the Ministry of Education in 2009 is utilized to render the data. The tone diacritics are presented as 1 for *yingping*, 2 for *yinshang*, 3 for *yinqu*, 4 for *yinru*, 5 for *yangping*, 7 for *yangqu*, and 8 for *yangru*.[4]

2 Relevant Studies on Mandarin Modality

Possibility can be expressed not only by deontic modals but also by potential constructions. Wei (2004) investigates the object position in verb-complement potential constructions in early Mandarin from a diachronic perspective. The default position of the object in Modern Chinese is after the complement in the V-C potential constructions such as *kan4 de jian4 yue4 liang4* (看得見月亮) 'be able to see the moon' and *kan4 bu jian4 yue4 liang4* (看不見月亮) 'be unable to see the moon'. However, the data in the Tang and Song dynasties shows that the object is often preposed. In Wei's analysis, the preposed object is in the "type A" construction while the object placed after the complement is in the "type B" construction. Both are illustrated in (5):

(5) Type A construction: V-得/不-C-O
Type B construction: V- O-得/不-C

In the Tang and Song dynasties, the structure of V- O-得/不-C is found in prevalence, while that of V-得/不-C-O is limitedly utilized. Nevertheless, both are developed due to the contraction of sub-clauses. Consider the following examples (Wei 2004: 671, 673):

a. Type A construction: [V-得/不-C-O]
(6) 故學者多看不見這般所在。(《朱子語類・論語十一》)
gu4 xue2zhe3 duo1 kan4 bu jian4 zhe4-ban1 suo3zai4
so scholar many see NEG see this-type place
'So the scholars are incapable to see the point mostly.'

b. Type B construction: [V-O-得/不-C]
(7) 如今趕他不上，回去了罷。(《平妖傳》二十七回)
ru2jin1 gan3 ta1 bu shang4, hui2qu1 le ba
Nowadays catch he NEG up back PART PART
'Since (we/you) can not catch him up, (let's) go back.'

In Wei's research, the complements in verb-complement potential constructions are all transitive verbs. Type A construction is contracted by two subclauses : [(S)V-Oi] ((學者)看這般所在) and [(S)不-R-Oi] ((學者)不見這般所在). In other words, the position of O is not concerned with any movement. In a similar fashion, the first subclause [V-O] (趕他) in Type B construction: [V-得/不-C-O] denotes conditions while the second subclause [不-C] (不上) signifies results. When the construction is fixed to express potentiality, the two subclauses are contracted into one sentence. In this way, the two subclauses construct a verbal phrase which specifies potentiality.

Hsieh (2006) utilizes Chinese corpus to analyze Chinese modal verbs and adverbs which denote epistemic modality, deontic modality, dynamic modality and evaluative modality, with each of them including two subsystems. The study analyzes both affirmative modals and

[4] The tone system of *Hoi2liuk7* dialect is tabled as follows:

調號(tone number)	1	2	3	4	5	7	8
調值(pitch value)	falling	rising	low level	short high	high level	mid level	short low
Example	*song* (霜)	rhi (雨)	*zi* (齋)	*siet* (雪)	*lui* (雷)	*tien* (電)	*pok* (雹)

negative ones. For instance, deontic modality encompasses affirmative ones such as *neng2* (能) 'can, be able to', *ke3 yi3* (可以) 'can', and *hao3* (好) 'can, be able to' and negative ones like *bu2 bi4* (不必) 'need not', *bu2 yong4* (不用) 'need not', *wu2 fang2* (無妨) 'may as well', *mian3* (免) 'need not', and *beng2* (甭) 'need not'. However, little discussion has been put on items that can express either affirmative or negative usages. While the deontic modal *neng2* (能) 'can, be able to' denotes possibility, its negative form *bu4 neng2* (不能) 'can't' expresses necessity instead. For instance, the sentence *ni3 bu4 neng2 tou1 ren4 he2 dong1 xi1* (你不能偷任何東西！) 'You can't steal anything!' signifies prohibition. The mismatching mapping between possibility, necessity and negation therefore is needed to be further investigated.

3 Logical Structure of Modality

In the extant framework, quite many efforts have been made regarding the classification of modality into various types and the different syntactic and semantic manifestations of these types (cf. Lyons 1977; Palmer 1979, 2001; Bybee et al. 1994; Talmy 1988, Sweetser 1991, among others).The extant knowledge has also shown that the negation of modal sentences can affect the semantic manifestation of modality. One of the famous achievements of Aristotle is the Square of opposition which provides a foundation in logic.

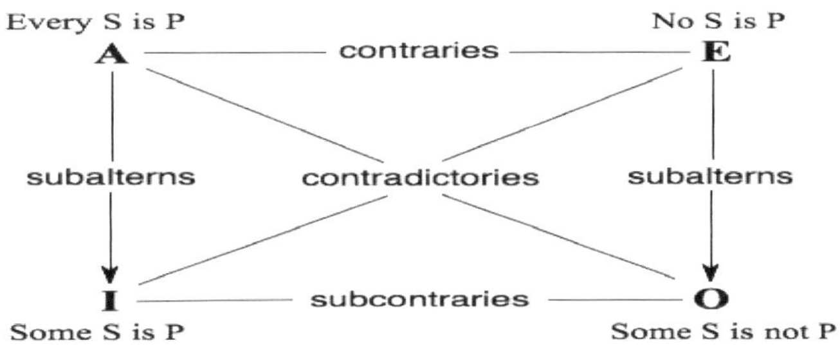

To clarify the mapping of modals onto logical structures, five sentences are given by De Haan (2005) as below. The relationship between necessity and possibility can be represented by certain logical notations, where "p" stands for proposition, "◊" for possibility, "□" for necessity, "¬" for negation, and "≡" for equivalence.

(8) a. John must be a bachelor. $\Box p$
b. John may be a bachelor. $\Diamond p$
c. John must not be a bachelor. $\Box \neg p$
d. John need not be a bachelor. $\neg \Box p$
e. John may not be a bachelor. $\Diamond \neg p$ (or $\neg \Diamond p$[5]) (De Haan 2005:53)

Radden (2007) also signifies the logical equivalent relationship between possibility, necessity and negation, as demonstrated in (9)[6]:

(9) a. poss p ≡ ~nec~ p
b. nec p ≡ ~poss~ p
c. ~poss p ≡ nec~ p
d. ~nec p ≡ poss~ p

5 Palmer (2003) claims that there is logical equivalence between "possible not" and "not necessary" (Palmer 2003:9). The logic notations of "◊¬p (or ¬◊p)" for (8e) therefore need further consideration.

6 "~" is the notation for negation (cf. "¬"(De Haan 2005)) in Radden's article.

With the four pairs of equivalence relations, the basic system of modality is provided. Following De Haan (2005) and Radden (2007), the logic concept is adopted to deal with the interrelationship between possibility and negation exemplified by Hakka deontic modals *zo3-ded4* (做得) and *sii2- ded4* (使得).

4 Possibility and Negation

In this section, we will demonstrate the interaction of possibility and negation. The two lexicalized modals *zo3-ded4* (做得) and *sii2-ded4* (使得) express possibility. The corresponding semantic logic notation is "◊p".

(10) 你愛先請假正做得走。

ngi5	*oi3*	*sen1*	*ciang2-ga2*	*zhang1*	*zo3-ded4*	*zeu2*
you	have to	first	ask-for-leave	only-then	can	leave

'You have to ask for leave first so then you are permitted to leave.'

(11) 這領衫使得送分你。

lia2	*liang1*	*sam1*	*sii2-ded4*	*sung3*	*bun1*	*ngi5*
this	CL	shirt	can	send	to	you

'(I) can send the shirt to you.'

To negate the modality, a negator is assigned before the modal verb. The negative form of "◊p" therefore is "¬◊p". Take *zo3-ded4* (做得) for example; the negative form consequently should be the combination of *m5* (毋) and *zo3-ded4* (做得) as **m5-zo3-ded4* (*毋做得). However, this is not the correct form in TH. The corresponding negative form of *zo3-ded4* (做得) is *zo3-m5-ded4* (做毋得) instead. The negative operator *m5* (毋) is infixed in the modal verb *zo3-ded4* (做得). The phenomena exhibited here can be captured by the analysis proposed by Wang (2005) on his application of reanalysis to deal with the Mandarin data of *hen4-bu4-de2* (恨不得) 'to itch to'. Reanalysis refers to a mechanism whereby the syntactic structure of a syntactic pattern is changed without changing its surface form (cf. Harris 2005). Wang (2005) proposes that the modern usage of the construction *hen4-bu4-de2* (恨不得) 'to itch to' undergoes such a reanalysis whereby a syntactic structure has become a lexicalized item. The source construction and the innovative one are shown below:

(12) a. Source construction:

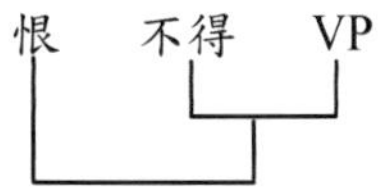

b. Innovative construction:

In other words, *hen4-bu4-de2* (恨不得) 'to itch to' experiences the process of lexicalization which is a linguistic change that "results in the production of new lexical/contentful items"(Brinton and Traugott 2005:96). By the same token, we can argue that *zo3-ded4* (做得)/*zo3-m5-ded4* (做毋得) in TH undergo the same kind of reanalysis in which lexicalized items with both affirmative and negative forms produced.

Now let us focus on the deontic modality of *zo3-ded4* (做得)/*zo3-m5-ded4* (做毋得). In TH *ded4* (得) carries deontic meaning of permission and occurs post-verbally; the case in (13) shows an affirmative potential complement construction, and that in (14), a negative one:

(13) 該條魚仔食得。
gai5 tiau5 ng5 shid8 ded4
that CL fish eat DED
'(You are) permitted to eat the fish.'

(14) 該條魚仔臭風了，食毋得。
gai5 tiau5 ng5 chiu3fung1 le1, shid8 m5 ded4
that CL fish smelly PART eat NEG DED
'(You) can't eat the fish since it is smelly.'

Ded4 (得) can also occur in the V-*de*(得)-C constructions as in (15):

(15) 佢食得/毋飽。
gi5 shid8 e[7]*/m5 bao2*
he eat PM/NEG full
'He can/cannot be full.'

It is observed that the V-*de*(得)-C constructions indicate the state of results while the potential complement constructions denote potentiality in a semantic account. The complement *bao2* (飽) 'full' here denotes a stative result. Nevertheless, the element follows the morpheme *ded4* (得) can also be an active verb as exemplified in (16):

(16) 你愛先請假正做得走。
ngi5 oi3 sen1 ciang2-ga2 zhang1 zo3-ded4 zeu2
you have to first ask-for-leave only-then can leave
'You have to ask for leave first so then you are permitted to leave.'

Following the patterns of (13) and (14), the negative form of *zo3-ded4* (做得) therefore is presented as *zo3-m5-ded4* (做毋得) instead of **m5-zo3-ded4* (*毋做得), as in (17). The linguistic performance of *zo3*(做)-type modals is shown in Table 2.

(17) 你無請假**做毋得**走。
ngi5 mo5 ciang2-ga2 zhang1 zo3-m5-ded4 zeu2
you no ask-for-leave only-then can't leave
'You can't leave without asking (for leave).'

Table 2: The linguistic performance of *zo3*(做)-type modals

	Examples	Logic notation	
		Possibility	Necessity
possible	做得(V)	◊p	
possible not	做得毋(V)	◊¬p	¬□p
not possible	*毋做得(V) 做毋得(V)	¬◊p	□¬p

The negation can affect the modality or the proposition. As introduced above, the negative forms of *zo3-ded4* (做得) and *sii2-ded4* (使得) are *zo3-m5-ded4* (做毋得) and *sii2-m5-ded4* (使毋得), respectively. While the two lexicalized negative forms are symmetrical structurally,

[7] A phonetic bleaching occurs on morpheme *ded4* (得), which pronounced as *e* (得).

the semantic interpretation of them is in diversity. The modal meanings of *zo3-m5-ded4* (做毋得) and *sii2-m5-ded4* (使毋得) are related to prohibition as in (18) and (19). The semantic logic notation therefore is "$\neg\Diamond p \equiv \Box\neg p$".

(18) 內容𠊎做毋得講出來。
nui7rhung5 ngai5 zo3-m5-ded4 gong2 chud4-loi5
content I can't speak out-come
'I can't say anything about the content.'

(19) 垃圾使毋得儘採亂丟。
la2sab4 sii2-m5-ded4 cin2cai2 lon7-diu1
trash can't random litter
'Don't litter at random.'

The performance of *zo3-m5-ded4* (做毋得) and *sii2-m5-ded4* (使毋得) which represent the concept of necessity[8] (that is, prohibitive in semantic field) does not imply the absence of the negation of possibility. The logical form of *m5-sii2* (毋使) is supposed to be "$\neg + \Diamond p$". However, the semantic logic interpretation is "$\neg\Box p$" instead. In other words, (20) expresses the idea that "it is not necessarily the case that this is true and it is possible that this is not true" (Radden 2007:226). The linguistic performance of *sii2*(使)-type modals therefore is exhibited in Table 3.

(20) 有麼个需要，隨時摎𠊎講，毋使細義。
rhiu1 ma2gai3 si1rau3, sui5shi5 LAU ngai5 gong2, m5- sii2 se3ngi7
have what need anytime LAU I speak need-not courteous
'Tell me what you need anytime. Make yourself at home.'

Table 3: The linguistic performance of *sii2*(使)-type modals

	Examples	Logic notation	
		Possibility	Necessity
possible	使得(V)	$\Diamond p$	
possible not	*使得毋(V) 毋使(V)	$\Diamond\neg p$	$\neg\Box p$
not possible	*毋使得(V) 使毋得(V)	$\neg\Diamond p$	$\Box\neg p$

Table 4 depicts the comparison of *zo3*(做)-type and *sii2*(使)-type modals in TH[9].

[8] The modal verbs which denote necessity in Taiwanese Hakka are *tin3 chog8* (定著). However, while the lexicalized forms composed of the elements to denote possibility and negation can be observed (such as *zo3-m5-ded4* (做毋得) and *sii2-m5-ded4* (使毋得)), the ones composed of the elements to denote necessity and negation cannot.

[9] One specific「NEG+M+NEG+VP」 construction is also observed here, which denotes the idea of "$\neg\Diamond\neg p \equiv \Box p$" as well. However, while the [不得不-V] construction in Mandarin Chinese implies unwillingness of the speaker, the [做毋得毋-V] construction does not.

(23) 講了恁多好話，缺點也**做毋得毋**提。
gong2 le1 an2 do1 ho2 fa3, kied4 diam2 rha7 zo3-m5-ded4-m5 ti5
speak PART so many good word defect too must mention
'While (I) have spoken so many good words, I must mention the defects too.'

Table 4: The comparison of *zo3*(做)-type and *sii2*(使)-type modals

Logic notation	做 type	使 type	TOTAL
◊p Number/Percentage	做得 229 / 92%	使得 20 / 8%	249 /100%
¬◊p ≡ □¬p Number/Percentage	做毋得 43 / 77%	使毋得 13 / 23%	56 / 100%
¬□p Number/Percentage	*毋做 0 / 0%	毋使 118 / 100%	100 / 100%

With different linguistic forms, the information processing of possibility and negation can be presented in various ways. To express the meaning of '◊p (possible)', both *zo3-ded4* (做得) and *sii2- ded4* (使得) can be applied. *Zo3-m5-ded4* (做毋得) and *sii2-m5-ded4* (使毋得), undergone the interaction of possibility and negation, denote the meaning of prohibition which relate to necessity '¬◊p ≡ □¬p (not possible = necessary not)'. Furthermore, while *m5-sii2* (毋使) indicates '¬□p (not necessary)', the linguistic form of *m5-zo3* (毋做) does not have the modal function. In other words, *m5-sii2* (毋使) predominates in the usage of '¬□p (not necessary)'. This paper therefore offers an analysis of the interaction of possibility and negation with logical information processing.

5 Concluding Remarks

TH modality has been paid little attention to in the literature, not to mention the interaction of possibility and negation. Exemplified via deontic modals, this paper attempts to shed light on the issue under the manipulation of logic. Both the two lexicalized deontic modals *zo3-ded4* (做得) and *sii2-ded4* (使得) denote possibility, and *zo3-m5-ded4* (做毋得) and *sii2-m5-ded4* (使毋得) signify prohibition which relates to necessity. However, some differences can be observed in a distributional account. *Zo3-ded4* (做得) and *zo3-m5-ded4* (做毋得) dominate in Taiwanese Hakka usage. In other words, the members of *zo3* (做) types are in predominance. On the contrary, the application of *sii2-ded4* (使得) and *sii2-m5-ded4* (使毋得) are fewer in linguistic use. Though it seems that the members of *sii2* (使) types may suffer the situation of fading out, only *m5-sii2* (毋使) can express the sense of 'it is not necessarily the case that this is true' or 'it is possible that this is not true'. In other words, *zo3* (做) types and *sii2* (使) types occupy different functional statues in TH modality. In line with the concept of lexicalization, this study analyzes the intricate syntactic and semantic features exhibited by modal verbs in Taiwanese Hakka.

Selected References

Brinton, Laurel J, and Elizabeth Closs Traugott. 2005. *Lexicalization and Language Change*. Cambridge: Cambridge University Press.

Bybee, Joan. 2005. Mechanisms of change in grammaticalization: The role of frequency. In Brian D. Joseph and Richard D. Janda, eds., *The Handbook of Historical Linguistics*, pp.602-623. Oxford: Blackwell.

Bybee, Joan, Revere Perkins, and William Pagliuca. 1994. *The Evolution of Grammar: Tense, Aspect and Modality in the Languages of the World.* Chicago: The University of Chicago Press.

Chu, Chauncey C. 1998. *A discourse Grammar of Mandarin Chinese.* New York and Berne: Peter Lang Publishing.

Chui, Kawai, and Hueiling Lai. 2008. The NCCU Corpus of Spoken Chinese: Mandarin, Hakka, and Southern Min. *Taiwan Journal of Linguistics* 6.2:119-144.

De Haan, Ferdinand. 2005. Typological approaches to modality. In William Frawley, ed., *Approaches to Modality*, pp. 27-69. Berlin: Mouton de Gruyter.

De Haan, Ferdinand. 1997. *The interaction of negation and modality: A typological study*. New York: Garland.

Fischer, Olga, M. Norde, & H. Peridon. (eds.) 2004. *Up and Down the Cline: The Nature of Grammaticalization*. John Benjamins.

Frawley, William. (ed.) 2005. *The expression of modality*. Berlin: Mouton de Gruyter.

Givon, T. 1995. *Functionalism and Grammar*. Amsterdam: John Benjamins.

Harris, Alice C. 2005. Cross-linguistic perspectives on syntactic change. In Brian D. Joseph and Richard D. Janda, eds., *The Handbook of Historical Linguistics*, pp. 529-551. Oxford: Blackwell.

Heine, Bernd. 2005. Grammaticalization. In Brian D. Joseph and Richard D. Janda, eds., *The Handbook of Historical Linguistics*, pp.575-601. Oxford: Blackwell.

Hopper, Paul J. and Elizabeth Closs Traugott. 2003. *Grammaticalization*. Cambridge: Cambridge University Press.

Huang, Lillian M.-J. 1980. *The Resultative Complement in Mandarin Chinese*. M.A. thesis, University of Florida

Johnson, Mark. 1987. *The body in the mind*. Chicago: University of Chicago Press.

Lyons, John.1982. Deixis and Subjectivity. Loquor, Ergo Sum? In Robert J. Jarvella and Wolfgangt Klein, eds., *Spech, Place, and Action: Studies in Deixis and Related Topics*, pp.101-124. New York: John Wiley and Sons, Ltd.

Lyons, John. 1977. *Semantics*. Cambridge: Cambridge University Press.

Nuyts, Jan. 2005. The modal confusion: On terminology and the concepts behind it. In A. Klinge and Henrik H. Müller, eds., *Modality: Studies in form and function*, pp.5-38. London: Equinox.

Palmer, Frank R. 2001. *Mood and modality* (Cambridge Textbooks in Linguistics), 2nd edition. Cambridge: Cambridge University Press.

Palmer, Frank R. 1979. *Modality and the English modals*. London: Longman.

Radden, Günter. 2007. Interaction of modality and negation. In Władysław Chłopicki, Andrzej Pawelec, and Agnieszka Pokojska, eds., *Cognition in Language: Volume in Honour of Professor Elżbieta Tabakowska*, pp.224-254. Kraków: Tertium.

Sun, C.F. and T. Givon. 1985. On the so-called SOV word-order in Mandarin Chinese: A quantified text study and its implications. *Language* 61(2), 329-351.

Sweetser, Eve. 1991. *From Etymology to Pragmatics: Metaphorical and Cultural Aspects of Semantic Structure*. Cambridge: Cambridge University Press.

Talmy, Leonard. 1988. Force dynamics in language and cognition. *Cognitive Science* 2, 49-100.

Traugott, Elizabeth Closs. 2005. Constructions in Grammaticalization. In Brian D. Joseph and Richard D. Janda, eds., *The Handbook of Historical Linguistics*, pp.624-647. Oxford: Blackwell.

Traugott, Elizabeth Closs. 1995. Subjectification in grammaticalization. In D. Stein and S. Wright, eds., *Subjectivity and Subjectivisation*, pp.31-54. Cambridge: Cambridge University Press.

Yue, Anne O. 2001. The verb complement construction in historical perspective with special reference to Cantonese. In Hilary Chappell, ed., *Sinitic Grammar: Synchronic and diachronic perspectives*, pp.232-265. Oxford: Oxford University Press.

屈承熹. 2010.《漢語功能篇章語法—從認知、功能到篇章結構》，文鶴出版社。

鍾榮富. 2001.《福爾摩沙的烙印-臺灣客家話導論（上、下冊）》。行政院文化建設委員會。

董秀芳. 2002. 〈論句法結構的詞彙化〉，《語言研究》3: 56-65.

何石松, 劉醇鑫. 2004.《現代客語詞彙彙編序篇》。臺北：台北市政府客家事務委員會。

謝佳玲. 2006.〈漢語情態詞的語意界定：語料庫為本的研究〉,《中國語文研究》1: 45-63.

蔣紹愚. 1994.《近代漢語研究概況》。北京：北京大學出版社。

柯理思. 1995.〈北方官話裡表示可能的動詞詞尾“了”〉,《中國語文》1995.4(總 247): 267-278。

羅肇錦. 1990.《客語語法》。臺北：臺灣學生書局。

沈家煊. 2003.〈現代漢語“動補結構”的類型學考察〉,《世界漢語教學》2003.3: 17-23。

宋永圭. 2007.《現代漢語情態動詞否定研究》。北京：中國社會科學出版社。

曹逢甫, 蕭素英. 2002.〈論漢語兩種關聯句式的語法與語意〉,《語言暨語言學》3.4: 811-838。

王燦龍. 2005.〈詞彙化二例—兼談詞彙化和語法化的關係〉,《當代語言學》7.3: 225-236.

魏培泉. 2004.〈近代漢語能性動補結構中賓語的位置〉,《語言暨語言學》5.3: 663-704。

吳福祥. 2002.〈漢語能性述補結構「V得/不C」的語法化〉,《中國語文》2002.1: 29-40。

The Syntax-Semantics Interface of Resultative Constructions in Mandarin Chinese and Cantonese

Pui Lun Chow

Department of Linguistics, University of Hong Kong,

MB126, Main Building, The University of Hong Kong, Hong Kong (852), China

h08dezi@hku.hk

Abstract. The mapping between grammatical functions and thematic roles of resultative constructions has been widely discussed in different frameworks of syntax, and theories have been proposed to account for the mismatches between them. The question behind the construction of these mapping theories always lies in the choice of suppressing one of the two competing roles or fusing them in order to maintain the Consistency Principle or Uniqueness Condition. However, these mechanisms always involve ad hoc additional mapping rules which need further justification or they may not be applicable to other mapping phenomena. In this paper, I am going to analyze the mapping phenomenon of resultative constructions in Mandarin Chinese and Cantonese by drawing insights from conceptual semantics (Jackendoff, 1990). I will show how conceptual structures can capture the special properties of resultative constructions and handle the mapping phenomenon mentioned above naturally.

Keywords: resultative constructions, mapping, conceptual semantics structure, verb-copying constructions, syntactic-semantic interface

Section 1 Introduction

The grammatical functions and thematic roles mapping phenomenon of resultative constructions has been widely discussed in different frameworks of syntax and mapping theories have been proposed to account for the mismatches between grammatical functions and thematic roles (the Causative Hierarchy account (Li 1995); Lexical Mapping Theory ((Levin 1986) and (Bresnan and Zaenen 1990)); Event Structure Account (Alsina 1992), etc.). The question behind the construction of these mapping theories always lies in the choice of suppressing one of the two competing roles or fusing two component roles in order to maintain the Consistency Principle or Uniqueness Condition, which says a particular attribute in a functional structure must have one and only one value (Dalrymple, 2001). However, the mechanisms of suppressing one of the competing roles or fusing two component roles always involve ad hoc additional mapping rules which need further justification or they may not be applicable to other mapping phenomena.

In this paper, I am going to show how the semantics of resultative constructions in Mandarin Chinese and Cantonese can be linked to the syntax by drawing insights from conceptual semantics (Jackendoff, 1990). Along with a demonstration of the application of conceptual structures in accounting for the mapping phenomenon in Mandarin Chinese and Cantonese resultative constructions, the paper will focus on the strange or marked mapping phenomenon of a Mandarin Chinese sentence discussed in Her's (2006) paper, "張三 追-累-了 李四 *Zhāngsān zhuī-lèi-le Lǐsì*" (John chase-tired-ASP Lee)[1]. I will also show in this paper how the representation of conceptual structures can capture the special properties of resultative constructions and at the same time handle the relevant mapping phenomena, including that of the marked structure mentioned above, naturally.

Section 2 The Conceptual Semantics Approach

To handle the argument-function mapping of possible ambiguous interpretations of resultative constructions like the sentence above in Mandarin and Cantonese, an approach considering the conceptual semantics as proposed by Jackendoff (1990) seems suitable. Unlike Lexical Mapping Theory ((Levin 1986) and (Bresnan and Zaenen 1990)), which handles mapping by assigning intrinsic values to individual roles and grammatical functions, the conceptual semantics approach handles mapping by looking at the conceptual structure of the sentence as a whole. Thus, each interpretation of the sentence would possess its corresponding conceptual structure. The mapping is done according to the position each participant of the event denoted by the sentence is put.

One of the features of Mandarin and Cantonese resultative constructions is that the resulting predicate or the means verb, which is usually adjective-like in a resultative compound contributes to the core meaning of the sentence unlike modifying adjuncts, which only provide additional information. These adjuncts are called "*Superordinate Adjuncts*" (Jackendoff, 1990). According to Jackendoff's (1990) analysis, resultative sentences like:

(1-i) Peter swung the towel dry.

(2-i) The gardener watered the tulips flat.

(3-i) The man hit the dog dead.

can be rephrased as follows:

(1-ii) Peter made the towel dry by watering it.

(2-ii) The gardener made the tulips flat by watering them.

(3-ii) The man made the dog dead by hitting it.

---

[1] According to Her (2006), there are three acceptable interpretations for this sentence.
Interpretation 1: John chased Lee to the extent of making him (Lee) tired.
Interpretation 2 : John chased Lee and (John) got tired.
Interpretation 3 : Lee chased John and was made tired (by John).
Further discussion on the above interpretations will be done in Section 4.

Now that sentences (1-i), (2-i) and (3-i) are rephrased, with the *superordinate adjuncts* denoted by the 'by' phrases at the end. Jackendoff (1990) suggests that the rephrased constructions are more basic for formulation. We will take the first sentence as an example. The conceptual structure of the sentence is as follows,

(4) The conceptual structure of (1-i):

$$\begin{pmatrix} \text{CAUSE ([}\alpha\text{]), [INCH [BE ([}\beta\text{], [AT [DRY]])]])} \\ \text{AFF ([PETER]}^{\alpha}\text{, [TOWEL]}^{\beta}\text{)} \\ \text{[BY} \begin{bmatrix} \text{SWING ([}\gamma\text{], [}\delta\text{])} \\ \text{AFF ([}\alpha\text{]}^{\gamma}\text{, [}\beta\text{]}^{\delta}\text{)} \end{bmatrix} \text{]} \end{pmatrix}$$

The first line of the conceptual structure is the thematic tier. It says that an individual [α] causes (i.e. CAUSE) an internal change (i.e. INCH) to another individual [β] to be in a state of being dry (i.e. BE … [AT ["DRY"]]). The second line is the action tier which tells that the two participants (i.e. the actor [α] and the patient [β]) are "PETER" and "TOWL" respectively. The superordinate *adjunct* BY part states that the above action is caused by a swinging action (i.e. SWING) with two participants, i.e. [γ] and [δ]. [α] takes the first position in the action tier within the BY subpart, which states that "PETER", which is co-indexed with [α], is the actor; whereas [β] takes the second position in the action tier within the BY subpart, which states that "TOWEL", which is co-indexed with [β], is the patient.

In the above structure, the resultant is introduced by the conceptual function "BY". One important point is that the subpart "BY" is not adjunctive. This representation echoes with the property of predicates or complex predicates in resultant constructions that neither of the predicates is adjunctive to each other.

Section 3 Mapping of Mandarin and Cantonese Resultatives

Having demonstrated the representation of resultative constructions in the case of English, we are in a better position to engage in the analysis of Mandarin Chinese and Cantonese RVCs. We will look at three types of resultative sentences in each language.

The first type is the most unmarked case of resultative construction.

Example sentence in Mandarin Chinese:

(5) 這 個 男人 打- 死 了 那 條 狗。

zhè gè nán rén **dǎ-sǐ** le nà tiáo gǒu

This CL man hit-dead ASP that CL dog.

"This man hit the dog and made it dead."

Example sentence in Cantonese:

(6) 呢 個 男 人 打 死 左 嗰 隻 狗。

nei4 go3 naam4 jan4 **daa2-sei2** zo2 gwo2 zek3 gau2

This CL man hit-dead ASP that CL dog.

"This man hit the dog and made it dead."

The sentences in Mandarin and Cantonese have the same syntactic structure and can be represented in the conceptual structures below.

(7) Conceptual structure of (5):

$$\begin{pmatrix} \text{CAUSE (} [\alpha]_A \text{), [INCH [BE (} [\beta]_A \text{, [AT [``DEAD'']] )]] )} \\ \text{AFF ( [nán rén ``MAN'']}_A{}^{\alpha}\text{, [gǒu ``DOG'']}_A{}^{\beta} \text{)} \\ \text{[BY } \begin{bmatrix} \text{HIT (} [\gamma], [\delta] \text{)} \\ \text{AFF (} [\alpha]^{\gamma}, [\beta]^{\delta} \text{)} \end{bmatrix} \text{]} \end{pmatrix}$$

The Argument-marked (or A-marked) arguments in the above structure are ordered as [nán rén "MAN"] and [gǒu "DOG"] according to the thematic hierarchy[2]. The argument in the first position is the ACTOR while the second argument is the PATIENT. The first A-marked argument is linked to the external argument or the subject, whereas the second argument is linked to the object.

(8) Conceptual structure of (6):

$$\begin{pmatrix} \text{CAUSE (} [\alpha]_A \text{), [INCH [BE (} [\beta]_A \text{, [AT [``DEAD'']] )]] )} \\ \text{AFF ( [mannm4 jan4 ``MAN'']}_A{}^{\alpha}\text{, [gau2 ``DOG'']}_A{}^{\beta} \text{)} \\ \text{[BY } \begin{bmatrix} \text{HIT (} [\gamma], [\delta] \text{)} \\ \text{AFF (} [\alpha]^{\gamma}, [\beta]^{\delta} \text{)} \end{bmatrix} \text{]} \end{pmatrix}$$

Since the Cantonese sentence (6) has the same conceptual structure as the Mandarin Chinese sentence (5), the mapping from semantics to syntax is the same.

The second type involves inversion[3] in resultative constructions. Consider the sentence in Mandarin Chinese:

(9) 這 種 藥 會 吃-死 你。

zhè zhǒng yào huì **chī-sǐ** nǐ

This CL medicine will eat-dead you.

"Eating this medicine will kill you."

(10) Conceptual structure of (9):

$$\begin{pmatrix} \text{CAUSE (} [\alpha]_A \text{), [INCH [BE (} [\beta]_A \text{, [AT [``DEAD'']] )]] )} \\ \text{AFF ( [yào ``MEDICINE'']}_A{}^{\alpha}\text{, [nǐ ``YOU'']}_A{}^{\beta} \text{)} \\ \text{[BY } \begin{bmatrix} \text{EAT (} [\gamma], [\delta] \text{)} \\ \text{AFF (} [\alpha]^{\gamma}, [\beta]^{\delta} \text{)} \end{bmatrix} \text{]} \end{pmatrix}$$

The first line of the semantic structure above (i.e. the thematic tier) is basically the same as the thematic tiers in the conceptual structures for sentences (5) and (6). The second line is the action

[2] According to Jackendoff (1990:258), the thematic hierarchy is an order of "the A-marked arguments in the action tier from left to right, followed by the A-marked arguments in the main conceptual clause of the thematic tier, from least embedded to most deeply embedded". The ordered A-marked arguments can be listed as Actor > Patient (AFF^-) or Beneficiary (AFF^+) > Theme > Location, Source, Goal.

[3] The canonical linking maps the Actor, or EATER, to the subject, and the Patient, or the EATEE, to the object. However, (9) shows an inverse mapping in which the Actor is mapped to the surface object instead of the subject.

tier which states that the two participants (i.e. the actor [α] and the patient [β]) are "yào MEDICINE" and "nǐ YOU" respectively. The superordinate adjunct BY part states that the result is caused by an eating action (i.e. EAT) with two participants, i.e. [γ] and [δ]. [α] takes the first position in the action tier within the BY subpart, which states that "nǐ YOU", which is co-indexed with [α], is the actor; whereas [β] takes the second position in the action tier within the BY subpart, which states that "yào MEDICINE", which is co-indexed with [β], is the patient. Consider the sentence in Cantonese:

(11) 呢 隻 藥 會 食 死 你。

Nie4 zek3 joek6 wui6 **sik6-sei2** nei5

This CL medicine will eat-dead you.

"Eating this medicine will kill you."

(12) Conceptual structure of (11):

$$\left(\begin{array}{l} \text{CAUSE (} [\alpha]_A \text{), [INCH [BE ([}\beta]_A\text{, [AT ["DEAD"]])]])} \\ \text{AFF ([joek6 "MEDICINE"]}_A{}^{\alpha}\text{, [nei5 "YOU"]}_A{}^{\beta}\text{)} \\ \text{[BY } \left[\begin{array}{l} \text{EAT ([}\gamma\text{], [}\delta\text{])} \\ \text{AFF ([}\alpha]^{\gamma}\text{, [}\beta]^{\delta}\text{)} \end{array}\right] \text{]} \end{array}\right)$$

Again, the resultative sentences in both languages have the same conceptual semantic structure. In these two cases, *joek6 "MEDICINE"* is put in the first argument position in the action tier because it is the instigator of the result "dead". The two A-marked arguments are ordered as [joek6 "MEDICINE"]$_A{}^{\alpha}$, [nei5 "YOU"]$_A{}^{\beta}$ according to the thematic hierarchy. The first argument is linked to the external argument or subject whereas the second argument is linked to the object. The Cantonese sentence would have the same syntactic mapping as the case in Mandarin Chinese because of their identical conceptual structures.

The third type of resultative construction is a marked construction in Mandarin Chinese. The sentence "張三 追-累-了李四 *Zhāngsān zhuī-lèi-le Lǐsì*" (John chase-tired-ASP Lee) has been discussed in Her's (2006) paper, which claims that the sentence has three possible readings.

(13) 張三 追-累-了 李四

Zhāngsān zhuī-lèi-le Lǐsì

John chase-tired-ASP Lee

Interpretation (i) John chased Lee and Lee got tired.

Interpretation (ii) John chased Lee and John got tired.

Interpretation (iii) Lee chased John and (Lee) got tired.

However, the second interpretation is not readily accepted by native speakers. In what follows, I am going to (i) prove my point above by looking at its conceptual structure and (ii) provide an explanation for the possibility of the third interpretation. Let us start by looking at the first interpretation.

Interpretation (i): John chased Lee and Lee got tired.

Interpretation (i) can be rephrased as "John made Lee tired by chasing him (Lee)".

(14) Conceptual structure of interpretation (i):

$$\left[\begin{array}{l} \text{CAUSE}(\,[\alpha]_{A},\ [\text{INCH}\ [\text{BE}\ (\,[\beta]_{A},\ [\text{AT}\ [\text{TIRED}]]\,)]]\,) \\ \text{AFF}^{-}(\,[\text{Zhāngsān}\ (\text{“John”})]_{A}^{\alpha},\ [\text{Lǐsì}\ (\text{“Lee”})]_{A}^{\beta}) \\ [\text{BY} \left[\begin{array}{l} \text{CAUSE}\ (\,[\gamma],\ [\text{GO}\ ([\gamma],\ [_{\text{PATH}}\ \text{TO}\ [\delta]]\,)]\,) \\ \qquad \text{AFF}^{-}\ ([\alpha]^{\gamma},\ [\beta]^{\delta}) \end{array}\right] \ ] \end{array}\right]$$

The first line, i.e. the thematic tier, denotes that an individual $[\alpha]$ is causing (i.e. CAUSE) an internal change (i.e. "INCH") on another individual $[\beta]$ to be in a state of being tired (i.e. [BE...AT [TIRED]]). The instigator of the above causative action, which is found in the first position of the action tier is "[Zhāngsān ("John")]", whereas the patient of the CAUSE action, which is denoted in the second position of the action tier, is [Lǐsì ("Lee")]. The "chasing" action is expressed by using the functions "GO" and "PATH", since "chasing" involves *A* going along the path B takes and trying to catch B. The two A-marked arguments are ordered as [Zhāngsān ("John")], [Lǐsì ("Lee")]. The ACTOR, which is the first argument in the action tier, is mapped to the external argument or subject, whereas the PATIENT, which is the second argument in the action tier, is mapped to the object.

* Interpretation (ii): John chased Lee and John got tired.

The corresponding paraphrase of the intended interpretation of this sentence is "John got tired by chasing Lee." However, this interpretation is not readily accepted by native speakers of Mandarin Chinese. This can be explained by considering the conceptual structure of the interpretation. First, since there is no "external" causer involved in the internal change (INCH) of Zhāngsān ("John") being tired, the thematic tier only states that there is an individual $[\alpha]$, which is co-indexed with [Zhāngsān ("John")], undergoes an internal change of being tired. Accordingly, there is only a single A-marked argument (i.e. $[\text{Zhāngsān (“John”)}]_{A}$) in the action tier ready for mapping. According to the mapping described above, the A-marked arguments are ordered as $[\text{Zhāngsān (“John”)}]_{A}$, $[\alpha_{(\text{John})}]_{A}$ and $[\text{Lǐsì (“Lee”)}]_{A}$. Since the resultative compound is a transitive verb, only $[\text{Zhāngsān (“John”)}]_{A}$ and $[\alpha_{(\text{John})}]_{A}^{\gamma}$ will be mapped in the syntax. The conceptual structure of the intended interpretation and the mapping result shows the intended interpretation, i.e. "John chased Lee and John got tired." cannot be obtained from the sentence "張三 追-累-了 李四 *Zhāngsān zhuī-lèi-le Lǐsì*".

(15) Conceptual structure of interpretation (ii):

$$\left[\begin{array}{l} [\text{INCH}\ [\text{BE}([\alpha],\ [\text{AT}\ [\text{TIRED}]]\,)]]\,) \\ \text{AFF}(\,[\textit{Zhāngsān}\ (\text{“John”})]_{A}^{\alpha}) \\ [\ \text{BY} \quad \left[\begin{array}{l} \text{CAUSE}\ ([\gamma],\ [\text{GO}\ (\,[\gamma],\ [_{\text{PATH}}\ \text{TO}\ [\delta]]\,)]\,) \\ \text{AFF}\ ([\alpha]_{A}^{\gamma},\ [\textit{Lǐsì}\ (\text{“Lee”})]_{A}^{\delta}) \end{array}\right] \ ] \end{array}\right]$$

Interpretation (iii): Lee chased John and (Lee) got tired.

Interpretation (iii) can be rephrased as "Lee got tired by chasing John."

(16) Conceptual structure of interpretation (iii):

$$\begin{bmatrix} \text{CAUSE} ([\alpha]_{A}, [\text{INCH} [\text{BE}([\beta]_{A}, [\text{AT} [\text{TIRED}]])]]) \\ \text{AFF}^{-} ([\text{Zhāngsān ("John")}]_{A}{}^{\alpha}, [\text{Lǐsì ("Lee")}]_{A}{}^{\beta}) \\ [\text{BY} \begin{pmatrix} \text{CAUSE} ([\gamma], [\text{GO} ([\gamma], [_{\text{PATH}} \text{TO} [\delta]])]) \\ \text{AFF}^{-} ([\beta]^{\gamma}, [\alpha]^{\delta}) \end{pmatrix}] \end{bmatrix}$$

In this case, [Zhāngsān ("John")] is still the instigator of the action which causes someone tired, and thus is put in the first position of the action tier. The ACTOR [Zhāngsān ("John")] is linked to the external argument or subject whereas the PATIENT [Lǐsì ("Lee")] is linked to the object. The difference between the conceptual structure in (16) and that in (15) lies in the "BY" subpart or the superordinate adjunct. The action tier in the superordinate adjunct of the conceptual structure in (16) is "AFF^{-} ([β ("Lee")]$^{\gamma}$, [α ("John")]$^{\delta}$)" , while the action tier in the superordinate adjunct of the conceptual structure in (14) is "AFF^{-} ([α ("John")]$^{\gamma}$, [β ("Lee")]$^{\delta}$)". The analysis above demonstrates how grammatical function and argument role mapping of Mandarin resultative constructions, including the marked structure discussed above can be handled naturally by Jackendoff's (1990) conceptual semantics approach. In what follows, I am going to demonstrate the mapping of Cantonese resultative construction in the conceptual semantics approach.

Section 4 Mapping of Cantonese Resultatives with Verb-Copying Construction

The syntactic structure of the resultative sentences in Cantonese resembles that of Mandarin Chinese resultative constructions. However, one major difference is that certain causing verbs or main verbs are not adjacent to the means verbs or resulting predicates. Instead, the main verbs or the causing verbs are separated from the resulting predicates and the resultative sentences are only licensed in verb-copying constructions, for example, the proposition "John chased Lee and made Lee tired." can only be expressed in a verb-copying construction like (17):

(17) 張 三 追 李 四 追- 到 好 攰。

Zoeng3saam3 **zeoi1** Lei5sei3 **zeoi1** dou3 **hou2 gui6**

John chased Lee chased-ASP very tired

"John chased Lee to an extent that Lee got tired."

Unlike the corresponding resultative sentence in Mandarin Chinese, there is only one acceptable interpretation for the Cantonese sentence, i.e. *John chased Lee to an extent that Lee got tired.* Moreover, there is one important point to note about this type of Cantonese resultative construction. Since the above resultative sentence is a verb-copying construction, there are semantic and syntactic properties that are not found in resultative compounds. According to

Fang and Sells's (1997) study on verb-copying constructions in Chinese, verb-copying constructions (VCC) are considered as a type of construction in which VPs are co-ordinated. The paper argues that a VCC is "a double or multiple-headed coordinated VP, with each VP as a co-head" (Fang and Sells, 1997). The syntactic relation of a VCC is shown in (18):

(18) VP (VCC) → VP   VP +.

$\uparrow \in \downarrow$ $\uparrow \in \downarrow$

$\uparrow = \downarrow$

It is also proposed that the first VP is the head of the construction and it is in a subsumption relation to all other VPs, in other words, the syntactic information of every VP under the VCC construction is subsumed by the first VP head (Zaenen and Kaplan 2002). Semantically, the first VP head is considered more general than the following VP(s) (Fang and Sells, 1997). It is shown in Fang and Sells's (1997) paper that the first VP "serves pragmatically as the secondary topic" while the co-headed VPs, usually post-verbal adjuncts, "serves as the comment to the first VP" and are considered more specific.

Given the properties of VCCs discussed by Fang and Sells (1997), we shall now consider the conceptual structure of Cantonese resultative sentences which appear as verb-copying constructions.

(19) Conceptual structure of (17):

$$\begin{bmatrix} ([\alpha], [\text{GO}([\alpha], [_{\text{PATH}}\ \text{TO}\ [\gamma]])]) \\ \text{AFF}^{-}([\text{Zoeng3saam3 ("John")}]_{A}^{\alpha}, [\text{Lei5sei3 ("Lee")}]_{A}^{\gamma}) \\ \begin{bmatrix} ([\beta]_{A}, [\text{INCH}\ [\text{BE}([\beta]_{A}, [\text{AT}\ [\text{TIRED}]])]]) \\ \text{AFF}^{-}([\alpha]_{A}^{\beta}) \end{bmatrix} \end{bmatrix}$$

Sentence (17) involves two VPs as shown in (20)

(20) VP (VCC) →	VP	VP +.
	$\uparrow \in \downarrow$	$\uparrow \in \downarrow$
	張 三 追 李 四	追- 到 好 攰
	Zoeng3saam3 zeoi1 Lei5sei3	zeoi1-dou3 hou2 gui6
	John chased Lee	chase-ASP very tired
	"John chased Lee"	"(John) got (very) tired."

Since the first VP is considered semantically more general, it is represented in the first two lines, which represent the main clause of the conceptual structure. The first line, i.e. the thematic tier, denotes a chasing action in which [α] (i.e. "John") GOes along the PATH [β] (i.e. Lee) takes. The embedded conceptual structure represents the co-headed VP, which states that an individual [β] which is co-indexed with [α] (i.e. "John") undergoes an internal change of being tired. Again, since the main structure represents the more general information, it seems to be a more suitable starting place for mapping. The A-marked arguments are ordered as ([Zoeng3saam3 ("John")] $_{A}^{\alpha}$ and [Lei5sei3 ("Lee")] $_{A}^{\gamma}$).The Actor [Zoeng3saam3 ("John")] $_{A}^{\alpha}$ in the action tier is mapped to the external argument or subject, while the Patient [Lei5sei3 ("Lee")] $_A{}^{\gamma}$) is mapped to the object.

It is noted that the reflective pronoun 自己 ***zi6gei2*** (self) can be added to sentence (17) which becomes:

(21) 張 三 追 李 四 追 到 *自己* 好 攰

Zoeng3saam3 **zeoi1** Lei5sei3 zeoi1 dou3 ***zi6gei2*** hou2 gui6

John chased Lee chased-ASP ***self*** very tired

"John chased Lee to an extent that John himself is very tired."

The conceptual structure in (19) can also account for the above syntactic structure. Since the two A-marked arguments have been mapped to syntax, we have to look inside the embedded conceptual structure for an additional argument[4] for mapping, which is $[\alpha]_A{}^{\beta}$ in this case. As $[\alpha]_A{}^{\beta}$ is subsumed by the main conceptual structure or, in other words, $[\alpha]_A{}^{\beta}$ is bound by the main conceptual structure, the reflective pronoun 自己 zi6gei2(self) is mapped to the post-verbal position of the second VP.

Section 5 Conclusion

In this paper, I have adopted Jackendoff's (1990) conceptual semantics approach to handle the syntax-semantics interface of RVCs, which has been discussed by many researchers. The conceptual structure representation of resultative sentences with the superordinate adjunct denoted by the "BY" subpart captures the semantic and syntactic properties of resultative constructions.

There are two major findings in my paper. The first one is that the application of Jackendoff's (1990) conceptual semantics approach of mapping can successfully explain why the interpretation "John chased Lee and John got tired" for the sentence "張三 追-累-了李四 *Zhāngsān zhuī-lèi-le Lǐsì* (John chased Lee and John got tired.)" is odd if not unacceptable. The second is that the mapping of the Cantonese verb-copying construction, i.e."張三 追 李四 追 到 好攰 Zoeng3saam3 zeoi1 Lei5sei3 zeoi1 dou3 hou2 gui6 (John chased Lee to an extent that John himself is very tired.)" involves a different conceptual structure because of its special syntactic structure.

---

[4] See footnote 2.

References

Alsina, Alex. 1992. On the Argument Structure of Causatives. *Linguistic Inquiry*, 23(4):517--555.

Alsina, Alex. 1996b. Resultatives: A Joint Operation of Semantic and Syntactic Structures. *On-line Proceedings of the First LFG Conference*, ed. by Miriam Butt and Tracy Holloway King. http://www-csli.stanford.edu/publications/LFG/lfg1.html.

Bresnan, Joan (2001). *Lexical Functional Syntax.* Blackwell.

Dalrymple, Mary (2001). *Lexical Functional Grammar.* No. 42 in Syntax and Semantics Series. New York: Academic Press.

Dowty, David. 1979. *Word Meaning and Montague Grammar*. Dordrecht: Reidel.

Fang, Ji and Sells, Peter. 2007. A Formal Analysis of the Verb Copy Construction in Chinese. *On-line Proceedings of the LFG07 Conference*, ed. by Miriam Butt and Tracy Holloway King. http://csli-publications.stanford.edu/

Foley, William A., Van Valin, Robert D. 1984. *Functional Syntax and Universal Grammar*. Cambridge University Press.

Her, One-Soon. 2004. *Argument-Function Linking in Resultatives.* Concentric: Studies in Linguistic, 30.2: 1-34

Jackendoff, Ray. 1990. *Semantics Structures*. Cambridge, Mass.: MIT Press.

Li, Yafei. 1995. The Thematic Hierarchy and Causativity. *Natural Language and Linguistic Theories* 13:255-82.

Li, YaFei. 1999. Cross-componential Causativity. *Natural Language and Linguistic Theory* 27:455-497.

Simpson, Jane. 1983. *Resultatives. Papers in Lexical-Functional Grammar*, ed. by Lori Levin, Malka Rappaport, and Annie Zaenen, 143-57. Bloomington, IN: Indiana University Linguistics Club.

Yuzhi Shi. 1999. *The Formation of the Resultative Construction and Its Effects on the Establishment of Modern Chinese Grammar.* PhD dissertation submitted to the Department of Asian Languages of Stanford University.

Zaenen, Annie and Ronald M. Kaplan, 2002. Subsumption and Equality: German Partial Fronting in LFG. *In Proceedings of the LFG02 Conference.* M. Butt and T.H.King (eds.), CSLI Publications, Stanford, CA.

Automatic Wrapper Generation and Maintenance

Yingju Xia, Yuhang Yang, Fujiang Ge, Shu Zhang, Hao Yu

Fujitsu Research & Development Center Co.,LTD.
15F Tower A, Ocean International Center, No.56 Dong Si Huan Zhong Rd, Chaoyang District, Beijing, China ,100025
yjxia@cn.fujitsu.com

Abstract. This paper investigates automatic wrapper generation and maintenance for Forums, Blogs and News web sites. Web pages are increasingly dynamically generated using a common template populated with data from databases. This paper proposes a novel method that uses tree alignment and transfer learning method to generate the wrapper from this kind of web pages. The tree alignment algorithm is adopted to find the best matching structure of the input web pages. A kind of linear regression method is employed to get the weight of different tag-matching. A transfer learning method is adopted to find the most likely content block. A wrapper built on the most probable content block and the repeating patterns extracts data from web pages. The wrapper maintenance arises because web source may experiment changes that invalidate the current wrappers. This paper presents a wrapper maintenance method using a log likelihood ratio test for detecting the change points on the similarity series which gotten from the wrapper and input web pages. The wrapper generation method is applied to generate a wrapper once the web source change is detected. Experimental results show that the method achieves high accuracy and has steady performance

Keywords: Data extraction, Wrapper generation, Wrapper maintenance.

1 Introduction

Web-based information is typically formatted to be read by human users, not by computer applications. Information agents are being proposed which automatically extract information from multiple websites. Data is typically extracted from web sources by writing specialized programs, called wrappers (Laender et al. 2002), which identify data of interest and map them to a suitable format.

Many approaches have been reported in the literature for wrapper generation. Detailed discussions of various approaches can be found in several surveys (Chang et al., 2006; Laender et al., 2002).

Early approaches were based on manual techniques (Atzeni and Mecca, 1997; Crescenzi and Mecca, 1998; Huck et al., 1998; Sahuguet and Azavant, 1999). By observing a web page and its source code, the programmer find some patterns from the page and then write a program to extract data from the web pages. A key problem with manually coded wrappers is that writing them is a difficult and labor-intensive task, and tends to be brittle and difficult to maintain.

Other approaches have some degrees of automation. In semi-automatic approaches (Cohen et al., 2002; Irmak and Suel, 2006; Kushmerick, 2000; Muslea et al., 1999; Pinto et al., 2003; Wang and Hu, 2002; Zheng et al., 2007), a set of extraction rules are learnt from a set of manually labeled pages or data records. These rules are then used to extract data items from similar pages. This method still requires substantial manual efforts.

In automatic methods, Arasu and Hector (2003), Chang and Liu (2001) and Crescenzi et al. (2001) found patterns or grammars from multiple pages containing similar data records. Wang and Lochovsky (2003) treated the input pages as strings and employed an algorithm to discover the continuously repeated substrings using suffix trees. Lerman et al. (2004) utilized the detailed data in the page behind the current page to identify data records. Simon and Lausen (2005) identified and ranked potential repeated patterns using visual features. Then matched subsequences of the pattern with the highest weight was aligned with global multiple sequence alignment techniques.

Several methods were presented to address the wrapper maintenance problem. Kushmerick (1999) defined a problem called "wrapper verification," which checks if a wrapper stops extracting correct data. Their proposed solution analyzes pages and extracted information, and detects the page changes. If the pages have changed, the designer is notified, so that she can re-learn the wrapper from the pages with the new structure. Lerman et al. (2003) developed a method for repairing wrappers in the case of small mark-up changes. Chidlovskii (2001) presented an automatic maintenance approach to repairing wrappers under the assumption that there are only small changes. Raposo et al.(2005) made wrappers collect some results from valid queries during their operation, and when the source changes, use those results to generate a new training set of labeled examples to bootstrap the wrapper induction process again. Meng et al. (2003) presented a schema-guided approach which is based on the observation that despite various page changes, many important features of the pages are preserved, such as syntactic patterns, annotations, and hyperlinks of the extracted data items. Their approach uses these preserved features to identify the locations of the desired values in the changed pages, and repair wrappers correspondingly by inducing semantic blocks from the HTML tree.

Those previous methods focused on the list pages (Each of such pages contains lists of objects, for example, the pages in the shopping website such as Amazon.com.). This kind of web pages can be retrieved using queries which enable the "wrapper verification" procedure. But for the web pages from News, Forum and Blogs, the "wrapper verification" approach cannot be utilized because these web pages cannot be retrieved using queries and such no valid training set can be provided for the wrapper maintenance.

This paper presents a method that uses tree alignment to automatically build wrapper from web pages coming from News, Forums and Blogs websites. A kind of linear regression method is proposed to get the weight of different tag-matching. Based on the alignment, we merge the trees into one union tree whose nodes record the statistical information gotten from multiple web pages. We use a transfer learning method to find the most likely content block and use the alignment algorithm to detect the repeat patterns on the union tree. A log likelihood ratio test is adopted to the wrapper maintenance. Because the likelihood ratios describe evidence rather than embody a decision, they can easily be adapted to the various goals for which inferential statistics might be used. The likelihood ratios provide an intuitive approach to summarizing the evidence provided by an experiment in wrapper maintenance scenario.

2 Related Works

For the wrapper generation, in the sense of techniques used, the most relevant approaches are (Zhai and Liu, 2005; Zigoris et al., 2006).

Zhai and Liu(2005) used partial alignment method to align and extract data items from the identified data records. Zigoris et al.(2006) used Support Vector Machines (SVM) for learning the tree alignment parameters. With well-tuned parameters these models are resilient.

Compared with these methods, the wrapper generation method proposed in this study presents a kind of linear regression method to get the weight of different tag-matching. The algorithm is dedicated to adopt different node features and different matching weights while the others haven't take into account the categories of html tags, the properties of different level nodes and the text features.

Another major difference between the proposed method and the previous works is the way the alignment algorithm and the statistics are used. Zhai and Liu(2005) used the alignment algorithm to align the data items (data fields) from the identified data records. A link was created when a matching was found. The method proposed in this paper utilizes the alignment algorithm to obtain skeleton of the input trees, merges the trees into one union tree and records the statistical information. The proposed method employed the most probable content block finding step to locate the content blocks. The statistics recorded in the union tree makes this step more accurate because the heuristic is often used to differentiate the content from junk information.

We present a transfer learning method to get the weight of each feature when finding the most probable content block. The proposed method gets steady performance due to the statistics used.

For the wrapper maintenance, as mentioned in Section 1, the previous methods focused on the list pages. The "wrapper verification" approach cannot be utilized on the web pages from News, Forums and Blogs. There are no literature considering the wrapper maintenance on News, Forums and Blogs websites. In this paper, a log likelihood ratio test is adopted to wrapper maintenance.

3 Wrapper Generation

There are several steps in the proposed method.

(1) Wrapper generation. We use the tree alignment methods to calculate the similarity between input web pages and build a wrapper on tree alignment results. The tree alignment method is also used to calculate the similarity between wrapper and the input web pages. The input trees are merged into one union tree whose nodes record the statistical information such as the times a node has been aligned, the text length of the node. A heuristic method is employed to find the most probable content block. The alignment algorithm is utilized again to detect the repeating patterns on the union tree. The wrapper is generated based on the most probable content block and the repeating patterns.

(2) Similarity series generation. A similarity series was built by calculating the similarity between the input web pages and the current wrapper using the tree alignment algorithm proposed in this paper. The similarity series is in the order of the input web pages' timestamp.

(3) Change point detection and wrapper regeneration. A log likelihood ratio test is utilized to detect the change points on the similarity series. The wrapper generation method is applied again to generate a wrapper once a change point is detected.

In this study, we are interested in one specific type of tree called labeled ordered rooted tree. A rooted tree is a tree whose root vertex is fixed. Ordered rooted trees are rooted trees in which the relative order of the children is fixed for each vertex. We use the tree edit distance to evaluate the structural similarities between Web pages. In its traditional formulation, the tree edit distance problem considers three operations: node removal, node insertion and node replacement. The solution of this problem consists in determining the minimal set of operations to transform one tree into another. Another equivalent formulation of this problem is to discover a mapping with minimum cost between the two trees.

In this work, we focus on setting the weight (cost) of different node mapping (tag-matching). One of the major contributions of our work is a kind of linear regression method for getting the weight of different tag-matching. Another contribution of our work is the way we use the similarity between trees and the transfer learning method which is used for finding the most likely content block.

3.1 Automatically getting tag-matching weight

The main problem of the previous method is that they did not consider about employing different weights for various tag-matching. For example, the HTML tags are divided into two categories: block elements and inline elements. The block elements are elements that usually, but not always, contain other elements. They normally act as containers of some sort. The inline elements normally mark up the semantic meaning of something. Furthermore, the level of the different nodes should also be considered. The higher-level nodes should have higher weight as the higher-level nodes usually act as bigger structure block. Different weight should be assigned to different type of tag-matching.

In this study, a kind of linear regression method is employed to get the weight of different tag-matching. First, we found a collection of similar web pages belong to the same "class" (The web pages share the common format and layout characteristics, usually generated with the same template, for example, the web pages of the same board in one Forum website). It's feasible to get this kind of web pages collection automatically. Next, we will use this web pages collection for getting the optimal weighting schema.

Let w_i be the weight of tag-matching and $w_i > w_j$ for $i < j$. Let D_{mn} be the sum of the gains in the best alignment between the trees T_m and T_n. $D_{mn} = \sum_i w_i t_i^{mn}$ (1)

Where t_i^{mn} is the number of w_i occur in the alignment procedure.

The sum of the gains in the collection is:

$$f = \sum_{m,n} D_{mn} = \sum_{m,n}\sum_{i} w_i t_i^{mn} = \sum_{i} w_i \sum_{m,n} t_i^{mn} \quad (2)$$

Because the collection is the similar web pages belonging to the same "class", a set of w_i is selected which makes the maximum f.

To get $argmax_w \sum_i w_i \sum_{m,n} t_i^{mn}$, a constraint $\sum_i w_i^2 = 1$ is added. The group of equations is rewritten as: $f = \sum_i w_i C_i + \lambda(\sum_i w_i^2 - 1)$, $C_i = \sum_{m,n} t_i^{mn}$, $\sum_i w_i^2 = 1$ (3)

The solution of the above equations is used as the weight of each type of tag-matching (w_i).

Figure 1 illustrates an example of the weight setting method. For one collection of similar web pages belong to the same "class", we calculate the sum of the alignment gains (or the similarity) for each weighting schema. The best weighting schema is the one maximize the sum of the gains. That means to find a set of w_i that output the maximum f in the equations (3).

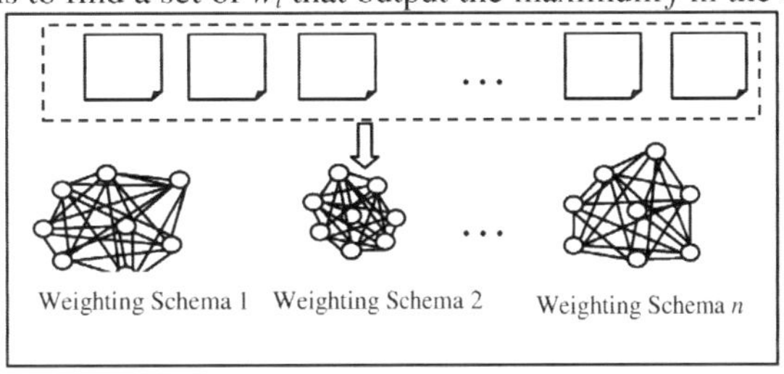

Figure 1: An example of weight setting

3.2 Transfer learning method for the most probable content block detecting

Using the alignment algorithm, we can find whether a node has been aligned. We then merge the two trees into one union tree and record the alignment information in each node. After processing several trees, we can use the statistic such as the ratio of the times a node has been aligned to make the decision whether this node should be kept or not. The union tree becomes more compact after deleting some useless nodes.

The next step is finding the most probable content block (the data in the content block is what we want to extract). In general cases, there is one content block in news page and several content blocks in forum and blog page. The content block detecting method is shown below:

$$\text{score} = \sum_i w_i f_i \quad (4)$$

Where, f_i is the feature and w_i is its weight.

There are many heuristic features (Christian , 2009) such as the variance of the text length of nodes, the ratio of the length of the link to the length of the text in the node, the ratio of the fixed text length and number of stop words inside the DOM node.

The remained issue is how to get the weight of each feature. Since there are three related types: News, Forums and Blogs. We can consider this problem as transfer learning (Jing, 2009). We are interested in getting the weight of target webpage type T and we have labeled instance for K auxiliary type A_1, ..., A_k. Let w^k denote the weight vector of the linear classifier for the auxiliary type A_k and w^T denote the weight vector for the target type T. we now assume that these weight vectors are related through a common component v:

$$\omega^T = \mu^T + v\,,\ \omega^k = \mu^k + v, \quad for\ k = 1,2,\ ...,\ K \quad (5)$$

If we assume that only weight of certain general features can be shared between different web page types, we can force certain dimensions of v to be 0. We use a square matrix F and set $Fv=0$. The entries of F are set to *0* except that $F_{i,i}=1$ if we want to force $v_i=0$.

Now we can learn these weight vectors in a transfer learning framework. Let x represents the feature vector of a candidate web page, and $y \in \{+1, -1\}$ represent a class label. Let $D_T = \{(x_i^T, y_i^T)\}_{i=1}^{N_T}$ denote the set of labeled instances for the target type T. Let $D_k = \{(x_i^k, y_i^k)\}_{i=1}^{N_k}$ denotes the labeled instance for the auxiliary type A_k.

We learn the optimal weight vectors $\{\hat{\mu}^k\}_{k=1}^K, \hat{\mu}^T$ and $\hat{v}$ by optimizing the following objective function:

$$(\{\hat{\mu}^k\}_{k=1}^K, \hat{\mu}^T, \hat{v}) = \arg\min_{\{\mu^k\}, \mu^T, v, Fv=0} [L(D_T, \mu^T + v) + \sum_{k=1}^{K} L(D_k, \mu^k + v) + \lambda_\mu^T \|\mu^T\|^2 + \sum_{k=1}^{K} \lambda_\mu^k \|\mu^k\|^2 + \lambda_v \|v\|^2] \quad (6)$$

Once we get the most probable content, we use the alignment algorithm to find the repeat patterns. We first split the union tree into several subtrees according to the content block nodes. The alignment algorithm is used to measure the similarity between subtrees. Also in the alignment, we consider about node's weight according to the level and category. This step is especially useful for the web pages coming from Forums and Blogs. In the News web pages, the content block itself is usually used as the extracting pattern.

Thus, by alignment, merging, finding content block and mining the repeat patterns, we can get a wrapper to extract the data from web pages.

4 Wrapper Maintenance

The wrapper maintenance arises because the template of the web source may experiment changes that invalidate the current wrappers.

Figure 2 shows an example of the template change detection. The x-axis shows the web pages of one website ordered by the timestamp. Let *time*(i) be the time of the webpage i, then *time*(i)<*time*(j) for $i<j$. The y-axis shows the similarities between the current wrapper and the input web pages. The similarities are calculated using the tree alignment algorithm presented in this paper. The website's template changed at *tc* which causes the low similarities between the current wrapper and the web pages after *tc*. This means that the wrapper should also change due to the change of the website's template. In this scenario, the wrapper maintenance includes two steps. The first step is the detection of the change points in the similarity series. The second step is repairing or re-generating the wrapper using the web pages after *tc*.

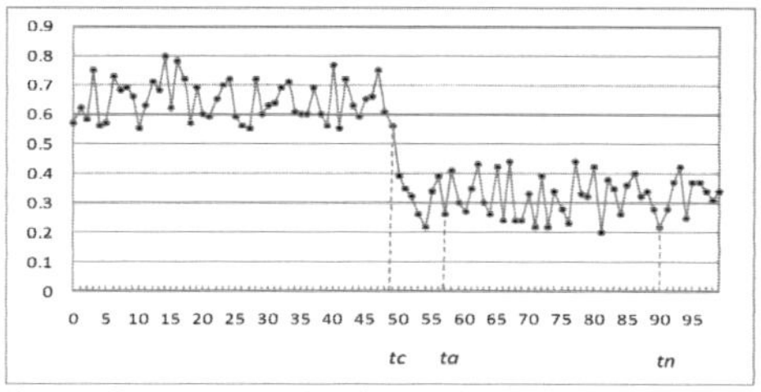

Figure 2: An example of template change detection

We use the log likelihood ratio test (Zeitouni et al., 1992) to detect the change points. Because the likelihood ratios describe evidence rather than embody a decision, they can easily be adapted to the various goals for which inferential statistics might be used. The likelihood ratios provide an intuitive approach to summarizing the evidence provided by an experiment in wrapper maintenance scenario. Let p be the actual distribution of the similarities series.

p_{θ_0} be the distribution under H_0 $p_{\theta 1}$ be the distribution under H_1

We use y_i to denote the similarity between the *i-th* web page and the current wrapper. Let us introduce the following hypotheses:

H_0: $p(y_i \mid y_{i-1}, \cdots, y_1) = p_{\theta_0}(y_i \mid y_{i-1}, \cdots, y_1)$

H_1: There is a time t_c such that

For $1 \le i \le t_c - 1: p(y_i \mid y_{i-1}, \cdots, y_1) = p_{\theta_0}(y_i \mid y_{i-1}, \cdots, y_1)$

For $t_c \le i \le k: p(y_i \mid y_{i-1}, \cdots, y_{t_c}) = p_{\theta_1}(y_i \mid y_{i-1}, \cdots, y_{t_c})$ (7)

We use the log of likelihood ratio $S_i = ln\frac{L_{\theta_1}(y_i)}{L_{\theta_0}(y_i)}$ to indicate the relative probability of the data.

S_j^k denotes the sum of log likelihood ratio. $S_j^k = \sum_{i=j}^{k} S_i$ (8)

To simplify, suppose that y_i are independent and normally distributed with common variance σ^2. Consider $y_i \sim N(\mu, \sigma^2)$.

$\mu = \mu_0$ under H_0 $\quad$ $\mu = \mu_1$ under H_1

We get $S_j^k = \frac{b}{\sigma}\sum_{i=j}^{k}(y_i - \mu_0 - \frac{v}{2})$ Where: $v = \mu_1 - \mu_0, b - \frac{\mu_1 - \mu_0}{\sigma}$

Hence, we get the following hypotheses:

H_0: $S_j^k \sim N(-\frac{mv^2}{2\sigma^2}, mb^2)$ $\quad$ H_1: $S_j^k \sim N(\frac{mv^2}{2\sigma^2}, mb^2)$ (9)

The problem becomes testing whether S_j^k is $N(-\frac{mv^2}{2\sigma^2}, mb^2)$. If H_1 holds, a change point is reported at *j-th* web pages. Take Figure 6 as an example, we use a window (size: m=(*tn-ta*)), and calculate the S_j^{j+m}. The H_1 holds at *i+m* will raise an alarm at *i*. for example, the H_1 holds at *tn* and raises an alarm at *ta*. There is (*ta-tc*) delay since the change point actually occurs at *tc*. In this paper, different window sizes were set to evaluate the change point detection performance.

As shown above, we assume *yi* are independent and normally distributed with common variance σ^2. This tends to be less flexible since it relies on a model assumption. In the community of statistics, some non-parametric density estimation is used for calculating the likelihood ratio (Brodsky and Darkhovsky, 1993). However, non-parametric density estimation is known to be a hard problem (Hardel et al. 2004; Huang et al., 2007), it may not be promising in the practice. The experimental results in Section 3 have shown this. One way to alleviating this difficulty is to directly estimate the ratio of probability densities, not the probability densities themselves. Recently, direct density-ratio estimation has been actively explored in the machine learning and the Kullback Leibler Importance Estimation Procedure (KLIEP)(Sugiyama et al., 2008). We also use the KLIEP and give the experimental results in Section 5.

5 Experimental Results

5.1 Evaluation of Wrapper Generation

The wrapper generation approach is compared with the Zhai and Liu(2005) (PA in Table 1) and Zigoris et al.(2006) (SVM in Table 1). For each web page category (News, Forum and Blog), 40 websites and 6000 web pages were selected for the experiments.

The experimental results are shown in Table 1. PA performs better in the news websites than in the forum and blog while our method gets the best performance in blogs. It's because that PA method is more suitable for news websites. The experimental results also showed that the transfer learning for tree alignment parameters outperform the SVM method.

We evaluated the system performance under different size of union tree. Figure 3 shows the experimental results. Here the 'news_p' and 'news_r' are the precision and recall gotten from the news corpus respectively, and 'forum_p' and 'forum_r' are the precision and recall gotten from the forum corpus respectively. The x axis shows number of the trees merged into the union tree. We can see that the system tend to convergence while the number is about 30. That means we can use about 30 samples to build the union tree and to get the extraction template, which will save much time.

We evaluated the impact of the size of the collection for getting the tag-matching weight. From the Figure 4, we can see that the system performance better on the blog corpus again. We should notice that the weight setting procedure needs more samples than the union tree building (50 web pages in the forum and blog corpus, 80 web pages in the news corpus). Since the weight setting is time-consuming (C_n^2 tree alignment on the collection of n web pages), we think it's better to get them in advance.

We also evaluated the annotated samples needed for the transfer learning method. The experiment results are shown in Figure 5. We can see that the more the annotated samples, the better the system performance. The system tends to convergence while the number of the annotated sample is about 200.

Table 1: The experimental results

		PA	SVM	Our method
News	Precision	0.912	0.892	**0.903**
	Recall	0.865	0.933	**0.956**
Forum	Precision	0.845	0.918	**0.932**
	Recall	0.891	0.946	**0.965**
Blog	Precision	0.848	0.921	**0.941**
	Recall	0.903	0.958	**0.969**

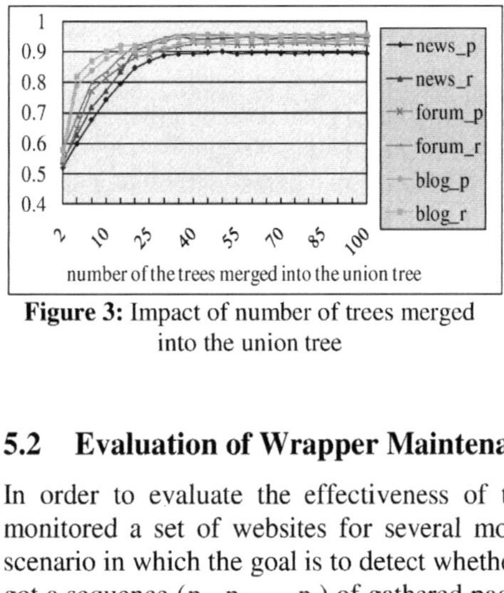

Figure 3: Impact of number of trees merged into the union tree

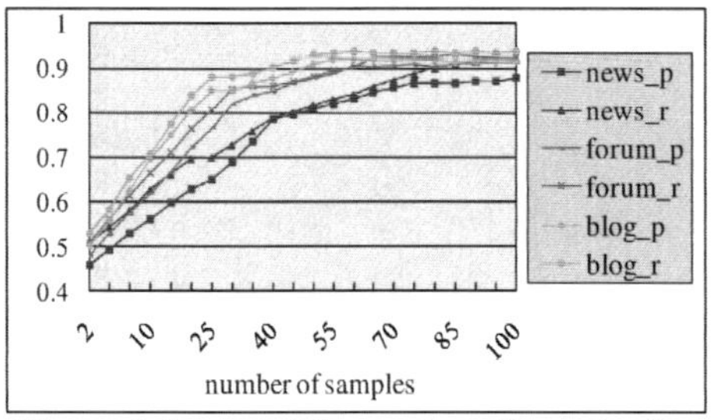

Figure 4: Impact of the number of samples for getting the tag-matching weight

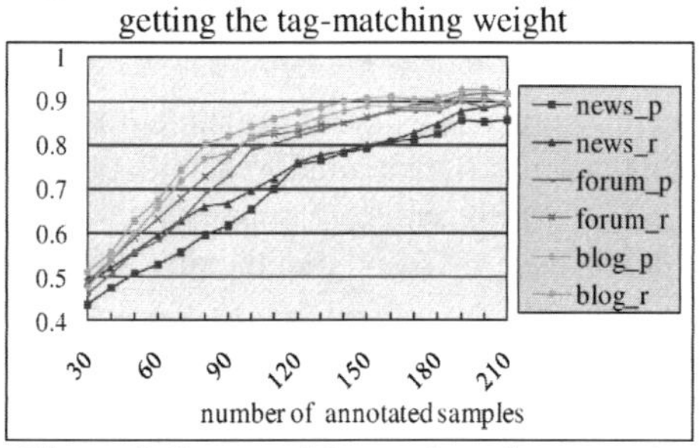

Figure 5: Impact of the number of annotated samples for transfer learning

5.2 Evaluation of Wrapper Maintenance

In order to evaluate the effectiveness of the proposed wrapper maintenance approach, we monitored a set of websites for several months. Our experiment was designed to model the scenario in which the goal is to detect whether a site's template has changed. For a fixed site, we got a sequence (p_1, p_2, ..., p_n) of gathered pages. The wrapper maintenance system should return TRUE iff the site's template changes at p_i which means $w_{i-1} \neq w_i$. Where the w_i is the wrapper for p_i. We measured the performance in term of 2*2 matrix shown in Table 2.

***Table 2:** Wrapper maintenance evaluation matrix*

	$w_{i-1}=w_i$	$w_{i-1} \neq w_i$
Predict TRUE	*n1*	*n2*
Predict FALSE	*n3*	*n4*

Several metrics are derived from this matrix.

$$Accuracy = \frac{n2 + n3}{n1 + n2 + n3 + n4} \qquad (10)$$

$$Precision = \frac{n2}{n1 + n2} \qquad Recall = \frac{n2}{n2 + n4} \qquad F = \frac{2 * Recall * Precision}{Recall + Precision} \qquad (11)$$

We manually made some data for wrapper maintenance evaluation because the real data is not enough (26, 30 and 35 for News, Forums and Blogs respectively). We made some test data manually. We change the template of website and put data in it to make some new pages. These kinds of data make the wrapper maintenance problem more difficult. We got 100 data sets for each type of websites (News, Forums and Blogs) including the real data gathered. Experimental results are shown in Figure 6. We can see that the performance on the merged test set (News_M, Forum_M, Blog_M) was worse than that on the real test set.

As shown in Section 4, there are parametric and non-parametric density estimation method and direct density-ratio estimation method for the log likelihood ration test. We compared these methods and got the experimental results shown in the Figure 7, 8 and 9. Here, the 'LLR-Norm' means the parametric method using normal distribution, 'LLR-Non' means the non-parametric method and 'KLIEP' means the direct density-ratio estimation method shown in (Sugiyama et al., 2008). The experimental results show that the LLR-Norm method outperforms the LLR-Non and KLIEP. As mentioned in Section 4, non-parametric density estimation is known to be a hard problem (Hardel et al. 2004; Huang et al., 2007), it may not be promising in the practice. The reason why the KLIEP is worse than LLR-Norm is that it is a batch algorithm and not suitable for the change point detection. The experiments follow the principles of Occam's Razor. In many cases, the simplest solution is usually the correct one.

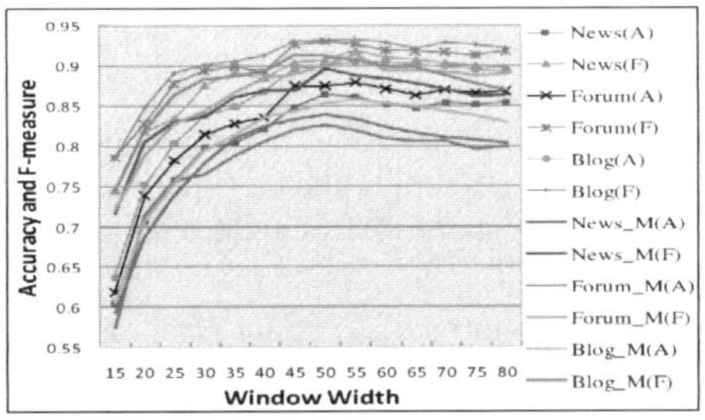

Figure 6: The experimental results on real and merged test set

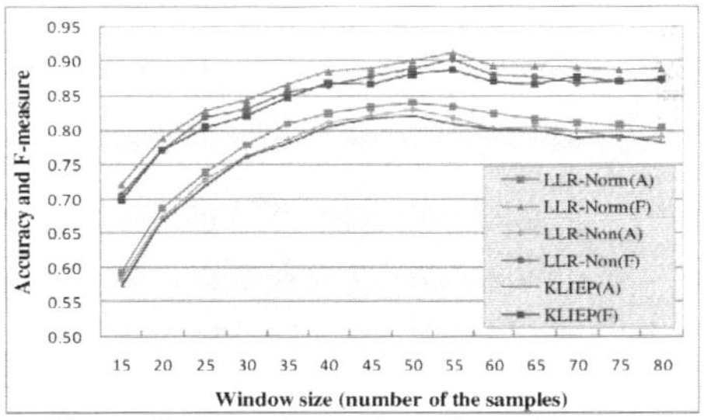

Figure 8: Experimental results on Forums

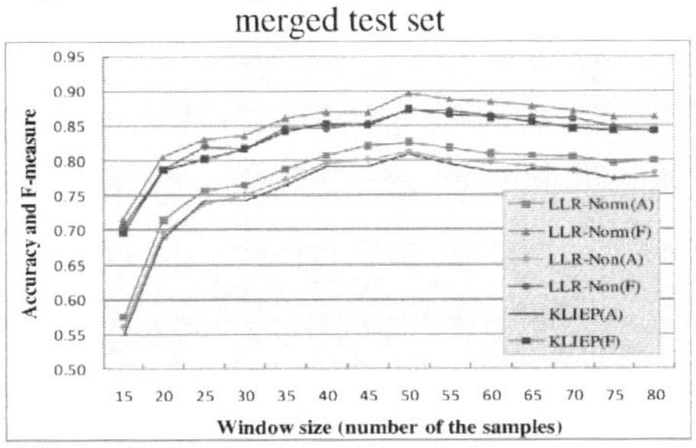

Figure 7: Experimental results on News websites

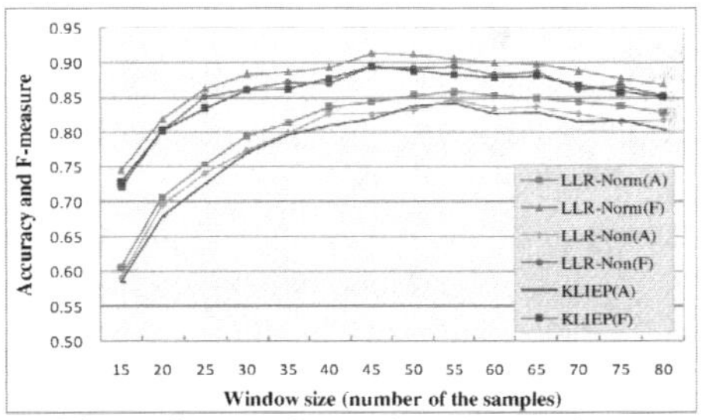

Figure 9: Experimental results on Blogs

6 Conclusions and Future Works

In this work, a method that uses tree alignment and transfer learning method is proposed to generate the wrapper from web pages of Forums, Blogs and News web sites. The tree alignment algorithm is adopted to find the best matching structure of the input web pages. A kind of linear regression method is employed to get the weight of different tag-matching. Based on the alignment, we merge the trees into one union tree whose nodes record the statistical information gotten from multiple web pages. We use a transfer learning method to find the most likely content block and use the alignment algorithm to detect the repeat patterns on the union tree. In the wrapper maintenance approach, the tree alignment algorithm is utilized as a metric of the similarity between wrapper and web pages. A log likelihood ratio test is adopted to detect the change points on the similarity series. The wrapper generation method is applied again to generate a wrapper once the web source change is detected. This joint wrapper generation and maintenance method can be applied to the kind of websites whose web pages are dynamically generated using a common template populated with data from databases. Experimental results show that the method achieves high accuracy and has steady performance.

There are several important issues remaining to be addressed in the future work. It is important to make the most probable content block detecting more accurately and thus enhance the repeating pattern mining procedure. In wrapper maintenance problem, it's a challenge to explore using fewer samples.

References

Arasu A and Hector GM. 2003. Extracting structured data from Web pages. Proceedings of the 2003 ACM SIGMOD international conference. San Diego, California. PP337-348.

Atzeni P and Mecca G. 1997. Cut and Paste. Proceedings of the sixteenth ACM SIGACT-SIGMOD-SIGART symposium. Tucson, Arizona, United States. PP144-153.

Chang C. and Lui SL. 2001. IEPAD: Information extraction based on pattern discovery. Proceedings of the 10th World Wide Web. Hong Kong. PP681-688.

Brodsky B and Darkhovsky B. Nonparametric Methods in Change-Point Problems, Kluwer Academic Publishers, 1993.

Chang CH, Kayed M, Girgis MR, Shaalan K. 2006. A survey of Web information extraction systems. IEEE Transactions On Knowledge and Data Engineering, 2006, pp1411-1428

Chidlovskii B. 2001. Automatic repairing of web wrap-pers. Proceedings of the 3rd international workshop on Web information and data management. Atlanta, Georgia, USA, 9 November 2001, PP24-30

Cohen W, Hurst M, and Jensen L. 2002. A flexible learning system for wrapping tables and lists in HTML documents. Proceedings of the 11th inter-national conference on World Wide Web. Honolulu, Hawaii, USA. PP232-241.

Crescenzi V and Mecca G. 1998. Grammars have ex-ceptions. Information Systems, 23(8), PP539-565

Crescenzi V, Mecca G and Merialdo P. 2001. Roadrunner: Towards automatic data extraction from large web sites. In proceedings of the 26th International Conference on Very Large Database Systems. Rome, Italy, 2001. PP 109-118.

Christian K. 2009. A Densitometric Analysis of Web Template Content. WWW 2009, April 20–24, 2009, Madrid, Spain. PP 1165-1166

Hardel W, Muller M, Sperlich S and Werwatz A. Non-parametric and Semi-parametric Models, Springer Series in Statistics, Springer, Berlin, 2004

Huck G, Frankhause P, Aberer K and Neuhold E J. 1998. Jedi: extracting and synthesizing information from the web. In Proceedings of 3rd IFCIS International Conference on Cooperative Information Systems. New York, USA, 20-22 Aug 1998. PP32-41.

Huang J, Smola A, Gretton A, Borgwardt K and Schol-kopf B, Correcting Sample Selection Bias by Unla-beled Data, In Advance in Neural Information Processing Systems, Vol. 19, MiT press, Cambridge, MA, 2007

Irmak U and Suel T. 2006. Interactive wrapper genera-tion with minimal user effort. In Proceedings of the 15th World Wide Web. Scotland, May 23-26, 2006. PP553-563.

Jing J. 2009. Multi-task Transfer Learning for Weakly-Supervised Relation Extraction. The 47 th Association for Computational Linguistics, August 2009, pp1012-1020.

Keogh E, Chu S, Hart D, and Pazzani M. 2003. Seg-menting time series: A survey and novel approach. In Data Mining in Time Series Databases. second ed. World Scientific, 2003.

Kushmerick N. 1999, Regression testing for wrapper maintenance. In Proceedings of the 14th National Conference on Artificial Intelligence (AAAI-1999), 1999, PP74-79

Kushmerick N. 2000. Wrapper induction: efficiency and expressiveness. Artificial Intelligence, 118(1-2), April 2000, PP15-68.

Laender AHF, Ribeiro Neto BA, da Silva AD, Teixeira JS, 2002. A Brief Survey of Web Data Extraction Tools. SIGMOD Record, 31(2), June 2002. pp84-93

Lerman K, Minton S N, Knoblock C A. 2003. Wrapper Maintenance: A Machine Learning Approach. Jour-nal of Artificial Intelligence Research 18(2003), PP149-181

Lerman K, Getoor L, Minton S and Knoblock C. 2004. Using the Structure of Web Sites for Automatic Segmentation of Tables. In Proceedings of the 2004 ACM SIGMOD international conference on Man-agement of data. Paris, France, 2004. PP119-130

Meng XF, Hu D D, Li C. 2003. Schema-Guided Wrap-per Maintenance for Web-Data Extraction, Proceedings of the 5th ACM international workshop on Web information and data management, November 7-8, 2003, New Orleans, Louisiana, USA.,PP1-8

Muslea I, Minton S and Knoblock C. 1999. A hierarchical approach to wrapper induction. In Proceedings of the third annual conference on Autonomous Agents, Seattle, Washington, United States, 1999. PP190-197.

Pinto D, McCallum A, Wei X and Bruce W. 2003. Table Extraction Using Conditional Random Fields. Proceedings of the 26th annual international ACM SIGIR conference on Research and development in information retrieval. Toronto, Canada, 2003. PP235-242.

Raposo J, Pan A, Álvarez M , Hidalgo J. 2005. Automatically maintaining wrappers for semi-structured web sources. Proceedings of the 9th International Database Engineering & Application Symposium. 25-27 July 2005, Montreal, Canada. PP 105- 114

Sahuguet A and Azavant F. 1999. Web ecology: Re-cycling HTML pages as XML documents suing W4F. In Proceedings of ACM SIGMOD Workshop, Pennsylvania, June 3-4, 1999.

Simon K and Lausen G. 2005. ViPER: Augmenting automatic information extraction with visual perceptions. In Proceedings of the 14th ACM international conference on Information and knowledge management. Bremen, Germany, 2005. pp 381-388.

Sugiyama M, Suzuki T, nakajima S, Kashima H, Von Bunau P and Kawanabe M. Direct Importance Estimation for Covariance Shift Adaptation, Annals of the Institute of Statistical Mathematics, 60(4), 2008

Wang JY, Lochovsky FH. 2003.Data extraction and label assignment for Web databases. In Proceedings of the 12th World Wide Web. Budapest,Hungary, 2003. PP187-196.

Wang Y and Hu J. 2002. A machine learning based approach for table detection on the Web. In Proceed-ings of the 11th World Wide Web. Honolulu, Hawaii, USA, 2002. PP242-250.

Zeitouni O, Ziv J and Merhav N. 1992. When Is the Generalized Likelihood Ration Test Optimal? IEEE Transactions on Information Theory, VOL 38, No. 5, PP1597-1602

Zhai YH and Liu B. 2005. Web data extraction based on partial tree alignment. In Proceedings of the 14th World Wide Web. Chiba, Japan, May 10-14, 2005, PP76-85.

Zhao HK, Meng WY, Wu ZH, Raghavan V and Yu C. 2005. Fully Automatic Wrapper Generation For Search Engines. In Proceedings of the 14th World Wide Web. Chiba, Japan, May 10-14, 2005, PP66-75

Zheng SH Y, Wu D, Song R H, Wen J R. 2007. Joint Optimization of Wrapper Generation and Template Detection. KDD 2007, August 12-15, 2007, San Jose, California USA, PP894-902

Zigoris P, Eads D, Zhang Y. 2006. Unsupervised Learning of Tree Alignment Models for Information Extraction. Sixth IEEE International Conference on Data Mining - Workshops 2006, PP.45-49

Evaluation *via Negativa* of Chinese Word Segmentation for Information Retrieval*

Mike Tian-Jian Jiang[ac], Cheng-Wei Shih[bc], Chan-Hung Kuo[c], Richard Tzong-Han Tsai[d], and Wen-Lian Hsu[abc]

[a]Department of Computer Science, National Tsing Hua University,
Hsinchu, Taiwan
[b] Institute of Information Systems and Application, National Tsing Hua University,
Hsinchu, Taiwan
[c] Institute of Information Science, Academia Sinica,
Taipei, Taiwan
{tmjanng, dapi, laybow, hsu}@iis.sinica.edu.tw
[d] Department of Computer Science & Engineering, Yuan Ze University,
Taoyuan, Taiwan
thtsai@saturn.yzu.edu.te

Abstract. Numerous studies have analyzed the influences of word segmentation (WS) performance on information retrieval (IR) for Mandarin Chinese and have demonstrated a non-monotonic relationship between WS accuracy and IR effectiveness. The usefulness of the compound words that have been a focus of the IR literature is not reflected by common WS evaluation metrics of word-based precision (P) and recall (R). This investigation proposes alternative measurements of WS accuracy, which are based on negative segments that are annotated against four standards of referenced corpora, called true negative rate (TNR) and negative predictive value (NPV), and compares with P and R through search engine simulation,. Accuracy-controlled WS systems segment queries for the simulation including NTCIR collections and "Sogou" logs. Mean average precision (MAP) estimates the similarity of search results between the original and segmented queries. The statistics demonstrate that TNR and NPV are generally more closely correlated with MAP than are P and R.

Keywords: Word segmentation, information retrieval, true negative rate.

1 Introduction

Word segmentation (WS) is an essential preparatory work for Chinese text processing applications and consequently has become a focus of research during the past two decades. Numerous researchers have urged the application of various algorithms to produce "accurate" tokenized text in which the segmentations are performed to match one of the standards of Chinese corpora, such as Academia Sinica Balanced Corpus (Huang *et al.*, 1997) and Chinese Treebank of University of Pennsylvania (Xia, 1999), and evaluated using various metrics, such as word-based precision (P), recall (R) and their harmonic average, termed F_1 measure score (F-score), popularized by SIGHAN Chinese WS bakeoffs (Sproat and Emerson, 2003; Emerson, 2005; Levow, 2006; Jin and Chen, 2007; Zhao and Liu, 2010). Subsequently, WS systems that

* This research was supported in part by the National Science Council under grant NSC 100-2631-S-001-001, and the research center for Humanities and Social Sciences under grant IIS-50-23. Ted Kony is appreciated for his editorial assistance. The authors would like to thank anonymous reviewers for their constructive criticisms.

perform strongly in terms of F-score have been considered reliable and are selected as the preprocessors for the commonly accepted notion that WS accuracy is directly related to the effectiveness of follow-up applications. However, this perspective has sometimes failed to win significant support, particularly in the Chinese IR area, because of the absence of strong evidence confirming the causation. As described later in Section 2.3, some previous studies demonstrated a non-monotonic relationship between the performances of WS and IR for Mandarin Chinese, implying that better WS results do not necessarily yield better IR outcomes (Foo and Li, 2004; Kwok, 2000; Peng *et al.*, 2002), while other studies have shown the opposite (He *et al.*, 2002; Nie *et al.*, 2000; Palmer and Burger, 1997). Although these investigations provide valuable information, they remain unable to reach consensus regarding the principles or metrics involved in selecting a proper WS system for IR applications.

Developing a credible method of measuring Chinese WS system requires error analysis. However, the mainstream of WS literature overlooked how incorrect identification of segments based on particular standards affects certain type of applications, and instead focused on improving segmentation accuracy. Consequently, this study annotates negative segment (NS) against segmented corpora, which may provide clues to help select Chinese WS systems for different purposes such as IR. Following definition, the NS forms supplementary WS evaluation metrics intuitively as the concept that already existed in binary classification test: true negative rate (TNR) and negative predictive value (NPV). This investigation designs a simulation on a commercial search engine, which demonstrates how to apply TNR and NPV and why they could be useful for analyzing the influences of WS performance on IR.

The remainder of this paper is organized as follows. Section 2 briefly introduces the literature on IR and WS for Mandarin Chinese. Section 3 then describes the proposed WS evaluation metrics using qualitative analysis. Next, Section 4 summarizes the quantitative analytical results of the simulation, while Section 5 discusses these same results. Finally, Section 6 presents conclusions, along with recommendations for future research.

2 Related Works

2.1 Evaluation of Chinese Information Retrieval

For various open evaluation tasks of Chinese IR, the test collections of TREC-5, TREC-6, and TREC-9 comprise 28, 26, and 25 queries in simplified Chinese, respectively, while NTCIR-2 comprises 50 queries in traditional Chinese. One problem is that the number of queries is small. Another problem with the TREC data is that the Chinese queries (topic titles) have too many keywords. According to Xu *et al.* (2010), the Chinese queries have an average length of 12.2 words; in contrast, the average length of English ad-hoc queries in TREC (English topics 251-350) is 4.7 words. Even the length of Chinese queries is measured using English translations, the average length still exceeds 7 words. Long queries introduce complex effects whose interactions are difficult to understand. These problems are part of a more general issue of sample pooling bias (Webber and Park, 2009). Common metrics for evaluating IR effectiveness include precision of top-*k* retrieval results (P@*k*), mean reciprocal recall (MRR), mean average precision (MAP), etc. These metrics of English *ad hoc* retrieval may suffer score standardization issues (Webber *et al.*, 2008). Alternative metrics were proposed and discussed, including geometric mean average precision (Robertson, 2006) or other popularity-based measurements (Mizzaro, 2008; Yilmaz and Aslam, 2006), but have not been adopted widely.

2.2 Evaluation of Chinese Word Segmentation

This study classifies known evaluation metrics of WS into three categories: boundary-based, token-based and constituent-based. Boundary recall is defined as the percentage of correct boundaries identified, while boundary precision is defined as the percentage of identified boundaries that are correct, discounting utterance boundaries (Fleck, 2008; Goldwater *et al.*, 2009; Palmer and Burger, 1997). Token-based recall (R) and precision (P) are defined analogously to their boundary-based counterparts, except the unit of measurement is tokens rather than boundaries, where tokens can be treated as morpheme instances (Ando and Lee, 2003), lexicon types (Fleck, 2008; Goldwater *et al.*, 2009), or word instances. For example, given an utterance "[[meta][data]] / is / the / data / of / data" as standard in five boundaries, seven morphemes (notice the case of [[meta][data]]), six words, and five lexicon types, one possible segmentation "meta / data / is / the / data / of / data" results in one boundary error, zero morpheme error, two word errors, and one lexicon type error. Ando and Lee (2003) proposed a constituent-based metric called compatible bracket error, which counts reasonable combinations of morphemes, estimate "[meta][data]" and "[metadata]" as interchangeable. Previous studies also counted word error rates (Chiang *et al.*, 1992; Teahan *et al.* 2000; Wong and Chan, 1996) and sentence accuracy (Chiang *et al.*, 1992) as complementary metrics of word-based recall and precision. Several other constituent-based metrics exist, and are usually close related to IR. For example, Liu *et al.* (2008) proposed an evaluation measure "RankPrecision" based on Kendall-tau distance, which compared the similarity between the predicted rankings of "Internal Association Strength (IAS)" and the ideally sorted rankings of IAS in descending order. Methodologies resemble IAS, which may be seen as constituent-based measurements, are "Phrase Inseparability" (Shi and Nie, 2009) and the "Tightness Continuum Measure" (Xu *et al.* 2010).

2.3 WS-to-IR Performance Relationship

The influence of different Chinese WS methods on IR has attracted extensive research attention (Foo and Li, 2004; He *et al.* 2002; Kwok, 2000; Liu *et al.*, 2008; Luk and Kwok, 2002; Nie *et al.*, 2000; Palmer and Burger, 1997; Peng *et al.*, 2002; Oard and Wang, 1999). For example, Foo and Li (2004) tested the effects of manual segmentation and various character-based segmentations and provided detailed analysis of query results. Foo and Li argued that a small test collection reduces the significance of the analytical results regarding the deduction of causal relation from WS accuracy to IR effectiveness. This argument might be considered as a Chinese-specific example of the issue of sample pooling bias mentioned in Section 2.1. Peng *et al.* (2002) compared various Chinese WS methods in IR by systematically examining retrieval effectiveness for different levels of accuracy of the word division. Experimental results indicated a non-monotonic relationship between Chinese WS accuracy (in terms of F-score) and retrieval effectiveness (in terms of average precision and R-precision), where retrieval performance increases steadily for WS accuracies between 44% and 70%, plateaus for WS accuracies between 70% and 77%, and finally decreases slightly for WS accuracies between 85% and 95%. The hypothesis is that although some Chinese WS systems tend to break compound words into smaller constituents, they cannot achieve the top F-score, but can improve the effectiveness of Chinese IR at some level. Kwok (2000) focused on various segmentation methods of query processing to obtain diverse IR results, while Luk and Kwok (2002) verified the influence of different segmentation approaches on document indexing. Kwok, sees more accurate segmentation as generally improving retrieval when content-bearing terms are involved, though exceptional cases exist that may average out the results, particularly for long queries where sufficient redundancies exist to remedy incorrect segmentations of short queries. However, the definitions for term types such as content-bearing and query lengths are unclear. Kwok also hypothesized that individual WS systems probably do not differ sufficiently in terms of accuracy to realize statistically significant differences in IR effectiveness in terms of P@*k*, MRR or MAP. Kwok thus suggested that a very high quality WS system, perhaps exceeding 95% in terms of both R and P, together with specially selected queries for query length and term type would display a different story. Subsequently, He *et al.* (2002) presented a different story, namely that a highly accurate WS system improves IR effectiveness, leaving the phenomenon of a non-monotonic performance relationship between WS and IR inconclusive. Additionally, those works do not apply the same evaluation methods, term types, or query lengths, thus and the relationship between WS and IR performance currently lacks the commensurability required to achieve a consensus among literature mentioned in this subsection.

3 Qualitative Analysis

3.1 Error Case Study

Chinese IR systems frequently employ WS systems as preprocessing tools. WS errors thus may propagate to follow-up Chinese IR systems. Kwok (2002) has investigated this issue and classified relationship between IR effectiveness and segmented terms for query or indexing into three categories. The first is insensitive: segmented terms whose errors do not influence IR effectiveness fall into this category. Most terms in this category are highly frequent and non-content-bearing terms, which are generally treated as stop-words and eventually removed in IR process. The second is monotonic: segmented terms in this category are high frequency content-bearing terms. WS accuracy is monotonically related to IR effectiveness. The third is non-monotonic. As the category named, IR effectiveness is not monotonically related to the accuracy of segmented terms in this category, which can be further divided into three sub-categories: 1) segmented terms are infrequent non-content-bearing terms that are segmented correctly and retained after stop-word removal, and that then may decrease IR effectiveness; 2) segmented terms that are semantically correct but do not help retrievals; 3) segmented terms are foreign names. Take the query phrase "1999 年西土耳其地震" (the 1999 Western Turkey Earthquake) for example, where "西土耳其" (Western Turkey) is the primary subject, which belongs to both the second and the third sub-classes. Correctly segmenting "西土耳其" (Western Turkey) as one term were observed that does not guarantee good IR effectiveness, because "西土耳其" is far less frequent than "土耳其" (Turkey). A particular observation is that "西土耳其" may not appear in some documents directly. Instead, "土耳其西部" (western part of Turkey) or "土耳其西部省分" (western provinces of Turkey) are mentioned in these documents that cannot be retrieved using the correctly segmented term "西土耳其".

Analysis of the above involves semantic and syntactical structures behind surface patterns of words, yet introduces potential debate regarding definitions such as "content-bearing term" and requires more complicated procedures such as sentence parsing that lie beyond the ability of simple WS systems. For example, "农作物" (agricultural plants) is segmented as two words "农" (agriculture) and "作物" (plants) and could be useful for recalling more relevant retrieval results, but is usually seen as an error from the perspective of WS accuracy. A more surprising case is "旱灾" (drought disaster). While one WS system segments it incorrectly into "旱" (drought) and "灾" (disaster) by following a certain standard, some IR systems actually welcome such queries because they have a better chance of recalling loosely relevant results such as "春旱" (Spring drought disaster) or "旱区" (area of drought disaster). In this case, surprises might result from semantic relations such as synonyms or hyponyms, which are frequently considered query expansions of IR rather than the duty of WS. Furthermore, the trade-off between IR recall and precision is also an issue. For instance, a single WS system may not recognize "皮纳图博火山" (Mount Minatubo) as a word and the resultant segmentation could be either "皮 / 纳 / 图 / 博 / 火山" as five words with "火山" (volcano) as one recognized word or simply "皮 / 纳 / 图 / 博 / 火 / 山" as six single-character words. These inaccurate segmentations in terms of WS performance evaluation metrics generally lead to the effective reduction of IR in terms of MAP. However, other studies may interpret similar segmentations as unexpected positive influences on IR in terms of MRR.

This study thus examines errors involving surface patterns rather than deep structures. Examples of the above imply that IR systems prefer segmentations as simple as containing some single-character words, but not as simple as consisting only of single-character words. This particular behavior could be visible in preferences regarding evaluation metrics, which leads this study to investigate properties of word-based WS evaluation metrics in Section 3.2.

3.2 Properties of Word-based WS Evaluation Metrics

Main WS events like the SIGHAN Chinese WS bakeoff traditionally apply word-based evaluation metrics such as recall (R), precision (P), and F_1-score (F) to both in-vocabulary and out-of-vocabulary data to measure participating system performance. Although these measurements are intuitive and uncomplicated, they still suffer the weakness of not considering incorrect segments that variously influence applications such as web search or text retrieval. This section presents qualitative analysis between word-based WS evaluation metrics and the proposed metrics. Notably, this study follows the naming convention proposed by Gao *et al.* (2005) and uses "segmentation unit" (segment in short, hereafter) rather than "word" as the conceptual element of qualitative analysis.

An input sequence "XYX" and its four possible segmentation gold standards G_1, G_2, G_3 and G_4 are "X/Y/X," "X/YX," "XY/X" and "XYX", respectively. Furthermore, four different systems S_1, S_2, S_3, and S_4 output "X/Y/X," "X/YX," "XY/X," and "XYX," respectively. Table 1 lists their recall (R) and precision (P).

Table 1: Performance Evaluation Samples of SIGHAN's Metrics

	S_1: X/Y/X		S_2: X/YX		S_3: XY/X		S_4: XYX	
	R	P	R	P	R	P	R	P
G_1: X/Y/X	3/3	3/3	1/3	1/2	1/3	1/2	0/3	0/1
G_2: X/YX	1/2	1/3	2/2	2/2	0/2	0/2	0/2	0/1
G_3: XY/X	1/2	1/3	0/2	0/2	2/2	2/2	0/2	0/1
G_4: XYX	0/1	0/3	0/1	0/2	0/1	0/2	1/1	1/1

One notable phenomenon listed in Table 1 is that the weighting of partial credits increases with the number of single-character segments in a system, which may mislead applications developers. The output of incorrect segments by different systems may influence the following applications such as IR with different degrees that P and R cannot reflect. For example, "施 / 政 / 偉" (*shih / zheng / wei*) and "施政 / 偉" (*shih-zheng*; *practice policy / wei*; *great*) are both treated as incorrect segments, but the former decreases IR effectiveness less than the latter, because the former only interprets "施政偉" vaguely, while the latter improperly alters the meaning of "施政偉" through its substring "施政." To reveal complementary facts besides R and P of a Chinese WS system, assuming a dictionary D contains segments {X, Y, XY, YX, XYX}, for an input sequence "XYX" in question and its four possible gold standards {X/Y/X, X/YX, XY/X, XYX}, namely G_1, G_2, G_3 and G_4, respectively, their corresponding positive segments (PS) and negative segments (NS) would be

- $PS_{G1} = \{X_1, Y_2, X_3\}$ and $NS_{G1} = \{XY_1, YX_2, XYX_1\}$;
- $PS_{G2} = \{X_1, YX_2\}$ and $NS_{G2} = \{X_2, X_3, XY_1, XYX_1\}$;
- $PS_{G3} = \{XY_1, X_3\}$ and $NS_{G3} = \{X_1, Y_2, YX_2, XYX_1\}$;
- $PS_{G4} = \{XYX_1\}$ and $NS_{G4} = \{X_1, Y_2, X_3, XY_1, YX_2\}$,

where digital subscriptions for segments of the above (such as $_1$ for X_1) denote the beginning position of that segment in the original input sequence. The general definitions of PS and NS are as follows.

- PS: For all segments a_i of a predefined dictionary D, a_i appears at position i of the input sequence and is identical to the segment at position i of the corresponding sequence from a particular gold standard.
- NS: For all segments a_j of a predefined dictionary D, a_j appears at position j of the input sequence and is **not** the same as the segment at position j of the corresponding sequence from a particular gold standard.

When a given gold standard of PS_G and NS_G compared with PS_S and NS_S obtained from a certain Chinese WS system, four true or false predictions form, as shown in Table 2, in the context of binary classification tasks. PS_G and PS_S symmetrically generate recall (also known as TPR) based on $|TP| / |PS_G|$ and precision (also known as PPV) based on $|TP| / |PS_S|$, yet since NS is defined, true negative rate (TNR) and negative predictive value (NPV) exist as $|TN| / |NS_G|$ and $|TN| / |NS_S|$, respectively. For consistency and readability, hereafter this study uses TPR and PPV rather than word-based recall and precision of WS evaluation, respectively. Using the same

Table 2: The Four Situations of Chinese WS as Binary Classification

	PS_S	NS_S	
PS_G	True positive (TP)	False negative (FN)	True positive rate (TPR) = $\|TP\| / \|PS_G\|$
NS_G	False positive (FP)	True negative (TN)	True negative rate (TNR) = $\|TN\| / \|NS_G\|$
	Positive predictive value (PPV) = $\|TP\| / \|PS_S\|$	Negative predictive value (NPV) = $\|TN\| / \|NS_S\|$	

Table 3: Performance Evaluation Samples of TNR and NPV

	S_1: X/Y/X		S_2: X/YX		S_3: XY/X		S_4: XYX	
	TNR	NPV	TNR	NPV	TNR	NPV	TNR	NPV
G_1: X/Y/X	3/3	3/3	2/3	2/3	2/3	2/3	2/3	2/5
G_2: X/YX	2/4	2/3	3/3	3/3	1/3	1/3	2/3	2/5
G_3: XY/X	2/4	2/3	1/3	1/3	3/3	3/3	2/3	2/5
G_4: XYX	2/5	2/3	2/5	2/3	2/5	2/3	5/5	5/5

assumptions as Table 1 and with the help of definitions of PS and NS, Table 3 lists simulated statistics of TNR and NPV.

For example, system S_1 segments "XYX" as "X/Y/X", suggesting its NS_{S1} are $\{XY_1, YX_2, XYX_1\}$. Comparing system S_1 with the gold standard G_4 "XYX" and NS_{G4} as $\{X_1, Y_2, X_3, XY_1, YX_2\}$, TN_{S1} is $\{XY_1, YX_2\}$, and thus TNR is $|TN_{S1}| / |NS_{G4}| = 2 / 5$ and NPV is $|TN_{S1}| / |NS_{S1}| = 2 / 3$. Simultaneously considering Table 1 and Table 3, TNR and NPV clearly balance some trends of TPR and PPV. For instance, according to the gold standard G_4, Chinese WS system S_1 gains no credits in TPR and PPV, yet obtains non-zero scores in TNR and NPV.

4 Quantitative Analysis

Reasonably good IR evaluation requires controlling an excessive number of variables. On the one hand, model indexing/retrieving involves numerous techniques such as stemming, stop-word elimination, word-based indexing, character-based n-gram indexing, hybrid indexing, vector space modeling, probabilistic modeling, etc. On the other hand, not only do test collections for ad-hoc retrieval have some unbalanced characteristics, such as mostly being involved in long queries, but choices must also be made between different IR evaluation metrics and their potential bias. This investigation respects these research difficulties and proposes a temporary solution based on popularity. Considering a real world search engine widely used in daily IR, indexing/retrieving approaches are considered a black box that is likely to be a reasonably good (and probably commercial confidential) set of treatments that includes all useful techniques. Each query and its ranked results based on this black box are paired as test collections. Original queries from different sources are collected to obtain a balanced simulation regarding term length and type. Different query representations are prepared by segmenting original queries using accuracy-controlled WS systems. Similarities in query results between original and correspondingly segmented queries should provide a series of numbers indicating the degree of how closely the segmented queries match the preferences of the black box. Calculating Pearson product-moment correlation coefficients between query result similarities and WS performance in several evaluation metrics can obtain a clearer picture of the influence of WS on IR effectiveness.

4.1 Query Collections

Owing to the sample pooling bias issues mentioned in Section 2.1, this study collected queries from two sources in the hope of obtaining a balanced samples: test sets of NTCIR CLIR 3, 4, 5 and 6 (NTCIR query as in short, hereafter) comprise 197 traditional Chinese queries with average length of 9.38 characters that may contains multiple query strings in a single query, representing academic samples of queries; meanwhile, query logs arranged by a commercial search engine company "Sogou" (Sogou query as in short, hereafter), written in simplified Chinese, comprising 432 consecutive query strings with an average length of 4.36 characters, provide a practical view of end users.

4.2 Accuracy-controlled WS Systems

This study implements several WS systems based on the-state-of-the-art approach that uses conditional random fields with a 6-tag labeling scheme in bi-directional unigram, bi-gram and pair contexts (Zhao *et al.*, 2006). Four gold standards involving Chinese WS corpus from SIGHAN 2005 WS bakeoffs, including Academia Sinica (AS), City University of Hong Kong (CityU), Microsoft Research (MSR), and Peking University (PKU), are adopted as training data (cf. footnote). By randomly dividing the training data into exponentially smaller parts ranging from 1/2 to 1/16384, WS systems trained using corresponding parts perform with linearly decreasing accuracy in TPR and PPV, just as demonstrated by Zhao *et al.* (2010).

4.3 Simulation Design

For traditional Chinese, NTCIR queries are segmented by the accuracy-controlled WS systems AS and CityU. For simplified Chinese, Sogou queries are segmented by the accuracy-controlled WS systems MSR and PKU. The average segment numbers of segmented NTCIR and Sogou queries are 5.8 and 3.1, respectively. All the segmented tokens of a query are quoted, adhered by white space, and formed a segmented query. The original query and all the segmented queries from different WS systems are forwarded to Google to retrieve the top-100 search results. Search results of original queries are considered as the gold standards of evaluating the consistency of querying popularity between original and segmented queries. The consistency evaluation result is measured by using mean average precision (MAP).

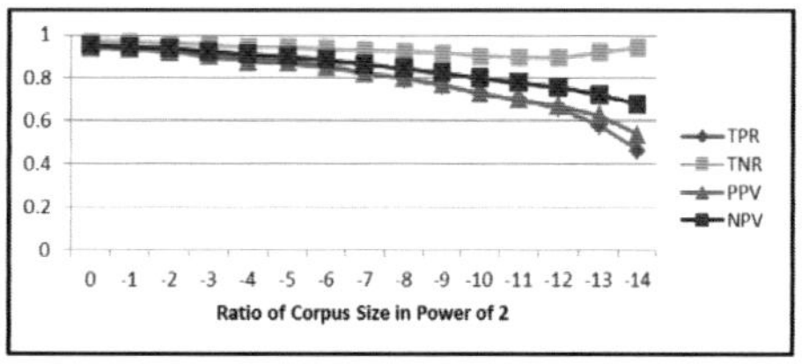

Figure 1: Performances of WS systems trained by different sizes of AS corpus.

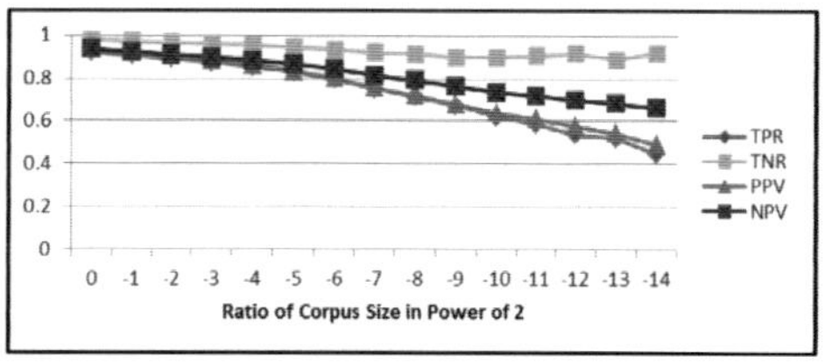

Figure 2: Performances of WS systems trained by different sizes of CityU corpus.

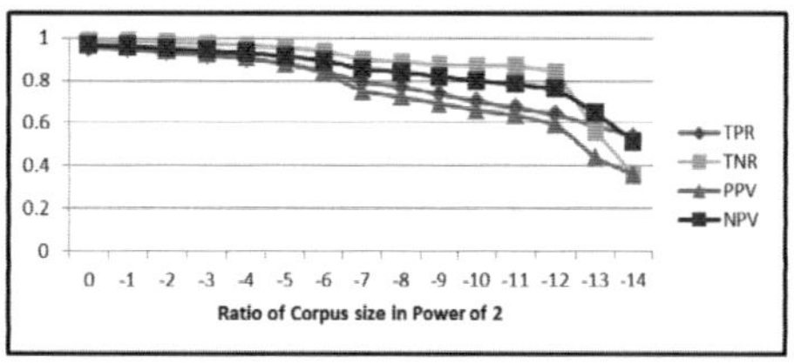

Figure 3: Performances of WS systems trained by different sizes of MSR corpus.

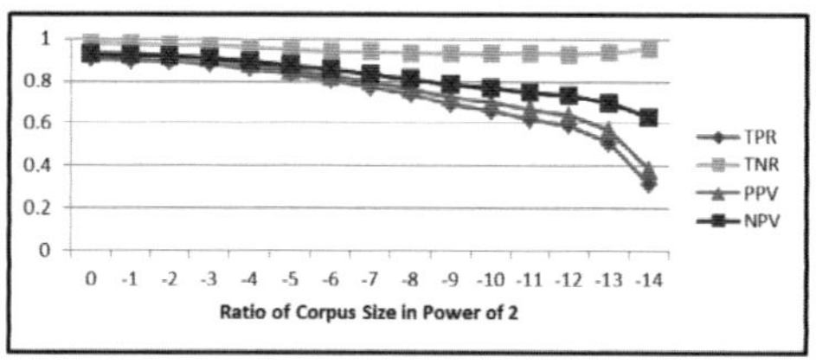

Figure 4: Performances of WS systems trained by different sizes of PKU corpus.

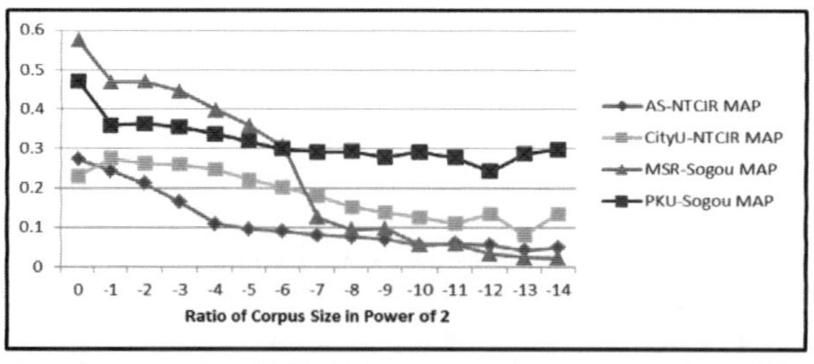

Figure 5: MAP of retrieval results of NTCIR/Sogou queries segmented by different WS systems.

4.4 Result of the Simulation

Figures 1 to 4 show the performances of accuracy-controlled WS systems in terms of TPR, TNR, PPV, and NPV. The MAP values of the search results retrieved by the original and segmented queries are illustrated in Figure 5. Finally, Table 4 compares correlation coefficients.

Table 4: Correlation between search similarities and WS metrics

	AS	CityU	MSR	PKU
TPR	0.742	0.916	0.933	0.615
TNR	0.836	0.944	0.649	0.870
PPV	0.788	0.931	0.901	0.634
NPV	0.800	0.940	0.819	0.692

5 Discussion

Table 4 shows that TNR and NPV are more closely correlated than TPR and PPV, except in the case of MSR. Notably, since Corpus quality assurance process (Sun *et al.*, 2005) and analysis for out-of-vocabulary issue (Li *et al.*, 2005) of MSR use similar definitions of NS, they provide a good demonstration that considering both the PS and NS oriented metric can identify differences between WS systems trained using different standards of corpora. For example, a Sogou query "上海滩" (*shang-hai-tan; The bund of Shanghai*) were segmented into "上海滩," "上海 / 滩" (*Shanghai / bund*), or "上 / 海 / 滩" (*up / sea / bund*) using the accuracy-controlled system MSR, while the same query were segmented into "上海滩," "上海 / 滩," or "上 / 海滩" (*go to / beach*) using the accuracy-controlled system PKU. The TPR and PPV values generally do not significantly differentiate "上 / 海 / 滩" and "上 / 海滩", but the TNR and NPV values do.

6 Conclusions and Future Work

Chinese WS achieve competitive performances based on TPR and PPV, meanwhile numerous academic studies have analyzed the influence of WS performance on IR and yet failed to reach a verdict since some of them demonstrate that WS accuracy is non-monotonically related to IR effectiveness. The usefulness of compounds and constituents of interest to the literature on Chinese IR might not be reflected by common WS evaluation metrics. This study thus develops alternative WS performance measurements, TNR and NPV, by defining negative segments, and then observes their correlation with results obtained using a major search engine. The experiment design aims to provide quantitative comparisons of Chinese search engine results that retrieved using different segmented query representations. The original queries are collected from NTCIR CLIR test sets and "Sogou" search engine logs. Segmented queries are generated using accuracy-controlled WS systems. Mean average precision (MAP) scores of Chinese IR results yield similarities between original and segmented queries. The statistics demonstrate that when obtaining comparisons using MAP, Chinese WS scores in TNR and NPV provide a complementary trend of correlation coefficient to traditional evaluation metrics TPR and PPV.

While Sproat and Emerson (2003) mentioned that WS performance on short Chinese strings has been only studied indirectly via IR evaluation of TREC, this study could also contribute to the research aspect on short Chinese strings since Sogou queries fall into this category. Although this study appears to omit the out-of-vocabulary (OOV) issue, the intention is to provide an alternative perspective in the form of token-based metrics based on NS, which can easily be expanded to cover specific token type of OOV. Sproat and Emerson believe that WS evaluation with alternative segmentation is straightforward, and this study thus roughly describes an implementation to serve this purpose. Assuming the definition of PS is relaxed, such that for a named entity "施政偉" as a gold standard, segments "施 / 政偉" and "施 / 政 / 偉" are also acceptable, the variations of NS are reduced to "施政 / 偉". Under this circumstance, a silver standard of WS can be developed using only highly unacceptable NS annotated in the corpus. Evaluation metrics tied up with this silver standard are naturally TNR and NPV, where traditional TPR and PPV can remain intact with the original gold standard that does not really include alternative segments of "施政偉". Evaluations thus could be more feasible for the WS system with customizable granularity of named entity (Wu, 2003; Gao *et al.*, 2005) or the concept of character combination (Dong *et al.*, 2010). Hence, not only the OOV issue could be transformed into character combination validation, but the word-hood debate regarding Chinese was perceived from different angles, thus probably reducing less disagreement, *via negativa*.

References

Ando, R. K. and L. Lee. 2003. Mostly-Unsupervised Statistical Segmentation of Japanese Kanji Sequences. *Natural Language Engineering*, 9(2), 127-149.

Chiang, T.-H., J.-S. Chang, M.-Y. Lin and K.-Y. Su. 1992. Statistical Models for Word Segmentation and Unknown Word Resolution. *Proceedings of ROCLING V*, 121-146.

Dong, Z.-D., Q. Dong and C.-L. Hao. 2010. Word Segmentation Needs Change – From a Linguist's View. *Proceedings of the First CIPS-SIGHAN Joint Conference on Chinese Language Processing*, 1-7.

Emerson, T. 2005. The Second International Chinese Word Segmentation Bakeoff. *Proceedings of the Fourth SIGHAN Workshop on Chinese Language Processing*, 123-133.

Fleck, M. M. 2008. Lexicalized Phonotactic Word Segmentation. *Proceedings of the 46th Annual Meeting of the ACL*. 130-138.

Foo, S. and H. Li. 2004. Chinese Word Segmentation and its Effect on Information Retrieval. *Information Processing & Management*, 40(1), 161-190.

Gao, J.-F, M. Li, A. Wu and C.-N. Huang. 2005. Chinese Word Segmentation and Named Entity Recognition: A Pragmatic Approach. *Computational Linguistics*, 31(4), 531-574.

Goldwater, S., T. L. Griffiths and M. Johnson. 2009. A Bayesian Framework for Word Segmentation: Exploring the Effects of Context. *Cognition*, 112(1), 21-54.

He, H.-Z., P.-L. He, J.-F. Gao and C.-N. Huang. 2002. Finding the Better Indexing Units for Chinese Information Retrieval. *Proceedings of the First SIGHAN Workshop on Chinese Language Processing*, 1-7.

Huang, C.-R., K.-J. Chen, F.-Y. Chen and L.-L. Chang. 1997. Segmentation Standard for Chinese Natural Language Processing. *International Journal of Computational Linguistics and Chinese Language Processing*, 2(2), 47-62.

Jin, G.-J. and X. Chen. 2007. The Fourth International Chinese Language Processing Bakeoff: Chinese Word Segmentation, Named Entity Recognition and Chinese POS Tagging. *Proceedings of the Sixth SIGHAN Workshop on Chinese Language Processing*, 69-81.

K. L. Kwok. 2000. Improving English and Chinese Ad-Hoc Retrieval: A Tipster Text Phase 3 Project Report. *Information Retrieval*, 3(4), 313-338.

Levow, G. A. The Third International Chinese Language Processing Bakeoff: Word Segmentation and Named Entity Recognition. *Proceedings of the Fifth SIGHAN Workshop on Chinese Language Processing*, 108-117.

Liu, Y.-X., B. Wang, F. Ding and S. Xu. 2008. Information Retrieval Oriented Word Segmentation based on Character Associative Strength Ranking. *Proceedings of the Conference on Empirical Methods in Natural Language Processing 2008*, 1061-1069.

Li, H.-Q., C.-N. Huang, J.-F. Gao and X.-Z. Fan. 2005. The Use of SVM for Chinese New Word Identification. *Proceedings of IJCNLP 2004*, 723-732.

Luk, R. W. P. and K. L. Kwok. 2002. A Comparison of Chinese Document Indexing Strategies and Retrieval Models. *ACM Transactions on Asian Language Information Processing*, 1(3), 225-268.

Mizzaro, S. 2008. The Good, the Bad, the Difficult, and the Easy: Something Wrong with Information Retrieval Evaluation? *Proceedings of the IR Research, 30th European Conference on Advances in Information Retrieval*, 642-646.

Nie, J.-Y., J.-F. Gao, J. Zhang and M. Zhou. 2000. On the Use of Words and N-grams for Chinese Information Retrieval. *Proceedings of the Fifth International Workshop on Information Retrieval with Asian Languages*, 141-148.

Oard, D. W. and J.-Q. Wang. 1999. Effects of Term Segmentation on Chinese/English Cross-Language Information Retrieval. *Proceedings of the String Processing and Information Retrieval Symposium & International Workshop on Groupware*, 149-157

Palmer, D. D. and J. D. Burger. 1997. Chinese Word Segmentation and Information Retrieval, *AAAI Spring Symposium on Cross-Language Text and Speech Retrieval.*

Peng, F. C., X.-J. Huang, D. Schuurmans and N. Cercone. 2002. Investigating the Relationship between Word Segmentation Performance and Retrieval Performance in Chinese IR. *Proceedings of the 19th International Conference on Computational Linguistics*, 1-7.

Robertson, S. 2006. On GMAP – and Other Transformations. Proceedings of the 15th ACM International Conference on Information and Knowledge Management, 78-83.

Shi, L. and J.-Y. Nie. 2009. Integrating Phrase Inseparability in Phrase-Based Model. Proceedings of the 32nd International ACM SIGIR Conference on Research and Development in Information Retrieval, 708-709.

Sproat, R. and T. Emerson. 2003. The First International Chinese Word Segmentation Bakeoff. *Proceedings of the Second SIGHAN Workshop on Chinese Language Processing*, 113- 143.

Sun, C.-J., C.-N. Huang, X.-L. Wang and M. Li. 2005. Detecting Segmentation Errors in Chinese Annotated Corpus. *Proceedings of the Fourth SIGHAN Workshop on Chinese Language Processing.*

Teahan, W. J., Y.-Y. Wen, R. McNab and I. H. Witten. 2000. A Compression-based Algorithm for Chinese Word Segmentation. *Computational Linguistics*, 26(3), 375-393.

Webber, W., A. Moffat and J. Zobel. 2008. Score Standardization for Inter-Collection Comparison of Retrieval Systems. *Proceedings of the 31st Annual International ACM SIGIR Conference on Research and Development in Information Retrieval*, 51-58.

Webber, W. and L. A. F. Park. 2009. Score Adjustment for Correction of Pooling Bias. Proceedings of the 32nd International ACM SIGIR Conference on Research and Development in Information Retrieval, 444-451.

Wong, P. and C. Chan. 1996. Chinese Word Segmentation Based on Maximum Matching and Word Binding Force. *Proceedings of the 16th Conference on Computational Linguistics*, 200-203.

Wu, A. 2003. Customizable Segmentation of Morphologically Derived Words in Chinese. *International Journal of Computational Linguistics and Chinese Language Processing*, 8(1), 1-27.

Xia, F. 1999. *Segmentation Guideline, Chinese Treebank Project.* Technical report, University of Pennsylvania.

Xu, Y., R. Goebel, C. Ringlstetter and G Kondrak. 2010. Application of the Tightness Continuum Measure to Chinese Information Retrieval. *Proceedings of the 23rd International Conference on Computational Linguistics*, 55-63.

Yilmaz, E. and J. A. Aslam. 2006. Estimating Average Precision with Incomplete and Imperfect Judgments. *Proceedings of the 15th ACM International Conference on Information and Knowledge Management*, 102-111.

Zhao, H, Y. Song and C.-Y. Kit. 2010. How Large a Corpus Do We Need: Statistical Method Versus Rule-based Method. *Proceedings of the Seventh conference on International Language Resources and Evaluation.*

Zhao, H, C.-N. Huang and M. Li. 2006. An Improved Chinese Word Segmentation System with Conditional Random Field. *Proceedings of the Fifth SIGHAN Workshop on Chinese Language Processing*, 162-165.

Zhao, H.-M. and Q. Liu. 2010. The CIPS-SIGHAN CLP2010 Chinese Word Segmentation Backoff. *Proceedings of the First CIPS-SIGHAN Joint Conference on Chinese Language Processing*, 199-209.

Factual or Satisfactory: What Search Results Are Better?[1]

Yu Hong, Jun Lu, Jianmin Yao, Guodong Zhou, Qiaoming Zhu
[a]School of Computer Science and Technology, Soochow University,
No.1 Shizi Street, Suzhou City and 215006, China
{hongy, 20104227066, jyao, gdzhou, qmzhu}@suda.edu.cn

Abstract. An interesting issue "whether the factual search result is better than the satisfactory one?" is discussed in this paper, and all effort is to illustrate the publicly recognized conception "the supreme satisfactory result is optimal" could lead Information Retrieval astray. By contrast, we propose a new hypothesis "the factually result should be the optimal although sometimes unsatisfactory". To implement the pilot study on this, we developed a search-engine (Google) based labeling platform and designed a new evaluation method involving user experiences. The results on the platform show the existence of bias on determining the optimal search results (factual or satisfactory). And the very different performances of NDCG and our evaluation metric demonstrate the weakness of current ranking algorithms in mining and recommending the long-term effective information.

Keywords: Factual search result, satisfactory search result, information retrieval, evaluation

1 Introduction

What services are current search engine providing? The universal search engines are mining and recommending all possible relevant information to users. Further, the personal search engines are learning the real intention of users and recommending the information that extremely satisfies the personal requirements. But whether are the satisfactory search results factually factual? The answer should be no. In detail, it can be sure that users aim to explore the unknown when using the search engine, and thus they should have little or even no prior knowledge to support their judgments on the satisfaction with the search results. This may result in the probability that any result with a little relation to the query (even wrong one) can be determined to be satisfactory. It just like that a lost visitor would always say "thank you" to the helpers even if he was shown the wrong way.

Both the explicit and the implicit feedbacks can reflect the user experience of search results (satisfied or not). So the feedbacks are normally used to adaptively learn user intention and iteratively improve the retrieval performance. However, as the discussion above, the judgment on the satisfaction might be imprecise. Thus the adaptive learning, as the most important component of personal search engines, is possibly using the unreasonable feedbacks to mislead the retrieval process.

The doubts mentions above raise two questions: 1) Whether are the satisfactory results always the helpful information for users to acquire knowledge? And whether can they consistently enhance the intelligence of information retrieval? 2) If the answer is no, whether does there exist other kind of information to compensate for the potential failings of users even or supersede the satisfactoriness?

In this paper, we propose a hypothesis that the better search results should be the factual information. The factualness mentioned here is not "users think something right or find it nice" but means the nature of information is really right. The best factual information should be the theorem, scientific laws, and all the knowledge that meets with the law of nature, e.g. "the

1 Supported by National Natural Science Foundation of China (Grant No. 60970057, 61003152) and Natural Science Foundation of Jiangsu Province Suzhou City (Grant No. SYG201030)

reason why an apple fell on Newton's head is because of the universal gravitation". Besides, the factual information should also include the centencyclopedism, common-sense knowledge and any principle that has been proved for centuries by human, e.g. "Not eating roughage will cause beriberi". The hypothesis supports the view that if we know the users' intention, we shouldn't indulge in satisfying their individual preferences or interests, but supply the tried and true knowledge for them to capture the essence of things.

The hypothesis implies a new way of knowledge acquisition: factualness-based information retrieval. And it should present new challenges to current retrieval techniques:

- Identify and mine the actual knowledge in large-scale information resource.
- Detect the target of knowledge acquisition and establish the corresponding query model.
- Involve factualness measurement into retrieval model.

But in this paper, as a pilot study on this issue, we focus on proving the hypothesis, viz., the factual search results should be better than the satisfactory ones. For this, we developed a search-engine (Google) based labeling platform and designed a new evaluation method to measure the precision along with user experiences. The results show strong differences of user opinions on satisfactoriness and factualness, and the factualness has more direct influences on user mood.

The paper is organized as follows: Section 2 discusses the difference between factual and satisfactory search results. Section 3 introduces the labeling platform. Section 4 gives the main labeling results. Section 5 gives the factualness-based evaluation metric and shows the performance of current retrieval model on acquiring the factual information.

2 Difference Between Factualness and Satisfactoriness

The factualness should be different from the relevance or satisfactoriness. For instance, suppose a query is "what is the Chinese Dragon", how can we classify the following search results (relevant, satisfactory and/or factual):

- *1) Do you want to know Chinese Dragon, see this book "Chinese History and Culture"*
- *2) Recently some researchers had proved the Chinese Dragon is but the crocodile*
- *3) Chinese Dragon is the totem of the Chinese nation*

Obviously, 1) is the relevant but not satisfactory information because it cannot reduce the effort of users in getting the answer. On the contrary, 2) normally can satisfy users by the forthright and seemingly authoritative answer although it is wrong, 3) is satisfactory if users have enough knowledge of the Chinese culture, otherwise and actually often it is undesirable although factual.

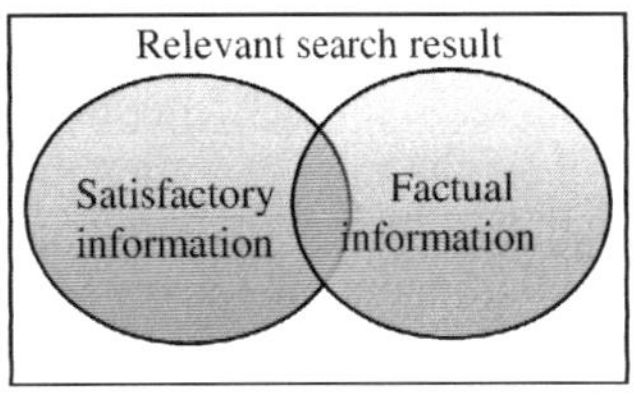

Figure 1: The intersection between factual and satisfactory search results.

It can be believed that both factual and satisfactory information normally are relevant search results. Therefore it is unreasonable to affirm that a search result is consequentially either factual or satisfactory. Actually they have the intersection as shown in the Figure 1. Obviously the search results in the intersection are the optimal because the satisfactoriness can persuade users to accept the knowledge in the results and meanwhile the factualness can ensure the knowledge is right. Thus the difference should occur in the two parts outside the intersection:

- Factual but not satisfactory (abbr., FNS) search results.
- Satisfactory but not factual (abbr., SNF) search results.

The main characteristic of FNS is that the results conflict with the preference, interest, sentiment or prior cognition of users. For example, if the query is "what is my test scores?", the following factual answers will receive different satisfactoriness (suppose the full mark is 5):

- *Your score is 5 (Satisfactory).*
- *Your score is 1 (Dissatisfactory).*

On the contrary, the main characteristic of SNF is that the results conflict with the truth. For example, if the query is "Daddy, will Santa Claus come tonight?", the satisfactory answers will involve different factualness:

- *Yes, but don't be surprised if he looks like me (factual).*
- *Yes, he will drive sled to our roof (untrue).*

As the discussion above, the search results in the intersection are obviously optimal. But which one of FNS and SNF is better? In the rest sections, we focus on introducing a google based labeling platform and the experiment results on it, by which to prove the initial hypothesis: factual information can improve user experience much more.

3 Factualness Labeling System and Results

In this section, we firstly introduce our search-engine based labeling platform for information factualness and satisfactoriness, and then we give the labeling results along with the corresponding analysis.

3.1 The Labeling Platform

The labeling platform includes three components: search engine, interaction interface and database. The search engine provides the service of information retrieval by remotely accessing Google. The interaction interface is used to display the search results and acquire user experiences. And the database is used to preserve the prepared queries and the corresponding factual results, and besides, it is also used to record the user experiences in real-time. Here we focus on introducing two key issues:

- How to obtain the queries having the corresponding factual results?
- How to collect the user experiences?

Considering the necessity for the first issue to ensure the factualness of the results, we regard encyclopedic knowledge of the Chinese language (We have only Chinese volunteers) as the best resources to obtain the queries. We extracted 279,576 items of knowledge from the Wikipedia and used the titles as the queries. Correspondingly the web pages which involve the knowledge are used to be the factual results. After filtering the ordinary and long queries which caused the difficulty for the factual results to be ranked at the top of the result list (users seldom can see them), we got 3,719 queries.

To ensure the realistic user experiments, we display the prepared queries on the interface for users to select the favorite ones. Also we make the displayed queries change in real-time to increase the likelihood of users finding their interests. To obtain the user experiments, we designed two forms to keep records of users' opinions on factualness, satisfactoriness and their mood for each clicked feedback. One form (FBC) includes 6 questions and opens before the click (see Table 1), the other form (FAC) includes 8 questions and opens after the click (see Table 2). The FBC is used to record the initial user experiences on a specific feedback, on the contrary, the FAC record the experiences when the users have gone deep into the details of the feedback. On the basis, a complete labeling process should be: Step 1: select and click a favorite query on the interface; Step 2: browse the feedbacks and select one of them; Step 3: fill out the form FBC and click the feedback; Step 4: fill out the form FAC; Step 5: go back to Step 2 or exist.

Table 1: The questions that should be answered before clicking a feedback.

Form before Click (FBC)
Q1: Whether is it the first feedback? *(Y/N)*
Q2: Whether have you the habit to neglect the first feedback and/or directly check the feedback on the current position? *(Y/N)*
Q3: Have you checked the feedbacks before this? *(Y/N)*
Q4: How satisfied are you with this feedback? *(Radio button)*
A. Very (5) B. just satisfied (4) C. A little (3) D. Hard to say (2) E. Dislike it (1)
Q5: Why did you check this feedback? *(Radio button)*
A. Must be factual (5) B. Should be factual (4) C. The abstraction looks right (3) D. Rank is high (2) E. At random (1)
Q6: How are you feeling now? *(Radio button)*
A. Feel good (5) B. Be interested (4) C. Struggle to continue (3) D. Anxiously (2) E. Be wearisome (1)

Table 2: The questions that should be answered after clicking a feedback.

Form after Click (FAC)
Q7: How satisfied are you with this feedback? *(Radio button)*
A. Very (5) B. just satisfied (4) C. A little (3) D. Hard to say (2) E. Dislike it (1)
Q8: How sure are you about the factualness of the feedback? *(Radio button)*
A. Very sure (5) B. Sure (4) C. Maybe (3) D. Hard to say (2) E. It is wrong (1)
Q9: How sure are you about the wrongness of the feedback? *(Radio button)*
A. Very sure (5) B. Sure (4) C. Maybe (3) D. Hard to say (2) E. It is factual (1)
Q10: What makes you think it is factual? *(Radio button)*
A. High authority B. Credible source C. Credible contents D. Seems reasonable E. I have the same thought
Q11: What satisfies you? *(Radio button)*
A. Provide everything I need (5) B. I can learn some knowledge (4) C. Interesting (3) D. Beautiful webpage (2) E. others (1)
Q12: Please rank all the results you have seen in the order of factualness.
Q13: Please rank all the results you have seen in the order of satisfactoriness.
Q14: How are you feeling now? *(Radio button)*
A. Feel good (5) B. Be interested (4) C. Struggle to continue (3) D. Anxiously (2) E. Be wearisome (1)

4 Main Labeling Results

There are 19 volunteers trained to use the labeling platform, and they submitted 1,659 FBC-click-FAC forms for 719 queries in a month. After filtering the incomplete forms and the errors caused by faulty operation, we finally got 1,238 forms for 539 queries.

Before the discussion on the main labeling results, we firstly give the frequently-used terminologies:

- FBC-click-FAC form: correspond to a click and include both FBC and FAC
- FBC form: a form need to be filled out before users clicking a feedback
- FAC form: a form need to be filled out after users having gone deep into the details of a feedback
- Patience level: an indicator of patience with the labeling process for a query. Here, we use the number of the FBC-click-FAC forms completed by users to indicate the level. For example, given a query, if users click 2 feedbacks and successfully submit the corresponding 2 FBC-click-FAC forms, the Patience level will equal to 2.

Additionally, to quantify the user opinions on the questions of factualness, satisfactoriness and experiments in the FBC-click-FAC form, we gave the answers scores from 1 to 5 according to the intensity (see Table 1 and Table 2). Finally, the quantitative data or/and trend curves that reported below are generated for different QA combinations, so we add the notations of the combinations (e.g. Q7+Q8) into the sub-headings for better discrimination.

4.1 Basic data distribution (Q1+Q2+Q3)

According to the data of the FBC-click-FAC forms, we find the volunteers reached the factual feedbacks of only 20.52 percent of the queries. But according to the prior records in the database, there are about 50.09 percent of the queries (viz. the queries selected by the volunteers) have factual feedbacks in the top 10 of the result list, and even all volunteers reported they at least browsed the whole feedbacks in the first page (viz. the top 10). So there are good reasons to believe that the volunteers missed the factual feedbacks of 29.57 percent of the queries.

Table 3: Recalls on different patience levels.

Patience level	*Recall (%)*	*Clicks (num)*
1	19.37	191
2	19.54	266
3	25.17	429
4	31.03	116
5	28.00	125
6	0.00	90

Besides, by inspecting the recalls on different patience levels (see Table 3), we find two interesting phenomenon:

- Users should have little patience to check more feedbacks (see the column of "Clicks" which gives the number of clicks on different patience levels)
- As the patience level increases, the recall of factual feedback rises (see Figure 2)

The phenomenon illustrate that users can gradually raise the capability of recognizing the factual feedbacks if they have the patience to check and learn more information. However, the truth is that most users only check 1 to 3 feedbacks (see Table 3), thus the probability of reaching factual feedbacks and successfully recognizing them are both low, especially when the factual feedbacks are far from the top.

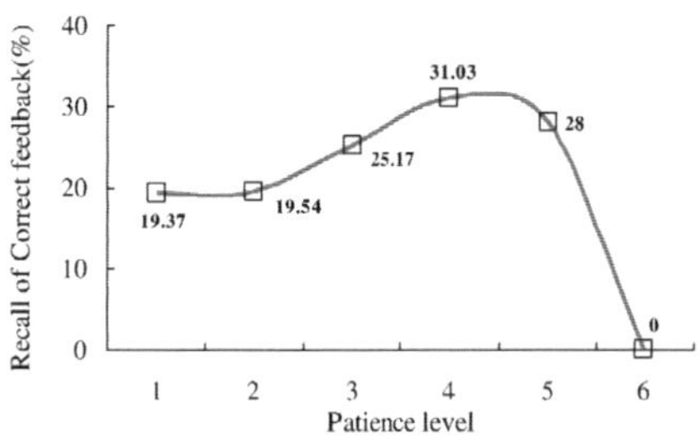

Figure 2: Recall rises as patience increases.

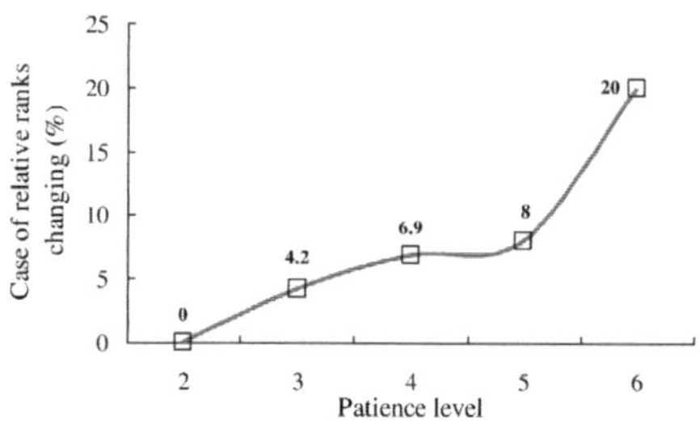

Figure 3: The probability of relative ranks changing.

4.2 Data of cognition transformation (Q12)

The basic data distribution also shows an exception that the recall weakens when the patience level increases up to 5. Then if the exception is not caused by the sparse data on the levels, a question is whether user cognition can be disturbed by over-learning. To answer the question, we inspected the "order of factualness" on different levels by using the data of Q12 in the FBC-click-FAC form. And we focus on surveying two issues:

- Whether does relative rank change as patience level increases?
- Whether will the ranks drop when users learn new things?

For the first issue, on every patience level, we calculated the average probability of relative rank changing as a new click occurs (see Figure 3). Here, the "relative rank changing" means the linear order of prior feedbacks is changed by volunteers according to their opinions on factualness. For instance, if the original order of the i-th and j-th clicked feedbacks is {i, j}, when user k-th clicks a feedback and arrange the feedbacks, within the possible orders {i, k, j}, {i, j, k} and {k, i, j}, the relative rank of {i, j} never changes, but the orders {j, k, i}, {j, i, k} and {k, j, i} change the rank.

This test is used to inspect the disturbance degree of new knowledge to user cognition on factualness. As shown in Figure 3, the disturbance does exist and its degree increases with the patience level. This phenomenon illustrates that users might be puzzled when they are confronted with lots of possible factual information. Thus, considering the little patience of users and the disturbance of over-learning, it is highly necessary for search engines to top-rank the factual information, otherwise users either miss the factual information or lose themselves in the redundant information. However, as reported in *1)*, actually only 50.09 percents of factual information appear in the top 10. This is really a big problem.

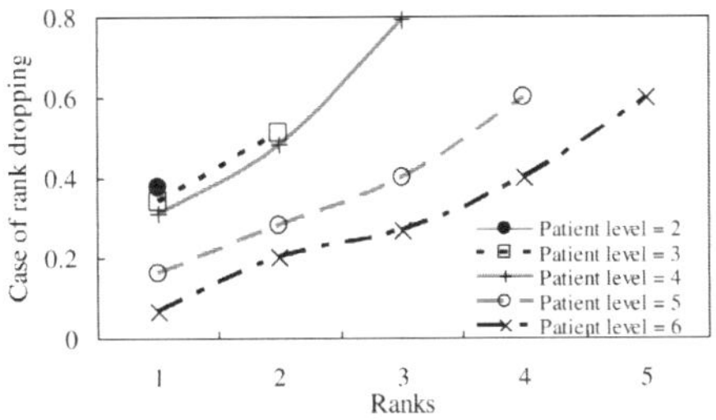

Figure 4: The probability of ranks dropping.

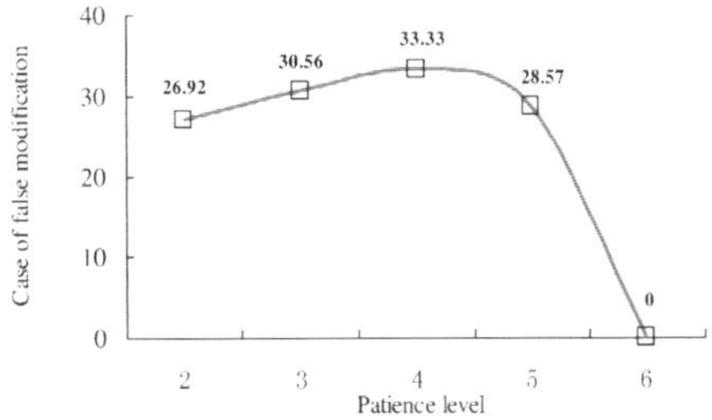

Figure 5: The probability of false modification.

For the second issue, we calculated the probability of rank dropping for every click at different patience levels (see Figure 4). Here, the "rank dropping" means the ranks of previously-clicked feedbacks is dropped by volunteers after a new click occurs. For instance, if the original order of the i-th and j-th clicked feedbacks is {i, j}, and the k-th clicked feedback is inserted into the linear order as {i, k, j}, then the rank of j-th click drops but the i-th doesn't.

This test is used to inspect the obstinacy of users to believe their opinions on factualness. As shown in Figure 4, whatever the patience level is, the probability of rank dropping at the first click is lowest. The labeling results illustrate that the users always persistently believe the feedback they initially clicked is factual. However, the factual precision of the first clicks is only 15.4%. Additionally if users cannot successfully reach the factual feedback at the first click, it will be harder for them to precisely recognize it in subsequent browsing process (see the whole precisions in Table 4). This supports the imagination discussed in the "eye tricks": users always easily accept what they learn or be taught initially and keep the cognition for a long time. But obviously current search engines seem to never consider the characteristics of users cognizing the unknown and the possible negative influence of the initial mistakes on the whole learning process.

Table 4: Precision at different clicks.

i-th click	*1st*	*2nd*	*3rd*	*4-th*	*5-th*
Precision (%)	15.40	6.32	5.12	1.39	0

Table 5: False modification at different patiences.

Patience level	*2*	*3*	*4*	*5*	*6*
False Modification	26.92	30.56	33.33	28.57	0.00

4.3 Data of false modification (Q12)

By the analysis in 1), we have found users can gradually raise the capability of obtaining the factual information if they have the patience to check and learn more search results (higher recall on high patience levels as shown in Figure 2). But it is still unknown for us how many mistakes they make before the factual click. For this, we checked the probabilities of false modification on each patience level (see Table 5). Here, the "false modification" means users mistakenly drop the rank of the factual feedback. Actually, besides of the false modification, the mistakes should also include the wrong clicks before users successfully reaching the factual feedback. But we regard the false modification as the more serious mistake because it happened after users having known the factual knowledge. It can be used to measure the confidence of users on factual feedbacks.

As shown in Table 5, nearly on all patience levels there exists false modification, and the corresponding probability increases as the patience level rise until up to 4 (see Figure 5). This illustrates the initial determination on factualness of users may often depend on intuition or indirectly relevant knowledge, which make it hard for users to confirm the factualness of information. And it can be believed that the false modification should be the main part of which causes the very low precisions on the subsequent clicks (see Table 4). But interestingly, the probability of false modification at the 2nd level is relatively low. It is actually because users always put more trust in their first selection and seldom to modify it, as the discussion in 2). Obviously it should be another challenge task for factualness-based information retrieval to identify and weaken the hesitation of users on the factual information.

4.4 Cognition consistency (Q4+Q5)&(Q7+Q8)

By the analysis in 1), 2) and 3), we concluded the characteristics of user recognizing the factual feedback: 1) Low precision and recall; 2) easy to be puzzled by wrong feedbacks; 3) persistently embrace the feedback they initially clicking; 4) be uncertain about the factualness of every determination. Thus, a necessary question is what makes the users to accept and embrace the wrong information and why they can be puzzled. As the discussion in section 1, one possibility to cause this may be the difference between the user cognitions on the factualness and satisfactoriness. In details, users may always concern with whether information meat their requirements but neglect the factualness, or/and even they cannot distinguish factualness from satisfactoriness. To verify this, we checked the answers of Q7, Q8, Q12 and Q13 in the FBC-click-FAC forms to survey the possible existence of the difference.

Table 6: Scores of satisfactoriness at different clicks.

i-th click	*SBC*	*SAC*	*Differenc*
1st click	3.183	3.646	0.517
2nd click	3.357	3.214	0.143
3rd click	4.000	2.556	1.434

Table 7: Scores of factualness at different clicks.

i-th click	*SBC*	*SAC*	*Difference*
1st click	3.366	3.556	0.068
2nd click	3.286	3.203	0.083
3rd click	2.333	2.258	0.075

We firstly inspected the average scores of satisfactoriness at the 1st, 2nd and 3rd clicked feedbacks before the clicks (Score-before-Click, abbr., SBC) and that after the clicks (Score-after-Click, abbr., SAC), see Table 6. The results show the average SBC of satisfactoriness continuously increases as the click number increases, but the average SAC continuously reduce. This illustrates the satisfactoriness is very different before and after the click. According to the difference, we can at least believe that users are always aware of what they need clearly. It is because they can completely demolish their prior opinions after go deep into the details of information.

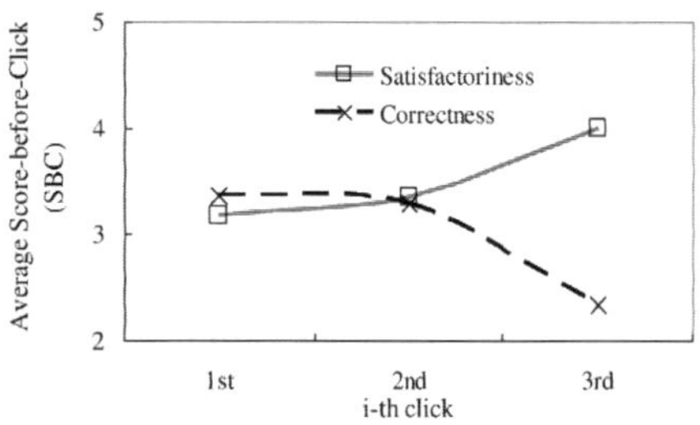

Figure 6: SBC distribution

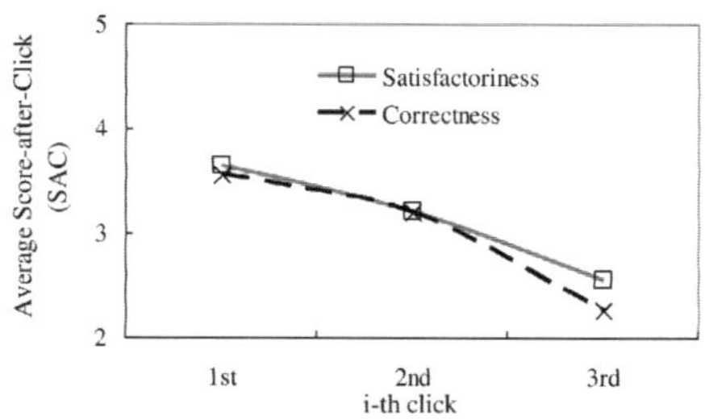

Figure 7: SAC distribution

On the contrary, the condition of factualness is very different. We inspected the average scores of factualness at the 1st, 2nd and 3rd clicked feedbacks before the clicks (SBC) and that after the clicks (SAC), see Table 7. The results show the average SBC of satisfactoriness and the SAC both continuously reduce as the click number increases. And especially, the differences between the SBC and SAC are very small. Thus, if it is right that users cannot determine the factualness by only checking the title or/and snapshot of feedback (actually the low precision has proved this), the small difference between the SBC and SAC may illustrate users normally are not aware of what is the factual information.

Secondly, we inspected the differences between the SBC of satisfactoriness and factualness at the 1st, 2nd and 3rd clicked feedbacks. The results show very different trends (see Figure 6). The rising trend of the satisfactoriness reflects the possibility that users can be easily satisfied so long as the information looks interesting, relevant or/and suiting their tastes. On the contrary, the reducing trend of the factualness illustrates that users may be more fastidious about the factual information. Thus it seems users have completely different cognitions on the satisfactoriness and factualness. However, by analyzing the differences between their SAC, we surprisingly found the cognitions are very similar (see Figure 7): both the SAC trends reduce as click number increases. This reflects the consistent meticulousness of users in evaluating the qualities of information when they go deep into the details.

As a conclusion, we can find following characteristics of users evaluating satisfactoriness and factualness: 1) Click a feedback with the low standard of satisfactoriness but high when checking the details uzzled by wrong feedbacks; 2)With high standard of factualness to select and evaluate the feedbacks Persistently embrace the feedback they initially clicking. Therefore, it can be believed that the relative random clicking creates the opportunity for wrong feedbacks to puzzle users. And if the users are puzzled at the beginning, they will easily embrace the mistake for a long time.

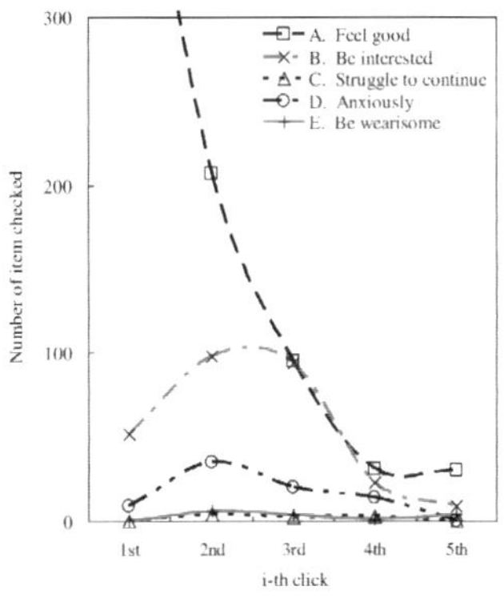

Figure 8: Mood swing before click (MBC).

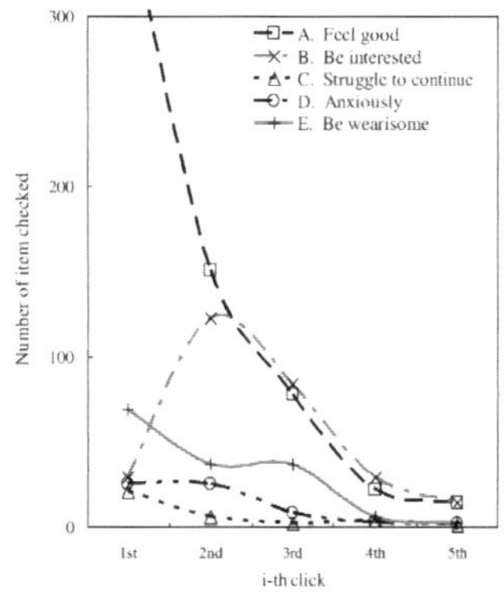

Figure 9: Mood swing after click (MAC).

4.5 Dada of mood swing (Q6+Q14)

In our experiments, we accordingly found the volunteers always have mood swings. In our imagination, the mood swings should be caused by the satisfactoriness or/and factualness. To verify this, we inspected the answers to Q6 (Mood-before-Click, abbr., MBC) and Q14 (Mood-after-Click, abbr., MAC) and counted the number of marks at from the 1st to 5th clicks. The whole trends of mood swings on the clicks are shown in Figure 8 (MBC) and Figure 9 (MAC). Here, it is necessary to note that the reducing trend of each curve in the figures should be neglected because the practical number of clicks at the higher patience level is really small. Thus the factual perspectives should be the height of the whole curve in the two-dimensional space and the height difference among the curves. By comparing the two figures, we found two characteristics: 1) The differences of curves A, B, C and D (viz., feel good, be interested, struggle to continue and anxiously) before and after click are not obvious; 2) The difference of curve E (viz., be wearisome) before and after click is big.

The characteristics illustrate that the mood swings of users normally occur after going deep into the details of feedbacks but not in the process of browsing the result list. Thus why will the details make users have the obvious mood swings? To answer the question, we exclusively extracted the feedbacks which caused the swings and inspected the probabilities of wrongness at different i-th click (see Table 8). It can be found that nearly all the feedbacks are wrong. Therefore, the mood swing should attribute to the frequently-occurring wrong information, especially that involving obvious errors or/and noises (others normally cannot move the users because their factualness are actually unknown to users at the beginning), e.g. advertisement, dead link, fraud page, irrelevant page, etc.

Table 8. Wrongness of the feedbacks causing mood swings.

i-th click	*1st click*	*2nd click*	*3rd click*
Wrong feedback	1	0.9126	0.9219

4.6 Factualness identification (Q10+Q11)

According to the quantitative evidences, we can conclude the main advantages of highly ranking factual feedbacks: 1) Help users cognize factual knowledge quickly; 2) Avoid to puzzle users in the process of surveying factual knowledge; 3) Reduce the probability of negative mood swings occurring. Therefore, compare to the satisfactory feedback, the factual one can not only supplies trustworthy information service but also improve the user experiments.

Table 9: Success rate of feature in factualness identifying.

Features	*A*	*B*	*C*	*D*	*E*
Factual	0.3439	0.3966	0.1304	0.0949	0.0343
Wrong	0.0796	0.3628	0.0531	0.0620	0.4425
Difference	**0.2643**	**0.0338**	**0.0773**	**0.0329**	**0.4082**

(**A**: *High authority*; **B**: *Credible source*; **C**: *Credible contents*; **D**: *Seems reasonable*; **E**: *I have the same thought*)

Table 10: Success rate of feature in satisfactoriness identifying.

Features	*A*	*B*	*C*	*D*	*E*
Satisfactory	0.2992	0.3333	0.1197	0.0855	0.0086
Dissatisfactory	0.1089	0.2657	0.2352	0.1237	0.0549
Difference	**0.1903**	**0.0676**	**0.1155**	**0.0382**	**0.0463**

(**A**: *Provide everything I need*; **B**: *I can learn some knowledge*; **C**: *Interesting*; **D**: *Beautiful webpage*; **E**: *others*)

Thus how can we identify the factual feedbacks? To answer this question, we inspected the opinions of volunteers on 5 features (see Q10 in Table 2): authority, credibility of source, credibility of contents, reasonability and the cognition consistency. We respectively calculated the probability of the features in being successfully used to determine the factualness (see Table 9). According to the difference between the success rates in factual and wrong feedbacks, we find the authority (A) and cognition consistency (E) should be the effective features.

They both have obvious difference between the success rates. However it is hard to automatically measure the cognition consistency. So the authority should be a feasible feature to identify factual feedbacks. Additionally, by checking the cognition consistency (viz. the users agree with the opinions in the feedbacks), we found its success rate is very low to identify factual feedback. It illustrates the users seldom agree with the opinions in the factual feedbacks. This further proved our hypothesis, users normally cannot precisely determine the factualness when they lack of enough priori or/and relevant knowledge. Besides, we also used the same method to detect the effect features in satisfactoriness identifying. The distributions of success rates are shown in Table 10. It can be found that the feature "providing everything users need" (A) is optimal. Obviously, the users indeed concern whether and how many information is consistent with their preferences, but lack of the consideration to factualness.

4.7 Evaluation Metric and Performance of Traditional IR

In this paper, we propose several new methods to evaluate the performance of information retrieval system in detecting and ranking the factual information. Based on the influences of factual feedbacks to the performance of information retrieval concluded in section 3.2, the factualness-focused evaluation metric should include three quantities to be measured: 1) *P@n*: indicates the precision of the top n feedbacks, which actually is the percentage of the factual feedbacks in the top n feedbacks; 2) NDCG@n[9][10][11]: is the normalized DCG@n which involves the tradeoff between the factualness degree and the ranking; 3) MCost@n: indicate the cost of negative mood swings in the top n feedbacks.

In information retrieval, the traditional DCG comprehensively considers the relevance level and the ranking: if a feedback which has higher relevance level is ranked highly, the DCG will increase, else will reduce. Here, we use the DCG to measure the tradeoff of the factualness level and the ranking: if a feedback which has higher factualness level is ranked highly, the DCG will increase, else will reduce. The third quantity, viz. MCost, is calculated like the DCG but focuses on measuring the tradeoff of the satisfactoriness level of wrong feedback and the ranking: if a wrong feedback which has higher satisfactoriness level is ranked highly, the MCost will increase, else will reduce.

We reproduced two personal information retrieval systems: one used Eye-tracking based user behavior analyzer[1] (abbr., E-sys); the other used click-through based user behavior analyzer[2] (C-sys). And we ran the two systems and evaluate their NDCG@10 and MCost@10 respectively. Besides, we used the metrics to measure the performance of manually labeling results and regarded that as baseline. The performances are shown in Table 11. It can be found that, compared to the baseline, the personal information retrieval systems E-sys and C-sys achieve better NDCG but worse Mcost (higher MCost score means worse user experience).

Table 11. Main performances

Features	*E-sys*	*C-sys*	*Baseline*
NDCG@10	0.2629	0.2816	0.1756
MCost@10	0.3521	0.3343	0.2212

5 Conclusion

This paper gives plenty of evidences achieved from a Google based labeling platform to prove the hypothesis that the factual feedback should be optimal in the search results. In future, we will firstly promote our search-engine based labeling platform. Current version only regards the Wikipedia webpage as the sole factual feedback. But there are indeed some other web pages involving the factual information, e.g. the Baidupedia pages, pages of knowledge bases, etc. Additionally, we will further survey the possible features for factualness identification. In our imagination, the logicality of information should be an effective feature. The logicality can be used to verify whether the relation of events, attribute of things, characteristics of things collaborating in information accord with the factual regularity. This should be a hard but necessary task in our works.

References

Laura, A. G., Thorsten, J., Geri, G. 2004. Eye-Tracking Analysis of User Behavior in WWW Search. The Proceedings of the 27th annual international ACM SIGIR conference on Research and development in information retrieval. New York: ACM Press, 478-479.

Xue, G-R., Zeng, H-J., Zheng, C., Yong, Y., Ma, W. Y., Xi, W-S., Fan, W-G. 2007. Optimizing Web Search Using Web Click-Through Data. CIKM'04. New York: ACM Press, 118-126.

A Graph-based Bilingual Corpus Selection Approach for SMT *

Wenhan Chao[a] and Zhoujun Li[a]

[a] School of Computer Science & Engineering, BeiHang University,
37# Xueyuan Rd, Haidian District, Beijing 100191, China
{chaowenhan, lizj}@buaa.edu.cn

Abstract. In statistical machine translation, the number of sentence pairs in the bilingual corpus is very important to the quality of translation. However, when the quantity reaches some extent, enlarging the corpus has less effect on the translation quality; whereas increasing greatly the time and space complexity to train the translation model, which hinders the development of statistical machine translation. In this paper, we propose a graph-based bilingual corpus selection approach, which makes use of the structural information of corpus to measure and update the importance of each sentence pair, and then selects a sentence pair with the highest importance each time. Our experiments in a Chinese-English translation task show that, selecting only 50% of the whole corpus by the graph-based selection approach as training set, we can obtain the near translation result with the one using the whole corpus.

Keywords: Statistical Machine Translation, Corpus Selection, Graph

1 Introduction

In statistical machine translation, large scale of bilingual corpus is very important. In order to improve the quality of translation, there are two viewpoints about the use of corpus.

One way is to collect more and more bilingual corpus to improve the quality of translation model, such as extracting the sentence pairs from the comparable corpus (Smith et al., 2010; Uszkoreit et al., 2010). However, some researchers found that, after the quantity of the sentence pairs (Han et al., 2009) in the corpus reaches some extent, adding more sentence pairs will not improve the quality of translation significantly. On the other hand, larger and larger corpus will consume more and more resources, which hinders the research progress of machine translation in some degree.

This type of approaches assumes the sentence pairs in the corpus are independent each other, not considering the relationship between sentence pairs and their effect on the translation.

The other view is to mine the potential of training corpus through corpus selection and optimization to improve the quality of the translation model. And it also includes three ways: the first one is to select and optimize the training corpus to adapt to the test set (Lu et al., 2007) or the domain (Yasuda et al,. 2008); the second one is to select the sentence pairs with high quality as training corpus (Chen et al., 2006; Han et al., 2009), in which the quality is measured through the features of the sentence pair itself, such as the number of words that can be translated each other in the sentence pair; the third one is to measure and sort the sentence pairs based on the number of unknown n-grams in the sentences, and then select the sentence pair with the highest scores each time (Eck et al. 2005).

This type of approaches considers the quality difference between the sentence pairs in the corpus. However, it still views the sentence pairs as independent.

---

* The work reported in this paper was supported by National Natural Science Foundation of China, Contract No. 61003111; and supported by Research Fund for the Doctoral Program of Higher Education of China (New teacher Fund), Contract No. 20101102120016

In this paper, we assume the quality of the translation model is related to the coverage and quality of the selected corpus, and expect to select the sentence pairs with high quality as possible when maximizing the coverage of the selected corpus. And we propose a graph-based bilingual corpus selection approach, which makes use of the structural information of corpus to measure and update the importance of each sentence pair, and then selects a sentence pair with the highest importance each time. The underlying principle is that we should select a sentence pair each time to maximize the coverage and quality of the selected sentence pairs.

In the rest of this paper, we first introduce how to measure the importance of each sentence pair based on the bilingual graph in Section 2, and then describe the framework of graph-based bilingual corpus selection approach in Section 3, emphasizing on corpus selection algorithm. Section 4 shows the results of the experiments, and we conclude in Section 5 and 6.

2 Graph-based Sentence Pair Ranking

2.1 Terminology and Notation

Monolingual Sub-Graph

Assume that the bilingual corpus ***BC*** is composed of a collection of sentence pairs $<f,c>$, which consists of two sentences that come from two languages F and C respectively and can be translated each other.

The monolingual sentences of each language in the collection of sentence pairs will construct an undirected graph, called *Monolingual Sub-Graph*. The two graphs are represented as $G_f=<V_f,E_f>$ and $G_c=<V_c,E_c>$ respectively.

Where $G_f=<V_f,E_f>$ represents the undirected graph constructed by the sentences of language F in the corpus, and a node $f\in V_f$ represents a sentence of language F, and if the similarity between two sentences f_1 and f_2 are greater than the threshold σ_f, i.e. $sim(e_1,e_2)\geq\sigma_f$, then there exists an edge $(e_1,e_2)\in E_f$.

Similarly, we use $G_c=<V_c,E_c>$ represents the undirected graph constructed by the sentences of language C in the corpus, and a nodes $c\in V_c$ represents a sentence of language C, and an edge $(c_1,c_2)\in E_c$ represents that the similarity between the two sentences c_1 and c_2 are greater than the threshold σ_c i.e. $sim(c_1,c_2)\geq\sigma_c$.

Bilingual Graph

Bilingual graph is an undirected graph constructed by the sentence pairs in the bilingual corpus ***BC***, represented as $G=<V_{f,c}, E_{f,c}>$, where $v\in V_{f,c}$ represents a sentence pair in the corpus. For each sentence pair $<f,c>\in V_{f,c}$, it will be $f\in V_f$ and $c\in V_c$.

An edge $(v_1,v_2)\in E_{f,c}$ represents the similarity between two sentence pairs v_1 and v_2 is greater than the threshold $\sigma_{f,c}$, i.e. $sim(v_1,v_2)\geq\sigma_{f,c}$, and the similarity between two sentence pairs can be calculated based on the similarities between the monolingual sentences.

If the node v does not connected to any other node, then we call the node v as an isolated sentence pair.

Quantity of Information (QI)

Given the set of selected sentence pairs $\boldsymbol{S}$, the *quantity of information* of a sentence pair is the quantity of the novel information it can provide, i.e. it represents the novelty of the sentence pair.

In the beginning, $S=\phi$, and the quantity of information for each sentence pair will be the largest value. And as the S increases, the quantity of information for each unselected sentence pair will be updated dynamically, removing the redundancy information between S and the sentence pair.

The quantity of information for the whole corpus will be the sum of quantity of information for all sentences pairs in the corpus, and it represents the coverage of the selected corpus.

Coverage of Sentence Pair (CSP)

For each unselected sentence pair, the *coverage* is the quantity of redundancy information between the sentence pair and all of the other unselected sentence pairs in the bilingual corpus. And it is the sum of redundancy information between the sentence pair and each unselected sentence pair in the corpus.

In the bilingual graph, the coverage for each sentence pair only considers the sentence pairs that connect to it.

The underlying principle is that the more the number of the similar sentence pairs with high quality is, the better of the quality of the sentence pair is. Thus, CSP represents the quality of the sentence pair.

Importance of Sentence Pair (ISP)

The *importance* of sentence pair consists of two parts: the *quantity of information* (*QI*) and the *coverage* (*CSP*) of the sentence pair.

The underlying assumption is that if the quantity of information and the coverage for the sentence pair is high, then importance of the sentence pair is high.

2.2 Importance Equation

After the bilingual graph has been constructed, our goal is to compute the importance for each sentence pair via the structural information of the corpus, and then make the sentence selection.

The importance of sentence pair (*ISP*) consists of two parts: the quantity of information *QI* and the coverage *CSP*. Given the bilingual corpus *BC* and the set of selected sentence pair *S*, the *QI* for a sentence pair v_a is equal to the initial quantity of information of v_a, represented as QI_0, subtracting the redundancy information contained in the *S* according to v_a:

$$QI(v_a, S) = QI_0(v_a) - RI(S, v_a) \quad (1)$$

Where $QI(v_a, S)$ represents the quantity of information for v_a when given *S*; $QI_0(v_a)$ is the initial *QI* for v_a, i.e. the *QI* for $S = \phi$.

$RI(S, v_a)$ represents the redundancy information contained in *S* according to v_a.

The importance of sentence pair *ISP* is the sum of the quantity of information *QI* and the coverage *CSP*.

$$ISP(v_a, S) = QI(v_a, S) + SRI(v_a, S, BC) \quad (2)$$

$$SRI(v_a, S, BC) = \sum_{\substack{v_b \in BC \\ v_a \neq v_b}} RI(v_a, v_b, S) = \sum_{\substack{v_b \in BC \\ v_a \neq v_b}} sim(v_a, v_b) \cdot QI(v_b, S) \quad (3)$$

Where $ISP(v_a, S)$ represents the importance of v_a when given *S*, $SRI(v_a, S, BC)$ represents the coverage of v_a in corpus *BC*, when given *S* and *BC*. $RI(v_a, v_b, S)$ represents the redundancy information contained in v_a according to v_b, when given *S*; $sim(v_a, v_b)$ represents the similarity between v_a and v_b; and $RI(v_a, v_b, S)$ equals the multiple of the $sim(v_a, v_b)$ and the *QI* of v_b.

Given the bilingual graph *G*, we assume that the redundancy information contained in *S* for v_a only be relevant to the sentence pairs that connect to v_a in *S*.

So, we rewrite the $RI(S, v_a)$ as follows:

$$RI_G(S, v_a) = sim(\bigcup_{v_b \in S} v_b, v_a) \cdot QI_0(v_a) \tag{4}$$

Where $sim(\bigcup_{v_b \in S} v_b, v_a)$ represents the similarity between the union of all of the similar sentence pairs of v_a in S and v_a.

Similarly, we can rewrite $RI(v_a, v_b, S)$ and $SRI(v_a, S, BC)$ as follows:

$$SRI_G(v_a, S, BC) = \sum_{(v_a, v_b) \in E_G} RI_G(v_a, v_b, S) = \sum_{(v_a, v_b) \in E_G} sim(v_b, v_a) \cdot QI_G(v_b, S) \tag{5}$$

Thus, our importance equation will be:

$$QI_G(v_a, S) = QI_0(v_a)[1 - sim(\bigcup_{v_b \in S} v_b, v_a)] \tag{6}$$

$$ISP_G(v_a, S) = QI_G(v_a, S) + \sum_{(v_a, v_b) \in E_G} sim(v_b, v_a) \cdot QI_G(v_b, S) \tag{7}$$

The underlying principle is: given the set of selected sentence pair S, the importance of sentence pair will be the sum of the quantity of information itself and the redundancy information between the sentence pair and all the unselected sentence pairs it connects to.

3 Graph-based Bilingual Corpus Selection

3.1 Framework

In order to implement the graph-based bilingual corpus selection, the graph-based bilingual corpus selection consists of three steps as shown in Figure 1:

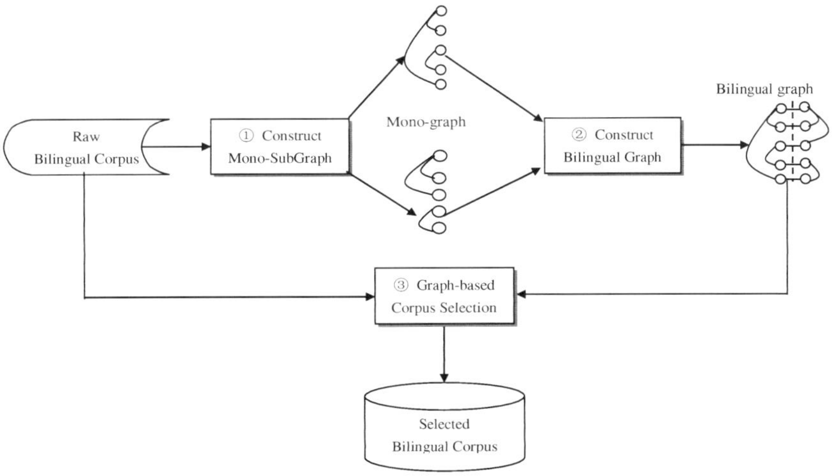

Figure 1: The graph-based corpus selection framework.

3.2 Construct Monolingual Sub-Graph

Measure the Similarity between Sentences

In order to construct the monolingual graph, we need to measure the similarities between the sentences. Considering the corpus is very large, we will take a very simple approach, which counts the number of co-occur words and obtain the similarity as follows:

$$sim(c_1, c_2) = \frac{2 \times |c_1 \cap c_2|}{|c_1| + |c_2|} \tag{8}$$

Where $|c_1 \cap c_2|$ represents the number of the co-occur words between the sentences c_1 and c_2, $|c_1|$ and $|c_2|$ represent the number of words in sentences c_1 and c_2 respectively.

Select the similarity threshold σ_f and σ_c

The similarity threshold will affect the structure of the monolingual graph, and then affect the computing of the importance of the sentence pair. If σ_f or σ_c is too large, it will decrease the edges in the graph, and make the isolated sentence pair increasing; on the other hand, if σ_f or σ_c is too small, there will be too many edges, weakening the ability of distinguishing the importance of sentence pair using the structural information.

Thus, we should try to find a balance between avoiding too many isolated sentence pairs and avoiding too many connected sentence pairs.

3.3 Construct Bilingual Graph

After constructing the two monolingual graphs respectively, we can construct the bilingual graph. We obtain the connection between two sentence pairs in the following way:

- For any two sentence pairs $v_a =< f_a, c_a >$ and $v_b =< f_b, c_b >$, if f_a connects to f_b and c_a connects to c_b in the two monolingual graph respectively, we say v_a connects to v_b, i.e. $(v_a, v_b) \in E_{f,c}$;
- The similarity between two sentence pairs is the average of the two similarities between the monolingual sentences:

$$sim(v_a, v_b) = \frac{1}{2} \times [sim(f_a, f_b) + sim(c_a, c_b)] \tag{9}$$

3.4 Graph-based Bilingual Corpus Selection

After constructing the bilingual graph, we can now make the corpus selection as follows:

1. **Initialize** the $QI_0(v_a) = 1$;
2. **Update** the importance of each unselected sentence pair by Equ.(6) and (7);
3. **Sort** the sentence pairs by the importance;
4. **Select** the sentence pair with the highest importance, and add it to the list S;
5. **Repeat** 2-4, until all of the sentence pairs in the corpus have been selected.
6. **Output** the sentence pairs in the list *S* in order.

When selecting a sentence pair each time, it need updated all the other sentence pairs that the selected sentence pair can reach through a connected path, and then sort all of the sentence pairs again. So the complexity of the selecting algorithm is very high.

We note when selecting a sentence pair, only the sentence pairs that the selected sentence connects will change their quantities of information, so we divide the updating of the importance into two steps:

Step 1: update the quantity of information using the following iterative way:

When t=k=0, $QI_G(v_a, \phi) = 1$, i.e. $QI_0(v_a) = 1$ for all of the v_a;

When t=k+1, assuming the new selected sentence pair is s_n, then only updating the quantity of information of each sentence pair v_a that s_n connects to:

$$QI_G^{k+1}(v_a, S \cup s_n) = QI_G^k(v_a, S) \times [1 - sim(v_a, s_n)] \tag{10}$$

The above equation will compute the quantity of information of v_a approximately.

Note that we set the initial quantity of information of each sentence pair QI_0 as 1 here, that is, all of the sentence pairs have the same *QI* in the beginning.

Step 2: in the selecting step, re-calculate the importance of the sentence pair with the highest importance by equation (7). If the importance has been changed, then sort it and test the next sentence pair with the highest importance; otherwise select the sentence pair, execute Step 1.

Taking the above two steps, it avoids updating and sorting the importance of each sentence pair that the selected sentence pair can reach through a connected path.

Thus the pseudo code of the final algorithm is shown as follows:

```
ALGORITHM:  Graph_Based_BiCorpus_Selection
INPUT:      Bilingual Graph G of Corpus BC
OUTPUT:     Selected Sentence List S
S = <> ;
FOR each Va in G DO
  Calculate the initial ISP_Va by equation (6) and (7);
  Insert into the list L in descending order;
WHILE L is not empty DO
   Va = L. RemoveHead();
   ISP_new = CalcISP(Va);      //by equation (7)
   IF  ISP_new < ISP_Va
       ISP_Va = ISP_new
       Insert into L in descending order
   ELSE
       S = S ∪ {Va}
       FOR each Vb that Va connects to DO
           Update QT_Vb by equation(10)
RETURN S
```

Figure 2: The pseudo code of graph-based corpus selection algorithm.

4 Evaluation

4.1 Data Set

We choose the training set in the Chinese-English news translation task in CWMT2009 as our bilingual corpus. After removing the sentence pairs in which one of the lengths of the monolingual sentences is greater than 50, we obtain a bilingual corpus containing about 2M sentence pairs, represented as *BC*.

In order to tune the translation model, we take one of the development sets in CWMT2009 as our development set, which is the test set in the Chinese-English news translation task in SSMT2007.

We also choose another develop set in CWMT2009 as our test set, the statistics of our data sets are shown in Table 1.

Table 1: The statistics of the data sets.

		Chinese	English
Train. corpus	Sentences	2,378,944	
	Words	34,362,755	34,921,267
	Vocabulary	193309	307095
Dev. Set	Sentences	1002	
	Words	26,285	
Test Set	Sentences	1006	
	Words	27,477	

4.2 Experiments

In order to analyze the efficiency of our graph-based corpus selection algorithm, we implement several different corpus selection algorithms and compare them with our selection algorithm.

In each experiment, we select a subset of the whole bilingual corpus by specifying the ratio via each selection algorithm, and take it as training set to train the translation model, and then compare the translation quality.

We take the state-of-the-art statistical translation system Moses[1] as the decoder, and BLEU as the evaluation metric.

Our experiments are designed as follows:

Method 1: Baseline I (Random Selection)

- Take the whole of the ***BC*** as training corpus to train the translation model;
- Random select specific ratios (10%, 30%, 50%, 60%, 70%, 80%) of the sentence pairs in the BC as training corpora to train the translation models respectively;

Method 2: Baseline II (Unseen gram-based Selection)

- Select the sentence pair with the highest weight each time, and we calculate the weight of the sentence using the $weight_{1,2}$ (Eck et al. 2005), which considered the length of the sentence and bi-grams, and generated the best results as reported in (Eck et al. 2005).
- Select specific ratios (10%, 30%, 50%, 60%, 70%, 80%) of the sentence pairs in the BC as training corpora to train the translation models respectively;

Method 3: Graph-based Corpus Selection (Considering the *QI* Only)

- Take the graph-based Corpus Selection algorithm, but it only consider the quantity of information of the sentence pair, i.e. the importance is equal to the quantity of information. So, the algorithm need not update the coverage.
- Select specific ratios (10%, 30%, 50%, 60%, 70%, 80%) of the sentence pairs in the BC as training corpora to train the translation models respectively;

Method 4: Graph-based Corpus Selection (Considering the *QI* and *CSP*)

- Take the graph-based Corpus Selection algorithm, here the importance is the sum of the quantity of information and the coverage;
- Select specific ratios (10%, 30%, 50%, 60%, 70%, 80%) of the sentence pairs in the BC as training corpora to train the translation models respectively;

Methods 3 and 4 need to construct the monolingual graphs and bilingual graph. We set the similarity threshold as 0.4, and the statistics of the graphs are shown in Table 2.

In table 2, the column 1 represents the three graphs (two monolingual graphs and a bilingual graph), the column 2 is the amount of edges in each graph, the column 3 is the average edge for each sentence or sentence pair in each graph, and the column 4 is the amount of the isolated nodes, which have no similar sentences or sentence pairs in the graph. Note the amount of the points is 2378944.

Table 2: The statistics of the graphs (N=2378944).

	Amount of Edges	Avg. Edge	Amount of Isolated Nodes
Mono. Graph (Chinese)	77,135,825	64.8	445,684 (18.7%)
Mono. Graph (English)	208,614,318	175.4	366,690 (15.4%)
Bilingual Graph	19,731,976	16.6	864,281 (36.3%)

From the table we can see that about 36.3% of sentence pairs in the bilingual graph are isolated sentence pairs. So we should adjust the thresholds to avoid so many isolated sentence pairs in the future.

After selecting the subsets of the corpus with specific ratios, the statistics of them are shown as Table 3.

[1] http://www.statmt.org

Table 3: The statistics of the subsets of the corpus.

Ratios	Method 1		Method 2		Method 3		Method 4	
	Avg.	OOV	Avg.	OOV	Avg.	OOV	Avg.	OOV
10%	14.4	389	11.9	191	15.2	361	13.5	359
30%	14.4	228	14.0	150	15.6	189	16.2	261
50%	14.4	186	14.8	148	15.8	158	16.3	156
60%	14.4	176	15.4	148	15.7	151	15.6	151
70%	14.4	165	14.6	148	15.1	150	15.2	149
80%	14.4	165	14.2	148	14.6	148	14.8	148
100%	14.4	148						

In table 3, the column 1 represents the specific ratios, the columns 2 to 5 represents the four selection methods, and each of them consists of two sub-columns, average length of the source sentences (Avg.) and the number of out of vocabulary words (OOV).

From the table, we can see that when using the random selection, the average lengths of the sentences are all near to the average sentence lengths of the whole corpus.

Both in method 2, 3 and 4, the numbers of OOV words decrease very quickly, and it can reflect the coverage of the selected corpus.

Finally, we obtained the translation results shown in Table 4.

Table 4: The test results for different selection methods(=BLEU%).

Ratios	Method 1	Method 2	Method 3	Method 4
10%	18.84	**20.03**	19.32	19.51
30%	19.91	20.68	**20.78**	20.30
50%	20.76	21.08	21.10	**21.25**
60%	20.96	21.00	21.00	**21.34**
70%	21.14	21.26	**21.54**	21.27
80%	21.25	21.26	21.30	**21.58**
100%	21.51			

In table 4, the column 1 represents the specific ratios, the columns 2 to 5 represents the BLEU% scores for four selection methods.

The results from the table 4 show, given the specific ratios of the training corpus, using unseen gram-based selection (Method 2) and graph-based corpus selection methods (Method 3 and 4) will obtain better results than using the random selection method.

The results obtained by Method 2 and Method 3 are similar, since both of them consider the *QI* when given the set of selected sentence pairs *S* only.

However, when comparing the Method 2 and 3 with Method 4, we find Method 2 and 3 obtained better results when selecting only 10% and 30% of the corpus, and after increasing the ratios, method 4 obtains the better results, especially it obtains the best results when selecting only 80% of the corpus.

We conclude that the quality of the translation model depends on both of the quality and coverage of the bilingual corpus. In the beginning, Method 2 and 3 obtain better coverage than Method 4 (see the number of the OOV in table 3); however, as enlarging the corpus, Method 4 can get similar coverage with Method 2 and 3, but it can obtain better sentence pairs, since it selects the sentence pair with best importance each time. Thus, it generates better results later.

And we can also see from the table 4 that, when using the method 4 to make corpus selection, selecting only 50% of the bilingual corpus will generate near result with selecting 60%~100% of the whole corpus. That is, when using more than 50% of the whole corpus, it does not obtain significant improvement. This shows the efficiency of our graph-based corpus selection approach.

Especially, when selecting 80% of the corpus, it will get the best results, overcoming the result using the whole corpus. This shows that there may be noisy data in the corpus, which decreases the quality of the translation, and Method 4 could filter the noisy sentence pairs.

5 Related Work

In statistical machine translation, there are three ways to make effective use of the bilingual corpus. One is assuming the sentence pair has different effects on the translation, so it need estimate the quality of each sentence pair, and sort them.

Chen et al. (2006) provided a quality sorting model for the sentence pair, which estimated the quality of each sentence pair via many features, such as language model, sentence length, word alignment etc. Their experiments showed that, when using the same number of sentence pairs as training corpus, selecting the sentence pairs with high quality would improve the quality of translation.

Han et al. (2009) provided another approach. They divided the sentence pairs in the corpus into two types: literal translation and free translation, the first was low-level word-word translation, and the latter was high-level translation. They assumed that SMT could be viewed as low-level translation system, which should be supervised by the sentence pairs with literal translation. So they provided word-match metric and grammar-match metric to find the sentence pairs with literal translation, and selected them as training corpus. Their experiments showed that, when taking the sentence pairs with literal translation as baseline, adding the sentence pairs with free translation would not improve the translation quality all the while.

These approaches considered the difference between the qualities of sentence pairs. However, they only used the features of each sentence pair itself, and the quality would not be updated as the selection process.

Our approach measures the importance of each sentence pair, which only uses the structural information, i.e. the relationship between sentence pairs, and the importance will be updated dynamically during the selection.

The other way is to select and optimize the corpus according to the test set. Lu et al. (2007) proposed the corpus selection and optimization approaches based on the information retrieval methods. The first one retrieved the similar sentence pairs in the corpus according to the test set, and took them as the training corpus; the latter increased the occur number for each similar sentence pair, so that the importance of the similar sentence pair in the translation model will be enlarged. These approaches made the translation model more adaptive to the test set. Their experiments showed the improvement in the translation quality.

The graph-based selection approach in this paper does not consider the test set at all; however, it just considers the corpus itself, especially the structural information within the corpus.

Eck et al. (2005) provided a simple way to sort and select the sentence pairs based on the number of unseen n-grams in the selected data set. The approach considered only the quantity of information between the selected data set and the unselected sentence pair.

6 Conclusion

In this paper, we proposed a graph-based bilingual corpus selection framework, which measures and updates the importance of each sentence pair based on the structural information of the bilingual corpus, and then selects the sentence pair with the highest importance each time, until it obtains the subset of the corpus with specific ratio.

Experiments showed that, through selecting only 50% of the corpus, we can obtain near translation quality with the whole corpus using the graph-based selection approach. We can even obtain better results than the whole corpus when selecting 80% of the corpus, which suggests that the corpus may contain noisy data and decrease the quality of the translation.

Thus, through the graph-based corpus selection approach, we can select only a part of corpus to train the translation model, which will reduce the time and space complexity largely when building machine translation system, while not decreasing the translation quality significantly.

However, since our approach is just a basic framework, we will improve the following issues in the future:

- Considering more effective approaches to build bilingual graph;
- Improving the graph-based selection algorithm, such as considering the difference between the sentence pairs' QI_0;
- Combining the other features with the structural feature to measure the importance.

References

Chen, Y.D., X.D. Shi and C.L. Zhou. 2006. Research on Filtering Parallel Corpus: A Ranking Model. *Journal of Chinese Information Processing*, Vol.20 Supplement, pp.66-70, 2006.

Eck, M., S. Vogel and A. Waibel. 2005. Low cost portability for statistical machine translation based on n-gram coverage. *Conference Proceedings: the tenth Machine Translation Summit (MT Summit X)* pp.227-234, *Phuket, Thailand, September 13-15,*2005.

Han, X.W., H.Z. Li and T.J. Zhao. 2009. Train the machine with what it can learn – corpus selection for SMT. *Proceedings of the 2nd Workshop on Building and Using Comparable Corpora*, Suntec, Singapore, 6 August 2009; pp.27-33, 2009.

Lü, Y.J., J. Huang and Q. Liu. 2007. Improving statistical machine translation performance by training data selection and optimization. *EMNLP-CoNLL-2007: Proceedings of the 2007 Joint Conference on Empirical Methods in Natural Language Processing and Computational Natural Language Learning*, June 28-30, 2007, Prague, Czech Republic; pp. 343-350, 2007.

Moore, R.C. and W. Lewis. 2010. Intelligent Selection of Language Model Training Data. *Proceedings of the ACL 2010 Conference Short Papers*, pp. 220–224, Uppsala, Sweden, 11-16 July 2010.

Smith, J.R., C. Quirk and K. Toutanova. 2010. Extracting Parallel Sentences from Comparable Corpora using Document Level Alignment. *Human Language Technologies: The 2010 Annual Conference of the North American Chapter of the ACL*, pp. 403–411, Los Angeles, California, June 2010.

Yasuda. K.J., R.Q. Zhang, H. Yamamoto and E. Sumita. 2008. Method of selecting training data to build a compact and efficient translation model. *IJCNLP 2008: Third International Joint Conference on Natural Language Processing*, January 7-12, 2008, Hyderabad, India; pp.655-660.

Yasuda. K.J., H. Yamamoto and E. Sumita. 2007. Method of selecting training sets to build compact and efficient language model. *MT Summit XI Workshop: Using corpora for natural language generation: language generation and machine translation*, 11 September 2007, Copenhagen, Denmark; pp.31-37, 2007.

Uszkoreit, J., J.M. Ponte, A.C. Popat, and M. Dubiner. 2010. Large Scale Parallel Document Mining for Machine Translation. *Proceedings of the 23rd International Conference on Computational Linguistics (Coling 2010)*, pp. 1101–1109, Beijing, August 2010.

Myanmar Phrases Translation Model with Morphological Analysis for Statistical Myanmar to English Translation System

Thet Thet Zin[a], Khin Mar Soe[b], and Ni Lar Thein[a]

[a] University of Computer Studies,Yangon,Myanmar
thetthetzin.ucsy@gmail.com
[b] Natural Language Processing Laboratory
University of Computer Studies, Yangon, Myanmar

Abstract. This paper presents Myanmar phrases translation model with morphological analysis. The system is based on statistical approach. In statistical machine translation, large amount of information is needed to guide the translation process. When small amount of training data is available, morphological analysis is needed especially for morphology rich language. Myanmar language is inflected language and there are very few creations and researches of corpora in Myanmar, comparing to other language such as English, French, and Czech etc. Therefore, Myanmar phrases translation model is based on syntactic structure and morphology of Myanmar language. Bayes rule is also used to reformulate the translation probability of phrase pairs. Experiment results showed that proposed system can improve translation quality by applying morphological analysis on Myanmar language.

Keywords: Morphological Analysis, Statistical Machine Translation, Bayes rule, Syntactic Structure.

1 Introduction

Machine translation (MT) is the task of automatically translating a text from one natural language into another. There exist different approaches to address the problem of machine translation. This paper presents translation model of Myanmar phrases for statistical Myanmar to English machine translation system. Target and source language model based on N-gram (trigram) and translation model based on Bayes' rule to reformulate translation probability P (f| e). N-gram method (trigram) based source language model is used to extract phrases for segmented Myanmar sentence.

Myanmar language likes other Southeast Asia languages that do not place spaces between words. Therefore, the system used Myanmar Word Segmenter (MWS) which is implemented in UCSYNLP Lab which is available for research purpose. Firstly, the system used translation probabilities without additional morphology analysis of Myanmar language. There are many unknown words in this process. Some of the unknown words occur due to the inflective nature of Myanmar Language. Languages may be divided into three broad categories: isolating, agglutinative and inflective languages. Isolating languages, such as Chinese, have little or no morphology and thus do not benefit from morphologically analysis. Agglutinative languages, also known as agglomerative or compounding languages, are those in which basic roots and words can be combined to make new words. These languages, such as Turkish or Finnish, tend to have many morphemes. Inflectional morphemes are used to modify a word to reflect information such as tense.

Myanmar language may be agglutinative language and inflective language because Myanmar word can be combined to make new word. When a form of a word does not occur in the training data, the system is unable to translate it. According to experimental result, the Out-of-Vocabulary (OOV) rate exceeds 50% for tested dataset with 2000 training sentences, which means that half of the words in test set are not present in the training set. Most of the OOV words appear in proper nouns, verb and noun phrases. Regardless of sparseness of the data, the statistical-based approaches have some difficulties with specific natural language processing tasks whereas the rule-based approaches have the advantage of providing analyses of Myanmar language. Therefore, translation model used some rules for syntactic structure and morphological analysis of Myanmar language to improve in translation direction and to reduce the number of unknown words in translation. The rest of this paper is organized as follows: In Section 2, previous works in statistical machine translation is presented. Section 3 presents analysis of Myanmar language. The proposed system is presented in section 4. Finally, Section 5 and 6 discusses translation results and conclusion.

2 Related Work

In this section, previous works in Statistical machine translation on different languages are reviewed. Various researchers have improved the quality of statistical machine translation system by using different methods on different language. Probabilistic, models is created for simulating the translation process, in the models using bilingual corpora and then decoding a test sentence by searching (Brown et al., 1990). In 1993, they took the translation process as a noisy-channel model. In terms of modeling Berger et al., 1996 appended context-based information based on the Maximum Entropy principle to enrich the word-based models. Alignment model which is based on phrase structure is firstly proposed by Wang and Waible in 1998, which was automatically acquired from parallel corpus. Och et al., 1999 used beam search algorithm, which could make use of pruning strategies for balancing efficiency and accuracy. In 2002, Och and Ney first introduced the log-linear model into SMT. In 2004 Koehn suggested using features of lexical weighting. In this year, the famous phrase-based decoder, Pharaoh, was released to be a free SMT toolkit by Philipp Koehn and further updated to Moses by Koehn et al., 2007. In 2003 Koehn, Och and Marcu, used noisy channel based translation model and beam search decoder. They achieved fast decoding, while ensuring high quality. They presented experiential result on many languages (English-German, French-English, Swedish-English, and Chinese-English). Log-linear based statistical machine translation model is proposed by Zens and Ney in 2004. They solve search problem using dynamic programming and beam search with three pruning methods. A comparison with Moses showed that the presented decoder is significantly faster at the same level of translation quality.

A few researches investigated the use of morphology to improve translation quality. If source language is morphology rich language (such as German, Spanish, Czech), phrase-based model has limitations. When a form of a word does not occur in the training data, current systems are unable to translate it. Data sparseness problem can be overcome by using large training data or morphology analysis of source or/and target languages. In 2005 Goldwater and McClosky used morphological analysis of Czech to improve a Czech-English statistical machine translation system. This system solve data sparse problem caused by the highly inflected nature of Czech. Their combine model achieved high BLEU score of development and test set. Nguyen and Shimazu, 2006 proposed morphological transformational rules and Bayes' formula based transformational model to translate English to Vietnamese. The score of their system is better than baseline score.

An ideal system for machine translation would take advantage of both empirical data and linguistic analysis. Different authors have different objectives that they attempt to achieve high translation precision on many languages. Our translation model aims is to get correct translation phrases with very limited bilingual corpus for Statistical Myanmar to English machine translation.

Because of the lack of prior research on this task, we are unable to compare to our results to those of other researches; but the results do seem promising.

3 Analysis of Myanmar Language

The Myanmar Language is the official language of Myanmar. It is also the native language of the Myanmar and related sub-ethnic groups of the Myanmar, as well as that of some ethnic minorities in Myanmar like the Mon. Myanmar Language is spoken by 32 million as a first language and as a second language by 10 million, particularly ethnic minorities in Myanmar and those in neighbouring countries. Myanmar language is a tonal and pitch-register, largely monosyllabic and analytic language, with a Subject Object Verb (SOV) word order. The language uses the Myanmar script, derived from the Old Mon script and ultimately from the Brāhmī script.

The language is classified into two categories. One is formal, used in literary works, official publications, radio broadcasts, and formal speeches. The other is colloquial, used in daily conversation and spoken. This is reflected in the Myanmar words for "language": စာ sa refers to written, literary language, and စကား sa-ka refers to spoken language. Therefore, Myanmar language can mean either "မြန်မာစာ mran-ma-sa" (written Myanmar language), or "မြန်မာစကား mran-ma-sa-ka:" (spoke Myanmar language). Much of the differences between formal and colloquial Myanmar language occur in grammatical particles and lexical items. Different particles (to modify nouns and verbs) are used in the literary form from those used in the spoken form. For example, the postposition after nouns is ၌ hnai: at in formal Myanmar language and မှာ hma: at in colloquial Myanmar language. The proposed system focuses on written Myanmar language.

Example: အမေသည်အိမ်၌ရှိသည်။ Mother is *at* home. (Formal form)
အမေအိမ်မှာရှိတယ်။ Mother is *at* home. (Spoken form)

4 Proposed System

Myanmar language does not place space between words. Thus, the proposed translation model use Myanmar Word Segmenter and phrase align Myanmar-English Bilingual corpus. The system created phrases by using N-gram method for input segmented sentence to search in the corpus. In this case, one segmented word is assumed one word. Example:

Myanmar Sentence: ဆရာများသည် သူတို့၏ တပည့်များ ကိုပညာရှိအောင်လုပ်ကြသည်။

"The teachers make their pupil wise."

After word Segmentation: ဆရာများ_သည်_သူတို့_၏_တပည့်များ_ကို_ပညာရှိ_အောင်_လုပ်_ကြ_သည်_။_

This sentence contains 11 words. ဆရာများ sa-yar-myar 'teachers' is one word. Left-to-right trigrams on segmented input sentence are used to create phrases for translation. If all trigram phrases have not been observed in the corpus, bigrams and unigram phrases are used. If unigram and trigram phrases have the same meaning, longer n-grams is selected. Therefore, the system generally gets less and less number of phrases. Phrases for input sentence according to the longest N-gram method are: ဆရာများ၊ သည် ၊ သူတို့၏ ၊ တပည့်များကို ၊ ပညာရှိအောင် ၊ လုပ်ကြသည်

The system used Bayes' rule to reformulate the translation probability for translating Myanmar phrases into English phrases. Among all possible target language phrases, we will choose the phrases with the highest probability:

$$E = \arg\max_{e} \{\Pr(e_1^I \mid f_1^J)\} \quad (1)$$

$$= \arg\max_{e} \{ \Pr(e_1^I) . \Pr(f_1^J \mid e_1^I) \} \quad (2)$$

This allows for a language model Pr (e) and a separate translation model Pr (f |e). The system are not focus on English phrase reordering. Rearranging the English phrases is implemented in separate part as a subsystem of statistical Myanmar to English translation system.

4.1 Problems in the System

No additional morphology for Myanmar language is applied to translation model. The system is unable to learn translations of words that do not occur in the data, because they are unable to generalize. Translation model knows nothing of morphology therefore it fail to connect different word forms. Myanmar verbs can have many suffixes and some suffixes have the same meaning by attaching the main verbs. This is difficult for translation. For instance; စားသည် sar-ti: 'eat'; စား၏ sar-ei: 'eat'; စားပါသည် sar- par-ti: 'eat' have different verb suffixes သည်: ti; ၏: ei; ပါသည်: par-ti. But they have the same meaning to translate English language. The root verb is စား sar: 'eat' and they are present tenses.

Unknown words can be reduce by using large training data or morphology analysis of source or/and target language. The large scale Myanmar Corpus is unavailable at present. Morphology analysis is complex and computationally expensive method. Therefore, we analyzed OOV words category for morphology analysis process. The system separately takes 215 parallel sentences as testing datasets and 12827 sentences is used as the training dataset. There is no overlap of parallel sentences between training and testing datasets. The effect of the rate of out-of-vocabulary (OOV) words on translation quality, the training dataset is divided into several different smaller sizes. Figure 1 shows the OOV rate of Myanmar-English testing dataset. We measure OOV based on types (each word in the vocabulary) as well as tokens (each word in the text).X-axis and Y-axis represent number of training sentences and OOV rate (%) respectively. According to the figure 1, the OOV rate increases as the number of training sentences decreases.

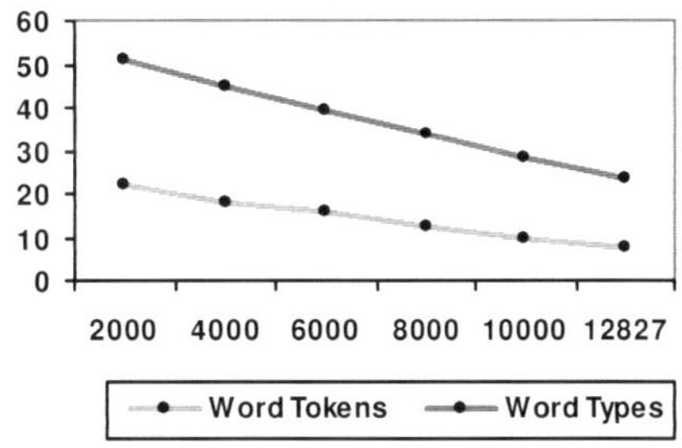

Figure 1: OOV Rate on Myanmar-English Test Set

Most of the unknown words occur in proper noun, noun and verb phrases. To reduce unknown words in noun and verb phrases, the system considers morphology analysis on number category of noun phrases, suffixes and particles of verb phrases for Myanmar language. Morphological analysis is applied on pre-processing phrase of translation process.

When translation model has learned multiple possible translations for a particular word or phrase, the choice of which translation to use is guided by conditional probability rather than by linguistic information. Sometimes linguistic factors like case marker, tense, or number categories of noun phrases are important determinants for what translation ought to be used in a particular context. Because phrase-based approaches lack linguistic information they do not have an appropriate means of choosing between alternative translations. The system selects one word according to conditional probability. Therefore, sometime translation result is incorrect.

Some postpositional markers have ambiguous meanings in translation. One way of helping the disambiguation of ambiguous words is use syntactic structure of language and to annotate words with their part-of-speech (POS). Example of ambiguous in postpositional markers (PPM) is shown in table 1.

Table 1: Ambiguous in Postpositional Markers

Myanmar Sentences	Postpositional Markers	English translation
မျက်မှန်နှင့်လူကလေးသည်တော်သည်။ 'The boy with glasses is clever.'	နှင့်	နှင့် (with)
အမေနှင့်မမသည်ဈေးမသို့သွားသည်။ 'Mother and Ma Ma go to the market'.	နှင့်	နှင့်(and)

In the first sentence, PPM နှင့် nint is used-PPM. Its meaning is နှင့် nint 'with. But in the second sentences, PPM နှင့် nint is similar-PPM. Its meaning is နှင့် nint "and". Therefore, translation of PPM is depended on sentence structure. We annotated Myanmar POS tags manually. We appended the Myanmar and English POS tags in training and test corpus to compare with the system without applying Myanmar POS.

4.2 Morphology of Myanmar Verb Phrases

The roots of Myanmar language verbs are almost always suffixed with at least one particle which conveys such information as tense, intention, politeness, mood, etc. These verb suffixes make us difficult in translation of Myanmar to English. Because some suffixes have the same tense and the same meaning. However, Burmese verbs are not conjugated in the same way as most European languages; the root of the Burmese verb always remains unchanged and does not have to agree with the subject in person, number or gender. The most commonly used verb particles and their usage are shown below with an example verb root ကစား ka-sa 'play'. The statement ကစား ka-sa 'play' is imperative.

- The suffix သည် ti (literary form) can be viewed as a particle marking the present tense and/or a factual statement: ကစားသည် ka-sa-ti 'play'
- The suffix ခဲ့ hkai denotes that the action took place in the past. The suffix သည် ti in this case သည် ti denotes a factual statement rather than the present tense: ကစားခဲ့သည် ka-sa-hkai- ti 'played'
- The particle နေ nay is used to denote an action in progression. It is equivalent to the English '-ing': ကစားနေသည် ka-sa-nay ti 'playing'
- The particle မည် mai (formal form: မည်) is used to indicate the future tense or an action which is yet to be performed: ကစားမည် ka-sa- mai 'will play'

Verbs are negated by the particle မ ma, which is prefixed to the verb. When the corpus contains only imperative verb ကစား ka-sa 'play', we can generally decide Myanmar verb tense by looking verb particles ခဲ့ hkai 'past tense', နေ nay 'continuous tense', မည် mai 'future tense'. Myanmar verb can be divided into three main categories: Individual Verb, Compound Verb and Adjective Verb. For example: individual verb: စားသည် sar-ti: 'eat'; compound verb: ပြေးဖက်သည် pye-pet-ti 'run and hug'; Adjective Verb: ပျော်သည် pw-ti 'is happy'. Some verbs can be used to support other verbs. For example: ပြောသည် pyaw-ti 'tell' and ပေးသည် pay-ti 'give' are individual verbs and can be used as main verbs in sentences. But in this verb ပြောပေးသည် pyaw-pye-ti 'tell', ပေး pye 'give' is not the main verb. It behaves particle to support the main verb ပြော pyaw 'tell'.

More than two individual English verbs can include in Myanmar compound verb. For example: three individual verbs: ကြွရောက် kyw-rwet 'come', အားပေး ar-pye 'encourage', ချီးမြှင့် khee-hmyint 'award' include in compound verb : ကြွရောက်အားပေးချီးမြှင့်သည် kyw-rwet-ar-pye-khee-hmyint-ti 'come and encourage and award'. 'ကြွရောက်အားပေးချီးမြှင့်သည်' is Myanmar Compound verb. It has three English individual verbs "come, encourage and award". Verb particle ကြ kyat can be omitted in the sentence. For example: ကျောင်းသားများ ကစားနေ ကြသည်။ 'Students are playing.' and ကျောင်းသားများ ကစားနေ သည်။ 'Students are playing'. Compound Verbs pose special problems to the robustness of a translation method, because the word itself must be represented in the training data: the occurrence of each of the components is not enough.

4.3 Verb Phrases Detection for Morphological analysis

Different languages may differ in their syntactic structure in general: for instance the placement of the verb in sentence or the use of postpositional markers in the sentences. Currently, no mature deep analysis that has been worked done is available for Myanmar language. The proposed system detects verb phrases in Myanmar sentence by using syntactical structure of sentence. Myanmar language is SOV pattern. Verb suffixes are at the end of Myanmar sentences and Myanmar verb (stem) is very complex to define. Example of Myanmar verbs are shown in Table 2.

Table 2: Examples of Myanmar Verbs

Myanmar Verbs	Main Verbs	Suffixes	English meaning
လုပ်အားပေးနေသည်။	လုပ်အားပေး	နေသည်	contributing
အားပေးနေသည်။	အားပေး	နေသည်	encouraging
ပေးနေသည်။	ပေး	နေသည်	giving
နေသည်။	နေ	သည်	live

Verb suffixes are mined from any Myanmar sentences by using N-gram method in the system. Main verb is in front of suffix. We will first provide some examples to illustrate this concept and conclude this section with a formal definition. The following sentences are collected from Myanmar grammar books. The main verbs are marked by parentheses and suffixes are marked by italics. Example:

(1)မောင်မြသည်သူမအားပန်းများကို(ပေး)*သည်*။(Mg Mya gives flowers to her.)

(2)မောင်လှသည်ကျောင်းသို့မြန်မြန်(သွား)*ခဲ့သည်*။(Mg Hla went to school quickly.)

(3)မောင်ဘသည်စာဖတ်ခြင်းကိုအလွန်(ကြိုက်နှစ်သက်)*သည်*။ (Mg Ba likes reading very much.)

According to syntactic structure of Myanmar language, generally verb phrases are always end of the sentence. Firstly verb suffixes are extracted and then define main verb. According to analysis, post positional markers or adverb phrases are in front of main verbs. In above examples post positional marker ကို:ko , adverb phrases မြန်မြန် myan-myan 'quickly', အလွန်:ar-lwan 'very' are in front of main verbs. The system defined five types of adverb, seventeen types of postpositional markers and thirteen types of verb particles according to Myanmar grammar rules to detect verb phrases in the sentences. The system does not consider complex sentences structure with the conjunction words. Some verb phrases are same in main verb category but different in suffixes category. But they have the same meaning in translation. The system solved this problem by defining possible verb suffixes groups.

4.4 Inflectional Form of Number Category of Noun

In Myanmar language, the particles "များ၊ တို့၊ တွေ" makes plural form of noun according to Myanmar grammar. In English, we don't want to explicitly store the plural of every noun, since there are mostly very predictable. The relatively few exceptions can be stored separately and rules used to generate the rest. The same applies to verb, where the addition of ***s, ing,*** and ***ed*** should be handled by morphological rules (although exceptions are somewhat more common). The regular plural of nouns (eg. book, class) is formed by adding ***s*** or ***es***. Example for one regular rule is:

Rule 1: Singular words which end in vowel + *y* add *s*

Examples: boy/boys, key/keys

Rule: *Vy*→*Vys* (V is any vowel.)

In either case, words not covered by the rules can be marked in the lexicon as having irregular plurals (eg. ***man/men***). Moreover some verbs have irregular forms (such as past tense of "**read**" is also "**read**"). Morphological rules cannot handle irregular verb forms. We also used lexicon as having irregular verb forms to handle irregular verb forms.

5 Translation Results

5.1 Corpus Statistics

For experiments, the corpus contains sentences from Myanmar text books, grammar books and websites. Corpus statistics are shown in table 3 and 4. Zawgyi-One Myanmar font is used for Myanmar Language. The system separately take 215 parallel sentences as testing datasets, and the remaining is used as the training dataset. There is no overlap of parallel sentences between training and testing datasets.

Table 3: Corpus Statistics

Myanmar-English		
Sentences Pairs	13042	
Language	Myanmar	English
Total Word	61824	56263
Vocubary Size	2713	2405
Average Sentence Length (Word)	18	10

Table 4: Statistics of the Myanmar-English datasets

Sentence Pairs of Datasets		Total Words		Vocabulary Size	
		Myanmar	English	Myanmar	English
Train	12827	60805	55335	2168	1965
Test	215	1019	928	545	440

5.2 Evaluation Criteria

Machine translation can be evaluated using the well-known measures precision, recall, and the F-measure. The F-measure has significantly higher correlation with human judgments than recently proposed alternatives. In this paper, we measure evaluation of the translation system in term of the standard measure of precision, recall and F-measure in equation 3, 4 and 5. Only single references are used in this measure. These reference sentences are manually translated. Our system does not consider word order of Myanmar and English language. Therefore, we ignore the word order of candidate and reference sentences.

$$\Pr eision\ (C \mid R) = \frac{|C \cap R|}{C} \quad (3)$$

$$\mathrm{Re}\ call\ (C \mid R) = \frac{|C \cap R|}{R} \quad (4)$$

$$F - measure = \frac{2 * (precision * recall)}{(precision + recall)} \quad (5)$$

C=set of candidate phrases
R=set of reference phrases

Table 5 shows the results for Myanmar-English translation with varying sizes of training sentences. According to the table, the proposed method begins to get some improvements over the corresponding baseline. When the size of training data sentences is less than 10000 sentences, morphology analysis method has good compared with the corresponding baselines. In proposed system, most errors occur in postpositional markers. Postpositional markers have ambiguous meaning in translation. One way of helping the disambiguation of ambiguous words is use syntactic structure of language and to annotate words with their part-of-speech (POS). Therefore, we annotated Myanmar POS tags manually. We appended the Myanmar and English POS tags in training and test corpus to compare with baseline system. By using POS tags, the system reduced ambiguous in postpositional markers.

Table 5: Translation Results

Corpu ssize (sent:)	Baseline (only probability) (%)			Baseline+ morpho (%)			Baseline+ morpho+POS (%)		
	Precisi on	Recall	F-Score	Precisi on	Recall	F-Score	Preci sion	Recall	F-Score
5000	67.3	68.3	67.8	69.2	68.5	68.8	70.1	71.8	70.9
10000	70.3	69.6	69.9	71.6	70.1	70.8	77.3	74.8	76
12827	73.2	71.5	72.34	76.1	71.6	73.8	79.7	80.7	80.2

The best results got by adding morphology and POS of Myanmar language to baseline system. We also analyzed OOV words in proposed system. The system reduced OOV words in noun and verb phrases. Compound verbs and proper nouns pose problems to the robustness of a translation method and increased unknown words rate in translation. OOV words reduction is shown in table 6.

Table 6: OOV reduction rate

Category of OOV words	OOV%	OOV words
Nouns	22.8	89
Verbs	22.3	87

5.3 Error Analysis

Compound verbs and proper nouns pose problems to the robustness of a translation method. For example: compound verb သွားစားသည် twe-sar-ti 'go and eat' has two meaning. သွားသည် thwr-ti; 'go', စားသည် sar- ti 'eat' and meaning of သွားစားသည် twe sar ti is 'go and eat'. Althoug the corpus contain သွားသည် thwr-ti 'go' and စားသည် sar-ti 'eat', we have difficult to translate these words သွားစားသည် twe-sar-ti 'go and eat' to get correct translation. Because the word itself must be represented in the training data: the occurrence of each of the components is not enough. Some errors occurred in adjective. Myanmar adjectives vary according to sentence patterns. There are 95 errors in tested sentences. The causes in detail are:

- Unknown words: The foreign word did not occur in the training corpus, so translation was not possible at all.
- Unknown translation: The word occurred in the training corpus, but fails to translate: fail to align the word to its correct translation, which often happens for rare words.
- Segmentation Error: Word Segmenter output is not suitable for correct translation result.
- Detecting verb phrases Error: Errors in finding verb phrases in the input sentence especially when input sentence is too long and include conjunction words.
- Untranslatable: Some phrases are not translatable into English phrase correctly.
- Others: missing English particle in noun phrases and so on.

6 Conclusion

We have shown that Myanmar-English phrase-based SMT can be improved by combining the syntactic structure, POS and morphological analysis of Myanmar Language. By adding these three features the system can achieve a better result than can be obtained with each individually. This improvement was primarily due to a reduction of the sparse data problem caused by the highly inflected nature of Myanmar language. An alternative method for reducing this problem is to use a larger parallel corpus. However, the large scale Myanmar Corpus is unavailable at present. For that reason, we believe that the approach presented in this paper is a promising one. In the future, we would like to apply other Myanmar morphological features in translation model and to test in more training data and domain specific corpus.

References

Brown Peter F., John .Cocke, Stephen.A.Della Pietra, Vincent J.Della Pietra, Fredrick. Jelinek, John.D. Lafferty, Robert.L. Mercer, and Paul.S. Roossin.1990. *A statistical approach to machine translation.* Computational Linguistics, 16(2), 79-85.

Brown Peter F., Vincent. J. Della Pietra, Stephen. A. Della. Pietra, and Robert. L. Mercer. 1993. *The mathematics of statistical machine translation: parameter estimation.* Computational Linguistics, 19(2), 263-311.

Berger, A. L., S. A. D. Pietra, and V. J. D. Pietra, *A maximum entropy approach to natural language processing,* Computational Linguistics 22(1), 39-72, 1996.

Department of the Myanmar Language Commission, Ministry of Education Yangon, 1998. *Myanmar-English Dictionary.*

Department of the Myanamar Languge Commission, Ministry of Education, Union of Myanmar. 2005. *Myanmar Grammar.*

Goldwater Sharon and McClosky David. 2005. *Improving Statistical MT through Morphological Analysis.* Proceedings of Human Language Technology Conference and Conference on Empirical Methods in Natural Language Processing (HLT/EMNLP), pages 676-683, Vancouver, October.

Htay Hla. H., G.Bharadwaja.Kumar, Kavi .N.Murthy. 26 march 2007. *Statistical Analyses of Myanmar Corpora,* Technical report, Department of computer and Information Science, University of Hyderabad. 26 march 2007.

Koehn Philipp. 2004. *Pharaoh: A beam Search Decoder for Phrase-Based Statistical Machine Translation Models.* In proceedings of the Sixth Conference of the Association for Machine Translation in the Americas..pp 115-124.

Koehn Philipp, Marcello, Cowan Brooke, Zens Richard, Dyer Chris, Bojar Ondrej, Constantin Alexandra and Herbst Evan.2007. *Moses: Open Source Toolkit for Statistical Machine Translation.* In proceedings of the ACL 2007 Demo and Poster Sessions, PP 177-180.

Koehn Philipp and Hoang Hieu 2007 June. *Factor Translation Models.* Proceedings of the 2007 Joint Conference on Empirical Methods in Natural Language Processing and Computational Natural Language Learning, PP.868-876, Pragun.

Koehn, P., F. J. Och, and D. Marcu, *Statistical phrase-based translation,* In proceedings of the Human Language Technology and North American Association for Computational Linguistics Conference (HLT/NAACL), Edomonton, Canada,2003.

Marcu Daniel and Wong William. 2002 Jul. *A phrase-based joint probability model for statistical machine translation.* In proceeding of EMNLP, pp 133-136.

Minkov, E., Toutanova, K., and Suzuki, H. 2007. *Generating complex morphology for machine translation.* In Proceedings of the 45th Annual Meeting of the Association for Computational Linguistics. Prague, Czech Republic, 128-135.

NieBen Sonja and Ney Hermann. 2004. *Statistical machine translation with scarce resources using morpho-syntactic information.* Computational Linguistics 30, 2, 181-204.

Nguyen Thai Phuong and Shimazu Akira. 2006 Augest. *Improving Phrase-Based SMT with Morpho-Syntactic Analysis and Transformation.* Proceedings of the 7th Conference of the Association for Machine Translation in the Americas, pages 138-147, Cambridge.

Och. Franz. J., Tillmann Christoph, and Ney Hermann. *Improved alignment models for statistical machine translation.* In proceedings of the Conference on Empirical Method in Natural Language Processing and Very Large Corpora, University of Maryland, College Park, MD, pp. 20-28.

Och.Franz. J and Ney. Hermann. *Discriminative training and maximum entropy models for statistical machine translation.* 2002. in proceedings of ACL, pp. 295-302.

Pa Pa Win, Thein Ni Lar. *Disambiguation in Myanmar Word Segmentation.* February 2009. Proceedings of the seventh international conference on computer applications, Pages 1-4.

Richard Zens and Hermann Ney, *Improvements in Phrase-Based Statistical Machine Translation,* 2004.

Thumana Ashin 2004. *New Method English Grammar.* Second Edition. Yangon, Myanmar.

Wang Ye-Yi and Waibel Alex.1998. *Modeling with structures in statistical machine translation.* In proceedings of COLING/ACL, Montreal, Quebec, Canada, pp. 1357-1363.

Context Resolution of Verb Particle Constructions for English to Hindi Translation

Niladri Chatterjee, Renu Balyan

Department of Mathematics, Indian Institute of Technology Delhi, India
{niladri.iitd, renu17775}@gmail.com

Abstract. Verb Particle Constructions (VPCs) are flexible in nature and hence quite complex and challenging to handle. As a consequence, VPCs generate a lot of interest for NLP community. Despite their prevalence in English they are not handled very well, and hence often result in poor quality of translation. In this paper we investigate VPCs for English to Hindi translation. An English VPC can have different meanings in Hindi based on what its neighboring entities are. The paper focuses on finding the correct Hindi verb for an English VPC. We also discuss some rules for VPC identification, and approaches for resolving the context of a VPC for English to Hindi machine translation.

Keywords: VPC, English to Hindi Machine Translation, Semantics, Separability.

1 Introduction

Quality of a translation often depends upon how correctly the verb of the source language sentence is translated into the target language. In a sentence the verb acts as the binding agent, and is therefore considered the most important component of a sentence. Consequently, verbs need to be handled in a more systematic way for a Machine Translation (MT) system. This is more pertinent with respect to translation from English to Indian languages, Hindi in particular. This is because English verbs are often polysemic, whereas Hindi has different verbs for each of the senses. For illustration, according to WordNet[1], the verb "break" has 59 senses, "make" has 49 senses, "give" has 44, "get" has 36 senses and so on. Almost for each of these senses a different and specific verb exists in Hindi. Consequently, selection of an appropriate Hindi verb is very important during translation from English to Hindi (or any other target language). This can be determined by identifying the sense in which the English verb is used. But it has been observed that this is not so straightforward, as often other features like semantics of other components of the sentence have to be looked into for correct translation.

English verbs can be classified as: "Single verbs" and "Phrasal verbs" (Singh, 2003). Single verbs are formed using only single words, e.g. "go", "decide", "take", and "give". Phrasal verbs are made of two or more words, like "take off", "make up", "do away with", "put up with" etc. Our focus in this paper is on translation of this special category of verbs, the 'phrasal verbs' from English to Hindi. The motive here is to capture the correct sense and hence provide correct translation of phrasal verbs in Hindi, as their structures. In the rest of the paper we shall be using the term VPC instead of "phrasal verb".

The difficulty in handling English VPCs is often due to their flexible syntactic structure in a sentence. Consider, for example, VPCs comprising a verb followed by a preposition. This can happen in two ways:

a) Intransitive verbs are followed by some prepositions e.g. "refer to", "look at".

b) Some VPCs have the structure of verb + preposition to convey some exact sense, e.g.

[1] http://wordnet.princeton.edu (Version 2.1)

"put out", "put off", and "run into".

Hence the primary difficulty is to understand the sense of the *verb + preposition* combination. But the difficulty here is that in some cases the prepositions in phrasal verbs can appear before or after an object, whereas in other cases they can appear only before the object and never after it. Some examples to illustrate this point are:

(a) She *switched off* the light vs. She *switched* the light *off*.

(b) The customer *threw away* the plates vs. The customer *threw* the plates *away*.

In examples (a) and (b) prepositions "off" and "away" can appear before as well as after the object (light in example (a) and plates in example (b)). However, in examples (c) and (d) below the preposition "out" can appear only before the object (change and solution, respectively) and not after it. It is worth noting that the preposition "out" in both the sentences is part of the VPC, and not because the verbs concerned are intransitive.

(c) The new manager *brought out* a change.

(d) The programmer *found out* a solution.

VPCs are generally not handled properly in the existing English to Hindi Machine Translation (MT) systems. Table 1 shows translations of VPCs for two simple sentences as given by some of the most commonly used English to Hindi MT systems, namely Google[2], MANTRA[3], MaTra2[4] and Anuvadaksh[5], which we shall refer to as MT1, MT2, MT3 and MT4, respectively in Table 1.

Table 1: Translation of VPCs by MT systems

Sentence	Hindi Translations	Problems encountered
He *switched on* the light.	MT1: *vah prakaash par bandh kar diyaa* He light on close did MT2: *vah ne roshni par badlaa* He light on changed MT3: *unhone prakaash par switch dabaayaa* By him light on switch pressed MT4: *unhone prakaash par badlaa kiyaa* By him light on change did	- Sense of "switch" is incorrect in MT1, MT2 and MT4. - The preposition "on" is taken as an entity independent of the verb "switch" by all the systems.
He *put on* the shoes.	MT1: *vah joote par daal diyaa* He shoes on spill did MT2: *vah joote daalte hein* He shoes wears MT3: *unhone jootain par daal* By him shoes on spill MT4: *unhone joote rakhtaa hai* By him shoes keeps	- "Put on" not treated as single unit by MT1 and MT3. - Incorrect Sense of "put" by all except MT2. - Incorrect tense by all the four systems.

This shows the need and necessity to look into these issues and thus design methods to handle these problems. In this work we focus on this aspect of English to Hindi MT in detail.

The paper is organized as follows. Section 2 discusses some of the previous works done for verb particle constructions (VPCs) and the problems faced during the English to Hindi translation of a VPC. A detailed analysis of the VPCs with their respective Hindi verbs based on the senses, and the VPC separability are also discussed in Section 2. Various rules for identification of a

[2] http://translate.google.com/

[3] http://mantra-rajbhasha.cdac.in/mantrarajbhasha/

[4] http://www.cdacmumbai.in/matra/

[5] http://tdil-dc.in/

VPC and some methods for resolving the context for VPCs for English to Hindi machine translation are discussed in Section 3. Section 4 concludes the paper.

2 Verb Particle Constructions

Verb particle constructions (VPCs) consist of a head verb and one or more obligatory particles, in the form of intransitive prepositions (e.g. "hand in", "take off"), adjectives (e.g. "cut short") or verbs (e.g. "let go", "let fly"). The focus of this paper is on prepositional particles due to their high frequency in text. VPCs cause significant problems for NLP systems. Semantically, they are seldom understood through the simple composition of their independent parts (Bannard *et al.*, 2003). The VPCs can display both a *joined* or *split* configuration. This prevents the systems from treating them as a single unit. Therefore, one prime requirement for an MT system is to be able to maintain the semantic bond between the components, even when they are non-adjacent (Constable and Curran, 2009).

The problem encountered for these prepositional VPCs has been shown for "put u*p*" in the following sentences: (1) Ram *put* the picture *up*. vs. (2) Ram was *put up* in a hotel. When we compare, sentences (1) and (2), the meaning in (1) seems to be that Ram *put* the picture somewhere and that as a consequence the picture was *up*. The verb and the particle, therefore, make independent contributions to the sentence. Sentence (2), on the other hand requires a rather different analysis. Ram can neither be said to have been *put* or be *up* in the hotel.

The major problem therefore is to identify whether the first or the second kind of semantic representation is appropriate? Previous research on VPCs has focused on their automatic extraction and classification (Baldwin and Villavicencio, 2002; Villavicencio, 2003). However, systematic study about how they should be handled during translation for a particular language is noticeably lacking.

2.1 Figuring out VPCs-The History

A lot of work has been done on actually figuring out the VPCs. According to Ramisch *et al.* (2008) a three way classification is adopted by Deh´e (2002), where a VPC can be classified as compositional, idiomatic or aspectual, depending on its sense.

- In compositional VPCs the meaning of the construction is determined by the literal interpretations of the particle and the verb. These VPCs usually involve particles with directional or spatial meaning, and these can often be replaced by the appropriate directional PPs. For illustration in the sentence "She carried the bags in the house", the particle "in" can be replaced with the directional preposition "into" without changing the sense of the sentence.
- Idiomatic VPCs, on the other hand, cannot have their meaning determined by interpreting their components literally (e.g. "get on", meaning to be on friendly terms with someone).
- Aspectual VPCs, which have the particle providing the verb with an endpoint, suggesting that the action described by the verb is performed completely, thoroughly or continuously (e.g. "tear up" meaning to tear something into a lot of small pieces).

Below we present some characterization of VPCs as discussed by Bolinger (1971):

C1: In a transitive VPC the particle may come either before or after the NP (e.g. He *backed up* the team vs. He *backed* the team *up*). However, whether a particle can be separated or not from the verb depends on the degree of bonding between them, the size of the NP, and the kind of NP. In some cases this separability is incorrect. For illustration, of the two sentences "He *got off* the bus", and "He *got* the bus *off*", the latter one is incorrect.

C2: Unstressed personal pronouns must precede the particle. For illustration, "They *ate* it *up*" is correct, but "They *ate up* it" is not.

C3: If the particle precedes a simple definite NP, the particle does not take the NP as its object. For example, consider the sentence "He *brought along* his friend". Here the particle "along" does not take the NP "his friend" as an object. Whereas in the sentence "He *slept* in the hotel" the particle "in" has a stronger bonding with the NP "the hotel". Hence it is not acting as a VPC. In this paper we have considered the semantics of the entities succeeding the VPC, or appearing in between the verb and the particle for VPC identification.

2.2 Translation of VPCs in Hindi and their problems

When it comes to translating these VPCs it proves to be more difficult. One VPC may have multiple possible translations based on its neighboring entities and their related semantics. Let us consider the VPC "*put on*" and different sentences with their Hindi translations as shown in Table 2.

Table 2: Different translations for the VPC "*put on*"

	English Sentence	Hindi Translation	Hindi Verb for "*Put on*"
a.	He *put on* the dress	*usne dress pahanii*	*pahannaa* → "to wear"
b	He *put on* the fan	*usne pankhaa chalaayaa*	*chalaanaa* → "to start"
c.	He *put on* the light	*usne light jalaayii*	*jalaanaa* → "to burn"
d.	He *put on* efforts	*usne mehanat karii*	*karnaa* → "to do"
e.	She *put on* make-up	*usne make-up lagaayaa*	*lagaanaa* → "to apply"
f.	She *put on* weight	*uskaa vajan badh gayaa*	*badhaanaa* → "to increase"
g.	She *put on* the tea	*usne chaay banayii*	*banaanaa* → "to prepare"
h.	She *put* the book *on* the table	*usne mej par kitaab rakhii*	"Non-VPC"

All the English sentences in Table 2 (except (h)) are structurally same. Hence it is expected that the translation of these sentences will also be similar. The structure of all the translated sentences is also similar (except (f) which is a translation divergence (Gupta and Chatterjee, 2003)). However, the Hindi verbs being used in the translations are different and depend on the object as well as its semantics used. Thus finding the object and its semantics will play a very important role in deciding what the Hindi verb for a particular VPC will be.

We have identified 22 VPCs for the present study which according to WordNet have large number of senses. Some example English sentences and their corresponding Hindi translations have been considered for each of these senses. In certain cases the number of WordNet senses and the possible Hindi verbs for a VPC are exactly the same. For example the VPC "break down" as shown in Table 3.

Table 3: Analysis for the VPCs "break down"

WordNet Sense	Hindi verb	Separa-bility	Related Verb exists	Semantics required
1, 5 (to analyze, to decompose)	*todnaa, baatnaa*	Yes	No	No
2 (make ineffective)	*samaapat karnaa*	Yes	No	No
3, 8 (lose control of one's emotion, collapse)	*ronaa, tootnaa*	No	No	No
4 (seize to work)	*kharaab honaa*	No	No	No
6, 7 (cause to fall, collapse)	*giraanaa, todnaa*	Yes	No	No

It has however been found that generally the number of verbs possible in Hindi for a VPC is less as compared to the senses found in WordNet. Some cases have also been found where a Hindi verb exists for a VPC, but no corresponding sense is available in WordNet. For example "break into" as discussed in Table 4. The VPC "*break into*" has only 2 senses in WordNet; whereas when we use it for translating to Hindi, more than 2 cases have been found. It has also been observed that "break into" is a non-separable VPC. In case this occurs in a sentence with some NP in between the words "break" and "into" then it is actually not behaving as a VPC. Table 4 presents a detailed analysis of "break into" with respect to its translation into Hindi.

Table 4: Analysis for the VPC "break into"

WordNet Sense	Hindi verb	Separability	Related Verb exists	Semantics required
1 (to cry)	*ronaa*	No	Yes	No
2 (change pace)	*daudnaa*	No	Yes	No
- (to laugh, smile)	*hansnaa, muskuraanaa*	No	Yes	No
- (to enter forcibly)	*ghusnaa*	No	No	Yes

The cases shown in Table 4 can all be generalized using the rule that needs to check the NP, and extract the verb form related to it. For illustration,

1) Tears would relate to verb "cry" and hence can be translated to "*ronaa*".
2) Laughter relates to "laugh" which is translated as "*hansnaa*" and so on.

However, for the last case discussed in Table 4 we cannot derive a verb directly for the NP following the VPC. Hence we need to find semantics of the object. For example, if the object is referring to a building/dwelling place then the corresponding Hindi verb would be "*ghusnaa*".

Another category of VPCs comprises the ones for which we need the semantics of the object in the sentence to get the Hindi verbs. One such example is "put on". The verb "put" has nine senses and so does the VPC "put on". We have found seven Hindi verbs for the VPC "*put on*". All these verbs do not actually match the senses found from WordNet. This has been shown in Table 5.

Table 5: Analysis for the "put on" VPC

WordNet Sense	Hindi verb	Separability	Related Verb exists	Semantics required
1 (to wear)	*pahannaa*	Yes	No	Yes
3 (to make/ prepare)	*banaanaa*	Yes	No	Yes
4 (to present)	*pesh/ prastut karnaa*	No	No	Yes
2, 5 (to add)	*jodnaa*	No	No	Yes
7 (to apply)	*lagaanaa*	No	No	Yes
9 (to get fat, increase weight)	*motaa honaa, vazan badhnaa*	No	No	Yes
6, 8 (mount, deceive)	-	-	-	-
- (to switch on, to start, to do)	*jalaanaa, chalaanaa, karnaa*	Yes, Yes, No	No	Yes

We could not find any corresponding Hindi verb for the senses 6 and 8 of "*put on*" in WordNet. Also three Hindi verbs (*jalaanaa, chalaanaa* and *karnaa*) have been found which do not have a relevant sense mentioned in WordNet. In these cases we find the semantics of the object and based on the semantics we use a relevant Hindi verb. This can be illustrated with the following example, "*Put on* the light/fan/TV".

A similar analysis has been done for other VPCs which have two or more Hindi verbs corresponding to the senses obtained for those VPCs from WordNet. This will prove helpful in the translation process and improve the quality of the translation in a machine translation system.

2.3 Separability of the VPCs

No standard technique is available for judging separability of a VPC. Our scheme for ascertaining separability for a VPC is the following. We have marked a VPC as separable or non-separable based on its frequency of occurrence in the text. We have used four search engines (Google, Bing, AltaVista and Lycos/ HotBot) for finding the frequency of occurrence of the VPCs. Some of these have been shown in Table 6 [6].

Table 6: Frequency of occurrence of some VPCs

	Example VPC	Google	Bing	AltaVista	Lycos/ HotBot
(1)	a. *Bring out* a change	91,4000	38,40,00,000	754	274,000,000
	b. *Bring* a change *out*	5	7	22	9
(2)	a. *Break into* the house	6,750,000	26,70,00,000	129,000	192,000,000
	b. *Break* the house *into*	10,400	54	221	223
(3)	a. *Switch on* the light	16,900,000	13,10,00,000	142,000	129,000,000
	b. *Switch* the light *on*	1,930,000	11,00,00,000	166,000	108,000,000
(4)	a. *Put on* efforts	12,600	1,99,00,000	650	20,400,000
	b. *Put* efforts *on*	80,900	16,00,00,000	5470	115,000,000

Three cases have been found to exist for most of the VPCs:

- The frequency of occurrence of split configuration is very low as compared to that of the joined configuration. As shown for example (1) and (2) in Table 6. Our conclusion is: the VPC is non-separable and it is incorrect to use the split configuration in a sentence.
- The frequency of occurrence of both configurations is high but the frequency of joined configuration is higher than the split configuration. This has been illustrated by example (3) in Table 6. We conclude that the VPC is separable and both the split as well as joined configurations can be used.
- The frequency of occurrence of both configurations is high but the frequency of split configuration is higher than the joined configuration. This case is illustrated with example (4) in Table 6. Our conclusion is that the split configuration is not a VPC. Some other factors are contributing to its high frequency of occurrence. The joined configuration is a VPC. It is to be noted that this conclusion is based on the set of sentences considered for our experiments only. A stronger conclusion in this regard can be achieved only after experimenting with a large set of examples.

[6] These experiments were carried out in August 2011.

3 VPCs for English to Hindi Translation

The first problem that an MT system needs to solve regarding translating VPCs is to decide whether the *verb + preposition* combination is a VPC. Since VPCs can occur in split as well as joined configurations in a sentence, it becomes mandatory to find when the verb and the particle are acting as a single unit, and when they are behaving as independent entities. Once this problem is solved, the correct Hindi verb can be found by considering the semantics of the object. The following methods have been suggested by different researchers:

- Lexical entry for expressions having fixed structure and meanings (Sinha and Thakur, 2004)
- Context - disambiguation rules (Sinha and Thakur, 2004; Bhandari *et al.*, 2002)
- Structural analysis of clauses (Sinha and Thakur, 2004)
- Use of Example-base approach for disambiguating the Phrasal verbs (Saha *et al.*, 2004)

In our approach the focus is more on the semantics of the object in a sentence. This helps in finding when a verb and a particle combination is a VPC and when it is not. Once it is known whether a VPC exists or not then the context of the VPC is resolved based on the same semantics. We first discuss certain rules based on which a VPC is identified and then describe various approaches that have been used for resolving the context of VPC if at all it exists.

3.1 Rules for VPC identification

The rules generated for identifying a VPC have been illustrated with some VPC examples, such as "put on", "keep on", "get off", "go on" in this section. In the following discussion we use <verb name> to indicate that various inflections of the verb have been considered.

- Put on - The semantics considered for direct object (Obj_1) that immediately follow this VPC are: {Electric appliance: light, fan; wearable: dress, shoes; Eatable: tea, coffee; Chemical: cosmetics, paint; Public activity: play, dance; Quantity: weight, distance; Act: physical, mental activity}. The semantics considered for the indirect object (Obj_2), if at all it is present in the sentence are: {Location: wall, roof; Object: table, bed; Event: picnic, trip}. The various inflections of "put" that have been considered are "put", "puts" and "putting". The rules are as follows:

  (a) IF *<put>* + *on* + Obj_1 (NP_1[7]). THEN a VPC.
  (b) IF *<put>* + Obj_1 (NP_1) + *on.* THEN a VPC.
  (c) IF *<put>* + Obj_1 (NP_1) + *on* + Obj_2 (NP_2). THEN not a VPC.

- Keep on - The semantic considered for object (Obj_1) is: {Thing: Living or Non- Living: fan, book, hat, dress, cosmetics, box, dog, cat etc.}. The semantics considered for the object (Obj_2), if at all it is present in a sentence are: {Location: wall, roof; Object: table, bed}. The semantic for the object (Obj_3) in rule (d) can only be some wearable item (e.g. hat, shoes, coat). The forms of the verb "keep" that have been used are: "keep" and "kept". The rules are as follows:

  (a) IF *<keep>* + *on* + [verb + ing] + ---. THEN a VPC.
  (b) IF *<keep>* + Obj_1 (NP_1) + *on* + Obj_2 (NP_2). THEN not a VPC.
  (c) IF *<keep>* + *on* + Obj_2 (NP_2). THEN not a VPC.
  (d) IF *<keep>* + Obj_3 (NP) + *on.* THEN a VPC.
  (e) IF *<keep>* + [verb + ing] + *on* + ---. THEN not a VPC.

[7] Noun Phrase

- Get off - The semantics considered for object (Obj_1) are: {Vehicle: Bus, train; Riding animal: horse, elephant; Act: penalty, punishment}. The semantics considered for the object (Obj_2), are: {Attribute: Dirty mark, stain; Human being}. The various forms of get that have been used are: "get", "got" and "getting". The rules are as follows:

  a) IF <*get*> + *off* + Obj_1 (NP_1) + ---. THEN a Non-separable VPC.

  b) IF <*get*> + Obj_2 (NP_2) + *off* + ---. THEN a Separable VPC.

  c) IF <*get*> + *off* + Obj_2 (NP_2) + ---. THEN a Separable VPC.

Similar rules have been formed for other VPCs that have been considered for study.

3.2 Context Resolution for VPCs translations

VPCs do not have a fixed behavior and exhibit different behavior in different contexts. The direct object in the sentence plays a key role in determining the sense of the VPC. The indirect object can also help in disambiguating the sense of the VPC (Saha *et al.*, 2004). In this section we suggest various methods for resolving the context of the VPCs for English to Hindi translation.

Lexical Entry

A number of VPCs (e.g. "go on", "move on", "call for", "catch up", "check in") have a single Hindi verb for them. These VPCs are entered into the lexicon with their meaning. However, one needs to make sure in what situation they are acting as a VPC. The rules discussed in Section 3.1 determine when a VPC can occur in a sentence. If a VPC exists then it is given priority and the meaning of the VPC is picked from the lexicon instead of picking meanings of the individual components.

Sense of VPC in WordNet

WordNet has been used to decide the sense of the VPC in a sentence. Based on WordNet senses and the possible Hindi verbs available for these senses, rules have been formed to decide which Hindi verb has to be used for a VPC. We discuss here the rules for the VPC "break down" that have eight senses as per WordNet and can be translated using eight Hindi verbs. The task can also be fulfilled using only five unique Hindi verbs that are sufficient to represent all the eight senses. Some of these rules for the "break down" VPC are:

- IF (sense of "*break down*" is 1 or 5) THEN Hindi verb is "*tohdanaa*" or "*baatnaa*" meaning to break or to divide. For example, consider "I *broke down* the problem into sub-parts".
- IF (sense of "*break down*" is 2) THEN Hindi verb is "*samaapat karnaa*" ~ to finish. For illustration, consider "The king tried to *break down* the racial discrimination".

This approach is successful for only those VPCs for which all the senses have equivalent Hindi verbs and all the Hindi verbs can be represented by some sense in WordNet as in the case of "*break down*". This approach fails for VPCs which have lesser number of senses in WordNet as compared to possible Hindi verbs, for instance the VPC "break into" and "put on". For VPCs of this kind knowing only the sense from WordNet is not sufficient. Other possibilities also need to be explored. The following approach is useful in such a situation.

Related Verb for a Noun

This is applied when for an English VPC the number of senses in WordNet is not sufficient to indicate the Hindi verb to be used. For example "break into". As discussed in Table 4, to deal with these cases one needs to check for the NP, if there is any, following the VPC. If the Noun in the NP has a related verb then translation of that verb is used to represent the Hindi for that VPC. For example, in the sentence "He *broke into* laughter/ tears" the VPC is followed by "laughter" which is associated with the verb "laugh" and hence the Hindi verb used is "*hansnaa*". Similarly "tears" is associated with the verb "cry" and the Hindi verb for this is "*ronaa*".

However, there are sentences, such as, "the thief *broke into* the house" in which we do not have a related verb for the NP ("the house"). In such a case the semantics of the object in the sentence is identified and then is used for context resolution. This method is explained below.

Semantics of the Object

If none of the approaches discussed above works, then we look for the object in the sentence and find its semantic. Based on the semantic of the object the Hindi verb that should be used to represent the VPC is found. Rules have been formed based on the semantics of the object. This has been illustrated for the VPC "put on" (see Table 5).

This VPC has nine senses in WordNet. Some senses (6 and 8) do not have corresponding Hindi verbs. Also three Hindi verbs were found where no corresponding sense occurs in WordNet. This is illustrated by the example "She *put on* the light". No sense for the VPC exists in WordNet for this type of occurrence. Consequently, we found semantics of the object and decided the Hindi verb to be used accordingly. In total 18 such rules were formed for cases where no WordNet sense exists for a VPC but a Hindi verb is available. One of these rules is:

- IF (sense of "*put on*" is [NIL] and semantic of object is [Electric device: source of illumination or that emits light]) THEN Hindi verb will be "*jalaanaa*" ~ to burn

We studied 22 VPCs which had multiple Hindi verbs for their senses as found in WordNet. In all 166 senses were obtained for these VPCs from WordNet. However, most of these senses could be accommodated by 82 unique Hindi verbs. The synonyms of Hindi verbs have not been counted here. We also found 12 Hindi verbs which contributed to more than one WordNet sense obtained for different VPCs. One such Hindi verb is "*lagaanaa*". This verb can be used for the VPC "put up" as well as "put on". WordNet sense 1 for "put up" is "to post a sign or warning"; and WordNet sense 7 for "put on" is "to apply, something on a surface". For illustration we consider the following two examples: (1) The college *put up* a notice for ragging. (2) She *put on* lipstick for the party. Both these senses can be represented by one Hindi verb "*lagaanaa*". Thus we have lesser Hindi verbs to accommodate WordNet senses.

4 Concluding Remarks

This paper deals with handling of VPCs while translating from English to Hindi (E-H). Existing E-H MT systems are often found wanting while translating English VPCs. A thorough analysis of the outputs of four of the major E-H MT systems reveals the fact clearly. In particular, the problem becomes more prominent when the VPCs take the structure *verb + preposition.* The problem can be of various types. As a consequence the solution scheme needs to find answers to the following questions:

- whether the *verb + preposition* combination is a true VPC, as opposed to the preposition being used to take care of an intransitive verb;
- how to identify the VPC even when the preposition is not adjacent to the underlying verb;
- how to identify the exact sense of the VPC, given that the same VPC may have multiple senses, as per WordNet;
- how to choose the proper translation in the target language. This becomes very important in E-H translation, as for most of the English VPCs there exists a specific verb in Hindi.

None of the major E-H MT systems are able to handle these problems in an efficient way. We propose a rule-based approach for solving this difficulty. The rules are formulated by identifying the semantic bonding between the VPC and other components of the source language sentence. The rules have been formulated by analyzing a large collection of English sentences and their Hindi translations to identify the following:

- Different senses that a VPC may have.

- In which situations the verb and preposition can have a joined structure, and in which cases a split structure is also possible.
- In which situations the *verb + preposition* is not a VPC.

The rules have been applied for different VPCs with multiple senses, and the results are promising. So far we have considered only *Verb + Preposition* type of VPCs. However, English VPCs may take other forms too. Some of the common VPC structures are *Verb + Adjective* (e.g. "*cut short*"), *Verb + Preposition + Preposition* (e.g. "*look down upon*"). We would like to extend our scheme to handle these VPCs as well. Also, we have considered only simple sentences so far. Our intuitive feeling is that a study for complex sentences for these VPCs may lead to further refinement of the rules that have been discussed for identification and context resolution of the VPCs. We are currently working in these directions.

The approaches described are not language dependent. We expect that similar techniques will prove to be helpful for other target languages by focusing on the lexicon and the verbs of that particular language.

References

Baldwin Timothy, Aline Villavicencio. 2002. Extracting the Unextractable: A Case Study on Verb-particles. *Proceedings of the 6th Conference on Natural Language Learning (CoNLL-2002)*, pp. 98-104. Taipei, Taiwan.

Bannard Colin, Timothy Baldwin, Alex Lascarides. 2003. A Statistical Approach to the Semantics of Verb-Particles. *Proceedings of the ACL-SIGLEX Workshop on Multiword Expressions: Analysis, Acquisition and Treatment*, Sapporo, Japan, pp. 65-72.

Bhandari Vartika, R.M.K. Sinha and Ajai Jain. 2002. Disambiguation of Phrasal Verbs for Machine Translation. *Proceedings of Symposium on Translation Support Systems (STRANS-2002)*, 15-17 March, Kanpur, India.

Bolinger Dwight L. 1971. *The Phrasal Verb in English*. Boston, USA: Harvard University Press.

Constable James W. D. and James R. Curran. 2009. Integrating verb-particle constructions into CCG parsing. *Proceedings of the Australasian Language Technology Association Workshop (ALTW)*, pp. 114–118.

Deh´e, Nicole. 2002. *Particle verbs in English: syntax, information structure and intonation*. John Benjamins, Amsterdam/Philadelphia.

Gupta Deepa and N. Chatterjee. 2003. Identification of Divergence for English to Hindi EBMT. *Proceedings of MT Summit IX*, New Orleans, LA, pp. 141 – 148.

Ramisch Carlos, Aline Villavicencio, Leonardo Moura, Marco Idiart. 2008. Picking them up and Figuring them out: Verb-Particle Constructions, Noise and Idiomaticity. *Proceedings of the Twelfth Conference on Computational Natural Language Learning*, pp. 49-56.

Saha Indranil, Ananthakrishnan R. and Sasikumar M. 2004. *Example-Based Technique for Disambiguating Phrasal Verbs in English to Hindi Translation*. Technical Report, KBCS Division, CDAC Mumbai.

Singh Suraj Bhan. 2003. *English-Hindi Translation Grammar (A Transfer Grammar based on Contrastive Analysis)*. Prabhat Publications, New Delhi.

Sinha R.M.K. and Anil Thakur. 2004. Multi-Word Expression in English and Hindi: Problems in Contextualization. *Proceedings of International Symposium on Machine Translaton NLP and TSS (iSTRANS-2004)*, Vol. 1. pp. 111-116.

Villavicencio Aline. 2003. Verb-Particle Constructions and Lexical Resources. *Proceedings of the ACL-SIGLEX Workshop on Multiword Expressions: Analysis, Acquisition and Treatment,* Sapporo, Japan.

Improving Sampling-based Alignment by Investigating the Distribution of N-grams in Phrase Translation Tables ⋆

Juan Luo[a], Adrien Lardilleux[b], and Yves Lepage[a]

[a]Graduate School of Information, Production and Systems, Waseda University,
2-7 Hibikino, Wakamatsu-ku, Kitakyushu, Fukuoka 808-0135, Japan
{juanluoonly@suou, yves.lepage@aoni}.waseda.jp
[b]TLP Group, LIMSI-CNRS,
BP 133, Orsay Cedex 91403, France
adrien.lardilleux@limsi.fr

Abstract. This paper describes an approach to improve the performance of sampling-based multilingual alignment on translation tasks by investigating the distribution of n-grams in the translation tables. This approach consists in enforcing the alignment of n-grams. The quality of phrase translation tables output by this approach and that of MGIZA++ is compared in statistical machine translation tasks. Significant improvements for this approach are reported. In addition, merging translation tables is shown to outperform state-of-the-art techniques.

Keywords: alignment, phrase translation table, statistical machine translation.

1 Introduction

Phrase translation tables play an important role in the process of building machine translation systems. The quality of translation table, which identifies the relations between words or phrases in the source language and those in the target language, is crucial for the quality of the output of most machine translation systems. Currently, the most widely used state-of-the-art tool to generate phrase translation tables is GIZA++ (Och and Ney, 2003), which trains the ubiquitous IBM models (Brown *et al.*, 1993) and the HMM introduced by (Vogel *et al.*, 1996), in combination with the Moses toolkit (Koehn *et al.*, 2007). MGIZA++, a multi-threaded word aligner based on GIZA++, is proposed by (Gao and Vogel, 2008).

In this paper, we investigate a different approach to the production of phrase translation tables: the sampling-based approach (Lardilleux and Lepage, 2009b). This approach is implemented in a free open-source tool called Anymalign.[1] Being in line with the associative alignment trend illustrated by (Gale and Church, 1991; Melamed, 2000; Moore, 2005), it is much simpler than the models implemented in MGIZA++, which are in line with the estimating trend illustrated by (Brown *et al.*, 1991; Och and Ney, 2003; Liang *et al.*, 2006). In addition, it is capable of aligning multiple languages simultaneously; but we will not use this feature here as we will restrain ourselves to bilingual experiments in this paper.

In sampling-based alignment, only those sequences of words sharing the exact same distribution (i.e., they appear exactly in the same sentences of the corpus) are considered for alignment.

⋆ Part of the research presented in this paper has been done under a Japanese grant-in-aid (Kakenhi C, A11515600: Improvement of alignments and release of multilingual syntactic patterns for statistical and example-based machine translation).

[1] `http://users.info.unicaen.fr/~alardill/anymalign/`

The key idea is to make more words share the same distribution by artificially reducing their frequency in multiple random subcorpora obtained by sampling. Indeed, the smaller a subcorpus, the less frequent its words, and the more likely they are to share the same distribution; hence the higher the proportion of words aligned in this subcorpus. In practice, the majority of these words turn out to be *hapaxes*, that is, words that occur only once in the input corpus. Hapaxes have been shown to safely align across languages (Lardilleux and Lepage, 2009a).

The subcorpus selection process is guided by a probability distribution which ensures a proper coverage of the input parallel corpus:

$$\mathrm{p}(k) = \frac{-1}{k\ \log(1-k/n)} \quad \text{(to be normalized)} \qquad (1)$$

where k denotes the size (number of sentences) of a subcorpus and n the size of the complete input corpus. Note that this function is very close to $1/k^2$: it gives much more credit to small subcorpora, which happen to be the most productive (Lardilleux and Lepage, 2009b). Once the size of a subcorpus has been chosen according to this distribution, its sentences are randomly selected from the complete input corpus according to a uniform distribution. Then, from each subcorpus, sequences of words that share the same distribution are extracted to constitute alignments along with the number of times they were aligned.[2]

Eventually, the list of alignments is turned into a full-fledged translation table, by calculating various features for each alignment. In the following, we use two translation probabilities and two lexical weights as proposed by (Koehn *et al.*, 2003), as well as the commonly used phrase penalty, for a total of five features.

One important feature of the sampling-based alignment method is that it is implemented with an *anytime* algorithm: the number of random subcorpora to be processed is not set in advance, so the alignment process can be interrupted at any moment. Contrary to many approaches, after a very short amount of time, *quality* is no more a matter of time, however *quantity* is: the longer the aligner runs (i.e. the more subcorpora processed), the more alignments produced, and the more reliable their associated translation probabilities, as they are calculated on the basis of the number of time each alignment was obtained. This is possible because high frequency alignments are quickly output with a fairly good estimation of their translation probabilities. As time goes, their estimation is refined, while less frequent alignments are output in addition.

Intuitively, since the sampling-based alignment process can be interrupted without sacrificing the quality of alignments, it should be possible to allot more processing time for n-grams of similar lengths in both languages and less time to very different lengths. For instance, a source bigram is much less likely to be aligned with a target 9-gram than with a bigram or a trigram. The experiments reported in this paper make use of the anytime feature of Anymalign and of the possibility of allotting time freely.

This paper is organized as follows: Section 2 describes a preliminary experiment on the sampling-based alignment approach implemented in Anymalign baseline and provides the experimental results from which the problem is defined. In Section 3, we propose a variant in order to improve its performance on statistical machine translation tasks. Section 4 introduces standard normal distribution of time to bias the distribution of n-grams in phrase translation tables. Section 5 describes the effects of pruning on the translation quality. Section 6 presents the merge of two aligners' phrase translation tables. Finally, in Section 7, conclusions and possible directions for future work are presented.

[2] Contrary to the widely used terminology where it denotes a set of links between the source and target words of a sentence pair, we call "alignment" a (source, target) phrase pair, i.e., it corresponds to an entry in the so-called [phrase] translation tables.

2 Preliminary Experiment

In order to measure the performance of the sampling-based alignment approach implemented in Anymalign in statistical machine translation tasks, we conducted a preliminary experiment and compared with the standard alignment setting: symmetric alignments obtained from MGIZA++. Although Anymalign and MGIZA++ are both capable of parallel processing, for fair comparison in time, we run them as single processes in all our experiments.

2.1 Experimental Setup

A sample of the French-English parts of the Europarl parallel corpus was used for training, tuning and testing. A detailed description of the data used in the experiments is given in Table 1. The training corpus is made of 100k sentences. The development set contains 500 sentences, and 1,000 sentences were used for testing. To perform the experiments, a standard statistical machine translation system was built for each different alignment setting, using the Moses decoder (Koehn *et al.*, 2007), MERT (Minimum Error Rate Training) to tune the parameters of translation tables (Och, 2003), and the SRI Language Modeling toolkit (Stolcke, 2002) to build the target language model.

As for the evaluation of translations, four standard automatic evaluation metrics were used: mWER (Nießen *et al.*, 2000), BLEU (Papineni *et al.*, 2002), NIST (Doddington, 2002), and TER (Snover *et al.*, 2006).

Table 1: Statistics on the French-English parallel corpus used for the training, development, and test sets.

		French	English
Train	sentences	100,000	100,000
	words	3,986,438	2,824,579
	words/sentence	38	27
Dev	sentences	500	500
	words	18,120	13,261
	words/sentence	36	26
Test	sentences	1,000	1,000
	words	38,936	27,965
	words/sentence	37	27

2.2 Problem Definition

In a first setting, we evaluated the quality of translations output by the Moses decoder using the phrase table obtained by making MGIZA++'s alignments symmetric in a second setting. This phrase table was simply replaced by that produced by Anymalign. Since Anymalign can be stopped at any time, for a fair comparison it was run for the same amount of time as MGIZA++: seven hours in total. The experimental results are shown in Table 2.

Table 2: Evaluation results on a statistical machine translation task using phrase tables obtained from MGIZA++ and Anymalign (baseline).

	mWER	BLEU	NIST	TER
MGIZA++	**0.5714**	**0.2742**	**6.6747**	**0.6170**
Anymalign	0.6186	0.2285	6.0764	0.6634

In order to investigate the differences between MGIZA++ and Anymalign phrase translation tables, we analyzed the distribution of n-grams of both aligners, The distributions are shown in

Table 7 (a) and Table 7 (b). In Anymalign's phrase translation table, the number of alignments is 8 times that of 1 × 1 n-grams in MGIZA++ translation table, or twice the number of 1 × 2 n-grams or 2 × 1 n-grams in MGIZA++ translation table. Along the diagonal (m × m n-grams), the number of alignments in Anymalign table is more than 10 times less than in MGIZA++ table. This confirms the results given in (Lardilleux *et al.*, 2009) that the sampling-based approach excels in aligning unigrams, which makes it better at multilingual lexicon induction than, e.g., MGIZA++. However, its phrase tables do not reach the performance of symmetric alignments from MGIZA++ on translation tasks. This basically comes from the fact that Anymalign does not align enough long n-grams (Lardilleux *et al.*, 2009).

3 Anymalign1-N

3.1 Enforcing Alignment of N-grams

To solve the above-mentioned problem, we propose a method to force the sampling-based approach to align more n-grams.

Consider that we have a parallel input corpus, i.e., a list of (source, target) sentence pairs, for instance, in French and English. Groups of characters that are separated by spaces in these sentences are considered as words. Single words are referred to as unigrams, and sequences of two and three words are called bigrams and trigrams, respectively.

Theoretically, since the sampling-based alignment method excels at aligning unigrams, we could improve it by making it align bigrams, trigrams, or even longer n-grams as if they were unigrams. We do this by replacing spaces between words by underscore symbols and reduplicating words as many times as needed, which allows to make bigrams, trigrams, and longer n-grams appear as unigrams. Table 3 depicts the way of forcing n-grams into unigrams.

Similar works on the idea of enlarging n-grams have been reported in (Ma *et al.*, 2007), in which "word packing" is used to obtain 1-to-*n* alignments based on co-occurrence frequencies, and (Henríquez Q. *et al.*, 2010), in which collocation segmentation is performed on bilingual corpus to extract *n*-to-*m* alignments.

Table 3: Transforming n-grams into unigrams by inserting underscores and reduplicating words for both the French part and English part of the input parallel corpus.

n	French	English
1	le debat est clos .	the debate is closed .
2	le_debat debat_est est_clos clos_.	the_debate debate_is is_closed closed_.
3	le_debat_est debat_est_clos est_clos_.	the_debate_is debate_is_closed is_closed_.
4	le_debat_est_clos debat_est_clos_.	the_debate_is_closed debate_is_closed_.
5	le_debat_est_clos_.	the_debate_is_closed_.

3.2 Phrase Translation Subtables

It it thus possible to use various parallel corpora, with different segmentation schemes in the source and target parts. We refer to a parallel corpus where source n-grams and target m-grams are assimilated to unigrams as an *unigramized n-m corpus*. These corpora are then used as input to Anymalign to produce phrase translation subtables, as shown in Table 4. Practically, we call Anymalign1-N the process of running Anymalign with all possible unigramized *n-m* corpora, with *n* and *m* both ranging from 1 to a given N. In total, Anymalign is thus run N × N times. All phrase translation subtables are finally merged together into one large translation table, where translation probabilities are re-estimated given the complete set of alignments.

Table 4: List of n-gram translation subtables (TT) generated from the training corpus. These subtables are then merged together into a single translation table.

		Target				
		unigrams	bigrams	trigrams	...	N-grams
Source	unigrams	TT 1 × 1	TT 1 × 2	TT 1 × 3	...	TT 1 × N
	bigrams	TT 2 × 1	TT 2 × 2	TT 2 × 3	...	TT 2 × N
	trigrams	TT 3 × 1	TT 3 × 2	TT 3 × 3	...	TT 3 × N
	...	...	...	...	...	...
	N-grams	TT N × 1	TT N × 2	TT N × 3	...	TT N × N

Although Anymalign is capable of directly producing alignments of sequences of words, we use it with a simple filter[3] so that it only produces (typographic) unigrams in output, i.e., n-grams and m-grams assimilated to unigrams in the input corpus. This choice was made because it is useless to produce alignment of sequences of words, since we are only interested in *phrases* in the subsequent machine translation tasks. Those phrases are already contained in our (typographic) unigrams: all we need to do to get the original segmentation is to remove underscores from the alignments.

3.3 Evaluation Results with Equal Time Configuration

The same experimental process (i.e., replacing the translation table) as in the preliminary experiment was carried out on Anymalign1-N with equal time distribution, which is, uniformly distributed time among subtables. For a fair comparison, the same amount of time was given: seven hours in total. The results are shown in Table 6. On the whole, MGIZA++ significantly outperforms Anymalign, by more than 4 BLEU points. The proposed approach, Anymalign1-N, produces better results than Anymalign in its basic version, with the best increase with Anymalign1-3 or Anymalign1-4 (+1.3 BP).

The comparison of Table 7 (c) (see last page) and Table 7 (a) shows that Anymalign1-N delivers too many alignments outside of the diagonal ($m \times m$ n-grams) and still not enough along the diagonal. Consequently, this number of alignments should be lowered. A way of doing so is by giving less time for alignments outside of the diagonal.

4 Time Distribution among Subtables

In order to increase the number of phrase pairs along the diagonal of the translation table matrix and decrease this number outside the diagonal (Table 4), we distribute the total alignment time among translation subtables according to the standard normal distribution:

$$\phi(n,m) = \frac{1}{\sqrt{2\pi}} e^{-\frac{1}{2}(n-m)^2} \qquad (2)$$

The alignment time allotted to the subtable between source n-grams and target m-grams will thus be proportional to $\phi(n,m)$. Table 5 shows an example of alignment times allotted to each subtable up to 4-grams, for a total processing time of 7 hours.

4.1 Evaluation Results with Standard Normal Time Distribution

We performed a third evaluation using the standard normal distribution of time, as in previous experiments, again with a total amount of processing time (7 hours).

The comparison between MGIZA++, Anymalign in its standard use, and Anymalign1-N with standard normal time distribution is shown in Table 6. Anymalign1-4 shows the best performance

[3] Option `-N 1` in the program.

Table 5: Alignment time in seconds allotted to each unigramized parallel corpus of Anymalign1-4. The sum of the figures in all cells amounts to seven hours (25,200 seconds).

		Target			
		unigrams	bigrams	trigrams	4-grams
Source	unigrams	3,072	1,863	416	34
	bigrams	1,863	3,072	1,863	416
	trigrams	416	1,863	3,072	1,863
	4-grams	34	416	1,863	3,072

in terms of mWER and BLEU scores, while Anymalign1-3 gets the best results for the two other evaluation metrics. There is an increase in BLEU scores for almost all Anymalign1-N, from Anymalign1-3 to Anymalign1-10, when compared with the translation qualities of Anymalign1-N with equal time distribution. The greatest increase in BLEU is obtained for Anymalign1-10 (almost +2 BP). Anymalign1-4 shows the best translation qualities among all other settings, but gets a less significant improvement (+0.2 BP).

Again, we investigated the number of entries in Anymalign1-N run with this normal time distribution. We compare the number of entries in Table 7 in Anymalign1-4 with (c) equal time distribution and (d) standard normal time distribution (see last page). The number of phrase pairs on the diagonal roughly doubled when using standard normal time distribution. We can see a significant increase in the number of phrase pairs of similar lengths, while the number of phrase pairs with different lengths tends to decrease slightly. This means that the standard normal time distribution allowed us to produce much more numerous useful alignments (a priori, phrase pairs with similar lengths), while maintaining the noise (phrase pairs with different lengths) to a low level, which is a neat advantage over the original method.

5 Translation Table Pruning

Until now, we were concerned with the shape of phrase translation tables in standard configurations. However, (Johnson *et al.*, 2007) have shown that substantially pruning the phrase translation tables can lead to slight but consistent improvements in translation quality.

They use Fisher's exact significance test to eliminate a substantial number of phrase pairs. The significance of the association between a (source, target) phrase pair is evaluated and their probability of co-occurrence in the corpus is calculated. The hypergeometric distribution is used to compute the observed probability of joint occurrence $C(\tilde{s},\tilde{t})$, with $\tilde{s}$ a source phrase and $\tilde{t}$ a target phrase:

$$p_h(C(\tilde{s},\tilde{t})) = \frac{\binom{C(\tilde{s})}{C(\tilde{s},\tilde{t})}\binom{N-C(\tilde{s})}{C(\tilde{t})-C(\tilde{s},\tilde{t})}}{\binom{N}{C(\tilde{t})}} \quad (3)$$

Here, N is the number of sentences in the input parallel corpus. The p-value is calculated as:

$$\text{p-value}(C(\tilde{s},\tilde{t})) = \sum_{k=C(\tilde{s},\tilde{t})}^{\infty} p_h(k) \quad (4)$$

Any phrase pair with a p-value greater than a given threshold will thus be filtered out. In practice, this mainly removes phrase pairs with different frequencies. A special case happens when a source phrase and a target phrase, hence the resulting phrase pair as well, occur only once in the corpus (called a 1-1-1 phrase pair in (Johnson *et al.*, 2007)). By considering a p-value of

$\alpha = \log(N)$, $\alpha + \varepsilon$ (where ε is very small) is the smallest threshold that results in none of the 1-1-1 phrase pairs being included, while $\alpha - \varepsilon$ is the largest threshold that results in those pairs being included.

We investigate the impact of pruning on Anymalign's translation tables in terms of n-gram distribution and final translation quality.

5.1 Evaluation Results with Pruning

In a fourth set of experiments, we thus compare the phrase translation tables of MGIZA++, and Anymalign1-N (standard normal time distribution), after applying this pruning. The $\alpha - \varepsilon$ filter was used.

Evaluation results on machine translation tasks with pruned translation tables are given in Table 6. The phrase table size reduction brings gains in BLEU scores. Among all Anymalign1-N, Anymalign1-4 once again gets the highest BLEU score of 0.2511 and shows the best performance in all evaluation metrics.

As an example, the number of entries in Anymalign1-4's translation table, after pruning, is shown in Table 7 (e). The largest difference when compared with the non-pruned translation table (Table 7 (d)) is visible in the cell corresponding to 1-1 entries: a substantial decrease of almost 200,000 entries is observed, which corresponds to a reduction of 76%. As a consequence, the most numerous entries are now 2-2 phrase pairs, which account for 19% of the total number of phrase pairs. On the whole, 54% of entries were filtered out from Anymalign1-4's translation table.

6 Merging translation tables

In order to check exactly how different the translation table of MGIZA++ and that of Anymalign are, we performed an additional set of experiments in which MGIZA++'s translation table is merged with that of Anymalign baseline and we used the union of the two translation tables. As for the feature scores in the translation tables for the intersection part of both aligners, i.e., entries in two translation tables share the same phrase pairs but with different feature scores, we adopted parameters computed either by MGIZA++ or by Anymalign for evaluation.

Evaluation results on machine translation tasks with merged translation tables are given in Table 6. This setting outperforms MGIZA++ on BLEU scores. The translation table with Anymalign parameters for the intersection part is slightly behind the translation table with MGIZA++ parameters. This may indicate that the feature scores in Anymalign translation table need to be revised.

7 Conclusions and Future Work

We have presented a method to improve the translation quality of the sampling-based subsentential alignment approach for statistical machine translation tasks. Our approach is based on adapting the number of n-grams by investigating their distribution in phrase translation tables. Furthermore, we inspected the influence of pruning the translation tables, a technique described in (Johnson *et al.*, 2007), and merging the translation tables from two aligners (i.e., Anymalign and MGIZA++). Adapting the number of n-grams leads to significantly better evaluation results than the original approach. Merging two translation tables outperforms MGIZA++ alone. As for future work, we plan to modify the computation of the feature scores in Anymalign's phrase translation tables to make them closer to those of MGIZA++.

Table 6: Evaluation results.

	mWER	BLEU	NIST	TER
MGIZA++	**0.5714**	**0.2742**	**6.6747**	**0.6170**
Anymalign	0.6186	0.2285	6.0764	0.6634

Anymalign1-N	equal time distribution				std.norm.distribution				pruning			
	mWER	BLEU	NIST	TER	mWER	BLEU	NIST	TER	mWER	BLEU	NIST	TER
Anymalign1-1	0.6818	0.1984	5.6353	0.7188	0.6818	0.1984	5.6353	0.7188	0.6871	0.1953	5.6042	0.7258
Anymalign1-2	0.6121	0.2406	6.2789	0.6536	0.6121	0.2404	6.2674	0.6535	0.6102	0.2425	6.3093	0.6515
Anymalign1-3	**0.6075**	0.2403	**6.3009**	**0.6507**	0.6079	0.2441	**6.2928**	**0.6517**	0.6117	0.2413	6.2501	0.6561
Anymalign1-4	0.6142	**0.2423**	6.2087	0.6583	**0.6071**	**0.2442**	6.2844	0.6526	**0.5978**	**0.2511**	**6.3985**	**0.6435**
Anymalign1-5	0.6099	0.2376	6.2331	0.6551	0.6134	0.2436	6.2426	0.6548	0.6076	0.2457	6.3120	0.6504
Anymalign1-6	0.6193	0.2349	6.1574	0.6634	0.6165	0.2403	6.1595	0.6589	0.6104	0.2459	6.2687	0.6545
Anymalign1-7	0.6157	0.2371	6.2107	0.6559	0.6136	0.2405	6.2124	0.6564	0.6079	0.2419	6.2569	0.6516
Anymalign1-8	0.6353	0.2253	5.9777	0.6794	0.6151	0.2366	6.1639	0.6597	0.6060	0.2446	6.2986	0.6496
Anymalign1-9	0.6279	0.2296	6.0261	0.6722	0.6136	0.2402	6.1928	0.6564	0.6078	0.2461	6.2974	0.6493
Anymalign1-10	0.6475	0.2182	5.8534	0.6886	0.6192	0.2361	6.1803	0.6587	0.6076	0.2459	6.3079	0.6490

Merge	mWER	BLEU	NIST	TER
Anymalign param.	**0.5671**	**0.2747**	**6.7101**	**0.6128**
MGIZA++ param.	**0.5685**	**0.2754**	**6.7060**	**0.6142**

References

Brown, Peter, Stephen Della Pietra, Vincent Della Pietra, and Robert Mercer. 1993. The mathematics of statistical machine translation: Parameter estimation. *Computational Linguistics*, 19(2), 263–311.

Brown, Peter, Jennifer Lai, and Robert Mercer. 1991. Aligning sentences in parallel corpora. In *Proceedings of the 29th Annual Meeting of the Association for Computational Linguistics (ACL'91)*, pp. 169–176, Berkeley (Californie, USA), jun.

Doddington, George. 2002. Automatic evaluation of machine translation quality using N-gram co-occurrence statistics. In *Proceedings of the Second International Conference on Human Language Technology Research*, pp. 138–145, San Diego. Morgan Kaufmann Publishers Inc.

Gale, William and Kenneth Church. 1991. Identifying word correspondences in parallel texts. In *Proceedings of the fourth DARPA workshop on Speech and Natural Language*, pp. 152–157, Pacific Grove, feb.

Gao, Qin and Stephan Vogel. 2008. Parallel implementations of word alignment tool. In Association for Computational Linguistics, ed., *Software Engineering, Testing, and Quality Assurance for Natural Language Processing*, pp. 49–57, Columbus, Ohio.

Henríquez Q., A. Carlos, R. Marta Costa-jussà, Vidas Daudaravicius, E. Rafael Banchs, and B. José Mariño. 2010. Using collocation segmentation to augment the phrase table. In *Proceedings of the Joint Fifth Workshop on Statistical Machine Translation and MetricsMATR*, WMT '10, pp. 98–102, Stroudsburg, PA, USA. Association for Computational Linguistics.

Johnson, J Howard, Joel Martin, George Foster, and Roland Kuhn. 2007. Improving translation quality by discarding most of the phrasetable. In *Proceedings of the 2007 Joint Conference on Empirical Methods in Natural Language Processing and Computational Natural Language Learning (EMNLP-CoNLL)*, pp. 967–975, Prague, Czech Republic.

Koehn, Philipp, Hieu Hoang, Alexandra Birch, Chris Callison-Burch, Marcello Federico, Nicola Bertoldi, Brooke Cowan, Wade Shen, Christine Moran, Richard Zens, Chris Dyer, Ondrej Bojar, Alexandra Constantin, and Evan Herbst. 2007. Moses: Open source toolkit for statistical machine translation. In *Proceedings of the 45th Annual Meeting of the Association for Computational Linguistics (ACL 2007)*, pp. 177–180, Prague, Czech Republic.

Koehn, Philipp, Franz J. Och, and Daniel Marcu. 2003. Statistical phrase-based translation. In *Proceedings of the 2003 Human Language Technology Conference of the North American Chapter of the Association for Computational Linguistics*, pp. 48–54, Edmonton.

Lardilleux, Adrien, Jonathan Chevelu, Yves Lepage, Ghislain Putois, and Julien Gosme. 2009. Lexicons or phrase tables? An investigation in sampling-based multilingual alignment. In Mikel Forcada and Andy Way, eds., *Proceedings of the third workshop on example-based machine translation*, pp. 45–52, Dublin, Ireland.

Lardilleux, Adrien and Yves Lepage. 2009a. Hapax Legomena : their Contribution in Number and Efficiency to Word Alignment. *Lecture notes in computer science*, 5603, 440–450.

Lardilleux, Adrien and Yves Lepage. 2009b. Sampling-based multilingual alignment. In *International Conference on Recent Advances in Natural Language Processing (RANLP 2009)*, pp. 214–218, Borovets, Bulgaria.

Liang, Percy, Ben Taskar, and Dan Klein. 2006. Alignment by agreement. In *Proceedings of the Human Language Technology Conference of the NAACL*, pp. 104–111, New York City, jun.

Ma, Yanjun, Nicolas Stroppa, and Andy Way. 2007. Bootstrapping word alignment via word packing. In *Proceedings of the 45th Annual Meeting of the Association of Computational Linguistics*, pp. 304–311, Prague, Czech Republic.

Melamed, Dan. 2000. Models of translational equivalence among words. *Computational Linguistics*, 26(2), 221–249, jun.

Moore, Robert. 2005. Association-based bilingual word alignment. In *Proceedings of the ACL Workshop on Building and Using Parallel Texts*, pp. 1–8, Ann Arbor, jun.

Nießen, Sonja, Franz Josef Och, Gregor Leusch, and Hermann Ney. 2000. An evaluation tool for machine translation: Fast evaluation for machine translation research. In *Proceedings of the Second International Conference on Language Resources and Evaluation (LREC)*, pp. 39–45, Athens.

Och, Franz Josef. 2003. Minimum error rate training in statistical machine translation. In *Proceedings of the 41st Annual Meeting on Association for Computational Linguistics - Volume 1*, ACL '03, pp. 160–167, Stroudsburg, PA, USA. Association for Computational Linguistics.

Och, Franz Josef and Hermann Ney. 2003. A systematic comparison of various statistical alignment models. In *Computational Linguistics*, volume 29, pp. 19–51.

Papineni, Kishore, Salim Roukos, Todd Ward, and Wei-Jing Zhu. 2002. BLEU: a method for automatic evaluation of machine translation. In *Proceedings of the 40th Annual Meeting of the Association for Computational Linguistics (ACL 2002)*, pp. 311–318, Philadelphia.

Snover, Matthew, Bonnie Dorr, Richard Schwartz, Linnea Micciulla, and John Makhoul. 2006. A study of translation edit rate with targeted human annotation. In *Proceedings of Association for Machine Translation in the Americas (AMTA 2006)*, pp. 223–231, Cambridge, Massachusetts.

Stolcke, A. 2002. SRILM-an extensible language modeling toolkit. In *Seventh International Conference on Spoken Language Processing*, volume 2, pp. 901–904, Denver, Colorado.

Vogel, Stephan, Hermann Ney, and Christoph Tillman. 1996. Hmm-based word alignment in statistical translation. In *Proceedings of the 16th International Conference on Computational Linguistics (Coling'96)*, pp. 836–841, Copenhagen, aug.

Table 7: Distribution of phrase pairs in translation tables.

(a) Distribution of phrase pairs in MGIZA++'s translation table.

		Target							
		unigrams	bigrams	trigrams	4-grams	5-grams	6-grams	7-grams	total
Source	unigrams	**89,788**	44,941	10,700	2,388	486	133	52	148,488
	bigrams	61,007	**288,394**	86,978	20,372	5,142	1,163	344	463,400
	trigrams	19,235	149,971	**373,991**	105,449	27,534	7,414	1,857	685,451
	4-grams	5,070	47,848	193,677	**335,837**	106,467	31,011	9,261	729,171
	5-grams	1,209	13,984	73,068	193,260	**270,615**	98,895	32,349	683,380
	6-grams	332	3,856	24,333	87,244	177,554	**214,189**	88,700	596,208
	7-grams	113	1,103	7,768	33,278	91,355	157,653	**171,049**	462,319
	total	176,754	550,097	770,515	777,828	679,153	510,458	303,612	3,768,417

(b) Distribution of phrase pairs in Anymalign's translation table (baseline).

		Target								
		unigrams	bigrams	trigrams	4-grams	5-grams	6-grams	7-grams	···	total
Source	unigrams	**791,099**	105,961	9,139	1,125	233	72	37	···	1,012,473
	bigrams	104,633	**21,602**	4,035	919	290	100	44	···	226,176
	trigrams	10,665	4,361	**2,570**	1,163	553	240	96	···	92,268
	4-grams	1,698	1,309	1,492	**1,782**	1,158	573	267	···	61,562
	5-grams	378	526	905	1,476	**1,732**	1,206	642	···	47,139
	6-grams	110	226	467	958	1,559	**1,694**	1,245	···	40,174
	7-grams	40	86	238	536	1,054	1,588	**1,666**	···	35,753
	···	···	···	···	···	···	···	···	···	···
	total	1,022,594	230,400	86,830	55,534	42,891	37,246	34,531	···	1,371,865

(c) Anymalign1-4 with equal time for each $n \times m$ n-grams alignments.

		Target							
		unigrams	bigrams	trigrams	4-grams	5-grams	6-grams	7-grams	total
Source	unigrams	**171,077**	118,848	39,253	13,327	0	0	0	342,505
	bigrams	119,953	**142,721**	67,872	24,908	0	0	0	355,454
	trigrams	45,154	75,607	**86,181**	42,748	0	0	0	249,690
	4-grams	15,514	30,146	54,017	**60,101**	0	0	0	159,778
	5-grams	0	0	0	0	0	0	0	0
	6-grams	0	0	0	0	0	0	0	0
	7-grams	0	0	0	0	0	0	0	0
	total	351,698	367,322	247,323	141,084	0	0	0	1,107,427

(d) Anymalign1-4 with standard normal time distribution.

		Target							
		unigrams	bigrams	trigrams	4-grams	5-grams	6-grams	7-grams	total
Source	unigrams	**255,443**	132,779	13,803	469	0	0	0	402,494
	bigrams	134,458	**217,500**	75,441	8,612	0	0	0	436,011
	trigrams	15,025	86,973	**142,091**	48,568	0	0	0	292,657
	4-grams	635	10,516	61,741	**98,961**	0	0	0	171,853
	5-grams	0	0	0	0	0	0	0	0
	6-grams	0	0	0	0	0	0	0	0
	7-grams	0	0	0	0	0	0	0	0
	total	405,561	447,768	293,076	156,610	0	0	0	1,303,015

(e) Distribution of phrase pairs in Anymalign1-4's translation table (after pruning).

		Target							
		unigrams	bigrams	trigrams	4-grams	5-grams	6-grams	7-grams	total
Source	unigrams	**60,297**	59,099	8,819	328	0	0	0	128,543
	bigrams	58,232	**110,415**	51,557	6,954	0	0	0	227,158
	trigrams	9,777	58,604	**69,431**	28,046	0	0	0	165,858
	4-grams	474	8,586	31,209	**31,666**	0	0	0	71,935
	5-grams	0	0	0	0	0	0	0	0
	6-grams	0	0	0	0	0	0	0	0
	7-grams	0	0	0	0	0	0	0	0
	total	128,780	236,704	161,016	66,994	0	0	0	593,494

Predicting Linguistic Difficulty by Means of a Morpho-Syntactic Probabilistic Model

Philippe Blache and Stéphane Rauzy

Aix-Marseille Univ & CNRS
LPL, 5 Avenue Pasteur, 13100 Aix-en-Provence, France
{blache;rauzy}@lpl-aix.fr

Abstract. We propose in this paper a new contribution to the evaluation of linguistic difficulty. At the opposite of classical approaches relying on syntax, we show that a probabilistic morpho-syntactic analysis provides information enough to calculate different parameters, including *surprisal*. This method constitutes an original and robust model to linguistic complexity. It constitutes a solution towards complexity experiments using spoken languages.

Keywords: Linguistic complexity, difficulty model, computational psycholinguistics, sentence processing.

1 Introduction

Linguistic complexity is an important problem both from linguistic, computational and cognitive perspectives: it is important to know for a given language what are the phenomena or the constructions that can lead to a processing problem for a human subject. Such knowledge is the basis of a better understanding of the cerebral mechanisms of language processing. It is also necessary in the persepctive of the development of a cognitively-plausible automatic parser. Today, several computational models have been developed in this perspective. However, most of them are partial, only take into account local phenomena, and are experimented on highly controlled written text (cf. (Gibson, 2000), (Vasishth, 2003) or (Lewis and Vasishth, 2005) for example). More recent works propose to go one step forward in experimenting models on larger corpora (see in particular (Demberg and Keller, 2008), making it possible to validate complexity models. One of the conclusion of these works is that generic models have to bring together many different complexity parameters in order to take into account a large variety of phenomena. Moreover, it still remains necessary to develop and validate generic computational models dealing with unrestricted linguistic material, in particular spoken languages.

Among the different parameters involved in its definition, the evaluation of the difficulty human subjects encounter in language production or perception plays a major role.

In the literature, one of the most frequently used approaches relies on surprisal effects that can occur when integrating a new word to the structure (cf. (Hale, 2001)): roughly speaking, surprisal is high when the probability for a word to occur in a specific context is low. This parameter is evaluated as the negative logarithm of the probability of a word w_t to appear in its context, taking into account the sequence $w_1...w_{t-1}$.

Surprisal is evaluated as a function of the probabilities of the possible parses when integrating the word w_t. When using a probabilistic grammar, evaluating surprisal consists in measuring the difference between the probability of all parses spanning the sequence $w_1...w_{t-1}$ and those spanning $w_1...w_t$:

$$SI_t = -\log \frac{P(w_1...w_t)}{P(w_1...w_{t-1})} \quad (1)$$

Surprisal has been shown by different studies as being correlated with difficulty. This has been demonstrated experimentally, in particular by several works relying on eye-tracking in reading tasks (cf. (Boston *et al.*, 2011), (Demberg and Keller, 2008) or (Mitchell *et al.*, 2010)). These last studies use results from the Dundee corpus (see (Kennedy *et al.*, 2003)) from which some short extracts have been chosen (20 texts read by 10 subjects). This corpus has been analyzed, surprisal values calculated and put in perspective with eye-tracking data. Results show a correlation between difficulty parameters (in particular reading time) and surprisal indexes.

One of the problems is that surprisal evaluation is sensible to the syntactic formalism. Moreover, from a computational point of view, surprisal also depends on the characteristics of the parser used in the evaluation. Surprisal being measured in terms of the probabilities of the possible parses, it is necessary first to build a probabilized grammar (which can be problematic) and second to correctly generate all candidate parses. We know that when parsing unrestricted linguistic material, it is not always possible to build parse trees. Robustness and precision are then pre-requisite properties of the parsers when evaluating surprisal. This also means that, because of the limitation of parsing technologies, it is not possible to measure difficulty for non-canonical or ill-formed construction (not to speak of spoken language).

We propose in this paper to explore a new direction for difficulty evaluation: syntax being problematic when dealing with unrestricted material, we propose to analyze precisely the contribution of morpho-syntactic information in surprisal evaluation. Our hypothesis is that surprisal effects appear at the lexical level, as corroborated by works on the impact of the lexicon on ambiguity or reanalysis phenomena (cf. (Fodor and Ferreira, 1998)). We propose to measure surprisal effects only by means of a probabilistic categorization task, without using parsing information. We use in this perspective a probabilistic morpho-syntactic tagger, taking into account at each step a variable-size context.

In the first section, we present the probabilistic method thanks to which we evaluate the different parameters entering in the difficulty model. In the second section, we describe how to calculate the parameters. Finally, the last section will present some results.

Before entering into the description of our approach, we want to underline the fact that this paper presents a theoretical proposal which still has to be validated experimentally. However, we propose in the last section preliminary results calculated from a large corpus showing a positive tendency.

2 The statistical model

The mechanism consists in evaluating a probability to any sequence of *tokens* (or part-of-speech). Each token is associated, thanks to a lexicon, to its corresponding lexical tags distribution, where tags take their values in the set of morphosyntactic categories C. An example of tags distribution is illustrated table 1.

Form	Lemma	Sampa	Tag	Proba.
est	être	E	`Auxiliary`	0.39
est	être	E	`Verb`	0.52
est	est	Est	`Noun`	0.09

Table 1: Tags distribution for the french lexical form *"est"* (meaning *"is"* in its verb or auxiliary use, or *"east"* in its noun use).

The tagging process is usually very ambiguous. This ambiguity generates an exploration tree space of potential solutions $\mathcal{S}ol$. Its cardinality card($\mathcal{S}ol$) is a function of the combinatory associated with the potential choices for each token of the sentence. The tokens being integrated step by step to the sentence, the cardinality card($\mathcal{S}ol(t)$) at position t in the sentence increases (or remains stable for tokens with one-to-one tag correspondence). For a given sentence, we denote hereafter by $S_i(t)$ the ith solution at position t ($i \in [1, \texttt{card}(\mathcal{S}ol)]$),

$$S_i(t) = c_{1,i}...c_{t,i} \tag{2}$$

where $c_{t,i}$ is the morphosyntactic category associated to the token at position t for solution $S_i(t)$. The probability of the solution $S_i(t)$ is obtained recursively by Bayes formulae :

$$P(S_i(t)) = P(c_{t,i}|S_i(t-1)) \times P(S_i(t-1)) \tag{3}$$

where $P(S_i(t-1))$ is the probability of the solution i at position $t-1$ and $P(c_{t,i}|S_i(t-1))$ is the conditional probability of category $c_{t,i}$ given the right context $S_i(t-1) = c_{1,i}...c_{t-1,i}$.

In order to calculate the probability of each solution of the space of solutions $\mathcal{S}ol$, we need a statistical model predicting the probability of each category c_t conditioned by each right context $c_1...c_{t-1}$, for all the combinatory cases found for each solution of the exploration tree :

$$\texttt{Model} \Rightarrow P(c_t|c_1...c_{t-1}) \quad , \quad c_1, ..., c_t \in \mathcal{C} \tag{4}$$

The probabilistic model may be limited to the sole use of morphosyntactic information (that is the strategy experimented in this paper), or makes use of higher syntactical information such like structure constituents and relations describing the context.

Given a model, the conditional probabilities of equation 4 allow to calculate for each added token the relative contribution of each solution $S_i(t)$ belonging to the space of solutions. The density function $\rho(t)$ associates to each solution at position t its relative probability $\rho_i(t)$:

$$\rho_i(t) = \frac{P(S_i(t))}{A_t}, \ \texttt{with} \ A_t = \sum_{\mathcal{S}ol} P(S_i(t)) \tag{5}$$

where $P(S_i(t))$ is computed from the model given equation 4 and the normalization factor A_t warrants the equality $\sum_{\mathcal{S}ol} \rho_i(t) = 1$. The evolution of the space of solutions and of its density is investigated in the following section. It provides us with the different parameters proposed for measuring the processing difficulty of a sentence at the morphosyntactic level.

The probabilities mentioned equation 4 are herein obtained using the *Pattern Model* (Blache and Rauzy, 2006), a Hidden Markov Model (HMM) more efficient than the standard *N-grams* models. For *N-grams*, the states of the automaton are characterized by sequence of categories of equal size $N-1$. The pattern model relaxes this constraint by accepting states identified by sequences of varying size. This property allows in practice to learn from the training corpus a set a states, the *patterns* of the model, which capture in an optimal way the morphosyntactic regularities found in the training corpus. The patterns model is seen as an approximation of the real statistical model describing the data, the approximation becoming more and more accurate as the training corpus size and coverage become larger.

The model is trained on the *GraceLPL* corpus, a version of the *Grace/Multitag* corpus (see (Paroubek and Rajman, 2000)) corrected by us. It is a French corpus containing about 700 000 words with morphosyntactic annotation following the tagset features Multext (Ide and Véronis, 1994). GraceLPL is regularly corrected and enriched in order to improve its tagging. The morphosyntactic information has been organized in an ad-hoc way in 50 tags (4 types of categories for punctuation marks, 1 for interjections, 2 for adjectives, 2 for conjunctions, 1 for determiners, 3 for nouns, 8 for auxiliaries, 4 for verbs, 5 for prepositions, 3 for adverbs and 15 for pronouns). In its current form, the tagset does not include gender, number and person features distinction nor tense and mood information for verbs.

The pattern model describing our tagger is composed of 2 841 patterns of varying size (the largest right context in the list of patterns counts 8 categories). The evaluation of the model is performed by comparing the tagged output with the reference. For the selected tagset of 50 categories mentionned above, the quality of the tagger (version 2011) reaches a score of 0.975 (F-measure).

3 The morpho-syntactic difficulty model

Surprisal is usually calculated thanks to a probabilistic grammar in building the set of possible parses (the number of parses being possibly limited to a given number). We propose to replace parses by the study of part-of-speech sequences, without any other information on structure nor relations.

The evolution of the surprisal with position t is herein defined for each solution $S_i(t)$ presented equation 2 as follows:

$$SI_i(t) = -\log \frac{P(S_i(t))}{P(S_i(t-1))} + \log(P(c_{t,i}|.)) \tag{6}$$

where the correction term $P(c_{t,i}|.)$ stands for the non-contextual probability of the morphosyntactic category $c_{t,i}$ associated to token at position t for solution $S_i(t)$. Following equation 3, the equation rewrites :

$$SI_i(t) = -\log \frac{P(c_{t,i}|c_{1,i}...c_{t-1,i})}{P(c_{t,i}|.)} \tag{7}$$

which is the negative logarithm of the ratio between contextual and non-contextual probabilities for category $c_{t,i}$. The higher this ratio, i.e. the category has a strong probability to occur within this context, the more negative is the surprisal index. This term aims at correcting asymmetry in category distribution. Some of them are densely populated (e.g. common noun) whereas some other are not (e.g. present participle of the auxiliary) without any consequence on human processing difficulty. With this correction, the overall surprisal $SI(t)$ is the same as proposed in the literature (see for example (Demberg and Keller, 2008)):

$$SI(t) = \sum_{Sol} \rho_i(t)\, SI_i(t), \tag{8}$$

which is the weighted average of individual surprisal values for each solution, weighted by their relative contribution $\rho_i(t)$ (see equation 5). Surprisal measures a function of these two difficulty parameters: one related to sparseness of the POS sequences, the other coming from the number of solutions to take into account at the same time (consequence of the lexical forms ambiguity).

This observation leads us to propose a second parameter making it possible to separate these two effects. The consequence of morpho-syntacic ambiguity on processing difficulty can be directly measured. A good indication is for example entropy variation of the probability distribution $\rho_i(t)$ described equation 5:

$$AH(t) = -\sum_{Sol} \rho_i(t)\, \log \rho_i(t) \tag{9}$$

$$AI(t) = AH(t) - AH(t-1) \tag{10}$$

The value $AH(t)$ measures evolution of the effective size of solution space. Its derivative across time, the ambiguity index $AI(t)$, shows that integrating the lexical form at a position t locally contribute to solve ambiguity ($AI(t) < 0$) or to increase it ($AI(t) > 0$).

4 Experimentation

As mentioned in the introduction, this paper present a preliminary study and many work is still to be done in order to validate our hypothesis. First, we have to verify that our model is a good predictor for difficulty. In this perspective, corpora with eye-tracking data have to be collected (for French in particular). Moreover, a systematic comparison with results obtained with syntactically-based surprisal values has to be done. Finally, new kinds of data have to be created in the perspective of validating our model against spoken language corpora.

However, we propose in this section a preliminary study on real data, giving some indications on the efficiency of the model.

Our study relies on a French corpus, made of 317,258 tokens (14,545 sentences), collected from the GRACE corpus mentioned before (automatically generated and manually corrected). The sentence selected from the initial corpus are those which have no difference between the reference categorization (that of the corpus) and that of our tagger. For each token, *surprisal* and *ambiguity* values have been calculated. Moreover, each sentence is associated to a revision rate, which relies on the number of revisions (or backtrackings) occurring during the tagging process. More precisely, the *revision rate* is the ratio between the number of solutions with a maximal probability that have been abandoned and the number of tokens in the sentence.

4.1 Model Validation

We propose in this section to verify the validity of our proposal in applying *surprisal* and *ambiguity* parameters to two phenomena known to be complex: relatives (subjects vs. objects) and clitics (nominative vs. accusative).

Relatives Several psycholinguistic studies (cf. (Gibson, 1998; Gibson, 2000), (Just and Carpenter, 1992)) have shown the that object relatives are more complex in terms of processing than subject relatives. Different analysis have been given for this: subject relatives follow the canonical SVO order, object relatives require to memorize more information, etc. The complexity differences have been shown experimentally by means of reading times (see for example (Lewis and Vasishth, 2005), (Demberg and Keller, 2008)).

We obtain the same prediction with our morpho-syntactic model: object relative pronoun has a surprisal value significantly higher than subject. Moreover, we also observe a relation between surprisal and ambiguity: the object pronoun is more ambiguous than the subject and causes a higher surprisal.

POS	Occur.	Surprisal	Ambiguity
Subj	2507	-1,438	-0,076
Obj	1228	-0,953	0,202

Clitics Language acquisition studies show a later acquisition of accusative clitics than nominative ones (see (Jakubowicz, 2003)), underlying higher complexity for the accusative case. This difference is predicted by our model: accusative clitics have surprisal values twice higher than nominative ones.

POS	Occur.	Surprisal	Ambiguity
Nomin.	9682	-1,586	0,003
Acc.	1857	-0,701	0,261

These results tend to confirm our hypothesis stipulating that surprisal evaluation on a morpho-syntactic basis is a good predictor of processing difficulty, as the syntactic-based surprisal model.

4.2 Surprisal

The following examples underline the effects of surprisal and ambiguity values, obtained on a morpho-syntactic basis. The figures show the evolution by words of the two parameters. In the first example, the maximal surprisal value is reached with the preposition "*de*", located between two determiners (a cardinal and a demonstrative). In this case, category sequence sparseness is the cause of the surprisal, more than ambiguity. This last parameter show a peak on the previous token, whereas the token associated to the surprisal peak corresponds to a negative ambiguity value.

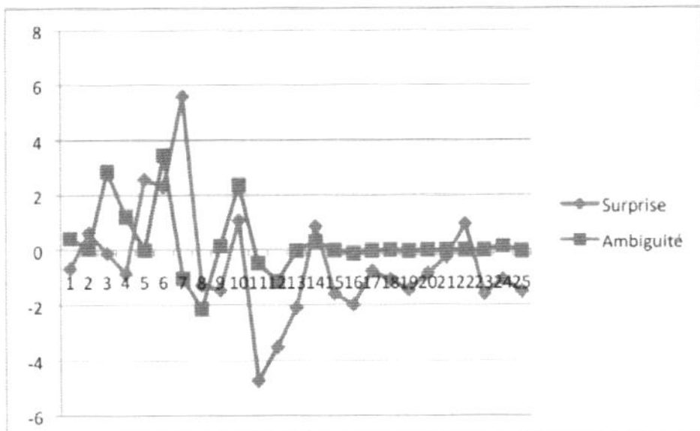

"Ainsi pour Le Seuil, quarante-sept de ces droits ont t acquis par des diteurs de langue allemande."

"So, for Le Seuil, 47 of these rights have been acquired by German-speaking editors."

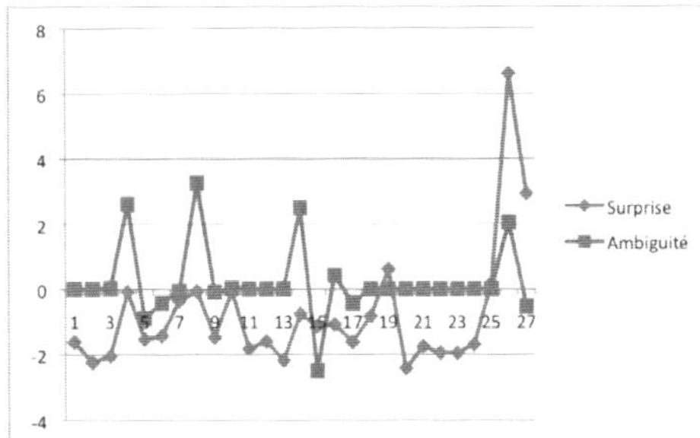

"On parle aussi d'étoiles de l'Opéra : Noella Pontois, qui est à la retraite, Michael Denard, qui va bientôt l'être ..."

"We also talk about Opera stars: Noella Pontois, who is retired, Michal Denard, who will be soon too ..."

Figure 1: Surprisal examples

In the second example, the surprisal peak is located on the infinitive verb "*être*". This value is related to the categorization of the preceding word "*l'*" as a determiner. It reveals a syntactic difficulty related to the elliptic construction. Moreover, at the difference with the previous example, surprisal comes with high ambiguity value.

These two examples show that the contribution of the ambiguity parameter to surprisal is not direct. Nevertheless, we have observed on the entire corpus a correlation between surprisal and ambiguity (Pearson correlation coefficient of 0.4).

Ambiguity, parallelism: A frequently discussed question in the literature concerning human processor is to know whether it works on a sequential or parallel manner (cf. (Gibson, 1991; Boston *et al.*, 2011)). This question is important and has consequences on complexity study, and more particularly on memorization costs. A parallel parser requires to store all possible parses at the same time whereas a sequential parser memorizes less states, but relies on backtracking. This question is still open, even with the massive use of probabilistic approaches in language processing that could militate in favor of a parallel processing.

(Brants and Crocker, 2000) have shown that the choice of an adequate hierarchization factor renders the parallelization process almost useless. The study of revision rates obtained in the corpus tends to confirm this result: surprisingly, the categorization process is almost deterministic. More precisely, we measured on the corpus 7,133 sentences (49% of the total) that do not present backtrack: the choice of the most probable solution at each step leads to the right solution. The overall revision rate is 4.3%.

In other words, the tagger behavior confirms the hypothesis of a very limited parallelism in language processing. It is an interesting result not only from a cognitive perspective, but also for automatic language processing: parsing techniques relying on a "*beam search*" strategy seems to constitute an adapted answer.

5 Conclusion

The analysis of language processing difficulty by human subjects necessarily has to take into account language in *natural situation*, which means the necessity of treating spoken language. The methods and models used in such studies must then deal with different uses in order to be general and reusable, which is not the case with current difficulty models. In particular, evaluating automatically difficulty parameters means tools able to process non canonical or even ill-formed sentences.

The solution we propose in this paper consists in using low-level information: morpho-syntax features can been calculated with a good performance, even for spoken language transcriptions. This means that automatic tools can always provide some information, whatever the structure (which is not the case with syntactic models). Our approach constitutes a first answer towards natural language difficulty modeling for mainly for two reasons:

- The approach is formalism-independent and theoretical-neutral: evaluating difficulty on the basis of morpho-syntactic information avoids the use of syntactically-annotated resources as well as parsers. It becomes the possible to adapt this technique to other languages, even those without syntactic resources.
- Robustness: the efficiency of modern taggers makes it possible to process all kinds of linguistic material, including spoken language.

The results we obtained on corpus analysis have to be generalized by means of experimentations on human subjects leading to reading-time, eye-tracking and evoked potentials data.

References

Blache, P. and S. Rauzy. 2006. Control mechanisms for parsing in property grammars. In *Proceedings of TALN*.

Boston, M. F., J. T. Hale, S. Vasishth, and R. Kliegl. 2011. Parallelism and syntactic processes in reading difficulty. *Language and Cognitive Processes*, 26, 301–349.

Brants, T. and M. Crocker. 2000. Probabilistic parsing and psychological plausibility. In *Proceedings of the 18th International Conference on Computational Linguistic*, Saarbrcken/Luxembourg/Nancy.

Demberg, V. and F. Keller. 2008. Data from eye-tracking corpora as evidence for theories of syntactic processing complexity. In *Cognition*, volume 109, Issue 2, pp. 193–210.

Fodor, J. D. and F. Ferreira. 1998. *Reanalysis in sentence processing*. London: Kluwer Academic Publishers.

Gibson, E. 1991. A computational theory of human linguistic processing: Memory limitations and processing breakdown. In *Doctoral dissertation*. Carnegie Mellon University.

Gibson, E. 1998. Linguistic complexity: locality of syntactic dependencies. *Cognition*, 68, 1–76.

Gibson, E. 2000. The dependency locality theory: A distance-based theory of linguistic complexity. In *Image*. A. Marantz, Y. Miyashita, W. O'Neil (Edts).

Hale, J. 2001. A probabilistic earley parser as a psycholinfuistic model. In *Proceeding of 2nd Conference of the North American Chapter of the Association for Computational Linguistics*, Pittsburgh, PA.

Ide, N. and J. Véronis. 1994. MULTEXT: Multilingual text tools and corpora. In *Proceedings of the 15th. International Conference on Computational Linguistics (*COLING 94*)*, volume I, pp. 588–592, Kyoto, Japan.

Jakubowicz, C. 2003. Computational complexity and the acquisition of functional categories by french-speaking children with SLI. *Linguistics*, 41(2).

Just, M. A. and P. A. Carpenter. 1992. A capacity theory of comprehension: Individual differences in working memory. *Psychological Review*, 99(1), 122–149.

Kennedy, A., R. Hill, and J. Pynte. 2003. The dundee corpus. In *Proceedings of the 12th European Conference on Eye Movements*.

Lewis, R. L. and S. Vasishth. 2005. An activation-based model of sentence processing as skilled memory retrieval. *Cognitive Science*, 29, 375–419.

Mitchell, J., M. Lapata, V. Demberg, and F. Keller. 2010. Syntactic and semantic factors in processing difficulty: An integrated measure. *Proceedings of the 48th Annual Meeting of the Association for Computational Linguistics*, pp. 196–206.

Paroubek, P. and M. Rajman. 2000. Multitag, une ressource linguistique produit du paradigme d'évaluation. In *Actes de Traitement Automatique des Langues Naturelles*, pp. 297–306, Lausanne, Suisse, 16-18 octobre.

Vasishth, S. 2003. Quantifying processing difficulty in human sentence parsing: The role of decay, activation, and similarity-based interference. In *Proceedings of the European Cognitive Science Conference 2003*.

Tibetan Word Segmentation as Syllable Tagging Using Conditional Random Field *

Huidan Liu[a,b], Minghua Nuo[a,b], Longlong Ma[a], Jian Wu[a], and Yeping He[a]

[a] Institute of Software, Chinese Academy of Sciences,
No.4 South Fourth Street, Zhong Guan Cun, Haidian District, Beijing 100190, China
[b] Graduate University of the Chinese Academy of Sciences,
No.80 Zhongguancun East Road, Haidian District, Beijing 100190, China
{huidan, minghua, longlong, wujian, yeping}@iscas.ac.cn

Abstract. In this paper, we proposed a novel approach for Tibetan word segmentation using the conditional random field. We reformulate the segmentation as a syllable tagging problem. The approach labels each syllable with a word-internal position tag, and combines syllable(s) into words according to their tags. As there is no public available Tibetan word segmentation corpus, the training corpus is generated by another segmenter which has an F-score of 96.94% on the test set. Two feature template sets namely TMPT-6 and TMPT-10 are used and compared, and the result shows that the former is better. Experiments also show that larger training set improves the performance significantly. Trained on a set of 131,903 sentences, the segmenter achieves an F-score of 95.12% on the test set of 1,000 sentences.

Keywords: Tibetan word segmentation, Tibetan, syllable tagging, CRF.

1 Introduction

During the 7th Century AD, Thume Sambota reputedly devised a script for Tibetan based on the Devanagari model. At present, Tibetan script is used to write both Tibetan language and Dzongkha (Bhutanese) language. The former is a language spoken by about 6 million people in China, India, Bhutan, Sikkim, Ladakh and Nepal, while the later is spoken by about 130,000 people in Bhutan as a national and official language.

Just like Chinese, Tibetan text is written without natural word delimiters, so word segmentation is an essential, fundamental and foremost step in Tibetan language processing. Researchers mainly use maximum matching method and some grammar rules to segment Tibetan text at present.

In this paper, we reformulate Tibetan word segmentation as a syllable tagging problem, and propose an approach using the conditional random field (CRF) for Tibetan word segmentation. The paper is organized as follows: In Section 2 we recall related work on Tibetan word segmentation and Chinese word segmentation methods by character tagging. In Section 3, we simply introduce Tibetan script. We propose the approach in Section 4. Then, in Section 5 we make experiments to evaluate the segmenter, compare it with other Tibetan segmenters. Section 6 concludes the paper.

2 Related Work

In this section, we first recall the research history and current situation on Tibetan/Dzongkha word segmentation. We also recall research on Chinese word segmentation by character tagging which we have drawn inspiration from.

* The research is partially supported by National Science & Technology Major Project (No.2010ZX01036-001-002, No.2010ZX01036-001-002) and CAS Action Plan for the Development of Western China (No.KGCX2-YW-512).

2.1 Tibetan/Dzongkha Word Segmentation

Chen *et al.* (2003a; 2003b) proposed a method based on case auxiliary words and continuous features to segment Tibetan text. Caizhijie (2009a; 2009b) designed and implemented the Banzhida Tibetan word segmentation system based on Chens method, using reinstallation rules to identify Abbreviated Words. Qi (2006) proposed a three level method to segment Tibetan text. Sun *et al.* (2009; 2010) researched Tibetan Automatic Segmentation Scheme and disambiguation method of overlapping ambiguity in Tibetan word segmentation. Dolha *et al.* (2007), Zhaxijia *et al.* (2007), Cairangjia (2009), Gyal and Zhujie (2009) made researches on the word categories and annotation scheme for Tibetan corpus and the part-of-speech tagging set standards.

Norbu *et al.* (2010) described the initial effort in segmenting the Dzongkha scripts. They proposed an approach of Maximal Matching followed by bigram techniques. Experiment shows that it achieves an overall accuracy of 91.5% on all 8 corpora in different domains. Chungku *et al.* (2010) described the application of probabilistic part-of-speech taggers to the Dzongkha language, and proposed a tag set containing 66 tags which is applied to annotate their Dzongkha corpus.

Models which are used in Chinese word segmentation, such as HMM, ME, CRF, need to be trained with corpus. However, there is no public available corpus for Tibetan word segmentation at present. So people mainly use maximum matching method based on dictionary in Tibetan word segmentation(Chen *et al.*, 2003a; Chen *et al.*, 2003b; Caizhijie, 2009a; Caizhijie, 2009b; Sun *et al.*, 2009; Sun *et al.*, 2010), accompanying with some grammar rules sometimes.

2.2 Chinese Word Segmentation by Character Tagging

Xue reformulated Chinese word segmentation as a tagging problem (Xue and Converse, 2002; Xue, 2003; Xue and Shen, 2003), which is a reform of Chinese word segmentation. The approach uses the maximum entropy tagger to label each Chinese character with a word-internal position tag, and then combines characters into word according to their tags. Ng and Low (Ng and Low, 2004; Low *et al.*, 2005) used the same method in their segmenter.

Peng *et al.* (2004) first used the CRF for Chinese word segmentation by treating it as a binary decision task, such that each character is labeled either as the beginning of a word or the continuation of one.

Tseng *et al.* (2005) presented a Chinese word segmentation system submitted to the closed track of Sighan bakeoff 2005. This segmenter uses a conditional random field sequence model which provides a framework to use a large number of linguistic features such as character identity, morphological and character reduplication features.

To give a comprehensive comparison of Chinese segmentation on common test corpora, two International Chinese Word Segmentation Bake-offs were held in 2003 and 2005, and there were 12 and 23 participants respectively (Sproat and Emerson, 2003; Emerson, 2005). In all of proposed methods, character based tagging method quickly rose in two Bakeoffs as a remarkable one with state-of-the-art performance. As reported by Emerson (2005), the results of Bakeoff-2005 shows a general trend to a decrease in error rates from 3.9% to 2.8% compared to the results of Bakeoff-2003. Especially, two participants, Ng (Ng and Low, 2004; Low *et al.*, 2005) and Tseng (Tseng *et al.*, 2005) gave the best results in almost all test corpora.

Zhao (2006a; 2006b) considered both feature template selection and tag set selection, instead of feature template focused only method. They made an empirical comparison study of performance among different tag sets, and found that there is a significant performance difference as different tag sets are selected. Based on the proposed method, their system gave the state-of-the-art performance several years ago. They also proposed a criterion called "average weighted word length distribution" to choose tag set.

In this paper, we will adopt the method used in Chinese word segmentation by tagging to segment Tibetan text.

3 Tibetan Script at a Glance

3.1 Delimiters in Tibetan

The Tibetan alphabet is syllabic, like many of the alphabets of India and South East Asia. Each letter has an inherent vowel /a/. Other vowels can be indicated using a variety of diacritics which appear above or below the main letter. A syllable contains one or up to seven character(s). Syllables are separated by a marker known as "tsheg", which is simply a superscripted dot. Linguistic words are made up of one or more syllables and are also separated by the same symbol, "tsheg", thus there is a lack of word boundaries in the language. Consonant clusters are written with special conjunct letters. Figure 1 shows the structure of a Tibetan word which is made up of two syllables and means "show" or "exhibition".

Figure 1: Structure of a Tibetan word.

ཁ་ས་མི་ཕྱུག་པོ་འདིའི་ཁང་པ་གོང་ཆེན་པོ་ཞིག་གཟིགས་སོང་།									
ཁ་ས་	མི་	ཕྱུག་པོ་	འདིའི་	ཁང་པ	གོང་ཆེན་པོ་	ཞིག་	གཟིགས་	སོང་	།
Yesterday	man	rich	this	house	expensive	an	bought	did	.
Yesterday this rich man bought an expensive house.									

Figure 2: A Tibetan sentence and its translation.

Tibetan sentence contains one or more phrase(s), which contain one or more words. Another marker known as "shed" indicates the sentence boundary, which looks like a vertical pipe. Figure 2 shows a Tibetan sentence.

3.2 Abbreviated Syllables

In Tibetan text, some words, including "འི", "ས", "ར", "འང", "འམ", "འོ"(We call them abbreviation marker (AM) in this paper), can glue to the previous word without a syllable delimiter "tsheg", which produce many abbreviated syllables. For example, when the genitive case word "འི" follows the word "རྒྱལ་པོ" (king), we dont put a "tsheg" between them and get the fused form "རྒྱལ་པོའི" (king[+genitive]), in which "པོའི" is an abbreiated syllable. When the ergative case word "ས" follows the word "ང་ཚོ" (we), it forms "ང་ཚོས" (we[+ergative]), in which "ཚོས" is an abbreviated syllable. In the above two examples, either abbreviated syllable should be broken into two parts while segmenting, and the left part has to be combined with the previous syllable(s) to form a word, while the right part is a 1-syllable word. In addition, the word before the AM can be 1-syllable word. For instance, if "འི" follows "ང" (I), it forms "ངའི" (I [+genitive]), and the abbreviated syllable should be broken into two 1-syllable words.

4 Proposed Method

4.1 Reformulating Tibetan Word Segmentation as a Syllable Tagging Problem

Just like Chinese hanzi which is analysed by Xue (2003), many Tibetan syllables can also occur in different positions within different words. Table 1 shows how the Tibetan syllable "ཁ" (mouth) can occur in four different positions.

Table 1: The Tibetan syllable can occur in multiple word-internal positions.

Position	Example	Meaning	Tag
Word by itself	ཁ་	mouth	S
Begin	ཁ་གསབ་	supplement	B
Middle	མི་ཁ་ཤས་	someone	M
End	གྲུ་ཁ་	ferry	E

Before applying the machine-learning algorithm, we convert the segmented words in the corpus into a tagged sequence of Tibetan syllables. We tag each syllable with one of the four tags, B (Begin), M (Middle), E (End) and S (Single) depending on its position within a word.

- It is tagged B if it occurs on the left boundary of a word, and forms a word with the syllable(s) on its right side.
- It is tagged M if it occurs in the middle of a word.
- It is tagged E if it occurs on the right boundary of a word, and forms a word with the syllable(s) on its left side.
- It is tagged S if it forms a word by itself.

As presented in section 3.2, Abbreviated syllable should be broken into two parts, thus we need another two tags ES (End and Single) and SS (Single and Single):

- It is tagged ES if it comes from a multiple-syllable word and an AM.
- It is tagged SS if it comes from a single-syllable word and an AM.

Then tags for the syllable "ཁ" in the former example are shown in the last column in Table 1.

Then we can use the tags to label Tibetan word. The usage of the tags on words in different length is shown in Table 2. Using the above tags, the Tibetan sentence in (a) can be tagged as (c),

Table 2: Usage of the tag set.

Word Type	Example	Tag Sequence	Word Type	Example	Tag Sequence
1-syllable	ཁ་	S	1-syllable + AM	ངས་	SS
2-syllable	ཁ་གསབ་	B-E	2-syllable + AM	གནས་པའི་	B-ES
3-syllable	མི་ཁ་ཤས་	B-M-E	3-syllable + AM	མ་བྱས་པའམ་	B-M-ES
4-syllable	རིས་མེད་རྒོལ་རྫུང་	B-M-M-E	N/A	N/A	N/A

and the segmentation result is in (d):

(a) ངཚོས་སྤྱི་ཚོགས་རིང་ལུགས་ཀྱི་སྤྱི་ལ་དབང་བའི་ལམ་ལུགས་དང་རྩོལ་བསྟུན་ཐོབ་སྐྱོད་ཀྱི་རྩ་དོན་མཐའ་འཁྱོངས་བྱས་ཡོད།

(b) We have always followed the principles of socialist public ownership and distribution according to work.

(c) ང/B ཚོས་/ES སྤྱི་/B ཚོགས་/M རིང་/M ལུགས་/E ཀྱི་/S སྤྱི་/B ལ་/M དབང་/M བའི་/M ལམ་/M ལུགས་/E དང་/S རྩོལ་/S བསྟུན་/S ཐོབ་/S སྐྱོད/S ཀྱི་/S རྩ་/B དོན/E མཐའ་/B འཁྱོངས་/E བྱས་/S ཡོད/S །/S

(d) ངཚོ/ ས་/ སྤྱི་ཚོགས་རིང་ལུགས་/ ཀྱི་/ སྤྱི་ལ་དབང་བའི་ལམ་ ལུགས་/ དང་/ རྩོལ་/ བསྟུན་/ ཐོབ་/ སྐྱོད/ ཀྱི་/ རྩ་དོན/ མཐའ་འཁྱོངས་/ བྱས་/ ཡོད/ །/

4.2 Tag Set Selection

In the former subsection, we presented our basic idea with a tag set B, M, E, S, ES, SS. In this subsection, we will decide how many tags to use. In Chinese word segmentation, people used different tag sets as shown in Table 3.

Table 3: Definitions of different tag sets.

Tag set	Tags	Words in tagging
2-tag	B, E	$B, BE, BEE, ...$
4-tag	B, M, E, S	$S, BE, BME, BMME, ...$
5-tag	B, B_2, M, E, S	$S, BE, BB_2E, BB_2ME, BB_2MME, ...$
6-tag	B, B_2, B_3, M, E, S	$S, BE, BB_2E, BB_2B_3E, BB_2B_3ME, BB_2B_3MME, ...$

Zhao *et al.* (2006b) proposed an effective method to choose the best tag set. They used a criterion called "average weighted word length distribution" to decide the tag set. They define L_k as follow:

$$L_k = \frac{1}{N}\sum_{i=k}^{K} i \times N_i \tag{1}$$

where L_k is the average weighted word length for all $i \geq k$; N_i is the word count with word length i, and K is the maximum word length in the corpus. N is the total word count. Then L_1 is the average weighted word length of the whole corpus.

Statistics on 8 Chinese word segmentation corpora shows that the average weighted word lengths of the 8 corpora are between 1.51 and 1.71, thus they chose a 6-tag set in their system. It can represent a 5 characters context window which can contain 3 words in average: $(1.51, 1.71) \times 3 = (4.53, 5.13)$. Experiments show that the 6-tag set is more effective when it acts in concert with an appropriate template(Zhao *et al.*, 2006a; Zhao *et al.*, 2006b).

Table 4: Statistical data on Tibetan corpus.

Word Length	L_k	Cumulative frequency	Word Length	L_k	Cumulative frequency
1	1.5294	0.5735	4	0.1432	0.9946
2	0.9559	0.9396	5	0.0307	0.9975
3	0.2238	0.9665	6	0.0161	0.9994

Base on this method, we made statistics on Tibetan corpus, and the data are shown in Table 4. In the corpus, the average weighted word length is 1.5294, which is also in the interval of [1.51, 1.71], so the 6-tag set is also suitable to Tibetan, and it can label 99.75% words in the corpus with different tags to every syllable in each word.

Table 5: Usage of the 8-tag set.

Word Type	Example	Tag Sequence
1-syllable	ཁ་	S
2-syllable	ཁ་གསབ་	$B-E$
3-syllable	མི་ཁ་ཤས་	$B-B_2-E$
4-syllable	རེས་མེད་རྒྱལ་རྫུང་	$B-B_2-B_3-E$
5-syllable	གཙོ་ཁྲིད་ཀྱི་གོ་གནས་	$B-B_2-B_3-M-E$
6-syllable	སྤྱི་ལ་དབང་བའི་ལམ་ལུགས་	$B-B_2-B_3-M-M-E$
1-syllable + AM	ངས་	SS
2-syllable + AM	གནས་པའི་	$B-ES$
3-syllable + AM	མ་བྱས་པའམ་	$B-B_2-ES$
4-syllable + AM	འཛམ་གླིང་གསུམ་པའི་	$B-B_2-B_3-ES$

As analysed in former subsection, we need another 2 tags ES and SS for abbreviated syllables. Actually, it forms an 8-tag set: B, B_2, B_3, M, E, S, ES, SS. The usage of the 8-tag set on words in different length is shown in Table 5. With the 8-tag set, the Tibetan sentence mentioned in the former subsection is tagged as (e):

(e) ང/B ཚོས་/ES སྤྱི་/B ཚོགས་/B_2 རིང་/B_3 ལུགས་/E ཀྱི་/S སྤྱི་/B ལ་/B_2 དབང་/B_3 བའི་/M ལམ་/M ལུགས་/E དང་/S རྩོལ་/S བསྟུན་/S ཐོབ་/S སྤྱོད་/S ཀྱི་/S རྩ་/B དོན་/E མཐའ་/B འཁྱོངས་/E ཐུས་/S ཡོད་/S །/S

4.3 CRF Tagger for Tibetan

Maximum Entropy (ME) tagger was used in early character-based tagging for Chinese word segmentation (Xue and Converse, 2002; Xue, 2003; Xue and Shen, 2003; Ng and Low, 2004; Low *et al.*, 2005), In recent years, more and more people choose linear-chain CRF as the learning model in their studies (Peng *et al.*, 2004; Tseng *et al.*, 2005; Zhao *et al.*, 2006a; Zhao *et al.*, 2006b).

CRF is firstly introduced into language processing by Lafferty (2001). Peng *et al.* (2004) first used this framework for Chinese word segmentation by treating it as a binary decision task, such that each Chinese character is labeled either as the beginning of a word or not.

The probability assigned to a label sequence for a syllable sequence by a CRF is:

$$p_\lambda(Y|W) = \frac{1}{Z(W)} exp\left(\sum_{t \in T}\sum_{k} \lambda_k f_k(y_{t-1}, y_t, W, t)\right) \tag{2}$$

where $Y = y_i$ is the label sequence for the sentence, W is the sequence of unsegmented syllables, $Z(W)$ is a normalization term, f_k is a feature function, and t indexes into syllables in the label sequence.

4.4 Feature Templates

The probability model and corresponding feature function is defined over the set $H \times T$, where H is the set of possible contexts (or any predefined condition) and T is the set of possible tags. Generally, a feature function can be defined as follow:

$$f(h,t) = \begin{cases} 1, & if \ \ h = h_i \ \ and \ \ t = t_j \\ 0, & otherwise \end{cases} \tag{3}$$

where $h_i \in H$ and $t_j \in T$.

Table 6: The two template sets TMPT-6 and TMPT-10.

Template Set	Type	Feature	Function
TMPT-6	Unigram	$C_n,\ n = -1, 0, 1$	The previous, current and next syllable
	Bigram	$C_nC_{n+1},\ n = -1, 0$	The previous (next) syllable and current syllable
		$C_{-1}C_1$	The previous syllable and next syllable
TMPT-10	Unigram	$C_n,\ n = -1, 0, 1$	The previous, current and next syllable
		C_{-2}	*The syllable before the previous syllable*
		C_2	*The syllable after the next syllable*
	Bigram	$C_nC_{n+1},\ n = -1, 0$	The previous (next) syllable and current syllable
		$C_{-1}C_1$	The previous syllable and next syllable
		C_1C_2	*The next two syllables*
		$C_{-2}C_{-1}$	*The previous two syllables*

In Chinese word segmentation by character tagging, their are two often used template sets (Xue and Converse, 2002; Xue, 2003; Xue and Shen, 2003; Ng and Low, 2004; Low *et al.*, 2005; Peng *et al.*, 2004; Tseng *et al.*, 2005; Zhao *et al.*, 2006a; Zhao *et al.*, 2006b), namely TMPT-6 and TMPT-10, which are shown in Table 6. In this work, we use and compare the two template sets to see their effect on the segmentation results. Note that there is a slight difference, the character "*C*" in the templates denotes a Tibetan *syllable* rather than a *character* like in Chinese word segmentation.

5 Experiments and Results

In this paper, we evaluate the approach by the Precision (P), Recall (R) and F-score (F1). Their definitions are the same as which are used in Chinese word segmentation. We used the CRF++ toolkit 0.54 from sourceforge `http://crfpp.sourceforge.net`.

5.1 Corpora

At present, there is no public available Tibetan segmentation corpus. In out experiments, the training set are machine-generated, and the test set is manually segmented.

Test Set: We randomly selected 1000 out of more than 230,000 Tibetan sentences from our Tibetan text corpus which consists of several political books and many news stories, legal texts and articles, then manually segmented them to form the test set.

Combining methods used by Chen (2003a, 2003b), Caizhijie (2009a, 2009b) with Sun (2009, 2010), we implemented a Tibetan word segmenter (SegT). Experiment on the test set shows that the precision, recall and the F-score are 96.99%, 96.91% and 96.94% respectively. SegT is used to generate the training set.

Corpus A: We get 1990 web pages in the domain of Tibetan arts, news, notice, religious, traditional culture, and history from the website `http://tb.tibet.cn`, and get 64,419 Tibetan sentences after preprocessing, which takes 9,739 K bytes in UTF-8 encoding plain text.

Corpus B: We get another 3292 web pages in the domain of news from another website `http://tb.chinatibetnews.com`. The preprocessing is similar to Training set A. and we get 67,484 Tibetan sentences which takes 18,372 K bytes in UTF-8 encoding plain text.

With SegT, the sentences are segmented into words to form the training set. We haven't made any manual corrections. As a machine-generated corpus, it includes about 3% words which are not correctly segmented. The two training set will be used to inspect the effect of training set scale change on the segmentation performance.

5.2 Comparison of TMPT-6 and TMPT-10

While training the model with the command crf_learn, we tried different values of the two parameters c and f. The former (c) trades the balance between overfitting and underfitting. The results will significantly be influenced by this parameter. The latter (f) sets the cut-off threshold for the features. CRF++ uses the features that occurs no less than f times in the given training data.

We set $f = 2$ and change the value of c, make the training and test on TMPT-6 and TMPT-10 respectively. We assign c with the values from 1.0 to 10.0 with a step length of 1.0. The data are shown in Table 7 and Figure 3. The F-score is the highest one at $c = 4.0$ on both template sets. Figure 3 shows that the F-scores are significantly higher on TMPT-6 than on TMPT-10, which is similar to the result in Chinese word segmentation.

Table 7: F-scores with different values of c on TMPT-6 and TMPT-10.

	TMPT-6			TMPT-10		
c	P(%)	R(%)	F1(%)	P(%)	R(%)	F1(%)
1.0	92.44	93.67	93.05	92.26	93.37	92.81
2.0	92.57	93.71	93.13	92.39	93.33	92.86
3.0	92.55	93.72	93.13	92.42	93.49	92.95
4.0	92.58	93.70	**93.14**	92.46	93.50	**92.98**
5.0	92.54	93.66	93.10	92.40	93.45	92.93
6.0	92.57	93.65	93.10	92.38	93.40	92.88
7.0	92.50	93.47	92.98	92.42	93.40	92.90
8.0	92.57	93.63	93.10	93.34	93.34	92.84
9.0	92.51	93.53	93.02	92.39	93.39	92.89
10.0	92.45	93.48	92.96	92.39	93.41	92.90

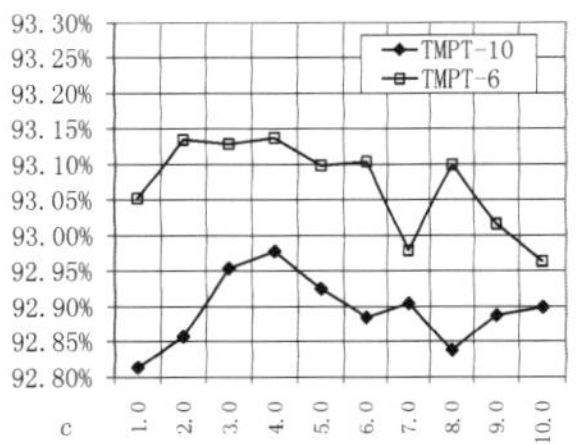

Figure 3: F-scores on TMPT-6 and TMPT-10.

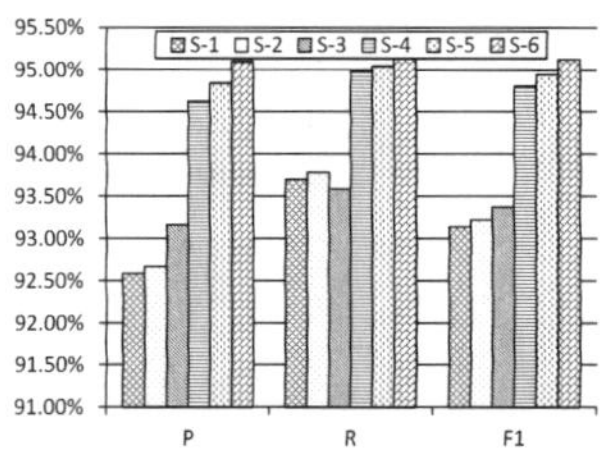

Figure 4: Performance with different settings.

5.3 Effect of Training Set Scale

As we get a better performance on TMPT-6 than TMPT-10, we make further experiments on it. We make the training and test with different f, c and training sets. The data are shown in Table 8 and

Figure 4. With $f = 2$, we get the highest F-score (93.22%) at $c = 4.9$ on Corpus A (S-2). With the same f and c, we train the segmenter with Corpus B, and the performance improves slightly (S-3). Then we use both Corpus A and Corpus B in the training, and get significant performance improvement (S-4). The best performance is achieved at $f = 1$ and $c = 4.0$.

Table 8: Performance of CRF-SegT with different settings.

Setting	Training Set	f	c	P(%)	R(%)	F1(%)
S-1	Corpus A	2	4.0	92.58	93.70	93.14
S-2	Corpus A	2	4.9	92.67	93.78	93.22
S-3	Corpus B	2	4.9	93.16	93.58	93.37
S-4	Corpus A+B	2	4.9	94.63	94.98	94.80
S-5	Corpus A+B	1	4.9	94.84	95.04	94.94
S-6	Corpus A+B	1	10.6	**95.09**	**95.15**	**95.12**

5.4 Comparison with other segmenters

We collected the test data of several Tibetan segmenters from related papers, and they are shown in Table 9. Chen and Sun evaluate their segmenters only by accuracy (Recall actually), so we can compare them only by recall. Compared with them, CRF-SegT outperforms only two of these sgementers. However, these segmenters are evaluated on different test sets, so it's not much meaningful to directly compare the Recalls here. All the segmenters are using maximum-matching method based on dictionary except our CRF-SegT. All of them have inherent weakness on segmentation disambiguation and Out-Of-Vocabulary word identification. Our CRF-SegT doesn't have those weakness. Considering these factors and the low quality of the training corpus, our approach is effective and acceptable though it doesn't have the highest F-score compared with other Tibetan segmenters.

Table 9: Comparison of different Tibetan/Dzongkha segmenters.

	Sentence Count	Word Count	P(%)	R(%)	F1(%)
Chen 2003a	N/A	N/A	N/A	≥ 0.96	N/A
Chen 2003b	500	5890	N/A	97.21	N/A
Sun 2009	435	4067	N/A	87.02	N/A
Norbu 2010	N/A	714	N/A	91.50	N/A
Our/SegT	1000	13977	96.99	96.91	96.94
Our/CRF-SegT	1000	13977	94.09	95.15	95.12

As collected by Zhao et al. (2006b), the F-scores of a state-of-art Chinese segmenter on most of 8 corpora are up to 95.3%-97.4%. Compared with them, CRF-SegT achieves a lower F-score. It mainly results from the low quality of the training corpus. As the F-score of SegT and CRF-SegT are 0.9694 and 0.9512 respectively, it means the latter $0.9512/0.9694 = 0.9812$ fits the former. Thus, the CRF-SegT fits the training corpus at a percentage of 98.12%. It's already greater than the upper bound of the interval 95.3%-97.4%, which shows that the result is acceptable.

6 Conclusion

In this paper, we reformulate Tibetan word segmentation as a syllable tagging problem and implemented a Tibetan word segmenter (CRF-SegT) which is trained by the CRF model on a corpus generated by another Tibetan word segmenter (SegT). Two feature template sets namely TMPT-6 and TMPT-10 are used and compared, and the result shows that the former is better. Experiments also show that larger training set improves the performance significantly. Trained on a set of 131,903 sentences, the segmenter achieves an F-score of 95.12% on the test set of 1,000 sentences. At present, almost all Tibetan segmenters are using maximum matching method based on dictionary except the proposed one. All of them have inherent weakness on segmentation disambiguation and Out-Of-Vocabulary word identification. The proposed approach doesn't have those weakness. What is more, our segmenter is test on a larger test set. Considering these factors, our approach is effective and acceptable.

References

Cairangjia. 2009. Research on the Word Categories and Its Annotation Scheme for Tibetan Corpus. *Journal of Chinese Information Processing*, 23(04):107-112

Caizhijie. 2009a. Identification of Abbreviated Word in Tibetan Word Segmentation. *Journal of Chinese Information Processing*, 23(01):35-37.

Caizhijie. 2009b. The Design of Banzhida Tibetan word segmentation system. *the 12th Symposium on Chinese Minority Information Processing*.

Yuzhong Chen, Baoli Li and Shiwen Yu. 2003a. The Design and Implementation of a Tibetan Word Segmentation System, *Journal of Chinese Information Processing*, 17(3): 15-20.

Yuzhong Chen, Baoli Li, Shiwen Yu and Lancuoji. 2003b. An Automatic Tibetan Segmentation Scheme Based on Case Auxiliary Words and Continuous Features, *Applied Linguistics*, 2003(01): 75-82.

Chungku Chungku, Jurmey Rabgay and Gertrud Faa. 2010. Building NLP Resources for Dzongkha: A Tagset and a Tagged Corpus. *Proceedings of the 8th Workshop on Asian Language Resources*. pp.103-110. Beijing, China.

Dolha, Zhaxijia, Losanglangjie and Ouzhu. 2007. The parts-of-speech and tagging set standards of Tibetan information process. *the 11th Symposium on Chinese Minority Information Processing*.

Thomas Emerson. 2005. The Second International Chinese Word Segmentation Bakeoff. *Proceedings of the Fourth SIGHAN Workshop on Chinese Language Processing*, pp.123-133. Jeju Island, Korea.

Jianfeng Gao, Mu Li, Andi Wu and Chang-Ning Huang. 2005. Chinese Word Segmentation and Named Entity Recognition: A Pragmatic Approach. *Computational Linguistics*, 31(4): 531-574.

Tashi Gyal and Zhujie. 2009. Research on Tibetan Segmentation Scheme for Information Processing, *Journal of Chinese Information Processing*, 23(04):113-117.

John Lafferty, Andrew McCallum and Fernando Pereira. 2001. Conditional Random Fields: Probabilistic Models for Segmenting and Labeling Sequence Data. *Proceedings of the Eighteenth International Conference on Machine Learning*, pp.282-289.

Jin Kiat Low, Hwee Tou Ng and Wenyuan Guo. 2005. A Maximum Entropy Approach to Chinese Word Segmentation. *Proceedings of the Fourth SIGHAN Workshop on Chinese Language Processing*, pp.161-164. Jeju Island, Korea.

Hwee Tou Ng and Jin Kiat Low. 2004. Chinese part-of-speech tagging: one-at-a-time or all-at-once? word-based or character-based. *Proceedings of 2004 Conference on Empirical Methods in Natural Language Processing*, pp.277-284.

Sithiar Norbu, Pema Choejey, Tenzin Dendup, Sarmad Hussain and Ahmed Mauz. 2010. Dzongkha Word Segmentation. *Proceedings of the 8th Workshop on Asian Language Resources*. pp.95-102. Beijing, China.

Fuchun Peng, Fangfang Feng and Andrew McCallum. 2004. Chinese Segmentation and New Word Detection Using Conditional Random Fields. *Proceedings of the 20th International Conference on Computational Linguistics*, pp.562-568. Geneva, Switzerland.

Kunyu Qi. 2006. On Tibetan Automatic Participate Research with the Aid of Information Treatment. *Journal of Northwest University for Nationalities (Philosophy and Social Science)*, 2006(04):92-97.

Richard Sproat and Thomas Emerson. 2003. The First International Chinese Word Segmentation Bakeoff. *Proceedings of the Second SIGHAN Workshop on Chinese Language Processing*, pp.133-143. Sapporo, Japan.

Yuan Sun, Luosangqiangba, Rui Yang and Xiaobing Zhao. 2009. Design of a Tibetan Automatic Segmentation Scheme, *the 12th Symposium on Chinese Minority Information Processing*.

Yuan Sun, Xiaodong Yan, Xiaobing Zhao and Guosheng Yang. 2010. A resolution of overlapping ambiguity in Tibetan word segmentation. *Proceedings of the 3rd International Conference on Computer Science and Information Technology*, pp.222-225.

Huihsin Tseng, Pichuan Chang, Galen Andrew, Daniel Jurafsky and Christopher Manning. 2005. A Conditional Random Field Word Segmenter for Sighan Bakeoff 2005. *Proceedings of the Fourth SIGHAN Workshop on Chinese Language Processing*, pp.168-171. Jeju Island, Korea.

Hanna M. Wallach. 2004. Conditional Random Fields: An Introduction. *Technical Report MS-CIS-04-21*. Department of Computer and Information Science, University of Pennsylvania,

Kun Wang, Chengqing Zong and Keh-Yih Su. 2009. Which is more suitable for Chinese word segmentation, the generative model or the discriminative one? *Proceedings of the 23th Pacific Asia Conference on Language, Information and Computation*, pp.827-834, Hong Kong, China.

Nianwen Xue and Susan P. Converse. 2002. Combining classifiers for Chinese word segmentation. *Proceedings of the First SIGHAN Workshop on Chinese Language Processing*, pp.63-70. Taipei, Taiwan.

Nianwen Xue and Libin Shen. 2003. Chinese Word Segmentation as LMR Tagging. *Proceedings of the Second SIGHAN Workshop on Chinese Language Processing, in conjunction with ACL03*, pp.176-179. Sapporo, Japan.

Nianwen Xue. 2003. Chinese word segmentation as character tagging. *Computational Linguistics and Chinese Language Processing*. 8(1): 29-48.

Ruiqiang Zhang, Genichiro Kikui and Eiichiro Sumita. 2006. Subword-based Tagging for Confidence-dependent Chinese Word Segmentation. *Proceedings of the joint conference of the International Committee on Computational Linguistics and the Association for Computational Linguistics*, pp.961-968, Sydney, Australia.

Yue Zhang and Stephen Clark. 2007. Chinese Segmentation with a Word-Based Perceptron Algorithm. *Proceedings of the 45th Annual Meeting of the Association for Computational Linguistics*, pp.840-847, Prague, Czech Republic.

Hai Zhao, Chang-Ning Huang and Mu Li. 2006a. An Improved Chinese Word Segmentation System with Conditional Random Field. *Proceedings of the Fifth SIGHAN Workshop on Chinese Language Processing*, pp.108-117. Sidney,Australia.

Hai Zhao, Changning Huang, Mu Li and Baoliang Lu. 2006b. Effective tag set selection in Chinese word segmentation via conditional random field modeling. *Proceedings of the 20th Pacific Asia Conference on Language, Information and Computation*, pp.87-94 Wuhan, China.

Zhaxijia, Dolha, Losanglangjie and Ouzhu. 2007. The theoretical explanation on "the parts-of-speech and tagging set standards of Tibetan information process". *the 11th Symposium on Chinese Minority Information Processing*.

Plural Problems in the Nominal Morphology of Marathi*

Shalmalee Pitale[a], Vaijayanthi Sarma[a]

[a]Department of Humanities and Social Sciences, IIT Bombay,
Powai, Mumbai-400076, India
{shalmaleep, vsarma}@iitb.ac.in

Abstract. In this paper, we describe the two tests developed and designed for Marathi using *non-words*, a) plural formation for *non-words* b) intuition test for gender assignment in which subjects were asked to assign gender to non-words. We look at the distribution of nouns across noun classes and genders and discuss the congruence between the problematic classes as observed in the tests and the actual class distribution and frequency in the language.

Keywords: Marathi, plurals, gender, non-words, morphological rules

1 Introduction

Marathi, an Indo Aryan language, makes a two-way number distinction, singular and plural. The number feature is synthetically marked on the noun itself. Two linguistic factors determine the plural formation of Marathi nouns: (a) grammatical gender, whether a noun is masculine, feminine or neuter and (b) the final segment of the noun. As a part of our ongoing research on the acquisition of Marathi morphology, we developed tests to see whether Marathi speaking children and adults apply tacitly known rules of inflectional morphology to new-coined words.

One of the tests we developed was designed for plural formation with *non-words*. In this test, subjects were required to choose the correct plural suffix for a given non-word. Ample agreement cues for gender were also provided. This test was adapted from Jean Berko's classic study on the acquisition of the inflectional morphology of English (1958) and Bettina Spreng's work on the acquisition of plural morphology in German (2004). We also developed an intuition test for gender assignment in which subjects were asked to assign gender to non-words to measure the effect of the phonological shape of the token on the choice of gender. This test was inspired by A. Mill's (1986) work on acquisition of gender in German.

The results of these two tests indicated that the performance of the subjects, both adults and children, is better for some noun classes compared to others. In other words, phonological cues were reliable for some of the noun classes and facilitated gender choice, but this was not a reliable or unique cue, and led us to study the distribution of nouns into gender classes in Marathi.

In this paper, we describe the two tests and analyze their results in brief. We look at the distribution of nouns across the noun classes and genders and discuss the congruence between the problematic classes as observed in the tests and the actual distribution of the same in the language.

---

*We would like to thank the three anonymous reviewers for their reviews. We have tried to address their comments and incorporate their suggestions in this version. Any errors are, of course, the authors.

2 Testing Plural morphology

Singular/bare forms of countable nouns in Marathi may end in a vowel or a consonant. The phonological ending of different nouns and their corresponding plural suffixes across all three genders in Marathi are given with examples in Table 1. It may be seen that there is significant overlap of both the phonological form and affixes across classes. Some nominal shapes are restricted to a single gender class. Thus, -ə or -u ending nouns are always masculine and e/ə alternating nouns are always neuter. However such one-to-one map is not seen with other shapes. Consonant final nouns could potentially belong to any of the three gender classes. Further, -a could either mark the bare noun shape (feminine or masculine) or the plural form of certain classes (the C or ī ending feminine nouns). The cells in grey indicate null classes, for example, there are no feminine or neuter nouns that end in -ə or in -u.

Table 1: Noun classes in Marathi[1]

Gender	Masculine	Feminine	Neuter
Singular	**Plural**		
ə	Ø mitrə 'friend'		
C	Ø hat 'hand'	C →a /ī (i) vaT → vaTa 'path' (ii) vihir →vihirī 'well'	C →e/ə ghər→ ghəre/ə 'house'
ī	Ø məNī 'bead'	ī →a nədī → nədya 'river'	
ū	Ø laDū 'a sweet'	Ø or a (i) vəstū 'thing' (ii) pisū → piswa 'a mosquito'	ū → e/ə limbū→limbe/ə 'lemon'
a	a→ e vaDa→vaDe 'mansion'	Ø šaLa 'school'	
e/ ə			e/ə → ī təLe/ə → təLī 'pond'
u	Ø šətru 'enemy'		

Based on this classification of nouns, we developed the tests for plural formation. Subjects were asked to provide appropriate plurals of given tokens, all *non-words*. Testing with non-words show us how subjects treat words for which they have no prior knowledge and permits inferences about the default assumptions that are made about words in the language and how morphological rules are applied. The picture material and procedures for the study were adapted from Berko's *wug* test (1958). While gender was (and is) not directly marked on nouns, it is marked morphologically through gender agreement. Agreement cues were given to facilitate the choice of gender and the selection of the corresponding plural form. The test groups consisted of ten Marathi speaking (invariably bilingual) adults (5 male, 5 female) and ten (monolingual or marginally bilingual) Marathi-speaking children (5 male, 5 female).[2]

Table 2 contains the results of the tests for both groups of subjects per gender class. Some of the tokens used are also provided per class.

1 The capital letters indicate retroflex consonants and grey cells indicate absence of lexical items in that class.

2 While the sample group appears small, it is usually sufficient to determine how rules are used by speakers. We do plan to test with a larger test group to address concerns of sample size quirks, once we have a general understanding of the kinds of difficulties that Marathi morphology poses for its speakers.

Table 2: Results for test of *non-words*

Gender/ Noun Class	Number		Token	Results (%)	
	Sg	Pl		Children sg to pl	Adults sg to pl
M1	ə	no change	pūmbə	100	100
M2	C		tšag	100	100
M3	ī		pəNī	100	100
M4	ū		maTū	100	100
M5	a	e	tuDa	80	80
F1	a	no change	gaTa	100	100
F2	ū		bhakū	100	100
F3	ī	a	sakvī	60	100
F4	C	a	raT	10	30
F5	C	ī	Dhak	0	20
N1	C	ə/e	khaD	20	80
N2	ū	ə/e	jambū	0	20
N3	ə/e	ī	bhəLə	0	30

Both children and adults appear to have no difficulty with the non-changing classes (M1-4, F1&2). The results are also encouraging for F3 and M5 classes. However, consonant final feminine classes (F4& F5) and the three neuter classes prove less tractable. Spreng's (2004) conclusions that some plural types are easier than others and those that are difficult remain so for both adults and children also holds true for Marathi. Children's performance is worse than the adults' performance for the difficult classes and, is particularly poor for the tokens simulating the neuter classes. These classes appear difficult for both groups. When in doubt, all subjects typically leave the nouns unmarked, substituting a zero suffix, though this is less frequent with adults than with children who opt for this strategy in providing answers. Other errors are restricted to the *potential* suffixes available for that particular gender class. For example, choosing ə/e where ī is required. The error is restricted to a specific gender class; in other words, gender drives affix selection but the target affix selected is incorrect though appropriate to the gender class. Though gender cues were provided, children as well as adults sometimes chose an affix that may apply to multiple genders though still relevant to the gender under consideration.

We can conclude that since the match between the phonological shape and the gender of the words is not unique, this makes the task of choosing the affixes for non-words complicated. The task reveals the high degree of ambiguity that is built into the system and is suggestive of the degree of difficulty in acquiring this system. Additionally, neuter nouns appear more problematic for both children and adults.

3 Intuiting Gender

Gender[3] in Marathi is morphologically unmarked and is reflected primarily through agreement of the noun with phrasal elements such as adjectives, demonstratives and verbs. Grammatical gender is congruent with natural sex distinctions (male versus female) for animate nouns but is otherwise arbitrarily selected and not associated with readily identifiable phonological or semantic features.

[3] Marathi along with Gujarati and Konkani are the only Indo-Aryan languages to have retained the three-gender system of Sanskrit where gender is arbitrarily assigned. Most languages have either shifted to the two-gender system or map grammatical gender with natural gender straightforwardly. Even loanwords in Marathi are reassigned arbitrarily to gender classes. In this Marathi resembles German more than its sister languages.

In this test, the subjects were asked to 'guess' the gender of non-words to measure the effect of the phonological shape of the noun on gender assignment. This test was inspired by A. Mill's (1986) work on the acquisition of gender in German where she developed a test using non-words for German speaking adults in order to study the psychological status of morphological and phonetic rules in German.

The test group consisted of ten Marathi speaking adults (5 M and 5 F) from Mumbai. The pictures used for the *wug* test (Berko 1958) were modified for our purposes. These simple, coloured pictures of some unfamiliar objects were associated with non-words which adhered to the phonotactic rules of Marathi. We created multiple tokens to rule out possible form-specific problems. The results are given in Table 3.

Table 3: Gender assignment and its frequency

Singular Ending	Potential Gender Preference (in %)	
a	M	75
	F	25
ī	M	5
	F	90
	*N	5
ū	M	35
	F	0
	N	65
ə	M	20
	N	75
	*F	5
Consonant	M	50
	F	30
	N	20

The first column provides possible singular endings for nouns in Marathi. The second column describes the *potential* gender/s possible for each ending of the singular form. For example, consonant ending tokens can be masculine, feminine or neuter. The third column shows the preference of the subjects (in %) while assigning gender to these non-words.

The cells in grey show the preferred gender for the choices possible per class – the winning gender as it were. Most subjects assigned masculine gender to '-a' ending tokens, feminine gender to '-ī' ending tokens and neuter gender to '-ə' ending tokens. No one assigned feminine gender to '-ū' ending tokens. For the -ī and the -ə classes, one subject also chose a gender that should have been ruled out by its shape; this is indicated in the table above with an asterisk (*).

In the absence of any other information (semantic or real-world), phonological shape biases the choice of gender and subjects attempt to distinguish classes given that cue. So we see that (a) subjects preferentially associate particular phonological shape(s) with particular genders and (b) that their responses allow other for other/alternate possibilities that we expect.

4 Frequency and Class Size

From the results above, we conclude that the match between the phonological shape and the gender of the words is not unique in Marathi and that this makes the task of choosing the affixes complicated. Further, of the three gender classes, neuter nouns appear more problematic in all tests for both children and adults. It thus becomes important to consider the frequency of these nominal classes in Marathi and consider whether the difficulties associated with both plurals in general and neuter nouns in particular shows class frequency effects. Since such frequency lists are not readily available for Marathi, we chose a contemporary dictionary compiled for students, the Navneet Marathi-English Dictionary, from which to cull the tokens for our analysis. This dictionary contains approximately 40,000 words. It represents a standard vocabulary of Marathi speakers. We collected all the nouns from this dictionary, approximately 18,000 tokens. The data needed some cleaning in order to address issues such as gender mismatch, compound words removal, manual inspection/verification of gender assignment by native Marathi speakers etc. At a final count, we had 17,840 nouns marked for gender. We further classify these nouns into 5 classes based on the phonological endings *viz*, a, ī, ə, ū and C (consonant). Table 4 shows the basic distribution of nouns across the three genders.

Table 4: Distribution of nouns across genders

Gender	Number of nouns	%
Masculine	7594	42.6
Feminine	6365	35.7
Neuter	3878	21.7
Total	17837	100.0

Nouns in Marathi are not distributed equally among the three genders. Masculine nouns occur most frequently (42.47%) in the data. Neuter nouns are least frequent and the difference between the frequency of neuter nouns and masculine or feminine nouns is significant.

In Table 5, we show the distribution of nouns across each nominal class and for all three genders. The first column describes the phonological ending of the nouns. Columns 2, 3 and 4 describe masculine, feminine and neuter nouns respectively. These columns are further divided to show the number of nouns allotted to each sub-class (phonological shape matched to one of the three genders) and their relative frequency (in %).

Table 5: Distribution of nouns within classes

Singular	Masculine nouns		Feminine nouns		Neuter Nouns	
	No.	%	No.	%	No.	%
C	3983	52.4	1887	29.6	3434	88.5
a	2029	26.7	1254	19.7	0	0
ī	623	8.2	3168	49.8	0	0
ū	226	3.0	56	0.9	63	1.6
ə/e	0	0	0	0	381	9.9
ə	733	9.7	0	0	0	0
Total	7594	100	6365	100	3878	100

There are six classes of masculine nouns. The consonant final one is the most frequent, followed by the 'a' class. Classes ending in 'ī', 'ū' and 'ə' are marginal classes of the masculine gender and it is observed that most of the nouns of these classes are borrowed from Sanskrit. The most frequent feminine class is the 'ī' class, followed by consonant and 'a' final nouns. The feminine class ending in 'ū' is marginal, constituting less than 1% of the total number of nouns. Of the three neuter gender classes, the consonant final class is the most frequent (88% of all neuter nouns). The other two classes are much less frequent.

Table 6 (read horizontally) is derived from the data shown in Tables 4 and 5. It represents the categorization of nouns into different classes based on their phonological endings. The first column shows the phonological ending of nouns. Columns 2, 3 and 4 describe masculine, feminine and neuter nouns respectively. These columns are further divided to show the numbers of nouns allotted to each class and their relative frequency For example, in row 2, for the 'a' ending noun class 61.8% of the words are masculine, 38.2% of the nouns are feminine and none belong to the neuter gender. Further, as seen in the last column, this class constitutes 18.4 % of the total number of nouns.

Table 6: Distribution of nouns based on phonological ending

Singular	Masculine		Feminine		Neuter		Total Nouns	% Total Nouns
	No.	%	No.	%	No.	%		
C	3983	42.8	1887	20.3	3434	36.9	9304	52.0
a	2029	61.8	1254	38.2			3283	18.4
ī	623	16.4	3168	83.6			3791	21. 4
ū	226	65.5	56	16.2	63	18.3	345	2.0
ə	733	65.8			381	34.2	1114	6.2
	Total						17837	100

We see that the consonant final nouns are the most frequent (52% of total nouns) and the nouns ending 'a' and 'ī' are much less so. Consonant final nouns are distributed among all three genders, but this distribution is not equal, masculine nouns being more frequent (42.8%) than either the feminine (20.28%) or the neuter (36.92%). Nouns ending in 'a' are distributed among masculine and feminine classes in a ratio of almost 2:1. The low frequency 'ə' and 'ū' classes contribute a fair number of neuter nouns. Thus neuter nouns are both less frequent in absolute numbers and also not uniquely identifiable. The insights we gain from a study of the lexical distribution of the classes now explains some of the difficulties faced by subjects in the previous tasks. We discuss this in the next section.

4.1 Comparison of tests

A comparison of the results of the previous tests and the class distribution that we just saw yields several generalizations. In Table 7, we present a comparison of class distribution with the intuition test, and in Table 8, a comparison of class distribution with the test for plural marking.

Table 7: Comparison of results of intuition test with distribution of nouns

Singular	Potential gender and its frequency - results of intuition test (%)		frequency of gender given a noun class (%)	frequency of noun class in all nouns (%)
a	M	75	61.8	18.4
	F	25	38.2	
ī	M	5	16.4	21.4
	F	90	83.6	
ū	M	35	65.5	2.0
	F	0	16.2	
	N	65	18.3	
ə	M	20	65.8	6.2
	N	75	34.2	
C	M	50	42.5	52.0
	F	30	20.3	
	N	20	36.9	

In Table 7, column 1 gives the potential phonological endings of the nouns in Marathi, column 2, the results of the intuition test (the potential gender given a particular phonological ending, column 3, the frequency of nouns allotted to a particular gender based on the phonological ending and column 4, the frequency of a noun class based on phonological ending given the total number of nouns.

It is noteworthy that the results for the '-a' ending tokens in the intuition test correlates with the distribution of the nouns ending in 'a' (cells marked in grey). Masculine gender is preferred by the subjects (potential genders being M&F) and 'a' ending masculine nouns are indeed more frequent (61.80%) than 'a' ending feminine nouns (38.2%).

A similar correlation is observed for the nouns ending in 'ī' (cells marked in grey). Feminine nouns ending in 'ī' are more frequent than masculine nouns and subjects preferred the feminine to masculine gender when intuiting gender for such tokens. Thus, nouns ending in 'ī' are intuited to be feminine and 'ī' ending nouns are predominantly feminine. For consonant ending nouns, a similar pattern is observed to some extent. All three classes occur equally frequently in the overall distribution of nouns.

The 'ə' and 'ū' ending nouns are judged to be neuter though their distribution indicates that they are more frequently masculine rather than neuter. It is observed that these two classes are marginal in the overall distribution of nouns and therefore preclude or limit more successful correlation between phonology and gender.[4]

In Table 8 which is very similar to Table 2 but contains an additional column which describes the frequency of nouns for a particular class, given the total number of nouns in Marathi we compare the results of the plural marking test with class distribution.

Table 8: Comparison of results of plural marking test with distribution of nouns

Gender	Sg	Pl	Non- words			% frequency of noun class
			Token	Results (%)		
				Children	Adults	
				sg to pl	sg to pl	
M1	ə	no change	pūmbə	100	100	4.1
M2	C		tšag	100	100	22.3
M3	ī		pəNī	100	100	3.5
M4	ū		maTū	100	100	1.3
M5	a	e	tuDa	80	80	11.4
F1	a	no change	gaTa	100	100	7.0
F2	ū		bhakū	100	100	0.3
F3	ī	a	sakvī	60	100	17.8
F4	C	a	raT	10	30	10.6
F5	C	ī	Dhak	0	20	
N1	C	ə/e	khaD	20	80	19.2
N2	ū	ə/e	jambū	0	20	3.5
N3	ə/e	ī	bhəLə	0	30	2.1

It may be observed that for non-changing classes the results of the test is 100%. The results do not reflect the pattern of distribution of nouns in the lexicon. For changing classes, the results of '-a' ending masculine and '-ī' ending feminine tokens correlate with the distribution of nouns. The higher frequency of nouns leads to better performance for both adults and children. It is interesting to observe that though the incidence of consonant final neuter nouns in the overall distribution of nouns is considerable (19.24 %), children are not able to select the correct plural affix (20%). However, the performance of adults for the same class of nouns is encouraging (80%). This suggests that there is some effect of maturation in the acquisition of the rules of plural morphology. Children may defer inducing or applying the rules till such time as they have ample evidence for the same.

The frequency of the other two subclasses of neuter gender (N2 and N3) is significantly low ('ū' ending nouns 3.53% and 'ə' ending nouns 2.13%) and both children and adult are unable to mark the plural suffix correctly. The less frequent classes of masculine and feminine gender do not inflect overtly for number. Only the less frequent classes corresponding to neuter gender inflect overtly for number. Hence, low frequency probably accounts for the poor performance of

[4] As remarked by one reviewer, we cannot rule out that something other than class marginality may be going on. We are increasing the number of tokens in all these tests and expect to reevaluate our results per class with this larger sample.

the subjects for these classes. Class F4 and F5 (consonant ending feminine nouns) also show poor performance in the selection of plural affixes. These noun classes are distributionally frequent but the ambiguity of affix selection accounts for the poor performance. The comparison shows not a straightforward correlation between noun distribution/frequency of nouns but a nuanced one where frequency, uniqueness of affix assignment and zero-suffixation all play a role in the performance of children and adults.

5 Conclusion

We have shown through a series of studies that the plural morphology of neuter gender nouns is difficult for subjects, both children and adults. When we relate the performance data to the distribution of nouns we gain several insights into this problem. While speakers do have an internalized system of rules and apply it appropriately, the performance and rule application is limited by other factors. It can be seen that nouns marked for neuter gender are the least frequent in the overall distribution of nouns. Hence, it is possible that the low overall frequency of neuter nouns triggers the poor performance in selecting plural suffixes. It can be concluded that while assigning gender, the gender classes which are distributionally most frequent are preferred over others. This effect is restricted to the classes which contribute a larger proportion of nouns in the overall distribution of nouns in Marathi. When the overall frequency of a class is low, that class also demonstrates problems with plural morphology assignment if, in addition, it also changes in the plural and its shape is class ambiguous. We can also infer that the rules for noun classes with high frequency are easy to acquire than those classes which have fewer nouns in it. Finally, since Marathi is one of the few Indo-Aryan languages with the three gender system, there may be additional pressure on the language to move towards a two-gender or an attenuated gender system as may be seen in other languages of this family.

References

Berko, J. 1958. The Child's learning of English Morphology. *Word*, 17 (2-3), pp.150-177.

Corbett, G. 1991. *Gender.* Cambridge: Cambridge University Press.

Damle, M. K. 1970. *Shastriya Marathi Vyakaran (A scientific grammar of Marathi).* K. S. Arjunwadkar (ed). Pune, India: Deshmukh & Company.

Dhongde, R. V. 1983. *Arwatsīn Marathi.* Pune, India: Continental Prakashan.

Kelkar, A. R. 1958. *The Phonology and Morphology of Marathi.* Ph.D Dissertation, Cornell University.

Lust, B. 2006. *Child Language Acquisition and Growth.* Cambridge: Cambridge University Press.

Mills, A. 1986. *The Acquisition of Gender.* Berlin and New York: Springer-Verlag.

Pandharipande, R. 1997. *Marathi.* London and New York: Routledge

Pinker, S. 1994. On the Acquisition of Grammatical Morphemes. *Journal of Child Language,* 8, pp.477-484.

Prabhudesai, S. 2011. Navneet Marathi – English Dictionary. Naveet Publication: Mumbai

Spreng, B. (2004). Error patterns in the acquisition of German plural morphology: Evidence for the relevance of grammatical gender as a cue. *Toronto Working Papers in Linguistics* 23(2), pp.147-172.

Child Language Data Exchange System (CHILDES). 2003. wugs.pdf retrieved from http://childes.psy.cmu.edu/topics/

The L1 Acquisition of the Imperfective Aspect markers in Korean: a Comparison with Japanese*

Ju-Yeon Ryu

Department of Cross-cultural Education, Tohoku University,
41 Kawauchi, Aoba-ku, Sendai, 980-8576 Japan
juyeonryu@gmail.com

Abstract. This study investigates the L1 acquisition of the Korean imperfective aspect markers *-ko iss-* and *-a iss-*, and attempts to identify language-general and language-specific acquisition patterns through comparison with Japanese. In cross-linguistic research on the acquisition of tense-aspect marking, children have been observed to associate progressive marking with activity verbs in early stages of development. This study aims to test whether or not Korean children will actually follow the acquisition pattern and acquire progressive marking with activity verbs earlier than resultative marking with achievement verbs. Longitudinal interaction data from three Korean boys was collected and analyzed. The results indicate that there was no common pattern in the three children's acquisition, which differences from the results of similar tests with Japanese children. This suggests that neither universal predisposition nor the distribution bias hypothesis can explain the L1 acquisition of Korean aspect markers, and that individual variation plays a much larger role.

Keywords: First language acquisition, Korean imperfective aspect markers, the Aspect Hypothesis, the distribution bias hypothesis, individual variation

1. Introduction

The acquisition of tense-aspect morphology has shown an interesting universal pattern in both first and second language acquisition (Andersen and Shirai, 1996). This universal tendency is referred to as the Aspect Hypothesis (Andersen and Shirai, 1994; Robison, 1995), which claims that there is a universal developmental sequence of tense-aspect markers: past tense forms start with achievement verbs, and progressive forms start with activity verbs.

Correlations between tense-aspect markers and the inherent aspect of verbs have been verified in the first language acquisition of various languages (for example, Bloom *et al.*1980 in English, Antinucci and Miller 1976 in Italian, Bronckart and Sinclair 1973 in French, Weist *et al.* 1984 in Polish, Stephany 1981 in Greek, Aksu-koc 1988 in Turkish). However, only a few studies were conducted on the L1 acquisition of Asian languages, such as Shirai (1993, 1998) and Shirai and Suzuki (in print) for Japanese, and Seda and Lee (2002) for Korean. In their study on the L1 acquisition of Korean, Seda and Lee (2002) found that both Korean and Turkish children use past marking predominantly with accomplishment and achievement verbs first, supporting the Aspect Hypothesis. However, they only focused on the acquisition of past tense . Further research is needed to verify the Aspect Hypothesis completely, including the acquisition of the progressive tense.

This study tests whether the universal developmental pattern proposed by Andersen and

* The work reported in this paper was supported by Grant-in-Aid for JSPS Fellows and the Tohoku University International Advanced Research and Education Organization.

Shirai (1996) holds true for the L1 acquisition of Korean, and also compares it to the L1 acquisition of the Japanese imperfective marker *-te i-* in order to discover what determines children's acquisition of aspect: universal predisposition, the distribution bias hypothesis or individual variation.

2. The Imperfective Aspect System in Korean

Imperfective aspect markers in Korean can express two meanings: the progressive and the resultant state (Lee, 1993; Martin, 1992). When expressing an action-in-progress meaning, Korean takes *-ko iss-* as the progressive marker. Meanwhile, when expressing a resultant state meaning, Korean takes *-ko iss-* or *-a iss-*. Syntactically, when expressing a resultative state, both *-ko iss-* and *-a iss-* are used, depending on the transitivity of the main verbs. As shown in Table 1, *-ko iss-* is used with transitive verbs, whereas *-a iss-* is used with intransitive verbs (Lee, 1991).

Table 1 Imperfective markers *-ko iss-* and *-a iss-*

	Intransitive verbs	Transitive verbs
The progressive marker	*-ko iss-*	
The resultant marker	*-a iss-*	*-ko iss-*

-ko iss- has been generally treated as a progressive marker similar to the English progressive marker *be -ing*, as shown in (1a). However, it is not obligatory to employ the Korean *-ko iss-* to describe an ongoing event, unlike with *be -ing* in English and *-te i-* in Japanese. The simple present form in Korean, in fact, can encode an ongoing event like the Romance languages as well as others, as shown in (1a) and (1b).

(1a) Pap-ul mek-ko iss-ta (AN 1;11)
lunch-Acc eat-Prog-Dec
"He(or She) is eating a lunch"
(1b) Pap-ul mek-nun-ta
lunch-Acc eat-Prs-Dec
"He(or She) is eating a lunch"

In addition to its progressive meaning, *-ko iss-* can also describe a resultant state with transitive verbs, such as verbs of wearing, carrying, and body posture (Ahn, 1995; Kim, 1993; Lee, 1991) .

(2) Wangkwan-ul ssu-ko iss-eyo (JONG 1;11)
crown-Acc wear-Resl-Dec
"He(or She) is wearing a crown." or "He(or She) is putting on a crown"

In (2), *-ko iss-* can be interpreted either as an ongoing event or as a resultant state. This is because in the case of transitive verbs, only *-ko iss-* can be chosen as the imperfective aspect marker in both the describing of the progressive and the resultant state.

-a iss- has been defined as the resultative marker in Korean (Ahn, 1995; Lee, 1993; Martin, 1992). However, whereas *-ko iss-* is compatible with all transitive verbs, *-a iss-* can only be used with intransitive verbs in describing a persisting state resulting from a completed action, as in (3) (Lee, 1991).

(3) Khokkili anc-a iss-e (JONG 1;11)
elephant sit-Resl-Dec
"The elephant is sitting."

Since we compare the results of Korean L1 acquisition with those of Japanese L1 acquisition, it is necessary to describe the aspectual system of Japanese. It has an aspectual system quite similar to Korean in that the Japanese imperfective marker *-te i-* can denote both progressive and stative meanings. Generally speaking, the meaning of *-te i-* is dependent on the inherent aspectual value of the verbs to which *-te i-* is attached. Dynamic durative verbs (i.e. Vendler's (1957) activity and accomplishment verbs) combine with *-te i-* to express progressive meanings, whereas punctual change of state verbs (Vendler's achievement verbs) express a resulting state. The Korean imperfective marker *-a iss-*, which covers the resultative state meaning denoted by *-te i-* with achievement verbs in Japanese, is attached almost exclusively to intransitive change-of-state verbs.[1] On the other hand, The Korean imperfective marker *-ko iss-*, which denotes progressive meaning with activity and accomplishment verbs as in Japanese, can have resultative meaning with transitive achievement verbs, as Shown in Table 2.

Table 2 Comparison of Japanese and Korean imperfective aspect markers

	Progressive	Resultative	
Japanese	*-te i-* Activity, Accomplishment	*-te i-* Achievement	
Korean	*-ko iss-* Activity, Accomplishment	*-ko iss-* transitive Achievement	*-a iss-* intransitive Achievement

3. Previous studies on the acquisition of aspect

Previous studies on the acquisition of tense/aspect have claimed that the development of tense/aspect morphology in language acquisition is strongly influenced by the inherent semantic aspect of the verbs to which the inflections are attached. This hypothesis, generally referred to as the Aspect Hypothesis (Andersen and Shirai, 1994, 1996; Shirai, 1991; Bardovi-Harlig, 1999, 2000; Li and Shirai, 2000; Salaberry and Shirai, 2002), claims the following:

1. Learners use (perfective) past marking on achievement/accomplishment verbs, eventually extending use to activity and stative verbs.
2. In languages that encode the perfective/imperfective distinction morphologically, the imperfective past appears later than the perfective past, and the imperfect past marking begins with stative and activity (i.e., atelic) verbs, then extends to accomplishment and achievement (i.e., telic) verbs.
3. In languages that have a progressive aspect, progressive marking begins with activity verbs, and then extends to accomplishment/achievement verbs.
4. Progressive marking is rarely incorrectly overextended to stative verbs (in L1 acquisition).

Although researchers generally agree on this descriptive observation (e.g. Shirai, Slobin and Weist, 1998), the explanation for this observation is not fully understood. One important hypothesis appeals to a universal predisposition (e.g., Bickerton, 1981), which presupposes that children have a bias to map tense-aspect markers with particular semantic content. Namely, he argued that children use past tense marking to denote punctuality, or telicity in aspectology, and progressive/imperfective marking to mark the lack of telicity, because the Punctual-NonPunctual Distriction (PNPD) is a distinction that has a special status in his bio-program hypothesis.. Meanwhile, the Distributional Bias Hypothesis (e.g. Shirai and Andersen, 1995) argues that children make particular associations based on input frequency. In other words, it

[1] Korean *-a iss-* is often treated as perfective (e.g. K-D. Lee 1980; Sohn 1995; McClure 1993). This is in a sense understandable because there is a close affinity between resultative, perfect, and perfective. However, in this paper, resultative markers are treated as imperfective markers that focus on the duration after the punctual point of change-of-state, following Shirai (1998).

suggests that associations in acquisition are based on a skewed distribution of such combinations in input, which was supported by analyzing input data of mother-child interaction in English(Shira and Andersen, 1995).

Seda and Lee (2002) focused on the development of tense-aspect morphology in L1 Korean acquisition. Their data was collected from thirty Turkish children and three Korean children. They found that (i) both Korean and Turkish children use past marking predominantly with accomplishment and achievement verbs first, (ii) the same children frequently used verbs involving telicity in their past references and (iii) Turkish children start using adverbs predominantly with accomplishment verbs. Their results suggest that the L1 acquisition of past markers shows similarity cross-linguistically. However, there has been no study focused on the development of Korean imperfective aspect markers.

In Japanese, which is known to be very similar to Korean in morphology, syntactic structures, and other typological criteria, this predicted developmental pattern has not been observed (Shirai 1993, 1998, Shirai and Suzuki, in print). Shirai (1993) surveyed whether the universal acquisition pattern holds true for the Japanese progressive *-te i-* and past tense *-ta-*. He found that the Japanese children in his study followed the same universal pattern found in previous studies. However, Shirai (1998) reported different results from Shirai (1993). Shirai (1998) investigated the emergence and later development of three tense-aspect markers in Japanese: *-ta* (past), *-te* i- (durative), and *-ru* (non-past). This data was taken from three Japanese children. He found that the emergence of tense-aspect morphology in Japanese does not necessarily follow the prediction of the Aspect Hypothesis, but is mediated by typological factors of Japanese, and that there is individual variation in the acquisition of the morphology. Shirai and Suzuki (in print) investigated the acquisition of *-te* i- again, including an analysis of the caretaker's speech data. The results indicated that there is no preponderance of activity verbs and thus progressive meaning does not occur more frequently. For all three children, the use of *-te i-* with achievements was more frequent than with activities. They suggested that frequency is more important than universal predisposition in the acquisition of tense-aspect markers, thus supporting the distribution bias hypothesis, and the usage-based model in general.

This paper is a contribution to the existing literature in two respects. First, research done so far has been predominantly on the L1 acquisition of aspect morphology of Indo-European languages. The Aspect Hypothesis states that in languages that have a progressive aspect, progressive marking begins with activity verbs, and then extends to accomplishment/ achievement verbs. This has been confirmed in research on Indo-European languages. However, Shirai and Suzuki (in print) reported that in Japanese, the progressive marking of *-te i-* emerges with achievement verbs rather than with activity verbs. This suggests that early use of *-te i-* is associated with activity verbs to mark non-punctuality, contrary to the universal prediction , and that children's use of *-te i-* is more strongly associated with achievements. In order to claim universal status for the Aspect Hypothesis, more evidence from non-Indo-European languages is needed. The current study offers vital information about how the Korean tense/aspect system is acquired, which until now has not been studied in depth, and will be the first attempt to clarify the developmental process of the imperfective aspect morphology for L1 Korean.

Second, this study will provide evidence to address the issue of whether tendencies in tense-aspect acquisition can be attributed to universal predisposition or input. Bickerton (1981, 1984) attributed such universal tendencies to his proposed bio-program, assuming that children's language acquisition is influenced by innate tendencies such as the PNPD (the Punctual-NonPunctual Distinction). Shirai and Andersen (1995) proposed an alternative account for the phenomena, which they called the Distributional Bias Hypothesis, based on the analysis of input frequency in child-directed speech. Shirai and Suzuki (in print) suggest that contrary to the bio-program hypothesis, *-te i-* was not associated with activities by Japanese children, and they argue that children follow the distributional pattern observed in the input language. In this paper, we investigate not only the children's use of the imperfective markers *-ko iss-/-a iss-*, but also the mother's use of them, in order to verify the validity of the Distributional Bias Hypothesis.

The research questions addressed in this study are:

(1) Is children' use of *-ko iss-/-a iss-* associated more with activity verbs than with achievement verbs?
(2) Is caretakers' use of *-ko iss-/-a iss-* associated more with activity verbs than with achievement verbs?
(3) Does the input in the child-directed speech influence the distributional pattern of imperfective aspect marking in the children's speech?

4. Study

4.1 Method and Participants

The Korean data used for the purpose of this study consists of longitudinal video-recoded speech samples from three children, as shown in Table 3 below. The data collection period was one and a half years. All data was taken from video-recordings during adult-child interaction at the children's homes. Videos were recorded every two weeks. The length of each session was 30min.

Table 3 Children for the Longitudinal Data

Children	Age range	Sex and Sibling	Age of first use
AN	1;7~3;1	M, no siblings	1;11
JONG	1;3~2;6	M, no siblings	1;11
YUN	2;3~3;9	M, no siblings	2;7

This data covered an extended period of acquisition, and includes relatively early stages of development, which was necessary to see the emergence and subsequent development of aspectual marking in both children's speech and child-directed speech. The child-directed speech (input) includes the utterances from all of the caretakers, including not only their parents but also their grandparents. In total, about 56hr of data was analyzed. The total number of utterances was 22,642: 10,361 utterances from the child YUN, 7,952 from JONG, and 4,329 from AN. The total number of utterances in the caretakers' speech was 48,240: 17,028 utterances from input to YUN, 17,821 to JONG, and 13,391 to AN (see Table 4).

4.2 Data Analysis and Results

The three children produced 114 predicate tokens with the imperfective aspect markers *-ko iss-/-a iss-*, and their caretakers produced 1173 tokens. Table 4 is a summary of the tokens we analyzed.

Table 4 Tokens of *-ko iss-/-a iss-* Produced by Children and Caretakers

	Target Tokens		Total Tokens		Frequency (target/total)	
	child	caretaker	child	caretaker	child	caretaker
AN (1;7~3;1)	20	229	4,329	13,391	0.005	0.017
JONG(1;3~2;6)	26	287	7,952	17,821	0.003	0.016
YUN (2;3~3;9)	68	657	10,361	17,028	0.007	0.039

The frequency (the mean number of imperfective aspect markers per utterance) was 0.005~0.007 for the children and 0.016~0.039 for the caretakers. These figures suggest that both the children and the adults overall used imperfective aspect markers quite infrequently across all contexts. YUN and his caretaker use *-ko iss-/-a iss-* more frequently than other two children and their caretakers. The frequency of imperfective aspect marker usage by YUN and his caretaker was almost two times that of the other two children and their respective caretakers. This could suggest that if a child's caretakers use *-ko iss-/-a iss-* very frequently, the child may also use them frequently because the child is getting adequate input to acquire aspectual marking properly.

4.2.1 RQ1: Children's Use of *-ko iss-/-a iss-*

Table 5 shows the usage of the three imperfective markers by the children and caretakers. We can see the longitudinal development of *-ko iss-/-a iss-* over time. We also separated the caretaker usage into "pre-emergence" and "post-emergence" in the table. YUN and JONG use not only the progressive *-ko iss-*, but also the resultative *-ko iss-/-a iss-* from early stages of development (Table 5.) JONG even uses the resultative *-ko iss-/-a iss-* predominantly more than the progressive *-ko iss-*. However, for over 1 year AN uses only the progressive *-ko iss-* from the first emergence of his use of imperfective markers. The results indicate that there was no common pattern in three children's acquisition. This can be seen in the fact that YUN and JONG didn't seem to associate imperfective aspect marking more with activity verbs, while AN exhibited a tendency to use imperfective aspect marking with activity verbs.

Table 5 Use of the three imperfective markers by the children and caretakers (token count)

AN	Pre-emergence		Post-emergence													
	Child 1;7-1;10	caretakers (percentage)	Child 1;11	2;0	2;1	2;3	2;4	2;5	2;6	2;7	2;8	2;9	2;10	3;1	sum(%)	caretakers (percentage)
PRG-ko iss-	N/A	38(64)	2	0	0	4	0	6	0	1	0	0	7	0	20(100)	121(71)
RSL-ko iss-	N/A	5(8)	0	0	0	0	0	0	0	0	0	0	0	0	0	17(10)
RSL-a iss-	N/A	16(27)	0	0	0	0	0	0	0	0	0	0	0	0	0	32(19)
Sum	0	59(100)	2	0	0	4	0	6	0	1	0	0	7	0	20(100)	170(100)

JONG	Pre-emergence		Post-emergence									
	Child 1;3-1;10	caretakers (percentage)	Child 1;11	2;0	2;1	2;2	2;3	2;4	2;5	2;6	sum(%)	caretakers (percentage)
PRG-ko iss-	N/A	53(66)	2	1	2	0	0	2	0	0	7(27)	92(44)
RSL-ko iss-	N/A	7(9)	3	1	2	3	0	0	0	0	9(35)	26(13)
RSL-a iss-	N/A	20(25)	2	3	2	1	0	2	0	0	10(38)	89(43)
Sum	0	80(100)	7	5	6	4	0	4	0	0	26(100)	207(100)

YUN	Pre-emergence		Post-emergence														
	Child 2;3-2;6	caretakers (percentage)	Child 2;7	2;8	2;9	2;10	2;11	3;0	3;1	3;2	3;5	3;6	3;7	3;8	3;9	sum(%)	caretakers (percentage)
PRG-ko iss-	N/A	35(42)	1	3	4	1	1	2	1	6	0	1	7	3	0	30(44)	289(50)
RSL-ko iss-	N/A	15(18)	4	0	0	2	2	0	2	0	0	0	0	0	0	10(15)	79(14)
RSL-a iss-	N/A	33(40)	0	1	0	0	2	2	0	0	2	9	2	9	1	28(41)	206(36)
Sum	0	83(100)	5	4	4	3	5	4	3	6	2	10	9	12	1	68(100)	574(100)

Note. In the Tables, PRG = Progressive, RSL = Resultative. The token frequency is in parentheses. In the data of AN, 2;2, 2;11, 3;0 was not recorded.

4.2.2 RQ2: Caretakers' Use of *-ko iss-/-a iss-*

Caretaker speech also showed the same tendencies as that of the children. Table 6 shows the usage of the three imperfective markers by the caretakers. YUN and JONG's caretakers use progressive *-ko iss-* and resultative *-ko iss-/-a iss-* equally (use of progressive *-ko iss-*: 49% for YUN and 51% for JONG). However, AN's caretaker uses the progressive *-ko iss-* more frequently than the resultative *-ko iss-/-a iss-* (use of the progressive *-ko iss-*: 69%). The results indicate that there was no common pattern in three caretakers' speech and that they did not use more progressive marking with activity verbs than resultative marking with achievement verbs.

Table 6 Use of the three imperfective markers by the caretakers (token count)

	YUN's caretaker		JONG's caretaker		AN's caretaker	
	token	percentage	token	percentage	token	percentage
PRG-ko iss-	324	49%	145	51%	159	69%
RSL-ko iss-	94	14%	33	11%	22	10%
RSL-a iss-	239	36%	109	38%	48	21%
Sum	657	100%	287	100%	229	100%

4.2.3 RQ3: Relationship Between Caretakers and Their Children

Figure 1 shows the children's and caretakers' use of *-ko iss-/-a iss-*. YUN's usage closely reflects the frequency of his caretaker, although YUN uses the resultative *-a iss-* 8 % more frequently than his caretaker. JONG uses the resultative *-ko iss-* 3 times more than his caretaker, and the progressive *-ko iss-* less (51% vs. 27% for the progressive *-ko iss-*). Thus, JONG's usage of imperfective aspect markers leaned more towards resultative markers than his caretaker. AN, however, uses only the progressive *-ko iss-* for over 1 year from the first emergence of imperfective markers. His caretaker's also shows a very high percentage of progressive marker usage compared to the other caretakers (69% vs. 51% and 49%). However, in the English data, the initial restriction of the past tense form to achievements is almost absolute (95% or higher), whereas in the mothers' speech the association is about 60% (Shirai and Andersen, 1995). Thus, the results found in this experimentation are quite striking, even though some differences between English and Korean must be accounted for.

Figure 1 Children's and Caretakers' Usage pattern of the imperfective markers

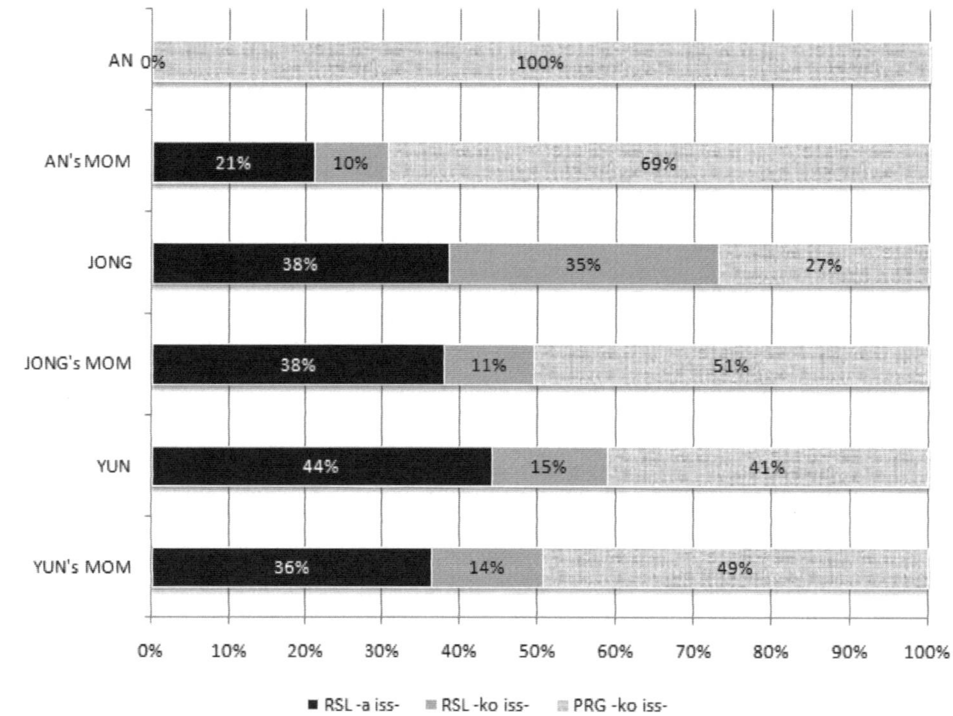

Looking at the relationship between the caretakers and their children, two patterns can be observed in our experimentation. One pattern, as in the case of YUN and JONG, shows caretakers using resultative and progressive marking equally, in which case their children also

show a tendency to use resultative marking with achievement verb. The other pattern shows caretakers using progressive marking predominantly (almost 70%), in which case the children show a tendency to use progressive marking with activity verbs. It is undeniable in the results of this experiment that children will show an overall distribution of *-ko iss-/-a iss-* similar to their caretakers. Thus, we can conclude that the input a child receives plays a decisive role in their use of imperfective aspect markers.

5. Discussion

The results obtained in this study answer the research questions stated earlier, as follows:

(1) There was no association found between children's use of *-ko iss-/-a iss-* and activity or achievement verbs.
(2) There was no association found between caretakers' use of *-ko iss-/-a iss-* and activity or achievement verbs.
(3) The input from the child-directed speech given by the caretaker seems to influence the distributional pattern of imperfective aspect marking in the children's speech.

The results found in our experimentation show that there was no universal pattern in the three children's acquisition. Two of them associated imperfective aspect marking with achievement verbs early on, but one child associated imperfective aspect marking with activity verbs. Thus, our results don't support the Aspect Hypothesis. We also suggest that the acquisition of the Korean imperfective aspect cannot be explained by the universal predisposition. We did, however, found that caretaker speech showed the same tendencies as that of their children. The analysis of the overall input indicates that if input is skewed in one direction or the other, children will show the same usage preference. Thus, frequency in the input appears to be more important in the acquisition of tense-aspect markers than any universal predisposition. Children were not observed to associate progressive marking with activity verbs at the early stages of development as the Aspect Hypothesis would predict. Rather, it would seem that there is a large amount of individual variation in the acquisition of morphology, as suggested by Budwig (1996) in his study of pronominal case acquisition in English. His research showed that of the six children he tested, half of them underwent a different acquisition order than the other half.

We suggest, for a number of reasons, that the main cause of the differences in acquisition seen in our experimentation is the input the children receive. We make this claim for a number of reasons. First, Shirai and Suzuki (in print) indicate that in L1 Japanese acquisition, there is a tendency for the resultative state to be acquired first. However, we achieved different results in Korean L1 acquisition in our study. They mention that because of the frequency in the input, children use *-tei-* with achievements more than with activities. According to their results, caretaker speech showed a skewed distribution, exhibiting more frequent use of achievements. This differs from the results of our study in Korean as well as those reported in Shirai (1993) and (1998). If we look at the total results of Shirai and Suzuki (in print), Shirai (1993), and Shirai (1998), we can see that three of nine children showed some preference for linking activity verbs to the progressive, while five of them showed some preference for linking achievement verbs to the resultative, and one didn't show any preference at all. In looking at the overall results of these three studies, individual variation can be observed in Japanese as it was in Korean in our experiments. In addition, if we look at the combined results of the three studies in Japanese mentioned above, it shows that the children's aspectual preferences coincide with that of their caretakers. This leads us to believe that the emergence of imperfective aspect markers in Korean and Japanese does not follow the predictions of the Aspect Hypothesis, and that there is individual variation in the acquisition of morphology, the distributional pattern of which is highly influenced by the input received.

6. Conclusion

This study investigated the acquisition of the imperfective aspect markers *-ko iss-/-a iss-* in Korean to address the issue of whether or not Korean children would actually follow the acquisition pattern predicted by the Aspect Hypothesis: progressive marking with activity verbs being acquired earlier than resultative marking with achievement verbs. The results clearly indicate that contrary to the Aspect Hypothesis, there was no common pattern in our test subject's acquisition, and that individual variation is plays a larger role in the early acquisition of tense-aspect markers than universal predisposition.

References

Ahn, Y. 1995. *The aspectual and temporal system of Korean: from the perspective of the two-component theory of aspect.* Unpublished doctoral dissertation, University of Texas at Austin.

Aksu-Koç, A. 1988. *The Acquisition of Aspect and Modality: The Case of Past Reference in Turkish.* Cambridge: Cambridge University Press.

Andersen, R.W. and Y. Shirai. 1994. Discourse motivations for some cognitive acquisition principles. *Studies in Second Language Acquisition* 16: 133-156.

Andersen, R.W. and Y. Shirai. 1996. The primacy of aspect in first and second language acquisition:The pidgin-creole connection. In W C Ritchie and T K Bhatia (eds.), *Handbook of Second Language Acquisition*, 527-570. San Diego, CA: Academic Press.

Antinucci, F., and R. Miller. 1976. How Children Talk about What Happened. *Journal of Child Language* 3:169-189.

Bardovi-Harlig, K. 1999. From morpheme studies to temporal semantics. *Studies in Second Language Acquisition, 21,* 341–382.

Bardovi-Harlig, K. 2000. *Tense and aspect in second language acquisition: Form, meaning, and use.* Oxford: Blackwell.

Bickerton, D. 1981. *Roots of Language.* Ann Arbor, MI: Karoma Publishers.

Bickerton, D. 1984. The Language Bioprogram Hypothesis. *The Behavioral and Brain Sciences* 7:173-188.

Bloom, L., K. Lifter, and J. Hafitz. 1980. Semantics of Verbs and the Development of Verb Inflection in Child Language. *Language* 56:386-412.

Broncart. J. P. and H. Sinclair. 1973. "Time, tense and aspect": Cognition 2.107-30.

Budwig, N. 1996. What influences children's patterns of forms and functions in early child language? In D. I.Slobin, J. Gerhardt, A.Kyratzis, and J. Guo (Eds.), *Social interaction, social context, and language* (pp. 143–156). Mahwah, NJ: Erlbaum.

Kim, Y. 1993. The resultative progressive in Korean. Paper of the 29th Regional Meeting. *Chicago Lingustic Society*, 251-265

Lee, H. S. 1991. *Tense, aspect and modality: A discourse-pragmatic analysis of verbal suffixes in Korean from a typological perspective.* Unpublished doctoral dissertation, University of California, Los Angeles.

Lee, K. 1993. *A Korean grammar on semantic-pragmatic principles.* Seoul: Hankwuk Mwunhwasa.

Li, Ping and Y. Shirai. 2000. *The acquisition of lexical and grammatical aspect*. Berlin: Mouton de Gruyter.

Martin, S. 1992. *A reference grammar of Korean.* Tokyo: Charles E. Tuttle Company.

Robison, R. E. 1995. The aspect hypothesis revisited: A cross-sectional study of tense and aspect marking in interlanguage. Applied *Linguistics* 16: 344-370

Salaberry, Rafael M. and Y. Shirai. 2002. *The L2 acquisition of tense-aspect morphology (pp. 1-20).* Amsterdam: John Benjamins..

Seda G. and C.M. Lee. 2002. Aspects of the acquisition of (past) tense and (telic) aspect in

Turkish and Korean. *Language Research* 38(4): 1317-1347
Shirai, Y. 1991. *Primacy of aspect in language acquisition: Simplified input and prototype.* Unpublished doctoral dissertation, University of California, Los Angeles.
Shirai, Y. 1993. Inherent Aspect and the Acquisition of Tense/Aspect Morphology in Japanese. *Argument Structure: Its Syntax and Acquisition*, eds. H. Nakajima and Y. Otsu, 185-211. Tokyo: Kaitakusha.
Shirai, Y. 1998. The Emergence of Tense-Aspect Morphology in Japanese: Universal Disposition? *First Language* 18:281-310.
Shirai, Y. and R. W. Andersen. 1995. The Acquisition of Tense-aspect Morphology: A Prototype Account. *Language* 71:743-762.
Shirai, Y. and Y. Suzuki. (in print). The acquisition of the Japanese imperfective aspect marker: universal predisposition or input frequency? In Bjarke Frellesvig and Peter Sells (Ed.), *Japanese/Korean Linguistics, 20*. Stanford, CA: CSLI Publications.
Shirai, Y., D. Slobin and R. M. Weist. 1998. Introduction: The Acquisition of Tense-Aspect Morphology. *First Language* 18:245-253.
Stephany, U. 1981. Verbal Grammar in Modern Greek Early Child Language. *Child Language: An International Perspective*, eds. P. S. Dale and D. Ingram, 45-57. Baltimore, MD: University Park Press.
Vendler, Z. 1957. *Linguistics in Philosphy*. Ithaca,NY: Cornell University Press.
Weist, R.M., H. Wysocka, K. Witkowska-Stadnik, E. Buczowska and E. Konieczna. 1984. The defective tense hypothesis: on the emergence of tense and aspect in child Polish. *Journal of Child Language*, 11, 347-374

APPENDIX 1

Verbs of the first 10 samples of imperfective aspect marker usage by each child

Child	Word	Meaning
AN	먹다(4) mek-ta	'eat'
	치다(4) chi-ta	'hit'
	주다(1) cwu-ta	'give'
	뜯다(1) ttut-ta	'(the cattle) graze'
JONG	낚시하다(1) naksiha-ta	'fish'
	타다(2) tha-ta	'ride'
	앉다(1) anc-ta	'sit'
	쓰다(1) ssu-ta	'wear'
	되다(2) toy-ta	'become'
	붙다(1) pwuth-ta	'stick'
	하다(1) ha-ta	'do'
	밀다(1) mil-ta	'push'
YUN	타다(1) tha-ta	'ride'
	모르다(1) molu-ta	'do not know'
	하다(1) ha-ta	'do'
	가다(3) ka-ta	'go'
	울다(1) wul-ta	'cry'
	쓰다(1) ssu-ta	'write'
	사다(1) sa-ta	'buy'
	놀다(1) nol-ta	'play'

Semi-Automatic Identification of Bilingual Synonymous Technical Terms from Phrase Tables and Parallel Patent Sentences

Bing Liang[a], Takehito Utsuro[b], and Mikio Yamamoto[b]

[a] Graduate School of Systems and Information Engineering, University of Tsukuba, Tsukuba, 305-8573, JAPAN
[b] Faculty of Engineering, Information and Systems, University of Tsukuba, Tsukuba, 305-8573, JAPAN

Abstract. In the research field of machine translation of patent documents, the issue of acquiring technical term translation equivalent pairs automatically from parallel patent documents is one of those most important. We take an approach of utilizing the phrase table of a state-of-the-art phrase-based statistical machine translation model. In this task, we consider situations where a technical term is observed in many parallel patent sentences and is translated into many translation equivalents. We apply SVM to the task of identifying synonymous translation equivalent pairs and achieve almost 98% precision and over 40% F-measure. Then, in order to improve recall, we introduce a semi-automatic framework, where we employ the strategy of selecting more than one seeds for each set of candidates bilingual synonymous term pairs. By manually judging whether each pair of two seeds is synonymous or not, we achieve over 95% precision and 50% recall.

Keywords: Bilingual Lexicon Acquisition, Synonyms, Phrase Tables

1 Introduction

For both high quality machine and human translation, a large scale and high quality bilingual lexicon is the most important key resource. Since manual compilation of bilingual lexicon requires plenty of time and huge manual labor, in the research area of knowledge acquisition from natural language text, automatic bilingual lexicon compilation have been studied. Techniques invented so far include translation term pair acquisition based on statistical co-occurrence measure from parallel sentences (Matsumoto and Utsuro, 2000), translation term pair acquisition from comparable corpora (Fung and Yee, 1998), compositional translation generation based on an existing bilingual lexicon for human use (Tonoike *et al.*, 2006), and translation term pair acquisition by collecting partially bilingual texts through the search engine (Huang *et al.*, 2005).

Among those efforts of acquiring bilingual lexicon from text, Morishita *et al.* (2008) studied to acquire technical term translation lexicon from phrase tables, which are trained by a phrase-based statistical machine translation model with parallel sentences automatically extracted from parallel patent documents. Recently, we further studied to require the acquired technical term translation equivalents to be consistent with word alignment in parallel sentences and achieved 91.9% precision with almost 70% recall. This technique has been actually adopted by a Japanese organization which is responsible for translating Japanese patent applications published by the Japanese Patent Office (JPO) into English, where it has been utilized in the process of semi-automatically compiling bilingual technical term lexicon from parallel patent sentences. In this process, persons who are working on compiling bilingual technical term lexicon judge whether to accept or not candidates of bilingual technical term pairs presented by the system.

Based on the achievement so far, in this paper, we consider situations where a technical term is observed in many parallel patent sentences and is translated into many translation equivalents. More specifically, in the task of acquiring technical term translation equivalent pairs, this paper studies the issue of identifying synonymous translation equivalent pairs. First, we collect candidates of synonymous translation equivalent pairs from parallel patent sentences. Then, we analyze features for identifying synonymous translation equivalent pairs. Finally, we apply the Support Vector Machines (SVMs) (Vapnik, 1998) to the task of identifying bilingual synonymous technical terms, and achieve the performance of almost 98% precision and over 40% F-measure. Then, in order to improve recall, we introduce a semi-automatic framework, where we employ the strategy of selecting more than one seeds for each set of candidates bilingual synonymous term pairs. By manually judging whether each pair of two seeds is synonymous or not, we achieve over 95% precision and 50% recall.

2 Japanese-English Parallel Patent Documents

In the NTCIR-7 workshop, the Japanese-English patent translation task is organized (Fujii *et al.*, 2008), where parallel patent documents and sentences are provided by the organizer. Those parallel patent documents are collected from the 10 years of unexamined Japanese patent applications published by the Japanese Patent Office (JPO) and the 10 years patent grant data published by the U.S. Patent & Trademark Office (USPTO) in 1993-2000. The numbers of documents are approximately 3,500,000 for Japanese and 1,300,000 for English. Because the USPTO documents consist of only patent that have been granted, the number of these documents is smaller than that of the JPO documents. From these document sets, patent families are automatically extracted and the fields of "Background of the Invention" and "Detailed Description of the Preferred Embodiments" are selected. This is because the text of those fields is usually translated on a sentence-by-sentence basis. Then, the method of Utiyama and Isahara (2007) is applied to the text of those fields, and Japanese and English sentences are aligned.

3 Phrase Table of an SMT Model

As a toolkit of a phrase-based statistical machine translation model, we use Moses (Koehn *et al.*, 2007) and apply it to the whole 1.8M parallel patent sentences. In Moses, first, word alignment of parallel sentences are obtained by GIZA++ (Och and Ney, 2003) in both translation directions and then the two alignments are symmetrised. Next, any phrase pair that is consistent with word alignment is collected into the phrase table and a phrase translation probability is assigned to each pair. More specifically, we construct a phrase table in the direction of Japanese to English translation, and another one in the opposite direction of English to Japanese translation. In the direction of Japanese to English translation, we finally obtain 76M translation pairs with 33M unique Japanese phrases, i.e., 2.29 English translations per Japanese phrase on average, with Japanese to English phrase translation probabilities $P(p_E \mid p_J)$ of translating a Japanese phrase p_J into an English phrase p_E. For each Japanese phrase, those multiple translation candidates in the phrase table are ranked in descending order of Japanese to English phrase translation probabilities. In the similar way, in the phrase table in the opposite direction of English to Japanese translation, for each English phrase, multiple Japanese translation candidates are ranked in descending order of English to Japanese phrase translation probabilities.

Those two phrase tables are then referred to when identifying a bilingual technical term pair, given a parallel sentence pair $\langle S_J, S_E \rangle$ and a Japanese technical term t_J, or an English technical term t_E. In the direction of Japanese to English, given a parallel sentence pair $\langle S_J, S_E \rangle$ containing a Japanese technical term t_J, the Japanese to English phrase table is referred to when identifying a bilingual technical term pair. From the Japanese to English phrase table, candidates of translating t_J into English which are consistent with word alignment are collected. Then, those English translation candidates are matched against the English sentence S_E of the parallel sentence pair, and those which are not found in S_E are filtered out. Finally, among the remaining translation candidates, $\hat{t}_E$ with the largest translation probability $P(t_E \mid t_J)$ is selected and the bilingual technical term pair $\langle t_J, \hat{t}_E \rangle$ is identified. The precision of identifying bilingual technical term pair here is 91.9%. Similarly, in the opposite direction of English to Japanese, given a parallel sentence pair $\langle S_J, S_E \rangle$ containing an English technical term t_E, the English to Japanese phrase table is referred to when identifying a bilingual technical term pair.

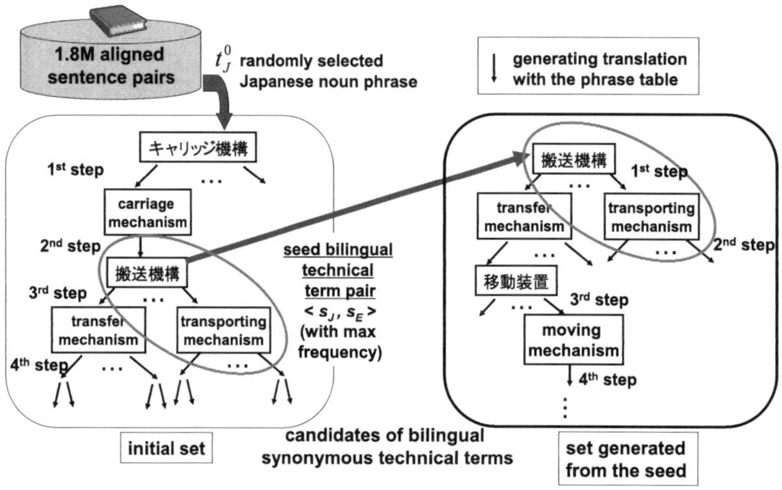

Figure 1: Developing a Reference Set of Bilingual Synonymous Technical Terms

4 Developing a Reference Set of Bilingual Synonymous Technical Terms

Table 1: Number of Bilingual Technical Terms: Candidates and Reference of Synonyms

	# of bilingual technical terms for the total 134 seeds	average per seed
Candidates of Synonyms	$\left\| \bigcup_{s_J} CBP(s_J) \right\| = 22{,}473$	167.7
Reference of Synonyms	$\left\| \bigcup_{s_{JE}} SBP(s_{JE}) \right\| = 1{,}680$	12.5

The following describes the procedure of developing a reference set of bilingual synonymous technical terms from the whole 1.8M parallel patent sentences and the Japanese to English / English to Japanese phrase tables. Figure 1 illustrates the whole procedure.

1. First, a initial Japanese noun phrase t_J^0 is randomly selected from the Japanese part of the 1.8M parallel patent sentences.
2. Then, to the initial Japanese noun phrase t_J^0, the following "Iteration: Generating Candidates Bilingual Synonymous Term Pairs" is applied, where the iteration is repeated steps of translation generation from the 1.8M parallel patent sentences and the Japanese to English / English to Japanese phrase tables[1]. Next, the initial set $CBP(t_J^0)$ of candidate bilingual

[1] The number of iteration 6 here is based on our preliminary evaluation, and is decided so that most synonymous bilingual technical terms are generated from the initial Japanese phrase t_J^0, while the number of candidates other than true synonyms is minimized. Throughout those steps, we simply avoid duplicate generation of terms.

synonymous term pairs is generated as in the left half of Figure 1.

Iteration: Generating Candidates of Bilingual Synonymous Term Pairs

1st step Given the input Japanese term t'_J, collect all the parallel sentence pairs which contain t'_J from the 1.8M parallel patent sentences. Next, from each parallel sentence pair, t'_J is translated into English according to the procedure in the previous section, referring to the Japanese to English phrase table. Then, all the bilingual term pairs $\langle t'_J, t^i_E \rangle$ are collected into the initial set $CBP(t'_J)$ of candidates bilingual synonymous term pairs[2].

2nd step Similarly, for each English term t_E in $CBP(t'_J)$, collect all the parallel sentence pairs which contain t_E from the 1.8M parallel patent sentences, and translate t_E into Japanese, referring to the English to Japanese phrase table. Then, all the bilingual term pairs $\langle t^i_J, t_E \rangle$ are added to $CBP(t'_J)$.

3rd step Similarly, for each Japanese term t_J in $CBP(t'_J)$, collect all the parallel sentence pairs which contain t_J from the 1.8M parallel patent sentences, and translate t_J into English, referring to the Japanese to English phrase table. Then, all the bilingual term pairs $\langle t_J, t^i_E \rangle$ are added to $CBP(t'_J)$.

4th step Repeat the procedure of the "2nd step".

5th step Repeat the procedure of the "3rd step".

6th step Repeat the procedure of the "2nd step".

After the candidate generation iteration, we restrict the set $CBP(t^0_J)$ as having more than or equal to 10 members (i.e., $\mid CBP(t^0_J) \mid \geq 10$). In the evaluation of this paper, out of 4,000 randomly selected initial Japanese noun phrases and corresponding initial sets $CBP(t^0_J)$, about 350 sets satisfy the lower bound of the number of members.

3. Next, out of the members of the initial set $CBP(t^0_J)$ of candidates bilingual synonymous term pairs for the initial Japanese noun phrase t^0_J, we select the seed bilingual term pair $s_{JE} = \langle s_J, s_E \rangle$ as below:

   First, in order to distinguish technical terms and general terms and to select bilingual technical term pairs as seeds, we assume the candidates of seeds to satisfy at least one of the following requirements:

   (a) The co-occurring frequency of the bilingual term pair in the 1.8M parallel patent sentences is less than 500.

   (b) The character length of the Japanese term is more than two when it contains kanji (Chinese characters) or hiragana (Japanese characters). The Japanese term consists of more than one morpheme when all of its characters are katakana (Japanese characters for foreign words).

   (c) The English term consists of more than one word.

   Then, we manually examine the bilingual term pair with the largest co-occurring frequency in the 1.8M parallel patent sentences. If the one with the largest co-occurring frequency is appropriate as a pair of technical terms, we select it as seed. Otherwise, we manually examine all the members of the initial set $CBP(t^0_J)$ and select the most appropriate pair as seed. If the initial set $CBP(t^0_J)$ does not include any pair of bilingual technical terms, we discard the set $CBP(t^0_J)$ at this step.

   In the evaluation of this paper, out of all the initial sets $CBP(t^0_J)$, for about 29% of the initial sets, we keep the bilingual term pair with the largest co-occurring frequency as seed, for about 14% of them, we manually select as seed the pair other than the one with the largest

[2] Throughout the steps from the "1st" to the "6th", we only keep bilingual term pairs which satisfy the lower bound 6 as well as the upper bound 800 of the co-occurring frequency in the 1.8M parallel patent sentences.

co-occurring frequency, and for the remaining 57%, we discard the initial sets $CBP(t_J^0)$. It took about 5.5 minutes on average to manually examine all the members of each initial set $CBP(t_J^0)$.

4. To the Japanese technical term s_J of the seed bilingual technical term pair $s_{JE} = \langle s_J, s_E \rangle$, "Iteration: Generating Candidates Bilingual Synonymous Term Pairs" is applied. As the result of this iteration, the set $CBP(s_J)$ of candidates of bilingual synonymous technical term pairs is generated as in the right half of Figure 1. Here, we again restrict the set $CBP(s_J)$ as having more than or equal to 10 members (i.e., $\mid CBP(s_J) \mid \geq 10$). In the evaluation of this paper, about 90% of the sets $CBP(s_J)$ satisfy the lower bound of the number of members. Finally, we have 134 seed bilingual technical term pairs, where the number of bilingual technical terms in total and their average are shown in Table 1.
5. Finally, for each seed bilingual technical term pair $s_{JE} = \langle s_J, s_E \rangle$, we manually divide the set $CBP(s_J)$ of candidates of bilingual synonymous technical term pairs into $SBP(s_{JE})$, those of which are synonymous with s_{JE}, and the remaining $NSBP(s_{JE})$. As in Table 1, the number of bilingual technical terms included in $SBP(s_{JE})$ in total for all of the 134 seed bilingual technical term pairs is 1,680, which amounts to 12.5 per seed on average.

5 Automatic Identification of Bilingual Synonymous Technical Terms by Machine Learning

In this section, we apply the SVMs to the task of identifying bilingual synonymous technical terms, which we originally proposed in Liang *et al.* (2011).

5.1 The Procedure

First, let CBP be the union of the sets $CBP(s_J)$ of candidates of bilingual synonymous technical term pairs for all of the 134 seed bilingual technical term pairs. In the training and testing of the classifier for identifying bilingual synonymous technical terms, we first divide the set of 134 seed bilingual technical term pairs into 10 subsets. Here, for each i-th subset ($i = 1, \ldots, 10$), we construct the union CBP_i of the sets $CBP(s_J)$ of candidates of bilingual synonymous technical term pairs, where $CBP_1, \ldots, CBP_{10}$ are 10 disjoint subsets[3] of CBP.

As a tool for learning SVMs, we use TinySVM (`http://chasen.org/~taku/software/TinySVM/`). As the kernel function, we use the polynomial (2nd order) kernel. In the testing of a SVMs classifier, we regard the distance from the separating hyperplane to each test instance as a confidence measure, and return test instances satisfying confidence measures over a certain lower bound only as positive samples (i.e., synonymous with the seed). In the training of SVMs, we use 8 subsets out of the whole 10 subsets $CBP_1, \ldots, CBP_{10}$. Then, we tune the lower bound of the confidence measure with one of the remaining two subsets (henceforth named as the *development set*). With this subset, we also tune the parameter of TinySVM for trade-off between training error and margin. Finally, we test the trained classifier against another one of the remaining two subsets (henceforth named as the *evaluation set*). We repeat this procedure of training / tuning / testing 10 times, and average the 10 results of test performance.

5.2 Features

Table 2 lists all the features used for training and testing of SVMs for identifying bilingual synonymous technical terms. Features are roughly divided into two types: those of the first type $f_1, \ldots, f_6$ simply represent various characteristics of the input bilingual technical term $\langle t_J, t_E \rangle$,

[3] Here, we divide the set of 134 seed bilingual technical term pairs into 10 subsets so that the numbers of positive (i.e., synonymous with the seed) / negative (i.e., not synonymous with the seed) samples in each CBP_i ($i = 1, \ldots, 10$) are comparative among the 10 subsets.

Table 2: Features for Identifying Bilingual Synonymous Technical Terms by Machine Learning

class	feature	definition (where X denotes J or E, and $\langle s_J, s_E\rangle$ denotes the seed bilingual technical term pair)
features for bilingual technical terms $\langle t_J, t_E\rangle$	f_1: frequency	log of the frequency of $\langle t_J, t_E\rangle$ within the whole parallel patent sentences
	f_2: rank of the Japanese term	given t_E, log of the rank of t_J with respect to the descending order of the conditional translation probability $\mathrm{P}(t_J \mid t_E)$
	f_3: rank of the English term	given t_J, log of the rank of t_E with respect to the descending order of the conditional translation probability $\mathrm{P}(t_E \mid t_J)$
	f_4: number of Japanese characters	number of characters in t_J
	f_5: number of English words	number of words in t_E
	f_6: number of times generating translation by applying the phrase tables	the number of times repeating the procedure of generating translation by applying the phrase tables until generating t_E or t_J from s_J, as in $s_J \rightarrow \cdots \rightarrow t_J \rightarrow t_E$, or, $s_J \rightarrow \cdots \rightarrow t_E \rightarrow t_J$
features for the relation of bilingual technical terms $\langle t_J, t_E\rangle$ and the seed $\langle s_J, s_E\rangle$	f_7: identity of Japanese terms	returns 1 when $t_J = s_J$
	f_8: identity of English terms	returns 1 when $t_E = s_E$
	f_9: edit distance similarity of monolingual terms	$f_9(t_X, s_X) = 1 - \frac{ED(t_X, s_X)}{\max(\lvert t_X\rvert, \lvert s_X\rvert)}$ (where ED is the edit distance of t_X and s_X, and $\lvert\, t \,\rvert$ denotes the number of characters of t.)
	f_{10}: character bigram similarity of monolingual terms	$f_{10}(t_X, s_X) = \frac{\lvert bigram(t_X) \cap bigram(s_X)\rvert}{\max(\lvert t_X\rvert, \lvert s_X\rvert)+1}$ (where $bigram(t)$ is the set of character bigrams of the term t.)
	f_{11}: rate of identical morphemes (for Japanese) / words (for English)	$f_{11}(t_X, s_X) = \frac{\lvert const(t_X) \cap const(s_X)\rvert}{\max(\lvert const(t_X)\rvert, \lvert const(s_X)\rvert)}$ (where $const(t)$ is the set of morphemes (for Japanese) / words (for English) in the term t.)
	f_{12}: subsumption relation of strings / variants relation of surface forms (for Japanese terms)	returns 1 when the difference of t_J and s_J is only in their suffixes, or only whether or not having the prolonged sound "—", or only in their hiragana parts.
	f_{13}: identical stem (for English terms)	returns 1 when the numbers of constituent words of t_E and s_E are the same, and their corresponding constituents have the same stem.
	f_{14}: hyphen / space (for English terms)	returns 1 when the difference of t_E and s_E is only whether having hyphen or space.
	f_{15}: compositional translation with an existing bilingual lexicon	returns 1 when s_J can be compositionally generated by translating constituents of t_E with an existing bilingual lexicon, or, s_E can be compositionally generated by translating constituents of t_J with an existing bilingual lexicon (Tonoike *et al.*, 2006).
	f_{16}: translation by the phrase table	returns 1 when s_J can be generated by translating t_E with the phrase table, or, s_E can be generated by translating t_J with the phrase table.

while those of the second type $f_7, \ldots, f_{16}$ represent relation of the input bilingual technical term $\langle t_J, t_E\rangle$ and the seed bilingual technical term pair $s_{JE} = \langle s_J, s_E\rangle$.

Among the features of the first type are the frequency (f_1), ranks of terms with respect to the conditional translation probabilities (f_2 and f_3), length of terms (f_4 and f_5), and the number of times repeating the procedure of generating translation with the phrase tables until generating input terms t_J and t_E from the Japanese seed term s_J (f_6).

Among the features of the second type are identity of monolingual terms (f_7 and f_8), edit distance of monolingual terms (f_9), character bigram similarity of monolingual terms (f_{10}), rate of identical morphemes / words (f_{11}), string subsumption and variants for Japanese (f_{12}), identical stems for English (f_{13}), hyphen / space of English terms (f_{14}), compositional translation with an existing bilingual lexicon[4] (f_{15}), and translation by the phrase tables (f_{16}).

5.3 Evaluation Results

Table 3: Evaluation Results of Automatic Identification of Bilingual Synonymous Technical Terms (%)

		Precision	Recall	F-measure
Baseline (t_J and s_J are identical, or, t_E and s_E are identical.)		67.0	54.3	60.8
SVM	Maximum Precision	**97.5**	28.7	43.9
	Maximum F-measure	73.5	68.1	**70.5**

Table 4: Examples of Improvement in Automatic Identification of Bilingual Synonymous Technical Terms by SVM

(a) Correctly Judging as "Synonym" only by SVM

seed $\langle s_J, s_E \rangle$	$\langle t_J, t_E \rangle$	Reference	Baseline	SVM (Maximum Precision)
⟨ホールド回路, hold circuit⟩	⟨保持回路, holding circuit⟩	synonym	not synonym	synonym

(b) Correctly Judging as "Not Synonym" only by SVM

seed $\langle s_J, s_E \rangle$	$\langle t_J, t_E \rangle$	Reference	Baseline	SVM (Maximum Precision)
⟨転写器, transfer unit⟩	⟨搬送ユニット, transfer unit⟩	not synonym	synonym	not synonym

Table 3 shows the evaluation results for a baseline as well as for SVMs. As the baseline, we simply judge the input bilingual term pair $\langle t_J, t_E \rangle$ as synonymous with the seed bilingual technical term pair $s_{JE} = \langle s_J, s_E \rangle$ when t_J and s_J are identical, or, t_E and s_E are identical. When training / testing a SVMs classifier, we tune the lower bound of the confidence measure of the distance from the separating hyperplane in two ways: i.e., for maximizing precision and for maximizing F-measure. When maximizing precision, we achieve almost 98% precision where F-measure is over 40%. When maximizing F-measure, we achieve over 70% F-measure with over 73% precision and over 68% recall.

Table 4 also show examples of improving the baseline by SVMs.

Table 4 (a) shows the case of correctly judging as "synonym" only by the proposed method. Here, the baseline judges as "not synonym", since neither t_J and s_J nor t_E and s_E are identical. With the proposed method, on the other hand, f_{13} returns 1 since "holding" and "hold" have the same stem. Also, f_{16} returns 1 since, by the phrase tables, "ホールド回路" can be generated by translating "holding circuit", and "保持回路" can be generated by translating "hold circuit".

Table 4 (b) shows the case of correctly judging as "not synonym" only by the proposed method. Here, the baseline judges as "synonym", since t_E and s_E are identical. With the proposed method,

[4] As the existing Japanese-English bilingual lexicon, Eijiro (`http://www.eijiro.jp/`, Ver.79, with 1.6M translation pairs, is used.

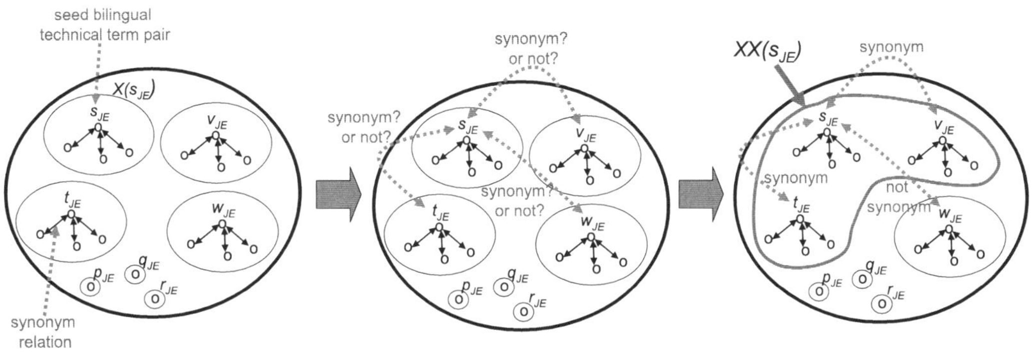

(a) Identifying synonymous pair by SVM

(b) Manually judging whether u_{JE} is synonymous with the seed if $|X(u_{JE})| > 1$

(c) Collect the members of $X(u_{JE})$ into $XX(s_{JE})$

Figure 2: The Procedure of Semi-Automatic Transitive Identification of Bilingual Technical Terms

on the other hand, both edit distance similarity f_9 and character bigram similarity f_{10} return 0 for the Japanese terms "転写器" and "搬送ユニット". Also, f_{15} returns 0 since, by compositional translation with an existing bilingual lexicon, '転写器" cannot be generated by translating "transfer unit", nor "搬送ユニット" cannot be generated by translating "transfer unit".

6 Semi-Automatic Approach to Transitive Identification of Bilingual Synonymous Technical Terms

Evaluation results of the previous section is satisfactory in terms of precision of identifying bilingual synonymous technical terms. However, its recall is relatively low, which needs to be improved. In this section, we allow semi-automatic approach to the task of identifying bilingual synonymous technical terms. In this approach, we assume that the SVM classifier trained by the procedure of section 5.1 is tuned so that it can achieve high precision against relatively easier instances, while it judges relatively harder instances as not synonymous, resulting in relatively low recall. Based on this assumption, we design a manual process which is responsible for examining whether pairs of bilingual technical terms judged by the SVM classifier as not synonymous are not actually synonymous.

6.1 The Procedure

The detailed procedure of the semi-automatic approach is presented in this section.

1st step Suppose that we are given the SVM classifier trained by the procedure of section 5.1. Then, for a set $CBP(s_J)$ of candidates of bilingual synonymous technical terms, apply the SVM classifier to every pair $u_{JE} = \langle u_J, u_E \rangle$ and $v_{JE} = \langle v_J, v_E \rangle$ of the members of $CBP(s_J)$.

2nd step Next, for each member $u_{JE} = \langle u_J, u_E \rangle$ of $CBP(s_J)$, collect u_{JE} itself and other member $v_{JE} = \langle v_J, v_E \rangle$ of $CBP(s_J)$ judged as synonymous with u_{JE} by SVM into a set $X(u_{JE})$ (Figure 2 (a))[5].

$$X(u_{JE}) = \Big\{ v_{JE} = \langle v_J, v_E \rangle \, (\in CBP(s_J)) \;\Big|\; v_{JE} = u_{JE}, \text{ or, } v_{JE} \text{ is judged as synonymous with } u_{JE} \text{ by SVM.} \Big\}$$

[5] Here, if both u^1_{JE} and u^2_{JE} are judged as synonymous with v_{JE}, but u^1_{JE} and u^2_{JE} are judged as not synonymous, we simply include both u^1_{JE} and u^2_{JE} in $X(v_{JE})$.

3rd step For each bilingual technical term pair $u_{JE} = \langle u_J, u_E \rangle$ ($\in CBP(s_J)$), if $|X(u_{JE})| > 1$ holds[6], then manually examine whether u_{JE} is synonymous with the seed bilingual technical term pair s_{JE}, i.e., whether $u_{JE} \in SBP(s_{JE})$ holds (Figure 2 (b)). If so, then collect the members of $X(u_{JE})$ into $XX(s_{JE})$ (Figure 2 (c)).

Finally, the set $XX(s_{JE})$ can be regarded as the final output of the procedure for semi-automatic transitive identification of bilingual technical terms that are judged as synonymous with the seed bilingual technical term pair s_{JE}, and can be denoted as the following formula:

$$XX(s_{JE}) = \bigcup_{u_{JE} \in SBP(s_{JE})} X(u_{JE})$$

6.2 Evaluation Results

In the evaluation, for each of the 134 seed bilingual technical term pairs, we evaluate the precision, recall, and F-measure of the set $XX(s_{JE})$. As in the case of the procedure of section 5.1, with the development set, we tune the lower bound of the confidence measure as well as the parameter of TinySVM for trade-off between training error and margin, so that we can control the precision of the set $XX(s_{JE})$ as over 80%, 85%, 90%, and 95%. Evaluation results against the evaluation set are shown in Table 5. Here, we achieve over 95% precision with more than 50% recall, and over 90% precision with almost 70% recall. As can be clearly seen from these results, by simply transitively merging the results of identifying bilingual synonymous technical terms by SVM, we can improve the recall of bilingual synonym identification task[7].

Table 5: Evaluation Results of Transitive Identification of Bilingual Synonymous Technical Terms (%)

Requirement for Precision against the Development Set	Precision	Recall	F-measure
> 80%	81.3	89.9	85.1
> 85%	86.9	80.9	83.4
> 90%	91.3	69.1	78.2
> 95%	95.2	53.1	67.9

7 Related Works

Among related works on acquiring bilingual lexicon from text, Itagaki *et al.* (2007) focused on automatic validation of translation pairs available in the phrase table learned by a statistical machine translation model, where their study differs with this paper in that Itagaki *et al.* (2007) did not study the issue of synonymous bilingual technical terms. Tsunakawa and Tsujii (2008) is mostly related to our study, in that they also proposed to apply machine learning technique to the task of identifying synonymous bilingual technical terms and that the features of machine learning studied in Tsunakawa and Tsujii (2008) are closely related those studied in this paper. However, Tsunakawa and Tsujii (2008) studied the issue of identifying synonymous bilingual technical terms only within manually compiled bilingual technical term lexicon and thus are quite limited in its applicability. Our study in this paper, on the other hand, is quite advantageous in that we start from parallel patent documents which continue to be published every year and then, that we can generate candidates of synonymous bilingual technical terms automatically.

[6] This condition means that at least one technical term pair v_{JE} is judged as synonymous with u_{JE} by SVM. Otherwise, we skip the process of manually examining the pair v_{JE}.

[7] In this evaluation, we simply measure the average number of the members u_{JE} of $SBP(s_{JE})$ for each of which $\left|X(u_{JE})\right| = 1$ holds. This number represents that, for how many members of $SBP(s_{JE})$, we can actually skip examining whether u_{JE} is synonymous with the seed bilingual technical term pair s_{JE}. Out of the average 12.5 members per seed, in Table 5, the numbers are 0.9 for "> 80%", 1.4 for "> 85%", 2.2 for "> 90%", and 4.0 for "> 95%", respectively.

Our study in this paper is also different from previous works on identifying synonyms based on bilingual and monolingual resources (e.g. Lin and Zhao (2003)) in that we learn synonymous bilingual technical terms from phrase tables of a phrase-based statistical machine translation model trained with very large parallel sentences.

In Liang *et al.* (2011), we proposed the framework of applying machine learning technique to the task of identifying bilingual synonymous technical terms in the process of acquiring technical term translation equivalent pairs from parallel patent documents. The major drawback of the framework of Liang *et al.* (2011) is in its low recall when preferring precision as over 90%. The framework proposed in Liang *et al.* (2011) is also employed in the first half of this paper, where the major contribution of this paper is in showing that the approach of manually merging synonym candidate sets identified by SVM in the first half of this paper is quite effective in improving low recall reported in Liang *et al.* (2011).

8 Conclusion

In the task of acquiring technical term translation equivalent pairs, this paper studied the issue of identifying synonymous translation equivalent pairs. We applied the SVMs to this task and achieved the performance of almost 98% precision and over 40% F-measure. Then, in order to improve recall, we simply introduced a semi-automatic framework, where we employed the strategy of selecting more than one seeds for each set of candidates bilingual synonymous term pairs. By manually judging whether each pair of two seeds is synonymous or not, we achieved over 95% precision and 50% recall. We are planning to incorporate the results of judgment by SVM when judging whether each pair of two seeds is synonymous or not.

References

Fujii, A., M. Utiyama, M. Yamamoto, and T. Utsuro. 2008. Toward the evaluation of machine translation using patent information. In *Proc. 8th AMTA*, pp. 97–106.

Fung, P. and L. Y. Yee. 1998. An IR approach for translating new words from nonparallel, comparable texts. In *Proc. 17th COLING and 36th ACL*, pp. 414–420.

Huang, F., Y. Zhang, and S. Vogel. 2005. Mining key phrase translations from Web corpora. In *Proc. HLT/EMNLP*, pp. 483–490.

Itagaki, M., T. Aikawa, and X. He. 2007. Automatic validation of terminology translation consistency with statistical method. In *Proc. MT Summit XI*, pp. 269–274.

Koehn, P., H. Hoang, A. Birch, C. Callison-Burch, M. Federico, N. Bertoldi, B. Cowan, W. Shen, C. Moran, R. Zens, C. Dyer, O. Bojar, A. Constantin, and E. Herbst. 2007. Moses: Open source toolkit for statistical machine translation. In *Proc. 45th ACL, Companion Volume*, pp. 177–180.

Liang, B., T. Utsuro, and M. Yamamoto. 2011. Identifying bilingual synonymous technical terms from phrase tables and parallel patent sentences. In *Proc. 12th PACLING*, #7.

Lin, D. and S. Zhao. 2003. Identifying synonyms among distributionally similar words. In *Proc. 18th IJCAI*, pp. 1492–1493.

Matsumoto, Y. and T. Utsuro. 2000. Lexical knowledge acquisition. In R. Dale, H. Moisl, and H. Somers, eds., *Handbook of Natural Language Processing*, ch. 24, pp. 563–610. Marcel Dekker Inc.

Morishita, Y., T. Utsuro, and M. Yamamoto. 2008. Integrating a phrase-based SMT model and a bilingual lexicon for human in semi-automatic acquisition of technical term translation lexicon. In *Proc. 8th AMTA*, pp. 153–162.

Och, F. J. and H. Ney. 2003. A systematic comparison of various statistical alignment models. *Computational Linguistics*, 29(1), 19–51.

Tonoike, M., M. Kida, T. Takagi, Y. Sasaki, T. Utsuro, and S. Sato. 2006. A comparative study on compositional translation estimation using a domain/topic-specific corpus collected from the web. In *Proc. 2nd Intl. Workshop on Web as Corpus*, pp. 11–18.

Tsunakawa, T. and J. Tsujii. 2008. Bilingual synonym identification with spelling variations. In *Proc. 3rd IJCNLP*, pp. 457–464.

Utiyama, M. and H. Isahara. 2007. A Japanese-English patent parallel corpus. In *Proc. MT Summit XI*, pp. 475–482.

Vapnik, V. N. 1998. *Statistical Learning Theory*. Wiley-Interscience.

Automatic Error Analysis Based on Grammatical Questions*

Tomoki Nagase[a], Hajime Tsukada[b], Katsunori Kotani[c],
Nobutoshi Hatanaka[d], Yoshiyuki Sakamoto[e]

[a]Fujitsu Laboratories,
1-1, Kamikodanaka, 4-chome, Nakahara-ku, Kawasaki, 211-8588, Japan
nagase.tomoki@jp.fujitsu.com
[b]NTT Communication Science Laboratories,
2-4, Hikaridai, Seika-cho, Soraku-gun, Kyoto 619-0237, Japan
tsukada.hajime@lab.ntt.co.jp
[c]Kansai Gaidai University,
16-1 Nakamiyahigashino-cho, Hirakata, Osaka 573-1001, Japan
kkotani@kansaigaidai.ac.jp
[d]Tokyo University of Information Sciences,
4-1 Onaridai,Wakaba-ku,Chiba,265-8501 Japan
hatanaka@rsch.tuis.ac.jp
[e]5-38-7, Akatsutsumi, Setagaya-ku, Tokyo, 156-0044, Japan
ysakanlp@ka2.so-net.ne.jp

Abstract. The present paper proposes automatic error analysis methods that use patterns representing grammatical check points. Our method is comparable to or slightly outperforms conventional methods for automatic evaluation metrics. Different from the conventional methods, our method enables error analysis for each grammatical check point. While our method does not depend on languages, we experimentally show its validity by using a Japanese-to-Chinese test set. Errors in existing Japanese-to-Chinese translation systems are also analyzed.

Keywords: automatic evaluation, machine translation, error analysis

1 Introduction

In the machine translation (MT) field, human evaluators subjectively evaluate the results of MT systems from the viewpoints of adequacy and fluency. However, two problems in subjective evaluations have been noted. The first is that the time and cost consumption of such evaluations is high. The second is that the evaluations have poor reproducibility due to the difficulty of reaching agreement on the scoring criteria among the evaluators. Thus, in the past decade, evaluation methods that automatically evaluate MT quality based on its similarity to a reference translation have become common (Papineni et al., 2002; Doddington, 2002; Banerjee and Lavie, 2005; Snover, et al., 2006; Melamed et al., 2007; Isozaki et al., 2010; Birch and Osborne, 2011).

Error analysis that investigates the strengths and weaknesses of a translation system is required for developing more accurate translation systems. According to the error analysis, system developers improve the translation rules/dictionaries of rule-based MT systems or add bilingual corpora/dictionaries to statistical MT systems. However, all the evaluation methods mentioned that include human subjective evaluation provide less information for error analysis because they give only one score for each document or sentence. Thus, evaluation methods have been proposed that present questions to human evaluators asking whether a sentence contains

* This work was conducted as an activity of **AAMT** (Asia-Pacific Association for Machine Translation) working group

grammatical error(s) or other type of errors (Isahara, 1995; Joans et al., 2007; Uchimoto et al., 2007; Nagase et al., 2009). These question-based evaluation methods have several features that enable the provision of new viewpoints for evaluation, the evaluation of grammatical coverage, and the provision of better metrics for evaluation combined with conventional automatic evaluation metrics.

Joans et al. (2007) used the Defense Language Proficiency Test (DLPT), which was originally developed to measure human language skills in their method. Their method enables MT quality to be evaluated from the viewpoint of "comprehension". Isahara (1995) developed the JEIDA test set, which contains example sentences and questions corresponding to each grammatical item, and proposed using it to find grammatical faults in MT systems. Nagase et al. (2009) developed a test set for a Japanese-to-Chinese MT system that expanded the JEIDA test set, and they showed that the test set was effective for analyzing the grammatical problems in Japanese-to-Chinese MT systems. Uchimoto et al. (2007) showed that an evaluation method combining question-based evaluations with conventional automatic evaluations outperforms the conventional automatic evaluation methods. All these works except that by Uchimoto et al. (2007) require human evaluators to answer the questions. Uchimoto et al. (2007) also showed that it was possible to replace question-based evaluation with matching of grammatical patterns with no performance loss. By using the pattern-matching approach, we can conduct question-based evaluation automatically without human evaluators. Uchimoto et al. (2007) aimed to improve automatic evaluation methods to use in scoring a given set of translated sentences, not for error analysis.

In this paper, we show that automatic question-based evaluation based on pattern matching can be used for error analysis, where achievement of a score for each grammatical check point is displayed. This is not obvious because the patterns for automatic evaluation are approximations of the questions for human evaluation. We reveal that the grammatical question-based evaluation can be replaced with a pattern-matching approach for the purpose of grammatical error analysis. Furthermore, we actually evaluated six existing Japanese-to-Chinese MT systems, and show the performance of our method from the viewpoint of grammatical error analysis.

2 Test Set for Evaluating Japanese-to-Chinese MT Quality

In this section, we describe the process of creating questions that enable the quality of Japanese-to-Chinese MT systems to be automatically evaluated. Section 2.1 describes the questions in previous research on manual evaluation, section 2.2 describes the concretization of the questions to reduce ambiguities, and section 2.3 explains the expansion of the questions for automatic evaluations. In this paper, we propose an evaluation method that includes both concretization and expansion of the questions.

2.1 Test Set

The JEIDA test set (Isahara 1995) is used in a method for MT quality evaluation that sheds light on the grammatical problems of MT. This test set is characterized by its yes/no questions for assessing translation results. An example of a test set sample is given below.

(1-4) Complex Predicates	Grammatical Category
私たちは研究開発をする。[1]	Japanese Sentence
We do research and development. We are carrying out research and development.	Reference Translations
The words 「研究[2]」 and 「開発[3]」 should be identified as parallel verbs.	Grammatical Check Point

1 "watashitachi wa kenkyukaihatsu wo suru." [we research&development do]
2 "kenkyu" [research]
3 "kaihatsu" [development]

Each example consists of a grammatical category, a Japanese sample sentence, its reference translation(s), and a yes/no question. Here, the yes/no questions are considered to be checked by human evaluators, not by computers.

Our first test set for Japanese-to-Chinese MT evaluation (AAMT 2008/2009, called "ver. 1" in this paper) was made based on the JEIDA test set (Japanese-to-English version) according to the following steps.

1. Translate the Japanese example sentences into Chinese (where a source sentence partially corresponds to two Chinese sentences).
2. Add a yes/no question checking the quality of the Chinese translation to each sample sentence, according to the grammatical point of the example.
3. Translate the yes/no questions into Chinese.

An example from test set ver. 1 is in Fig. 1.

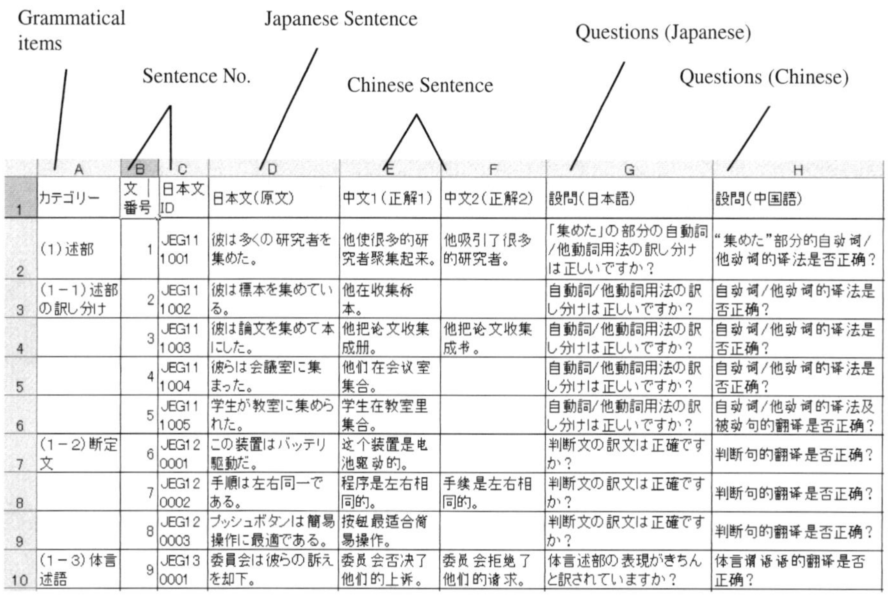

	A	B	C	D	E	F	G	H
1	カテゴリー	文番号	日本文ID	日本文(原文)	中文1(正解1)	中文2(正解2)	設問(日本語)	設問(中国語)
2	(1)述部	1	JEG111001	彼は多くの研究者を集めた。	他使很多的研究者聚集起来。	他吸引了很多的研究者。	「集めた」の部分の自動詞/他動詞用法の訳し分けは正しいですか?	"集めた"部分的自动词/他动词的译法是否正确?
3	(1−1)述部の訳し分け	2	JEG111002	彼は標本を集めている。	他在收集标本。		自動詞/他動詞用法の訳し分けは正しいですか?	自动词/他动词的译法是否正确?
4		3	JEG111003	彼は論文を集めて本にした。	他把论文收集成册。	他把论文收集成书。	自動詞/他動詞用法の訳し分けは正しいですか?	自动词/他动词的译法是否正确?
5		4	JEG111004	彼らは会議室に集まった。	他们在会议室集合。		自動詞/他動詞用法の訳し分けは正しいですか?	自动词/他动词的译法是否正确?
6		5	JEG111005	学生が教室に集められた。	学生在教室里集合。		自動詞/他動詞用法の訳し分けは正しいですか?	自动词/他动词的译法及被动句的翻译是否正确?
7	(1−2)断定文	6	JEG120001	この装置はバッテリ駆動だ。	这个装置是电池驱动的。		判断文の訳文は正確ですか?	判断句的翻译是否正确?
8		7	JEG120002	手順は左右同一である。	程序是左右相同的。	手续是左右相同的。	判断文の訳文は正確ですか?	判断句的翻译是否正确?
9		8	JEG120003	プッシュボタンは簡易操作に最適である。	按钮最适合简易操作。		判断文の訳文は正確ですか?	判断句的翻译是否正确?
10	(1−3)体言述語	9	JEG130001	委員会は彼らの訴えを却下。	委员会否决了他们的上诉。	委员会拒绝了他们的请求。	体言述部の表現がきちんと訳されていますか?	体言谓语语的翻译是否正确?

Figure 1: Example of Japanese-to-Chinese test set ver. 1

2.2 Improvement of Test Set

Test set ver. 1 did not contain enough examples; several important Chinese grammatical phenomena could not be checked in the test set because the set was based on a Japanese-to-English test set. For example, the word "not" should be translated as "不 ("bu" in Chinese)" or "没 ("mei" in Chinese)". Correctly selecting the two words "不" or "没" is important, but this point could not be checked using test set ver. 1. Thus, after review of the test set by Chinese linguists, 251 sentences for 39 newly defined grammatical check points were added to test set ver. 1. The resultant expanded test set is called ver. 2.

Table 1: Size of test set.

Test set	Number of sentences
Ver. 1	325
Ver. 2	576 (additional 251 sentences)

The answer to a question is either "Yes" or "No", and this answer must be consistent. However, when two native Chinese speakers actually evaluate MT systems using the test set, 25.7% of their answers to the questions differ (AAMT 2008/2009). For this reason, most of the questions are considered to be composed of abstract terms. The question in test set ver. 1 "Is the translation of the idiomatic expression appropriate?" is an example of an abstract question. The answer to this type of question depends on the evaluator's language skills. Thus, the questions newly added to test set ver. 2 were created based on pattern-matching questions such as "Is the expression xxxxx included in the translation?" When test set ver. 2 is applied, the rate of difference between the two evaluators is reduced to 16.1% from 25.7% (Nagase et al. 2009). This indicates that pattern-matching-based questions help to increase the objectivity of evaluations.

2.3 Expansion of Test Set for Automatic Evaluation

The test set we introduce in this section is an approximate test set with test set ver. 2 Thus, it is not logically ensured that the corresponding questions between an approximate test set and test set ver. 2 are completely consistent. As mentioned in section 2.2, the objectivity of evaluations could be increased through using questions that check whether certain words or phrases are included in the translated text. However, if compatible words (synonyms) are not included in the test set, the evaluators judge the text by their own standards. All synonyms and paraphrases must thus be prepared in advance, and they are added to each question in order to achieve a fully automatic evaluation. Examples of questions before and after rewriting are shown in Table 2.

Table 2: Examples of expanded questions.

Original questions	Expanded questions
「病気で」が「因为生病」で訳されていますか？[4]	「病気で」が「因为生病」または「由于生病」または「因为毛病」または「由于毛病」または「因为病」または「由于病」または「因病」で訳されていますか？[5]
「木で」が「用木头」で訳されていますか？[6]	「木で」が「用木头」または「拿木头」で訳されていますか？[7]

An example of a program (pseudo code) for automatic evaluation is shown in Fig. 2. It represents synonyms and phrases that should exist (or not exist) using regular expressions. Synonyms and paraphrases are exhaustively defined in the program so that an answer to a question is close to a human's evaluation.

One advantage of our method is that tokenization of Chinese sentences, which is required by conventional automatic evaluation methods, is not needed. Chinese word boundaries are very ambiguous and difficult to define, different from in western languages. Therefore, we segmented Chinese sentences by each character to calculate the scores of conventional evaluation metrics in our experiment.

---

4 Is the phrase "病気で" (byoki-de, [due to illness]) in Japanese translated as "因为生病" (yin wai sheng bin) in Chinese?

5 Is the phrase "病気で" in Japanese translated as either "因为生病", "由于生病" (you yu sheng bin), "因为毛病" (yin wai mao bin), "由于毛病" (you yu mao bin), "因为病" (in wai bin), "由于病" (you yu bin), or "因病"'(yin bin) in Chinese?

6 Is the phrase "木で" (ki-de, [by wood]) in Japanese translated as "用木头" (yong mu tou) in Chinese?

7 Is the phrase "木で" in Japanese translated as "用木头" or "拿木头" (na mu tou) in Chinese?

```
read a line;
if the line matches /严|严厉|严格|厉害/ then
    print "Yes";
else
    print "No";
endif

read a line;
if the line matches /去买东西|去购物|去逛街|去逛商店/ then
    print "Yes";
else
    print "No";
endif
```

Figure 2: Pseudo codes for automatic evaluation.

3 Experiments and Discussion

3.1 Experimental Method

In this section, we describe the experiment carried out to verify the effectiveness of our automatic evaluation method proposed in section 2. In this experiment, we used the test set consisting of 251 examples (39 grammatical items) that were added for checking grammatical phenomena specific to Chinese. Using our experimental results, we discuss the performance of our automatic evaluation method from the perspective of correlation with a human's objective evaluations, in comparison with those of traditional automatic evaluation methods. Moreover, we discuss the degree of agreement between our proposed method and a human's evaluation (both being question-based). To discuss the above points, the experiment was carried out as follows.

(1) Manual evaluation by human:
- Manual evaluation by human: 2 people (native Chinese speakers)
- Points of evaluation
  - Adequacy: rating on a 1–5 scale by referring to the source sentence and the translation result
  - Fluency: rating on a 1–5 scale by referring to the translation result
  - Question: answering "yes" or "no" to the question by referring to the translation result

(2) Automatic evaluation by program:
- Conventional automatic evaluation metrics based on characters: BLEU, NIST, WER, PER
- Automatic evaluation answering the questions

The two evaluators were native Chinese speakers having linguistic knowledge who had achieved mastery of the Japanese language. Six Japanese-to-Chinese MT systems accessible on the Internet were used as the targets of the experiments. Four out of the six systems use a rule-based MT (RBMT), and two use a statistical MT (SMT).

3.2 Results and Discussion

The coefficients of correlation (Pearson product-moment correlation coefficient) for the MT evaluation scores were examined for six evaluation methods. This was to ensure that our method shows adequate performance compared to conventional automatic evaluation methods. The average score of two evaluators for each sample sentence was used in the comparisons and analyses.

The coefficients of correlation in every combination were very high (Table 3). The reason could be that the lengths of the source sentences were fairly short, in contrast to those in the normal test sets.

Table 3: Coefficients of correlation between automatic evaluations and conventional subjective evaluations.

Methods	Adequacy	Fluency
BLEU	0.9453	0.9588
NIST	0.9783	0.9123
WER	-0.9801	-0.9267
PER	-0.9707	-0.8986
Questions (human)	0.9793	0.9334
Questions (automatic)	0.9902	0.9208

As shown in Tables 3, 4, and 5, our question-based methods highly correlated with subjective evaluations from the viewpoints of fluency and adequacy. The results of a t-test indicate that the correlations between our method and subjective evaluation (fluency and adequacy) achieved statistical significance with a 1% significance level. The correlation coefficients obtained by our methods exceed those of the conventional automatic evaluations. Considering from the above results, our methods may supplement and be a possible alternative to current subjective evaluations. In addition, the performance of our methods compares favorably with that of the conventional automatic evaluations.

Table 4: Frequency distribution of answered pattern (Auto-Human1)

Same	Yes-Yes	425	1181	0.784
	No-No	756		
Different	Yes-No	222	325	0.216
	No-Yes	103		

Table 5: Frequency distribution of answered pattern (Auto-Human2)

Same	Yes-Yes	473	1179	0.783
	No-No	706		
Different	Yes-No	174	327	0.217
	No-Yes	153		

Table 6: Frequency distribution of answered pattern (Human1-Human2)

Same	Yes-Yes	456	1264	0.839
	No-No	808		
Different	Yes-No	170	242	0.161
	No-Yes	72		

Tables 4 and 5 show the number of scoring patterns ("Yes-Yes", "No-No", "Yes-No", and "No-Yes") scored automatically and manually. Table 6 shows the number of scoring patterns for the two human evaluators. All evaluators must answer a question with either "Yes" or "No". When the answering pattern is "Yes-Yes" or "No-No", the pattern type is "the same"; in other cases, it is "different". Between the automatic evaluation and manual evaluation, the rates of "the same" were 74.8 and 78.3% for "Yes-Yes" and "No-No" respectively. Between the two evaluators, it is 83.9%, which slightly exceeds the rates in Tables 4 and 5. Table 7 shows the

Kappa coefficients calculated using the values in Tables 4, 5, and 6. They are all considerably high, exceeding 0.5.

Table 7: Kappa coefficients between automatic and human evaluation-based questions.

Methods	Kappa coefficient
Automatic : Human (Evaluator-1)	0.5494
Automatic : Human (Evaluator-2)	0.5552
Human (Evaluator-1) : Human (Evaluator-2)	0.6616

The results of a t-test indicate that the agreement of yes/no answering between the automatic evaluation and human evaluation achieved statistical significance with a 1% significance level. This indicates that the automatic question-based method can be used on behalf of human question-based method although the questions of both methods are not exactly the same.

3.3 Evaluation of Grammatical Achievement of Japanese-to-Chinese MT Systems

The question-based evaluation method not only enables MT quality to be quantified but also brings out the strengths and weaknesses of a MT system. The scores of the questions in six Japanese-to-Chinese MT systems (labeled A–F) were averaged, where the answers "Yes" and "No" correspond to the scores "1" and "0", respectively. Figure 3 graphs the evaluation scores with the averages of the six systems according to each grammatical item.

The averages for each system greatly varied among the grammatical items shown in Table 8. For example, most systems were accurate for items No. 9 (sentences including "有" ("*you*" in Chinese)) and No. 10 (adjectival predicates), while almost no systems worked well for items No. 31 (expressions of possibility) and No. 32 (expressions of voluntary) among others. From the low-scored items, there might be problems common among Japanese-to-Chinese MT systems. As a whole, the current Japanese-to-Chinese MT systems are considered to have much room for development because the averages exceeded 0.5 only in 10 items out of the 39.

Comparing the systems, a big difference exists between systems A–D and systems E and F. It is noteworthy that the first- and second-lowest scored systems (E and F) are Statistical MT systems, while the others are rule-based ones. The properties of SMT might limit the improvement of the translation quality. Fifteen and twelve items in systems E and F respectively scored zero, and eleven of these items were the same. In these eleven items, it is possible that the particularly badly scored items, such as No. 15 (expressions of desire), No. 22 (expressions of experience), No. 30 (passive sentences), and No. 37 ("越-越" ("*yue-yue*" in Chinese) according to "すればするほど" ("*sureba suruhodo*" in Japanese) phrases) contain characteristic problems of SMT.

From Fig. 3, we can see that system D obtained a high score for almost all the items, but for No. 34 (honorific) and No. 19 ("了" ("*la*") and "着" ("*zhe*" in Chinese) according to "--ている"("*--teiru*" in Japanese)), the scores were exceptionally below the average for the six systems. In contrast, the scores for systems E and F were relatively bad, but for items No. 16 (prepositions), No. 14 (expressions of permission), and No. 39 (idiomatic phrases), the scores exceeded the average for the six systems.

These data examined above would be quite useful for developers of MT systems. Such data were not obtained by previous automatic evaluation methods. Developers can recognize the strengths and weaknesses of their own systems from the graphs, which can be used as feedback to the developers for deciding the approach to and priority of development candidates.

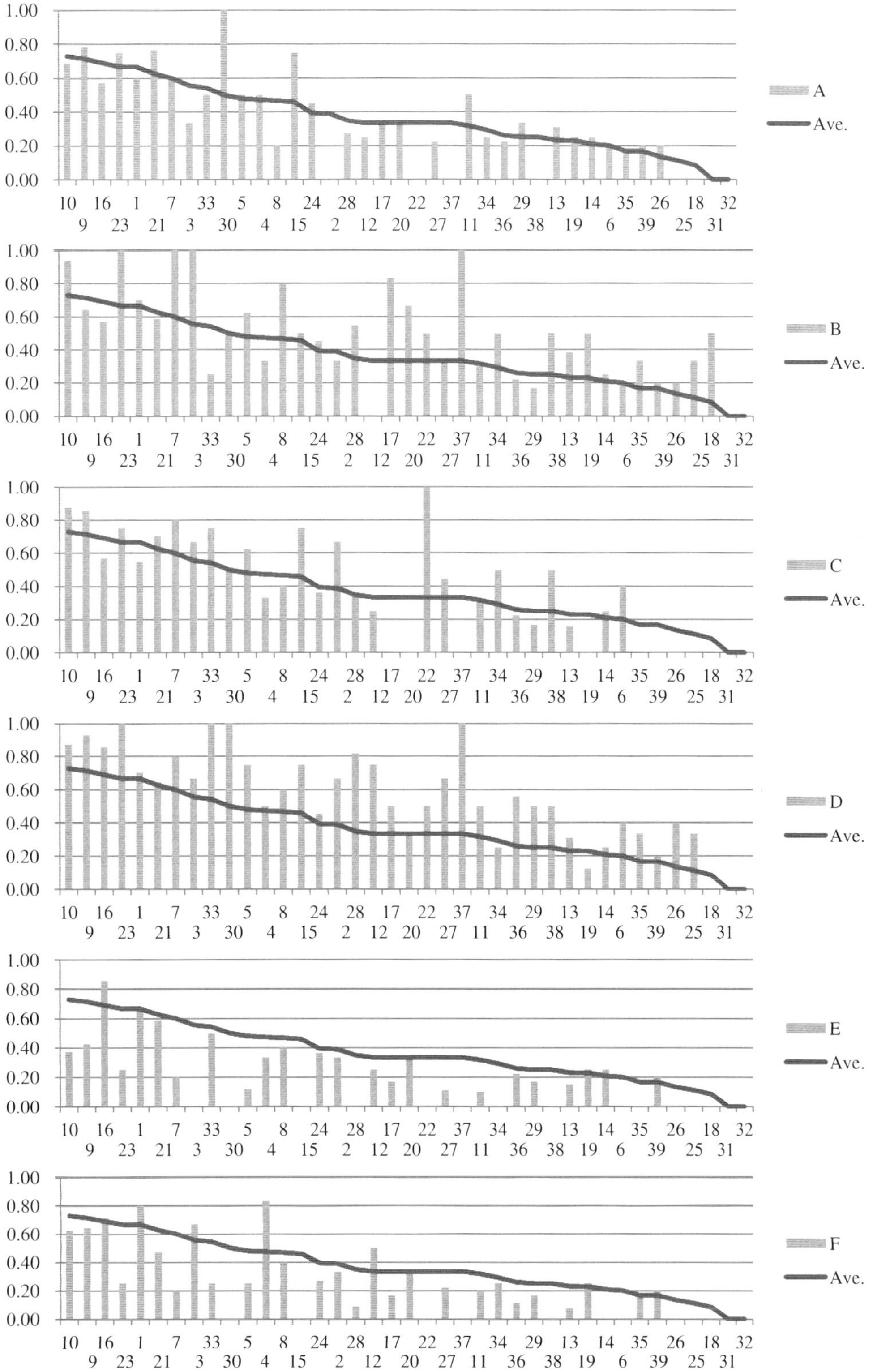

Figure 3: Average scores of question-based evaluation for each grammatical item.

Table 8: Grammatical items.

1	"的" (de) according to "の" (no)	21	Expressions according to "--ている" (--teiru)
2	"的" (de) according to "V た" (da)	22	Expressions of experience
3	"的" (de) according to "もの" (mono)	23	Transitive/Intransitive verbs
4	Location words	24	Particles
5	Interrogatives	25	Sentences ending with "のだ" (noda)
6	Negative sentences	26	Sentences including "把" (ba)
7	Selecting "不" (bu) and "没" (mei)	27	Complements
8	Sentences including "在" (zai)	28	Causative Sentences
9	Sentences including "有" (you)	29	Passive sentences using "被" (bei)
10	Adjectival predicates	30	Passive sentences not using "被" (bei)
11	Pivotal sentences	31	Expressions of possibility
12	Verb phrases with two objects	32	Expressions of voluntariness
13	Auxiliary verbs	33	Respectful phrases
14	Expressions of permission ("可以" (keyi))	34	Honorific expressions
15	Expressions of wish	35	Sentences ending with "ようだ・そうだ" (youda/souda)
16	Prepositions	36	Expressions of solicitation
17	Expressions of comparison	37	"越-越" (yue-yue) according to "すればするほど" (surebasuruhodo)
18	"刚刚" (gang gang) according to "--したばかり" (--shitabakari)	38	Prepositions
19	"着" (zhe) "了" (la) according to "ている" (--teiru)	39	Idiomatic phrases
20	Sentences including "了" (la)		

4 Conclusion and Future Work

We proposed a question-based automatic evaluation method that does not depends on languages, validated out our method in Japanese-to-Chinese translation, and showed its effectiveness by the error analysis of existing six translation systems. Our method has high correlation with subjective evaluations by humans, even when only our method is used (which is comparable to conventional automatic evaluation methods and question-based evaluation by humans). We verified that the results of our automatic evaluation method are consistent with that of human evaluation for each question, and clarified that our method can be used for error analysis of grammatical items. In particular, by visualizing the scores for each grammatical item on a graph, valuable information related to the characteristics of each MT system became visible. We are planning to provide a web service that automatically evaluates MT quality and to provide information on the strengths and weaknesses of an MT system through a cobweb chart and others.

The automatization of question-based evaluation yields not only increased efficiency due to the reduced number of evaluators, but also enhanced reliability of the evaluation by improving objectivity. In an evaluation using a question-based method, 16.1% of the answers of two evaluators differed. However, in the case of automatic evaluation, the answers are always the same. Our experiment indicated that a question-based automatic evaluation method could be closer to a human subjective evaluation than a question-based human evaluation.

Problems of a question-based evaluation method are that sentences must be prepared that include grammatical items for conducting error analysis, and that questions must be prepared that include the words to be checked as well as sets of synonyms and paraphrases. If these preparations could be done automatically, the efficiency of the evaluation process would be dramatically enhanced. In addition, the grammatical items, which are useful for error analysis, are also defined by a human. In the future, a method for automatically preparing test sentences, the grammatical items, and their questions should be investigated.

References

AAMT Working Group. 2008. Toward Building of AAMT Test-sets for Quality Evaluation of Machine Translation. *AAMT Journal No.42*, 18-24.

AAMT Working Group. 2009. Toward Publication of AAMT Test-sets for Quality Evaluation of Machine Translation. *AAMT Journal No.45*, 29-30.

Banerjee, S. and A. Lavie. 2005. METEOR: An Automatic Metric for MT Evaluation with Improved Correlation with Human Judgments. *Proc. of the ACL Workshop on Intrinsic and Extrinsic Evaluation Measures for Machine Translation and/or Summarization*, 65–72.

Birch,. A. and M. Osborne, Reordering Metrics for MT. 2011. *Proc. of ACL-HLT,* 1027–1035.

Doddington G. 2002. Automatic Evaluation of Machine Translation Quality using N-gram Co-occurrence Statistics. *Proc. of HLT*, 138–145.

Isahara, H. 1995. JEIDA's Test-Sets for Quality Evaluation of MT Systems --Technical Evaluation from the Developer's Point of View--. *Proceedings of MT Summit V.*

Isozaki, H., T. Hirao, K. Duh, K. Sudoh and H. Tsukada. 2010. Automatic Evaluation of Translation Quality for Distant Language Pairs. *Proc. of EMNLP,* 944–951.

Melamed, D., Green, R., and Turian, J. P. 2007. Precision and Recall of Machine Translation. *Proc. of NAACL-HLT,* 61–63.

Nagase, T., K. Kotani, M. Nagata, N. Hatanaka, Y. Sakamoto, E. Sumita and K. Uchimoto. 2009. Evaliation of Japanese-Chinese MT System using AAMT's Test-Set. *Proc. Of The 5th China Workshop on Machine Translation*, 211-218.

Papineni K., S. Roukos, T. Ward, and W. Zhu. 2002. BLEU: A Method for Automatic Evaluation of Machine Translation. *Proc. of ACL*, 311–318.

Snover, Matthew., B. Dorr, R. Schwartz, L. Micciulla, and J. Makhoul. 2006. A Study of Translation Edit Rate with Targeted Human Annotation. *Proc. of AMTA*, 223–231.

Uchimoto, K., K. Kotani, Y. Zhang and H. Isahara. 2007. Automatic Evaluation of Machine Translation Based on ate of Accomplishment of Sub-goals. *Proceedings of NAACL HLT*, 33-40.

Maximum Entropy Based Lexical Reordering Model for Hierarchical Phrase-based Machine Translation

Zhongguang Zheng, Yao Meng, Hao Yu

Fujitsu R&D Center CO., LTD.
15/F, Tower A, Ocean International Center, No.56 Dongsihuan Zhong Rd.
Chaoyang District, Beijing, 100025, China
{zhengzhg, mengyao, yu}@cn.fujitsu.com

Abstract. The hierarchical phrase-based (HPB) model on the basis of a synchronous context-free grammar (SCFG) is prominent in solving global reorderings. However, the HPB model is inadequate to supervise the reordering process so that sometimes positions of different lexicons are switched due to the incorrect SCFG rules. In this paper, we consider the order of two lexicons as a classification problem and propose a novel lexical reordering model based on a maximum entropy classifier. Our model employs the word alignment and translation during the decoding process. Experimental results on the Chinese-to-English task showed that our method outperformed the baseline system in BLEU score significantly. Moreover, the translation results further proved the effectiveness of our approach.

Keywords: hierarchical phrase-based model, reordering, maximum entropy model

1 Introduction

Reordering is a big challenge for statistical machine translation (SMT). The hierarchical phrase-based (HPB) translation model (Chiang, 2005), which adopts a synchronous context-free grammar (SCFG), is considered to be prominent in capturing global reorderings. However, the HPB model is weak in controlling the reordering process. Arbitrary reorderings frequently come up during the decoding phase, worsening the translation quality, such as the example shown in Figure 1(a). The non-terminal "X_2" is reordered with "X_1" and "*anshui rongye*", but the punctuation "、" indicates that the phrase should be translated monotonously.

This kind of reordering error frequently occurs when target phrases contain similar lexicons, which include both terminals and non-terminals, with different permutations, e.g., the rules in Figure 1(b). We believe that there are mainly two reasons that the HPB model can not distinguish such ambiguous rules properly.

- The extraction of SCFG rules is merely based on the word alignment information. Thus any form of rules could be obtained. As shown in Figure 1, the same Chinese part "X_1 *anshui rongye* X_2" corresponds to different target rules "X_2 X_1 ammonia solution" and "X_1 ammonia solution X_2", which contain the same English words but differ in word order. The order of non-terminals should depend on their concrete translations and contexts. However, the decoder does not take into account those factors when reorderings happen.
- There are not enough features to evaluate the correctness of word order for SCFG rules. Conventionally, the HPB model has 8 features (Chiang, 2005), including language model, constituent feature, word penalty, phrase penalty, bi-direction translation weights $P(\gamma|\alpha)$ and $P(\alpha|\gamma)$, bi-direction lexical weights $P_w(\gamma|\alpha)$ and $P_w(\alpha|\gamma)$, but none of them is responsible for the rationality of word order. Although language model evaluates the fluency of target

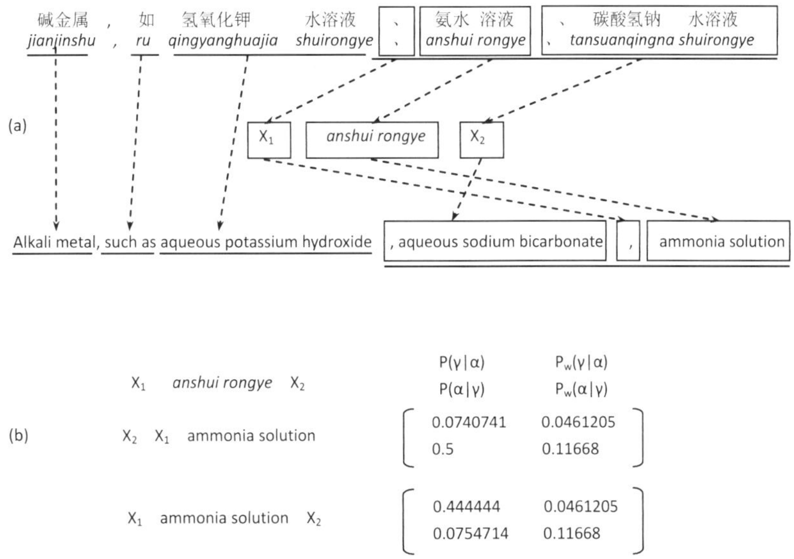

Figure 1: Incorrect reordering.

string, it considers the target words only. As shown in Figure 1(b), the two SCFG rules have different probabilities given by $P(\gamma|\alpha)$, $P(\alpha|\gamma)$ and language model, but they do not yield correct result.

Various methods have been proposed in order to solve the reordering problem for HPB model. Some of them focus on the sentence rewriting in the preprocessing stage (Xia and McCord, 2004; Collins *et al.*, 2005; Wang *et al.*, 2007; Tromble and Elsner, 2009; Du and Way, 2010). The main idea of those studies is to rewrite source language in order to make the source word sequence close to the target language before training and testing by various syntactic methodologies. Those offline rewriting methods are independent of the decoder. Thus other useful information such as word translation generated in the decoding process cannot be utilized. Moreover, offline methods require syntax analysis which does not always produce convincing result on certain languages. The parsing error will result in wrongly reordered sentences so that the translations cannot be correct.

Shen *et al.* (2008, 2009) proposed a string-to-dependency language model to capture long-distance word order. He *et al.* (2010) classified SCFG rules into different patterns and built a maximum entropy classifier to select proper translation rules during decoding. Analogously, Cui *et al.* (2010) proposed a joint model for SCFG rule selection. Four sub-models which include context free model and context based model are used to predict proper rules. Both source and target strings are considered simultaneously in the model. Hayashi *et al.* (2010) integrated the method of (Tromble and Elsner, 2009) into the decoder as a source language model. Those online methods are involved in the decoding phase as a soft constraint to bias the decoder toward certain SCFG rules that are considered appropriate. This paper proposes a lexical reordering model based on the maximum entropy model for the HPB model, and we also integrate our model into the decoder to exploit various information during decoding.

The rest of this paper is organized as follows. Section 2 introduces the related work. In Section 3, we describe the implementation of the maximum entropy based lexical reordering model and the integration into the decoder. Experiment on the Chinese-to-English task is shown in Section 4, followed by a discussion in Section 5. The conclusion and future work are presented in Section 6.

2 Previous Related Work

2.1 Online Reordering Methods

Comparing with the offline method, online method is able to utilize various useful information during decoding. Shen *et al.* (2008) proposed a string-to-dependency target language model to capture long distance word orders. Furthermore, Shen *et al.* (2009) extended the work by applying more features such as phrase length distribution and context language model. Shen *et al.* (2009) also intended to build a dependency language model on the source language, but the result reported a decline with this feature. He *et al.* (2010) classified SCFG rules into several fixed patterns. For example, the rule $<X_1$ *anshui rongye* X_2, X_2 X_1 ammonia solution$>$ belongs to the pattern $<X_1\mathrm{F}X_2$, $X_2X_1\mathrm{E}>$. A maximum entropy classifier is trained to select rules according to the patterns on the both source and target sides. This method is insensitive to the terminal order.

Our work is somewhat similar to the word-based reordering model proposed by Hayashi *et al.* (2010). In order to differ from their work, we name our approach a lexical reordering model, and the differences between the two methods are described below.

- Our method does not change the original HPB model. The former research changes HPB model from Equation 2 to

$$X \longrightarrow < \gamma, \gamma', \alpha, \sim > \tag{1}$$

  where γ' is the rewriting string of γ.

- Former research needs to consider the positions of unaligned words after rewriting a source string. But there is no such a problem with our model since we do not rewrite sentences.
- During the decoding process, our model employs the target language and word alignment information which are not included in the former research. The translation and alignment information will benefit the word order disambiguation to some extent. For example, Chinese phrase "A 的(*de*) B" can be translated into English phrases "A 's B" and "B of A". The order between "A" and "B" is determined by the translation of "*de*".

  Furthermore, word alignment information is also useful. Recall the example of Figure 1, "*anshui*" and "、" are ambiguous words for the rewriting method, since both "*anshui* 、" and "、 *anshui*" are reasonable phrases that should be translated without reordering. However, if a rule reorders "*anshui*" and "、" according to the word alignment, it is probably incorrect and should not be used here.
- The former research worked on the Japanese-to-English task, while ours works on the Chinese-to-English task.

2.2 Hierarchical Phrase-Based Model

The hierarchical phrase-based (HPB) model (Chiang, 2005), which is based on a synchronous context-free grammar (SCFG), is presented in the form

$$X \longrightarrow < \gamma, \alpha, \sim > \tag{2}$$

where X is a non-terminal, γ and α denote source and target strings, which contain both terminals and non-terminals. $\sim$ is the one-to-one correspondence between terminals and non-terminals in γ and α. Chiang (2005) integrated all the features mentioned in the first section into the log-linear framework (Och and Ney, 2002)

$$P(e|f) \propto \sum_i \lambda_i h_i(\gamma, \alpha) \tag{3}$$

where $h_i(\gamma, \alpha)$ is a feature function and λ_i is the weight of h_i. One merit of the log-linear framework is that we are able to adopt various features into the HPB model conveniently. Hence we intend to complement the HPB model with our proposed method as a new feature.

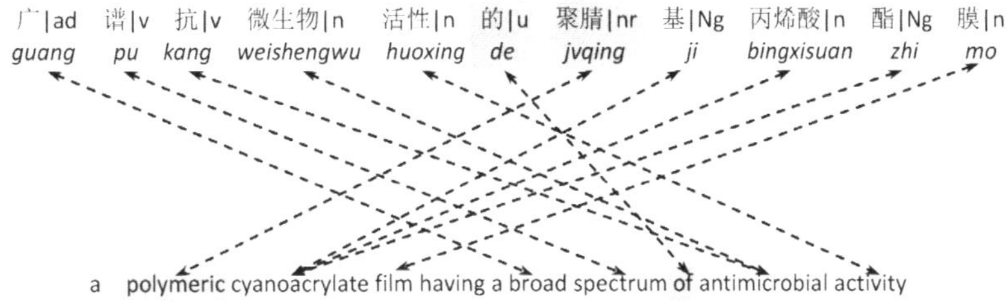

Figure 2: Sentence pair with word alignment.

Table 1: Features extracted from "*de*" and "*jvqing*".

Feature	Feature Value
Feat1	order=0 lw=*de* lp=u lt=of rw=*jvqing* rp=nr rt=polymeric
Feat2	order=0 lw=*de* lp=u lt=of rw=*null* rp=nr rt=polymeric
Feat3	order=0 lw=*null* lp=u lt=of rw=*jvqing* rp=nr rt=polymeric

3 Maximum Entropy Based Lexical Reordering Model

3.1 Overview of the Model

A score S_{re} is calculated using the maximum entropy based lexical reordering model for each SCFG rule

$$S_{re}(r) = log(\prod_{i,j:1 \leq i < j \leq n} P_{re}(order_{i,j}|\phi_{i,j})) \tag{4}$$

where i and j are subscripts of the source words in rule r. $\phi_{i,j}$ is a set of features extracted from w_i and w_j. $order_{i,j}$ presents the position relationship between w_i and w_j. According to the word alignment, $order_{i,j}$ equals "0" when w_i and w_j are reordered, otherwise $order_{i,j}$ equals "1".

3.2 Feature Extraction

The feature extraction is carried out together with SCFG rule extraction. We use GIZA++ (Och and Ney, 2003) to obtain word alignment on the training set. Given a word aligned sentence pair $\langle f, e \rangle$, where $f = \{w_0, ..., w_n\}$, we select translations, part of speech (POS) tags and the order relationship of w_i and w_j as features. Firstly, we employ a non-linguistic constraint to limit the distance between w_i and w_j, which is described as follows.

Constraint 1. Non-linguistic constraint.

- w_i and w_j must be in the same $initial\ phrase\ pair$ defined by Chiang (2005).
- $|j - i| \leq Threshold\_Word\_Scope$.

$Threshold\_Word\_Scope$ is an empirical threshold used to avoid arbitrary selection of word pairs in case of useless information. We also adopt linguistic rules to capture collocations that reveal word order explicitly when they violate the non-linguistic constraint.

There are many linguistic phenomena between Chinese and English that indicate the word order explicitly, even though they often violate the $initial\ phrase\ pair$ constraint. Du and Way (2010) studied the reorderings of "*de*" structures for Chinese to English translation and their experiment reported a significant improvement. Linguistic knowledge acquisition generally requires language analysis tools such as dependency parser. However, the "*de*" structure is relatively easier to capture without parsing the sentence in that word "*de*" is closely related to its context words. Therefore,

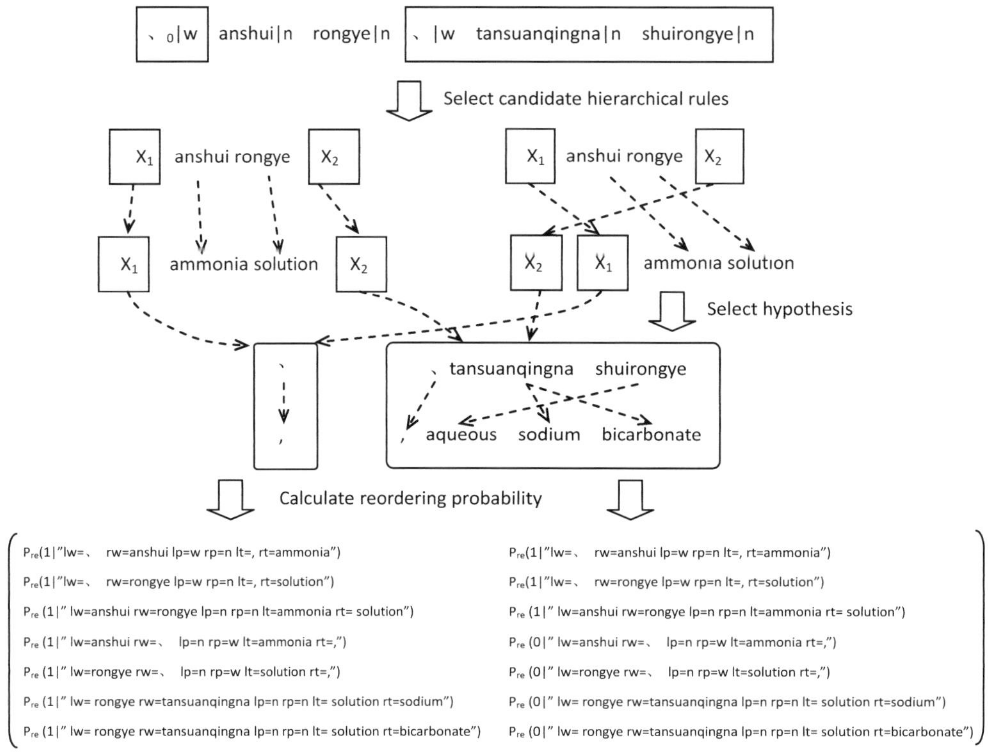

Figure 3: The process of computing reordering probabilities for SCFG rules.

we especially propose a linguistic constraint based on the Chinese word "*de*" when the word pair violates the non-linguistic constraint.

Constraint 2. Linguistic constraint.

- w_i or w_j is Chinese auxiliary word "*de*".
- $|j - i| \leq Threshold\_Word\_Scope.$

The linguistic constraint is simple but effective. Figure 2 shows a sentence pair with word alignments. If confine an initial phrase pair to the maximum coverage of 10 source words, we will lose the collocations such as "*de*" and "*jvqing*", which indicates a reordering, by only considering the non-linguistic constraint. In this case, the linguistic constraint is helpful to complement the lost collocations. Table 1 lists all the features extracted from word pair "*de*" and "*jvqing*", where "w", "p" and "t" stand for word, POS and translation, respectively. "*null*" denotes empty word. Note that there is a default precondition that w_i and w_j must both have alignments.

3.3 Model Training

There is a simple way to calculate the reordering probability using maximum likelihood estimation (MLE) method, which is in the form

$$P_{re}\left(order_{i,j}|\phi_{i,j}\right) = \frac{count\left(order_{i,j}, \phi_{i,j}\right)}{count\left(\phi_{i,j}\right)} \quad (5)$$

where $count\left(*\right)$ is the occurrence of $*$ in the training set, and $\phi_{i,j}$ is a set of features. However, MLE method faces the severe data sparsity.

Table 2: Information of our data sets.

Data Set		Sentence Number	Word Number
Training Set	Ch	100k	3.7M
	En	100k	4.4M
Development Set	Ch	1.0k	37.5K
	En	1.0k	33.8K
Test Set	Ch	1.0k	38.8K
	En	1.0k	34.2K

Table 3: Experiment results of different settings of $Threshold\_Word\_Scope$.

$Threshold\_Word\_Scope$	MLE	ME
2	30.05%	30.17%
3	30.32%	30.66%
4	29.76%	29.96%

On the other hand, the order of two words is either monotone or inverse which means it belongs to a binary classification task. The maximum entropy (ME) classifier is suitable for solving this kind of problem and has been successfully applied in many previous studies. The ME model we trained is in the form

$$p_{re}(o|w_l, w_r) = \frac{\exp(\sum_i \lambda_i h_i(o, w_l, w_r))}{\sum_o \exp(\sum_i \lambda_i h_i(o, w_l, w_r))} \tag{6}$$

where o denotes the order of two source words w_l and w_r, h_i is a feature function and λ_i is the weight of h_i.

3.4 Integrating Our Model into the Decoder

Given a source sentence s, candidate SCFG rules are first selected from the rule table. For one candidate rule r, all the source words it covers are easy obtained according to the rule span. Since word alignments are also known beforehand, it is easily to extract features described in 3.2 for each two terminals in r. As to non-terminals, we extract features from their boundary terminals in each hypothesis during the cube-pruning. The reordering probability of r is then calculated using Equation 4. Here, again, we limit the computational scope with the following constraints.

Constraint 3. Suppose w_i and w_j are source words containing either terminals or non-terminals of r. The subscripts denote the word positions in r. We calculate reordering probability of that word pair only when

- Neither w_i nor w_j aligns to empty word.
- There is at most one non-terminal between w_i and w_j.
- $\left|j' - i'\right| \leq Threshold\_Word\_Scope$, where j' and i' denote the original positions of w_i and w_j in s.

Figure 3 depicts the process of distinguishing the two rules of Figure 1(b) by our method with the setting $Threshold\_Word\_Scope = 2$. The incorrect rule will be assigned with a lower order probability so that it is probably ignored in the cube pruning.

4 Experiment

4.1 Data Set

We conducted experiments on Chinese-to-English patent translation. On the one hand, word order is different between Chinese and English, thus it is a sensible testbed for our model. On the other

Table 4: Experiment results of all the systems. "*" denotes significant better than the baseline system at $p < 0.01$.

System ID	Language Model	BLEU
Baseline system	4-gram	29.74%
Baseline 5-gram	5-gram	30.37%
Baseline 6-gram	6-gram	30.27%
MLE	4-gram	30.32%*
ME-no-de	4-gram	30.28%*
ME-all	4-gram	30.66%*

Table 5: The ambiguous SCFG rules.

	Source Rules	Ambiguous Target Rules	
Sentence 1	(X_1	(X_1	X_1 (
Sentence 2	X_1 texing	X_1 characteristic	characteristic X_1

hand, since the language of patent text is well organized and constrained in expression, our model would be more suitable for this kind of data.

Our data set is a part of NTCIR-9 Patent Machine Translation Task (PatentMT) Document Data provided by NTCIR-9 Workshop[1]. We selected 100,000 sentence pairs randomly from the whole data set as our training set, and then divided the original development set into our development set and test set respectively. Table 2 shows the information of our data sets in detail.

4.2 Experimental Setup

Our experiments were on Chinese-to-English patent translation. Chinese word segmentation and POS tagging was implemented using an in-house Chinese word segmentation toolkit. The English tokenization was implemented using our own script.

GIZA++ (Och and Ney, 2003) was run in both translation directions to obtain the word alignment on the training set, and then the alignment result was refined by "grow-diag-final" method (Koehn, 2003).

For the language model, we used the SRI Language Modeling Toolkit (SRILM) (Stolcke, 2002) to train three language models from 4-gram to 6-gram on the target portion of the training set. Considering that long distance language models may influence the word order on the target string, it makes sense to compare our model with those long distance language models.

We used the minimum error rate training algorithm (MERT) (Och, 2003) for tuning the feature weights of the log-linear model, and adopted BLEU (Papineni *et al.*, 2002) as our evaluation metric. An open source Maximum Entropy Toolkit (Zhang, 2004) was employed to train our lexical model.

We implemented two systems based on maximum likelihood estimation (MLE) and maximum entropy (ME) model, respectively. Our experiments were carried out in two steps.

Firstly, in order to find out the most effective model settings, we tested different values of the threshold $Threshold\_Word\_Scope$ on the both systems. The results are shown in Table 3.

From the results, the ME based systems produce better results than the MLE based systems. This indicates that the ME classifier is more suitable for our approach. The best performance is achieved by setting $Threshold\_Word\_Scope = 3$, which was adopted as the final setting in the rest of the experiments. It is a reasonable result that we could not get enough features in a smaller scope and may obtain too much noise in a larger scope.

[1] http://research.nii.ac.jp/ntcir/index-en.html

Src1	weishengyongpin[*hygiene article*] , tebieshi[*particular*] niaobu[*diaper*] (yinger[*infant*] 、 shijin[*incontinent*] chengren[*adult*]) 、 nvxing[*feminine*] weishegnyongpin [*hygiene article*] ,
BL	Hygiene products, in particular (baby diapers, incontinent adult), feminine hygiene products,
MEL	Hygiene products, particular diapers (baby, incontinent adult), feminine hygiene products,
RF	Sanitary articles, in particular diapers (infant, incontinent adult), feminine hygiene products,
Src2	kepeizhi[*configurable*] canshu[*parameter*] 375 (liru[*such as*] shujv[*data*] leixing[*category*] , shujv[*data*] dingxiang[*orientation*], he[*and*] shujv[*data*] texing[*characteristic*]) ,
BL	configurable parameters 375 characteristics (e. g., data type, orientation and data),
MEL	configurable parameters 375 (e. g., data type, data orientation and data characteristics),
RF	configurable parameters 375 (such as data categories, data orientations and data characteristics),
Src3	canzhao[*refer*] tu[*figure*] 7 , yonghu[*user*] dui[to] caidan[*menu*] xuanxiang[*option*] 607 de[*'s*] xuanze[*selection*] (tu[*figure*] 6)
BL	Referring now to Figure 7, the user selects to menu options 607 (Figure 6)
MEL	Referring to FIG.7, user selection of the menu options 607 (Figure 6)
RF	Referring to FIG. 7, the user's selection of menu option 607 (FIG. 6)

Figure 4: The actual influence of our method on translation results. Src: The source sentence. BL: Translation of Baseline system. MEL: Translation of ME-all system. RF: Reference.

Then, to evaluate the effectiveness of our model, we conducted experiments on six systems.

- Baseline system: an in-house hierarchical phrase-based machine translation system (Chiang, 2007) with 4-gram language model.
- Baseline 5-gram: baseline system using 5-gram language model.
- Baseline 6-gram: baseline system using 6-gram language model.
- MLE: proposed method using maximum likelihood estimation.
- ME-no-de: proposed method using maximum entropy model, but was trained with the features merely satisfying the non-linguistic constraint.
- ME-all: proposed method using maximum entropy model using all sorts of features.

Note that all the MLE and ME systems are trained with 4-gram language model only.

4.3 Results

The experimental results are shown in Table 4. We can observe that all the proposed methods outperformed the baseline system. The improvements are all statistically significant at $p < 0.01$ according to the significant test method described in (Koehn, 2004). The fact that our methods yield better results than the long distance n-gram language model illustrates that information on the source side is useful to judge the word order. Moreover, as applying the simple linguistic constraint, the BLEU score rises accordingly. We can observe that the ME-all system outperformed ME-no-de systems at the significance $p < 0.05$. This proves that the linguistic constraint is effective.

We compared the translation results between the baseline system and ME-all system to investigate the actual influence of our method. Figure 4 shows some examples. From the first two sentences we can see that incorrect reorderings occur in the *BL* system due to the ambiguous SCFG rules, which are listed in Table 5, while *MEL* system is able to produce correct results. The third sentence demonstrates that *MEL* system is prone to produce more proper result than *BL* system since translation is considered when measuring the word order.

5 Discussion

The experiment result confirms us that the application of linguistic knowledge is beneficial. In our experiment we also tried to exploit more linguistic knowledge from training set, such as collocations of preposition and verb (pv). We used pv as an alternative linguistic constraint to capture more reordering relationships, since such collocations frequently trigger reorderings. For example, Chinese phrase "*yong(with)*$_1$|p A *fugai(cover)*$_2$|v B" always corresponds to English phrase "$cover_2$|v B $with_1$|p A". And those pv collocations are prevalent in the training set.

However the result turned out a decline on BLEU score. We believe that there are mainly two reasons for this.

- Sometimes the preposition and verb are far from each other so that they exceed the coverage of one hierarchical rule, e.g., 10 words conventionally. Thus they are split into different SCFG rules. Our model can not calculate reordering scores between two rules.
- We did not apply any kind of parser to analyze the Chinese sentence. It is too ambiguous to capture collocations only referring to the POS tags. As a result, too much noise was obtained when training our model.

Therefore, though linguistic knowledge is beneficial, if we want to employ more useful linguistic rules, language analysis toolkit must be involved.

6 Conclusion and Future Work

In this paper we proposed a maximum entropy based lexical reordering model for the hierarchical phrase-based translation model. Our model employs useful features, e.g., word alignment and translation, during the decoding process to measure the correctness of word order for SCFG rules. The experimental results showed that our method outperformed baseline system significantly on the Chinese-to-English patent translation.

Although we only use a simple linguistic constraint, the experimental result shows a significant improvement. This is a positive signal that our model will become much stronger by exploiting more sophisticated linguistic knowledge. Furthermore, the maximum entropy model makes it convenient to incorporate various features. Thus in the future, we will apply language analysis tools to extract more beneficial features to improve our model.

References

Andreas Stolcke. 2002. SRIM - An Extensible Language Modeling Toolkit. In *Proceedings of the 7th International Conference on Spoken Language Processing (ICSLP),* pages 901-904.

Chao Wang, Michael Collins and Philipp Koehn. 2007. Learning linear ordering problems for better translation. In *Proceedings of the 2007 Joint Conference on Empirical Methods in Natural Language Processing and Computational Natural Language Learning,* pages 737-745.

David Chiang. 2005. A hierarchical phrase-based model for statistical machine translation. In *Proceedings of the 43rd Annual Meeting of the Association of Computational Linguistics,* pages 263-270.

David Chiang. 2007. Hierarchical phrase-based translation. In *Computational Linguistics,* pages 201-228.

Fei Xia and Michael McCord. 2004. Improving a Statistical MT System with Automatically learned Rewrite Patterns In *Proceedings of the 18th ICON,* page 508-514.

Franz Josef Och. 2003. Minimum Error Rate Training in Statistical Machine Translation. In *Proceedings of the 41st Annual Meeting of the Association of Computational Linguistics,* pages 160-167.

Franz Josef Och and Hermann Ney. 2002. Discriminative training and maximum entropy models for statistical machine translation. In *Proceedings of the 40th Annual Meeting of Computational Linguistics (ACL),* pages 295-302.

Franz Josef Och and Hermann Ney. 2003. A system comparison of various statistical alignment models. *Computational Linguistics,* pages 19-51.

Jinhua Du and Andy Way. 2010. The Impact of Source-Side Syntactic Reordering on Hierarchical Phrase-based SMT. *2010 European Association for Machine Translation.*

Katsuhiko Hayashi, Hajime Tsukada, Katsuhito Sudoh, Kevin Duh and Seiichi Yamamoto. 2010. Hierarchical Phrase-based Machine Translation with Word-based Reordering Model. In *Proceedings of the 23rd International Conference on Computational Linguistics (Coling 2010),* pages 439-446.

Kishore Papineni, Salim Roukos, Todd Ward, and WeiJing Zhou. 2002. BLEU: a Method for Automatic Evaluation of Machine Translation. In *Proceedings of the 40th Annual Meeting of the Association of Computational Linguistics,* pages 311-318.

Le Zhang. 2004. Maximum Entropy Modeling Toolkit for Python and C++. available at http://homepages.inf.ed.ac.uk/lzhang10/maxent_toolkit.html

Lei Cui, Dongdong Zhang, Mu Li, Ming Zhou, and Tiejun Zhao. 2010. A Joint Rule Selection Model for Hierarchical Phrase-based Translation. In *Proceedings of the ACL 2010 Conference Short Papers,* pages 6-11.

Libin Shen, Jinxi Xu and Ralph Weischedel. 2008. A New String-to-Dependency Machine Translation Algorithm with a Target Dependency Language Model. In *Proceedings of ACL 08,* pages 577-585.

Libin Shen, Jinxi Xu, Bing Zhang, Spyros Matsoukas and Ralph Weischedel. 2009. Effective Use of Linguistic and Contextual Information for Statistical Machine Translation. In *Proceedings of the 2009 Conference on Empirical Methods in Natural Language Processing,* pages 72-80.

Michael Collins, Fhilipp Koehn and Ivona Kucerova. 2005. Clause Restructuring for Statistical Machine Translation. In *Proceedings of the 43rd Association of Computational Linguistics,* page 531-540.

Philipp Koehn, Franz Josef Och and Daniel Marcu. 2003. Statistical phrase-based translation. In *Proceedings of the 40th Annual Meeting of HLT-NAACL 2003,* pages 127-133.

Philipp Koehn. 2004. Statistical Significance Tests for Machine Translation Evaluation. In *Proceedings of EMNLP 2004,* pages 901-904.

Roy Tromble and Jason Elsner. 2009. Learning linear ordering problems for better translation. In *Proceedings of the Conference on Empirical Methods in Natural Language Processing,* pages 1007-1016.

Zhongjun He, Yao Meng and Hao Yu. 2010. Maximum entropy based phrase reordering for hierarchical phrase-based translation. In *Proceedings of the 2010 Conference on Empirical Methods in Natural Language Processing,* pages 555-563.

A Bare-bones Constraint Grammar

Eckhard Bick

Institute of Language and Communication, University of Southern Denmark
Campusvej 55, DK 5230 Odense M
eckhard.bick@mail.dk

Abstract. This paper presents a solution for overcoming the lexical resource gap when mounting rule-based Constraint Grammar systems for minor languages, or in the face of licensing and financing limitations. We investigate how the performance of a CG disambiguation grammar responds to shifting input parameters, among them lexicon limitations of various degrees, the lack a morphological analyzer or both. We propose solutions for a bare-bones system, introducing endings heuristics and so-called morphological APPEND rules. For English, even with an unadapted disambiguation grammar, our bare-bones tagger achieved F-scores of 90-96% for part of speech, and 94-97% for lemmatization, depending on the modules and mini-lexica used.

Keywords: Less-resourced languages, PoS-tagging, Constraint Grammar, morphological analyzer, lexicon generation

1 Introduction

Conventional wisdom has it that in the realm of natural language parsing (NLP), statistical methods are more cost-efficient and easier to build than rule-based systems. However, the latter are dependent on training data, and machine learning of morphosyntactic analysis relies on the existence of a fair-sized annotated corpus for the language in question. If no such corpus exists, manual annotation of a boot-strapping corpus will be necessary, eliminating part of the cost-effectiveness advantage. Furthermore, in the face of Zipf's law, the limited availability of large linguist-revised corpora (especially treebanks) makes it difficult to achieve good lexical coverage. Rule-based NLP systems, on the other hand, while not dependent on training data, generally require extensive lexica and/or morphological analyzers as input modules. As it would seem, both statistical and rule-based approaches are resource-sensitive and can run into difficulties with minor languages, or in the face of licensing and financing limitations. What we are addressing in this paper, is the assumption that these problems are especially difficult to solve for rule-based systems, among them our own methodology of choice, Constraint Grammar (CG). At the disambiguational level, early work by Chanod & Tapanainen (1995) showed that even a small set of CG rules can compete with an off-the-shelve statistical tagger. However, in their experiment, both systems had access to an extensive lexicon an a mature morphological analyzer (a finite-state transducer). All published CG parsers to date (Karlsson et al. 1995 and Bick 2000) have included extensive lexico-morphological resources as input to their grammatical rules (as have other rule-based approaches like HPSG and LFG). To the best of our knowledge, no previous research has been done on how to build a CG in the absence of such resources.

2 Related work and methodological focus

A great deal of methodological inspiration on the corpus-based creation of lexico-morphological resources can be found in recent research literature, and the different approaches can be clustered into two distinct groups - on the one hand linguistically pre-structured corpus work with an emphasis on paradigm completeness and validation (e.g. Clément, Sagot & Lang 2004 or Forsberg et al. 2006), on the other hand machine learning techniques designed to deduce lexical information from raw text data in an unsupervised fashion (e.g. Goldsmith 2001 or Creutz & Lagus 2005). Automatic extraction techniques have also been suggested for higher level lexical information (e.g. Nikuládóttir & Whelpton 2009 for semantic relations), but the focus of this paper will be on the lexico-morphological level. Though our goal is a full inflexional analysis, we don't intend to build full morphological paradigms like Forsberg et al. or Clément et al. Rather, the idea is to find a balance between fullform mini-lexica from small annotated corpora on the one hand (chapter 5.3) and what Piasecki and Radzieszewski (2007) in their work on Polish call a statistical *a tergo index* on the other hand - a list of corpus- or lexicon-derived pseudo-suffixes or -endings, capturing inflexional and other patterns of word formation at the surface level (chapter 3). While Piasecki and Radzieszewski use a letter tree to spawn individual morphological tags, in our own work on English we investigated complete endings strings of various lengths, each associated not with individual tags, but complete tag chain readings, assuming that for a poorly inflecting language like English the line between analytical morphology and derivation is blurred, and that it is more important to capture possible patterns in word class changes or ethymology at the same time. As a third module, supplementing and modifying suggested readings from both mini-lexica and endings heuristics, we use a new type of Constraint Grammar rules (chapter 4), which are morphologically productive in nature, running counter to the traditional use of CG as reductionist disambiguation technique.

3 Simulating a full form lexicon

Depending on typological characteristics of the language in question, the balance of importance between a morphological analyzer and its lexicon may shift considerably. Thus, a language with a rich and completely regular inflexion and affixation system can be annotated for part of speech (PoS), number, tense etc. with an analyzer alone, and would need a lexicon only to resolve compounding and root-affix ambiguities. Highly irregular, non-compounding languages with an underspecified morphological system (such as English), on the other hand, can be handled with a so-called fullform list alone, where every word form is associated with one or more reading lines providing PoS and other linguistic categories.

Consider the following (ambiguous) input to a CG disambiguation grammar:

```
The
        "the" <def> ART S/P              (definite article singular/plural)
test
        "test" N S NOM                   (noun, singular, nominative)
        "test" V PR -3S                  (verb present tense, non-third-person)
        "test" V INF                     (verb, infinitive)
        "test"  V IMP                    (verb, imperative)
showed
        "show"  V IMPF                   (verb, past tense)
        "show"  V PCP2                   (verb, past participle)
        "show"  V IMPF                   (verb, past tense)
interpretable
        "interpretable"  ADJ POS         (adjective)
 results
        "result"  N P NOM                (noun, plural, nominative)
        "result"  V PR 3S                (verb, third person singular)
$.
```

In this example, the word form *'results'* can either be looked up in a full form list providing both noun and verb readings, or it can be analyzed as *result+s,* with the s-morpheme triggering the plural and third person inflexional readings, and the root *result* being verified in a separate base form lexicon. Even without lexicon support, there is a fair chance that an English word ending in *-s* will be a plural noun or a third person verb, while such guesses are impossible for uninflected and closed-class words.

In the full form list approach, inflected forms can be generated from lemma-lists using paradigmatic information about the language, or by using an FST in generative mode. But while only generation will ensure the inclusion of all forms of a lemma, many of these forms may be very rare, and a reasonable fullform list may be built simply by extracting all unique word forms (and their different analyses) from an annotated corpus. In a unix environment this can be done with an extremely simply command pipe. Assuming a corpus in .txt format with line-separated tokenization:

```
cat corpus | sort | uniq -c | sort -r -n
```

In the analyzer approach, for languages with a rich inflexion, a full FST can be approximated by pairing a lexeme list (for instance from a translation dictionary) and small analyzer program for all possible inflexion endings, but without paradigmatical information. Such an analyzer will come up with many overgenerated readings, but for each reading the hypothetical root can be checked against the lexeme lexicon, and a certain amount of false readings due to paradigmatical confusion can be weeded out by contextual disambiguation at the CG grammar stage.

In the absence of lexica and analyzers, and with only a small annotated corpus available, we still think a rule-based system can be bootstrapped just as well as a statistical one. What we propose is to combine a mini-lexicon with an word-endings guesser. Though requiring a minimum of manual linguistics, and a text book or other, the mini-lexicon is necessary to cover highly frequent closed-class words (conjunctions, pronouns, functional adverbs) and irregular verb or noun forms. And because, in general, this kind of words is overrepresented in the high-frequency bracket, a large portion may actually be covered by even a small toy corpus. In order to bypass the rest of the lexicon and the morphological analyzer, a second mini-lexicon is compiled from *all* words in the corpus - or even selectively those words in the corpus that are *not* part of the irregular and closed-class first mini-lexicon. Depending on the size of this word inventory, we will regard the last 3-5 letters of each word form as an "endings" string - a heuristic guess at real world inflexion or affixation endings or ethymological word class regularities. The adjective *interpretable,* for instance, can be guessed at from the following 4pattern, derived from more common words, like *available, considerable, acceptable, capable, valuable, unable:*

xxxable ADJ

Using a frequency breakdown of these "endings", we can then assign PoS and linguistic categories to unknown word forms, using a longest match strategy. For endings with multiple readings, only the most frequent ones will be included in the annotation and passed on to the CG disambiguation grammar. As a consequence of this strategy, corpus errors, misspellings and hapaxes will automatically be weeded out, and the noisy frequency tail of the word inventory ignored. For our English miniature test corpus with only 4.000 words, the top frequency end of the resulting 3-letter endings lexicon looked like this (with prefixed frequency counts):

```
50 xxxion,  N S NOM
44 xxxing,  V PCP1
30 xxxons,  N P NOM
21 xxxing,  N S NOM
18 xxxers,  N P NOM
17 xxxity,  N S NOM
15 xxxlly,  ADV
14 xxxnts,  N P NOM
```

14 xxxies, N P NOM
14 xxxent, N S NOM
13 xxxnce, N S NOM
12 xxxble, ADJ POS
10 xxxing, ADJ POS
10 xxxely, ADV
10 xxxcal, ADJ POS
9 xxxess, N S NOM
8 xxxtes, N P NOM
8 xxxted, V PCP2 PAS
8 xxxent, ADJ POS
8 xxxces, N P NOM

As can be seen, the list nicely manages both inflexion (*-ion/-ions)* and derivation *(-ble,-lly)*. For *-ing*, verbonominal ambiguity is covered, as is the N/ADJ ambiguity of *-ent*.

In principle, there are two diffent sources for endings patterns and their statistics. On the one hand, corpora can be used, leading to an emphasis on tokens and true frequency. On the other hand a dictionary can be used, with a type focus, and "frequency" meaning that there are many words in a language with a given ending. While the former is a better model for a bare-bones system relying heavily on endings also for common words, the latter is better suited to predict the analysis of a small remaining percentage of rarer, unknown words. Therefore, in out evaluation, we used one method for the lexicon-free system, and the other for experiments with lexicon sizes.

4 A Constraint Grammar analyzer

A classical CG rule, as allowed in the cg-1 (LingSoft Oy) and cg-2 (Tapanainen 1996) formalisms, is a disambiguation rule that discards or selects reading lines from a readings cohort, or individual tags from a single readings line:

REMOVE (VFIN) IF (-1C ART OR DET) ; # remove a finite verb reading if the word to the left is a safe (C) article or determiner

SELECT (VFIN) IF (NOT *-1 VFIN) (NOT *1 VFIN) ; # select a finite verb reading if there is no other finite verb neither left (*-1) or right (*1)

This reductionist methodology was complemented by ADD and MAP rules used for adding syntactic function tag canditates (subject, object etc.) for higher level disambiguation. However, in the original formalism, these tag-adding rules could not make reference to word form string elements, and could not be used to add entire reading lines to unknown tokens. In our own, new CG rule formalism, cg-3, we therefore implemented a new rule type, APPEND, specifically targeting morphological work in the face of lacking or incomplete lexical resources. We also added full support for regular expressions and string variables in both target and context matches. Apart from the obvious application, morphological analysis of the target word, regular expression matches can also be used for on-the-fly reference to grammatical sets of words in context conditions, at least for features with some form of regular surface representation, such as using the *'-ize'* affix as a marker for verb transitivity in English, or aspect prefixes in slavic languages.

For closed-class words like prepositions and uninflecting words like adverbs, an APPEND rule is very simpel, and equivalent to a full form list:

APPEND ("$1"v <atemp> ADV) TARGET ("<(always|ever|never|now|soon|today|tomorrow|yesterday)>"r) ;

For affixation[1], as in the adjective example below, we use <safe> and <heur> (heuristic) markers, the idea being that safe mappings will prevent later rules from adding further, heuristic readings for competing word classes:

```
APPEND ("$1"v <safe> ADJ) TARGET ("<(.*(ic|oid|ous))>"r) ; # spastic, android, gaseous
APPEND ("$1"v <heur> ADJ) TARGET ("<(.*(al))>"r) ; # accidental
```

Here, the second rule will allow a later noun mapping for *-al (e.g. withdrawal).*

Obviously, rule order is important, and more specific rules, with more morphological information to draw on, must precede default rules, the last of which will be a singular noun reading for most languages, given the dominance and productivity of nouns in the lexicon. The following noun rules show how a certain amount of root alterations can be handled, overriding more general rules:

```
APPEND ("$1y"v <heur> N P NOM) TARGET ("<(.*)ies>"r) (NOT 0 <lex>) ; # flies
APPEND ("$1"v <safe> N S GEN) TARGET ("<(.*)'s>"r) (NOT 0 <lex> OR (N)) ; # fly's
APPEND ("$1"v <safe> N P GEN) TARGET ("<(.*s)'>"r) (NOT 0 <lex> OR (N)) ; # flies'
APPEND ("$1"v <heur> N P NOM) TARGET ("<(.*)s>"r) (NOT 0 <lex> OR (N)) ; # pies
```

Note the ie->y change in the analysis of "flies", and the fact that the genitive-s analysis, deemed <safe>, will overrule the general plural s-stripping in the fourth rule.

All in all, for English, some 20 APPEND rules can provide very good morphological coverage on top of a small lexicon of irregular base forms, and with no analyzer in the program chain. A certain degree of unavoidable over-generation of ambiguity can be handled by an ordinary disambiguation CG - the same contextual rules working for true ambiguity (e.g. N/V for *tests*) will also tackle heuristic ambiguity (e.g. N/V for *xxxs*). For inflecting or agglutinating languages, more APPEND rules will be needed, but they will also be much more precise and be less prone to systematic heuristic ambiguity. We have evaluated the performance effect of our morphological CG heuristics for English, but expect it to be better rather than worse, for these other language types.

5 Evaluation

In order to evaluate the various suggested setups for a bare-bones CG system, we are using our English CG system as a chain of replaceable black box modules. Thus, we reduced the original morphological analyzer to a mere look-up program with access only to a mini-lexicon of irregular and closed-class words, inactivating the real, verbo-nominal lexicon. Likewise, the disambiguation CG was not allowed access to valency or semantic class tags from the main lexicon. To maintain tokenization compatibility, and thus matchability with the gold standard annotation, we retained the system's own preprocessor, but for a new language a working version could be produced with a few lines of code, basically line-breaking on space and punctuation, with a few exceptions for abbreviations and - depending on the language - contractions, enclitics and possibly names.

All experiments were performed on a random text chunk from the English Wikipedia (en.wikipedia.org), with 3957 tokens (3510 functional words, 1699 word form types). 48.6% of running word form tokens (1705 words), or 80% of word form types (1368) were "unknown" once the main lexicon had been inactivated.

[1] Rules like these can be improved considerably, and be made to include much longer and more fine-grained lists of derivational morphemes. On the other hand, many suffixes will also be captures by a good endings heuristics (cp. below), which is why our rule was not made more elaborate in the current setup.

5.1 The effect of APPEND rules and endings heuristics

In all evaluation scenarios we used a small CG module with about 40 APPEND rules for the heuristic assignment of part of speech (PoS) and inflexion tags to unknown words. Without a lexicon or analyzer, this module alone permitted the disambiguation CG a part-of-speech F-Score of 87. Without a lexicon, the original analyzer helped only a little (89.6 for PoS), and its effect could be matched and surpassed by using a bare-bones analyzer using endings heuristics learned from a corpus:

Table 1: performance with various input combinations for CG disambiguation grammar

	No lexicon no analyzer	No lexicon but analyzer	No lexicon but endings heuristics	Full system
full lexicon				+
base lexicon	+	+		+
original analyzer		+		+
mini-analyzer with endings heuristics (4 letters)			+ (3.5 - 310 M words)	
morph. APPEND cg	+	+	+	
CG disambiguation	+	+	+	+
PoS F-score	87	89.6	89.1-89.8	99.6
Morphology F-score	85.1	84.8	84.1-86.4	98.5
Base form F-score	93.1	93.4	93.3-94.6	99.2

Since endings heuristics are a very cheap resource to produce, we searched for the optimal number of letters to use, and investigated the effect of the size of the corpus used for learning endings patterns. In the table below, we looked at the last 2,3,4,5 or 6 letters, respectively, and distinguish between 3 different corpus sources:

1. Wikipedia test chunk endings (ca. 3.500 tokens revised), i.e. same corpus
2. Leipzig Internet corpus[2] (ca. 3.500 words revised), i.e. small, but different corpus
3. Leipzig Internet corpus (ca. 310.000 words unrevised), i.e. moderate treebank size

Table 2: performance with various input combinations for CG disambiguation grammar (full disambiguation or choose first reading)

endings heuristics number of letters	2	3	4	5	6
PoS F-score	87.3 84.2 87.7	89.3 86.1 89.2	91.9 **89.1** **89.8**	**92.8** **89.1** 89.6	92.1 88.6 89.5
Morphology F-score	86.4 83.6 86.4	88.2 83.2 **86.7**	90.3 **84.1** 86.4	**90.6** **84.1** 85.4	88.2 83.2 84.8
Base form F-score	92.2 91.9 92.1	93.9 92.7 93.7	95 **93.3** **94.6**	**95.6** **93.3** 94.1	94.9 92.9 93.

[2] (Quaesthoff et al. 2006)

As one might expect, the use of same-corpus data performed best, both for genre and lexicon reasons, but this is not a realistic scenario outside the realm of Wall Street Journal linguistics. Interestingly, the best cross-corpus F-Score for PoS was achieved with 4-letter endings[3]. The likely reason for this is that fewer letters will not capture enough morphemes, and leave too much ambiguity, while using too many letters may lead to a lower level of "abstraction", and hence, coverage problems. Performance rose when using more corpus data[4], even though we used unrevised annotations for the larger data set, and revised annotation for the small one.

Base form recognition performed better than PoS, and morphology worse, but both was to be expected, since, for instance, English verbs and nouns may share a common base form *(a house - to house),* while especially verbs have a great deal of 0-morpheme inflexion in English *(e.g. house V INF, house V -3S, house V IMP),* allowing for morphological mistaggings even in the face of a correctly recognized V part of speech.

5.2 Recall ceilings before disambiguation

All of the above tests targeted overall performance, through the optics of an existing English disambiguation grammar. However, the rules in this grammar were written for input from a regular analyzer drawing on a large lexicon (> 200.000 lexemes) complete with valency and semantic class information. In order to get an idea about the potential performance ceiling of a new grammar, optimized for the kind of heuristic, over-ambiguous input our bare-bones setup is providing, it is interesting to know the point of departure for a disambiguation grammar, i.e. the recall and precision of a bare-bones analyzer with access only to an endings heuristics and morphological APPEND rules.

Table 3: Recall / precision / F-score for bare-bones analyzer **without** disambiguation CG (endings lexicon from unrevised 310.000 word corpus)

endings heuristics	3 letters Recall/Prec./F-score	4 letters Recall/Prec./F-score	5 letters Recall/Prec./F-score
PoS	**95.6** /47.7 / 63	95 / 50.6 / 66	94.3 / 51.5 / 66.6
Morphology	**93.9** / 46.9 / 62.6	92.7 / 49.4 / 64.5	91.4 / 49.9 / 64.6
Base form	95.6 / 81.6 / 88	**96.1** / 84.8 / 90.1	95.4 / 85.3 / 90.1

The numbers show that for writing a disambiguation grammar from scratch, it might actually be a good idea to use shorter ending strings for heuristics, since the implicit over-generation will ensure a higher recall. Conversely, precision is higher with the longer 5-letter endings heuristics, giving an existing (reductionist) disambiguation grammar less room to make errors. The latter effect, however, is dependent on a sufficiently large corpus base - with a small corpus, even a manually revised one (!), *both* recall and precision will be higher with the more generalizing 3-letter endings:

Table 4: recall / precision / F-score for bare-bones analyzer without disambiguation CG (endings lexicon from different, revised 3.500 word corpus)

endings heuristics	3 letters	4 letters	5 letters
PoS F-score	**93.9** / 53 / 67.8	93.6 / 51.9 / 66.8	93.6 / 51.6 / 66.6

[3] For same-corpus training, the optimal number of letters may be a little higher, since longer string matches may mean a more narrow modeling of individual, frequent words in the corpus.

[4] Still, this is also true of full form lexica built from the same corpora, so with bigger corpora available, the need to have endings heuristics in the first place will decrease.

Morphology F-score	**91.4** / 51.6 / 66	90.5 / 50.2 / 64.6	90.6 / 49.9 / 64.4
Base form F-score	**94.5** / 84.7 / 89.3	94.2 / 84.6 / 89.1	94.1 / 84.6 / 89.1

5.3 The effect of fullform mini-lexica

Finally, we simulated the availability of a corpus-derived fullform lexicon, to enhance our bare-bones system, assuming that no real lexicon resource would be available, and that available corpora would not be human-revised. For this experiment we used the English Leipzig Internet corpus (2 million words, Quaesthoff et al. 2006), automatically annotated with the EngGram parser (Bick 2009). The corpus contained a maximum of 180.000 different non-hapax word form types, not counting numerical expressions and compound names. Of these, we used the 1000, 10,000 and 100,000 most frequent forms to enhance the base lexicon of the bare-bones system. As before, we used both an endings-based heuristics and morphological APPEND rules to handle remaining unknown forms, and ran the evaluation metrics after disambiguation. For the endings heuristics we settled for a string length of 4, and used the same frequency chunk to build the endings lexicon, i.e. combining the 1.000 word min-lexicon with an endings lexicon likewise built from only 1.000 word forms, etc. One important difference between a fullform lexicon derived from a small corpus, and one generated from complete lexical paradigms (or simply written by hand) is that the former does not guarantee cohort completeness - for instance, the most frequent analyses of the word *'close'* (say, adjective and infinitive) may be represented in the corpus, while others (say, finite verb and imperative) are missing. To simulate a generated cohort-complete resource for comparison, we ran an alternative evaluation where rarer forms below the chosen frequency threshold were added, *if* another, more frequent reading for the same form had been found *above* the threshold. Figures for both scenarios are given in the table below, the cohort-complete results in parentheses.

Table 5: The influence of mini-lexicon size (endings files built from same lexicon size)

mini lexicon size in words	1 000	10 000	100 000	180 000 (all)
PoS F-score	90 (89.8)	93.7 (93.3)	**95.3** (95.2)	95.2 (95.2)
Morphology F-score	87 (87.2)	91.8 (91.7)	**94.1 (94.1)**	**94.1 (94.1)**
Base form F-score	93.6 (93.3)	96 (95.8)	**96.8 (96.8)**	**96.8 (96.8)**

The figures show the expected performance increase with bigger corpora, but also that growth is asymptotic - the Zipf tail of the frequency, i.e. frequencies close to the hapax level, do not contribute. An interesting finding is that completing cohorts with rarer readings does not help. The expected beneficial recall effect is canceled out either by the loss of implicit statistical disambiguation, or by corpus annotation errors found in the low frequency bracket. In this light, it must be emphasized that no human revision of either corpus or lexicon was involved, and that cohort-completeness was simulated from corpus data. In a development setting, better results might be achieved with revised corpora (treebanks), or by manually cohort-completing the top frequency bracket of a corpus-derived lexicon.

6 Conclusions and Outlook

We have shown how the necessary morphological input for the disambiguation rules of a Constraint Grammar tagger can be generated in a resource-poor environment. To bypass the usual lexico-analytical setup (analyzers, lexica, finite state machines), we compared and combined 3 methods - (a) morphological APPEND rules, (b) endings heuristics and (c) corpus derived mini-lexica. With an annotated, but unrevised 2-million word corpus as "maximal resource", the best combination of a-c achieved F-scores of 95.3 for PoS and 96.8 for lemmatization, respectively, even in a cross-genre evaluation. Even with a lexicon of only closed-class words, a combination of (a) and (b) came close to 90% correctness for PoS, with a theoretical recall ceiling of 95.6 without disambiguation. Future research should determine if using a newly written, tailor-made disambiguation grammar could exploit this recall ceiling better than the existing grammar made for non-heuristic lexico-analytical input.

An important lesson learned, and a nice aspect for resource-savers, was the fact that for generating data-driven lexica, corpus size matters more than whether the corpus annotation has been human-revised - this being true both for full form lexica and endings heuristics. For the latter, we established 4 letters as the optimal string length to use for English[5].

We chose English for our experiments not because CG has a special affinity or effectiveness for English, but simply to make our research maximally accessible for the research community as a whole. However, our intuition is that the effectiveness of both endings-based heuristics and morphological APPEND rules should be higher for languages with a richer morphology, as would be the case for most other Indo-European languages, for instance. On the other hand, the coverage of same-size fullform lexica should be lower for those languages. In a bare-bones setting we believe the treatment of unknown word forms to be more important than lexicon coverage, but this intuition need to be corroborated by future research on representative members of various language families.

References

Bick, Eckhard. 2000. *The Parsing System Palavras - Automatic Grammatical Analysis of Portuguese in a Constraint Grammar Famework,* Aarhus: Aarhus University Press

Bick, Eckhard. 2009. "Introducing Probabilistic Information in Constraint Grammar Parsing". *Proceedings of Corpus Linguistics 2009, Liverpool, UK.* Electronically published at: ucrel.lancs.ac.uk/publications/cl2009/

Chanod, Jean-Pierre and Pasi Tapanainen. 1995. *Tagging French – comparing a statistical and a constraint-based method.* In Proceedings of the Seventh Conference of the European Chapter of the Association for Computational Linguistics, pp. 149–156, Dublin, Ireland, March. ACL.

Clément, Lionel, Benoît Sagot and Bernard Lang. 2004. Morphology based automatic acquisition of large-coverage lexica. In *Proceedings of the 4th Language Resources and Evaluation Conference* (LREC'04), pages 1841–1844, Lisbon, Portugal.

Creutz, Mathias and Krista Lagus. 2005. Inducing the morphological lexicon of a natural language from unannotated text. In Proceedings of the International and Interdisciplinary Conference on Adaptive Knowledge Representation and Reasoning (AKRR'05), pp 106–113, Espoo, Finland.

Forsberg, Markus, Harald Hammarström and Aarne Ranta. 2006. Morphological Lexicon Extraction from Raw Text Data. In *Proceedings of FinTAL'2006.* pp.488~499

Goldsmith, John A. 2001. Unsupervised learning of the morphology of a natural language. Computational Linguistics, 27(2): pp. 153–198.

Karlsson, Fred, Atro Voutilainen, Juha Heikkilä, and Arto Anttila, editors. 1995. *Constraint Grammar: A Language-Independent System for Parsing Unrestricted Text.* Natural Language Processing, No 4. Mouton de Gruyter, Berlin and New York

Nikulásdóttir, Anna Björk and Matthew Whelpton. 2009. Automatic Extraction of Semantic Relations. In: Pedersen, Bolette Sandford et al. (eds): *Proceedings of the NODALIDA 2009 workshop WordNets and other Lexical Semantic Resources -*

[5] Without disambiguation, in pure recall terms, 3 letters were better, but at too high a price in terms of ambiguity.

between Lexical Semantics, Lexicography, Terminology and Formal Ontologies. NEALT Proceedings Series, Vol 7. ISSN 1736-6305

Quasthoff, U.; M. Richter; C. Biemann. 2006. "Corpus Portal for Search in Monolingual Corpora". *Proceedings of the fifth international conference on Language Resources and Evaluation, LREC 2006, Genoa.* pp. 1799-1802

Piasecki, Maciej and Adam Radziszewski. 2007. Polish Morphological Guesser Based on a Statistical A Tergo Index . In: *Proceedings of the International Multiconference on Computer Science and Information Technology*. pp. 247–256 . ISSN 1896-7094

Tapanainen, Pasi. 1996. *The Constraint Grammar Parser CG-2.* No 27, Publications of the Department of General Linguistics, University of Helsinki.

Spring Cleaning and Grammar Compression: Two Techniques for Detection of Redundancy in HPSG Grammars

Antske Fokkens[a], Yi Zhang[b] and Emily M. Bender[c]

[a] Department of Computational Linguistics, Saarland University
Saarland University Campus, 66123 Saarbrücken, Germany
afokkens@coli.uni-saarland.de
[b] LT-Lab, German Research Center for Artificial Intelligence
Stuhlsatzenhausweg 3 / Building D3, 66123 Saarbrücken, Germany
yizhang@dfki.de
[c] Department of Linguistics, University of Washington,
Box 354340, Seattle, WA 98195-4340, USA
ebender@uw.edu

Abstract. This paper presents two approaches that identify which parts of an implemented grammar are used and which parts are computationally inactive. Our results lead to the following insights: even small grammars contain noise due to revised analyses, removing superfluous types from a grammar may help to detect errors in the original grammar and at least half of the types defined in the grammars we investigated do not play a role in the computational process of the grammar.

Keywords: Implemented grammars, HPSG, typed feature structures.

1 Introduction

Grammars of natural language are highly complex objects. This complexity is reflected in implementations of linguistically motivated precision grammars. Understanding the role of a specific element in a broad coverage precision grammar is therefore not always straightforward, even for the engineer who implemented the grammar. Implementations for different phenomena interact, and revisions to the grammar may change the role of existing parts of the grammar. In this paper, we present two techniques for investigating the role that specific types play in implemented HPSG (Pollard and Sag, 1994) grammars. The first, dubbed 'spring cleaning', focuses on identifying portions of the grammar that do not play any role in the set of sentences it recognizes or the structures it assigns to them. Such artifacts can accrue in a grammar because abandoned analyses are not completely removed or because the grammar is built on a cross-linguistic resource but does not use all of the infrastructure that resource provides. Spring cleaning is intended to be used in the course of grammar development and as such must leave the grammar in a state that is still easy to maintain. In contrast, the second technique, 'grammar compression', computes the smallest subset of a type hierarchy that can assign the same structures to the same sentences as the original grammar. In grammar compression, we remove not only the types taken out in spring cleaning, but also those that exist only to express generalizations over their subtypes.

We use these techniques to explore the degree of redundancy in a range of DELPH-IN[1] grammars, including the two grammars of Wambaya (Bender, 2010), the BURGER grammar of Bulgarian (Osenova, 2010), the ManGO grammar[2] of Mandarin Chinese, all built with the LinGO

[1] http://www.delph-in.net/

[2] http://wiki.delph-in.net/moin/MandarinGrammarOnline

Grammar Matrix (Bender *et al.*, 2002; Bender *et al.*, 2010), and two much larger grammars, the English Resource Grammar (Flickinger, 2000) and German Grammar (Müller and Kasper, 2000; Crysmann, 2005).

This paper is structured as follows: First, we describe the overall structure of the grammars under consideration. This section is followed by an overview of the first approach under examination: removing superfluous types from the grammar. Section 4 provides the details of our second investigation of relevant types: maximally reduced computationally equivalent grammars. The next section presents our quantitative results and their implications. Finally, we conclude by suggesting avenues for future research.

2 General structure of DELPH-IN grammars

The grammars under consideration are HPSG-based grammars that can be used for parsing and generation with the LKB (Copestake, 2002) and for parsing with the PET parser (Callmeier, 2002).

The grammars we work with are all written in the DELPH-IN joint reference formalism (Copestake, 2000), known as TDL. TDL grammars consist of one or more files defining a type hierarchy as well as a collection of files defining instances: phrase structure rules, lexical rules, lexical entries, node labels and initial symbols. The instances are manipulated by the parsing and generation algorithms during processing, while the types are used to define the instances. The type hierarchy consists of typed feature structures, i.e., types which are arranged into a subsumption relation and associated with (complex) feature structures.

The definition of a type consists of an identifier for the type, one or more supertypes, and optionally one or more type constraints. Type constraints are feature-path value pairs, where the values are drawn from the type hierarchy. The value of a feature can be atomic (i.e., a type with no further features of its own) or complex (i.e., a type with future features that are appropriate to it). The value of two features may be identified, creating reentrancies. Thus the feature structures are DAGs (cycles are disallowed). Any given feature is associated with exactly one type for which it is appropriate. All other types that bear constraints on the value of that feature must inherit from the type for which the feature is declared appropriate.

An example TDL type definition, drawn from the Wambaya grammar, is shown in Figure 1. The string before the symbol := is the type identifier (`noun-lex`). After :=, four supertypes are specified. The remainder of the type definition (enclosed in square brackets) provides the type constraints. `#spr` labels a reentrancy between the values of two features.[3]

```
noun-lex := basic-noun-lex & basic-one-arg &
            no-hcons-lex-item & non-wh-lex &
  [ SYNSEM.LOCAL.CAT [ MC na, HEAD.MOD <>,
                        VAL [ SPR < #spr & [ LOCAL.CAT.HEAD det, OPT + ] >,
                              COMPS < >, SUBJ < >, SPEC < > ]],
    ARG-ST < #spr > ] .
```

Figure 1: Sample type definition from Wambaya grammar

The parsing and generation algorithms require that the type hierarchy be a bounded complete partial order (BCPO), i.e., for any two types that share subtypes, there must be one unique most general such type, called the 'greatest lower bound (glb)'. However, grammar engineers are not required to make sure that the type hierarchy has this property. Rather, the glb types are created programmatically at compile time: if any two types have more than one mutual subtype, the grammar compiler creates an additional type, as shown in Figure 2.

[3] Note that the < > notation is syntactic sugar that simplifies the expression of lists. Lists are underlying treated as feature structures with FIRST and REST as appropriate features.

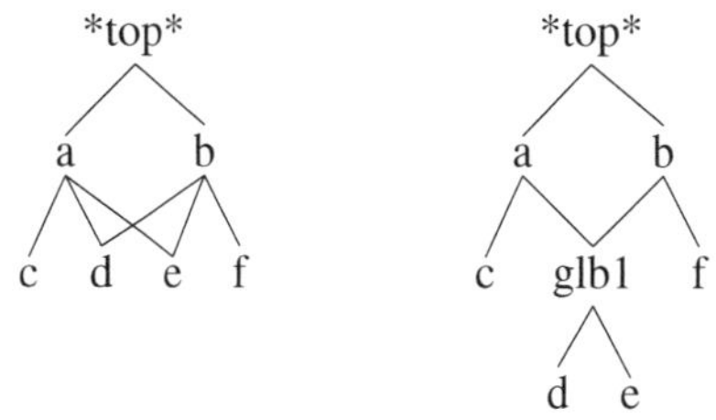

Figure 2: Sample hierarchy as written by grammar engineer (left) and augmented with glb type by compiler (right)

When working with the LKB, the grammar is compiled when it is loaded into the system. The grammar engineer can then interact with the grammar, using it to parse and generate but also exploring the type hierarchy through a GUI. With PET, grammar compilation is handled via a program called 'flop', resulting in a file storing the compiled version of the grammar. The parser, called 'cheap', reads in the flopped grammar for runtime parsing.

3 Spring cleaning: Removing superfluous types

This section describes a process for removing types that do not have an impact on the competence of the grammar. By **competence**, we mean the set of analyses that the grammar provides for any possible input strings; for strings the grammar does not recognize, this will be the empty set. In practice, we can only test this competence with some finite set of strings. In the experiments reported below, we use the testsuites associated with each grammar.

As explained in the previous section, the LKB and PET parsers and LKB generator take instances as starting points for parsing and generation. Instances thus have a direct influence on the competence of the grammar. There are several ways in which types may be **relevant**, i.e., play a role for instances. The first and most direct way is if a type is an **instantiated type**, meaning that it either has an instance or has a subtype that has an instance. Instantiated types thus directly define the instances of the grammar. The second way a type has an impact on instances is by defining **features** or **values** that are part of the definition of one or more instantiated types. Finally, a type may be relevant to instances, because it defines a **lower bound** between two relevant types. In this case, the type influences the possibility of unification, i.e. if a type t forms the only lower bound between types t_1 and t_2, t permits unification between t_1 and t_2, which can no longer take place when t is removed from the grammar.

Types that do not influence instances in any of the three possible ways defined above do not have an impact on the competence of the grammar. Our 'spring cleaning' algorithm goes through the type definition files and identifies such irrelevant types. This process takes place in two stages. In the first stage, we identify types that are necessary for the definition of the instantiated types. This means types that either (i) are instantiated types, (ii) define values of features of instantiated types, or (iii) introduce features used to define an instantiated type. Errors occurring in this stage can be tested at **compile time** of the grammar: if a type is removed that is required for the definition of an instantiated rule or lexical entry, the grammar will not load in LKB. Similarly, the PET 'flop' command will fail (and report an error) on a grammar missing such a type.

Types that permit unification between other types, but play no direct role to other type's definitions, are only relevant at **runtime**. These types are identified in the second stage of the process. After separating types needed to define instantiated types from those that are not, our algorithm checks for relevance at runtime of the latter types. We create a hierarchy h of types that lead to instances and their values. For each type from the original grammar that is not defined in h, our algorithm checks whether it permits the unification of types from h that would otherwise fail. In order to test this stage for correctness, we use the grammar to parse some set of strings. In addition, we use grammar compression, explained in the next section, to verify if all relevant types are kept in the grammar.[4]

The final output of our algorithm is three sets of files: (i) modified versions of the files of the original grammar, in which the definition files include only those types that are either in h or identified as relevant at runtime, (ii) copies of the original definition files and (iii) files that list removed types for each definition file. The structure of the original grammar is preserved by this process. This includes types that are used to capture generalizations so that a given constraint need be stated in only on place. Thus the result is a grammar that is 'cleaned up' with respect to the input without being made more compact in ways that might make it more opaque to the grammar engineer or introduce redundancy at the level of the statement of constraints. As we will see below, exploring which types are eliminated can be illuminating for the grammar engineer as well.

4 Grammar compression: Maximally reduced computationally equivalent grammars

While the 'spring cleaning' algorithm safely removes types that do not have an impact on the competence of the grammar, it does not guarantee the maximal reduction of the grammar. More specifically, the supertypes in an inheritance hierarchy represent generalizations on various levels, but many of them serve no computational purpose, and will never show up in the analysis. This section describes our algorithm that identifies computationally relevant types of the grammar. The compression algorithm removes a superset of types to those reduced by the 'spring cleaning' method, hence can be used to verify the equivalence of the grammars achieved by the less-invasive reduction method from the previous section. The main practical difference between the algorithm applied in this section and the one in the previous section is that this algorithm operates on a compiled grammars, i.e. grammars that have been compiled to be used by the PET parser. The consequence of this difference is that this algorithm can also identify supertypes of instantiated types and relevant values that are not strictly necessary for the grammar from a computational point of view. Note, however, that types that are not computationally relevant can play an important role in the maintainability of the grammar or, from a linguistic point of view, in capturing cross-grammar similarity. We will explain these two differences in the coming subsections. The explanation of the grammar compression algorithm is followed by a formal proof of the equivalence between the original and the maximally reduced grammar.

4.1 Reducing compiled grammars

Before a grammar written in TDL can be interpreted by the PET parser, the grammar has to be compiled. There are several significant differences between a compiled grammar and its original that have an impact on identifying types that are relevant for the grammar. First, as mentioned above, a compiled grammar defines a type hierarchy that is a bounded complete partial order (BCPO), which means that all possible greatest lower bounds of existing compatible types are already included in the inheritance hierarchy. Second, all constraints on each defined type are expanded, including those inherited from supertypes. Moreover, the potential subsumption relations between pairs of types are encoded in a bit-matrix, so the immediate supertype-subtype relations become insignificant so long as the subsumption relations do not change. Because each type definition contains all constraints inherited from supertypes as well as direct information about all types that it subsumes, compatibility between types can be checked by applying bit-vector AND. This procedure allows us to identify types that are not strictly necessary for computational purposes (though they may be useful for reasons of grammar maintainability). For instance, a type that serves to define a set of constraints for all its subtypes is no longer required in a grammar where each subtype already contains these constraints.

[4] Note, however, that neither test (compiling or parsing) ensures that all redundant types have been removed.

This is illustrated in Figure 3, which displays the subsumption table for the BCPO in Figure 2. Each row in this table denotes the types subsumed by the current type. Therefore, even without the direct inheritance information from Figure 2, we can tell from Figure 3 that type *b* is equal to or more general than type *b*, *d*, *e*, *f*, and *glb1*.

	top	*a*	*b*	*c*	*d*	*e*	*f*	*glb1*
top	1	1	1	1	1	1	1	1
a	0	1	0	1	1	1	0	1
b	0	0	1	0	1	1	1	1
c	0	0	0	1	0	0	0	0
d	0	0	0	0	1	0	0	0
e	0	0	0	0	0	1	0	0
f	0	0	0	0	0	0	1	0
glb1	0	0	0	0	1	1	0	1

Figure 3: Example of subsumption table in a compiled grammar

Our grammar compression algorithm goes through the instantiated types of the grammar and marks the instantiated type itself plus the type value of each expanded constraint. Our grammar compression algorithm goes through the instantiated types of the grammar and marks the type value of each expanded constraint. Once this is done, it further marks the glbs of the marked types to complete the sub-BCPO. The unmarked types which are identified as having no computational impact on the grammar are a superset of those identified by our spring cleaning algorithm, including both types that are not related to instantiated types in any manner, as well as types that may play a role in representing linguistic generalizations and in maintainability of the grammar, but could be removed from the grammar in a compression process where constraints are pushed down on subtypes. The maximally reduced grammar then will only contain the marked types, with the constraints on the removed types specified on the subtypes directly. We provide a proof in the next subsection that such grammar reduction does not change the grammar behavior.

4.2 Proof of equivalence

Definition 1. *For a TFS grammar G, an* analysis *is a TFS created by unifying the TFSes of instances defined in G.*

Definition 2. *TFS grammars G and G′ are* A-equivalent *iff they always produce the same type feature structure analyses for any inputs.*

Note that the notion of *A-equivalence* is similar to the *tree-language equivalence* for CFG or TAG where two grammars not only yield the same sequences, but also the complex structures that produce those sequences.

Assuming a type inheritance hierarchy T is a bounded complete partial order (BCPO), we define a reduced type inheritance hierarchy $R(T)$ as an order-preserving hierarchy containing all the types that (i) are directly mentioned in one or more instances in G; or (ii) serve as the greatest lower-bound (glb) in T for the types included in $R(T)$. A reduced TFS grammar $G(R(T))$ contains the same instances in $G(T)$, and a reduced hierarchy $R(T)$ from T.

Theorem 1. *Given a BCPO type hierarchy* $T = \langle \mathcal{T}, \wedge_T \rangle$ *and its reduction* $R(T) = \langle \mathcal{T}', \wedge_{T'} \rangle$ $(\mathcal{T}' \subseteq \mathcal{T})$*, if two types from* $R(T)$ *are compatible, their greatest lower bound is the same, i.e.,* $\forall t_1, t_2 \in \mathcal{T}', t_1 \wedge_{T'} t_2 = t_1 \wedge_T t_2$,

The proof is obvious from the definition, due to the glb-preserving nature of the mapping of types from $R(T)$ to T.

Theorem 2. *$G(T)$ and $G(T')$ are* A-Equivalent *if T' = R(T).*

Proof. An analysis with grammar $G(T)$ is produced by unifications with instances. The analysis with $G(T')$ involves the unification of the same set of instances. Since the unification of types mentioned in the instances yields the same glb (Theorem 1), the unifications of the same instances on T and $R(T)$ produce the same TFSes. □

5 Results

5.1 Spring cleaning Matrix based grammars

We tested our algorithm by removing superfluous types from the BURGER grammar of Bulgarian [bul] (Osenova, 2010), the ManGO grammar[5] of Mandarin [cmn] and two grammars of Wambaya [wmb] (Bender, 2010). The Wambaya grammars represent two branches of development on the same grammar, built around two separate analyses of the auxiliaries in the language: an (older) grammar with an argument composition analysis ('arg-comp') and a new grammar which uses a verbal cluster approach ('aux+vc').

We checked whether the reduced grammar was equivalent to the original grammar by comparing the results of the spring cleaning algorithm to those of the grammar compression algorithm, which we have proven to lead to an equivalent grammar. If the reduced grammar contains all types of the compressed grammar, it is guaranteed that all types that have instances as well as types that influence their ability to unify are present in the grammar. This only leaves the question of whether all required supertypes were correctly identified by the algorithm. This can be verified by compiling the grammar, since missing supertypes lead to compilitation errors. We verified the two biggest spring cleaned grammars, the Wambaya grammars, this way, which both passed the test.

In addition, we verified equivalence by parsing associated testsuites with the original and newly created grammar. The set of syntactic trees and semantic interpretations produced for each grammar were compared using [incr tsdb()] (Oepen, 2001). Equivalence was confirmed for all grammars, though not immediately with the Wambaya grammars. As discussed below (§5.2), we discovered that the value hierarchy associated a semantic feature was not a BCPO in the grammars as written. Once this was fixed, we were able to confirm equivalence. As mentioned in Section 1, all four grammars are further developments of grammars originally created by the LinGO Grammar Matrix customization system. This means that types identified as being superfluous can be divided in two main categories: language specific types and types from the cross-linguistic component.

Table 1 presents the results for all grammars. The types removed from Wambaya (arg-comp) form a subset of those removed from Wambaya (aux+vc).

Source	Wambaya (arg-comp)	Wambaya (aux+vc)	BURGER	ManGO
Multilingual Component	178	178	138	131
Language Specific	17	26	226	62
Total	195	204	364	213

Table 1: Number of redundant types identified for each grammar

In general, most of the removed types come from the multilingual core. BURGER forms the only exception, but this result is misleading. The bulk of the language specific types removed from BURGER are lexical types (183 of 226). The lexicon of the publicly available version of BURGER[6] is relatively small (BURGER only has 183 lexical items), and a grammar with a

[5] http://wiki.delph-in.net/moin/MandarinGrammarOnline
[6] http://www.bultreebank.org/BURGER/index.html

bigger lexicon currently exists (Osenova, p.c.). Taking this in consideration, it is likely that the real number of superfluous language specific types in BURGER lies around 40.

It is expected that most removed types would be multilingual types for several reasons. First, the multilingual core may contain types that are not relevant for the particular language. Second, the grammars we investigated are relatively small. This has two consequences that may lead to a relatively high number of superfluous multilingual types as compared to language specific types. The multilingual core may, to begin with, contain types that support phenomena that the grammar does not yet cover. In addition, a small to medium sized grammar will not have too many revised analyses that would lead to noise in the grammar.

5.2 Further observations from Spring cleaning

In order to get a clearer idea of the way the Grammar Matrix multilingual component is used, we compared the set of types removed from each grammar. We looked at which types where removed from all grammars, from two grammars or just one grammar. All types were classified according to whether they correspond to a phenomenon not covered by the grammar (Not Covered), whether they represent a phenomenon that does not occur cross-linguistically generally (Not Applicable), or represent an abandoned analysis (Abandoned). Note that the types from the first category may potentially be used in the grammar in the future. The Grammar Matrix contains one type that serves as an example and is not meant to be used (Example). Table 2 presents this classification.[7]

Grammars where removed	Not Covered	Not applicable	Example	Abandoned	Total
Wambaya, BURGER, ManGO	63	29	1	6	99
Wambaya, BURGER	2				2
BURGER, ManGO	18	6			24
Wambaya	10	36		15	61
BURGER	12	1		2	15
ManGO	4	4			8
Total	109	76	1	23	209

Table 2: Classification of redundant types from LinGO Grammar Matrix

As mentioned above, we parsed associated testsuites of each grammar with the original version of the grammar, as well as the reduced grammar in order to verify the equivalence between the two grammars. This additional test lead to another, unforeseen, benefit of our investigation for the Wambaya grammars. Namely, we identified missing types in the hierarchy of the semantic values for person and number. The reduced grammars produced the same number of readings and the same trees as the original grammars, but revealed differences in semantic representations for a small set of analyses. Upon closer inspection, it turned out that some semantic feature values of the feature PERNUM (person and number) had glb-types (greatest lower bound types) as their value. These types are automatically introduced by the LKB when compiling the grammar to make sure the type hierarchy is bounded complete partially ordered (BCPO). They may play a role as a syntactic component of a derivation, but they should not appear in semantic representations. The LKB uses numbers to assign each added glb-type a unique name. These numbers, and thus the name given to a specific type, may differ if the size of the grammar changes. Because of different number of the glb-types representing person and number values in Wambaya, we were able to identify the missing types and improve the Wambaya grammars.

[7] The grammars were not based on the same version of the Grammar Matrix, leading to some divergence. Specifically, five of the types removed from BURGER and ManGO because they are not cross-linguistically valid were not present in the Grammar Matrix that Wambaya is based on.

5.3 Grammar Compression

We ran our grammar compression algorithm on the ERG, GG, JaCY, Wambaya (arg-comp) and BURGER grammars. The results are presented in Table 3.

Grammar	required types	defined types	reduction rate
ERG	4030	7772	48.1%
GG	5211	10778	51.7%
JaCY	1232	2497	50.7%
Wambaya (arg-comp)	751	3400	77.9%
BURGER	3325	5280	37.0%

Table 3: Superfluous Types according to Grammar Compression

Our results show that all tested grammars contain a great number of types that do not have an impact on the behavior of the grammar. Furthermore, a significant difference is observed between the grammars, with the large grammars like ERG, GG and JaCY having about half of their types playing a computational role in the grammar's competence, and the Wambaya grammar using only slightly above 20%. The high amount of unused types in Wambaya can be explained by the fact that it contains the multilingual component from the Grammar Matrix. The Matrix-based BURGER grammar, on the other hand, implements a sophisticated morphological system with over 2700 inflectional rules, outweighing the unused types provided by the Matrix core grammar.

The results presented in Section 5.1 showed that most superfluous types in the Wambaya grammar are found in the multilingual component. Moreover, the multilingual core of the Grammar Matrix makes heavily use of generic types used to define more specific types further down the hierarchy. The purpose of this structure is to make the core more modular and hence provide more flexibility to ensure cross-linguistic applicability. In a monolingual grammar, the grammar engineer can restrict this usage to generic types known to be useful for the particular language.

6 Conclusion and Future Work

We have presented two approaches that investigate which types in an HPSG grammar are used. The first approach examines the type hierarchy as it is defined in TDL. It identifies types that do not define properties of any instantiated types, nor influence their ability to unify and removes such types from the grammar. As such, this approach respects the original structure in the grammar. The second approach looks at the minimum number of types that is required to create a grammar that is equivalent to the grammar that is defined in TDL.

One can learn a variety of things by examining the types that are removed, both for monolingual projects and for cross-linguistic projects. For monolingual projects, cleaning out the unused types improves grammar maintainability. In a multilingual context, systematically exploring what gets used and what doesn't is useful feedback for developers of the multilingual core. These insights shed light both on which analyses aren't working crosslinguistically and on where Matrix users are apparently failing to discover relevant infrastructure provided by the Matrix.

In future work, we plan to extend our spring cleaning algorithm to identify constraints that do not affect the grammar's competence. Furthermore, we aim to continue our investigation of the Grammar Matrix by comparing the formal properties of type hierarchies. For this investigation, we plan to compare hierarchies that represent a grammar at different stages of its development, which should lead to more exact insights on how multilingual components are used in individual grammars.

References

Bender, Emily M. 2010. Reweaving a grammar for Wambaya: A case study in grammar engineering for linguistic hypothesis testing. *Linguistic Issues in Language Technology*, 3(3), 1–34.

Bender, Emily M., Scott Drellishak, Antske Fokkens, Laurie Poulson, and Safiyyah Saleem. 2010. Grammar customization. *Research on Language & Computation*, 8(1), 23–72.

Bender, Emily M., Dan Flickinger, and Stephan Oepen. 2002. The grammar matrix: An open-source starter-kit for the rapid development of cross-linguistically consistent broad-coverage precision grammars. In John Carroll, Nelleke Oostdijk, and Richard Sutcliffe, eds., *Proceedings of the Workshop on Grammar Engineering and Evaluation at the 19th International Conference on Computational Linguistics*, pp. 8–14, Taipei, Taiwan.

Callmeier, Ulrich. 2002. Preprocessing and encoding techniques in PET. In Stephan Oepen, Daniel Flickinger, J. Tsujii, and Hans Uszkoreit, eds., *Collaborative Language Engineering. A Case Study in Efficient Grammar-based Processing*. CSLI Publications, Stanford, CA.

Copestake, Ann. 2000. Appendix: Definitions of typed feature structures. *Natural Language Engineering*, 6, 109–112.

Copestake, Ann. 2002. *Implementing Typed Feature Structure Grammars*. CSLI Publications, Stanford, CA.

Crysmann, Berthold. 2005. Relative clause extraposition in German: An efficient and portable implementation. *Research on Language and Computation*, 3(1), 61–82.

Flickinger, Dan. 2000. On building a more efficient grammar by exploiting types. *Natural Language Engineering*, 6 (1) (Special Issue on Efficient Processing with HPSG), 15 – 28.

Müller, Stefan and Walter Kasper. 2000. HPSG analysis for German. In Wolfgang Wahlster, ed., *Verbmobil: Foundations of Speech-to-Speech translation*, pp. 238 – 253, Berlin, Germany. Springer.

Oepen, Stephan. 2001. [incr tsdb()] — competence and performance laboratory. Technical report, DFKI, Saarbrücken, Germany.

Osenova, Petya. 2010. BUlgarian Resource Grammar – Efficient and Realistic (BURGER). ms, Stanford University.

Pollard, Carl and Ivan A. Sag. 1994. *Head-Driven Phrase Structure Grammar*. Studies in Contemporary Linguistics. The University of Chicago Press and CSLI Publications, Chicago, IL and Stanford, CA.

Developing a Chunk-based Grammar Checker for Translated English Sentences

Nay Yee Lin[a], Khin Mar Soe[b], and Ni Lar Thein[c]

[a,c]University of Computer Studies,Yangon, Myanmar
{nayyeelynn, nilarthein}@gmail.com
[b]Natural Language Processing Laboratory,
University of Computer Studies,Yangon, Myanmar
kmsucsy@gmail.com

Abstract. Machine Translation systems expect target language output to be grammatically correct. In Myanmar-English statistical machine translation system, target language output (English) can often be ungrammatical. To address this issue, we propose an ongoing chunk-based grammar checker by using trigram language model and rule based model. It is able to solve distortion, deficiency and make smooth the translated English sentences. We identify the sentences with chunk levels and generate context free grammar (CFG) rules for recognizing grammatical relations of chunks. There are three main processes to build a grammar checker: checking the sentence patterns in chunk level, analyzing the chunk errors and correcting the errors. According to experimental results, this checker can detect simple, compound and complex sentence types for declarative and interrogative sentences. This system is useful for reducing grammar errors of target language in Myanmar-English machine translation system.

Keywords: Statistical Machine Translation System, Trigram Language Model, Rule based Model.

1 Introduction

A language checker, typically, has two basic components, a spell-checker and a grammar checker. Whereas the spell-checker, usually, limits its operation to the inspection and correction of individual text words, the grammar checker has to cope with errors that can only be detected in contexts that are larger than the word (Anna).

Grammar is the set of structural rules that govern the composition of clauses, phrases, chunks and words in any given natural language. Grammar checking is one of the most widely used tools within natural language processing (NLP) applications. Grammar checkers check the grammatical structure of sentences based on morphological processing and syntactic processing. These two steps are part of natural language processing to understand the natural languages. Morphological processing is the step where individual words are analyzed into their components and non-word tokens such as punctuation. Syntactic processing is the analysis where linear sequences of words are transformed into structures that show grammatical relationships between the words in the sentence (Rich and Knight 1991).

Three main approaches are widely used for grammar checking in a language; syntax-based checking, statistics-based checking and rule-based checking. In syntax based grammar checking, each sentence is completely parsed to check the grammatical correctness of it. The text is considered incorrect if the syntactic parsing fails. In statistics-based approach, POS tag sequences are built from an annotated corpus, and the frequency, and thus the probability, of these sequences are noted. The text is considered incorrect if the POS-tagged text contains POS sequences with frequencies lower than some threshold. The statistics based approach essentially learns the rules from the tagged training corpus. In rule-based approach, the approach is very similar to the statistics based one, except that the rules must be handcrafted (Naber, 2003).

Grammar checkers are most often implemented as a feature of a larger program, such as a word processor. However, such a feature is not available as a separate free program for machine translation. Therefore, we propose a grammar checker as a complement of Myanmar-English machine translation by using trigram language model and rule based model. In this approach, the translated English sentence is used as an input. Firstly, this input sentence is tokenized and tagged POS to each word. Then these tagged words are grouped into chunks by parsing the sentence into a form that is a chunk based sentence structure. After making chunks, these chunks relationship for input sentence are detected by using trained sentence patterns. If the sentence pattern is incorrect, we analyze the chunk errors and then correct the errors using English grammar rules.

The rest of the paper is organized as follows. Section 2 presents the related work of this paper. Section 3 describes the overview of Myanmar-English Statistical Machine Translation System. In section 4, the proposed chunk based grammar checker is explained. Section 5 reports the experimental results of our proposed system and finally section 6 concludes the paper.

2 Related Work

This section presents the related works of the grammar checking in natural language processing for many languages.

Alam et al. (2006) proposed an approach which based on n-gram statistical grammar checker for both Bangla and English. It considered the n-gram based analysis of words and POS tags to decide whether the sentence is grammatically correct or not. Sharma and Jaiswal (2010) developed a model for reducing errors in translation using Pre-editor for Indian English Sentences. They have used a major corpus in tourism and health domains. This was incorporated in the AnglaBharti Engine and gave significant improvement in the Machine Translation output.

A user model can be tailored to different types of users to identify and correct English language errors. It is presented in the context of a written English tutoring system for deaf people. The model consists of a static model of the expected language and a dynamic model that represents how a language might be acquired over time. Together these models affect scores on a set of grammar rules which are used to produce a "best interpretation" of the user's input (McCoy et al., 1996).

Stymne and Ahrenberg (2010) checked the Swedish grammar for evaluation tool and post processing tool of Statistical Machine Translation. They have performed experiments for English-Swedish translation using a factored phrase-based statistical machine translation (PBSMT) system based on Moses (Koehn et al., 2007) and the mainly rule-based Swedish grammar checker Granska (Domeij et al., 2000; Knutsson, 2001)..

The ongoing developments in the LRE-2 project SECC (A Simplified English Grammar and Style Checker/Corrector) check if the documents comply with the syntactic and lexical rules; if not, error messages are given, and automatic correction is attempted wherever possible to reduce the amount of human correction needed (Adriaens,1993).

An approach based on hybrid approach that presents an implemented hybrid approach for grammar and style checking, combining an industrial pattern based grammar and style checker with bidirectional, large-scale HPSG grammars for German and English 2 (Crysmann et al., 2008).

Buscail and Dizier (2009) presented an analysis of the most frequently encountered style and text structure errors produced by a variety of types of authors when producing texts. They showed an argumentation system can be used so that the user can get arguments for or against a certain correction.

3 Myanmar-English Statistical Machine Translation System

Input for Myanmar-English statistical machine translation system (SMT) is Myanmar sentence and the target output is English sentence. Myanmar-English statistical machine translation system has developed source language model, alignment model, translation model and target language model to complete translation.

- **The source language model** includes making Part-of-Speech (POS) tags and function tags for each Myanmar word and searching grammatical relations of Myanmar sentence.
- **The translation model** includes phrase extraction, translation from Myanmar sentences to English sentences by using Myanmar-English bilingual corpus. This model also interacts with Word Sense Disambiguation (WSD) system to solve ambiguities when a phrase of a Myanmar sentence has more than one sense.
- **The alignment model** is working parallel with the other models. Its main work is to build the word and phrase aligned Myanmar-English bilingual corpus.
- **The target language model** includes two parts such as reordering the translated English sentences and smoothing it by using English grammar checker to reduce grammar errors.

Our proposed system is concerned with the target language model to check the grammar errors for translated English sentences. After input sentence has been processed in three models (source language model, alignment model and translation model), the translated English sentence is obtained in target language model. This sentence might be incomplete in grammar because the syntactic structures of Myanmar and English language are totally different. For example, after translating the Myanmar sentence "ပန်းခြံထဲမှာ သစ်ပင်များ ရှိကြသည်။", "pan chan htae hmar thet pin myar shi kya thi", the translated English sentence might be "*are trees in park.*". This sentence has missing words "*There*" and "*the*" for correct English sentence "*There are trees in the park.*". As an another input "သူသည် လက်ဖက်ရည်တစ်ခွက် သောက်နေသည်။", "thu thi laphet yae ta khwit thauk nay thi", the translated output is "*He is drinking a cup tea.*". In this sentence, "of" (preposition) is omitted from "*a cup of tea*". These examples are just simple sentence errors. When the sentence types are more complex, grammar errors detection and correction are more needed. There are many English grammar errors to correct ungrammatical sentences. This grammar checker currently detects and provides the following errors:

- If the sentence has missing words such as preposition (PPC), conjunction (COC), determiner (DT) and existential (EX) then this system suggests the required words according to the chunk types.
- In Subject-Verb agreement rule, if the subject is plural, verb has to be the plural. Verbs vary in form according to the person and number of the object.
- Sentence can contain inappropriate determiner. Therefore grammatical rules have been identified several kinds of determiner for appropriate noun.
- Translated English sentences can have the incorrect verb form. The system has to memorize all of the commonly used tenses and suggest the possible verb form.

4 Chunk-based Grammar Checker

In SMT system, there are very few spelling errors in the translation output, because all words are come from the corpus. Therefore, this system proposes a target-dominant grammar checker for Myanmar-English statistical machine translation system as shown in Figure 1.

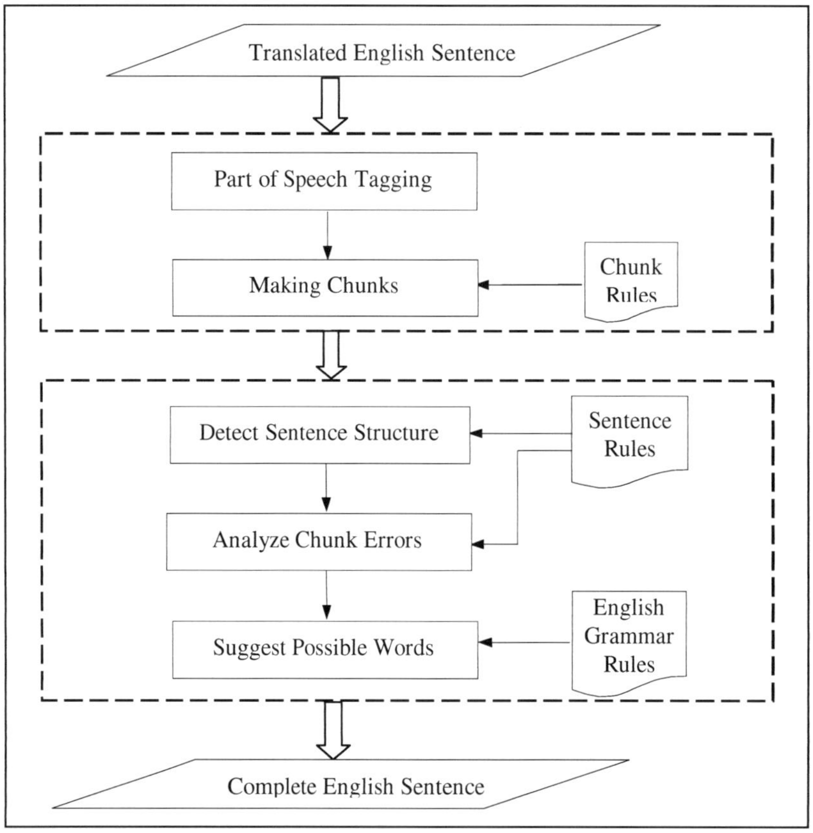

Figure 1: Overview of Proposed System.

4.1 Part-of-Speech (POS) Tagging

POS-tagging is the main process of making up the chunks in a sentence as corresponding to a particular part of speech. POS tagging is the process of assigning a part-of-speech tag such as noun, verb, pronoun, preposition, adverb, adjective or other tags to each word in a sentence. Nouns can be further divided into singular and plural nouns, verbs can be divided into past tense verbs and present tense verbs and so on.

There are many approaches to automated part of speech tagging. In this system, each word is tagged by using Tree Tagger which is a Java based open source tagger. However, Tree Tagger often fails to tag correctly some words when one word has more than one POS tag. For example, POS tags of the word "sweet" are "JJ" and "NN". In this case, refinement of the POS tags for these words is made by using the rules based on the position of the neighbor words' POS tags. The example for refinement tags is shown in Table 1.

Table 1: Example of refinement tags

Sentence	POS Tagging	Refine Tag by rules
He eats a ***sweet***.	He[PP] eats[VBZ] a[DT] ***sweet[JJ]*** . [SENT]	If previous tag is "DT", current tag is "JJ" And current word is "sweet", then change sweet[JJ] to ***sweet[NN].***
He is a ***tailor***.	He[PP] is[VBZ] a[DT] ***tailor[VB]*** .[SENT]	If previous tag is "DT", current tag is "VB" And current word is "tailor", then change tailor[VB] to ***tailor[NN].***

He ***bit*** a rope.	He[PP] ***bit[RB]*** a[DT] rope[NN] .[SENT]	If previous tag is "PP", current tag is "JJ" And current word is "bit", then change bit[RB] to ***bit[VBD].***

4.2 Making Chunk-based Sentence Patterns

Making chunks is a process to parse the sentence into a form that is a chunk based sentence structure. A chunk is a textual unit of adjacent POS tags which display the relations between their internal words. Input English sentence is made in chunk structure by using hand written rules. It represents how these chunks fit together to form the constituents of the sentence.

Context Free Grammar (CFG): CFGs constitute an important class of grammars, with a broad range of applications including programming languages, natural language processing, bio informatics and so on. CFG's rules present a single symbol on the left-hand-side, are a sufficiently powerful formalism to describe most of the structure in natural language.

A context-free grammar G = (V, T, S, P) is given by

- A finite set V of variables or non terminal symbols.
- A finite set T of symbols or terminal symbols. We assume that the sets V and T are disjoint.
- A start symbol $S \in V$.
- A finite set $P \subseteq V \times (V \cup T)^*$ of productions.

A production (A, α), where $A \in V$ and $\alpha \in (V \cup T)^*$ is a sequence of terminals and variables, is written as $A \rightarrow \alpha$. CFGs are powerful enough to express sophisticated relations among the words in a sentence. It is also tractable enough to be computed using parsing algorithms (Thurimella, 2005).

NLP applications like Grammar Checker need a parser with an optional parsing model. Parsing is the process of analyzing the text automatically by assigning syntactic structure according to the grammar of language. Parser is used to understand the syntax and semantics of a natural language sentences confined to the grammar.

There are two methods for parsing such as Top-down parsing and Bottom-up parsing. Top-down parsing begins with the start symbol and attempt to derive the input sentence by substituting the right hand side of productions for non terminals. Bottom-up (shift–reduce) parsing begins with the input sentence and combines words into higher-level chunks until the unit finally becomes a sentence. Bottom-up parsers handle a large class of grammars (Cooper et al., 2003). In this system, Bottom-up parsing is used to parse the sentences.

Parsing chunks by using CFG: Chunking or shallow parsing segments a sentence into a sequence of syntactic constituents or chunks, i.e. sequences of adjacent words grouped on the basis of linguistic properties (Abney, 1996). The syntactic chunk structure of a sentence is necessary to determine its grammar correctness. In the proposed system, ten general chunk types are used to make the chunk structure as shown in Table 2.

Table 2: Chunk Types

Chunk Types	Description	Example
NC	Noun Chunk	a young boy, the girls
VC	Verb Chunk	is playing, goes, went
AC	Adjective Chunk	more beautiful, younger, old
RC	Adverb Chunk	usually, quickly
PTC	Particle Chunk	up, down
PPC	Prepositional Chunk	at, on, in, under
COC	Conjunction Chunk	and, or, but
QC	Question Chunk	Where, Who, When
INFC	Infinitive Chunk	to
TC	Time Chunk	tomorrow, yesterday

The proposed grammar checker identifies the chunks using CFG based bottom-up parsing for assembling POS tags into higher level chunks, until a complete sentence has been found. For example, a simple sentence "*The students are playing football in the playground.*" is chunked as follows:

NC_VC_NC_PPC_NC_END (Chunk-based Sentence Pattern)

NC_VC_NC_PPC_NC_[SENT]

NC_VC_NC_PPC_[DT_NN][SENT]

NC_VC_NC_[IN][DT][NN][SENT]

NC_VC_[NN][IN][DT][NN][SENT]

NC_ [VBP_VBG][NN][IN][DT][NN][SENT]

[DT_NNS][VBP][VBG][NN][IN][DT][NN][SENT]

The[DT]students[NNS]are[VBP]playing[VBG] football[NN]in[IN]the[DT]playground[NN].[SENT]

Chunk-based sentence patterns are widely used in this system for detection sentence patterns. The larger the trained sentence patterns, the better the detection errors. The system has currently trained on about 6000 number of sentence patterns for simple, compound and complex sentence types. Some sample sentence rules are shown in Table 3.

Table 3: Chunk-based Sentence Patterns

NC_VC_END=S
NC_VC_NC_END=S
NC_VC_AC_PPC_NC_END=S
NC_RC_VC_PTC_RC_END=S
NCS_PRV2_RC_NCB2_END_END=S
VC_NC_PPC_NC_END=S
VC_NC_VC_TC_END=S
VC_NC_VC_TO_NC_END=S
QC_VC_NC_VC_IEND=S
QC_VC_NC _IEND=S
QC_VC_NC_AC_PPC _IEND=S
QC_VC_NC_VC_PPC _IEND=S
QC_VC_NC_PPC_TC _IEND=S

4.3 Detecting and Analyzing Chunk Errors

After making chunks, these chunks relationship for input sentence are detected and analyzed chunk errors using trigram language model and rule based model.

Trigram Language Model: The simplest models of natural language are n- gram Markov models. The Markov models for any n-gram are called Markov Chains. A Markov Chain is at most one path through the model for any given input (Saul and Pereira, 1997). N-gram models are the examples of statistical model. N-grams are traditionally presented as an approximation to a distribution of strings of fixed length.

N-grams of words or POSs are widely used but are not the only type of patterns used in previous work. Sun et al. (2007) extended n-grams to non continuous sequential patterns allowing arbitrary gaps between words. Sjöbergh (2006) used sequences of chunk types, for example, "NP_VC_PP." The parse trees returned by a statistical parser are used by Lee and Seneff (2008) to detect verb form errors.

According to the n-gram language model, a sentence has a fixed set of chunks, $\{ c_0, c_1, c_2, \ldots, c_n \}$. This is a set of chunks in our training sentences, e.g., {NC, VC, AC,…,

END}. In N-gram language model, each chunk depends probabilistically on the n-1 preceding words. This is expressed as shown in equation 1.

$$p(c_{o,n}) = \prod_{i=0}^{n-1} p(c_i | c_{i-n+1}, \ldots, c_{i-1}) \qquad (1)$$

where (c_i) is the current chunk of the input sentence and it depends on the previous chunks. In trigram language model, each chunk (c_i) depends probabilistically on previous two chunks (c_{i-1}, c_{i-2}) and is shown in equation 2.

$$p(c_{o,n}) = \prod_{i=0}^{n-1} p(c_i | c_{i-1}, c_{i-2}) \qquad (2)$$

Given a sentence, a trigram is a sequence of three chunks (c_i, c_{i+1}, c_{i+2}) where a generic chunk c_i is either the i-th chunk of the sentence.

Trigram language model is most suitable due to the capacity, coverage and computational power (3 Roark and Chamiak, 2000). The trigram model is used in a greater level of some advanced and optimizing techniques such as smoothing, caching, skipping, clustering, sentence mixing, structuring and text normalization. This model makes use of the history events in assigning the current event some probability value and therefore, it suits for our approach.

Rule-Based Model: Rule-based model has successfully used to develop natural language processing tools and applications. English grammatical rules are developed to define precisely how and where to assign the various words in a sentence. Rule-based system is more transparent and errors are easier to diagnose and debug.

It relies on hand-constructed rules that are to be acquired from language specialists, requires only small amount of training data and development could be very time consuming. It can be used with both well-formed and ill-formed input. It is extensible and maintainable. Rules play major role in various stages of translation: syntactic processing, semantic interpretation, and contextual processing of language (Charoenpornsawat et al., 2002). Therefore, the accuracy of translation system can be increased by the product of the rule based correcting ungrammatical sentences.

4.4 Grammar Error Correction

The final step of our proposed system is controlled by grammar rules to determine proper corrections. These rules can determine syntactic structure and ensure the agreement relations between various chunks in the sentence. POS tags for each chunk type are used to correct grammar errors. There are about 1800 sentence patterns and 1300 English grammar rules for correction at present. When the sentence patterns increased, the grammar rules will be improved. Some rules for correcting subject-verb agreement are presented in Table 4.

Table 4: Some Rules for Subject Verb Agreement

Rules (NC_VC)	**Example**
NNS +VBP	We go
NNS +VBD	We went
NNS +VBP_VBG	We are going
NNS +VBD_VBG	They were going
NNS +VBP_VBD	They have worked
NNS +MD_VB	They will come
NN +VBZ	She goes
NN +VBD	She went
NN +VBZ_VBG	She is going
NN +VBD_VBG	She was going
NN +VBZ_VBD	He has walked
NN +MD_VB	He will come

4.5 Example

For an incorrect translated sentence "*A man a woman went to their house*", the following sentence pattern and probability values are obtained.

POS Tagging :
A[DT] man[NN] a[DT] woman[NN] went[VBD] to[TO] their[PP$] house[NN] .[SENT]

Making Chunks :
NC [DT_ NN] => [A man]
NC [DT_NN] => [a woman]
VC [VBD] => [went]
INFC [TO] => [to]
NC [PP$_NN] => [their house]
END [SENT] => [.]

Chunk based Sentence :
NC_NC_VC_INFC_NC_END

Probabilities of each chunk from trained sentences
P(NC/none, none) = 0.586
P(NC/none, NC) = 0.0
P(VC/NC, NC) = 0.0
P(INFC/NC, VC) = 0.483
P(NC/VC, INFC) = 0.364
P(END/INFC, NC) = 0.675

P(S) =0.586 * 0.0 * 0.0 * 0.483 * 0.364 *0.675 =0.0

The product of the whole sentence is 0.0 by equation (2). In this case, we search the sequence of chunks P(NC/none, NC) which has zero probability. We get the probability values for possible chunks depend on previous chunks (none, NC) as follows:

P(VC/none, NC)=0.54
P(RC/none, NC)=0.01
P(COC/none, NC)= 0.01

According to these probabilities, RC, VC and COC can be in the second place. Firstly, VC (verb chunk) is substituted as the maximum probability. Then the sentence pattern NC_VC_ NC_VC_INFC_NC_END is obtained. However, this rule is incorrect by comparing the trained sentence patterns. Therefore, RC and COC are also substituted. When COC is substituted, the correct sentence rule NC_COC_NC_VC_INFC_NC_END is resulted for our system. From this example, the proposed system can search the correct chunk type (COC) by using trigram language model and rule based model.

Thereafter, the proposed system fills up a word in the missing place depending on grammar rules to correct the error. The missing chunk (COC) represents POS tag CC which corresponds to English words ('and', 'or', ',') according to the chunk rules. The correct sentence pattern might include 'and' between two noun chunks ([NC_COC_NC] [A man and a woman]) according to the English grammar rules.

5 Experimental Results

The proposed system is tested on about 1800 number of sentences. For each input sentence, the system has classified the kinds of sentence such as simple, compound and complex and then described whether the sentence type is interrogative or declarative. The grammar errors mainly found in the tested sentences are subject verb agreement, missing chunks and incorrect verb form. The performance of this approach is measured with precision, recall and F-score according to equation 3, 4 and 5. The resulting precision, recall and F-score of chunk-based grammar checker on different sentence types are shown in Table 5.

$$\text{PRECISION}=\frac{NumberofCorrectlyReducedErrors}{Numberof\ ReducedErrors}\times 100\% \quad (3)$$

$$\text{RECALL}=\frac{NumberofCorrectlyReducedErrors}{NumberofErrors}\times 100\% \quad (4)$$

$$\text{F score}=2\times\frac{Precision\times Recall}{Precision+Recall} \quad (5)$$

Table 5: Experimental Results

Sentence Type	Actual	Reduce	Correct	Precision	Recall	F-score
Simple	650	570	512	89.83 %	78.77 %	83.94%
Compound	530	480	402	83.75 %	75.85 %	79.61%
Complex	560	530	440	83.02%	78.57%	80.73%

6 Conclusion

A chunk-based grammar checker for translated English sentences which makes use of trigram language model and rule based model. Context Free Grammar rules are also used for identifying the sentence patterns and to divide a text into chunk types which correspond to certain syntactic units. We use our own training sentence patterns. We expect this grammar checker will get the benefits for Myanmar-English machine translation system. Moreover, we plan to improve the accuracies of detection, analyzing and correction grammar errors. In the future, we will expand the sentence rules to fully assess all sentence types and detect the semantic errors.

References

Abney, S. 1996. Tagging and Partial Parsing, In: Ken Church, Steve Young, and Gerrit Bloothooft (eds.), Corpus-Based Methods in Language and Speech. Kluwer Academic Publishers, Dordrecht.

Adriaens, G. November, 1993. Simplified English Grammar and Style Correction in an MT Framework, *Translation and the Computer 15 conference*, pp. 8-19, (London:Aslib).

Alam, J., N. UzZaman and M. Khan. 2006. N-gram based Statistical Grammar Checker for Bangla and English, *Proceedings of 9th International Conference on Computer and Information Technology (ICCIT 2006)*, Dhaka, Bangladesh.

Buscail, L. and P. Saint-Dizie. 2009. Textual and Stylistic Error Detection and Correction: Categorization, Annotation and Correction Strategies, *IEEE English International Symposium on Natural Language Processing.*

Charoenpornsawat, P., V. Sornlertlamvanich and T. Charoenporn. 2002. Improving Translation Quality of Rule-based Machine Translation, *In 19th International Conference on Computational Linguistics (Coling2002),* Workshop on Machine Translation in Asia. Taipei, Taiwan.

Cooper, K.D., K. Kennedy and L. Torczon. 2003. "*Bottom-up Parsing*".

Crysmann, B., N. Bertomeu, P. Adolphs, D. Flickinger and T. Kluwer. August 2008. Hybrid processing for grammar and style checking, *Proceedings of the 22nd International Conference on Computational Linguistics,* pp. 153-160, Manchester.

Domeij, R., O. Knutsson, J. Carlberger, and V. Kann. 2000. Granska-an efficient hybrid system for Swedish grammar checking, *In Proceedings of the 12th Nordic Conference on Computational Linguistics (Nodalida'99)*, pp.49-56, Trondheim, Norway.

Hein, A.S. "A Chart-Based Framework for Grammar Checking Initial Studies", Linguistics Department, Uppsala University, http://guagua.echo.lu/langeng/en/le3/scarrie/scarrie.html.

Koehn, P. and H. Hoang. 2007. Factored translation models, In Proceedings of the 2007 Joint Conference on Empirical Methods in Natural language Processing and Computational Natural Language Learning, pp. 868-876, Prague, Czech Republic.

McCoy, K.F., C. Pennington and L.Z. Suri. January, 1996. English Error Correction: A Syntactic User Model Based on Principled Mal-Rule Scoring, *In Proceedings of the Fifth International Conference on User Modeling*, Kailua-Kona, Hawaii.

Naber, D. 2003. "A Rule-Based Style and Grammar Checker" Faculty of Engineering, University of Bielefeld.

Rich, E. and K. Knight. 1991. *Artificial Intelligent.* Second edition. New York: McGraw Hill, Inc.

Roark, B. and E. Charniak. 2000. Measuring Efficiency in High-Accuracy, Broad-Coverage Statistical Parsing, *In Proceedings of the International Conference on Computational Linguistics (COLING) 2000* Workshop on Efficiency in Large-Scale Parsing Systems, pp. 29-36.

Saul, L. and F. Pereira. 1997. Aggregate and mixed order Markov models for statistical language processing, *Proceedings of the Second Conference on Empirical Methods in Natural Language Processing*, pp. 81-89. ACM Press, New York.

Sharma, A. and N. Jaiswal. 2010. Reducing Errors in Translation using Pre-editor for Indian English Sentences, *Proceedings of Annual Seminar of CDAC-Noida Technologies (ASCNT)*, Noida, pp.70-76, India.

Sjöbergh, J. 2006. Chunking: An unsupervised method to find errors in text, *In Proceedings of the 15th Nodalida Conference*, pp.180-185. Joensuu, Finland: University of Joensuu electronic publications in linguistics and language technology.

Stymne, S. and L. Ahrenberg. 2010. Using a Grammar Checker for Evaluation and Postprocessing of Statistical Machine Translation, *In Proceedings of the International Conference on Language Resources and Evaluation (LREC)* 2010. Valetta, Malta.

Sun, G., X. Liu, G. Cong, M. Zhou, Z. Xiong, J. Lee and C. Lin. 2007. Detecting erroneous sentences using automatically mined sequential patterns, *In Proceedings of the 45th Annual Meeting of the Association for Computational Linguistics,* pp. 81-88. Prague, Crech Republic: Association for Computational Linguistics.

Thurimella, R. 2005. "Context Free Grammars".

Creating the Open Wordnet Bahasa*

Nurril Hirfana Mohamed Noor and Suerya Sapuan and Francis Bond

School of Humanities and Social Sciences
Nanyang University of Technology
hirfananoor@yahoo.com, suerya.sapuan@gmail.com, bond@ieee.org

Abstract. This paper outlines the creation of the Wordnet Bahasa as a resource for the study of lexical semantics in the Malay language. It is created by combining information from several lexical resources: the French-English-Malay dictionary **FEM**, the KAmus Melayu-Inggeris **KAMI**, and wordnets for English, French and Chinese. Construction went through three steps: (i) automatic building of word candidates; (ii) evaluation and selection of acceptable candidates from merging of lexicons; (iii) final hand check of the 5,000 core synsets. Our Wordnet Bahasa is only in the first phase of building a full fledged wordNet and needs to be further expanded, however it is already large enough to be useful for sense tagging both Malay and Indonesian.

Keywords: Wordnet, Malaysian, Indonesian, Hyponymy, Open Source

1 Introduction

The dictionary is a very important lexical resource in any field of studies. However, WordNet, originally created by academics at Princeton University, is just as important if not greater (Fellbaum, 1998). In fact, it is a source of reference that takes the traditional dictionary to a whole new level. While a dictionary can provide information such as the meaning, synonyms and parts of speech, and can organise them in alphabetical order, a wordnet is able to organise the words into a set of cognitive synonyms (synsets) which express distinct concepts. This reason has been the motivation for the creation of the various wordnets for various languages.

There is currently no wordnet available for Malay despite the great number of wordnets available for many languages. Hence, this paper will attempt to create a lexical database for the Malay language based on alignments with other lexical resources — the French-English-Malay (**FEM**) dictionary, the English wordnet, **KAMI** and wordnets for Chinese and French. Crossing lexicons over several languages contributes to the accuracy of the Wordnet Bahasa. This wordnet will be released under an open source license (Creative Commons Attribution) in order to make it fully accessible to all potential users.

Bahasa Melayu "the Malay language" is one that had been standardized over time with the aim of formal usage of the language. It derived from the variety of Malay languages that exist in the different parts of the Malay Archipelago, and is now widely used in Malaysia, Singapore, parts of Thailand and Brunei. The language spoken in Indonesia (Bahasa Indonesia) is very similar, and largely mutually intelligible. In this paper we will use **Malay** for standard Malay (the official language of Malaysia, ISO 639-3 code **zsm**), **Indonesian** to refer to the official language of Indonesia (**ind**) and **Bahasa** to refer to the generic Malay language that includes both (**msa**). Bahasa is the official language of four South Eastern Asian countries, namely Malaysia, Indonesia, Brunei and

* We would like to thank Key-Sun Choi for allowing us to use the Goi-Taikei–CoreNet–Wordnet mappings; Nippon Telegraph and Telephone Corporation for allowing us to use **KAMI**, the **FEM** developers for allowing us to use **FEM**, and all the developers of the various Wordnets. This research was supported in part by the joint JSPS/NTU grant on *Revealing Meaning Using Multiple Languages*.

Singapore. Some people from The Philippines, Thailand, Burma, Sri Lanka, Cocos Island and Christmas Island also use it. There are about 40 million native Bahasa speakers worldwide.[1]

Spelling reforms in the 1970s harmonized the orthographic conventions of Malay and Indonesian, making the written forms very similar (Asmah Haji Omar, 1975). Because of the enormous overlap in vocabulary (close to 98% by our measure, see Section 4.3) we decided it was possible to create a single wordnet for both languages: the Wordnet Bahasa. The vast majority of words are usable for both Malay and Indonesian and we specially mark those words that are used exclusively in one language. We hope that by building a single, open wordnet for both Malay and Indonesian we can help to create a strong lexical resource for the region.

2 Previous Work

The most common approaches to building a wordnet for a new language are automatic or semi automatic approaches. There are two main methods: the merge and the extend approach (Vossen, 2005). The merge approach would require the construction of an independent lexicon for a certain language based on monolingual resources, after which, it is mapped to other wordnets. The extend approach on the other hand is executed by obtaining a set of synsets from Princeton WordNet (PWN), and then translating it into the target language. This method allows the preservation of the original structure of the wordnet. We have opted for the extend approach both because of its simplicity and because the resulting wordnet is automatically aligned to all other wordnets.

The idea of extending the synsets with reference from not just the PWN but at least one other wordnet in a different language provides a much stronger foundation laid before the construction of a new wordnet. In Bond *et al.* (2008), the authors pointed out that by using wordnets in multiple languages to disambiguate the target language (Japanese in their study), a more reliable prototype could be provided. This multiple-pivot technique was then adapted to suit the needs of the Wordnet Bahasa, as will be explained in the next section.

There has already been some work on building wordnets for Malay and Indonesian. Lim and Hussein (2006) serves as a good head start for the building of a Malay wordnet. The paper suggests finding the prototype based on sense alignments with Kamus Inggeris Melayu Dewan (KIMD) and the English wordnet.

According to Lim and Hussein (2006), this "… fast prototyping exercise (would require the creation of) semantic relations between the Malay synsets based on the existing relations between their English equivalents". This method is an elaboration of the merge methodology. Lim and Hussein (2006) managed to build 12,429 noun synsets and 5,805 verb synsets. While this is by no means exhaustive, it is at the very least a rough gage of the minimum possible range of words in a Malay wordnet. In the final discussion of the paper, Lim and Hussein (2006) point out that the bottleneck for their prototype "is in the dictionary used". Unfortunately, we do not have access to the same Malay lexicon, so we cannot directly implement their approach.

There have been two approaches to building an Indonesian wordnet. The first was an expand approach, and created a small prototype (Putra *et al.*, 2008). The second also used an expand approach, and then corrected entries using the infrastructure from the Asian Wordnet Project (Riza *et al.*, 2010). The Indonesian Wordnet at the Asian Wordnet currently has 33,726 synsets; 38,394 words and 65,206 senses (word-synset pairs).[2] The lexicons used to expand were bilingual English-Indonesian and thus did not enable the use of multiple pivots.

3 Resources

We used two lexicons: **FEM**, which contains entries with French, English and Malay as well as hypernyms in French; and **KAMI**, which contains Malay, English and Chinese as well as semantic classes from the Goi-Taikei ontology.

[1] `http://www.ethnologue.com/show_language.asp?code=msa`

[2] `http://id.asianwordnet.org/`

We used four wordnets: one for English, one for Chinese and two for French as the original French Wordnet has not been maintained, so we supplemented it with the new Wordnet Liberé du Français (WOLF). As these map to different versions of the English WordNet, we used mappings to harmonize them (Daude *et al.*, 2003). To map between the Goi-Taikei ontology and wordnet, we used the mappings produced by CoreNet (Kang *et al.*, 2010).

3.1 Malay Lexicons

We used two lexicons **FEM** and **KAMI**.

The Malay-English Dictionary **KAMI**: KAmus Melayu-Inggeris was compiled by NTT-MSC (Quah *et al.*, 2001), based on a dictionary produced originally by a translation company. The dictionary currently has 67,670 Malay words with English translations. 69% have only one translation, 19% have two, 7% have three; the average number of translations is 1.57, giving 106,558 Malay-English pairs.

Each entry in the dictionary consists of the following fields: (1) Malay index word; (2) Malay root word; (3) Malay POS; (4) detailed syntactic features; (5) semantic classes; (6) English translation; (7) English comments; (8) Chinese translation. All entries have values for fields 1,2 and 3; most have syntactic features. 22% have Chinese translations and 28% have semantic classes from the Goi-Taikei (**GT**) ontology (Ikehara *et al.*, 1997). The Goi-Taikei ontology consists of 2,710 semantic classes, providing an upper level ontology. It was originally designed for Japanese, but has also been used for Chinese, English, Korean and Malay.

English and Chinese translations and comments are provided for use in a machine translation system, as well as an aid for non-Malay speakers. Semantic classes were automatically produced from a variety of sources, including deducing them from the associated classifiers and finding them in other lexicons or resources such as International Standard Organization (ISO) language and currency names (Quah *et al.*, 2001), and still contains some errors.

We also used **FEM**: the French-English-Malay Lexicon (Lafourcade *et al.*, 2003). We combined the general lexicon and a specialist lexicon of computational terms, giving 33,022 lexical entries. Each entry comes with: (1) French headword; (2) pronunciation; (3) part of speech; (4) superordinate term in French (46% of entries); (5) English equivalent; (6) Malay equivalent; (7) French example (30%); (8) English example (30%); (9) Malay example (30%). The dictionary had been automatically compiled and hand-corrected with some errors remaining, especially in the Malay equivalents.

We converted both lexicons to the following format (ignoring fields that we won't use):

(1)
$$\begin{bmatrix} \textit{lexical entry} & \\ \text{Malay} & m_0, \ldots m_n \\ \text{English} & e_0, \ldots e_m \\ \text{French/Chinese} & f_0, \ldots f_o \\ \text{Part-of-Speech} & \left\{\text{noun, verb, adjective, adverb, other}\right\} \\ \text{Hypernym} & \left\{\text{French word} \mid \textbf{GT} \text{ class}\right\} \end{bmatrix}$$

Each entry has one or more words in Malay, English and French/Chinese plus possibly a hypernym, expressed either as a French word or as Goi-Taikei semantic class. They also have a part-of-speech which we map into either one of the four open classes used in WordNet, or the class **other** which is used for closed class words.

3.2 WordNets and Mappings

Because we had dictionaries linking Malay to English, Chinese and French, we needed wordnets for these three languages, summarized in Table 1. For English, we used the Princeton WordNet

(Fellbaum, 1998), the original wordnet, and the largest so far. For Chinese, we used the Chinese Wordnet created by (Xu *et al.*, 2008), with some normalization (removing bracketed data, leading and trailing punctuation and white space, removing affixes attached to adjectives and adverbs such as 的 *de* and 地 *zi*). For French, we created a new wordnet (which we will just call the French Wordnet) by combining entries from the French part of Euro WordNet (Vossen, 1998) and the Wordnet Liberé du Français (Sagot and Fišer, 2008). The combined wordnet had considerably better coverage than either of its components.

All of the wordnets were linked to some version of the English wordnet (shown in Table 1) We used the mappings produced by Daude *et al.* (2003) to harmonize them.

Language	English	Chinese		French	
Wordnet	Princeton		Combined	Euro WordNet	WOLF
Synsets	117,659	109,140	44,914	31,601	21,951
Senses	206,941	161,655	77,015	44,920	32,689
Words	155,287	102,364	49,420	37,364	18,787
version	3.0	2.0	3.0	1.5	2.0

Table 1: Wordnet Sizes

To map between the Goi-Taikei (**GT**) ontology and PWN, we used the mappings produced by CoreNet (Kang *et al.*, 2010). CoreNet is an extension of Goi-Taikei to Chinese and Korean. These consist of a table matching CoreNet classes to one or more wordnet synsets. We were also given a table matching **GT** classes to CoreNet classes. The **GT**-CoreNet mapping is very accurate, as CoreNet design was strongly influenced by Goi-Taikei (Korterm, 2005). The CoreNet-wordnet mapping is automatically produced, we found it quite accurate. We crossed the two tables to get a single **GT**-corenet-wordnet mapping.

The combined wordnets can be thought of as having entries like the following (ignoring irrelevant information).

(2)
$$\begin{bmatrix} \textit{synset} & \\ \text{Lexemes} & \begin{bmatrix} \text{English} & e_0, \ldots e_m \\ \text{Chinese} & c_0, \ldots c_n \\ \text{French} & f_0, \ldots f_o \end{bmatrix} \\ \text{Part-of-Speech} & \left\{ \text{noun, verb, adjective, adverb} \right\} \\ \text{Relations} & \begin{bmatrix} \text{Hypernym} & \textit{synset} \\ \text{Meronym} & \textit{synset} \\ \ldots & \end{bmatrix} \end{bmatrix}$$

4 Method

Building the Wordnet Bahasa was done in three steps: (i) automatically building candidates; (ii) evaluating and selecting acceptable groups; (iii) hand correcting the 5,000 most common concepts (core synsets).

4.1 Automatic Construction

The construction broadly follows the matching through multiple pivot approach of Bond and Ogura (2007). We want to match lexical entries (which have Malay words associated with them) to wordnet synsets.

For each word in the lexicon, we try to link to each synset that has the same part-of-speech. We have three pivots for this: the English term, the French or Chinese term and the hypernym.

We first link through the terms, and then, for each synset that matched, we see if the hypernym is compatible with the synset's hypernyms.

We will give an example for the following entries.

(3) Entry in **FEM**

lexical entry	
Malay	busur
English	bow
French	arc
Part-of-Speech	noun
Hypernym	arme "weapon"

(4) Entry in **KAMI**

lexical entry	
Malay	busur
English	bow
Chinese	弓
Part-of-Speech	noun
Hypernym	⟨940 : *worktool*⟩

(5) Wordnet candidates (only two of many)

a.

synset	
Lexemes	English bow; Chinese 弓; French arc
Part-of-Speech	noun
Relations	Hypernym *weapon*; …
Definition	a weapon for shooting arrows, …

b.

synset	
Lexemes	English bowing, obeisance, bow; Chinese 鞠躬, 弯腰, 运弓法[3]; French révérence
Part-of-Speech	noun
Relations	Hypernym *reverence, motion*; …
Definition	bending the head or body or knee as a sign of reverence …

Considering the **FEM** entry for {busur, bow, arc} (3), we look up the combined wordnet and find one entry (5a) that matches in two languages, and several that match in only one (we only show 5b). We then look at the semantic class, and using the combined wordnet, find that *arme* "weapon" gives a synset which is a hypernym of (5a), but not (5b). We thus have a strong match to the correct synset.

When we come to the **KAMI** entry for {busur, bow, 弓} (4), we look up wordnet and also find one entry (5a) that matches in two languages, and several that match in only one (we only

[3] This is in fact an error, it means "archery" and should be in a different sysnet.

show 5b). When we look up the semantic class, the **GT**-corenet-wordnet mapping leads to the synset for `tool` "an implement used in the practice of a vocation", which is not a hypernym of any of the candidates.[4] We thus have a reasonable link to the correct synset, and only weak links to the others.

The process of matching is straightforward, the major effort was in getting all the lexical resources into compatible formats. As was shown in this example, typically there would be small errors in one or more of the resources. Actual matching was done with a series of one-off python scripts using the Natural Language Toolkit's wordnet interface (Bird *et al.*, 2009) to calculate the hypernym relation.

4.2 Selection

After matching all the candidates, we wanted to identify those that could be used as is, with an acceptable level of error. We considered the following criteria in selection:

uniq lexical entry matched only one synset
in this case we considered it monosemous so the match should be good

multi lexical entry matched through two languages
as ambiguity is expressed differently in different languages, matching through two gives a much stronger match

more lexical entry matched more than one word (in one languages)
for entries with multiple words in the same language, if these all matched the same synset it suggests it is a better match

sem lexical entry's hypernym was compatible
If a word and its hypernym both match, then it should be semantically compatible

We took a random sample of a hundred entries from each combination of these features. The major groups are shown in Table 2, including those entries that just matched through one word (one) which we did not check for accuracy as we expected the accuracy to be low. Any combination that had fewer than 100 candidates was completely hand checked, there were 417 examples of these (such as **sem+uniq+multi**). Checking was done by the first and second authors, who are bilingual in Malaysian and English. When one author was unsure, they checked with the other, with standard reference lexicons for Malaysian and Indonesian (Dewan Bahasa dan Pustaka, 2005; Pusat Bahasa, 2008) and by checking usage examples on-line.

Lexicon	**KAMI**		**FEM**	
Match	Size	Accuracy (%)	Size	Accuracy (%)
one	340,537	—	210,443	—
more	5,920	75	409	78
sem	7,137	69	**12,208**	**93**
uniq	**7,381**	**85**	4,723	79
sem+uniq	**1,340**	**86**	204	79
multi	**8,870**	**96**	**21,213**	**85**
sem+multi	**684**	**93**	**2,533**	**89**

Table 2: Lexical Entry-Synset Match Accuracy
Subsets marked in bold were included in the Wordnet Bahasa as good.

We chose the fairly low threshold of 85% accuracy, as we judged coverage to be extremely important, and it is easier to remove bad entries than add new ones.

[4] The semantic class in **KAMI** is incorrect, it should be the immediate hypernym of this class

We merged the candidates from the two dictionaries, grouping things in to only four groups: **good** according to the selection above. **ok** in that it matched two or more criteria and — if there was only one supporting match.

When we merged if each dictionary marked a sense as **ok**, we upgraded it to **good**, based on a random sample of a 100 such entries. This happened to a further 3,533 entries.

Type	Senses
—	497,911
ok	23,257
good	42,050

Table 3: Merged results of the automatic construction

Because of overlap in the two resources, the numbers in the merged lexicon are less than the sum of the individual lexicons.

4.3 Correction

In order to make sure of the reliability of the most common synsets, we hand corrected the 5,000 core synsets: the most common synsets used in the British National Corpus[5] (Fellbaum and Vossen, 2007). After mapping to WordNet 3.0, the actual list has the 4,960 synsets. All candidates for these entries were hand-checked, regardless of how well they matched. There were a total of 99,061 sense candidates, of which 15,951 were judged to be good.

Type	Senses	
rejected	83,365	
—	413,899	
ok	18,172	
good	30,805	Release
checked	17,524	Release

Table 4: Merged results of the automatic construction

During this process, candidates that were only used in either Malay or Indonesian were marked as such. The default assumption is that a sense (synset-word) mapping can be used in either Malay or Indonesian (which we tag as Bahasa). If it is restricted to use in one or the other, then we tag it as Malay or Indonesian.

5 Results and Discussion

The resulting Wordnet Bahasa counting hand-checked and high-quality automatic candidates has 19,207 synsets, 48,111 senses and 19,460 unique words. This is still quite small, in terms of types, but as the high frequency synsets are all in, it should have high token coverage when used to tag text. The average ambiguity is high ($\frac{|\text{senses}|}{|\text{words}|} = 2.47$), but this because of the high frequency (and thus highly polysemous) entries. If we take out the high frequency synsets and consider just the average ambiguity of the high-quality automatic candidates it is only 1.05.

Looking at the results in section 4.2, we can see that adding the hypernym matching gave us over a quarter of the good entries (the **sem** cell for **FEM** in Table 2). The hypernym matching was less useful for **KAMI**— an analysis of errors showed that this was mainly due to errors in the (automatically assigned) semantic classes. The classes tended to be too general, and this gave them little disambiguating power. Matching through multiple pivots was much more effective for **KAMI**. In this case, we hypothesize that the more different language (Chinese) gives more disambiguating power than French, when combined with English. Because French and English are closely related, they often show the same ambiguity.

[5] `http://wordnet.cs.princeton.edu/downloads.html`

We measured how close Malay and Indonesian are by calculating the distribution of the language tags. These only exist for the hand checked entries, of these 17,150 (97.9%) were marked as acceptable in both languages, 158 (0.9%) as acceptable only in Indonesian and 216 (1.2%) as acceptable only in Malay.

(6)

synset		
Lexemes	English	dragonfly, mosquito hawk, …
	Chinese	蜻蜓
	French	libellule
	Bahasa	capung
	Malay	sibur-sibur
	Indonesian	sibar-sibar
Part-of-Speech	noun	
Relations	Hypernym	*odonate*

Further investigation in this phenomenon shows that differences in Malay and Indonesian words mostly lie with nouns, other than minor spelling differences of various words. (6) is an example of this.

As can be seen above, a dragonfly in translated as *sibur-sibur* which is identified only as a Malay word, since in Indonesian, a dragonfly is a *sibar-sibar*. However, in both languages *capung* can also be used to describe this insect, showing that the two languages are highly interrelated in terms of meaning and spelling.

Another example of a difference is in translation of worms. When translated in Bahasa (both Malay and Indonesian), a worm is *cacing*. However, once the basic word divides in subordinate categories, the two Bahasa languages also divide. The Indonesian language has *cacing parasit* "roundworm" as a subordinate word for *cacing* whereas the Malay language uses *cacing keruit/cacing kerawit* "threadworm" to describe the same creature. In wordnet, *threadworm* is a hyponym of *roundworm*. This shows that on top of having slight variations in spelling and nouns, the two languages sometimes have different hierarchies.

This research was made possible by the availability of a wide variety of lexical resources: the original lexicons, wordnets of various languages, mappings between different versions of wordnet and wordnet and different ontologies. Many of these have been released freely, some of these we were granted permission to use for research. Granting access to resources makes possible entirely new applications and so should be encouraged.

The Wordnet Bahasa is released under the MIT license[6] (equivalent to the original wordnet license: it allows the rights to use, copy, modify, merge, publish, distribute, sublicense, and/or sell copies so long as copyright is attributed to the original authors). It can be freely downloaded from `wn-msa.sourceforge.net`. We have three reasons for choosing an open license. The first is practical, creating the wordnet was a significant investment in time and labor, so we want it to be used as widely as possible, getting us the highest return on our investment. The second is moral, we were able to create the Wordnet Bahasa quickly and accurately due to the wealth of lexical resources people allowed us to use, therefore feel we should also let others build upon our work. The final reason is also practical, maintaining and extending a lexical resource is an unending struggle, by making it open we hope to get more useful feedback and user contributions.

[6] `http://www.opensource.org/licenses/mit-license.php`

6 Further Work

As this is only the first phase step toward creating a wordnet for Malay and Indonesian, much more can be done to improve it. Firstly, the Malay languages have very rich derivational morphology — we would like to extend the Wordnet Bahasa to cover derivational morphology and link the words to their stem form (which may require an extension of the data structure, the root form does not fit cleanly into the part of speech categories). Secondly, we intend to add numeral classifier relations. Thirdly, we would like to add Malay and Indonesian definition sentences. Finally, tagging a corpus with this WordNet will allow us both to get frequency information and also to check for gaps in coverage.

Currently we under-specify the language for most entries in our master database, and output two fully specified versions of the dictionary (Malay and Indonesian) for applications. As these are 98% the same, this is inefficient. We would like to enhance our lexical search interface so that we can have a combined wordnet, and extend the **`domain:usage`** relation to languages, linking individual senses to the synsets for either Malay or Indonesian as required.

Finally, we intend to continue our research on the Wordnet Bahasa in cooperation with other groups in Indonesia and Malaysia, so that we can all contribute to a single rich lexical resource.

7 Conclusions

We were able to make a rapid start in building the Wordnet Bahasa using several existing lexical resources (**FEM**, **KAMI** and many wordnets). We extend the standard matching through multiple pivot languages to also consider hypernym compatibility. We also combine Standard Malay and Indonesian into a single Wordnet Bahasa only marking those entries where the Malay language and Indonesian language were differentiated. This wordnet will serve as a platform for further work in those two languages and we intend to cooperate with teams in both Malaysia and Indonesia for future expansion.

References

Asmah Haji Omar. 1975. Supranational standardisation of spelling system: the case of Malaysia and Indonesia. In *Essays in Malaysian Linguistics*, pp. 84–101. Dewan Bahasa dan Pustaka, Kuala Lumpar.

Bird, Stephen, Ewan Klein, and Edward Loper. 2009. *Natural Language Processing with Python.* O'Reilly. (`www.nltk.org/book`).

Bond, Francis, Hitoshi Isahara, Kyoko Kanzaki, and Kiyotaka Uchimoto. 2008. Boot-strapping a WordNet using multiple existing WordNets. In *Sixth International conference on Language Resources and Evaluation (LREC 2008)*, Marrakech.

Bond, Francis and Kentaro Ogura. 2007. Combining linguistic resources to create a machine-tractable Japanese-Malay dictionary. *Language Resources and Evaluation*, 42(2), 127–136. (Special issue on Asian language technology).

Daude, Jordi, Lluis Padro, and German Rigau. 2003. Validation and tuning of Wordnet mapping techniques. In *Proceedings of the International Conference on Recent Advances in Natural Language Processing (RANLP'03)*, Borovets, Bulgaria.

Dewan Bahasa dan Pustaka. 2005. *Kamus Dewan [The Institute Dictionary]*. Dewan Bahasa dan Pustaka, Kuala Lumpar, 4 edition.

Fellbaum, Christiane and Piek Vossen. 2007. Connecting the universal to the specific: Towards the global grid. In *First International Workshop on Intercultural Collaboration (IWIC-2007)*, pp. 2–16, Kyoto.

Fellbaum, Christine, ed. 1998. *WordNet: An Electronic Lexical Database*. MIT Press.

Ikehara, Satoru, Masahiro Miyazaki, Satoshi Shirai, Akio Yokoo, Hiromi Nakaiwa, Kentaro Ogura, Yoshifumi Ooyama, and Yoshihiko Hayashi. 1997. *Goi-Taikei — A Japanese Lexicon*. Iwanami Shoten, Tokyo. 5 volumes/CDROM.

Kang, In-Su, Sin-Jae Kang, Se-Jin Nam, and Key-Sun Choi. 2010. Linking CoreNet to WordNet through KorLex — some aspects and interim consideration. In Pushpak Bhattacharyya, Christiane Fellbaum, and Piek Vossen, eds., *5th Global Wordnet Conference: GWC-2010*, Mumbai.

Korterm. 2005. *CoreNet: Multilingual WordNet*. KAIST Press. (in Korean).

Lafourcade, M., G. Sérasset, L. Metzger, A. Rahman, and C. K. Chuah. 2003. Dictionnaire Français-Anglais-Malais (FeM) - version 2. CD-ROM, Dictionnaire en version XML et Application Java. (online at `http://www-clips.imag.fr/cgi-bin/geta/fem/fem.pl?lang=en`).

Lim, Lian Tze and Nur Hussein. 2006. Fast prototyping of a Malay wordnet system. In *Proceedings of the Language, Artificial Intelligence and Computer Science for Natural Language Processing (LAICS-NLP) Summer School Workshop*, pp. 13–16.

Pusat Bahasa. 2008. *Kamus Besar Bahasa Indonesia*. Pusat Bahasa, Jakarta, 3 edition.

Putra, Desmond Darma, Abdul Arfan, and Ruli Manurung. 2008. Building an Indonesian wordnet. In *Proceedings of the 2nd International MALINDO Workshop*, CyberJaya.

Quah, Chiew Kin, Francis Bond, and Takefumi Yamazaki. 2001. Design and construction of a machine-tractable Malay-English lexicon. In *Asialex 2001 Proceedings*, pp. 200–205, Seoul.

Riza, Hammam, Budiono, and Chairil Hakim. 2010. Collaborative work on Indonesian wordnet through Asian wordnet (awm). In *Proceedings of the 8th Workshop on Asian Language Resources*, pp. 9–13, Beijing.

Sagot, Benoît and Darja Fišer. 2008. Building a free French wordnet from multilingual resources. In European Language Resources Association (ELRA), ed., *Proceedings of the Sixth International Language Resources and Evaluation (LREC'08)*, Marrakech, Morocco.

Vossen, Piek, ed. 1998. *Euro WordNet*. Kluwer.

Vossen, Piek. 2005. Building wordnets. `http://www.globalwordnet.org/gwa/BuildingWordnets.ppt`.

Xu, Renjie, Zhiqiang Gao, Yuzhong Qu, and Zhisheng Huang. 2008. An integrated approach for automatic construction of bilingual Chinese-English WordNet. In *3rd Asian Semantic Web Conference (ASWC 2008)*, pp. 302–341.

Automatic identification of words with novel but infrequent senses*

Paul Cook and Graeme Hirst

Department of Computer Science
University of Toronto
{pcook,gh}@cs.toronto.edu

Abstract. We propose a statistical method for identifying words that have a novel sense in one corpus compared to another based on differences in their lexico-syntactic contexts in those corpora. In contrast to previous work on identifying semantic change, we focus specifically on infrequent word senses. Given the challenges of evaluation for this task, we further propose a novel evaluation method based on synthetic examples of semantic change that allows us to simulate differing degrees of sense change. Our proposed method is able to identify rather subtle simulated sense changes, and outperforms both a random baseline and a previously-proposed approach.

Keywords: Neologisms, semantic change, word senses, lexical semantics

1 New word senses

The meanings of words are not static, but can vary and change in a number of ways. In particular, words can undergo diachronic change—change over time—and come to be used in new senses. Contemporary examples of sense change can be seen in the following usages of *rock*, *sick*, and *text*, all of which correspond to relatively new senses of these words.

1. *Marvez has rocked the mullet* [hair-style] *for years as a style statement.* [*rock* = 'display with pride']
2. *LeBron has one of the sickest vertical leaps in the game, yet how many alley-oops have you seen him convert in his career?* [*sickest* = 'best']
3. *After she ignored the first few texts and phone calls, I gave up.* [*text* = 'text message']

Furthermore, new word senses are not necessarily frequent. For example, the above usages are taken from the enTenTen corpus,[1] a very large corpus containing a wide variety of text types, but the corresponding senses of these words appear to be rare in this corpus.

The identification of new word senses is an important task in lexicography, and is necessary to keep dictionaries up-to-date. But lexical semantic change has only recently been studied from a computational perspective, and only to a limited extent (e.g., Sagi et al., 2009; Cook and Stevenson, 2010; Gulordava and Baroni, 2011). Furthermore, despite the low frequency of many novel word senses, no work to date has specifically considered the identification of words with novel infrequent senses. In contrast, in this paper we focus specifically on this issue

The manual identification of novel senses is becoming increasingly difficult nowadays due to the vast quantities of text being produced (e.g., through online social media) that must be searched.

* We thank Afsaneh Fazly, Diana McCarthy, Suzanne Stevenson, and the members of the University of Melbourne Language Technology Group for their feedback on earlier versions of this work. This work was financially supported by MITACS. Paul Cook is now a McKenzie Postdoctoral Fellow in the Department of Computer Science and Software Engineering at the University of Melbourne.

[1] http://trac.sketchengine.co.uk/wiki/Corpora/enTenTen

The methods we propose could form the basis for a lexicographical tool to aid in the identification of new word senses that are particularly difficult to find due to their relatively low frequency.

Evaluating approaches to identifying diachronic semantic change is difficult; indeed, most previous studies have relied on rather small datasets (e.g., Sagi et al., 2009; Cook and Stevenson, 2010) or human judges' intuitions about changes in meaning, which might not accurately reflect changes in meaning observed in corpora (e.g., Gulordava and Baroni, 2011). Therefore, taking inspiration from evaluation approaches in word sense disambiguation that make use of artificially-ambiguous words (e.g., Schütze, 1992; Gale et al., 1992), we propose evaluation methods that use synthetic examples of semantic change. Crucially, this enables us to to carefully control for the frequency of senses; this allows us to assess how rare a word sense may be, and yet still be identified by our method.

One further consideration is that methods for identifying semantic change must be applicable to relatively small corpora. Although there is a move towards using ever-larger corpora in computational linguistics, many historical corpora and corpora for specific time periods are rather small. For example, one year of text from the New York Times Annotated Corpus (Sandhaus, 2008) consists of roughly 50 million words, which is small compared to contemporary corpora which often contain billions of words. In this study, we therefore focus on relatively small corpora.

We discuss some related work in Section 2, and then present our model for identifying words with differing senses in Section 3. In Sections 4 and 5 we empirically evaluate our model on synthetic examples of semantic change created from Senseval data and near synonyms. We then offer some concluding remarks in Section 6.

2 Related work

Sagi et al. (2009) and Cook and Stevenson (2010) focus on identifying specific types of diachronic change—widening and narrowing, and amelioration and pejoration, respectively—and exploit properties of these phenomena in their methods for identifying them. Gulordava and Baroni (2011) consider the identification of diachronic changes in meaning from an *n*-gram database, but in contrast to Sagi et al. and Cook and Stevenson, do not focus on specific types of semantic change. Others have studied differences in meaning between dialects and domains, instead of over time. Peirsman et al. (2010) consider the identification of lectal markers—words typical of one dialect versus another, either because of their marked frequency or sense—in Belgian and Netherlandic Dutch. McCarthy et al. (2007) consider the identification of predominant word senses in corpora, focusing on differences between domains. This method can be applied to not only identify the words that differ in predominant sense in two corpora, but also the specific predominant senses of those words. Nevertheless, none of these studies has specifically considered the identification of words with novel infrequent senses, the focus of this study.

Given the challenges of evaluating methods for identifying semantic change—namely a lack of suitable resources—we propose the use of synthetic examples of semantic change for evaluation. Gaustad (2001) showed that evaluations using pseudowords (artificially-ambiguous words) can over-estimate the accuracy of a word sense disambiguation system on real data. Gaustad suggests this is because word senses are typically related (i.e., words are polysemous) whereas pseudowords are usually created from words with distinct senses. Nakov and Hearst (2003) and Otrusina and Smrz (2010) propose methods for constructing more-realistic pseudowords by taking into account information about lexical categories, and lexical or distributional information, respectively. In this work we propose a new use for pseudowords—evaluating methods for identifying semantic change—and attempt to address concerns about the use of pseudowords, such as those raised by Gaustad, by creating our pseudowords (discussed in Sections 4 and 5) from real word senses and words with related senses.

3 Model

The input to our method is two corpora which represent different text varieties, e.g., different time periods. The output is a set of words—in this study, either nouns or verbs—that are hypothesized by the method to have different senses in one of the corpora compared to the other.

We consider a statistical model similar to one that Peirsman et al. (2010) used for automatically identifying lectal markers. This approach assumes that usages of different senses of a word will occur in different contexts, and that the aggregated contexts of a word in two corpora will differ if the senses of that word differ in those corpora. The model is based on a distributional representation of meaning that draws on work on automatically clustering similar words (Lin, 1998) that has been incorporated into tools used by lexicographers to identify word senses (Kilgarriff and Tugwell, 2002). Specifically, this method measures the similarity of two lexico-syntactic representations of the aggregated contexts of a target word; these two representations would typically come from different corpora representing, for example, different time periods. The lexico-syntactic representations capture the association of a target word with dependency triples, and the similarity between two target word representations is determined with a number of metrics. We propose some variations to Peirsman et al.'s model—specifically a novel association measure (Section 3.1) and similarity metric (Section 3.2)—that are found to improve its performance (discussed in Section 5).

3.1 Association measures

We use the following information-theoretic association measure proposed by Lin (1998):

$$I(w_1, r, w_2) = \log\left(\frac{||w_1, r, w_2||\ ||*, r, *||}{||w_1, r, *||\ ||*, r, w_2||}\right) \tag{1}$$

where w_1, r, and w_2 are a head, dependency relation, and dependent, respectively; $||\cdot||$ is the frequency of some tuple (e.g., w_1, r, w_2); and $*$ refers to any item (e.g., $w_1, r, *$ is a tuple with head w_1, relation r, and any dependent).

In some cases I is not an appropriate association measure. For small corpora, counts for many dependency triples will be very low and hence unreliable. To avoid these data sparseness problems we therefore consider a second, and much simpler, association measure. Joanis et al. (2008) found that the frequency of a verb occurring in specific syntactic relations, as well as the frequency with which that verb co-occurs with specific prepositions, are useful features in verb classification. Our conditional probability-based association measure (cprob), captures information similar to that used by Joanis et al., and is calculated as below:

$$\text{cprob}(w_1, r, w_2) = \begin{cases} \dfrac{||w_1, r, w_2||}{||w_1, *, *||} & \text{if } r = \text{preposition or particle} \\[2ex] \dfrac{||w_1, r, *||}{||w_1, *, *||} & \text{otherwise} \end{cases} \tag{2}$$

Prepositions and particles both often indicate the meaning of a verb. Because these parts-of-speech are frequent, and other dependents are ignored, this association measure can be estimated from smaller corpora more accurately than I.

3.2 Similarity metrics

We refer to the usages of a given word w in a corpus C as w_C. We define the salient tuples T_C for a word w_C to be the set of all head, dependency relation, dependent tuples t in corpus C having w as head and frequency in C greater than a threshold, which we set to 5. Peirsman et al. (2010) find cosine to slightly outperform several other metrics—including the similarity metric proposed by

Lin (1998)—in a cross-varietal synonymy detection task, and use cosine in their experiments on identifying lectal markers; we therefore also consider cosine and define the similarity for usages of tuples in corpora A and B as follows:

$$\text{Cosine}(w_A, w_B) = \frac{\sum_{t \in T_A \cap T_B} A_A(t) * A_B(t)}{\sqrt{\sum_{t \in T_A} A_A(t)^2} * \sqrt{\sum_{t \in T_B} A_B(t)^2}} \tag{3}$$

where $A_A(t)$ and $A_B(t)$ correspond to the association—either I or cprob—computed for corpora A and B, respectively.

Cosine is a symmetrical similarity metric, but an asymmetrical metric may be more appropriate in some cases. For example, one method used by lexicographers to search for neologisms is to compare a corpus of recent texts to a reference corpus representing standard usage (O'Donovan and O'Neil, 2008). In this case, focusing on salient usages in the corpus of newer texts that are less salient, or unattested, in the reference corpus may be more appropriate for identifying novel senses. We therefore propose the following asymmetrical metric—Newness—in which R is considered to be a reference corpus, and N a corpus of newer texts:[2]

$$\text{Newness}(w_N, w_R) = \frac{\sum_{t \in T_N - T_R} A_N(t) + \sum_{t \in T_N \cap T_R} \max(A_N(t) - A_R(t), 0)}{\sum_{t \in T_N} A_N(t)} \tag{4}$$

The first part of the numerator ($\sum_{t \in T_N - T_R} A_N(t)$) focuses on tuples that are in N but unattested in R. The second part of the numerator ($\sum_{t \in T_N \cap T_R} \max(A_N(t) - A_R(t), 0)$) focuses on tuples that have stronger association in N than R; the max prevents tuples with stronger association in R than N from impacting the score. The denominator ensures the final score is in $[0, 1]$.

Cosine is a similarity metric—words that have similar usages in two corpora will receive high scores. However, Newness is a dissimilarity metric which assigns high scores to words that have novel usages in one corpus compared to a reference corpus. We use Cosine and Newness to produce a ranking of lemmas, and account for this difference between the measures by simply negating Cosine scores to reverse the rankings for Cosine.

3.3 Inter-corpus and intra-corpus similarity

To determine the extent to which the meanings of a word differ between two corpora, we could simply compute inter-corpus similarity for that word directly, using any of the above similarity metrics; e.g., to compute the difference in the meanings of *click* between corpora A and B using the Newness similarity metric, we could compute Newness$(click_A, click_B)$. However, as Peirsman et al. (2010) observe, it may also be important to take into account the extent to which the meanings of a word vary *within* a corpus. For example, suppose we observe that the computed difference in meaning is large for some word w between corpora A and B. Taking B as a reference corpus, suppose that we also observe that the computed difference in meaning for w between two random samples of usages from B alone is large. In this case we should not necessarily believe that w differs in meaning between A and B because, based on w's distribution in B, we expect its computed meaning to vary. However, if the computed difference in meaning of w between two random samples from B were small, then the observed computed difference for w between A and B might be more indicative of w having different senses in A and B.

We operationalize the above intuition as follows: we randomly 2-partition the documents of B—the reference corpus—10 times. For a given word w, this allows us to compute 10 intra-corpus B similarities. However, corpus size can influence association measures.[3] In order to make

[2] In this case, following Lin (1998), we additionally restrict the salient tuples to those having positive association.

[3] I is known to assign high association to low frequency items; a given item will tend to have lower frequency in a smaller corpus.

comparisons between similar-size corpora, we randomly 2-partition the documents of A once.[4] This allows us to compute a total of 40 inter-corpus similarities for w. We then compute the difference between w's average inter-corpus and average intra-corpus similarity.

4 Synthetic examples of semantic change from Senseval data

In this section we use Senseval data to create synthetic examples of words which have undergone semantic change, and evaluate our model on these items. Specifically, we simulate words taking on a novel sense. We do so by dividing the usages for a given word into two parts such that one sense—the "novel" sense—is present in only one of the parts. We can further vary the frequency of the novel sense to simulate more or less drastic changes in sense. Crucially, using manually sense-annotated data allows us to create synthetic examples of semantic change based on real word senses; the resulting synthetic examples are constructed from related word senses, increasing our confidence that they are plausible examples of semantic change.

4.1 Data and preprocessing

We use the 32 verbs and 20 nouns in the data from the Senseval-3 English lexical sample task (Mihalcea et al., 2004) to create synthetic examples of semantic change. We restrict ourselves to the training portion of this data, which consists of from 26 to 266 manually sense-annotated usages of each word. We refer to the set of senses of each word w as S_w. We select the second most frequent sense, $s \in S_w$, ignoring instances which are assigned multiple senses or annotated as unknown. (We select the second most frequent sense because it tends to be moderately frequent, but does not account for the majority of usages.) We then partition the sense-tagged usages of w into three approximately equal-sized parts w_A, w_B, and w_C. In this discussion, w_A and w_B consist of instances whose corresponding manually-tagged senses are in $S_w - \{s\}$. They are used to simulate w *not* undergoing semantic change; the frequency of any given sense of w is approximately the same in both w_A and w_B. We refer to this as the "no change" condition.

By contrast, w_C consists of usages of w with any sense in S_w such that the percentage of usages of s is approximately r. These usages are used to simulate w undergoing semantic change, namely w acquires a novel sense; specifically, sense s is not present in w_A, but accounts for roughly $r\%$ of the usages in w_C. We refer to this as the "change" condition.

The usages of w are divided into w_A, w_B, and w_C in such a way that as much of the Senseval data as possible is used while still maintaining the appropriate ratio of senses in w_C and keeping the sizes of w_A, w_B and w_C approximately equal.

When a word changes in meaning by taking on a new sense, it typically goes through a period where it also maintains its original senses (Campbell, 2004, Chapter 9). For example, the predominant meaning of *gay* has changed from 'merry' to 'homosexual', but the 'merry' sense is still understood. Furthermore, *gay* has taken on another sense—often considered offensive—meaning roughly 'of poor quality'. We model this aspect of semantic change in our synthetic examples through the choice of r (the percentage of usages of the novel sense in the "change" condition). Values of r close to 100 simulate a word that has lost its original senses and taken on an entirely new meaning, while values of r closer to 0 correspond to a novel but relatively infrequent sense.

We tag all sentences in our dataset with their part-of-speech using the TreeTagger (Schmid, 2004), and then parse the sentences using the MALT dependency parser (Nivre et al., 2007) with the provided pre-trained linear model for English.[5] For each dependency triple w_1, r, w_2 in the resulting parses we add a corresponding triple $w_2, r\text{-inverse}, w_1$. Then for each word w, we extract all dependency triples with head w, and compute the similarity between w_A and w_B, and w_A and

[4] Here we assume A and B are approximately equal in size. Differences in corpus size could be accounted for through a partitioning scheme that ensures that comparisons are made between equal-size corpus parts.

[5] `http://maltparser.org/`

Table 1: Average % accuracy over 32 verbs and 20 nouns using the Cosine and Newness similarity metrics for differing values of r—the percentage of usages of the novel sense in the "change" condition. Items marked * are significantly better ($p < .05$) than a random baseline.

	Average % accuracy			
	Verbs		Nouns	
r	Cosine	Newness	Cosine	Newness
100	85*	78*	82*	79*
80	79*	70*	81*	79*
60	75*	66*	77*	74*
40	67*	57*	71*	67*
20	58*	51	60*	54

w_C, using the cprob association measure.[6] In this first set of experiments we compute similarity directly—i.e., not taking into account intra-corpus similarity—due to the rather small number of tokens for each item in these experiments.[7]

4.2 Experimental setup and results

For each value of r in $\{20, 40, ..., 100\}$, we randomly repeat the process described in Section 4.1 100 times. For each word w and each trial, we compute the difference between the "change" and "no change" conditions using each similarity metric, e.g., for Newness we compute $\text{Newness}(w_A, w_B) - \text{Newness}(w_A, w_C)$. If this difference is positive, the method is scored as correct, and as incorrect otherwise. We compute the accuracy over the 100 trials for each word, and then compute the average accuracy over all verbs and nouns separately. In Table 1 we report the average accuracy over all verbs and nouns in our dataset for each similarity metric and value of r.

As expected, the accuracies are higher for experimental setups with higher values of r, i.e., words with more-frequent novel senses are easier to identify. For each similarity metric and each value of r, we compare the accuracies to a chance baseline of 50% accuracy using a one-sided one-sample Wilcoxon signed-rank test (a non-parametric alternative to a one-sample t-test). The differences are significant ($p < .05$) in all cases except those not marked with * in Table 1. This encouraging result demonstrates that—under the conditions of the present experiment—this method is better able to identify whether a given word has acquired a novel sense than a random baseline, even if that novel sense accounts for only 20% of the usages.

It is not clear how to statistically test the difference between Cosine and Newness over all values of r. Because the results using different values of r are based on the same usages of the experimental items, the paired differences obtained for different values of r are not independent. Therefore statistical tests such as the paired t-test and the Wilcoxon signed-rank test are not appropriate. We can, however, test the difference between the similarity metrics for a *specific* value of r. For the 32 verbs, the accuracy using Cosine is significantly better ($p < .05$) than that using Newness according to a two-sided paired Wilcoxon signed-rank test, for each value of r. For the 20 nouns, Cosine is significantly better than Newness in 1 case ($r = 20$).

5 Synthetic examples of semantic change from near synonyms

Many words have multiple related senses; i.e., many words are polysemous. Therefore, when a word takes on a novel sense, it is often related to its older senses. For example, the relatively recent sense of *post* referring to online message boards and social media is related to its older senses

[6] Because we are using a dataset of usages, as opposed to a corpus, we cannot compute the marginal frequencies required for I here.

[7] Although the similarity of w_A and w_B could be viewed as a measure of intra-corpus similarity, here we are using these samples to simulate two corpora in which w has the same set of senses.

referring to physical message boards. In this section we use this knowledge of semantic change to construct plausible synthetic examples of lexical semantic change based on near synonyms. By replacing varying numbers of usages of a given word in a corpus with a near synonym, we can simulate different degrees of sense change; i.e., we simulate different degrees of a word acquiring a novel, but related, sense. This corresponds to the view that semantic change is gradual, with words taking on new senses, and their original senses remaining or fading from usage over time. Moreover, these synthetic examples can be viewed as a type of *widening*, a common type of semantic change in which the use of a word is extended to additional contexts (Campbell, 2004). In contrast to the experiments in Section 4, here we have access to usages of our synthetic examples of semantic change in a corpus, and are able to calculate association measures such as I that require marginal frequencies; however, this comes at the expense of our synthetic examples of semantic change no longer being based on manually-identified word senses.

5.1 Data and experimental items

For these experiments we use the New York Times Annotated Corpus (Sandhaus, 2008) for the year 1990, a sample of approximately 50 million words of non-newswire text from the *New York Times*. We tag and parse this corpus using the TreeTagger and MALT parser as in Section 4.1.

We require a set of words to use in the creation of our synthetic examples of semantic change. These should be frequent words—so that we can accurately estimate our association measures—but not very frequent and highly polysemous words, such as light verbs, e.g., *give*, *take*, and *make*. We select the 1000 verbal lemmas and 1000 nominal lemmas in our corpus with frequency rank 101–1100 amongst verbal and nominal lemmas, respectively. From this set of words we then identify all words w such that the first WordNet (Fellbaum, 1998) synset of w has at least one lemma, near_synonym(w), that is not w and has frequency greater than 500; in the case that multiple lemmas satisfy these conditions, we randomly choose one.[8] For example, near_synonym(*propose*) is *suggest*. Of the 1000 verbs and nouns, 252 verbs and 214 nouns, respectively, satisfy these conditions. These items are used to create synthetic examples of semantic change. The remaining 748 verbs and 786 nouns are used as examples of words that do not undergo semantic change.

5.2 Synthetic example creation

We randomly partition the documents in our corpus into two parts, referred to as A and B. For a given word w, we refer to its usages in corpus parts A and B as w_A and w_B, respectively.

A synthetic example of semantic change is formed from w_A, a random sample of $(1 - \frac{r}{100}) \cdot |w_B|$ usages from w_B, and $\frac{r}{100} \cdot |w_B|$ usages of near_synonym(w) from corpus part B.

We consider values of r—the proportion of usages in corpus part B that correspond to a novel sense—in $\{10, 20, 30, 40\}$. As an example, to form a synthetic example for *propose* with $r = 20$, we use all usages of *propose* in A, a sample of 80% of the usages of *propose* in B, and a sample of usages of *suggest* in B of size equal to 20% of the number of usages of *propose* in B.

5.3 Experimental setup

In these experiments, we consider both of the association measures (I and cprob) and both of the similarity metrics (Cosine and Newness) discussed in Sections 3.1 and 3.2. We further consider similarity computed directly between two corpora, and taking into account intra-corpus similarity (Section 3.3).

We randomly repeat the process described in Section 5.2 5 times. For each of the 5 trials, we compute the similarity of each synthetic example of semantic change between the corpus parts (using both association measures, both similarity metrics, and both computing inter-corpus similarity directly and taking into account intra-corpus similarity). We similarly compute similarity for

[8] Although for a given word w we choose near_synonym(w) from the same synset, these words will typically differ somewhat in their usage and in the contexts in which they appear.

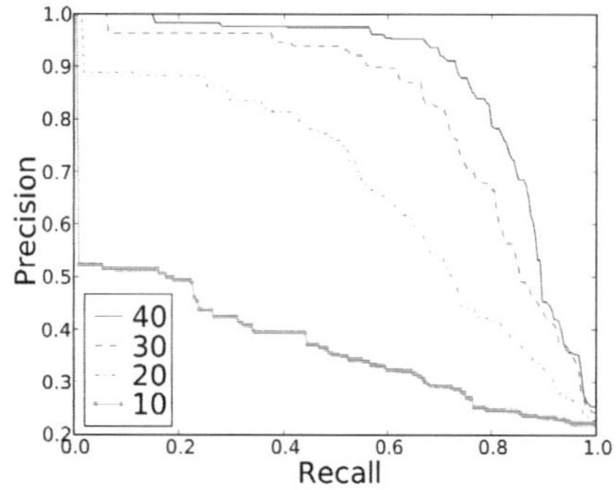

r	Top-100 % accuracy Nouns	Verbs
40	97	94
30	93	76
20	81	55
10	48	36
Baseline	25	21

Figure 1: Left: Interpolated precision–recall curves for identifying synthetic examples of nouns using the association measure I and Cosine similarity metric. Results for experiments in which the novel sense accounts for 10–40% of the usages of a noun are shown. Right: Top-100 % accuracy for identifying synthetic examples of nouns and verbs using the association measure I and Cosine similarity metric in experiments where the novel sense accounts for 10–40% of the usages of a word. The performance of a random baseline is also shown

the examples of words that do not change in meaning. We compute the average similarity of each item across the 5 trials. For both types of synthetic semantic change—nouns and verbs—we rank all experimental items—synthetic examples of semantic change, and examples of words that don't undergo semantic change—by average similarity. We then compute interpolated precision–recall curves for the synthetic examples of semantic change.

5.4 Results

The left panel of Figure 1 presents interpolated precision–recall curves for identifying synthetic examples of nouns using the association measure I, Cosine similarity metric, and taking intra-corpus similarity into account, an experimental setup similar to one considered by Peirsman et al. (2010). Results for experiments using $r = 10$–40 (i.e., the percentage of usages corresponding to the novel sense) are shown. As in the experiments in Section 4.2, stronger instances of semantic change are easier to identify. Results using synthetic examples of verbs (not shown) are similar.

Because we expect the candidates returned by our method to be manually examined by a lexicographer, we are particularly interested in whether the top-ranked items are correct. We therefore also consider the accuracy of our method on the top 100 ranked items. Top-100 % accuracy for the same experimental conditions as above, and also for experiments using synthetic examples of verbs, is shown in the right panel of Figure 1; a random baseline is also shown.[9] In all cases, the accuracy is significantly better than the random baseline using a one-tailed binomial test ($p < .05$). For the rest of this study we focus on experiments with $r = 10$ because we are especially interested in cases where the novel sense is relatively infrequent.

We now consider whether the cprob association measure, and newly-proposed similarity metric Newness, are an improvement over the measures I and Cosine. The left panel of Figure 2 shows results on nouns using both association measures and similarity metrics—taking intra-corpus similarity into account—in experiments with $r = 10$. The methods using cprob outperform those using I. In terms of top-100 accuracy, cprob and Newness (93%), and cprob and Cosine (77%), are both significantly better than the best method using I (I and Cosine—48%) using a two-tailed binomial test ($p \ll .05$ in both cases). The best performance is achieved using cprob in combination with Newness; the top-100 accuracy of this method is significantly better than that of the next best

[9] The baseline is calculated as the number of synthetic examples of semantic change divided by the total number of items.

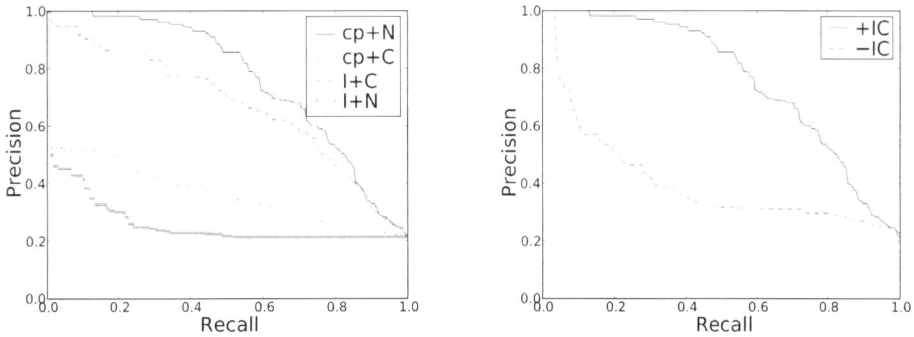

Figure 2: Left: Interpolated precision–recall curves for identifying synthetic examples of nouns with $r = 10$ using the association measures cprob (cp) and I, and the Cosine (C) and Newness (N) similarity metrics. Right: Interpolated precision–recall curves for identifying synthetic examples of nouns with $r = 10$ using the cprob association measure and Newness similarity metric, computing similarity based on intra-corpus similarity (+IC) and directly (−IC).

performing method—cprob and Cosine—using a two-tailed binomial test ($p \ll .05$). In the case of verbs (not shown) the methods using cprob are again significantly better than those using I; however, in this case the accuracy using cprob and Newness (72%) is not significantly different than that using cprob and Cosine (64%, $p > .05$).

In all the experiments so far in this section, we have taken intra-corpus similarity into account. We now examine the impact of this process on performance. The right panel of Figure 2 shows results using our best performing method—cprob in combination with Newness—for synthetic examples of nouns in experiments with $r = 10$. (Results using verbs—not shown—are similar.) The results taking intra-corpus similarity into account are much better than those for which similarity is computed directly. The top-100 accuracy using intra-corpus similarity (93%) is significantly better than that calculating similarity directly (47%) using a two-tailed binomial test ($p \ll .05$). These results confirm Peirsman et al.'s (2010) observation that it is important to take into account information about intra-corpus variation when identifying differences between corpora.

6 Conclusions

We have proposed a method for identifying words that are used in a novel sense in one corpus with respect to another. In contrast to previous work in this area, we focused specifically on infrequent novel senses, the identification of which is a challenge in lexicography due to the vast amount of text being produced nowadays. Our proposed method outperformed random baselines, even when evaluated on rather subtle changes in sense. Furthermore, the combination of a very simple association measure (cprob) and our newly-proposed asymmetrical similarity metric (Newness) outperformed methods using a standard association measure and symmetrical similarity metric.

Given the challenges of evaluation for this task—namely a lack of gold standard data—we further proposed the use of two different types of synthetic examples of semantic change to empirically assess performance on this task. Sense-tagged data was used to construct a small number of synthetic examples of semantic change based on real word senses, while near synonyms were used to build greater numbers of synthetic examples of semantic change.

Although we motivated this work in the context of identifying novel senses, these methods can be applied to any pair of comparable corpora to identifying words with different senses in those corpora. In our ongoing work we are applying our methods to pairs of corpora to manually assess its performance. Given the expense of this manual evaluation, synthetic examples of semantic change remain attractive as a means for determining the strengths and weaknesses of approaches to this task, and for selecting approaches for further manual evaluation.

References

Campbell, L. 2004. *Historical Linguistics: An Introduction*. MIT Press, Cambridge, MA.

Cook, P. and S. Stevenson. 2010. Automatically identifying changes in the semantic orientation of words. In *Proceedings of the Seventh International Conference on Language Resources and Evaluation (LREC 2010)*, pages 28–34, Valletta, Malta.

Fellbaum, C., editor. 1998. *WordNet: An Electronic Lexical Database*. MIT Press, Cambridge, MA.

Gale, W. A., K. W. Church, and D. Yarowsky. 1992. Work on statistical methods for word sense disambiguation. In Goldman, R., Norvig, P., Charniak, E., and Gale, B., editors, *Working Notes of the AAAI Fall Symposium on Probabilistic Approaches to Natural Language*, pages 54–60. AAAI Press, Menlo Park, CA.

Gaustad, T. 2001. Statistical corpus-based word sense disambiguation: Pseudowords vs. real ambiguous words. In *Companion Volume to the Proceedings of the 39th Annual Meeting of the Association for Computational Linguistics (ACL 2001) – Proceedings of the Student Research Workshop*, pages 61–66, Toulouse, France.

Gulordava, K. and M. Baroni. 2011. A distributional similarity approach to the detection of semantic change in the Google Books Ngram corpus. In *Proceedings of the GEMS 2011 Workshop on GEometrical Models of Natural Language Semantics*, pages 67–71, Edinburgh, Scotland.

Joanis, E., S. Stevenson, and D. James. 2008. A general feature space for automatic verb classification. *Natural Language Engineering*, 14(3):337–367.

Kilgarriff, A. and D. Tugwell. 2002. Sketching words. In Corréard, M.-H., editor, *Lexicography and Natural Language Processing: A Festschrift in Honour of B. T. S. Atkins*, pages 125–137. Euralex, Grenoble, France.

Lin, D. 1998. Automatic retrieval and clustering of similar words. In *Proceedings of the 36th Annual Meeting of the Association for Computational Linguistics and the 17th International Conference on Computational Linguistics (ACL/COLING 1998)*, pages 768–774, Montreal, Canada.

McCarthy, D., R. Koeling, J. Weeds, and J. Carroll. 2007. Unsupervised acquisition of predominant word senses. *Computational Linguistics*, 33(4):553–590.

Mihalcea, R., T. Chklovski, and A. Kilgarriff. 2004. The Senseval-3 English lexical sample task. In *Senseval-3: Third International Workshop on the Evaluation of Systems for the Semantic Analysis of Text*, pages 25–28, Barcelona, Spain.

Nakov, P. I. and M. A. Hearst. 2003. Category-based pseudowords. In *Companion Volume of the Proceedings of HLT-NAACL 2003 - Short Papers*, pages 67–69, Edmonton, Canada.

Nivre, J., J. Hall, J. Nilsson, A. Chanev, G. Eryiğit, S. Kübler, S. Marinov, and E. Marsi. 2007. MaltParser: A language-independent system for data-driven dependency parsing. *Natural Language Engineering*, 13(2):95–135.

O'Donovan, R. and M. O'Neil. 2008. A systematic approach to the selection of neologisms for inclusion in a large monolingual dictionary. In *Proceedings of the 13th Euralex International Congress*, pages 571–579, Barcelona, Spain.

Otrusina, L. and P. Smrz. 2010. A new approach to pseudoword generation. In *Proceedings of the Seventh International Conference on Language Resources and Evaluation (LREC 2010)*, pages 1195–1199, Valletta, Malta.

Peirsman, Y., D. Geeraerts, and D. Speelman. 2010. The automatic identification of lexical variation between language varieties. *Natural Language Engineering*, 16(4):469–491.

Sagi, E., S. Kaufmann, and B. Clark. 2009. Semantic density analysis: Comparing word meaning across time and space. In *Proceedings of the EACL 2009 Workshop on GEMS: GEometrical Models of Natural Language Semantics*, pages 104–111, Athens, Greece.

Sandhaus, E. 2008. The New York Times Annotated Corpus. Linguistic Data Consortium, Philadelphia, PA.

Schmid, H. 2004. Probabilistic part-of-speech tagging using decision trees. In *Proceedings of the International Conference on New Methods in Language Processing*, pages 44–49, Manchester, UK.

Schütze, H. 1992. Automatic word sense discrimination. *Computational Linguistics*, 24(1):97–123.

Annotating the Structure and Semantics of Fables *

Oi Yee Kwong

Department of Chinese, Translation and Linguistics, City University of Hong Kong,
Tat Chee Avenue, Kowloon, Hong Kong
Olivia.Kwong@cityu.edu.hk

Abstract. This paper outlines an annotation scheme we developed for a corpus of fables. Reference is made to previous studies on discourse structure and story grammar, as well as discourse relations and text coherence. The applicability and adequacy of the various frameworks for annotating and analysing fables are considered. The current work addresses several issues including the basic units for discourse segments, the distinction between structure and semantics in stories, the characteristics of fables, and the practicality and annotator-friendliness of the annotation scheme. A concise set of structural and semantic tags is thus synergised and applied. Some interim results and future directions are discussed.

Keywords: Corpus annotation, Discourse relations, Narrative structure, Fables.

1 Introduction

Stories are distinguished from other genres of discourse by their unique coherent structures and discourse relations. As a special kind of stories, fables share the typical structural and semantic properties of stories, and are often associated with a moral. It is thus even more cognitively demanding to understand fables than stories in general. Apart from the temporal and causal relations among the events happening in the story, one needs to figure out the lesson intended by the storyteller. Interestingly, the same fable could be retold in different ways, where storytellers deploy a wide range of lexico-grammatical constructions, rhetorical devices, and discourse strategies, within specific narrative structures, to convey the moral invariably. Hence, fables are often semantically deep despite their apparently simple structures.

To provide a useful resource for research on story understanding, a corpus containing various published versions of the Aesop's Fables in English and Chinese is compiled. In this paper, we discuss the annotation scheme developed for marking up the discourse structure and semantics of the fables. In Section 2, we briefly review related work on discourse structure and story structure, and evaluate the applicability and adequacy of the various frameworks for annotating and analysing fables. The issue of basic analysis unit is addressed in Section 3. A concise set of structural and semantic tags is synergised, as described in Section 4 and Section 5. The paper is concluded with the work in progress and future directions in Section 6.

2 Related Work

2.1 Discourse Structure and Relation

Grosz and Sidner's (1986) computational model suggests that discourse structure comprises (1) a linguistic structure consisting of the discourse segments and some embedding relationship

* The work described in this paper was supported by a grant from City University of Hong Kong (Project No. 7008064).

that can hold between them, (2) an intentional structure accounting for the discourse purpose and individual discourse segment purposes, and (3) an attentional state dynamically recording the objects, properties and relations salient to the participants' focus of attention as their discourse unfolds. The intentional structure is essential for understanding, but it is the most difficult to identify as it might or might not be readily indicated by surface linguistic devices, and is closely related to discourse participants' beliefs and shared knowledge.

Mann and Thompson's (1987) Rhetorical Structure Theory (RST) is considered closely related to the intentional structure in Grosz and Sidner's model, while it is more functionally oriented. RST aims at giving a descriptive account of discourse relations holding between adjacent text spans, indicating the coherence and structure exhibited among natural text. A text is thus divided into units, essentially clauses, hierarchically structured and functionally organised with respect to a set of discourse relations, e.g. EVIDENCE, ELABORATION, CONCESSION, etc. Each relation defines how the two involved text spans, the nucleus and the satellite, functionally relate to each other with respect to the effect on the reader. RST relations are annotated in many corpora, e.g. the Potsdam Commentary Corpus (Stede, 2004).

Also centering on discourse relations, the annotation in the Penn Discourse Treebank (PDTB) emphasises less on the effect intended on the reader, but focuses on the semantic link between discourse segments. The annotation is mostly lexically triggered with discourse connectives including explicit connectives like subordinating conjunctions, coordinating conjunctions and adverbials, as well as implicit ones inferred by readers (Miltsakaki et al., 2008). A discourse connective is viewed as a predicate taking two abstract objects such as propositions, events, or situations as its arguments (Arg1 and Arg2), the simplest syntactic realisation of which is taken to be a clause. Arg1 and Arg2 are determined by how they are syntactically bound to the discourse connective, which indicates certain directionality as the nucleus/satellite distinction in RST. But unlike RST, PDTB has no restriction on how far an argument can be from its corresponding connective. The sense tags for the discourse connectives fall into four classes: TEMPORAL, CONTINGENCY, COMPARISON and EXPANSION, which are further fine-grained into types and subtypes. Pragmatic sense tags are also defined for rhetorical or pragmatic uses of connectives.

2.2 Story Structure and Story Point

Story structure is a generally accepted notion (e.g. since Propp's (1968) analysis of Russian folktales), and its psychological validity has been demonstrated (e.g. Mandler and Johnson, 1977; Thorndyke, 1977). But structure alone is not enough to account for the interestingness of stories, which Wilensky (1982a) attributes to the presence of story "point" arising from the goals and plans of the protagonists, and the conflicts therein.

Although story structure is deemed important, its representation has remained controversial. Rumelhart (1975) put forth a "story schema" defining "grammatical" stories by a set of phrase structure rules, e.g. Story → Setting + Episode, Episode → Event + Reaction, etc. These rules are to be interpreted with a set of semantic interpretation rules, e.g. ALLOW (Setting, Episode). The "grammar" was later revised and extended with transformational rules by Mandler and Johnson (1977), to give more flexibility in the precise ordering of the story constituents in practice. This grammar was further adapted for fables by Ryan (1991, cited in Ryan (2008)).

Hasan (1996), on the other hand, describes the plausible structure of nursery tales in a concise one-line pattern, called Generic Structure Potential (GSP), containing elements like Placement, Initiating Event, Sequent Event, Final Event, Finale, and Moral, with their optionality, ordering, and repetition shown. The meanings associated with individual structural elements and how they are realised by various lexico-grammatical patterns have been analysed for different kinds of stories (e.g. Sano and Thomson, 2007; Tan, 2009).

The notion of story grammar has triggered a series of discussions and debates (e.g. Black and Wilensky, 1979; Mandler and Johnson, 1980; Rumelhart, 1980; Beaugrande, 1982;

Fillmore, 1982; Mandler, 1982; Wilensky, 1982b). Wilensky (1982a) argued strongly against story grammar as a "grammatical" story is not necessarily an interesting story. Structure alone does not account for "storiness". It is not the physical ordering of propositions but features such as goals and plots in a story which should be responsible for a good story. Interesting stories have a "point", which often arises from conflicting goals. Obviously it involves very sophisticated inference to uncover such conflict, and it is thus more realistic to start our annotation with the semantic relations holding among discourse segments.

2.3 Applicability and Adequacy for Fables

The various analytical frameworks above are important pointers for our current work, but it appears that none of them is directly adaptable for annotating fables. Some might be underspecified for actual annotation, while others might be inadequate to cover the features specific to fables. For instance, the intentional structure should be important for revealing how the storyteller gets the message across in a fable, and thus story comprehension, but the nature of the intentional structure (as in Grosz and Sidner) has not been very precisely defined and its recognition would involve too much subjective judgement from an annotator.

The elements used in individual frameworks might have mixed different levels of analysis. For example, Rumelhart's (1975) story schema has been criticised for not being entirely structural, as many components like Consequence and Goal Path can only be determined semantically. Mann and Thompson (1987) also pointed out that the discourse relations in RST like ELABORATION and CONDITION are more semantic or ideational while others like MOTIVATION and ANTITHESIS are more pragmatic or presentational in nature.

The previous studies also worked on different text types, such as simple narratives involving only one protagonist, nursery tales, news reportage, etc. Most are monologues. Nevertheless, fables often involve more than one protagonist and dialogues are abundant. Hence the structural components in story schemas and the discourse relations like those in RST or PDTB may not be all relevant or adequate for fables. Although Grosz and Sidner's discourse model was intended to account for dialogues, it lacks precise definitions of the structural components and is not ready to be used in annotation directly.

Hence we need to draw on the various frameworks and synergise an annotation scheme addressing our requirements and the features of fables. It is particularly important to separate the structural components from the semantic relations, which would be the focus in this paper. Ideally we also need to take care of the dialogues in fables and the pragmatics therein, but this would be left for the next step. On the practical front, it is also important to ensure the relevant linguistic properties can be feasibly and reliably annotated by most annotators with minimal training. The annotation schemes and the labels used should be relatively straightforward and unambiguous, and the subjective judgment should be minimised, or at least sufficiently guided.

3 Discourse Segmentation

The first thing we need to operationalise is the unit of analysis. The many previous studies on story structure and discourse models would analyse the structural and semantic relations among *discourse segments*, locally or globally, but the actual unit often remains vague. Few state very precisely what counts as a discourse segment. For example, in Rumelhart's (1975) analysis, the stories are said to be "parsed into single propositions". Nevertheless, the resulting segments might include things which do not exist in the surface text but are only inferred by the reader, e.g. sadness. Mandler and Johnson (1977) pointed out that it may take several sentences in a text or only part of a sentence to form a proposition corresponding to a terminal node in the story structure. RST emphasises the consecutiveness of the text spans and the relation therein (Mann and Thompson, 1987), but the unit under analysis is apparently arbitrary and not precisely defined linguistically. Hence, though discourse segments are often roughly taken to be clausal units, they effectively include different linguistic units like clauses, sentences, or paragraphs, even within the same analytical framework. This flexibility might be convenient for analysis, but it is not systematic enough especially for computational purposes, and the fuzziness often confuses human annotators in practice.

In our annotation, we stick to mostly clausal units as our minimal unit of analysis. Since *events* and *states* are important building blocks in a story, clauses expressing individual events and states are the basic discourse segments for our annotation and analysis. Currently only independent clauses, coordinate clauses, and specific types of adverbial clauses[1] are treated as separate discourse segments. Others including complement clauses, relative clauses, subject or object clauses, etc. are kept together with the main clause in which they are embedded.

4 Structural Annotation

It is observed that many of the terminal nodes in Rumelhart's (1975) schema are absorbed into the intermediate level nodes in Mandler and Johnson's (1977) schema which eventually all boil down to either state or event[2]. In fact, apart from the high level nodes which can really be considered "structural" in nature, revealing the grouping of individual discourse segments into larger chunks, the other nodes are relatively semantic. States and events can possibly be suggested by the lexical items (particularly verbs) in individual discourse segments, but the rest require a lot more inference and sometimes subjective judgement. They can hardly be straightforwardly determined from the lexico-grammatical patterns of the surface text, but rely mostly on the reader's interpretation of the temporal and causal chains underlying a sequence of events and/or states. Short versions of the fables might have a lot of such intermediate level structural components missing and these gaps would have to be filled by the reader.

To reduce the burden on the annotators so that the structural annotation can be more reliably done, our structural level tags are restricted to a few high level nodes and the terminal nodes, as explained in Table 1. Those at the intermediate level mostly involving semantic interpretation will be incorporated into the semantic annotation as discussed in the next section.

Table 1: Labels for Structural Annotation

Structural Tag	Definition
Setting	Setting introduces the background information of a story such as the main protagonists, the context in which the story takes place, etc.
Episode	An episode corresponds to a self-contained description of a single incident happening to the protagonists in the story. Setting and Episode can cover multiple discourse segments, but are only marked at the first segment of each group.
Internal Event	An internal event corresponds to the cognitive functions of a protagonist, including thoughts and plans, perceptions, etc.
Internal State	An internal state corresponds to the emotion and state of mind of a protagonist.
Event	An (external) event corresponds to any occurrence or happening in a story such as an action or a change of state in the world.
State	A state corresponds to the condition of the world or of a person.
Speech	All verbal exchanges among the protagonists in the form of conversations and expressed as direct speech are categorised as speech.
Moral	The moral is the lesson of the story, often appearing as an additional sentence at the end to convey the message.

---

[1] Adverbial clauses indicating *condition, temporal relation, reason, result, purpose, concession, and contrast* are treated as individual discourse segments. Other kinds such as those indicating time and place are currently not treated separately.

[2] For example, the terminal nodes in Rumelhart's (1975) scheme include *State*, *Event*, *Change-of-state*, *Emotion*, *Desire*, *Action*, *Plan*, and *Subgoal*, whereas Mandler and Johnson's (1977) scheme has only four terminal nodes, namely *State*, *Event*, *Internal Event*, and *Internal State*. Others like *Plan* and *Action* appear as intermediate level nodes instead, which also include *Simple Reaction*, *Complex Reaction*, *Goal Path*, *Attempt*, *Outcome*, etc.

5 Semantic Annotation

Our semantic annotation focuses on the relation between adjacent text spans which may contain single or composite discourse segments, but we do not force annotators to build a complete hierarchical structure for any story.

As mentioned in the last section, many of the intermediate level nodes in the story schemas are not simply structural, but often involve semantic interpretation. Hence we try to absorb them into the semantic level annotation. With reference to PDTB and RST, as well as story schemas, the discourse semantic relations that are often found in fables and essential for their comprehension are identified and consolidated into a set of semantic labels. Similar to RST, we mark up the relations between two consecutive spans of text, and each span can cover multiple discourse segments. But instead of distinguishing between satellite and nucleus as in RST, or Arg1 and Arg2 as syntactically bound to the discourse connectives like PDTB, we simply identify the two spans bearing a relation, and render them in a tuple like <DSa> (is) <RELATION> (to) <DSb> where DSa can physically precede DSb in the text, or vice versa. In this way, the directionality is preserved, independent of the particular lexical and syntactic realisation of the relation. Hence complementary relations like CAUSE and RESULT can be merged into one, allowing us to use a more compact set of labels to streamline the annotation.

Practicality and annotator-friendliness are also very important. To enable the annotation to be done within a reasonable timeframe, we need to simplify the semantic labels and keep their number manageable, and to make them self-explanatory and easy to apply. So in the current annotation, we use a dozen semantic relation labels drawn from PDTB and RST. They fall into the four classes as in PDTB, namely TEMPORAL, CONTINGENCY, COMPARISON and EXPANSION, but we only maintain two levels of tags. This was done either by renaming the second-level tags in PDTB more specifically, or making them more encompassing, depending on the relevance of the relations to fables and the ease for annotators to identify them. The semantic labels are described below, with their correspondence in PDTB and RST indicated.

5.1 TEMPORAL

Sequence (PDTB: Asynchronous, RST: SEQUENCE) indicates that the events/states in the two spans are related temporally, the one in DSb after the one in DSa, as in (1).

(1) DS1 *a crane ventured her long neck down the wolf's throat*
DS2 *and drew out the bone.*
<DS1> <Sequence> <DS2>

Synchronous (PDTB: Synchronous, RST: N/A) indicates that the events/states in the two spans happen (almost) simultaneously, as in (2).

(2) DS1 *the cock flew up into a tree*
DS2 *and perched himself on a high branch,*
DS3 *while the dog dozed below at the foot.*
<DS1> <Sequence> <DS2>
<DS1-DS2> <Synchronous> <DS3>

Circumstance (PDTB: N/A, RST: CIRCUMSTANCE) indicates that DSa is the situation where the event in DSb occurs, but they do not really happen in sequential order, as in (3).

(3) DS1 *When he finally had to admit defeat,*
DS2 *he retreated*
DS3 *and muttered to himself ...*
<DS2> <Sequence> <DS3>
<DS1 > <Circumstance> <DS2-DS3>

5.2 CONTINGENCY

Reaction (PDTB: Cause – reason / result involving reaction, RST: VOLITIONAL CAUSE / VOLITIONAL RESULT / PURPOSE) indicates that the event/state in DSb is an external or internal response or action caused by the event/state in DSa, which could indicate some goal or desire or other things triggering the reaction, as in (4).

(4) DS1 *Moved by his pleas as well as the prospect of the money,*
DS2 *a crane ventured her long neck down the wolf's throat ...*
<DS1> <Reaction> <DS2>

Causal (PDTB: Cause – remaining cases of reason / result, RST: NON-VOLITIONAL CAUSE / NON-VOLITIONAL RESULT) indicates that the event/state in DSb is caused by the event/state in DSa in general, which might not be intended, as in (5).

(5) DS1 *A wolf devoured his prey so ravenously*
DS2 *that a bone got stuck in his throat ...*
<DS1> <Causal> <DS2>

Condition (PDTB: Condition – general, RST: subset of CONDITION) indicates that the event/state in DSa is a condition which will lead to the event/state in DSb in general, as in (6).

(6) DS1 *If you tell lies once,*
DS2 *nobody will believe you the next time.*
<DS1> <Condition> <DS2>

Hypothetical (PDTB: Condition – hypothetical / unreal present / unreal past / factual present / factual past, RST: subset of CONDITION) indicates that the event/state in DSa is a condition which will lead to the event/state in DSb, and this is known to be applicable to the current situation but it may not always work this way, as in (7).

(7) DS1 *Had you been satisfied with your own feathers,*
DS2 *you would have escaped the punishment of your betters, and also the contempt of your equals.*
<DS1> <Hypothetical> <DS2>

Fantasy (PDTB: N/A, RST: N/A) is similar to Hypothetical, but the consequence is not likely to be true even if the condition is true in reality. This is something new in our annotation. The logical relationship involving condition is usually taken simply as if X is true then Y is true, but the truth or reality of Y is often ignored. We specify this in our annotation to capture the unrealistic expectation or false conception of the protagonists and the lies they tell, as in (8).

(8) DS1 *If I double my hen's allowance of barley,*
DS2 *she'll lay twice a day.*
<DS1> <Fantasy> <DS2>

5.3 COMPARISON

Contrast (PDTB: Contrast – juxtaposition / opposition, RST: CONTRAST / ANTITHESIS) compares two things with respect to some dimension, as in (9).

(9) DS1 *But the one in front is full of his neighbor's faults;*
DS2 *the one behind, full of his own.*
<DS1> <Contrast> <DS2>

Concession (PDTB: Concession – expectation / contra-expectation, RST: CONCESSION) indicates that the event/state in DSb is not expected to arise from the event/state in DSa, but it happens somehow, as in (10).

(10) DS1 *the fox jumped and sprang many times*
DS2 *but failed in all his attempts.*
<DS1> <Concession> <DS2>

5.4 EXPANSION

Elaboration (PDTB: Conjunction / Instantiation / Restatement / List, RST: ELABORATION / RESTATEMENT) indicates that DSb provides additional information for DSa by giving examples, restating or generalising the situation, etc., as in (11).

(11) DS1 *A bear used to boast of his excessive love for humankind,*
DS2 *saying that he never touched or mauled a human corpse.*
<DS1> <Elaboration> <DS2>

Justification (PDTB: Pragmatic Cause, RST: EVIDENCE / JUSTIFY) indicates that DSb gives evidence or justifies for DSa, as in (12).

(12) DS1 *but I don't see how I could have done anything to the water*
DS2 *since it runs from you to me, not from me to you.*
<DS1> <Justification> <DS2>

6 Progress, Future Work and Conclusion

We have thus outlined the annotation scheme that we have developed for marking up the structure and semantics of fables. To better distinguish between these two levels of analysis, and to increase annotator-friendliness, we have reformulated previous models on discourse and story structure, and consolidated a set of simplified labels for annotating the structural components and discourse relations in our corpus. The scheme has been applied by two annotators on an English version of the Aesop's Fables, which contains 135 fables, with about 15.7K word tokens, 2.73K word types, and an average of about 116 words per story. Some quantitative comparison between the two annotators in this initial attempt is shown in Table 2 and Table 3 for structural and semantic annotation respectively. As Table 2 shows, despite the difference in the number of discourse segments (DS) excluding morals, the two annotators produced a comparable amount of Events and Speech, but they apparently agree less on States, Internal States and Internal Events. As Table 3 shows, although the two annotators identified a different amount of semantic relations (SR), the distribution over the four major classes of relations is quite similar. Their agreement on the subtypes, however, appears less consistent. More qualitative analysis to reveal the detailed difference in their conception is in progress.

Table 2: Comparison between Annotators on Structural Annotation

Annotator	DS	Event	Int.Event	State	Int.State	Speech
1	1644	68.5%	4.0%	2.3%	0.4%	24.9%
2	1478	65.2%	1.8%	5.7%	1.7%	25.6%

Table 3: Comparison between Annotators on Semantic Annotation

Annotator	SR	TEMPORAL	CONTINGENCY	COMPARISON	EXPANSION
1	1120	51.3%	12.7%	5.8%	30.2%
2	912	51.8%	11.3%	9.2%	27.7%

Future development of the annotation needs to account for dialogues and pragmatics. For example, considerable usages of "if" in the fables, especially within dialogues, do not really indicate conditions, but rather, pragmatic conditions. This is especially obvious when the if-condition is followed by a rhetorical question (e.g. *if a mere messenger can do as much damage as he's already done, how shall I withstand the attack of the man who sent him?*) which does not really indicate the consequence but rather some assertions. The moves within dialogues and the pragmatics therein, such as warning, sarcasm, regret, lecture, etc., will merit in-depth investigation in their own rights, particularly with respect to the intention of the storyteller. Hence one important future direction we anticipate is to enhance the current structural and semantic annotation with pragmatic annotation. The resulting annotated corpus is expected to contribute a valuable resource for researchers with diverse linguistic interests.

References

Beaugrande, R. de. 1982. The Story of Grammars and the Grammar of Stories. *Journal of Pragmatics, 6*:383-422.

Black, J.B. and R. Wilensky. 1979. An evaluation of story grammars. *Cognitive Science, 3*:213-229.

Fillmore, C.J. 1982. Story grammars and sentence grammars: some considerations. *Journal of Pragmatics, 6*:451-454.

Grosz, B.J. and C.L. Sidner. 1986. Attention, Intention, and the Structure of Discourse. *Computational Linguistics, 12(3)*:175-204.

Hasan, R. 1996. The Nursery tale as a genre. In C, Cloran, D. Butt and G. Williams (Eds), *Ways of Saying: Ways of Meaning*. London: Cassell.

Mandler, J.M. 1982. Another story of grammars: Comments on Beaugrande's "The story of grammars and the grammar of stories". *Journal of Pragmatics, 6*:433-440.

Mandler, J.M. and N.S. Johnson. 1977. Remembrance of things parsed: story structure and recall. *Cognitive Psychology, 9*:111-151.

Mandler, J.M. and N.S. Johnson. 1980. On throwing out the baby with the bathwater: A reply to Black and Wilensky's evaluation of story grammars. *Cognitive Science, 4*:305-312.

Mann, W.C. and S.A. Thompson. 1987. *Rhetorical Structure Theory: A Theory of Text Organization*. ISI Research Report ISI/RS-87-190, University of Southern California.

Miltsakaki, E., L. Robaldo, A. Lee and A. Joshi. 2008. Sense Annotation in the Penn Discourse Treebank. *Computational Linguistics and Intelligent Text Processing, Lecture Notes in Computer Science, Vol 4919*, pp.275-286.

Propp, V. 1968. *Morphology of the Folktale (translated by Laurence Scott).* University of Texas, Austin.

Rumelhart, D. 1975. Notes on a schema for stories. In D. Bobrow and A. Collins (Eds.), *Representation and Understanding: Studies in Cognitive Science*. New York: Academic Press.

Rumelhart, D.E. 1980. On Evaluating Story Grammars. *Cognitive Science, 4*:313-316.

Ryan, M-L. 2008. Story Grammars. In D. Herman, M. Jahn and M-L. Ryan (Eds.), *Routledge Encyclopedia of Narrative Theory*. Routledge Ltd.

Sano, M. and E. Thomson. 2007. Japanese Folk Tales: text structure and evaluative expressions. In *Proceedings of ASFLA Annual Conference 2007.*

Stede, M. 2004. The Potsdam Commentary Corpus. In *Proceedings of the ACL-2004 Workshop on Discourse Annotation*, Barcelona, Spain, pp.96-102.

Tan, X. 2009. Semantic Attributes and Lexicogrammatical Patterns: Genre Analysis of the Event Sections of Grimm's Fairy Tales. *Journal of Cambridge Studies, 4(1): 50-63.*

Thorndyke, P.W. 1977. Cognitive structures in comprehension and memory of narrative discourse. *Cognitive Psychology, 9(1)*:204-215.

Wilensky, R. 1982a. Points: A theory for the structure of stories in memory. In W. Lehnert and M. Ringle (Eds.), *Strategies for Natural Language Processing*. Hillsdale, NJ: Lawrence Erlbaum, pp.345-375.

Wilensky, R. 1982b. Story Grammars Revisited. *Journal of Pragmatics, 6*:423-432.

Verbal Inflection in Hindi: A Distributed Morphology Approach*

Smrti Singh[a], Vaijayanthi Sarma[b]

[a]Department of Humanities and Social Sciences, IIT Bombay,
Powai, Mumbai-400076, India
smritismriti@gmail.com
vsarma@iitb.ac.in

Abstract. In this paper, we provide a complete description of Hindi verbal inflection within the framework of Distributed morphology. We discuss the categories that are visible on the verb itself and on associated auxiliaries. We show how both analysis and generation are possible using this model. We also discuss the implementation of such linguistically motivated analysis in a morphological analyzer for Hindi, one of the several NLP tools that we have developed for Hindi, and discuss the outcomes of such an implementation.

Keywords: Hindi, Distributed Morphology, verbal inflection, morphological analyzer

1 Introduction

In this paper, we present an analysis of Hindi verbal inflection in the framework of Distributed Morphology (DM) (Halle and Marantz 1993 1994, Harley and Noyer 2003). The analysis presented in this paper demonstrates how DM may be used to provide a systematic and economical account of verbal inflection in Hindi. This DM analysis also lends itself straightforwardly to implementation in a Hindi Morphological Analyzer. We begin by detailing the different inflectional categories of Hindi verbs and the morphemes that realize them. Using the tools of DM we demonstrate how Hindi verbal forms can be both generated and analysed. The Hindi Morphological Analyzer that implements this analysis, produces the root, the suffixes and the morpheme analyses for any given verbal form. We would like to show that a linguistically motivated analysis provides a completely natural and successful way of implementing NLP tools.

2 Inflectional Categories of Hindi Verbs

There has been much debate about the number of tenses, aspects, moods and modal auxiliaries that may be expressed by a single verb in Hindi. Many grammarians and morphologists including Kellogg (1875), Vajpeyi (1958), Guru K P (1920), Kachru (1966), Olphen (1975), Shapiro (2000) have discussed the inflectional categories of Hindi verbs but these studies are either pedagogical or structural in approach. Singh and Agnihotri (1997) give a word-based description of Hindi verb morphology discounting the concepts of stem, roots or affixes and using word-formation strategies to express lexical relatedness between word forms. Across all approaches, there is much agreement on the kinds of inflectional categories that are seen on Hindi verbs. These categories and their exponents are given in Table 1.

---

* The authors would like to thank the three anonymous reviewers for their reviews. We have tried to address their comments and incorporate their suggestions in this version. We would also like to thank Shalmalee for help with getting the manuscript ready. Any errors are, of course, the authors.

Table 1: Inflectional categories and their markers for Hindi verbs

Verbal Form	Grammatical Category		Exponents
Finite	Tense	Present	ho
		Past	th-
		Future	-g-
	Aspect	Habitual	-t-
		Progressive	rəh
		Perfective	-(y)ā, -(y)ī, -(y)ĩ, -(y)e
		Completive	cuk
	Mood	Imperative	null, -o, -iye, -jiye, -nā
		Subjunctive (root)	-ũ, -o, -(y)e, -(y)ẽ
		Subjunctive (auxiliary)	ho
		Presumptive	ho-g-
		Root conditional	-t-
		Condition (auxiliary)	ho-t-
	Gender-Number	Masculine-singular	-(y)ā
		Masculine-plural	-(y)e
		Feminine-singular	-(y)ī
		Feminine-plural	-(y)ĩ
	Person-Number	1st p-singular	-ũ
		1st p-plural	-(y)ẽ
		2nd p-singular	-(y)e -o (semi-honorific)
		2nd p-plural	-o (semi-hon) -(y)ẽ (honorific)
		3rd p-singular	-(y)e
		3rd p-plural	-(y)ẽ
	Voice	Passive	Perfective + auxiliary 'jā'
Non-Finite	Infinitive		-n-
	Past Participle		-(y)ā, -(y)ī,-(y)ĩ,-(y)e
	Present Participle		-t-

The inflection on Hindi verbs may appear as suffixes or as auxiliaries as shown in the examples in 1-4. In 1 and 2, the habitual and perfective aspects are marked on the verbs using suffixes. In 3, the progressive aspect is marked by the auxiliary *'rəh'*. Present and past tense are marked by the auxiliary form of the verb *to be* in 1, 2 and 3. The future tense is marked directly on the verbal root (if the tense auxiliary is absent, as shown in 4).

1) vəh khā-**tā** hai
he eat-participle-sg-m be-3s-present
He eats

2) us-ne khā-**yā** hai
he-ERG eat-en-sg-m be-3s-present
He has eaten

3) vəh khā **rəh**-ā **hai/thā**
he eat progressive-sg-m be-3s-present/be-3s-past-m
He is/was eating

4) vəh khāe-**g**-ā
he eat-fut-3sm
He will eat

Morphemes of all languages are subject to constraints while they combine to form words or word groups or phrases. These constraints can be syntactic, phonological or semantic. For example, the Hindi future morpheme *-g-* cannot be attached to a verb stem unless the *person-number* morpheme is already present. Further, the verbal stem must be closed using a *gender-number* marker if the future morpheme *-g-* is present. These constraints reject forms such as *khāgā (eat-Future), sogī (sleep-Future)* or *soũg (sleep-1p, sg-Future)* while permitting *khāyegā (eat-3p,masc-Future-3p,sg), soũgī (will sleep-1p,fem-Future-3p,sg).* Morpheme arrangement rules enable us to identify valid word forms and rule out invalid ones. The order in which the primary Hindi verbal elements arrange themselves is Verb-Aspect-Tense/Mood. The order for all inflectional categories for Hindi verbs (or the template of the verbal group) is given below.

5) Template for verbal inflection
Main Verb > infinitive > passive marker > person-number > Modal > Aspect > Tense/Mood > gender-number

In Table 2, we provide a complete list of the various verb forms (all aspects, moods, tenses, etc.) for the 3rd person, singular for different kinds of verbal roots as a sample of the kinds of inflections that are found in Hindi.

Table 2: Inflections marked on Hindi verbal roots

Root ending ⟶ Aspect/Mood/Tense ↓	**ā** *khā* 'eat'	**ī** *pī* 'drink'	**e** *de* 'give'	**ū** *chū* 'touch'	**o** *so* 'sleep'	**C** *b^{h}āg* 'run'
Perfective Aspect	khāyā	piyā	diyā	chuā	soyā	b^{h}āgā
Habitual Aspect	khātā	pītā	detā	chūtā	sotā	b^{h}āgtā
Infinitive	khānā	pīnā	denā	chūnā	sonā	b^{h}āgnā
Subjunctive	khāye	piye	de	chuye	soye	b^{h}āge
Conditional	khātā	pītā	detā	chūtā	sotā	b^{h}āgtā
Future	khāyegā	piyegā	degā	chuegā	soyegā	b^{h}āgegā
Imperative/intimate	khā	pī	de	chū	so	b^{h}āg
Imperative (semi-hon)	khāo	piyo	do	chūo	soo	b^{h}āgo
Imperative (hon)	khāiye	pījīye	dījīye	chuiye	soiye	b^{h}āgiye

3 Hindi Verbal inflection in Distributed Morphology

The Distributed Morphology framework states that terminal nodes are organized into hierarchical structures at the level of SS by syntactic operations. These nodes contain a complex of semantic and syntactic features but lack any phonological content. After syntax, the nodes may undergo changes as a result of various morphosyntactic operations (such as *merger, fusion, fission, impoverishment,* etc.) at the level of MS (morphological structure). Phonological content is supplied at PF through vocabulary insertion to these modified terminals. This yields the phonetic form of the utterance (and the surface structure of a word/phrase) through sequential derivation (Halle and Marantz 1994). There are two kinds of terminal nodes available at syntactic structure. The first kind of terminal node is typically filled by root entries. Root entries contain phonological and semantic features but no grammatical category features. They acquire a category only after insertion into the syntactic structure. For example, the root terminal combines with the category head as shown in 6 below to produce a V that represents the verb *khā* 'eat'.

6)

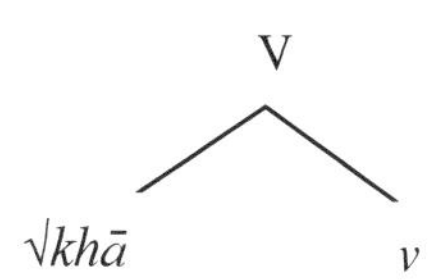

The second kind of terminal node has grammatical features but no phonological form. The phonological form is supplied through the process of Vocabulary Insertion. Some features, however, may never be expressed phonologically and are thus *phonologically null.* For example, the verbal form in the imperative mood to indicate intimacy (between the speaker and the addressee) in Hindi is not marked using any specific suffix. Thus, [+imperative, +intimate] is realised as the bare root verb in Hindi, as in */jā/* 'Go!', */ā/* 'Come!', etc. Conversely, a single grammatical feature may have multiple phonological realizations. In this case, competition among the possible phonetic exponents dictates the final selection based on their feature specifications. For example, the 'plural, direct' form of the nouns in Hindi is marked through the suffixes *-ẽ, -yā̃, -e* or the *null* morpheme and the selection is driven by the gender and the phonological ending of the noun root. The selection of one of these suffixes is based on the features that best match those present at the terminal node. The framework of Distributed Morphology (DM) relies on *late insertion, underspecification* and *isomorphism between structures at all levels in the grammar of a language.* As was mentioned earlier, the terminal nodes in the structure that syntax provides to the level of MS are manipulated using certain morphological operations before vocabulary insertion. These operations work under strict adjacency principles and can *split, fuse* or *merge* terminal nodes. These operations account for the mismatches between syntactic structure and the morphological structure of word forms. In English, the verbal form in the past tense is generated by assuming a syntactic structure in which T(ense) and the V(erb) appear as separate nodes. T(ense) first lowers (known as Tense lowering) in the tree and then merges with the main verb (V). Merger may or may not lead to fusion of the adjacent morphemes. For example, in English past tense, T(ense) and V(erb) nodes fuse to give rise to a single terminal node. If the two adjacent morphemes fuse into a single terminal node, they are represented using a single exponent. And, if the two nodes do not fuse, different exponents are inserted at each of the two merged nodes.

In Hindi, verbs are cumulatively marked for gender and number (*e.g., bhāg-ī̃* (ran-feminine-pl)) or person and number (*bhāg-ũ* (run-1st person-singular)) as the nodes for the two features fuse before vocabulary insertion. These fused nodes then merge with that of verbal head and make slots available for two vocabulary items. Hindi offers a case where unlike English, the verbal head raises to tense or aspect or mood in order to adjoin to the higher syntactic head(s). We give the example of the verb *'khāyā'* (ate) where a single exponent *-yā* represents aspect and agreement (gender-number). Figure 1 provides a diagrammatic representation of merger and fusion in Hindi verbs. Note that Hindi is right-headed and syntactic heads appear stacked one above the other.

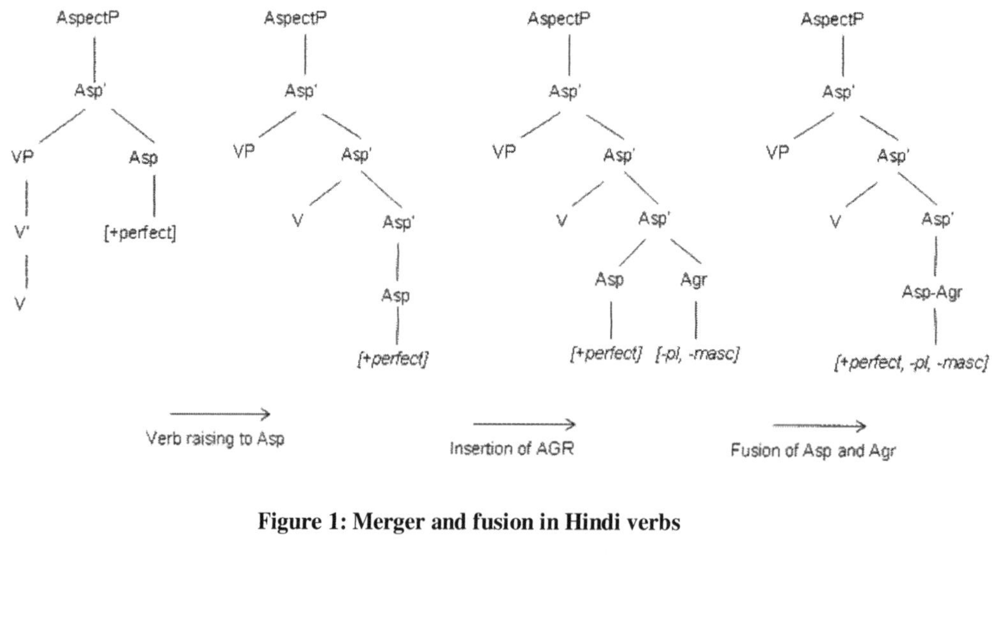

Figure 1: Merger and fusion in Hindi verbs

Vocabulary items (affixes) also carry information about the contexts of their phonological realization (Halle and Marantz 1993). In addition, their form or shape may either be contextually determined by neighbouring morphemes or trigger changes in those morphemes. These typically yield phonologically conditioned allomorphs, stem alternations or deletion or modification of particular features of the morphemes (impoverishment). In the following, we discuss each of these processes in Hindi verbal morphology.

An allomorph is a contextually determined variant of a given morpheme. The phonological shape of a particular morpheme (verb root here) may affect the choice of other morphemes (a suffix, for example) that may be inserted in adjacent nodes. Roots that are inserted prior to affixal entries may have different phonological shapes. The interaction of the root and the suffix may trigger changes in the shape of a suffix or the root itself. In Hindi, the verbal roots that end in consonants or in the vowel */ū/* select suffix *-ā* in the features [+perfect, +masc, -pl]. But, for the verbal roots ending in the vowels */ā/, /ī/, /e/* or */o/,* the glide */y/* is inserted between the suffix and the final vowel of the verbal stem. The suffix *-yā* is thus an allomorph of the suffix *-ā*. Stem alternation is seen when a stem undergoes phonological modification that is triggered by the presence of an adjacent suffixal morpheme. The shortening or the lengthening of root final vowels, sandhi or suppletion (either partial or complete), constitute typical changes as shown in 7. The readjustment rules in DM are designed to account for these changes post-syntactically.

7)	**Root**	**Root-Suffix**	**Final Form**	**Phonological Change**
	pī (drink)	*pī-yā*	*piyā*	*Vowel shortening*
	chū (touch)	*chū-ā*	*chuā*	*Vowel shortening*
	le (take)	*le-yā*	*liyā*	*e → i*
	jā (go)	*jā-yā*	*gəyā*	*Complete suppletion*
	kər (do)	*kər-ā*	*kiyā*	*Partial suppletion*

Certain verbal features may be deleted or modified in the presence of other features and this is known as impoverishment in DM. Impoverishment allows insertion of default or underspecified entries at a node as entries specified for the deleted feature are taken out of the competition. In Hindi, verbs are marked cumulatively for the perfective aspect and the gender-number feature. The fused gender-number feature appears at a number of places where perfective is absent but not vice-versa. This can be represented using the rule given in 8 below that says that the feature [+perfect] is deleted in the presence of the gender-number features at a node. This results in the insertion of entries that are specified only for gender and number features. Another impoverishment rule is given in 9 which blocks the insertion of */ho/* for the subjunctive and inserts the person-number morpheme instead.

8) *[+perfect] → null / [gender-number]*
9) *[+subjunctive] → ϕ / [person-number]*

3.1 Vocabulary Insertion

The insertion of verbal affixes and auxiliaries can be understood in terms of vocabulary items (both root and affixal) given below in Table 3. The symbols *Vī, Ve, Vā, Vū* denote different vowel endings of verbal roots. The vocabulary items compete for insertion at the terminal nodes, and are chosen based on their feature specification. The auxiliary insertion entries in Table 3 insert auxiliaries while all other entries insert suffixes at the terminal nodes. The first six suffixal rules mark Hindi verbs for the imperative mood and the sixth rule is the default rule for the imperative mood. The suffixal rules are arranged in the order of their proximity to the verbal stem. The suffixes that appear closest to the stem are placed first in the list followed by those that appear after them (more distally). For example, the person-number marking rules must be applied before the application of the rule that inserts the future morpheme. Similarly, the future morpheme *-g-* must be inserted before any *gender-number* morpheme is inserted. The future morpheme insertion rule entails a necessary condition that should be fulfilled first – that a person-number marker must be inserted before the future morpheme is inserted. The conditional mood, the infinitive, and the habitual aspect are all followed by the insertion of the gender-number morpheme.

3.2 Readjustment Rules

Hindi verb roots may end in a consonant (b^h*āg* 'run', *cəl* 'walk') or in a vowel such as */ā/ (khā* 'eat', *jā* 'go'*), /ī/ (pī* 'drink', *sī* 'sew'*), /e/ (de* 'give', *le* 'take'*), /ū/ (*c^h*ū* 'touch'*),* or */o/ (so* 'sleep', *ro* 'weep'*).* The V-V sequences are resolved by glide insertion (a), vowel shortening (b and c), vowel modification (d), or vowel nasalization (e). The readjustment rules given in 10(a-e) pertain to these changes that are made to the inflecting verb.

10) Rules:
   a) Root final Vā or Vī or Ve or Vo → Glide insertion / [+perfect] (pīyā-piyā)
   b) Root final ī [Vī] → i / gender-number (pīyā-piyā)
   c) Root final ū [Vū] → u / gender-number (chūā-chuā)
   d) Root final e [Ve] → i / gender-number (deyā-diyā)
   e) Root final e [Ve] → nasal / person-number (de-dẽ)

Table 3: Rules to account for verbal inflection in Hindi

Auxiliary Insertion Rules	Suffix Insertion Rules
[+passive, -past] ↔ jā	*[+imperative, +neutral] ↔ nā*
[+subjunctive] ↔ /ho/	*[+imperative, -intimate, +polite] ↔ /-jiye/ /Vī or Ve*
[+ability] or [+probability] ↔ sək	*[+imperative, -intimate, +polite] ↔ /-iye/*
[+ability] ↔ pā	*[+imperative, -intimate, -polite] ↔ -o*
[+obligation] ↔ /pəR/ / vInfinitive	*[+imperative] ↔ null*
[+necessity] ↔ cāhiye / vInfinitive	*[2p] ↔ -o*
[+permissive] ↔ de / vInfinitive	*[1p, -pl] ↔ -ũ*
[-perfect, -habitual] ↔ rəh	*[-masc] ↔ -ī*
[+completive] ↔ cuk	*[+pl] ↔ -ẽ*
[-past] ↔ /ho/	*[-pl] ↔ -e*
	Future ↔ -g- (person, ±pl)
	Conditional ↔ -t-
	[-perfect, +habitual] ↔ -t-
	Infinitive ↔ -n-
	[+perfect, +pl, -masc] ↔ -ĩ
	[+pl, +masc] ↔ -e
	[-pl, +masc] ↔ -ā

3.3 Rules for Irregular Roots

The phonological changes that occur as a result of the association of the verb stem and a suffix can be explained using the rules given above. However, there are cases when stems undergo some modifications that cannot be explained phonologically as in suppletive or irregular forms. The irregular behaviour of certain verb stems in Hindi is accounted for as shown below.

11) Rules:
   i. *jā → /g-/ / [+perfect]*
   ii. *kər → /ki-/ / [+perfect, +masc]*
   iii. *kər → /k-/ / [-masc]*
   iv. *ho → /h/ / [-past, 1p, -pl]*
   v. *ho → /hai/ / [-pl]*
   vi. *ho → /hãĩ/ / [+pl]*
   vii. *(ho) subjunctive → /hõ/ / [+pl]*

The analysis presented is a comprehensive one and is expected to describe and generate all and only the grammatically acceptable forms of the Hindi verbs. The analysis economises on the descriptive classes that are generated and relates roots and affixes in an unambiguous and complete way. We expect that any new root that enters the language can also be treated straightforwardly with this account which attempts to capture native speakers' intuitions about the formation of verbal forms. We implement this analysis in a morphological analyzer to demonstrate its accuracy and competences and to develop an NLP tool that is independently required for the language.

4 Implementation of Hindi Morphological Analyzer

The DM-based Morphological analyser uses a set of ordered contextual rules to isolate and extract the suffixes from a given word form. For implementation purposes, the vocabulary entries developed for nouns, adjectives, quantifiers, ordinals and verbs (discussed in the previous section) were converted into *if-then* rules and arranged in order of specificity of inflectional and contextual features. These rules being bidirectional can both synthesize and analyse word forms. Although, we have not implemented a synthesizer or a word generator, we would like to point out that the implementation does not require a new set of rules. The internal processes of the DM-based morphological analyser are shown in Figure 2. The rules are applied from right to left iteratively until no suffixes remain and only the base root (that is identified from the root lexicon) is left. Readjustment rules apply wherever applicable to produce the correct root which is then matched with the incorporated root-list to determine a match or matches. The three distinct steps that are used in the analyzer are as follows:

12) <u>Morphological Analyzer</u>
    a) Stemming
    b) Root formation and lexicon look up
    c) Morphological analysis

The system produces a detailed morpheme analysis for each word and provides the root, the grammatical category, the inflectional class and the feature values associated with the word. The system also produces a detailed morphological analysis for each morpheme that constitutes the word form. The sample output format of the system is given in 13.

13) Input Token: X/Y/Z
    Possible Root 1: class: category: suffix: morphemes (morpheme1, morpheme 2, ...): Morpheme analysis (morpheme 1, morpheme 2, ...)
    Possible Root 2: category: suffix: morphemes (morpheme1, morpheme 2, ...): Morpheme analysis (morpheme 1, morpheme 2, ...)

The morpheme analysis of each suffix is produced in a seven field with values for the features *gender, number, person, case, tense, aspect,* and *mood* with the applicable values completed as appropriate to the grammatical category. Therefore, for verbs, the values for the case feature are not applicable while the other six fields will include the values that are present. If an input word form could yield multiple roots through multiple analyses (within or across grammatical categories), all such analyses are offered by the analyser. Since, a morphological analyser deals only with words, all analyses offered are retained for the use of higher processing tasks such as POS Tagging or Word Grouping. The analysis for verbs that we presented has been used to develop a DM based Morphological Analyzer for Hindi. An Analyzer extracts suffixes from a word form and outputs its possible morphemes and their analyses. We used a lexicon with approximately 1500 verbal roots. In Figure 2 we show how stemming and morphological analysis is done for the input word *pāegā* (पाएगा) 'will get' (masculine, singular). The vocabulary rules that are applied in the analysis of a word such as *pāegā* are:

14) *[-pl, +masc] ↔ /ā/*
[+Future] ↔ /-g-/
[-pl] ↔ /-e/ / V
[+ability] ↔ pā

The verb root */pā/* can be a main verb or a modal auxiliary. The system outputs both options. In 15 we provide the details of both possibilities. Features with no exponents are marked 'x':

15) *Token: pāegā, Total Outputs: 2*

Output 1:

[Root 1: pā, Category: verb main, Suffix: egā]

[Gender: +masc, Number: -pl, Person: 2p, Tense: +future, Aspect: x, Mood: x]
[Gender: +masc, Number: -pl, Person: 3p, Tense: +future, Aspect: x, Mood: x]

Output 2:

[Root 2: pā, Category: verb_auxiliary, Suffix: egā]

[Gender: +masc, Number: -pl, Person: 2p, Tense: +future, Aspect: x, Mood: +ability]
[Gender: +masc, Number: -pl, Person: 3p, Tense: +future, Aspect: x, Mood: +ability]

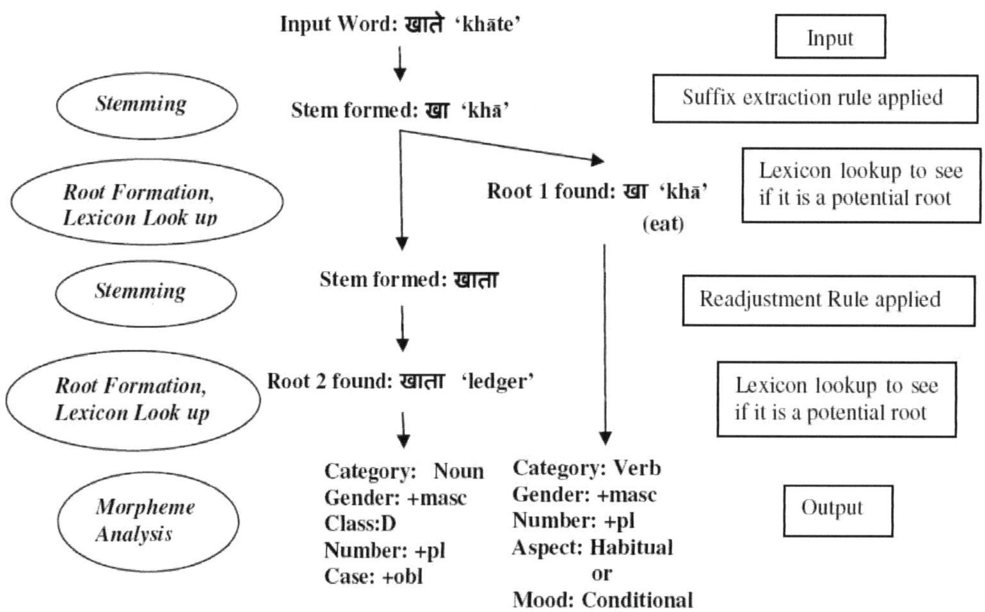

Figure 2: Processes of the DM-based Hindi Morphological Analyser

5 Evaluation, Results and Future Work

We tested the analyser on 13160 Hindi verb forms and manually verified the outputs of the system. The performance of the system on Hindi verbs is very good. The results are given in Table 4. The system fails to identify only 116 forms. The system was able to correctly analyse most of the regular and irregular forms when the root verb is found in the lexicon.

Table 4: Results of the DM-based MA on Hindi verbs

Total number of words	13160
Total number of verbs correctly analysed	13044
Total number of unidentified verbs	116

The main reasons for the errors encountered are (a) incorrect spelling, (b) hyphenated word forms, (c) missing roots and (d) extra/incorrect characters in the word form. We provide the details of the unidentified words with examples in Table 5.

Table 5: Error report of DM-based MA on Hindi verbs

Error Type	Example 1	Example 2	Example 3	Example 4
Root missing in lexicon	मंगा 'məŋā' (order)	धंस 'dhəns' (sink)	भव 'bhəv' (happen)	धड़धड़ा 'dhəDdhəDā' (make noise)
Hyphenated words	आने-जाने 'āne-jāne' (coming-going)	चलते-चलते 'cəlte-cəlte' (walking-reduplication)	रो-धोकर 'ro-dhokər' 'crying etc.'	खाने-पीने 'khāne-pīne' (eating-drinking)
Incorrect/ variant spelling	रक्खा 'rəkhā' (kept)	उड़ाय 'uDāe' (flew-pl)	जायँगे 'jāẽge' (go-fut-pl)	पावें 'pāvẽ' (get-subjunctive)
Words with extra characters	देखने- 'dekhane'	बैठे- 'bæThe-'	है... 'hai…'	लगे- 'lẽge-'

6 Conclusions

In this paper, we have presented a comprehensive analysis of Hindi verb inflection and its implementation in a DM-based Morphological Analyser. The system was able to completely and correctly analyze both regular and irregular verb forms. The system failures were driven primarily by external factors. The output of the system is quite detailed as it produces morpheme analyses for both root and suffixes for a word form. This analysis can easily be done in the reverse to generate verbal forms as well.

The linguistic analysis that was presented in the earlier part of the paper is economical in descriptive terms. Traditional paradigm analyses proliferate paradigms based on features such as gender or number or verb class. Distributed Morphology allows for morphology to work in tandem with syntax (so a parser based on this system can easily incorporate the analyzer) and at the same time allows for the quirks of morphology to be dealt with in specific ways (fusion, fission etc.) NLP tools that are developed on well-argued linguistic analyses are arguably intuitively more appealing, but also, as we have just shown, capable of providing good results.

We have also extended the current analysis to Verb Group Identification (main verb and its auxiliaries). This module selects one analysis out of potentially possible multiple analyses for a word using its contextual information. Strict morphotactical constraints are used to identify verb groups in a sentence and to rule out invalid groups. The DM-based analyser is currently being used in the CRF based POS Tagger and Word Group Identifier for Hindi and deals with all categories of words. It is also being plugged into the Hindi Wordnet and in the Word Sense Disambiguation (WSD) engine to stem the input words and to use their morphological information for sense disambiguation. We hope that this will present a strong case for NLP tools based on well-reasoned and well-argued linguistic analyses.

References

Guru, K. P. 1920. *Hindi Vyakaran.* Kashi: Lakshmi Narayan Press. (1962 edition)

Halle, M. and A. Marantz. 1993. Distributed morphology and the pieces of inflection. In K. Hale and S. J. Keyser (eds.), *The View from Building 20*, pp.111–176. Cambridge, MA: MIT Press.

Halle, M. and A. Marantz. 1994. Some Key Features of Distributed Morphology. In A. Carnie and H. Harley (eds.) *Papers in Phonology and Morphology*, pp275-288. MITWPL 21.

Harley, H. and R. Noyer.1999. Distributed Morphology. *GLOT International 4(4),* pp.3-9.

Kachru, Y. 2006. *Hindi.* Amsterdam and Philadelphia: John Benjamins.

Olphen, H. 1975. Aspect, Tense, and Mood in the Hindi Verb. *Indo-Iranian Journal* 16(4), pp.284-301.

Shapiro, M. 2000. *A Primer of Modern Standard Hindi Grammar.* Delhi: Motilal Banarsidass Publications.

Singh, R. and Agnihotri, R. 1997. *Hindi Morphology: A Word-Based Description.* Motilal Banarsidass Series in Linguistics, Volume IX. Delhi: Motilal Banarsidass.

Upreti, M. L. 1964. *Hindi me Pratayay Vichar.* Agra: Vinod Pustak Mandir.

Vajpeyi, K. 1958. *Hindi Shabdanushasan.* Kashi: Nagri Pracharni Sabha.

Word classes in Indonesian: A linguistic reality or a convenient fallacy in natural language processing?

Meladel Mistica[a], Timothy Baldwin[b], and I Wayan Arka[a]

[a] CHL, The Australian National University,
Canberra, Australia
meladel.mistica@gmail.com
wayan.arka@anu.edu.au
[b] CSSE, The University of Melbourne,
Parkville, Australia
tb@ldwin.net

Abstract. This paper looks at Indonesian (Bahasa Indonesia), and the claim that there is no noun-verb distinction within the language as it is spoken in regions such as Riau and Jakarta. We test this claim for the language as it is written by a variety of Indonesian speakers using empirical methods traditionally used in part-of-speech induction.

In this study we use only morphological patterns that we generate from a pre-existing morphological analyser. We find that once the distribution of the data points in our experiments match the distribution of the text from which we gather our data, we obtain significant results that show a distinction between the class of nouns and the class of verbs in Indonesian. Furthermore it shows promise that the labelling of word classes may be achieved only with morphological features, which could be applied to out-of-vocabulary items.

Keywords: Indonesian, Word class, Word class induction, Morphology

1 Introduction

The notion of word classes, such as the nouns, verbs and adjectives, is fundamental in both linguistics and computational linguistics. Word classes are the basis for the labels in part-of-speech tagging, and also the building blocks for parsing. In grammar engineering, they are the primitives upon which context-free grammar rules are written. In linguistics, they are considered the categories that shape the organisation of the language, and the way the world is conceived through language. These categories may not align across languages: what is expressed as a verb in one language may be expressed as an adjective or noun in another. But one linguistic universality hypothesis that remains despite these variations is that the categories *noun* and *verb* exist in all languages (Croft, 2003).

This paper examines the noun–verb distinction specifically for Indonesian (*Bahasa Indonesia*) as, at least in spoken Indonesian in particular regions such as Riau and Jakarta, it has been claimed that open class categories are indistinguishable (Gil, 2001; Gil, 2010). If correct, this would refute the universality of the noun–verb distinction in Linguistics, with significant implications for Linguistic Typology and Theoretical Syntax.

The primary aim in this paper is to apply unsupervised data-driven analysis of Indonesian text to determine whether we can automatically learn the noun–verb distinction, and in doing so, shed light on whether Indonesian conforms to Croft's noun–verb universality hypothesis, or is indeed a counter-example to the hypothesis as claimed by Gil. In addition, these experiments are a litmus test to see if "morphological signatures", as used by Goldsmith (2001), are sufficient in determining parts-of-speech, and can be used to determine the part-of-speech of out-of-vocabulary items (OOV) in Indonesian text processing. One assumption we make throughout this work is that the same basic word class distinctions are invariant across different styles, genres and registers (such as spoken vs. written) of a given language. That is, a conclusion on word class distinctions drawn based on written data should apply equally to spoken data, for example.

This paper is laid out as follows. In Section 2 we look at how word classes are determined, both qualitatively in Linguistics and statistically in the field of part-of-speech induction. Next, we look at the formal properties of Indonesian, and we give examples to show how the distinction between nouns and verbs can be illusive. In the next two sections (Sections 4 and 5) we describe the data, tools and method for our experiments, followed by the results in Section 6. Finally, we discuss our findings and the impact and contribution to both Linguistics and Computational Linguistics, particularly in natural language processing for Indonesian (Sections 7 and 8).

2 Determining Word Classes

In the following sections, we outline the linguistic methodology for determining word classes, and how we emulate this computationally using methods borrowed from part-of-speech induction.

2.1 Linguistic Categories

Within a descriptive framework, the current methodology for determining word classes is rather formal, relying on the combinatorics of the form. At the clausal or phrasal level, we look at the syntagmatic possibilities of the units within the phrase or clause. When looking at the word level, we look at how each of the morphological components combine. The heuristics for this *combinatorics* approach are outlined by Evans (2000), which takes into consideration semantic properties as a way of labelling these classes rather than determining them.

There are of course problems in taking an overly formal approach, without any reference to the semantics of the word or stem, or its function, as outlined by Croft (2000), using the English adjective class as a case in point: the adjective *big* in its superlative form is *biggest*, whereas the adjective *beautiful* cannot combine with the *-est* suffix to form a superlative. Instead, it must be formed analytically with the adverb *most*, as in *the* ***most beautiful*** *sunset*. Even given this fact about these two stems/words, it may be difficult to argue that these are not of the same word class because in this instance they do not combine in the same way morphologically. One could concede that these form sub-classes of adjectives.

Our assumption is that the two aforementioned levels, phrasal/clausal and word level, to some extent have their own localised characteristics and constraints on combination. However the predictions we make at the word level, by and large, have consequences at the phrasal/clausal level, and vice versa. For example, if we decide that, at the word level, the stem *stool* is a noun, we then assume that within a phrase it will behave like other nouns and therefore form a group with other terms that are like it; i.e., it will combine with other terms in the same way that other nouns do.

In an article that led to many responses, Evans and Osada (2005) argue against the claim that Mundari (an Austroasiatic language from India) has no noun–verb distinction. They outline three criteria for establishing the lack of word classes within a language, as summarised in Figure 2.1. Additionally, Evans and Osada state that these criteria must apply *exhaustively* throughout the language. We address each of the issues in Figure 2.1 for Indonesian in Section 3 to show how one could possibly analyse Indonesian as being a language that had no noun–verb distinction.

2.2 Part-of-speech Induction

According to Biemann (2009), part-of-speech induction aims to approximate syntactic labels based on unlabelled token sequences, usually resulting in the discovery of categories that are not considered linguistically motivated. It is traditionally approached using unsupervised methods,

I. Equivalent combinatorics
"Members of what are claimed to be merged classes should have identical distributions in terms of both morphological and syntactic categories."

II. Compositionality
"Any semantic differences between the uses of a putative 'fluid' lexeme in two syntactic positions (say argument and predicate) must be attributable to the function of that position."

III. Bidirectionality
"[T]o establish that there is just a single word class, it is not enough for Xs to be usable as Ys without modification: it must also be the case that Ys are usable as Xs."

Figure 1: Criteria for determining word classes by Evans and Osada (2005)

otherwise known as clustering, and then assigning labels after the fact. However in this study we use linguistic features in order to induce linguistically motivated clusters.

A recent survey of systems developed for part-of-speech (POS) induction by Christodoulopoulos *et al.* (2010) shows that these systems are notoriously difficult to evaluate due to the nature of the task. Rather than focusing on the individual learners developed in these systems, for our purposes, we observe that two main feature types were utilised in all the systems that were surveyed: morphological, and collocational (or pseudo-syntactic). Of the seven systems surveyed, five developed systems based on solely on collocational or distributional properties of tokens in a text, while two systems (Clark, 2003; Biemann, 2006) additionally included morphological features.

Relevant to the morphological features we develop in this study is the research of Goldsmith (2001), and his use of the term **signatures** to mean a collection of morphological patterns relevant to a stem. He employs the MDL (minimum description length) algorithm as a way of discovering and grouping verbs that inflect in the same way. Although this field focuses on collocational or distributional features that emulate syntactic position, Goldsmith's work focuses solely on morphological patterns as a way of grouping *inflectional categories*. Rather than inducing the signatures in the way the Goldsmith does, we derive them from a corpus using a non-class biased morphological analyser (See Section 5 for more details).

3 Formal Properties of Indonesian

In this section, we discuss the properties of Indonesian in terms of the criteria set up by Evans and Osada (2005), as summarised in Section 2.1. We show how the combinatorics of lexical items could lead one to analyse the language as having one catch-all open class lexical category, i.e. have no distinction between nouns and verbs or other open word classes such as adjectives or adverbs.

First we address the issue of *equivalent combinatorics*. The following examples focus on the word *lari* "run". As is evident in Examples (2) and Example (1) , *lari* can occur in both the *subject* and the *predicate* position.

(1) *Ia* *lari.*
(S)he run
"(S)he runs."

(2) *Lari* *menyehatkan.*
run cause.to.be.healthy
"Running is healthy."

The examples below employ the stems *bunyi* "sound" and *bangun* "to wake up", and show how words that can be traditionally thought of as noun and verb, respectively, can occur in the same morphological environment, by combining with the same morphological affixes:

(3) *membunyikan*
mem-bunyi-kan
AV-sound-CAUS
"make X make a sound (instrument)"

(4) *membangunkan*
mem-bangun-kan
AV-wake.up-CAUS
"make X wake up (someone)"

Take first the issue of *Compositionality* from Section 2.1, which states that given a word in a position, we should be able to predict its semantics. We see that in Examples (1) and (2), the predicative or referential function of *lari* "run" is simply determined by its position in the clause, unlike English that requires us to employ derivational morphology.[1]

In Examples (3) and (4), the semantic and morpho-syntactic effects of the affixes are predictable: the suffix *-kan* CAUS is a **causative**, meaning that it will have causative semantics associated with it. The prefix *mem-* AV simply tells us that the agent is the subject, which would be true for both examples above. In other words these examples satisfy the semantic predictability criterion stipulated by the *Compositionality* requirement.

Testing the criterion of *Bidirectionality* is not a trivial task simply because we would have to rely on grammaticality judgements, which can be subjective and continuous rather than binary in nature (Keller, 2001). Assuming that there is no distinction between open word classes in Indonesian, this criterion states that those classes traditionally labelled as nouns must be able to behave as all other parts of speech in the open class category, and vice versa. We have an example of what would be traditionally analysed as a verb in a syntactic slot normally reserved for nouns in Example (2) . However, we would also have to find possibilities of traditional nouns in verbal positions, without the need for morphological affixation to license its usage in that position.

Rather than rely on grammaticality judgements, we analyse how the language is used by the Indonesian speaking population in publicly available web data.

4 Data and Tools

This section outlines how we gathered our data and developed our data set, obtained our evaluation data, and modified existing tools for the task in order to create our morphological features.

4.1 Getting the Word-forms for Morphological Analysis

The text we use for this study is the Indonesian Wikipedia[2] because not only is it a large source of naturally-occurring text, but also because the data is produced and curated by many authors; it is representative of the way the language is used throughout the Internet-connected areas of Indonesia, and Indonesian speakers throughout the world.

We gathered approximately 2 million Indonesian tokens from Wikipedia articles. After removing markup using WikiPrep[3], we sorted the data and counted token frequencies, leaving capitalisation untouched and preserving any errors in the removal of mark-up. We then ran the morphological analyser over all tokens that occurred 5 or more times, mainly to eliminate typographic or other errors. In actuality this is only around 17% of all word forms found, with a long tail of singleton occurrences.

4.2 Stem lexicon

The method we employ in discovering the word class clusters is fully unsupervised, and does not incorporate any possibly biasing information on word class distinctions. In order to ascertain whether the induced word clusters reflect the noun–verb distinction, however, we require evaluation data that we consider to encode the conventional definition of noun and verb. For this, we

[1] In English we can say: *I run.* but not: **Run is healthy.*

[2] We used the dump produced on October 15, 2009, downloaded on October 19, 2009 from `http://dumps.wikimedia.org/idwiki/`

[3] `http://www.cs.technion.ac.il/~gabr/resources/code/wikiprep`

PART-OF-SPEECH	COUNT
Noun	8,096
Verb	821
Other (Prep, Pron, Num, etc.)	1,770
TOTAL	10,687

Table 1: Part-of-speech distribution in the stem lexicon for the morphological analyser.

PREFIX	Active Voice; Passive Voice; Causative; Passive *Ter/ter; ber; OrdKe/ke; pe/peN; se*
CIRCUMFIX	*ke_an; per_an; pe/peN_an*
SUFFIX	*an; i; kan; wi*
CLITICS	*ku; mu; nya*
OTHER	Reduplication

Figure 2: Types of affixes from the morphological analyser.

extract the lexicon from a morphological analyser which encodes a hard distinction between the two word classes, in a manner which is compatible with the criteria of Evans and Osada (2005) and word class definitions of Croft (2003). As can be seen in Table 1, the lexicon is biased towards nouns, having almost ten times as many nouns as there are verbs. The class labelled "Other" consists of all stems not marked as a noun or verb, and includes adjectives, pronouns, prepositions, numbers, determiners, etc.

4.3 Morphological Analyser

Due to Indonesian being a morphologically rich language, we need some way of mapping word forms onto lexemes, to capture as complete a signature as possible for each lexeme. For this, we used the same morphological analyser as provided the source of the stem lexicon, but altered the analyser to remove all distinctions between word classes, to avoid biasing the clustering results. For example, we defined the (verbal) circumfix *peN+..+an* (e.g. such as *pem+bakar+an* peN+burn+an, meaning "the process of incinerating") to be able to flank any stem. This leads to uninhibited over-generation, but it also enables the possibility of analysing all classes of stems in a uniform manner.

We obtained the original morphological analyser by Mistica *et al.* (2009), which was built using XFST (Beesley and Karttunen, 2003) and includes the 10,687 lexicalised stems from Table 1. We then merged all stems in the lexicon into a single undifferentiated word class. The set of affixes the morphological analyser can process is outlined in Figure 2.

5 Method

5.1 Feature Engineering

We perform two kinds of experiments, based on two distinct feature representations: multinomial and binomial. Multinomial features take into account the number of occurrences of a morphological pattern, and the binary features record the existence of a particular morphological pattern (irrespective of how often it occurs). Linguists conventionally manually classify lexemes into morpho-syntactic categories using a binomial representation, i.e. testing (often using elicited data or intuition) whether a given lexeme is compatible with each of a range of morpho-syntactic configurations. Computational linguistic methods, on the other hand, tend to use a multinomial lexeme representation. Part of our interest in comparing these two feature representations is to empirically test the relative expressiveness of the two approaches.

		STEM	STEM+S	un+STEM+ed	STEM+ed
bird	a.	10	20	0	0
	b.	1	1	0	0
plug	a.	1	3	5	15
	b.	1	1	1	1

Figure 3: An example of features extracted from *bird*, *birds*, *plug*, *plugs*, *unplugged* and *plugged*.

DATA	# **Features**	**N**	**V**	**O**	**TOTAL**
All POS (All parts-of-speech)	259	8,096	821	1,770	10,687
Noun & Verbs	250	8,096	821	-	8,917
All POS, NoRR (No Reduplication)	208	8,096	821	1,770	10,687
Nouns and Verbs, NoRR (No Reduplication)	200	8,096	821	-	8,917

Table 2: Part-of-speech distribution for the 'Clustering' experiments, with number of features.

The morphological patterns are collated from the output of the morphological analyser. That is, we do not just note which suffixes are appended to each stem, but we look at each word form in its entirety, i.e. what combinations of morphs occur with stem. The combination of these morphs make up each feature.

If, for example, we were looking at an English corpus and found the tokens *bird*, *birds*, *plug*, *plugs*, *unplugged* and *plugged* in the corpus 10, 20, 1, 3, 5, 15 times respectively, then the features for this set would be as shown in Figure 3, wherein the **a.** rows indicate the multinomial values and the **b.** rows are the binary values.

5.2 Clustering

For our clustering experiments, we use two basic datasets: (1) lexemes from all word classes (noun, verb and other) in the stem lexicon, and (2) lexemes from just the noun and verb classes in the stem lexicon. We additionally experiment with reduplication either enabled or disabled in the morphological analyser, as it has been claimed that reduplication is the only instance of non-derivational morphology in Indonesian, and leads to marked differences in semantic effect between predicates and nominals (Musgrave, 2001). We hypothesise that this may have an influence on the assignment of instances to clusters, and test this by optionally disabling analysis of reduplication.

Table 2 shows the breakdown of data across the different logic possibilities of word class composition in the stem lexicon, and reduplication in the morphological analyser (with "NoRR" indicating that reduplication is disabled). In each case, "N", "V" and "O" indicate the breakdown of nouns, verbs and other word classes in the dataset in question. We also observe that, of the possible combinations of morphs (from Figure 2) for a given stem, a relatively small number is attested in the actual data (as indicated in the column "# Features").

Rather than apply a hard clustering algorithm such a k-means, we decided to employ a soft probabilistic clustering algorithm, namely the EM algorithm, as a way of modelling the fact that these categorial distinctions are not necessarily absolute. The first component of the EM algorithm (the *Expectation Step*) is the same as the process by which k-means assigns a data point to a cluster, however in the second step of EM (the *Maximisation Step*), the cluster centroids are recomputed such that the likelihood of the parameters of the distributions are maximised. The expectation and maximisation steps are repeated iteratively until the parameters do not change or reach a specified threshold (Tan *et al.*, 2006).

We used the EM implementation in the Weka package,[4] (Witten and Frank, 2005) maintaining the default parameters for the maximum number of iterations ($I = 100$), the minimum allowable standard deviation in log-likelihood ($1e - 6$), and the number of random seeds initially selected ($S = 100$). We ran the EM cluster either with no pre-defined cluster number ($N = -1$, where the number of clusters is dynamically optimised by maximising the log-likelihood) or exactly 2 clusters ($N = 2$).

5.3 Experimental Set-up

We perform 2 groups of experiments, which we term "All Clustering" and "Subsampling". For "All Clustering", we use all available data in a given dataset, across each of the full datasets described in Table 2. The stem lexicon is biased towards nouns, with 75.8% of the stems being nouns in the All POS case, and 90.8% being nouns in the Nouns & Verbs case, as shown in Table 2.

For the "Subsampling" experiments, we aimed for a noun–verb split which is more representative of the split seen in actual text, based on hand-analysing an Indonesian document external to our document collection.[5] For each unique word token in the article (except English words, words in the footer, the menu, and tab items not relevant to the document), we looked up that word form in the Indonesian government's official dictionary *Kamus Besar Bahasa Indonesia* "The Big Indonesian Language Dictionary" (Sugiono, 2008). If the dictionary lists it and gives a POS or multiple POSs, we count oncee for each POS listing. We found that the proportion of nouns to verbs was 65:35 (with 30 noun and 16 verb types). Equipped with this knowledge, we created a sub-sampled dataset with these proportions of nouns and verbs, in two datasets: (1) a 650–350 mix of nouns to verbs, and (2) a 1300–700 mix of nouns and verbs.

As briefly discussed in Section 4.2, we evaluate the discovered clusters against the classes in the original stem lexicon. We do this in accordance with the evaluation methodology adopted in word class induction (Clark, 2003; Biemann, 2006), by first mapping each lexeme to the cluster with the highest probability for that instance. In the 2-class ($N = 2$) clustering case, we assign one cluster noun and one cluster verb, according to the assignment which maximises the F-score relative to the labels in the original stem lexicon; in the $N = -1$ case where the number of clusters is automatically determined, we determine the assignment of labels to classes which maximises F-score (accepting that the same class can be used to label multiple classes) subject to the constraint that each class is used to label at least one cluster.

In all cases, we use computationally-intensive *randomised shuffling* to test statistical significance (Yeh, 2000).

6 Results

6.1 All Clustering

As can be seen in Table 3, the experiments over all parts of speech, fared rather poorly, with F-scores (F) falling below the (supervised) majority class baseline, as can be seen in Table 3. Bear in mind, however, that our primary question is whether nouns and verbs can be distinguished in Indonesian, where these results are over the much harder task of differentiating nouns, verbs and a heterogeneous assortment of closed- and open-class words. We thus move directly on to consider the results for the binary "Noun & Verb" case, and observe that our precision (P), recall (R), and F-score (F) are all above the majority class baseline, for both the multinomial and binomial feature representations.

[4] `http://www.cs.waikato.ac.nz/ml/weka`

[5] The Indonesian *Linguistik komputasional* "Computational Linguistics" stub article, as accessed in May, 2011 at the URL: `http://id.wikipedia.org/wiki/Linguistik_komputasional`; this article was not contained in the 2009 dump of Indonesian Wikipedia.

Data Type	ALL POS			NOUNS & VERBS					
	$N = -1$			$N = 2$			$N = -1$		
	P	R	F	P	R	F	P	R	F
Multinomial	.985	.588	.737	.930	.931	.930	.990	.990	.990
Binary	.977	.579	.727	.914	.915	.915	.973	.973	.973
Random	.623	.341	.441	.512	.512	.512	.512	.512	.512
Majority Class	.756	.756	.756	.908	.908	.908	.908	.908	.908
Multinominal (NoRR)	.989	.591	.740	.942	.942	.942	.942	.942	.942
Binominal (NoRR)	.940	.556	.699	.918	.918	.918	.971	.971	.971
Random	.616	.338	.436	.501	.502	.502	.501	.502	.502
Majority Class	.757	.757	.757	.908	.908	.908	.908	.908	.908

Table 3: Results for the "All Clustering" experiments.

Data	$N = 2$				$N = -1$					
	650–350	p	**1300–700**	p	**650–350**	N-V	p	**1300–700**	N-V	p
Multinomial	.783	.184	**.788**	**.043**	**.808**	3-1	**.000**	**.788**	1-1	**.044**
−NoRR	.778	.452	**.803**	**.000**	.780	2-1	.490	**.793**	3-1	**.003**
Binomial	**.812**	**.000**	**.825**	**.000**	**.822**	3-3	**.000**	**.848**	5-4	**.000**
−NoRR	**.812**	**.001**	**.828**	**.000**	**.824**	3-4	**.000**	**.849**	3-5	**.000**
Random	.538		.529		.538			.529		
Majority Class	.650		.650		.650			.650		

Table 4: F-score for "Subsampling" experiments

The results we found most surprising were the data that had no morphological reduplication (NoRR). These were consistently outperformed by the systems that had reduplicated stems. This is unexpected because reduplication has different interpretations across word classes in Indonesian, and as mentioned previously is the only morphologically inflectional process (Musgrave, 2001).

At this stage, none of the differences in results over the Majority Class baseline are statistically significant ($p > 0.05$), although all of the differences over the random baseline are significant ($p < 0.001$).

6.2 Subsampling

We next move on to experiments with the subsampling data, which is a better reflection of the relative occurrence of nouns and verbs in actual text. We run two types of experiments: one with a 650–350 mix of nouns to verbs, and another with a 1300–700 mix of nouns to verbs, as described in Section 5.3. This ratio is based on manual analysis of the rate of occurrence of nouns and verbs in a held-out document.

Firstly, all F-scores surpassed the 0.650 majority class baseline, as shown in Table 4. Secondly, almost all of these results were significant based on our random sampling method. As with the previous "All Cluster" experiments, all F-scores exceeded the random baseline.

The column "n-v" indicates how many clusters were found, and how they were merged for evaluation. For example 3-1 indicates that 4 (3+1) clusters were induced, with three of them combining to form the "N" class and the other forming the "V" class.

The boldfaced figures in Table 4 highlight the results that exceed the majority-class baseline at a level of statistical significance ($p < 0.05$). As can be seen, in most cases there was a significant improvement over the baseline for both the smaller and larger datasets. This provides strong weight to the claim that the noun–verb distinction is discernible for Indonesian, refuting the claims

Features with Greatest Probability Density as a Proportion per Class			
Noun		Verb	
STEM+NYA	SE+STEM	STEM+PEN_AN	TER+STEM
REDUP[STEM]	STEM+I+NYA	Passive+STEM+KAN	Active+STEM+KAN+NYA
STEM		Active+STEM+KAN	Passive+STEM+I
BER+STEM		STEM+AN+NYA	STEM+KAN
REDUP[STEM]+NYA		STEM+AN	Active+STEM+I

Figure 4: Morphological patterns associated with nouns and verbs.

of Gil (2001, 2010). With the exception of Multinomial $N-1$, the results for the larger dataset were slightly better than the smaller dataset, and the binomial feature representation was superior to the multinomial feature representation. Again, the experiments containing no reduplicated stems (NoRR) either did not fare better than those without, or were only slightly better.

7 Discussion

One experimental question we had was whether using only morphological features would suffice in determining word classes, and whether syntactic features were a requirement for this kind of experiment. We were also curious to see (given that our experiments were successful) if there were morphological signatures or a group of morphological patterns that defined a class. For each of our features in the 1300–700 binomial experiment, we collected the accumulated probabilities for each class and compared them to each other. We found that there were about 10 morphological patterns that we could associate with verbs, and 7 with nouns. These are shown in Figure 4.

From a linguistic perspective, one result that we feared was that the multinomial experiments, which took into account the number of times a pattern occurred with a stem, would fare better than the binomial experiments. The implications of this would suggest that the means by which linguists determine word classes, by adding to their inventory of possible combinatorics, would not suffice. However, we see that the binomial features have the same score or do better than the multinomial features, and therefore seeing a token only once, or simply having the knowledge that particular forms are possible, is enough to assist in analysing and determining classes of stems.

These morphological signature experiments look promising in determining the class of unknown words or out of vocabulary items, as a means of extending the lexicons. For future experiments we would like to mix syntactic features with the morphological features used in this study. We would also like to extend the study to see how different the morphological signatures are from one source of text to another.

8 Conclusion

We had designed an experiment that applied the linguistic criteria based on Evans and Osada (2005) in determining word classes for Indonesian, focusing specifically on the question of whether the noun–verb distinction is discernible to an unsupervised word class induction system. The results have shown that there are certainly distinguishable properties between nouns and verbs in Indonesian, even when we restrict ourselves to only examining features at the morphological level. The experiments used solely morphological features based on Goldsmith's (2001) signatures, showing promise that the labelling of word classes may be achieved only with morphological features, with potential application to out-of-vocabulary items.

From a natural language processing perspective, the labels 'nouns' and 'verbs' may be used felicitiously, and not merely as 'convenient labels' in Indonesian text processing. On a broader, more general note, this study has shown how issues in linguistics can be tackled using methods developed and used in the field of computational linguistics.

References

Biemann, Chris. 2006. Chinese Whisper - An efficient graph clustering algorithm and its application to natural language processing problems. In *Proceedings of the HLT-NAACL-06 Workshop on Textgraphs-06*, New York, USA.

Biemann, Chris. 2009. Unsupervised part-of-speech tagging in the large. *Research on Language and Computation* 7.101–135.

Christodoulopoulos, Christos, Sharon Goldwater, and Mark Steedman. 2010. Two decades of unsupervised pos induction: How far have we come? In *Proceedings of the 2010 Conference on Empirical Methods in Natural Language Processing*, 575–584, Massachusetts, USA.

Clark, Alexander. 2003. Combining distributional and morphological information for part of speech induction. In *Proceedings of the 10th Annual Meeting of the European Association for Computational Linguistics (EACL)*, 59–66, Budapest, Hungary.

Croft, William. 2000. Parts of speech as language universals and as language-particular categories. In *Approaches to the typology of word classes*, ed. by P. Vogel and Bernard Comrie, 65–102, Berlin, Germany. Mouton de Gruyter.

Croft, William. 2003. *Typology and Universals*. Cambridge University Press.

Beesley, Kenneth and Lauri Karttunen. 2003. *Finite State Morphology*. CSLI Publications.

Evans, Nicholas. 2000. Word classes in the world's languages. In *Morphology: a handbook on inflection and word formation*, ed. by Christian Lehmann and Geert Booij and Joachim Mugdan, 708–732, Berlin, Germany. Mouton de Gruyter.

Evans, Nicholas and Toshiki Osada. 2005. Mundari: The myth of a language without word classes. *Linguistic Typology* 9.351–390.

Gil, David. 2001. Escaping eurocentrism: fieldwork as a process of unlearning. In *Linguistic Fieldwork*, ed. by Paul Newman and Martha Ratliff, chapter 5. Cambridge, UK: Cambridge University Press.

Gil, David. 2010. The acquisition of syntactic categories in Jakarta Indonesian. In *Part of Speech: Empirical and theoretical advances*. John Benjamins Publishing Company.

Goldsmith, John. 2001. Unsupervised learning of the morphology of a natural language. *Association for Computational Linguistics* 27.153–198.

Keller, Frank, 2001. *Gradience in Grammar: Experimental and Computational Aspects of Degrees of Grammaticality*. The University of Edinburgh dissertation.

Mistica, Meladel, I Wayan Arka, Timothy Baldwin, and Avery Andrews 2009. Double Double, Morphology and Trouble: Looking into Reduplication in Indonesian. In *Proceedings of the 2009 Australasian Language Technology Workshop (ALTW 2009)*, 44–52.

Musgrave, Simon, 2001. *Non-subject Arguments in Indonesian*. Melbourne, Australia: The University of Melbourne dissertation.

Sugiono, Dendy (ed.) 2008. *Kamus Besar Bahasa Indonesia - Pusat Bahasa*. Departemen Pendidkan Nasional, Jakarta, Indonesia: PT Gramedia Pustaka Utama, edisi keempat edition.

Tan, Pang-Ning, Michael Steinbach, and Vipin Kumar. 2006. *Introduction to Data Mining*. Boston, USA: Addison Wesley.

Witten, Ian H. and Eibe Frank. 2005. *Data Mining: Practical Machine Learning Tools and Techniques*. Data Management Systems. Morgan Kaufmann Publishers Inc.

Yeh, Alexander. 2000. More accurate tests for the statistical significance of result differences. In *Proceedings of the 18th of Conference on Computational Linguistics COLING*, 947–953.

Automated Proof Reading of Clinical Notes

Jon Patrick and Dung Nguyen

School of Information Technology, University of Sydney,
1 Cleveland St, Sydney 2006, NSW, Australia
{jonpat, nguyend}@it.usyd.edu.au

Abstract. Misspellings, abbreviations and acronyms are very popular in clinical notes and can be an obstacle to high quality information extraction and classification. In addition, another important part of narrative reports is clinical scores and measurements as doctors infer a patient's status by analyzing them. We introduce a knowledge discovery process to resolve unknown tokens and convert scores and measures into a standard layout so as to improve the quality of semantic processing of the corpus. System performance is evaluated before and after an automatic proof reading process by comparing the computed SNOMED-CT codes to the coding created originally by the clinical staff. The automatic coding of the texts increased the coded content by 15% after the automatic correction process and the number of unique codes increased by 4.7%. Accuracy of the automatic coding and annotations in the notes which have not been coded by the clinical staff is suggested by the system output.

Keywords: clinical, proof reading, spelling, normalization, standardization.

1 Introduction

Clinical notes contain valuable information about patients' status, however, retrieving information from them is challenging because they may comprise up to 30% non-word tokens, idiosyncratic spellings, abbreviations and acronyms, and poor grammatical structure. Besides resolving misspellings, knowing the correct expansions of abbreviations and acronyms is critical to the understanding of the document for both automatic natural language understanding and human comprehension and interpretation (Pakhomov et al., 2005).

Proof reading is a process whereby a clinical text is validated to identify unknown tokens/words and their valid forms. Proof correcting is modifying the proofed text to make it notionally "correct" text and thereby more readily processible by automatic means. There are two principal tasks to be achieved, these are `normalization` and `standardization`. The normalization process changes the texts in a way so that a human reader would consider it as normal, such as correcting spelling, expanding abbreviations and acronyms. The standardization process converts the text into certain formats that an expert community has defined as standard; a good example is converting scores and measures into a standard layout.

At first glance it would seem that standardization should be done initially before normalization, however it is more likely that both will need to be performed multiple times in a repeated cycle of processing as there is interaction between the two processes. Standardization converts various instances of the same scores and measures into standard forms so that the system does not need to be concerned about their details for later processing steps such as normalization. For example: "HR 70" and "HR 78" are standardized to the representation of heart rate. However, most measurements and scores contain acronyms or abbreviations which may need to be expanded during the normalization process. Normalization could improve the standardization process by correcting misspelling and other token error within standard forms. If normalization is executed first, a large amount of tokens within standard layouts will need to be processed while they could be excluded if they were ringfenced by a standardization process.

Once both these tasks are completed the result is a corpus that is annotated by all of these processes. The final act is `proof correcting` or `transformation` which is to change the raw corpus into a proofed corpus, that is, the text can be read as a fully corrected corpus. The important process is to use the annotation properties of each token to change its representation in the source file to the correct form. This produces two versions of the source file, the uncorrected form and the corrected form. The former form has a set of annotations with properties defining the changes that needed to be made in the proof correcting process, and the latter form has all the text corrected and a set of annotations that define the original form of the token(s) and structure(s).

2 Related Work

The normalization process contains misspelling corrections, abbreviation and acronym expansions. Spelling error detection and correction can be classified into two categories (Ruch et al., 2003). The first category is word-based or context-free spelling correction which resolves errors for words that cannot be found in the lexicon (such as 'medicla' is a misspelling of medical). The second category is context-based or context sensitive spelling correction which concerns a valid word but misspelt within the context (for example, in 'a peace of paper' where 'piece' is misspelt).

The classical word-based spelling correction algorithm is minimum edit distance which ranks suggestion candidates by the minimal number of insertions, deletions, substitutions and transpositions needed to transform one string into the other (Levenshtein 1966). The Metaphone algorithm uses consonant symbols which represent their usual English pronunciations, the vowels 'AEIOU' are also used, but only at the beginning of the word (Philips 1990). In more recent research, Kukick (1992) maps every string into a key such that similarly spelt strings will have identical keys; this method is called similarity key. Some spelling suggestion tools such as Aspell and Gspell which combine multiple algorithms are now available for use and research. Aspell is a combination of the Metaphone algorithm and near-miss strategy by its predecessor Ispell (Atkinson 2006; Kuenning 2006). The mix of algorithms in Gspell includes the NGrams, metaphone, common misspellings, and homophone retrieval tools. Candidates are evaluated by the Levenshtein edit distance, and similar ranked candidates are re-ordered by use of word based corpus frequencies (Divita, 2003).

Much research on normalization has been developed in the medical domain due to a high frequency of misspellings, abbreviations and acronyms. A frequency-based technique combining a comprehensive and a medical dictionary configuration was developed to improve suggestion ranking of Aspell and Gspell (Crowell et al., 2004). Without a comprehensive dictionary, Turchin et al. (2007) identified misspelt words using prevalence analysis. Senger et al. (2010) used Aspell and user behavior to analyze drug misspelling characteristics in a drug query system.

Spelling correction is more effective when the method takes into account the context in which the word occurs. To improve spelling correction in the electronic patient record, Ruch et al. (2003) uses lexical disambiguation and named-entity recognition, and shows how a set of natural language processing (NLP) tools can be combined to improve the processing of clinical records. Emphasis on first suggestion accuracy in Patrick et al. (2010) introduced a high accuracy spelling corrector for clinical notes which uses a combination of rule-based suggestion generation and a context-sensitive ranking algorithm.

A comparative study of supervised acronym disambiguation in a corpus of clinical notes, using three machine learning algorithms: the naïve Bayes classifier, decision trees and Support Vector Machines (SMVs) has been conducted by Joshi et al. (2006). Instead of using three machine learners, Joshi el al. (2006) also developed three kernels for SVMs – one that makes use of knowledge derived from unlabeled text, the second using semantic knowledge from ontologies, and finally a third, additive kernel consisting of the first two kernels – and studied their effect on the tasks of word sense disambiguation and automatic expansion of ambiguous acronyms. A method for collecting training data for supervised machine learning approaches to disambiguating acronyms has been introduced by Pakhomov S. (2002). The approach is based on the assumption that the expansion of an acronym and the acronym itself usually occur in similar contexts. The closest work to clinical document normalization is Wong et al. (2006), who integrated scores for spelling error correction, abbreviation expansion and case restoration.

Measurements and scores are text patterns that need to be identified in the clinical notes. Finite State Automata (FSA) is a pattern matching approach that is used in our standardization process. FSA have many applications in NLP such as pattern matching, named-entity recognition and partial parsing. A language-independent method of finite-state surface syntactic parsing and word-disambiguation is introduced and discussed in (Koskenniemi, 1990). In this work, finite-state machines represented syntactic constraint rules where each constraint excludes certain types of ungrammatical readings. From the view of computational efficiency, the use of finite-state automata is motivated by taking into account optimal time and space (Mohri, 1997). Abney (1996) used cascaded FSAs to parse free text while Aït-Mokhtar and Chanod (1997) utilized incremental finite-state machines to build a shallow parser. Both of these researchers highlighted the efficiency of the FSA in that they can be extended at modest cost, maintain broad coverage and linguistic granularity and do not necessarily involve trading off accuracy against speed. This characteristic of an FSA is very useful in recognition of scores & measurements in the clinical domain where there is a large number of different patterns and new incoming examples which require rapid re-training of FSA. Furthermore, Finite-state transducers are used for deterministic part-of-speech tagging and semi-structured data extraction from the web (Roche and Schabes, 1995; Hsu and Dung, 1999). For probabilistic FSA, CSSR is an algorithm that generates weighted FSA from training data used to identify named-entities in text (Padro and Padro, 2007). In the CSSR algorithm, the model changes its structure to satisfy new training data.

To our knowledge, our system is the first automated proof reading system for clinical data which combines normalization and standardization into the cycle of processing with evaluation of the result using a SNOMED-CT[1] concept identifier versus clinical staff's assigned codes.

3 Method

The important system requirement is to create a process for the automated proof reading of a clinical corpus so that it can be used to improve the information retrieval accuracy of clinical knowledge in the text.

The combination of normalization and standardization guarantees that standard expressions (scores and measures) are captured and each token contains its lexical verification information (abbreviation, acronym expansion and misspelling correction) whether the token is standing outside or within multi-token expression.

The result of normalization and standardization process will be stored as annotations in the notes. This approach enables different subsets of annotation type to be used in specific processing tasks or experiments (detailed in section 4).

3.1 Corpus Description

The corpus used in our experiment is the Concord hospital's clinical progress summary which contains 43712 anonymised records from 2003 to 2008. Each record contains information about Principle diagnosis, Additional diagnosis, SNOMED-CT Description Identifier (DID),

---

[1] Systematized Nomenclature of Medicine - Clinical Terms (SNOMED-CT). Available at http://www.ihtsdo.org/snomed-ct

Description and Progress working text. 22974 of the 43712 notes contain SNOMED-CT DID and description (one for each note) which are assigned manually by clinical staff.

3.2 Tokenization

Three kinds of tokenizing strategies for different levels of tokenization are utilized: the standard morphology tokenizer splits text into single tokens for lexical verification, while the ring-fencing tokenizer recognizes multi token expressions as standard types of scores or measurements, and the combined tokenizer. For example, the standard tokenizer can split "HR 72" into the word "HR" and number "72" so that HR can be further verified and classified into the acronym with expansion "Heart Rate". Then the ring-fencing tokenizer recognizes the phrase "HR 72" as a standard measurement of type heart rate. The combined annotation will have two overlapping levels: "HR" is an acronym, "72" is a number and "HR 72" annotated as a measurement of type HR (heart rate).

The standard tokenizer uses morphology defined by regular expressions (REs) for basic classification of word and non-word tokens. This tokenizer classifies non-word tokens into sub-classes: date (e.g. 3/7/02), time (e.g. 11.30am), range (e.g. 0.01->0.49), complex digit (e.g 0.52/0.44), digit (e.g 652), separator (e.g. ##, **), operator (e.g. +, -), punctuation (e.g. !, ?). Word tokens are divided into single word (e.g. patient) and compound words such as two_word_slash (e.g. d/c), two_word_hyphen (e.g beta-blockers), two_word_apostrophe (e.g. didn't) and more_than_two_words (e.g. behind-the-wheel). The lexical processing of each word component in compound words is similar to single word.

The ring-fencing tokenizer is a Finite State Recognizer (FSR) which uses training example patterns to recognize token patterns constituting a score or measurement that requires standardization (Patrick and Sabbagh, 2011). There are a large number of different scores and measurements in clinical notes. When using REs to describe patterns as more rules are developed to capture missed items, the rules became so complicated that it makes them difficult to update as any change has the risk of losing previously recognized patterns or introducing new false positives. Another problem is that the rule updating task requires an exhaustive knowledge about REs and a considerable amount of time modifying the rules. Consequently, the automated learning process to capture patterns using REs is particularly difficult. On the other hand, a trainable FSR can be built directly from training examples of data with high accuracy and efficient computational time. Some other types of measurements and scores in the training patterns are illustrated in table 1. The FSR training file has a simple format and contains two columns, first is the type and second is the span of the text which expresses the pattern. Training examples are then generalized so that the FSR can capture all the similar forms of these patterns.

Table 1: A subset of training Types.

Type	Pattern	Type	Pattern
BP	BP 140/65(84)	ABG	ABG's: 0355 7.41/41/103/26/2
SaO2	O2 sats 91%	Measurement	7mg/hr
Temp	37.6	O2-measurement	2L O2
Lipids	Lipids 10% at 20mls/hr	DRNAME	Dr. <:[A-Z][a-zA-Z]*<: [A-Z][a-zA-Z]*:>

The combined tokenizer uses the standard and ring-fencing tokenizer. It uses both morphology defined by REs and FSRs to tokenize text where measurements and scores can be recognized as multi-word expressions with no separated tokens, other tokens are split and classified by REs method.

3.3 Proof Reading and Proof Correcting

After standard tokenization, each token is passed through the lexical verification process and then inserted into the Lexicon Management System (LMS) which supports automated and manual resolution of unknown tokens. The LMS is a system developed to store the accumulated lexical knowledge and contains categorizations of spelling errors, abbreviations, acronyms and a variety of non-word tokens. It also has a web interface that supports rapid manual correction of unknown words with a high accuracy clinical spelling suggestor plus the addition of grammatical information and the categorization of such words into gazetteers (Patrick et al., 2010). The method of the clinical spelling suggestor is based on combining heuristic-based suggestion generation and ranking algorithms based on word frequencies and trigram probabilities. This approach achieved high accuracies on test data sets with over 93.5% for the Concord corpus. By using the LMS to resolve unknown words, the Concord lexicon database contains approximately 15000 tokens that have been manually corrected. Figure 1 illustrates the lexical verification process supported by our resources which includes 7 checking steps (1) Misspellings (2) Abbreviations (3) Acronym (4) Gazetteers (5) Moby lexical verifier for English[2] (6) UMLS dictionary of medical terms[3] (7) SNOMED-CT dictionary.

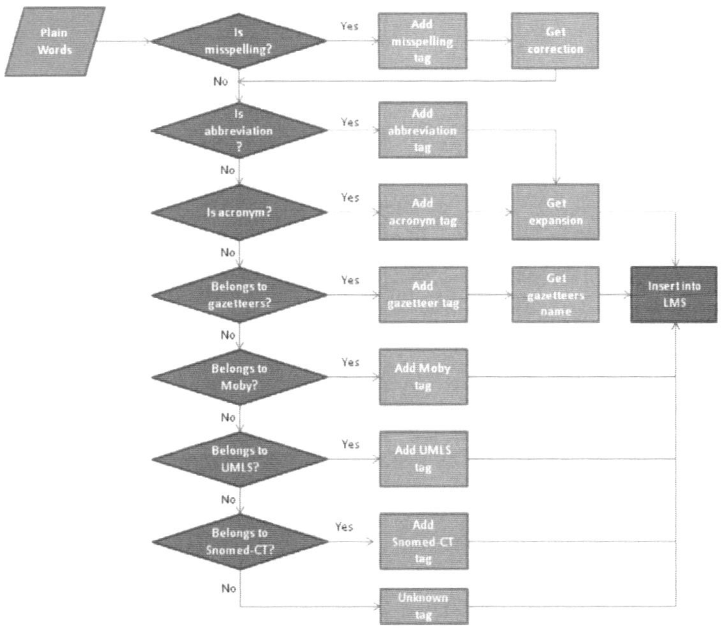

Figure 1: Lexical verification process.

The lexical verification process contains an additional step to resolve misplaced whitespace and punctuation. The LMS manages a developed process for manual spell correcting but it only considers single tokens hence errors of misplaced white space are not processed in it. The misplaced whitespace problem is dealt with in an external computational process. For example: "looka fter" should be "look after", and the LMS will give suggestions for each word. However, these words should be resolved together. The rate of this kind of error is not high in a single

[2] The Institute for Language, Speech and Hearing. Available at http://icon.shef.ac.uk/Moby

[3] Unified Medical Language System (UMLS). U.S National Library of Medicine, National Institutes of Health. Available at http://www.nlm.nih.gov/research/umls

document but for a large corpus, they are costly to manually resolve. Examples of incorrect punctuation problems are "natio;n" where it should be "nation" and "nation.The" has missing whitespace. Currently the LMS tokenizes each string on the left and right of the punctuation and so a correction has to be made in another process.

At the end of the proof reading step, annotation files which contain lexical information from a corpus are generated. This means every token is annotated so any correction or expansion can be made when needed. The misspelt words will have correction information while abbreviations and acronyms come with expansion within their annotations. If a token is correct, it should contain information about the resource where the token was validated and mapped to the name of gazetteer or dictionary. Table 2 shows tag type statistics used in the proof reading process.

Table 2: Frequencies of tag types used in the proof reading process.

Tag type	Frequency
Abbreviation	47,564
Acronym	149,372
Misspelling	93,477
Non-word	1,385,184
Unknown	3,162
Valid Words	4,608,664
Total	6,287,423

The proof correcting process generates the proof-corrected annotation files. They contain annotations that enable the user to see which tokens have been changed from the original corpus. In order to evaluate the effect of specific normalization types, proof correcting can generate corrected text files from annotation files with a selected set of annotation tags (misspellings, abbreviation, and acronym).

3.4 SNOMED-CT Code Annotating and Comparison

To evaluate the effect of the proof reading and correcting process, an algorithm for converting Text to SNOMED-CT (TTSCT) is used to annotate the corpus before and after the proof reading process to see the improvement and identify the distribution of SNOMED-CT concepts over the corpus (Patrick et al., 2007). TTSCT was developed so that SNOMED-CT concepts can be identified in free text narratives and to annotate them with the clinical reference terms. The accuracy of TTSCT is approximately 70% on a test corpus. Its improvement is ongoing research conducted by the authors. This evaluation is based on the assumption that if TTSCT can identify many more clinical terms in the proofed corpus than the original one, the proof reading process is considered effective because terms in the misspelt words, acronyms and abbreviations are now revealed. The measurements and scores patterns usually contain abbreviations and/or acronyms; so, we would expect there are more patterns after executing proof correcting using the misspelt tag only.

Another purpose for computing SNOMED-CT codes for the corpus is to compare with assigned DIDs from clinical staff and generate suggestions codes for unassigned DID notes. In the SNOMED-CT resource, each Concept Identifier (CID) may contain several DIDs. This step checks whether the manually assigned DID belongs to a computed SNOMED-CT concept in each note and generates CID candidates for unassigned notes (20738 unassigned notes / 43712 notes). When computing candidates for unassigned notes, we are especially interested in the two most popular assigned and computed classes: Clinical finding and Body structure.

4 Experiment Result and Discussion

Generally, when using all corrections and expansions, we found more SNOMED-CT codes instances (over 150,000 or 14.3%) and distinct concepts (842 new concepts or 4.7%) in every SNOMED-CT category except Record artifact (Table 3). When only applying the misspelling tag in the proof correcting process, there are only around 22,000 new SNOMED-CT instances and 268 new concepts. Consequently, most new SNOMED-CT codes come from expansion of abbreviations and acronyms (85.4%) as the SNOMED-CT recognizer could not map these concepts. We can conclude that when applying an automated proof reading process, the clinical note is more informative as more medical concepts and instances are revealed.

Table 3: Frequency of SNOMED-CT upper-level categories before and after proof reading. The figures in brackets show the number of distinct concepts in each category.

Category	Before	After	Difference
Clinical finding	441,498 (8,673)	497,486 (9,052)	55,988 (379)
Body structure	184,679 (2,462)	199,748 (2,542)	15,069 (80)
Procedure	93,267 (2,181)	108,165 (2,345)	14,898 (164)
Substance	75,630 (1,050)	79,509 (1,096)	3,879 (46)
Observable entity	74,229 (792)	86,926 (836)	12,697 (44)
Social context	70,243 (439)	104,141 (455)	33,898 (16)
Physical object	32,623 (556)	38,003 (567)	5,380 (11)
Situation with explicit context	26,275 (402)	32,531 (452)	6,256 (50)
Environment or geographical location	22,516 (287)	22,936 (305)	420 (18)
Pharmaceutical / biologic product	15,472 (467)	16,331 (486)	859 (19)
Event	10,576 (158)	12,407 (162)	1,831 (3)
Staging and scales	7,377 (19)	7,407 (21)	30 (2)
Physical force	7,026 (39)	8,364 (42)	1,338 (3)
Organism	5,450 (289)	5,475 (292)	25 (3)
Specimen	676 (35)	770 (39)	94 (4)
Record artifact	221 (13)	221 (13)	0 (0)
Total	1,067,758 (17,862)	1,220,420 (18,705)	152,662 (842)

On the other hand, most ring-fencing patterns contain abbreviations or acronyms. When using ring-fencing after misspelling corrections and abbreviation expansion, we lost more than 3000 patterns in the corpus (for example BP is an acronym which is widely used in most blood pressure ring-fencing examples, if we expand BP we may lose some of these patterns). When applying misspelling corrections only, we found slightly more patterns. Table 4 indicates the detailed number of high frequency types in scores & measurements before and after processing, other types with low frequency (<50) are PaO2, ST, Ward, F, Alb, PaCO2, PS, SiO2, RENAL, FiO2, BSL, Creat, TV.

Another experiment with the Concord database was to check the coincidence of manually assigned SNOMED-CT codes for each note from the principle diagnosis, additional diagnosis and progress text with values returned by TTSCT; we found 10465 over 22974 (45.48%) matches before proof reading with 1200 distinct concepts. After proof reading, the proportion of matched DIDs increased to 48.41% (10981 matches/ 22974 notes with DID) with the addition of 25 new concepts. From the experiments, it was found that the two most popular DID classes are Clinical finding (82.1%) and Body structure (6.2%). Furthermore, a maximum of 8 different DIDs were referenced to a single CID. In addition, some assigned DIDs can only be found in the progress working text (1785 before and 1834 after proof reading process), this means in this case the clinicians may need to pay more attention to the content of the patient's note to decide the representative DID for that note rather than solely based on diagnosis sections. In approximately 12,000 notes that the system could not find any match between the assigned codes and the computed codes, some examples were analyzed and the common explanation for the mismatch is that the assigned DID is a general term (parent class) of the computed codes which are found in the notes. Combining multiple codes of the same class to infer the possibility of parent class could be a future enhancement for the system. Table 5 shows the distribution of matched DID within the notes.

Table 4: High frequency scores & measurements before and after proof reading using misspelling tags only.

Tag	Before	After	Difference
Measurement	13,638	13,650	12
BP	4,004	4,006	2
GCS	3,227	3,231	4
O2-Measurement	3,220	3,220	0
RR	2,988	2,988	0
HR	2,584	2,585	1
SaO2	2,270	2,276	6
Temp	1,836	1,846	10
Hb	846	847	1
PEARTL	838	846	8
PR	810	810	0
K	289	289	0
pH	142	142	0
Total	36,692	36,736	44

Finally, most of the unassigned notes contain information about at least one of two of the most popular classes which have been found in both assigned and computational SNOMED-CT codes. Within 20738 unassigned notes, 98.9% contain a clinical finding and 90.1% contains Body structure (86.2% contain both classes). This result means that many notes with unassigned SNOMED-CT DIDs might have the relevant codes computed from the annotated corpus. A list of CID candidates for each note is generated by the system and will be validated by clinical staff as well as the correctness of assigned DIDs against computed DIDs.

Table 5: Locations of matched DIDs in notes.

Section	Before	After
Principle Diagnosis	8594 (82.12%)	9058 (82.49%)
Additional Diagnosis	219 (2.09%)	251 (2.29%)
Working Progress	5315 (50.79%)	5670 (51.63%)

5 Conclusion

In this study, a general approach for proof reading of clinical notes is developed and evaluated. This work also introduces and illustrates the necessity of combining standardization and normalization into the cycle of the proof reading process in the clinical domain. The combination of REs and trainable FSR guarantees general classification of tokens and clinical pattern recognition. Automated lexical verification and high accuracy clinical spelling suggestion are supported in the LMS interface which then enable high accuracy and efficiency at manual resolution of unknown tokens. As a result, the proofed corpus becomes much more informative for automatic information extraction as well as human comprehension and interpretation. Finally, the method is easily adapted to other domains or others languages by re-defining the training patterns for FSR and central resources used in the proof reading process (dictionaries, gazetteers ...).

The limitation in our work is that most abbreviations and acronyms are mapped directly from the accumulated dictionaries or manually expanded by using the LMS. The future development for our system is to apply an automated context-sensitive and probabilistic abbreviation, acronym expansion suggestion to support the lexical verification process and the LMS. A more general method for extracting and comparing computed SNOMED-CT codes with assigned codes to enable hierarchical inference is currently has our attention for future research. Furthermore, the clinical staffs will be involved in the evaluation process to have a better estimation of system performance.

References

Abney, S. 1996. Partial parsing via finite-state cascades. *Journal of Natural Language Engineering,* 2(4), 337-344.

Aït-Mokhtar S. and J.P. Chanod. 1997. Incremental finite-state parsing. *In Proceedings of the fifth conference on Applied natural language processing (ANLC). Association for Computational Linguistics*, pp. 72-79.

Atkinson, K. 2006. Gnu aspell 0.60.4, http://aspell.sourceforge.net/.

Crowell, J., Q. Zeng, L. Ngo and E.M. Lacroix. 2004. A Frequency-based technique to improve the spelling suggestion rank in medical queries. *Journal of the American Medical Informatics Association*, 11:179-185.

Divita, G. 2003. SPECIALIST Spelling Suggestion Tools (Gspell), produced by National Library of Medicine. Available at http://lexsrv3.nlm.nih.gov/LexSysGroup/Projects/gSpell/current/GSpell.html

Hsu C.N. and M.T. Dung. 1999. Generating finite-state transducers for semi-structured data extraction from the Web. *Journal of Information Systems,* 23(8), 521-538.

Koskenniemi, K. 1990. Finite-state parsing and disambiguation. *Proceedings of the 13th conference on Computational linguistics,* 2, 229-232.

Kuenning, G. 2006. International ispell 3.3.02. Available at http://lasr.cs.ucla.edu/geoff/ispell.html.

Kukich, K. 1992. Technique for automatically correcting words in text. *Association for Computing Machinery (ACM) Computing Surveys*, 24(4), 377-439.

Levenshtein, V. 1966. Binary codes capable of correcting deletions, insertions, and reversals. *Soviet Physics Doklady*, 10(8), 707–710.

Mohri, M. 1997. Finite-state transducers in language and speech processing. *Journal of Computational Linguistics,* 23(2), 269-311.

Padro, M. and L. Padro. 2007. ME-CSSR: an extension of CSSR using maximum entropy. *Proceeding of the Conference on Finite-State Methods for Natural Language Processing (FSMNLP)*, pp. 161-165.

Pakhomov S., T. Pedersen and C.G. Chute. 2005. Abbreviation and Acronym Disambiguation in Clinical Discourse. *Proceedings of the Annual Symposium on Biomedical and Health Infomatics (AIMA)*, 2005:589-593.

Pakhomov S. 2002. Semi-Supervised Maximum Entropy Based Approach to Acronym and Abbreviation Normalization in Medical Texts. *Proceedings of the 40th Annual Meeting on Association for Computational Linguistics (ACL)*, pp. 160-167.

Patrick J. and M. Sabbagh. 2011. An Active Learning Process for Extraction and Standardization of Medical Measurements by a Trainable FSA. *In Tokyo-Japan: Springer Berlin / Heidelberg*, pp. 151-162.

Patrick J., M. Sabbagh, S. Jain and H. Zheng. 2010. Spelling correction in Clinical Notes with Emphasis on First Suggestion Accuracy. *2nd Workshop on Building and Evaluating Resources for Biomedical Text Mining*, pp. 2-8.

Patrick J., Y. Wang and P. Budd. 2007. An automated system for conversion of clinical notes into SNOMED clinical terminology. *Proceedings of the 5th Australasian Symposium on Australasian Computer Science Week (ACSW) frontiers*, 68:219-226.

Philips, L. 1990. Hanging on the metaphone. *Computer Language Magazine*, 7(12), 38–44.

Roche E. and Y. Schabes. 1995. Deterministic part-of-speech tagging with finite-state transducers. *Journal of Computational Linguistics*, 21(2), 227-253.

Ruch, P., R. Bauda and A. Geissbuhlera. 2003. Using lexical disambiguation and named-entity recognition to improve spelling correction in the electronic patient record. *Artificial Intelligence in Medicine*, 29(2003), 169–184.

Senger C., J. Kaltschmidt, S.P.W. Schmitt, M.G. Pruszydlo and W.E. Haefeli. 2010. Misspellings in drug information system queries: Characteristics of drug name spelling errors and strategies for their prevention. *International Journal of Medical Informatics*, 79(2010), 832–839.

Turchin, A., J.T. Chu, M. Shubina and J.S. Einbinder. 2007. Identification of misspelled words without a comprehensive dictionary using prevalence analysis. *Proceedings of the Annual Symposium on Biomedical and Health Infomatics (AIMA)*, 11:751-755.

Modelling Word Meaning using Efficient Tensor Representations

Mike Symonds[a], Peter Bruza[a], Laurianne Sitbon[a], and Ian Turner[b]

[a]Department of Computer Science, Queensland University of Technology, Brisbane, Queensland, Australia
{m.symonds, p.bruza, l.sitbon}@qut.edu.au
[b]Department of Mathematics, Queensland University of Technology, Brisbane, Queensland, Australia
i.turner@qut.edu.au

Abstract. Models of word meaning, built from a corpus of text, have demonstrated success in emulating human performance on a number of cognitive tasks. Many of these models use geometric representations of words to store semantic associations between words. Often word order information is not captured in these models. The lack of structural information used by these models has been raised as a weakness when performing cognitive tasks.

This paper presents an efficient tensor based approach to modelling word meaning that builds on recent attempts to encode word order information, while providing flexible methods for extracting task specific semantic information.

Keywords: Semantic Space, Unsupervised Learning, Tensor, Word Order

1 Introduction

Research in the area of natural language processing has demonstrated that psychologically relevant models of word meaning can be learnt from exposure to natural language (Landauer and Dumais, 1997; Lund and Burgess, 1996; McRoy, 1992; Turney, 2008). Many of these models are based on vector representations built from word co-occurrence statistics that aim to model various semantic relationships. Even though these semantic space models appear to identify words with similar meanings, it has been argued that they do not incorporate syntax or achieve other basic cognitive language abilities (Perfetti, 1998).

Recently, a number of semantic space models, that learn directly from unstructured text, have been developed that encode word order into the semantic space, hence capturing more structural information about word associations (Jones and Mewhort, 2007; Sahlgren *et al.*, 2008). Jones and Mewhort (2007) concluded that a model that pays attention to both context and word order while learning, stands a greater chance of matching the trends found in human data. The strength of a geometric approach to encode word order is in the ability to work within a mathematically well defined framework, including the availability of many existing operators from linear algebra, such as Kronecker products. However, to our knowledge there has been very few efficient methods for implementing uncompressed Kronecker products when encoding word order information within a semantic space.

The main contribution of this paper is to present a novel, efficient approach to using Kronecker products to encode word order information within a semantic space. The other significant contribution is to demonstrate how applications can use our single representation to access various task specific semantic information.

2 Related Work

The main areas of research that provide a theoretical framework for our model include: (i) the structuralist approaches to defining word meaning, and (ii) the use of semantic spaces to model word meaning.

2.1 Word Meaning

Ferdinand de Saussure (1916) argued that meaning arose from the relationships between words. He called the two types of relationships that created this meaning: (i) syntagmatic and (ii) paradigmatic associations. Saussure's structuralist ideas provide a relatively clean linguistic framework, free of psychology, sociology and anthropology, within which we can distinguish between two types of word associations that can be used to model word meaning (Holland, 1992). This structuralist approach to linguistics has been used to motivate other semantic space models (Sahlgren *et al.*, 2008).

A syntagmatic association exists between two words if they co-occur more frequently than expected from chance. Some common examples may include "coffee-drink" and "sun-hot". A paradigmatic association exists between two words if they can substitute for one another in a sentence without affecting the grammaticality or acceptability of the sentence. Some common examples may include "drink-eat" and "quick-fast" (Rapp, 2002).

2.2 Semantic Space Models

Linked to structuralist ideas of linguistics, researchers have argued that word meaning can be modelled by comparing the distributions of words within text (Schütze, 1993). A popular approach to representing these word distributions is to collect word occurrence frequencies and place them in high-dimensional *context* vectors (Turney and Pantel, 2010). This approach allows techniques from linear algebra to be used to model relationships between objects, including semantic associations, within the geometric space.

Two of the most well-known semantic space models in literature are HAL (Hyperspace Analogue to Language; Lund and Burgess (1996)) and LSA (Latent Semantic Analysis; Landauer and Dumais (1997)). These two models differ in the way they build their context vectors. HAL builds context vectors by storing pre- and post-order word co-occurrence frequencies in a word-by-word matrix. Consider the HAL matrix, shown in table 1, created by the sentence "*a dog bit the mailman*", using a sliding context window with radius 2. The co-occurrence information preceding and post-ceding each word are recorded separately by the row and column vectors.

Table 1: Example HAL Space

	a	dog	bit	the
dog	2	0	0	0
bit	1	2	0	0
the	0	1	2	0
mailman	0	0	1	2

LSA differs from HAL in that LSA's context vectors are formed by collecting the word occurrence frequencies within each document to create a word-document matrix. A costly technique, known as single value decomposition (SVD), is then used to reduce the dimensions of the word-document matrix to the k most significant latent concepts. Even though models based on LSA and HAL have been shown to simulate human performance on a number of cognitive tasks, it has been argued by Perfetti (1998) that these models do not capture concepts such as syntax or achieve other basic cognitive language abilities. A relevant example, includes the fact that LSA chose *nurse* over *doctor* when asked to determine the closest match to *physician* in a synonym judgement test. The lack of word order information in LSA is a result of the way in which it builds its context vectors, however, even though HAL would appear to hold word order information, it has been argued by Jones and Mewhort (2007) that HAL does not explicitly encode order information.

A number of recent semantic space models have tried to increase the amount of structural information encoded within the representations. These include the *Bound Encoding of the Aggregate Language Environment* (BEAGLE) model (Jones and Mewhort, 2007) and a permutation model (Sahlgren *et al.*, 2008) based on Random Indexing (RI) (Kanerva *et al.*, 2000). Both BEAGLE and the permuted RI model build their semantic spaces from a set of *fixed length* environment vectors. This approach allows the dimensionality of the semantic space to be contained. These fixed dimension approaches rely on the random assignment of environment vectors to create an approximately orthogonal basis, which is required to use many of the popular geometric distance measures.

In addition to forming context vectors, by summing environment vectors for terms that co-occur within the sliding context window, both BEAGLE and the permuted RI model create *order* vectors. To build order vectors BEAGLE binds the environment vectors using a circular convolution operation ($\circledast$), which is a mathematical function that compresses the Kronecker (outer) product of two vectors. The compression avoids the explosion in tensor order associated with Kronecker products, and is achieved by summing along the trans-diagonal elements of the outer product, giving rise to a vector dubbed a *holographic reduced representation* (HHR) (Plate, 1991). The resulting HHR created by the n-grams within the context window are added to the term's order vector. Circular convolution is non-commutative, such that $\boldsymbol{a} \circledast \boldsymbol{b} \neq \boldsymbol{b} \circledast \boldsymbol{a}$ for distinct vectors $\boldsymbol{a}, \boldsymbol{b}$. Non-commutativity is crucial as word order is usually not commutative.

The main drawback of BEAGLE's encoding method comes from the cost of the binding process and the loss of information through compression of the Kronecker products (Mitchell and Lapata, 2010). In the case of the permuted RI model, word order encoding is performed by rotating the coordinates of the sparse environment vectors in the direction of the co-occurrence (with preceding opposite to post-ceding) before summing the result with the order vector. This approach is much more efficient than circular convolution. The results of both BEAGLE and the permuted RI model show that including order information improves performance on a synonym judgement task over context information alone. We now present a model that formally encodes word order and provides the ability to compute semantic associations that underpin word meaning.

3 Building the Tensor Encoding Model's Semantic Space

Our tensor encoding (TE) model builds its semantic space using an efficient binding process based on Kronecker products of *theoretically* unbounded unit vectors. The result contains both context and order information in a single representation we call the *memory tensor*.

3.1 The TE Binding Process

The way in which the TE model encodes word order is illustrated by considering our binding process for the following example sentence, "*A dog bit the mailman*", where *A* and *the* are considered to be stop words (noisy, low information terms that are ignored) and hence will not be included in the vocabulary. The resulting vocabulary includes:

Term-id	Term	Environment vector
1	dog	$\boldsymbol{e}_{dog} = (1 \quad 0 \quad 0)^T$
2	bit	$\boldsymbol{e}_{bit} = (0 \quad 1 \quad 0)^T$
3	mailman	$\boldsymbol{e}_{mailman} = (0 \quad 0 \quad 1)^T$

The *memory tensor* for each term in the vocabulary is constructed by summing the resulting Kronecker products of the environment vectors within a sliding context window over the text. The number of environment vectors bound using Kronecker products impacts the order of the memory tensors. For this research a second order binding process was used, and results in second order tensors (matrices) being formed. Higher order TE models, which capture the co-occurrence frequencies of n-tuples, are left for future work. The second order binding process for the TE model is defined by:

$$\boldsymbol{M}_w = \sum_{k \in CW}^{k \prec w} \boldsymbol{e}_k \otimes \boldsymbol{e}_w^T + \sum_{k \in CW}^{k \succ w} \boldsymbol{e}_w \otimes \boldsymbol{e}_k^T, \tag{1}$$

where w is the target term, k is a non-stop word found within the sliding context window (CW), $k \prec w$ indicates that term k appears before term w in the context window, and $k \succ w$ indicates that term k appears after term w. Note, stop words are not bound, but they are included when determining the window boundaries. Consider the memory matrices created for the vocabulary terms using a sliding context window with radius 2.

Binding Step 1: $\overbrace{A_s \ [dog] \ bit \ the_s}$ $mailman$

$$\boldsymbol{M}_{dog} = \boldsymbol{e}_{dog} \otimes \boldsymbol{e}_{bit}^T = \begin{pmatrix} 1 \\ 0 \\ 0 \end{pmatrix} (0 \quad 1 \quad 0) = \begin{pmatrix} 0 & 1 & 0 \\ 0 & 0 & 0 \\ 0 & 0 & 0 \end{pmatrix}.$$

Binding Step 2: $\overbrace{A_s \ dog \ [bit] \ the_s \ mailman}$

$$\boldsymbol{M}_{bit} = \boldsymbol{e}_{dog} \otimes \boldsymbol{e}_{bit}^T + \boldsymbol{e}_{bit} \otimes \boldsymbol{e}_{mailman}^T = \begin{pmatrix} 1 \\ 0 \\ 0 \end{pmatrix} (0\ 1\ 0) + \begin{pmatrix} 0 \\ 1 \\ 0 \end{pmatrix} (0\ 0\ 1) = \begin{pmatrix} 0 & 1 & 0 \\ 0 & 0 & 1 \\ 0 & 0 & 0 \end{pmatrix}.$$

Binding Step 3: $A_s \ dog$ $\overbrace{bit \ the_s \ [mailman]}$

$$\boldsymbol{M}_{mailman} = \boldsymbol{e}_{bit} \otimes \boldsymbol{e}_{mailman}^T = \begin{pmatrix} 0 \\ 1 \\ 0 \end{pmatrix} (0 \quad 0 \quad 1) = \begin{pmatrix} 0 & 0 & 0 \\ 0 & 0 & 1 \\ 0 & 0 & 0 \end{pmatrix}.$$

The resulting pattern is that all non-zero elements are situated on the row or column corresponding to the target term's term-id. If this vocabulary building process was performed over the entire corpus the general form of a *memory matrix* would be:

$$\boldsymbol{M}_w = \begin{pmatrix} 0, \ \ldots, 0, \ f_{1w}, \ 0, \ \ldots, 0 \\ \cdots \\ 0, \ \ldots, 0, \ f_{(w-1)w}, \ 0, \ \ldots, 0 \\ f_{w1}, \ldots, f_{w(w-1)}, f_{ww}, f_{w(w+1)}, \ldots, f_{wN} \\ 0, \ \ldots, 0, \ f_{(w+1)w}, \ 0, \ \ldots, 0 \\ \cdots \\ 0, \ \ldots, 0, \ f_{Nw}, \ 0, \ \ldots, 0 \end{pmatrix},$$

where f_{iw} is the value in row i column w of the matrix which represents the ordered co-occurrence frequencies of term i before term w, f_{wj} is the value in row w column j of the matrix that represents the ordered co-occurrence of term j after term w, and N is the number of unique terms in the vocabulary.

3.2 Capturing Stronger Proximity Information

Similar to HAL, our TE model captures stronger proximity information by weighting the strength of a co-occurrence inversely proportional to the distance between the target term and the interacting term. Formally, the binding process in equation (1) becomes:

$$\boldsymbol{M}_w = \sum_{k \in CW}^{k \prec w} (R - d_k + 1).\boldsymbol{e}_k \otimes \boldsymbol{e}_w^T + \sum_{k \in CW}^{k \succ w} (R - d_k + 1).\boldsymbol{e}_w \otimes \boldsymbol{e}_k^T, \tag{2}$$

where R is the radius of the sliding context window, and d_k is the distance between term k and target term w. To demonstrate, consider our previous example sentence, noting *bit* and *mailman* are 2 words apart in the sentence (as stop words are included when calculating distance within the context window):

$$\textbf{Binding Step (with proximity scaling):}\quad \overbrace{A_s \quad dog \quad [bit] \quad the_s \quad mailman}$$

$$\boldsymbol{M}_{bit} = 2 \times \boldsymbol{e}_{dog} \otimes \boldsymbol{e}_{bit}^T + \boldsymbol{e}_{bit} \otimes \boldsymbol{e}_{mailman}^T = 2 \times \begin{pmatrix} 1 \\ 0 \\ 0 \end{pmatrix} (0\ 1\ 0) + \begin{pmatrix} 0 \\ 1 \\ 0 \end{pmatrix} (0\ 0\ 1) = \begin{pmatrix} 0 & 2 & 0 \\ 0 & 0 & 1 \\ 0 & 0 & 0 \end{pmatrix}.$$

3.3 Flexible use of Word Order

Unlike BEAGLE and the permuted RI model, the TE model has the ability to access explicit context and order information within the one geometric representations. This means that order information can be easily ignored by combining rows and columns of the memory tensors. This can be efficiently achieved within similarity measures, as will be demonstrated in section 4.

3.4 Efficient Implementation of Tensor Computations

By using environment vectors that are unit vectors, our second order binding process creates sparse N-by-N memory matrices, with the percent sparseness proportional to $1 - \frac{2}{N} + \frac{1}{N^2}$. This sparseness, along with the fact that no multiplication of elements is required in the binding process, allows memory matrices to be efficiently computed and stored at an implementation level. To demonstrate, consider the memory matrix for *bit* in the proximity scaled example above. M_{bit} can be stored as a fixed dimensional vector of term-id (T), co-occurrence frequency (CF) pairs, (T CF):

$$\text{Storage vector for } \boldsymbol{M}_{bit} = [(-1 \quad 2) \quad (3 \quad 1)],$$

where parenthesis have been added to illustrate implicit grouping of (T CF) pairs, and the sign of the T component is used to capture the word order. Knowing that a context window of radius 2 was used, the storage vector above indicates that the word *dog* (term 1) appeared directly before (as indicated by the negative sign) the word *bit*, and the word mailman (term 3) occurred two words after *bit*. By storing the memory matrix in this way, the process of building memory matrices is achieved by searching the (T CF) pair list in the focus term's storage vector, to find a matching, ordered term-id. If a match is found then the co-occurrence frequency element of the pair is incremented.

Even for applications where the vocabulary is small and the context window radius is small, there will be a number of noisy terms that co-occur with many terms. These co-occurrences with noisy terms will quickly fill the storage vectors. To ensure the model is scalable and these noisy terms are managed a number of methods are used:

1. **Stop-list**: A stop-list is used to remove common high frequency terms.
2. **Co-occurrence frequency ratio cut-offs**: Frequency cut-offs are commonly used in semantic space models (Rohde *et al.*, 2006). Traditionally, the cut-off is applied to the collection frequency of a term. In contrast, our approach is to use a *co-occurrence frequency ratio* (CFR) cut-off, and apply it during the vocabulary building process when a storage vector is full and no match on term-id exists. The CFR is used to identify a (T CF) pair to be replaced, and is determined by comparing $\frac{CF}{F_w}$, where F_w is the collection frequency of the target term w, to a threshold value. If the CFR is below the threshold value the pair is moved to the end of the list and updated with the (T CF) details of this new co-occurrence.

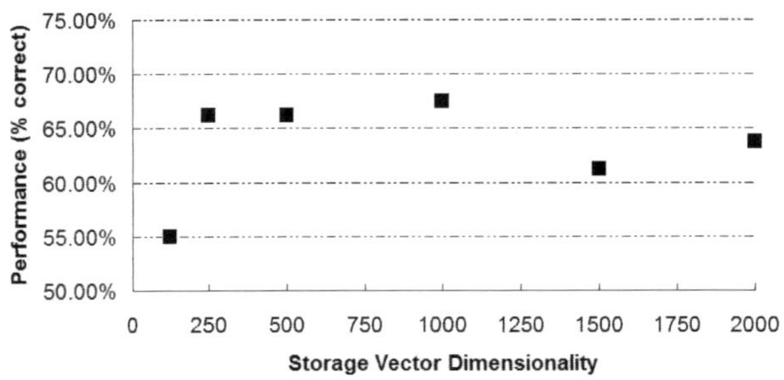

Figure 1: Performance on a synonym judgement task for storage vectors of various dimensions.

The success of these storage vector management methods can be evaluated by considering their impact on the model's performance on a synonym judgement task when the dimensionality of the storage vector is varied, as shown in figure 1. The task was taken from the synonym-finding part of the *Test of English as a Foreign Language* (TOEFL). TOEFL is a standardized test employed by American universities to evaluate foreign applicants' knowledge of the English language, and is further explained in section 4.2.

The superior performance achieved by the TE model for lower dimensionality vectors is particularly beneficial when contrasting computational complexity of the various models. Both BEAGLE and RI have been shown to achieve improved performance as the environment vector dimensionality is increased, often greater than 2000 (Sahlgren *et al.*, 2008). The relatively superior effectiveness for storage vectors with dimensionality between 250 and 1000, compared to those greater than 1000 may be due to our storage vector management technique removing low information items when the storage vector becomes full. At larger dimensions we predict that these low information terms are not removed and this may introduce noise into the TE model's synonym judgement.

The time complexity of the TE model's vocabulary building operation is determined by considering the worst case, in which the storage vector is full and a replacement operation is needed. In this case, the basic operation of the binding process becomes a full search of the (T CF) list, giving: $T_{TE}(n) = O(\frac{D_{SV}}{2})$, where D_{SV} is the storage vector dimensionality. For the synonym judgement task, optimal performance is when $D_{SV} = 1000$. The binding operation of the permuted RI model involves the summing of an environment vector with a context vector and a permuted environment vector with an order vector. Assumng the dimensionality of the vectors are D_{RI}, the time complexity of the permuted RI model would be $T_{RI}(n) = O(2.D_{RI})$, and from our discussion above $D_{RI} \geq 2000$. Therefore, our approach is argued to build the semantic space more efficiently than the permuted RI approach on the synonym judgement task.

4 Computing Word Meaning

One of the major advantages of our approach to encoding word order, compared to BEAGLE and the permuted RI model, is that it captures explicit word co-occurrence frequencies. This allows probabilistic measures to be used in addition to geometric measures when extracting information from the semantic space. The following section outlines two features that effectively measure the strength of syntagmatic or paradigmatic associations crucial in modelling word meaning.

When developing these measures we have tried to generalise the result to support the similarity between a sequence of priming words $Q = (q_1, \ldots, q_p)$ and any vocabulary term w. This was done so that the TE model could be more easily applied to a wider range of information processing tasks. The memory matrix for the sequence of priming terms is formed by summing the memory matrices of these terms, $\boldsymbol{M_Q} = \boldsymbol{M_{q_1}} + \ldots + \boldsymbol{M_{q_p}}$.

4.1 A Measure of Syntagmatic Associations

One of the most popular measures of similarity between two geometric representations is the cosine of the angle formed between them. For the unique structure of the memory matrices used in our model, two interesting results were identified when developing a cosine measure: (i) that there exists a very efficient expression for calculating the cosine of the angle between memory matrices, and (ii) the resulting expression provides an excellent measure of the strength of syntagmatic associations between the terms.

For the extended general case and using linear algebra techniques, the cosine of the angle θ between memory matrices, $\boldsymbol{M_Q}$ and $\boldsymbol{M_w}$, is defined as:

$$\cos\theta = \frac{\sum_{\substack{j=1\\ w\in Q}}^{N} s_w^2 f_{jw}^2 + \sum_{\substack{j=1\\ j\neq w\\ w\in Q}}^{N} s_w^2 f_{wj}^2 + \sum_{\substack{i=q_1\\ i\neq w}}^{q_m} (s_i^2 f_{iw}^2 + s_i^2 f_{wi}^2)}{\sqrt{\sum_{i=q_1}^{q_m}\left[\sum_{j=1}^{N} s_i^2 f_{ji}^2 + \sum_{\substack{j=1\\ j\neq i}}^{N} s_i^2 f_{ij}^2\right]}\sqrt{\sum_{j=1}^{N} f_{jw}^2 + \sum_{\substack{j=1\\ j\neq w}}^{N} f_{wj}^2}}, \quad (3)$$

where $q_1, \ldots, q_m$ are the list of m unique priming terms found in the sequence of all priming terms Q having $m \leq p$, s_i is the number of times term q_i appears in Q, f_{ab} is the co-occurrence frequency of term a appearing before term b in the vocabulary, f_{ba} is the co-occurrence frequency of term a appearing after term b.

The time complexity of this measure would appear to be linear with N, the size of the vocabulary. However, the storage vectors hold a maximum of $\frac{D_{SV}}{2}$ (T CF) pairs, where D_{SV} is the dimensionality of the storage vector. This means that the cosine measure has maximum time complexity when the storage vector is full and hence $T(n) = O(\frac{D_{SV}}{2}.|Q|)$, where $|Q|$ is the number of priming terms. An additional saving when computing the cosine scores for the vocabulary terms is gained by noting that the numerator in equation (3) will only be non-zero if term w has at least one interaction with a priming term $(q_1, \ldots, q_p)$, or is a priming term itself. Therefore, equation (3) will only need to be computed for term-ids found in the storage vectors of the priming terms, $(q_1, \ldots, q_p)$.

Nearest neighbours: Due to the unique construction of our memory matrices, it can be seen from equation (3) that the cosine measure extracts primarily syntagmatic associations of the priming terms and the focus term w. Access to syntagmatic relationships can be useful for many tasks including the identification of terms most likely to precede or succeed a target term. Within our representations, this can be achieved by isolating co-occurrence frequencies in the direction of interest, effectively setting elements to 0 on the row or column not of interest in the memory matrices, $\boldsymbol{M_Q}$ and $\boldsymbol{M_w}$. For example, to identify the term w that most likely precedes a sequence of priming terms Q, equation (3) becomes:

$$\cos_{\text{pr}}\theta = \frac{\sum_{\substack{j=1\\ w\in Q}}^{N} s_w^2 f_{jw}^2 + \sum_{\substack{i=q_1\\ i\neq w}}^{q_m} s_i^2 f_{iw}^2}{\sqrt{\sum_{i=q_1}^{q_m}\sum_{j=1}^{N} s_i^2 f_{ji}^2}\sqrt{\sum_{j=1}^{N} f_{jw}^2}}, \quad (4)$$

with an equivalent expression, using f_{wx} instead of f_{xw}, created to calculate most likely succeeding terms. Table 2 provides a list of most likely preceding and succeeding terms produced by the TE model for a list of target words identified in Jones and Mewhort (2007) for the BEAGLE model. The results illustrate the influence of the asymmetric nature of the memory matrices, and the effectiveness of the cosine measure to identify the strongest ordered syntagmatic associations.

Table 2: Top 6 lexical representations produced for a word preceding or succeeding a target word.

KING		PRESIDENT		WAR		SEA	
___ king	king ___	___ president	president ___	___ war	war ___	___ sea	sea ___
luther:0.419	jr:0.945	vice:0.905	roosevelt:0.948	civil:0.989	ii:0.918	mediterran-ean:0.995	level:0.972
martin:0.288	midas:0.695	elected:0.834	kennedy:0.927	world:0.851	ended:0.298	caribbean:0.857	anemone:0.315
dr:0.185	arthur:0.419	former:0.14	nixon: 0.876	revolution-ary: 0.524	effort: 0.056	baltic:0.738	urchins:0.256
french:0.146	minos:0.307	new:0.07	johnson:0.613	spanish-american:0.306	began:0.038	caspian:0.714	captains:0.252
rex:0.03	queen:0.193	our:0.036	lincoln:0.522	during:0.122	between:0.024	aegean:0.675	gull:0.157
english:0.025	myron:0.165	twenty-seventh:0.012	carter:0.386	declare:0.085	broke:0.024	sargasso:0.592	gulls:0.154

4.2 A Measure of Paradigmatic Associations

One of the main advantages of our TE model, over BEAGLE and the permuted RI model, is the ability to capture explicit co-occurrence frequencies within the geometric representations. This result provides the model with the ability to use the element values of the geometric representations to calculate direct probabilistic measures between vocabulary terms. As an example, we developed an expression to estimate the strength of paradigmatic associations between a sequence of priming terms $Q = (q_1, \ldots, q_p)$ and a vocabulary term w. The measure is based on enhancing terms that co-occur with the same terms as Q, and is defined as:

$$P_{\text{par}}(w|Q) = \frac{1}{Z_{\text{par}}} \sum_{j=q_1}^{q_p} \sum_{i=1}^{N} \frac{f_{ij} f_{iw} + f_{ji} f_{wi}}{f_j f_w}, \tag{5}$$

where f_j is the vocabulary frequency of term j, f_{ji} is the ordered co-occurrence frequency of term j before term i, N is the size of the vocabulary, and $Z_{\text{par}} = \sum_{w \in V_k} \left[\sum_{j=q_1}^{q_p} \sum_{i=1}^{N} \frac{f_{ij} f_{iw} + f_{ji} f_{wi}}{f_j f_w} \right]$. Since the storage vector holds a maximum of $\frac{D_{SV}}{2}$ (T CF) pairs, the worst case time complexity of this paradigmatic measure is $T(n) = O(\frac{D_{SV}^2}{4}.|Q|)$, where D_{SV} is the dimensionality of the storage vector.

Synonym judgements: Paradigmatic associations are heavily used in the process of making synonym judgements. Therefore, we will evaluate our paradigmatic measure on the synonym-finding task in the TOEFL, after using the TASA (Touchstone Applied Science Associates, Inc.) corpus to build our semantic space. TASA contains 12-million words, and is a collection of English text articles that are reportedly equivalent to what the average college-level student has read in his or her lifetime. It has been extensively used to learn semantic relationships within semantic space models evaluated on TOEFL (Landauer and Dumais, 1997; Jones and Mewhort, 2007; Sahlgren *et al.*, 2008). In the synonym-finding part of TOEFL the participant is asked to choose one of four provided words as the most similar to the question word. It was reported that for a large sample of applicants to U.S. colleges, coming from non-English speaking countries, the average result on the synonym test was 51.6 items correct out of 80 (or 64.5%) (Landauer and Dumais, 1997).

A review of past papers using the TOEFL synonym test as a benchmark [1], suggests that the corpus used, preprocessing of documents and resulting vocabulary size may impact the performance achieved (Stone *et al.*, 2008). Therefore, comparisons of TOEFL performance between papers is likely unreliable. A more robust comparison may be achieved by

[1] http://aclweb.org/aclwiki

evaluating the models of interest on the same data configuration, hence we built BEAGLE and the permuted RI model.[2] In our experiments a 416 word stop list[3] was used, with the exception of the words *enough*, *often* and *alone*, which were present as a question or answer within TOEFL. We did not use any stemming on the vocabulary, however, the TOEFL question, *expeditiously*, was not found in the TASA corpus, whereas *expeditious* was, therefore that TOEFL question was updated to use *expeditious*. We also chose to remove TASA terms that contained numerics. These steps resulted in a vocabulary size of 134,054 unique terms. The performance achieved by each model is shown in figure 2.

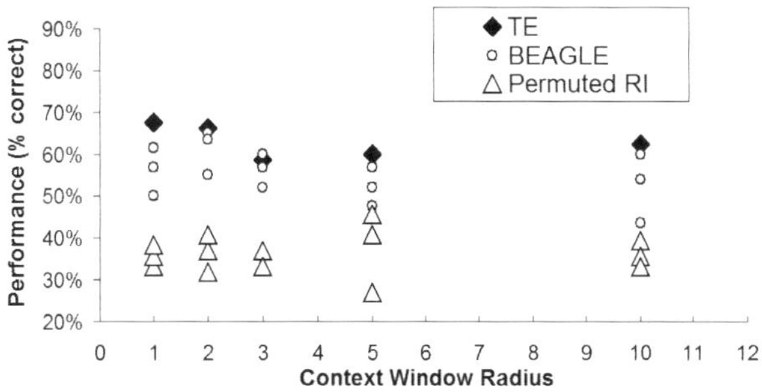

Figure 2: TOEFL performance for the Tensor Encoding, BEAGLE and permuted RI model.

Since BEAGLE and the permuted RI model use random environment vectors, a number of runs were performed to calculate the average score. The best average results were: (i) BEAGLE=61.25% (49/80) using a context window radius (cwr) of 2, and environment vector length (evl) of 2048, and (ii) permuted RI model=38% (30/80) using cwr=5 and evl=2,000. The best TE model result was 67.5% (54/80) using cwr=1 and a storage vector length of 1,000. The BEAGLE results were similar to those reported in Jones and Mewhort (2007), with any improvement likely due to the reduced context window length used in our experiments. The permuted RI model result is much lower than that reported in Sahlgren *et al.* (2008), possibly due to the difference in vocabulary size. Their TASA vocabulary was reduced to 74,100 terms by using stemming and high frequency cut-offs.

Addressing weaknesses in LSA: Landauer and Dumais (1997) indicated that some of the TOEFL errors produced by LSA, that were not made by students, may be attributed to the fact that LSA was more sensitive to paradigmatic associations, and not syntagmatic. For example, Perfetti (1998) commented that on the TOEFL, LSA chose *nurse* (0.47) over *doctor* (0.41) for the question word of *physician*. Even though this is Perfetti's selective example, we found that the TE model was more likely to choose *doctor* ($P(w|Q)$=**0.01926**) over nurse ($P(w|Q) = 0.01818$) for the same question.

5 Conclusions and Future Work

The aim of this paper has been to present a model of word meaning that goes beyond existing semantic space models by using Kronecker products to capture word order and co-occurrence information. Our TE model overcomes weaknesses in previous models attempting to encode greater structural information by reducing the information loss without computational cost. It also provides applications with more flexibility when extracting task specific semantic information without relying on existing knowledge or POS taggers.

[2] The permuted RI model functions were supplied by http://code.google.com/p/semanticvectors/

[3] Stoplist taken from the Lemur toolkit for information retrieval: http://www.lemurproject.org

The ability to extend the evaluation of this model to other information processing tasks, such as word sense disambiguation, query expansion, and document retrieval, is an area for future research. Another area for further investigation includes extending the current vocabulary binding process to form higher order tensors that would allow larger n-tuple associations to be encoded in the representations underpinning the semantic space. Using higher order TE models may have advantages similar to those highlighted by Baroni and Lenci (2010).

References

Baroni, Marco and Alessandro Lenci. 2010. Distributional memory: A general framework for corpus-based semantics. *Computational Linguistics*, 36, 673–721.

Holland, Norman N. 1992. *The Critical I*. Columbia University Press, New York, USA.

Jones, Michael N. and Douglas J. K. Mewhort. 2007. Representing word meaning and order information in a composite holographic lexicon. *Psychological Review*, 114, 1–37.

Kanerva, Pentti, Jan Kristoferson, and Anders Holst. 2000. Random indexing of text samples for latent semantic analysis. *In Proceedings of the 22nd Annual Conference of the Cognitive Science Society*, p. 1036.

Landauer, T. K. and S. T. Dumais. 1997. A solution to plato's problem: The latent semantic analysis theory of the acquisition, induction, and representation of knowledge. *Psychological Review*, 104, 211–240.

Lund, K. and C. Burgess. 1996. Producing high-dimensional semantic spaces from lexical co-occurrence. *Behavior research methods, instruments and computers*, 28, 203–208.

McRoy, S. W. 1992. Using multiple knowledge sources for word sense discrimination. *Computational Linguistics*, 18(1), 1–30.

Mitchell, Jeff and Mirella Lapata. 2010. Composition in distributional models of semantics. *Cognitive Science*, 34(8), 1388–1429.

Perfetti, Charles A. 1998. The limits of co-occurrence: Tools and theories in language research. *Discourse Processes*, 25, 363–377.

Plate, Tony. 1991. Holographic reduced representations: Convolution algebra for compositional distributed representations. In *International Joint Conference on Artificial Intelligence*, pp. 30–35. Morgan Kaufmann.

Rapp, Reinhard. 2002. The computation of word associations: comparing syntagmatic and paradigmatic approaches. In *Proceedings of the 19th international conference on Computational linguistics - Volume 1*, pp. 1–7, Morristown, NJ, USA. Association for Computational Linguistics.

Rohde, Douglas L. T., Laura M. Gonnerman, and David C. Plaut. 2006. An improved model of semantic similarity based on lexical co-occurence. *Communications of the ACM*, 8, 627–633.

Sahlgren, Magnus, Anders Holst, and Pentti Kanerva. 2008. Permutations as a means to encode order in word space. In V. Sloutsky, B. Love, and K. Mcrae, eds., *Proceedings of the 30th Annual Conference of the Cognitive Science Society*, pp. 1300–1305. Cognitive Science Society, Austin, TX.

Schütze, Hinrich. 1993. Word space. In *Advances in Neural Information Processing Systems 5*, pp. 895–902. Morgan Kaufmann.

Stone, Benjamin P., Simon J. Dennis, and Peter J. Kwantes. 2008. A systematic comparison of semantic models on human similarity rating data: The effectiveness of subspacing. In *Proceedings of the Thirteeth Conference of the Cognitive Science Society*. Cognitive Science Society.

Turney, Peter D. 2008. A uniform approach to analogies, synonyms, antonyms, and associations. In *Proceedings of the 22nd International Conference on Computational Linguistics - Volume 1*, COLING '08, pp. 905–912, Stroudsburg, PA, USA. Association for Computational Linguistics.

Turney, Peter D. and Patrick Pantel. 2010. From frequency to meaning: vector space models of semantics. *Journal of Artificial Intelligence Research*, 37, 141–188, January.

A Study of Sense-disambiguated Networks Induced from Folksonomies

Hans-Peter Zorn and Iryna Gurevych

Ubiquitous Knowledge Processing Lab
Technische Universität Darmstadt
Hochschulstraße 10
64289 Darmstadt, Germany

Abstract. Lexical-semantic resources are fundamental building blocks in natural language processing (NLP). Frequently, they fail to cover the informal vocabulary of web users as represented in user-generated content. This paper aims at exploring folksonomies as a novel source of lexical-semantic information. It analyzes two prototypical examples of folksonomies, namely BibSonomy and Delicious, and utilizes NLP and word sense induction techniques to turn the folksonomies into word sense–disambiguated networks representing the vocabulary and the word senses found in folksonomies. The main contribution of the paper is an in-depth analysis of the resulting resources, which can be combined with conventional wordnets to achieve broad coverage of user-generated content.

1 Introduction

Lexical-semantic resources are fundamental building blocks of natural language processing systems. For a long time, WordNet has been widely deployed in a great variety of tasks. A few years ago, the attention of researchers has turned to the so-called collaboratively created lexical-semantic resources such as Wikipedia[1] and Wiktionary[2] (Gurevych and Wolf, 2010). They have been found to perform well as sources of background knowledge in multiple NLP tasks.

While collaboratively created resources represent an excellent addition to conventional lexical-semantic resources, their coverage is insufficient in terms of the represented domains. Also, there is often lack of contextual information about individual sense descriptions. This is why, in this paper, we turn to folksonomies as a promising source of lexical-semantic information. *Folksonomy* is a term used first by Vander Wal (2004) and defined as "tagging is ontology that works", in reference to social bookmarking systems like Delicious. Such applications allow users to assign tags to web sites or other resources. By doing so, they create a structure consisting of the three entities, "tag, the object being tagged and [the user's] identity" which is referred to as a folksonomy.

Our goal is to derive a resource that can effectively complement conventional resources, *e.g.*, WordNet, as folksonomies are known to contain special vocabulary reflecting users' interests, current trends, or neologisms typically lacking in conventional resources. To achieve this, we investigate two widely deployed folksonomies, Delicious and BibSonomy. We constructed three types of tag-based graphs utilizing the tag co-occurrence with resources, users, and other tags. Then, we apply graph clustering techniques to perform word sense induction and obtain a word sense–disambiguated lexical-semantic network. Based on this graph, we present a detailed analysis of the resulting networks in terms of their graph-theoretic properties and compare them with the properties of conventional resources. We also compare their coverage and find that a folksonomy-derived resource includes web-specific vocabulary that is lacking in other resources. Furthermore,

[1] `http://wikipedia.org`

[2] `http://wiktionary.org`

we investigate the nature of the resulting word sense distributions for individual lexemes and relate them to the word senses encoded in WordNet and Wiktionary.

There has been work on inducing hierarchies (Heymann and Garcia-Molina, 2006) and ontologies (Schmitz, 2006) from folksonomies based on co-occurrence patterns. Recently, work has been published on clustering and disambiguating tag similarity graphs. Yeung *et al.* (2009) employ the Girvan–Newman algorithm (Girvan and Newman, 2002) to optimize the betweenness of nodes by incrementally removing edges and recalculating betweenness. They only look at a small data set of ten exemplary tags. Our goal is to go beyond simple clustering and do actual disambiguation, meaning to instantiate the different readings of a tag as individual nodes within the network. Jurgens (2011) presents a way to use community detection to induce word senses from word collocations. He builds a graph from word co-occurrences and then applies a community detection algorithm. In contrast to the approach in this work, they do not split the nodes into different senses but use a clustering algorithm that deals with nodes belonging to multiple communities. The algorithm is a hierarchical agglomerative clustering operating on a similarity measure defined for edges, not vertices.

The paper is structured as follows: First, we describe how to derive a tag similarity graph from folksonomies and introduce our approach for sense disambiguation of individual tags (Section 2) . We analyze the resulting graphs in terms of their properties (Section 3) and coverage (Section 4). With this analysis we are laying ground to combine traditional LSRs and folksonomies in applications.

2 From Folksonomies to Lexical-Semantic Resources

2.1 Datasets

We explore two datasets for our investigations, Delicious and BibSonomy, which are available for research purposes.

The first dataset was extracted by TU Berlin from the Delicious social bookmarking site (Wetzker *et al.*, 2008). Delicious is a general-purpose social bookmarking system founded in 2003. TU Berlin crawled about 142 million bookmarks resulting in more than 450 million tag assignments. We used the first 30 million tag assignments for our experiments, a number where the vector representation fits in about 12 GB of RAM. The Delicious system is generally open to everyone, but the users seem to be mostly technical and IT people, resulting in a higher coverage in these domains. We choose Delicious because of its size and its broad coverage.

BibSonomy (Benz *et al.*, 2010) is a social bookmarking system for both publications and web sites. It was created by the Knowledge and Data Engineering research group at the University of Kassel to provide a useful service to the research community and to collect data for their social bookmarking research. Therefore the dataset[3] is available for research purposes and has been used in various studies on tag recommendation. We choose BibSonomy as a reference dataset in the field of folksonomies. We perform only light preprocessing by removing special characters[4] because we see concatenations by hyphens, underscores, and colons as possibly emerging neologisms or Internet jargon that we are actually interested in.

2.2 Graph Representation of Lexical-Semantic Resources

Previously, folksonomies have been principally considered a tool to recommend tags to users, and have been studied with regard to their semantic properties. The contribution of our work is the conversion of a folksonomy to a lexical-semantic resource (LSR) that could be used alongside other LSRs. LSRs can be represented as graph structures that contain words and their relations to

[3] Knowledge and Data Engineering Group, University of Kassel: Benchmark Folksonomy Data from BibSonomy, version of January 1, 2009

[4] `[!#?%/&+,;]`

each other. By interpreting the LSR as a graph, we can identify three types of LSRs that differ in what the vertices represent. In a **lexical graph**, each vertex denotes exactly one *lexical item*. For example, there is exactly one vertex for the lexeme "order" even though this word has multiple meanings. **Disambiguated lexical graphs** represent each *reading* of every word as a separate vertex. In this case, there is a vertex for "order" as a command, and for "order" as a "ranking". Finally, a **semantic graph** represents each *meaning* as a vertex. In such a structure, there is exactly one vertex combining (for example) the common meaning of the lexemes "order" and "command".

We will describe and apply a multi-stage process to transform folksonomies to an LSR. We first create a *lexical graph* based on the tags in a folksonomy. Then, we split the lexical nodes with the help of community detection techniques to create a *disambiguated lexical graph*. As future work, we plan to apply graph clustering methods to transform the resulting graph to a *semantic graph*.

2.3 Creating a Tag Similarity Graph

As a first step, we create a lexical graph from tags, where each vertex represents a tag. Next, we calculate similarities between tags to create edges between similar tags. Cattuto *et al.* (2008) and Markines *et al.* (2009) summarize the state of the art in similarity measures on folksonomies. We choose one specific category from those distributional measures that represent tags in a vector space. These measures work with the disambiguation algorithm proposed in Section 2.4.

Resource Similarity. We create a vector space over all resources (*e.g.*, web sites) and represent each tag as the number of resources it has been assigned to by users. Then

$$\mathrm{sim}_{\mathrm{res}}(t_1, t_2) = \frac{v_{r1} \cdot v_{r2}}{|v_{r1}| \cdot |v_{r2}|}, \tag{1}$$

where $v_{rn} \in \{R\}$ is the vector space representation of all resources t_n has been assigned to.

Tag Context Similarity. The tag context similarity is a global co-occurrence similarity. Each tag is represented as the frequency of tags it appears with. This can be seen as a global co-occurrence measure. Then

$$\mathrm{sim}_{\mathrm{tag}}(t_1, t_2) = \frac{v_{t1} \cdot v_{t2}}{|v_{t1}| \cdot |v_{t2}|}, \tag{2}$$

where $v_{tn} \in \{T\}$ is the vector-space representation of all tags that have been assigned to resources where t_n has also been assigned.

Because each resource usually has multiple tags assigned by different users, feature vectors in this space are more dense than in the resource space. The tag context feature space can be limited by looking at only the N most popular tags. N has been chosen empirically as $N = 10\,000$ to achieve a good balance between performance and coverage.

User Similarity. This measure is similar to resource similarity but represents each tag by the users it has been used by:

$$\mathrm{sim}_{\mathrm{user}}(t_1, t_2) = \frac{v_{u1} \cdot v_{u2}}{|v_{u1}| \cdot |v_{u2}|}, \tag{3}$$

where $v_{un} \in \{U\}$ is the vector-space representation of all users that have been tagging the resources with t_n.

To create the tag similarity graph, we compute the neighborhood for each tag and create edges between the tag and its neighbor. The neighborhood is defined by a similarity threshold δ, after the application of which we can compute the average number of edges per vertex. Based on this we set the value of δ to 0.4 for the following experiments.

Table 1 shows the influence of the threshold on the average degree of nodes to the resulting graph for BibSonomy.

Table 1: Influence of δ on average degree of the nodes in the graph

δ	tag context similarity	resource similarity	user-similarity
0.4	99.51	6.20	96.06
0.5	74.53	3.70	85.51
0.6	42.84	2.38	72.46
0.7	18.34	1.60	58.47

2.4 Identifying Word Senses of Tags: Disambiguated Lexical Graphs

The second step is to transform the tag similarity graph to a disambiguated lexical graph. To do so, we first need to determine how many different senses a tag has and then to split each tag into new vertices representing those. Lastly, we need to modify the vector representation of each tag in a way that it only reflects its specific sense. Each ambiguous tag has a neighborhood of similar tags that have been calculated by one of the similarity measures discussed above. We assume that each neighboring tag belongs to one of the senses of the tag to be disambiguated. As discussed, each tag is represented by a feature vector. In the following procedure, for each sense of a tag, new feature vectors are created which contain only those features contributing to the specific sense.

Assuming we want to split tag t_i into a set of disambiguated tags, we define its *neighborhood* as

$$\text{neighborhood}(t_i) = \{t_j \in T \mid \text{sim}(t_i, t_j) > \delta\}$$

given a similarity measure sim() and a similarity threshold δ.

The threshold δ is chosen in such way that it produces a large neighborhood. In this case, the neighbors are not relations in a resource but are used as contexts for disambiguation. We then represent the tags in the neighborhood by their respective resource vectors and apply single-link hierarchical agglomerative clustering (HAC) (Manning *et al.*, 2008) on this neighborhood. We choose this algorithm because it is straightforward to implement, and because it does not require previous knowledge about the number of clusters like k-means does. The number of clusters determines the number of senses which is what we want to induce. This algorithm starts with each tag in its own cluster and iteratively merges the most similar clusters until a similarity threshold δ_{hac} is reached. For sparse feature spaces, such as in the resource domain, we have to choose $\delta_{hac} = 0$, as the neighbors are often only similar to t_0 but have only very low similarity to each other. By choosing $\delta_{hac} = 0$, we group all tags that have at least one feature in common. For tags t_1 and t_2 that are located in different clusters, the similarity $\text{sim}(t_1, t_2)$ is zero.

Now we apply the actual sense induction algorithm:

- For each cluster, we create a new tag t_n and assign it the feature-vector $\overrightarrow{f}$ of the original tag.
- For each cluster, we add its tags' feature-vectors together to create a masking vector $\overrightarrow{m}$.
- We set

$$f_i = \begin{cases} f_i & \text{if } m_i > 0 \\ 0 & \text{if } m_i = 0 \end{cases} \tag{4}$$

where f_i is the ith component of vector $\overrightarrow{f}$, and m_i is the ith component of vector $\overrightarrow{m}$. This way, the newly created tag is represented by only those features that are also present in the feature vectors of all the tags in the same cluster. Now we reconstruct the graph by applying the process described in Section 2 again to create a new, much larger tag similarity graph in which all senses of a tag are represented as a separate vertex.

Table 2: Graph-theoretic properties of the tag similarity graph based on BibSonomy

	$\|V\|$	$\|E\|$	$\#CC$	$\|V_{LCC_1}\|/\|V\|$	$\|V_{LCC_2}\|/\|V\|$	L	$\overline{k}$	C_{LCC}
bib-res	13,275	107,101	4941	0.63	< 0.01	3.23	12.85	0.19
bib-tag	13,275	91,518	157	0.99	< 0.01	2.41	40.00	0.40
bib-user	13,274	466,740	4902	0.63	< 0.01	3.31	56.55	0.31
bib-res-da	62,461	1,181,465	1572	0.96	< 0.01	4.29	19.53	0.57
bib-tag-da	21,160	91,101	2	1.00	< 0.01	3.04	58.80	0.42
bib-user-da	15,721	846,421	81	0.99	< 0.01	1.00	54.12	0.53
del-res	31,166	122,090	15,298	0.48	< 0.01	6.57	7.93	0.16
del-tag	32,724	2,327,591	111	0.99	< 0.01	3.45	40.00	0.36
del-user	15,766	416,688	7,253	0.54	< 0.01	0.00	48.99	0.25
del-res-da	133,497	1,567,909	17,003	0.82	< 0.01	6.02	14.15	0.39
del-tag-da	133,505	1,567,898	16,999	0.82	< 0.01	6.02	14.16	0.39
del-user-da	33,281	1,457,235	362	0.97	< 0.01	8.87	44.96	0.64
WiktG	20,011	33,650	8,214	0.57	< 0.01	5.03	5.80	0.0822
GNG	42,129	99,130	355	0.67	0.21	8,77	2.82	0.0155

3 Analyzing Network Properties of Tag Similarity Graphs

To investigate the potential value value of the generated resources, we now compare graph-theoretic properties to traditional LSRs. Topological analysis can help to understand the structure of the resource. Furthermore, it helps to understand if the tag similarity graph is structurally similar to conventional LSRs. We understand that manually crafted LSRs such as WordNet aim to be linguistically and psychologically sound, while the bottom-up characteristics of folksonomies are much more domain-specific and unbalanced. However, analyzing similarities and differences between those resources will help to understand if and how they could be used in combination in certain application scenarios. Last but not least, many LSR-based applications and algorithms operate on the graph, and they are likely to work with a resource based on a folksonomy if they work on a conventional, topologically similar resource.

Since the construction of tag similarity graphs is dependent on a set of empirically derived parameters as described in Section 2, it should be noted that many graph properties can be related to those parameters. If parameters are changed at this step, the graph-theoretic properties will change. In this work, we focus on an analysis of the automatically induced resources constructed with fixed parameters. An in-depth study of how the parameters are correlated with the resulting resources is left to future work.

Table 2 shows the results for tag similarity graphs induced from BibSonomy and Delicious. The table cover the graphs created by using three similarity measures as described in Section 2.3: resource (res), tag context (tag), and user (user) for both the tag similarity graph and the disambiguated version (-da). For comparison we include the values reported by Garoufi *et al.* (2008) for the German Wiktionary (WiktG) and GermaNet (GNG), the German wordnet.

The **size of the resource** in terms of the number of vertices ($|V|$) and edges ($|E|$) directly influences the coverage, and the ratio between vertices and edges is a measure for the density of lexical-semantic relations. While the Delicious-derived graphs are larger than BibSonomy in terms of vertices, they have more edges for each node. The number of **connected components** ($\#CC$) is the number of distinct subgraphs in which all vertices are connected to each other. A high number of CCs means a lot of nodes are not reachable from each other. If the largest connected component ($|LCC_1|$) is magnitudes higher than the second largest component ($|LCC_2|$), then LCC_1 can probably be used as a resource and all the small outliers may be simply ignored. If the CCs have all similar sizes, then the graph is fragmented, which hinders traversal-based algorithms. In our case, all graphs are highly connected and feature one, large set of nodes covering almost all nodes aside from some outliers. This means that random-walk or graph-traversal algorithms should work properly on the folksonomy-induced resource proposed in this paper.

The following properties refer to LCC_1 of the respective graph only. The **average path length** L denotes the average distance between all vertices. It is an indication of whether the graph is a small-world network. The **average degree** $\overline{k}$ is the average number of all edges entering and leaving a node. The **network clustering coefficient** C_{LCC} is the average of all local clustering coefficients C_i. The local clustering coefficient is calculated as the proportion of all actual existing edges between the neighbor vertices of a vertex and the possible edges. BibSonomy is a much smaller resource than Delicious, even though we only use a fraction of the data available from Delicious. However, the structure in terms of connected components is about the same and depends only on the used similarity measure. The ratio between largest CC and second-largest is also similar. BibSonomy has a smaller average path length. The average degree is slightly larger in BibSonomy, the clustering coefficient is about the same. This means in terms of graph properties there is no large difference between the both datasets even though they are of such different size - the influence of the similarity measure is much larger. Tag and user similarity produce graphs with much higher average degrees and clustering coefficients. The disambiguated graphs are much larger, they have a smaller average degree and higher clustering coefficients. The smaller average degree comes from the fact that relations are now distributed between the newly created senses.

4 Analyzing the Vocabulary of Automatically-induced Tag Similarity Graphs

4.1 Vocabulary Coverage

Since the folksonomies under investigation can be freely edited by users without any editorial control, we expect to find large differences from the conventional resources like WordNet on the one hand and from collaboratively constructed dictionaries like Wiktionary on the other hand. Our expectations regarding the vocabulary found in folksonomies can be summarized as follows:

Mixed natural languages. Users can specify tags in any language they are comfortable with.

Free-form. Tags do not need to be constrained to natural language words; they can be any symbols which the users find useful.

Creative. People can use neologisms such as novel portmanteau words.

To analyze the multilingual vocabulary of the folksonomies, we calculated the overlap with the Hunspell spelling dictionaries provided by OpenOffice.org[5] covering 36 languages. Figures 1a and 1b show that the most of the tags could not be assigned to any language. The most common language is English, followed by German, Dutch, French and Czech. Note that the coverage is overlapping and in some languages loanwords are more common.

Table 3 shows the term overlap between the folksonomy-derived resources and two common LSRs, WordNet and Wiktionary. A node is considered as overlapping if the strings are exactly the same. Because folksonomies are multilingual, and we make no attempt to separate languages, these statistics only indicate which part of the LSR's vocabulary is found in a folksonomy-induced resource and not the other way round. However, both the English Wiktionary and WordNet include some foreign-language vocabulary, which is why the coverage is higher than the coverage for US English detected by Hunspell. Table 4 shows the categories of folksonomy-specific tags we discovered in our analysis of the folksonomy vocabulary not found in other resources.

This lexical-semantic information is complementary to the knowledge in common LSRs and can be directly utilized to analyze user texts in order to achieve better coverage in automatic language analysis and induce semantic knowledge about user-specific vocabulary.

[5] `http://wiki.services.openoffice.org/wiki/Dictionaries`

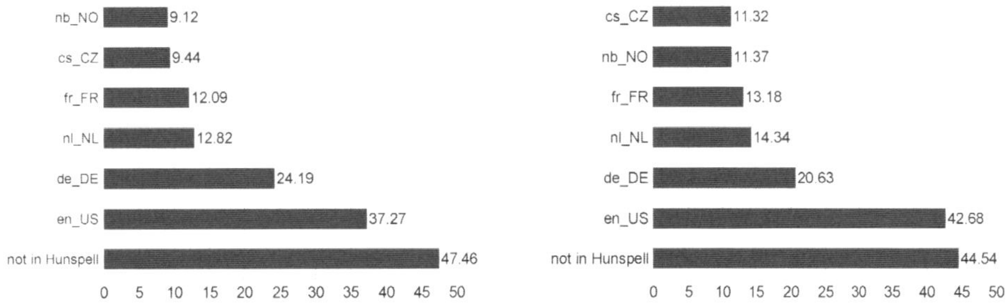

(a) BibSonomy (b) Delicious

Figure 1: Percentage of tags matched by Hunspell

Table 3: Percentage of folksonomy vocabulary that is also contained in WordNet or Wiktionary.

	BibSonomy	Delicious
WordNet	40.68	53.65
Wiktionary	58.13	61.59

4.2 Word Sense Distribution

Meyer and Gurevych (2010) study the distribution of senses per lexeme in Wiktionary and WordNet. We follow their approach to analyze the distribution of senses per lexeme and calculate $\omega_r(\ell)$, the number of word senses per lexeme (Table 5). The sense distribution $d_r(k) = |\{\ell|\omega_r(\ell) = k\}|$ specifies the number of occurrences of lexemes with a certain number of senses. While the majority of lexemes in WordNet 3.0 and in Wiktionary[6] (70% and 83%, respectively) have only a single sense, the sense distribution in the folksonomy-induced resources strongly depends on the employed similarity measure and other parameters, as described in Section 2.3. For example, user similarity on the BibSonomy dataset has a sense distribution that resembles that of WordNet and Wiktionary. If used with resource similarity, the average number of senses is much higher. Due to the sparseness of the resource space, many of a tag's neighboring tags feature no similarity to each other and will therefore end up in separate clusters yielding more senses.

Next, we turn to a qualitative analysis of polysemous lexemes found in the both generated disambiguated graphs from Section 2.3. Table 6 shows the number of senses for six lexemes

[6] The English edition from June 5, 2011, accessed using JWKTL 0.14.1 (Zesch *et al.*, 2008)

Table 4: Examples of words found in the folksonomy but not in Wiktionary

Category	**Examples**
abbrevations	cvs, pda, tdd, dhtml, nyc
concatenations	real_estate, bayarea, zipcode
meta-tags	mek:untagged, firefox:import
multiword expressions	milkandcookies, home_improvement,
spelling errors	acadamia
neologisms	hometheater, pilates, howto, etext, bioinformatics, portscan
named entities	junit
other	hamradio

Table 5: Sense distribution for different tag similarity graphs and other resources in percent

	bib-res	bib-user	del-res	del-user	WKT	WN
$d_r(1)$	15.45	83.75	44.81	62.99	70.16	82.68
$d_r(2)$	15.62	13.74	22.16	8.75	16.68	10.70
$d_r(3)$	14.68	2.12	12.74	26.83	6.49	3.33
$d_r(4)$	12.05	0.32	7.25	0.92	2.97	1.40
$d_r(\geq 5)$	42.20	0.08	13.04	0.50	3.71	1.88

Table 6: Number of senses in tag similarity graphs compared to WordNet and Wiktionary

	del-res	del-user	bib-res	bib-user	synsets in WN	senses in WKT
bank	5	1	6	1	18	12
life	5	3	5	1	14	14
order	8	2	8	1	24	16
sf	2	1	4	1	0	2
table	3	1	10	1	8	8
tree	9	2	9	1	7	10

(*table*, *bank*, *sf*, *order*, *tree* and *life*) in the Delicious and BibSonomy graphs constructed with the user and resource similarity measures, along with those for WordNet and Wiktionary.

We see that, for some of the selected words, there have been more senses created in BibSonomy, and for others more in Delicious. Thus, the number of senses does not seem to depend much on the size of the resource. Sense splitting using user similarity does not work at all in BibSonomy while it does produce some senses in Delicious. In comparison to WordNet and Wiktionary, the folksonomies produce quite different number of senses. For *table* and *tree*, for example, the folksonomy-derived LSRs have more senses than WordNet, but for *bank*, *life*, and *order* there are fewer. The abbreviation *sf* for "science fiction" or "San Francisco" is not contained in WordNet. To better understand the nature and granularity of word senses encoded in the analyzed resources, we look closer at the clusters for *sf* and *table* in the two resources derived from Delicious and BibSonomy. We choose resource similarity because besed on the resulting sense distribution this one looks most similar to the conventional resources.

The word *table* has three senses in Delicious, one of them refers to HTML tables, one of them refers to the periodic table, and one of them is an artifact which probably should have been merged into another cluster. The sense of *table* as a piece of furniture does not appear at all in the folksonomy. We see from Figures 2a-2d that the folksonomies are very unbalanced. Some topics are covered extensively, some meanings are not contained at all. If course, this depends on the way people use the Internet. The absence of the "furniture" meaning of *table* may come from the fact that furniture is one of the things people do not yet buy on-line so much and as a result do not annotate web sites about this topic.

5 Conclusions

In this paper, we presented experiments on inducing sense-disambiguated lexical-semantic networks based on two popular folksonomies, BibSonomy and Delicious. We apply a multi-step process to analyze the tags assigned by users to resources and construct a tag similarity graph which is further processed to induce word senses. We compare the resources resulting from a set of different system configurations with conventional lexical-semantic resources such as WordNet and Wiktionary. Regarding the graph-theoretic properties, we find that the induced resources have similar properties as traditional resources in terms of connectivity. Furthermore, we analyze the coverage of different resources and observe that folksonomies overlap in large part with existing

novel, via:boingboing, reality, charles, etext, culture, worldbuilding, webzine, utopia, ebook, starwars, science.fiction, popularmedia, writing, lovecraft, zine, read, writing, short, horror, california, transhumanism, future, science-fiction, author, singularity, sanfrancisco, fantasy, science-fiction, science, sci-fi, sciencefiction, fiction, scifi
francisco, bay, san, california, bayarea, sanfrancisco

(a) *sf* in Delicious

chemistry, elements
tables
sequence, sequences
robot
convert, latex, converter, openoffice,
data, presentation, liste, table, elements, year2006, tree, graphs, informationdesign, visualization, übersicht, phawk, methoden, knowledgevisualization

(b) *table* in Bibsonomy

writing, storytelling, fiction, tricks, plot, scifi, stories, fiction, sciencefiction
frameworks, codegeneration, sourceforge

(c) *sf* in Bibsonomy

webauthoring, webdevelopment, sorted, programming/javascript, data, web, example, cssgalleries, cssgalleries, web, dev, web.design, voorbeeld, css.example, xhtml,js
table, elements, periodictable, periodic, chemistry
absolute

(d) *table* in Delicious

Figure 2: Induced senses of the tags *sf* and *table*

resources but also contribute vocabulary that is not included in them. Finally, we compare the word senses encoded in the individual resources and find that the proposed sense induction algorithm detects many of the senses that are encoded in the folksonomy, although due to the folksonomies' nature, they differ substantially from the senses in traditional LSRs.

In summary, the folksonomy-induced resources show good potential to complement the knowledge in conventional resources because they directly encode information regarding non-standard terms frequently found in user-generated content and lacking in conventional resources. The resulting lexical-semantic knowledge can be directly utilized for example in query expansion, or for personalized information management in the context of Web applications. For such applications we plan to look into how to couple folksonomies with traditional LSRs to extend their domain-specific vocabulary.

An interesting by-product of our research is a parameterizable framework for word sense induction. Such a framework is not limited to folksonomies, but can be applied to any network based on term distributions, such as those based on n-gram statistics from the Web or other corpora or the co-occurrence of terms in a semantically structured corpus such as Wikipedia. While current methods, such as Explicit Semantic Analysis (Gabrilovich and Markovitch, 2007), operate on the term co-occurrence vectors lacking sense disambiguation, our framework can be applied to construct a sense-disambiguated resource. We plan to explore this direction in the future. Another important issue to systematically study is the relation between empirically set parameters for similarity graph construction and the properties of the resulting lexical-semantic networks. While we experiment with a set of predefined parameters in this paper, we plan to conduct an in-depth study of this issue in the future. Utilizing the resulting resources in NLP applications as mentioned above is another important avenue of research.

6 Acknowledgements

We thank Tristan Miller and Christian M. Meyer for their helpful comments. This work has been supported by the Volkswagen Foundation as part of the Lichtenberg Professorship Program under grant № I/82806.

References

Benz, Dominik, Andreas Hotho, Robert Jäschke, Beate Krause, Folke Mitzlaff, Christoph Schmitz, and Gerd Stumme. 2010. The Social Bookmark and Publication Management System BibSonomy. *The VLDB Journal*, 19(6), 849–875.

Cattuto, Ciro, Dominik Benz, Andreas Hotho, and Stumme Gerd. 2008. Semantic Grounding of Tag Relatedness in Social Bookmarking Systems. In *Proceedings of the 7th International Conference on The Semantic Web*, ISWC '08, pp. 615–631, Berlin, Heidelberg. Springer-Verlag.

Gabrilovich, Evgeniy and Shaul Markovitch. 2007. Computing Semantic Relatedness using Wikipedia-based Explicit Semantic Analysis. *Proceedings of the 20th International Joint Conference on Artificial Intelligence*, pp. 6–12.

Garoufi, Konstantina, Torsten Zesch, and Iryna Gurevych. 2008. Graph-theoretic analysis of collaborative knowledge bases in natural language processing. In Christian Bizer and Anupam Joshi, eds., *International Semantic Web Conference (Posters & Demos)*.

Girvan, Michelle and Mark E J Newman. 2002. Community Structure in Social and Biological Networks. *Proceedings of the National Academy of Sciences of the United States of America*, 99(12), 7821–7826.

Gurevych, Iryna and Elisabeth Wolf. 2010. Expert-Built and Collaboratively Constructed Lexical Semantic Resources. *Language and Linguistics Compass*, 4(11), 1074–1090.

Heymann, Paul and Hector Garcia-Molina. 2006. Collaborative Creation of Communal Hierarchical Taxonomies in Social Tagging Systems. Technical Report 2006-10, Stanford InfoLab.

Jurgens, David. 2011. Word Sense Induction by Community Detection. In *Proceedings of the 49th Annual Meeting of the Association for Computational Linguistics Human Language Technologies*, pp. 24–28. ACL.

Manning, Christopher D, Prabhakar Raghavan, and Hinrich Schütze. 2008. *Introduction to Information Retrieval*. Cambridge University Press.

Markines, Benjamin, Ciro Cattuto, Filippo Menczer, Dominik Benz, Andreas Hotho, and Stum Gerd. 2009. Evaluating Similarity Measures for Emergent Aemantics of Social Tagging. In *Proceedings of the 18th international conference on World wide web*, WWW '09, pp. 641–650, New York, NY, USA. ACM.

Meyer, Christian M. and Iryna Gurevych. 2010. How web communities analyze human language: Word senses in wiktionary. In *Proceedings of the Second Web Science Conference*, Raleigh, NC, USA.

Schmitz, Patrick. 2006. Inducing Ontology from Flickr tags. In *Proceedings of the Collaborative Web Tagging Workshop at WWW '06*, Edinburgh.

Vander Wal, Thomas. 2004. Folksonomy Coinage and Definition. `http://vanderwal.net/folksonomy.html`.

Wetzker, Robert, Carsten Zimmermann, and Christian Bauckhage. 2008. Analyzing Social Bookmarking Systems: A del.icio.us Cookbook. In *Proceedings of the ECAI 2008 Mining Social Data Workshop*, pp. 26–30. IOS Press.

Yeung, Ching Man Au, Nicholas Gibbins, and Nigel Shadbolt. 2009. Contextualising Tags in Collaborative Tagging Systems. In *20th ACM Conference on Hypertext and Hypermedia*, Torino, Italy. ACM Press.

Zesch, Torsten, Christof Mueller, and Iryna Gurevych. 2008. Extracting lexical semantic knowledge from Wikipedia and Wiktionary. In *Proceedings of the Conference on Language Resources and Evaluation*. (electronic proceedings).

Unsupervised Word Sense Disambiguation Using Neighborhood Knowledge[1]

Huang Heyan[1,2], Yang Zhizhuo[1,2], and Jian Ping[1,2]

[1]Beijing Engineering Applications Research Center of High Volume Language Information Processing and Cloud Computing, Beijing Institute of Technology,
No.5 Yard, Zhong Guan Cun South Street Haidian District,Beijing, 100081,China
[2]Department of Computer Science, Beijing Institute of Technology,
No.5 Yard, Zhong Guan Cun South Street Haidian District,Beijing, 100081,China
{hhy63,10907029,pjian}@bit.edu.cn

Abstract. Usually ambiguous words contained in article appear several times. Almost all existing methods for unsupervised word sense disambiguation make use of information contained only in ambiguous sentence. This paper presents a novel approach by considering neighborhood knowledge. The approach can naturally make full use of the within-sentence relationship from the ambiguous sentence and cross-sentence relationship from the neighborhood knowledge. Experimental results indicate the proposed method can significantly outperform the baseline method.

Keywords: Unsupervised WSD, Neighborhood Knowledge, Similarity Measure, Graph-based Ranking Algorithm.

1. Introduction

Word Sense Disambiguation (WSD), the task of indentifying the intended meaning (sense) of words in context is one of the most important problem in natural language processing. Though it is often characterized as an intermediate task rather than an end in itself, it has the potential to improve the performance of many applications including information retrieval, machine translation and so on.

Existing methods conduct WSD usually using only the information contained in the ambiguous sentence to be disambiguated. They utilize context words within predefined window in sentence together with other syntactic information. It has been proved that expanding context window size around the target ambiguous word can help to enhance the WSD performance.

[1] This work is supported by the National Natural Science Foundation of China under Grant No.61132009, the Cloud Computing for High Volume Language Information Intelligent Processing, the Primary Funds of National Defense ,Open Project Program of National Laboratory of Pattern Recognition ,BIT Fundamental Research Projects No.3070012210917

However, expanding window size unboundedly will bring not only useful information but also some noise which may finally deteriorate the WSD performance. Can we find other way to expand context words without bringing too much noise?

In this study, we proposed to conduct WSD using collaborative techniques. One common assumption of existing methods is that the sentences are independent of each other, and WSD is carried out separately without interactions among the sentences. However, some ambiguous words contained in article appear more than one time, the multiple sentences contain the same ambiguous word within the article actually have mutual influences and contain useful clues which will helpful to deduce word sense from each other. For example, sentence containing *program design* commonly shares similar topic with the sentence containing *computer program*, thus the meaning of the ambiguous words *program* in those two sentences can be deduced from each other. The idea is borrowed from the observation that ambiguous words appear in topic related sentences contained in the same article often share common meanings. Therefore, we can retrieve a small number of sentences containing the ambiguous word from the same article. These neighbor sentences can be used in the disambiguation process and help to disambiguate word sense for the specified sentence.

This study proposes to construct an appropriate knowledge context for unsupervised WSD method by making use of a few neighbor sentences closed to the ambiguous sentence in the article. The framework for WSD consists of the step of neighborhood knowledge building and the step of word sense disambiguation. In particular, the neighborhood knowledge context is obtained by applying the similarity algorithm on the article. The graph-ranking based algorithm is employed to disambiguate word sense in a specified knowledge context. Instead of leveraging only the word relationships in a single sentence, the algorithm can incorporate the relationship in multiple sentences, thus making use of global information existing in the whole article.

Experiments are carried out on dataset and the results confirm the effectiveness of our method. The neighborhood knowledge can significantly improve the performance of single sentence WSD. Furthermore, how the size of the neighborhood influences the WSD performance is also investigated. It has been reported that a small number of neighbor documents are sufficient to elevate the performance.

The rest of paper is organized as follows: Section 2 briefly introduces the related work. The proposed method is described in detail in Section 3, and experimental results are presented in Section 4. Lastly we conclude this paper in Section 5.

2. Related Work

Generally speaking, Word Sense Disambiguation methods are either knowledge-based or corpus-based. In addition, the latter can further be further divided into two kinds: unsupervised ones and supervised ones. In this paper we focus on unsupervised WSD method.

Knowledge-based method disambiguates words by matching context with information from a prescribed knowledge source. These methods include Lesk's algorithm (Lesk, 1986), Walker's algorithm (Walker and Amsler, 1986), Yarowsky's algorithm (Yarowsky, 1992) and so on. Unsupervised methods cluster words into some sets which indicate the same meaning, but they cannot give an exact meaning of the target word, these methods can be categorized into methods based on word clustering (Lin, 1998) and co-occurrence graphs (Widdows and Dorow, 2002).

Supervised method learns form annotated sense examples, the learning algorithms including: SVM (Escudero et al, 2000a), naïve Bayesian learning (Escudero et al, 2000b) and maximum entropy (Tratz et al, 2007). Though corpus-based approach usually has better performance, the mount of words it can disambiguate essentially relies on the size of training corpus, while knowledge-based approach has the advantage of providing larger coverage. Knowledge based methods for word sense disambiguation are usually applicable to all words in the text, while corpus-based techniques usually target only few selected word for which large corpora are available.

More recently, graph-based methods for WSD have gained much attention in the NLP community (Veronis, 2004, Sinha and Mihalcea, 2007, Navigli and Lapata, 2007, Mihalcea, 2005, Agirre E, 2006). The HyperLex (Veronis, 2004) algorithm is entirely corpus-based, which uses small-world properties of co-occurrence graphs. TexRank (Mihalcea, 2005) creates a complete weighted graph formed by the synsets of the words in the input context, and the weight of the edge linking two synsets is calculated by executing Lesk's algorithm. These methods have been proposed to rank word sense based on the "vote" or "recommendations" between each other. When a word sense links to another one, it is basically casting a vote for that word sense. The higher the number of vote that is cast for a sense, the higher the importance of the sense is. Moreover, how important of the word sense is casting the vote determines how important the vote itself is.

All the above WSD methods make use of only information within the ambiguous sentence. It is noteworthy that collaborative techniques have been successfully used in tasks of information filtering (Xue et al., 2005), document summarization (Wan et al., 2007), web mining (Wong et al., 2006) and keyword extraction (wan et al., 2008). To the best of our knowledge, collaborative techniques have been never applied in WSD task. In other words, applying neighbor sentences to improve single sentence WSD has not been investigated yet.

3. Proposed Approach

3.1. Disambiguation Framework

The proposed disambiguation method consists of two steps: neighborhood knowledge building and word sense disambiguation. The first step aims to obtain a few neighbor sentences that topically related to the ambiguous sentence. In the step of word sense disambiguation, the knowledge context expanded by these neighbor sentences is utilized to a better disambiguation of the specified word sense in the ambiguous sentence. The second step can be further divided into two steps: affinity graph building and word sense score computation. First, a global affinity graph G is built based on all sentences related to the ambiguous sentence. The graph will not only reflect the within-sentence relationships (local information) but also the cross-sentence relationships (global information) between words. Then, based on the global affinity graph G, the score of each word sense is computed through the graph-ranking based algorithm. The score calculated here quantifies the importance of the word sense.

The proposed approach first expands knowledge context by finding a few sentences closed to ambiguous sentence, which can provide more knowledge and clues for word sense disambiguation, then an affinity graph is constructed to model both the within-sentence relationships and cross-sentence relationships respectively, finally the saliency score of word sense based on the graph is iteratively computed. Each word gets its saliency score after the algorithm converges and the ambiguous word sense with higher saliency score is chosen to represent the final sense of the ambiguous word.

3.2. Neighborhood Knowledge Building

Usually an ambiguous word occurs in article several times. Which sentences should priority considered to build neighborhood knowledge context? Given an ambiguous sentence, neighborhood knowledge building seeks to select a few nearest neighbors for the sentence from the same article. The neighbor sentences from expanded sentences set can be considered as the expanded knowledge context for the ambiguous sentence.

The performance of neighborhood sentences selection relies on the measurement for sentence similarity evaluation. Given the word collection of a sentence, the semantic similarity between two sentences relies on word's similarity. Distance between words can be computed by either knowledge-based or corpus-based approach. Knowledge-based measure tries to quantify the degree to which two words are semantically related using information drawn from semantic networks. WordNet (Fellbaum, 1998) is a lexical database where each unique meaning of a word is represented by a synonym set. Each synset has a gloss which defines the concept it represents. Synsets are connected to each other through explicit semantic relations that are defined in WordNet. Many graph-based WSD methods have been presented to measure semantic relatedness based on WordNet. Corpus-based methods try to identify the degree of similarity between words using information exclusively derived from large corpora. Such measures as mutual information (Turney 2001) has been proposed to evaluate word semantic similarity based on the co-occurrence information on a large corpus. An advantage of using corpus-based methods is that they reflect the characteristics of the corpus and are potentially better suited for capturing word relation across genres and domains, whereas knowledge-based methods neighbors are corpus-invariant. In this study, we choose the mutual information to compute the semantic similarity between words and as follows:

$$mi(w_k, w_m) = \log \frac{M \times p(w_k, w_m)}{p(w_k) \times p(w_m)} \tag{1}$$

which indicates the degree of statistical dependence between w_k and w_m, Here, M is the total number of words in the corpus and $p(w_k)$ and $p(w_m)$ are respectively the probabilities of the occurrences of w_k and w_m respectively, i.e. $count(w_k)/M$ and $count(w_m)/M$, where $count(w_k)$ and $count(w_m)$ are the frequencies of w_k and w_m. $p(w_k, w_m)$ is the probability of the co-occurrence of w_k and w_m within a window with a predefined size k, i.e. $count(w_m, w_k)/M$, where $count(w_m, w_k)$ is the number of the times w_k and w_m co-occur within the window.

The most popular similarity measure in literature is cosine measure which calculates similarity score though common words between two sentences. However, we notice that ambiguous sentence usually have fewer words than document, and a lot of topic related sentences can barely share same word except some empty words. Therefore, if we use cosine measure to compute similarity between sentences, we cannot differentiate similarity between sentences pairs and thus fall back on a reasonable knowledge context for ambiguous sentence. In this study we proposed to use a new method based on corpus to calculate similarity between sentences, which use mutual information score to record the semantic similarity between words. The formula is as follows:

$$sim(s_i, s_j) = \frac{\sum_{w_k \in s_i} \sum_{w_m \in s_j} mi(w_k, w_m) * tf_{w_k} * isf_{w_k} * tf_{w_m} * isf_{w_m}}{\left\| \vec{s_i} \right\| \times \left\| \vec{s_j} \right\|} \quad (2)$$

where s_i and s_j are the corresponding term vectors of sentences s_i and s_j respectively. The weight associated with term t is calculated with $tf_t * isf_t$, where tf_t is the frequency of term t in the sentence and isf_t is the inverse sentence frequency of term t, i.e. $1 + \log(N / n_t)$, where N is the total number of sentences and n_t is the number of sentences containing term t in a background corpus. w_k and w_m are the corresponding words contained in sentences s_i and s_j respectively. The formula indicates the degree of statistical dependence between sentences s_i and s_j, it will get a large value if the feature words contained in two sentences are strongly related with each other, and vice versa.

In this study, we use corpus-based measure to compute similarity value between the ambiguous sentence s_0 and the sentences in the corpus, and sentences with similarity value exceeding the threshold will be chosen as nearest neighbors for s_0. At last, the expanded sentences set $S = \{s_0, s_1, ..s_{k+1}\}$ is composed by the $k+1$ selected sentences. We will investigate how the size of neighbor sentences k influences the WSD performance in the experiments.

3.3. Word Sense Disambiguation

Affinity graph building: It has been proved that the words within a predefined window around ambiguous word are more effective for disambiguating ambiguous word sense. The words within predefined window around the ambiguous word are chosen as context words. Moreover, because not all words in the document are good indicators for word sense, the words chosen as context words are restricted with syntactic filters, i.e., only the words with a certain part of speech are added. In our experiment, only nouns and verbs are chosen as context words.

Given the expanded sentences set S, let $G = (V, E)$ be an undirected graph reflecting the relationships between words in S. V is the set of vertices and each vertex represents a context word. E is the set of edges, which is a subset of $V \times V$. Each edge in E is associated with an affinity weight between words if their affinity weight exceeds 0. The affinity weight is calculated using formula (1). The links between words in graph G can be categorized into two classes: within-sentence link and cross-sentence link. If both the end words v_i and v_j of a link come from the same sentence, the link is regarded as within-sentence link; otherwise, it is a cross-sentence document link. Actually, the within-sentence link reflects the local information in a sentence, while the cross-sentence link implies the global information in expanded sentences set. In the experiment we will investigate how the combination size of the two types of links between words influence the WSD performance. We use an adjacency matrix $\mathbf{M}$ to describe G with each entry corresponding to the weight of a link in the graph. $\mathbf{M} = (M_{i,j})_{n \times n}$ is defined as following:

$$M_{i,j} = \begin{cases} mi(v_i, v_j), if\,(i \neq j) \\ 0, \text{otherwise} \end{cases} \quad (3)$$

then $\mathbf{M}$ is normalized to make the sum of each row equal to 1. Note that we use the same notation to denote a matrix and its normalized matrix.

Word sense score computation: The computation of important score is based on the following three intuitions: 1) the more neighbors a word sense has, the more important it is; 2) the more important a word sense's neighbor are, the more important it is; 3) the more heavily a word sense is linked with other word senses, the more important it is. Based on the above intuitions, the importance score $ipscore(v_i)$ for word sense v_i can be deduced from those of all other word senses linked with it and further formulated in a recursive form like PageRank (Page et al., 1998) as follows:

$$ipscore(v_i) = (1-d)/n + d * \sum ipscore(v_j) * M_{i,j} \quad (4)$$

where n is the number of vertexes contained in the graph, and d is the dumping factor usually set to 0.85.

We can use the Markov chain model and random reader to formulate the iterative process. In the Markov model, G is treated as the Markov chain, each word as a state and each edge as a transition from one state to another. The random reader continually browses and reads words following the transition matrix $(1-d)\mathbf{e}/n + d\widetilde{\mathbf{M}}$, where e is the vector with all elements equaling to 1. Usually the algorithm will converge after less than 50 times jump. A threshold can be set to control the time of iteration.

4. Experiment

4.1. Experimental Setup

In the experiment, Sogou Chinese collocation relation[2] was used to compute mutual information of words. The collocation corpus involves more than 20 million collocation relations and more than 15000 high-frequency words, which was extracted from over 100 million internet pages on web in October 2006.

To our knowledge, there was no gold standard All-words Chinese word sense disambiguation dataset for evaluation. So we manually annotated an article randomly chosen from internet for evaluation. The article was firstly preprocessed by word segmentation, and then three graduate students were employed to manually label the word sense for each ambiguous word. The extended TongYiCiCiLin[3] was used as the sense inventory. The annotation process last for two days and the annotation conflicts between three annotators were solved by discussion. Finally, the datasets consisted of 76 testing instances for 24 ambiguous words, the average number of meanings for ambiguous word is 2.54, and the average number of sentences for each ambiguous word is 3.16.

Macro-average precision (Liu et al., 2007) was used to evaluate word sense disambiguation performance. Here is the formula: $p_{mar} = \sum_{i=1}^{N} p_i / N, p_i = m_i / n_i$, where N is the number of all ambiguous words, m_i is the time that the ambiguous word is labeled with the correct sense, and n_i is the number of all test instances for this ambiguous word.

2 http://www.sogou.com/labs/dl/r.html

3 It is located at http://ir.hit.edu.cn/.

4.2. Evaluation Results

The proposed approach (i.e. CollaDisam) is compared with the baseline method (i.e. OrigDisam) which only relies on the information of ambiguous sentence and applies graph-based algorithm to rank ambiguous word senses.

Table 1: WSD performance.

	OrigDisam	CollaDisam
Average precision	0.4268	0.4594
Improving Performance (%)	3.26	0

Table 1 gives the comparison results of baseline methods and the proposed CollaDisam (within-sentence window size=1, cross-sentence window size=1) methods when using 2 neighbor sentences. We can see from the figures that CollaDisam obtains improvement over OrigDisam method, which indicates its effectiveness.

In order to investigate how the size of the neighborhood influences the WSD performance, we conduct experiments with different values of the neighbor number k and different values of window size n .Figure 1 shows the performance curves for the CollaDisam method. In the figure, k ranges from 0 to 5. Note that when $k=0$, the CollaDisam method degenerates into baseline OrigDisam method. In the experiment, we set within-sentence and cross-sentence window size the same number n except when $k=0$. For example, the best performance is achieved when set $n=1$ and $k=2$ which means that two words around ambiguous word in three sentences (including one original sentence and two neighbor sentences) will be added to the graph and determine the sense of the ambiguous word.

We can see from the figure that almost all performances of CollaDisam can outperform the baseline OrigDisam method (when $k=0$), no matter how many neighbor sentences are used. We can also observe that the performances of CollaDisam first increase and then tend to be relatively stable, finally decreased with the increase of k . We can notice that very few neighbors will deteriorate the results, because they cannot provide sufficient knowledge. However, it is not necessary to provide too many neighbors due to the computational complexity problem.

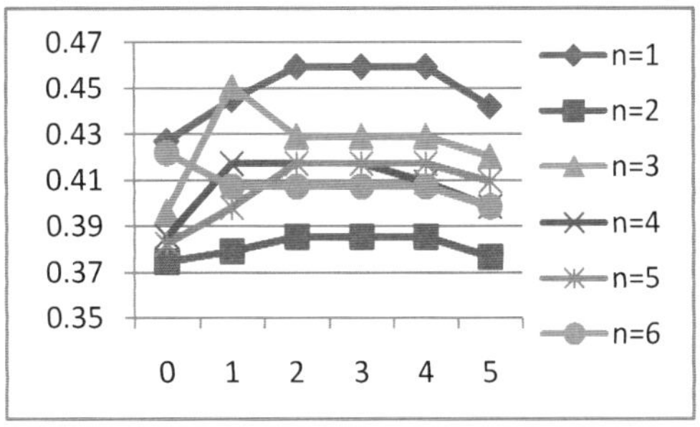

Figure 1: CollaDisam(within-sentence window size= cross-sentence window size) WSD Performance vs. neighbor sentences number

As can be Seen from the figure 1, when k ranges from 2 to 4, the curves tends to be relatively stable, it means that add neighbor sentence into expanded sentences set does not influence the final result, that is partly because some ambiguous words only occur two times in testing article, it seem that all the sentences contain same ambiguous words are useful for determining final sense of ambiguous word and the similarity measure does not play its role, but we argue that similarity measure is extremely important for sentence selection especially for the long article which contain more sentences than short one, since there are some ambiguous word contained in sentence have different meaning compare to other ones, the similarity method can guide us to obtain suitable neighborhood knowledge to improve disambiguation performance.

In order to investigate how the window sizes around the ambiguous word influences WSD performance, we conduct experiment with different values for within-sentence window size $n1$ and cross-sentence window size $n2$. Figure 2 and Figure 3 shows the curves for CollaDisam method with different window sizes. In both figures, window size ranges from 1 to 6 and k represents the different value of neighbor sentences used in experiment. In the experiment, within-sentence window size is fixed at 1 in Figure 2 and cross-sentence window size is fixed at 1 in Figure 3. It can be seen from both figures that almost all curves decline as the window size increasing which means that the context words near ambiguous word have the best disambiguation capacity and enlarging window size will bring noisy information. We can also observe that enlarging neither within-sentence nor cross-sentence window size can improve the WSD performance. The best WSD performance was achieved when both type of window sizes are fixed at 1.

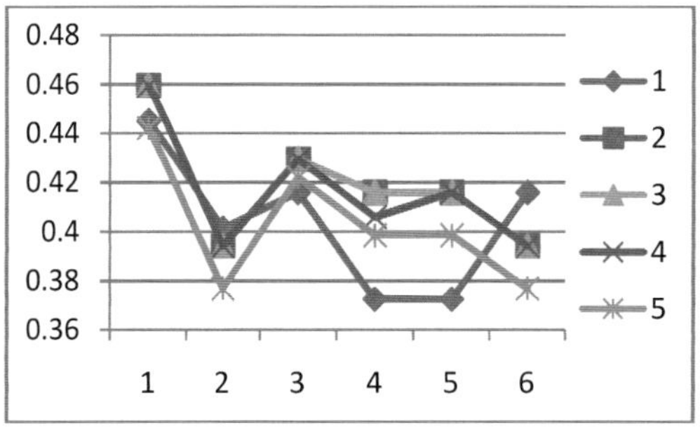

Figure 2: CollaDisam (within-sentence window size=1) WSD Performance vs. cross-sentence window size $n1$

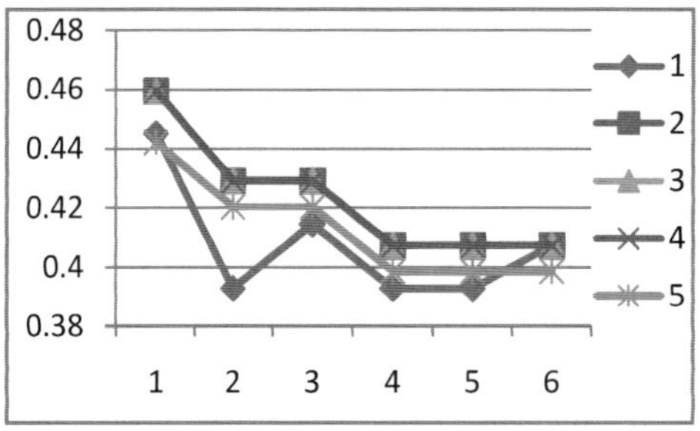

Figure 3: CollaDisam (cross-sentence window size=1) WSD Performance vs. within-sentence window size $n2$

From above experiments, we can draw the conclusion that the two words around ambiguous word have the best disambiguation capability, and the specified words (near ambiguous word) in several similar neighbor sentences is better than the other words (far from ambiguous word) in ambiguous sentence when conducting WSD task. Since the specified words (near ambiguous word in neighbor sentences) would have fewer noisy information than the other words (far from ambiguous word in ambiguous sentence), we can exploit context words in neighbor sentences to improve WSD performance.

5. Conclusion and Future work

In this paper, we proposed a novel approach for unsupervised word sense disambiguation by leveraging neighborhood knowledge of the ambiguous sentence. The within-sentence information and cross-sentence information are incorporated into the graph-based ranking algorithm. The experimental results on dataset demonstrate the good effectiveness of our method.

In current study, we consider sentences in the same article as neighborhood knowledge. Actually the granularity is relatively small. In future work, we will investigate larger granularity including topic and domain, that is to say exploit neighbor sentences in same topic or domain to enhance disambiguation performance, it is very useful for some ambiguous words which appear only one time in small granularity, moreover we will do more experiment in larger dataset to test our method.

References

Michael Lesk. 1986. “Automatic sense disambiguation using machine readable dictionaries: how to tell a pine cone from an ice cream cone”, in Proceedings of the 5th annual international conference on Systems documentation, Toronto, Ontario, Canada, 1986.

Walker D. and Amsler R. 1986. "The Use of Machine Readable Dictionaries in Sublanguage Analysis", in Analyzing Language in Restricted Domains, Grishman and Kittredge (eds), LEA Press, pp. 69-83, 1986.

Yarowsky, David. 1992. "Word sense disambiguation using statistical models of Roget's categories trained on large corpora", in Proceedings of the 14th International Conference on Computational Linguistics (COLING), Nantes, France, 454-460, 1992.

LIN,D. 1998a. Automatic retrieval and clustering of similar words. In Proceedings of the 17th International Conference on Computational linguistics (COLING, Montreal, P.Q., Canada). 768–774.

WIDDOWS, D. AND DOROW, B. 2002. A graph model for unsupervised lexical acquisition. In Proceedings of the 19th International Conference on Computational Linguistics (COLING, Taipei, Taiwan). 1–7.

ESCUDERO, G., M`ARQUEZ, L., AND RIGAU, G. 2000b. Naive Bayes and exemplar-based approaches to word sense disambiguation revisited. In Proceedings of the 14th European Conference on Artificial Intelligence (ECAI, Berlin, Germany). 421–425.

ESCUDERO, G., M`ARQUEZ, L., AND RIGAU, G. 2000. On the portability and tuning of supervised word sense disambiguation. In Proceedings of the Joint SIGDAT Conference on Empirical Methods in Natural Language Processing and Very Large Corpora (EMNLP/VLC, Hong Kong, China). 172–180.

TRATZ, S., SANFILIPPO, A., GREGORY, M., CHAPPELL, A., POSSE, C., AND WHITNEY, P. 2007. PNNL: A supervised maximum entropy approach to word sense disambiguation. In Proceedings of the 4th InternationalWorkshop on Semantic Evaluations (SemEval, Prague, Czech Republic). 264–267.

V´ERONIS, J. 2004. Hyperlex: Lexical cartography for information retrieval. Comput. Speech Lang. 18, 3,223–252.

Page, L., Brin, S., Motwani, R., and wingorad, T., 1998.The pagerank citation ranking: Bringing order to the web Technical report, Stanford Digital Library Technologies Project.

R. Mihalcea. 2005. Unsupervised large-vocabulary word sense disambiguation with graph-based algorithms for sequence data labeling. In Proceedings of HLT05, Morristown, NJ, USA.

R. Navigli and M. Lapata. 2007. Graph connectivity measures for unsupervised word sense disambiguation.In IJCAI.

R. Sinha and R. Mihalcea. 2007. Unsupervised graph based word sense disambiguation using measures of word semantic similarity. In Proceedings of ICSC 2007, Irvine, CA, USA.

Agirre E., Lopez de Lacalle O., Martinez D., Soroa A. 2006 Two graph-based algorithms for state-of-the-art WSD Proceedings of the Conference on Empirical Methods in Natural Language Processing (EMNLP). Pages 585–593.

Xiaojun Wan, Jianguo Xiao: CollabRank: Towards a Collaborative Approach to Single-Document Keyphrase Extraction. COLING 2008: 969-976

Xiaojun Wan, Jianwu Yang: CollabSum: exploiting multiple document clustering for collaborative single document summarizations. SIGIR 2007: 143-150

Wong, T.-L.; Lam, W.; and Chan, S.-K. 2006. Collaborative information extraction and mining from multiple web documents. SDM2006.

Xue, G.-R.; Lin, C.; Yang, Q.; Xi, W.; Zeng, H.-J.; Yu, Y.; and Chen, Z.2005. Scalable collaborative filtering using cluster-based smoothing. SIGIR2005.

C. Fellbaum. 1998. WordNet: An Electronic Lexical Database.The MIT Press.

P. Turney. 2001. Mining the web for synonyms: PMI-IR versus LSA on TOEFL. In Proceedings of ECML-2001.

Liu PY，Zhao TJ，Yang MY. mT-WSD：Using search engine for multilingual Chinese-English lexical sample task. SemEval-2007. Madison：Omni Press，2007. 169-172.

Dependency-based Analysis for Tagalog Sentences *

Erlyn Manguilimotan and Yuji Matsumoto

Graduate School of Information Science
Nara Institute of Science and Technology
8916-5, Takayama, Ikoma, Nara, Japan, 630-0192
{erlyn-m, matsu}@is.naist.jp

Abstract. Interest in dependency parsing increased because of its efficiency to represent languages with flexible word order. Many research have applied dependency-based syntactic analysis to different languages and results vary depending on the nature of the language. Languages with more flexible word order structure tend to have lower performances compared to more fixed word order languages. This work presents, for the first time, a dependency-based parsing for Tagalog language, a free word order language. The parser is tested using manually assigned POS and auto-assigned POS data. Experiment results show an average of about 78% accuracy on unlabeled attachment scores, and about 24% on complete dependency scores. As the position of the sentence head is not fixed, we look into sentence head accuracy as assigned by the parser. Results show that around 83% - 84% of the sentence head are assigned correctly.

Keywords: Dependency parsing, Tagalog, free word order, morphological information

1 Introduction

Morphologically rich languages (MRL) are languages where word-level information affects syntactic relations (Tsarfaty et al., 2010). Recently, MRL have drawn attention in statistical parsing. While state-of-the-art parsers brought high performance scores for languages such as English and Japanese, this is not true for MRLs. Dependency parsing techniques and approaches are developed for languages with relatively fix word orders; however, they are not successful when applied for MRL. In the 2007 CoNLL Shared Task on Dependency parsing, languages such English and Catalan have top scores while languages with free word order and higher degree of inflection have lower scores (e.g. Arabic, Basque)(Nivre et al., 2007). Although factors such as small data can contribute to the degradation of the parser performance, linguistic factors such as morphological inflection and freeness in word order have made it difficult to parse MRL with models and techniques developed with languages like English (Tsarfaty et al., 2010).

In this paper we look into a state-of-art dependency parser applied on Tagalog language. Prior to this work, there is no known data-driven dependency-based parsing for Tagalog. Tagalog is the national language of the Philippines and is a member of the Austronesian language family. It is a morphologically rich language which has affixations, stress shifting, consonant alteration, and reduplication (Nelson, 2004). Affixations include prefixation, infixation, suffixation and circumfixation, where two or three affixes are attached to a root word. Highly inflected verbs show verbal focus *(actor, object, etc.)* and aspect *(perfective, imperfective, and contemplated).*

Aside from its morphological complexity, sentences are word order free. In Tagalog sentences, predicate comes first for pragmatically unmarked clauses but the NP complements take flexible positions in the sentence (Kroeger, 1993). Figure 1 showing possible orders of the complements

* The authors would like to thank the Center for Language Technologies of De La Salle University, Manila, Philippines for allowing us to use the Tagalog POS annotated data used in this work.

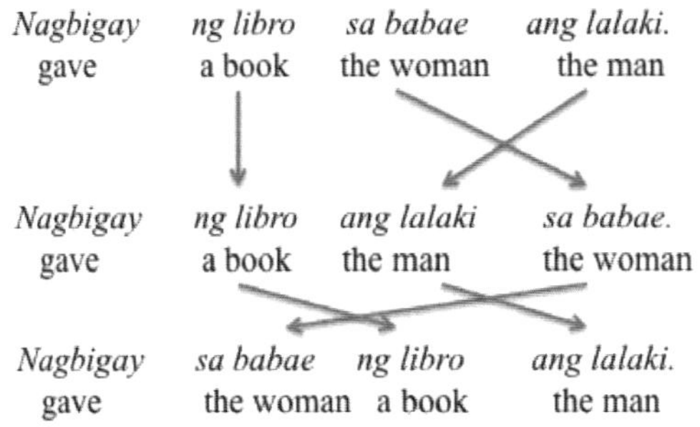

Figure 1: Three (3)of the possible translations of the sentence *"The man gave the woman a book"*

in the Tagalog sentence *"Nagbigay ng libro sa babae ang lalaki"* (The man gave the woman a book). According to Schachter and Otanes (1972) as mentioned in Kroeger (1993), *"the sentences include exactly the same components, are equally grammatical, and are identical in meaning"*. On the other hand, as briefly explained in Section 3, adverbial and nominal phrases may take pre-verbal position.

For Tagalog sentences, dependency-based syntactic parsing is preferred over phrase-structure based analysis because dependency analysis does not rely on word positions(Tsarfaty et al., 2010), instead, sentence representations are based on links between words, called dependencies.

Due to limited resource, this work deals only with unlabeled data. Our corpus are annotated with dependency heads but do not include dependency relations of the word (e.g.NMOD, ROOT). We look into the *unlabeled attachment scores* (UAS), or the number of correct heads, as well as *complete scores*. We also look into the number of sentence heads correctly predicted. The free word order nature of Tagalog may put a verb at the initial position or after a nominal or adverbial element in the sentence.

We briefly introduce dependency parsing in section 2, section 3 briefly explains sentence structures in Tagalog and section 4 discusses the how heads are assigned to words in a sentence. Sections 5 describes the experiment set-up and results. Finally, we discuss some issues found in the parsing results in section 6.

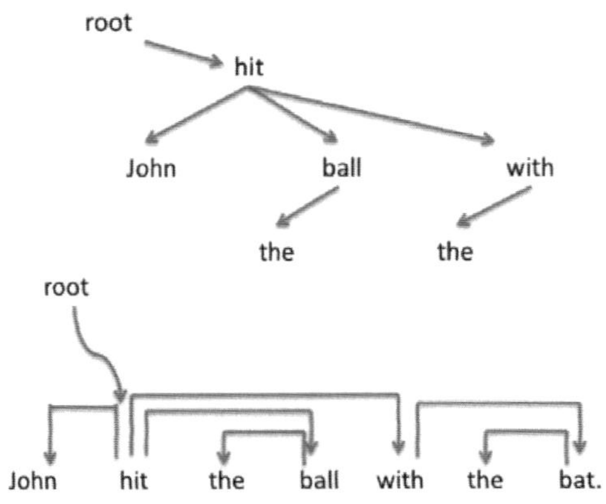

Figure 2: An example of a dependency structure. (Source: McDonald and Pereira, 2006)

2 Dependency Parsing

Dependency analysis creates a link from a word to its dependents. When two words are connected by a dependency relation, one takes the role of the *head* and the other is the *dependent* (Covington, 2001). The straightforwardness of dependency analysis has been used in other NLP tasks such as word alignment (Ma et al., 2008) and semantic role labeling (Hacioglu, 2004). Dependency parsers developed were either graph-based (McDonald and Pereira, 2006) or transition-based parsers (Nivre and Scholz, 2004; Yamada and Matsumoto, 2003). Syntactic analysis for different languages also use dependency parsers such as in Japanese (Kudo and Matsumoto, 2001; Iwatate et al., 2008), English (Nivre and Scholz, 2004), Chinese (Chen et al., 2009; Yu et al., 2008) to mention some.

The task of dependency-based parsing is to construct structure for an input sentence and identify the syntactic head of the word in the sentence(Nivre et al., 2007). Figure 2 shows a sentence with dependency arcs (below) and its equivalent dependency tree structure(top). Each word in the sentence has one syntactic head except for the root or the head of the sentence. Dependency trees can be projective or non-projective. It is projective if no arcs cross over when drawn above the sentence, while it is non-projective when there are edges crossing each other. Non-projective dependency is a result of parsing languages with more flexible word order such as German and Czech(McDonald and Pereira, 2005).

In this work, we applied the graph-based maximum spanning tree(MST) parser of McDonald and Pereira (2006) on Tagalog language. In MST, a sentence as $\boldsymbol{x} = x_1 \cdots x_n$ is represented as a set of vertices $V = v_1 \cdots v_n$ in a weighted directed graph G. A dependency tree y of a sentence is a set of edges (i, j), where $(i, j) \in E$ in the graph G, $E \subseteq [1 : n] \times [1 : n]$ and edge (i, j) exists if there is a dependency from word x_i to word x_j in the sentence. The *maximum spanning tree* of graph G is a rooted tree $y \subseteq E$ that maximizes the score $\sum_{(i,j)\in y} s(i, j)$, where $s(i, j)$ is the score of a dependency tree y. For detailed explanation of MST, please refer to McDonald and Pereira (2006).

3 Tagalog Sentences

3.1 Pre-verbal Position

As shown in Fig. 1, Tagalog NP complements take flexible position in the sentence. However, nominal and adverbial elements may take pre-verbal position (Kroeger, 1993) such as the sentences in Fig. 3.

Itong	*tasa*	*ay*	***binili***	*ko*	*sa pamilihan.*
This=LNK	*cup*	*INV*	*PERF=buy*	*SG.GEN.*	*DAT=market*

I bough this cup at the market.

(a) *ay*-inversion

Itong	*tasa,*	***binili***	*ko*	*sa pamilihan.*
This=LNK	*cup*	*PERF=buy*	*SG.GEN.*	*DAT=market*

This cup, I bought at the market.

(b) Topicalization

Figure 3: Sentences with pre-verbal elements (Source: Kroeger, 1993, p. 123)

3.2 Non-verbal Predicates

In addition to verbs, prepositional, nominal and adjectival phrases take predicate positions in the sentence (Kroeger, 1993) . Figure 4 shows two sentences with non-verbal predicates. Sentence

Bago	*ang mga kotse=ng*	*iyon.*
New	*NOM=PL=car=LNK*	*that.*

Those cars are new.

(a) Predicate Adjective

Opisyal	*sa=hukbo*	*ang panganay.*
Officer	*DAT=army*	*NOM=eldest.*

The eldest child is an officer in the army.

(b) Predicate NP

Figure 4: Examples of sentences with non-verbal predicate (Source: Kroeger, 1993, p. 131)

4a has an adjective *"bago"* (new) as predicate while sentence 4b has the NP *"opisyal sa hukbo"* (officer in the army) as predicate.

Other linguistic explanations of Tagalog structures can be found in (Kroeger, 1993). Nagaya (2007) also explains Tagalog syntax and pragmatics and how they interact in Tagalog clauses.

4 Dependency Heads

From the part-of-speech annotated corpora available, we manually assigned heads to words in the sentences. Deciding *"What heads what?"* may sound simple, however, often it is not. Nivre (2005) discussed some criteria in distinguishing the head and dependent relations. For Tagalog, we applied a *head-complement*, *head-modifier*, *head-specifier* relations principle.

In general, predicate comes before its complements, thus, annotating such sentences is straightforward, such as in Fig. 5 for the sentence *"Bumili ang lalaki ng isda sa tindahan"* (The man bought a fish at the store). The verb *bumili* (bought, actor focus) heads the complements *lalaki*(man), *isda* (fish) and *tindahan* (store) and *ang*, *ng* and *sa* are dependents of the noun they specify. Head-specifier relation refer to the determiner and noun relation.

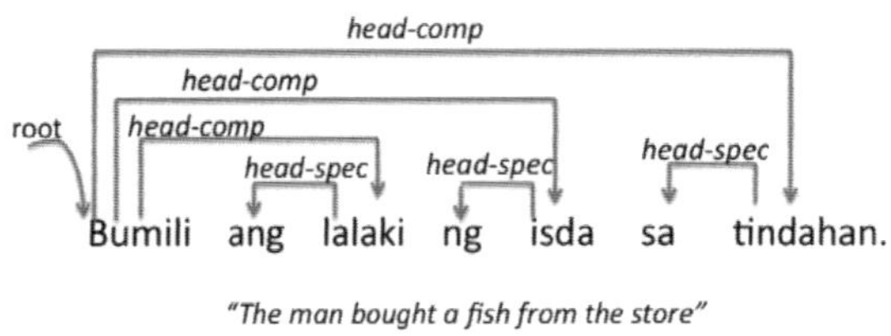

Figure 5: Dependency relations between words in the sentence *"Bumili ang lalaki ng isda sa tindahan"*

4.1 Modifiers

Modifiers may appear in a linear order relative to the modified phrase (noun phrase or verb)(Kroeger, 1993). They are connected with the noun phrase using a linker "na" such as in "mabait *na* bata" (good kid). However, when a modifier ends with a vowel or the letter "N" such as "matalino" (smart) and "antokin" (sleepy), the modifier is suffixed with *-ng* or *-g* (i.e. *"matalinong bata"*(smart kid), *antoking bata*(sleepy child)). The latter case has a more direct annotation, while the former has to be decided which heads linker *"na"*. In this case, since the existence of linker "na" depends on the modifier, we assigned the modifier as the head of the linker. Figures 6a and 6b illustrates these dependencies.

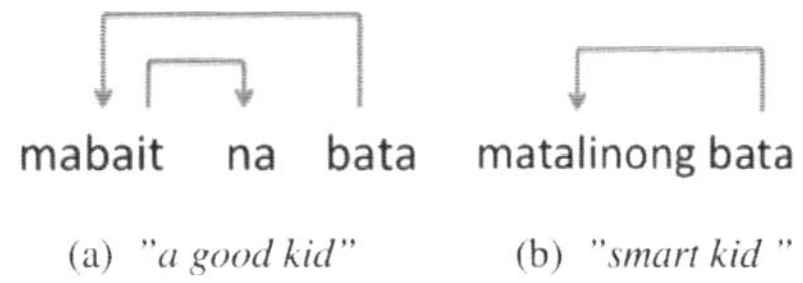

Figure 6: Dependencies for modifiers and nouns

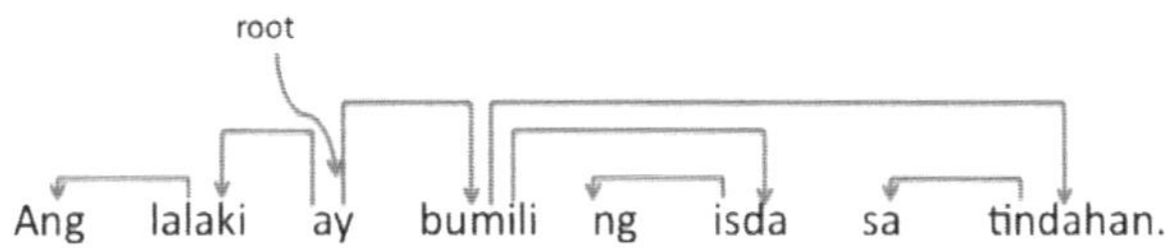

Figure 7: Dependency structure for the sentence with "ay"- inversion

4.2 Sentence Head

In case of a verbal predicate, the head of the VP phrase is the head of the sentence. However, Section 3 explains different positions of verb in a sentence. One pre-verbal position of a sentence is the use of lexeme *ay*. The sentence in Fig. 5 can be written as *"Ang lalaki* ***ay bumili*** *ng isda sa tindahan"* as in Fig. 7. The meaning of the sentence did not change; however, the nominative argument *ang lalaki* is placed before the verb *bumili*(bought). According to Kroeger (1993), *ay* could be treated as a kind of sentence-level auxiliary. In this case, if a sentence is in an *ay*-inversion format, *ay* is assigned as the *head* of the sentence instead of the verb. The nominative argument marked by determiner *ang* becomes a sibling of the verb. Sentences with non-verbal predicates follow the basic head-modifier rule in case it is adjectival or PP predicates, making the head of the modified phrase the head of the sentence.

5 Experiment

5.1 Data

The sentences used in the experiment were extracted from POS annotated Tagalog corpora consisting of novels and short articles. We only chose sentences of lengths L, for $4 \geq L \leq 20$. Longer sentences have tendencies of lower accuracies while shorter sentences tend to perform better (McDonald and Nivre, 2008). A total of 2,741 sentences were used for the experiments. The total number of sentences were then divided into 5 parts for a 5-fold cross validation. Table 1 gives the data distribution in the 5-fold cross validation while Table 2 shows the distribution of the Test and Training data by sentence lengths. Compared to other treebanks, Tagalog data set is relatively small; however, this is the start in building Tagalog Dependency Treebank for future work.

Table 1: 5-fold Cross Validation Data Distribution

Data	Test	Train
1	548	2,192
2	548	2,192
3	548	2,192
4	546	2,194
5	550	2,190

Number of Sentences per Part

Table 2: Test Data Distribution by Length

	Test Data			Train Data		
Data/Lengths	4-10	11-15	16- 20	4-10	11-15	16- 20
1	295	148	105	1,192	569	432
2	297	145	106	1,190	572	430
3	260	159	129	1,227	558	407
4	302	141	103	1,186	576	433
5	333	124	93	1,155	593	443

Table 3: POS Tagging Results

Test Data	POS Accuracy
1	89.09
2	87.18
3	88.84
4	89.37
5	90.46
average	88.96

5.2 Experiment Set-up

5.2.1 POS Tagging. Auto-assigned part-of-speech (POS) tagging is done using a conditional random fields (CRF) based tool CRF++[1]. We used a hierarchical tag set for Tagalog with 88 specific tags derived from 10 word categories (verb, noun, adjective, etc.)[2]. The same data set described in Section 5.1 are used in training and testing the POS tagger. POS tagging result is given in Table 3.

5.2.2 Parsing. We performed dependency parsing using McDonald and Pereira (2006)'s MST Parser. To be able to run the parser with morphological features, we used the CoNLL-X shared task format[3]. The parser is trained with fine-grained and coarse-grained POS tags. Coarse-grained POS, fine-grained POS, word stem (lemma) and morphological features (affixes and reduplication) are used as input to the parser. In our experiments, we used two word related feature settings. First, we run the parser with word stem feature and no morphological features, which we refer as MST 1 in Table 4; then we run the parser using word stem and morphological features (affixes and reduplication) (MST 2 in Table 4). Summary of features for the parser is presented in Table 4. We also run our parsers with *first - order* and *second - order* dependencies. *First-order* dependency scores are limited to single edge dependency while *second-order* dependency takes the score of two adjacent edges. Please refer to McDonald and Pereira (2006) for further explanations on first-order and second-order dependencies.

5.3 Result

The Tagalog parsers are tested using manually assigned POS tags and automatically tagged POS data. The manually assigned data is considered as the gold data in this work. Dependency parsing results are shown in Table 5 for the manually assigned POS tags and Table 6 for the auto-tagged POS. The parser is evaluated using unlabeled attachment score (*UAS*), or the accuracy of the total

[1] CRF++ by Taku Kudo http://crfpp.sourceforge.net/
[2] Unpublished work
[3] CoNLL-X website http://ilk.uvt.nl/conll/

Table 4: Parser Features

**CPOSTAG =coarse-grained POS tag, POSTAG=fine-grained POS tag*

MST1	*word form (or punctuation), lemma (word stem), CPOSTAG, POSTAG*
MST2	*word form (or punctuation), lemma (word stem), CPOSTAG, POSTAG , morphological info (affixes, reduplication)*

Table 5: Test results using manually assigned POS tags

	MST 1				**MST 2**			
Test Data	1st Order		2nd Order		1st Order		2nd Order	
	UAS	Complete	UAS	Complete	UAS	Complete	UAS	Complete
1	0.787	0.253	0.792	0.246	0.788	0.239	0.790	0.239
2	0.785	0.251	0.788	0.261	0.772	0.228	0.775	0.242
3	0.781	0.206	0.783	0.204	0.771	0.201	0.777	0.202
4	0.779	0.222	0.783	0.250	0.779	0.248	0.777	0.231
5	0.755	0.230	0.761	0.246	0.759	0.241	0.755	0.235
Ave	0.777	0.232	**0.781***	**0.241**	0.773	0.231	0.774	0.229

* *at* $\alpha = 0.05$, *MST1 2nd order UAS is significant*

number of correct heads assigned to each word. *Complete* dependency analysis is also computed, or the number of sentences with (all) correct dependencies.

Affixes and reduplication information have helped in deciding the POS tags (Manguilimotan and Matsumoto, 2009), thus we expected the same for parsing. However, this is not the case. In Table 5, results show that 2nd-order MST1 features obtained the highest accuracy in both *UAS* and *complete* scores for manually-tagged data compared to the test results using MST2 features. It is to be noted that MST1 features do not include affix and reduplication information while MST2 has these features as described in Table 4. This may imply that correct POS information have helped choose the head of the word and the use of other morphological information have harmed the performance of the parser. On the other hand, the auto-tagged POS data in Table 6 shows different results. The 2nd-order MST2 has the highest *UAS* but 2nd-order MST1 and 1st-order MST2 has the highest in *complete scores*. The error in POS tagging (about 11%) have affected the parsing results, but the morphological information (MST2) may have helped in choosing the correct head of the word.

Aside from dependency accuracies, we also looked at the sentence head selection accuracy. Here, we only considered correct sentence heads as chosen by the MST parser. Results are presented in Tables 7 and 8. The parser is about 84% accurate in choosing the sentence head for test data with gold POS tags and about 83% for auto-tagged POS. Heads of shorter sentences were mostly chosen correctly by the parser compared to those of longer sentences. Also, sentences with heads in initial positions have mostly predicted correctly than those with pre-verbal elements such as adverbial phrases, except for sentences with lexeme *"ay"* as heads where they were mostly correctly predicted.

Table 6: Test results using auto-assigned part-of-speech tags

	MST 1				MST 2			
Test Data	1st Order		2nd Order		1st Order		2nd Order	
	UAS	Complete	UAS	Complete	UAS	Complete	UAS	Complete
1	0.767	0.213	0.770	0.218	0.767	0.218	0.778	0.211
2	0.756	0.228	0.760	0.233	0.758	0.226	0.756	0.220
3	0.761	0.178	0.761	0.187	0.753	0.187	0.761	0.184
4	0.748	0.217	0.749	0.213	0.759	0.222	0.760	0.215
5	0.733	0.202	0.737	0.219	0.741	0.221	0.740	0.219
Ave	0.753	0.207	0.755	**0.214**	0.756	**0.214**	**0.759***	0.209

* *at $\alpha = 0.05$, MST2 2nd order UAS is NOT significant*

Table 7: Sentence Head Selection Accuracy with Manually Tagged POS

	MST 1		MST 2	
Test Data	1st Order	2nd Order	1st Order	2nd Order
1	85.40	86.50	85.95	86.86
2	82.66	82.30	81.39	80.84
3	84.12	84.12	83.21	83.39
4	81.45	81.27	80.73	80.73
5	88.12	87.93	88.48	88.85
Ave	84.35	84.43	83.95	84.13

6 Discussions

We looked at some words that we believed to have lower chances of ambiguity, for example, determiners (DT) *ang* (the) and *mga* (plural marker for noun) considering that these do not require morphological information. These two function words come together often to indicate plurality, such as in "**ang mga** bata" *(the children)* or "**ang mga** bahay" *(the houses)*. However, when there are modifiers between the determiner *ang* or *ang mga* and the noun, the parser assigned wrong head to the determiners. These cases may be isolated accounting part of the 10% error for determiners in our data; however, this is still observable considering that distances between head and dependent should not be a problem in MST parser.

Word categories that topped the errors in head selection are noun(NN), conjuncts(CC), adjective(JJ) and adverb(RB). For NN, proper nouns such as titles (e.g. "doktor tiburcio" *(doctor tiburcio)*, "kapitan basilio" *(captain basilio)*) or a noun modifying another noun (e.g. "balkonahe=ng kawayan" *(bamboo balcony or balcony made of bamboo)*) are some cases that are found to be inconsistent.

On the other hand, lexeme "ng" is seen as ambiguous since it can function as a genetive marker in "kumain **ng** pan ang bata" *(the child ate bread)*, where "ng" is dependent on "pan/NN" (bread), or as a possessive marker in "ang ina **ng** bata" *(the child's mother)*; in this case, "ng" is dependent on "ina/NN" (mother). In both cases "ng" is headed by a noun. The same is observed with "sa", which can be a dative marker as in sentences in Fig. 3 or as part of an adverbial head phrase such as in "para sa" (*for* – benefactive), "dahil sa" (*because of* – causative).

Although we did not include in Section 5.3, we initially run our parsers with sentence lengths of greater than 30 words. Scores of those experiments are lower than the reported results in this paper. This reiterates that shorter sentences perform better than longer sentences (McDonald and Nivre, 2008). MST parser should not have a problem with distance, however, ambiguities in sentences cannot be helped.

Table 8: Sentence Head Selection Accuracy with Auto-Assigned POS Tags

	MST 1		**MST 2**	
Test Data	1st Order	2nd Order	1st Order	2nd Order
1	86.31	84.85	86.49	85.95
2	78.83	79.56	80.65	79.92
3	85.40	84.12	83.94	83.94
4	80.65	81.38	81.56	81.75
5	86.91	85.27	88.00	88.72
Ave	83.62	83.03	84.12	84.05

7 Summary

This paper introduces the first dependency-based syntactic analysis of Tagalog, a morphologically rich and word order free language. We described the scheme we used in assigning the head of the word. A state-of-the art dependency parser, MST parser, is used in our experiment. Experiments are performed manually assigned POS, which is considered as the gold data, and automatically tagged POS. When gold POS information are used, the parser tends to perform better when there are no morphological information used as features. However, when auto-tagged POS are used, the parser with morphological information has higher accuracy. This may indicate that morphological information helps when POS tagging is not accurate.

Morphological information will be more interesting to examine in labeled dependency analysis, especially verb affixes, because this will determine what kind of relationship does the verb have with its arguments. However, our work only deals with unlabeled dependencies, thus semantic relations of words are not included in our work.

Although dependency parsing is a more fitting framework than phrase-structure analysis in dealing with languages with flexible word order it still does not perform better compared to languages with a more fixed word order. Parsing morphologically complex languages with free word order gives rise to issues on the right data annotation, or what kind of morphological features are to be included in the parser(Tsarfaty et al., 2010).

The parsing results for Tagalog is still not high enough compared to other languages. Whether the factors of dependency parsing for Tagalog is the small sized data or the inadequacy of features, we still have to know. As our future work, we aim to increase the size of the Tagalog dependency treebank we have started. And since our current work deals only with unlabeled data, the next step is to run parser with labeled dependency relations and see which morphological features best solve issues in Tagalog dependency parsing.

References

Bonus, D.E. 2003. *The Tagalog Stemming Algorithms (TagSA).* In the Proceedings of the Natural Language Processing Research Symposium, DLSU, Manila.

Chen, W., D. Kawahara, K. Uchimoto, Y.Zhang, and H. Isahara. 2009. *Using Short Dependency Relations from Auto-Parsed Data for Chinese Dependency Parsing.* ACM Transactions on Asian Language Information Processing (TALIP), volume 8 issue 3.

Covington, M. 2001. *A Fundamental Algorithm for Dependency Parsing.* In Proceedings of the 39th Annual ACM Southeast Conference, pp. 95-102.

Iwatate, M., M. Asahara, and Y. Matsumoto. 2008. *Japanese Dependency Parsing Using a Tournament Model.* In Proceedings of the 22nd International Conference on Computational Linguistics (Coling 2008), pp. 361-368.

Hacioglu, K. 2004. *Semantic Role Labeling Using Dependency Trees* In Proceedings of the 20th International Conference on Compurational Linguistics.

Kroeger, P. 1993. *Phrase Structure and Grammatical Relations in Tagalog.* Center for the Study of Language and Information, Stanford California.

Kudo, T. and Yuji Matsumoto. 2002. *Japanese Dependency Analysis using Cascaded Chunking* In Proceedings of the Conference on Computational Natural Language Learning (CoNLL-2002).

Ma, Y., S. Ozdowska, Y. Sun, and A.Way. 2008. *Improving Word Alignment Using Syntactic Dependencies.* In Proceedings of the Second ACL Workshop on Syntax and Structure in Statistical Translation (SSST-2), pp. 69-77.

Manguilimotan, E. and Matsumoto, Y. 2009. Factors Affecting POS Tagging for Tagalog. *In the Proceedings of the 23rd Pacific Asia Conference on Language, Information and Computation,* pp. 803-810 (2009).

McDonald, R. and F. Pereira. 2005. *Non-projective Dependency Parsing using Spanning Tree Algorithms.* In the Proceedings of Human Language Technology and Empirical Methods in Natural Language Processing(HLT-EMNLP), pp. 523-530.

McDonald, R. and F. Pereira. 2006. *Online Learning of Approximate Dependency Parsing Algorithms.* In the Proceedings of the European Chapter of the Association for Computational Linguistics (EACL).

McDonald, R. and J. Nivre. 2008. Integrating Graph-based and Transition-based Dependency Parsers. *Association for Computational Linguistics (ACL).*

Miguel, D. and Roxas, R.E.. 2007. *Comparative Evaluation of Tagalog Part-of-Speech Taggers.* In the Proceedings of the Proceedings of the 4th National Natural Language Processing.

Nagaya, N. 2007. *Information Structure and Constituent Order in Tagalog.* Language and Linguistics 8.1:343-372, 2007.

Nelson, H. 2004. *A Two-Level Engine for Tagalog Morphology and a Structured XML Output for PC-KIMMO.* Available : [Online: http://contentdm.lib.byu.edu/ETD/image/etd465.pdf] .

Nivre, J. and M. Scholz. 2004. *Deterministic Dependency Parsing of English Text* In Proceedings of the 20th International Conference on Compurational Linguistics.

Nivre, J. 2005. *Dependency Grammar and Dependency Parsing.* MSI report 05133 MSI report 05133. VŁxj University: School of Mathematics and Systems Engineering.

Nivre, J., J. Hall, S. Kubler, R. McDonald, J. Nilsson, S. Riedel, and D. Yuret. 2007. *The CoNLL 2007 Shared Task on Dependency Parsing.* Proceedings of the CoNLL Shared Task Session on EMNLP-CoNLL 2007, pp 915-932.

Schachter, P. and F. Otanes. 1972. Tagalog Reference Grammar. *University of California Press.*

Tsarfaty, R., et al. 2010. Statistical Parsing of Morphologically Rich Languages (SPMRL) What, How and Whither. *In Proceedings of the NAACL HLT 2010 First Workshop on Statistical Parsing of Morphologically Rich Languages*, pp. 1-12.

Yamada, H. and Y. Matsumoto. 2003. *Statistical Dependency Analysis with Support Vector Machines.* In Proceedings of 8th International Workshop on Parsing Technologies, pp. 195-206.

Yu, K., D. Kawahara, and S. Kurohashi. 2008. *Chinese Dependency Parsing with Large Scale Automatically Constructed Case Structures.* In the Proceedings of the 22nd International Conference on Computational Linguistics (Coling 2008), pp. 1049-1056.

Case study of BushBank concept

Marek Grác

Faculty of Informatics
Masaryk University
Czech Republic

Abstract. In this paper, we present a new type of annotated corpus, called BushBank, which improves handling of ambiguity in natural language. Unlike in traditional approaches where data are directly disambiguated, in a BushBank, disambiguation is done later, based on application needs. This has major impact on the structures used in the corpus, since ordinary syntactic trees disallow ambiguity. Our approach was tested on 10.000 sentences and more than a hundred annotators when creating Czech BushBank. The paper contains information about creating such a resource and the methods used to obtain high inter-annotator agreement.

Processing natural language is one of those areas where the quality and the quantity of lexical resources distinguish a great project from an inferior one. Lexical resources for major languages tend to address both these requirements, but the situation for smaller languages varies a lot. Thanks to various projects like WebBootCat [1], it is possible to build large corpora from documents available on the internet. Unfortunately this approach can't help us in the process of building high-quality annotated corpora. The most noticeable examples of annotated corpora are the PENN Treebank [11] and PDT [7]. Sentences in these corpora are parsed, i.e. annotated with (at least) syntactic structures. These structures are offered to users in the form of syntactic trees and they are unambiguous. In order to obtain high quality, unambiguous annotation of natural language (which is ambiguous on every level), skilled annotators and hundreds of pages of manuals [8] are needed. Building such complex lexical resources is out of reach for most of the less-used languages.

This paper focuses on a new type of annotated corpus named BushBank and an example study performed on Czech language that belongs to the Slavic languages together with Russian or Polish. Slavic languages tend to very good for such experiments as they have rich morphology and fairly free word order. Czech language is one of the most described European languages and there are already several high quality resources like Prague Dependency Treebank [7] or a Czech version of EuroWordNet [13]. This gives us a reference to compare our results to.

1 General overview of BushBank

Language resource, from our experience, tend to focus on complex and clear description of a language. Such description is extremely useful for language research and theory observation, but its usage in NLP applications is limited. Bushbank (derived from TreeBank) was created to fulfill those needs and is almost purely application-driven. We are aware that different applications have different needs and thus several levels of annotation are needed. Various levels of annotation are already used in other language resources. The main difference is that ambiguity in annotations is not resolved on the corpus level, but we offer tools to obtain *correct* annotations based on different needs for the quality/quantity ratio of the data.

1.1 Annotation principles

Annotation of linguistic data is considered to be an expert task. This is especially true for those corpora that attempt to cover several layers of a language. Extensive training for annotators is required, together with an exhaustive annotation manual (annotation layer for syntactic level of PDT2.0 spans 301 pages). Our funding situation and the lack of trained annotators did not allow us to use any of the existing heavy-weight approaches.

We had to find a more light-weight approach that will be affordable even for smaller budget and less-widely-used languages. Inspired by existing projects, we decided to replace experts by untrained annotators. These techniques, called crowdsourcing, are widely used on the internet (e.g. Wikipedia) and we have observed use of these approaches for partial linguistic annotation [12]. However we are not aware of any attempts to build annotated corpora entirely via crowdsourcing.

In order to be able to use crowdsourcing we need access to a crowd that exceeds critical mass. This may be a problem even for large languages, but for these it is possible to use paid services, lika Amazon Mechanical Turk. For smaller languages (e.g. Czech - 10 million speakers), we are unable to target a suitable crowd even when using such paid services, since these simply do not exist. These constraints lead us to the decision to target students who were taking courses related to NLP. Our annotators were mostly in their first year at the university, they have very limited amount of deeper linguistic knowledge and no previous experience with annotation. We believed that their interest in the topic of NLP should provide better results compared to a *general* crowd. Students should complete their projects in 10-20 hours, meaning that extensive manuals had to replaced by much simpler rules, which can't cover less frequent or borderline cases in any way other than the intuitive one.

We assume that an annotation standard is usually an attempt to approximate several mutually exclusive and contradictory constrains [9]:

1. **completness**: the annotation should provide complete linguistic insight into the particular area

2. **consistency**: the annoation should be consistent, i.e. same or similar language phenomena should be handled in same or similar ways
3. **usability**: the annotation should enable straightforward usage in the intended application
4. **simplicity**: the annotation should be as simple as possible to make high inter-annotator agreement achievable.

In our experience, most language resources try to find a trade-off among the constrains by prioritizing them in order given above. They prefer completness over consistency and both of them over simplicity. Following the so-called KISS principle, we are strongly convinced that the reverse order of those constrains represents a much better priority list. Thus our priorities are:

1. **simplicity**: so that annotators do not err too often and can rely on their introspection for simple cases
2. **usability**: annotated data have to be easily applied to other NLP applications
3. **consistency**: if annotators do not err and rules are simple, consistency follows
4. **completness**: it will be nice but we do not rely on it

Main objection against this new order of priorities can be that consistency is crucial in most NLP applications. This applies to using the data both for testing/development and for machine learning. From our perspective, natural language is too ambiguous and flexible to be easily and consistenly annotated. In real world, even with trained annotators and exhaustive annotation manuals, we have to face situations where annotators encounter the possibility of using more than one correct annotation. We do not attempt to force selection of one preferred annotation, but face the fact that preferred solution is intuitively different per annotator. Inconsistencies between annotators are traditionally resolved by an expert who decides which annotation is correct [14]. Such qualified opinion improves consistency of annotations. Our approach to building corpora does not believe in experts and border-line cases have to be selected by the annotator according to their introspection and intuition. Inconsistencies between annotators are not handled directly in the corpus, but in an external framework where the user, on a per-application basis, selects the proper resolution model that gives him the desired results. For some applications, it is optimal to use all results that are confirmed by 5 out of 7 annotators, but for other purposes we want 100% agreement. We offer all annotations with the corpus, which makes it easy to create a new resolution model based on our unique requirements. The fact that we do not offer ultimate correct annotation leads to an impossibility of *completness* for non-trivial cases. To obtain completness we will have to offer annotators superset of all valid answers what is not possible with automatic tools and obtain perfect inter-annotator agreement. Therefore, the last position that completeness occupies on the priority list is in fact a necessity.

Simplicity as a top priority is, on the other hand, necessitated by the fact that our annotators do not have enough time for training and that they will annotate for only a few hours. Their ability to understand their task is crucial to success of our project. In order to obtain high quality and high speed of annotation, we have decided to constrain the annotators as much as possible, even if completness will be hurt (we expect that to happen anyway). Annotators can only select the correct answer from a list, which is generated by existing automated NLP tools. This means that there is no way for the annotator to add a correct answer if it is missing. In our existing work, the annotators had to choose among two (valid/invalid noun phrase), or among up several answers (select verb to which the noun phrase relates). Limiting creativity and working with pre-processed data helps us to speed up the process, to increase inter-annotator agreement and (therefore) also to increase consistency.

1.2 Annotation manual

The lack of time for exhaustive training of annotators has to be supplemented by an annotation manual. We have developed and tested manuals for two tasks. The first one is the identification of syntactic elements (short noun phrases, coordinations, verb phrases and clauses) and the second is creating dependencies between noun phrases and their parent elements. In our case study, manual for identification of syntactic elements was at first based on just first two hundred sentences and it contained 21 rules and 13 examples. It is clear that a manual of this size does not even try to describe what a noun phrase is. Instead, it just describes some of the most common borderline cases where annotators are not sure about the correct answer. After a year of development and more than a hundred annotators, we ended up with a manual consisting of 48 rules (most of them are defined by a single clause) and 70 examples.

The second annotation manual should help annotators to find dependencies between identified valid noun phrases and their parents elements. This task is much more ambiguous than the previous one but we have found that most of the cases can be solved by annotator introspection and we do not have to define exact rules for them. First version of the manual contained just 6 rules and the current one contains 8. In our view, examples are at least as important as the rules themselves.

1.3 Corpus structure

BushBank is a concept that extends TreeBanks, which are sets of annotated syntactic trees, by reducing the requirements for unambiguity and making them closer to real language. Like other modern corpora, bushbank usually covers several layers of lingusitic annotation. For this reason, we have decided to use NXT NITE [3], which was developed for multimodal corpora. We do not plan to have a multimodal corpus, but using existing libraries for complex search queries and the XML format persuaded us. On top of this toolkit, we have built our own library which maps elements in the corpus to objects, so that programmers do not need to care about the internal NXT NITE structures or about XML elements.

One of our main objections against existing annotated corpora is the fact that they treat language as an unambigious structure and possible ambiguities are solved by the annotation manual or by expert decision. This leads to a situation when corpora users are not able to determine whether they are handling cases that were easy to determine or cases where even human annotators were not really sure. For various NLP applications, it is crucial to know whether the application can handle correctly at least the clear cases and only later focus on areas which are hard even for humans.

Ambiguity in a bushbank is one of its main advantages. In fact, only the first layer has to be disambiguated. This layer contains marks for sentences and a token for every word in the corpus. We are aware that even on this layer, it is possible to have ambiguities but both simplicity and usability will be corrupted if we introduce ambiguity at this level. Currently for the Czech BushBank (as first case-study of bushbank concept) we have the following layers:

1. **tokens**: contains tokens and marks for begin/end of sentence.
2. **morphology**: defines lemma and morphologic tag for tokens.
3. **syntactic structures**: defines short noun phrases, verb phrases, coordination and clauses. This structures uses the token layer.
4. **relations between syntactic structures**: for every short noun phrase we define its dependency parent.

We believe that corpus users should be able to select proper resolution model for their needs and thus they should have access to the existing annotation also in the form of raw data. All our results are easily reproducible and can be reproduced by anyone interested in doing so. To showcase the importance of access to raw data and deducing *correct answer* on the application level, we would like to present two existing applications. The first one uses the Czech BushBank as a test suite for the rule based syntactic analyser SET [10], where we want to determine its success only on those syntactic structures and their relations which are identified correctly by all (number vary from 3 to 7) annotators, as the cases where human annotators differ in opinion are the difficult cases and can be handled after the simpler part is done. The other is the project Shallow Ontology based on Valency Frames [6], where semantic network is created manually from candidates obtained by mapping noun phrases to possible semantic roles. In this case, we are interested in the semantic head of a noun phrase and as the annotator has no access to the context of the noun phrase, we do not care whether the noun phrase is a longest correct one or not (eg. the blue little rabbit and little rabbit belongs to same semantic group).

2 Obtaining high inter-annotator agreement

One of the main features of an annotated corpus is the quality and thus reliability of its data. In the previous section, we have shown that it is possible to choose a tradeoff between quality and quantity on an application level. However, we still plan to obtain data as good as possible (given the constraints of time, experience and training). To prove our theory in practice, we have created a case study. In this study, we have built the Czech BushBank, which contains 10.000 sentences annotated by more than one hundred annotators and where each sentence is annotated at least three times. The experiment was divided into several stages and we tried to make the conditions the same for every person during any given stage. Experience from previous stages was incorporated into later ones, usually in form of an upgraded annotation manual.

Using unskilled annotators makes interpretation of the results even more difficult than when working with classical models. We really can't (and don't want) to say which answer is correct but we wish to know that this answer is really preferred by annotators and it is not just a random coincidence. This can be a major problem when dealing with identification of syntactic elements as annotator answers are just yes/no. In our case, if we expect to have 80% of the pre-processed data correct, then if two annotators will select answers randomly (and ratio of valid/invalid answers remains) then they can obtain $0.8 * 0.8 + 0.2 * 0.2 = 64.04\%$ agreement. These reasons lead us to use a more standard solution for computing the inter-annotator agreement.

Problems of agreement by chance are especially pertinent when we are using Cohen's kappa [4] to measure inter-annotator agreement. This coefficient takes into account the number of possible answers and frequency of their usage. Cohen's kappa can be applied to evaluate agreement between two or more annotators. For illustration purposes, we have decided to compute it only for pairs of annotators as these are the numbers that are usually published and can therefore be compared readily. Interpreting the obtained numbers can be difficult for those who are unfamiliar with Cohen's kappa. For this reason, several benchmark scales were developed (table 1 presents most used metrics).

Table 1. Example of Benchmark Scales for Cohen's Kappa

Landis and Koch		Fleiss	
Kappa Statistics	Strength of Agreement	Kappa Statistics	Strength of Agreement
< 0.0	Poor		
0.0 to 0.20	Slight		
0.21 to 0.40	Fair	< 0.40	Poor
0.41 to 0.61	Moderate		
0.61 to 0.80	Substantial	0.40 to 0.75	Intermediate to Good
0.81 to 1.00	Almost Perfect	0.76 to 1.00	Excellent

Since we have no gold standard, we have to compare the quality of annotation just between the annotators themselves. If the inter-annotator agreement is high, we can assume that the annotators are able to work consistently and according to the annotation manual and their linguistic knowledge. If agreement is low then the whole data set is unreliable and our resolutions model won't help us.

The threshold of acceptability varies among authors, but the general consensus seems to be that Cohen's kappa over 0.67 is reliable enough ([2], [5].

For the sake of simplicity, we will focus just on identification of syntactic elements in the first and the last stage of our project. In the first stage, the annotators had a simple annotation manual based on annotations of two hundred sentences. All of these sentences were annotated with a rule-based syntactic analyser, making the ratio between valid and invalid elements fairly high. Cohen's kappa obtained in this stage was on average on the border of acceptability. In table 2 we can see the worst, one of the average and the best results of annotation. In the worst case the annotator did not understand the concept of verb phrases and there were 3 – 5 times as many errors as usually. Although these data are not reliable enough when used directly adding a third annotator helps us to make these results reliable enough for practical application. But we do need 50% more annotators and the price of an annotated sentence has raised considerably.

Table 2. Annotatition results 1st stage

valid by annotator A/B	invalid by annotator A/B	agreement	cohen kappa	max kappa
2377/2604	975/793	79.04%	0.50	0.85
3009/2669	326/685	88.43%	0.66	0.81
2473/2431	678/713	92.68%	0.76	0.96

In the last stage of our case study, annotators had access to an annotation manual which was more detailed and mainly consisted of more examples and also the graphical interface was optimized to suit their needs better. The rules in the manual were just described in more detail and in the case of *easy* to identify elements there were no changes relative to previous annotations. Additionaly an output from three more syntactic grammars was added, so they had to identify more elements and ratio between valid/invalid has lowered, since many of the correct elements were found multiple times but the errors produced by different grammars were mostly disjoint.

Results of the last stage are presented in table 3. In this case, we did not detect any noticeably bad or great annotations. For that roason, we have decided to show a table containing three annotators working on the same data set. The consistency between those is on high level and easily exceed an acceptability treshold of 0.67.

3 Conclusions

In this paper, we have presented a new type of corpus, BushBank, that attempts to cover ambiguity in a natural language more precisely. We have described the

Table 3. Annotatition results 3rd stage

annotators	agreement	cohen kappa	max kappa
D vs M	0.91	0.77	0.92
D vs P	0.94	0.85	0.99
M vs P	0.90	0.77	0.92

basic ideas and the structure of such corpora, together with our experience on applying this theory. As a case study, we have presented Czech BushBank that contains 10.000 sentences and which was built entirely through the presented techniques. We have shown that even with a small annotation guide and annotators without proper training, it is possible to obtain high inter-annotator agreement and create high-quality data.

The infrastructure for building this type of annotation corpus is freely available at `http://www.bushbank.org` and we will gladly help with creation of a similar resource for other languages. We believe that this can help even smaller languages in obtaining valuable linguistic resources, using a very low-cost approach.

Acknowledgments

This work has been partly supported by the Ministry of Education of CR within the Center of basic research LC536 and by the Czech Science Foundation under the project P401/10/0792.

References

1. M. Baroni, A. Kilgarriff, J. Pomikálek, and P. Rychlý. Webbootcat: instant domain-specific corpora to support human translators. In *Proceedings of EAMT*, pages 247–252. Citeseer, 2006.
2. J. Carletta. Assessing agreement on classification tasks: the kappa statistic. *Computational linguistics*, 22(2):249–254, 1996.
3. J. Carletta, S. Evert, U. Heid, and J. Kilgour. The nite xml toolkit: data model and query language. *Language resources and evaluation*, 39(4):313–334, 2005.
4. Jacob Cohen. A coefficient of agreement for nominal scales. In *Educational and Psychological Measurement*, volume 20, pages 37–46, 1960.
5. B.D. Eugenio and M. Glass. The kappa statistic: A second look. *Computational linguistics*, 30(1):95–101, 2004.
6. M. Grác. Shallow ontology based on verbalex. In *Slovko 2009*, page 114, 2009.
7. J. Hajič. Complex Corpus Annotation: The Prague Dependency Treebank. Bratislava, Slovakia, 2004. Jazykovedný ústav Ľ. Štúra, SAV.
8. J. Hajič, J. Panevová, E. Buráňová, Z. Urešová, J. Štěpánek, P. Pajas, and J. Kárník. Anotace na analytické rovině – Návod pro anotátory, 2005.

9. Miloš Jakubíček, Vojta Kovář, and Marek Grác. Through low-cost annotation to reliable parsing evaluation. In *PACLIC 24 Proceedings of the 24th Pacific Asia Conference on Language, Information and Computation*, 2010.
10. V. Kovář, A. Horák, and M. Jakubíček. Syntactic analysis as pattern matching: The SET parsing system. In *Proceedings of the 4th Language & Technology Conference*, pages 100–104, Poznań, Poland, 2009.
11. M.P. Marcus, M.A. Marcinkiewicz, and B. Santorini. Building a large annotated corpus of english: The penn treebank. *Computational linguistics*, 19(2):313–330, 1993.
12. Robert Munro, Steven Bethard, Victor Kuperman, Vicky Tzuyin Lai, Robin Melnick, Christopher Potts, Tyler Schnoebelen, and Harry Tily. Crowdsourcing and language studies: the new generation of linguistic data. In *Proceedings of the NAACL HLT 2010 Workshop on Creating Speech and Language Data with Amazon's Mechanical Turk*, CSLDAMT '10, pages 122–130, Stroudsburg, PA, USA, 2010. Association for Computational Linguistics.
13. K. Pala and P. Smrž. Building Czech WordNet. *Romanian Journal of Information Science and Technology*, 7(2-3):79–88, 2004.
14. B. Snyder and M. Palmer. The english all-words task. In *Senseval-3: Third International Workshop on the Evaluation of Systems for the Semantic Analysis of Text*, pages 41–43, 2004.

Building and Annotating the Linguistically Diverse NTU-MC (NTU– Multilingual Corpus)*

Liling Tan and Francis Bond

Division of Linguistics and Multilingual Studies, Nanyang Technological University, 14 Nanyang Drive, Singapore, 637332, Singapore
alvations@gmail.com, bond@ieee.org

Abstract. The NTU-MC compilation taps on the linguistic diversity of multilingual texts available within Singapore. The current version of NTU-MC contains 375,000 words (15,000 sentences) in 6 languages (English, Chinese, Japanese, Korean, Indonesian and Vietnamese) from 6 language families (Indo-European, Sino-Tibetan, Japonic, Korean as a language isolate, Austronesian and Austro-Asiatic). The NTU-MC is annotated with a layer of monolingual annotation (POS tags) and cross-lingual annotation (sentence-level alignments). The diverse language data and cross-lingual annotations provide valuable information on linguistic diversity for traditional linguistic research as well as natural language processing tasks. This paper describes the corpus compilation process with the evaluation of the monolingual and cross-lingual annotations of the corpus data. The corpus is available under the Creative Commons – Attribute 3.0 Unported license (CC by).

Keywords: Multilingual, Corpus, Parallel text

1 Introduction

"The rapidly growing gap between the demand for high-quality multilingual content and the lag in the supply of language professionals is driving the requirement for technology that can dramatically improve translation turnaround time while maintaining exceptionally high output quality" (McCallum, 2011). Cross-lingual training using parallel corpora has been gaining popularity in NLP application tasks such as word sense disambiguation (e.g. Sarrafzadeh et al. 2011; Saravanan et al. 2010; Mitamura et al. 2007), information retrieval and question-answering. In addition, parallel corpora are valuable resources for advancing linguistic annotations morphologically, syntactically and semantically (e.g. Snyder and Barzilay; 2008, Hwa et al. 2005; Resnik, 2004).

The essential knowledge resource in building these language technologies are grounded on parallel corpora. The present pool of resources holds a sizable amount of European parallel corpora (e.g. Ralf et al. 2006; Erjavec, 2004), an increasing interest in building Asian languages-English bitexts (e.g. Xiao, 2004) but only a handful of parallel Asian language corpora (e.g. Zhang, 2005).

To fill the lack of parallel corpora of Asian languages, the NTU–Multilingual Corpus (NTU-MC) taps on the array of multilingual texts available in Singapore; ranging from the multilingual sign boards with official languages of Singapore (English, Chinese, Malay, Tamil) to posters, signs and guides targeted towards migrants, expats and tourists (in Indonesian, Japanese, Korean, Vietnamese, Thai, Tagalog, etc.). Singapore's multicultural and multilingual

* The authors of this paper thank Ms Joan Lee, New Media Manager of the Singapore Tourist Board, for granting permission to use and redistribute text from their multilingual websites (www.yoursingapore.com.sg). This research was partially funded by a joint JSPS/NTU grant on *Revealing Meaning through Multiple Languages.*

society has necessitated the use of parallel text for signboards, public announcements and information dissemination. The NTU-MC presents multilingual data from a modern cosmopolitan city where people interact in different languages. Empirically, the NTU-MC represents unique societal linguistic diversity; computationally, the NTU-MC provides diverse parallel text for NLP tasks. The NTU-MC presents a wealth of data to inform our analysis of language in a modern multicultural city from the traditional and computational linguistic point of view. This paper discusses the compilation of the NTU-MC from data collection to the present state of POS tagged and sentence-aligned parallel texts.

The rest of the paper is structured as follows: Section 2 describes the sub-tasks in the corpus compilation, the monolingual annotation and cross-lingual annotation process; Section 3 present the NTU-MC outputs and evaluates the layers of annotations; Section 4 presents future work on the NTU-MC and Section 5 concludes.

2 Corpus Construction

The NTU Multilingual Corpus adopts an opportunistic data collection approach and it is representative of the linguistically diverse data available within the Singapore language habitus. Currently, the corpus data contains the tourism domain of Singapore where multiple foreign languages are used on Singapore Tourism Board's website to entreat the tourism from the countries that speaks the respective languages. The NTU-MC is built on a Linux operating system with UTF-8 as the standardized encoding for its outputs.

2.1 Data Collection

The corpus project was granted the permission to use the websites[1] that are published by Singapore Tourism Board (STB). In the initial phase we have built a corpus totaling 375,000 words (15,000 sentences) in 6 languages (English, Chinese, Japanese, Korean, Indonesian and Vietnamese), from 6 language family trees[2] (Indo-European, Sino-Tibetan, Japonic, Korean as a language isolate, Austronesian and Austro-Asiatic) based on texts from the Singapore Tourism Board's *www.yoursingapore.com* website.

2.2 Crawling and Cleaning

`Httrack` (Roche, 2007) was used for data-collection and it was completed with a single command `httrack http://www.yoursingapore.com -o +*.yoursingapore.com/content/traveller/*/*.html -p1` .The raw HyperText Markup Language (HTML) files were downloaded without the embedded media files (e.g. images, flash files, embedded videos, etc.) from the webpages. As the markup language used to construct the websites were consistent, a custom-made perl script was created to extract the main body paragraph instead of using the commonly used Condition Random Field (CRF) algorithm (Marek et al. 2007). The markup cleaning extracted the text bounded by `<p>...</p>` within the `<div class = paragraph section>...</div>` attributes. The perl script successfully extracted the main body text from each webpage and ignored the subtexts that were headers to other pages.

During the annotation tasks, non-break spaces (`0xa0`) were found in the extracted text. These caused errors in POS tagging and sentence alignment. They appear before the start of the sentence and after the full stops in the sentence. A second round of cleaning was carried out to

---

[1] STB hosts a series of tourism related websites in particular websites with parallel texts, viz. *http://www.singaporemedicine.com/index.asp* , *http://app.singaporeedu.gov.sg/asp/index.asp* and *www.yoursingapore.com*

[2] Language family in this paper refers to the highest level of language classification from the Ethnologue (Lewis, 2009)

remove non-break spaces and the texts were then re-tokenized and re-annotated. All the textfiles were saved in UTF-8 encoding.

2.3 Sentence Segmentation

The English, Korean and Indonesian Texts use the same punctuation and the Natural Language Tool Kit (NTLK) `sent_tokenize` module (Bird et al, 2009) was sufficient to segment the English, Korean and Indonesian text. The `sent_tokenize` program uses stop punctuations (i.e. ! ? .) to identify the end of the sentence and it also correctly segmented sentence with websites by differentiating the sentence end full stop and full stops within a website.

The multi-byte Chinese and Japanese sentences were separated by the same sets of ！？。 punctuations. Thus the `nltk.RegexpTokenizer(u'[^！？。]*[!?。]')` was used to segment the Chinese and Japanese sentences. The Japanese regex has a minor tweak from the common `nltk.RegexpTokenizer(u'[^「」！？。]*[！？。]')`, as recommended by the Hagiwara's Japanese chapter of the 「入門 自然言語処理」*nyumon shizen gengo shori* "Japanese Natural Language Processing with python" (Bird et al, 2010). The tweak was necessary to include non-sentence phrases bounded by「...」 brackets. Normally the Japanese「」brackets would have an individual sentence within the bracket, the text from www.yoursingapore.com used the 「」differently by embedding not only sentence but also proper names (e.g. 「マリーナ貯水池」*mari-na chosuichi* "Marina Reservoir"; 「スターバックス」*suta-bakkusu* "Starbucks") or loan phrases(e.g.「三歩一拝」*san ho ichi hai* "three step a bow" - a Chinese Buddhism term; 「ハラール」 *hara-u* "halal"; 「カルーセル」*karu-seru* "carousal") .

2.4 Tokenization

The tokenization (i.e. word level segmentation) tasks splits sentences up into individual "meaningful units" and these meaningful units are dependent on the philological stance of different word segmenter programs. In this paper, the term word and token will be used interchangeably to refer to the individual tokens output by the POS taggers and tokenizers.

For English and Indonesian data, whitespaces are the delimiter for the tokens. Although Vietnamese words are separated by whitespaces in the orthography, sometimes two "words" separated by whitespace are supposed to mean a single thing. For example, the Vietnamese word 'quốc tế' mean international but the individual "word" separated by the space does have its meaning ('quốc' means country and 'tế' means to run). Thus the JVnSegmenter module within JVnTextPro (Nguyen and Phan, 2007) was used to tokenize the Vietnamese data.

For the Japanese and Korean word level segmentation, the segmenter is incorporated into the POS-taggers that this corpus project is using. The Stanford Chinese word segmenter was used to segment the Chinese sentences in this corpus (Tseng et al, 2005).

Mis-segments generated from Stanford segmenter were local street names that were transliterated from English to Chinese. For example, the Stanford Chinese word segmenter wrongly tokenized 乌节路 *wujielu* "Orchard road" as 乌 节路 *wu jielu* "black joint-road". These topological terms were re-segmented with a manually crafted dictionary built using Wikipedia's Chinese translations of English names of Singapore places and streets.

2.5 Monolingual Annotation – Part Of Speech (POS) Tagging

Different programs were used to tag the individual languages with their respective POS tag sets. Due to the lack of an open source POS-tagger for Bahasa Indonesian, the Indonesian texts were not POS-tagged. All the tagged output was formatted into the Corpus Work Bench (CWB) verticalized text format with eXtensible Markup Language (XML) tags to encode the start and end of a sentence (i.e. <s>...</s>). Table 1 presents a brief summary of the sentence segmentation and POS-tagging task for the corpus compilation.

Table 1: Summary of Tokenization and Monolingual Annotation (POS tagging) Task

Language	Sentence Segmenter	Word Segmenter	POS-tagger (Tagger Encoding)	Tagset
English (en)	NLTK sent_tokenize	Whitespaces	HunPos (ISO-8859-1)	Penn Treebank II
Japanese (ja)	NLTK RegexpTokenizer	MeCab	MeCab (UTF-8)	IPAdic
Korean (ko)	NLTK sent_tokenize	POSTAG/ Sejong	POSTAG/Sejong (EUC-KR)	Sejong
Vietnamese (vi)	NLTK sent_tokenize	JVnSegmenter	JVnTagger (UTF-8)	VSLP
Chinese (zh)	NLTK RegexpTokenizer	Stanford Segmenter	Stanford POS tagger (UTF-8)	Penn Chinese Treebank
Indonesian (in)	NLTK sent_tokenize	Whitespaces	–	–

The HunPos tagger applied the Penn Treebank II POS annotations to the English texts (Halacsy et al, 2007). The pre-trained Wall Street Journal English (`en_wsj.model`) model was used with the HunPos tagger to tag the English data.

The Japanese data was tagged by the MeCab tagger (Kudo et al, 2004). The MeCab tagger was used with the `-Ochasen` model, which was trained by the ChaSen tagger (Matsumoto et al. 1999). Different from the other POS-tagger used in this project, the MeCab morphological analyser provided more than a layer of POS annotations; MeCab output adheres to the IPADIC 2.7.0 standards (Matsumoto and Asahara, 2004).

The POSTech TAGger –Korean (POSTAG/Sejong) was used to tag the Korean text. As an agglutinative language, POSTAG/Sejong tagged the tokens at a morpheme level rather than a word level. A custom tagset with 41 tags was used by POSTAG/Sejong to suit the Korean morphemes. The POSTAG/Sejong tagger is only available on Microsoft Windows OS but we managed to run it under the WINE emulator (scripts for this are available with the corpus).

The JVnTagger (part of the JVnTextPro tool) with the `MaxEnt` model was used to annotate the Vietnamese text. The tagset used by JVnTextpro sets the standards for Vietnamese NLP as they pioneered the VLSP project (2006-2010) to "building basic resources and tools for Vietnamese language and speech processing", a five year long project from 2006 – 2010.

The Stanford Chinese POS tagger tags the Chinese data with the `chinese.tagger` model; the Chinese Penn Treebank tagset were used by the Stanford tagger (Tseng et al, 2005).

The primary issues with multilingual corpus POS annotation is the difference in encoding of the sources and the encoding that the POS tagger accepts as input and produce as output. When feeding data into the English (HunPos) and the Korean (POSTAG/Sejong) tagger, the encoding needed to be changed to the respective encoding that the tagger accepts (ISO-8859-1 and EUC-KR respectively). This caused some problems for Korean, as the input text contained characters that cannot be represented in the EUC-KR encoding used by POSTAG/Sejong (such as the –, é and © characters). We mapped them to - , e and (C) during the POS-tagging task for the Korean texts. We hope that more systems will produce UTF-8 versions of their morphological analyzers in the future.

Table 2: A sample of the monolingual annotation from the NTU-MC

Language	Segemented, Part of Speech tagged Text
English	<s>If_IN you_PRP only_RB have_VBP time_NN for_IN one_CD club_NN in_IN Singapore_NN ,_, then_RB it_PRP simply_RB has_VBZ to_TO be_VB zouk_JJ ._.</s>
Japanese	<s>シンガポール_名詞-固有名詞-地域-国 で_助詞-格助詞-一般 一つ_名詞-一般 の_助詞-連体化 クラブ_名詞-一般 に_助詞-格助詞-一般 しか_助詞-係助詞 行く_動詞-自立 時間_名詞-副詞可能 が_助詞-格助詞-一般 なかっ_形容詞-自立 た_助動詞 と_助詞-格助詞-引用 し_動詞-自立 たら_助動詞 、_記号-読点 間違い_名詞-ナイ形容詞語幹 なく_助動詞 、_記号-読点 この_連体詞 ズーク_名詞-一般 に_助詞-格助詞-一般 行く_動詞-自立 べき_助動詞 です_助動詞 。_記号-句点 </s>
Korean	<s>싱가포르_NNP 에서_JKB 클럽_NNP 한_NNP 군데_NNB 밖에_JX 가_VV ㄹ_ETM 시간_NNG 이_JKS 없_VA 다면_EC ,_SP Zouk_SL 를_JKO 선택_NNG 하_XSV 시_EP 어요_EF ._SF</s>
Vietnamese	<s>Nếu_C bạn_N chỉ_R có_V thời_gian_N ghé_V thăm_V một_M câu_lạc_bộ_N ở_E Singapore_Np ,_, hãy_R đến_V Zouk_Np ._.</s>
Chinese	<s>如果_CS 您_PN 在_P 新加坡_NR 只_AD 能_VV 前往_VV 一_CD 间_M 俱乐部_NN ，_PU 祖卡_NN 酒吧_NN 必然_AD 是_VC 您_PN 的_DEG 不二_JJ 选择_NN 。_PU </s>

2.6 Cross-lingual Annotation - Sentence-level Alignment

As machine-readable dictionaries are only available for certain languages in the NTU-MC, the dictionary and length based hunalign tool is suitable for aligning the NTU-MC as the algorithm "remains completely meaningful even in total absence of a dictionary" (Varga et al. 2005). The alignments generated by hunalign are bi-directionally equivalent. The sentence-level alignment task was carried out with four different conditions:

- –dic – hunalign outputs without language pair dictionary,
- +dic – hunalign outputs with language pair dictionary,
- +human – manually aligned Gold Standard,
- +pivot – alignments generated by transitive relation using 2 +human alignments

Only sentences from the textfiles that were available in all 6 languages were sentence-aligned. Two native Chinese and Japanese speakers were enlisted to correct the +dic alignments for the English-Chinese and English-Japanese data. The English-Chinese, English-Japanese and English-Korean were generated with the `CC-CEDICT` (MDBG, 2011), `JMDICT` (Breen, 2004) and enhanced `engdic` (Paik and Bond, 2003) respectively.

By extending the idea of exploiting existing resources to building and extending valency dictionaries, we used the +human alignments to produce +pivot alignments. Using English as the pivot language, we aligned Chinese-English-Japanese.

3 Corpus Evaluation

The corpus evaluation is based on the data availability, corpus outputs and its monolingual and cross-lingual annotations. The monolingual annotations were evaluated extrinsically by measuring Inter-annotator Agreement (IAA) between the POS-taggers and human annotators. The lack of in-depth knowledge about the tagsets deters the human annotators to use sophisticated tags thus intrinsic evaluation (i.e. using human Gold Standard) is not viable. The quality of the parallel text alignments was intrinsically evaluated by computing the F-score of the hunalign outputs against manually aligned data.

Corpus Availability

For a corpus to be a valuable resource, it must be both useful and accessible (Ishida et al. 2006). The owners of the source data (Singapore Tourism Board) have allowed the redistribution of this data, licensed by the Creative Commons (CC) Attribution 3.0 Unported License. Users of the corpus are able to share (i.e. copy, distribute and transmit) and remix (i.e. to adapt) the corpus under the condition of attributing the work to the NTU-MC project. The data is available from http://linguistics.hss.ntu.edu.sg/ResearchinLMS/Pages/NTUMultilingualCorpus.aspx

Corpus Outputs

The NTU-MC project compiled a foundation text of 375,000 words (15,000 sentences) for the NTU-MC in 6 languages from 6 language family trees. The breakdown of the monolingual annotation is as followed (the number. of tokens excludes punctuations and symbols):

Table 3: Monolingual Annotation Outputs

Language (language code)	Language Family	#Texts	#Sentences	#Tokens	POS Tagged
English (en)	Indo-European	398	3,255	76,339	✓
Japanese (ja)	Japonic	267	2,648	72,797	✓
Korean (ko)	Language Isolate	266	2,407	67,341	✓
Vietnamese (vi)	Austro-Asiatic	269	2,236	56,535	✓
Chinese (zh)	Sino-Tibetan	280	2,365	52,047	✓
Indonesian (id)	Austronesian	270	2,185	50,315	✗
Total:	6 Families	1750	15,096	375,374	

The main alignment task for NTU-MC focused on the English-Asian Languages alignments due to the amount of lexical resources available for English bitext. The corpus produced 2 Gold Standard (+human) alignments, 3 +dic alignments, 1 +pivot alignment and 11 -dic alignments generated with the `null.dic` option on hunalign.

Table 4: Cross-lingual Annotation Outputs

	en	id	ja	ko	vi	zh
en						
id	–dic					
ja	+human / +dic	–dic				
ko	+dic	–dic	–dic			
vi	–dic	–dic	–dic	–dic		
zh	+human / +dic	–dic	+pivot	–dic	–dic	

3.1 Monolingual Annotation Evaluation

The `fish-head-curry.txt` from the NTU-MC was selected at random for human annotators to verify the POS-taggers' accuracy. The human annotators were assigned to verify the POS tags and mis-segmented tokens. The accuracy of the human annotation might be primed by what the POS tagger had tagged. Therefore the human verifications were not treated as the "gold standard" but an inter-annotation agreement (IAA) score that was derived from the annotators' identification of the mis-segmented and mis-tagged tokens[3]. For the Japanese POS

[3] This excludes punctuation and both the number of mis-segments and mis-tagged tokens.

evaluation, there was no human annotator available. Thus a different POS tagger, ChaSen morphemic analyzer, was used to calculate IAA. Both programs uses the ipadic POS, but the noticeable difference is that ChaSen is more conservative when tagging unknown words: ChaSen applied the 未知語 *michigo* "unknown word" tag to tokens for unseen words whereas MeCab forces the closest fit POS to the unknown tokens. The 12 instances of 未知語 tags in `fish-head-curry.txt` were not included in the IAA calculation.

Table 5: Summary of Segmentation and POS Annotation Task

Lang-uage	Sentence Order	#Tokens	#Sent-ences	#Mis-segments	#Mis-tagged	IAA	Reported accuracy
en	SVO	235	7	-	18	92.23%	96.58% (Halacsy et al, 2009)
ja	SOV	293	14	3	8	96.25%	97.66 % (Kudo et al, 2004)
ko	SOV	374	14	44	27	81.02%	90.7% (Lee et al, 2002)
vi	SVO	225	7	14	10	89.33%	93.32% (Nguyen et al, 2010)
zh	SVO	249	9	19	16	85.94%	93.65% (Tseng et al, 2005)

The IAA reported in table 4 serves as a gauge, an error bar, of the reported accuracy reported by the individual taggers. The IAA is measured as such:

non-matches = no. of mis-segment + no. of mis-tagged (1)
matches = no. of tokens – non-matches (2)
IAA = matches / (matches + non-matches) * 100% (3)

3.2 Cross-lingual Annotation Evaluation

A subset of 9 text files was selected to evaluate the quality of the hunalign outputs for language pairs with English sentences. The evaluation metrics adheres to standards set by the ARCADE II project (Chiao et al. 2006); the recall, precision and F-score is computed on the hunalign output of word segmented sentences. F-scores were computed using sentence and character granularity (with and without space).

From Figure 1, the alignment task on Japanese, Korean and Chinese is a much more difficult task than aligning Indonesian or Vietnamese data; even with the dictionaries' input, alignments for non-Latin character-based languages are poorer in alignments. Possibly, it is the difference in sentence order (refer table 4) that affected the lexicon quality of the Japanese-English and Korean-English alignments. Nevertheless, +human alignments were manually crafted for English-Japanese and English-Chinese sentences and the English-Korean alignment is reasonably good in terms of character granularity.

Figure 1: F-measure of `hunalign` on English-Asian Language alignments

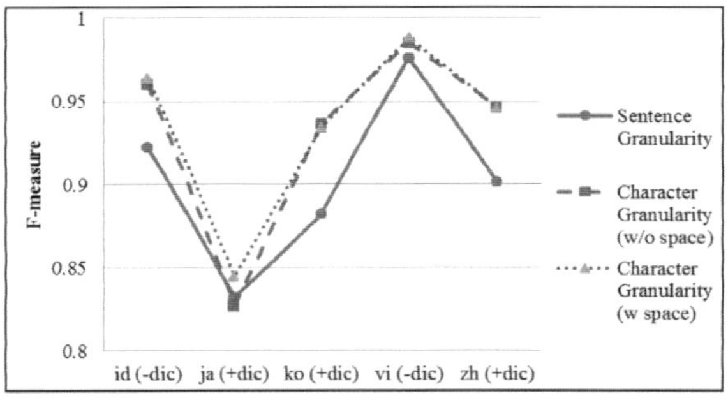

The primary advantage of pivoting alignments to generate other language-pairs alignments is the simplicity to leverage on Gold Standard alignments to produce alignments where the

bilinguals of the language pairs are scarce. Similar to the idea of increasing number of language pairs quadratically by sourcing parallel sources with more languages (Eisele & Yu, 2010), +pivot alignments can produce +human like alignments quadratically with each +human alignments. Although it is possible to create more alignments through other pivoting permutations, generating pivoted alignments from crude -dic alignments will be perpetuating the original mis-alignments that hunalign had produced. Thus only the pivoted Gold Standard alignments was worth the effort as it can be able to produce word-level alignments of similar quality to the +human alignments.

4 Discussion and Future work

A comparable corpus to the NTU-MC is OPUS which taps open source parallel text (Tiedemann, 2009). The OPUS is representative of a global open source enthusiast's community, while the NTU-MC targets data from a specific cosmopolitan society. The OPUS covers a wider range of domains with large sub-corpora and it provides automated monolingual (POS tags and syntactic parses) and cross-lingual (sentence and word level alignments) annotations; whereas the NTU-MC is a corpus of a smaller size but more diverse in Asian language data with deeper annotations. Over time we intend to achieve Gold Standard annotations beneficial for NLP tasks.

The NTU-MC is an ongoing effort to add content, layers of annotation and usability as it continues to make multilingual resources machine readable for NLP tasks. Future work on the NTU-MC involves increasing the amount of data, the layers of monolingual annotations and cross-lingual annotations. The immediate expansion of the corpus would be to use the parallel texts (English, Malay, Chinese and Tamil) distributed by National Environment Agency of Singapore (NEA) and Sembawang Town Council (SBTC).[4] Also, we are constantly requesting for parallel public informational text from other governmental authorities.

Although we have exploited prior knowledge put into the design of the POS tag sets and token segmentations using different (ad-hoc) tools, the philological perspective on segmentations and POS varies within each individual language and across languages. To fill these philological and cross-lingual gaps in the monolingual annotations, we are working to provide syntactic annotation with the Deep Linguistic Processing with HPSG Initiative (DELPH-IN)[5] and semantic annotation with the Global WordNet Association (GWA).[6] From the parses of the individual languages, the multi-layered annotation will allow extraction of the syntactic annotations (e.g. POS from HPSG word classes, word boundary from HPSG lexicon) and semantic annotations (e.g. semantic constraints from HPSG lexicon and its corresponding word senses mapped to WordNet).

For cross-lingual annotation, sentence-level and word-level alignments will be carried out as resources permits; then alignment pivoting will be done in a mesh manner to achieve Gold Standard sentence alignments for all language pairs and proceed with word-level alignments. These word alignments from the hitherto under-represented language pairs should provide rich data for language technologies like MT and IR.

5 Conclusion

This project has produced the initial text collection of the NTU Multilingual Corpus, small in size but rich in language diversity. The NTU-MC contains a layer of monolingual annotation

[4] The authors thank Ms Dorothy Cheung, Public Relations Manager of Sembawang Town Council (SBTC) and Mr Edrick Chua, Assistant Director of Corporate Communications from National Environment Agency (NEA) for their permission and aid in providing access to their data. Though the data from SBTC and NEA is not used for the current phase of NTU-MC compilation, we hope to use it for the future extension of the corpus.

[5] `http://www.delph-in.net/`

[6] `http://www.globalwordnet.org/`

(POS tags) on all language data except Indonesian and a layer of cross-lingual annotation (sentence-level alignments) valuable for cross-lingual NLP tasks. The texts and annotation will be released under an open license (CC by). In any cosmopolitan city like Singapore, the wealth of parallel text remains untapped for corpora building. This project urges future research to continue to draw diverse data through readily available yet untapped resources for corpus compilation. By progressively extending the NTU-MC with a larger dataset and multiple layers of annotation, it expands the scope of the usage and becomes a better corpus for general or computational linguistics researches. By building corpora of more diverse cross-lingual nature, it provides information on the unique sociolinguistic situation in linguistically diverse societies (e.g. translatability researches, language choice and language domain researches); also it pushes the state-of-the-art NLP techniques through more robust cross-lingual training (Matsumoto et al. 1993).

References

Bird, S., Klein, E., Loper, E., 萩原正人 (Hagiwara, M.), 中山敬広 (Nakayama, T.) and 水野貴明 (Mizuno, T.) (translation). 2010. *入門 自然言語処理 (Introduction to Natural Language Processing).* O'Reilly, Japan (translation, with one extra chapter, of Bird *et al.* 2009).

Bird, S., Ewan, K., and Loper, E. 2009. *Natural Language Processing with Python*. O'Reilly Media.

Breen, J.W. 2004. JMDict: a Japanese-multilingual dictionary. In *COLING 2004 Workshop on Multilingual Linguistic Resources*, Geneva. pp, 71–78.

Chiao, Y.C., Kraif, O., Laurent, D., Nguyen, T.M.H., Semmar, N., Stuck, F., Veronis, J. and Zaghouani,W. 2006. Evaluation of multilingual text alignment systems: the ARCADE II project. *Proceedings of the LREC 2006 Conference*.

Eisele, A. and Chen, Y. 2010. MultiUN: A multilingual corpus from United Nation documents. *Proceedings of the Seventh conference on International Language Resources and Evaluation (LREC'10).*

Erjavec, T. 2004. MULTEXT-East Version 3: Multilingual Morphosyntactic Specifications, Lexicons and Corpora. *Fourth International Conference on Language Resources and Evaluation, LREC'04, (ELRA)*, pp. 1535-1538.

Halácsy, P., Kornai, A. and Oravecz, C. 2007. HunPos - an open source trigram tagger In Proceedings of the 45th Annual Meeting of the Association for Computational Linguistics Companion Volume *Proceedings of the Demo and Poster Sessions. Association for Computational Linguistics*, pp.209--212.

Hwa, R., Resnik, R., Weinberg, A., Cabezas, C., and Kolak,C. 2005. Bootstrapping parsers via syntactic projection across parallel texts. *Natural Language Engineering, 11(3)*, pp.311–325

Kudo T., Yamamoto, K., and Matsumoto, Y. 2004. Applying conditional random fields to Japanese morphological analysis. In *Proceedings of the 2004 Conference on Empirical Methods in Natural Language Processing*. pp.230–237.

Lewis, P.M. 2009. *Ethnologue: Languages of the World, Sixteenth edition*. Dallas, Tex.: SIL International. Online version: http://www.ethnologue.com/.

Marek, M., Pecina, P. and Spousta, M. 2007. Web page cleaning with conditional random fields. In *Proceedings of the Web as Corpus Workshop (WAC3), Cleaneval Session*.

Matsumoto, Y., Ishimoto, H. and Utsuro, T. 1993. Structural matching of parallel texts. In *31st Annual Meeting of the Association for Computational Linguistics: ACL-93*, pp.23–30.

Matsumoto, Y., Takaoka, K. and Asahara, M. 1999. *ChaSen Morphological Analyzer version 2.4.0 User's Manual.* NAIST Technical Report, Nara Institute of Science and Technology

Technical Report 99009. Retrieved on 07 Jan 2011 from http://sourceforge.jp/projects/chasen-legacy/docs/chasen-2.4.0-manual-en.pdf/en/1/chasen-2.4.0-manual-en.pdf.pdf

MDGB. 2011. *CC-CEDICT [Machine-Readable Dictionary].* Netherlands : MDGB, Retreived May 03, 2011 from http://www.mdbg.net/chindict/chindict.php?page=cedict

McCallum, B. 2011. Translation Technology at the United Nations. *MultiLingual Computing & Technology, 15(2)*, pp. 62.

Mitamura, T., Lin, F., Shima, H., Wang, M., Ko, J., Betteridge, J., Bilotti, M., Schlaikjer, A., and Nyberg, E. 2007. JAVELIN III: Cross-Lingual Question Answering from Japanese and Chinese Documents. *Proceedings of NTCIR-6 Workshop Meeting*, Tokyo, Japan.

Paik, K. and Bond, F. 2003. Enhancing an English/Korean Dictionary. In *Papillon 2003 Workshop on Multilingual Lexical Databases*, Sapporo, Japan.

Nguyen, C.T. and Phan, X.H. 2007. *JVnSegmenter: A Java-based Vietnamese Word Segmentation Tool*. Retrieved on 30 Jan 2011 from http://jvnsegmenter.sourceforge.net/

Ralf, S., Pouliquen, B., Widiger, A., Ignat, C., Erjavec, T., Tufiş, D., Varga, D. 2006. The JRC-Acquis: A multilingual aligned parallel corpus with 20+ languages. *Proceedings of the 5th International Conference on Language Resources and Evaluation (LREC'2006)*,Genoa, Italy.

Resnik, P. 2004. Exploiting Hidden Meanings: Using Bilingual Text for Monolingual Annotation. In Alexander Gelbukh (ed.), *Lecture Notes in Computer Science 2945: Computational Linguistics and Intelligent Text Processing*, pp. 283-299.

Roche, X. 2007. *Httrack Website Copier - Offline Browser*. [Computer Software]. Retrieved Jan 30, 2011. Available from http://www.httrack.com/

Sarrafzadeh, B., Yakovets, N., Cercone, N., & An, A. 2011. *Cross Lingual Word Sense Disambiguation for Languages with Scarce Resources. (Technical Report CSE-2011-01).* Ontario: Department of Computer Science and Engineering.

Saravanan, K., Udupa, R., and Kumaran, A. 2010. Crosslingual Information Retrieval System Enhanced with Transliteration Generation and Mining, In *Forum for Information Retrieval Evaluation (FIRE-2010) Workshop*, Kolkata, India.

Snyder, B. and Barzilay, R. 2008. Cross-lingual propagation for morphological analysis. In *AAAI'08: Proceedings of the 23rd national conference on Artificial intelligence*, pp. 848–854.

Ishida, T. 2006. Language Grid: An Infrastructure for Intercultural Collaboration. In *IEEE/IPSJ Symposium on Applications and the Internet (SAINT-06)*, pp.96-100, keynote.

Tiedemann, J. 2009. News from OPUS - A Collection of Multilingual Parallel Corpora with Tools and Interfaces. In *Proceedings of RANLP'09*, Borovets, Bulgaria. pp.237–248.

Tseng, H., Jurafsky, D. and Manning, C. 2005. Morphological features help POS tagging of unknown words across language varieties. In *Proceedings of the Fourth SIGHAN Workshop,* Jeju Island, Korea.

Varga, D., Nemeth, L., Halacsy, P., Kornai, A., Tron, V. and Nagy, V. 2005. Parallel corpora for medium density languages. In *Proceedings of the Recent Advances in Natural Language Processing 2005 Conference,* Borovets. Bulgaria. pp.590–596.

VLSP Project (2006-2010). *VLSP Project – Vietnamese Language Processing*. Retrieved on 02 Jan 2010 from http://vlsp.vietlp.org:8080/demo/?page=about .

Xiao, Z., McEnery, A., Baker, P. and Hardie, A. 2004. Developing Asian language corpora: standards and practice. In *Proceedings of the 4th Workshop on Asian Language Resources, Sanya, Hainan Island.* pp. 1-8.

Zhang, Y., Uchimoto, K., Ma, Q. and Isahara, H. 2005. Building an Annotated Japanese-Chinese Parallel Corpus – A Part of NICT Multilingual Corpora. *Second International Joint Conference on Natural Language Processing*, Jeju Island, Republic of Korea. pp 85-90.

In Situ Text Summarisation for Museum Visitors

Timothy Baldwin[a], Patrick Ye[a b], Fabian Bohnert[b], and Ingrid Zukerman[b]

[a]Department of Computer Science and Software Engineering
The University of Melbourne, Australia
tb@ldwin.net ye.patrick@gmail.com
[b]Faculty of Information Technology
Monash University, Australia
{fabian.bohnert, ingrid.zukerman}@monash.edu

Abstract. This paper presents an experiment on in situ summarisation in a museum context. We implement a range of standard summarisation algorithms, and use them to generate summaries for individual exhibit areas in a museum, intended for in situ delivery to a museum visitor on a mobile device. Personalisation is relative to a visitor's preference for summary length, the visitor's relative interest in a given exhibit topic, as well as (optionally) the summary history. We find that the best-performing summarisation strategy is the Centroid algorithm, and that content diversification and customisation of summary length have a significant impact on user ratings of summary quality.

1 Introduction

With the increasing saturation of mobile technology, museums and other cultural heritage institutions are increasingly looking to deliver content to visitors via their personal mobile device. This has led to a move away from a traditional mode of content delivery via static information on placards in the museum space, to interactive applications on mobile devices supporting path finding, social networking and personalised content delivery (Burnette *et al.*, 2011; Filippini-Fantoni *et al.*, 2011).

This paper explores the feasibility and utility of in situ personalised content delivery in a museum context, focusing on document summarisation. Museums provide a compelling context for in situ summarisation, as visitors often wish to access key information relevant to their immediate surroundings, but want to avoid information overload. Personalised summarisation is an integral component of museum content delivery, as exhibits are typically associated with vast amounts of curated information, predominantly in textual form. This can range from simple tabular information such as the date of acquisition of an exhibit, to full-length research articles published by museum curators/researchers relating to the exhibit. Personalised summarisation offers the possibility to present the most salient facets of information to a visitor, according to their interests and preferences. The pragmatic choice of a mobile device such as a smart phone to deliver the content poses challenges in terms of the amount of content that can be effectively presented to the visitor (Yang and Wang, 2003; Otterbacher *et al.*, 2006).

Personalised summarisation should ideally be coupled with tracking/geolocating technology to be situation aware (Bohnert *et al.*, 2008; Bohnert and Zukerman, 2009; Bickersteth and Ainsley, 2011) and take place interactively (Callaway *et al.*, 2005). In principle, any evaluation should take place in situ as part of an actual museum visit. However, in this preliminary research, we present the results of a web-based user study targeted at members of Melbourne Museum (Melbourne,

** This research was supported in part by grant no. DP0770931 from the Australian Research Council. The authors thank Carolyn Meehan and her team from Museum Victoria for their assistance.

Australia), based on a fixed path through the museum. To partly overcome this limitation, we elicit the participants' interest in an exhibit topic, and generate a summary which takes into account this interest level. In this way, we examine the impact of interest level on summary length and different summarisation strategies, as a guide for future research.

Our contributions are: (1) we deploy a range of extractive summarisation methods over a fixed path through a museum, focusing on generating summaries for individual exhibit areas, personalised in length according to visitor preferences and interest levels, and diversification of summary content; (2) we carry out a medium-scale user study over the generated summaries, to determine the relative utility of the summaries and the effectiveness of the various strategies trialled; and (3) we present the results of a web-based museum visitor questionnaire on opportunities for in situ personalisation in a museum environment.

2 User Study

The goal of this research is to investigate whether automatic text summarisation techniques can be harnessed for in situ personalised content delivery in a museum. We explore this in a two-part web-based survey, where we: (1) presented participants with a questionnaire regarding their interest in mobile device-based personalised content delivery in a museum; and (2) asked participants to rate automatically generated summaries for individual exhibit areas in the museum space. The survey was advertised to members of Melbourne Museum via the official e-newsletter. It was completed outside the museum, but the participant group can reasonably be expected to be very familiar with the museum. In total, we received 34 valid responses to the survey, which form the basis of the results in this paper.

2.1 Questionnaire on Personalised Content Delivery

Survey participants were provided with a brief description of the project, asked a few questions on demographics and their museum visiting patterns, and then asked specific questions about personalised content delivery.

The broad findings of the poll are as follows: (1) over two thirds of participants are very likely or likely to actively interact with a mobile device in the museum for personalised content delivery, and would consent to being tracked for user modelling purposes; (2) two thirds or more of the participants are likely to make use of images, videos or sound bites on the mobile device, but participants are considerably less likely to use (museum-related) games or (external) websites; and (3) most participants are at least likely to use recommendations across a range of content types during a visit, excluding recommendations of games. These survey findings show that there is broad support and scope for personalised content delivery within the museum context.

Participants were also provided with the facility to provide comments. Specific reasons cited for being interested in personalised content delivery (with or without tracking) were: the desire for personalised learning, difficulties in accessing placards in crowded exhibitions, and frustration with "unfathomable" static displays. Primary reasons for participants not being interested in mobile devices were their unsuitability for smaller children (especially in a group setting), the feeling that mobile devices would be a distraction, and also concerns over data privacy and security. There were also comments suggesting that a personalised post-visit follow-up on topics of interest was superior to in situ content delivery.

In sum, participants were generally supportive of in situ personalised content delivery of various types, lending support to the basic premise of this research.

2.2 Rating of Summaries

The second stage of the web survey was to rate the quality of automatically generated summaries. Participants were first presented with three manually generated summaries of varying length (short $\approx$ 50 words; mid-length $\approx$ 75 words; long $\approx$ 100 words) for the Dinosaur Walk exhibit area in

Melbourne Museum, and asked to state their preference for summary length relative to the pre-prepared summaries. This was intended to reduce the effect of summary length bias on summary preference. Next, participants were given the following instructions:

> *Imagine yourself in front of a series of exhibits at Melbourne Museum. First you will be asked about your relative interest level in an exhibit. Assuming a non-zero response (i.e. you have some interest in the exhibit area), you will be presented with three descriptions of the exhibit, and asked to rate each one. Your rating should reflect your response to the quality of the content as well as the language used.*

The participants were then shown four exhibit areas in Melbourne Museum. For each exhibit area, they were given an indication of its location on a map, and a photo of the exhibit area. The rating of interest level in each exhibit area was on a scale of 0 ("Not interested at all") to 3 ("Extremely interested"). If a participant indicated a non-zero interest level in an exhibit area, they were provided with three summaries and asked to rate each on a scale of 1 ("Horrible") to 5 ("Excellent"); if the participant indicated no interest, they were taken directly to the next exhibit area without being shown any summaries. Summary lengths were tailored to both the indicated preference for summary length, and the relative interest level in the exhibit area (Section 3.4).

All participants were shown the same four exhibit areas in the same order. The first two exhibit areas were from the same gallery ("Bugs Alive") with a strong thematic connection relating to insects. The next two exhibit areas were deliberately selected from galleries that have little connection with any of the other three exhibit areas (relating to deep sea life and horse racing, respectively). This was done to explore the impact of exhibit area "theming" (i.e., thematic relation) on content differentiation, as described in Section 3.2 (with the first pairing of exhibit areas being themed, and the second two pairings being "unthemed").

3 Automatic Summarisation

The setting where we apply automatic summarisation is characterised by the following properties:

- **Per-exhibit sequenced summaries:** a stand-alone summary is generated for each exhibit area, for presentation to the visitor in situ, in sequence of the order in which the exhibit areas are visited; each summary is personalised to the summary length preference and interest level of the participant, and optionally based on "content diversification" over preceding summaries.
- **Short summaries:** the summaries need to be relatively short, in order to display them effectively on the small screen of a mobile device.
- **Single primary document:** the amount of text associated with a given exhibit area varies, but is generally of the order of slightly over 1000 words, in a single primary document authored by museum curators; this is complemented with a secondary document from Wikipedia which is anywhere from 600 to slightly over 3000 words in length.

The secondary Wikipedia document is determined by manual alignment for each exhibit area. It is intended to be the document of best fit within Wikipedia, which can vary from a Wikipedia page dedicated to the exact museum artefact to an article which is only thematically related (e.g., an article on gold mining, to represent a historical diorama of a particular gold mine). Our motivation in including these secondary documents is to reduce data sparseness in the sentence ranking, without allowing the content of the Wikipedia article to be included in the summary, as the article often diverges significantly from the context of presentation of the exhibit area.

Our summarisation task is differentiated from conventional document summarisation in: (1) the segmentation into discrete exhibit areas, and generation of short individuated summaries per exhibit area for in situ delivery; (2) the relative sparsity of text (multi-document summarisation is typically based on at least 10 documents); and (3) the interaction between the physical movements of the visitor and summary generation, in terms of the sequentiality of the exhibit area summaries (mirroring the physical path through the museum), and potential interplay between the summaries generated for different exhibit areas. A primary interest in this research is the determination of the utility of established multi-document summarisation algorithms for our novel summarisation task.

In the following sections, we outline the summarisation algorithms trialled in this research, describe how we personalise summary length, and outline a simple method for content diversification, to avoid repetition in the summaries for individual exhibit areas.

3.1 Summarisation Algorithms

For our experiments, we implemented five standard extractive summarisation algorithms from the literature (Radev *et al.*, 2002):

- First-N sentence algorithm (FIRSTN): select the first N sentences of each document.
- Lead-based algorithm (LEAD): select the first N sentences of each paragraph.
- Centroid algorithm (CENTROID): cluster the document collection using a variant of TF·IDF, and rank sentences through a weighted sum of token weights based on the cluster centroid, a sentence positional weight, and similarity with the first sentence (Radev *et al.*, 2000).
- LexRank algorithm (LEXRANK): cluster the document collection, and rank sentences using a variant of PageRank (Brin and Page, 1998) over the component words (Erkan and Radev, 2004).
- Manifold-ranking algorithm (MANIFOLD): score each sentence based on a manifold-ranking process, and rerank sentences based on a diversity penalty (Wan *et al.*, 2007).

Each algorithm was run over the primary and secondary document for a given exhibit area. All sentences were ranked, but only sentences from the primary document (that authored by Melbourne Museum) were candidates for selection in the final summary. In this sense, the task we are performing is not, strictly speaking, multi-document summarisation so much as document condensation, using a secondary document (and optionally summary context) to bias the sentence selection. Any findings on the relative successes of the summarisation algorithms should be interpreted accordingly.

3.2 Content Diversification

The task of generating in situ content for museum visitors on an exhibit-by-exhibit basis has an inherent segment granularity (summarise one exhibit area at a time) and chronological order, neither of which is found in generic multi-document summarisation tasks. Exhibit areas vary greatly in similarity (Grieser *et al.*, 2011), and for closely-related exhibit areas (e.g., those found in the same gallery, as is the case with our "themed" exhibit area pairing), there is significant potential for generating overlapping content. Due to the strict chronological ordering, we can of course access content previously delivered to the visitor, and personalise the summary to ensure "content diversity", akin to result diversification in personalised web search (Radlinski and Dumais, 2006). That is, we can reduce redundancy in the information presented to the museum visitor by explicitly dispreferring sentences similar to those the visitor has already seen.

We adopt the following rather simple approach: for preceding exhibit area pairs, we bias the sentence ranking by including the summary for the preceding exhibit area as an extra secondary document. Similarly to the Wikipedia document, sentences from this summary are included in the sentence ranking, but cannot be included in the final summary. This has the effect of demoting sentences for the current exhibit area which are very similar to those for the preceding exhibit area, hence leading to diversification.

Preferred	Interest Level		
length	1	2	3
Short	25	50	75
Medium	50	75	100
Long	75	100	125

Table 1: Summary lengths in number of words

3.3 Pronoun Filtering

Many sentences in the museum documents associated with a given exhibit area contain personal or possessive pronouns, which may not be resolvable out of context, or may resolve to an unintended antecedent. To avoid this, we considered the following strategies: (1) remove all sentences containing pronouns from the sentence ranking step, but include them in the clustering step (to avoid exacerbating the effects of data sparseness); and (2) allow sentences containing pronouns, but recursively include the preceding sentence from the original document if a selected sentence includes a pronoun.

3.4 Personalisation and Summary Length

In prior work, Berkovsky *et al.* (2008) found a strong correlation between summary length and interest level, i.e., the more interested a user is in a topic, the greater the likelihood they will prefer a longer summary. To explore this effect further, we first asked participants to state their overall preference for summary length (short, medium or long), prior to presenting them with any exhibit area summaries. For each exhibit area, we generated summaries of varying length for each of three interest levels (1, 2 or 3) and the three summary length preferences, as indicated in Table 1. For each algorithm — optionally in combination with content diversification and pronoun filtering — we fashioned a summary of each of the indicated lengths by monotonically adding sentences from the sentence ranking determined by the summarisation strategy, and selecting the summary which best approximated the required summary length.

When presenting a participant with the summaries for a given exhibit area, we show them a summary of the requested length, in addition to a shorter and longer summary, to determine the relative impact of variance in length on their summary ratings. For example, if a visitor's summary length preference were "mid-length" and they indicated an interest level of 1 ("Have a tiny bit of interest") in a given exhibit area, a summary of length of 50 words would be selected; a summary of length 25 and a summary of length 75 words would then be added (for a total of three summaries per exhibit area).

Our motivation for varying the summary lengths in this manner was to explore the interaction between summary length and perceived quality for different summarisation strategies, hoping to validate the findings of Berkovsky *et al.* (2008). Naturally, in a fully deployed in situ summarisation system, we would hope to dynamically learn the level of user interest (Bohnert and Zukerman, 2009) and customise the summarisation length accordingly. In our current research, we simply hope to establish the need for user interest prediction for the purposes of summary length personalisation.

3.5 Summary Selection

To recap, we generate summaries based on five summarisation algorithms, optional pronoun exclusion, and optional content diversification, for a total of 20 basic summarisation configurations over nine possible summary lengths. These are evaluated over four separate exhibit areas, for each of which we present three summaries of differing length; one pairing of the four exhibit areas is themed, and two are unthemed. All summaries were pre-generated to minimise time lag in the trial. Due to content diversification being conditioned on the previous summary, the total number of pre-generated summaries was $180 + 180^2 + 180^3 + 180^4 = 1,055,624,580$.

To expose each participant to as many summarisation configurations as possible, over their visit, we performed random selection without replacement over the 20 summarisation configurations. Additionally, for each exhibit area, we randomly varied the order in which the "correct" length summary vs. the short and long summaries were presented to the visitor.

4 Results

4.1 Clustering of Summarisation Configurations

To determine the relative differentiation in content between the pre-generated summaries for each exhibit area, we performed a pairwise summary comparison using the ROUGE-2 metric (Lin and Hovy, 2003). For each pairing of the 20 summarisation configurations, we averaged across the different summary lengths and exhibit areas to generate an overall similarity. Based on these similarity values, we clustered the summarisation configurations using "oblivious" hierarchical agglomerative clustering over the three attributes of summarisation algorithm (binarised into the individual algorithms), pronoun filtering and content diversification. That is, we calculated the single attribute which leads to the (weighted) purest partitioning of the data at each level of the dendrogram in a bottom-up fashion.

Overall, the greatest differentiating factor was the choice of summarisation algorithm, followed by the inclusion/exclusion of sentences with pronouns, and finally, content diversification. Comparing the individual algorithms, LEAD was the most different to the other four algorithms, and CENTROID and FIRSTN generally produced very similar summaries (all irrespective of the pronoun and content differentiation settings). MANIFOLD without pronouns produced summaries similar to CENTROID, while MANIFOLD with pronouns was more differentiated.

4.2 User Study

As stated in Section 2, we received a total of 34 valid responses to the web survey. In terms of the summary ratings, this amounted to up to 12 rated summaries per participant,[1] and a total of 357 summary ratings. This breaks down into two overlapping subsets: 62 summary ratings for the "themed" exhibit area pairing, and 326 ratings for the two "unthemed" exhibit area pairings.

The different factors that potentially impact on the summary ratings are as follows:

- Actual summary length (*act_length* $\in \{-1, 0, 1\}$): the selected summary length, based on the summary length preference, exhibit area interest level, and the shorter ("-1") and longer length ("1") variations over the selected length.
- Summarisation algorithm (*algorithm* $\in$ {LEAD, FIRSTN, CENTROID, LEXRANK, MANIFOLD}): the choice of the summarisation algorithm.
- Interest level (*indicated* $\in \{1, 2, 3\}$): the participant's indicated interest level in the exhibit.
- Summary length preference (*pref_length* $\in \{1, 2, 3\}$): the participant's indicated preferred summary length ("1" = short; "2" = mid-length; "3" = long).
- Content diversification (*diversification* $\in \{0, 1\}$): is content diversification used in the summarisation ("1") or not ("0")?
- Pronoun filtering (*pronoun* $\in \{0, 1\}$): is pronoun filtering used in the summarisation ("1") or not ("0")?

To investigate the interaction between the various factors and the summarisation ratings, as well as the interactions between the factors, we perform a factorial ANOVA (Tabachnick and Fidell,

[1] Participants were not presented with summaries for exhibit areas where they indicated they had no interest. Additionally, it was possible for participants to submit an incomplete set of summary ratings for a given exhibit area.

Combination of factors	All (p-value)	Themed (p-value)	Unthemed (p-value)
{*algorithm,diversification,indicated*}	**0.00**	NaN	**0.00**
{*pref_length*}	**0.00**	0.62	**0.00**
{*algorithm,act_length,indicated,pronoun*}	**0.01**	NaN	**0.03**
{*indicated*}	**0.01**	**0.05**	**0.05**
{*act_length,pronoun*}	**0.01**	0.64	**0.02**
{*diversification*}	**0.02**	0.54	**0.00**
{*algorithm,pref_length,indicated*}	**0.04**	0.94	**0.03**
{*algorithm,pref_length,diversification,indicated,pronoun*}	**0.05**	NaN	**0.05**
{*algorithm,pref_length,act_length,diversification,indicated*}	**0.05**	NaN	**0.03**
{*algorithm,pref_length,indicated,pronoun*}	0.06	NaN	0.06
{*algorithm,pref_length*}	0.07	0.47	**0.04**
{*algorithm,act_length,diversification,indicated*}	0.07	NaN	0.31
{*pref_length,act_length,indicated*}	0.07	0.21	**0.04**
{*pronoun*}	0.07	0.38	0.07
{*algorithm,pref_length,act_length,pronoun*}	0.07	NaN	**0.02**

Table 2: Top-15 combinations of factors for "All" exhibit areas, based on factorial ANOVA, compared to the subset of "Themed" exhibit areas and the subset of "Unthemed" exhibit areas (**boldfacing** indicates a statistically significant combination of factors, $p \leq 0.05$)

2006) for each combination of factors over the participants' ratings. In this, we perform separate factorial ANOVAs for each of: (1) the overall set of exhibit areas ("All"); (2) the themed exhibit areas ("Themed"); and (3) the unthemed exhibit areas ("Unthemed"), to investigate whether thematic relations between exhibit areas have any effect on the relative impact of the factor combinations. Table 2 shows the top-15 factor combinations for "All" exhibit areas (i.e., the factor combinations with the lowest p values). Not all feature combinations are represented in the "Themed" data, leading to gaps in the table (labelled as "NaN"). It is worth noting that there are no statistically significant ($p \leq 0.05$) factor combinations for "Themed" and "Unthemed" outside the top-15 factor combinations for "All" presented in the table.

Looking first at the individual factors, we see that *indicated* is the only factor that universally affects a participant's rating (for all of "All", "Themed" and "Unthemed"). This suggests that, despite the instructions provided to the participants, they found it hard to judge the intrinsic quality of the summaries independently of their relative interest level in the exhibit area. This effect was particularly notable for the CENTROID algorithm (Figure 1).

Content diversification (*diversification*) has a significant impact on "All" and "Unthemed" summaries, but no impact on "Themed" ones ($p = 0.54$ in isolation). Analysis of the data indicates that this is due to diversification negatively affecting unthemed exhibit area pairings (which account for the majority of the data in "All"), but having negligible impact on themed exhibit area pairings. Manual analysis of the summaries for the unthemed exhibit area pairs indicates that this negative impact may be due to *diversification* artificially removing lead sentences (because of the boilerplate structure of the curated documents); the effect was felt less for themed exhibit area pairs, as even if the lead sentence for the second exhibit was dropped, the similarity in content with what had already been presented to the participant meant that the summary was still coherent. It is disappointing that diversification has no impact on the visitors' assessment of themed exhibit summaries, despite the fact that it has a noticeable effect on the summaries themselves, by incorporating extra content (and removing content that overlaps with that provided for the preceding exhibit area, including the lead sentence). However, as participants rated the quality of the summaries, rather than the cumulative novel content delivered over the series of the summaries,

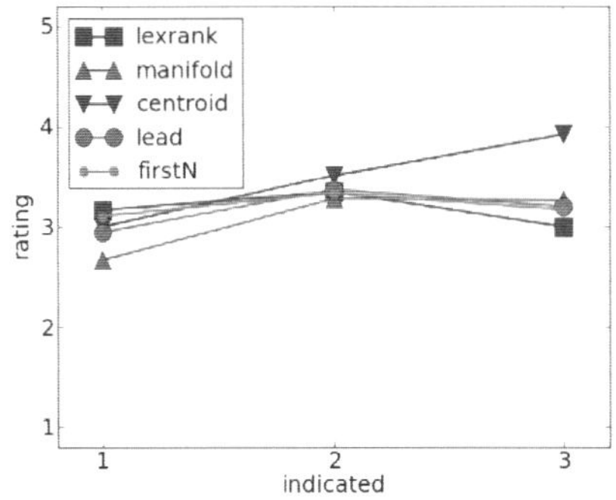

Figure 1: Graph of *indicated* vs. user rating for the different summarisation algorithms

Algorithm	Marginal means
LEAD	3.10 ± 0.51
FIRSTN	3.00 ± 0.42
CENTROID	3.50 ± 0.38
LEXRANK	2.89 ± 0.48
MANIFOLD	3.46 ± 0.53

Table 3: Estimated marginal means for individual summarisation algorithms, with 95% confidence interval

this difference was not reflected in the ratings.

Summary length preference (*pref_length*) has a significant impact on "All" and "Unthemed", but not "Themed". Analysis of the data shows that for "Themed", the choice of algorithm has a highly variable effect on a participant's rating, particularly for participants who indicated they preferred longer summaries (with CENTROID performing strongly), while with the other two datasets, the results were more consistent. Whether this is an effect of data sparseness for the "Themed" data or can be replicated over other pairings of themed exhibit areas is left for future work.

None of *pronoun*, *act_length* and *algorithm* had a significant impact on the participants' ratings. The fact that *act_length* had no impact on results is surprising given the high impact of *indicated*, suggesting that the participants' ratings were biased heavily by their relative interest level and don't reflect subtle variations in summary length. It would be interesting to carry out follow-up experiments with greater differentiation in summary length, and a clearer separation between the rating of exhibit area interest level and intrinsic summary quality.

Table 3 shows the breakdown of estimated marginal means across algorithms (based on "All"). It is evident that CENTROID and MANIFOLD rate better on average than the other methods, but not statistically significantly ($p > 0.05$). Despite strong results in other contexts (Erkan and Radev, 2004), LEXRANK was, surprisingly, the worst performer.

It is harder to tease out any strong trend from the combinations of factors which show up as having a significant impact on ratings, other perhaps than *algorithm* and *indicated* tending to have a significant impact when combined (including other factors). Also, the impact of *pref_length* tends to be dampened when combined with other factors.

Reflecting back on our original question of whether automatic summarisation methods can be applied to personalised content delivery in a museum domain, the answer would appear to be yes, in that the best-performing methods produced summaries which were rated around 3.5 on average (with 3 indicating "Not bad" and 4 "Good"). Contrary to our clustering results from Section 4.1, the choice of algorithm was found to have no significant effect on summary rating, with *indicated*, *pref_length* and *diversification* having a greater individual impact on summary quality. Finally, the correlation observed by Berkovsky *et al.* (2008) between interest level and preferred summary length was not strongly evident in our results.

5 Related Work

While multi-document summarisation has been a highly active research area, personalised summarisation over single documents has received considerably less attention.

There has been work on personalized document search and summarisation in the medical domain for clinicians and patients, based on semantically-enhanced extraction of snippets and terminology standardisation (McKeown *et al.*, 2001; McKeown *et al.*, 2003). Here, however, the personalisation was at the level of two discrete user profiles, and not truly individualised.

Radev *et al.* (2001) present the design of a search engine which supports recommendation, clustering, and personalised summarisation, but do not include any technical details or evaluation. Goren-Bar and Prete (2005) report on a preliminary situated experiment on content delivery in a museum, but found that the simple static text delivery method was preferred to the adaptive method.

Berkovsky *et al.* (2008) present a method for generating summaries of different length, and demonstrate a correlation between the level of user interest in a topic area, and the preferred summary length. However, their method relies on hand-compiled summaries of expanding length, and no attempt was made to automate the summary generation.

The content differentiation aspect of our work is somewhat related to the TAC 2008 Update Summarization Task (Dang and Owczarzak, 2008), where participants were provided with a set of 10 documents and a pre-prepared summary, in addition to a set of 10 update documents containing new information, from which a summary was to be generated. In the TAC 2008 task, the update summary was for the same topic as the original summary, and the task was specifically to highlight novel content. In our setup, the exhibit areas overlap in content to varying degrees (depending on theming), and the relative importance of differentiation is more subtle (partly because the museum visitor sees the summaries in discrete chunks, in the context of different exhibit areas).

6 Conclusions

We have presented a user study on personalised summarisation for a museum visit. We implemented a range of summarisation algorithms, and used them to generate summaries for individual exhibit areas in a museum, intended for in situ delivery to a museum visitor on a mobile device. Personalisation took the form of adjustment of summary length on the basis of the visitor's indicated interest level in a given exhibit area, as well as (optionally) diversification over previously-delivered summaries. We found that museum visitors are largely supportive of personalised content delivery, and explored the impact of a range of summarisation parameters on visitors' ratings of summaries.

References

Berkovsky, Shlomo, Timothy Baldwin, and Ingrid Zukerman. 2008. Aspect-based personalized text summarization. In *Proceedings of the 5th International Conference on Adaptive Hypermedia and Adaptive Web-Based Systems (AH 2008)*, pp. 267–270, Hanover, Germany.

Bickersteth, Julian and Christopher Ainsley. 2011. Mobile phones and visitor tracking. In *Museums and the Web 2011: Proceedings*, http://conference.archimuse.com/mw2011/papers/mobile_phones_and_visitor_tracking.

Bohnert, Fabian and Ingrid Zukerman. 2009. Non-intrusive personalisation of the museum experience. In *Proceedings of the 17th International Conference on User Modeling, Adaptation, and Personalization (UMAP-09)*, pp. 197–209, Trento, Italy.

Bohnert, Fabian, Ingrid Zukerman, Shlomo Berkovsky, Timothy Baldwin, and Elizabeth Sonenberg. 2008. Using interest and transition models to predict visitor locations in museums. *AI Communications*, 21(2–3), 195–202.

Brin, Sergei and Larry Page. 1998. The anatomy of a large-scale hypertextual web search engine. In *Proceedings of the Seventh World Wide Web Conference*, pp. 107–117, Brisbane, Australia.

Burnette, Allegra, Rich Cherry, Nancy Proctor, and Peter Samis. 2011. Getting on (not under) the Mobile 2.0 bus: Emerging issues in the mobile business model. In *Museums and the Web 2011: Proceedings*. http://conference.archimuse.com/mw2011/papers/getting_on_not_under_the_mobile_20_bus.

Callaway, Charles, Tsvi Kuflik, Elena Not, Alessandra Novello, Oliviero Stock, and Massimo Zancanaro. 2005. Personal reporting of a museum visit as an entrypoint to future cultural experience. In *Proceedings of the 2005 International Conference on Intelligent User Interfaces (IUI 2005)*, pp. 275–277, San Diego, USA.

Dang, Hoa Trang and Karolina Owczarzak. 2008. Overview of the TAC 2008 update summarization task. In *Proceedings of 2008 Text Analysis Conference*, pp. 1–16, Gaithersburg, USA.

Erkan, Günes and Dragomir R. Radev. 2004. Lexrank: Graph-based lexical centrality as salience in text summarization. *Journal of Artificial Intelligence Research*, 22, 457–479.

Filippini-Fantoni, Silvia, Sarah McDaid, and Matthew Cock. 2011. Mobile devices for orientation and way finding: the case of the British Museum multimedia guide. In *Museums and the Web 2011: Proceedings*. `http://conference.archimuse.com/mw2011/papers/mobile_devices_for_wayfinding`.

Goren-Bar, Dina and Michela Prete. 2005. Report on a museum tour report. In *Proceedings of INTETAIN 2005: INtelligent TEchnologies for interactive enterTAINment*, pp. 230–234, Madonna di Campiglio, Italy.

Grieser, Karl, Timothy Baldwin, Fabian Bohnert, and Liz Sonenberg. 2011. Using ontological and document similarity to estimate museum exhibit relatedness. *ACM Journal on Computing and Cultural Heritage*, 3(3), 1–20.

Lin, Chin-Yew and Eduard H. Hovy. 2003. Automatic evaluation of summaries using n-gram co-occurrence statistics. In *Proceedings of the 3rd International Conference on Human Language Technology Research and 4th Annual Meeting of the NAACL (HLT-NAACL 2003)*, pp. 71–78, Edmonton, Canada.

McKeown, Kathleen R., Shih-Fu Chang, James Cimino, Steven K. Feiner, Carol Friedman, Luis Gravano, Vasileios Hatzivassiloglou, Steven Johnson, Desmond A. Jordan, Judith L. Klavans, André Kushniruk, Vimla Patel, and Simone Teufel. 2001. PERSIVAL, a system for personalized search and summarization over multimedia healthcare information. In *Proceedings of the 2001 Joint Conference on Digital Libraries (JCDL)*, Roanoke, USA.

McKeown, Kathleen R., Noemie Elhadad, and Vasileios Hatzivassiloglou. 2003. Leveraging a common representation for personalized search and summarization in a medical digital library. In *Proceedings of the 3rd ACM/IEEE-CS Joint Conference on Digital Libraries*, pp. 159–170.

Otterbacher, Jahna, Dragomir Radev, and Omer Kareem. 2006. News to go: hierarchical text summarization for mobile devices. In *Proceedings of 29th International ACM-SIGIR Conference on Research and Development in Information Retrieval (SIGIR 2006)*, pp. 589–596, Seattle, USA.

Radev, Dragomir R., Weiguo Fan, and Zhu Zhang. 2001. Webinessence: A personalized web-based multi-document summarization and recommendation system. In *NAACL Workshop on Automatic Summarization*, Pittsburgh, USA.

Radev, Dragomir R., Eduard Hovy, and Kathleen McKeown. 2002. Introduction to the special issue on summarization. *Computational linguistics*, 28(4), 399–408.

Radev, Dragomir R., Hongyan Jing, and Malgorzata Budzikowska. 2000. Centroid-based summarization of multiple documents: sentence extraction, utility-based evaluation, and user studies. In *Proceedings of the 2000 NAACL-ANLP Workshop on Automatic Summarization*, pp. 21–30, Seattle, USA.

Radlinski, Filip and Susan Dumais. 2006. Improving personalized web search using result diversification. In *Proceedings of 29th International ACM-SIGIR Conference on Research and Development in Information Retrieval (SIGIR 2006)*, pp. 691–692, Seattle, USA.

Tabachnick, Barbara G. and Linda S. Fidell. 2006. *Using Multivariate Statistics*. Allyn & Bacon, Boston, USA, 5th edition.

Wan, Xiaojun, Jianwu Yang, and Jianguo Xiao. 2007. Manifold-ranking based topic-focused multi-document summarization. In *Proceedings of the 20th International Joint Conference on Artificial Intelligence (IJCAI-2007)*, pp. 2903–2908, Hyderabad, India.

Yang, Christopher C. and Fu Lee Wang. 2003. Fractal summarization for mobile devices to access large documents on the web. In *Proceedings of the 12th International Conference on World Wide Web*, pp. 215–224, Budapest, Hungary.

Iteratively Estimating Pattern Reliability and Seed Quality With Extraction Consistency *

Yi-Hsun Lee[a,b], Chung-Yao Chuang[b], and Wen-Lian Hsu[a,b]

[a] Institue of Information Systems and Applications, National Tsing Hua University, 101, Section 2, Kuang-Fu Road, Hsinchu, Taiwan, R.O.C.
[b] Institute of Information Science, Academia Sinica, 128 Academia Road, Sec.2, Nankang, Taipei, Taiwan, ROC
{rog, cychuang, hsu}@iis.sinica.edu.tw

Abstract. In this paper, we focus on the task of distilling relation instances from the Web. Most of the approaches for this task were based on provided seed instances or patterns to initiate the process. Thus, the result of the extraction depends largely on the quality of the instances and patterns. For this matter, we propose an iterative mechanism that estimates the reliability of a pattern by the consistency of its extractions, and reevaluate the usefulness of seed instance based on estimated pattern reliability. The resulting system is a semi-supervised method that can take a large quantity of seed instances with diverse quality. To evaluate the effectiveness of our approach, we experimented on 8 types of relationships. The empirical results show that our system performs quite consistency in different relationships while maintaining high precision and recall value.

Keywords: consistency estimation, relation extraction, semi-supervised approach, seed quality

1 Introduction

The rapid growth of the World Wide Web has attracted a lot of research effort on designing methods that automatically extract knowledge or useful information from large, unstructured text. Different from the conventional corpus, the magnitude and noisy natural of the Web has prohibited analytical approaches to be effective. Consequently, most of the systems that took this challenge proceed in a semi-supervised fashion with a human-provided starting point, such as a few instances of the desired extraction(Mann and Yarowsky, 2005; Muslea, 1999; Ravichandran and Hovy, 2002; Pantel and Pennacchiotti, 2006).

In this paper, we focus on the extraction of relation instances. In this scenario, the system needs to be fed with prepared pairs, such as *<Barack Obama, Auguest 4th>*, or initial extraction patterns to bootstrap. Kozareva and Hovy (2010) mentioned that seed selection plays an important role in this kind of semi-supervised approaches. Therefore, how to select high quality seeds in the initial stage is a critical issue. Most researchers select seeds manually to avoid this problem, but the scalability of such manual selection is not promising. Then, these approaches utilize the given instances, called seeds, and generate extraction patterns that has the potential to locate more instances of the desired type in the text. For example, Ravichandran and Hovy (2002) use surface text patterns like `<Person> was born on <Date>` to answer questions about birth dates.

* This research was supported in part by the National Science Council under grant NSC 100-2631-S-001 -001, and the research center for Humanities and Social Sciences under grant IIS-50-23.

```
{{Infobox NBA Player
| name = Kobe Bryant
| position = [[Shooting guard]]
| team = Los Angeles Lakers
| salary = 23,034,375
| nationality = [[United States|American]]
| birth_date = {{Birth date and age|1978|8|23}}
| birth_place = [[Philadelphia]], [[Pennsylvania]]
| highschool = [[Lower Merion High School|Lower Merion HS]]}}
```

Figure 1: An example of Wikipedia Infobox

Different from those approaches that heavily depend on the quality of the initial seeds, in this paper, we took an alternative direction that focuses more on the quantity of the seed instances. Such a pursuit is made possible by the advent of rich knowledge sources such as Wikipedia[1] and CIA Fact Book[2]. For example, Wikipedia Infoboxes[3] provide an opportunity to easily gather a vast amount of seed instances because the data is stored in a template form as illustrated in Figure 1. Using such sources, we can harvest a large number of pairs like <*Kobe Bryant, Pennsylvania*> from the below infobox as seed instances for birth place extraction. However, using arbitrary seeds to retrieve sentences from the Web will potentially result in a large number of irrelevant content, which will in turn hamper pattern production.

To demonstrate such a situation, we conducted an experiment on seeds gathered from Wikipedia infobox. The results are presented in Table 1. For each relation type, we randomly select 200 seed instances for forming queries and for each query, evaluate first ten snippets returned from search engine. The relevance of the retrieved snippets are judged by two human annotators. We can see that the relevance ratio is not perfect even we have used both entities in the pair for forming the query. One factor behind such imperfection is that the open and voluntary nature of Wikipedia allows editors to fill in information of different specificity. For example, the birth place field of some people contains only less detailed information such as the country instead of more specific description like county or city. Moreover, as can be seen in Table 1, the relevance ratio is not consistent among different relation types and may be surprisingly low such as the type of death place. Such a situation will affect the performance of semi-supervised approaches greatly(Xu *et al.*, 2007).

Fortunately, having abundant seed instances offers us an opportunity to mitigate such a problem. In this paper, we propose a mechanism that iteratively assesses both the quality of seed instances and induced extraction patterns. Our strategy is to estimate the reliability of an extraction pattern by the consistency of its extractions, and alternately, reevaluate the usefulness of seed instances based on estimated pattern reliability. The resulting system works best when it is fed with a large number of seeds, so that the reliability of the induced pattern can be better estimated.

In the next section, we review several semi-supervised approaches that are comparable

[1] http://www.wikipedia.org

[2] http://www.cia.gov/library/pulications/the-world-factbook

[3] http://en.wikipedia.org/wiki/Help:Infobox

Table 1: Relevance ratio of snippets retrieved by submitting seed instances as queries.

Type	Birth Date	Birth Place	Birth Year	Death Date	Death Place	Death Year	Nobel Prize	Spouse
Ratio	0.96	0.768	0.955	0.939	0.107	0.888	0.879	0.889

to our system. We introduce the proposed CEPRA method in Section 3. In Section 4, we describe the experimental settings; and in Section 5, we discuss the experiments conducted to evaluate the performance of different selection approaches. We summarize the results in Section 6. Then, in Section 7, we provide some concluding remarks and consider avenues for future research.

2 Related Works

Semi-supervised approaches start with manually prepared patterns or seeds, and then generate surface text patterns, which are syntactic patterns that connect two entities in one relationship. Surface text patterns are widely used for information extraction. For example, `<Person> was born in <Year>` is an intuitive pattern for matching the birth year of someone. This pattern connect the person and the corresponding year as a semantic relation (birth year) and thus can be used to effectively extract the information. For binary relation extraction, such as the above example of *<Person, Birth Year>*, the first term is often called the *hook* term(e.g. *Person*), and the second one the *target* term(e.g. *Birth Year*) (Alfonseca *et al.*, 2006; Mann and Yarowsky, 2005; Ravichandran and Hovy, 2002).

Most pattern-based approaches for relation extraction are implemented as follows. First, a set of seed instances are prepared in the form of pairs of hook and target terms serving as examples of the intended relation type. For instance, *<Kobe Bryant, 1978>* could be one of the seed instances that fed into a relation extraction system for learning how to extract the birth year of someone. The seed instances are then used as queries for retrieving sentences containing both the hook and the target terms, most popularly from the Web. The retrieved sentences are subsequently used for generating extraction patterns. Several approaches for this step have been proposed such as the longest common substring (Agichtein *et al.*, 2001), substrings in suffix trees (Ravichandran and Hovy, 2002; Ruiz-Casado *et al.*, 2007) and edit distance based alignment (Ruiz-Casado *et al.*, 2007). However, a portion of the retrieved sentences can be, to a certain degree, not relevant in describing the intended relation. Thus, the patterns built on top of them can deviate from the original goal. To overcome this problem, most approaches place an evaluation step in which patterns are assessed using certain criteria. Such an evaluation is usually done using a sentence collection different from the one used for producing the extraction patterns. When using the Web as our extraction source, one apparent choice of this testing collection is the sentences retrieved by only submitting the hook terms to the search engine. In this paper, we denote such a sentence collection as $\mathbf{S}_H$, and the sentence collection gathered using both hook and target terms as $\mathbf{S}_{\langle H,T\rangle}$.

With an additional sentence collection, we can assess the utility of the generated patterns. A simple way to estimate the usefulness of an extraction pattern, p, is based on the extraction frequency of that pattern. This frequency-based estimation (FE) method counts how many terms (regardless correct or not) that pattern, with hook-term slot filled, is able to extract from $\mathbf{S}_H$,

$$f_{FE}(p) = \sum_{h \in \mathbf{H}} |p_h(\mathbf{S}_H)|$$

where $\mathbf{H}$ is the set of all hook terms, p_h is the pattern p with hook term h, $p_h(\mathbf{S}_H)$ is the bag of terms that p_h extracted from $\mathbf{S}_H$, and $|p_h(\mathbf{S}_H)|$ denotes the size of that bag of terms.

Another intuitive approach for evaluating extraction patterns is based on estimated accuracy. The accuracy can only be estimated because of the noisy nature of the Web. For example, in the Chinese portion of Wikipedia, the birth place of Kobe Bryant extracted from infoboxes is "賓夕法尼亞州 (Pennsylvania)" and "費城 (Philadelphia)". However, there are several translations other than the above for "Pennsylvania" and "Philadelphia" in Chinese, which all could appear in the retrieval. Besides the translation problem that we encountered frequently in this work, the voluntary nature of Wikipedia renders automatic evaluation vulnerable to specificity mismatches. For instance, the extracted information may be more detailed than the information provided in the infobox, however, there is no general and convenient way to adjust such a mismatch. For these reasons, rather than calling this approach accuracy-based, we refer it as confidence-based estimation (CE), and is formulated as

$$f_{CE}(p) = \frac{\sum_{\langle h,t\rangle \in \langle \mathbf{H},\mathbf{T}\rangle} |p_h(\mathbf{S}_H) = t|}{\sum_{h \in \mathbf{H}} |p_h(\mathbf{S}_H)|}$$

where $\langle \mathbf{H}, \mathbf{T} \rangle$ is the set of seed instances in which each $\langle h, t \rangle$ is a pair of hook and target terms, and $|p_h(\mathbf{S}_H) = t|$ is the number of terms in $p_h(\mathbf{S}_H)$ that matches t. Both frequency and confidence-based approaches rely heavily on the seed quality. In order to alleviate that, Pantel and Pennacchiotti (2006) proposed a method called *Espresso* which uses point-wise mutual information (PMI) to evaluate the strength of association between a pattern and its extractions,

$$f_{ES}(p) = \frac{\sum_{\langle h,t\rangle \in \langle \mathbf{H},\mathbf{T}\rangle} \frac{pmi(\langle h,t\rangle,p)}{\max_{pmi}} \times g_{ES}(\langle h,t\rangle)}{|\langle \mathbf{H},\mathbf{T}\rangle|}$$

where $pmi(\langle h, t\rangle, p)$ is the point-wise mutual information between pattern p and a relation instance $\langle h, t\rangle$, $\max_{pmi}$ is the largest PMI observed, and $g_{ES}(\langle h, t\rangle)$ is an estimate of the quality of instance $\langle h, t\rangle$,

$$g_{ES}(\langle h,t\rangle) = \frac{\sum_{p \in \mathbf{P}} \frac{pmi(\langle h,t\rangle,p)}{\max_{pmi}} \times f_{ES}(p)}{|\mathbf{P}|}$$

where $\mathbf{P}$ is the set of all patterns. These two formulas are calculated iteratively to adjust the weights of both patterns and seed instances. This approach utilizes the co-occurrence as an indication. However, patterns frequently co-occurred with some instances may still have no relevance to the targeted relation. For example, in (Blohm *et al.*, 2007), *Espresso* got a low precision result in birth year extraction. Xu *et al.* (2007) noted that a factor for pattern-based approach to be effective is the ratio of relevant sentences within the text collection for generating the patterns. In this paper, we gather many seeds extracted from Infoboxes in the initial stage. Due to the seed quality is not consistent, we propose a new approach for evaluating both the patterns and seed instances. Different from the above approaches which only evaluate performance based on $\mathbf{S}_H$, our proposal further utilizes the statistical similarity between extractions from $\mathbf{S}_{\langle H,T\rangle}$ and extractions from $\mathbf{S}_H$, which we believe is a good indicator of pattern reliability.

3 Proposed Approach

In this section, we focus on the main concept about estimating pattern's reliability with consistency measurement between different sentence collections and measure the seed's quality by reliable patterns, described in the following sub-sections.

As pattern generation process can potentially produce a large number of extraction patterns, we need a strategy to find the most reliable patterns. To explain the intuition behind our approach, consider an "oracle collection", $\mathbf{S}_O$, which contains all sentences describing the targeted relation that we can find on the Web. Figure 2 shows the relationship between $\mathbf{S}_H$, $\mathbf{S}_{\langle H,T\rangle}$ and $\mathbf{S}_O$. Ideally, $\mathbf{S}_O$ and $\mathbf{S}_{\langle H,T\rangle}$ would be subsets of $\mathbf{S}_H$ if we could retrieve all sentences containing hook terms from the Web. As depicted in Figure 2, $\mathbf{S}_{\langle H,T\rangle}$

is not a subset of $\mathbf{S}_O$ because the sentences retrieved by using hook and target terms will contain some noisy results as discussed in Section 1 and demonstrated in Table 1. When generating patterns, $\mathbf{S}_{\langle H,T\rangle} \setminus \mathbf{S}_O$ will cause relevance problems, which makes the pattern induction procedure producing deviated patterns. On the other hand, $\mathbf{S}_O \setminus \mathbf{S}_{\langle H,T\rangle}$ will cause specificity problems, which undermines useful patterns in evaluation.

Manually selecting seed instances could reduce the extent of these two kinds of problems. However, the scalability of such an approach is not promising. Thus, we need an approach to automatically assess the utility of each seed instance in evaluating the extraction patterns. Supposedly, high utility seed instances are the ones which distribute high scores into the reliable patterns. In this work, we assume that the reliability of a pattern can be measured by looking into the performance similarities between applying that pattern to $\mathbf{S}_H$ and $\mathbf{S}_{\langle H,T\rangle}$. We consider such a similarity because if a pattern extract mostly in the intersection of $\mathbf{S}_H$, $\mathbf{S}_{\langle H,T\rangle}$ and $\mathbf{S}_O$, then its performance will be consistent regardless extracting from $\mathbf{S}_H$ or $\mathbf{S}_{\langle H,T\rangle}$. Once those highly reliable patterns are found, we could in turn assessing the quality of each seed instance.

In this work, we use the *extended Jaccard coefficient*(Strehl and Ghosh, 2000) (EJAC) to evaluate the consistency in performance when applying to two different sentence collection

$$J(p) = \frac{V_{\mathbf{S}_H}(p) \bullet V_{\mathbf{S}_{\langle H,T\rangle}}(p)}{\parallel V_{\mathbf{S}_H}(p) \parallel^2 + \parallel V_{\mathbf{S}_{\langle H,T\rangle}}(p) \parallel^2 - V_{\mathbf{S}_H}(p) \bullet V_{\mathbf{S}_{\langle H,T\rangle}}(p)} \tag{1}$$

where $V_X(p)$ is the performance vector of p under sentence collection X which comprises the pattern's weighted precision estimates for each seed instance

$$V_X(p) = \left(\ \lambda_{\langle h_1,t_1\rangle}(p,X), \quad \lambda_{\langle h_2,t_2\rangle}(p,X), \quad ..., \quad \lambda_{\langle h_n,t_n\rangle}(p,X) \ \right)$$

where $\lambda_{\langle h_i,t_i\rangle}(p,X) = A_{\langle h_i,t_i\rangle}(p,X) \times w_{\langle h_i,t_i\rangle}$ in which $w_{\langle h_i,t_i\rangle}$ is the weight of seed instance $\langle h_i, t_i\rangle$ (described below), and $A_{\langle h_i,t_i\rangle}(p,X)$ is the estimated precision of p,

$$A_{\langle h_i,t_i\rangle}(p,X) = \frac{|p_{h_i}(X) = t_i|}{|p_{h_i}(X)|}$$

When binding to some hook terms, a pattern may not be able to extract anything from $\mathbf{S}_H$ or $\mathbf{S}_{\langle H,T\rangle}$. In this case, we use the *expected target accuracy* (ETA), μ_X, as the missing value,

$$\mu_X(p) = \frac{\sum_{\langle h,t\rangle \in \langle \mathbf{H},\mathbf{T}\rangle} A_{\langle h,t\rangle}(p,X) \times w_{\langle h,t\rangle}}{\sum_{\langle h,t\rangle \in \langle \mathbf{H},\mathbf{T}\rangle} w_{\langle h,t\rangle}} \tag{2}$$

where X can be $\mathbf{S}_H$ or $\mathbf{S}_{\langle H,T\rangle}$. However, using only Equation 1 is not sufficient because inferior patterns would have similar low precision distribution in both $\mathbf{S}_H$ and $\mathbf{S}_{\langle H,T\rangle}$.

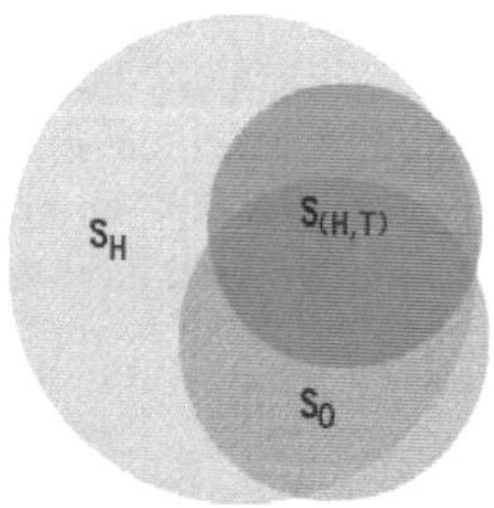

Figure 2: Overlap Diagram between $\mathbf{S}_H$, $\mathbf{S}_{\langle H,T\rangle}$ and $\mathbf{S}_O$

Therefore, we combine Equation 1 and 2 to form our evaluation metric

$$f_{CEPRA}(p) = \alpha \times \mu_{\mathbf{S}_{\langle H,T \rangle}}(p) + \beta \times J(p)$$

In this paper, we set both α and β to 0.5.

As mentioned earlier, the quality of the seed instances is an important aspect of this task. Intuitively, the utility of a seed instance can be assessed by the frequency that it is matched by extraction patterns. This assumes that the more inbound links to a seed, the higher quality it gets. However, there may be some overly-general patterns that are characterized by high coverage and low precision. Therefore, we need to prune those possibly unreliable patterns and utilize the remaining ones to evaluate the quality of seed instances. It is conceivable that if the reliable patterns cannot extract correct target term for a specific hook term, then the quality of this seed instance is questionable. In other word, the more reliable the patterns matching the instance, the higher will be the quality of that instance. Hence, we derive our formula for weighing seed instance as

$$v_{\langle h,t \rangle} = \sum_{p \in \mathbf{P}} \begin{cases} A_{\langle h,t \rangle}(p, \mathbf{S}_{\langle H,T \rangle}), & \text{if } f_{CEPRA}(p) > \varepsilon \\ 0, & \text{otherwise} \end{cases}$$

where $\varepsilon = 0.7$ in this work. This value is normalized to obtain the final weight

$$w_{\langle h,t \rangle} = \frac{v_{\langle h,t \rangle} - \min_i v_{\langle h_i,t_i \rangle}}{\max_i v_{\langle h_i,t_i \rangle}/c}$$

where $c = 20$ in this work.

$w_{\langle h,t \rangle}$'s and $f_{CEPRA}(p)$'s are calculated iteratively. Initially, we compute $f_{CEPRA}(p)$'s using $w_{\langle h,t \rangle} = 1$. Then, we collect patterns with high f_{CEPRA} values to determine $w_{\langle h,t \rangle}$'s. After setting the seed weights, we can re-calculate the f_{CEPRA}'s with reduced influence from inferior seeds. As this process iterates, only patterns whose f_{CEPRA} values higher than a threshold are retained. Note that we also keep patterns with high ETA value if it can extract several seed instances with high $w_{\langle h,t \rangle}$ and their f_{CEPRA} is set to its $\mu_{\mathbf{S}_{\langle H,T \rangle}}$.

4 System Architecture and Experimental Environment

In this section, we describe our system, Consistent Estimation Pattern-based Relation Acquirer (CEPRA), which runs briefly as follows. Based on the seed instances gathered from the infoboxes in Chinese portion of Wikipedia, we collect two sentence collections $\mathbf{S}_H$ and $\mathbf{S}_{\langle H,T \rangle}$ from the Web. The retrieved sentences are preprocessed with segmentation and parts-of-speech tagging. Next, extraction patterns are generated with an alignment-based approach (Sung *et al.*, 2009) based on sentences in $\mathbf{S}_{\langle H,T \rangle}$. Those patterns are then evaluated by the approach described in Section 3. Finally, we utilize the retained patterns to extract relation instances.

To assess the performance of our method, we performed experiments on 8 types of relations. The experimental settings are described below:

Experiment Data: We collected our seed instances from the infoboxes in the Chinese portion of Wikipedia. The collected instances are biographical relations and of 8 different types. To compile the training $\mathbf{S}_{\langle H,T \rangle}$, for each relation type, we used 1000 seed instances and submitted the hook and target terms of each training seed to retrieve 50 snippets from Google. Among those 1000 seed instances, we randomly picked 50 instances and used their corresponding sentences retrieved from the Web to run pattern generation. The produced patterns are evaluated using whole training sentence collection. A testing sentence collection[4] is formed by using a separate set of 200 instances from each relation type. This testing set contains 3768 sentences and is annotated by two human annotators (the relevance statistics are shown in Table 1.)

Evaluation and Comparisons: We compared our method with three other approaches described in Section 2. In this paper, we want to evaluate the difference in pattern selection, thus, we use the same pattern generation procedure for all 4 approaches. The results are compared both in recall and precision.

5 Evaluation of Pattern Estimation Approaches

Figure 3 shows the precision value of the eight relationships for top N ranked patterns. In this figure, we can observe that none of the approaches performs well on the *Death Place* relationship. In Table 1, we can find although the relevant ratio is quite low in the *Death Place* relationship, which affects the performance of the pattern-based systems. However, on this relationship, our approach achieves a higher precision score (0.67) than the compared approaches. In the *Birth Place* relationship, the *FE*, *CE* and *Espresso* approaches would get a lower precision at top 500 ranked patterns. In contrast, our approach achieves a perfect precision score of 1 on the top 500 and 1000 patterns. In these relationships with lower relevant ratio, our approach still performs better than other approaches. Next, in some relationships with high quality seeds like *Birth Date, Birth Year, Nobel Prize* and *Spouse*, the *CE* and our approach both achieve good performance. But we can find the *CE* approach with a significant drop when N increased in *Death Date* and *Death Year* relationships. Contrast to our approach, we still get a stable and good performance, higher than 0.9, in these relationships. It means that our approach would gather more reliable patterns than other approaches. Finally, unlike other approaches, the *Espresso* approach only considers the relationships between the targets and the patterns. It did not perform well in our experiments.

Next we observe the methods' distribution of precision value between these eight relationships is quite different In Figure 3. Our approach achieves the highest precision score on the top 500 ranked patterns, but the score decreases slightly as N increases. In contrast, the *Espresso's* precision score increases with N ranked patterns. However, this phenomenon presents that the top N ranked patterns would not be the good choice. Figure 3 also shows that the *CE* approach performs quite unstable in different relationships. This approach is easily influenced on the quality of seeds. Next, we discuss the recall and precision value derived by the compared approaches on the eight relationships.

Table 2 shows the highest recall value of the eight relationships with precision value above γ, range from 0.7 to 0.9. Because the *Espresso* and *FE* approaches get lower

[4] http://140.109.17.85/cepra/

Table 2: Highest recall value with different precision threshold, γ, in these eight relationships.

Type	Method	γ			Type	Method	γ		
		0.9	**0.8**	**0.7**			**0.9**	**0.8**	**0.7**
Birth Date	CE	0.68	0.70	0.74	Birth Place	CE	0.17	0.35	0.43
	CEPRA	0.71	0.74	0.74		CEPRA	0.17	0.35	0.43
Birth Year	CE	0.71	0.73	0.73	Death Date	CE	0.57	0.58	0.58
	CEPRA	0.71	0.72	0.73		CEPRA	0.56	0.58	0.58
Death Place	CE	0	0	0	Death Year	CE	0.28	0.33	0.35
	CEPRA	0	0	0		CEPRA	0.33	0.41	0.43
Nobel Prize	CE	0.39	0.42	0.43	Spouse	CE	0	0.14	0.43
	CEPRA	0.38	0.42	0.43		CEPRA	0	0.4	0.48

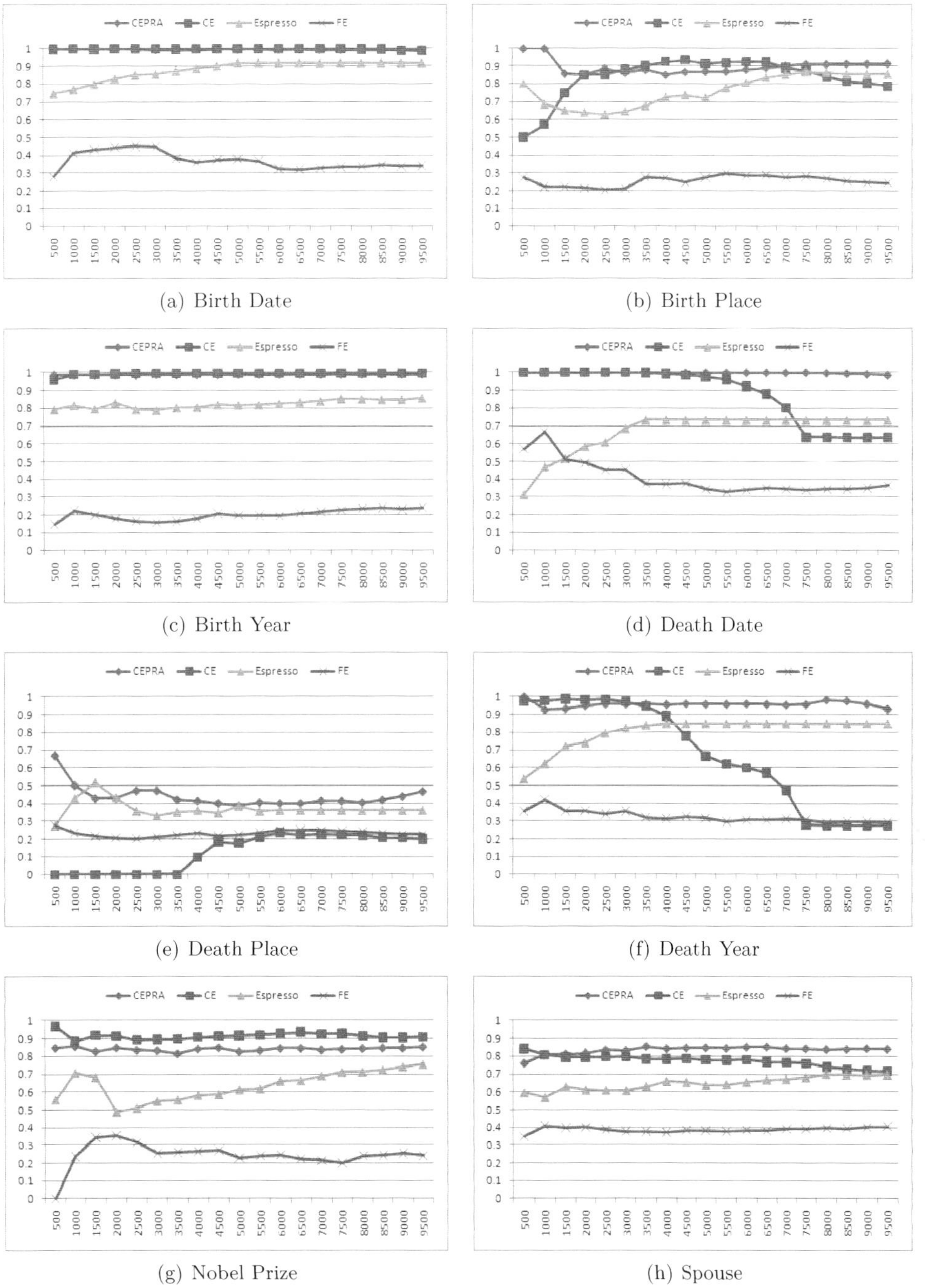

(a) Birth Date (b) Birth Place

(c) Birth Year (d) Death Date

(e) Death Place (f) Death Year

(g) Nobel Prize (h) Spouse

Figure 3: Precision of the Top N ranking patterns of the four compared approaches, *CEPRA*, *CE*, *FE* and *Espresso*. The x-axis represents the precision value and the y-axis represents the number of N.

precision values at top N ranked patterns, we do not consider these two approaches in this table. First of all, in the *Death Year* relationship, we can find our approach achieves a higher recall value than the CE approach. As shown in Figure 3, the CE would encounter a significant drop in this relationship at top 6000 to 7000 ranked patterns. Compared to our approach, we not only retain more reliable patterns but we also get a higher recall value. In the *Spouse* relationship, although our approach get a bit lower precision value, we get a higher recall value 0.4 compared to 0.14 for the CE approach. Generally speaking, in this empirical experiment, our approach would retain more reliable patterns while maintaining stable and high performance in different relationships.

6 Discussion

As mentioned in Sections 5, the performance of CE approach is not stable on different relationships. We assume that the problem is caused by 1) insufficient information to judge whether the target is correct, which means that the CE approach yields a biased confidence score because of the influence of low quality seeds; 2) the lack of relevant sentences in the $\mathbf{S}_H$. In the FE approach, the precision value of the top N patterns is quite low because a pattern with a high frequency is always a general pattern. In some domains, highly frequent patterns may be useful for finding new instances. However, in relation extraction tasks, we need to find some related or specific patterns instead of highly frequent patterns. Next, we consider the performance of the $Espresso$ approach. In this paper, we utilize collections comprised of sentences retrieved from the Web. This factor may affect the performance of the $Espresso$ approach. However, the patterns highly occurred with some targets possible describe different relationships. Besides, how to compile a training set is an important issue when utilizing the $Espresso$ approach. In this paper, we propose an approach to estimate a pattern's reliability between different sets. We use an iteratively pattern-seed evaluation method to prune irrelevant patterns and low quality seeds. In Sections 5, we noted that the $CEPRA$ achieved a stable performance on different relationships. However, we still need to resolve the following issues. 1) Because our approach was based on utilizing many seeds extracted from Wikipedia Infoboxes, we need to observe more details about the seed sets like the learning curve with different sizes of seed sets or the performance on different ratio of inferior quality seeds. 2) Currently, we do not consider the issue about pattern generation. Maybe we need to concern about utilizing more complex linguistic tools to generate frequent patterns and check our validation performance is consistent or not.

7 Conclusion

Unlike other semi-supervised approach utilizing manually prepared seeds in the beginning, we proposed a method to estimate pattern's reliability by abundant seeds extracted from Wikipedia Infoboxes automatically. First, we employ an automatic approach to select sentences, and then use an alignment-based pattern generation approach. Next we apply consistency measurement to estimate pattern's reliability and utilize an iteratively approach to find high quality seeds and reliable patterns. Finally, we use the derived patterns to find precise targets. Based on our experimental result, our system has a more stable and better performance than other approaches. In our future work, we will discuss more experiments about the sizes of seed sets and how to utilize a deep linguistic tool to improve the system's performance.

References

Agichtein, Eugene, Luis Gravano, Jeff Pavel, Viktoriya Sokolova, and Aleksandr Voskoboynik. 2001. Snowball: a prototype system for extracting relations from large text collections. In *Proceedings of the 2001 ACM SIGMOD international conference on Management of data*, SIGMOD '01, p. 612, New York, NY, USA. ACM.

Alfonseca, Enrique, Pablo Castells, Manabu Okumura, and Maria Ruiz-Casado. 2006. A rote extractor with edit distance-based generalisation and multi-corpora precision calculation. In *Proceedings of the COLING/ACL on Main conference poster sessions*, COLING-ACL '06, pp. 9–16, Stroudsburg, PA, USA. Association for Computational Linguistics.

Blohm, Sebastian, Philipp Cimiano, and Egon Stemle. 2007. Harvesting relations from the web: quantifiying the impact of filtering functions. In *Proceedings of the 22nd national conference on Artificial intelligence - Volume 2*, pp. 1316–1321. AAAI Press.

Kozareva, Zornitsa and Eduard Hovy. 2010. Not all seeds are equal: measuring the quality of text mining seeds. In *Human Language Technologies: The 2010 Annual Conference of the North American Chapter of the Association for Computational Linguistics*, HLT '10, pp. 618–626, Stroudsburg, PA, USA. Association for Computational Linguistics.

Mann, Gideon S. and David Yarowsky. 2005. Multi-field information extraction and cross-document fusion. In *Proceedings of the 43rd Annual Meeting on Association for Computational Linguistics*, ACL '05, pp. 483–490, Stroudsburg, PA, USA. Association for Computational Linguistics.

Muslea, Ion. 1999. Extraction patterns for information extraction tasks: A survey. In *AAAI-99 Workshop on Machine Learning for Information Extraction*, pp. 1–6.

Pantel, Patrick and Marco Pennacchiotti. 2006. Espresso: leveraging generic patterns for automatically harvesting semantic relations. In *Proceedings of the 21st International Conference on Computational Linguistics and the 44th annual meeting of the Association for Computational Linguistics*, ACL-44, pp. 113–120, Stroudsburg, PA, USA. Association for Computational Linguistics.

Ravichandran, Deepak and Eduard Hovy. 2002. Learning surface text patterns for a question answering system. In *Proceedings of the 40th Annual Meeting on Association for Computational Linguistics*, ACL '02, pp. 41–47, Stroudsburg, PA, USA. Association for Computational Linguistics.

Ruiz-Casado, Maria, Enrique Alfonseca, and Pablo Castells. 2007. Automatising the learning of lexical patterns: An application to the enrichment of wordnet by extracting semantic relationships from wikipedia. *Data Knowl. Eng.*, 61, 484–499, June.

Strehl, Alexander and Joydeep Ghosh. 2000. Value-based customer grouping from large retail data-sets. In *In Proceedings of the SPIE Conference on Data Mining and Knowledge Discovery*, pp. 33–42.

Sung, Cheng-Lung, Cheng-Wei Lee, Hsu-Chun Yen, and Wen-Lian Hsu. 2009. Alignment-based surface patterns for factoid question answering systems. *Integr. Comput.-Aided Eng.*, 16, 259–269, August.

Xu, Feiyu, Hans Uszkoreit, and Hong Li. 2007. A seed-driven bottom-up machine learning framework for extracting relations of various complexity. In *Proceedings of the 45th Annual Meeting of the Association of Computational Linguistics*, pp. 584–591, Prague, Czech Republic, June. Association for Computational Linguistics.

The Effect of Answer Patterns for Supervised Named Entity Recognition in Thai *

Nutcha Tirasaroj and Wirote Aroonmanakun

Department of Linguistics, Chulalongkorn University,
Bangkok, Thailand
pernn39@gmail.com, awirote@chula.ac.th

Abstract. In this paper, we present Thai named entity recognition (NER) systems using supervised Conditional Random Fields (CRFs) with various answer patterns to find out whether different answer patterns would affect the performance of the systems. Every system used the same set of features except the answers in the training corpus. There are 5 patterns of answer used in this study. The results show that the answer tags having more information can help improve the system performance than those having less information.

Keywords: Named entity recognition, Conditional Random Fields, Supervised machine learning, Thai language processing

Introduction

Named entity recognition (NER) was first introduced in MUC-6 in 1990's. According to MUC, NER is divided into 3 main groups. The first one is entity names including person, organization, and location names. The second one is temporal expressions and the last one is numerical expressions which are monetary values and percentages. Among these 3 groups, the first one is the most difficult to be recognized because the structures of the names are complicated and the contexts they occur are varying. As a result, a number of research on NER as well as this study have focused on the first group.

Most research on NER using statistical models mainly focused on feature selection since features are the most important part of the models and directly affect the performance of the systems. It was assumed that the answer given to the models has no effect on the system performance. However, in Chinese, some research on NER (Mao *et al.*, 2008; Yu *et al.*, 2008), the work of Yu *et al.* (2008) proved that the number of answer tags can help improve the system performance. The use of more tags yields better results because it gives more information of entity names' boundaries to the system for learning. For machine learning, it tends to be that the more information is provided, the better the performance of the system is. Research on Thai NER using statistical models such as SVMs (Suwanno *et al.*, 2007), HMM (Sansing and Prayot, 2010), ME (Chanlekha and Kawtrakul, 2004), CRFs (Tepdang *et al.*; Tirasaroj and Aroonmanakun, 2009), etc. also focused on feature selections. None has studied the effect of answer patterns for their supervised systems. The answer pattern is the way we give the answer in the training corpus for supervised machine learning system. The answer suggests how much information of NEs provided for the systems. For example, the answer can be only the information of NE types or it can include the NE boundaries. In addition, most of previous

* The work reported in this paper was supported by The Thailand Research Fund (TRF) under grant no MSG53Z0008, and partially supported by Chulalongkorn University Centenary Academic Development Project. Moreover, we would like to thank NECTEC for their BEST 2009 corpus and reviewers for their suggestions and comments.

research did not distinguish metonymic names, which are location names referring to organizations and organization names referring to locations.

Thus, apart from presenting the NER systems, this study is conducted to find out if the more informative answers can improve the system performance of Thai NER like in Chinese or not. In addition, we will find out the differences of results when metonymic names are marked. Our NER systems are based on CRF models. Recently, there was a comparative study on Thai word segmentation approaches (Haruechaiyasak *et al.*, 2008). The results showed that CRFs yielded the best performance when compared with other machine learning methods, Naïve Bayes, decision tree, and Support Vector Machine. CRFs were also applied to Thai NER (Tepdang *et al.*; Tirasaroj and Aroonmanakun, 2009) and yielded about 80% of recognition rate or F-measure. In this study, we used CRF++0.53 implemented by Taku Kudo.

Related Work

There are a number of research focusing on Thai named entity recognition. Charoenpornsawat *et al.* (1998) used feature-based approach such as context words, collocations, and heuristic rules to extract the candidates and then used Winnow algorithm to recognize the entity names. The accuracy was 92.17%. Chanlekha *et al.* (2002) applied statistical and heuristic rule-based model to POS tagged data. The results showed that the model did have much problem when extract the names from magazines but when the model was applied to the newspapers, the accuracy was quite low. It was due to the written style of magazines that the names were usually in regular patterns.

Tirasaroj and Aroonmanakun (2009) compared the performance of the systems between word-based and syllable-based system by applying CRF. The results showed no significant difference. Although in their work, they mentioned about the NE tags that differentiated between common named entities – person, organization, and location names - and metonymic names, the organization names referring to the locations and vice versa. Their answers did not divided into five categories like their tags but just three categories as other previous research.

In Thai NER, the researchers have never mentioned about their answer patterns used in their systems but in Chinese, there are some research proving that the number of tag types does have an effect on supervised learning systems. The amount of tags used in 2008 is more than those used in 2006. In 2006, Feng *et al.* (2006) used BIO tags; B for the beginning of names, I for the inside of names, and O for others. In 2008, Mao *et al.* (2008) used BIOE and Yu *et al.* (2008) used BIOES instead of BIO. They added E and S; E for the end of names and S for single character names. From their research, giving more tags could help improve the system performance. In our study, we will apply NE type tags like in Tirasaroj and Aroonmanakun's work and for NE boundaries, we will adapt from BIOE. We will explain in more detail in the section about patterns of answer.

Conditional Random Filed Models

Conditional Random Fields (CRFs) (Lafferty *et al.*, 2001), which are developed from MEMMs, is a discriminative undirected graphical model. They are usually used for segmenting and labeling sequence data. CRF models the conditional distribution P(Y|X), where Y is the hidden label sequence or output and X is the observation or input. A linear chain CRF defines the conditional probability of sequence Y when given the observation sequence X as follows:

$$p(y|x) = \frac{1}{Z(x)} \exp\left(\sum_{t=1}^{T}\sum_{k=1}^{K} \lambda_k f_k(y_{t-1}, y_t, x, t)\right) \quad (1)$$

Z is a normalization factor defined as:

$$Z(x) = \sum_{y} \exp\left(\sum_{t=1}^{T} \sum_{k=1}^{K} \lambda_k f_k(y_{t-1}, y_t, x, t)\right) \quad (2)$$

where $f_k(y_{t-1}, y_t, x, t))$ is an arbitrary feature function, λ_k is a learned weight for each feature function.

Corpus

The corpus used in this study is taken from BEST 2009 corpus. BEST 2009 is the corpus created for training and testing word segmentation systems in "BEST 2009: THAI WORD SEGMENTATION SOFTWARE CONTEST." Many genres of data were collected in BEST but only news genre was used in our study because in the news there are all three kinds of named entities- person, organization, and location names- and the number of entities are much more various than those found in other genres like fictions and encyclopedia. Thai word segmentation program (Aroonmanakun, 2002) was used to segment all data in our corpus. The number of tokens is about 367,600 tokens.

As we applied supervised learning system, we tagged all answers in the corpus. The data from BEST 2009 had been tagged the NE boundaries but not NE types. We then had to add NE types manually. As one of the main purposes of this study was to compare the answer patterns of the systems, we tried to give as much information of answers as possible. We followed Tirasaroj and Aroonmakun (2009) so that there were five NE types in our corpus. Apart from common NE types, person, organization, and location names, there were two more tags for metonymic names, organization names referring to locations and vice versa. The followings were NE tags in our corpus:

1. <persName>…</persName> is for person names including first names, last names, nicknames, alias, etc. The titles and honorifics right before the names are also included such as

<persName>ลุงสมหมาย</persName>

Uncle Sommai

2. <orgName>…</orgName> is for organization names. In case that the full names are followed by their abbreviated names, they are tagged separately like

<orgName>กระทรวงสาธารณสุข</orgName><orgName><abb>สธ.</abb></orgName>

Ministry of Public Health MOPH

3. <placeName>…</placeName> is for location names such as

ที่<placeName>นครปฐม</placeName>

at Nakornpathom

4. <orgName ref="loc">…</orgName> is for organization names used to refer to locations. Generally, if the locations do not have their specific names, their names would undoubtedly be the same as the organization situated in that place. For example,

เข้ามารักษาโรคที่<orgName ref="loc">โรงพยาบาลสัตว์</orgName>

had exam at Veterinary hospital

5. <placeName ref="org">…</placeName> is for location names used as organization names. Mostly, this kind of names is used to refer to an organization, especially official offices and the government such as

<placeName ref="org">ประเทศไทย</placeName>ได้แจ้งไปยังองค์การระหว่างประเทศเรียบร้อยแล้ว

Thailand has already informed International Organizations

Besides NE tags, there is a tag for abbreviations. The tag <abb>…</abb> is used to tag every abbreviation in the corpus. In case of the abbreviations like titles or honorifics which are parts of names, the abbreviation tags would be tagged inside NE tags like the example in the organization tag above.

Features and Patterns of Answer

In this study, we applied both open and closed features. The open features are the knowledge we got outside the corpus while the closed features are those extracted from the training and testing data. There are 7 features used in this study; two open features, three closed features, and two baseline features. The open and closed features are all binary features. In this study, the deep linguistic features such as POS, functional features were not used because this is the preliminary stage of our study and these features take a lot of time in preparing the training corpus. The followings are the details of each feature used in this study.

The open features: applying only closed features may not be enough for the system as the entity names sometimes occur in ambiguous context or without any clue words. The gazetteers were used to help extract this kind of names. Our gazetteers include the lists of person, organization, and location names, abbreviated organization names, and personal titles and honorifics. If the token matched with any part of the names in the list, this feature would be set to 'Y'.

Another outside knowledge is a general word list. This feature was set from the patterns of names that the names can composed of known and unknown strings. However, although those known strings are words found in dictionary, they are sometimes not words used in daily life. For example, "อัปสร" (Upsorn) is a synonym of 'นางฟ้า' (Nang-faa); both mean an angel, but no one generally calls the angel as "อัปสร" except in literature. Then, words that are not frequently found in daily life are possibly a name or a part of the name. So, in this case, the feature for the token not found in the list was set to 'Y'.

The closed features: there were three closed features we got from the corpus, including abbreviation, context clues, and repeated NE. The details of each feature are as follows:

The abbreviation feature was considered from the characteristic of Thai entity names that they are usually preceded by the abbreviation. Person names usually co-occur with titles and honorifics such as น.ส. (Miss), ดร. (Ph.D), organization names with company designators such as บจ. (company limited), and location names with location indicators like ถ. (Road), จ. (province). Those abbreviations can help indicate not only named entities' boundaries but also their types. For this feature, the sequence of three tokens would be set to 'Y' if one of them was an abbreviation.

The context clues are the key factors in assigning the types of metonymic names. For example, the location names, in fact, could not co-occur with verbs since only persons and organizations can do some actions. Thus, whenever the location names co-occur with verbs, it implies that these names are used as metonymic names referring to the organization. The list of context clues was extracted from the three tokens before and after the entity names in the training corpus. If the token matched with any token in the list, the feature was set to 'Y'.

Repeated NE is set from our assumption that most named entities do not occur once in the text. Then, if the strings of words appeared several times in the text, we assumed that they would probably be entity names. For this feature, if the three tokens, including the current token and the tokens before and after, occurred together more than three times in the text, they would be set to 'Y'.

The baseline features: apart from the open and closed features, there were baseline features used as templates for running CRF. Our baseline features were unigram and bigram.

Besides feature selection, we have to set the patterns of answer. There are 5 answer patterns used in this study. Each pattern has different information of named entities' boundaries and types. The details are as shown in Table 1:

Table 1: Answer patterns

No	Pattern
1	P, O, L, X
2	B, I, X – PER, ORG, LOC
3	B, I, X – P, O, L, LO, OL
4	B, I, E, X – PER, ORG, LOC
5	B, I, E, X – P, O, L, LO, OL

Pattern 1 has the least information and Pattern 5 has the most information. Pattern 1 has no information of named entities' boundaries but only basic entity types. The entity boundaries are BIEX, B for the beginning of a name, I for a token inside a name, E for the end of a name, and X for others. The answer pattern 1, 2, and 4 have basic entity types. The metonymic names are included in their referred types. The pattern 3 and 5 have all 5 entity types.

An example of training data, including features and answer, is shown in figure 1.

กระทรวง	N	N ..	B-ORG
สาธารณสุข	N	N ..	E-ORG
<s>	N	N ..	X
องค์การ	N	N ..	B-ORG
อนามัย	N	Y ..	I-ORG
โลก	N	Y ..	E-ORG
และ	N	Y ..	X
…			

Figure 1: Example of training data with the 4th answer pattern

The first column is the token. From the second column to the one before the last column, they are features which are all binary features. The last column is the answer given to CRF. Every answer pattern uses the same set of features.

Experimental Results

In this experiment, we used 10-fold cross validation and evaluated our systems with precision (P), recall (R), and F-measure (F). Only exactly matched answer is counted as correct answer. Table 2 shows the experimental results of all systems.

The performances of the systems with answer pattern 2 to 5 are almost indifferent, the difference of the values of f-measure is less than 1%. However, when compared with pattern 1, their performances are about 3% better. From all of the answer patterns, f-measure of pattern 4 is the highest while pattern 1 is the lowest. The results show that the patterns containing more information tend to improve the systems' performances than those having less information.

Although pattern 5 has most information, it is not the one getting the best performance. The main reason may be that the training corpus is not large enough. Since the named entities are divided into 5 categories, the system, therefore, needs a large number of examples of names in each category for training. However, from all of the entity types, the organization names referring to the locations have the lowest number of examples (147 instances), while the highest number of entity names is 5,672 instances which are person names. As a result, the f-measures of this kind of names, both in pattern 3 and 5, are low when compared with other named entity types.

Table 2: Experimental results

NE	P(%)	R(%)	F(%)
1. P, O, L, X			
PER	85.69	83.93	84.77
ORG	77.28	70.55	73.75
LOC	76.82	70.57	73.52
ALL	80.39	75.26	77.73
2. B, I, X – PER, ORG, LOC			
PER	90.59	86.37	88.41
ORG	82.68	74.61	78.42
LOC	80.72	70.71	75.31
ALL	85.24	77.67	81.26
3. B, I, X – P, O, L, LO, OL			
P	90.14	86.17	88.08
O	82.57	75.15	78.65
L	80.44	73.26	76.55
LO	81.43	67.32	73.43
OL	75.39	43.71	54.89
ALL	84.82	77.09	80.75
4. B, I, E, X – PER, ORG, LOC			
PER	92.05	86.50	89.16
ORG	82.19	74.23	77.99
LOC	79.92	70.77	74.98
ALL	85.37	77.64	81.30
5. B, I, E, X – P, O, L, LO, OL			
P	91.52	86.47	88.89
O	82.67	75.38	78.83
L	80.04	73.35	76.45
LO	81.04	68.00	73.72
OL	77.35	43.57	55.35
ALL	85.29	77.37	81.12

Another main problem of metonymic names is that the systems are confused about common names and metonymic names. The influential factor that can differentiate them is the context in which they occur. For instance, if the location names are followed by verbs or the organization names are preceded by prepositions, they tend to be metonymic names rather than common names. However, in this study, we did not use the deep linguistic features like POS tagging, so the systems could not know the part of speech of each word. Moreover, one word can have more than one part of speech. As a result, considering only forms of words like in our work is not enough for recognizing the differences between common names and metonymic names. We believe that the problem of metonymic name classification may be one factor that more or less affects the accuracy of organization and location name recognition of many previous studies.

The main problem of pattern 1 is the boundaries of named entities. Although classifying the entities' types correctly, the system tended to merge 2 named entities that were separated by a space but in the same category into a name. The examples are as follows:

<persName>จอย</persName><s><persName>รินลณี</persName>

<placeName>ตะกั่วทุ่ง</placeName><s><placeName>ตะกั่วป่า</placeName>

Form the performance of all systems shown in table 2, we can see that the answer given to the system more or less affect the system performance. Many researchers give importance to feature selection and overlook the answer designed for the system. However, from this study, it indicates that every process is important to the system.

Discussion

When considered overall performance in table 2, we will see that the f-measures of person names in every system are much higher than others. Apart from the highest number of samples in the corpus, the person names usually appear in regular patterns such as occurring with the titles, the first names separated from the last names by spaces, etc. As a result, the systems could easily recognize the person names rather than other NE types. For the organization names, although they do not appear in the regular patterns like person names, the way they appear in the text seems like a pattern. The organization names that have abbreviated forms are usually first introduced with the full names in the text and later appear with their abbreviated names. Thus, the f-measures of organization names are better than those of location names in every system.

In addition to f-measures, the recalls were quite low. The main problem is that the systems could hardly extract the names appearing without clue words such as person names appearing without the titles or honorifics or the names that are in ambiguous context. For example, "ส่งเสริม" in "ผศ. น.สพ. ดร. ทวีศักดิ์ ส่งเสริม" (Assistant Prof. Dr. Taweesak Songserm) is in fact a last name but has the same form like a verb "ส่งเสริม", which means 'support' in Thai. As a result, the system could extract only "ผศ. น.สพ. ดร. ทวีศักดิ์" (Assistant Prof. Dr. Taweesak) and cut off his last name.

Moreover, in Thai, lots of names, especially location and organization names, are in the same forms as general phrases. Consequently, if they do not appear in the obvious context which can indicate that they are actually proper names, the systems could not differentiate between them and general phrases. For example, the system could not recognize "ศูนย์ปฏิบัติการโรคไข้หวัดนก" (Bird Flu Operation Centre) or "องค์การเฝ้าระวังโรคระบาดในสัตว์" (The Animal Disease Surveillance Organization) as the organization names. This explains why the accuracy of person names is higher than those of other names. It is possible to enhance the system performance by using more syntactic features like part of speeches, but for cases in which named entities have the same word forms and syntactic structures like general words, whether those named entity would be recognized is still a question.

Conclusion

In this study, we present Thai named entity recognition system using CRFs as well as comparing the performance of the systems applying different answer patterns. The results show that the answer pattern does have an effect on the performance of the system. The answer patterns having more information can help improve the system performance than those having less information. Nevertheless, the systems have the problem of extracting names without clue words or in ambiguous context. Thus, for future work, we may consider using POS as a feature in our model.

References

Aroonmanakun, W. 2002. Collocation and Thai Word Segmentation. *Proceedings of SNLP-Oriental COCOSDA 2002*. pp.68-75. Prachuapkhirikhan.

Chanlekha, H., and A. Kawtrakul. 2004. Thai Named Entity Extraction by incorporating Maximum Entropy Model with Simple Heuristic Information. *International Joint Conference of Natural Language Processing (IJCNLP-2004)*. Hainan Island.

Chanlekha, H., A. Kawtrakul, P. Varasrai and I. Mulasas. 2002. Statistical and Heuristic Rule Based Model for Thai Named Entity Recognition. *Proceeding of SNLP- Oriental COCOSDA 2002*. Hua Hin.

Charoenpornsawat, P., B. Kijsirikul and S. Meknavin. 1998. Feature-based Proper Name Identification in Thai. *Proceedings of National Computer Science and Engineering Conference*. Bangkok.

Feng, Y., L. Sun and Y. Lv. 2006. Chinese Word Segmentation and Named Entity Recognition Based on Conditional Random Fields Models. *Proceeding of the Fifth SIGHAN Workshop on Chinese Language Processing*, pp. 181-184. Sydney.

Haruechaiyasak, C., S. Kongyoung and M. N. Dailey. 2008. A Comparative Study on Thai Word Segmentation Approach. *Proceedings of ECTI-CON.* Krabi.

Lafferty, J., A. McCallum, and F. Pereira. 2001. Conditional Random Fields: Probabilistic Models for Sequence Data. *Proceeding of 18thICML.* San Francisco.

Mao, X., S. He, S. Bao, Y. Dong and H. Wang. 2008. Chinese Word Segmentation and Named Entity Recognition Based on Conditional Random Fields. *Proceeding of the Sixth SIGHAN Workshop on Chinese Language Processing*, pp. 90-93. Hyderabad.

Sansing, Y., and A. Prayot. 2010. Thai Named Entity Recognition using Hidden Markov Model. *Proceedings of the Second Conference on Knowledge and Smart Technologies.* Chonburi. [in Thai]

Suwanno, N., Y. Suzuki and H. Yamazaki. 2007. Selecting the optimal feature sets for Thai named entity extraction. *Proceedings of ICEE-2007 & PEC-5.* Phuket.

Tepdang, S., C. Haruechaiyasak, and R. Kongkachandra. (n.d.) *Thai Named Entity Recognition by using Conditional Random Fields.* (n.p.)

Tirasaroj, N. and W. Aroonmanakun. 2009. Thai Named Entity Recognition Based on Conditional Random Fields. *Proceedings of the Eighth International Symposium on Natural Language Processing.* Bangkok.

Yu, X., W. Lam, S. Chan, Y. Wu and B. Chen. 2008. Chinese NER Using CRFs and Logic for the Fourth SIGHAN Bakeoff. *Proceeding of the Sixth SIGHAN Workshop on Chinese Language Processing*, pp. 102-105. Hyderabad.

A Listwise Approach to Coreference Resolution in Multiple Languages

Oanh Thi Tran, Bach Xuan Ngo, Minh Le Nguyen, and Akira Shimazu

School of Information Science, JAIST,
1 - 8 Asahidai, Nomi, Ishikawa, Japan 923 - 1211
{oanhtt, bachnx, nguyenml, shimazu}@jaist.ac.jp

Abstract. This paper presents a listwise approach as an alternative to commonly used pairwise approaches to the task of coreference resolution in multiple languages. In this listwise approach, all antecedent candidates are examined simultaneously and assigned corresponding scores expressing the probability that each candidate is coreferent with a given mention. The experimental results on the corpora of SemEval-2010 shared task 1 showed that our proposed system gave the good results in English and Spanish, and comparative results in Catalan when compared to previous participating systems. These results prove that this approach is appropriate and quite efficient for Coreference Resolution in Multiple Languages.

Keywords: listwise approach, coreference resolution, multiple languages.

1 Introduction

Reference resolution (Jurafsky and Martin, 2009) (chapter 21, section 21.4) is a task of determining to which entities are referred by which linguistic expressions. This task plays an important role in a large number of NLP applications such as Information Retrieval, Question Answering and Machine Translation. Therefore, it has attracted many attentions within the NLP community. Many works on various aspects (linguistic features (Ng, V., 2007), (Haghighi and Klein, 2009); machine learning models (Soon *et al.*, 2001); multiple languages (Recasens *et al.*, 2010a); and so on) of the coreference resolution task have been published.

Until the release of the SemEval-2010 task 1 (Recasens *et al.*, 2010a), there has no competition or public corpus that allows evaluating different coreference resolution systems in multiple languages. Most published systems only focus on a specific language and use the same data sets for example ACE or MUC corpora to train and test the systems. This makes the systems easy to unintentionally adapt themselves to the corpus but not to the problem in general. Therefore, this SemEval-2010 task 1 (Recasens *et al.*, 2010a) made it possible to evaluate and compare various automatic coreference resolution systems in the aspects of: (i) the portability of systems across languages, (ii) the relevance of different levels of linguistic information, and (iii) the behavior of scoring metrics.

This shared task attracted lots of researchers' attentions, but finally only six teams submitted their final results. The participating systems differed in terms of architecture, machine learning methods, etc. These systems mostly based on pairwise models, graph partitioning and entity-mention models. Unfortunately, these models suffered from an important weakness (Ng, V., 2010). In these models, each antecedent candidate is resolved independently with the other candidates. So the models could not determine the best candidate in the relation with the other candidates. To address this drawback, ranking models were proved to be a useful solution (Denis and Baldridge, 2007), (Ng, V., 2005), (Yang *et al.*, 2003). Motivated from ranking models, in this paper, we present our proposal approach for learning-based reference resolution task in multiple languages.

We exploit the listwise approach, which is originally proposed for learning to rank task in information retrieval (Cao *et al.*, 2007), to solve the SemEval-2010 Task on Coreference Resolution in Multiple Languages. This method allows the system to choose the best candidate for a given mention in the relation with other candidates. This means that all candidates will be examined simultaneously and the candidate with the highest score will be selected as a correct antecedent. This listwise approach has been successfully applied to information retrieval task (Cao *et al.*, 2007). Our experimental results on the corpora of SemEval-2010 shared task 1 showed that when applied to coreference resolution task, this new listwise approach usually gave the better results than previous approaches. When estimated on the latest metric BLANC, our proposed system got the state-of-the-art performance.

The rest of the paper is organized as follows. Section 2 reviews related work proposed for this shared task. Section 3 describes our listwise approach to this shared task. Section 4 presents experimental results on the corpora of this SemEval-2010 shared task. Finally, section 5 gives some conclusion and future work.

2 Related Work

In this section, we preview previous approaches of the systems participated in the SemEval-2010 shared task 1. The experimental results of these systems are also used to make an experimental comparison with our proposed approach's results. Here, we preview four systems: (1) RelaxCor system (Sapena *et al.*, 2010); (2) SUCRE system (Kobdani and Schutze, 2010); (3) TANL-1 system (Attardi *et al.*, 2010); and (4) UBIU system (Zhekova and Kubler, 2010). Table 1 presents an overview of the systems, their architecture and machine learning methods.

Table 1: Main characteristics of the previous systems.

Systems	System Architecture	Machine learning methods
RelaxCor	Graph Partitioning (solved by relaxation labeling)	Decision trees, Rules
SUCRE	Best-first clustering, Relational database model, Regular feature definition language	Decision trees, Nave Bayes, SVM, MaxEnt
TANL-1	Highest entity-mention similarity	MaxEnt
UBIU	Pairwise model	MBL

2.1 RelaxCor system

RelaxCor (Sapena *et al.*, 2010) is a constraint-based graph partitioning approach to coreference resolution solved by relaxation labeling. The approach combines the strengths of groupwise classifiers and chain formation methods in one global method. This system includes three phases:

Phase 1: Graph representation

Let $G = G(V, E)$ be an undirected graph. Each mention m_i in the document is presented as a vertex $v_i \in V$ in G. An edge $e_{ij} \in E$ is added to the graph for pairs of vertices (v_i, v_j) representing the possibility that both mentions corefer. A subset of constraints $C_{ij} \in C$ is used to compute the weight value w_{ij} of the edge connecting v_i and v_j.

Phase 2: Training process

Each mention pair (m_i, m_j) in training document is evaluated by the set of feature functions which form a positive example if the mention pair corefers, and a negative otherwise. For each type of mention mj (for example: pronoun, named entity or nominal), a decision tree is generated and a set of rules is extracted with C4.5 rule-learning algorithm.

Given the training corpus, the weight of a constraint C_k is related with the number of examples where the constraint applies and how many of them corefer.

Phase 3: Resolution Algorithm

The algorithm solves weighted constraint satisfaction problem dealing with the edge weights w_{ij}. In this manner, each vertex is assigned to a partition satisfying as many constraints as possible. The algorithm assigns a probability for each possible label of each variable (corresponding to each vertex in G). The process updates the weights of the labels in each step until convergence. Finally, the assigned label for a variable is the one with the highest weight.

2.2 SUCRE system

This system developed a feature engineering which can help reducing the implementation effort for feature extraction. SUCRE has a novel approach to model an unstructured text corpus in a structured framework by using a relational database model and a regular feature definition language to define and extract the features.

In learning, there are four classifiers integrated in SUCRE: Decision tree, Nave bayes, Support vector machine and maximum entropy. However, finally the best reported results were achieved with Decision tree. In decoding, the coreference chains are created. The system uses best-first clustering. It searches for the best predicted antecedent from right-to-left starting from the end of the document.

2.3 TANL-1 system

The system is built based on highest entity-mention similarity. The authors applied Maximum Entropy classifier to determine whether two mentions refer to the same entity. The classifier is trained using the features extracted for each pair of mentions. If the pairwise classifier assigns a probability greater than a given threshold to the fact that a new mention belongs to a previously identified entity, it is assigned to that entity. In the case that more than one entity has a probability greater than the threshold; the mention is assigned to the one with highest probability by using best-first clustering strategy.

2.4 UBIU system

Classification in UBUI is based on mention pairs. The UBIU system used a combination of machine learning, in the form of memory-based learning (MBL) in the implementation of TiMBL (Daelemans *et al.*, 2007), and language independent features. MBL uses a similarity metric to find the k nearest neighbors in the training data in order to classify a new example.

Despite of the difference in feature engineering, learning methods and some processing techniques, it can be seen that three later systems - SUCRE, TANL-1, and UBIU - belong to the approach called pairwise approach. The typical machine learning approach of these three systems includes two steps:

- Classification: systems evaluate whether each pair of mentions is coreferent with each other or not.
- Formation coreference chain: Given the previous classification, the systems form coreference chain (mostly based on best-first clustering).

The approach presented in RelaxCor system joined classification and chain formation into the same step. In this manner, decisions are taken considering the whole set of mentions, ensuring consistency and avoiding that classification decisions are independently taken.

3 A listwise approach to coreference resolution task

3.1 Coreference resolution as a ranking problem

In previous models, a classifier is trained to determine whether two NPs are coreferent or not. Instances are created based on mention to be resolved and an antecedent candidate. However, those models suffer from an important weakness. Since each antecedent candidate for an anaphoric NP is considered independently of the others, it cannot determine how good an antecedent candidate is relative to other candidates. To address this drawback, ranking models were proved to be useful solutions (Denis and Baldridge, 2007), (Ng, V., 2005), (Yang *et al.*, 2003). In the ranking model, most authors use tournament by (Iida, 2003) and twin-candidate model by (Yang *et al.*, 2003) and cluster-ranking by (Rahman and Vincent, 2009) to solve the problem of ranking antecedent candidates. However, this weakness is not fully solved in the aspect that these models cannot examine all antecedent candidates at the same time. They only directly compare pairs of antecedent candidates by building a preference classifier based on triples of NP mentions.

In the next sub-section, we will present a new listwise approach - ListNet method - to this task in multiple languages. It addresses the drawback of previous approaches to this coreference resolution task as discussed above.

3.2 ListNet method

This sub-section briefly presents ListNet method - a listwise approach with Neural Network as the model and Gradient Descent as the optimization algorithm. This method was proposed by (Cao *et al.*, 2007) for the task of learning to rank. We first state the learning problem in listwise approach to learning to rank task. Then, we present ListNet method and the learning algorithm of ListNet. In the following description, we use superscript to denote the id of the mention to be resolve and subscript to denote the id of a candidate in the antecedent candidate list.

In listwise approach to learning to rank, a set of m samples $S = s^{(1)}, s^{(2)}, \ldots, s^{(m)}$ is given. Each sample $s^{(i)}$ consists of an object list $o^{(i)} = o_1^{(i)}, o_2^{(i)}, \ldots, o_{n^{(i)}}^{(i)}$, where $o_j^{(i)}$ denotes the jth object and $n^{(i)}$ denotes the number of objects in i^{th} sample. Furthermore, each object list $o^{(i)}$ is associated with a list of scores $y^{(i)} = y_1^{(i)}, y_2^{(i)}, \ldots, y_{n^{(i)}}^{(i)}$, where $y_j^{(i)}$, a real number, is the score of the object $o_j^{(i)}$. In coreference resolution task, for example, a sample $s^{(i)}$ is associated with a mention $m^{(i)}$to be resolved, each object $o_j^{(i)}$ corresponds to an antecedent candidate $c_j^{(i)}$, and score $y_j^{(i)}$ denotes the judgment on an antecedent candidate $c_j^{(i)}$ with respect to the mention $m^{(i)}$ (the value of $y_j^{(i)}$ expresses how relevant coreference an antecedent candidate $c_j^{(i)}$ is with a mention $m^{(i)}$ to be resolved).

A feature function ϕ will produce a real-valued feature vector for each object $x_j^{(i)} = \phi(o_j^{(i)})$, $i = 1, 2, \ldots, m$; $j = 1, 2, \ldots, n^{(i)}$. A list of feature vectors $x^{(i)} = x_1^{(i)}, x_2^{(i)}, \ldots, x_{n^{(i)}}^{i}$ and the corresponding list of scores $y^{(i)} = y_1^{(i)}, y_2^{(i)}, \ldots, y_{n^{(i)}}^{(i)}$ will form a training instance $(x^{(i)}, y^{(i)})$. The training set can be represented by the following set: $D = (x^{(i)}, y^{(i)})_{i=1}^{m}$.

In training phase, we want to learn a ranking function f, that produces a real-valued score $f(x_j^{(i)})$ for each feature vector $x_j^{(i)}$.

Suppose that $z^{(i)} = \left(f(x_1^{(i)}), f(x_2^{(i)}), \ldots, f(x_{n^{(i)}}^{(i)})\right)$ is the list of scores produced by f on a list of feature vectors $x^{(i)} = x_1^{(i)}, x_2^{(i)}, \ldots, x_{n^{(i)}}^{(i)}$, and L is a loss function defined on two lists of scores $y^{(i)}$ and $z^{(i)}$. We want to minimize the total losses on the training data:

$$\sum_{i=1}^{m} L(y^{(i)}, z^{(i)}) \tag{1}$$

In ranking phase, given a new sample $s^{'}$ (a list of new objects $o^{'}$), we first construct a list of feature vectors $x^{'}$ using feature function ϕ, and then produce a list of scores $y^{'}$ using ranking function f. Finally, objects are ranked in descending order of the scores.

ListNet is a listwise method for learning to rank task. ListNet uses Cross Entropy metric as loss function, Neural Network as model, and Gradient Descent as learning algorithm. If we use a linear Neural Network model, the score of a feature vector can be calculated as follows:

$$f_\omega(x_j^{(i)}) = \left\langle \omega, x_j^{(i)} \right\rangle \quad (2)$$

where $\langle ., . \rangle$ denotes an inner product.

The following algorithm 1 shows learning steps of this ListNet method.

Algorithm 1 Learning Algorithm of ListNet method (cited from the paper of (Cao *et al.*, 2007))

Input: Set of training instances: $(x^{(i)}, y^{(i)})_{i=1}^{m}$
Parameter: iteration number T and learning rate η
Initialize parameter ω
  for $t = 1 \to T$ **do**
    for $i = 1 \to m$ **do**
      Input $x^{(i)}$ to Neural Network and Compute score list $z^{(i)}(f_\omega)$ with current value of ω
      $z^{(i)}(f_\omega) = \left(f_\omega(x_1^{(i)}), \ldots, f_\omega(x_{n^{(i)}}^{(i)})\right)$
      Compute gradient $\Delta\omega$ using equation (3)
      Update $\omega = \omega - \eta \times \Delta\omega$
    end for
  end for
Output: Neural Network model ω

$\Delta\omega$ is computed using the following formula:

$$\Delta\omega = \frac{\delta L(y^{(i)}, z^{(i)}(f_\omega))}{\delta\omega} =$$

$$-\frac{1}{\sum_{j=1}^{n^{(i)}} exp(y_j^{(i)})} \sum_{j=1}^{n^{(i)}} exp(y_j^{(i)}) \frac{\delta f_\omega(x_j^{(i)})}{\delta\omega} + \frac{1}{\sum_{j=1}^{n^{(i)}} exp(f_\omega(x_j^{(i)}))} \sum_{j=1}^{n^{(i)}} exp(f_\omega(x_j^{(i)})) \frac{\delta f_\omega(x_j^{(i)})}{\delta\omega} \quad (3)$$

3.3 Modeling the listwise approach to coreference resolution task

In previous models, they only determine how good a candidate antecedent is relative to the anaphoric NP, but not how good a candidate antecedent is relative to other candidates. In other words, they fail to answer the question of which candidate antecedent is the most probable. Our proposed model will allow us to determine which candidate antecedent is the most probable given an NP to be resolved. For example, we have four mentions named A, B, C, and D in the order of their occurrence in the document. Given that we are resolving an anaphoric mention D to determine a true antecedent among A, B, and C.

The following describes our training and resolution phase of the system.

Training phase

In this phase, trained instance is created as follows:

The training instances for this listwise approach are built based on a mention to be resolved D and a list of its antecedent candidates together with their scores. The candidate set includes all mentions occurring before an anaphoric mention D. The score denotes whether each candidate corefers with mention D and whether each candidate is closest to mention D if they corefer. The way of getting our training data is a way to rank candidates based on coreference and distance criterion. This way is somewhat like a way of human score. In learning, the system has to induce the model that determines these rankings based on not only the distance but also other criteria such as other features and relations between them. In the above example, if we create an instance corresponding to mention D, we have an instance in the form of $(D - A : Pr(D - A); D - B : Pr(D - B); D - C : Pr(D - C))$. In that $Pr(D - x)$ is determined as follows:

$$Pr(D-x) = \begin{cases} 0 & \text{if } D \text{ is not coreferent with } x \\ 1 & \text{if } D \text{ is coreferent with } x \text{ and } x \text{ is closest to } D \\ 0.5 & \text{if } D \text{ is coreferent with } x \text{ and } x \text{ is not closest to } D \end{cases}$$

These training instances are used to learn parameters of the Neural Network model ω according to the algorithm 1.

Resolution phase

Figure 1 visualizes the resolution phase. In our listwise approach, we create instance as a list of candidates in learning and the learning function will assign a score for each candidate in that list. The candidate is chosen as a true antecedent is the one that has the highest score. To allow a mention to be non-anaphoric, we set up a threshold θ to determine whether a given mention is anaphoric or not. This parameter will be chosen using the development set. In figure 1, we assume that B is selected as an exact antecedent of mention M among the candidate list of A, B, C, and so on.

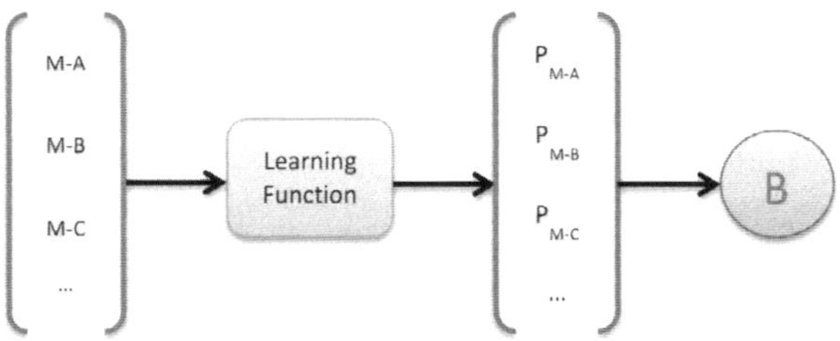

Figure 1: Visualizing the resolution phase.

4 Experiments

4.1 Describing the corpus and evaluation metrics

In these experiments, we used the corpora of SemEval-2010 task 1 on Coreference Resolution in Multiple Languages. We tested our system using three different languages (Catalan, English, and Spanish). The size of the task datasets are provided in the table 2:

Table 2: Size of the task datasets.

Languages	Training			Development			Testing		
	#docs	#sents	#tokens	#docs	#sents	#tokens	#docs	#sents	#tokens
Catalan	829	8,709	253,513	142	1,445	42,072	167	1,698	49,260
English	229	3,648	79,060	39	741	17,044	85	1,141	24,206
Spanish	875	9,022	284,179	140	1,419	44,460	168	1,705	51,040

In the experiments, we evaluate our system using closed gold-standard setting. It means that we use the gold-standard columns with true mention boundaries and our system was built strictly with the information provided in the task datasets. This is because our system focuses on evaluating various approaches of previous participating systems versus our proposed listwise approach.

To evaluate our system, we also use four metrics which are CEAF (Luo, 2005), MUC (Vilain *et al.*, 1995), BCUB (Bagga and Baldwin, 1998) and BLANC scores (Recasens and Marti, 2010b) provided by this shared task. The first three measures have been widely used, while BLANC is a proposal of a new measure interesting to test.

MUC-6/7 (Vilain *et al.*, 1995)

This is the oldest and most widely-used metric measure. This metric is based on coreference links. First, we count the number of common links between the reference (or "truth") and the system output (or "response"). The link precision is the number of common links divided by the number of links in the system output, and the link recall is the number of common links divided by the number of links in the reference.

BCUB (Bagga and Baldwin, 1998)

The MUC metric yields unintuitive results because of two main shortcomings. First, it does not give any credit for single-mention entities since no link can be found in these entities. Second, all errors are considered to be equal because in some tasks, some coreference errors do more damage than others. These drawbacks lead to the proposal of BCUB metric. This metric first computes a precision and recall for each individual mention, and then takes the weighted sum of these individual precisions and recalls as the final metric. The choice of the weighting scheme is determined by the task for which the algorithm is going to be used.

CEAF (Luo, 2005)

The BCUB metrics still has its own problems: for example, the mention precision/recall is computed by comparing entities containing the mention and therefore an entity can be used more than once. Thus, they proposed Constrained Entity-Aligned F-measure or CEAF metric. It finds the best one-to-one mapping entities between the subsets of reference and system entities. They are aligned by maximizing the total entity similarity under the constraint that a reference entity is aligned with at most one system entity, and vice versa. After that, it computes the recall, precision and F-measure.

BLANC (Recasens and Marti, 2010b)

BLANC, a measure obtained by applying the Rand index (Rand 1971) to coreference resolution and taking into account the shortcomings of above previous metrics. The Rand index seems to be especially adequate for evaluating coreference since it allows us to measure 'non-coreference' as well as coreference links. Despite of its shortcomings, it addresses to some degree the drawbacks of previous metrics.

4.2 Feature Sets

In this task, the feature sets were selected from the feature pool presented in (Haghighi and Klein, 2009). We selected 22 features which are divided into 3 groups as described in more detail in table 3. These features are popular and available in all languages of this SemEval-2010 shared task 1.

4.3 Experimental results

By implementing ListNet, our system had to choose the set of three parameters which are (1) number of iteration T; (2) learning rate η; and (3) the threshold θ to determine a candidate is coreferent with a given mention or not. To determine the best parameter set, we varied their values and selected parameters that maximize the sum of four metrics based on the development sets. After that, we used these parameters to evaluate our proposed system on the test sets. The best parameter sets for three languages are presented in the table 4.

The experimental results are compared with four models which are (1) RelaxCor system (Sapena *et al.*, 2010); (2) SUCRE system (Kobdani and Schutze, 2010); (3) TANL-1 system (Attardi *et al.*, 2010); and (4) UBIU system (Zhekova and Kubler, 2010). Table 4 shows our experimental results of the proposed model for three languages using four metrics.

For Catalan language, our system got the best result on BLANC F-scores. It beat TANL-1 and UBIU systems in all four F-scores. In comparison with RelaxCor system, MUC and BLANC F-score increase significantly from 42.5 to 55.42 and from 59.7 to 67.13; CEAF and BCUB F-score decrease from 70.5 to 67.15, and from 79.9 to 76.35. In comparison with SUCRE system, our system only increases on BLANC F-scores and decreases on three remaining F-scores.

Table 3: The feature set for all languages.

Features describing m_j, a candidate antecedent	
1. PRONOUN_1	Y if m_j is a pronoun; else N
2. SUBJECT_1	Y if m_j is a subject; else N
3. NESTED_1	Y if m_j is a nested NP; else N
Features describing m_k, the mention to be resolved	
4. NUMBER_2	SINGULAR or PLURAL, determined using a lexicon
5. GENDER_2	MALE, FEMALE or UNKNOWN, determined using a list of common first names
6. PRONOUN_2	Y if m_k is a pronoun; else N
7. NESTED_2	Y if m_k is a nested NP; else N
8. SEMCLASS_2	The semantic class of m_k
9. HEAD_MATCH	C if the mentions have the same head noun; else I
10. STR_MATCH	C if the mentions are the same string; else I
11. SUBSTR_MATCH	C if one mention is a substring of the other; else I
12. NUMBER	C if the mentions agree in number; I if disagree; NA if numbers for one or both mentions cannot be determined
13. GENDER	C if the mentions agree in gender; I if disagree; NA if genders for one or both mentions cannot be determined
14. AGREEMENT	C if the mentions agree in both gender and number; I if they disagree in both number and gender; else NA
15. BOTH_PRONOUNS	C if both mentions are pronouns; I if neither are pronouns; else NA
16. SEMCLASS	C if the mentions have the same semantic class; I if they don't; NA if the semantic class information for one or both mentions cannot be determined
17. DISTANCE	Binned values for sentence distance between the mentions
Additional features describing the relationship between m_j, m_k	
18. NUMBER'	The concatenation of the NUMBER_2 feature values of m_j and m_k
19. GENDER'	The concatenation of the GENDER_2 feature values of m_j and m_k
20. PRONOUNS'	The concatenation of the PRONOUN_2 feature values of m_j and m_k
21. NESTED'	The concatenation of the NESTED_2 feature values of m_j and m_k
22. SEMCLASS'	The concatenation of the SEMCLASS_2 feature values of m_j and m_k

For English language, our system got the best results on three F-scores of CEAF, BCUB and BLANC and got the second best on the remaining MUC F-score. In that, CEAF and BLANC F-scores increase significantly from the previous highest scores 75.6 to 78.58, and from 70.8 to 75.66. Our system also overcomes three systems of RelaxCor, TANL-1 and UBIU in all four metrics.

For Spanish language, our system got the best results on two F-scores of BLANC and MUC. For the two remaining F-scores of CEAF and BCUB, we got the results which are comparative to previous best scores (CEAF: 69.15 in comparison with 69.8; and 77.81 in comparison with 78.2). Our system beat TANL-1 and UBIU system. Compared with RelaxCor, our system got higher results on three F-scores of CEAF (from 66.6 to 69.15), MUC (from 24.7 to 57.82) and BLANC (from 55.6 to 67.38) which are all significant increase. For the remaining BCUB F-score, our system decreases insignificantly (from 78.2 to 77.81). Compared to SUCRE system, our system increases the F-score of MUC, BCUB and BLANC and decrease insignificantly on the CEAF F-score.

4.4 Discussion

The experimental results on these corpora showed that our proposed system gave the good results in English and Spanish; and comparative results in Catalan when compared to previous participating systems. When applied to coreference resolution task in multiple languages, this new listwise approach overcomes most of previous approaches for all four available metrics. For other systems which our system cannot overcome, usually we got the comparative results or insignificantly decrease in one metric and significantly increase in other remaining metrics.

Among lots of metrics proposed for evaluating a coreference resolution system, none of them is fully adequate. Each metrics has its own strong points as well as weak points as we discussed

Table 4: Experimental results of the proposed model for three languages and four metrics.

Languages	Systems	MUC			BCUB			CEAF			BLANC		
		R	P	F1	R	P	F1	R	P	F1	R	P	F1
English	RelaxCor	21.9	72.4	33.7	74.8	97.0	84.5	75.6	75.6	75.6	57.0	83.4	61.3
	SUCRE	68.1	54.9	**60.8**	86.7	78.5	82.4	74.3	74.3	74.3	77.3	67.0	70.8
	TANL-1	23.7	24.4	24.0	74.6	72.1	73.4	75.0	61.4	67.6	51.8	68.8	52.1
	UBIU	17.2	25.5	20.5	67.8	83.5	74.8	63.4	68.2	65.7	52.6	60.8	54.0
	Our system 2 - 0.005 - 0.25	48.62	62.4	54.66	81.29	89.19	**85.05**	78.17	78.99	**78.58**	73.75	77.92	**75.66**
Spanish	RelaxCor	14.8	73.8	24.7	65.3	97.5	**78.2**	66.6	66.6	66.6	53.4	81.8	55.6
	SUCRE	52.7	58.3	55.3	75.8	79.0	77.4	69.8	69.8	**69.8**	67.3	62.5	64.5
	TANL-1	16.6	56.5	25.7	65.2	93.4	76.8	66.9	64.7	65.8	52.5	79.0	54.1
	UBIU	9.6	18.8	12.7	46.8	77.1	58.3	45.7	59.6	51.7	52.9	63.9	54.3
	Our system 5 - 0.01 - 0.25	58.15	57.49	**57.82**	78.5	75.9	77.81	69.13	69.16	69.15	71.69	64.62	**67.38**
Catalan	RelaxCor	29.3	77.3	42.5	68.6	95.8	**79.9**	70.5	70.5	**70.5**	56.0	81.8	59.7
	SUCRE	51.4	58.4	**56.2**	76.6	77.4	77.0	68.7	68.7	68.7	72.4	60.2	63.6
	TANL-1	17.2	57.7	26.5	64.4	93.3	76.2	66.0	63.9	64.9	52.8	79.8	54.4
	UBIU	8.8	17.1	11.7	47.8	76.3	58.8	46.6	59.6	52.3	51.6	57.9	52.2
	Our system 2 - 0.001 - 0.15	55.28	55.56	55.42	77.11	75.6	76.35	67.13	67.16	67.15	70.79	64.67	**67.13**

in section 4.1. This situation makes it hard to successfully compare systems. Getting the state-of-the-art performance based on all this four common metrics seems to be a difficult task. Until now there is no common agreement on a standard measure for coreference resolution task.

However, based on formulas and characteristics of each metric, we saw that later-proposed metrics usually give the better quality than metrics proposed early. If using this criterion, we saw that we got the highest F-score for the latest proposed BLANC metric in all three languages. In other words, our proposed system got the state-of-the-art performance for coreference resolution task in multiple languages.

5 Conclusion and Future Work

In this paper, we present a new listwise approach to the task of SemEval-2010 task 1 on coreference resolution in multiple languages. This new listwise approach allows all candidate antecedents are considered simultaneously and therefore brings in more benefit than traditional pairwise approaches. The experimental results on the public corpora showed that this new proposed approach gave relatively good performance in all three languages. For the latest proposed metric BLANC, we got the state-of-the-art performance for this coreference resolution task in multiple languages.

For the future works, we will continue to do experiments using other settings of the SemEval-2010 task 1 to fortify the strength of this listwise approach.

A straightforward generalization of twin-candidate model is the ranker model proposed by (Denis and Baldridge, 2007). In this ranker model, the computation of the model's expectation of a feature is directly based on the probabilities assigned to the different candidates by using supervised maximum entropy ranking approach. In the future, we also would like to investigate other ranker models like this one on the corpora of this SemEval-2010 shared task number 1.

Acknowledgments

This work was partly supported by the 21st Century COE program 'Verifiable and Evolvable e-Society', Grant-in-Aid for Scientific Research, Education and Research Center for Trustworthy e-Society.

References

Attardi, G., Rossi, S. D., and Simi, M. 2010. TANL-1: coreference resolution by parse analysis and similarity clustering. *SemEval-2*, pp.108-111.

Bagga, A. and Baldwin, B. 1998. Algorithms for scoring coreference chains. *LREC Workshop on Linguistic coreference*, pp.563-566.

Cao Z., Qin T., Liu T.Y., Tsai M.F., Li H. 2007. Learning to rank: from pairwise approach to listwise approach. *ICML*, pp. 129-136.

Daelemans, W., Zavrel, J., Sloot, K., and Bosch, A. 2007. TiMBL: Tilburg memory based learner version 6.1 reference guide. *Technical Report ILK 07-07, Induction of Linguistic Knowledge, Computational Linguistics, Tilburg University.*

Denis, P. and Baldridge, J. 2007. A ranking approach to pronoun resolution. *International Conference on Artificial Intelligence*, pp.1588-1593.

Haghighi, A., Klein, D. 2009. Simple Coreference Resolution with rich syntactic and semantic features. *Empirical methods in Natural Language Processing*, pp.1152-1161.

Iida, R., Inui, K., Takamura, H., and Matsumoto, Y. 2003. Incorporating contextual cues in trainable models for coreference resolution. *EACL Workshop on the computational Treatment of anaphora*, pp.23-30.

Jurafsky D., Martin J.H. 2009. Speech and Language Processing. *Prentice Hall Series in Artificial Intelligence*, 2nd Edition.

Kobdani, H. and Schutze, H. 2010. SUCRE: Modular system for coreference resolution. *SemEval-2*, pp.92-95.

Luo, X. 2005. On coreference resolution performance metrics. *HLT-EMNLP*, pp.25-32.

Ng, V. 2005. Supervised ranking for pronoun resolution: Some recent improvements. *AAAI*, pp.1081-1086.

Ng, V. 2007. Semantic class induction and co-reference resolution. *ACL*, pp.536-543.

Ng, V. 2010. Supervised Noun phrase coreference research: The first fifteen years. *Annual Meeting of the Association for Computational Linguistics*, pp.1396-1411.

Rahman, A. and Vincent Ng. 2009. Supervised models for coreference resolution. *Empirical Methods in Natural Language Processing*, pp.968-977.

Recasens, M., Marquez, L., Sapena, L., Marti, M., Taule, M., Hoste, V., Poesio, M., Versley, Y. 2010a. SemEval-2010 Task 1: Co-reference Resolution in Multiple Languages. *International Workshop on Semantic Evaluation, ACL*, pp.1-8.

Recasens, M. and Hovy, E. 2010b. BLANC: Implementing the Rand Index for coreference evaluation. *In prep.*

Soon W.M., Ng H.T., Lim D.C.Y 2001. A machine learning approach to co-reference resolution of noun phrases. *Computational Linguistics*, pp.521-544.

Sapena, E., Padr, L., and Turmo, J. 2010. RelaxCor: A Global relaxation labeling approach to coreference resolution for the SemEval-2 Coreference Task. *SemEval-2*, pp.88-91.

Vilain, M., Burger, J., Aberdeen, J., Connolly, D., and Hirschman, L. 1995. A model-theoretic coreference scoring scheme. *MUC-6*, pp.45-52.

Yang, X., Zhou, G., Su, J. and Tan, C.L. 2003. Coreference resolution using competitive learning approach. *ACL*, pp.176-183.

Zhekova, D., and Kubler, S. 2010. UBIU: A language-independent system for coreference resolution. *SemEval-2*, pp.96-99.

Combining Dependency and Constituent-based Syntactic Information for Anaphoricity Determination in Coreference Resolution

Fang Kong[a,b] and Guodong Zhou[a,b]

[a] JiangSu Provincial Key Lab for Computer Information Processing Technology

[b] School of Computer Science and Technology Soochow University, Suzhou(215006) ,China

{kongfang, gdzhou}@suda.edu.cn

Abstract. This paper systematically explores the effectiveness of dependency and constituent-based syntactic information for anaphoricity determination. In particular, this paper proposes two ways to combine dependency and constituent-based syntactic information to explore their complementary advantage. One is a dependency-driven constituent-based structured representation, and the other uses a composite kernel. Evaluation on the Automatic Content Extraction (ACE) 2003 corpus shows that dependency and constituent-based syntactic information are quite complementary and proper combination can much improve the performance of anaphoricity determination, and further improve the performance of coreference resolution.

Keywords: Dependency Relation, Constituent Parser, Anaphoricity Determination, Coreference Resolution, Tree Kernel, Composite Kernel

1 Introduction

Coreference resolution plays a critical role in many NLP applications. It identifies which noun phrases (NPs) refer to the same entity in the real world and can be divided into two subtasks: anaphoricity determination and antecedent identification. The first subtask, anaphoricity determination, determines whether a given noun phrases (NP) is anaphoric or not. Here we say an NP is anaphoric if it has any antecedent in the context preceding it, and non-anaphoric otherwise. The second subtask, antecedent identification, identifies the antecedent of a given anaphoric NP. Although machine learning approaches have performed reasonably well in coreference resolution without explicit anaphoricity determination (e.g. Soon et al. 2001; Ng and Cardie 2002b; Yang et al. 2003, 2008; Kong et al. 2009), knowledge of NP anaphoricity is expected to much improve the performance of a coreference resolution system, since a non-anaphoric NP does not have an antecedent and thus does not need to be resolved.

Recently, anaphoricity determination has been the subject of increased attention in coreference resolution. A variety of techniques have been proposed to address anaphoricity determination as an independent task (e.g. Paice and Husk 1987; Lappin and Leass 1994; Kennedy and Boguraev 1996; Denber 1998; Bean and Riloff 1999; Vieira and Poesio 2000; Evans 2001; Cherry, Cherry and Bergsma 2005; Bergsma et al. 2008). Since then, more studies have been done to incorporate anaphoricity determination into coreference resolution in a pipeline way (e.g. Ng and Cardie 2002a; Yang et al. 2005; Kong et al. 2010) or in a joint way (e.g. Denis and Balbridge 2007; Luo 2007; Finkel and Manning 2008; Zhou and Kong 2009; Ng 2009), and achieved promising results.

While it is well known that NP anaphoricity interacts with various kinds of structured factors, most of previous studies only consider constituent-based syntactic information and there are few studies on exploring dependency-based syntactic information for anaphoricity determination. In this paper, we first study the effectiveness of dependency-based syntactic information for anaphoricity determination. Then, we propose different ways to combine dependency and constituent-based syntactic information for anaphoricity determination in better exploring their complementary nature. Our study shows that dependency and constituent-based syntactic information are quite complementary and proper combination can much improve the performance of anaphoricity determination and that of coreference resolution as a whole even when simply integrating the anaphoricity determination module into a coreference resolution system as a filter.

The rest of this paper is organized as follows. Section 2 describes some background knowledge about this task. Section 3 briefly overviews related work. Section 4 describes dependency and constituent-based syntactic information and different ways of combining them for anaphoricity determination. Section 5 reports the experimental results. Finally, we conclude our work in Section 6.

2 Background Knowledge

For better understanding, we first describe some background knowledge in this section.

2.1 Anaphoricity determination

As a subtask in coreference resolution (Webber 1979), anaphoricity determination is responsible for determining whether a given NP is anaphoric or not. In principle, anaphoricity determination can work through either filtering out non-anaphoric NPs or keeping anaphoric NPs. From the viewpoint of the former, the simplest way is to include certain patterned syntactic constructions where non-anaphoric NPs often occur. From the viewpoint of the latter, the simplest way is to include the antecedent along with necessary syntactic constructions in the parse tree structure as much as possible.

2.2 Dependency parse tree and constituent parse tree

Both the dependency and constituent parse tree structures are widely used to represent the structure of a sentence. Figure 1 shows an example. In the dependency parse tree structure, the dependency relationship between two words is represented by an arrow along with its name. In accordance with the convention adopted in the literature, the word pointed by the arrow is the dependent word, and the word outpointed by the arrow is the head word.

```
(2-1) Congressman Sonny Bono was first a songwriter in the
nineteen sixties and then a popular entertainer.
```

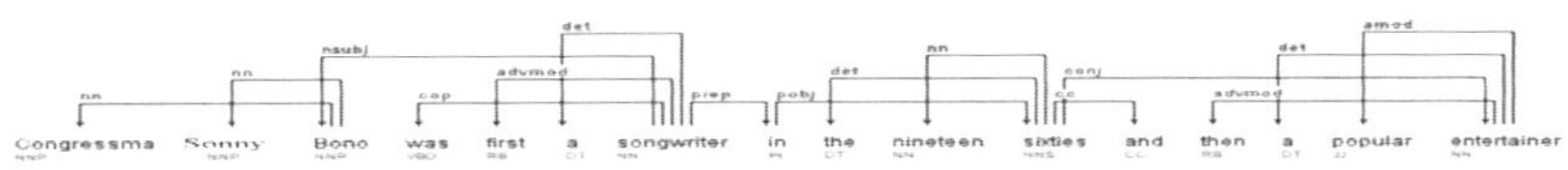

(a) Dependency parse tree

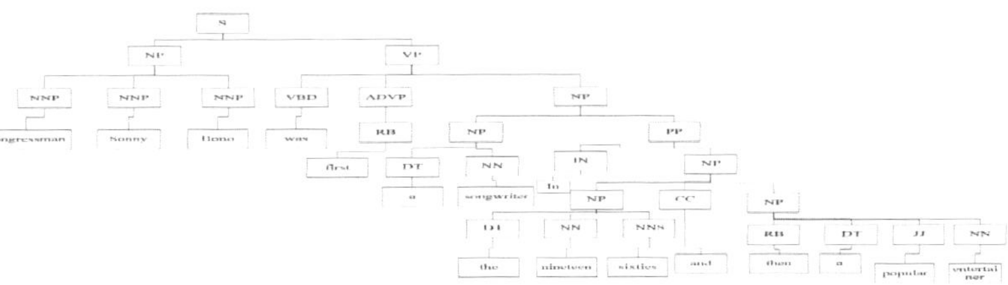

(a) Constituent parse tree

Figure 1: Example of dependency and constituent parse trees with regard to sentence "Congressman Sonny Bono was first a songwriter in the nineteen sixties and then a popular entertainer."

However, there exist some important differences between the dependency and constituent parse tree structures. On the one hand, the constituent parse tree structure is normally derived from the phrase structure grammar, which employs linguistic labels (such as part-of-speech and phrase tags) and has dominated the research of syntactic analysis in the literature. On the other hand, the dependency parse tree structure is derived from the dependency grammar, which does not employ linguistic labels and has drawn more and more attention in recent years due to its conciseness and clearness. While the constituent parse tree structure represents the syntactic structure of a sentence in a way of nested multi-word phrase constituents, the dependency one directly represents the dependency relationship between individual words. That is to say, the dependency parse tree structure mainly concerns the dependency relationship between individual words, instead of the phrase structure contained in the constituent parse tree structure. Therefore, these two kinds of syntactic parse tree structures may behave quite differently in capturing different aspects of syntactic phenomena.

Normally, the constituent parse tree structure is more effective at filtering out non-anaphoric NPs and keeping the anaphoric NPs whose anaphoricity is only related with a local antecedent. For example, as illustrated by the Government and Binding theory, a reflexive (e.g. "himself" in 2-2) often works as a short-distance anaphor and is locally bound by its antecedent (e.g. "John" in 2-2). Such locality can normally be effectively captured by the constituent parse tree structure.

```
(2-2) John likes pictures of himself.
```

In comparison, the dependency parse tree structure is more effective at determining the anaphoricity of those NPs which is not bound locally. (2-1) gives an example where it is easy for the dependency parse tree structure to determine the anaphoricity of the NP "a popular entertainer".

Obviously, dependency and constituent parse tree structures have their own advantages in either filtering out non-anaphoric NPs or keeping anaphoric NPs. This paper focuses on improving the performance of anaphrocity determination and coreference resolution by combining useful structured information in both the dependency and constituent parse tree structures.

3 Related Work

This section briefly overviews related work on anaphoricity determination.

Traditionally, anaphoricity determination has been tackled independently of coreference resolution using a variety of techniques. Representative studies include: Kennedy and Boguraev (1996), Bean and Riloff (1999), Evans (2001), Cherry and Bergsma (2005), and Bergsma et al. (2008).

Kennedy and Boguraev (1996) looked for modal adjectives (e.g. "necessary") or cognitive verbs (e.g. "It is thought that..." in a set of patterned constructions) in identifying pleonastic it. Bean and Riloff (1999) automatically identified existential definite NPs which are non-anaphoric. The intuition behind is that many definite NPs are not anaphoric since their meanings can be understood from general world knowledge, e.g. "the FBI". They found that existential NPs account for 63% of all definite NPs and 76% of them could be identified by syntactic or lexical means. Evans (2001) automatically identified the anaphoricity of pronoun "it" using various kinds of lexical and syntactic features. Cherry and Bergsma (2005) extended the work of Lappin and Leass (1994) for large-scale anaphoricity determination by additionally detecting pleonastic "it". Bergsma et al. (2008) proposed a distributional method in detecting non-anaphoric pronouns. They first extracted the surrounding context of the pronoun, then gathered the distribution of words that occurred within the context from a large corpus, and finally identified the pronoun either anaphoric or non-anaphoric based on the word distribution.

Recently, anaphoricity determination has been incorporated into coreference resolution in a pipeline way. Representative studies include: Ng and Cardie (2002a), Ng (2004), Yang et al. (2005), and Kong et al. (2010). Ng and Cardie (2002a) employed various domain-independent features in identifying anaphoric NPs. Experiments showed that their method improved the performance of coreference resolution by 2.0 and 2.6 in F1-measure to 65.8 and 64.2 on the MUC-6 and MUC-7 corpora, respectively. Ng (2004) further examined the representation and optimization issues in using anaphoricity information to improve the performance of coreference resolution. Yang et al. (2005) made use of non-anaphors to create a special class of training instances in the twin-candidate model (Yang et al. 2003) and improved the performance of coreference resolution by 2.9 and 1.6 to 67.3 and 67.2 in F1-measure on the MUC-6 and MUC-7 corpora, respectively. Kong et al. (2010) proposed a dependency-driven scheme to dynamically determine the constituent parse tree structure for tree kernel-based anaphoricity determination. This was done by exploiting constituent dependencies from both the syntactic and semantic perspectives to distinguish necessary evidence from noisy information in the syntactic parse tree. Experiments showed that this scheme outperformed all previous syntactic parse tree structures on anaphoricity determination, and improved the performance of coreference resolution.

Alternatively, anaphoricity determination and antecedent identification have been modeled as a joint task more recently. Representative studies include: Denis and Balbridge (2007), Luo (2007), Finkel and Manning (2008), Zhou and Kong (2009), and Ng (2009). Denis and Balbridge (2007) employed an integer linear programming (ILP) formulation for joint anaphoricity determination and antecedent identification by informing each other the final assignments. Experiments on the ACE 2003 corpus showed that this joint ILP formulation improved the F1-measure by 3.7-5.3 on various domains. However, their experiments assume true ACE mentions (i.e. all the mentions are already known from the annotated corpus). Therefore, the actual effect of this joint ILP formulation on fully automatic coreference resolution is still unclear. Luo (2007) proposed a twin-model for coreference resolution: a link component, which models the coreferential relationship between an anaphor and a candidate antecedent, and a creation component, which models the possibility that a NP is not coreferential with any candidate antecedent. This twin-model combined the probabilities returned by the creation component (an anaphoricity model) with those returned by the link component (a coreference model) to score a coreference partition, such that a partition was penalized whenever an anaphoric mention was resolved. Finkel and Manning (2008) showed that transitivity constraints could be incorporated into an ILP-based coreference resolution system and much improved the performance. Zhou and Kong (2009) employed a global learning method in determining the anaphoricity of NPs via a label propagation algorithm to improve the performance of coreference resolution. Experiments on the ACE 2003 corpus demonstrated the effectiveness of such a global learning method with performance improvement of 2.4, 3.1 and 4.1 in F1-meaure on the NWIRE, NPAPER and BNEWS domains, respectively. Ng (2009) presented a graphic approach to anaphoricity determination based on graph minimum cuts and demonstrated its effectiveness in overall coreference resolution. Experiments on the ACE 2003 corpus showed that his method improved the overall F1-measure by 2.8, 2.2 and 4.5 to 54.5, 64.0 and 60.8 on the NWIRE, NPAPER and BNEWS domains, respectively.

This paper proposes a new approach to determining NP anaphoricity by combining dependency and constituent-based syntactic information, and studies the application of an explicit anaphoricity determination module in coreference resolution.

4 Combining Dependency and Constituent-based Syntactic Information

In this section, we first introduce the representation of dependency-based syntactic information and the presentation of constituent-based syntactic information individually in tree kernel-based anaphoricity determination. Then we propose two ways to combine these two kinds of structured syntactic information.

4.1 Representation of Dependency-based Syntactic Information

Given a NP in consideration, one key issue is to choose a proper dependency tree span to well cover necessary dependency-based syntactic information for anaphoricity determination in the tree kernel computation. The basic idea is to keep various dependencies related with the focus NP in the same sentence. For this purpose, a dependency relations tree (DRT) is constructed as follows: (Figure 2 illustrates an example dependency relations tree for sentence (2-1).)

(a) Root path with "a popular entertainer" as focus NP

(b) After attaching all the immediate dependencies except "det"

Figure 2: DRT: Representation of dependency-based syntactic information

From the dependency parse tree, as shown in Figure 1(a), we first extract the path between the focus NP and the topmost node along the reverse direction of the arrows from the focus NP. We call this path as root path. Figure 2(a) shows an example root path with "a popular entertainer" as focus NP.

Attaching all the nodes which have the immediate dependency relationship with a node (except the "det" relation) in the root path. Figure 2(b) shows the result after such dependency attachment.

Attaching the dependency relation type to the dependent word. In every dependent word node, we also record its corresponding POS.

4.2 Representation of Constituent-based Syntactic Information

It is well proven that constituent-based syntactic information plays an important role for anaphoricity determination. In this paper, we adopt the state-of-the-art Dynamic Expansion Tree (DET) extraction scheme, as proposed in Zhou and Kong (2009). DET takes predicate- and antecedent candidates-related information and right siblings into consideration (For details, please refer to Zhou and Kong, 2009). Generally, the more a parse tree structure includes, the more structured syntactic information would be provided, at the expense of more noisy information. In this paper, we limit the window size to 5 chunks (either NPs or non-NPs), including previous two chunks, current chunk and following two chunks.

Figure 3 illustrates a dynamic expansion tree example for the example sentence (2-1). Obviously, the antecedent "a songwriter" of the focus NP "a popular entertainer" is not bound locally and fails to be covered in DET.

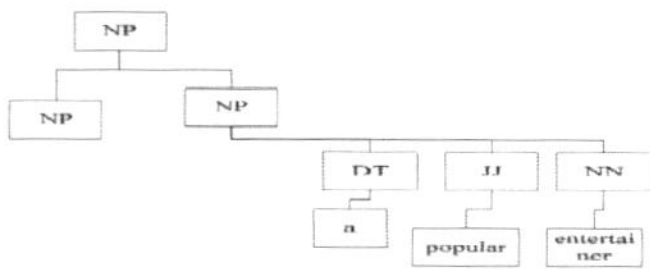

Figure 3: DET: Representation of constituent-based syntactic information

4.3 Combining Dependency and Constituent-based Syntactic Information

Just as described above, both dependency and constituent-based syntactic information have their own advantages and are helpful for anaphoricity determination. In this subsection, we propose two ways to combine dependency and constituent-based syntactic information. One is to generate a better representation of constituent-based syntactic information with the guidance of dependency relations and the other is to combine them via a composite kernel.

Dependency-driven constituent parse tree

Given a full constituent parse tree, the root path from the focus NP to the root node is first kept. Then, all the nodes with the immediate dependency relationship with the focus NP, and their corresponding paths are attached to the root path. The intuition behind is that immediate dependencies normally carry major contextual information of the focus NP. Figure 4 illustrates the dependency-driven constituent parse tree (DCPT) of the example sentence (2-1) with the focus NP "a popular entertainer".

nn(Bono-3, Congressman-1)
nn(Bono-3, Sormy-2)
nsubj(songwriter-7, Bono-3)
cop(songwriter-7, was-4)
advmod(songwriter-7, first-5)
det(songwriter-7, a-6)
det(sixties-11, the-9)
nn(sixties-11, nineteen-10)
prep_in(songwriter-7, sixties-11)
advmod(entertainer-16, then-13)
det(entertainer-16, a-14)
amod(entertainer-16, popular-15)
prep_in(songwriter-7, entertainer-16)
conj_and(sixties-11, entertainer-16)

(a) Dependencies achieved by Stanford Parser

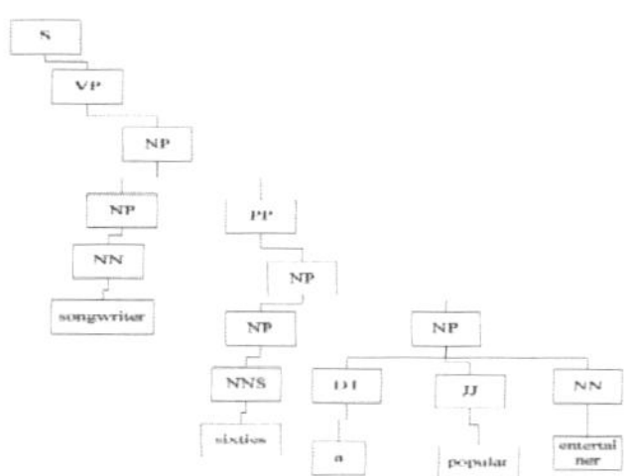

(b) DCPT: Depdendency-driven constituent parse tree

Figure 4: Example of DCPT

Composite kernel

For simplicity, this paper only adopts a simple linear kernel to equally combine a dependency-based tree kernel K_{dep} and constituent-based tree kernel K_{con} with normalization

$$K_{comp}(x_1, x_2) = \frac{K_{dep}(x1, x2)}{|K_{dep}(x1, x2)|} + \frac{K_{con}(x1, x2)}{|K_{con}(x1, x2)|}$$

In particular, we use the composite kernel to combine the dependency-based representation DRT and the constituent-based representation DET. We also consider the combination of DRT with the dependency-driven constituent-based representation DCPT to further capture the complementary nature of dependency and constituent-based syntactic information.

5 Experimentation

This section systematically evaluates our proposal on anaphoricity determination and its application in coreference resolution using the ACE 2003 corpus.

5.1 Experimental Setting

The ACE 2003 corpus contains three domains: newswire (NWIRE), newspaper (NPAPER), and broadcast news (BNEWS). For each domain, there exist two data sets, training and devtest, which are used for training and testing respectively.

For preparation, all the documents in the corpus are preprocessed automatically using a pipeline of NLP components, including tokenization and sentence segmentation, named entity recognition, part-of-speech tagging and noun phrase chunking. Among them, named entity recognition, part-of-speech tagging and noun phrase chunking apply the same state-of-the-art Hidden Markov Model (HMM) based engine with error-driven learning capability (Zhou and Su, 2000 & 2002). In addition, all the texts are parsed using the Charniak parser (Charniak 2001) to get the constituent parse tree structure while the dependency parse tree structure is achieved by the Stanford Parser (Marie et al. 2006). Finally, we use the SVM-light toolkit (Joakim, 1998) [1] with the convolution tree kernel function SVM^{light}–TK (Moschitti, 2004)[2] as the classifier. For comparison, the training parameters C (SVM) and λ (tree kernel) are simply set to 2.4 and 0.4 respectively, as adopted in Zhou and Kong (2009).

For anaphoricity determination, we report the performance in Acc+ and Acc-, which measure the accuracies of identifying anaphoric NPs and non-anaphoric NPs, respectively. Obviously, higher Acc+ means that more anaphoric NPs would be identified correctly, while higher Acc- means that more non-anaphoric NPs would be filtered out. For overall coreference resolution, we report the performance in terms of recall, precision, and F1-measure using the commonly-used model theoretic MUC scoring program (Vilain et al. 1995).

5.2 Experimental Results

Performance of anaphoricity determination

Table 1 compares the performance of anaphoricity determination using different settings. It shows that:

Table 1: Comparison of different settings on anaphoricity determination

Corpus	DRT		DET		DRT+DET		DCPT		DRT+DCPT	
	Acc^+	Acc^-	Acc^+	Acc^-	Acc^+	Acc^-	Acc^+	Acc^-	Acc^+	Acc^-
NWIRE	69.3	71.6	72.1	79.8	78.7	78.9	83.3	77.1	85.4	79.7
BNEWS	73.7	62.4	81.9	66.4	82.7	72.0	86.8	70.3	84.7	79.5
NPAPER	75.8	60.8	80.8	61.1	84.7	66.8	90.0	64.2	91.1	68.8

1) The constituent-based representation DET noticeably outperforms the dependency-based representation DRT on both keeping anaphoric NPs and filtering out non-anaphoric NPs. This indicates the advantage of the constituent-based representation over the dependency-based one on anaphoricity determination.

---

[1] http://svmlight.joachims.org/

[2] http://ai-nlp.info.uniroma2.it/moschitti/

2) The combination of DRT and DET via a simple composite kernel significantly improves the performance in both keeping anaphoric NPs and filtering out non-anaphoric NPs by about 4-8% in accuracy. This justifies the complementary nature of dependency and constituent-based syntactic information.

3) Although dependency-driven constituent-based representation DCPT performs worse than the composite kernel combination of DRT and DET by about 2% in filtering out non-anaphoric NPs, DCPT significantly outperforms the composite kernel combination by about 4-6% in keeping anaphoric NPs. Actually, this characteristic is preferred since a coreference resolution system can often detect some non-anaphoric NPs when failing to find their antecedent candidates while it is almost impossible to recover those filtered anaphoric NPs caused by anaphoricity determination. Therefore, keeping more anaphoric NPs is always preferred over filtering out more non-anaphoric NPs in anaphoricity determination from the viewpoint of overall coreference resolution.

4) The composite kernel combination of DCPT with DRT outperforms the composite kernel combination of DET with DRT on both keeping anaphoric NPs and filtering out non-anaphoric NPs. This further indicates the effectiveness of dependency-based syntactic information.

Performance of coreference resolution

We have evaluated the effectiveness of our anaphoricity determination module with different settings on coreference resolution by including it as a preprocessing step to a state-of-the-art baseline coreference resolution system without explicit anaphoricity determination. This is done by filtering out those non-anaphoric NPs according to the anaphoricity determination module. To see whether an improvement is significant, we also conduct significance testing using paired t-test. In this paper, '***', '**' and '*' denote p-values of an improvement smaller than 0.01, in-between (0.01, 0,05] and bigger than 0.05, which mean significantly better, moderately better and slightly better, respectively. Here, the baseline system employs the same set of features, as adopted in the single-candidate model of Yang et al. (2003) and uses a SVM-based classifier with the feature-based RBF kernel. Table 2 presents the detailed performance of the coreference resolution system with different anaphoricity determination settings. It shows that:

Table 2: Performance of anaphoricity determination on coreference resolution

System	NWIRE			NPAPER			BNEWS		
	R%	P%	F	R%	P%	F	R%	P%	F
Without anaphoricity determination (Baseline)	55.0	63.8	59.1	62.1	65.0	63.5	53.2	60.5	56.6
With DRT -based anaphoricity determination	53.5	68.6	60.1	60.0	69.5	64.4	50.8	66.7	57.7
With DET-based anaphoricity determination	53	73.8	61.7	58.1	74.5	65.3	50	70.8	58.6
With anaphoricity determination using the combination of DRT and DET	52.8	75.6	62.2	57.8	77.5	66.2	49.8	78.4	60.9
With DCPT -based anaphoricity determination	52.4	79.6	63.2	58.1	80.3	67.4	50.1	79.8	61.6
With anaphoricity determination using the combination of DRT and DCPT	52.7	82.1	64.2	57.6	83.3	68.1	49.5	83.9	62.3
With golden anaphoricity determination	54.6	81.7	65.5	60.4	82.1	69.6	51.9	82.1	63.6

There is a large performance gap of 6.4, 6.1 and 7.0 in F1-measure on the NWIRE, NPAPER and BNEWS domains, respectively, between the coreference resolution system with golden anaphoricity determination and the baseline system without anaphoricity determination. This suggests the necessity of proper anaphoricity determination.

Compared to the baseline system without anaphoricity determination, the DRT-based anaphoricity determination module improves the F1-measure by 1.0(***), 0.9(***) and 1.1(***) to 60.1, 64.4 and 57.7 on the NWIRE, NPAPER and BNEWS domains, respectively, while the DET-based anaphoricity determination module improves the F1-measure by 2.6(***), 1.8(***) and 2.0(***) to 61.7, 65.3 and 58.6 on the NWIRE, NPAPER and BNEWS domains, respectively. This indicates the effectiveness of automatic anaphoricity determination using both dependency and constituent-based syntactic information, respectively, and the superiority of the constituent-based one over the dependency-based one.

Compared to the baseline system, the anaphoricity determination module with the combination of DRT and DET via a composite kernel improves the F1-measure by 3.1(***), 2.7(***) and 4.3(***) to 62.2, 66.2 and 60.9 on the NWIRE, NPAPER and BNEWS domains, respectively. This proves the complementary nature of a dependency-based anaphoricity determination module and a constituent-based anaphoricity determination module on overall coreference resolution.

The coreference resolution system with the DCPT-based anaphoricity determination module consistently performs better than the one with anaphoricity determination using the composite kernel combination of DRT and DET by 1.0(***), 1.2(***) and 0.7(***) in F1-measure on the NWIRE, NPAPER and BNEWS domains, respectively. This justifies our claim on the preference of keeping more anaphoric NPs over filtering out more non-anaphoric NPs.

Compared to the coreference resolution system with DCPT-based anaphoricity determination, the further combination of DCPT with DRT via the simple composite kernel consistently improve the F1-measure by 1.0(**), 0.7(**) and 0.7(**), on the NWIRE, NPAPER and BNEWS domains, respectively. Although there are still some performance gaps with 1.3, 1.5 and 1.3 in F1-measure compared to the coreference resolution system with golden anaphoricity determination, our gains over the baseline system without anaphoricity determination are much more obvious with 5.1, 4.6 and 5.7 in F1-measure, on the NWIRE, NPAPER and BNEWS domains, respectively.

Table 3: Comparison of different anaphoricity determination on overall coreference resolution

System		NWIRE			NPAPER			BNEWS		
		R%	P%	F	R%	P%	F	R%	P%	F
Zhou and Kong (2009)	without anaphoricity determination	53.1	67.4	59.4	57.7	67.0	62.1	48.0	65.9	55.5
	with DET -based anaphoricity determination in a pipeline way	51.6	77.2	61.8	55.2	78.6	65.2	47.5	80.3	59.6
	performance gain			2.4			3.1			4.1
Ng (2009)	without anaphoricity determination	59.1	58.	58.6	60.8	62.6	61.7	57.7	52.6	55.0
	with graph minimum cut-based anaphoricity determination in a joint way	54.1	69.0	60.6	57.9	71.2	63.9	53.1	67.5	59.4
	performance gain			2.0			2.2			4.4
Ours	without anaphoricity determination	55.0	63.8	59.1	62.1	65.0	63.5	53.2	60.5	56.6
	with DRT+DCPT-based anaphoricity determination in a pipeline way	52.7	82.1	64.2	57.6	83.3	68.1	49.5	83.9	62.3
	performance gain			5.1			4.6			5.7

Comparison with other anaphoricity determination approaches

Table 3 compares the contribution of different anaphoricity determination approaches on overall conference resolution. Here, Zhou and Kong (2009) use the same set of features with ours in the baseline system and apply a DET-based anaphoricity determination module in a pipeline way. Ng (2009) builds his baseline system using 33 features as described in Ng (2007) and integrates anaphoricity determination into coreference resolution in a joint way using a graph minimum cut algorithm. From Table 3, we can find that:

The overall performance of our baseline system is almost as good as that of Zhou and Kong (2009) and a bit better than Ng's (2009).

Using DET-based anaphoricity determination in a pipeline way, Zhou and Kong (2009) improve the F1-measure of overall coreference resolution by 2.4, 3.1 and 4.1 on the three domains of NWIRE, NPAPER and BNEWS, respectively. Integrating anaphoricity determination into coreference resolution in a joint way using a graph minimum cut algorithm, Ng (2009) improves the F1-measure of overall coreference resolution by 2.0, 2.2 and 4.4 on the three domains, respectively. In comparison, our approach is much more effective with the performance gain of 5.1,4.6 and 5.7 on the three domains, respectively.

6 Conclusion and Further Work

This paper systematically explores the effectiveness of dependency-based syntactic information for anaphoricity determination. Furthermore, we study two ways of integrating dependency-based syntactic information with constituent-based syntactic information for anaphoricity determination. Evaluation on the ACE 2003 corpus indicates the usefulness of both dependency-based and constituent-based syntactic information in anaphoricity determination. It also shows that dependency and constituent-based syntactic information complement each other in capturing different aspects of syntactic phenomena for anaphoricity determination and coreference resolution.

To our best knowledge, this is the first systematic research on exploring the effectiveness of dependency-based syntactic information and its combination with constituent-based syntactic information for anaphoricity determination.

For future work, we will explore more kinds of structured syntactic information in anaphoricity determination and their application in overall coreference resolution. In addition, we will study better ways of integrating anaphoricity determination and antecedent identification.

Acknowledgments

This research was supported by Projects 60873150, 90920004 and 61003153 under the National Natural Science Foundation of China, Project KJS1025 under the Open Projects Fund of Jiangsu Provincial Key Laboratory for Computer Information Processing Technology.

References

D. Bean and E. Riloff 1999. Corpus-based Identification of Non-Anaphoric Noun Phrases. *ACL*' 1999

S. Bergsma, D. Lin and R. Goebel 2008. Distributional Identification of Non-referential Pronouns. *ACL*'2008

E. Charniak. 2001. Immediate-head Parsing for Language Models. *ACL*' 2001

C. Cherry and S. Bergsma. 2005. An expectation maximization approach to pronoun resolution. *CoNLL*'2005

M. Collins and N. Duffy. 2001. Covolution kernels for natural language. *NIPS*' 2001

M. Denber 1998. Automatic Resolution of Anaphoria in English. *Technical Report*, Eastman KodakCo.

P. Denis and J. Baldridge. 2007. Global, joint determination of anaphoricity and coreference resolution using integer programming. *NAACL/HLT*'2007

R. Evans 2001. Applying machine learning toward an automatic classification of it. *Literary and Linguistic Computing*, 16(1):45-57

F. Kong, G.D. Zhou and Q.M. Zhu. 2009 Employing the Centering Theory in Pronoun Resolution from the Semantic Perspective. *EMNLP*'2009

F.Kong, G.D. Zhou, L.H. Qian and Q.M. Zhu. 2010. Dependency-driven Anaphoricity Determination for Coreference Resolution. *COLING*'2010

S. Lappin and J. L. Herbert. 1994. An algorithm for pronominal anaphora resolution. *Computational Linguistics*, 20(4)

X. Luo. 2007. Coreference or not: A twin model for coreference resolution. *NAACL-HLT*'2007

M.C. Marneffe, B. MacCartney and C.D. Manning. 2006. Generating Typed Dependency Parses from Phrase Structure Parses. *LREC* 2006.

V. Ng and C. Cardie 2002. Identify Anaphoric and Non-Anaphoric Noun Phrases to Improve Coreference Resolution. *COLING*'2002

V. Ng and C. Cardie 2002. Improving machine learning approaches to coreference resolution. *ACL*'2002

V. Ng 2004. Learning Noun Phrase Anaphoricity to Improve Coreference Resolution: Issues in Representation and Optimization. *ACL*' 2004

V. Ng 2009. Graph-cut based anaphoricity determination for coreference resolution. *NAACL*'2009

V. Ng 2010. Supervised Noun Phrase Coreference Research: The First Fifteen Years. *ACL*'2010

W. M. Soon, H. T. Ng and D. Lim 2001. A machine learning approach to coreference resolution of noun phrase. *Computational Linguistics*, 27(4):521-544.

V. Stoyanov, N. Gilbert, C. Cardie and E. Riloff. 2009. Conundrums in Noun Phrase Coreference Resolution: Making Sense of the State-of-the Art. *ACL*'2009

B. L. Webber. 1979. A Formal Approach to Discourse Anaphora. *Garland* Publishing, Inc.

X.F. Yang, J. Su and C.L. Chew. 2005. A Twin Candidate Model of Coreference Resolution with Non-Anaphor Identification Capability. *IJCNLP*'2005

X.F. Yang, J. Su and C.L. Tan 2008. A Twin-Candidate Model for Learning-Based Anaphora Resolution. *Computational Linguistics* 34(3):327-356

G.D. Zhou and F. Kong. 2009. Global Learning of Noun Phrase Anaphoricity in Coreference Resolution via Label Propagetion. *EMNLP*'2009

G.D. Zhou and J. Su. 2002. Named Entity recognition using a HMM-based chunk tagger. *ACL*'2002

Sentiment Classification in Resource-Scarce Languages by using Label Propagation

Yong Ren[a], Nobuhiro Kaji[b], Naoki Yoshinaga[b], Masashi Toyoda[b], and Masaru Kitsuregawa[b]

[a] Graduate School of Information Science and Technology, University of Tokyo, Japan
renyong@tkl.iis.u-tokyo.ac.jp
[b] Institute of Industrial Science, University of Tokyo, Japan
{kaji,ynaga,toyoda,kitsure}@tkl.iis.u-tokyo.ac.jp

Abstract. With the advent of consumer generated media (e.g., Amazon reviews, Twitter, etc.), sentiment classification becomes a heated topic. Previous work heavily relies on a large amount of linguistic resources, which are difficult to obtain in resource-scarce languages. To overcome this problem, we investigate the usefulness of label propagation, which is a graph-based semi-supervised learning method. Extensive experimental evaluation on three real datasets demonstrated that label propagation performs more stable than support vector machines (SVMs) and transductive support vector machines (TSVMs) in a document-level sentiment classification task for resource-scarce languages (Chinese in our case).

Keywords: sentiment classification, label propagation, semi-supervised learning

1 Introduction

Over the last decade, document-level sentiment classification has attracted much attention from NLP researchers; its potential applications include opinion summarization and opinion mining (Pang and Lee, 2008). Most of the existing methods locate sentiment classification as a supervised classification problem and train a reliable classifier from a large amount of labeled data (Pang *et al.*, 2002; Mullen and Collier, 2004; Matsumoto *et al.*, 2005; Gamon, 2005). The main disadvantage of such supervised approaches is that it is quite expensive in both time and labor to annotate a large amount of training data.

Unfortunately, in some languages such as Chinese and Hindi, a sufficient amount of training data is not always available. Sentiment classification becomes a quite challenging problem for such resource-scarce languages. While some studies have tackled this problem (Wan, 2009; Dasgupta and Ng, 2009), they still require substantial human efforts or specific linguistic resources that are only available in particular languages as we will see later in Section 2. We therefore want to develop a low-cost, general method that can be readily applicable to sentiment classification in any languages.

In this paper, we explore the use of label propagation (LP) (Zhu and Ghahramani, 2002) in building a document-level sentiment classifier under a minimally-supervised setting, where we have only a small number of labeled reviews other than the target reviews that we want to classify. Having a similarity graph whose vertices are labeled or unlabeled instances (reviews, here) and edges represent the similarity between the vertices, LP infers the label (sentiment polarity) of unlabeled (target) reviews based on labeled reviews that are similar to the target reviews. The key in applying LP to document-level sentiment classification is therefore in the way to represent reviews on the graph and to define the similarity between the them. We thus investigate the impact of the review representation and the similarity measure on the classification performance.

The main contributions of our work are summarized as follows:

- We evaluate LP on document-level sentiment classification in a resource-scarce language. Our method can be applied to any languages in which a small number of labeled reviews are available.
- We run LP with different review representations[1] (content words, phrases, and adjectives), and various similarity measures (dice coefficient, overlap coefficient, Jaccard, cosine similarity) (Manning and Schütze, 1999). We thereby reveal their impact on the classification performance.
- We compare our method with support vector machines (Vapnik, 1995) and transductive support vector machines (Joachims, 1999), and demonstrate the stability of the classification performance of our method in this task.

The rest of this paper is organized as follows: Section 2 introduces related work, Section 3 explains LP algorithm in detail. Section 4 evaluates our method. Section 5 concludes this study and discusses future direction.

2 Related Work

Several researchers attempted to solve a sentiment classification task in languages without abundant training instances (Dasgupta and Ng, 2009; Wan, 2009; Yanyan Zhao and Liu, 2010). In what follows, we briefly introduce those studies.

Dasgupta and Ng (2009) used transductive SVM (Joachims, 1999) to exploit unlabeled reviews in a document-level sentiment classification task. Basically their work is divided into three steps: firstly they perform spectral clustering to identify unambiguous reviews from unlabeled reviews. Second, they employ active learning to label the remaining ambiguous reviews. Third, they use the resulting labeled reviews and the remaining unlabeled reviews to train a transductive SVM classifier. Unlike our method, this study assumes manual intervention in the active learning step.

Wan (2009) employed co-training (Blum and Mitchell, 1998) to exploit labled reviews for a resource-rich language (English) in a document-level sentiment classification task in Chinese. Co-training assumes two independent classifiers that solve the target task, and use the output of one classifier to train the other classifier. With the help of machine translation, they could train two document-level sentiment classifiers in Chinese and English alternately. Their method can be applied to only resource-scarce languages that have a machine translation system between the target resource-scarce languages and a resource-rich language (e.g, English) and the classification performance could be heavily affected by the translation quality.

Yanyan Zhao and Liu (2010) adopted a graph-based propagation approach called Potts model (Wu, 1982) to solve a sentence-level sentiment classification task. Similar to label propagation we used in this study, Potts model uses the relationship among instances, and each instance arrives a probability state through the process of propagation until the whole graph stabilizes. We should mention that the motivation of their study is not to obtain high classification performance in a minimally-supervised setting but to make use of intra- and inter-document evidences in sentence-level sentiment classification. The usefulness of a graph-based semi-supervised algorithm in a minimally-supervised setting remains to be investigated.

3 Proposed Method

3.1 Method Overview

We adopt label propagation (Zhu and Ghahramani, 2002), which is a graph-based semi-supervised learning method, to solve a document-level sentiment classification task. Label propagation owns a

[1] hereafter referred to as sentiment features

Table 1: POS patterns and example sentiment features that match them

POS pattern	Sentiment features
AD VA	真的不错 (really not bad) 太困难 (too difficult)
AD VV	很生气 (very angry) 不犹豫 (do not hesitate)
AD JJ	太慢 (too slow) 那么简单 (so simple)
NN JJ	环境一流 (environment excellent) 设施旧(facilities old)
NN VA	态度不错 (attitude OK) 语言简洁 (language concise)

Table 2: Reviews and their sentiment phrases

Reviews	Sentimental features extracted
房间很小，很冷，不满意！	很小 很冷 不满意
The room is very small and cold. Unsatisfying!	Very small, very cold, Unsatisfying
服务态度不错，吃的很好。	态度不错 很好
Service attitude is OK. The food is very good.	Attitude is OK, very good

lot of advantages including convergence and a well defined objective function. It has been successfully employed in several NLP tasks, such as sentiment lexicon induction (Rao and Ravichandran, 2009) and word sense disambiguation (Niu *et al.*, 2005). To the best of our knowledge, there is no previous work that uses this algorithm in document-level sentiment classification where there are only a few amount of training data available.

Our method is divided into three steps:

Step 1: We extract from each review *sentiment features*, which are words/phrases with sentiment polarity, and then represent the review with a vector of extracted sentiment features (*sentiment feature vectors*).

Step 2: We construct a similarity graph by regarding the reviews (sentiment feature vectors) as vertices. The edge (weight) between two vertices (reviews) represents a degree of similarity between their sentiment polarity.

Step 3: Having a few vertices labeled as seeds, each vertex iteratively propagates its label to its neighboring vertices according to their similarity; seeds (initially labeled vertices) thereby behave like sources that push out labels to unlabeled vertices.

In the following sections, we explain each step in detail.

3.2 Step1: Extract Sentiment Feature

Feature selection plays an important role in label propagation, since the similarity score (label consistency) is directly affected by the design of feature vector. We therefore try the following three different ways to obtain the feature vector. Prior to extraction, Stanford Chinese Word Segmenter[2] and Stanford Log-linear Part-Of-Speech Tagger[3] are used to pre-process each review. In what follows, AD, VV, VA, JJ and NN refer to adverb, verb, predicative adjective, adjective and noun, respectively.

content words: We extract content words with the exception of words with pronoun (PN), measure word (M), cardinal number (CD), proper noun (NR), which do not convey sentiment.

phrases: We extract phrases that are likely to express sentiment by using manually-tailored POS patterns. Table 1 lists five POS patterns that we used to extract phrases, along with corresponding phrases extracted by them. These POS patters motivates from an intuition that

[2] http://nlp.stanford.edu/software/segmenter.shtml
[3] http://nlp.stanford.edu/software/tagger.shtml

Table 3: Similarity measure methods

Name	Computing formula
Dice	$\frac{2\|A\cap B\|}{\|A\|+\|B\|}$
Jaccard Index	$\frac{\|A\cap B\|}{\|A\cup B\|}$
Overlap	$\frac{\|A\cap B\|}{\|min(A,B)\|}$
Cosine (tf-idf)	$\frac{A\cdot B}{\|A\|\|B\|}$
Cosine (binary)	$\frac{\|A\cap B\|}{\sqrt{(\|A\|\times\|B\|)}}$

they are common indicators to identify sentiment expressed in reviews. Note that negation is tagged as AD. Turney (2002) used similar feature extracting strategy.

adjective: We extract only adjective words with POS tag VA and JJ.

Table 2 lists two examples of sentiment features extracted from reviews in the dataset we used in our experiment. They are positive and negative reviews in hotel domains, respectively.

3.3 Step 2: Build Similarity Graph

We try several similarity measures to define the similarity between the feature vectors extracted from reviews in Step 1. We assume that the more similar the sentiment polarity of two reviews is, the higher the similarity score between them is. Table 3 lists similarity measures we have used, where A and B are two reviews represented as feature vectors.

Then we construct a similarity graph from both labeled reviews (seeds) and unlabeled target reviews to be classified. In this study, when the similarity score between two reviews is above 0, we create an edge between two vertices corresponding to the two reviews in the graph, and the edge weight is computed by the similarity score. We should note that this graph construction procedure is performed in a totally parameter-free fashion. We do not require precious labeled data (as development set) to tune hyper-parameters as other (semi-)supervised methods do.

3.4 Step 3: Learning on Similarity Graph

Having the similarity graph obtained in step 2, label propagation (LP) (Zhu and Ghahramani, 2002) iteratively propagates a label from the labeled instances to their neighbors. LP can assign labels to the vertices that are connected to labeled vertices on the graph. In other words, if the graph is well-connected, we need a few labeled data to provide a label to a large amount of unlabeled data.

The similarity graph $G=\{V, E, W\}$ consists of vertices V, edges E, and an $n \times n$ weighted similarity matrix $W = [w_{ij}]$, where $n = |V|$. The edge weight w_{ij} is calculated by similarity score between review i and review j. When similarity score w_{ij} between x_i and x_j is larger, they are more likely to have the same label.

Mathematically speaking, LP aims to minimize the following objective function (Rao and Ravichandran, 2009), where l is the number of labeled data, u is the number of unlabeled data, and y_i is a binary label that takes 1 if the vertex is positive and 0 if the vertex is negative.

$$\sum_{i,j=1}^{l+u} w_{ij}(f(x_i) - f(x_j))^2 \text{ subject to } f(x_i) = y_i \text{ for } i = 1, 2, \ldots, l \quad (1)$$

The solution to this problem satisfies the following stationary conditions:

$$f(x_i) = y_i, i = 1...l \;\; f(x_j) = \frac{\sum_{k=1}^{l+u} w_{jk} f(x_k)}{\sum_{k=1}^{l+u} w_{jk}} \quad (2)$$

Algorithm 1: Label Propagation

Input : $G = \{V, E, W\}$ is the similarity graph built in section 3.1;
w_{ij} is the elements of W

1 $T_{ij} = P\{j- > i\} = \frac{w_{ij}}{\sum w_{kj}}$
2 Initialize label matrix Y by using seed examples
3 **while** *Y not converge* **do**
4     $Y = T * Y$
5   Row-normalize Y
6   Clamp the seed examples in Y to their original values
7 **end while**

Output : label Matrix Y

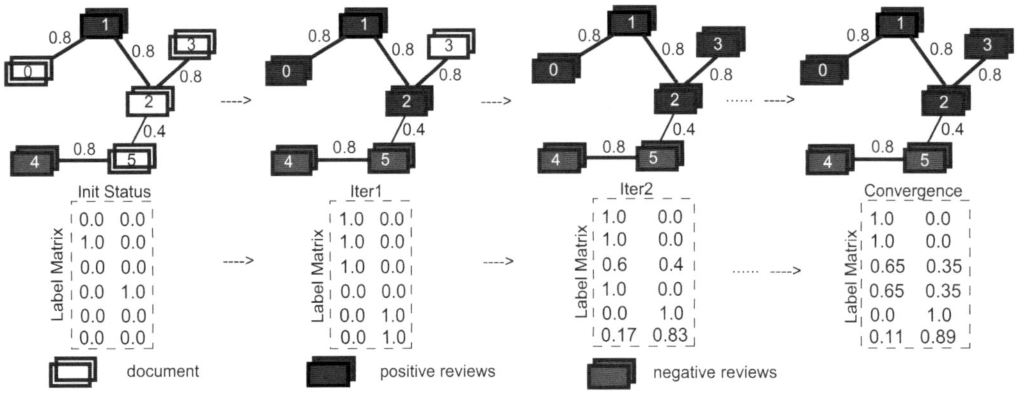

Figure 1: LP illustration

Intuitively, label propagation seeks $f(x_i)$ $(i = l + 1, \ldots, l + u)$ that satisfies in the Equation 2 in iterative manner.

Algorithm 1 depicts the label propagation algorithm in detail. There are mainly three steps: it first transforms the given similarity matrix by column normalization (line 1 in Algorithm 1). Each element w_{ij} in similarity matrix W represents the similarity score between review i and review j. After this step we could get a new matrix T whose element T_{ij} represents the transition probability between vertex j and vertex i. Next, the algorithm initializes the label matrix Y, which has N lines and two columns matrix, where N is the number of reviews including both positive and negative ones (line 2 in Algorithm 1). Here we define column 0 and column 1 are used to store a positive value and a negative value respectively. Label matrix Y is also the output of the algorithm. Each line in this matrix is the sentiment polarity score (one positive value and one negative value). The score of labeled positive seed is initialized to (1,0), while negative one is initialized to (0,1). The initialization of the rows of Y corresponding to unlabeled data points is not important (Zhu and Ghahramani, 2002). We initialize the value to (0.5,0.5) which stands for the unlabeled reviews have equal probability to below to positive or negative class. Then, LP propagates labels through the graph, in essence it is an iterative matrix computation. At each interaction, the label matrix Y is row normalized so that each line could be maintained as probability value which stands for the probability that the corresponding review belongs to one specific class. At the end of each iteration, the seeds are re-adjusted to original value, so that we could take seeds as energy sources.

When label matrix Y converges, the propagation process ends and unlabeled target reviews receive both positive and negative polarity value, and both of them are a probability value (the sum is 1). They are categorized according to the two values: for each review, if the value of column 0 (positive polarity value) is larger than column 1 (negative polarity value), the review is classified as positive and vice versa.

Table 4: Classification performance with label propagation

Domain	Sentiment features	Dice	Jaccard	Overlap	Cosine (tf-idf)	Cosine (binary)
Notebook	Adjective words	0.514	0.520	0.507	0.590	0.509
	Content words	0.584	0.681	0.690	0.685	0.611
	Phrases	0.820	0.819	0.819	**0.826**	0.821
Hotel	Adjective words	0.501	0.501	0.501	0.507	0.503
	Content words	0.544	0.534	0.502	0.528	0.532
	Phrases	0.712	0.759	0.735	0.752	**0.764**
Book	Adjective words	0.501	0.501	0.501	0.507	0.503
	Content words	0.626	0.604	0.535	0.626	0.619
	Phrases	**0.641**	0.623	0.627	0.598	0.631

The process of the algorithm is exemplified in Figure 1[4]. Each rectangle stands for one vertex (review). The weight value is the similarity score computed by using similarity measures introduced in Table 3 in Step 1. Here we define blue vertices as positive reviews and red ones as negative reviews.

Algorithms 1 process this graph as follows: Firstly, vertex 1 and vertex 4 are initialized as positive seed and negative seed, respectively. The corresponding label matrix Y is also shown. Then after the the first iteration (Iter1), label from vertex 1 is propagated to vertex 0 and vertex 2. Similar behavior happens between vertex 4 and vertex 5. After the second iteration (Iter2), positive label is also propagated to vertex 3 from vertex 2. Although vertex 2 could also receive negative label from vertex 5, in the corresponding label matrix Y, we could find positive value ($Y[2, 0]$) is larger than negative value ($Y[2, 1]$). Vertex 2 is still be categorized as positive review according to the classifying criteria we mentioned before. Finally the state of label matrix Y is stabilized (Convergence). The classifying process ends.

4 Evaluation and Discussion

We firstly investigate the performance of sentiment classification using different sentiment features and various similarity measures to define edges in the LP's similarity graph. We then compare LP with representative supervised and semi-supervised algorithms in terms of classification performance when we change the number of labeled reviews.

4.1 Data Set

The dataset we used is ChnSentiCorp[5]. It consists of reviews from three different domains: notebook, hotel, and book. The sentiment polarity of each review has been manually labeled. In each domain, we randomly selected 300 reviews as test dataset. The ratio between positive and negative reviews in the test data is 1:1, so that random baseline achieves accuracy of 0.5. We divided the remaining reviews into two parts: labeled seeds and unlabeled data. The number of labeled seeds is varied from 10 to 300 to control the amount of supervision.

In order to decrease the effect of seed selection, we conduct a ten-rounds experiment for the same number of labeled seeds. In each round, different labeled seeds are used. We report the average classification accuracy as a final result.

4.2 Sentiment Feature and Similarity Graph Selection

In this section we present classification results of our method when using different sentiment features and similarity graphs. The number of labeled seeds is fixed to 300. The classification results are summarized in Table 4. We have marked the best results using bold characteristics.

[4] Due to the space limitation, we preclude the similarity matrix transformation.

[5] http://www.searchforum.org.cn/tansongbo/corpus-senti.htm

Table 5: Similarity graphs statistics

Domain	Number of vertices	Number of edges	Density	LCS size
Notebook	3632	189,271	0.03	3433
Hotel	3544	346,127	0.06	3372
Book	3631	266,265	0.04	3495

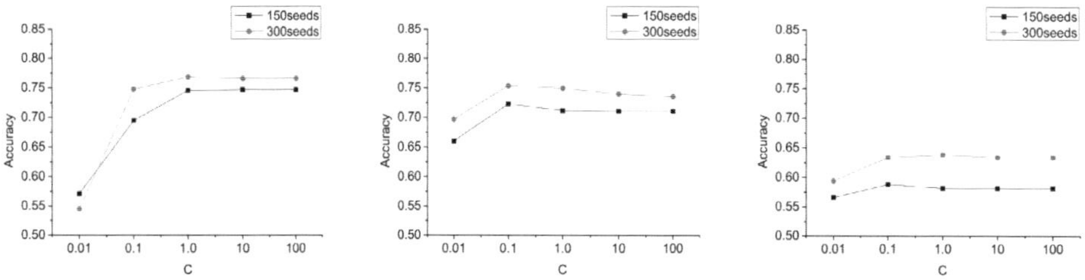

(a) Notebook reviews (b) Hotel reviews (c) Book reviews

Figure 2: C parameter sensitivity in SVM

We observe that when we use phrases as sentiment features, we obtained the best classification performance. On the other hand, when we use adjectives or content words as sentiment features, the classification accuracy drops significantly. We guess that the polarity of adjective can be affected by their contexts (which noun they modify or which adverb they are modified by), while the POS patterns could capture such contexts. Some of the content words (nouns) convey no polarity into the sentence, and they wrongly connect reviews that are in the opposite polarity but share the topics (nouns).

We could find that, in the same domain, the classification performance is not greatly affected by the choice of similarity measures. In the following experiments, we use cosine (binary) as similarity measure.

After determining review representation and similarity measure, we build the similarity graph for reviews in each domain. The statistics of similarity each graph are presented in Table 5.

We could see in all the three domains the largest connected subgraph (LCS) contains most of the vertices, which means the similarity graphs we built are well-connected.

4.3 Performance Comparison

We compare our method with the following two baseline methods:

Support Vector Machines (SVM) (Vapnik, 1995) is a well-known supervised learning algorithm; it tries to construct a hyperplane that classifies positive and negative training examples and then use it for classification. A good separation is achieved by the hyperplane that has the largest distance to the nearest training data points of any class. It has a hyper-parameter C which controls the trade-off between training error and margin. SVM has been already used in a document-level sentiment classification task(Mullen and Collier, 2004).

Transductive Support Vector Machines (TSVM) (Joachims, 1999) is a semi-supervised extension of traditional SVM so that it can exploit unlabeled data in semi-supervised learning. In addition to SVM hyper-parameter C, TSVM has additional hyper-parameter p, which specifies the ratio of positive/negative examples in unlabeled data.

We used SVMlight[6] as implementations of SVM and TSVM used in our experiments.

[6] http://svmlight.joachims.org/

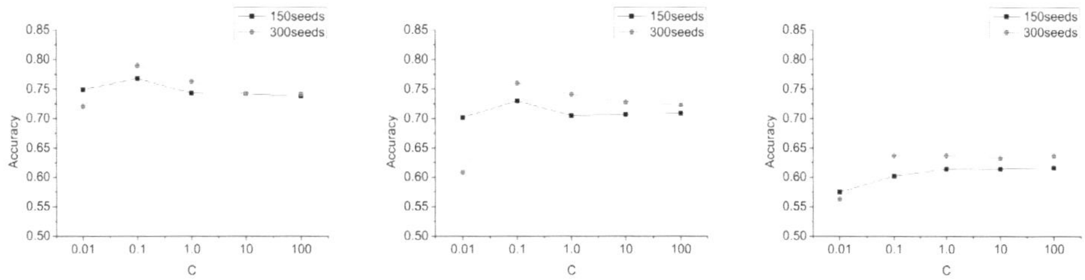

(a) Notebook reviews (b) Hotel reviews (c) Book reviews

Figure 3: C parameter sensitivity in TSVM (p is fixed to 0.5)

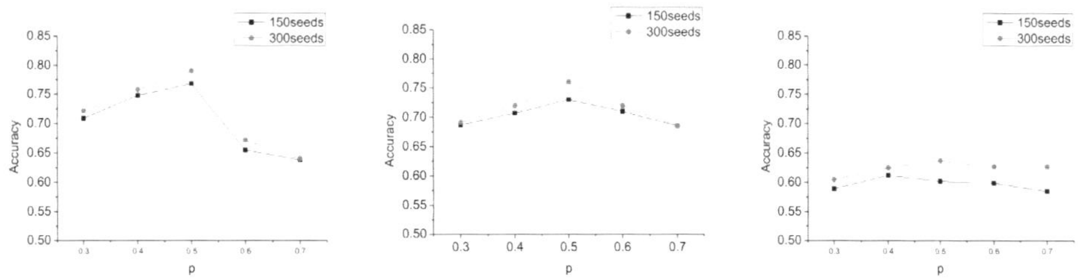

(a) Notebook reviews (b) Hotel reviews (c) Book reviews

Figure 4: p parameter sensitivity in TSVM (c is fixed to 0.1)

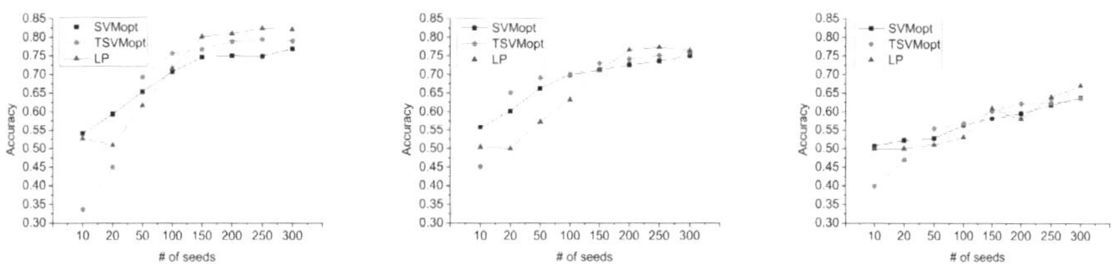

(a) Notebook reviews (b) Hotel reviews (c) Book reviews

Figure 5: Performance Comparison between LP and optimized SVM ($c = 1.0$)/TSVM ($c = 0.1, p = 0.5$) (SVMopt/TSVMopt)

4.3.1 Parameter Sensitivity We first investigate the effect of the hyper-parameters of SVM and TSVM. The effect of parameter C in SVM and TSVM are shown in Figure 2 and Figure 3 respectively. The vertical axis indicates the accuracy, while the horizontal axis indicates the value of parameter C. The effect of parameter p in TSVM is presented in Figure 4. The vertical axis indicates the accuracy, while the horizontal axis indicates value of parameter p.

We could find the performance of SVM and TSVM are sensitive to the changes of parameter C; they perform worse when the value of C is small. Also, the optimal C value is different in each domain. The performance of TSVM is further affected by hyper-parameter p. It behaves best in the most of situations with p equals to 0.5. This is probably because the unlabeled data we use during the experiment is nearly balanced in positive and negative sentiment. While in the situation where we have no prior knowledge in characteristics of unlabeled data, it is hard to tune hyper parameter p. When we make performance comparison, the value of parameter C in SVM is set to 1.0; the value of C and p in TSVM are set to 0.1 and 0.5, respectively. We found the they perform best in most of situations with these settings. And we should point out that it is usually quite difficult to tune the parameters without development set, which are precious in a minimally-supervised setting.

4.3.2 Performance Comparison The comparison of classification performance is shown in Figure 5; the vertical axis indicates the accuracy, while the horizontal axis indicates the number of labeled seeds. The performance of LP is comparable with SVM and TSVM with optimal hyper-parameter setting (referred to as SVMopt and TSVMopt int Figure 5) and even outperforms them when an appropriate number of seeds are provided. We should note that label propagation is a parameter-free method. It performed reasonably well across all the three domains without tuning hyper-parameters.

We could find that, with the increase of labeled instances, the performance of all of three methods were improved. For SVM and TSVM, the increase of labeled instances means more labeled data are available, so the classifiers perform better. On the other hand, for label propagation when more seeds take part in the label propagating process, unlabeled vertices could get more reliable sources so that LP could become more confident to decide the label one specific vertex belongs to.

Finally, all the three methods do not perform well in book domain. Because in book reviews people would discuss various aspects including the story, the writing style of author, the figures in the book and even the publisher. Sometimes the sentiment those aspects are not consistent. Turney (2002) reported similar findings on movie reviews.

5 Conclusion and Future Work

In this paper we explore the use of label propagation (LP) for a document-level sentiment classification task in resource-scarce languages. We exhaustively investigate the performance of label propagation in this task while varying the way to build the task similarity graph. We found the similarity graph built on phrases is an excellent choice for label propagation for this task. And based on phrases, conine (binary) could be used to measure the sentimental similarity well.

We compared our method with supervised learning and semi-supervised learning methods on real Chinese reviews classification in three domains. Experimental results demonstrated that label propagation showed a competitive performance against SVM or Transductive SVM with best hyper-parameter settings. Considering the difficulty of tuning hyper-parameters in a resource-scarce setting, the stable performance of parameter-free label propagation is promising.

We plan to further improve the performance of LP in sentiment classification especially when we only have a small number of labeled seeds. We will exploit the idea of restricting the label propagating steps when the available labeled data is quite small. Besides, according the work (Velikovich *et al.*, 2010) label propagation suffers a problem when there are dense subgraphs in the similarity graph. Because in label propagation a vertex with multiple paths to a seed will be influenced by all these path, when the label information comes into a dense subgraphs a reinforcement effect will happen. We plan to adopt the idea of damping factor used in PageRank (Brin and Page, 1998) to solve the problem. Finally, we will also explore sentiment feature extracting approaches and different similarity graphs combining methods.

References

Blum, Avrim and Tom Mitchell. 1998. Combining labeled and unlabeled data with co-training. In *Proceedings of the eleventh annual conference on Computational learning theory*, COLT' 98, pp. 92–100. ACM.

Brin, Sergey and Lawrence Page. 1998. The Anatomy of a Large-Scale Hypertextual Web Search Engine. *Computer Networks and ISDN Systems*, 30(1-7), 107–117, April.

Dasgupta, Sajib and Vincent Ng. 2009. Mine the easy, classify the hard: a semi-supervised approach to automatic sentiment classification. In *Proceedings of the Joint Conference of the 47th Annual Meeting of the ACL and the 4th International Joint Conference on Natural Language Processing of the AFNLP: Volume 2 - Volume 2*, ACL '09, pp. 701–709.

Gamon, Michael. 2005. Sentiment classification on customer feedback data: noisy data, large feature vectors, and the role of linguistic analysis. In *In COLING*, pp. 841–847.

Joachims, Thorsten. 1999. Transductive inference for text classification using support vector machines. pp. 200–209. Morgan Kaufmann.

Manning, Christopher D. and Hinrich Schütze. 1999. *Foundations of statistical natural language processing*. MIT Press.

Matsumoto, Shotaro, Hiroya Takamura, and Manabu Okumura. 2005. Sentiment classification using word sub-sequences and dependency sub-trees. In *PAKDD'05*, pp. 301–311.

Mullen, Tony and Nigel Collier. 2004. Sentiment analysis using support vector machines with diverse information sources. In *In Proceedings of Conference on Empirical Methods in Natural Language Processing*.

Niu, Zheng-Yu, Dong-Hong Ji, and Chew Lim Tan. 2005. Word sense disambiguation using label propagation based semi-supervised learning. In *Proceedings of the 43rd Annual Meeting on Association for Computational Linguistics*, ACL '05, pp. 395–402.

Pang, Bo and Lillian Lee. 2008. Opinion mining and sentiment analysis. *Found. Trends Inf. Retr.*, 2, 1–135, January.

Pang, Bo, Lillian Lee, and Shivakumar Vaithyanathan. 2002. Thumbs up? sentiment classification using machine learning techniques. In *EMNLP '02: Proceedings of the ACL-02 conference on Empirical methods in natural language processing*, pp. 79–86. Association for Computational Linguistics.

Rao, Delip and Deepak Ravichandran. 2009. Semi-supervised polarity lexicon induction. In *Proceedings of the 12th Conference of the European Chapter of the Association for Computational Linguistics*, EACL '09, pp. 675–682.

Turney, Peter D. 2002. Thumbs up or thumbs down?: semantic orientation applied to unsupervised classification of reviews. In *Proceedings of the 40th Annual Meeting on Association for Computational Linguistics*, ACL '02, pp. 417–424.

Vapnik, Vladimir N. 1995. *The nature of statistical learning theory*. Springer-Verlag New York, Inc.

Velikovich, Leonid, Sasha Blair-Goldensohn, Kerry Hannan, and Ryan McDonald. 2010. The viability of web-derived polarity lexicons. In *Human Language Technologies: The 2010 Annual Conference of the North American Chapter of the Association for Computational Linguistics*, HLT '10, pp. 777–785.

Wan, Xiaojun. 2009. Co-training for cross-lingual sentiment classification. In *Proceedings of the Joint Conference of the 47th Annual Meeting of the ACL and the 4th International Joint Conference on Natural Language Processing of the AFNLP: Volume 1 - Volume 1*, ACL '09, pp. 235–243.

Wu, F. Y. 1982. The potts model. *Rev. Mod. Phys.*, 54(1), 235–268, Jan.

Yanyan Zhao, Bing Qin and Ting Liu. 2010. Integrating intra- and inter-document evidences for improving sentence sentiment classification. *ACTA AUTOMATICA SINICA*, 36(10), 1417–1425.

Zhu, Xiaojin and Zoubin Ghahramani. 2002. Learning from labeled and unlabeled data with label propagation. Technical report.

A Hybrid Extraction Model for Chinese Noun/Verb Synonym bi-gram Collocations *

Wanyin Li and Qin Lu
Department of Computing, The Hong Kong Polytechnic University,
Hung Hom, Kowloon, Hong Kong
csclaireli@gmail.com, csluqin@comp.polyu.edu.hk

Abstract. Statistical-based collocation extraction approaches suffer from (1) low precision rate because high co-occurrence bi-grams may be syntactically unrelated and are thus not true collocations; (2) low recall rate because some true collocations with low occurrences cannot be identified successfully by statistical-based models. To integrate both syntactic rules as well as semantic knowledge into a statistical model for collocation extraction is one way to achieve a high precision while keeping a reasonable recall. This paper designs a cascade system which employs a hybrid model by integrating both syntactic and semantic knowledge into a statistical model for Chinese synonymous noun/verb collocations extraction. The grammatically bounded noun/verb collocations are extracted first from a syntactic-rule based module, which is then inputted to a semantic-based module for further retrieval of low frequent bi-gram collocations.

Keywords: Collocation extraction, statistical model, syntactic rules, semantic relationship, similarity calculation, HowNet.

1. Introduction

According to (Benson, 1990), "collocation is an arbitrary and recurrent word combination", and (Manning, 1999), "A collocation is an expression consisting of two or more words that corresponds to some conventional way of saying things". The definitions imply the feasibility of statistics calculation on collocation identification, which has been widely employed by traditional collocation extraction systems (Dunning, 1993; Smadja, 1996; Sun, 1997; Manning, 1999). These statistical models which depended on word frequencies and association strength of co-occurrence (bi-grams) made them difficult to detect bi-gram collocations with lower frequencies. Moreover, bi-grams which occur with high frequencies may not be syntactically related. For example, "这/r 就/d 要/v 从/p 各自/r 的/u 实际/n 情况/n 出发/v" (It should be thought about according to the real condition). The bi-gram "实际(…)出发" bears a higher co-occurrence frequency from the corpus based on statistical models. However, it is syntactically ill-formed as a noun/verb phrases. (Choueka, 1993) defined collocations as "a sequence of two or more consecutive words, that has characteristics of a syntactic and semantic unit", and (Cowie, 1978) defined them as "co-occurrence of two or more lexical items as realizations of structural elements within a given syntactic pattern". This paper investigates how to extract the so called bi-gram synonym collocations which satisfy the synonym substitution rule in which a co-word or head-word of a given bigram can be replaced by another synonym word (Liu, 2002) and the substituted bigram is also existed. For example "重要/位置" and "主要/位置" are one synonym collocation pair because "重要" and "主要" are synonyms and "重要/位置" and "主要/位置" co-occurs in Chinese corpus. "重要/位置" and "重要/地位" is another synonym collocation pair because "位置" and "地位" are synonyms. Based on the

* Acknowledgments "The work is partially supported by a grant from The Chiang Ching-kuo Foundation for International Scholarly Exchange under the project RG013-D-09" .

previous work (Li et. al., 2005; Li and Lu, 2006), this work proposes a hybrid approach to employ the syntactic, semantic and statistical information for the extraction of syntactically bound synony bi-gram collocations. This paper focuses on collocation extraction in noun/verb phrases. A sub-model of HowNet based similarity calculation is proposed to identify bi-gram synonymous collocations derived from a base noun/verb phrase structure, say in the distance of [-5, +5], especially the ones in low frequency from a monolingual corpora. Our pattern generation process from the actual training data is similar to the works in (Seretan, 2005). The named syntactic patterns in this paper are automatically learned from the actual training data according to the *F*-score of the final extracted collocations by re-applying each pattern on the training corpus. Hence the syntactic patterns are corpus independent while most of the previous works arbitrarily choose the patterns in advance.

The rest of the paper is organized as follows. Section 2 studies related works. Section 3 describes the design of the system. Section 4 presents performance analysis. Section 5 is the conclusion.

2. Related Works

Researches on collocation extraction which make use of syntactic knowledge usually employ chunk-based approach to detect the syntactic patterns such as the constructions of <PP + Verb> (Krenn, 2001; Villada Moirón, 2004), <Verb + Noun> (Wu, 2003; McCarthy *et al.*, 2003; Jian, 2004), <Noun + Noun> (Wang, 2003; Seretan, 2005), and <Adjective + Noun> (Seretan *et al.*, 2004). Jian (Jian, 2004) performed a *logarithmic Likelihoood Ratio* statistics with the integration of chunks, PoS tagging and clause knowledge achieved an average precision of 89.3% in the types of <Verb+Noun> collocation extraction. Drawbacks exist in the self-confliction of rules themselves as well as the parser precision. To deal with this, *t*-test is employed to measure the co-occurrence strength of the lexical pairs which satisfy the syntactic templates learned from the actual training data.

Researches on synonymous collocation extraction using semantic knowledge are mainly based on the similarity calculation. Lin (Lin, 1997) proposed a distributional hypothesis that if two words have similar sets of collocations, they are considered similar. According to (Miller, 1992), two expressions are synonymous in a context *C* if the substitution of one for the other in *C* does not change the truth-value of a sentence in which the substitution is made. Liu Qun (Liu *et al.,* 2002) defined word similarity as two words that can substitute for each other in a context and keep the sentence consistent in syntax and semantic structure. Researchers (Lin, 1997; Pearce, 2001; Wu and Zhou, 2003) have applied similarity-based calculation for collocation identifications. Pearce identified collocations by relying on a mapping from one word to its synonyms for each of its senses. (Wu and Zhou, 2003) are the first researches to extract synonymous collocations by mapping synonyms relationships between two different languages to automatically acquire English synonymous collocations. However, this method needs a parallel corpus which is difficult to be obtained in real case.

3. System Design

Figure 1 shows the system framework consisted of two cascaded modules. Module I, labeled as BNP/BVP bi-gram Candidates Extractor, presents a syntax model from the chunked training corpus to generate collocation patterns of Base Noun Phrase (BNP) and Base Verb Phrase (BVP). To achieve this task, the model requires certain training data with base phrase chunking information although though it does not require the targeted collocations to be annotated. After successfully extraction of the patterns, the extracted patterns are then applied to extract candidate bi-grams which are further evaluated by *t*-test. The candidate collocations from Module I will be inputted into the Module II, Synonym BNP/BVP bi-grams Extractor, in which a HowNet based similarity model is employed to extract the synonym noun/verb bi-gram collocation candidates.

Two text corpuses are utilized in the paper. One million training corpus, named corpusTrain (Xu, 2005), tokenized by linguists with chunking information as well as PoS tagging and another testing corpus with half a year People's Daily newspaper prepared by Peking University (PKU corpus), named corpusTest which contains 11 million words with PoS tags information only, which is also the training corpus used in Module II .

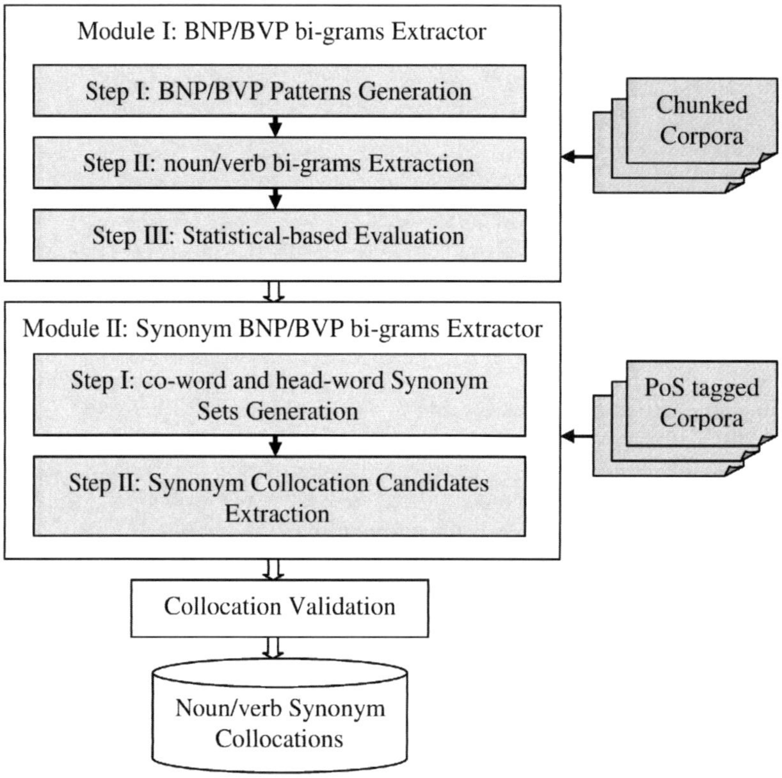

Figure 1: System Framework.

3.1 Module I – BNP/BVP bi-gram Collocations Extraction Model

Three steps are included in this Module:

- Step One: The syntactic pattern sets of noun/verb phrases are generated from the POS chunked corpusTrain with a raw pattern precision attached.
- Step Two: Taking a randomly selected Noun/Verb as an input word, named head-word $w_{h,}$ apply the syntactic patterns on corpusTest to extract candidate noun/verb phrases with respect to w_h. For example, given the head-word "新闻/n" and the syntactic pattern of [/n /n], the noun phrase" 新闻/n 媒介/n" will be such a candidate. The same candidate extracted when taking the head-word "媒介/n" as input will be eliminated.
- Step Three: Apply *t*-test to candidate noun/verb bi-grams of w_h to obtain syntactically bound bi-gram collocation candidates (w_h, w_c), where w_c identifies the collocated word of w_h.

3.2 BNP/BVP bi-gram Patterns Generation

BNP/BVP is a Noun/Verb Phrase that does not contain a Noun/Verb Phrase nor any Noun/Verb Phrase post-modifier. The syntactic bi-gram patterns of noun and verb phrases are automatically learned from the base phrase chunked training corpus corpusTrain. Then they are re-tested on corpusTrain in which the chunking information is removed. After which each pattern is attached with a pattern precision score such as the ones showed in the second column of Table 1. The precision threshold of the final syntactic patterns is determined from F-score of final extracted collocations, which is 30% for noun collocation patterns and 20% for verb collocation patterns. Table 1 contains the noun/verb bi-gram patterns which will be applied on corpusTest to extract the candidate noun/verb collocations.

Table 1: Bi-gram noun/verb phrases patterns.

Instances	Precision tested on corpusTrain	BNP Patterns
27,484	0.41	[/n /n]
10,856	0.53	[/vn /n]
8,421	0.38	[/n /vn]
7,198	0.62	[/a /n]
3710	0.61	[/b /n]
Instances	Precision tested on corpusTrain	BVP Patterns
22,267	0.22	[/v /n]
20,164	0.66	[/d /v]
19,548	0.43	[/v /v]
16,001	0.26	[/v /u]
3,681	0.69	[/ad /v]
2323	0.37	[/d /v /u]

3.3 Noun/Verb bi-gram Collocation Candidates Extraction

t-score is used to measure the co-occurrence strength of the syntactic bound bi-gram candidates because *t*-score achieves better performance than *z-score*, *MI*, χ^2 and *log-likelihood* for noun/verb phrase collocation extractions on Chinese corpus (Li and Lu, 2006). The first N-best from the output will be the syntactically bound noun/verb bi-gram collocations (w_h, w_c).

$$t-score = \frac{p(w_h, r, w_c) - p(w_h) \times p(w_c)}{\sqrt{\frac{p(w_h, r, w_c)}{N}}} = \frac{\frac{f(w_h, r, w_c)}{N} - \frac{f(w_h)}{N} \times \frac{f(w_c)}{N}}{\sqrt{\frac{f(w_h, r, w_c)}{N^2}}} \quad (1)$$

$f(w_h,r,w_c)$: frequency of collocations with head-word as w_h, co-word as w_c and relationship as r;
$f(w_h)$: frequency of head-word w_h; $f(w_c)$: frequency of co-word w_c
N : of the total instances of BNP/BVP;

3.4 Module II- Synonym BNP/BVP bi-gram Candidates Extraction Model

Two steps are included in this Module:

Step 1: For each Noun/Verb bi-gram collocation candidates (w_h, w_c) from Section 3.3, the synonyms against w_h and w_c are acquired respectively using the word similarity calculation based on HowNet (See Section 3.5 for details). Any word in HowNet having a similarity value above the threshold is considered a synonym head-word $w_{sh,}$ or a synonym collocated word w_{sc} for further extractions in Step 2.

- **Step 2**: For each synonym head-word w_{sh} of w_h and the collocated word $w_{c,}$, the bi-gram (w_{sh}, w_c) is taken as a synonym collocation if the pair appear at least once in the corpus. The same processing is applied to each of the synonym collocated word w_{sc} of w_c, for the bi-gram (w_h, w_{sc}).

3.5 Similarity Model Based on HowNet

The definition of synonyms in this Module is similar with the word similarity given by (Liu, 2002). A word in HowNet is defined as a set of concepts, and each concept is represented by its up to four different primitives classified as: *basic independent primitive* (weighted by β_1 in formula (4)), *other independent primitive* (weighted by β_2), *relation primitive* (weighted by β_3), and *symbol primitive* (weighted by β_4), where basic independent primitive and other independent primitive are used to calculate the semantic relationship between two concepts and the another two primitives are used to measure the syntactic relationships between two concepts. The definition of HowNet is described as a collection W of n words as below:

$$W = \{w_1, w_2, \ldots w_n\}$$

Each word w_i is described by a set of concepts S_{ij},

$$w_i = \{S_{i1}, S_{i2}, \ldots S_{ix}\}$$

Each concept S_i is described by a set of primitives p_{ij}:

$$S_i = \{p_{i1}, p_{i2}, \ldots p_{iy}\}$$

For each word pair w_1 and w_2, the similarity function is defined by:

$$Sim(w_1, w_2) = \max_{i=1 \ldots n, j=1 \ldots m} Sim(S_{1i}, S_{2j}) \quad (2)$$

S_{1i} is the concept lists associated with w_1 and S_{2j} is the concept lists associated with w_2. Considering the semantic tree structure of HowNet, the primitive similarity for any two nodes p_1 and p_2 of the same primitive type can be expressed by the following formula:

$$Sim(p_1, p_2) = \frac{\min(d(p_1), d(p_2))}{Dis(p_1, p_2) + \min(d(p_1), d(p_2))} \quad (3)$$

where $d(p_i)$ is the depth of node p_i in the tree, $Dis(p_1, p_2)$ is the path length between p_1 and p_2 based on the semantic tree structure.

To integrate both semantic and syntactic information, the similarity between two concepts S_1 and S_2 is taken into consideration of all the four primitive types in weighted as:

$$Sim(S_1, S_2) = \sum_{i=1}^{4} \beta_i \prod_{j=1}^{i} Sim_j(p_{1j}, p_{2j}) \quad (4)$$

$\beta_{i,i=1..4}$ is a weighting factor (Liu, 2002), where $\beta_1 + \beta_2 + \beta_3 + \beta_4 = 1$ and $\beta_1 \geq \beta_2 \geq \beta_3 \geq \beta_4$. The similarity model given here is the basis for building the synonym set where β_1 *and* β_2 represent the semantic information, and β_3 *and* β_4 represent the syntactic relationship.

3.6 Synonym Set

The synonyms set W_{syn_h} against the head-word w_h based on the similarity formula (4) is defined as below:

$$W_{syn\_h} = \{w_s : Sim(w_h, w_s) > \theta\} \quad (5^a)$$

The same definition against the co-word w_c of w_h to build up the synonyms set W_{syn_c} is:

$$W_{syn\_c} = \{w_s : Sim(w_c, w_s) > \theta\} \quad (5^b)$$

where $0 < \theta < 1$ is tuned from experiments (see Figure 3).

3.7 Synonym Collocations

We follow the idea from (Wu and Zhou, 2003) to define the synonym collocation pair as two collocations that are similar in meaning, but may not identical in wording. For a given collocation (w_{sh}, w_c, d), if $w_{sh} \in W_{syn\_h}$, then we deem the triple (w_{sh}, w_c, d) as a synonym collocation with respect to the collocation (w_h, w_c, d) if (w_{sh}, w_c, d) appears at least once in the corpus, d identifies the position distance of [-5,+5] between w_h and w_c with respect to w_h within the running text line. Hence, the set of synonym collocations C_{syn_h} is defined as:

$$C_{syn\_h} = \{(w_{sh}, w_c, d) : Freq(w_{sh}, w_c, d) >= 1\} \quad (6^a)$$

Similarly, for $w_{sc} \in W_{syn\_c}$, the set of synonym collocations C_{syn_c} is:

$$C_{syn\_c} = \{(w_h, w_{sc}, d) : Freq(w_h, w_{sc}, d) >= 1\} \quad (6^b)$$

4. Experiments

To evaluate the proposed methodology, i.e., the effectiveness of true named collocations extraction. The strategies of a collocation dictionary and human judgment are applied. Firstly, the N-best bigrams are evaluated against the collocation dictionary built up from the colleagues in our NLP laboratory. Secondly, the remainder bi-gram candidates are then judged manually to evaluate how many among the N-best scored bi-grams are true collocations. The performance of the hybrid approach is evaluated by N-best strategies supplemented with precision and a so called local recall defined as below:

$$Local\ Recall = \frac{\text{The number of Correctly Identified Collocations}}{\text{Toal number of True Collocations}} \quad (7)$$

Where total number of true collocations is defined by adding the extracted collocations from both the hybrid and statistical-based approaches and then sorted in N-best without duplication. The performance of the proposed approach is compared with the pure statistical-based approach, the syntax-based approach and the semantic-based approach.

4.1 Evaluation of Module I

30 nouns and 30 verbs are randomly selected as the head-words. Table 2 shows the performance by comparing with the statistical-based model (Xu, 2003) in which the returned word list have been further processed against the 30 nouns and verbs with the syntax-based model.

Table 2: Comparison of syntactic & statistical models.

		Extracted bigrams	Prec. Rate	Local Recall	F-Score
30 Noun Head-words					
Rule Prec. >30%	Rule-Based	3,497	81.01%	59.63%	68.69%
	Refined by *t*-test	3,114	83.26%	58.08%	68.43%
Statistical Model Only		1,484	78.84%	26.15%	39.27%
30 Verb Head-words					
Rule Prec. >20%	Rule-Based	2,615	71.74%	62.62%	66.87%
	Refined by *t*-test	2,398	75.43%	64.25%	69.39%
Statistical Model Only		818	73.15%	21.24%	32.92%

Figure 2 shows the precision variation against the local recall by the *t*-test which achieves the precision rate up to 88.39% in noun collocations and up to 83.21% in verb collocations when taking the first 70% of each respectively.

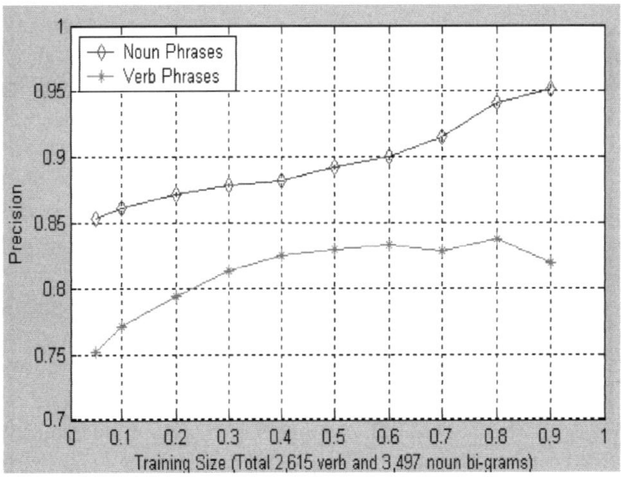

Figure 2: Variation of precision and local recall.

4.2 Evaluation of Hybrid Model

Module II aims to extract the collocations in lower co-occurrence frequency especially the ones appear less than three times in the corpus (Li et. al., 2005).

Taking total 4,278 (3,497*0.7+2,615*0.7) bi-gram noun and verb collocations from Module I as the input to Module II, total 2,573 synonym head-words and co-words are acquired with the tuned value of θ = 0.9. After Step 2 of Module II, additional 6,051 bi-gram synonym collocation candidates are extracted. 5,417 of them are true collocations to a evaluate set of manually checked "true positive" (Table 3).

Table 3: Precision of synonym collocations extraction.

Head-words in Noun	30
Synonym head-words	1,129
Synonym bi-grams extracted in Step 2 of Module II	3,078
True synonym collocations obtained in Step 2 of Module II	2,802
Precision Rate	91.03%
Head-words in Verb	30
Synonym head-words	1,444
Synonym bi-grams extracted in Step 2 of Module II	2,973
True synonym collocations obtained in Step 2 of Module II	2,615
Precision Rate	87.95%
Overall Precision Rate	89.49%

Figure 3 shows the variation of the value of θ in equation 5 with F-value, which has its best value of 0.9.

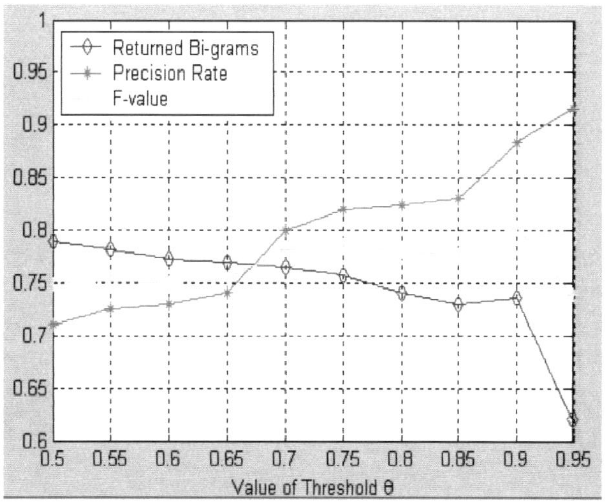

Figure 3: The choice of θ.

Table 4 presents the performance comparison for statistical-based approach, syntactic integrated approach (Module I), semantic integrated approach (Module II), and finally the hybrid approach.

Table 4: Comparison of statistical-based, Module I, II and cascade hybrid approaches.

	Models	Extracted bi-grams	Precision Rate	Local Recall Rate	F-Score
	Statistical-based	1,484	78.84%	15.52%	25.93%
	Module I Only	2,948	86.39%	33.78%	48.57%
	Module II Only	3,078	91.03%	37.16%	52.78%

Noun	Hybrid (I+II)	6,026	88.77%	70.94%	78.86%
Verb	Statistical-based	818	73.15%	10.34%	18.12%
	Module I Only	2,058	78.21%	31.24%	44.65%
	Module II Only	2,973	87.95%	45.19%	59.70%
	Hybrid (I+II)	5,031	87.91%	76.43%	81.77%
Noun + Verb		11,057	88.34%	73.69%	80.35%

5. Conclusion

The paper proposes a hybrid model to identify Chinese Noun and Verb synonym bi-gram collocations. The system achieves an average precision of 88.34% and local recall of 73.69%. The approach, aimed at low frequency word pairs which lead up to poor performance in pure statistical-based associate measure approaches, proposes distinct models reflecting diverse linguistic knowledge to improve both precision rate and recall rate.

The paper is focused on the extraction of bi-gram noun/verb synonym collocations, especially the ones may have a lower co-occurrence of less than 3 times in the running texts. Fu (Fu et al., 2010) made use of semantics of n-grams as the set of all the texts containing it to measure the information distance of n-grams which makes the n-grams of any length to their semantics applicable. To extend the current work in this paper to n-grams of free length is one valuable inspiration in the future.

References

Benson M., 1990. Collocations and General Purpose Dictionaries. *International Journal of Lexicography,* 3(1), pp. 23-35.

Choueka Y., 1993. Looking for Needles in a Haystack or Locating Interesting Collocation Expressions in Large Textual Database. *Proceedings of RIAO Conference on User-oriented Content-based Text and Image Handling*: 21-24, Cambridge.

Cowie A. P., 1978. The place of illustrative material and collocations in the design of a learner's dictionary. *In P. Strevens, editor, In Honour of A. S. Hornby*, pages 127—139. Oxford University Press.

Dunning Ted, 1993. Accurate methods for the statistics of surprise and coincidence. *Computational Linguistics*, 19(1):61–74.

Fan Bu, Xiaoyan Zhu and Ming Li, Measuring the Non-compositionality of Multiword Expressions (2010).*COLING '10 Proceedings of the 23rd International Conference on Computational Linguistics*.

Jian, J. Y., Chang, Y. C., & Chang, J. S., 2004. Collocational Translation Memory Extraction Based on Statistical Linguistic Information. *ROCLING 2004, Conference on Computational Linguistics and Speech Processing*, Taipei.

Krenn B. and Evert S., 2001. Can we do better than frequency? a case study on extracting pp-verb collocations. *In Proceedings of the ACL Workshop on Collocations*, Toulouse, France.

Li W.Y, Lu Q. and Xu R. F., 2005. Similarity based Chinese Synonyms Collocation Extraction. *International Journal of Computational Linguistics and Chinese Language Processing*, vol.10, no.1, pp.123-144.

Li W.Y., Lu Q., 2006. Collocation Extraction for Noun Phrases using Shallow Parsing Rules and Statistical Models. *In Proceeding of 20th Paclic Asia Conference on Language, Information and Computation*, pp. 99-106, Wuhan, China.

Lin, D. K., 1997. Using Syntactic Dependency as Local Context to Resolve Word Sense Ambiguity. *Proceedings of ACL/EACL-97*, pp. 64-71, Madrid, Spain.

Liu, Q., 2002. The Word Similarity Calculation on <<HowNet>>. *Proceedings of* 3rd *Conference on Chinese lexicography*, TaiBei.

Manning C. and Sch¨utze H., 1999. Foundations of Statistical Natural Language Processing. *MIT Press*, Cambridge.

McCarthy, D., B. Keller and J. Carroll (2003) `Detecting a continuum of compositionality in phrasal verbs'. *In Proceedings of the ACL-SIGLEX Workshop on Multiword Expressions: Analysis, Acquisition and Treatment*, Sapporo, Japan.

Miller, G and C. Fellbaum, 1992. Semantic networks of English. *In Beth Levin & Steven Pinker (eds.)*, Lexical and conceptual semantics, pp. 197-229.

Villada Moirón, M. B., 2004. Acquisition of Dutch support verb collocations: a model comparison .ms. Groningen University. URL: http://www.let.rug.nl/~begona/papers/svcmodels.ps.

Pearce, D., 2001. Synonymy in Collocation Extraction. Proceedings of NAACL'01 Workshop on Wordnet and Other Lexical Resources: Applications, Extensions and Customizations, 2001.

Smadja Frank, Kathleen R., Mckeown, Vasileios H., 1996. Translation collocations for bilingual lexicons: a statistical approach. *Computational Linguistics*, 22:1-38.

Sun, M. S., C. N. Huang and J. Fang, 1997. Preliminary Study on Quantitative Study on Chinese Collocations. *ZhongGuoYuWen*, No.1, 1997, pp. 29-38.

Violeta Sereran, Luka Nerima, Eric Wehrli, 2004. Using the Web as a Corpus for the Syntactic-Based Collocation Identification. *In Proceedings of International Conference on Language Resources and Evaluation* , Lisbon, Portugal, pp. 1871-1874

Violeta Seretan, 2005. Induction of Syntactic Collocation Patterns from Generic Syntactic Relations. *In Proceedings of Nineteenth International Joint Conference on Artificial Intelligence (IJCAI 2005)*, Edinburgh, Scotland, pp. 1698-1699.

Wang Xinglong, Carroll J., 2003. Acquisition Of Collocations. *Technical Report for the MEANING Project (IST-2001-34460)*. University of Sussex, UK.

Wu H. and Zhou M., 2003. Synonymous Collocation Extraction Using Translation Information. *Proceeding of the 41st Annual Meeting of ACL.*

Wu Andi., 2003. Learning Verb-Noun Relations to Improve Parsing. *In Proceedings of the Second SIGHAN Workshop on Chinese Language Processing*, pp. 119-124.

Xu R. F., Lu Q., and Li Y., 2003. An automatic Chinese Collocation Extraction Algorithm based on Lexical Statistics. *In Proceedings of IEEE International Conference on Natural Language Processing and Knowledge Engineering*, Beijing, china, 321-326.

Xu R. F., Lu Q., Li Y., Li W. Y., 2005. The design and construction of the PolyU Shallow Treebank. *International Journal of Computational Linguistics and Chinese Language Processing*, Vol.10, no.3.

Word-order and argument-marking: Japanese vs Chinese vs Naxi*

Paul Law

Department of Chinese, Translation and Linguistics, City University of Hong Kong
Tat Chee Ave, Kowloon Tong, Hong Kong
paul.law@cityu.edu.hk

Abstract. It is argued that varying word-order is related not to the marking on the arguments indicating their grammatical relations but to the syntax of object. The flexible word-order in Japanese and the lack thereof in Chinese may be attributed to the presence or absence of argument-marking, but evidence from Naxi shows that although argument-marking may help identify the semantic roles of the arguments from the processing point view, it is syntax that decides the word-order. Insofar as the relative positioning of the object and adverbs cannot be reduced to argument-marking, the mechanism allowing movement of the object past the verb from a universal order derives both the verb-final property and the varying word-order.

Keywords: movement, processing, syntax of object, Universal Order Hypothesis.

1 Introduction

A common view about word-order is that if the arguments of a predicate are overtly marked, e.g., for Case, leading to the identification of their grammatical relations (subject, object and obliques), then the arguments may be ordered in more than one way. The semantic roles of the arguments can be recognized by their grammatical relations in conjunction with the voice of the predicate (active, passive). Conversely, if such marking is lacking, then linear order is the crucial means to identify the grammatical relations of the arguments and their interpretations with respect to their semantic roles.

The processing point of view above works well for the comparison of a language like Japanese (or Korean) with one like Chinese (or English). The picture becomes a bit more complicated when Naxi comes into the picture. Naxi is a verb-final language like Japanese and Korean. It too marks the arguments to the effect that their grammatical relations may be identified. But the marking is optional; yet, the varying word-order is largely the same.

In this paper I argue that for certain word-orders syntax must be appealed to since they do not fall under the processing account. If the underlying phrase structure is universally the same (Kayne 1994), then the superficial variation with respect to the relative positioning of the object and the verb must be due to movement. This account both derives the verb-final property, which evidently has no bearing on processing, and the varying position of the object.

Processing nevertheless has a role to play, insofar as the parser needs to select more than one derivation for the same surface form.

---

* I am grateful to Masayuki Hirata and Yurie Hara for sharing their native judgment of Japanese with me, and to He Lijuan, He Wanchuan, He Zhili, Yang Yunfang and Zhao Qinglian for being patient language consultants for Naxi. I thank three anonymous reviewers for insightful comments, constructive criticisms and helpful suggestions. The work reported in this paper is supported by a GRF grant from the Research Grants Council of the Hong Kong Special Adminstrative Region government, for which I am very grateful. I assume responsiblity for any inadequacy that remains.

2 Word-order and argument-marking

In Japanese, the arguments in a great many cases (see also note 5) are followed by the nominative marker *ga* for subject, and the accusative marker *o* for object. The subject may appear before or after the object; in either order, the sentence has the same meaning:[1]

(1) a. Taro-ga hon-o yonda (koto). (Japanese)
-NOM book-ACC read fact
'Taro read books.'
b. hon-o Taro-ga yonda (koto).
'Taro read books.'

With the marking on the arguments indicating their grammatical relations, there is no difficulty in identifying the semantic roles of the arguments. This is why the two orders in (1) have the same meaning.

In this light, the rigid word-order in Chinese is understandable, there being no marking on the arguments for their grammatical relations. Different word-orders result in different, possibly pragmatically odd interpretations (indicated by #):

(2) a. Zhangsan xihuan Lisi. (Chinese)
like
'Zhangsan likes Lisi.'
b. Lisi xihuan Zhangsan.
'Lisi likes Zhangsan.'

(3) a. Zhangsan kan shu.
read book
'Zhangsan read books.'
b. #shu kan Zhangsan.
'Books read Zhangsan.'

Absent the marking on the argument indicating their grammatical relations, the only means to identify the grammatical relations and semantic roles of the arguments is linear order. The argument to the left of the verb is the subject, and the argument to the right of it is the object.

The varying word-order in Japanese applies to the object and an adverb as well. The object may appear to the right or left of an adverb:

(4) a. Taro-ga tokidoki hon-o yonda (koto). (Japanese)
-NOM sometimes book-ACC read fact
'Taro sometimes read books.'
b. Taro-ga hon-o tokidoki yonda (koto).
'Taro sometimes read books.'

It is conceivable that the object in (1a) and (4a) is in a position inside the VP, and ends up in a position to the left of the subject in (1b) by movement, possibly via the intermediate position in (4b), as in (5) (the derivation in (5) will be later revised):

(5) hon-o_i Taro t_i (tokidoki) t_i yonda.

---

1 Japanese root clauses generally require a topic, a phrase followed by the topic marker *wa*. To control for this complication, the morpheme *koto* 'fact' is added to turn the preceding clause into an embedded one, as is standard in the formal analysis of Japanese syntax. Abbreviations: ACC=accusative, C=complementizer, EXP=experiential, NOM=nominative, Q=question, REL=relativizer.

Given the word-order facts in (2)-(3), it comes as no surprise that the object in Chinese cannot occur in any position between the subject and the verb: [2]

(6) a. Zhangsan jingchang kan shu. (Chinese)
often read book
'Zhangsan often read books.'
b. *Zhangsan jingchang shu kan.
c. *Zhangsan shu jingchang kan.

The ungrammaticality of the examples in (6b,c) surely has nothing do with the failure to identify the grammatical relation and semantic role of the object. Given its appearance after the subject, it is in principle possible to identify the grammatical relation and semantic role of the object. The exclusion of the examples in (6b,c) is clearly due to the syntax of Chinese restricting the object to postverbal position (see note 2, however).

Even though the flexible word-order in Japanese and the rigid word-oder in Chinese can be attributed to their independent difference with respect to argument-marking, this account is incomplete. It cannot explain why the object may appear either to the left or right of an adverb in Japanese in (4), but not in Chinese in (6). There is no possible processing difficulty distinguishing the object from the adverb. Clearly it is syntax that determines the position of the object.

That varying word-order need not be related to the marking on the arguments indicating their grammatical relations is clear from Naxi, a minority language spoken in Yunnan, China. Much like Japanese, the verb comes at the end of the sentence. The arguments in Naxi, like those in Japanese, may be marked. The subject may be followed by the marker *nee* and the object the marker *dol* (or *gol*) (cf. He 1987:90):

(7) a. Aka nee Ahua dol meil. (Naxi)
NOM ACC teach
'Aka taught Ahua.'
b. Ahua dol Aka nee meil.
'Aka taught Ahua.'

(8) a. Aka nee ddee ni ggug ddee ni Ahua dol meil.
NOM one day and one day ACC teach
'Aka taught Ahua everyday.'
b. Aka nee Ahua dol ddee ni ggug ddee ni meil.
'Aka taught Ahua everyday.'

The grammatical relations of the arguments can accordingly be identified and their semantic roles can be recognized.

In contrast with that in Japanese, however, the marking on the arguments in Naxi is optional. The sentences in (7) are also grammatical if one of the arguments is not marked. Regardless of word-order, the meanings of the sentences are the same:

---

2 The object may occur between the subject and the verb if it is preceded by a morpheme that does not appear in postverbal position, e.g., *ba*:

(i) ta ba zheben shu kan wan le.
he this book read finish PAST
'He finished reading the books.'

I return to the case where the object unaccompanied by the morpheme *ba* occurs before the subject in section 4.

(9) a. Aka nee Ahua meil. (Naxi)
NOM teach
'Aka taught Ahua.'
b. Ahua Aka nee meil.

(10) a. Aka Ahua dol meil.
ACC teach
'Aka taught Ahua.'
b. Ahua dol Aka meil.

For the sentences in (8), the marking on either argument or both may be absent:

(11) a. Aka nee ddee ni ggug ddee ni Ahua meil. (Naxi)
NOM one day and one day teach
'Aka taught Ahua everyday.'
b. Aka nee Ahua ddee ni ggug ddee ni meil.
'Aka taught Ahua everyday.'

(12) a. Aka ddee ni ggug ddee ni Ahua dol meil.
one day and one day ACC teach
'Aka taught Ahua everyday.'
b. Aka Ahua dol ddee ni ggug ddee ni meil.
'Aka taught Ahua everyday.'

(13) a. Aka ddee ni ggug ddee ni Ahua meil.
one day and one day teach
'Aka taught Ahua everyday.'
b. Aka Ahua ddee ni ggug ddee ni meil.
'Aka taught Ahua everyday.'

The marking on the arguments evidently has little bearing on the word-orders in (9)-(13).

When neither argument is marked, however, word-order seems to be crucial in determining the grammatical relations of the arguments. Thus, in contrast with the pairs of the sentences in (9)-(12) where one of the arguments is marked or the pair in (13) where an adverb occurs between the arguments, it is quite difficult to interpret the pair of sentences in (14) to have the same meaning:

(14) a. Aka Ahua meil. (Naxi)
teach
'Aka taught Ahua.'
b. Ahua Aka meil.
'Ahua taught Aka.' NOT 'Aka taught Ahua.'

Speakers take the first argument to be the subject and the second the object.

We may fall back on the observation earlier that without the marking on the arguments, the grammatical relations are determined by word-order. But this move is ill-advised from the perspective of the syntax of object. I return to this point section 4.

3 The universal base hypothesis and the syntax of object

Suppose the underlying basic clause structure is universally as in (15) (Kayne 1994):

(15) Universal Order Hypothesis
Spec-Head-Complement

Then, the order in which the object, a complement, appears before the verb must be due to it moving past the verb (the precise position where the object moves to need not concern us here):

(16) O_i ... [$_{VP}$ V t_i]

The verb-final property is thus a direct consequence of the object moving past the verb. This would also explain why the object does not appear in a postverbal position in Japanese:

(17) *Taro-ga yonda hon-o. (Japanese)
-NOM read book-ACC
'Taro read a book.'

Whatever sanctions the movement of the object past the verb, the same will sanction leftward movement of the object to any other clause-internal position. In other words, if the object can make the first move, then it can make the subsequent move. On this view, then, the word-orders in (1) and (4) are all related to the same leftward movement of the object.

The Japanese examples in (4) and (1b) would be more accurately represented as in (18):

(18) a. Taro ga tokidoki hon-o$_i$ [$_{VP}$ yonda t_i] (Japanese)
b. Taro ga hon-o$_i$ tokidoki t_i [$_{VP}$ yonda t_i]
c. hon-o$_i$ Taro ga t_i (tokidoki) t_i [$_{VP}$ yonda t_i]

The object originates in the position after the verb, by the Universal Order Hypothesis. If movement is subject to the Minimal Link Condition (Chomsky 1995), i.e., movement must be to the closest available position, then the object in (18c) conceivably moves through two intermediate positions before it lands in a position before the subject. Examples (18a,b) may be taken to be independent evidence for two intermediate positions.

For verb-medial languages like Chinese, the mechanism that derives the verb-final property is not at work. The object hence does not move past the verb. Whatever principle prevents the object from moving leftward in (6b) would also prevent it from moving further in (6c):[3]

(19) *O_i ... t_i ... [$_{VP}$ V t_i]

Naxi is a verb-final language, much like Japanese. The sentences in (7)-(8) can thus be derived in the same way as those in Japanese in (18):

(20) a. Aka nee Ahua dol$_i$ [$_{VP}$ meil t_i] (=(7))
NOM ACC teach
'Aka taught Ahua.'
b. Ahua dol$_i$ Aka nee t_i [$_{VP}$ meil t_i]
'Aka taught Ahua.'

(21) a. Aka ddee ni ggug ddee ni Ahua dol$_i$ [$_{VP}$ meil t_i] (=(8))
one day and one day ACC teach
'Aka taught Ahua everyday.'

[3] What is meant here is that the object does not move past the verb in surface structure. It is conceivable that the object moves past the verb at some stage in the derivation and the verb subsequently moves past the object, yielding the verb-object order (see Huang, Li and Li 2009).

b. Aka Ahua dol_i ddee ni ggug ddee ni t_i [$_{VP}$ meil t_i]
'Aka taught Ahua everyday.'

The leftward movement of the object explains its non-occurrence after the verb:

(22) *Aka nee meil Ahua dol. (Naxi)
NOM teach ACC
'Aka taught Ahua.'

The examples in (9)-(10) too can be similarly derived, despite the marking is absent on one of the arguments:

(23) a. Aka nee $Ahua_i$ meil t_i (Naxi)
NOM teach
'Aka taught Ahua.'
b. $Ahua_i$ Aka nee t_i meil t_i
'Aka taught Ahua.'

(24) a. Aka Ahua dol_i meil t_i
ACC teach
'Aka taught Ahua.'
b. Ahua dol_i Aka t_i meil t_i
'Aka taught Ahua.'

It is therefore clear that varying word-order has more to do with the syntax of object rather than with argument-marking.

4 Processing strategy

From the perspective of the analysis of word-order discussed in the last section, there is apparently no reason why the object cannot move across the subject deriving (25b) from (25a) preserving the same meaning the same way the object moves across the subject in (23b) and (24b), a problem noted in section 2:

(25) a. Aka $Ahua_i$ meil t_i (=(14))
teach
'Aka taught Ahua.'
b. $Ahua_i$ Aka t_i meil t_i
'Ahua taught Aka.' NOT 'Aka taught Ahua.'

Indeed, given that the subject need not be marked for its grammatical relation (see (24a)) and the object moving over the subject need not be marked for its grammatical relation (see (23b)), it is difficult to see why the derivation in (25b) should be syntactically impossible.

The obvious difference between the sentences in (25) and those in (23) and (24) is that none of the arguments in (25) is marked for their grammatical relations, while one of the arguments in (23) and (24) is marked. We can impose a constraint on movement of the object to the effect that the object may move over the subject only if either one of them is marked. This would derive the correct result, but at the expense of making the movement operation less general. There seems to be no principled reason why a syntactic operation like movement should be constrained by argument-marking, especially when movement of the object over an adverb is not subject to such a constraint:

(26) a. Aka ddee ni gguq ddee ni Ahua$_i$ meil t_i (Naxi)
one day and one day teach
'Aka taught Ahua everyday.'
b. Aka Ahua$_i$ ddee ni gguq ddee ni t_i meil t_i
'Aka taught Ahua everyday.'

The adverb in (26b) is not marked for it being an adverb, inasmuch as the subject in (25b) is not marked for it being a subject. Yet, the object may move across the adverb. We can certainly make the distinction between arguments and adverbs and bring it to bear on the movement operation. Nevertheless, to the extent no other syntactic operation is conditioned by argument-marking, it is hard to think of a syntactic reason for why the movement operation should be subject to the marking on the arguments. As we will see below, imposing such a constraint would lead to certain empirical problems.

If we are to maintain the full generality of the movement operation, then the derivation in (25b) is syntactically possible. I would like to suggest that it is processing that explains why the example is not taken by speakers to have the same meaning as that of the underlying sentence in (25a). The surface form of (25b) co-incides with that of a sentence that can be independently generated in which the object is not moved over the subject:

(27) Ahua Aka$_i$ meil t_i (Naxi)
teach
'Ahua taught Aka.'

Without the marking on the arguments indicating their grammatical relations, the parser has no reason to take the first argument to be the object moving across the subject. Moreover, as the surface form in (25b) can readily be derived as in (27), the parser would select this derivation instead of the derivation in (25b) where the object moves over the subject.

This processing account has both conceptual and empirical advantages. Conceptually, the generality of the movement operation can be fully maintained. Empirically, it can explain why the examples in (28a,b) where the argument in the relative clause is marked are unambiguous, whereas the example in (28c) where it is not marked is ambiguous:

(28) a. Aka nee meil gge xi. (Naxi)
NOM teach C person
'The person who Aka taught.'
b. Aka dol meil gge xi.
ACC teach C person
'The person who taught Aka.'
c. Aka meil gge xi.
teach C person
'The person who Aka taught.' OR 'The person who taught Aka.'

In the movement analysis of relative clauses (Chomsky 1977) the head noun is related to the relativized argument by a (possibly empty) operator (Chomsky 1986, Browning 1987). In English, it is plausible that in relative clauses there is an empty operator performing the same function as the relative pronoun *who* or *which*. It moves to SpecCP much like *who* and *which*:

(29) a. The person [$_{CP}$ who$_i$ [$_{IP}$ John taught t_i]]
b. The person [$_{CP}$ O_i [$_{IP}$ John taught t_i]]

Along these lines, the Naxi examples in (28a,b) would be derived as in (30a,b) respectively:

(30) a. [$_{CP}$ O_i [$_{IP}$ Aka nee t_i meil t_i] gge] xi (=(28a))
b. [$_{CP}$ O_j [$_{IP}$ t_j Aka dol$_i$ meil t_i] gge] xi (=(28b))

The empty operator in (30a) originates as the object of the verb, and that in (30b) as the subject of the verb.[4] In (30c) the argument in the relative clause is not marked for its grammatical relation; hence, the operator can either be the object or the subject of the verb. The representations in (31) reflect this ambiguity:

(31) a. [$_{CP}$ O_i [$_{IP}$ Aka t_i meil t_i] gge] xi.
'The person who Aka taught.'
b. [$_{CP}$ O_j [$_{IP}$ t_j Aka$_i$ meil t_i] gge] xi.
'The person who taught Aka.'

In (31) neither the argument in the relative clause nor the empty operator are marked. If movement of the object across the subject is possible only if either argument is marked, then the derivation in (31a) would be impossible, for neither the operator nor the other argument in the relative clause are marked for their grammatical relations. Consequently, the ambiguity of the surface form in (28c) cannot be represented, the derivation in (31a) being excluded by the constraint restricting movement over the subject only if either argument is marked for its grammatical relation.

A question that arises is to what extent the processing account for the interpretation of the example in (25b) bears on the ambiguous interpretation of the example in (28c). More specifically, we might wonder whether the way the parser selects one derivation over the other for the same surface form in (25b) would apply to (28c) as well. After all, the two derivations in (31) have the same surface form.

An obvious difference between the surface form in (25b) and that in (28c) is that the former is a declarative clause and the latter is a relative clause. On the one hand, in declarative clauses, the first argument unmarked for its grammatical relation can be taken to be the subject (see (24a)), unless the following argument is marked to be the grammatical subject (see (23b)). If both arguments are unmarked for their grammatical relations, then the derivation in which the first argument is the subject requires less time to complete than the derivation in which it is taken to be the object, since it does not involve movement of the object over the subject.

On the other hand, in relative clauses, there is always an empty operator in SpecCP c-commanding the rest of the clause. Regardless of it being the subject or object, the empty operator must move to SpecCP. The task of the parser is to locate the gap of the operator. In principle, it can be the subject or object; it can even be in an embedded clause arbitrarily far away from the head noun it is related to:

(32) a. Ahua shel mei Aka nee meil gge xi. (Naxi)
say C NOM teach REL person
'The person Ahua said Aka taught'
b. Alia vq Ahua shel mei Aka nee meil gge xi.
think say C NOM teach REL person
'The person Alia thinks Ahua said Aka taught.'

If the parser has no problem locating the gap arbitrarily far away from the head noun in (32), then it should have no problem in locating the object gap in (31).

To the extent an additional syntactic constraint imposing an argument-marking condition on movement incorrectly rules out one of the readings of the example in (28c), it clearly cannot be

[4] Like Chinese, Naxi has no overt relative pronouns. It is therefore not possible to determine empirically where the empty operator in (30) moves to. The analysis in the text remains the same, if it turns out that SpecCP is to the right, contra the Universal Order Hypothesis.

an adequate account for the unambiguous interpretation of the example in (25b). Processing is a more plausible explanation, however, for the interpretation is obtainable from the same surface form whose derivation is independently possible and requires less time to complete.[5]

5 Topic structure

The claim that the object having the same form as that occurring in the postverbal position cannot appear before the verb may seem to be problematic in light of the examples in (33):

(33) a. Zhangsan kan wan zheben shu le. (Chinese)
read finish this book PAST
'Zhangsan finished reading books.'
b. Zheben shu, Zhangsan kan wan le.

There are reasons to suppose that the example in (33b) is not derived by fronting the object, but by base-generating the object in its surface position as some sort of topic.

First, if the object in (33b) is moved from a postverbal position, then there would no reason why Chinese should differ from Japanese and Naxi in not allowing the object to move to a position between the subject and the verb (see (6b,c)) (see also note 2).

Second, the clause-initial phrase in (33b) can be related to an argument that lies in a relative clause, a syntactic island for extraction (Ross 1967) (the empty operator related to the head noun is left out for simplicity):

(34) a. Zheben shu$_i$, Zhangsan renshi [[$_{CP}$ hen duo kan guo *pro*$_i$] de ren]
this book know very many read EXP C person
'This book, Zhangsan knows many people who read.' (Chinese)
b. ?*ano hon-o$_i$ John-ga [[$_{CP}$ t_i katta] hito] ni aitagatte iru rasii.
that book-ACC -NOM bought person to meet seem
'It seems that John wants to see the person who bought that book.' (Japanese)
c. *chee tee'ee dol$_i$ Aka nee [[$_{CP}$ jjaif bbeeq t_i xaq gge] xi] see.
this book ACC NOM very many buy C person know
'This book, Aka knows many people who bought.' (Naxi)

The Chinese example in (34a) is grammatical, since the clause-initial phrase is not moved out of the relative clause but is related to an empty pronoun *pro* in argument position. By contrast, the Japanese example in (34b) (Saito 1985:307) and the Naxi example in (34c) are ruled out as ungrammatical, as the accusative object moves out of the relative clause, a syntactic island.

Third, the clause-initial phrase in (33b) cannot be a *wh*-phrase, while there is no such restriction in Japanese or Naxi:

(35) a. *shenme Zhangsan kan wan le? (Chinese)
what read finish PAST
'What did Zhangsan finish reading?'
b. nani-o Taro-ga yonde shimatta no? (Japanese)
what-ACC -NOM read finish Q
'What did Taro finish reading?'

[5] This processing analysis for Naxi carries straightforwardly to cases in Japanese where the subject and object are marked identically, e.g., *Taro-ga Hanako-ga suki da* 'Taro likes Hanako'. Much like in (27), the first NP is understood to be the subject and the second the object. The relative clause *Taro-ga suki na hito* too is ambiguous, meaning either 'the person who Taro likes' or 'the person who likes Taro'. Space limitation prevents me from discussing the morphosyntax of these cases. I thank a reviewer for drawing my attention to this point.

c. eqzee Aka nee lvq seiq? (Naxi)
what NOM read finish
'What did Aka finish reading?'

If a non-subject clause-initial phrase in Chinese is a base-generated topic, then the example in (35a) would be straightforwardly excluded. Topics must carry old information and *wh*-phrases carry no new information. By contrast, the fronted object in Japanese and Naxi is not a base-generated topic; therefore, it may be a *wh*-phrase.

In sum, despite appearance, the example in (33b) is not evidence that the object in Chinese may move past the verb.

6 Conclusion

In this paper, I show that varying word-order has little to do with argument-marking. It is the syntax of object that accounts for the varying position of the object. On the one hand, if the object can move past the verb, deriving the verb-final property, then it may move further leftwards to a structurally higher position above the subject. On the other hand, if the first move past the verb fails, then it is impossible for it to move to a structurally higher position.

The obligatory argument-marking in Japanese and the lack thereof in Chinese gives the impression that varying word-order correlates with argument-marking. The optional argument-marking in Naxi shows that this impression does not exactly correspond to all the facts. Word-order may vary even when argument-marking is not obligatory. One case where the absence of argument-marking seems to restrict word-order possibilities is in fact related to the processing strategy whereby the parser discards a derivation with movement in favor of one without.

The account for varying word-oder in terms of the syntax of object is most sensible only if the basic clause structure is as in (15). Thus, to the extent that varying word-order cannot be derived in any other principled way, the Universal Order Hypothesis has some empirical basis. Moreover, insofar as the ambiguity of the example in (28c) and the lack thereof in the example in (25b) can be explained in structural terms, the existence of the empty operator in relative clause is empirically justified.

References

Browning, M. 1987. Null operator constructions. Doctoral dissertation. MIT.

Chomsky, N. 1977. On *wh*-movement. In P. Culicover, T. Wasow and A. Akmajian (eds.), *Formal syntax*, 72-132. New York: Academic Press.

Chomsky, N. 1986. *Barriers*. Cambridge, MA: MIT Press.

Chomsky, N. 1995. *The Minimalist program*. Cambridge, MA: MIT Press.

He, Z. W. 1987. Naxi Yu Jichu Yufa [Basic grammar of Naxi]. Kunming: Yunnan Minzu Chuban She.

Huang, J., A. Li and Y. Li. 2009. *The syntax of Chinese*. Cambridge, UK: Cambridge University Press.

Kayne, R. 1994. *The antisymmetry of syntax*. Cambridge, MA: MIT Press.

Ross, J. R. 1967. Constraints on variables in syntax. Doctoral dissertation. MIT.

Saito, M. 1985. Some asymmetries in Japanese and their theoretical implications. Doctoral dissertation. MIT.

Classification of Filipino Speech Rhythm Using Computational and Perceptual Approach

Timothy Israel D. Santos [a], Rowena Cristina L. Guevara Ph.D. [b]

Digital Signal Processing Laboratory, Electrical and Electronics Engineering Institute, University of the Philippines, Diliman

[a]tdsantos1@up.edu.ph
[b]gev@eee.upd.edu.ph

Abstract. This study incorporates computational and perceptual methods to classify Filipino speech rhythm. Speech rhythm may be described as a language's distinguishing durational sound pattern, resulting from the complexity of the language's syllable inventory.[1] Computational methods involve the correlation of rhythm-types to acoustic features such as the vocalic and consonantal intervals, one of which is the implementation of Multivariate Discriminant Analysis (MDA). Perceptual methods involve contrasting the rhythm of an unclassified language from prototype syllable-timed and stress-timed sentences. In order to isolate rhythm from speech, a data-stripping technique called *flat sasasa* resynthesis was implemented wherein the consonants are replaced with /s/ and vowels with /a/, producing a resynthesized alternating "sasasa" sounds at a constant pitch (F0). The rhythm discrimination and classification were closely examined for consistency between the data modeling and listening test results. The computational experiment was able to show that an MDA classifier trained to distinguish English and Japanese sentences tend to label Filipino sentences as Japanese 67% of the time, vis-à-vis the perceptual experiment showing that the listeners perceive Filipino to be more similar with Japanese, this study shows computational and perceptual validation that Filipino is syllable-timed, just like Japanese.

Keywords: Computational Linguistics, Natural Language Processing, Psychoacoustics, Speech Analysis, Speech Rhythm

1 Introduction

Speech prosody is an important aspect of natural speech. Pitch, duration, and intensity are some of the prosodic components that dictate the naturalness of speech and differentiate contextual meaning. The objective of this study is to present computational analyses and perceptual experiments to confirm the existence and applicability of rhythm classes to Filipino; to find their salient features for computational classification; and to find the rhythm typology of Filipino speech. Among the prosodic characteristics of speech, this study focuses on the temporal or the duration aspect.

Speech prosody or suprasegmentals refer to the features of speech that can modify the meaning and information being carried by the words not found in the lexicon. Speech intensity, duration, pitch, and rhythm are the most common features that differentiate one prosodic unit from another. Embedded in the human perception is the distinction of speech rhythm or timing to discriminate between languages. Languages are traditionally classified as stress-timed or syllable-timed where syllable-timed language were said to exhibit near-equal duration for each syllable, and stress-timed languages were said to have near-equal duration between stresses or

---

[1] Some languages allow a variety of complex syllables C^nV, CVC, etc., while some languages strictly adhere to simpler CV syllables (C-consonant, V-vowel).

what is called isochrony (Pike, 1943). Years of research on the subject has shown development in which evidences have been piling up against isochrony theory, and there emerged other rhythm classes such as Mora-timing (Abercrombie, 1967; Benadon, 2009). New models have been developed to accommodate intermediate languages, and a continuous language distribution plane was proposed (Dauer, 1983).

Instead of actually having equal duration between stresses and syllables, Dauer observed that the impression of syllable saliency for stress-timed and equal-saliency for syllable-timed is a result of the phonetic inventory, specifically syllable structures, of a language. Dauer's continuously-distributed model of rhythm postulates that a characteristic typical to stress-timed languages is a wider syllable inventory (occurrence of C^nV, CVC, etc.) resulting in heavier intervals. As a result, there are more frequent vowel reductions in the unstressed syllables, in a manner of speaking a *compensation* for the lengthening. These elements are consistent with stress-timed language's underlying concept of syllable stress that makes some syllables longer than others. For languages that seem to be more syllable-timed, it's just the opposite of the stress-timed. The simplicity of syllable (frequency of the simpler CV syllables) and fewer vowel reduction results in more *controlled* syllable durations (Fenk & Fenk-Oczlon, 2006). From these characteristics, some prefer the term *compensating* and *controlling* instead of the traditional syllable and stress timing, respectively.

Despite Japanese being classified as a distinct rhythm class called Mora (Bloch, 1950), in the course of this paper, we refer to Japanese as "syllable-timed," in adherence to the phonological model where we considered Japanese Mora as an extreme case of syllable-timing. As shown in (Ramus, Nespor, & Mehler, 1999), Japanese is located at the extreme syllable-timed side of the syllable/stress-time spectrum. Similarly, English was chosen since it has a great degree of stress-timing characteristic (Tajima , 1998).

2 Material

For this project, 120 sentences were taken each from Filipino and two other rhythmically distinct prototype languages. English was chosen as the prototype for highly-compensating rhythm or stress-timed, and Japanese for highly-controlling rhythm or syllable-timed. Most of the sentences are declarative, only less than 20 percent are interrogative. The selection was done with a couple of guidelines in mind. Syllables were kept at around 11 to 19 per sentence; as much as possible, and the average duration was kept at about 3 seconds per sentence, ranging from 2 to 4 seconds.

2.1 Corpora

The sentences came from the Filipino Speech Corpus (FSC), TIMIT English Corpus, and the Japanese Multext-J corpus. The mentioned language corpora contained phonetically transcribed sentences done by native speakers of the respective language. The following are more specific criteria since each corpus had different design and content:

TIMIT

- The sentences taken were the 5 phonetically-balanced sentences (SX sentences) for 24 speakers.
- To minimize dialectal differences within the speakers, the selected sentences came from the North Midland dialect region, considered to be the most neutral accent for American English.

MULTEXT-J

- Since there are only 6 speakers in all, 20 sentences were taken from each speaker's recordings.

- The corpus contained read-speech and emotionally performed speech. To simulate the natural language rhythm, sentences were taken from the semi-natural or emotionally performed set.

FILIPINO SPEECH CORPUS

- The 5 sentences taken were from 24 speakers.
- The selection was based on the average time of 2.5 seconds per sentence, after which sentences with 11 to 19 syllables were then chosen.

2.2 Transcription

Phoneme-labeled transcription files of the sentences were already available in the TIMIT and MULTEXT-J, transcribed by native speakers. The researcher, being a native speaker of Filipino, transcribed the sentences from the Filipino Speech Corpus using the PRAAT-Txtgrid tool. The DSP46 phoneme set in Table 1 was used, which was determined to be the unique phonetic inventory found in the Filipino Language (Guevara, et al., 2002).

Table 1: DSP 46 Phoneme Set

B	D	G	K	P	T	J	Ts	F	S	Sh	V	Z	M	N	Ng
Q	L	R	W	Y	A	E	I	O	U	Ag	At	Ak	Ad	Og	Hu
Aw	V	Ay	Oy	Iw	El	Em	En	Ha	He	Hi	Ho	Pau	Epi	Ow	

3 Experiment 1: Computational Analysis

The 120 sentence transcription in Filipino, English, and Japanese was processed to extract the duration for each phoneme. Each phone was labeled as either vowel or consonant, with the following rules to be applied: Pre-vocalic glides (as in Filipino /wa/: "wa·lâ" or /yâ/: "kan·yâ") was treated as consonants, whereas post-vocalic glides (as in Filipino /áw/: "i·káw" or /áy/: "ka·máy") were treated as vowels. This convention was based on the assumption that infants rely on a coarse segmentation of speech; the infant only distinguishes clusters of vowels and non-vowels. Adults have more perceptual cues taken into consideration since they have knowledge of phonotactics and have more linguistic memory. However, the rudimentary vowel-consonant coarse segmentation becomes apparent in situations where the sentences are lexically unintelligible to the adult listener. There are studies done to confirm this inherent human capability (Narayan, 2006), but a simple thought experiment could give us an idea. For example, when listening to a speaker of a completely unfamiliar language, the listener tends to just recognize an alternating pattern of the salient vowels and consonants while maintaining very minimal recognition of specific phonetic sounds. This is the reason why when one tries to mimic a foreign language, just a very small phoneme set is used whereas rhythm is actually retained; case in point, when one tries to mimic a speaker using *'blah blah blah.'*

3.1 Acoustic Correlates

For each i-th sentence with N_i and M_i vocalic and consonantal intervals respectively, the duration of the n-th vocalic interval ($V_{i,n}$) and the duration of the m-th consonantal interval ($C_{i,m}$) were taken from the phonemic transcriptions. The interval values were then used to calculate the Proportion of Vocalic Interval (%V), and the standard deviation of the Vocalic (ΔV) and Consonantal (ΔC) Interval.

$$\%V = \frac{\sum_{n=1}^{N(i)} V(i,n)}{\sum_{n=1}^{N(i)} V(i,n) + \sum_{m=1}^{M(i)} C(i,m)} \quad (1)$$

$$\Delta V(i) = \sqrt{\frac{1}{N(i)-1}\sum_{n=1}^{N(i)}(V(i,n) - \bar{V}(i))^2} \quad (2)$$

$$\Delta C(i) = \sqrt{\frac{1}{M(i)-1}\sum_{m=1}^{M(i)}(C(i,m) - \bar{C}(i))^2} \quad (3)$$

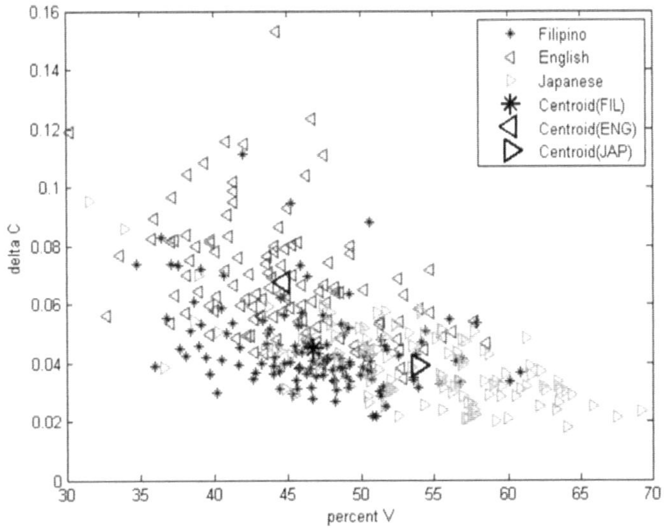

Figure 1: Rhythm distribution plane (using %V, ΔC). Each point is a representation of a sentence in the feature plane.

Table 2: Acoustic Correlates

Language	%V	ΔC	ΔV
English	44.8	6.74	5.34
Filipino	46.8	4.482	3.94
Japanese	54.0	3.91	3.90

Figure 1 is the mapping of the correlates of each sentence on a continuous rhythmic scale as proposed by Dauer (1983). Further to the right is the region for syllable-timed characteristic and further to the left is the stress-timed characteristic. The location of the Filipino sentences on the rhythmic scale suggests that Filipino may be an intermediate language, neither being extremely stress-timed nor syllable-timed as supported by Nespor (1990). With the Filipino situated in the middle of the extreme cases, it would be more suitable to describe Filipino Speech rhythm in terms of linguistic distance or similarity to the two rhythm classes.

3.2 Multivariate Discriminant Analysis (MDA)

MDA tries to predict the classification of an observation by fitting multivariate normal density using different covariance estimates. MDA was performed on a 2-group and 3-group MDA which can estimate the discriminant functions such as Linear, Diagonal-Linear, and Quadratic.

Three-group MDA

To confirm the predictive significance of the acoustic correlates on the rhythm discrimination, we performed 3-group MDA beginning with previously established 2-features (%V, ΔC), adding up to 5 features (%V, ΔC, ΔV, duration, syllables). Table 3 is the summary of performance of the quadratic classifier using different feature sets. It can be observed that aside from %V and ΔC, ΔV is also a good predictor for rhythm classification which is consistent with (Ramus, Nespor, & Mehler, 1999). It can be said that the results support the suggestion of the Phonological model of rhythm that the variation of rhythm types is a product of respective phonological properties, and that these properties can be independent and cumulative in forming the distinction of a language's rhythm.

Table 3: Classifier performance & Feature Evaluation

Features	(%V ΔC)	(%V ΔC) + n_{syll}	(%V ΔC) + t_{sent}	(%V ΔC) + ΔV	(%V ΔC) + ΔV, t_{sent}	(%V ΔC) + ΔV t_{sent}, n_{syll}
$Error_{Eng}$	19.17	16.67	15.83	22.5	21.67	20.83
$Error_{Fil}$	46.67	50	50	45.83	42.5	35
$Error_{Jap}$	32.5	31.67	25.83	20.83	17.5	17.5
$P_{Correct}$	67.22	67.22	69.44	70.28	72.78	75.56

Two-group MDA

Using 2-group MDA, the probability that the rhythm of a Filipino sentence was classified as English or Japanese was evaluated. It is basically looking for the intersection of the distribution space of Japanese and English to that of Filipino. Fig. 2 shows the 2-group linear classifier trained using %V and ΔC labeling Filipino sentences as Japanese 66.7% of the time. From this result, the computational experiment suggests that Filipino intersects more with the Japanese distribution space and is therefore more similar with the Japanese syllable-timed rhythm.

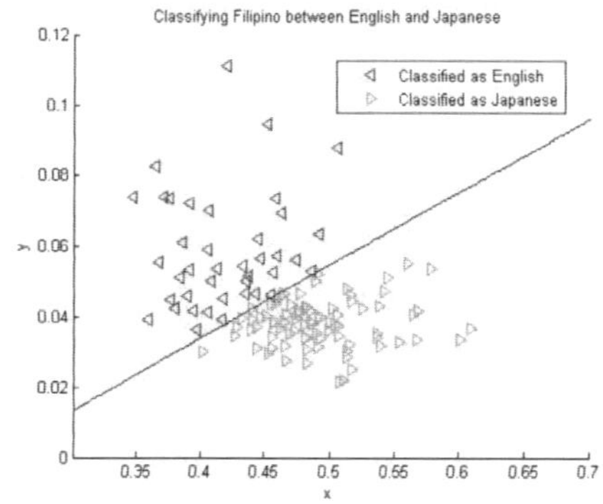

Figure 2: English-Japanese classifier with Filipino test data. The graph shows that the trained classifier identifies Filipino as Japanese 67% of the time.

4 Experiment 2: Perceptual Analysis

Auditory Signal Processing and Mathematical Psychoacoustics, the foundation of the subjective test performed in this study are widely used in pattern- classification, human auditory perception, and listener performance analyses (Leijon, 2008) (Green & Swets, 1966). Psychoacoustics tries to find the significant relationship between physical variables and its effects on psychological response. This psychoacoustic test was designed to compare the performance of a generated classifier to what is considered the ideal classifier, the human brain (Leijon, 2008), in order to validate or reject findings from the computational analysis.

4.1 Flat Sasasa Resynthesis

The Flat Sasasa Resynthesis is a data-stripping method to isolate the rhythmic characteristic of speech. It is composed of two phases, translation and synthesis. Firstly, the phonetic transcription was translated into unintelligible transcriptions, and then the original speech recordings were reproduced based on the transcriptions.

For the transcription translation, adjacent vowels were transformed into a long /a/ and adjacent consonants to one long /s/ sound, while maintaining the duration of the original vocalic and consonantal clusters. The outcome was a transcription of alternating vocalic and consonantal intervals, from which each vocalic interval was replaced by 'a' and each consonantal interval was replaced by 's.' As an example, the phrase "higit sa lahat" will have the following *sasasa* translation : /h/ /i/ /g/ /i/ /ts/ /a/ /l/ /a/ /h/ /a/ /t/ - /s/ /a/ /s/ /a/ /s/ /a/ /s/ /a/ /s/ /a/ /s/.

The resynthesis was done by simply truncating and concatenating pre-recorded /s/ and /a/ segments, using the sasasa transcription as basis. The pitch was held constant by using only one source of /s/ and /a/ sound taken from one recording of the diphone /sa/. In order to lessen the effect of boundary mismatch, the duration of each /s/ and /a/ were controlled by dropping samples at the head and tail of the /sa/ diphone recording.

4.2 Listening Test

The listening test followed the AAX perceptual test developed by (Ramus, Dupoux, & Mehler, The psychological reality of rhythm classes: perceptual studies., 3 August 2003). It is a modified 2-Interval 2-Alternative Choice (2I2AFC) Test and Same-Different Test (SD), described by the confusion matrix Fig. 3 (a). For each language pair, the subjects were asked to listen to 3 resynthesized (*flat sasasa*) sentences per trial. The first two sentences were of the same language (AA in AAX), and functions as the context. The third was either the same or a different group (X in AAX). After listening to each AAX group, the subject was asked whether the third sentence (X) was the same language as the previous two (AA). The two alternatives being ***same*** and ***different***, makes it basically a Same-Different (SD) test despite taking the form of 3-Interval 2-Alternative Choice (3I2AFC). The inter-stimuli-interval was 500ms as prescribed by RNM which was consistent with the suggestions from (Levitt, 1971) for psychoacoustic tests. The test subjects were given visual cues on the GUI as to which sentence was playing.

		Actual Value	
		Same	Different
Predicted outcome	Same	True Negative (P_{FA}')	False Negative (P_{FA})
	different	False Positive (P_H')	True Positive (P_H)

(a)

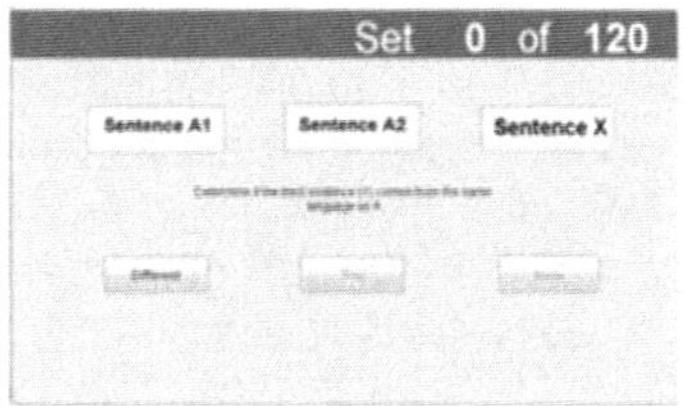

(b)

Figure 3: AAX Listening Test (a) Confusion Matrix (b) GUI.

There were 40 AAX triplets for each language pairing of the three languages: Filipino-Japanese (FJ), Japanese-English (JE), and Filipino-English (FE). The trials were randomly distributed in the test, for a total of 120 trials.

It is a basic assumption in psychophysical experiments that there is a level of observer fallibility wherein the observer does not only 'miss' the presence of a response, but also can falsely assume a positive response (Green & Swets, 1966). Hit and false alarm rates are computed from the correct percent scores. Hit rate (P_H) is the proportion of correct "same" trials and false alarm rate (P_{FA}) is the proportion of incorrect "different" trials as indicated in Fig. 3-a. Without going through the intricacies of the complex internal processing procedures of perception, we simplify the analysis of the listening test results from Table 3 by establishing a baseline for discriminability between two disjoint rhythm groups in the JE experiment, and looking for a language pair that has almost a chance-level or "good-as-guess" result of 50%.

Table 3: Listening Test Results

	Fil-Eng(FE)	Fil-Jap (FJ)	Jap-Eng(JE)
P_{FA}'	64.47 %	59.47 %	73.16 %
P_H	57.11 %	52.89 %	62.63 %
P_{Cmax}	60.79 %	56.18 %	67.89 %

The listening test is comprised of 19 listeners, 12 were male and 7 were female. As expected, listeners have performed well in distinguishing Japanese from English just by rhythm alone. Higher discriminability scores for JE test than both the FE and FJ tests is consistent with the result from the objective feature-plane that Filipino rhythm is in-between Japanese and English. For the discrimination of Filipino from English and Japanese, listeners have performed relatively higher for the FE tests. This suggests that Filipino is more similar with the Japanese rhythm, causing the confusion as manifested by the 52% true-positive score (P_H), very near the 50% 'good as guess' performance.

5 Conclusions

Placing the results on the feature plane, Filipino sentences lie in between Japanese and English, consistent with the suggestion that instead of discrete rhythm classes, rhythm is continuously distributed where opposite sides represent extreme and ideal conditions of syllable and stress timing. On a computational perspective, the acoustic correlates were shown to contribute cumulatively to the distinction of the rhythm of a language. A 3-group, 2-feature to 5-feature MDA classifier was able to identify the languages without the aid of lexical or semantic information at a rate of 67% to 75% accuracy. This characteristic of rhythm, and the significance of the features selected is valuable for Language Identification (LID) systems at the front-end of multilingual speech recognition systems. We have shown that the features for speech rhythm investigated may be used for objective speech rhythm and accent discrimination; hence, the speech rhythm features extraction may be automated to be used in modern automatic speech systems. It can be further expanded to not just discriminate between language, but to be able to distinguish whether a certain sentence is spoken in either its natural rhythm or in a different 'accent' due to the interference of another language (probably a speaker's native tongue). This is especially useful in the context of second-language learning. Language development, historical linguistics, and other linguistic issues can benefit from similarly-done studies to observe the changes in the natural rhythm of Filipino from recordings a couple of years ago to the modern globally-influenced Filipino language.

The computational and perceptual experiments yielded supporting results where the MDA predictive model classified the Filipino sentences as Japanese 67% of the time, despite Filipino being closer to English in the sense of Eucledian-mean distance. The perceptual experiment showed that human listeners have a hard time of telling the difference between Japanese and Filipino when presented with the rhythm-isolated sentence, where the correct distinction 52% was very near the chance-level of 50%. Both experiments done in respective objective and subjective manner were showing compelling evidence that Filipino is rhythmically similar to the rhythm of Japanese which is syllable-timed.

Table 4: Computational and Perceptual Results Analysis

	Filipino is Similar to English therefore **Stress-Timed if:**	Filipino is Similar to Japanese therefore **Syllable-Timed if:**
Objective Test: Multivariate Discriminant Analysis (MDA)	P (Eng|x=Fil) > P(Jap|x=Fil)	P(Jap|x=Fil)> P (Eng|x=Fil)
Subjective Test: Same-Different Test	P(correct|Fil-Jap) > P(correct|Fil-Eng)	P(correct|Fil-Eng) > P(correct|Fil-Jap)

The combination of computational and perceptual analysis, as summarized in Table 4, can be used as a good interdisciplinary template for resolving some of the issues in Filipino language standardization, and for performing similar tasks for other Philippine-type languages.

Acknowledgement

We would like to thank the Department of Science and Technology's Philippine Council on Industry, Energy, and Emerging Technology Research & Development (PCIEERD) and Engineering Research and Development for Technology (ERDT) for supporting this research endeavor.

References

Abercrombie, D. (1967). Elements of General Phonetics. Chicago: Aldine.

Benadon, F. (2009). Speech Rhythms and Metric Frames. *Communications in Computer and Information Science, 38*, 22-31.

Bloch, B. (1950). Studies in colloquial Japanese IV: Phonemics. *Language 26*, 86-125.

Dauer, R. (1983). Stress-timing and Syllable-timing Reanalyzed. *Journal of Phonetics 11*, 51-69.

Fenk, A., & Fenk-Oczlon, G. (2006). Crosslinguistic Computation and a rhythm-based classification of languages. Data Information Analysis to Knowledge Engineering. *Proceedings of the 29th Annual Conference of the Gesellschaft für Klassifikation*, (pp. 350-357). Berlin/Heidelberg:Springer.

Green, D., & Swets, J. (1966). *Signal Detection Theory and Psychophysics.* Cambridge: John Wiley & Sons, Inc.

Guevara, R., Co, M., Tan, E., Garcia, I., Espina, E., Ensomo, R., et al. (2002). Development of a Filipino Speech Corpus. *3rd National ECE Conference.*

Leijon, A. (2008, May 14). *Auditory Signal Processing-Mathematical Psychoacoustics.* Retrieved September 29, 2010, from KTH Electrical Engineering: www.ee.kth.se/sip/courses/FEN3100/

Levitt, H. (1971). Transformed up-down methods in psychoacoustics. *J. Acoustic Society Am., 49(2)*, 479-483.

Narayan, C. (2006). Acoustic-perceptual salience and developmental speech perception.

Nespor, M. (1990). On the rhythm parameter in phonology. *Logical issues in language acquisition*, (pp. 157-175). Dordrecht: Foris.

Pike, K. L. (1943). *Phonetics: a critical analysis of phonetic theory and a technic for the practical description of sounds.* Ann Arbor: University of Michigan.

Ramus, F., Dupoux, E., & Mehler, J. (3 August 2003). The psychological reality of rhythm classes: perceptual studies. *15th International Congress of Phonetic Sciences*, (pp. 337-342). Barcelona.

Ramus, F., Nespor, M., & Mehler, J. (1999). Correlates of Linguistic Rhythm in the Speech Signal. *Cognition*.

Ramus, F., Nespor, M., & Mehler, J. (1999). Correlates of Linguistic Rhythm in the Speech Signal. *Cognition*.

Disfluencies in Consecutive Interpreting among Undergraduates in the Language Lab Environment[1]

Kexiu Yin
College of Education, De La Salle University
2401 Taft Avenue, Manila, 1004, Philippines
yinkexiu@gmail.com

Abstract: Consecutive interpreting (CI) has gained increasing popularity and application in today's world. Fluency is a criterion for CI output assessment. Although disfluencies among CI professionals were investigated in previous studies, little research has been done on the disfluency prevalence among CI undergraduate learners. Nor is the advantage of the language lab facilities studied in terms of helping beginning learners to improve speech fluency. Based on the analysis of 28 recorded CI outputs produced by students in a Chinese university, this paper attempts to identify clearly the frequencies of difluencies. The results show that the problems of overusing fillers and repeated words may be prevalent among CI beginning learners, while notable pause seems to be better controlled in the language lab environment. Then, the causes of the difluencies are explored and pedagogical suggestions are offered.

Keywords: Consecutive interpreting, pause, fillers, repetition, language lab

Introduction

Consecutive interpreting (CI) is "a process in which adequate information is orally presented and transferred into another linguistic and cultural system" (Hu, 2006, p. 3). Among the forms of interpreting, e.g. simultaneous interpreting (SI) featured by the dependence on high-tech booth facilities and remote interpreting (RI) featured by the reliance on high speed internet connection, CI is the most frequently adopted for its low cost and moderate requirement on technical support. It is applied in interpreter-on-site business negotiations, press conferences, parent teacher meetings, interviews, and individual consultations. Responding to the increasing social demand for CI interpreters and English users of certain CI skills, a number of universities and colleges in China have offered CI as a compulsory core course for English majors.

In the assessment of CI output, fluency is an important criterion. Since CI output can be regarded as a natural speech delivered in the form of the target language and featured by spontaneous production, CI researchers share the findings on fluency in natural speech studies. Although categorized as disfluencies (Engelhardt et al., 2010; MacGregor et al., 2009; Corley & Stewart, 2008; Shriberg, 1999; Clark & Wasow, 1998), pause, fillers and repetition are by no means tantamount to fluency hindrance. Studies have shown that pause, fillers and repetition may help smooth speech, facilitate understanding and serve different communicative functions (Brennan & Schober, 2001, in Xu, 2010; Tissi, 2000; Hieke, 1981). Further, Clark & Tree (2002) propose moving the status of the fillers *um* and *uh* toward that of an interjection. The positive role of disfluecies in spontaneous speech is undeniable. However, it is also beyond dispute that disfluencies impair speech fluency when they exceed acceptable limits. Goffman states that

[1] **Acknowledgements** I owe my thanks to the School of Foreign Languages, Yunnan University, China for the support of the study. I am also thankful to Professor Leonisa A. Mojica at De La Salle University-Manila and three anonymous reviewers of PACLIC 25 for their insightful comments and suggestions. Any errors, in both form and substance, are my own responsibility.

"[natural speech] segments must be patched together without exceeding acceptable limits of pauses, restarts, repetitions, redirections, and other linguistically detectable faults" (1981 in Mead, 2002, p. 78). Evidence also shows that disfluencies can affect language comprehension (Arnold & Tanenhaus, 2011; Xu, 2010; MacGregor, et al., 2009).

The studies aforementioned are based on the corpora of natural conversation and output of professional interpreters. Few, if any, investigations have focused on CI beginning learners. It is clear that these would-be interpreters are not professionals --- hence the limited applicability of the research findings in CI teaching. Besides, the objectives of CI courses at the beginner's level vary in mainland China, as is the case in Taiwan. Kuo's (2001) research shows that some of the schools in Taiwan offering CI courses aim to enhance students' proficiency in listening comprehension and oral expression while some plan to prepare their students for advanced interpreting training at the graduate level. CI beginning learners in mainland China, mostly English majors in universities and colleges, demonstrate considerable difference in learning motivation and language proficiency. Further, had the previous studies investigated the frequencies of disfluencies, it would have been clearer whether pause, fillers and repetition are prevalent among the speakers, interpreters and learners.

This investigation aims at filling this gap. Based on the examination of the frequencies of pause, fillers, and repetition in 28 CI outputs produced by Chinese undergraduates, the investigation attempts to answer the following research questions:

1) What is the frequency of pause occurring in CI learners' output?
2) What is the frequency of fillers occurring in CI learners' output?
3) What is the frequency of repetition occurring in CI learners' output?
4) What pedagogical suggestions can be made to improve CI learner's fluency?

Methodology

Participants

A total of 28 students – 14 females and 14 males – participated in the study. These students were third-year English majors, taking up the course Interpretation 2, and enrolled in the English Department, Dianchi College, Yunnan University, Kunming, China. They had learned English for 9 years and passed the course Interpretation 1 by the time the study was conducted. The sampling validity is ensured by the ratio of 5:5:4 on their English proficiency as high: average: low in female and male groups respectively based on their performance in the courses of English listening, speaking and writing.

Instruments and Environment

The instruments used were the final exam of the course Interpretation 2 and the unstructured interview on their interpretation difficulties. The validity of the exam could be ensured without a pilot test, since it followed the test design of Intermediate-Level Shanghai Interpretation Accreditation, which gains nationwide recognition and is pursued by students at the level of third-year English majors in China. There were two tasks in the exam (see Appendix), Chinese-into-English (C-E) interpretation and English-into-Chinese interpretation (E-C). In the C-E task, a Chinese paragraph was read by the teacher at the normal speed, and then part by part with an interval of about 1 minute for the students to interpret. The paragraph was divided into 4 parts, each containing 2 or 3 sentences. The E-C task followed the same procedure, with a slight difference in that the paragraph was separated into 5 parts.

The other instrument – unstructured interview – was conducted throughout the semester and after the final exam among those who were willing to share their difficulties in practicing the interpretation.

The exam was conducted in an audio-visual language lab, where a total of 60 student booths were connected with the teacher console. Each student booth was equipped with a headset with integral microphone, a monitor and a PC.

Data Gathering Procedure

The language lab for the exam was the place where the participants had the practice, training and lectures of the course Interpretation 2 in the semester. The facilities of the language lab ensured that all the participants took the exam in the same environment, i.e. they heard the original utterance to be interpreted exactly at the same time through the headphone and then interpret into the microphone within the same duration for interpreting. The exam lasted for 15 minutes, with the entire process audiotaped and automatically stored on the computers of each booth. The participants were arranged in every four booths so as to minimize the possible influence from her/his classmates, and they were familiar with the environment and the equipment operation in the lab. Also, they had sufficient knowledge of the exam procedure, because there had been similar practices before the final exam. Altogether 28 CI outputs were selected for data analysis with the informed consent of the participants.

Interrating

An M.A. student from the Department of English and Applied Linguistics at De La Salle University was invited to interrate the 28 CI outputs. Since the investigation involves only frequency count, his lack of experience in teaching CI presented no problem for him to be a qualified rater after a short training. The two of us recorded the frequencies of notable pause, fillers, and repetition in the CI outputs independently and then convened to check the results.

Data Analysis

The learners' use of pause, fillers, and repetition were investigated at two levels: the part level and the task level. There were 4 parts in the C-E task, and 5 parts in the E-C task. Each output contained both tasks. First, the part in which a pause of more than 5 seconds occurred was recorded as "with notable pause". The ground of setting the criterion in the rating lies in the wide agreement on CI assessment that a pause longer than 5 seconds may be unacceptable to the audience and affect the on-site atmosphere (Lei & Chen, 2006). Second, the frequency of the fillers, *er*, *um*, and *uh*, was counted and recorded in each part. Third, based on the "typical and less typical disfluencies" criteria (Yaruss, 1998), the part was recorded as "with notable repetition" when the same word(s) got repeated adjacently three times or more, e.g. the part with the output that "the Duanwu Festival, also called the Dragon Boat Festival, falls *on the*, *on the*, *on the* fifth day of the fifth months of the Chinese lunar calendar". Fillers were not taken as a type of repeated words for the purpose of this investigation, although some researchers (Clark & Wasow, 1998; Schachter et al., 1991) classify them under the category of repetition.

Findings and Discussion

Pause occurring in CI learners' output

Pause is a dimension in evaluating speech fluency. As is specified above, a CI part containing a pause of more than 5 seconds was recorded as "with notable pause" in the investigation. Table 1 shows the frequency of the part with notable pause in task C-E and task E-C respectively.

Table 1: Frequency of the part with notable pause

Task	F		M		Total%
	f	%	*f*	%	
C-E	9	16.1	18	32.1	24.1
E-C	7	10	10	14.3	12.1

NOTE: C-E: *N* = 4 parts * 14 outputs = 56 parts;
E-C: *N* = 5 parts * 14 outputs = 70 parts (F& M respectively).

As can be seen, the total frequencies of the part with notable pause in both tasks are less than 25% and thus are not alarming. However, the total frequency in task C-E is almost twice higher than that of task E-C, consistent with the result that the frequencies in task C-E in both female and male groups are much higher than those in task E-C. Also, the frequencies in male group are much higher than those in female group. Accordingly, three inferences may be drawn. First, the problem of notable pause seems to be not prevalent among the participants; second, both female and male participants tend to be more likely to make notable pause in task C-E than in task E-C; and third, female participants appear to perform better than male participants in controlling the pause.

While Table 1 presents a general picture of the occurrence of notable pause in the outputs, Table 2 further shows the frequency of the output with no notable pause.

Table 2: Frequency of the output with no notable pause

Task	F		M		Total %
	f	%	*f*	%	
C-E	8	57.1	3	21.4	39.3
E-C	9	64.3	7	50	57.1

NOTE: C-E: $N = 14$; E-C: $N = 14$ (F& M respectively).

With the exception of the frequency in task C-E in male group, other frequencies of the output with no notable pause are much higher than 50%. Besides, the frequencies in task E-C are higher than those in task C-E, and the frequencies in both tasks in female group are higher than those in male group. The data indicate that a) most participants were able to produce CI output with no notable pause; b) they performed better in task E-C than in C-E in this regard; and c) female participants had a better control of pause duration.

The results of Table 2 are consonant with those of table 1. The participants' use of pause could be discussed in three ways. First, the satisfactory control of notable pause by the participants may be attributable to the adequate stress they felt in the exam. In the follow-up interview, participants said they were clearly aware that they could not afford a long pause in such exams as with fixed duration set for interpretation; they also said that when they vaguely heard others around start interpreting they would force themselves to start as well even without a full preparation. Therefore, it seems that adequate stress from the exam may play a positive role in controlling pause. Second, the general better performance in controlling pause in task E-C may relate to the participants' higher language proficiency of the target language, i.e. Chinese as their L1. Under the exam stress, the participants forced themselves to say something even if they didn't fully understand the original English utterance. It seems less difficult for them to extemporarily organize sentences in their L1 than in English. Third, the better performance of female group in both tasks may reflect that female participants tend to be more sensitive to the exam stress. In contrast, male learners might be less driven by the fixed time for interpreting and less affected by the environment. It is also possible that the female participants in the study were more proficient in speaking or other relevant language skills.

Fillers occurring in CI learners' output

Fillers often occurring in speech include *er*, *um*, *uh* and other words of this kind. Table 3 gives the specific averages of fillers in the output used at the task level and the part level.

Table 3: Averages of fillers used at the task level and the part level

Task	F			M			Total	
	$\sum f$	Mean 1	Mean 2	$\sum f$	Mean 1	Mean 2	Mean 1	Mean 2
C-E	268	19.1	4.8	320	22.9	5.7	21	5.25
E-C	209	14.9	3.0	142	10.1	2.0	12.5	2.5

It is noted that the averages of fillers used in C-E at both the task and part levels in total as well as in both female and male groups are almost as twice as those in task E-C. Meanwhile, the averages in both tasks and at both levels present only slight difference between female and male groups. The data indicate that statistically in C-E task each participant tended to use about 5 fillers in each part and thus about 20 in total, and in E-C task each participant tended to employ about 3 fillers in each part and thus about 13 fillers in total. Since there seems to be no available specific criterion of acceptable frequency of fillers in CI assessment, a further examination of the output is necessary. Given that each part in both tasks consists of only 2 or 3 sentences, it is proposed to take an output containing less than 10 fillers in a task as an output with no notable fillers in that task. Table 4 provides the said frequencies in both tasks and the frequencies of the output with no fillers.

Table 4: Frequencies of the output with no notable fillers

Task	*f1*	%	*f2*	%
C-E	7	25	2	7.1
E-C	14	50	2	7.1

NOTE: *f1*= frequency of the output containing less than 10 fillers; *f2* = frequency of the output containing no fillers; C-E: $N = 28$; E-C: $N = 28$.

As shown in Table 4, there are less than 10% of outputs containing no fillers in both tasks, and exactly twice as many outputs in E-C task are free of notable fillers. With reference to the findings in Table 3, Table 4 suggests that about half of the participants tended to have the problem of overusing fillers in both C-E and E-C tasks, and the problem may be more prevalent in task C-E. However, it is possible for CI beginning learners to reduce the use of fillers, given the inspiriting finding that approximately one out of ten participants successfully avoided using any filler in the investigation.

Repetition occurring in CI learners' output

Repetition in most data for the study adds little wanted information in speech and thus affects speech fluency. In the investigation, the part in which reiteration of the same word(s) occurs three times or more was regarded as "with notable repetition." Table 5 presents the frequency of such parts.

Table 5: Frequency of the part with notable repetition

Task	F		M		Total %
	f	%	*f*	%	
C-E	33	58.9	36	64.3	61.6
E-C	17	24.3	27	38.6	31.4

NOTE: C-E: $N = 56$; E-C: $N = 70$ (F& M respectively).

It can be noted that in Table 5, over a half of the parts in task C-E and about one third of the parts in task E-C were found with notable repetition. The frequencies in female group and male group present unremarkable difference. Accordingly, it seems that repetition may be overused by a majority of participants, both females and males, and in C-E task in particular. Complementarily, Table 6 provides the frequency of the output free of notable repetition.

Table 6: Frequency of the output with no notable repetition

Task	F		M		Total %
	f	%	*f*	%	
C-E	2	14.3	3	21.4	17.9
E-C	5	35.7	5	35.7	35.7

NOTE: C-E: $N = 14$; E-C: $N = 14$ (F & M respectively).

As shown in Table 6, about 18 percent of C-E outputs and over 35 percent of E-C outputs were found with no notable repetition, and the frequencies present no remarkable differences between female and male groups. The frequencies display the possibility that notable repetition could be avoided by CI learners. Based on the results of Table 5 and Table 6, it seems that the problem of repetition may be prevalent among the participants in task C-E. Yet, there seems to be a lack of supportive data to identify whether the problem is prevalent in task E-C, because the frequency of outputs with notable repetition is roughly the same as that of the outputs free of notable repetition. However, it may be asserted that the problem of repetition could not be neglected in E-C task.

According to Clark & Wasaw (1998), repeated words, as well as fillers, are regarded as forms impairing fluency in spontaneous speech, most of which seem to reflect planning problems (p. 201). This statement explains the finding of the investigation that both repetition and fillers occur more frequently in task C-E than in E-C. In the tasks, the paragraphs to be interpreted were read at normal speed to the students before the part-by-part reading and interpreting so that the students had a general idea of the message to be interpreted. Apart from listening comprehension and memory, the difficulty in planning the CI output may be their proficiency of the target language. Since in E-C task, the target language is their L1, it seems natural that the participants used less fillers and repeated words than in C-E.

Implications

Abused pause, fillers and repetition exceeding acceptable limits are factors impairing speech fluency. The investigation shows that the problems of overusing fillers and repeated words may be prevalent among CI beginning learners, while notable pause seems to be under the participants' better control in the language lad environment. Thus, pedagogical implications of the study can be gained in the following aspects.

First, adequate stress could help students avoid making notable pause. Selye (1956 in Riccardi, et al., 1998) points out that stress is not a merely negative phenomenon as there is also a positive stress (p. 95-96). In order to realize the positive function of stress in the CI process, a proper design of the practice and exam is of great importance. The mimic environment of a conference, court, interview and situations in which CI is applied could generate adequate stress. Jones (1998) points it out that professional public speaking ability tends to be considered part and parcel of the interpreter's skills (p. 40). Moreover, a limit of maximum duration of pause could be worked out with the beginning learners and then strictly followed in the routine practice for the purpose of class training, i.e. a pause beyond the limit is to be avoided. Similarly, it is useful for the leaners to appreciate to what extent fillers can detract from fluency, though over-zealous outlawing of all fillers should not be encouraged (Mead, 2005, p. 54). It is worth mentioning that over stress may bring problems as well. With a lack of adequate planning, a rushing start may lead to the abuse of fillers and repeated words.

Second, the prevalence of overusing fillers and repetition calls for the attention and efforts of both undergraduate learners and instructors. It seems necessary to help students realize the problems in their CI output. As Schachter et al. (1991) has observed that one could be shocked by his/her apparent verbal clumsiness characterized by fillers, repeated words, false starts, to name but a few when listening to a tape recording his/her remarks (p. 362). The instructor could suggest that the students listen to the recorded tapes of their own CI output and record the frequencies of fillers and repetition. Then, the students could be suggested to keep a self-evaluation journal on their progress in overcoming the problems of fillers and repetition. In this way, the students may better aware of their problems and make more effective self-regulation.

Third, the general less satisfactory performance of the participants in task C-E than in task E-C reveals the need to improve their English proficiency. Although pause, fillers and repetition distribute and function differently in the speech, research has shown that disfluencies are associated with planning difficulty (Brennan & Schober, 2001, in Xu, 2010; Schachter et al., 1991). It seems safe to infer that notable disfluencies may be related to language incompetence which leads to planning difficulty. Therefore, regular practice on English speaking seems necessary and could be required as routine assignment. Also, memorizing words and reciting essays on topics relevant to C-E tasks may help students improve their language proficiency as well as familiarity with the topics.

Fourth, the language lab environment can be explored for both instructor-on-site training and student autonomous learning (instructor-off-site). Since all the computers in the student booths are connected with the teacher console in a language lab, the instructor is able to monitor the interpreting process of several learners at the same time and provide immediate guidance. The facilities also ensure easy grouping and mimic working conditions. On the other hand, the language lab helps improve autonomous learning efficiency. The activities in the lab can be either audio-taped or video-taped, which brings at least two advantages in autonomous learning. One advantage is that the learners may keep adequate stress with the awareness of being recorded. This can be regarded as a positive stimulus compensatory for the absence of the instructor and the classmates as audience. After all, in actual consecutive interpreting the speaker, the interpreter and the audience are generally on-site. The other advantage is that learners can retrieve the record conveniently and then evaluate their own performance. Accurate self-assessment and the awareness of the problems could help learners make adjustment in the autonomous learning.

In addition, the study reveals a tendency that female participants performed better than male participants in controlling disfluencies. Further research can be made on whether and how gender, language competence and other variables work on the production of disfluencies.

Based on the above findings and discussion, the study calls for the recognition of disfluency as a fundamental problem in CI learning at the beginner's level. Despite the constraints that the results can be hardly generalizable due to the limited data and that other variables such as accuracy are excluded from the data analysis, the study at least provides the specific frequency of disfluencies and thus clearly presents the problems among some Chinese undergraduates in CI learning.

References

Arnold, J. E. and Tanenhaus, M. K. 2011. Disfluency effects in comprehension: How new information can become accessible. In E. Gibson and N. Perlmutter (Eds.) *The processing and acquisition of reference* (pp. 197-217). Cambridge: MIT Press.

Clark , H. H. and Wasow, T. 1998. Repeating words in spontaneous speech. *Cognitive psychology,* 37, 201-242.

Clark, H. H. and Tree, J. E. F. 2002. Using *uh* and *um* in spontaneous speaking. *Cognition,* 84, 73-111.

Corley, Martin and Stewart, Oliver W. 2008. Hesitation disfluencies in spontaneous speech: The meaning of *um*. *Language and Linguistics Compass*, (4)2, 589-602.

Engelhardt, P. E., Corley, M., Nigg, J. T., and Ferreira, F. 2010. The role of inhibition in the production of disfluencies. *Memory and Cognition*, (38)5, 617-628.

Hieke, A. 1981. A content-processing view of hesitation phenomena. *Language and Speech*, (24)2, 147-160.

Hu, Gengsheng. 2006. Adaptation in consecutive interpreting. *Perspectives: Studies in Translatology*, 14 (1), 3-21.

Jones, R. 1998. *Conference interpreting explained.* Manchester: St Jerome Press.

Kuo, Hsing-hsiu. 2001. *A Cognitive model of consecutive interpretation for teaching undergraduate students*. Unpublished Master's thesis. Taiwan: National Yunlin University of Science & Technology.

Lei, Tianfang and Chen, Jing. 2006. *Challenging interpreting: A coursebook of interpreting skills*. Shanghai: Shanghai Foreign Language Education Press.

MacGregor, L. J., Corley, M., and Donaldson, D. I. 2009. Not all disfluencies are equal: The effects of disfluent repetitions on language comprehension. *Brain & Language*, (111)1, 36-45.

Mead, Peter. 2002. Exploring hesitation in consecutive interpreting. In Giuliana Garzone and Maurizio Vizzi (Eds.), *Interpreting in the 21st century* (pp.73-82). Philadelphia: John Benjamins North America.

Mead, Peter. 2005. Methodological issues in the study of interpreters' fluency. *The Interpreters' Newsletter*, 13, 39-63.

Riccardi, A., Marinuzzi, G., and Zecchin, S. 1998. Interpretation and stress. *The Interpreters' Newsletter*, 8, 93-106.

Schachter, S., Christenfeld, N., Ravina, B., and Bilous, F. 1991. Speech disfluency and the structure of knowledge. *Journal of Personality and Social Psychology*, 60(3), 362-367.

Shriberg, E. 1999. Phonetic consequences of speech disfluency. *Proceedings of International Congress of Phonetic Science (ICPhS)*, 1, 619-622. San Francisco.

Tissi, Benedetta. 2000. Silent pauses and disfluencies in simultaneous interpreting: A descriptive analysis. *The Interpreters Newsletter*, 10, 103-127.

Xu, Haiming. 2010. Pauses in conference consecutive interpreting from English into Chinese: An empirical study. *Foreign Languages Research (119)*1: 64-71.

Yaruss, J. Scott (1998). Real-time analysis of speech fluency procedures and reliability training. *American Journal of Speech-Language Pathology (7)*2, 25-37.

Appendix Transcript of the Final Exam for Interpretation 2

Task 1 C-E Interpretation

（1）端午节，也叫龙舟节，每年农历 5 月初 5 举行，为了纪念不向权贵屈服而投江的屈原。//（2） 端午节最重要的活动是赛龙舟，比赛的队伍在热烈的鼓声中划着他们多彩的龙舟前进。这项活动的灵感来自当时汨罗江畔的居民在江中划船，试图拯救投江的屈原。//（3）端午节时最受欢迎的食物是粽子。粽子用糯米包肉、花生、蛋黄和其它材料，再以竹叶似的粽叶包裹。屈原投江后，江边的渔民做粽子投入江中，希望鱼虾不要将屈原吃掉。//（4）端午节时人们还会互赠香袋，在自家大门前挂上一种特别的草，喝雄黄酒，在门上贴钟馗像，以驱走病魔，祈求平安。

Task 2 E-C Interpretation

(1) Perhaps the most interest development of music in the 20th century is jazz. It is unique, totally different from other music types, such as gypsy music, brass band music, and rock music. // (2) Nobody seems to know for sure where jazz got its name. It is said that jazz is derived from a Negro slang *to jazz something*, which means to play with it, alter it, and mess it up. // (3) However, it is clear that jazz began when the black slaves were brought from the Africa to work in the cotton plantations of the US. These people brought their strong sense of rhythm to the continent. // (4) The early songs of the slaves were sad, as they had little to be happy about. From these, grew the blues, which included bitter-sweet songs. // (5) Apart from the sad life, there must also have been happy occasions. The cheerfulness and high spirits added variation into the blues. Here was the birth of jazz.

About the author

Kexiu Yin obtained her M.A degree in English Language and Literature from Yunnan University, China in 2005 and now she is a PhD candidate in De La Salle University-Manila, the Philippines. She is currently a lecturer in the School of Foreign Languages, Yunnan University, China. Her research interests include translation and interpretation studies and sociolinguistics.

An English-Chinese Cross-lingual Word Semantic Similarity Measure Exploring Attributes and Relations *

Lin Dai and Heyan Huang

Department of Computer, Beijing Institute of Technology
Beijing 100081, China.
{dailiu,hhy63}dailiu@bit.edu.cn

Abstract. Word semantic similarity measuring is a fundamental issue to many NLP applications and the globalization has made an urgent request for cross-lingual word similarity measure. This paper proposed a word semantic similarity measure which is able to work in cross-lingual scenarios. Basically, a concept can be defined by a set of attributes. The basic idea of this work is to compute the similarity between words by exploring their attributes and relations. For a given word pair, we first compute similarities between their attributes by combining distance, depth and relation information. Then word similarity are computed through a combination scheme. The algorithm is implemented based on an English-Chinese bilingual ontology *HowNet*. Experiments show that the proposed algorithm results in high correlation against human judgments, which encourages its broad application in cross-lingual applications.

Keywords: Word semantic similarity, Cross-lingual, Natural Language Processing, Computing linguistics.

1 Introduction

Word semantic similarity measure plays a fundamental role in many natural language processing (NLP) applications such as information retrieval (IR), machine translation (MT) and word sense disambiguation (WSD). Many research efforts have been made in the past decades to improve the effectiveness of word semantic similarity measures. With the progress of the globalization, information emerged from a variety of languages to the Internet. Under this circumstance, cross-lingual applications such as machine translation, cross-lingual information retrieval, cross-lingual text categorization and clustering etc., become more and more attractive. Consequently, cross-lingual word semantic similarity measure becomes a meaningful research topic.

Although there are some statistical and hybrid measures which have good overall performance (Li *et al.*, 2003; Xia *et al.*, 2011; Hassan and Mihalcea, 2009), the knowledge-based measures, to us, is still an important method. Even in a hybrid measure, the knowledge-based part is still a key part. Furthermore, if a large scale ontological knowledge base is available, the knowledge-based measures can be further improved if the knowledge base is comprehensively investigated and the similarity measures are elaborately designed.

In this work, we "re-examine" merely knowledge based word similarity measure and a cross-lingual semantic similarity measure is proposed. As we know, concepts are language-independent and it is natural that each concept can be defined by several aspects, i.e., attributes. For example, the concept of the animal *dog* can be roughly defined by a *kind-of* attribute with value *livestock* and a *modifier* attribute with value *domesticated*. If all the words in this world are defined in this way, it is possible to compute the semantic similarity of any pair of words in spite of their

* The authors would like to thank Prof. Z.D. Dong for his valuable advices.

language. This is the basic idea of this work. In this work, this idea is implemented by utilizing a bi-lingual ontology, HowNet (Dong and Dong*et al.*, 2006), to locate attributes and concepts.

Although the proposed method can deal with English and Chinese solo-lingual word pairs, this paper focuses on cross-lingual ones. To evaluate our method, a series of experiments were conducted on a cross-lingual benchmark data sets with human ratings. A conclusion could be safely drawn from experimental results that the proposed measure is promising when compared with previous solo-lingual and cross-lingual word similarity measure.

The rest of this paper is organized as follows. Section 2 discusses the related works. The methodology of our method is presented in Section 3. Brief introduction of HowNet and its attribute network are introduced in Section 4. The implementation of the method is presented in Section 5. We evaluate the method in Section 6 before concluding this paper in Section 7.

2 RELATED WORKS

Previous researches of word semantic similarity measure mainly focus on monolingual settings. Early research efforts have been devoted to design the knowledge-based measures, in which word synonym set in thesaurus plays an elementary role to word similarity calculation. In particular, WordNet (Fellbaum, 1998) has been widely adopted in word similarity measures for English due largely to the hierarchically organized synsets for English words. Researchers investigate taxonomic structure or ontological framework, and attempt to calculate the word similarity by counting conceptual distance. For example, (Yang *et al.*, 2005; Alvarez *et al.*, 2007).

Some research efforts have been made to develop the corpus-based measures (jarmasz, 2003; Terra *et al.*, 2003; Bollegala *et al.*, 2007; Alvarez *et al.*, 2007) or hybrid measures (Li *et al.*, 2003; Strube *et al.*, 2006). The basic idea is to measure dependence between words by using statistics extracted from corpora. As a result, the corpus-based measures are found less effective than the knowledge-based ones in most word similarity measuring evaluations due to coverage problem.

In recent years, HowNet has been investigated by more and more researchers in several applications including word semantic similarity measuring. For example, (Liu and Li, 2005; Lin *et al.*, 2009; Fan and Chen, 2009). These works focused on mono-lingual context and were not evaluated on data sets with human ratings. Newly works began to apply HowNet on English data set (Dai *et al.*, 2008). Xia *et al.* (2011) combine HowNet and parallel corpus to mearsure cross-lingual word similarity. But their algorithms ignore the relations between sememes, which is proven to be very informative in this paper.

3 BASIC IDEA

Human beings judge similarity and dissimilarity between objects by their attributes. For example, when concept *automobile* and *bicycle* are concerned, people think they are similar because both of them have the *is-a* attributes with value *vehicle*. At the same time, people think they are different because an automobile is *automatic* while a bicycle is *manual*.

There are numerous concepts in this world which are represented by different languages. To define concepts in an efficient and standard manner and make the definitions easy to be handled by computers, we can use a set of fundamental and language independent concepts to define other concepts. We call them meta-concepts. Furthermore, the real world is complex and there are abstract concepts as well as concrete concepts. To define all the concepts properly, meta-concepts must be organized into hierarchial trees.

Because concepts are defined by meta-concepts, meta-concept similarity is extremely important to concept similarity. For a given concept pair $\{c_1, c_2\}$, we propose that the similarity between them $s(c_1, c_2)$ is a function of their feature sets as follows:

$$s(c_1, c_2) = f(fs_1, fs_2) \tag{1}$$

where fs_1 and fs_2 is the feature set of concept c_1 and c_2 respectively.

Meta-concept similarity is the basis of similarity between feature (i.e., attribute) sets. Distance and depth information of meta-concepts in meta-concept hierarchies are fundamental evidences for computing meta-concept similarities. Given two meta-concepts in a hierarchy, there must exist the shortest path between them, which connects their hypernyms. We call their common hypernym on the shortest path the $subsumer$ of them and the length of the shortest path the *distance* between them. Intuitively, meta-concept similarity is a monotonically decreasing function of the distance a monotonically increasing function with respect to the depth of subsumers.

Besides, when computing meta-concept similarity, the impact of various relations should be considered. Actually, besides hypernym-hyponym relation which forms tree hierarchies, there are many other kinds of relations between concepts.

Now, we propose that the similarity between meta-concept mc_1 and mc_2 is a function of the distance l, depth h, and relatedness r, as follows:

$$s(mc_1, mc_2) = f(f_l(l), f_h(h), f_r(r)) \tag{2}$$

where $f_l(\cdot)$, $f_h(\cdot)$ and $f_r(\cdot)$ is the contribution of distance, depth and relation respectively. $f(\cdot)$ is the framework that combine the three parts into final measure.

It worth noting that values of both the distance and depth may cover a large range, while the interval of similarity should be finite with extremes of exactly the same or not similar at all. If we assign exactly the same with a value 1 and no similarity as 0, then the interval of similarity is [0, 1].

4 ATTRIBUTE AND RELATION SYSTEM IN HOWNET

To fulfill the task of this paper, a well structured knowledge base in which concepts are defined by feature(s) is demanded. In this section we briefly introduce the attribute and relation system of HowNet, which meets our request.

As a knowledge base for natural language processing, HowNet provides plenty of taxonomically semantic knowledge as well as real-world knowledge. As a knowledge system that describes relations between concepts, HowNet attempts to construct a net structure of its knowledge base from the inter-concept relations and inter-attribute relations. This is the fundamental distinction between HowNet and other tree-structured lexical databases. The philosophy of HowNet entails its unique structure.

The meta-concept in HowNet is called *sememe*, which is the smallest semantic unit that can't be reduced further and used to define concepts. Through combining sememes selected from a finite sememe set, HowNet can describe infinite concepts. There are 2219 basic sememes in the current version of HowNet which are organized into five taxonomies and four subsidiary taxonomies.

As the sememes are concerned, in addition to being fundamental description units, there are complicated relations among them. The relations include hypernym-hyponym, antonym, converse, whole-part, material-product, etc. These relations are given in two ways. One way is the tree structure which represents hypernym-hyponym in taxonomies. The other way is the definition of sememes themselves. Although sememes are the meta-concepts used to define other concepts, the sememes are again made up by sememes. For example[1], the frame of sememe *bird* is: {*animal:materialOf=*{*edible*}, {*eat:patient=*{~}}, {*fly:agent=*{~}}}, and the frame of sememe *food* is: {edible:{cook:PatientProduct ={~}}}. Both of these two frames have a sememe *edible*. By this way, HowNet gives a strong relation between sememe *bird* and *food*.

[1] The current version of HowNet is bilingual, i.e., English and Chinese. Sememes are identified by English sememes and Chinese sememes at the same time. Both English version and Chinese version of sememe set is competent to define words of any language. We only give the English version of the sememes.

From the relations among sememes we can see that the actual structure of HowNet is indeed a net rather than merely a tree. Although there exist tree hierarchies in it, HowNet is totaly different to a traditional thesaurus. In a traditional thesaurus such as WordNet, concept is the minimum unit for word sense description and each concept is a node in a hierarchy. But in HowNet, sememes are nodes in hierarchies and each concept is defined by sememes.

HowNet uses *Knowledge Database Markup Language* (KDML, in short) to construct the semantic expression of concepts and sememes. KDML consists of a set of grammar rules and keywords. The detailed introduction of KDML is beyond this work. We give several definition examples in Table 1.

Word	Definition
cock	{bird:modifier={domesticated}{male}}
fruit	{fruit}
asylum	{InstitutePlace:domain={medical},{doctor:content={disease:CoEvent ={mad}},location={~}}}
grin	{CausePartMove:PatientPart={part:PartPosition={mouth},whole= {AnimalHuman}}}
jewel	{material:MaterialOf={treasure}}
stove	{tool:{WarmUp:instrument={~}},{burn:location={~}}}

Table 1: The examples of definition expression of concepts in HowNet

From the examples we can conclude several rules that are necessary for similarity computing.

- The first sememe in any definition expression gives the most essential sense, i.e., *is-a* attribute of corresponding concept.
- A concept has one or more features. Each feature is defined by an attribute-value pair. The attribute symbols are in the front of the equal sign and values go after the equal sigh.
- The sign ~ is a special and frequently used meta-concept which means the defined concept itself.

The current version of HowNet includes 100,168 English words and 96,370 Chinese words. Its large coverage makes it competent to act as a knowledge base in many NLP researches.

5 IMPLEMENTATION

From section 4 we know that the nature of HowNet matches the methodology proposed in section 3 very well. This section gives the detailed implementation of the methodology.

5.1 Sememe Similarity

As already discussed, the sememe is the basic unit of word definition and sememe similarity is extremely important to word similarity. We will use function (2) to compute sememe similarity. In (2), there are three information resources, i.e., distance, depth and relation. The performance of different strategies for formula (2) will be experimentally investigated in section 6.3.

5.2 Concept Similarity

Because concepts are defined by frames, concept similarity can be calculated from their definitions. From section 4 we know that a frame is constructed with sub-frames in a nested manner. The first sub-frame of a frame, which is always a simple sememe without attribute label, points out the essential feature of the corresponding concept. It specifies the *is-a* attribute of each concept. Meanwhile, the other sub-frames describe other necessary attributes.

To simplify the computation and make full use of the semantic information provided by frames, we break a frame into a set of *features*. Sememes in all levels are reserved in this feature set.

Each feature is a {*attribute-label, value*} pair. We name the feature from the first sub-frame as *primary feature* and the corresponding sememe as *primary sememe*. And other features are called *secondary feature* and corresponding sememes are called *secondary sememe*. The attribute-label of a secondary feature reserves the attribute-labels of upper features. For example, the feature set of *grin* is {{*CausePartMove*},{*PatientPart,part*},{*PatientPart-PartPosition,mouth*},{*PatientPart-whole,AnimalHuman*}}.

Similarity of feature pairs is measured by:

$$s_{ft}(ft_1, ft_2) = k * s(s_1, s_2) \tag{3}$$

where $s(\cdot)$ is the similarity of the corresponding sememe pair, and k is a scaling factor decided by their attribute labels. If their attribute labels are the same, k is set to 1.0, or it is set as a decimal with value from 0.0 to 1.0, which reflects the strength of their relations.

Now, frame similarity is converted to similarity between feature sets. When computing the similarity between two given feature sets, following principles are considered.

- Primary features are more informative than secondary features.
- Attribute-label *modifier* and *null* are equal to other attribute-labels.
- For two features both have value of the sign ˜, the similarity between them is 1 if their attribute-label is the same. Otherwise the similarity is a small value, which is experientially set to 0.1 in this work.
- Similarity between any feature set and empty set is 0.

To satisfy the above principles, we use the following formula to compute concept similarity.

$$SimC(C_1, C_2) = \begin{cases} s_{set}(fs_1, fs_2) & \text{if } s_{ft}(pft_1, pft_2) = 0 \\ s_{ft}(pft_1, pft_2) \cdot s_{set}(fs_1, fs_2) & \text{if } s_{ft}(pft_1, pft_2) > 0 \end{cases} \tag{4}$$

where fs_1, fs_2 is the feature set of concept C_1 and C_2, pft_1 and pft_2 is the primary feature of concept C_1 and C_2.

At last we compute the similarity of two feature sets $s_{set}(\cdot)$. The measure of feature-set similarity must satisfies two basic requirements.

(1) Similarity between two exactly same sets should be 1.

(2) Given two sets, both have n elements and there are z identical elements. Their similarity should be z/n.

Based on the understanding of above principles, we use following steps to compute feature-set similarity.

(1) Find the feature-pair with the highest similarly from two feature sets. Accumulate their similarity value to sim_{sum}.

(2) Delete the two features from their original feature sets.

(3) Repeat 1 and 2, until any one feature set is empty.

(4) The final similarity is: $2 * sim_{sum}/(m + n)$, where sim_{sum} is the accumulated feature-pair similarly, m and n are the size of two feature sets respectively.

5.3 Word Semantic Similarity

Word semantic similarity is decided by concepts carried by them. For the case of polysemy, we select the maximum concept similarity as word similarity, which matches the psychology of human beings. Let $C_1 = \{C_{1i}\}(i = 1, .., m)$ and $C_2 = \{C_{2j}\}(j = 1, .., n)$ denote concept sets of word W_1 and W_2, respectively. The similarity between word W_1 and W_2 is:

$$SimW(W_1, W_2) = \arg\max_{i,j}\{SimC(C_{1i}, C_{2j})\} \tag{5}$$

6 Evaluation and Discussion

6.1 Data Set

To evaluate an algorithm for word semantic similarity, we should investigate its performance against human common sense. A commonly used word-pair set is constructed by Rubenstein *et al.* (1965) for evaluating word semantic similarity measures (denoted as RG65). Twenty five years later, Miller *et al.* (1991) selected 30 pairs(denoted as MC30) from RG65 data set to form another data set. Earlier researchers use the 28 word pairs (denoted as MC28) of the Miller-Charles set due to the absence of two word pairs from WordNet.

The data sets mentioned above are monolingual which can't be directly used in this work. Up to now, there is a critical lack of a benchmark set for the evaluation of cross-lingual similarity measures. To evaluate the performance of our algorithm under cross-lingual circumstances, we constructed a English-Chinese bilingual data set (denoted as EC62) from RG65. For each word pair, we form 2 pairs by translating the first and second word into Chinese respectively. There are 2*62 word pairs because the word *oracle* is not presented in the current version of HowNet. To make EC62 reliable, Native speakers of Chinese who are also highly proficient in English, were asked to translate the words in the two data sets. They were asked to disambiguate the words and avoid multi-word expressions, slang or culturally-biased terms in their translations.

6.2 Tasks

As discussed above, useful information for measuring word similarity includes the distance between sememes, depth of consumers, and relations between concepts. We believe that, to get a good similarity measure, all these information should be taken into account trough a reliable scheme. This section experimentally investigates the contribution of different information to deduce a good combination strategy of these information.

Researchers evaluated the performance of word similarity measures on benchmark data sets. The best way of evaluate similarity measure on a data set is to perform training-testing framework. But the size of RG65 is limited, to train and test algorithms on fixed subsets of it will causes overfitting and bias. In this work, a cross-validation scheme is used to get the performance. We randomly divide EC62 into training set and testing set. The size of training sets is 84 and the size of testing sets is 40. For each strategy, its parameters are tuned on training sets, and it is tested on testing sets. Similar to most works, we adopt the correlation coefficient[2] as evaluation criteria. Each strategy will be evaluated 10 times and the average correlation on testing set is recorded as its performance.

6.3 Experimental Results

From section 5.2 we know that sememe similarity is the key part of word similarity measure. In this section, we experimentally investigate the performance of sememe similarity strategies. The parameter k of feature similarity function (3) is fixed at 0.8 through out the experiments according to our previous experiences.

Strategy 1. Sememe similarity measure is linear and exclusively decided by the shortest distance between sememes. A segmental linear function is investigated and sememe similarity is defined as

$$S_1(s_1, s_2) = max\{0, 1 - \frac{l}{L}\} \tag{6}$$

where L is a parameter which makes sememe similarity to be 0 when l is larger than L. This formula ensures the sememe similarity value falls into [0, 1]. The correlation coefficient with optimal L between this strategy and human judgments of Rubenstein-Goodenough's is 0.8594.

[2] Let x and y the variables with covariance σ_{xy} and standard deviations σ_x and σ_y. The correlation coefficient between x and y is $\rho_{xy} = \frac{\sigma_{xy}}{\sigma_x \sigma_y}$.

This value proves that the shortest path length is an effective information source for word similarity measure.

Strategy 2. Sememe similarity measure is linear and exclusively based on the depth of the subsumer of given sememe pair. A segmental linear functions is used in this strategy.

$$S_2(s_1, s_2) = min\{1, \frac{h}{H}\} \tag{7}$$

where H is a parameter which makes sememe similarity being 1 when h is larger than H. This formula ensures that sememe similarity value falls into [0, 1]. This strategy is plausible because it reflects the truth that higher subsumer results in more abstract meaning the two sememes share and vice versa. The correlation coefficient with optimal H between the results of this strategy and human ratings is 0.8443. This value proves that the depth of subsumers is an effective information source for word similarity measure.

Strategy 3. Sememe similarity is merely decided by the relationship between given sememe pair. We can simply model the contribution of relations between two sememes as a segmental linear function:

$$S_3(s_1, s_2) = \min\{1, \frac{D_r}{R}\} \tag{8}$$

where D_r is the depth of the deepest relation-sememe, R is a parameter that makes similarity to be 1 when D_r is larger than R. D_r is set to zero if there is no relation-sememe. The correlation coefficient with optimal R between the results of this strategy and human ratings is 0.8343. This value proves that the relation between sememes should be considered when designing word similarity measure.

Strategy 4. Strategy 1 is nonlinearly combined with Strategy 2 through multiplication. This strategy considers both the shortest path and depth of subsumer.

$$S_4(s_1, s_2) = S_1(s_1, s_2) \cdot S_2(s_1, s_2) \tag{9}$$

The average correlation coefficient between the results of this strategy and human ratings is 0.8713, greater than that of Strategy 1, 2 and 3. This experiment illustrates that a simple combination of the shortest path length and the depth of subsumers using multiplication can significantly increase the accuracy of the similarity measure.

Strategy 5. Similar to Strategy 4, sememe similarity measure is a function of the length of the shortest path and the depth of subsumer. But exponential functions are considered in this strategy. the sememe similarity is defined as

$$S_5(s_1, s_2) = e^{-\alpha l} \cdot \frac{e^{\beta h} - e^{-\beta h}}{e^{\beta h} + e^{-\beta h}} \tag{10}$$

where $\alpha \geq 0$ and $\beta \geq 0$ are parameters scaling the contribution of the shortest path and the depth of subsumer, respectively. The average correlation coefficient between this strategy and human judgments of Rubenstein-Goodenough's is 0.8861, which is greater than that of Strategy 4.

Strategy 6. To consider the shortest path, depth and relation at a same time, Strategy 3 is linearly combined with Strategy 4.

$$S_6(s_1, s_2) = \lambda \cdot S_3(s_1, s_2) + (1 - \lambda) \cdot S_4(s_1, s_2) \tag{11}$$

where λ is the parameter which leverages the weight of S_3 and S_4. The average correlation coefficient with optimal λ between this strategy and human judgments of Rubenstein-Goodenough's is 0.8372. This value is less than Strategy 4, so this combination of relation contribution with length and depth cannot produce a better similarity measure.

Strategy 7. Strategy 3 is linearly combined with Strategy 5.

$$S_7(s_1, s_2) = \lambda \cdot S_3(s_1, s_2) + (1 - \lambda) \cdot S_5(s_1, s_2) \tag{12}$$

where λ is a parameter which leverages the contribution of S_3 and S_5. The average correlation coefficient between this strategy and human judgments of Rubenstein-Goodenough's is 0.8499, which does not bring a better correlation than using S_5 alone.

Strategy 8. Strategy 3 is used as a modifier of Strategy 4.

$$S_8(s_1, s_2) = min\{1, S_4(s_1, s_2) \cdot (1 + \lambda \cdot S_3)\} \tag{13}$$

where λ is a parameter which leverages the impact of S_3 on S_4. When λ is 0, this strategy is equal to S_4. The average correlation coefficient between this strategy and human judgments of Rubenstein-Goodenough's is 0.8945. This measure performs nearly at a level of human replication, where correlation between individuals is 0.9015 (Resnik, 1999). The strongest correlation against human similarity judgments is obtained at λ=2.

Strategy 9. Strategy 3 is used as a modifier of Strategy 5.

$$S_9(s_1, s_2) = min\{1, S_5(s_1, s_2) \cdot (1 + \lambda \cdot S_3)\} \tag{14}$$

where λ is a parameter which leverages the impact of S_3 on S_5. When λ is 0, this strategy is equal to S_5. The average correlation coefficient between this strategy and human judgments of Rubenstein-Goodenough's is 0.8667, less than that of S_5.

Strategy 10. Relation between sememes is used to improve Strategy 4. An exponential non-linear function is involved in this strategy.

$$S_{10}(s_1, s_2) = min\{1, S_4(s_1, s_2) \cdot exp(\lambda \cdot D_r)\} \tag{15}$$

where D_r is the depth of the deepest relation-sememe, λ is a parameter which adjusts the contribution of relation. When λ is set to 0, this strategy is equal to S_4. The average correlation coefficient between this strategy and human ratings is 0.8469, , less than that of S_4.

Strategy 11. Relation between sememes is used to improve Strategy 5. The same exponential nonlinear function in Strategy 10 is involved.

$$S_{11}(s_1, s_2) = min\{1, S_5(s_1, s_2) \cdot exp(\lambda \cdot D_r)\} \tag{16}$$

This strategy is equal to S_5 when λ is set to 0. The average correlation coefficient between this strategy and human judgments of Rubenstein-Goodenough's is 0.9035, which is greater than Strategy 8 and a little bit greater than individual average. The strongest correlation against human similarity judgments is obtained at λ=0.22.

6.4 DISCUSSION

Referring to results in Section 6.3, we can reach several observations. From the results of S_1, S_2 and S_3, we can see that the shortest path, depth of subsumer, and relation between concepts all contributes a lot to word similarity. When compared with previous research results, we can see that with any single factor, the performance is comparable to early work. It is particular worth noting that the results of Strategy 3 indicate the importance of relations in computing word similarity. Strategy 4 and Strategy 5 combines the shortest path length and the subsumer depth in different ways. They have better performance than Strategy 1 and 2 which uses single factor. This proves that combining effective information sources with a proper strategy will produce higher performance. Strategy 6 and Strategy 7 explores three kinds of information at the same time in different ways. But both of them produce lower performance than Strategy 4 and Strategy 5.

This explains that relationship can not be linearly combined with distance and depth to improve algorithm's performance. From Strategy 8 to Strategy 11, relationship is used as a modifier of Strategy 4 or Strategy 5. When we use a linear function of relation to modify Strategy 4 in which distance and depth are used in linear manner (Strategy 8), or when we use a nonlinear function of relation to modify Strategy 5 in which distance and depth are used in nonlinear manner (Strategy 11), we can get higher performance. Otherwise, lower performance will be reached (Strategy 9 and Strategy 10). As Strategy 4 and Strategy 5 are concerned, we can see that Strategy 5 is better than Strategy4. It also can be seen that Strategy 11 is better than Strategy 8. This proves that nonlinear exponential function works better than linear function on this problem.

As a conclusion, we propose an algorithm for word semantic similarity measuring using Strategy 11 to compute sememe similarity. According to the experimental results, optimal parameters are α=0.3, β=0.4, λ=0.22. However, since our method combines three kinds of information in a intuitive and experimental way, we believe the performance could be further improved if better combination strategies are found.

The state-of-the-art monolingual algorithms (Alvarez *et al.*, 2007) (Yang *et al.*, 2005) get correlation values around 0.90 against Rubenstein-Goodenough's human ratings, which is very close to the human performance. On the English-Chinese data set EC62, our algorithm reaches an average correlation of 0.9035, which is comparable to monolingual measures of similarity, higher than (Xia *et al.*, 2011)'s result. This grade of performance encourages the use of word similarity measuring algorithms in various cross-lingual applications.

It is worth noting that the proposed method can be competent to English or Chinese sololingual word similarity measure, with fairly better performance than cross-lingual context. Due to the lacking of space, we won't give out the detailed result here.

7 CONCLUSION AND FUTURE WORK

This paper presents an attribute and relation based measure to calculate semantic similarity of English-Chinese word pairs. The key feature of this work which differs from the previous ones is that our algorithm explores attributes and semantic relations that connect sememes and concepts. Experiments on English-Chinese cross-lingual data sets show that the performance of the new measure is close (i.e. correlation coefficient value of 0.9035) to human judgments as well as comparable to monolingual word similarity measures. It can thus be concluded that attribute and semantic relation contribute a great deal to word similarity measuring and HowNet is applicable and effective in the task for English-Chinese cross-lingual scenarios.

The inspiring results stimulate a few future works. For instance, we will explore the feasibility to integrate our measure in real NLP applications such as word sense disambiguation, cross-lingual information retrieval, and machine translation.

References

Alvarez, M.A., and S. Lim. 2007. A Graph Modeling of Semantic Similarity between Words. *ICSC '07: Proceedings of the International Conference on Semantic Computing*, pp.355-362. IEEE Computer Society.

Bollegala, D., Y. Matsuo, M. Ishizuka. 2007. Measuring semantic similarity between words using web search engines. *WWW '07: Proceedings of the 16th international conference on World Wide Web*, pp.757-766. ACM.

Dai, L., B. Liu, Y. Xia and S. Wu. 2008. Measuring Semantic Similarity between Words Using HowNet. *ICCSIT '08: Proc. of the International Conference on Computer Science and Information Technology*, pp.601-605. IEEE.

Dong, Z., and Q. Dong. 2006. Hownet And the Computation of Meaning. World Scientific Publishing Co., Inc..

Fan, X., and J. Chen. 2009. Similarity Computation of Low-frequency Chinese Words. *FSKD '09. Sixth International Conference on Fuzzy Systems and Knowledge Discovery*, pp.524-528. IEEE.

Fellbaum, C. 1998. WordNet: An Electronic Lexical Database (Language, Speech, and Communication). The MIT Press.

Hassan, S., and R. Mihalcea 2009. Cross-lingual Semantic Relatedness Using Encyclopedic Knowledge. *Proc. EMNLP'09*, pp.1192-1201.

Jarmasz, M., S. Szpakowicz. 2003. Roget's Thesaurus and Semantic Similarity. *Proceedings of Conference on Recent Advances in Natural Language Processing (RANLP 2003)*, pp.212-219.

Li, Y., Bandar, A. Zuhair and D. McLean. 2003. An Approach for Measuring Semantic Similarity between Words Using Multiple Information Sources. *IEEE Trans. on Knowl. and Data Eng.*, pp.871-882. IEEE Educational Activities Department.

Lin, P., Y. Zhang and T. Zhang. 2009. Research on HowNet-based Chinese Word Lexical Semantic Similarity Measurement. *Proceedings of the Eighth International Conference on Machine Learning and Cybernetics*, pp.282-287.

Liu, Q., and S. Li. 2005. Word Semantic Similarity Computation based on HowNe. *The 3rd Chinese lexical and semantic proseminar*, pp.17-30.

Miller, G.A., and W.G. Charles, 1991. Contextual correlates of semantic similarity. *Language and Cognitive Processes*, pp.1-28. Psychology Press.

Resnik, P. 1999. Semantic Similarity in a Taxonomy: An Information-Based Measure and its Application to Problems of Ambiguity in Natural Language. *Journal of Artificial Intelligence Research*, pp.95-130.

Rubenstein, H. and J.B. Goodenough. 1965. Contextual correlates of synonymy. *Commun*, pp.627-633. ACM Press.

Strube, M., and S. Ponzetto. 2006. WikiRelate! computing semantic relatedness using wikipedia. *AAAI'06: proceedings of the 21st national conference on Artificial intelligence*, pp.1419-1424. AAAI Press.

Terra, E. and C. Clarke. 2003. Frequency estimates for statistical word similarity measures. *NAACL '03: Proceedings of the 2003 Conference of the North American Chapter of the Association for Computational Linguistics on Human Language Technology*, pp.165-172. Association for Computational Linguistics.

Yang, D., and D. Powers. 2005. Measuring semantic similarity in the taxonomy of WordNet. *ACSC '05: Proceedings of the Twenty-eighth Australasian conference on Computer Science*, pp.315-322. Australian Computer Society, Inc..

Xia, Y., T. Zhao, J. Yao, and P. Jin. 2011. Measuring Chinese-English Cross-Lingual Word Similarity with HowNet and Parallel Corpus. *Proc. CICLing 2011, Part II*, pp.221-233. LNCS.

Learning-to-Translate Based on the S-SSTC Annotation Schema

Tang Enya Kong
Enyakong1@gmail.com

Zaharin Yusoff
University Sarawak Malaysia, Sarawak, Malaysia
zarinby@gmail.com

Christian Boitet
Université Joseph Fourier, Grenoble, France
Christian.Boitet@imag.fr

Abstract

We present the S-SSTC framework for machine translation (MT), introduced in 2002 and developed since as a set of working MT systems (SiSTeC-ebmt). Our approach is example-based, but differs from other EBMT approaches in that it uses alignments of string-tree alignments, and in that supervised learning is an integral part of the approach. Our model directly deals with three main difficulties in the traditional treatment of MT that stem from its separation from the "translation task" (the 'world'). First, by allowing the system to learn from real translation examples directly, we avoid the need to indefinitely pursue the elusive goal of writing grammars to exactly describe intermediate syntactico-semantic monolingual representations and their correspondences. Second, we make explicit the dependence of the MT system performance on the input from the environment. That is possible only because the learning process uses feedback from the real translation knowledge when constructing its knowledge representation. Third, such MT systems using an inductively learned knowledge base yield a desirable non-regressive behavior by using translation mistakes to improve their knowledge base.

1. Introduction

The S-SSTC-based framework for the construction of MT systems has been introduced in 2002 [Mosleh et. al. 2002] and developed since to an operational state (SiSTeC-ebmt for English-Malay and English-Chinese). In this article, we would like to stress a particular aspect, namely that this approach is better capable of modeling the translation knowledge of human translators than other example-based approaches. Because the translation knowledge is represented as alignments (synchronizations) between string-tree alignments (SSTCs, or structured string-tree correspondences), it is more natural to translators (and post-editors) than direct word-word, string-string or chunk-chunk correspondences used in classical SMT and EBMT models. It is also totally static, hence more understandable than procedural knowledge embedded in almost all RBMT approaches.

The learning process which is an integral part of the development of SiSTeC-ebmt MT systems can in fact be viewed as a special case of the study of reasoning reported in [Khardon&Roth 94], because it combines the interfaces to the 'world' used by known learning models with the reasoning task and a performance criterion suitable for it. In such a framework, the intelligent agent is given access to its learning interface, and is also given a grace period in which it can interact with this interface and construct its representation Knowledge Base (KB) of the 'world'. Its reasoning performance is measured only after this period, when it is presented with 'queries' from some query language, relevant to the 'world', and has to answer whether such 'queries' are implied by the learned 'world' model. In our case, the 'world' is the 'translation task' captured in terms of the parallel texts produced by human translators and enriched by their S-SSTCs, and the 'queries' are simply modeled by a predicate `Translate(ST,TT)` where ST is the source language text and TT is a variable to be instantiated by a target language text if the 'translation' model learned is capable of performing such translation.

Our model directly deals with three main difficulties in the traditional treatment of MT which stem from its separation from the "translation task" (the 'world'). First, by allowing the system to learn from real translation examples directly, we avoid the need to indefinitely pursue the elusive goal of writing grammars to exactly describe intermediate syntactico-semantic monolingual representations and their correspondences. Second, we make explicit the dependence of the MT system performance on the input from the environment. This is possible only because the learning process uses feedback from the real translation knowledge when constructing its knowledge representation. Third, such MT systems using an inductively learned knowledge base yield a desirable non-regressive behavior by using translation mistakes to improve their knowledge base.

Learning to translate is just like any other machine learning task; it is concerned with modeling and understanding learning phenomena with respect to the 'world' — a central aspect of cognition. Traditional theories of Machine Translation systems, however, have assumed that such cognition can be studied separately from learning. It is assumed that the knowledge is given to the system, stored in some representation language with a well-defined meaning, and that there is some mechanism which can be used to determine what source language text can be translated with respect to the given knowledge; the question of how this knowledge might be acquired and whether this should influence how the performance of the machine translation system is measured is not considered. We prove the usefulness of the 'learning-to-translate' approach by showing that through interaction with the world, the agent truly gains additional translating power, over what is possible in more traditional settings.

2. The bilingual knowledge bank base as a set of S-SSTCs

Bilingual parallel texts which encode the correspondences between source and target sentences have been used extensively in implementing the so called example-based machine translation systems [Sato 91, Richardson et. al. 2001, Menezes et. al. 2001, Kawahara & Kurohashi 2010]. In order to enhance the quality of example-based systems, sentences of a parallel corpus are normally annotated with their constituent or dependency structures [Sadler&Vendelmans 90], which in turn allows correspondences between source and target sentences to be established at the structural level. Here, we annotate parallel texts based on the Structured String-Tree Correspondence (SSTC) [Boitet&Zaharin 88]. The SSTC is a general structure that can associate, to strings in a language, arbitrary tree structures as desired by the annotator to be the interpretation structures of the strings, and more importantly is the facility to specify the correspondence between the string and the associated tree which can be interpreted for both analysis and synthesis in the machine translation process. These features are very much desired in the design of an annotation scheme, in particular for the treatment of certain non-standard linguistic phenomena, such as unprojectivity or inversion of dominance [Tang&Zaharin 95].

In this paper, we show how to use the good properties of the SSTC annotation scheme for S-SSTC-based MT, using the example of the SiSTeC-ebmt English-Malay Machine Translation system. We have chosen dependency structures as linguistic representations in the SSTCs, since they provide a natural way of annotating both the tree associated to a string as well as the mapping between the two [Goh 96]. We also give a simple means to denote the translation elements between the corresponding source (English) and target (Malay) SSTCs. Similar arguments also appeared in [Sadler&Vendelmans 90] and [Maxwell&Schubert 89]. The dependency structure used here is in fact quite analogous to the use of abstract syntax tree in most of the compiler implementation. However, we note that the SSTCs can easily be extended to keep multiple levels of linguistic representation (e.g. syntagmatic[1], functional and logical structures) if that is considered important to enhance the results of the machine translation system. Naturally, the more information annotated in an SSTC, the more difficult is the annotation work; that is why one should try to keep only the annotations contributing most to the task at hand.

In the general case, let S be a string (usually a sentence) and T a tree (its linguistic representation). Instead of simply write (S,T), we want to decompose that 'large' correspondence into smaller ones (S1, T1)...(Sn, Tn) in a hierarchical fashion; hence the adjective 'structured' in 'SSTC'. If T is an abstract representation of S, some nodes may represent discontinuous words or constituents (e.g. He gives the money back to her), or some words are not directly represented (e.g. auxiliaries, articles), or some words omitted (elided) in S may have been restored in T. [Boitet&Zaharin 88] have shown how to encode such string-tree correspondences in the tree part (T), through 2 functions, SNODE and STREE, even if the trees are 'abstract', but provided they obey some formal constraints that are in effect verified by all known kinds of linguistic trees. In the SSTC diagrams presented here, any tree node N bears a pair X/Y where X = SNODE(N) and Y = STREE(N). X and Y are generalized (not necessarily connex) substrings of the string S, and are written as minimal[2] left-to-right lists of usual intervals, like 1_3+4_5). SNODE(N) denotes the substring that corresponds to the lexical information contained in

---

[1] by constituents.

[2] That means that any occurrence of $n_1\_n_2+n_2\_n_3$ is replaced by $n_1\_n_3$, n_i being a position between two typographical words, or more generally (to handle writing systems without word delimiters such as Chinese, Japanese, Korean, Vietnamese, Thai, Lao, or Khmer), between two characters.

node[3], while STREE(N) denotes the (again possibly discontinuous) substring that corresponds to the whole subtree rooted at node N.

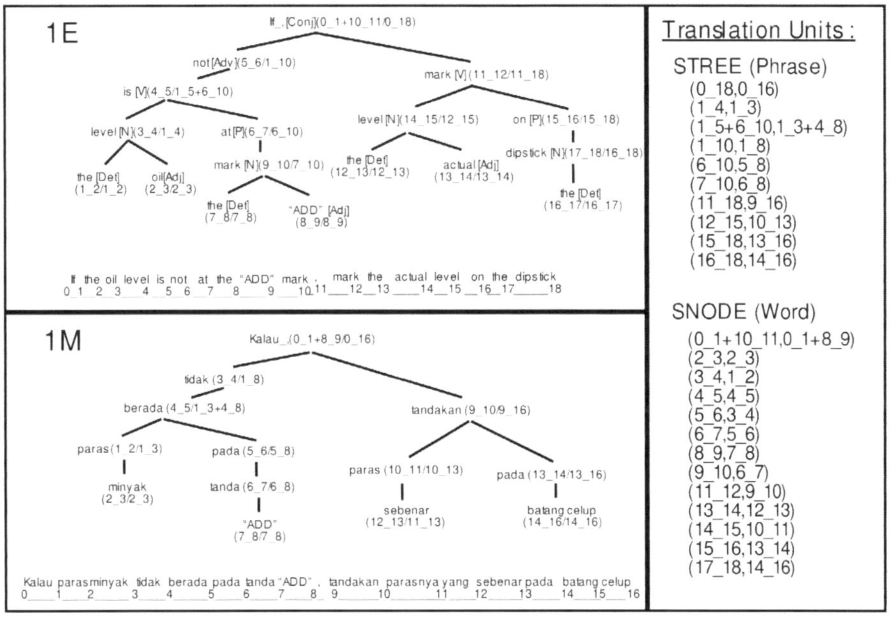

Figure 1: An example pair of English - Malay SSTCs and the corresponding translation elements

As for the correspondences between the source (English) and target (Malay) SSTCs, the translation elements[4] between phrases and words are coded in terms of STREE pairs and SNODE pairs, respectively. To illustrate this, we show in Figure 1 a pair of source (English) and target (Malay) SSTCs and the corresponding translation elements. In the example SSTCs given, an interval is assigned to each word in the sentence, i.e. 0_1 to "if", 1_2 to "the", etc. The node "not" has SNODE = 5_6, meaning that its lexeme corresponds to the word "not" in the sentence. Similarly, the node bearing "is" has STREE = 1_5+6_10, meaning that the subtree it dominates corresponds to the discontinuous substring "the oil level is" + "at the ADD mark".

Figure 2 gives another example of correspondence between source sentence 2E and target sentence 2M. Both translation pairs, (1E, 1M) and (2E, 2M), will serve as running examples of annotated bilingual parallel sentences in the rest of the discussion.

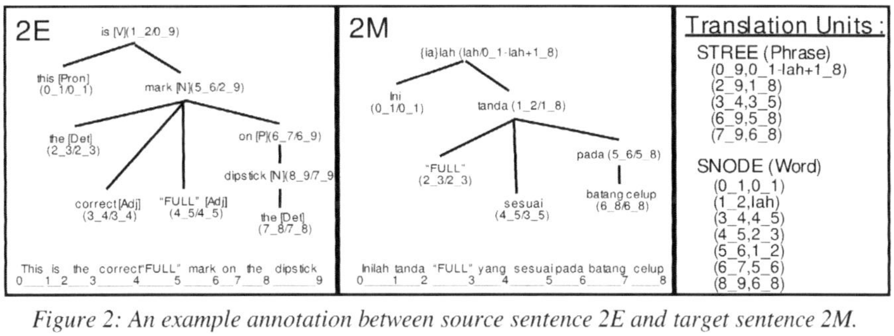

Figure 2: An example annotation between source sentence 2E and target sentence 2M.

---

[3] A lexeme for leaves and nothing for internal nodes in syntagmatic structures, and a lexeme for each node in a dependency structure, where a lexeme might be a compound corresponding to a discontinuous substring, such as *give_back, neither_nor, if_then_else*, etc.

[4] The term 'translation units' (TUs) has been used in previous publications, but, as the normal sense of TU is 'a minimal unit for human translation', that is, a sentence or a title, an exclamation, etc., we replace it here by 'translation element'.

3. A learn-to-translate process based on a bilingual knowledge bank (BKB)

The process of *learning-to-translate* begins with the construction of a shared forest structure based on the representation structure of the used source sentences (here 1E and 2E) together with its words index as illustrated in Figure 3 below. The shared forest structure together with its words index is then used to parse a new input source sentence by extracting from the BKB the related substructure of the shared forest, using the words index as a guide. An example of a shared forest for the new source sentence 3E, constructed based on the shared forest structure of sentences 1E and 2E, is given in Figure 3 below.

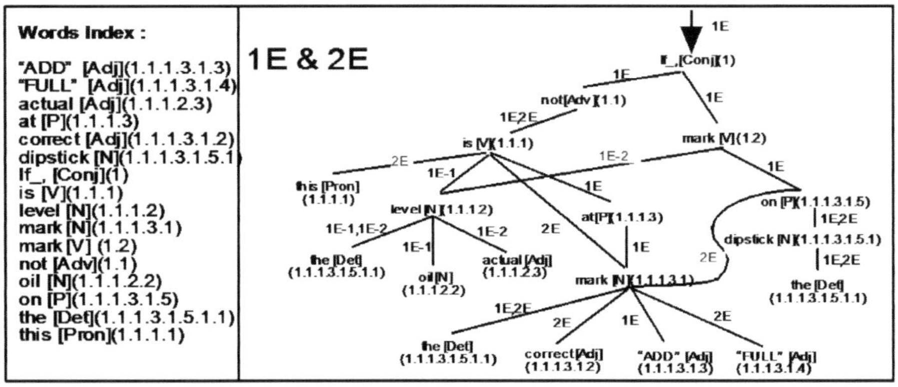

Figure 3: A shared forest structure constructed based on the representation structures of source sentence 1E and 2E with their word index.

The shared forest structure together with its words index is then used to parse a new input source sentence by mean of extracting out the related substructure of the shared forest through the guidance of words index. An example of a shared forest for a new source sentence 3E, constructed based on the shared forest structure of sentences 1E and 2E, is given in Figure 4. The resulting shared forest is then used to construct the corresponding dependency tree of sentence 3E as well as the substring to subtree mappings, as shown on the top part of Figure 5 — the analysis task [Tang 94].

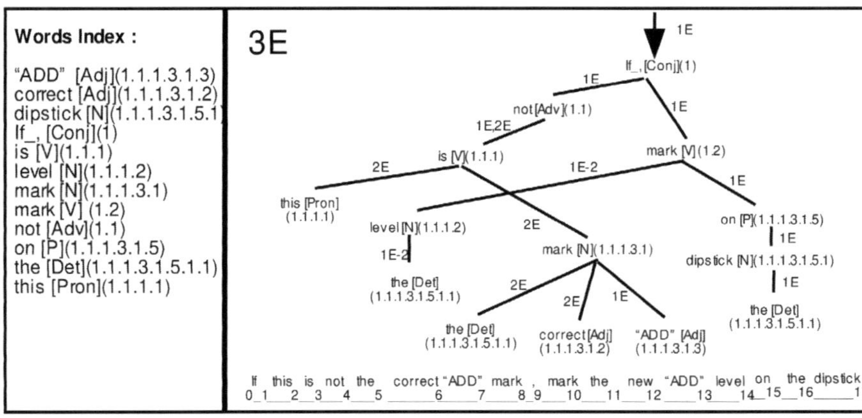

Figure 4: An example shared forest structure for sentence 3E constructed based on structures created in Figure 3.

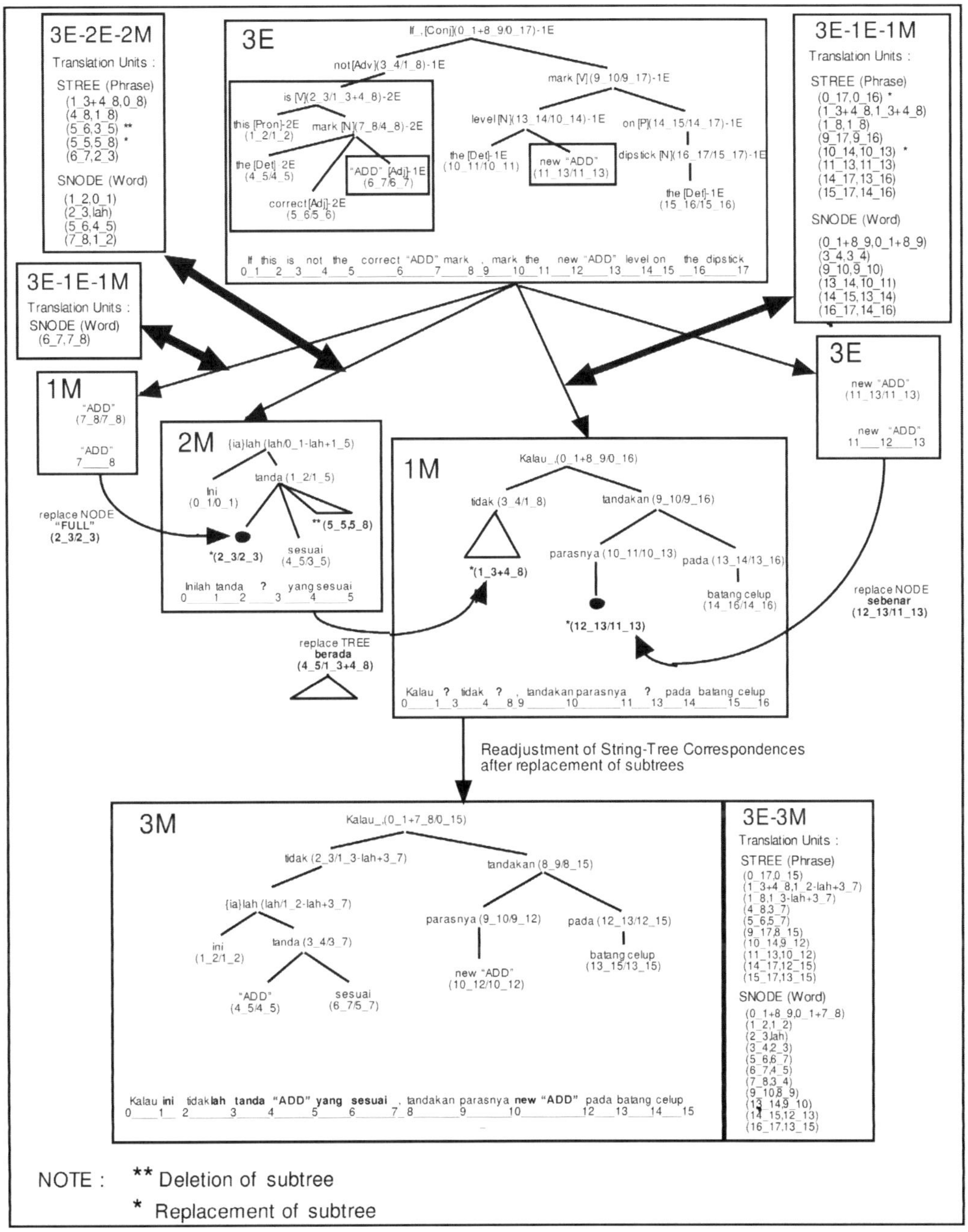

Figure 5: Learn-to-translate process based on the bilingual knowledge bank and guided by the shared forest structure of Figure 4.

Note that the dependency tree is constructed by extracting the related subtrees from the dependency trees of both sentences 1E and 2E. Note also that a substring which has not been treated before, e.g. "new ADD", will be set to correspond to a node in the dependency tree; the location of this node in the dependency tree is decided based on its context (i.e. the surrounding words). The resulting sub-SSTC of sentence 3E is then used to retrieve the related target language sub-SSTC based on the translation elements stored in the bilingual knowledge bank — the transfer task. The target sub-SSTCs are then merged to form a complete SSTC for the translated sentence, as shown at the bottom of Figure 5. Such a merging process can be considered as a kind of synthesis process in order to construct the target sentence [Heng 95].

4. Learning from corrected translation mistakes

In order to improve the performance of an MT system, not only do we need to fix detected errors, we also need to increase at the same time the translation knowledge (encoded in the bilingual knowledge bank). To do that, we feed back to the system the information as to whether the previous translation has been done correctly or not. In the case of error translation, it is also necessary to correct the BKB by making the necessary adjustments to reflect the error correction process (hence the need for an integrated post-editing environment), so that a similar error will not occur again. In the case of perfect translation, we may reinforce scores attached to the used translation elements, or do nothing, treating the result as a simple confirmation. In the given example, the resulting target SSTC appears to have some errors and it is corrected as highlighted in Figure 6. The corrected SSTC is then added to the system in order to enrich the bilingual knowledge bank. Here, we add a shared forest structure constructed from the representation structures of source sentences 1E, 2E and 3E, as shown in Figure 7.

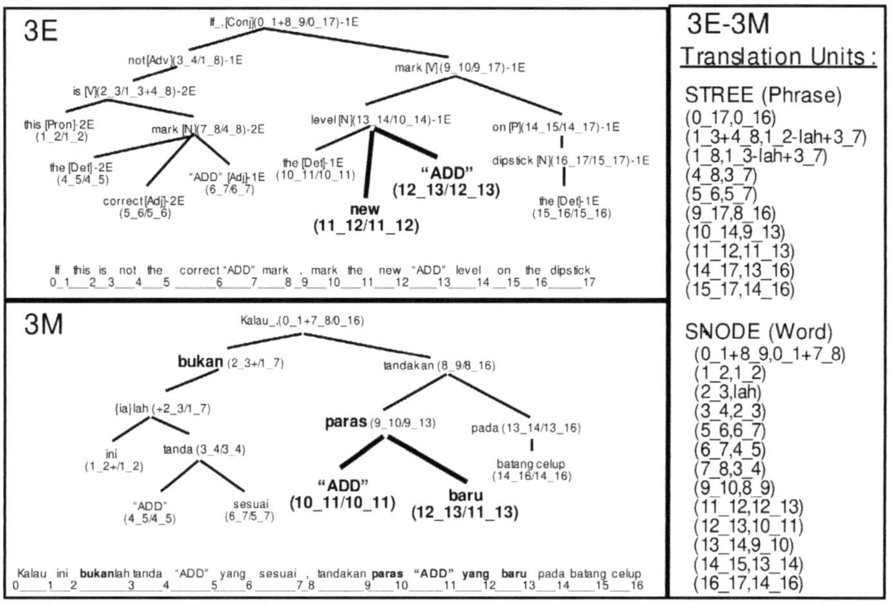

Figure 6: An example annotation between source sentence 3E and target sentence 3M after going through the correction done by the linguist on the improper annotations produced by the MT system.

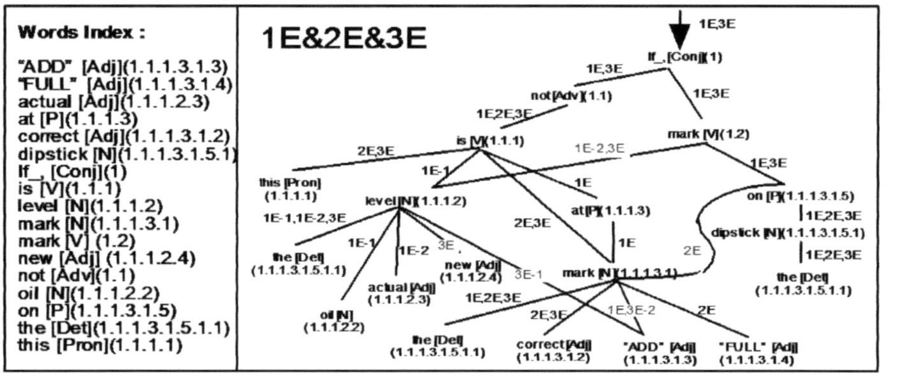

Figure 7: A shared forest structure constructed based on the representation structures of source sentence 1E, 2E and 3E with its words Index

5. Implementation notes

The main purpose of the project described in this paper is to build a general software package that provides an integrated environment for the construction of S-SSTC-based EBMT systems. In this project, we put emphasis on the development of an English->Malay MT system in the domain of computer science texts. However, the same methodology can be adapted to develop MT systems for any other typology of texts, and naturally also for any other language pairs. The current SiSTeC-ebmt platform consists of four major subcomponents (as shown by the diagram given in Figure 8), namely (1) the preparation of an annotated bilingual parallel texts to be used for the initial learning process, (2) a set of acquisition tools used to construct the initial bilingual knowledge bank, (3) a general MT system to translate new input sentences (using the bilingual knowledge bank) into the target language, together with all the related annotation, (4) the post-editing process to make corrections (if any) on the translation as well as on the annotations, which in turn will be used by the learning tools to confirm the well translated parts and adjust the translation elements of the BKB corresponding to the corrected parts.

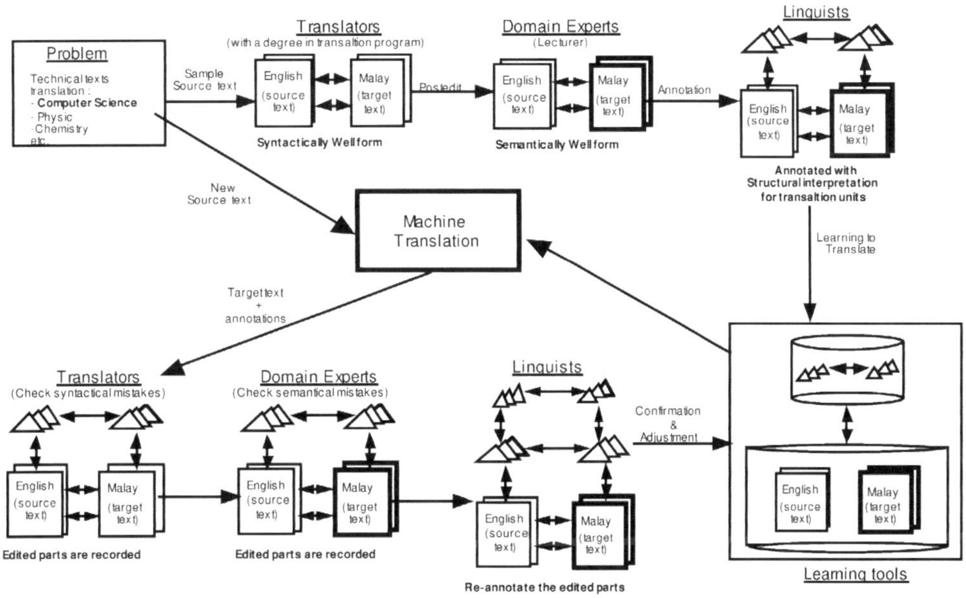

Figure 8: An overview of the implementation for the "learn-to-translate" S-SSTC-based model

An English->Malay MT system with 100,000 translation examples annotated in the S-SSTC has been constructed based on the implementation frame as described above. To provide an overview of the performance of this system, a quick comparison of the MT results produced by Google Translate and our SiSTeC-ebmt is given in the table below.

Sample English Text	**Translation to Malay by Google Translate**	**Translation to Malay by SiSTeC-ebmt (100,000 S-SSTCs)**
The main purpose of the project described in this paper is to build a general software package that provides an integrated environment for the construction of S-SSTC based EBMT systems. In this project, we put emphasis on the development of an English->Malay MT system in the domain of computer science texts. However, the same methodology can be adapted to develop MT systems for any other typology of texts, and naturally also for any other language pairs.	Tujuan utama projek yang dihuraikan dalam kertas kerja ini adalah untuk membina satu pakej perisian umum yang menyediakan persekitaran bersepadu bagi pembinaan sistem S-SSTC EBMT berasaskan. Dalam projek ini, kami meletakkan penekanan kepada pembangunan bahasa Inggeris> MT sistem bahasa Melayu dalam domain teks sains komputer. Walau bagaimanapun, kaedah yang sama boleh disesuaikan untuk membangunkan sistem MT bagi mana-mana tipologi teks lain, dan secara semulajadi juga untuk mana-mana pasangan bahasa lain.	Tujuan utama daripada projek itu digambarkan di dalam kertas ini untuk membina perisian umumnya pakej yang menyediakan mengintegrasikan S-SSTC persekitaran bagi pembinaan berdasarkan EBMT sistem. Dalam projek ini, kami meletakkan teks sains sistem menekankan pembangunan English->Malay MT di domain komputer. Walau bagaimanapun, metodologi sama boleh disesuaikan mengikut merangka sistem Tm untuk tipologi lain teks, dan secara semula jadi juga untuk sebarang pasang bahasa-bahasa lain.

We provide also in the following table a comparison of the results produced by our SiSTeC-ebmt system with different size of its bilingual knowledge bank.

Translation to Malay by SiSTeC-ebmt (1,500 S-SSTCs)	**Translation to Malay by SiSTeC-ebmt (25,000 S-SSTCs)**	**Translation to Malay by SiSTeC-ebmt (100,000 S-SSTCs)**
Tujuan utama projek itu memerikan dengan kertas ini untuk membina bungkusan perisian jeneral yang memberikan mengintegrasikan persekitaran untuk pembinaan S-SSTC menempatkan sistem EBMT. Dalam projek ini, kami menyimpan penekanan terhadap perkembangan-perkembangan English->Malay MT sistem dalam kawasan kekuasaan komputer teks sains. Walau bagaimanapun, metodologi sama boleh menjadi disadur untuk berkembang MT sistem untuk sebarang typology yang lain (-lain) teks, dan semula jadinya juga untuk sebarang pasangan bahasa yang lain (-lain).	Tujuan sesalur projek itu dikatakan dengan kertas ini untuk membina perisian jeneral bungkusan memberikan yang mengintegrasikan persekitaran untuk senibina S-SSTC berasaskan sistem EBMT. Dalam projek ini, kami meletakkan penekanan terhadap perkembangan English->Malay MT sistem dalam domain komputer teks sains. Walau bagaimanapun, perkaedahan yang sama boleh menjadi disesuaikan memajukan sistem MT untuk typology yang lain (-lain) teks, dan semula jadinya juga untuk bahasa yang lain (-lain) pasang.	Tujuan utama daripada projek itu digambarkan di dalam kertas ini untuk membina perisian umumnya pakej yang menyediakan mengintegrasikan S-SSTC persekitaran bagi pembinaan berdasarkan EBMT sistem. Dalam projek ini, kami meletakkan teks sains sistem menekankan pembangunan English->Malay MT di domain komputer. Walau bagaimanapun, metodologi sama boleh disesuaikan mengikut merangka sistem Tm untuk tipologi lain teks, dan secara semula jadi juga untuk sebarang pasang bahasa-bahasa lain.

Acknowledgments

The work reported in this paper is supported by a Brain Gain Research Grant from the Malaysian Ministry of Science, Technology & Innovation. We thank also to the French Embassy at Malaysia and the ANR Traouiero project for the supports provided to the first author to have one month stay at Université Joseph Fourier (UJF) as a visiting researcher.

References

[Boitet&Zaharin 88] Zaharin bin Yusoff, Christian Boitet, Representation trees and string-tree correspondences, COLING-88, Budapest, August 1988, pp. 59-64.

[Goh 96] Goh Chooi Ling, Pengunting Papan, Laporan Projek Tahun Akhir Sains Komputer, USM, 1996.

[Heng 95] Heng Ai Looi, Natural Language generation in Machine Translation (MT) Based on the String-Tree Correspondence Grammar (STCG), Dissertation submitted in fulfillment of the M.Sc., 1995.

[Kawahara & Kurohashi 2010] Daisuke Kawahara and Sadao Kurohashi, Acquiring Reliable Predicate-argument Structures from Raw Corpora for Case Frame Compilation, In Proceedings of the 7th International Conference on Language Resources and Evaluation (LREC2010), 2010.

[Khardon&Roth 94] Roni Khardon, Dan Roth, Learning to Reason, Proceedings of AAAI-94.

[Maxwell&Schubert 89] Dan Maxwell, Klaus Schubert (eds), Metataxis in practice: Dependency syntax for multilingual machine translation. Dordrecht/Providence : Foris. DLT 6, 1989.

[Menezes et. al. 2001] Menezes, A., Richardson, S.: A Best-first alignment algorithm for automatic extraction of transfer mappings from bilingual corpora. In: Proceedings of the Workshop on Data-Driven Machine Translation, ACL 2001, Toulouse, France, 2001.

[Mosleh et. al. 2002] Mosleh H. Al-Adhaileh & Tang Enya Kong & Zaharin Yusoff. "A Synchronization Structure of SSTC and ITS Applications in MachineTranslation". COLING 2002 Post-conference Workshop "Workshop on Machine Translation in Asia", Taipei, Taiwan, September, 2002

[Richardson et. al. 2001] Richardson, S., Dolan, W., Menezes, A., Pinkham, J.: Achieving commercial-quality translation with example-based methods. In: Proceedings of MT Summit VIII, Santiago de Compostela, Spain, 2001

[Sadler&Vendelmans 90] Victor Sadler, Ronald Vendelmans, Pilot Implementation of a bilingual Knowledge Bank, COLING 90, Helsinki, 1990.

[Sato 91] Sato, S., Example-Based Translation Approach to Machine Translation, Proceedings of the International Workshop on Fundamental Research for Future Generation of Natural Language Processing, ATR interpreting Telephony Research Laboratories, 1991.

[Tang 94] Tang Enya Kong, Natural Language Analysis In Machine Translation (MT) Based On The String-Tree Correspondence Grammar (STCG), Dissertation submitted in fulfillment of the Ph.D., 1994.

[Tang&Zaharin 95] Tang Enya Kong, Zaharin Y., Handling Crossed Dependecies with the STCG, proceedings of NLPRS'95, Sofitel Ambassador Hotel, Seoul, Korea, Dec. 4-6, 1995.

Translating English Names to Arabic Using Phonotactic Rules *

Faisal Alshuwaier[a] and Ali Areshey[a]

Computer Research Institute, King Abdulaziz City for Science and Technology
P.O.Box 6086, Riyadh 11442, Kingdom of Saudi Arabia
{shuwaier, aareshey}@kacst.edu.sa

Abstract. With the increasing numbers of the arrivals to the Arabian countries; it is necessary to use Arabic language in writing names on official documents. Because of the difference in writing English names in Arabic language, many methods have been spread for translating English names which led to first, duplication in every single English name written in Arabic and this will lead to negative effects security and property rights. The second difference is that even if the transliteration of Arabic names is standardized, it is difficult for a layperson to implement it. This paper is to provide algorithms based on some rules that can be used in programming a system to transliterate English names automatically. The system uses only plan for Translate English Names to Arabic, and that can be processed and printed easily. Moreover, the Translated names can be read and recognized by ordinary people.

Keywords: Automatic Translation, Phonotactic Rules, Phonemes, Arabic, English, Diacritized Arabic Phone.

1 Introduction

With the rapid increase of the published information, it is difficult to rely on human translation to translate such information from one language to another and translation of appropriate names is generally realized as a significant issue in many multi-lingual text and speech processing applications. In our work, a set of hand-crafted transformations for locally editing the phonemic spelling of an English word to conform to rules of Arabic syllabification are used to seed a transformation-based learning algorithm. The algorithm examines some data and learns the proper sequence of application of the transformations to convert an English phoneme sequence to a Arabic syllable sequence. Our paper describes a data driven counterpart to this technique, in which a cascade model is used to go from English names to Arabic transliteration. The system uses only plan for Translate English Names to Arabic, and that can be processed and printed easily. Moreover, the Translated names can be read and recognized by ordinary people. This paper also discusses the problem background and provides solutions to Arabize almost all English Names. In section 2, we briefly highlight some related works. In section 3, we introduce description of translation system. In section 4, some specific phonotactic rules are shown. In section 5, the evaluation experiment for auto transliteration is presented. Finally, in Section 6, we draw some concluding remarks.

2 Related Works

Transliteration has been of interest to researchers in automatic lexicon creation and cross-language information retrieval involving radical differences in writing systems, such as English/Arabic, English/Korean, English/ Chinese and Japanese/English. (Knight and Graehl, 1998) have relied on the probabilistic mappings between English phones and Japanese phones generated. (Mansur

* The authors would like to acknowledge the reviewers for their valuable comments, which contributed to the clarity of the paper and in particular for their suggestions for the statements of rules.

et al., 1994) developed an algorithm at IBM for the automatic forward transliteration of Arabic personal names into the Roman alphabet. (Knight and Graehl, 1997) describe a back transliteration system for Japanese. (Lee et al. 1998) used a specific formula to generate a transliterated Korean word K for a given English word E. (Paola and Sanjeev, 2003) demonstrate the application of statistical machine translation techniques to translate the phonemic representation of an English name, obtained by using an automatic text-tospeech system, to a sequence of initials and finals, commonly used sub-word units of pronunciation for Chinese. (Stalls and Knight, 1998) present an Arabic-to- English back-transliteration system based on the source-channel framework.

3 Translation System Description

The procedure for constructing English-Arabic pairs is as follows: First, beginning with English name list which obtains each words English phonetic representations since these seemed to be most common English pronunciation symbol. Then the English pronunciation symbols are mapped to Arabic phonetic using a mapping table between the English phonetic characters. Then the Arabic phonetic sequences are mapped into diacritized Arabic name. Each diacritized symbol is mapped to the corresponding character. In Arabic language, the scripts are written right-to-left (RTL), so the system also manipulates the text direction. Finally, The Arabic name is represented without the Arabic diacritization.

3.1 English Name to English Phone

There are two general methods to mapping English names stored in the Database which contains over 133 thousand names to phonetic representations. The simplest one, if lexicon exists translating each name to its phonetic representations, then one can simply look up the corresponding phonetic stored in the Database which contains 84 symbols. However, this method will not work if a name is not existed. A more general method is to use a model of the English syllables to the phonetic sequences, and to choose the sequences that maximize the occurrence. In our model, we translated the names with known pronunciations from a pronunciation dictionary. We also used the Carnegie Mellon University (CMU) Speech Pronunciation Dictionary which applies 39 phonemes, each written as a sequence of Latin symbols (Carnegie Mellon University Project, 2007). We obtain the following English phonetic as an example for the name Obama:

OBAMA $\longrightarrow$ OW2-B-AA1-M-AH0

Where each phone is separated by a hyphen "-". The CMU dictionary also provides the name representation since this seemed to be the most common pronunciation (Yan et al., 2003).

3.2 English Phone to Diacritized Arabic Phone

For mapping from an English phonetic existed in the CMU dictionary to an Arabic phonetic representation, we used phonotactic rules for mapping from English sounds to Arabic sounds. First, the system should map the English phonetic symbols to the Diacritized Arabic Phonetic symbols which a scan has been made for the universal phonetic symbols for (vowels), and linked it with the audio symbols for Vowels in Arabic so that we can convert the English names to the universal phonetic symbols, and then convert the universal phonetic symbols to the Arabic phonetic symbol. An obvious target inventory is the Arabic syllabary itself, shown in Table 1 as the short vowel symbols which are typically not written. Short vowels may be written with diacritics placed above or below the consonant that precedes them in the syllable, called *harakat* or *diacritics*. All Arabic vowels, long and short, follow a consonant; in Arabic, words like "Ali" or "alif".

In the fully vocalized Arabic text found in texts such as *Quran*, a long ā following a consonant other than a *hamzah* is written with a short a sign (*fatah*) on the consonant plus an *alif* after it; long is written as a sign for short i (*kasrah*) plus a ya ; and long ū as a sign for short u (*ammah*) plus a *waw*. Briefly, ^{a}a = ā, ^{i}y = $\bar{\text{i}}$ and ^{u}w =ū. Long ā following a *hamzah* may be represented by an *alif maddah* or by a free *hamzah* followed by an *alif* (Wikipedia).

Table 1: The values of Long and Short Vowels in Arabic

Symbols	Name	Trans.	Value
بِ	kasrah	*i*	/i/
بَ	fathah	*a*	/a/
بُ	dammah	*u*	/u/
ا	fathah alif	*ā*	/a:/
ى	fathah alif maqsura	*ā/aȳ*	/a/
وُ	dammah waw	*ū/ uw*	/u:/
يِ	kasrah ya	*ī/ iy*	/i:/

Table 2 provides the listing of the phoneme set and the corresponding phoneme symbols used in the system training . The table also shows illustrative examples of the vowel usage.

Table 2: The phoneme set

Arabic	Phoneme	Arabic	Phoneme	Arabic	Phoneme	Arabic	Phoneme
dammah/waw → ضمة/واو	/AO0/	fatha/alif → فتحة/ألف	/AA0/	Qaf → ق	/G/	Jeem → ج	/ZH/
dammah/waw → ضمة/واو	/UH0/	fatha/alif → فتحة/ألف	/AE0/	Qaf → ق	/R	Dal → د	/D/
dammah/waw → ضمة/واو	/UW0/	fatha/alif → فتحة/ألف	/AH0/	Kaf → ك	/K/	Daj → دج	/JH/
dammah/waw → ضمة/واو	/OY0/	fatha/alif → فتحة/ألف	/EH0/	Lam → ل	/L/	Thal → ذ	/DH/
dammah/waw → ضمة/واو	/OW0/	fatha/alif → فتحة/ألف	/EH2/	Meem → م	/M/	Reh → ر	/ER0/
dammah/waw → ضمة/واو	/UW1/	fatha/ya → فتحة/ي	/AY0/	Heh → هـ	/HH/	Reh → ر	/ER2/
wawya → وي	/OY1/	fatha/ya → فتحة/ي	/EY0/	Waw → و	/W/	Zain → ز	/Z/
Beh → ب	/B/	fatha/waw → فتحة/و	/AW0/	Noon → ن	/N/	Seen → س	/S/
Beh → ب	/P/	kasrah/ya → كسرة/ياء	/IH0/	Noon → ن	/Y/	Sheen → ش	/SH/
Ghain → غ	/NG/	Teh → ت	/T/	Feh → ف	/PH/	kasrah/ya → كسرة/ياء	/IY0/
Feh → ف	/F/, /V/	Teh Sh → تش	/CH/	dammah/waw → ضمة/واو	/UX/	kasrah/ya → كسرة/ياء	/IX/

The regular Arabic short vowels are /AE/. /IH/, and /UH/ corresponding to the Arabic diacritical marks Fatha, Kasra and Damma, respectively. The /AA/ is the pharyngealized allophone of /AE/. Similarly, the /IX/ and /UX/ are the pharyngealized allophones of /IH/ and /UH/ respectively. When /AE/ appears before an emphatic letter, its allophone /AH/ is used instead. The regular Arabic long vowel allophones are /AE:/ /IY/ and /UW/ respectively. The length of a long vowel is normally equal to two short vowels. The allophones /AY/ and /AW/ are actually two vowel sounds in which the articulators move from one post to another. These vowels are called Diphthongs. The allophone /AY/ appears when a Fatha comes before an undiacritized Yeh. Similarly, /AW/ appears when a Fatha comes before an undiacritized Waw. The Arabic voiced stops phonemes /B/ and /D/ are similar to their English counter parts. /DD/ corresponds to the sound of the Arabic Dhad letter. The Arabic voiceless stops /T/ and /K/ are basically similar to their English counter parts. The sound of the Arabic emphatic letter Qaf is represented by the phone /Q/. The Hamza plosive sound is represented by the phone /E/, and the sound of Jeem (in many dialects) is represented by /G/. The voiceless fricatives are produced with no vibration of the voice cords (Mohamed, et al., 2007). The set of symbols is called International Phonetic Alphabet (IPA) (International Phonetic Association, 2005) which its symbol is based on the Roman letters as shown in Figure 1.

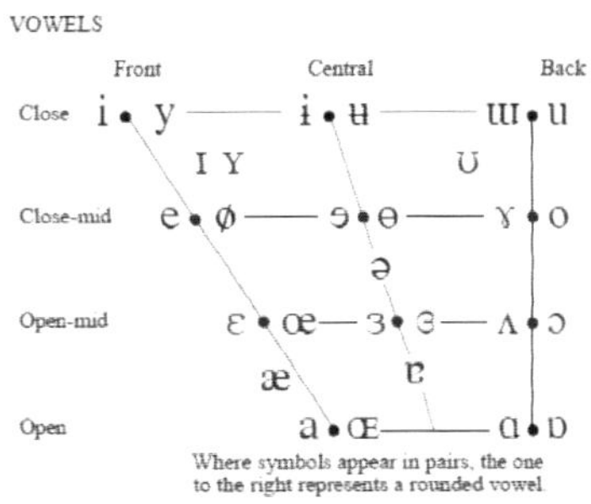

Figure 1: International Phonetic Alphabet

In addition, IPA does not have symbols for the emphatic sounds:

ص - ض - ط - ظ

So, to make it possible for researcher and Arab linguists and who work on language sounds, a new alphabet has been created. Arabic International Phonetic Alphabet (AIPA) consists of symbols that are based on Arabic orthographic system. (Mansour Alghamdi et al., 2004; Wikipedia; Alghamdi, 2003). Figure 1 presents the phonetic symbols as they are the IPA which consists of 28 sounds, however, in Arabic has 3 sounds symbols as:

إ، آ، أ

For the phonetic sequence OW2-B-AA1-M-AH0, this step creates the diacritized Arabic sound sequence as follows:

OW2-B-AA1-M-AH0 ⟶

آ - م - آ - ب - و - أ

3.3 Diacritized Arabic Phone to UnDiacritized Arabic Phone

For mapping from a diacritized Arabic phone representation to undiacritized Arabic phone representation, we use traditional mappings between the diacritized symbols, corresponding characters as shown in Table 1 and the phonetics rules that will be explained in the next section. Because short vowels (diacritics) are commonly not presented in Arabic orthography, this creates a problem in transliterating unknown proper names (Out Of Vocabulary) since these missing diacritics should be deduced before transliteration to obtain the appropriate pronunciation. For the phonetic sequence:

آ - م - آ - ب - و - أ

This step creates the undiacritized Arabic sound sequence as follows:

أ و ب ا م ا ⟵ آ م آ ب و أ

The steps in English-to-Arabic transliteration of names are depicted in Figure 2.

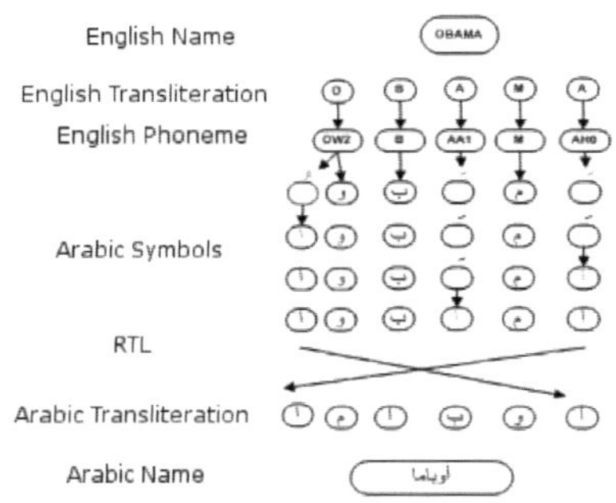

Figure 2: The steps in English-to-Arabic transliteration of names

4 Phonotactic Rules

Using the selected phoneme set, we developed a set of rules that are used to automatically generate the phonetic pronunciations for Arabic words. Each rule tries to match certain conditions on the context of the letter and provide a replacement from the phoneme list. Replacements can be one or more phonemes. Some letters dont have an effect on pronunciation or, depending on context, they might not be pronounced; in this case, the replacement will be empty (Mohamed et al., 2007). Each rule follows this format:

/ # (pre_rule) ⟶ / # (post_rule)

<u>or</u>

$$(pre\_rule)\,\#\,/ \longrightarrow (post\_rule)\,\#\,/$$

To facilitate understanding of the Phonotactic Rules, the Table 3 explains the symbols used in. The left hand side of the rule is pre-replacement and each letter in the pre-replacement is referenced by its name as defined in the Unicode standard. Multiple classes are defined to simplify the rules syntax. The right hand side of the rule defines the post-replacement, which can either be a phoneme or a sequence of phonemes from the phoneme list, or the letter might not have a matching phoneme and will be omitted from pronunciation.

Table 3: Symbols used in the Phonotactic Rules

Symbol	Significance	Symbol	Significance
/ #	Beginning of the word	( )	Character between brackets optional
# /	End of the word	[ ]	It corresponds to another character
C & V	Consonant & Short Vowels	$\longrightarrow$	Become
_	Character of the applicable rules	Cn	A series of consonants

4.1 First Rule

Short vowels can be normal ones or either emphatic or pharyngeal, depending on the surrounding letters. We developed rules that take care of all these situations. If the name starts with Arabic diacritization it will be transferred to corresponding Characters. For instance, Fatha will be transferred to Fathah Alif as described in the condition 1, Dammah will be transferred to Dammah Alif as shown in the condition 2 and Kasrah will be transferred to Kasrah Alif as described in the condition 3.

/# [◌َ] → /# [أَ] (1)   /# [◌ُ] → /# [أُ] (2)   /# [◌ِ] → /# [إِ] (3)

4.2 Second Rule

The vowels (A, E, I, O, U and sometimes Y) are sometimes treated as semi-vowels and other times it is treated as a long vowel, depending on its context. The condition 4 describes the second rule. If the name ended with one of these vowels will be transmitted to the following letters depending on the pronunciation of the letter in Arabic : "Alif" or "Waw" or "Ya".

_v #/ → _ [ا / و / ي] #/ (4)

4.3 Third Rule

In the case of a vowel at the beginning of the word optional (v) followed by consonant and then a vowel v as shown in the condition 5, the second vowel to be switched to the following letters depending on the pronunciation of the letter in Arabic : "Alif" or "Waw" or "Ya".

/# (v) c v → /# (v) c [ا / و / ي] (5)

4.4 Fourth Rule

In the case of a vowel at the beginning of the word optional (v) followed by consonant and then a vowel v as shown in the condition 6, the second vowel to be switched to the following letters depending on the pronunciation of the letter:

(أ) ، (و) ، (ي)

/# (v) c_n v → /# (v) c_n [ا و ي] (6)

4.5 Fifth Rule

In the case of a vowel at the beginning of the word optional (v) followed by consonant and then a vowel v as shown in the condition 7, the second vowel to be switched to the following letters depending on the pronunciation of the letter in Arabic : "Alif" or "Waw" or "Ya".

/# (v) c NG #/ → /# (v) c نغ#/ (7)

4.6 Sixth Rule

In the case of a vowel at the beginning of the word optional (v) and then followed by the letter N and G and then a fixed character as shown in the condition 8, the letters (NG) together are switched to the following:

(ڽ)

/# (v) NG c → /# (v) ڽ c (8)

4.7 Seventh Rule

In the case of a vowel at the beginning of the word optional (v) and then fixed character C1 followed by fatah or dammah or kasrah and then followed by same fixed character C1 as shown in the condition 9, then fatah or dammah or kasrah will be converted to the following character:

(أَ)، (أُ)، (إِ)

/# (v) c1 [ـَ ـُ ـِ] c1 → /# (v) c1 [ا و ي] c1 (9)

4.8 Eighth Rule

In the case of a vowel at the beginning of the word optional (v) and a fixed character C1 followed by fatah or dammah or kasrahand then followed by same fixed character C1 as shown in the condition 10, only one character from C1 to be written in addition to:

(آ).

/# (v) c1 [ـَ ـُ ـِ] c1 → /# (v) c1[ـَّ] (10)

5 Evaluation Experiment

In order to evaluate the correctness of our system in term of agreement and ordering handling, we have developed an evaluation methodology based on a comparison between the system outputs with the original translation of the input text. The following steps describe the evaluation methodology:

(1) Run the system. (2) Compare the original translation with the system output. (3) Classify the problems that arise from the mismatches between the two translations. (4) Assign a suitable score for each problem. A range of score between 0 and 10 determines the correctness of the translation. While 0 indicates absolutely incorrect translation and 10 indicates absolutely correct (matched) translation. (5) When a situation belongs to multiple problems compute its score average. (6) Determine the correctness of the test case by computing the percentage (%) of the total scores (T.S.).

5.1 Extracting Named Entity Transliteration Experiment

The purpose of this experiment is to investigate whether the following machine translation systems (MTS), namely, Google, Bing and our system, are sufficiently robust for handling the word agreement and ordering in the translation the names from English to Arabic. The evaluation methodology is applied on 100 independent test examples. The experiment gives the following results between our system and Google & Bing as shown in Table 4. Figure 3 presents the matching chart bet. Google (a) and Bing (b) with our system.

Table 4: Experiment Results bet. System and Google & Bing

MTS	Matches	Mismatches	T.S. of Matches	T.S. of Mismatches	T.S.	%
Google	41	59	410	405	815	81.5%
Bing	40	60	400	421	821	82.1%

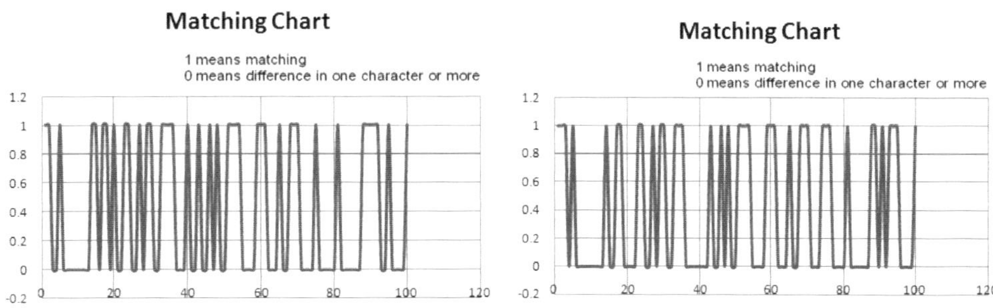

(a) Google with Our System

(b) Bing with Our System

Figure 3: Matching Charts

The percentage of the total score for each system has been found by dividing the total score by 1000; as we have 100 test examples and each is evaluated out of 10. The mismatches test examples have problems that arise from the mishandling the word agreement and ordering in the target language. The following steps classifies these problems and assigns suitable scores for them; we have classified the problems to either agreement or ordering problems as following: (1) Difference in one symbol is evaluated out of 9. (2) Difference in two symbols is evaluated out of 8. (3) Difference in three symb. is evaluated out of 7. (4) Difference in four symb. is evaluated out of 6.

6 Conclusion

We proposed an English-Arabic transliteration model using phonetic rules and pronunciation. We provided algorithms based on phonetic rules that can be used in programming a system to transliterate English names automatically. Since Arabic transcription is playing an increasingly important role in a variety of practical applications, it is necessary to pursue efforts to develop more language-specific transcription systems based on linguistic knowledge.

References

Algamdi, Mansour. 2003. *KACST Arabic Phonetics Database.* The Fifteenth International Congress of Phonetics Science, Barcelona, 3109-3112.

Carnegie Mellon University Project. *Cmusphinx, Free Pronouncing Dictionary of English.* https://cmusphinx.svn.sourceforge.net/

Helen M. Meng, Wai-Kit Lo, Berlin Chen, and Karen Tang. 2001. *Generating Phonetic Cognates to Handle Named Entities in English-Chinese Cross-Language Spoken Document Retrieval.* Proceedings of ASRU.

International Phonetic Association. *THE INTERNATIONAL PHONETIC ALPHABET.* http://www.langsci.ucl.ac.uk/ipa/IPA_chart_(C)2005.pdf/

Kevin Knight and Jonathan Graehl. 1997. *Machine transliteration.* In Proceedings of the 35th Annual Meeting of the Association for Computational Linguistics, pages 128-135.

Khaled Shaalan. 2004. *Machine Translation of English Noun Phrases into Arabic.* International Journal of Computer Processing of Oriental Languages Vol. 17, No. 2.

Knight, K. and Graehl, J. 1998. *Machine Transliteration.* Computational Linguistics: 24(4).

Lee, J. S. and K. S. Choi. 1998. *English to Korean Statistical transliteration for information retrieval.* Computer Processing of Oriental Languages,12(1):17-37.

Mansour M. Alghamdi. *Arabic International Phonetic Alphabet.* http://www.mghamdi.com/AIPA%20.pdf/

Mansour Alghamdi, Husni Almuhtasib and Mustafa Elshafei. 2004. *"Arabic Phonological Rules".* King Saud University Journal: Computer Sciences and Information. Vol. 16, pp. 1-25.

Mansur Arbabi, Scott M. Fischthal, Vincent C. Cheng, and Elizabeth Bart. 1994. *Algorithms for Arabic name transliteration.* IBM Journal of Research and Development, 38(2):183-193.

Mohamed Ali, Moustafa Elshafei, Husni Al-Muhtaseb, and Mansour Al-Ghamdi. 2007. *Automatic Segmentation of Arabic Speech.* Workshop on Information Technology and Islamic Sciences, Imam Mohammad Ben Saud University, Riyadh, March.

Paola Virga and Sanjeev Khudanpur. 2003. *Transliteration of proper names in cross-lingual information retrieval.* MultiNER '03 Proceedings of the ACL 2003 workshop on Multilingual and mixed-language named entity recognition - Volume 15.

Rached Zantout and Ahmed Guessoum. 2000. *Arabic Machine Translation: A Strategic Choice for the Arab World*, Vol. 12, Comp. and Info Sci., pp. 117-144. King Saud University, KSA.

Soudi A., Bosch A. and Neumann G. 2007. *Arabic Computational Morphology: Knowledge-based and Empirical Methods, Text and Language Technology.* Vol 38. Springer, New York.

Stalls, Bonnie G. and Kevin Knight. 1998. *"Translating Names and Technical Terms in Arabic Text".* In Proceedings of the COLING/ACL on Comput. Approaches to Semitic Lang. 19.

Sung Young Jung, SungLim Hong, and Eunok Paek. 2000. *English to Korean Transliteration Model of Extended MarkovWindow.* Proceedings of COLING.

Yan Qu, Gregory Grefenstette and David A. Evans. 2003. *Automatic Transliteration for Japanese-to-English Text Retrieval.* SIGIR03, July 28August 1, 2003, Toronto, Canada.

Translating Common English and Chinese Verb-Noun Pairs in Technical Documents with Collocational and Bilingual Information

Yi-Hsuan Chuang[†] Chao-Lin Liu[§] Jing-Shin Chang[↑]
[†§] National Chengchi University, Taiwan; [↑]National Chi Nan University, Taiwan
{[†]g9804, [§]chaolin}@cs.nccu.edu.tw, [↑]jshin@csie.ncnu.edu.tw

Abstract. We studied a special case for the translation of English verbs in verb-object pairs. Researchers have studied the effects of the linguistic information about the verbs being translated, and many have reported how considering the objects of the verbs will facilitate the quality of translations. In this study, we took an extreme venue – assuming the availability of the Chinese translations of the English objects. We explored the issue with thousands of samples that we extracted from 2011 NTCIR PatentMT workshop. The results indicated that, when the English verbs and objects were known, the information about the object's Chinese translation could still improve the quality of the verb's translations but not quite significantly.

Keywords: Machine Translation, Feature Comparison

1 Introduction

Researchers have studied extensively the problems related to verbs (e.g., Dorr *et al.*, 2002; Lapata and Brew, 2004) and phrases-based translations (e.g., Chuang *et al.*, 2005; Koehn *et al.*, 2003). Some techniques were developed for text of special domains (Seneff *et al.*, 2006). The techniques are applicable in many real-world problems, including computer-assisted language learning (Chang *et al.*, 2008) and cross-language information retrieval (Chen *et al.*, 2000).

We work on the processing of patent documents (Lu *et al.*, 2010; Yokoama and Okuyama, 2009), and present an experience in translating common verbs and their direct object based on bilingual contextual information. In this study, we took an extreme assumption of the availability of the Chinese translations of the English objects to examine whether the extra information will improve the quality of verbs' translation. The proposed methods are special in that we are crossing the boundary between translation models and language models, by considering information of the target language in the translation task. The purpose of conducting such experiments was to investigate how the availability of such bilingual and collocational information might contribute to the translation quality. It is understood and expected by many that the Chinese translations of English objects might not be available for all cases and that such information should be applied with many other features to achieve high translation quality.

The experiments were conducted with the training data available to the participants of the 2011 NTCIR Patent MT task. The corpus contains one million pairs of Chinese and English pairs. We explored four different methods to determine the verb's Chinese translation. These methods utilized the bilingual and contextual information about the English verb in different ways. Effects of these methods were compared based on experimental evaluation which conducted with 35 thousands of verb-object pairs extracted from the NTCIR corpus. (Since objects are nouns, we will refer to verb-object pairs as verb-noun pairs or VN pairs to simplify the wording.)

We provide a broad outline of our work in Section 2, present our methods for aligning the bilingual VN-pairs in Section 3, explain how we build lexicons with extra information to serve the needs of VN-pair alignment in Section 4, delineate the design of our experiments in Section 5, and discuss the experimental results in Section 6.

2 The Big Picture

Our work consisted of two major stages. We extracted the VN pairs from the original corpus. Then, we applied our translation methods to translate English words to Chinese and vice versa,

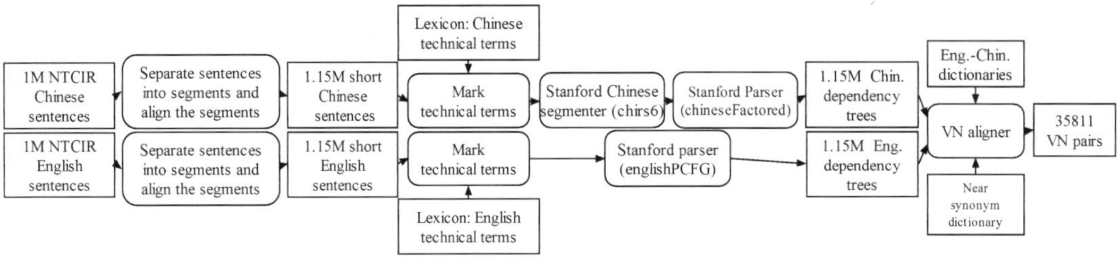

Figure 1: The flow for extracting VN pairs from the original corpora

and compared the translation quality achieved by using different combinations of contextual and bilingual information.

Figure 1 shows how the VN pairs were extracted from the 1 million parallel sentences, which we obtained from the NTCIR 9 PatentMT task in 2011[1]. The process started from the left of the figure. Most of the original sentences were very long. A sentence has 34 words on average, and the longest sentence has 141 words. Since our goal was to extract VN pairs from the corpus, not doing a full-scale research in machine translation, we choose to segment the sentences into shorter parts at commas and periods. Normally, VN pairs will not cross the punctuations, and, even if some VN pairs did, we afforded to neglect them because we had 1 million pairs of long sentences.

We then re-aligned the short English and Chinese segments with a sentence aligner (Tien *et al.*, 2009) that we implemented based on the concept of Champollion (Ma, 2006). We treated the original long sentence pairs as aligned paragraphs, and ran our aligner on the sentences. Like the Champollion, we computed probabilistic scores for the sentence pairs, so we could choose those pairs with higher scores to achieve higher confidence on the aligned pairs. More specifically, we kept only the leading 33% of the short sentence pairs, and obtained 1148632 short sentence pairs.

We employed the Stanford Chinese segmenter[2] to segment the Chinese text. This segmenter allows us to mark the technical terms so that the segmenter will treat the words belonging to technical terms as a unit, preventing them from being segmented again. In addition, currently, our technical terms are nouns, so they are annotated accordingly. When there were more than one possible ways to mark the technical terms in a string, we preferred the longer choices. English texts were tokenized by the Stanford parser[3]. Technical phrases and compound words in English were also marked and would not be treated as individual words either. The special terms came from the glossary that will be explained in Section 4.1.

Based on these short sentence pairs, we aligned VN pairs with the method to be explained in Section 3. This process employed an English-Chinese glossary for technical terms, which we will discuss in Section 4.1, and a bilingual dictionary enhanced with Chinese near synonyms, which we will discuss in Section 4.2. In the end, we accepted 35811 VN pairs for experiments at the second stage.

During the second stage of our work, we split the VN pairs into training and test data. Useful statistics were collected from the training data, and were applied to select Chinese translations for the English words in question.

3 VN Pair Alignment

We employed the Stanford parsers (SPs, henceforth) for English and Chinese to compute the dependency trees for the parallel texts. We extracted the `dobj` relations from the trees and align the VN pairs.

[1] http://ntcir.nii.ac.jp/PatentMT/

[2] http://nlp.stanford.edu/software/segmenter.shtml, version 1.5

[3] http://nlp.stanford.edu/software/lex-parser.shtml, version 1.6.5

3.1 Dependency Trees

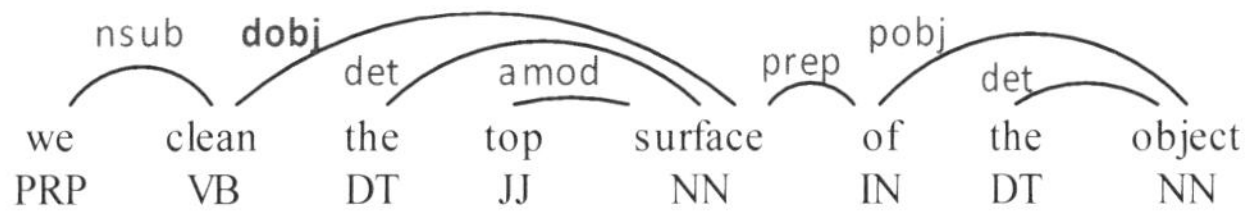

Figure 2: A sample dependency tree with POS tags

Based on the general recommendations on the Stanford site3, we parsed English with the englishPCFG.ser.gz grammar, and parsed Chinese with the chineseFactored.ser.gz grammar.

Figure 2 shows the dependency tree for a simple English sentence "`we clean the top surface of the object`". SPs can provide the part of speeches (POSes) of words and recognize the relationships between the words. POSes are shown below the words, and the relationships are attached to the links between the words. The **`dobj`** link between "`clean`" and "`surface`" indicates that "`surface`" is a direct object of "`clean`", and we could rely on such `dobj` links to identify VN pairs in the corpus.

3.2 VN Pair Alignment

We found 375041 `dobj` links in the 1.15M English sentences and 465866 `dobj` links in the Chinese part. However, not all of the words participating in a `dobj` link were real words. Hence, we looked up the words in our bilingual lexicon, which we will explain in Section 4.2. If the lexicon did not contain the words, we would not use the words in the corresponding `dobj` links as VN pairs. After this step, we had 254091 and 249591 VN pairs in English and Chinese, respectively.

We then tried to align the remaining English and Chinese VN pairs, noting that only those VN pairs that originated from the same pair of long sentence pairs can be aligned.

The alignment method can be quite simple. Let (EV, EN) and (CV, CN) denote an English and a Chinese VN pair, respectively, where EV, EN, CV, and CN denote an English verb, an English noun, a Chinese verb, and a Chinese noun. We just had to check whether CV is a possible translation of EV and whether CN is a possible translation of EN. If both answers are positive, then we aligned the VN pairs.

However, even when an English verb can carry only one sense, there can be multiple ways to translate it into Chinese, and there is no telling whether a dictionary will include all of the possible translations to contain the Chinese translations that were used in the Patent MT corpus. For instance, (improve, quality) can be translated to (改善(gai3 shan4), 品質(pin3 zhi2)) or (改進(gai3 jin4), 品質). If an English-Chinese dictionary only lists "改善" as the translation for "improve" and does not include "改進" as a possible translation, than we could not use that dictionary to align (improve, quality) and (改進, 品質). We need a way to tell that "改進" and "改善" are similar.

Therefore, we expanded the set of possible Chinese translations in a given dictionary with near synonyms, and employed the expanded dictionary to enhance the accuracy of VN pair alignment. The process of constructing such expanded dictionary is provided in Section 4.2.

After completing the VN pair alignment, we obtained 35811 aligned VN pairs, cf. Figure 1.

4 Lexicon Constructions

We explain (1) how we built the glossary of technical terms and (2) how we constructed a bilingual dictionary that contains information about near synonyms in this section.

4.1 Creating a Glossary of Technical Terms

As explained in Section 2, we built a glossary of technical terms so that we can separate technical terms from normal text, thereby achieving higher quality of parsing.

We downloaded 138 different kinds of domain technical term pairs from Taiwan National Academy for Educational Research[4]. The files were stored in excel format, and the total file size is 177MB.

The format of English-Chinese technical term pairs is not always in one-to-one relationship; some English technical terms have more than one translation in Chinese. We converted such pairs into multiple one-to-one pairs, and acquired 804068 English-Chinese technical term one-to-one pairs.

To validate the reliability of the glossary, we conducted a small experiment; that is, to segment patent sentences with the glossary. The results showed that the coverage of these "technical term" pairs was too broad, and almost all of words were considered as technical terms.

We alleviated this problem with E-HowNet[5] (Chen *et al.*, 2005) and WordNet[6]. Treating the words listed in E-HowNet and WordNet as ordinary words, we used them to identify normal words in our technical term pairs. If the original pairs contained any normal Chinese or English words, then the pairs would be removed.

As a result, we removed 14% of the original pairs, and kept 690640 technical term pairs.

4.2 The English-Chinese Dictionary and Near Synonyms

As announced in Section 3.2, we built a bilingual dictionary and enhanced it with information about near synonyms to improve the recall rates of the VN pair alignment.

A good English-Chinese dictionary is the basis for the task of VN pair alignment. We collected and combined the Chinese translations of English words in the Concise Oxford English Dictionary and the Dr.eye online dictionary[7], and acquired 99805 pairs of English words and their translations.

As we explained in Section 3.2, the Chinese translations listed in the dictionaries might not be complete, so we enhanced the merged dictionary with information about near synonyms. We employed two sources of relevant information to obtain near synonyms in this study.

The Web-based service of Word-Focused Extensive Reading System[8] (Cheng, 2004) is maintained by the Institute of Linguistics of the Academia Sinica in Taiwan. The service allows us to submit queries for the near synonyms of Chinese words for free, so we collected the near synonyms from the web site.

Given an entry in our bilingual dictionary, we queried the near synonyms for each of the Chinese translations of an English word, and added the results to the Chinese translations of the English word.

E-HowNet is another source that we could compute and obtain near synonyms. E-HowNet is a lexicon for Chinese. The lexicon contains two levels of detailed semantic information for words: TopLevelDefinition and BottomLevelExpansion. The semantic definitions provided in these two entries come from the E-HowNet Ontology[9], and can be used to compute similarity scores between word senses.

We determine whether two Chinese words are near synonyms with the following procedure. Given a Chinese word, CW, we looked up the E-HowNet for its senses. Let $S_i(CW)$ be one of CW's senses. We combined the semantic definitions listed in the TopLevelDefinition and BottomLevelExpansion of $S_i(CW)$, which might include multiple words. Denote this set by $U_i(CW)$, and let CWW_{ij} be a word in $U_i(CW)$. We looked up the E-HowNet for the senses of CWW_{ij}. Let $S_k(CWW_{ij})$ denote one of the senses of the CWW_{ij}, and $V_{ijk}(CWW_{ij})$ denote the combined semantic definitions listed in the TopLevelDefinition and BottomLevelExpansion of $S_k(CWW_{ij})$. Finally, we computed the union of $U_i(CW)$ and $V_{ijk}(CWW_{ij})$ as a sense vector of CW. Note that

[4] http://terms.nict.gov.tw/
[5] http://ckip.iis.sinica.edu.tw/taxonomy/taxonomy-edoc.htm
[6] http://wordnet.princeton.edu/
[7] http://www.dreye.com/index_en.html
[8] http://elearning.ling.sinica.edu.tw/c_help.html
[9] http://ckip.iis.sinica.edu.tw/taxonomy/taxonomy-edoc.htm

due to lexical ambiguity, a Chinese word might have multiple such vectors. Two Chinese words were considered as near synonyms if the cosine value of any of their sense vectors exceeded 0.7.

Given an entry in our bilingual dictionary, we compute the near synonyms of the Chinese translations of each English word. This was carried out by comparing the sense vectors of a Chinese translation with 88074 Chinese words in E-HowNet. The qualified words were added to the Chinese translations of the English word in our dictionary.

The purpose of adding information about near synonyms into our bilingual dictionary was to increase the recall rates of VN-pair alignment. More complex methods for identifying synonyms, e.g. (Bundanitsky and Hirst, 2006; Chang and Chiou, 2010) will be instrumental for the study.

5 Design of the Experiments

We have conducted experiments to translate from English to Chinese and from Chinese to English. In addition, we have tried to find the best translations of verbs, and tried to find the best translations of objects of the verbs given their contexts. Nevertheless, we present only the experiments of translating English verbs to Chinese verbs in this paper.

5.1 Statistics about the Aligned VN pairs

We calculated the frequencies of the verbs in the 35811 aligned VN pairs, and ranked the verbs based on the observed frequencies. Table 1 shows the 20 most frequent English verbs and their frequencies. We identified the 100 most frequent English verbs and the corresponding aligned VN pairs in our experiments. In total, there were 30376 such aligned VN pairs. The most frequent English verb appeared 4530 times, as shown in Table 1. The 100th most frequent English verb is "lack", and it appeared 47 times.

Some of the English verbs are relatively easier to translate than others. We can calculate the frequencies of the Chinese translations of verbs to verify the differences. For instance, "add" was translated in five different ways: "增加"(zeng1 jia1) 48 times, "添加"(tian1 jia1) 44 times, "加入"(jia1 ru4) 43 times, "加上"(jia1 shang4) 2 times , and "增添"(zeng1 tian1) 1 time. The distribution, (48, 44, 43, 2, 1), is not very skewed, and the frequencies of the most frequent translation and the second most frequent translation are close. Therefore, we would not achieve very good results, if we should choose to use the most frequent translation for all occurrences of "add".

Based on this observation, we defined the *challenging index* of a word as the ratios of the frequency of their most frequent translation against the frequency of their second most frequent translation. The challenging index of "add" mentioned in the previous paragraph is 1.09.

This challenging index is not a scientifically-proven index for difficulty for translation, but could serve as a heuristic. The larger the index; the easier to achieve good translation by using the most frequent translation to translate. Table 2 lists 22 verbs that had the smallest challenging indexes.

5.2 Translation Decisions

Given the aligned VN pairs, we could compute conditional probabilities, and apply the condi-

Table 1: 20 most frequent English verbs in the aligned VN pairs

Verb	have	provide	use	include	comprise	contain	form	receive	reduce	perform
Freq.	4530	3345	1993	1954	1588	1080	914	863	774	616
Verb	increase	produce	maintain	determine	represent	show	obtain	achieve	improve	allow
Freq.	465	453	397	382	373	352	329	329	322	287

Table 2: 22 most "challenging" English verbs and their indexes

Verb	make	exhibit	add	represent	retain	leave	enhance	reduce	lack	improve	achieve
	1.00	1.09	1.09	1.21	1.21	1.22	1.25	1.26	1.27	1.33	1.39
Verb	employ	reach	create	give	replace	take	apply	adjust	obtain	carry	explain
	1.41	1.43	1.50	1.54	1.69	1.69	1.69	1.72	1.76	1.82	2.00

tional probabilities to determine the Chinese translation of English words.

Table 3: Translation decisions

$\arg\max_{CV_i} \Pr(CV_i \mid EV)$	(1)
$\arg\max_{CV_i} \Pr(CV_i \mid EV, EN)$	(2)
$\arg\max_{CV_i} \Pr(CV_i \mid EV, EN, CN)$	(3)
$\arg\max_{CV_i} \Pr(CV_i \mid EV, CN)$	(4)

Table 3 lists four possible ways to choose a Chinese translation for an English verb in a VN pair. Equation (1) is the most simplistic. Let EV denote a specific English verb, and CV_i be one of EV's translations observed in the training data. Given the English verb, the equation chooses the CV_i that maximizes the conditional probability. Namely, it prefers the most frequent Chinese translation of EV in the training data.

We could obtain the conditional probability $\Pr(CV_i|EV)$ by dividing the frequency of observing the VN pair (EV, CV_i) in the training data by the frequency of observing EV in any VN pairs. Using the data for "add" that we mentioned in Section 5.1 for example, we observed 135 occurrences of "add". Therefore, Pr("增加" | "add") = 48/135=0.356 and Pr("加上" | "add") = 2/135=0.015.

Let EN be a specific English noun, Equation (2) considers the object of the verb when choosing the verb's translation. Let $C(\bullet)$ denote the frequency of a given event. The conditional probability in Equation (2) is defined below.

$$\frac{C(EV,EN,CV_i)}{C(EV,EN)} \tag{5}$$

The remaining equations, (3) and (4), take an extreme assumption. We assumed the availability of the Chinese translation of the English object at the time of translation, and used this special information in different ways. Equation (3) considers the words EV, EN, and CN. In a strong contrast, Equation (4) considers only EV and CN to determine the translation of the English verb. The conditional probabilities in Equations (3) and (4) were calculated using Equation (6) and (7), respectively.

$$\frac{C(EV,EN,CV_i,CN)}{C(EV,EN,CN)} \tag{6}$$

$$\frac{C(EV,CN,CV_i)}{C(EV,CN)} \tag{7}$$

We considered the exploration of using the information about the Chinese translation of the English noun is interesting. Would the information about CN provide more information, given we had information about EV and EN? How would we achieve when we had information about only EV and CN but not EN?

In all of the experiments, we used 80% of the available aligned VN pairs as the training data, and the remaining 20% as test data. The training data were randomly sampled from the available data.

As a consequence, it was possible for us to encounter the zero probability problems. Take Equation (6) for example. If, for a test case, we needed C(EV, EN, CN) in (6), but we happened not to have observed any instances of (EV, EN, CN) in the aligned VN pairs in the training data, then we would not be able to compute (6) for the test case. When such cases occurred, we chose to allow our system to admit that it was not able to recommend a translation, rather than resorting to the smoothing technologies.

6 Experimental Results

Using the formula in Table 3 would allow our systems to recommend only one Chinese translation. In fact, we relax this unnecessary constraint by allowing our systems to consider that largest *k* conditional probabilities and to recommend *k* translations.

Although we have been presenting this paper with the 1 million parallel sentences in NTCIR PatentMT data as the example, we have run our experiments with the English-Chinese bilingual version of Scientific American. Moreover, we ran experiments that aimed at finding the best Chinese translations of English objects. The formulas were defined analogously with those listed in Table 3.

6.1 Basic Results for the Top 100 Verbs in Patent Documents

When we conducted experiments for the top 100 verbs (cf. Section 5.1), we had 24300 instances of aligned VN pairs for training and 6076 instances of aligned VN pairs for test.

We measured four rates as the indication of the performance of using a particular formula in Table 3. The *rejection rate* is the percentage of not being to respond to the test cases. This is due to our choosing not to smooth the probability distributions as we explained in Section 5.2.

Table 4: Inclusion rates for top 100 verbs

inclusion	*k*=1	*k*=3	*k*=5
Eq1	0.768	0.953	0.975
Eq2	0.786	0.913	0.918
Eq3	0.795	0.911	0.916
Eq4	0.791	0.910	0.916

Table 5: Average number of recommendations

recommend	*k*=1	*k*=3	*k*=5
Eq1	1.000	2.919	4.614
Eq2	1.000	1.923	2.225
Eq3	1.000	1.847	2.107
Eq4	1.000	1.920	2.244

Table 6: Average ranks of the answers

ranking	*k*=1	*k*=3	*k*=5
Eq1	1.000	1.241	1.310
Eq2	1.000	1.166	1.185
Eq3	1.000	1.151	1.168
Eq4	1.000	1.153	1.173

It is not surprising that the rejection rates increased as we considered more information in the formulas. The rejections rates were 0, 0.201, 0.262, and 0.218 when we applied Equations (1) through (4) in the experiments. As expected, we encountered the highest rejection rate when using (3). Note that using (4) resulted in a higher rejection rate than using (2). This was because that there were no less than one possible Chinese translations for any English verbs. Hence, the distributions for $\Pr(CV_i \mid EV\ CN)$ would be more sparse than $\Pr(CV_i \mid EV\ EN)$ on average.

Table 4 shows the rates of the correct answers were included in the recommended *k* translations. We did not consider the cases that our systems could not answer in computing the statistics in Table 4. Hence, the data show the average inclusion rates when our systems could answer. As one may have expected, when we increased *k*, the inclusion rates also increased.

It may be surprising that the inclusion rates for Equations (2) through (4) seem to have saturated when we increase *k* from 3 to 5. This was because our systems could not actually recommend 5 possible translations, when they were allowed. Although we had hundreds or thousands of aligned VN pairs for an English verb, cf. Table 1. Including more conditioning information in Equations (2) through (4) still reduced the amount of VN pairs qualified for training and testing, thereby limiting the actual numbers of recommended translations. Table 5 shows the average number of actual recommendations in the tests.

The main advantage of using Equations (2) through (4) is that they were more precise, when they could answer. Table 6 shows the average ranks of the correct translation in the recommended translations. The average ranks improve as we considered more information from Equation (1) to (2) and to (3). Using (2) achieved almost the same average rank with using (4), but using (4) led to slightly better performance.

6.2 Improving Results for the Top 100 Verbs in Patent Documents

Results reported in the previous subsection indicated that Equation (4) is robust in that it could offer candidate answers all the time. Methods that employed more information could choose translations more precisely, but were less likely to respond to test cases. Hence, a natural question is whether we could combine these methods to achieve better performance. To answer this question, we conducted all of the combinations of the basic methods listed in Table 3.

In Tables 7 and 8, we use the notation EqX+EqY to indicate that we used EqX to find as many candidate translations as possible, before we reached a total of *k* recommendations. If applying EqX could not offer sufficient candidate translations, we applied EqY to recommend more candidate translations until we acquired *k* recommendations.

Using Eq1 is sufficiently robust in that the conditional probabilities would not be zero, unless the training data did not contain any instances that included the English verb. Hence, in our experiments, the rejection rates for "Eq2+Eq1", "Eq3+Eq1", and "Eq4+Eq1" became zero. In other words, our systems responded to all test cases when we used these combined methods by allowing all methods to recommend up to *k* candidates.

We compare the performance of these combined methods with the best performing methods in Tables 7 and 8. We copy the inclusion rates of Eq1 from Table 4 to Table 7 to facilitate the comparison, because Eq1 was the best performer, on average, in Table 4. The combined methods improved the inclusion rates, although the improvement was marginal.

Table 7: Inclusion rates (combined methods)

inclusion	*k*=1	*k*=3	*k*=5
Eq1	0.768	0.953	0.975
Eq2+Eq1	0.772	0.960	0.979
Eq3+Eq1	0.778	0.960	0.979
Eq4+Eq1	0.776	0.959	0.978

Table 8: Average ranks of the correct answers (combined methods)

ranking	*k*=1	*k*=3	*k*=5
Eq1	1.000	1.241	1.310
Eq3	1.000	1.151	1.168
Eq2+Eq1	1.000	1.240	1.301
Eq3+Eq1	1.000	1.234	1.294
Eq4+Eq1	1.000	1.233	1.296

Moreover, we copy the average ranks for Eq1 and Eq3 from Table 6 to Table 8. Using Eq1 and using Eq3 led to the worst and the best average ranks in Table 6, respectively. Again, using the combined methods, we improve the average ranks marginally over the results of using Eq1.

Statistics in Table 7 suggest that using machine-assisted approach to translating verbs in common VN pairs in the PatentMT data is feasible. Providing the top five candidates to a human translator to choice will allow the translator to find the recorded answer s nearly 98% of the time.

It is interesting to find that using Equation (2) and Equation (4) did not lead to significantly different results in Tables (4) through (8). The results suggest that using either the English nouns or the Chinese nouns as a condition contributed similarly to the translation quality of the English verbs. More specifically, the translation of the English verb may be conditionally independent of the information about the noun's Chinese translation given the English verb and the English noun. This does not imply that the translation of the English verb is unconditionally independent of the information of the English noun's translation. That Eq4 performed better than Eq1 in Table 6 offered a reasonable support.

6.3 Results for the Most Challenging 22 Verbs in Patent Documents

We repeated the experiments that we conducted for the top 100 verbs for the most challenging 22 verbs (cf. Section 5.1). Tables 9 through 13 correspond to Tables 4 through 8, respectively. The most noticeable difference between Table 9 and Table 4 is the reduction of the inclusion rates achieved by Eq1 when *k*=1. Although the inclusion rates reduced noticeably when we used Eq2, Eq3, and Eq4 as well, the drop in the inclusion rate for Eq1 (when *k*=1) was the most significant.

Although we did not define the challenging index of verbs based on their numbers of possible translations, comparing the corresponding numbers in Table 10 and Table 5 suggest that the challenging verbs also have more possible translations in the NTCIR data.

Corresponding numbers in Table 11 and

Table 9: Inclusion rates for 22 challenging verbs

inclusion	*k*=1	*k*=3	*k*=5
Eq1	0.449	0.865	0.923
Eq2	0.561	0.818	0.820
Eq3	0.564	0.827	0.829
Eq4	0.550	0.827	0.829

Table 10: Average number of recommendations

recommend	*k*=1	*k*=3	*k*=5
Eq1	1.000	2.977	4.756
Eq2	1.000	2.090	2.364
Eq3	1.000	2.022	2.230
Eq4	1.000	2.106	2.411

Table 11: Average ranks of the answers

ranking	*k*=1	*k*=3	*k*=5
Eq1	1.000	1.607	1.773
Eq2	1.000	1.365	1.373
Eq3	1.000	1.374	1.383
Eq4	1.000	1.394	1.400

Table 6 supports the claim that translating the 22 challenging words is relatively more difficult. The average ranks of the answers became worse in Table 11.

Data in Tables 12 and 13 repeat the trends that we observed in Tables 7 and 8. Using the combined methods allowed us to answer all test cases, and improved both the inclusion rates and the average ranks of the answers.

If we built a computer-assisted translation system for these 22 verbs, the performance would not be as good as if we built a system for the top 100 verbs. When the system suggested the leading 3 translations (k=3), the inclusion rates dropped to around 0.90 in Table 12 from 0.96 in Table 7.

Table 12: Inclusion rates (combined methods)

inclusion	*k*=1	*k*=3	*k*=5
Eq1	0.449	0.865	0.923
Eq2+Eq1	0.512	0.896	0.940
Eq3+Eq1	0.503	0.894	0.940
Eq4+Eq1	0.508	0.900	0.942

Table 13: Average ranks of the correct answers (combined methods)

ranking	*k*=1	*k*=3	*k*=5
Eq1	1.000	1.607	1.773
Eq3	1.000	1.374	1.383
Eq2+Eq1	1.000	1.537	1.662
Eq3+Eq1	1.000	1.546	1.677
Eq4+Eq1	1.000	1.547	1.664

Again, using either the English nouns or the Chinese nouns, along with the English verbs, in the conditions of the methods listed in Table 3 did not make significant differences, as suggested by the results in Tables 9 through 13.

6.4 More Experimental Results

We repeated the experiments that we conducted for the top 100 verbs for the top 100 nouns in the PatentMT data. For experiments with the nouns, we had only 3952 test instances. The goals were to find the best Chinese translation of the English objects, given its contextual and bilingual information. More specifically, in addition to the English verbs and the English nouns, we were interested in whether providing the Chinese translations of the English verbs would help us improve the translation quality of the English objects.

Due to the page limits, we could not show all of the tables as we did in Section 6.1. The statistics showed analogous trends that we reported in Section 6.1. Namely, the availability of the Chinese translation of the English verbs did not help, when we already considered the English verbs and objects in the translation decisions.

Scientific American is a magazine for general public. The writing style is more close to ordinary lives. We ran a limited scale of experiment with available text from Scientific American. We had about 1500 training instances and 377 test instances for 25 verbs. The results indicated that using the Chinese translations of the English objects influenced the translation quality of the English verbs. However, the observed differences were not significant. A side observation was that it was relatively harder to find good translation of English verbs in Scientific American than in the PatentMT data. When providing five recommendations, only about 88% of the time the recommendations of our system can include the correct translation. In contrast, we had achieved inclusion rates well above 90% in Tables 7 and 12.

7 Concluding Remarks

We designed a procedure to extract and align VN pairs in a bilingual corpus of patent documents. The corpus contains 1 million pairs of English and Chinese sentences, and we aligned 35811 VN pairs. We employed the VN pairs to investigate whether the availability of the Chinese translations for nouns in English VN pairs would improve the translation quality of the English verbs. Experimental results suggest that the Chinese translation of the English noun is marginally helpful when both the English verbs and English nouns are already available. Choosing the best Chinese translation of the English verb based on the constraint of its English object or based on the information about the object's Chinese translation achieved similarly in the experiments.

Additional and analogous experiments were conducted with the PatentMT data. In these new experiments, we aimed at the translations of the nouns in the English VN pairs, given different combinations of the bilingual and contextual information. Again, we observed that, after putting the English verb and English noun in the conditions in the attachment decision formulas (analogous to but slightly different with those in Table 3), the Chinese translations of the English verbs did not offer extra help. In addition, using (1) the English verb and the English noun or (2) the Chinese verb and the English noun achieved similar experimental results.

Acknowledgments

The work was supported in part by the funding from the National Science Council in Taiwan under the contracts NSC-99-2221-E-004-007 and NSC-100-2221-E-004-014. The authors are obliged to the anonymous reviewers for their valuable comments because we could not respond satisfactorily to all comments due to the page limits on this paper.

References

Bundanitsky, A. and G. Hirst. 2006. Evaluating WordNet-based measures of lexical semantic relatedness. *Computational Linguistics*, 32(1):14–47.

Carpuat, M., P. Fung and G. Ngai. 2006. Aligning word senses using bilingual corpora. *ACM Trans. on Asian Language Information Processing*, 5(2):89–120.

Chang, J.-S. and S.-J. Chiou. 2010. An EM algorithm for context-based searching and disambiguation with application to synonym term alignment. *Proc. of the 23rd Pacific Asia Conf. on Language, Information and Computation*, 2:630–637.

Chang, Y. C., J. S. Chang, H. J. Chen and H. C. Liou. 2008. An automatic collocation writing assistant for Taiwanese EFL learners: A case of corpus-based NLP technology. *Computer Assisted Language Learning*, 21(3):283–299.

Cheng, C. C. 2004. Word-focused extensive reading with guidance. *Selected Papers from the 13th International Symposium and Book Fair on English Teaching*, 24-32. http://elearning.ling.sinica.edu.tw/WordFocused%20Extensive%20Reading%20with%20Guidance.pdf

Chuang, T. C., J.-Y. Jian, Y.-C. Chang and J. S. Chang. 2005. Collocational translation memory extraction based on statistical and linguistic information. *Int'l J. of Computational Linguistics and Chinese Language Processing*, 10(3):329–346.

Chen, A., H. Jiang and F. Gey. 2000. Combining multiple sources for short query translation in Chinese-English cross-language information retrieval. *Proc. of the 5th Int'l Workshop on Information Retrieval with Asian Languages*, 17–23.

Chen, K.-J., S.-L. Huang, Y.-Y. Shih and Y.-J. Chen. 2005. Extended-HowNet: A representational framework for concepts. *Proc. of the 2005 IJCNLP Workshop on Ontologies and Lexical Resources*, 1–6.

Dorr, B. J., G.-A. Levow and D. Lin. 2002. Construction of a Chinese-English verb lexicon for machine translation and embedded multilingual applications. *Machine Translation*, 17:99–137.

Koehn, P., F. J. Och and D. Marcu. 2003. Statistical phrase-based translation. *Proc. of the 2003 Conf. of the North American Chapter of the Association for Computational Linguistics on Human Language Technology*, 48-54.

Lapata, M. and C. Brew. 2004. Verb class disambiguation using informative priors. *Computational Linguistics*, 30(1):45–73.

Lu, B., B. K. Tsou, T. Jiang, O. Y. Kwong and J. Zhu. 2010. Mining large-scale parallel corpora from multilingual patents: An English-Chinese example and its application to SMT. *Proc. of the 1st CIPS-SIGHAN Joint Conf. on Chinese Language Processing*.

Ma, X. 2006. Champollion: A robust parallel text sentence aligner. *Proc. of the 5th Int'l Conf. of the Language Resources and Evaluation*, 489–492.

Seneff, S., C. Wang and J. Lee. 2006. Combining linguistic and statistical methods for bi-directional English Chinese translation in the flight domain. *Proc. of the 7th Conf. of the Association for Machine Translation in the Americas*, 213–222.

Tien, K.-W., Y.-H. Tseng and C.-L. Liu. 2009. Sentence alignment of English and Chinese patent documents, *Proc. of the 21st Conf. on Computational Linguistics and Speech Processing*, 85–99.

Yokoama, S. and M. Okuyama. 2009. Translation disambiguation of patent sentences using case frames. *Proc. of the 3rd Workshop on Patent Translation*, in Machine Translation Summit XII, 33–36.

System for Flexibly Judging the Misuse of Honorifics in Japanese*

Tamotsu Shirado[a], Satoko Marumoto[b], Masaki Murata[c], and Hitoshi Isahara[d]

[a]National Institute of Information and Communications Technology,
Kyoto, 619-0289 Japan
shirado@nict.go.jp

[b]The Institute of Behavioral Sciences,
Tokyo, 162-0845 Japan
smarumoto@ibs.or.jp

[c]Tottori University,
Tottori, 680-8550 Japan
murata@ike.tottori-u.ac.jp

[d]Toyohashi University of Technology,
Aichi, 441-8580 Japan
isahara@tut.ac.jp

Abstract. We propose a system for flexibly judging the misusage of honorifics in Japanese sentence. The system can point out misused words and phrases, and can also indicate how they are misused. The system uses judgment rules whose degrees of validity in modern Japanese society are quantified by psychological experiments. The system can judge sentences flexibly based on the learner's linguistic level by tuning thresholds regarding the degree of validity. The proposed system is expected to be applied in practical computer-aided education.

Keywords: Japanese, honorifics, misuse, judgment, education

1 Introduction

In Japan, linguistic honorifics play an important role in social activities, especially in conversations. There are few languages in which such linguistic honorifics are as highly developed as Japanese.

One important function of linguistic honorifics is to awaken in each person a consciousness of the social-relationship among speakers, listeners, and individuals being addressed or referred to. Here, social-relationship is assumed to be represented by a combination of {relative social position among in the people in same group} and {in-group/out-group relationship} in our study.

The correct usage of honorific expressions is indispensable to maintain appropriate social distance between individuals and assists smooth communication in Japanese society.

Recently, however, increasing misusage of honorific expressions has been noted. One origin of such misusage may be poor education regarding linguistic honorifics. So, development of a computer-aided learning system for linguistic honorifics has been needed.

Recently, Shirado (2007) proposed a system to judge the misusage of honorific expressions in Japanese. The system uses judgment rules constructed from textbooks of Japanese honorifics. However, these textbooks are not necessarily consistent with the awareness among the people regarding normative honorific expressions in modern Japanese society. Most of these textbooks

* This research was supported by JSPS KAKENHI 21520424.

are based on traditional studies even though linguistic norms change over time. So, more practical system to learn linguistic honorifics is needed.

In this paper, we propose a system to flexibly judge the misusage of honorific expressions in Japanese sentences. This system uses the framework of the system proposed by Shirado, but our system is more practical than the previous one due to the following points:

1. The judgment rules are generalized.
2. The degrees of the validity of rules are quantified.
3. Judgments are performed flexibly based on the learner's linguistic level.

2 Misusage of Japanese Honorific Expressions

2.1 Types of the Japanese Honorific Expressions

Japanese honorific expressions can be divided into the following types:

Sonkeigo (in Japanese) shows respect toward a person, who is usually the subject of sentence's predicate, by elevating the person's status. *Sonkeigo* principally includes: (1) such honorific titles as "*san*"/"*sama*," (2) respectful forms of verbs, (3) verb stems + auxiliary verbs, and (4) "*o*"/ "*go*" (prefixes) + verb stems + auxiliary verbs.

Kenjougo-I (in Japanese) shows respect toward a person, who is usually the object of the sentence's predicate, by humbling the speaker or the predicate's subject. *Kenjougo*-I principally includes: (1) humble forms of verbs, (2) verb stems + auxiliary verbs, and (3) "*o*"/"*go*" (prefixes) + verb stems + auxiliary verbs.

Kenjougo-II (or *Teichougo*) (in Japanese) shows politeness, but not necessarily respect, toward the listener by using humbling form of predicates regarding the speaker's action etc. *Kenjougo*-II includes "*mousu*"/"*mairu*"/ "*itasu*," etc.

Teineigo (in Japanese) shows politeness, but not necessarily respect, toward a person, who is usually the listener. *Teineigo* includes an auxiliary verb at the end of a sentence, such as "*desu*"/"*masu*"/"*gozaimasu*," etc.

Table 1 show examples of morphemes corresponding to each honorific type.

Table 1: Honorific type.

Morphemes	Honorific type
"A" "*san*"	honorific title of person A
"B" "*sama*"	honorific title of person B
"*osharu*"	*sonkeigo*
verb stem "*rareru*"	*sonkeigo*
"*o*" verb stem "*kudasaru*"	*sonkeigo*
"*go*" verb stem "*kudasaru*"	*sonkeigo*
verb stem "*itasu*"	*kenjougo-I*
"*o*" verb stem "*suru*"	*kenjougo-I*
"*go*" verb stem "*suru*"	*kenjougo-I*
"*mousu*"	*kenjougo-II*
"*go*" "*suru*" "*te*" "*kudasaru*"	*kenjougo-I* + *sonkeigo*
"*desu*" "."	*teineigo*
"*masu*" "."	*teineigo*

2.2 Categories of Misusage of Honorific Expressions

The misusage of honorific expressions can be divided into two categories:

Misusage in word form: The word form is not normative; i.e., the word form differs from the normative word forms mentioned in Section 2.1. For example, "*o*"(a pre-fix) + verb stem +

"*rareru*" (an auxiliary verb) is a misusage in word form because "*rareru*" is not allowed to be used in this word form.

Misusage in performance: The word form is normative, but is not consistent with the social-relationship among the speakers, listeners, and individuals being addressed or referred to in the sentence. For example, a sentence that does not contain *Teineigo* is usually considered a misusage in performance when the listener's social position is higher than the speaker's.

The misusage in word form can be avoided simply by preparing a sufficient list of normative and non-normative word forms. The present study concentrated on misusage in performance.

3 Framework

3.1 Restriction

In our study, each input sentence is assumed to satisfy the following conditions:

1) at most, four persons - speaker, listener, and two others (denoted as "A" and "B") being addressed or referred to - are involved in the sentence,

2) one predicate in the sentence that has one subject person and one object person

3.2 Honorific Feature

Since all sentences inputted to the system are assumed to satisfy the restrictions stated in Section 3.1, the honorific features of the sentence can be represented by the set of *s*, *o*, *e*, and *p* defined in Table 2. For example, the honorific features of sentence "*A ga kimi ni gosetsumei suru*," ("person A explains something to you") is s=0, o=0, e=0, p=2, because the subject is person A, the object is listener ("*kimi*"), there are no honorific titles for the subject and object persons, the honorific type of the auxiliary verb ("*suru*") at the end of the sentence is not polite, and the honorific type of the predicate ("*gosetsumei*") is *kenjougo*-I.

Table 2: Honorific features.

Honorific value	Explanation
s=0	No honorific title for subject
s=1	Honorific title for subject
o=0	No honorific title for object
o=1	Honorific title for object
e=0	Honorific type of auxiliary verb at end of sentence is not polite. / No auxiliary verb at end of sentence
e=1	Honorific type of auxiliary verb at end of sentence is polite
p=0	Honorific type of predicate is neither *sonkeigo* nor *kenjougo-I* nor *kenjougo-II*
p=1	Honorific type of predicate is *sonkeigo*
p=2	Honorific type of predicate is *kenjougo-I*
p=3	Honorific type of predicate is *kenjougo-I + senkeigo*
p=4	Honorific type of predicate is *kenjougo-II*

3.3 Judgment Rules

We constructed rules for judging the misusage of honorific expression based on the existing rule proposed by Shirado. Our rules are more general than the existing one because our rules can be applied for any number (up to two, three, or four) of persons. But the existing rules were divided into three kinds for two, three, and four persons. The experimental results using the test sets adapted by Shirado show that our rules are identical to the existing rules regarding the judgment ability.

Table 3 shows part of the judgment rules, which define the honorific consistency between the social-relationship among persons (and specifications of the subject/object persons in some of them) and the honorific feature of sentence that is honorifically consistent with the social-relationship.

Table 3: Part of judgment rules.

Rule No.	Explanation	Social-relationship among persons	Specification of subject / object	Honorific feature s=0/1 o=0/1 e=0/1 p=0/1/2/3/4
1	Rules regarding honorific title of subject (honorific feature s)	(S)(subject)	no	s=1
2		(subject > S) and (S, L)	no	s=1
3		(subject, S)(L)	no	s=0
4		(S => subject)	no	s=0
5		Any	S is subject	s=0
6	Rules regarding honorific title of object (honorific feature o)	(object)(S)	no	o=1
7		(object > S) and (S, L)	no	o=1
8		(object, S)(L)	no	o=0
9		(S => object)	no	o=0
10		Any	S is object	o=0
11	Rules regarding politeness of end of sentence (honorific feature e)	(L > S)	no	e=1
12		(S)(L)	no	e=1
13		(S => L)	no	e=0
14	Rules regarding type of predicate (honorific feature p)	(subject > S) and (S, L)	no	p=1
15		(S => L)(object) and (S => subject)	no	p=0 or 2
16		(S => L)(object)	S is subject	p=0 or 2
17		(S => subject) and (S => object) and (S => L)	no	p=0

In Table 3, symbols "S", "L", "subject", and "object" indicate the speaker, the listener, the subject person of the predicate, and the object person of the predicate, respectively. {"X>Y" / "X=>"Y"} means that the social position of the person corresponding to symbol X {is higher than / is higher than or equal to} that of the person corresponding to symbol Y. {"(X)(Y)"/ "(X)(Y)(Z)"} means that {X and Y / X and Y and Z} are the out-group, {"(X,Y)" / "(X,Y,Z)"} means that {X and Y / X and Y and Z} are the in-group and there is no restriction as to the relative social position between them, where X/Y/Z are S (speaker)", "L (listener)", "A (person A)", or "B (person B)" and are different.

Table 3 consists of four kinds of rule groups, each of which corresponds to each of honorific features s, o, e, p. For example, the top rule in Table 3 means that honorific feature s of the sentence must be 1 (i.e., the honorific title of the subject must appear in the sentence) when the speaker and the subject are the out-group.

4 Quantification of Degree of Validity of Judgment Rules by Psychological Experiments

4.1 Experiment

For all the honorific features (*s*, *o*, *e*, *p*) of each rule, we quantified the degree of validity by a psychological experiment using Scheffe's paired comparison method (1952).

One hundred and three peoples, all of them are over thirty years old and non-experts in Japanese linguistics, participated in the experiment.

Figure 1 shows an example of an answer sheet. The social-relationship among persons ("speaker > person A > listener"), speech intention ("person-A explains something to you"), and a pair of different types of predicates of "*setsumei suru*" (i.e., non-honorific) and "*gosetsumei suru*" (i.e., *kenjougo*-I) are described in the sheet. Each subject answered which honorific type of predicate was more honorifically appropriate to use and to what extent by marking the answer sheets with an O. If the subjects felt that both predicates were equally appropriate or inappropriate, they marked the O halfway between them.

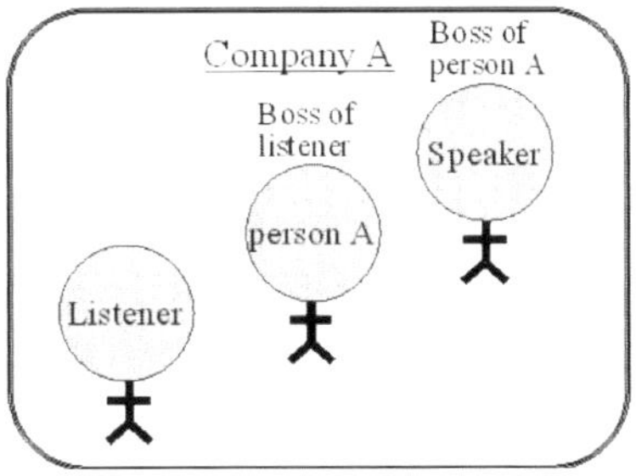

[Question]
A social-relationship among persons is given in the figure above.
Assume that a speaker is talking to a listener.
The speech intention is "person A explains something to you."
Answer which type of
non-honorific predicates (ex., "*setsumei suru*") and *kenjougo-I* (ex., "*gosetsumei suru*")
is more appropriate to express "explains"
by selecting among the following choices:

must be non-honorific	may be non-honorific	both good/bad	may be *kenjougo-I*	must be *kenjougo-I*

Figure 1: Example of answer sheet.

For all honorific features (*s*, *o*, *e*, *p*), all the pairs of the stimuli corresponding to each value of each honorific feature were presented one at a time to each subject. For example, all pairs of non-honorifics (p=0) / *sonkeigo* (p=1) / *kenjougo*-I (p=2) / *kenjougo*-I + *sonkeigo* (p=3) / *kenjougo*-II (p=4) were presented in the experiments regarding the honorific feature p.

All kinds of social-relationships, each of which represents a typical social-relationship described in each rule, are presented in the answer sheet. For example, we assumed that social-relationship "speaker > person A > listener" is the typical social-relationship described in rule No. 17 of Table 3.

4.2 Experimental Results

Table 4 shows part of the values of the degrees of validity obtained by the experiment. Common rule numbers are used between Tables 4 and 3. Each value of the degree of validity is shown in parentheses followed by each value of the honorific feature, where values with/without bold face mean that they are/are not described in Table 3. The larger the value, the more the degree of validity. Due to the quantification method, the value of the validity theoretically ranges from -2.0 to 2.0 for s=0, s=1, o=0, o=1, e=0, and e=1 and from -1.6 to 1.6 for p=0, p=1, p=2, p=3, and p=4.

Table 4: Part of values of degree of validity.

Rule No.	Honorific feature (value of degree of validity)				
1	s=0 (-1.592)	**s=1** (1.592)			
2	s=0 (-1.495)	**s=1** (1.495)			
3	**s=0** (0.883)	s=1 (-0.883)			
4	**s=0** (0.611)	s=1 (-0.611)			
5	**s=0** (0.922)	s=1 (-0.922)			
6	o=0 (-1.311)	**o=1** (1.311)			
7	o=0 (-1.417)	**o=1** (1.417)			
8	**o=0** (0.932)	o=1 (-0.932)			
9	**o=0** (0.340)	o=1 (-0.340)			
10	**o=0** (0.650)	o=1 (-0.650)			
11	e=0 (-1.282)	**e=1** (1.282)			
12	e=0 (-0.320)	**e=1** (0.320)			
13	**e=0** (-0.204)	e=1 (0.204)			
14	p=0(-0.111)	**p=1** (0.231)	p=2 (-0.295)	p=3 (0.214)	p=4 (-0.039)
15	**p=0** (0.633)	p=1 (-0.351)	**p=2** (0.039)	p=3 (-0.435)	p=4 (0.115)
16	**p=0** (0.664)	p=1 (-0.400)	**p=2** (0.039)	p=3 (-0.404)	p=4 (0.101)
17	**p=0** (0.920)	p=1 (-0.322)	p=2 (-0.216)	p=3 (-0.328)	p=4 (-0.054)

5 Algorithm

Figure 2 shows an example of the process flow of our system. In this example, the social-relationship among persons "(S>A>L)" and sentence "*A ga kimi ni gosetsumei suru*" ("person A explains something to you"), are given as input.

The honorific judgment is executed by the flowing steps.

Step 1 Obtain morphemes by analyzing the sentence using "ChaSen," the Japanese morphological analysis program.

Step 2 Identify subject / object of the predicate ("*gosetsumei*") using our parsing program (subject / object are identified as "A" (i.e., person-A) / "*kimi*"(i.e., listener (L)) for this example).

Step 3 Determine the honorific features of the sentence using the results of Steps 1 and 2 (s/o/e/p are determined to 0/0/0/2 for this example).

Step 4 Select all rules whose description regarding the social-relationship and the subject / object coincide with those obtained in Steps 1 and 2 (rules No. 4 (for s), No.9 (for o), No13 (for e), and No.17(for p) are selected for this example).

Step 5 Enable/disable rules whose degrees of validity are greater/less than thresholds, where the thresholds are set separately for each *s, o, e, p* (rules No. 4, No.9, and No.17 are enabled, rule No.13 is disabled for this example).

Step 6 If some misusages are detected by the rules enabled in Step 5, output all the misusages, otherwise, output "input sentence is correct" (only one misusage for Rule No.17 was detected for this example).

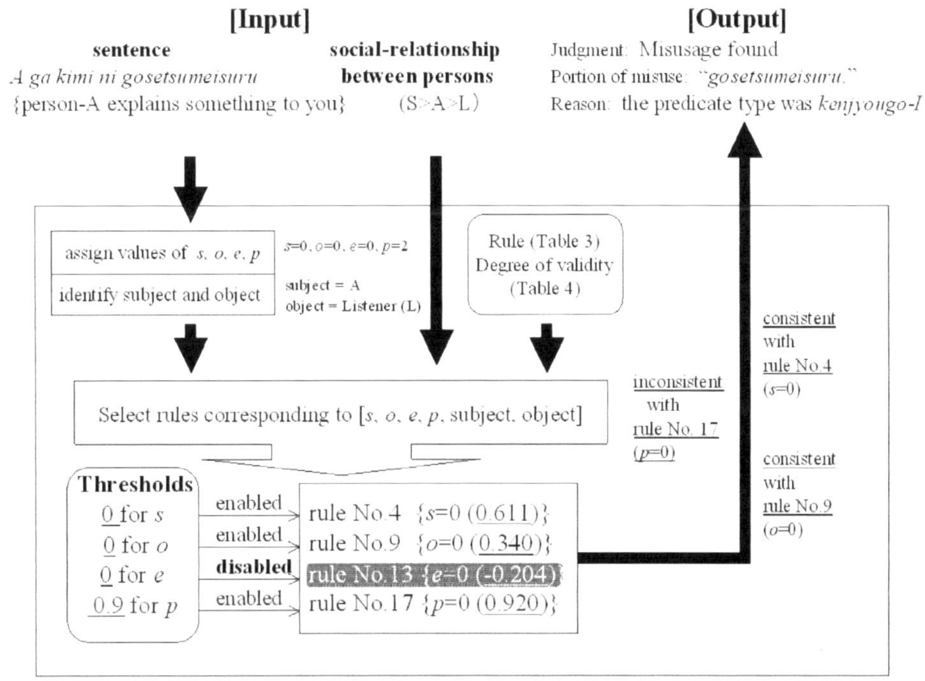

Figure 2: Process flow.

6 Tuning of Thresholds Based on Learner's Linguistic Level

As mentioned above, only rules whose degrees of validity exceed the thresholds of *s*, *o*, *e*, *p*, are enabled for judgment. The degree of validity is closely correlated with the importance to be learned in modern Japanese society. Our system can perform flexible judgments based on the learner's linguistic level by tuning these thresholds. For example, when the thresholds are set to appropriately large values, the system urges learners to learn only rules whose importance is large.

As a primitive study to investigate the appropriate tuning point of these thresholds, we introduce comprehensive index "*T*," which is related to these thresholds. Concretely, we defined the thresholds of *s*/*o*/*e* as $-2.0 + (2.0+2.0)/10*(10-T)$ and the thresholds of *p* as $-1.6 + (1.6 + 1.6) / 10 * (10-T)$, where they are normalized based on the ranges of the degrees of validity for *s*, *o*, *e*, *p* mentioned in Section 4.2. The thresholds of *s*/*o*/*e* decrease from 2.0 to -2.0 and the threshold of *p* decreases from 1.6 to -1.6 when *T* increases from 0 to 1.

Two kinds of test sets (each test set is a pair of a social-relationship and a speech sentence) were inputted to our system. One is called "low," which includes elementary level honorific misusages prepared by us. The other is called "middle," which was collected by non-experts of Japanese linguistics.

Figure 3 shows the number of sentences (percentage of all input included in each test set) judged as "misusage" versus *T*.

Figure 3 suggests that the system can urge elementary level learners to learn rules whose importance is in the upper half of all rules when *T* is set to around 2. It also suggests that the system can urge middle level learners to learn rules whose importance is in the upper half of the rules that haven't been learned yet (i.e., about 30% of rules in our study) when *T* is set to around 4, assuming that they have already learned rules whose importance is in the upper 70% of all rules.

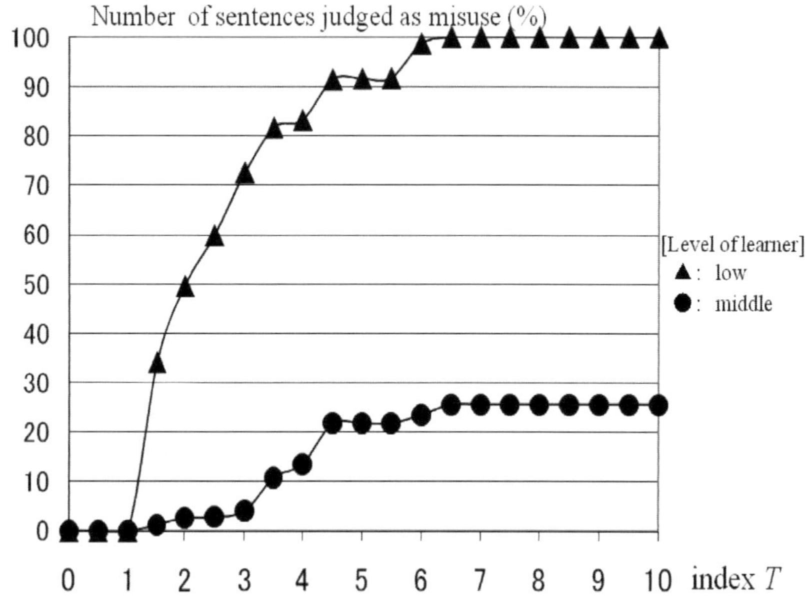

Figure 3: Dependency on *T*

7 Conclusion

We proposed a system that flexibly judges the misusage of honorifics in Japanese sentence. The system uses judgment rules whose degrees of validity in modern Japanese society were quantified by psychological experiments. The system can judge sentences flexibly based on the learner's linguistic level by tuning thresholds regarding the degree of validity. The proposed system is expected to be applied in practical computer-aided education.

References

Scheffe H. 1952. An analysis of variance for paired comparisons, *Journal of American Statistical Association*, 47, 381-400.

Shirado T., Marumoto S., Murata M., Uchimoto K., Kawahara D., and Isahara H. 2007. A System to Point Out Misuse of Honorific Japanese Expressions(in Japanese), *IEICE Transactions*, J90-A(11): 1-13.

Compound Event Nouns of the 'Modifier-head' Type in Mandarin Chinese

Shan Wang, Chu-Ren Huang

Dept. of Chinese and Bilingual Studies
The Hong Kong Polytechnic University
Hung Hom, Kowloon, Hong Kong
wangshanstar@gmail.com, churenhuang@gmail.com

Abstract. Event nouns can lexically encode eventive information. Recently these nouns have generated considerable scholarly interest. However, little research has been conducted in their morphological and syntactic structure, qualia modification, event representing feature, and information inheritance characteristics. This study has these main findings. 1) Morphologically, the modifier and the head is either free or bound morpheme. Syntactically the modifier is a nominal, adjectival, verbal or numeral morpheme, while the head is a nominal morpheme. 2) The modifier acts as a qualia role of the head. 3) All heads represent events, while the modifier is or is not an event. 4) The semantic information of a compound event noun can be inherited from the modifier or the head.

Keywords: compound event noun, modifier, head, qualia structure, information inheritance

1 Introduction

Event nouns are a subtype of nouns that lexically encode eventive information (Wang et al. 2011). In recent years, there has been growing interest in these nouns. Previous research in Mandarin Chinese includes patterns that they usually appear (Chu 2000; Han 2010; Ma 1995), their classifiers (Ma 1995; Wang & Zhu 2000; Wang & Huang 2011), internal and external temporal attributes (Liu 2004), semantic type system of the event noun *huìyì* (Wang et al. 2011). However, little attention has been devoted to the morphological and syntactic structure, qualia modification, event representing feature, and information inheritance characteristics of event nouns.

Compound nouns can be divided into seven groups according to their syntactic structure: modifier-head, coordinative, predicate-object, predicate-complement, subject-predicate (topic-comment), reduplicative, and abbreviatory compound nouns (Chang 1995). This study focuses on 'modifier-head' compound nouns that represent events.

The data in this study are from three sources. 1) The balanced modern Chinese corpus *Sinica Corpus*[1]. 2) *The Grammatical Knowledge-base of Contemporary Chinese——A complete Specification.* It is complied by *(Yu et al. 2003)* and includes more than 400 event nouns. 3) A few example sentences are searched online by using the search engines Google and Baidu.

The following sections are organized as follows. Section 2 discusses the structure of compound event nouns of the 'modifier-head' type. Section 3 examines the qualia role in an event noun. Section 4 is about the event representing ability of the modifier and the head. Section 5 demonstrates event ordering. Section 6 analyses information inheritance from the modifier and the head. Finally Section 7 draws the main conclusion and suggests future work.

2 Structure of the 'Modifier-head' Type Event Nouns

2.1 Morphological Structure

Either the modifier or the head can be a free or bound morpheme in a 'modifier-head' type event noun. 1) bound morpheme + free morpheme: 瑞雪 *ruì-xuě* 'auspicious snow', 劇痛 *jù-*

[1] http://db1x.sinica.edu.tw/kiwi/mkiwi/

tòng 'sharp pain'. 2) free morpheme + bound morpheme: 工作餐 *gōngzuò-cān* 'working lunch', 書法展 *shūf -zh n* 'handwriting exhibition'. 3) bound morpheme + bound morpheme: 便宴 *biàn-yàn* 'informal dinner', 蝗災 *huáng-zāi* 'plague of locusts'. 4) free morpheme + free morpheme: 海風 *h i-fēng* 'sea breeze', 團圓飯 *tuányuán-fàn* 'reunion dinner'.

2.2 Syntactic Structure

The modifier can be a nominal, adjectival, verbal or numeral morpheme, while the head is a nominal morpheme. 1) N+N: 核戰爭 *hé-zhànzhēng* 'nuclear war', 直腸炎 *zhícháng-yán* 'rectitis', 春汛 *chūn-xùn* 'spring flood'. 2) Adj+N: 大雨 *dà-y* 'heavy rain', 美餐 *měi-cān* 'delicious meal'. 3) V+N: 團圓飯 *tuányuán-fàn* 'reunion dinner', 搖擺舞 *yáob i-w* 'rock and roll'. 4) Numeral+N: 百戰 *b i-zhàn* 'hundreds of battles'.

2.3 Productive Right Morphemes

Compound event nouns are morphologically productive, with the right morpheme as an event stem. Examples are shown below.

~戰 *zhàn* 'battle': 資訊戰 *zīxùnzhàn* 'information warfare', 細菌戰 *xìjūnzhàn* 'germ warfare', 化學戰 *huàxuézhàn* 'chemical warfare', 貿易戰 *màoyìzhàn* 'trade war'

~賽 *sài* 'match': 世乒賽 *shìpīngsài* 'the world Table Tennis game', 象棋賽 *xiàngqísài* 'chess match'

~餐 *cān* 'meal': 番茄餐 *fānqiécān* 'tomato meal', 法國餐 *f guócān* 'French food', 學生餐 *xuéshengcān* 'student meal'

~會 *huì* 'meeting, gathering; *council*': 舞蹈會 w d ohuì 'dance council', 校董會 *xiàod nghuì* 'school direct council', 哲學會 zhéxuéhuì 'philosophy council'

~病 *bìng* 'disease': 心臟病 *xīnzāngbìng* 'heart disease', 心血管病 *xīnxuègu nbìng* 'cardiovascular disease', 胃病 *wèibìng* 'gastric disease'

These examples show that compound event nouns have double roots. The right root is the head of an event noun, expressing generic event types, while the modifying left root elaborates information on the event.

3 Qualia Modification of the 'Modifier-head' Type Event Nouns

Pustejovsky (1991, 1995) shows how lexical items encode semantic information in the qualia structure. There are four roles in the qualia structure, and each is associated with some values. 1) The constitutive role is the relation between an object and its constituents or parts. The role values include material, weight, parts and component elements. 2) The formal role can distinguish the object within a larger domain. Orientation, magnitude, shape, dimensionality, color, and position are its role values. 3) The telic role is about the purpose and function of the object. 4) The agentive role describes factors involved in the origin of an object, such as creator, artifact, natural kind, causal chain.

Under the theoretical framework of qualia structure, Johnston & Busat (1996) analyze the nominal compounding phrases in English and Italian. They find that the modifier can specify the type of an argument to a predicate in a telic, agentive or constitutive role. Lee et al. (2010) demonstrate the qualia modification within a noun-noun compound. Following (Johnston & Busat 1996; Lee et al. 2010), we examine the qualia roles involved between the modifier and head in event nouns.

Telic modification: the modifier is the function or aim of the head. For example, 淘汰賽 *táotài-sài* 'elimination game', 選拔賽 *xu nbá-sài* 'selective trial', 衛冕賽 *wèimi n-sài* 'championship fight'.

Agentive modification: the modifier is origin or cause of the head. For instance, 訂婚宴 *dìnghūn-yàn* 'a betrothal party', 答謝宴 *dáxiè-yàn* 'return Banquet'.

Constitutive modification: the modifier is the component of the head. For example, 橄欖球賽 *g nl nqiú-sài* 'rugby match', 帆船賽 *fānchuán-sài* 'yacht match'.

Formal modification: one type is the modifier is a subtype of the head, such as 鼾聲 *hān-shēng* 'snoring sound', 喊聲 *h n-shēng* 'shouting sound', 吼聲 *h u-shēng* 'roaring sound', 歡呼聲 *huānhū-shēng* 'acclamation sound'. The other type is the modifier is the scale of the head, such as 中雨 *zhōng-y* 'moderate rain', 大風 *dà-fēng* 'strong wind'.

4 Event Representing Ability of the Modifier and Head in Event Nouns

'Modifier-head' type event nouns have three types of event-representing patterns, depending on whether the modifier or the head represents an event.

1) Both the modifier and the head refer to events, such as 歌舞劇 *gēw -jù* 'song and dance opera'. The modifier 歌舞 *gēw* 'song and dance' is about the singing and dancing event. The head 劇 *jù* 'opera' is a performing event.

2) Only the head refers to an event, such as 海水浴 *h ishu -yù* 'sea bath', 木偶戲 *mù u-xì* 'puppetoon'. The heads 浴 *yù* 'bath' and 戲 'drama' are events themselves, while the modifiers 海水 *h ishu* and 木偶 *mù u* 'puppet' are entities.

3) The head refers to an event, and the modifier is coerced to be an event. An instance of this type is 冠軍賽 *guànjūn-sài* 'championships'. 賽 *sài* 'game' is an event in itself while 冠軍 *guànjūn*'' is coerced to be an event through the telic role 'competing for the champion'.

5 Event Ordering of Compound Event Noun with Two Events

When there are two events in a 'modifier-head' type event noun, there is an ordering issue between them.

TLINK is one type of the Time Markup Language tags. It is a temporal link which represents two temporal elements' relation. TLINK distinguishes 14 relation types: Before | After | Includes | Is_Included | During | Simultaneous | I-after | I-before | Identity | Begins | Ends | Begun_By | Ended_By | During_Inv[2]. TimeML does not have overlap relation, as this relation does not naturally occur in real texts (Verhagen 2004). However, in compound event nouns, overlap relation is common. We have detected two kinds of overlapping events in compound event nouns.

The first type is partially overlapping. For instance, 雪災 *xuězāi* 'snow disaster' contains both a snowing event and a disaster event. Snowing happens first. As time goes on, the heavy snow continues and consequently it becomes a disaster. The disaster lasts even after snowing ends. The relation between the two events is demonstrated in (1).

(1) 雪 *xuě* 'snow' ————————————
災 *zāi* 'disaster' ————————————

The second type is completely overlapping. In 冠軍賽 *guànjūn sài* 'championship', 冠軍 *guànjūn* 'champion' is coerced to be an event, meaning competing for the champion, and 賽 *sài* 'game' is having a match. The two events completely overlap with each other.

6 Information Inheritance of the 'Modifier-head' Type Event Nouns

6.1 Inheriting Information from the Modifier

[2] http://www.timeml.org/site/publications/timeMLdocs/timeml_1.2.1.html#tlink

Righthand Head Rule (RHR) states that the head of a morphologically complex word is the righthand member of that word (Williams 1981). This entails that the properties of a word is determined by the rightmost constituent. This section examines the compound 音樂會 *yīnyuèhuì* 'concert'. Different from RHR, the results demonstrate that in many cases the left side modifier contributes more semantic information than the right side head.

In *'Modern Chinese Dictionary'(Dictionary Editing Room of the Language Institute 2005)*, 會 *huì* 'meeting' has the following 6 senses, out of which only the first one is an event.

會 *huì* 'meeting'

1) Gathering with certain purpose. 2) Certain groups. 3) Temple fair. 4) Collective activities that are organized for civil pilgrim or praying for harvest, such as incense will, temple events, etc. 5) Small-scale mutual assistance economic organization that the joined members pay on average on schedule and they can use the organization in turn. 6) Primary cities.

The qualia structure of 會 *huì* 'meeting' is depicted below.

(2) *huì*'meeting'
QUALIA = [FORMAL = meeting
CONSTITUTIVE = attendee and topic
TELIC = certain purpose
AGENTIVE = organize]

The qualia structure of 音樂 *yīnyuè* 'music' is illustrated below.

(3) 音樂 *yīnyuè* 'music'
QUALIA = [FORMAL = auditory communication, entertainment
CONSTITUTIVE = songs
TELIC = listen
AGENTIVE = play; sing; compose]

The qualia structure of 音樂會 *yīnyuèhuì* 'concert' is shown below.

(4) 音樂會 *yīnyuèhuì* 'concert'
Qualia = [FORMAL = performance
CONSTITUTIVE = songs; audience, player
TELIC = listen
AGENTIVE = play, sing; organize]

In the following part, seven evidences show that 音樂會 *yīnyuè huì*'concert' usually inherits information from the modifier 音樂 *yīnyuè*'music'.

1) Nominal Modifier of **音樂會** *yīnyuè huì*'concert'

If we utter 貝多芬音樂會 *Bèiduōfēn yīnyuèhuì*'Beethoven concert' at present time, the nominal modifier 貝多芬 *Bèiduōfēn* 'Beethoven' is the composer.

貝多芬音樂會 *Bèiduōfēn yīnyuèhuì* 'Beethoven concert' is a concert which plays the music composed by 貝多芬 *Bèiduōfēn* 'Beethoven'. That is, 貝多芬 *Bèiduōfēn* 'Beethoven' is the composer.

(5) [貝多芬音樂會 *Bèiduōfēn yīnyuèhuì*'Beethoven concert'
Qualia = [AGENTIVE = play music composed by 貝多芬 *Bèiduōfēn* 'Beethoven']]

(5) shows that the agentive role of 貝多芬音樂會 *Bèiduōfēn yīnyuèhuì*'Beethoven concert' is the same as the 'compose' agentive role of 音樂 *yīnyuè* 'music' as shown in (3). This indicates that Beethoven modifies the modifier 音樂 rather than the head 會 in the compound 音樂會.

In 陳奕迅音樂會 *Chén yìxùn yīnyuèhuì* 'the concert of Eason Chan', the nominal modifier 陳奕迅 *Chén yìxùn* 'Eason Chan' is the singer. 陳奕迅音樂會 *Chén yìxùn yīnyuèhuì* 'the concert of Eason Chan' is a concert on which 陳奕迅'Eason Chan' sings.

(6) [陳奕迅音樂會 *Chén yìxùn yīnyuèhuì* 'the concert of Eason Chan'
Qualia = [AGENTIVE =陳奕迅 *Chén yìxùn* 'Eason Chan' sings on the concert]]

The agentive role of 陳奕迅音樂會 *Chén yìxùn yīnyuèhuì* 'the concert of Eason Chan' is the same as the 'sing' agentive role of 音樂 *yīnyuè* 'music' as shown in (3). Therefore, Eason Chan modifies 音樂 *yīnyuè* 'music' rather than 會.

In 小提琴音樂會 *xi otíqín yīnyuèhuì* 'violin concert', the nominal modifier 小提琴 *xi otíqín* 'violin' is the exclusive instrument used to play music on a concert. The constitutive role of 小提琴音樂會 *xi otíqín yīnyuèhuì* 'violin concert' is the songs played by violin, which is identical with the constitutive role 'songs' of 音樂 *yīnyuè* 'music'. Thus 小提琴 *xi otíqín* 'violin' modifies 音樂 *yīnyuè* 'music' instead of 會.

2) Adjectival Modifiers of **音樂會** *yīnyuèhuì*'concert'

精彩的音樂會 *jīngc ide yīnyuèhuì* 'splendid concert' expresses the splendid music on a concert, not a splendid meeting. Thus, 精彩 *jīngc i* 'splendid' inherits information from 音樂 *yīnyuè* 'music' rather than 會 *huì* 'meeting'.

3) Verbal Modifier of **音樂會** *yīnyuèhuì*'concert'

The agentive role of 獨唱音樂會 *dúchàng yīnyuèhuì* 'vocal recital' is 'sing'; the agentive role of 獨奏音樂會 *dúzòu yīnyuèhuì* 'instrumental recital' is 'play'. They are the same as agentive role of 音樂 *yīnyuè* 'music' as depicted in (3).

4) Nouns Modified by **音樂會** *yīnyuèhuì*'concert'

The constitutive role of 音樂會曲目 *yīnyuèhuì q mù* 'concert songs' is the songs on a concert, which is the same as the constitutive role of 音樂 *yīnyuè* 'music'.

5) **音樂會** *yīnyuèhuì*'concert' as a Subject

In 音樂會演出 *yīnyuèhuì y nchū/dúzòu* 'concert performance', the agentive role is 'play', which is identical with the agentive role of 音樂 *yīnyuè* 'music', not 會 *huì* 'meeting'.

6) **音樂會** *yīnyuèhuì* 'concert' as an Object

In 聆聽音樂會 *língtīng yīnyuèhuì* 'listen carefully to a concert', the constitutive role is songs, which shares the same constitutive role with 音樂 *yīnyuè* 'music'.

7) Classifiers of **音樂會** *yīnyuèhuì* 'concert'

In 這台音樂會 *zhè tái yīnyuèhuì* 'this concert', 台 *tái* is a stage where the performance takes place. Thus it is related to 音樂 *yīnyuè* 'music'. For 會 *huì* 'meeting', it is related to the gathering of audience who seats in the concert hall, not the 台 *tái* 'stage'.

In sum, contrary to RHR, the 'modifier-head' event noun 音樂會 *yīnyuèhuì* 'concert' indicates that the modifier, which is on the left, holds more semantic information gives the event structure of the whole noun, while the head, which is on the right, is more bleached and generic in meaning. Other similar examples are 舞蹈會 *w d o huì* 'dance party', 演奏會 *y nzòu huì* 'playing concert', 圖片展 *túpiàn zh n* 'photo exhibition'.

6.2 Inheriting Information from the Head

It is more conventional that the main information is inherited from the head, which is in conformity with RHR. Examples are shown in (7) and (8).

(7) 陽春 三月 京城 普 降 鵝毛 雪。
yángchūn sānyuè jīngchéng p jiàng émáo xuě。
spring March capital city widespread fall goose feather snow
'Goose feather like snow falls widely in the capital city in Spring March.'

(8) 成都 下起 了 鵝毛 雪。
chéngdōu xiàq le émáo xuě。
Chengdu begin ASP goose feather snow
'It began to snow goose feather like snow in Chengdu.'

In both (7) and (8), 降 *jiàng* 'fall' and 下 *xià* 'fall' selects 雪 *xuě* 'snow' rather than 鵝毛 *émáo* 'goose feather like snow' as their arguments. 鵝毛 *émáo* 'goose feather', as a modifier, gives the shape of the snow, which is the formal quale of snow.

6.3 Inheriting Information from Either the Modifier or the Head

The semantic information of some compound event nouns can be inherited either from the modifier or the head.

1) Inheriting information from the head

(9) 地雷 戰 英雄
dìléi zhàn yīngxióng
landmine warfare hero
'heroes in the landmine warfare'

(10) 地雷 戰 越 打 越 大
dìléi zhàn yuè d yuè dà
landmine warfare more fight more large
'The Landmine warfare becomes larger and larger.'

In 地雷戰 *dìléi zhàn* 'landmine war', the left morpheme 地雷 *dìléi* 'landmine' is a physical object, while the right morpheme 戰 *zhàn* 'war' is an event. (9) refers to heroes in 戰 *zhàn* 'wars' rather than 地雷 *dìléi* 'landmine'. In (10), 大 *dà* 'large' modifies the right morpheme 戰 *zhàn* 'wars' rather than the left morpheme 地雷 *dìléi* 'landmine'.

2) Inheriting information from the modifier

(11) 地雷 戰 炸 破 敵 膽
dìléi zhàn *zhà* *pò* *dí* *d n*
landmine warfare explode broken enemy gallbladder
'The landmine warfare frightens the enemy and defeats their morale. '

In (11), 炸 *zhà* 'explode' indicates the exploding event of 地雷 *dìléi* 'landmine' rather than the warfare event of the head 戰 *zhàn* 'wars'.

The above examples illustrate that the semantic information of 地雷戰 *dìléi zhàn* 'landmine warfare' can be inherited either from the modifier or the head. A similar example is 地道戰 *dìdào zhàn* 'tunnel warfare'.

7 Conclusion and Future Work

This study has the following findings for compound event nouns of the 'modifier-head' type. 1) Both the modifier and the head can be free or bound morphemes. Moreover, the modifier can be a nominal, adjectival, verbal or numeral morpheme, while the head is a nominal morpheme. Some compound event nouns have a morphologically productive right-side event morpheme. 2) The modifier is a telic, agentive, constitutive or formal role of the head. 3) The modifier can directly or be coerced to represent an event, while the head represents an event all the time. 4) In a compound, the head usually provides the semantic and syntactic information. However, this research finds that the modifier can sometimes provide more semantic information and gives the event structure.

For future work, compound event nouns with other syntactic structures, such as coordinative, subject-predicate, need to be investigated in order to get an overall view of event nouns.

Acknowledgments: The authors would like to thank Dr. Yurie Hara for her comments on The 7th Linguistic Society of Hong Kong Postgraduate Research Forum on Linguistics (PRFL-7). We also thank Dr. Lan LI for her suggestions on language use. The remaining errors are ours.

References

Chang, Shu-Min. 1995. *A study on Mandarin compounds (漢語複合詞的研究)*. Hsinchu: National Tsing Hua University.

Chu, Zexiang. 2000. *An Investigation on Nouns' Adaptation to Temporality (名词的时间适应性情况考察)*. Modern Chinese Grammar Studies that Face the Challenges of New Century:the International Conference on Modern Chinese Grammar,1998 (面临新世纪挑战的现代汉语语法研究：'98 现代汉语语法学国际学术会议论文集), ed. by J. Lu. Jinan: Shandong Education Press.

Dictionary Editing Room of the Language Institute, Chinese Academy of Social Sciences. 2005. Modern Chinese Dictionary (现代汉语词典). Beijing: The Commercial Press.

Han, Lei. 2010. Analysing the Word Class Status of Event Nouns (试析事件名词的词类地位). *Journal of Ningxia University (Humanities & Social Sciences Edition)* (1).

Johnston, Michael & Federica Busat. 1996. *Qualia Structure and the Compositional Interpretation of Compounds*. Proceedings of the ACL SIGLEX workshop on breadth and depth of semantic lexicons, 77-88. Santa Cruz, California.

Lee, Chih-yao, Chia-hao Chang, Wei-chieh Hsu & Shu-kai Hsieh. 2010. *Qualia Modification in Noun-Noun Compounds: A Cross-Language Survey*. Proceedings of the 22nd Conference on Computational Linguistics and Speech Processing (ROCLING-2010), 379-390. National Chi Nan University, Puli, Nantou, Taiwan.

Liu, Shun. 2004. A Study of Temporality of Common Nouns (普通名词的时间性研究). *Language Teaching and Linguistic Studies* (4).

Ma, Qingzhu. 1995. *Verbs with denotational Meaning and Nouns with Statement Meaning(指称义动词和陈述义名词)*. Research and Exploration of the Grammar (语法研究和探索). Beijing: The Commercial Press.

Pustejovsky, James. 1991. The Generative Lexicon. *Computational Linguistics* 17 (4).409-441.

Pustejovsky, James. 1995. *The Generative Lexicon*. Cambridge, MA: MIT Press.

Verhagen, Marc. 2004. *Times Between The Lines: Embedding a Temporal Closure Component in a Mixed-Initiative Temporal Annotation Framework* Waltham: Brandeis University.

Wang, Hui & Xuefeng Zhu. 2000. *Subcategorization and Quantitative Research on Modern Chinese Nouns (现代汉语名词的子类划分及定量研究)*. Modern Chinese Grammar Studies that Face the Challenges of New Century:the International Conference on Modern Chinese Grammar,1998 (面临新世纪挑战的现代汉语语法研究：'98 现代汉语语法学国际学术会议论文集). Jinan: Shandong Education Press.

Wang, Shan & Chu-Ren Huang. 2011. Event Classifiers and Their Selected Nouns. *Paper presented at the The 19th Annual Conference of the International Association of Chinese Linguistics (IACL-19)*, Nankai University, Tianjin, China.

Wang, Shan, Sophia Lee & Chu-Ren Huang. 2011. A Corpus-based Analysis of Semantic Type System of Event Nouns: A Case Study on *huìyì Paper presented at the North American Conference on Chinese Linguistics 23 (NACCL-23)*, Eugene, Oregon, USA

Williams, Edwin. 1981. On the notions 'Lexically Related' and 'Head of a Word'. *Linguistic inquiry* 12 (2).245-274.

Yu, Shiwen, Xuefeng Zhu, Hui Wang, Huarui Zhang, Yunyun Zhang & Dexi Zhu. 2003. In *the Grammatical Knowledge-base of Contemporary Chinese——A complete Specification (现代汉语语法信息词典详解)*. Beijing: Tsinghua University Press.

The Co-occurrence of Two Delimiters: An Investigation of Mandarin Chinese Resultatives

Jingxia Lin and Chu-Ren Huang

Department of Chinese & Bilingual Studies
The Hong Kong Polytechnic University, Hong Kong
ctjlin@polyu.edu.hk, churen.huang@inet.polyu.edu.hk

Abstract. Tenny (1987, 1994: 79) proposes the Single Delimiting Constraint that the event described by a verb can only be delimited once (cf. Goldberg 1991, 1995). The constraint applies the effects of delimitedness as an aspectual property to the mapping of semantics and syntax, and explains why sentences with two delimiters (e.g., **Martha wiped the table* $\underline{dry}_1$ $\underline{clean}_2$ Tenny 1994: 80) are unacceptable. The constraint is challenged with English counterexamples and modified by Matsumoto (2006) and Zhou (2008). However, this study proposes that the constraint holds for Mandarin Chinese resultatives, whereas the revised constraints do not. Furthermore, we point out that while two independent delimiters usually do not co-occur in Chinese, a second delimiter that further specifies or reinforces the endpoint/ endstate denoted by the first delimiter is allowed (cf. Tenny 1994, Goldberg 1991). The results of this study may shed light on event structure of Chinese.

Keywords: Single Delimiting Constraint; Unique Path Constraint; Mandarin Chinese resultatives

1 Introduction

Delimitednes[1] refers to "the property of an event's having a distinct, definite and inherent endpoint in time" (Tenny 1994: 4). For instance, *He ate an orange* describes a delimited event because eating an orange has a definite endpoint, that is, when the whole orange is eaten; in contrast, the event described in *He ran* is undelimited because a running event can take place forever if no endpoint is explicitly expressed (Tenny 1994: 4). Tenny (1987, 1994: 79) proposes the Single Delimiting Constraint (SDC) that an event described by a verb can be delimited only once. A similar constraint the Unique Path Constraint (UPC) is proposed by Goldberg (1991: 368-369, 1995) that only one "distinct path" can be predicated of an argument denoting a physical object. The path in the UPC can be understood in two senses, either as a path for physical motion, or as a metaphorical path where the object undergoes a change of state. And the notion of a distinct path entails that the physical object cannot be in two locations or in two states at a time, or in both a location and a state at a time (ibid.). Both the SDC and the UPC apply the effects of delimitedness as an aspectual property to the mapping of semantics and syntax, and explain why sentences such as (1) are not acceptable.

(1) a. *Shirley sailed into the kitchen into the garden. (Goldberg 1991: 368) (two locations)

[1] Delimitedness is also called "measuring-out" by Tenny (1994) or "scale" by Hay et al. (1999).

b. *Martha wiped the table dry$_1$ clean$_2$. (Tenny 1994: 80) (two states)
c. *Sam kicked Bill black and blue$_1$ out of the room$_2$. (Goldberg 1991: 368) (a location+ a state)

Before introducing counterexamples to the SDC and the UPC raised by linguists, we provide a few examples showing what elements can be delimiters, i.e. have a delimiting function. As illustrated in (1), prepositional directionals, e.g., *into the kitchen* and *into the garden* in (1a), and adjective resultatives, e.g., *dry* and *clean* in (1b), can be the delimiters contributing an endpoint or endstate for an event. In addition, telic verbs or verb phrases by themselves can be delimiting; these include achievements such as *arrive* and *die*, and accomplishments such as *break* and *walk three miles* (Tenny 1994, among others, cf. Goldberg 1991). According to the SDC and the UPC, no additional resultative is allowed if the verb in a clause is inherently delimiting. For instance, the box being open in (2) can only have a depictive reading, but cannot be understood as a result of the event of arrival (Rappaport Hovav and Levin 2010).

(2) The box arrived open.

Both the SDC and the UPC are found with counterexamples in English according to Matsumoto 2006, Zhou 2008, among others. For instance, two delimiters, e.g., *broke* and *into pieces* in (3a), or *into thick pieces* and *into the bowl* in (3b), can occur together for the same event.

(3) a. The vase broke$_1$ into pieces$_2$. (Zhou 2008: 229)
b. I sliced the cheese into thick pieces$_1$ into the bowl$_2$. (Matsumoto 2006: 7)

For this reason, Zhou (2008) modifies the SDC that changes can be understood on different dimensions (e.g., time, space, property, degree) and delimiters describing changes on different dimensions can co-occur. As in (3a), Zhou points out that *break* and *into pieces* can occur together because the former specifies a change on the dimension of property (from being a whole into broken), whereas the latter describes a change on the dimension of degree (e.g., broken into several bigger pieces or into many smaller pieces). Matsumoto (2006:16) also proposes a revised UPC that spatial and non-spatial delimiters can co-occur if they describe aspects of "a single line of development" that an entity follows. For instance, the non-spatial phrase *into thick pieces* and the spatial phrase *into the bowl* in (3b) can co-occur because they specify a change of state and a change of location that an entity can undergo in a natural temporal order, that is, cheese is usually placed into a container such as a bowl after it is sliced into pieces.

2 Chinese Resultatives Consistent with the SDC and the UPC

We propose that Mandarin Chinese resultatives conform to the SDC and the UPC whereas the revised constraints by Zhou (2008) and Matsumoto (2006) do not hold. For instance, in (4) and (5), the (a) sentences describe a change of state, and the (b) sentences describe a change of location, which according to Zhou (2008), can be understood on different dimensions, and thus are allowed to co-occur by Zhou's revised constraint. However, as (4c) and (5c) illustrate, these delimiters cannot co-occur for the event of cutting or the event of running.

(4) a. ba cai qie sui
BA food cut shattered
'cut the food into a state of shattered'

b. ba cai qie dao panzi-li
BA food cut arrive plate-inside
'cut the food into the plate'

c. *ba cai qie sui_1 dao $panzi\text{-}li_2$
BA food cut shattered arrive plate-inside
#'cut the food into a state of shattered and into the plate" (intended meaning)

(5) a. Zhangsan pao lei le
Zhangsanrun tired ASP
'Zhangsan became tired as a result of running.'

b. Zhangsanpao hui xuexiao le
Zhangsanrun return school ASP
'Zhangsan ran back to the school.'

c. *Zhangsan pao hui $xuexiao_1$ lei_2 le
Zhangsan run return school tired ASP
#'Zhangsan ran back to school and became tired as a result.' (intended meaning)

In addition, it can be understood as a single line of development for food to be chopped into pieces and then moved into a plate, or for a person to become tired after running back to school. Therefore, the ungrammaticality of (4c) and (5c) also indicate that Matsumoto's (2008) revision of the UPC does not hold for Chinese resultatives.

In contrast, (4c) and (5c) become acceptable only if the SDC and the UPC are satisfied. Specifically, for (4c) and (5c) where two delimiters delimit one event, we can add a verb denoting a new (sub)event so that each delimiter delimits only one (sub)event. As illustrated in (6a), when a second verb *fang* 'put' is added, the sentence in (4c) becomes grammatical: the subevent denoted by the first verb *qie* 'cut' is delimited by the first delimiter *sui* 'shattered', whereas the new subevent denoted by *fang* 'put' is delimited by the second delimiter *dao panzi-li* 'into the plate'. Besides serialization in (6a), verb copying is another means to satisfy the constraints (cf. Fang and Sells 2007). As in (6b), cf. (5c), the repeated verb contributes a (sub)event for the second delimiter *lei* 'tired' although the (sub)event overlaps with the that denoted by the first verb.

(6) a. ba cai **qie** sui_1 **fang** dao $panzi\text{-}li_2$
BA food cut shattered put arrive plate-inside
'Cut the food into a state of shattered and put it into the plate"

b. Zhangsan **pao** hui $xuexiao_1$ **pao** lei_2 le
Zhangsan run return school run tired ASP
'Zhangsan ran back to school and became tired as a result.'

Therefore, although it is claimed that the SDC and the UPC have counterexamples in English, the Chinese resultatives conform to these constraints in that they do not allow the co-occurrence of two expressions that can independently delimit the same event; two independent delimiters co-occur only when there are two (sub)events in a clause.

3 The Second Delimiter Further Specifying/Reinforcing the First

Both Tenny (1987, 1994) and Goldberg (1991, 1995) also discuss examples with two delimiters in English, but they argue that in these cases, there is still only one endpoint or endstate for the event. Following Gruber (1965), Tenny points out that a second delimiter is allowed only when it is to further specify the endpoint denoted by the first delimiter. In other words, when the first delimiter specifies a change of location and the resultant location can be "refined or elaborated upon" (Gruber 1965: 82, cf. Hay et al 1999, Kennedy & McNally 2005, among others), a second delimiter can occur in order to describe the location in more detail. For instance, (7a) has two *to* PPs to delimit the event of transferring the book: although New York in the first *to* PP can be understood as the endpoint for the path of book transfer, Bill, who is located in New York, is more specific than New York as the endpoint for the path, and thus it is possible for *to Bill* to occur as the second delimiter; in contrast, (7b) is not allowed because the second *to* PP is less specific than the first (Gruber 1965, Tenny 1994).

(7) a. John sent the book to New York to Bill.
b. *John sent the book to Bill to New York.
(Gruber 1965, cited in Tenny 1994: 78)

Goldberg (1991, 1995) also argues that two directional PPs or adjective resultatives can co-occur if they designate the same path or state. For instance, according to Goldberg (1991), the second PP *through the back door* modifies the first PP *out of the house* in (8a), and the two resultatives in (8b) form only one constituent because one is modifying the other.

(8) a. She kicked him out of the house through the back door.
b. He washed his face shiny clean.
(Goldberg 1991: 370)

In Chinese too, clauses can be found with two delimiting expressions. For instance, both *sui* 'shattered' in (9a) and *dao 3-limi zhi 8-limi* 'to 3-8 cm long' in (9b) describe the endstate of the event of cutting, and they can co-occur in (9c), cf. (4).

(9) a. ba xiaomai jiegan qie sui
BA wheat straw cut shattered
'cut the wheat straw into a state of shattered'
(http://news.sina.com.cn/c/2010-06-09/073717631393s.shtml)

b. ba xiaomai jiegan qie dao 3-limi zhi 8-limi$_2$
BA wheat straw cut arrive 3-cm to 8-cm
'cut the wheat straw to 3-8cm in length'

c. ba xiaomai jiegan qie sui$_1$ dao 3-limi zhi 8-limi$_2$
BA wheat straw cut shattered arrive 3-cm to 8-cm
'cut the wheat straw into a state of shattered to 3-8cm in length'
(http://info.china.alibaba.com/news/detail/v0-d1005654608.html)

Following Tenny and Goldberg, we argue that (9c) does not violate the SDC or the UPC. The wheat straw in (9) changes its state when it is shattered. However, "shattered" is not an absolute specification, but can be specified "in greater degrees of accuracy" (Gruber 1985: 82). Therefore, a second delimiter 'to 3-8cm long' can occur and provide more precise information for the event of cutting.

However, unlike English, in addition to the delimiter that further specifies the endpoint/endstate, Chinese allows another type of delimiter to follow an existing delimiter and function to reinforce the attainment of the endpoint/endstate denoted by first delimiter. In other words, the two delimiters in a clause provide the same degree of specification of an endpoint/endstate. For instance, the second delimiter *dao* 'arrive' in (10) does not add new information to the description of the event, but specifies the arrival at the endpoint (the school) which is also the endpoint of the event of returning denoted by *hui* 'return', a delimiting verb that *dao* 'arrive' follows.

(10) a. pao <u>hui</u> xuexiao
run return school
'run back to the school'

b. pao <u>dao</u> xuexiao
run arrive school
'run to the school'

c. pao <u>hui_1</u> <u>dao_2</u> xuexiao
run return arrive school
'run back to the school'

Two more examples are given in (11)-(12), where the state denoted by the second delimiting elements, *diao* 'away' and *guang* 'empty', is also a repetition of the endstate specified by the first delimiting elements: *diao* 'away' in (11b) reinforces the broken state of the vase (a broken vase is understood as a vase that is gone away); and *guang* 'empty' in (12b) reinforces the endstate of the event of forgetting, i.e. that person has been totally forgotten.

(11) a. na-ge huaping da <u>sui</u> le
that-CLF vase hit shattered ASP
'The vase was broken.'

b. na-ge heaping da <u>sui_1</u> <u>$diao_2$</u> le
that-CLF vase hit shattered away ASP
'That vase was broken.' (Zhou 2008: 236)

(12) a. Zhangsan ba na-ge ren <u>wang</u> le
Zhangsan BA that-CLF person forget ASP
'Zhangsan forgot that person.'

b. Zhangsan ba na-ge ren <u>$wang_1$</u> <u>$guang_2$</u> le
Zhangsan BA that-CLF person forget empty ASP
'Zhangsan [totally] forgot that person.'

The second delimiters such as those in (10)-(12) can occur after a delimiter that denotes a state which either can be absolute specification (e.g., *wang* 'forget') or non-absolute specification (e.g., *sui* 'shattered'), whereas the delimiters that further specify the endpoint/endstate of an event, as in

(9), are only allowed to follow a delimiter with a state that is non-absolute specification, i.e. a state that can be described in greater detail.

4 Conclusions and future study

This study shows that although further study is necessary for the inconsistency between the SDC/UPC and English data, Mandarin Chinese conforms to these constraints in that a verb can have only one delimiting expression. That is, the event denoted by the verb can only have one endpoint or endstate. When two elements with delimiting function are found in a predication in Chinese, the two actually express the same endpoint or endstate, with the latter either further specifying or reinforcing the endpoint or endstate denoted by the former. The results of this paper may illuminate the study of event structure of Chinese, especially the identification of delimited events and their constituents. The future study will verify our proposal through a corpus-based investigation of whether two expressions are found to independently delimit an event. Furthermore, the event types will also be analyzed when two delimiters co-occur and have one further specifying or reinforcing the other.

References

Fang, J. and P. Sells. 2007. A Formal Analysis of the Verb Copy Construction in Chinese. In T.H. King and M. Butt, eds., *Proceedings of the LFG07 Conference*. CSLI On-line Publications.

Goldberg, A. E. 1991. It can't go up the chimney down: Paths and the English resultative. In *Proceedings of the Berkeley Linguistic Society* 17, 368-378.

Goldberg, A. E. 1995. *Constructions: A Construction Grammar Approach to Argument Structure*. Chicago: University of Chicago Press.

Gruber, J. S. 1965. *Studies in Lexical Relations*. Doctoral dissertation, MIT, Cambridge, MA.

Hay, J., C. Kennedy and B. Levin. 1999. Scalar structure underlies telicity in "degree achievements". In T. Mathews and D. Strolovitch, eds., *Semantics and Linguistic Theory IX*, pp. 127-144. Ithaca: CLC Publications.

Kennedy, C. and L. McNally. 2005. Scale structure and the semantic typology of gradable predicates. *Language*, 81, 2: 345-381.

Mastumoto, Y. 2006. Constraints on the co-occurrence of spatial and non-spatial paths in English: A close look at the Unique Path Constraint. Paper presented at the *Fourth International Conference on Construction Grammar*, University of Tokyo, Tokyo, September 2006.

Rappaport Hovav, M. and B. Levin. 2010. Reflections on manner/result complementarity. In E. Doron, M. Rappaport Hovav, and I. Sichel, eds., *Syntax, Lexical Semantics, and Event Structure*, pp. 21-38. Oxford: Oxford University Press.

Tenny, C. 1987. *Grammaticalizing Aspect and Affectedness*. PHD dissertation, MIT, Cambridge.

Tenny, C. 1994. *Aspectual Roles and the Syntax-semantics Interface*. Dordrecht: Kluwer.

Zhou, C. 2008. Danyi jiehua xianzhi yu BREAK lei jieguo jushi de tuidao [The Single Delimiting Constraint and the derivations of BREAK-type resultative constructions]. *Xiandai Waiyu [Modern Foreign Languages]*, 31: 228-237.

The Order of Mandarin Chinese Motion Morphemes and the "Scalar Specificity Constraint" *

Jingxia Lin

Department of Chinese & Bilingual Studies
The Hong Kong Polytechnic University
GH618, The Hong Kong Polytechnic University, Hong Kong
ctjlin@polyu.edu.hk

Abstract. This study investigates semantic constraints affecting the order of motion morphemes in Mandarin multi-morpheme motion constructions (e.g., *tui-hui* recede-return). It classifies Chinese motion morphemes into three major types and proposes a "Scalar Specificity Constraint" to account for the order in multi-morpheme motion constructions. The constraint not only provides a better coverage of the data of Chinese motion constructions from the perspective of the syntax-semantics interface, but also illuminates the distribution of motion verbs in other serial verb languages.

Keywords: order of motion morphemes, Scalar Specificity Constraint, Mandarin Chinese

1 Introduction

Mandarin Chinese (hereafter "Chinese") often expresses directed motion events through a concatenation of verbal morphemes, e.g., *gun* 'roll' and *jin* 'enter' in *gun-jin shui-li* 'roll into the water'.[1] However, the order of these co-occurring motion morphemes is not flexible, e.g., **jin-gun shui-li* enter-roll water-inside. This paper first reviews previous studies on the order of Chinese motion morphemes, and then provides proposals that can better explain the order.

2 Previous Studies

This section reviews previous studies on the order of motion morphemes in Chinese MMMCs, and shows that a more refined proposal is still necessary.

2.1 RVC and the Morpheme Order

Previous studies (e.g., Li and Thompson (1981), among others) treat Chinese motion constructions as a type of resultative verbal compounds (RVC), in which the second morpheme specifies the direction of motion as a result of the action denoted by the first morpheme (Li and Thompson 1981). For instance, in (1a) and (1b), the second morpheme *luo* 'fall' and *jin* 'enter' are understood as the results of the event of rolling.

(1) a. huapo	chu	buduan	you	xuanshi	**gun-luo**
landslide	place	continuously	have	hanging.stone	roll-fall

*This paper is partially based on my dissertation. I would like to thank Beth Levin and Chaofen Sun for their insightful advice on the dissertation and Chu-Ren Huang for his helpful comments on the draft of the paper. The usual disclaimers apply.

[1] This paper uses the term "motion morphemes" instead of "motion verbs" because previous studies have not reached a consensus on the lexical status of some motion morphemes. The lexical status of Chinese motion morphemes is not the focus of this study.

'There were hanging stones continuously rolling and falling from the place of landslide' (PKU Corpus)[2]

b. na-kuai tiaoshi **gun-jin**-le yan-xia de shui-jian
that-CLF square.stone roll-enter-ASP cliff-below REL water.stream
'That square stone rolled into the stream under the cliff.' (PKU Corpus)

However, the RVC account cannot explain why when *luo* 'fall' and *jin* 'enter' co-occur, only *luo* precedes *jin* (2a), but not vice versa (2b), given that both morphemes can have a result understanding, as (1a) and (1b) illustrate.

(2) a. huran yi-kuai shizi **luo-jin**-le shui-li
suddenly one-CLF pebble fall-enter-ASP water-inside
'Suddenly, a pebble fell into the water.' (PKU Corpus)

b. *huran yi-kuai shizi **jin-luo**-le shui-li
suddenly one-CLF pebble enter-fall-ASP water-inside

2.2 Temporal Sequences and the Morpheme Order

Tai (1985: 50, also Li 1993) proposes that in Chinese, "the relative word order between two syntactic units is determined by the temporal order of the states" denoted by the units. While this principle holds for the order of motion morphemes denoting subevents with a sequential temporal relationship, it is unable to account for MMMCs where the motion morphemes denoting simultaneous subevents. For instance, a person can run and ascend stairs at the same time, especially if the person stands at the lower ends of the stairs before running, but only can *pao* 'run' occurs before *shang* 'ascend', but not vice versa, as in (3).

(3) a. ta pao-shang louti
he run-ascend stairs
'He went up the stairs running.'

b. *ta shang-pao louti
he ascend-run stairs

2.3 Two-way Classification of Motion Morphemes and the Morpheme Order

Talmy (1975, 2000) classifies motion morphemes into two types. One type is manner-of-motion morpheme that specifies how a motion event is carried out, e.g., *gun* 'roll', *pao* 'run'. The other is path morpheme that specifies in which direction a motion event is carried out, e.g., *luo* 'fall', *jin* 'enter'. When a manner-of-motion morpheme and a path morpheme occur together in a construction, the former must precede the latter, as in (1a) and (1b). However, as illustrated in (2), the two path morphemes *luo* 'fall' and *jin* 'enter' can occur together, and when they co-occur, *luo* can only occur before *jin*, but not vice versa. Therefore, the two-way classification is unable to account for the order of two co-occurring path morphemes.

2.4 Four-way Classification of Motion Morphemes and the Motion Morpheme Hierarchy

Based on recent study on "scale structure" (Rappaport Hovav and Levin 2010, Kennedy and McNally 2005), Lin and Peck (2011) classify Chinese motion morphemes into four types according to the type of scale each lexicalizes. A path is composed of contiguous points ordered between the starting point of motion and a reference object; the path can be understood as a scale because its ordered points indicate measurement values on the dimension of distance (Rappaport Hovav and Levin 2010). When the moving object change its location along the path,

---

[2] PKU Corpus in this paper refers to the corpus of Modern Mandarin Chinese constructed by the Center for Chinese Linguistics at Beijing University. The corpus has 307,317,060 characters updated on 7/20/2009. See http://ccl.pku.edu.cn/.

Abbreviations in this paper: ASP = Aspect marker; CLF = Classifier; REL = Relative clause marker.

the value changes too, so the change is understood as a scalar change which is measurable (Rappaport Hovav and Levin 2010). According to Lin and Peck, motion morphemes are first classified into scalar change (e.g., *luo* 'fall', *hui* 'return', *jin* 'enter', equivalent to Talmy's (1975) path verbs) and nonscalar change motion morphemes (e.g., *gun* 'roll', equivalent to Talmy's (1975) manner-of-motion verbs) depending on whether they lexicalize a scale or not. Scalar change motion morphemes are then classified into open scale (e.g., *luo* 'fall') and closed scale motion morphemes (e.g., *hui* 'return', *jin* 'enter') depending on whether the scales have endpoints or not. Closed scale motion morphemes are classified into multi-point (e.g., *hui* 'return') and two-point closed scale motion morphemes (*jin* 'enter') depending on whether the scales have only two points (starting point and end point) or multiple points, i.e. whether the motion is instantaneous or durative. A set of independent diagnostics is proposed by Lin and Peck to determine which type each Chinese motion morpheme falls into. Then, they propose a Motion Morpheme Hierarchy formed of the four types of morphemes to predict the order of motion morphemes. In this hierarchy, nonscalar change motion morphemes are located at the farthest left, followed by open scale, multi-point closed, and two-point closed scale motion morphemes, as in (4).

(4)

Nonscalar change (a):		**Open scale (b):**		**Multi-point closed scale (c):**		**Two-point closed scale (d):**
gun 'roll'	⇨	*luo* 'fall'	⇨	*hui* 'return'	⇨	*jin* 'enter'
pao 'run'		*shang* 'ascend'		*lai* 'come'		*chu* 'exit'
fei 'fly'		*xia* 'descend'		*qu* 'go'		*dao* 'arrive'
zou 'walk'		*tui* 'recede'		etc.		etc.
etc.		*sheng* 'ascend'				
		etc.				

According to Lin and Peck, in a motion construction, the motion morphemes are ordered from left to right according to how their types appear in the hierarchy. For instance, *gun* 'roll' is located to the left of *luo* 'fall' and *jin* 'enter' in the hierarchy, so *gun* 'roll' must occur before *luo* 'fall' and *jin* 'enter' when they co-occur, as in (1a) and (1b), respectively. Similarly, *luo* 'fall' is located to the left of *jin* 'enter' in the hierarchy, so *luo* 'fall' must precede *jin* 'enter', as in (2a). The hierarchy is able to account for a large amount of data in Chinese, as shown in the corpus studies by Lin and Peck.[3]

However, Lin and Peck do not provide explanation why this hierarchy emerges; in addition, the hierarchy is a generalization of the morpheme order in existing Chinese motion constructions, but it does not explain why some combinations of motion morphemes do not exist in Chinese although they are allowed by the hierarchy. For instance, the hierarchy predicts that *hui* 'return' as a multi-point closed scale motion morpheme can occur before *jin* 'enter', which is a two-point closed scale motion morpheme, but these two morphemes seldom co-occur in Chinese, as in *??hui-jin fangjian* return-enter room #'return into the room'. Therefore, a more refined explanation is necessary for the order of motion morphemes in Chinese.

3 Our proposal: Revised Motion Morpheme Hierarchy and the Scalar Specificity Constraint

In section 3.1, we propose a revised motion morpheme hierarchy that can better predict the order in MMMCs. The hierarchy is verified by two corpus-based studies of recent Chinese novels. In Section 3.2, we propose the Scalar Specificity Constraint to account for why the hierarchy holds.

[3] Lin and Peck (2011) do not treat the deictic motion morphemes *lai* 'come' and *qu* 'go' in construction-final position as real motion morphemes, as in *pao-jin-**lai*** run-enter-come 'run in towards the deictic center' and *pao-jin fangjian* ***lai*** run-enter room come 'run into the room towards the deictic center'. Therefore, their hierarchy does not include the distribution of such *lai* 'come' or *qu* 'go'.

3.1 Revised Motion Morpheme Hierarchy

We observe that multi-point and two-point closed scale motion morphemes usually do not co-occur, for instance, **lai-jin come-enter*, **hui-chu return-exit*. The only exception is the two-point closed scale motion morpheme *dao* 'arrive'; *dao* can occur after all types of motion morphemes, including morphemes of its own type, i.e. two-point closed scale motion morphemes such as *jin* 'enter' and *chu* 'exit', as in (5).

(5) gun/luo/hui/jin-dao xuexiao
roll/fall/return/enter-arrive school
'roll to/fall to/return to/enter the school'

Therefore, to better reflect the possible motion constructions that exist and do not exist in Chinese, we propose a revised Motion Morpheme Hierarchy in which multi-point and two-point closed scale motion morphemes are grouped together, whereas the special motion morpheme *dao* 'arrive' is listed separately in a box with dotted-line border in the rightmost position of the hierarchy; the new hierarchy is given in (6).

(6)

Nonscalar change (a):	→	**Open scale (b):**	→	**Multi-point closed scale (c):**	→	**Special motion morpheme (e):**
gun 'roll'		*luo* 'fall'		*hui* 'return'		*dao* 'arrive'
pao 'run'		*shang* 'ascend'		*lai* 'come'		
fei 'fly'		*xia* 'descend'		*qu* 'go', etc.		
zou 'walk'		*tui* 'recede'		**Two-point closed scale (d):**		
etc.		*sheng* 'ascend'		*jin* 'enter'		
		etc.		*chu* 'exit', etc.		

Two corpus-based studies of recent Chinese novels are carried out to verify the hierarchy. In the first study, we collect all MMMCs from selected chapters of four Chinese novels[4] and investigate whether the motion morphemes in those MMMCs are in an order consistent with the hierarchy. A total of 231 MMMCs are found consisting of two motion morphemes (the deictic motion morphemes *lai* 'come' and *qu* 'go' are not treated as a real motion morpheme, see Footnote 4).[5] Figure 1 illustrates the types of the 231 two-motion-morpheme MMMCs, along with their frequencies of occurrence.

As Figure 1 shows, the morpheme order in 230 MMMCs is consistent with the hierarchy, whereas one MMMC is in an order that is not predicted by the hierarchy, i.e. the MMMC consisting of an open scale motion morpheme followed by a nonscalar change motion morpheme. This exception is given in (7).

(7) yiwusuoyou de piaopiao **sheng-fei**
with.nothing MOD drifting scend-fly
'[She] is ascending and flying in a drifting manner; nothing is with her.' (*Kongzhong Xiaojie*)

[4] The corpus data includes the entire novel of *Taiyang Chushi* 'The Sun was Born' by Chi Li in 1992 (35,433 characters), the first six chapters from *Diqiu de Hong Piaodai* 'The Earth's Red Flying Ribbon' by Wei Wei in 1998 (34,108 characters), the entire novel of *Kongzhong Xiaojie* 'Flight Attendant' by Wang Shuo in 1985 (29,185 characters), the first twelve chapters of *Taiyang Zhao zai Sangganheshang* by Ding Ling in 1952 (28,935 characters).

[5] Thirteen MMMCs consisting of three motion morphemes (the final morpheme is not deictic *lai* 'come' or *qu* 'go') are found in the two corpus studies. For instance, *duo-hui-dao zhouzi-pang* stroll-return-arrive table-side 'stroll back to the table'. The morpheme order of all these MMMCs is found to be consistent with hierarchy. However, no further discussion is given in this paper because of space limit.

However, (7) does not represent a strong challenge to the hierarchy for two reasons. First, the study finds 36 MMMCs consisting of a nonscalar change (e.g., *zou* 'walk', *pao* 'run') and an open scale motion morpheme (e.g., *shang* 'ascend', *xia* 'descend'). *Sheng-fei* ascend-fly is the only instance in which the open scale motion morpheme precedes the nonscalar change motion morpheme. Second, in order to determine whether *sheng* 'ascend' must precede *fei* 'fly' whenever they occur together, both the orders, *sheng-fei* ascend-fly and *fei-sheng* fly-ascend, are searched for in the PKU Corpus. The results show that *fei* always precedes *sheng*. Therefore, it is likely that the instance of *sheng-fei* ascend-fly in (7) is a nonce use by the author.

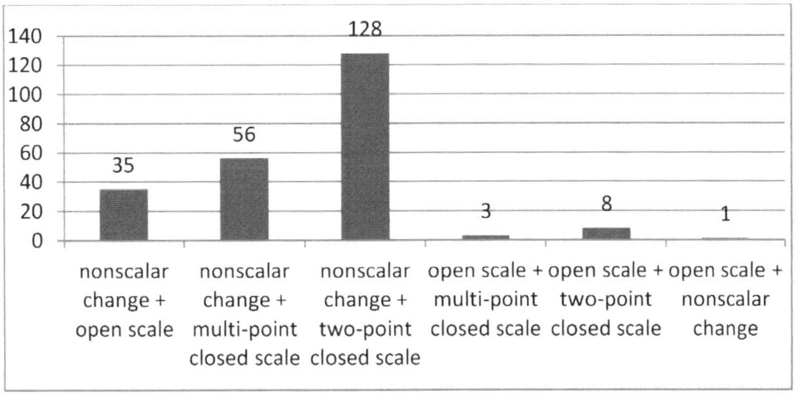

Figure 1. Frequencies of the types of two-motion-morpheme MMMCs

In the second corpus study, we choose the most frequently used motion morphemes from each type of motion morphemes found in Corpus Study 1. These morphemes are then searched for in the novel category of the PKU Corpus, and their relative order with the co-occurring motion morphemes are investigated.[6] Table 1 lists the morphemes investigated.[7]

Table 3 Motion morphemes to be investigated in Corpus Study 2

Morpheme types in the hierarchy	Nonscalar change motion morpheme	Open scale motion morpheme	(Multi-point /two-point) closed scale motion morpheme	*dao* 'arrive'
Motion morphemes investigated	*zou* 'walk' *pao* 'run'	*shang* 'ascend' *xia* 'descend'	*hui* 'return' *chu* 'exit'	*dao* 'arrive'

Figures 2-8 display the distribution of each key morpheme in two-morpheme MMMCs. In each figure, there are three columns, with the middle column representing the key morpheme, the column to its left representing the number of occurrences of different types of motion morphemes that precede the key morpheme, and the column to its right representing the number of occurrences of different types of motion morphemes that follow the key morpheme in MMMCs. Take Figure 2, for example: the motion morpheme in the middle column is *zou* 'walk', which is the key morpheme. In total, 334 instances of *zou* were found to occur in MMMCs. The column to its right represents the different types of motion morphemes that occur

[6] To make the manual analysis feasible, only the first 1,000 instances of each motion morpheme searched for in the novel category of the PKU Corpus were selected and analyzed. However, there are instances in which the morpheme searched for is not used in a MMMC, or even not used as a motion morpheme. Therefore, the numbers of MMMCs collected for analysis is much less than 7,000 (1,000 for each motion morpheme), as shown in Figures 2-8.

[7] Multi-point closed scale and two-point closed scale motion morphemes (other than *dao* 'arrive') do not co-occur, so they were grouped together as closed scale motion morphemes.

after *zou*: 99 instances of *dao* 'arrive', 201 instances of closed scale motion morphemes (including both multi-point closed and two-point closed scale motion morphemes, e.g., *hui* 'return' in *zou hui-lai* walk return-come, *jìn* 'enter' in *zou-jin shangdian* walk-enter store), and 34 instances of open scale motion morphemes (e.g., *shang* 'ascend' in *zou-shang che* walk-ascend car). The column to the left of the *zou* column represents the types of motion morphemes that precede *zou* in MMMCs. However, as illustrated in Figure 2, no motion morpheme occurring before *zou* was found in the corpus search.

The figures show that the distribution of the key motion morphemes in MMMCs is consistent with the revised hierarchy. Among them, Figure 8 shows that *dao* 'arrive' can follow any type of motion morphemes. Other than *dao*, two closed scale motion morphemes do not co-occur, as predicted by the hierarchy.

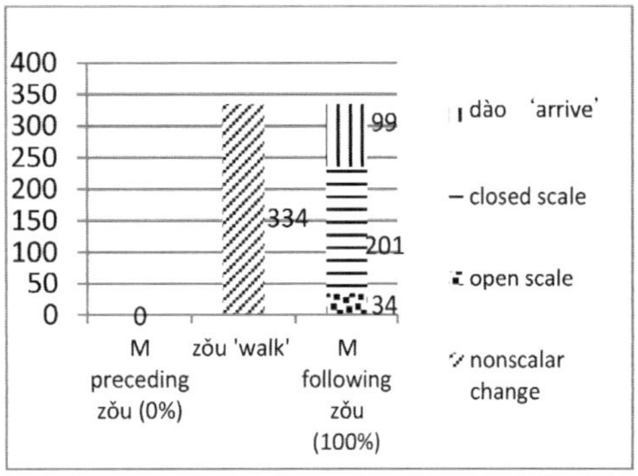

Figure 2. *Zou* 'walk'

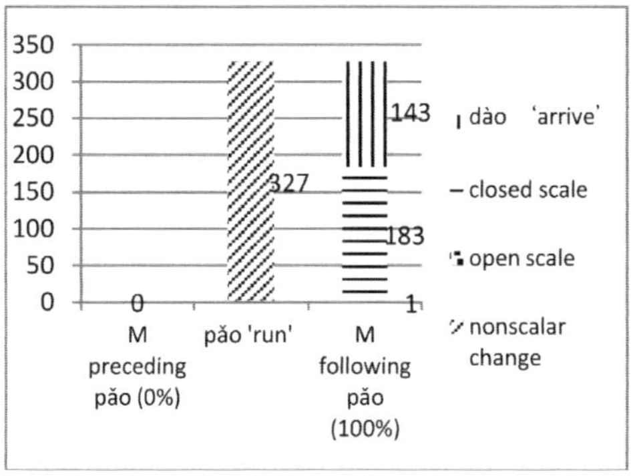

Figure 3. *Pao* 'run'

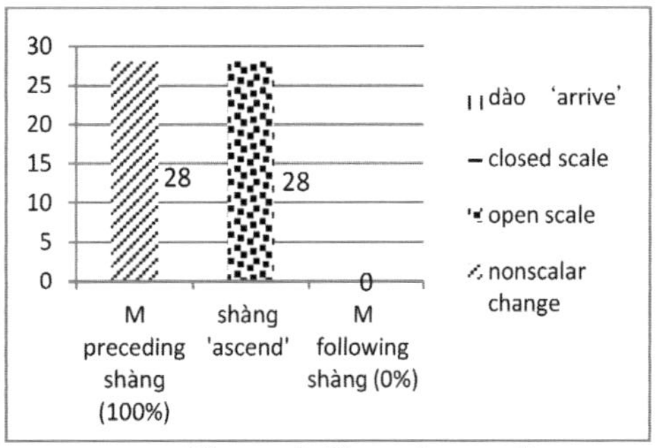

Figure 4. *Shang* 'ascend'

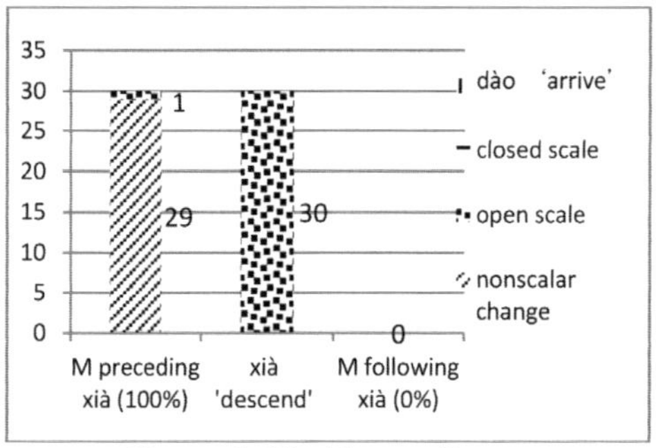

Figure 5. *Xia* 'descend'

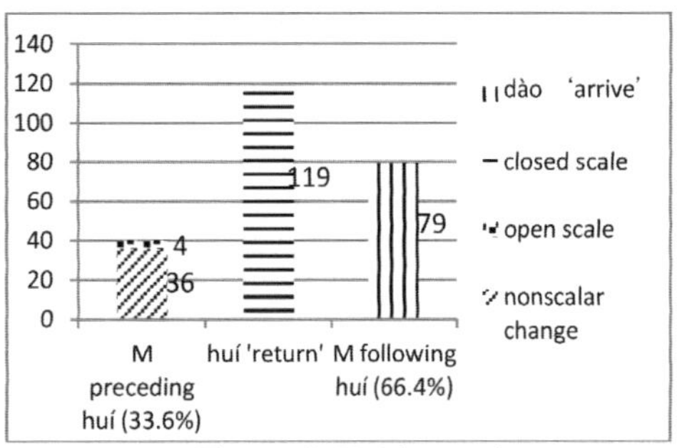

Figure 6. *Hui* 'return'

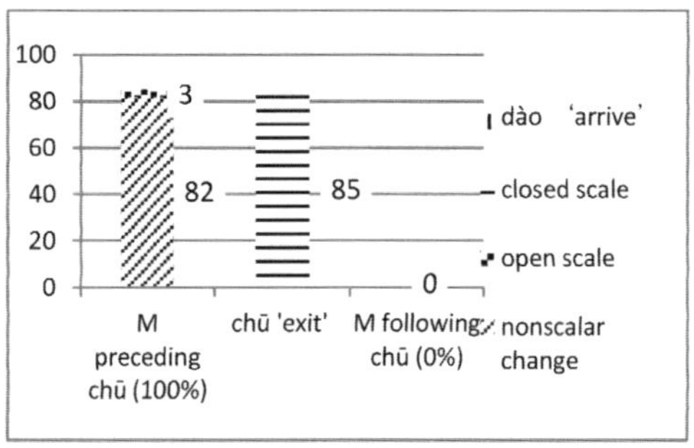

Figure 7. *Chu* 'exit'

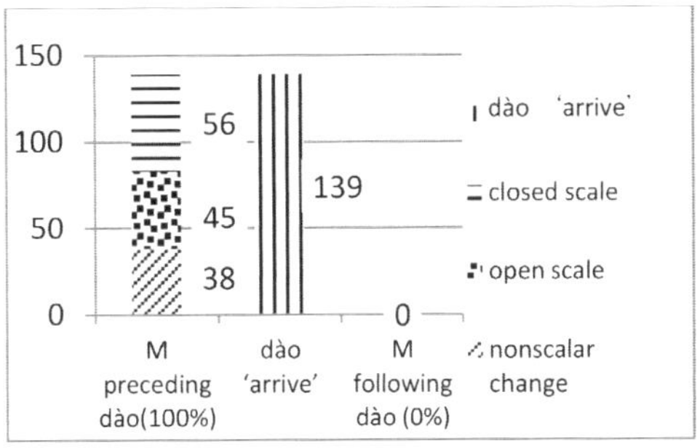

Figure 8. *Dao* 'arrive'

3.2 The Scalar Specificity Constraint

We propose the "Scalar Specificity Constraint" that explains why the hierarchy in (6) emerges: the morpheme that is less specific about the scale in a motion event must precede the morpheme with more specific scalar information. In the remainder of this section, we first elaborate how the constraint gives rise to the hierarchy, including why two closed scale motion morphemes usually do not co-occur, then turn to *dao* 'arrive' and give explanation why it can be exception.

-The Scalar Specificity Constraint gives rise to the Revised Motion Morpheme Hierarchy

The Scalar Specificity Constraint requires a morpheme with more specific information about the scale to follow the one with less information; this explains why the hierarchy in (6) emerges.

First, in terms of degree of specification about a scale, nonscalar change motion morphemes (e.g., *gun* 'roll') do not provide any information about the scale, open scale motion morphemes (e.g., *luo* 'fall') specify the existence of a scale, whereas (both multi-point and two-point) closed scale motion morphemes such as *hui* 'return' and *jin* 'enter' not only specify the existence of a scale, but also the existence of an endpoint for the scale. Therefore, to satisfy the Scalar Specificity Constraint, when these morphemes form a hierarchy to predict morpheme order, they must follow an order as represented by the three boxes with solid-line border in (6).

Second, in terms of the degree of specification of a scale, a two-point closed scale motion morpheme (e.g., *jin* 'enter)' is not more specific than a multi-point closed scale motion morpheme (e.g., *hui* 'return)', or vice versa: both specify the existence of a scale and the existence of an endpoint for the scale. Therefore, conforming to the Scalar Specificity Constraint, two closed scale motion morphemes do not co-occur, as in **hui-jin fangjian* return-enter room. This explains why the two types of morphemes should be grouped together in (6).

Compared with the Motion Morpheme Hierarchy proposed by Lin and Peck (2011), the revised hierarchy and the Scalar Specificity Constraint provide a more precise prediction of the morpheme order and a better coverage of the motion constructions in natural Chinese data.

-*Dao* 'arrive' as a special motion morpheme

The two-point closed scale motion morpheme *dao* 'arrive' can follow other closed scale motion morphemes, as in *hui-dao fangjian* return-arrive room 'return to the room' and *jin-dao fangjian* enter-arrive room 'enter the room', whereas other two-point closed scale motion morphemes such as *jin* 'enter' cannot follow another closed scale motion morpheme, as in **hui-jin fangjian* return-enter room and **lai-jin fangjian* come-enter room. In terms of the degree of specification of scale information, *dao* 'arrive' is as specific as other two-point closed scale motion morphemes, i.e. they all specify the existence of a scale, as well as the existence of an endpoint for the scale. Therefore, the fact that *dao* 'arrive' can follow closed scale motion morphemes represents an exception to the Scalar Specificity Constraint.

Lin (to appear) points out that although *dao* 'arrive' lexicalizes a closed scale, it does not specify information about the direction in which a moving object moves to the reference object, nor what kind of reference object is involved in the motion event. In contrast, the other two-point closed scale motion morphemes such as *jin* 'enter' and *chu* 'exit' are highly specific about the reference object and path: *jin* 'enter' expresses a boundary-crossing motion event involving motion from the outside to the inside of an enclosed region, whereas *chu* 'exit' expresses a similar event in a reverse direction. For instance, *jin* 'enter' and *chu* 'exit' only select NPs expressing enclosed regions (e.g., house, but not table) as their complements, as in (6), whereas *dao* 'arrive' can take any kind of reference object NPs as its complements, as in (7).

(6) xiaomao jin **fangzi-li/*zhuozi-shang** le
kitty enter house-inside/table-on.top.of ASP
'The kitty entered the house/#The kitty entered on top of the table.'

(7) xiaomao dao **fangzi-li/zhuozi-shang** le
kitty arrive house-inside/table-on.top.of ASP
'The kitty went inside the house/The kitty went onto the table.'

For this reason, when *dao* 'arrive' occurs with another closed scale motion morpheme, it does not add new information about the reference object or path that may be different from or incompatible with the information denoted by the co-occurring motion morpheme. This explains why *dao* 'arrive' can follow all kinds of motion morphemes, whereas *jin* 'enter' and *chu* 'exit' cannot. It also indicates that *dao* 'arrive' should be treated as a special motion morpheme that the Scalar Specificity Constraint does not apply to.

4 Conclusions

To conclude, this paper proposes a revised Motion Morpheme Hierarchy that can better predict the order of motion morphemes in the description of directed motion events. In addition, it proposes the Scalar Specificity Constraint that accounts for why the hierarchy is valid, and explains why *dao* 'arrive' behaves as an exception to the constraint. The results of this study not only shed light on the role of the scalar specificity a motion morpheme lexicalizes in determining the morpheme's distribution, but also may be extensible to the ordering of motion verbs/morphemes in other serial verb languages such as Thai (cf. Thepkanjana 1986, Muansuwan 2000) and Ewe (cf. Ameka and Essegbey 2001).

References

Ameka, F. and J. Essegbey. 2001. Serialising languages: satellite-framed, verb-framed or neither. Paper presented at *The 32nd Annual Conference on African Linguistics*. University of California, Berkeley.

Li, C. and S. Thompson. 1981. *Mandarin Chinese: a Functional Reference Grammar*. Berkeley: University of California Press.

Li, Y. 1993. Structural head and aspectuality. *Language* (69), 480-504.

Lin, J. To appear. The figure's final location must be identifiable: Localizer distribution in Chinese directed motion construction. *Proceedings of the 37th Annual Meeting of the Berkeley Linguistics Society.*

Lin, J. and J. Peck. 2011. The syntax of multi-morpheme motion construction in Chinese: An analysis based on scale structure. *Studies in Language*, 35(2), 337–379.

Muansuwan, N. 2000. Directional serial verb constructions in Thai. In *Proceedings of the 7th International HPSG Conference, UC Berkeley*. Stanford: CSLI Publications.

Rappaport Hovav, M. and B. Levin. 2010. Reflections on manner/result complementarity. In E. Doron, M. Rappaport Hovav, and I. Sichel, eds., *Syntax, Lexical Semantics, and Event Structure*, pp. 21-38. Oxford: Oxford University Press.

Tai, J. H-Y. 1985. Temporal sequence and word order. In John Haiman, ed., Chinese. *Iconicity in Syntax*, pp. 49-72. Amsterdam: John Benjamins.

Talmy, L. 1975. Semantics and Syntax of Motion. In John Kimball, ed., *Syntax and Semantics 4*, pp. 181-238. New York: Academic Press.

Thepkanjana, Kingkarn. 1986. *Serial Verb Construction in Thai*. Ph.D. Dissertation, University of Michigan, Ann Arbor.

Verbs and (sub)Event Structure: A Case Study from Italian *

Francesca Strik Lievers

Department of Chinese and Bilingual Studies, The Hong Kong Polytechnic University,
Hung Hom, Kowloon, Hong Kong
Dipartimento di Linguistica, Università di Pisa,
Via Santa Maria 36, Pisa, Italy
francesca.striklievers@gmail.com

Abstract. In this paper, I try to show the advantages of analyzing events in terms of subevent structure, by taking into consideration the case of a specific class of verbs: transitive and intransitive verbs which obligatorily require the presence of a predicative complement (e.g., English *seem*, *consider*). The proposed analysis is exemplified with data from Italian. Two verbs are described in detail: *rimanere*, 'remain' and *rendere*, 'make'. It is shown that subevent structure representation is useful for the description of the different uses and meanings of these verbs. This type of description can also be the basis for an accurate treatment in computational semantic lexica.

Keywords: event structure, Italian, predicative complement, verbs, Generative Lexicon.

1 Introduction

The relationship between events[1] and verbs is notoriously strong, since in most cases verbs lexicalize event predicates, and event predicates are lexicalized by verbs. However, the class of verbs is not uniform (although at least in Italian and in other European languages it is easily defined on the basis of morphological criteria). And, at the same time, it is not exclusively verbs that can be used to code events. A brief overview of some cases of mismatch between verbs and (lexicalizations of) events will be useful for defining the class of verbs with predicative complement in Italian.

2 The place of verbs with predicative complement in the verbal lexicon

The most relevant distinction is that between predicative verbs and verbs that are used to support other predicative elements. The label "predicative verbs" refers to verbs that function as nucleus of simple sentences (e.g., *sleep*, *eat*). Support (or "light") verbs, on the contrary, do not have the role of predicative nucleus of the sentence, but they can supply event nouns with the verbal morphology they lack, thus allowing the noun to act as predicative nucleus. Verbs can function as support to other predicative elements in at least two other cases: auxiliaries and the copula. In both cases the verb functions as the "skeleton" of a process, and "[a]n adjective, preposition, participle, or infinitive puts 'flesh' on the skeleton" (Langacker 1987: 77). Auxiliary and semi-auxiliary verbs occur with predicative verbs in non-finite form, contributing morphological information and eventually additional information such as modality or aspect. The copula *essere* ('to be') is also non-predicative: it enables a non-verbal predicate to function

* This work was supported by Erasmus Mundus Action 2 Strand 2 Lot 4 MULTI programme / agreement number 2009-5259/005-001-EMA2.

[1] As it is well known, the term "event" has been used in many different ways. In what follows, it has a meaning similar to what elsewhere in the literature is often called "eventuality" (after Bach 1986), that is, it refers to all types of situation (cf. Levin and Rappaport Hovav 2005).

as the main predicate of the clause. This means that it is the non-verbal predicate that determines the number and semantic type of arguments (cf. Hengeveld 1992: 29). The combination of the copula with the non-verbal predicate gives rise to a specific type of predication, where a referent is put into relationship with a class or property expressed by the non verbal predicate.

Also the so-called copular verbs, like English *seem* and *become*, are verbs that can be used only in association with a non-verbal predication, i.e., the predicative complement. These verbs are here analyzed together with transitive verbs that also obligatorily require an (object) predicative complement, such as English *consider*, *make*. Some verbs requiring a predicative complement in Italian are listed in (1):

(1) Subject predicative complement: *apparire* ('appear'), *diventare* ('become'), *finire* ('end'), *parere* ('appear'), *rimanere* ('remain'), *sembrare* ('seem'), *stare* ('stay'), *suonare* ('sound'), ...
Object predicative complement: *considerare* ('consider'), *credere* ('believe'), *fare* ('make'), *lasciare* ('leave'), *mantenere* ('maintain'), *rendere* ('make'), *vedere* ('see'), ...

As the copula, these verbs require a predicative complement. But, while the copula is not part of the predicate (cf. Hengeveld 1992: 32), verbs with predicative complement are part of the predicate, determining at least partly the content of the event and argument structure. However, differently from "regular" predicative verbs, in order to reach a complete semantic and syntactic independence they need a predicative complement. Verb and predicative complement form a complex predicate, describing a complete event. My proposal is that this event can be well described in terms of subeventual analysis.

As regards the type of event they describe, Italian verbs with predicative complement can be divided into two main classes: simple events (e.g., *sembrare*, 'seem'), and complex events (e.g., *diventare*, 'become') (see §3 for this distinction). The two verbs that will be analysed here in detail (*rimanere*, 'remain', and *rendere*, 'make') are both describing complex events, for which an analysis in terms of subevents shows to be particularly useful.

3 The Generative Lexicon and event representation

In the literature, there are of course different approaches to event structure and subeventual analysis (e.g., Grimshaw 1990, Pustejovsky 1991, Levin and Rappaport Hovav 2005, Goldberg 2010). Here I refer to that developed within the Generative Lexicon (henceforth, GL) framework developed by James Pustejovsky (1991, 1995), that is briefly introduced in the following paragraph.

Three main event types are recognized in GL: states, processes, transitions. While states are simple events, consisting of a single event, processes and transitions are complex events, where subevents can be ordered according to different temporal relations. Processes consist of a sequence of subevents that are identical and temporally ordered. Transitions consist of two subevents that can be ordered following different temporal relations and syntactic prominence relations called headedness (Pustejovsky 1995: 72). The event described in *to build a house* (an accomplishment, in classical *Aktionsart* terms), for example, is a transition where e_1 is a process and e_2 is a state; e_1 is the head subevent (marked with an asterisk in representations) and it precedes e_2. To complete the description of this event, another level of information is necessary: opposition structure. The resulting structural representation is the following (cf. Pustejovsky 2000: 459)[2]:

[2] The sum of two temporally overlapping (°) events e_1 and e_3 is here marked (following Pustejovsky 2000: 458, footnote 13) as the projection of the most prominent event e_1, noted as $\bar{e}_1$.

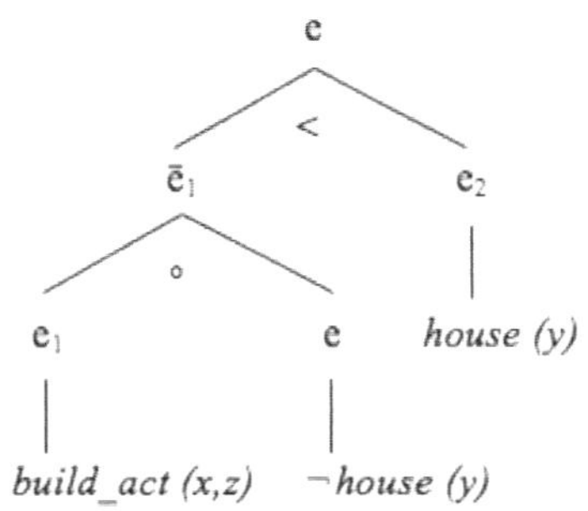

Figure 1: Structure of the event *to build a house* in GL.[3]

This representation accounts for the function (*gating function*) of the verb *build* in bringing into existence the referent of its direct object, *house*. Subevent e_3 (the non-existence of the object) is the precondition for the event to be true. The gating function can have four different consequences on the arguments of predicates (Pustejovsky 2000: 468):

1. The argument persists: *A man sat on a bench.*
2. The head of the argument does not persist: *Mary ate a cookie.*
3. The head of the argument persists, but there are properties of the head introduced by predication that do not persist: *Mary cleaned the table.*
4. The head of the argument persists, but there are properties of the head expressed in the referring expression that do not persist: *Mary fixed the flat tire.*

As it will emerge from the analysis below, depending on the type of the predicative complement that combines with the verb, the scope of the opposition introduced by the verb can be different: it may concern the head or a property of the argument the predicative complement applies to.

4 Case study 1: *rimanere* ('remain')

At a first glance, the verb *rimanere* ('remain') may appear as the 'prototypical' stative verb, therefore characterized by the simplest event structure. However, at a closer look the situation shows to be more complex. When it is used with a predicative complement, the contribution of the verb *rimanere* is mainly aspectual in nature. However, the aspectual properties of the predication are determined compositionally, depending also on the characteristics of the predicative complement. Let us consider the following examples:[4]

(2) *Ha ottant'anni ma è rimasta affascinante.*
'She is 80 years old, but she remained attractive'.

(3) *È rimasto ferito durante una sparatoria.*
'He was wounded during a firefight'.

It can immediately be noted that these two phrases are aspectually different one from the other. While the first one describes a lasting state, in the second one the state described by the predicative complement is seen as the result of an event that is "dynamic" (i.e., non-stative).

The question is then: what triggers one interpretation or the other? Considering the two examples given above, a first hypothesis could be that adjectives are related to the stative sense, while past participles are related to the dynamic sense. Although it is often so, things show to be more complex. For instance, it appears that: a) some adjectives allow a dynamic interpretation:

[3] "Gating will be defined as the introduction of termination or initiation conditions for the sort or properties of an argument" (Pustejovsky 2000: 457).

[4] Some examples are extracted from the *La Repubblica* corpus (http://sslmit.unibo.it/repubblica).

(4) *È rimasto sordo in seguito a un incidente.*
'He went deaf due to an accident'.

and b) some past participles allow a stative interpretation, as in:

(5) *Il traffico è rimasto bloccato per due ore.*
'The traffic remained blocked for two hours'.

There is therefore need for a more fine-grained analysis of the different predicative complements that can occur with the verb *rimanere*.

Rimanere: Adjectives

Let us start with adjectival predicative complements. The relevant distinction here is that between individual-level (IL) and stage-level (SL) adjectives. Looking at data, it comes out that when the adjective is classifiable as IL, the event is stative[5], as in this example:

(6) *Anna è rimasta bella come quando era giovane*
'Anna remained beautiful as when she was young'.

Stative predications are uniform (cf. Binnick 1991). However, *rimanere* has a complex event structure, at the level of presupposition. Following the representation proposed by Schlücker (2004) for German *bleiben* ('remain'), '*rimanere* + IL Adj' can be described as follows: it is asserted that state P (expressed by the adjective) holds at event time t, and it is at the same time presupposed[6] that P holds for time t' preceding t.[7]

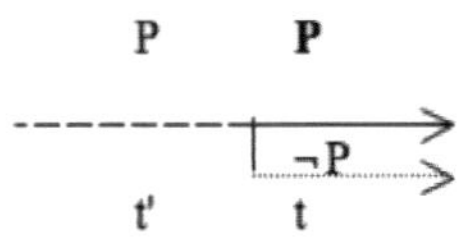

Figure 2: '*rimanere* + IL Adj'

Event structure for <*rimanere* + IL Adj> can be thus represented by modifying GL event structure representation to include also presupposed subevents, that are indicated by dotted lines.

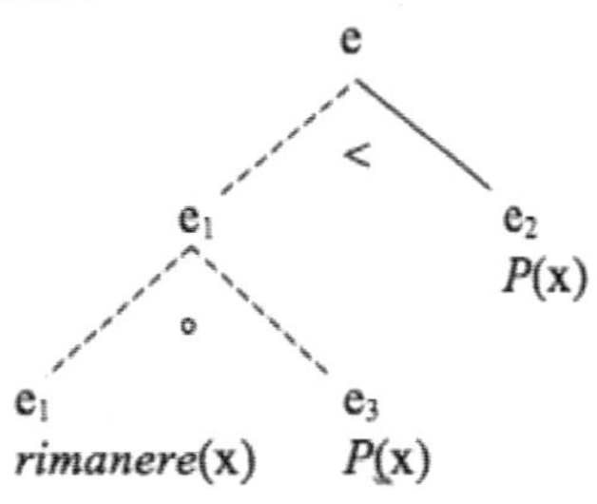

Figure 3: *Rimanere*: stative sense

[5] This is confirmed by the traditional stativity tests, such as the impossibility to occur with "in x time" adverbials (**Anna è rimasta bella in tre giorni*, 'Anna remained beautiful in three days) and aspectual operators like 'finish' (**Anna ha appena finito di rimanere bella*, 'Anna has just finished remaining beautiful').

[6] It is a semantic (vs. pragmatic) presupposition, holding under negation: *Anna è rimasta bella* presupposes that Anna was beautiful before event time; the same holds for *Anna non è rimasta bella*.

[7] Schlücker (2004) notes that German *bleiben* ('remain') appears in a context where the counterstate (¬P) would be expected to occur, instead of the asserted state. The same holds for *rimanere*, so that a sentence like *Anna è rimasta bella* would be interpreted as 'Anna did not become ugly'.

Only the state in e_2 is asserted. How do we account, then, for the difference between *Anna è bella* and *Anna è rimasta bella*? In both cases it is only asserted the state P expressed by the predicative complement (*bella*). In the sentence with *rimanere*, however, it is also presupposed a subevent preceding the event time, where the same state P holds.
The event structure represented in Figure 3 could also be applied to nominal predicative complements.

The event is in most cases stative also with SL adjectives. However, there are some differences that are worth mentioning. IL and SL adjectives behave differently with respect to some aspectual tests. For example, SLs can occur as complement of *force/persuade*, or can occur as imperative, as it is shown in (7a) and (7b). ILs usually cannot occur in these contexts, as shown in (8a) and (8b):

(7) a. *Lo hanno convinto a rimanere zitto*
'They persuaded him to remain silent'.
b. *Non rimanete svegli ad aspettarmi!*
'Don't stay awake to wait for me!'
(8) a. ?? *Ho convinto Anna a rimanere alta / intelligente ...*
'I persuaded Anna to remain tall / intelligent /...'
b. ??*Anna, rimani alta / intelligente / ...!*
'Anna, remain tall / intelligent /...!'

These tests are traditionally used to identify states (cf. Lakoff 1966), which usually cannot occur in these contexts. However, with reference to verb aspect, it has been noted (among others, by Dowty 1979: 183-184, Levin-Rapppaport Hovav 2005: 89) that classical stativity tests should instead be used to individuate non-agentive verbs. This fits well with Pustejovsky's interpretation of SL adjectives: "What distinguishes stage-level from the general class of stative predicates is the inherent reference to that factor that brings this state about; [...] there is reference to the "coming into being" factor, the AGENTIVE role in the qualia." (Pustejovsky 1995: 225). To summarize, then, '*rimanere* + Adj' is stative[8], but it is agentive with SL adjectives and non-agentive with IL adjectives.

Temporal adverbials such as 'for x time', 'from x time to x time' are usually odd with IL adjectives, since temporal restrictions can hardly apply to (in principle) permanent predicates. These adverbials can occur, and do frequently occur, with SL adjectives. Interestingly, temporal restrictions apply only to the asserted state, canceling at the same time the presupposition (in this case *rimanere* is thus almost equivalent to the copula *essere*, except for the presupposition that a counterstate would have been more likely to occur, see footnote 7).

(9) *I treni sono rimasti fermi dalle 8 alle 20.*
'The trains remained standing from 8 to 20'.

Rimanere: Past Participles

As it has been noted above, past participles can code both stative and dynamic events. Is it possible to identify different classes of past participles that can be associated to one or to the other sense?

[8] A dynamic interpretation is available only with a small number of SL adjectives (as in the following example: *La capitale è rimasta priva di elettricità.*'The capital remained lacking electricity'). These adjectives are usually qualifying the subject as lacking something, and the subject is interpreted as a patient in the event, as it is the case with past participles of highly transitive verbs described in what follows (they are also receiving a dynamic interpretation).

The first distinction that shows to be relevant is that between Target-states and Resultant-states (Parsons, 1990: 234-235), i.e., between (in principle) reversible states and states holding forever after the event that brings them about.

The stative sense occurs only when the participle is a Target state:

(10) *La pistola è rimasta nascosta nel cassetto.*
'The gun remained hidden in the drawer'.

The reason for that is that in the stative sense we find reference to a counterstate and, as Schlücker (2008: 362) notes, reference to a counterstate can obviously not be possible if the state expressed by the participle is not reversible, i.e., if there is no possibility of change.

The dynamic sense occurs with Resultant states. More specifically, it occurs with two subclasses of Resultant states: past participles of highly transitive verbs[9], and past participles of psychological verbs. These two subclasses are linked to two partially different dynamic senses.

The first class includes past participles of verbs such as *uccidere* ('kill'), *colpire* ('hit'), etc.

(11) *Per fortuna, nessun agente è rimasto ferito.*
'Fortunately, any policeman remained injured'.

The second class contains past participles of verbs such as *scioccare* ('shock'), *affascinare* ('charm'):

(12) *Anna è rimasta scioccata dal film.*
'Anna remained shocked by the film'.

It is now possible to describe the event structure of the dynamic sense of *rimanere*. It is a transition, since, as it has been pointed out, it describes a change of state. More precisely, aspectual tests[10] show that it behaves like achievements, i.e., it is a right-headed transition. Figure 4 highlights also the opposition introduced by the event: a property of the subject is modified from ¬P to P:

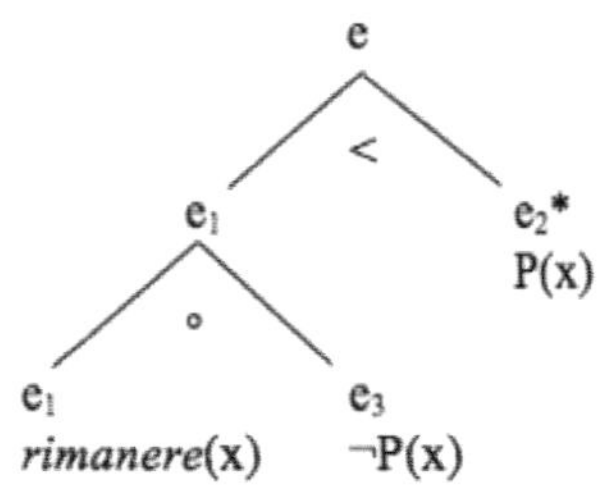

Figure 4: *Rimanere*: "dynamic" sense.

In the Qualia Structure, a Formal role corresponds to the state in e_2.

5 Case Study 2: *Rendere* ('make')

'*Rendere* + predicative complement' is found in phrases like the following:

[9] Prototipical transitive verbs can be defined as 'those verbs which describe an action that not only impinges on the patient but necessarily creates a change in it' (Tsunoda 1985: 387).

[10] For example, it does not allow verbs like *cominciare* ('to start'): **Ha cominciato a rimanere ucciso* ('He started remaining killed').

(13) *Fortissime e ripetute emicranie gli rendevano la vita impossibile.*
'Very strong and recurrent migraines made life impossible for him'.

It is a causative event, that can be represented as in Figure 5:

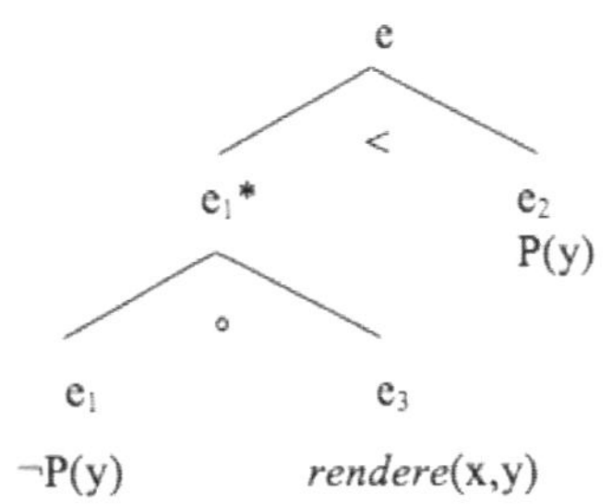

Figure 5: *Rendere*: event and opposition structure.

The structure is composed by two subevents e_1 and e_2, where e_1 is a process that temporally precedes, and is the cause of, the resulting state e_2. In the Qualia Structure, an Agentive role corresponds to e_1 and a Formal role corresponds to e_2. The event described by '*rendere* P' can be defined as a direct causative accomplishment[11] (Pustejovsky 1995: 187).

Unlike what happens with *rimanere*, with *rendere* different predicative complements are not associated to different event structures. They are instead associated to different opposition structures. It has been shown above that the event introduces an opposition between P and ¬P with respect to the direct object. When the predicative complement is adjectival, the culmination of the event implies a change in a property of the referent of the direct object. The changing property can be introduced by the predicative complement (opposition type 3), or it can be that explicitly expressed on the direct object (opposition type 4):

(14) *Hanno reso accogliente la stanza.*
'They made the room comfortable'.

(15) *Nessuna donna può rendere intelligente un uomo stupido.*
'Any woman can make intelligent a stupid man'.

When the predicative complement is a NP, what changes is not a property but the head of the direct object itself (opposition type 2):

(16) *Hanno reso l'informazione spettacolo.*
'They made information a show'.

In (16), when the event culminates, the referent of the direct object is not classified as 'information' any more, but as 'show'.

6 Concluding remarks: subevents and lexicographic description

Transitive (e.g., *rendere*) and intransitive (e.g., *rimanere*) verbs have been here considered as describing a single event together with the predicative complement they combine with. We focused on complex events, i.e., events composed by two subevents: it was shown that the first subevent is lexicalized by the verb, while the second subevent is lexicalized by the predicative

[11] The accomplishment interpretation is confirmed by aspectual tests (it can for example occur in imperative mood, it can be introduced by *cominciare*, etc.). Direct causative accomplishments are left-headed events, as it is the case for *rendere*.

complement. These verbs can thus be interpreted as the realization of an analytical strategy to lexicalize events, since the 'skeleton' of the event structure already emerges at the expression level.

The proposed interpretation can also give instruments to improve lexicographic description. Dealing with these (often semantically "light") verbs in computational lexica has proven to be difficult. Even in the SIMPLE lexicon (see Lenci *et al.* 2000), which is based on the GL model, the description that is provided for them appears to be problematic, since the event type that should be attributed to the "verb + predicative complement" complex is usually attributed exclusively to the verb (e.g., *diventare* 'become' is described as a transition, while it is actually '*diventare* + predicative complement' that denotes a transition; *diventare* is responsible only for the process subevent). Thanks to subevent analysis it is possible to isolate, and thus to represent, the contribution of the verb. This is in line with recent proposals drawing attention to the importance of marking subevent structure (Im and Pustejovsky 2010), which could possibly be extended to all eventive entries of computational lexica.

References

Bach, E. 1986. The Algebra of Events. *Linguistics and Philosophy* 9, pp. 5-16.

Binnick, R. 1991. *Time and the Verb*. Oxford. Oxford University Press.

Dowty, D. R. 1979. *Word Meaning and Montague Grammar*. Dordrecht. Kluwer.

Goldberg, A. 2010. Verbs, Constructions and Semantic Frames. In M. Rappaport Hovav *et al.* (eds.). *Syntax, Lexical Semantics and Event Structure*. Oxford University Press, pp. 39-58.

Grimshaw, J. 1990. *Argument Structure*. Cambridge, MA. MIT Press.

Hengeveld, K. 1992. *Non-verbal Predication. Theory, Typology, Diachrony*. Berlin / New York. Mouton de Gruyter.

Im, S. and J. Pustejovsky. 2010. Annotating Lexically Entailed Subevents for Textual Inference Tasks. In *Proceedings of FLAIRS* 2010, pp. 204-209.

Lakoff, G. 1966. Stative Adjectives and Verbs in English. Computation Laboratory, Harvard University Report No. NSF-17.

Langacker, R. 1987. *Nouns and Verbs*. *Language* 63, pp. 53-93.

Lenci, A. *et al.* 2000. *SIMPLE. Linguistic Specifications*, Deliverable D2.1.

Levin, B. and M. Rappaport Hovav. 2005. *Argument Realization*. Cambridge. Cambridge University Press.

Parsons, T. 1990. *Events in the Semantics of English*. Cambridge, Mass. MIT Press.

Pustejovsky, J. 2000. Events and the Semantics of Opposition. In C. Tenny and J. Pustejovsky (eds.). *Events as Grammatical Objects*. Stanford. CSLI Publications, pp. 445–482.

Pustejovsky, J. 1995. *The Generative Lexicon*. Cambridge, MA. MIT Press.

Pustejovsky, J. 1991. The syntax of event structure. *Cognition* 41, pp. 47-81.

Schlücker, B. 2008. Warum *nicht bleiben* nicht *werden* ist: Ein Plädoyer gegen di Dualität von *werden* und *bleiben*. *Linguistische Berichte* 215, pp. 345-371.

Schlücker, B. 2004. On the Event Structure of German *bleiben*. In C. Meier and M. Weisgerber (eds.). *Proceedings of the Conference "sub8 – Sinn und Bedeutung"*. Arbeitspapier Nr. 117. Universität Konstanz, FB Sprachwissenschaft, pp. 259-272.

Tsunoda, T. 1985. Remarks on transitivity. *Journal of Linguistics* 21(2), pp. 385-96.

The Effects of EFL Learners' Awareness and Retention in Learning Metaphoric and Metonymic Expressions

Yi-chen Chen[a], and Huei-ling Lai[b]

[a]Foreign Language Center, National Chengchi University,
NO.64, Sec.2, ZhiNan Rd., Wenshan District, Taipei City 11605, Taiwan (R.O.C)
yicc@nccu.edu.tw
[b]Department of English, National Chengchi University,
NO.64, Sec.2, ZhiNan Rd., Wenshan District, Taipei City 11605, Taiwan (R.O.C)
hllai@nccu.edu.tw

Abstract. Cognitive linguists contend that learners' awareness of motivations is the key in not only second language acquisition but also figurative language learning. Two cognitive-oriented methods are proposed to raise L2 learners' awareness on metaphoric/metonymic expressions and to enhance retention: instruction involving conceptual metaphors (CM) and instruction involving metaphoric mappings (MM). The present study aims to examine their effectiveness in an EFL context. The results show favorable influences on learners' awareness and retention, which confirm that cognitive-oriented instructions indeed can assist learners to make better sense of figurative language. Moreover, the instruction on metaphoric mappings seems to result in better awareness of expressions which involve more complicated and abstract mapping relationships. The findings of the study can shed light on the application of metaphor and metonymy to EFL teaching and learning of figurative language

Keywords: Conceptual metaphor, Metaphoric mappings, Cultural universality/specificity

1. Introduction

Researchers in the field of SLA contend that learners' awareness of motivations is the key in second language acquisition (Ammar, Lightbown, & Spada, 2010; O'Mally & Chamot, 1990; R. Ellis, 2002). Cognitive linguists, applying the idea to research on figurative language learning, demonstrate the beneficial effects of enhanced awareness (Boers, 2000ab, 2001; Boers & Lindstromberg, 2006; N. Ellis, 2006ab ; Chung & Ahrens, 2004; Deignan et al., 1997; Dong, 2004; Kövecses, 2001; Low, 1988, among others). These studies mainly implement metaphoric themes—called conceptual metaphor—during the learning processes in order to raise L2 learners' awareness of semantic motivation behind figurative expressions. The results have proved that L2 learners' enhanced awareness of conceptual metaphor is indeed beneficial in comprehension and retention.

However, the method of providing conceptual metaphor is not unproblematic. First of all, their method mainly focuses on *metaphor*; *metonymy* is seldom taken into consideration. The underestimation of the importance of metonymy may lead to an overlook of its effects on learning figurative expressions. *Metonymy* and *metaphor*, in extant literature, are believed to interact with each other in intricate ways and their boundary is fuzzy (Barnden, 2010; Goossens, 1990; Radden, 2003). Chen & Lai (in press), manifesting their interactions as a continuum, has found that L2 learners respond differently to figurative expressions locating on different spots of the continuum. However, with the significance of *metonymy* taken into consideration, whether L2 learners would respond to figurative expressions differently hasn't been determined.

Moreover, focusing mainly on awareness raising may lead to an underestimation of effects of one important element: the gaps caused by different cultures between native and target languages. In the early stage of learning, both similarities and differences between L1 and L2 may facilitate L2 learning (Kellerman,1977; Odlin, 1989; Ringbom, 1987); with the advance in L2 learning process, such as metaphor and metonymy learning which involve not only languages but also cultures and conventions, conflicts between L1 and L2 knowledge may cause greater difficulties (Kövecses, 2001).

In order to help numerous EFL learners around the world to be more aware of figurative language use, Kövecses' (2001) proposal of integrating metaphoric mappings seems very promising. Presumably, *ontological mappings* that characterize the correspondences between basic constituent elements in the source and in the target domain may help learners to create links between distinct linguistic expressions of the two languages; *epistemic mappings* that carry over knowledge about elements in the source domain onto elements in the target domain may help learners to relate their knowledge of the used and abstract half to the unused and concrete half. The idea of using metaphoric mappings as explicit instructions to facilitate domain linking processes between L1 and L2 figurative concepts not only follows the trend of cognitive linguistics but also deals with cultural gaps by utilizing learners' already-existent world knowledge and universal concepts. However, up till now the idea hasn't been empirically tested yet, and hence hasn't been able to claim its effects on L2 learning.

The present study, therefore, intends to compare the two methods in teaching EFL learners metaphoric and metonymic expressions, determine their effects on L2 figurative language learning, and find a compromising way for EFL learners with different native languages. The two methods are the method of conceptual metaphor (CM), which focuses on giving conceptual metaphors and has learners compare two domains to find associative characteristics, and the method of metaphoric mappings (MM), which emphasizes mapping processes and has learners map between domains and between cultures. The present study targets at Chinese native speakers who are learning English as a foreign language. Their ability of finding figurative expressions and their retention of what have learned are under investigation.

2. Methodology

2.1 Participants

The participants of the study were 68 first-year university students who were non-English majors with levels of English proficiency around intermediate to high-intermediate level. They were all native Chinese speakers, and had learned English for at least six years during their high school years; none of the participants had lived in foreign countries for over one year. The control of the participants' general English proficiency and experience in English is meant to mitigate the impact of factors identified as complicating in previous studies. They were divided into two groups: one group contained 32 participants, and received instruction in conceptual metaphor (the CM group). The other group contains 36 participants, and received instruction in metaphoric mappings (the MM group).

2.2 Instruments

To measure the participants' ability to recognize figurative language use, an awareness test was designed. The test consisted of 48 English sentences collected from dictionaries, a corpus (the British National Corpus), and the internet. The sentences were modified to maintain an average sentence length of 10 to 15 words to ensure that the stimuli were similar and would not influence learners' judgments. Among the 48 sentences, 24 sentences contained metaphoric or metonymic expressions and 24 counterparts contained no figurative intentions in the expressions. Moreover, the sentences that had metaphoric or metonymic expressions were further categorized into four groups based on the metonymy-metaphor continuum: metonymy (C1), metaphoric metonymy (C2), metonymic metaphor (C3), and metaphor (C4). Each category contained sentences that involved embodied descriptions or body-related expressions as well as sentences that did not.

Participants were asked to read each sentence first and determine whether the sentence contained metaphoric/metonymic expressions, or whether it needed to be understood by thinking figuratively. Participants were required to rate their certainty to their judgments on a scale of 1-5; to avoid reading problems caused by unknown vocabulary, one extra option (0) was given as well.

2.3 Procedures and Data Collections

The experiment required two successive weeks to complete. The first week was used to conduct the pretest and to teach, and the second week was used to conduct the posttest. The CM group and the MM group were led through the experiment respectively.

In the beginning of the first week, the participants were given the test in order to determine the participants' default level of awareness. The test took 15 minutes to complete. After the test, the CM group and the MM group received instructions about conceptual metaphors and metaphoric mappings, respectively, and were led to discussions in Chinese about the metaphoric/metonymic expressions used in a given article. The goals of the discussions were to lead the participants to be aware of the pervasiveness of metaphoric and metonymic expressions, to clarify an idea that *pì-yù* ('metaphor') includes not only idioms but words or phrases, and to draw their attention to the similarities and differences between Chinese and English. The teaching and discussing phase lasted 25 minutes. One week after, the participants were given the 15-minute test again to examine the effects on retention and in what ways the two instructions might cause different learning effects. The test used contained the same test items as the one used in the first week, but the orders of the items were reshuffled. Before taking the test, the participants were asked whether they had studied relevant subjects during the week to ensure that their performances would result from the effect of learning.

The results of the tests were calculated by SPSS 17. Some external factors, including the participants' scores in English on the JCEE, their time spent on learning English by themselves outside of classes, and their study of relevant subjects during the week, were calculated in order to exclude possible impacts of the participants' individual background differences.

3. Results

Table 1 shows the mean performance scores of the participants. The mean scores show that the participants of both CM and MM group had overall improvements. The improvements of scores also indicate that the participants became more certain about their judgments of recognizing metaphoric/metonymic expressions.

Table2 reports differences in participants' performances between pretest and posttest. Regarding the sentences containing metaphoric/metonymic expressions, the CM group showed no significant progress whereas the MM group showed significant differences between two tests. On the other hand, regarding the sentences containing no metaphoric/metonymic expressions, both groups performed no significant differences between the two tests. In sum, the results suggest that explicit instructions on metaphoric/metonymic expression indeed enhanced learners' awareness of figurative language use; however, the instruction on metaphoric mappings resulted in significantly better improvement on the participants' ability to recognize figurative expressions.

Table 3 reports the results of comparing the progress that the CM and the MM group made in evaluating sentences in the posttest. The results show that the CM group had better improvements than the MM groups did on evaluating both sentences with and without metaphoric/metonymic expressions; however, the differences between two groups were not significant.

In what specific ways could the instruction on metaphoric mappings facilitate steady learning requires further investigation. Thus, the finer-grained analyses based on metaphor-metonymy continuum were conducted and reported in Table 4. The CM-group participants did not make significant progress on any of the four categories, though they received higher scores averagely in the posttest. However, the MM-group participants made significant progress in Category Three (C3) and Category Four (C4).

Table 5 reports the results of cross-examination between sentences with/without body-related metaphoric/metonymic expressions and the four categories to further determine the effects of transparency and opaqueness on the participants. Regarding the sentences whose metaphoric/metonymic expressions contained body-related descriptions, the participants of both groups did not show any significant progress in the four categories of expressions. However, regarding the sentences whose metaphoric/metonymic expressions did not contain body-related descriptions, the CM-group participants did not make any significant progress in any of the four categories, while the MM-group participants made significant progress in C3 and C4.

4. Discussion

4.1. Effects on Awareness Raising

The first focus of the study is EFL learners' awareness of figurative language. The results of the Awareness Test, as reported in Table 1, show that both the participants of the CM group and of the MM group made progress on the Awareness Test after receiving the instructions. The improvements of scores indicate that the participants became more confident of their judgments of recognizing metaphoric/metonymic expressions; the enhanced certainty also indicates the participants' raised awareness of figurative language.

However, the results reported in Table 2 also show that the participants of the MM groups performed significantly better in the posttest than in the pretest while those of the CM groups did not. The significances suggest that instruction on metaphoric mappings were especially beneficial to the learners' awareness in some aspects. Table 3 reports the analyses on the participants' responses to expressions of different categories on the metaphor-metonymy continuum, and shows that the MM-group participants performed significantly better in evaluating metonymic-metaphoric (C3) and metaphoric expressions (C4), the two categories which were closer to the metaphoric end on the continuum and were considered more abstract in the concepts involved. The findings suggest that instruction on metaphoric mappings can help L2 learners to process abstract concepts and hence can be helpful in noticing and understanding expressions concerning abstract source or target domains.

Moreover, Table 4 reports the analyses on the participants' responses to body-related metaphoric/metonymic expressions, and shows that the MM-group participants received significantly higher scores in the posttest in evaluating metaphoric/metonymic expressions containing no bodily descriptions, expressions which were even more abstract and opaque than others due to lack of bodily experiences. The finding suggests that instruction on metaphoric mappings can help learners overcome difficulties resulting from abstractness of concepts and insufficiency of embodied experiences, and they become more aware of those expressions.

To sum up, both instructions were proved to be beneficial in improving EFL learners' awareness of figurative language use. Moreover, instruction on metaphoric mappings, owing to its structural, systematic, and logical mapping processes, was found to be especially helpful in facilitating learners' awareness of expressions involving more abstract concepts, such as expressions which involved complicated cross-domain mappings and expressions which were not grounded in embodied experiences.

4.2. Effects on Retention

The other focus of the study is EFL learners' retention of figurative language. The general improvements in the posttest demonstrate the effects of having explicit instructions during figurative language learning process. In other words, the improvements on mean scores of the tests give positive evidence of beneficial effects on cognitively-based instructions, including CM and MM instructions.

However, when comparing the participants' performances of the two groups, the degree of progress the MM group made was lower than the degree of progress the CM group made in judging sentences with or those without metaphors/metonymies, as shown in Table 3. Even though the MM group did not achieve higher average scores than the CM group, the results of the comparisons indicate that the MM-group participants did gain significantly higher overall improvements. In other words, the participants of the MM groups might have made more consistent progress on the posttest, and thus the variances of the changes resulted in significance in Table 2. Contrarily, the participants of the CM groups might have performed inconsistently on the posttest, so they did not show significant overall changes. The results of the comparisons answer the second research question: instruction involving metaphoric mappings can lead to longer-term effect than instruction involving conceptual metaphors.

To sum up, even though both instructions bring beneficial effects to EFL learners' awareness raising and comprehension improvement, instruction on metaphoric mappings can also bring relatively more consistent and steady progress. The findings assure the effects of meaningful learning on second language acquisition (Ausubel, 1963, 1968). Metaphoric mappings provide structural correspondence through ontological mappings as well as knowledge association through the epistemic mappings. The systematic elaborations can facilitate a deeper level of cognitive processing throughout the learning process (Ellis, 2002). In addition, the advantages of relating existing and concrete knowledge to new and abstract concepts through epistemic mappings can solve problems caused by cultural specificity.

5. Conclusion

The present study sheds light on the application of metaphor and metonymy to EFL teaching and learning of figurative language in three aspects. First, that explicit instructions on second language acquisition carry beneficial effects is validated. In addition, metonymy is suggested as equally important as metaphor, and should be included in EFL language learning programs. Moreover, instruction of metaphoric mappings should be incorporated with instruction of conceptual metaphor in order to assist figurative language learning in EFL classrooms.

6. Tables

Table 1: Mean Performance Scores of Participants in the Awareness Test

	CM group		MM group	
Type	Pretest	Posttest	Pretest	Posttest
With figurative expressions (k=24)	3.50 (.55)	4.17 (.43)	3.52 (.54)	3.97 (.60)
Without figurative expressions (k=24)	1.84 (.45)	2.20 (.66)	1.86 (.49)	2.05 (.62)
Sample size	32		36	

Notes. k: number of items. Standard deviations are in parentheses.

Table 2: Differences in Participants' Performances between Pretest and Posttest

Variables	Sentences with metaphoric/metonymic	Sentences without

	exp.		metaphoric/metonymic exp.	
	CM group	MM group	CM group	MM group
	β (t-value)	β (t-value)	β (t-value)	β (t-value)
Constant	2.15 (.98)	3.04 (2.50)**	.10 (.05)	1.10 (1.23)
Scores	-.12 (-.75)	-.20 (-2.14)$^+$	.00 (.00)	-.05 (-.72)
Self-learning time	-.03 (-.47)	.037 (.64)	.05 (.86)	-.08 (-1.95)$^+$
Review or not	.45 (1.93$^+$)	-.11 (-.54)	.28 (1.20)	-.07 (-.47)
R^2	.13	13	.09,	.15

$^+$ $p < .05$, one-tailed. ** $p < .01$, two-tailed.

Table 3: Differences in Participants' Performances between the CM and the MM Group

	Sentences with metaphoric/metonymic exp.	Sentences without metaphoric/metonymic exp.
Variables	β (t-value)	β (t-value)
(Constant)	2.15 (1.00)	.10 (.06)
Group (G)	-.29 (-1.81)	-.18 (-1.25)
Scores (S)	-.12 (-.76)	.00 (.01)
Self-learning (SL)	-.03 (-.48)	.05 (.99)
Review or not R)	.45 (1.98)	.28 (1.38)
G×S	-.08 (-.44)	-.05 (-.32)
G×SL	.07 (.79)	-.35 (-1.28)
G×R	-.57 (-1.81)	-.13 (-1.86)
R^2	.15	.13

Note: Group: The CM group is coded as 0, and the MM group is coded as 1.

Table 4: Differences in Performances on Four Categories between the Pretest and the Posttest

		CM group	MM group
	Variables	β(t-value)	β (t-value)
C1	Constant	-1.85 (-.49)	2.49 (1.67)
	Scores	.17 (.64)	-.14 (-1.26)
	Self-learning time	.03 (.34)	-.04 (-.50)
	Review or not	-.12 (-.31)	-.24 (-.92)
	R^2	.02	.09
C2	Constant	3.21 (.96)	2.30 (1.35)
	Scores	-.20 (-.84)	-.14 (-1.10)
	Self-learning time	-.06 (-.70)	-.01 (-.16)
	Review or not	.90 (2.53)*	-.11 (-.39)
	R^2	.19	.05

C3	Constant	2.40 (1.26)	2.86 (2.28)*
	Scores	-.13 (-.96)	-.19 (-2.01)
	Self-learning time	-.04 (-.79)	.02 (.40)
	Review or not	.01 (.05)	-.01 (-.02)
	R^2	.05	.11
C4	Constant	4.86 (1.46)	4.49 (2.38)*
	Scores	-.32 (-1.32)	-.31 (-2.19)$^+$
	Self-learning time	-.04 (-.48)	.17 (1.92)
	Review or not	1.03 (2.90) *	-.10 (-.31)
	R^2	.25	.18

+ $p < .05$, one-tailed. * $p < .05$, two-tailed.

Table 5: Cross-examination of Four Categories and Sentences with/without Body-related Expressions between the Pretest and the Posttest

		Sentences with body-related exp.		Sentences without body-related exp.	
		CM group	MM group	CM group	MM group
	Variables	β (t-value)	β (t-value)	β (t-value)	β (t-value)
C1	Constant)	-1.53 (-.38)	2.66 (.92)	-2.16 (-.47)	.08 (.03)
	Scores	.17 (.62)	-.14 (-.71)	.17 (.52)	-.53 (-1.44)
	Self-learning time	.01 (.17)	-.14 (-1.77)	.05 (.40)	-.07 (-.89)
	Review or not	-.19 (-.46)	.49 (1.51)	-.05 (-.10)	.08 (.52)
	R^2	.02	.14	.01	.09
C2	Constant	5.41 (1.64)	3.23 (.96)	1.00 (.18)	1.53 (.61)
	Scores	-.37 (-1.60)	-.21 (-.89)	-.01 (-.04)	.02 (.05)
	Self-learning time	.03 (.34)	-.09 (-1.01)	-.15 (-1.04)	-.09 (-.96)
	Review or not	.60 (1.73)	.39 (1.03)	1.18 (2.02$^+$)	-.02 (-.10)
	R^2	.17	.08	.14	.03
C3	Constant	2.46 (1.15)	-.05 (-.02)	2.33 (.85)	3.33 (2.43)*
	Scores	-.14 (-.95)	.01 (.05)	-.11 (-.59)	-.08 (-.38)
	Self-learning time	.00 (.11)	-.00 (-.02)	-.08 (-1.18)	-.07 (-1.31)
	Review or not	-.10 (-.45)	.26 (.85)	.12 (.42)	-.15 (-1.56)
	R^2	.04	.02	.06	.14
C4	Constant	1.59 (.36)	3.04 (1.11)	8.12 (1.53)	8.10 (3.09)*
	Scores	-.08 (-.28)	-.22 (-1.12)	-.54 (-1.43)	.15 (.35)
	Self-learning time	-.02 (-.22)	.03 (.47)	-.06 (-.42)	-.30 (-2.92$^+$)
	Review or not	.69 (1.51)	.34 (1.09)	1.36 (2.42)	-.31 (-1.64)
	R^2	.08	.09	.21	.29

* $p< .05$, two-tailed. + $p < .05$, one-tailed.

Selected References

Ammar, A., Lightbown, P. M., & Spada, N. (2010). Awareness of L1/L2 differences: Does it matter? *Language Awareness*, 19(2), 129-146.

Ausubel, D. (1963). *The psychology of meaningful verbal learning*. New York: Grune & Stratton.

Ausubel, D. (1968). Educational psychology: A cognitive view. New York: Holt, Rinehart & Winston.

Barnden, J. A. (2010). Metaphor and metonymy: Making their connections more slippery. *Cognitive Linguistics*, 21(1), 1-34.

Boers, F. (2000a). Enhancing metaphoric awareness in specialised reading. *English for Specific Purposes*, 19, 137-147.

Boers, F. (2000b). Metaphor awareness and vocabulary retention. *Applied Linguistics*, 21, 553-571.

Boers, F. (2001). Remembering figurative idioms by hypothesising about their origin. *Prospect*, 16, 35-43.

Boers, F., & Lindstromberg, S. (2006) Cognitive linguistic applications in second or foreign language instruction: rationale, proposals, and evaluation. In G. Kristiansen, M. Achard, R. Dirven & F. J. Ruiz de Mendoza Ibáñez (Eds.), *Cognitive linguistics: Current applications and future perspective* (pp.305-355). Berlin: Mouton de Gruyter.

Chen, Yi-chen & Lai, Huei-ling (In Press). EFL learners' awareness of metonymy–metaphor continuum in figurative expression. *Language Awareness*.

Chung, Siaw-Fong & Ahrens, K. (2004). Teaching Economy Metaphors: A Psycholinguistic Perspective through the CMM. *Proceedings of the Thirteenth International Symposium and Book Fair on English Teaching*. Taipei, Taiwan: English Teachers Association.

Deignan, A., Gabrys, D. & Solska, A. (1997). Teaching English metaphors using cross-linguistic awareness-raising activities. *ELT Journal, 51*(4), 352-60.

Dong, Y. (2004). Don't keep them in the dark! Teaching metaphors to English language learners. *English Journal*, *93*(4), 29-35.

Ellis, N. (2006a). Cognitive perspectives on SLA. *AILA Review*, 19, 100–121.

Ellis, N. (2006b). Language acquisition as rational contingency learning. *Applied Linguistics*, 27(1), 1–24.

Ellis, R. (2002). *The study of second language acquisition*. Oxford: Oxford University Press.

Goossens, L. (1990). Metaphonymy: The interaction of metaphor and metonymy in expressions for linguistic action. *Cognitive Linguistics*, 1, 323-340.

Kellerman, E. (1977). Towards a characterization of the strategy of transfer in second language learning. *Interlanguage Studies Bulletin*, 2, 58-145.

Kövecses, Z. (2001). A cognitive linguistic view of learning idioms in an FLT context. In M. Pütz, S. Niemeier & R. Dirven (Eds.), *Applied cognitive linguistics II: Language pedagogy* (pp. 87-115). Berlin: Mouton de Gruyter.

Low, G. (1988). On teaching metaphor. *Applied Linguistics*, *9*(2), 125-147. Retrieved February 4, 2009, from http://applij.oxfordjournals.org/cgi/reprint/9/2/125

Odlin, T. (1989). *Language transfer: Cross-linguistic influence in language learning*. Cambridge: Cambridge University Press.

O'Malley, J. M, & Chamot, A. U. (1990). *Leaning strategies in second language acquisition*. Cambridge: Cambridge University Press.

Radden, G. (2003). How metonymic are metaphors? In R. Dirven & R. Pörings (Eds.), *Metaphor and metonymy in comparison and contrast* (pp. 407-434). Berlin, New York: Mouton de Gruyter.

Ringbom, H. (1987). *The role of the first language in foreign language learning*. Clevedon, England: Multilingual Matters.

NERSIL: the Named-Entity Recognition System for Iban Language

Soo-Fong Yong[a], Bali Ranaivo-Malançon[b], Alvin Yeo Wee[b]

[a]Faculty of Computer Science and Information Technology, Universiti Malaysia Sarawak
94300 Kota Samarahan, Sarawak, Malaysia
soofong0629@gmail.com

[b]Faculty of Computer Science and Information Technology, Universiti Malaysia Sarawak
94300 Kota Samarahan, Sarawak, Malaysia
{mbranaivo, alvin}@fit.unimas.my

Abstract. This paper presents NERSIL, the first Iban named entity recognition using ANNIE, an information extraction tool available within GATE. We proposed a method for building rules and gazetteers for Iban language. Rules were determined based on named entities that were not recognized by ANNIE. Then, the investigation of the contexts of these non-recognized Iban named entities allowed us to write the rules. NERSIL achieves 76.4% F-measure.

Keywords: Named Entity Recognition, GATE, Information Extraction, Rules-based, Gazetteers

1 Introduction

Named entities (NEs) are recognized as an important source of information for many applications. In information retrieval, they improve the detection of relevant documents. In machine translation, post-editing is very expensive when the errors of a machine translation system are mainly due to NEs. Named entity recognition (NER) is the process of detecting NEs and classifying them into semantic categories. NERSIL is the first Iban NER. One of the policies of the Malaysian government is to develop more Malaysian digital contents by including indigenous languages like Iban. Presently, NER can accommodate only major languages such as English and Chinese. Indigenous languages are largely neglected. Hence, NER which can accommodate indigenous languages such as Iban is required. Besides the development of the tool itself, our project will provide access to indigenous knowledge. These may in turn encourage more research, which in long term will preserve the culture. In addition, the proposed method may help other under-resourced languages.

The paper is structured as follows. Section 2 presents the background and related works. Section 3 explains the proposed method for building Iban rules and gazetteers. Section 4 describes the experiment performed to evaluate NERSIL, and section 5 depicts the analysis of the errors. Section 6 concludes the presentation and highlights our plans for future work.

2 Background and Related Works

2.1 Iban language

According to *Dewan Bahasa dan Pustaka* (Malay for The Institute of Language and Literature) there are 63 indigenous languages in Sarawak, an east Malaysian state. Iban is the largest ethnic group making up about 44% of the population of Sarawak. Iban language is the vernacular for Iban people. The language is written using Latin alphabet. In 2008, Iban language was introduced as a new elective subject in the national fifth form examination.

The digitization and content processing of Iban texts are parts of our center research objective. Currently, we have already developed for Iban, a morphological analyzer and generator, a syntactic parser, a POS tagger, a spell checker, and an interactive alignment tool. The development of the Iban NER is in line with the research center objective. Even though a few processing tools have been developed for Iban, this language is still considered as an under-resourced language.

2.2 NER

NER process is divided into two successive parts. The first part consists of identifying proper names in a given text. The second part concerns the classification of these proper names into semantic categories such as Person, Organization, Location, Date, Time, Percentage, Monetary value and etc.

ANNIE is an information extraction tool widely used to identify NEs in different domains and languages (e.g., Maynard et al., 2003). ANNIE adopts a rule-based approach in recognizing NEs. A rule-based model consists of patterns (or rules) and gazetteers. Rules are manually written by language engineers. A gazetteer contains a list of words of the same kind of NE. Therefore, each type of NE will have its own gazetteer. In the literature, research on NER task for under-resourced languages is rare. In 2003, Maynard and her colleagues (Maynard et al., 2003) reported the development and evaluation of the first NER for Cebuano, a language used in the Philippines. They adapted ANNIE for Cebuano and achieved an F-measure of 77.5%. The authors reused the default setting (tokeniser, sentence splitter, POS tagger, gazetteer, NE grammar, and orthomatcher) and made some modifications by providing the Cebuano post-processor, Cebuano lexicon as well as Cebuano gazetteers. As ANNIE for Cebuano achieved high accuracy result, hence, it gives us some motivation to adapt also ANNIE for Iban language.

One of the difficulties of NER task is the identification of named entity variants. A named entity may be displayed in different formats. For instance, a date can be displayed as "10 Oct.", "10 October 2010", or "10/10/10". Another difficulty of NER task is language ambiguity. A named entity may belong to more than one semantic category. In "Malaysia won the Suzuki Cup 2010", "Malaysia" is considered as an organization. In "The Suzuki cup 2010 took place in Malaysia", "Malaysia" is a location. In addition, style, structure, domain, genre, punctuation, capitalization, spelling, spacing as well as formatting also can be considered as NER difficulties.

3 Proposed Method

Given that there is no large corpus available for the indigenous languages we are working with, we attempted to develop the Iban NER tool as depicted in Figure 1.

To determine Iban rules for the automatic recognition of NEs, we first look for missing rules. We said that a rule is missing in ANNIE, if a NE that occurs in the Iban texts has not been identified by ANNIE. The main purpose of this experiment is to highlight the NEs that can be recognized by ANNIE. Next, the NEs are investigated manually. The result of this investigation is the creation of a set of Iban rules and gazetteers.

We tested the accuracy of NERSIL by comparing its results against human annotated texts, which have been labeled by local Iban native speaker. They used the "Simple Named Entity Guidelines V6.5" as a reference. This guideline has been designed specifically for less commonly taught languages (LDC, 2006). Three metrics, available in GATE, were used for this evaluation: recall, precision, and F-measure.

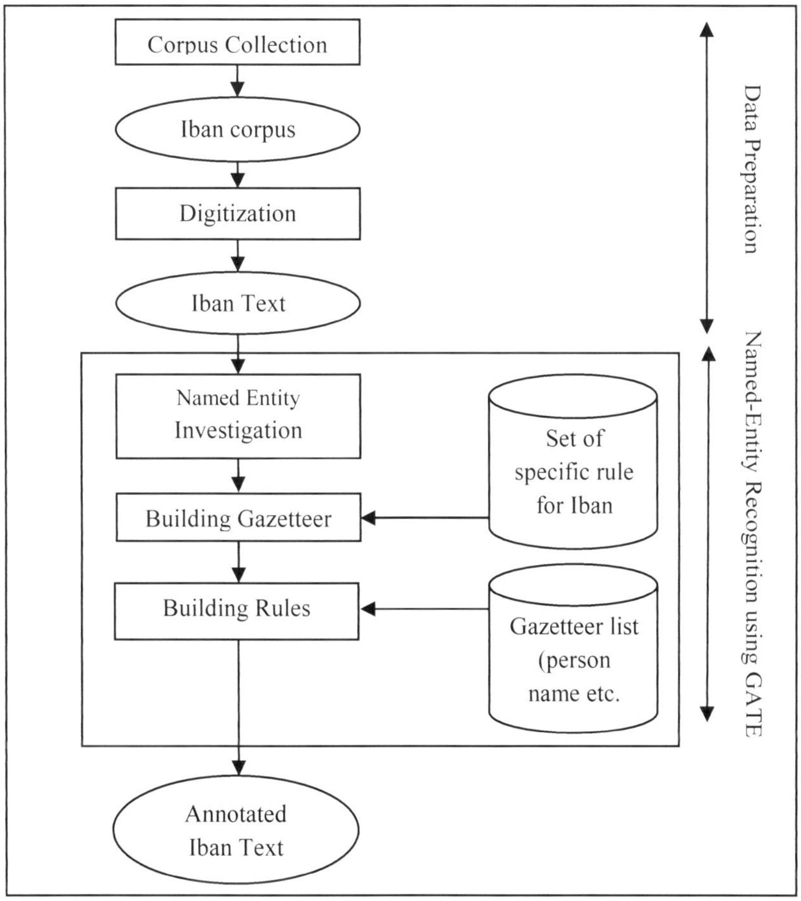

Figure 1: Proposed Method

Step1: Corpus Collection
The Iban texts corpus was collected from the Tun Jugah Foundation, which is one of the organizations carrying out research projects and activities on oral history and literature of Iban community.

Step2: Digitization
Since our Iban texts corpus is in paper format, we need to digitize it. We used as Optical Character Recognition (OCR) such as *ABBYY FineReader* software, which is able to recognize Malay texts. As Iban and Malay are close languages (Ng et al, 2010). We assume that this software will convert Iban corpus into electronic files with minimal errors.

Step3: Named Entity Investigation
In order to determine the best rules for the recognition of Iban NEs, we investigated the named entity of Iban. A known problem in the area of NER was found in our corpus that is cascaded NEs. This is the case when a named entity is embedded in another named entity. For instance, the whole

expression “Tuai CID Sibu [location] DSP Wong Chee Kiong” is tagged as a [Person]. However, “Sibu” will be tagged as a Location, “Wong Chee Kiong” as Person, and “Tuai CID” and “DSP” as Title. To make sure there are not duplicate rules happen, we can set the priority.

Step4: Building Gazetteers

The gazetteers are manually built. Although a somewhat tedious process, this was the only way to obtain accurate results. Besides that, due to the texts corpus is paper format. Thus, we have to manually check the validity. The gazetteers are the lookup list of NEs. During our corpus investigation, we have found that, like many language, Iban incorporates foreign words in its communication. These foreign words are mainly borrowed from English vocabulary. Therefore, we kept the English gazetteers available in ANNIE to ensure the recognition of all NEs, either native or foreign words, in Iban texts.

Step5: Building Rules

Rules in ANNIE are written using JAPE (Java Annotation Pattern Engine) (Maynard, 2011). Iban rules are built based on some contexts (Table2) and morphological features (Table3).

a. Person Rule

The identification of the entity Person, makes use of title information whether they are Malay titles (*Dato', Tan Sri*) or English Title (Dr., Mr.). Then, it checks the initial case status of the following words. A sequence of words is labeled as Person if it starts with a title followed by capitalized words. For example, “Tan Sri Dato” Sri Dr Lim Kok Wing” will be recognized as a Person. Knowing that “Tan Sri”, “Dato' Sri”, and “Dr.” are titles, any occurrence of “Lim Kok Wing” will be also tagged as Person. Table 1 shows some examples of rules for Person identification.

Each culture has its own system of naming. For example, Malay names have the following pattern: (<name> bin or binti <father's name>, where “bin” is for men or “binti” is for women, e.g., Musa bin Osman); Chinese names, as used in Malaysia, have three segments: (<surname>< name1><name2>, e.g., Chong Ai Ling); Indian names in Malaysia have similar pattern as Malay names. The difference is on the words used to express the relationship with the father. If Malay uses “bin” and “binti”, Indian uses “a/l”, for “anak lelaki” (“son of”) or a/p, for “anak perempuan” (“daughter of”), e.g., Anbuselvan a/l Ramanan Similarly, the names of Bumiputeras in Sarawak differ only on the middle word used in indicate the father's name. They use anak (“child of”), as in Jugah anak Rentap. When one look closely to all these patterns, they are quite similar. The difference is on the words used to introduce the father's name. Thus, we built a JAPE rule that can recognize the pattern <Name><Father's affiliation><Father's name>. By referring to the naming patterns, the naming patterns are quite similar. Thus, the naming patterns rules can simplified as generic rules, such as <Proper Noun><Unknown><Proper Noun>. We can try and predict the “unknown” words.

Table 1: Example of rules (Person)

Example of Rule	Explanation
Rule: Person	
({Token.kind !="number"})	Check whether it is number, to avoid address pattern is tagged.
(	
({Token.kind==word, Token.orth==upperInitial})	At least one Capital letter word
({Token.kind==word, Token.orth==upperInitial})?	? refer to Capital letter word exist anot
({Token.kind==word, Token.orth==upperInitial})?	? refer to Capital letter word exist anot
):label	
({Token.string==","})	
({Token.kind=="number"})	Number refer to the age
({Token.string==";") +	+ mean that repeat the pattern again
→	Match the LHS rules with RHS
:label.Person={rule="Person"}	label as Person

Table 2: List of contexts features for Iban (Budi, 2005)

Feature Name	Explanation	Example
PPRE	Person prefix	Tan, Teo (surnames)
PMID	Person middle	bin, b. binti, bt. (Malay names); a/l, a/p (Indian names); a/k, anak (Bumiputera names)
PTIT	Person title	Sapit Kepala Menteri Datuk Patinggi Tan Sri
OPRE	Organization prefix	Sekula/Sekula (School); Gerempong/ Gerempung (Community, association, cooperative); Kelab (Club); kunsil (council, Sarawak Administrative Officer); Kompeni (Company)
OSUF	Organization suffix	Sdn. Bhd /Sendirian Berhad (Incorporated); Beng/Bing (Bank)
OPOS	Position in organization	Tuai (Chief, head, leader)
LPRE	Location prefix	Jalai (road); Kampong (village); Bukit, Gunong (Mountain); Negeri/Nengeri (city); menoa/menua (settlement); Long (river mouth); Palan (resting place, camp, port)
POLP	Preposition that's usually followed by person	Oleh (by) , untuk (for)
LOPP	Preposition that's usually followed by location name	ba (at, in, on); di (at, in, on); dalam (in); ari (from); ngagai (towards); ke (for, to); enggau (with, together, and)
DAY	Day	Hari Senin (Monday)
MONTH	Month	Januari, Februari, Mac, Mei, Jun, Julai, Ogos, Oktober, Disember

Table 3: List of morphological features (Budi, 2005)

Feature Name	Explanation	Example
TitleCase	Begin with uppercase letter and followed by all lowercase letter	Soedirman
UpperCase	All uppercase letter	SHELL
LowerCase	All lowercase letter	Lemai (afternoon, evening)
MixedCase	Uppercase and lowercase letter	SaLT
CapStart	Begin with uppercase letter	-
ChartDigit	Letter and number	P3K
DigitSlash	Number with slash	12/5
Numeric	Number with dot or comma	20.5; 15,000
NumStr	Number in word	Sa/Satu (One)
Roman	Roman number	VII, XI
TimeForm	Number in time format	17:05; 19:30

b. Location Rule

Location entities are identified using location prefixes and preposition for places. For instance, "*Long Lamai*" is recognized as a Location since "Long" is a location prefix. In "*di Limbang*", "*Limbang*" is recognized as a Location because "*di*" is a locative preposition or <preposition><Proper Noun> -*di Limbang*.

c. Organization Rule

Organization is recognized by using the organization prefix or suffix. For example, "*kompeni Teras Kimia*" is an Organization because of the prefix "*kompeni*". "*Teras Kimia Sdn Bhd*" is an organization because of the suffix "Sdn Bhd" or <Organization prefix><Proper Noun><Organization suffix> - *kompeni Teras Kimia Sdn Bhd.* or <Proper Noun><Organization suffix> - *Teras Kimia Sdn Bhd* or <Organization prefix> <Proper Noun><Organization suffix> - *kompeni Teras Kimia Sdn Bhd.* In this case, there are 3 patterns of rules to identify the same entity. Thus, we use the most frequent used patterns. Besides that, we can identify organization by using the symbolic "()". For instance, Organization name (Abbreviation) - *Pengangkut Jalai Alun (JPJ).*

d. Date Rule

As for date, we can use the document Meta information. Meta means that the data in documents can be used directly most of times without further processing. For instance, news often starts with a location name plus date - *SIBU, 19 Jul.* Besides that, we can use the gazetteer lookup, lookup for the list of month. For instance, <Number><list of month> <Number> - *4 Disember 2004.*

e. Time Rule

As for time, we can identify time by using some trigger words such as 'pukul', 'pagi'(morning), 'tengah hari' (afternoon), 'lemai'(evening) . For instance, *pukul 6.45 pagi – pukul* [trigger words] *6.45* [Numeric] *pagi* [trigger words].

f. Percentage Rule

As for percentage, we can identify percentage by using the symbolic (%) or word (peratus). In Iban texts, they often use word compared to symbolic. For example, *3.8 peratus*. Besides that, we also can use some specific word such a "niki" (climb). E.g. *niki 14.5 peratus (increase 14. 5%).*

g. Monetary Rule

As for monetary, we can monetary by using the symbolic of currency or currency unit. Thus, we need to build the list for symbolic currency and currency unit. Example of symbolic currency such as 'RM', '$' and etc; currency unit - rupiah, ringgit and etc.

4 Experiment Setup and Metrics

4.1 Experimental Setup

To evaluate NERSIL, we used an Iban annotated corpus made of 100 texts (29837 words, average 298 per texts), 22 lists of entities, and a set of Iban Jape rules (Table 4 and Table 5). The lists of entities constitute the Iban gazetteers.

Table 4: Number of Iban Jape Rules

Entity	Number of Jape rules
Person	14
Organization	5
Location	5
Time	4
Monetary	4
Date	3
Percentage	3

Table 5: Number of Jape Rules which Reuse and Created for Iban

Entity	No. of rules in ANNIE	No. of ANNIE rules that reuse	No. of created rules for Iban
Person	15	2	12
Organization	20	1	4
Location	7	1	4
Time	12	1	3
Monetary	2	1	3
Date	21	1	2
Percentage	2	1	2

GATE provides some evaluation metrics to assess the accuracy of the NER tool (Maynard, 2011). Recall measure the number of correctly identified item as a percentage of the total of correct item. Precision measure the number of correctly identified items as a percentage of items identified. F-measure is the average of the recall and precision.

$$\text{Recall:} \quad \frac{\text{Correct} + 0.5\ \text{Partial}}{\text{Correct} + \text{Missing} + 0.5\ \text{Partial}} \tag{1}$$

$$\text{Precision:} \quad \frac{\text{Correct} + 0.5\ \text{Partial}}{\text{Correct} + \text{Spurious} + 0.5\ \text{Partial}} \tag{2}$$

$$\text{F-Measure: } \frac{(\beta^2 + 1) P * R}{(\beta^2) + P} \quad (3)$$

In these formulae, 'correct' is understood as the number of correct recognition performed by the test system. 'Partial' is the number of partial correct recognition performed by the tested system. For instance, "Annah Rais" should be recognizing as a PERSON but the system recognized just "Annah" or "Rais" as a PERSON.

4.2 Experiment

To test the accuracy of NERSIL, we compared its results against human annotated texts and also the results of ANNIE on the same set of texts. It is expected that ANNIE will recognize only English NEs.

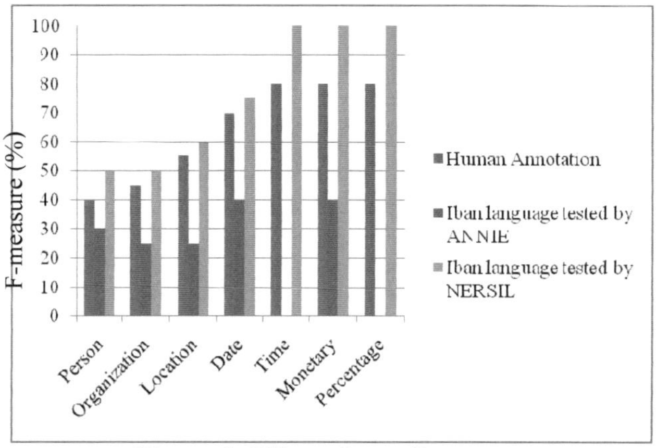

Figure 2: NE results on Iban texts

The overall results are shown in Figure 2. Human annotation achieves on F-measure of 64.3%, while Iban language tested by ANNIE achieves on F-measure of 22.8% and Iban language tested by NERSIL achieving on F-measure 76.4%. Based on these results, we noticed that ANNIE is also able to identify some NEs in Iban texts, which as we mentioned earlier are generally from English vocabulary. Therefore, we try to keep the default English gazetteers and add new named entities related to Malaysian locations to improve the performance of NERSIL. Besides, there are some common patterns we can find in English texts as well as in Iban texts such as date and monetary patterns. Hence, we can reuse the same JAPE rules for English and Iban. In the other hand, ANNIE is unable to identify NEs for time and percentage (Table 6), thus, we need to create specific rules for Iban texts.

Table 6: Difference between English language and Iban Language

Categories	English language	Iban language
Time	3:31:00 PM or 12:00 AM	Pukul 6 lemai or Pukul 10.30 malam
Percentage	10.0 %	10.0 peratus

Figure 3 shows the distribution of NEs in our Iban texts.

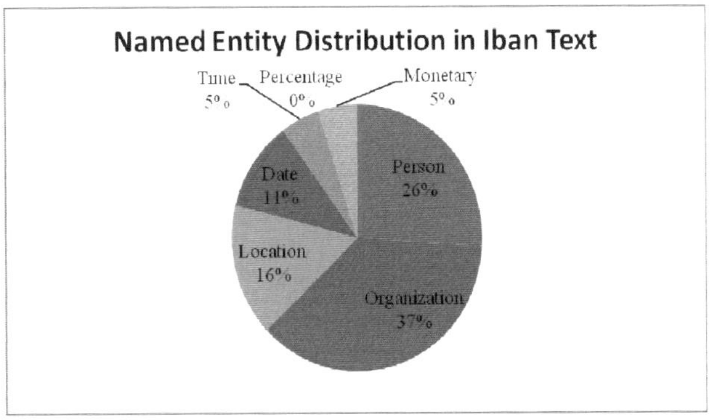

Figure 3: NEs Distribution in Iban Text

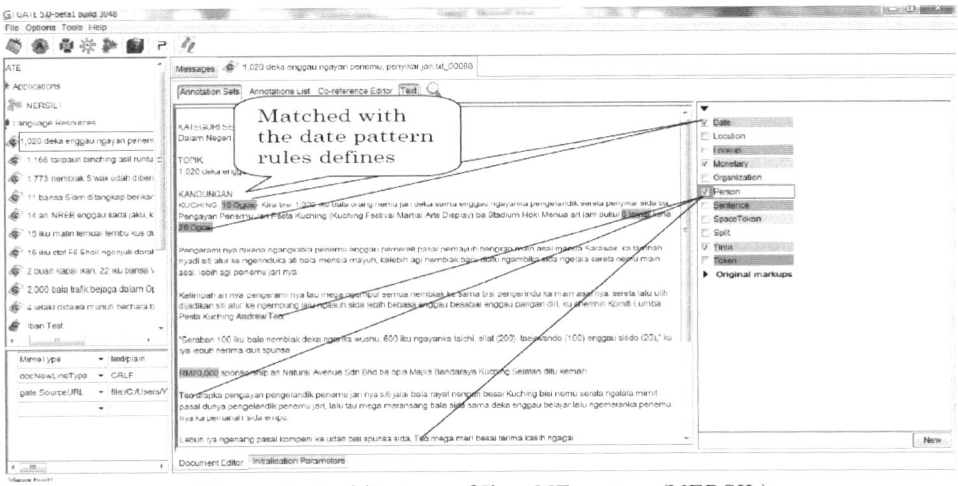

Figure 4: Architecture of Iban NE system (NERSIL)

5 Error Analysis

NERSIL is not perfect yet and some errors occurred during its testing.

- **Error in capital letters** – Some of the NEs was not capitalized. For example, chong ai ling. It should be Chong Ai Ling.
- **Spelling mistakes** – Some of the NEs was spelt incorrectly. For example, Cristopher Lee. The correct spelling is Christopher Lee. Both spelling mistakes and error in capital letters need another approach to solve it, for example, using a spelling checker for Iban language.
- **Incomplete gazetteers** – There are many NEs that occur in Iban texts and cannot be found in the current gazetteers especially Person, Location as well as Organization. Thus, this problem can be solved by improving the gazetteers.
- **Ambiguous words** – Homonymy is another source of errors. For example, Malaysia can be either a Location or an Organization. A Word Sense Disambiguation tool may solve this problem.
- **Missed tags by native speaker** – As our native speaker was not familiar with NEs and also GATE annotator, some tags were missing. Thus, the answer key annotations were inaccurate.

6 Conclusion and future work

In this project, we presented the development and testing of NERSIL, the first Iban NER tool. Based on our research, we can say that GATE is suitable for developing a NER tool for a new language. NERSIL was able to achieve 76.4% accuracy in identifying Person, Location, Organization, Date, Time, Percentage, and Monetary.

The contribution of this work is the creation of two language resources for Iban language that are NE rules and gazetteers. Moreover, we have adapted ANNIE to Iban. In addition, we have also helped in preserving an indigenous language.

While testing this Iban NER tool, few problems occurred. To overcome these problems, we propose, 1) Expanding the gazetteers, 2) Testing more Iban texts to discover more NEs, 3) Reducing negative effects on evaluation results – due to incomplete annotation of the test corpus, 4) Enhancing quality of transliterated names, 5) Using Iban texts with error free spelling, 6) Including all possible spelling variations used for names in Iban written texts.

References

Babych, B. and Hartley, A. 2003. *Improving Machine Translation Quality with Automatic Named Entity Recognition.* Proceedings of EACL-EAMT. Budapest. .

Budi, I. Bressan, S., Wahyudi, G., Hasibuna, Z.A. and Bazief, B.A.A. 2005. *Named Entity Recognition for the Indonesian Language: Combining Contextual, Morphological and Part-of-Speech Features into a Knowledge Engineering Approach.* Proceedings of 8th International Conference, DS 2005, Singapore, October 8-11, 2005

LDC. 2006. *Simple Named Entity Guidelines for Less Commonly Taught Languages, Version 6.5.* http://projects.ldc.upenn.edu/LCTL/Specifications/SimpleNamedEntityGuidelinesV6.5.pdf

Maynard, D., Valentin, T. and Hamish, C. 2003. *NE recognition without training data on a language you don't speak.* In Proceeding of the ACL 2003 Workshop on Multilingual and Mixed-language Named Entity Recognition, pp. 33-40

Maynard, D. 2011. *Developing Language Processing Components with GATE,Version 6* http://gate.ac.uk/sale/tao/tao.pdf

Ng, E.L., Chin, B., Yeo, A. & Bali, R.M. 2010. *Identification of Closely-Related Indigenous Languages: An Orthographic Approach.* Intertional Journal on Asia Language Processing 20(2):43-61

Improving PP Attachment Disambiguation in a Rule-based Parser *

Yoon-Hyung Roh[a], Ki-Young Lee[a], and Young-Gil Kim[a]

[a]Natural Language Processing Research Team, Electronics and Telecommunications Research Institute,
161 Gajeong-dong, Yuseong-gu, Daejeon, 305-350, Korea
{yhroh, leeky, kimyk}@etri.re.kr

Abstract. This paper deals with how to enhance the performance of a rule-based parser using statistical Information. PP (Prepositional Phrase) attachment ambiguity is one of the main ambiguities found in parsing. We therefore conducted some experiments on extracting statistical information for PP attachment from a corpus, and on applying such information to a rule-based parser. Two types of information are used: supervised learning data and unsupervised learning data. In this paper, we show how we apply these types of information and to what degree they contribute to the PP attachment as well as to the overall parsing performance. The final results show a 5.42% performance improvement in PP attachment, with an 8.7% error reduction ratio in the overall parsing performance.

Keywords: PP attachment, rule-based parsing, syntactic ambiguity, statistical information, lexical dependency

1 Introduction

For a rule-based parser using CFG as its grammar, syntactic ambiguity is a challenging problem as it becomes more difficult to resolve conflicts between rules as the number of rules increases. Certain methods to solve this problem have been suggested, and have generally introduced statistical approaches (Sagae and Lavie, 2003; Foth and Menzel, 2006).

Many recent parsing technologies have also taken statistical approaches, as we can get more linguistic data, such as the Penn Treebank (Collins, 1999; Collins, 2000; Charniak, 2000). These technologies have shown encouraging performances. But practically speaking, statistical parsing has efficiency and scalability problems. As a statistical parser generally uses a significant number of parameters, and the search space is large, the parsing speed is relatively low and is not adequate for a real-time application. In our previous research, we conducted some experiments on applying statistical information to a rule-based parser (Roh, 2009). The parsing performance was affected mainly in the attachment performance and by the attachment information. Therefore, we do not need to apply full statistical information.

The scalability problem indicates the difficulty in incorporating other types of knowledge for use in parsing. Usually, a practical parser uses various types of additional knowledge for parsing, such as lexical patterns or semantic patterns. However, it is not easy to incorporate other knowledge into a parsing system based on probability. It is also difficult to tune the parser minutely with respect to each sentence. Thus, we want to use a rule-based parser as a base parsing system, and selective statistical information for ambiguity resolution.

Our parsing system conducts bottom-up chart parsing using ACFG (Augmented Context Free Grammar) rules, which have many syntactic and semantic features and constraints for

* The work reported in this paper was supported by the IT R&D program of MKE, "Development of Machine Translation Technology for Korean/Chinese/English Spoken Language and Business Documents".

prohibiting implausible syntactic structures and prioritizing the rules. These parsing rules are initially extracted from the Brown Corpus in the Penn Treebank. Not only have the syntactic tags and bracketing style been modified, but the rules have also been revised and enlarged in the course of extending the target domain of the parser. Our parser shows a competitive performance in rule-based parsing. However, the parsing performance remains at a standstill, and we now need to resolve syntactic ambiguity for additional improvements in performance.

In the next section, we briefly introduce a PP attachment task, and in sections 3 and 4, we present ways to apply supervised learning data and unsupervised learning data for a PP attachment, respectively. In section 5, we show a method for applying two types of data. Finally, we conclude this paper with several remarks on our future work.

2 PP attachment Disambiguation

PP attachment disambiguation is a task used to determine which site a PP is attached to while parsing. There have been many researches regarding PP attachment disambiguation (Ratnaparkhi, 1998; Stetina and Nagao, 1997; Olteanuand and Moldovan, 2005; Foth and Menzel, 2006). The main issues are mainly concerned with data extraction, learning methods, disambiguation models, and the treatment of the data sparseness problem.

Most of them simplify the problem into selecting an attachment site between a noun and a verb. However, in real parsing, the situation is more complicated. There can be more attachment sites, and the impact of a PP attachment on the other part has to be considered.

A few researchers have dealt with multiple PP attachments (Merlo, 1997; Bharati, 2005). Foth and Menzel (2006) presented a more comprehensive disambiguation method using Lexical Attraction, which is a type of mutual information.

We solve this problem by simply giving an attachment weight to the existing chart weight. We focus on how we can calculate the attachment weight when a PP is attached to some other constituent.

3 Supervised Learning

In conducting supervised learning, we consider a PP attachment task as a process of full syntactic analysis, and we use the statistical model typically used in statistical parsing.

There are two different probabilistic models depending on how the probability is conditioned. One is a bilexical model (Collins, 1996), which is a kind of discriminative model, and the other is a generative model (Collins, 1999). In the bilexical model, given two words w_i and w_h, the probability that w_i is dependent on w_h is expressed as follows.

$$P(D \mid w_i, w_h), \qquad (1)$$

where D represents a dependency relation between w_i and w_j.

In the generative model, given a head, w_h, the probability that a dependent w_i will be generated is expressed as follows.

$$P(w_i \mid w_h) \qquad (2)$$

3.1 Generative Model

The state of the art model in statistical parsing is the generative model (Collins, 2000; Charniak, 2000). Therefore, we first consider this model in our analysis. The generative probability that the i-th dependent (child) d_i is dependent on head child h in a chart generated in chart parsing is expressed as follows.

$$P(d_i \mid h) \approx P(t(d_i), l(d_i) \mid t(h), l(h), dist(i)), \qquad (3)$$

where $t(x)$ represents the tag of x, $l(x)$ represents the lexical root of x, and $dist(i)$ represents the distance feature between the head child and i-th dependent in the chart.

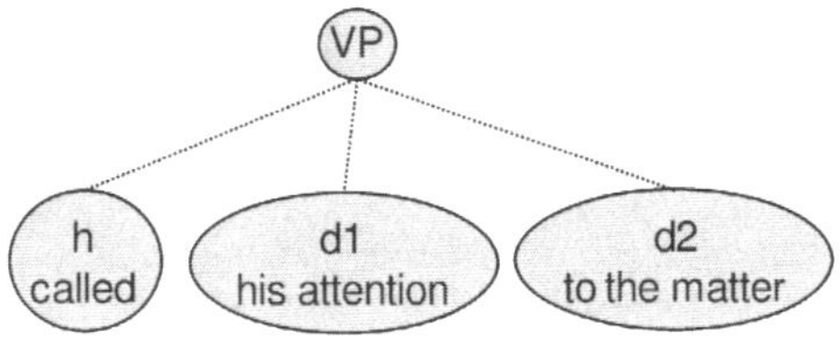

Figure 1: An example chart

Figure 1 shows a snapshot of the parsing process of the sentence, "President Bush called his attention to the matter." In the chart, the generative probability is as follows.

$$P(d_2 \mid h) = P(to, TO \mid call, VBD, 100) \quad (4)$$

The distance feature "100" captures how far the dependent is from the head child, and is a function of the surface string, as in Collins (1999). The problem of using such probability is that the generative probability is too low. This makes it difficult to apply other types of knowledge such as lexical or semantic patterns, or to apply statistical information selectively. The desirable characteristic of the lexical dependency weight is that the weight is 1 when the head child and its dependent have no preference, is a value greater than 1 when two words have a dependency preference, and is a value between 0 and 1 when they have a dependency dispreference. For this, we normalize the generative probability by dividing it with the generative probability given only the tag of the head child. The dependency weight is expressed as follows.

$$W(d_i \mid h) = \frac{P(t(d_i), l(d_i) \mid t(h), l(h), dist(i))}{P(t(d_i), l(d_i) \mid t(h), dist(i))} \quad (5)$$

Considering that the rule probability of PCFG reflects only the probability about a syntactic tag, the weight can be regarded as reflecting the variation through lexicalization.

The above method suffers from the data sparseness problem that the lexical statistical approach usually has. The following back-off method can be used.

$$W(d_i \mid h) = \frac{P(t(d_i) \mid t(h), l(h), dist(i))}{P(t(d_i) \mid t(h), dist(i))} \quad (6)$$

The total weight of rule r applied to a chart is then calculated by the following.

$$W(r) = P(r) * \prod_i W(d_i \mid h) \quad (7)$$

Generally, the probability of a parse tree is calculated by multiplying all rules applied to the parsed tree, such as $P(T) = \prod_i P(r_i)$. Likewise, the weight of a parse tree with statistical information is calculated by $W(T) = \prod_i W(r_i)$, and a parse tree with maximum weight is selected as the final result.

3.2 Bilexical Model

In the bilexical model, the dependency probability that i-th dependent d_i is dependent on head child h in a chart is expressed as follows.

$$P(D \mid h, d_i) \approx P(D \mid t(h), l(h), t(d_i), l(d_i), dist(i)) \quad (8)$$

In the chart in figure 1, the dependency probability is as follows.

$$P(D \mid call, to) = P(D \mid call, VBP, to, TO, 100)$$

As in the case of the generative model, the probability has to be applied in the form of a weight. The dependency weight is expressed as follows.

$$W(D \mid h, d_i) = \frac{P(D \mid t(h), l(h), t(d_i), l(d_i), dist(i))}{P(D \mid t(h), t(d_i), dist(i))} \quad (9)$$

This shows the ratio of the probability conditioned on particular lexical items to the probability conditioned on a more generalized tag.

In previous research, we conducted experiments on these two models and obtained better results from the generative model (Roh, 2009). However, in analyzing the errors in detail, we found that the dependency weight of the bilexical model has some problems.

First, the ratio is not adequate in this situation. For example, for $P(D|h,p)$ = 1.0 and $P(D|t(h1),t(p))$ = 0.5, the weight is 2.0, while for $P(D|h2,p)$ = 0.9 and $P(D|t(h2), t(p))$ = 0.3, the weight is 3.0. Here, p and $h2$ have greater weight, but it is obvious that p and $h1$ must have more weight based on the definition of bilexical dependency probability. In other words, the dependency weight should be purely dependent on the bilexical dependency probability, not on the ratio.

Second, p and $h1$ need to have much greater weight as $P(D|h,p)$ approaches 1. Thus, the weight should not be linearly proportional to $P(D|h,p)$. With this in mind, we can revise the expression as follows.

$$W(D \mid h, d_i) = (P(D|h, d_i) + 0.5)^n \quad (10)$$

In the above expression, when $P(D \mid h, d_i)$ = 0.5, the weight becomes 1.0, which has no effect as a weight. This is reasonable since we are unable to give either preference or dispreference if the probability that h and p have a dependency relation is one half. The value $P(D|h,p)+0.5$ then has a range of 0.5 to 1.5, and the weight decreases or increases as it distances itself from 1.0. The value n was determined experimentally, and we use 7.0 as its value.

3.3 Extracting Lexical Dependency Information

We use the Penn Treebank as the linguistic data source (Marcus, 1993). When extracting the dependency data from the Penn Treebank, there are certain points that we need to consider.

In the Penn Treebank, some coarse tags are used. For example, the part of speech (POS) tag "IN" includes both prepositions such as "in" and conjunctions such as "while." Also the Treebank does not distinguish the "TO" of a preposition from the "TO" of a to-infinitive. Moreover, SBAR represents all types of clauses including noun clauses such as that-clauses, adverbial clauses such as if-clauses, and relative clauses such as which-clauses. In addition, while our parser basically uses the Penn Treebank tags, we had to modify the syntactic and POS tags, which resulted in some mismatched tags. For example our parser distinguishes adverbial clauses (SBARV) such as if-clauses from that-clauses (SBAR).

Lastly, using a syntactic tag eliminates some important information. In the case of a verb, the syntactic tag "VP" (Verb Phrase) misses the form information of the verb, for example, whether it is in the gerund form or infinitive form. Thus, we distinguish between them by using different tags such as VPG (present participle VP), VPB (infinitive VP), VPN (past participle VP), etc, only when the verb is used as a dependent. When the verb is used as a head, we do not distinguish them.

For this problem, we do not use a POS tag but rather the syntactic tag of the parent of the pre-terminal in the syntactic tree, and we conduct a tag conversion.

The overall procedure is as follows:

- Find its heads in the pre-terminals using a tree structure. The heads are marked by '!'.

```
(SS (S!
    (NP (NNP President) (NNP Bush) )
    (VP! (VBD! called)
```

(NP (PRP$ his) (NN! attention))
(PP (TO! to)
(NP (DT the) (NN! matter))))
(. .)))

For example, from the parse tree below, "President/NNP Bush/NNP called/VBD his/PRP$ attention/NN to/TO the/DT matter/NN" is extracted.

- Conduct word/tag normalization, where the words are stemmed, and those tagged with "CD, NNP" are replaced by their tags, while the tags are replaced by their parent tags: (Bush/NNP called/VBD!) => (NNP/NNP called/VBD!)
- Count all the events of word pairs with the distance feature.
  From (call/VP! attention/NP to/PP), the following are generated.
  000 call/VP! attention/NP
  100 call/VP! to/PP
  100 call/VP
- Calculate all the lexical dependency weights according to the formulas used for the dependency weight.

3.4 Experiments

For the experiment, we use the standard data division (Collins, 1999). The lexical data was extracted from section 02-21 of the WSJ corpus. In addition, section 23 was reserved for the evaluation, and section 00 was used as a development set.

The common method used to evaluate the CFG style parsing performance is through matching bracketing. However, this method is heavily affected by the tags and bracketing style. Therefore, we use the dependency accuracy between words. Except for the headword of a sentence as a whole, all words in the sentence have their own headword. Therefore, the dependency accuracy is measured by obtaining and matching the headwords. The usual dependency accuracy includes the match of the relation between the head and its dependents (Lin, 1998). However, we do not consider the tags or any relation due to the tag disagreement and bracketing style. The dependency performance is measured by obtaining how many words are attached to its correct headword. Table 1 shows the results.

Table 1: Attachment accuracy of supervised learning

	PP attachment Accuracy	Dependency Accuracy
Base parsing system	79.23%	91.39%
generative model	83.04%	91.92%
bilexical model	83.44%	91.97%

Table 1 shows that the bilexical model is slightly better than the generative model. This is considered reasonable since the PP attachment problem is to find the attachment site when a sentence is given, and is better described by the bilexical model. The baseline for the experiments in this paper is our base parsing system, as our main concern is not PP attachment itself, but how we can improve the parsing performance using a statistical PP attachment disambiguation method.

4 Unsupervised Learning

4.1 Data Extraction

In an unsupervised learning method for PP attachment, the learning data is usually extracted heuristically (Ratnaparkhi, 1998). We followed a similar method. For the unsupervised learning data, the raw corpus is tagged and chunked, and all chunked NPs are replaced with their head words. Next, 4-tuples (*v*, *n*, *p*, *n2*) are extracted, where *v* is the closest verb occurring on the left of preposition *p*, and there is no conjunction except for a coordinate conjunction between v and *p*. In addition, *n* is the closest noun occurring on the left of preposition *p* with no verb between *n* and *p*. Finally, *n2* is the object noun of *p*. If there is not either *v* or *n*, it is denoted as *NULL*.

For example, the sentence "A man in the park saw a girl with a telescope" is tagged and chunked as follows:

A/DT man/NN in/IN the/DT park/NN saw/VBD a/DT girl/NN with/IN a/DT telescope/NN ./.
=>
man/NN in/IN park/NN saw/VBD girl/NN with/IN telescope/NN ./.

4-tuples: (*NULL*, man, in, park), (see, girl, with, telescope)

The number of triple (*v/n*, *p*, *n2*) is then counted as follows according to the ambiguity.

1) If a 4-tupe has the form of (*v*, *NULL*, *p*, *n2*), then add 1 to the number of triple (*v*, *p*, *n2*).
2) If a 4-tupe has the form of (*NULL*, *n*, *p*, *n2*), then add 1 to the number of triple (*n*, *p*, *n2*).
3) If a 4-tupe has the form of (*v*, *n*, *p*, *n2*), then several counting methods are considered.

Counting method 1: Add 0.5 to the number of triple (*v*, *p*, *n2*) and 0.5 to the number of triple (*n*, *p*, *n2*).

Counting method 2: Add *P(D|VERB, PREP)* to the number of triple (*v*, *p*, *n2*) and *P(D|NOUN, PREP)* to the number of triple (*n*, *p*, *n2*).

Counting method 3: Add *P(D|VERB, p)* to the number of triple (*v*, *p*, *n2*) and *P(D|NOUN, p)* to the number of triple (*n*, *p*, *n2*).

Counting method 4: Add *P(D|v, p)* to the number of triple (*v*, *p*, *n2*) and *P(D|n, p)* to the number of triple (*n*, *p*, *n2*).

In the above example sentence, the numbers of triples are as follows.

Counting method 1:
(man, in, park):1, (see, with, telescope):0.5, (girl, with, telescope): 0.5

Counting 2:
(man, in, park):1, (see, with, telescope):P(D|VERB, PREP) = 0.395, (girl, with, telescope): P(D|NOUN, PREP) = 0.691

Counting 3:
(man, in, park):1, (see, with, telescope): P(D|VERB, with) = 0.527, (girl, with, telescope): P(D|NOUN, with) = 0.632

For the linguistic source, the BLLIP WSJ corpus was used, which is composed of about 1.8 million automatically tree-tagged sentences. The pos-tagged results were extracted, the results of which were used to extract the triples. The number of triples extracted was 1,466,472.

4.2 Model

For the attachment weight, we used the generative model and its ratio to a more general case conditioned on tags as follows.

$$W(p,n2 \mid w) = \lambda \frac{P(p,n2 \mid w)}{P(p,n2 \mid t(w))} + (1-\lambda)\frac{P(p \mid w)}{P(p \mid t(w))}, \quad (11)$$

where *w* is a verb or a noun, *t(w)* is the tag of *w*, and λ is an interpolation constant for data sparseness. The method used to apply the weight is similar to that of the supervised learning.

$$W(r) = P(r) * \prod_i \alpha W(p,n2 \mid w), \quad (12)$$

where α is a proportional constant used for scaling the PP attachment weight in order to adjust the weight according to the parsing weighting mechanism, and is determined experimentally.

4.3 Experiments

As in the experiments on supervised learning, the evaluation was conducted using section 23 of the WSJ corpus. Table 2 shows the results.

Table 2: Attachment accuracy of unsupervised learning according to the counting methods of ambiguous data

	PP attachment Accuracy	Dependency Accuracy
Base parsing system	79.23%	91.39%
Counting method 1	82.33%	91.70%
Counting method 2	81.26%	91.65%
Counting method 3	81.71%	91.69%
Counting method 4	81.68%	91.70%
(v, p, n2): (n, p, n2) = 0.7:0.3	82.95%	91.78%

One puzzling result is that counting method 1 is better than the other cases where supervised learning data are applied. We assumed that a more informed case would have better results than the case of simply giving one half. Therefore, we conducted additional experiments, changing (*v*, *p*, *n2*) using the constant values of 0.6, 0.7, and 0.8. As a result, 0.7 gives the best results, and was thus selected as the final value. However, further analysis regarding these results is needed.

5 Combination

We considered two methods in combining supervised and unsupervised learning data.

1) We applied supervised learning data when supervised learning data was available for the attachment weight, and we applied unsupervised learning data only when there was no supervised learning data available (super > unsuper).
2) We applied the attachment weight using both supervised and unsupervised learning data at the same time (super + unsuper).

Table 3 shows the results.

Table 3: Attachment accuracy of combining supervised and unsupervised learning methods.

	PP attachment Accuracy	Dependency Accuracy
Base parsing system	79.23%	91.39%
supervised	83.44%	91.97%
unsupervised	82.95%	91.78%
super > unsuper	84.06%	92.09%
super + unsuper	84.65%	92.14%

Volk (2002) took the "super > unsuper" approach. It seems that these cases are different as they deal with PP attachment as a classification problem, while we deal with it as a weighting problem. Finally, using statistical information, the PP attachment performance was enhanced by 5.42% with an 8.7% error reduction ratio in the overall parsing performance.

6 Conclusion

This paper presented a method to enhance the PP attachment performance in a rule-based parser. We conducted a comparative experiment between the bilexical and generative models for supervised learning. We also applied the unsupervised learning method of PP attachment to the rule-based parser. The results show a 3.73% improvement in performance.

We also conducted simple experiments on combining two types of learning methods, the final results of which show a 5.42% performance improvement in PP attachment, with an 8.7% error reduction ratio in the overall parsing performance.

For future work, we obviously need to conduct more analysis and experiments on adding counts to ambiguous 4-tuples by applying the supervised learning method. In addition, we need a more elaborate method to combine the supervised and unsupervised learning methods. Finally, we plan to devise an efficient way to build a tagged corpus for PP attachment.

References

Bharati, A., U. Rohini, P. Vishnu, S. Bendre, and R. Sangal. 2005. A hybrid approach to single and multiple PP attachment using WordNet. *Proceedings of International Joint Conference on Natural Language Processing (IJCNLP) 2005*, pp. 211–222.

Charniak, E. 2000. A maximum-entropy-inspired parser. *Proceedings of the North American Chapter of the Association for Computational Linguistics*, pp. 132-139.

Collins, M. 2000. Discriminative Reranking for Natural Language Parsing. *Proceedings of the Seventeenth International Conference on Machine Learning*, pp. 175–182.

Collins, M. 1996. A New Statistical Parser based on Bigram Lexical Dependencies. *Proceedings of ACL '96*, pp. 184–191.

Collins, M. 1999. *Head-Driven Statistical Models for Natural Language Parsing*. Ph.D. thesis, University of Pennsylvania.

Foth, K. and W. Menzel. 2006. The benefit of stochastic PP attachment to a rule-based parser. *Proceedings of the COLING/ACL*, pp. 223–230.

Lin, D. 1998. A Dependency-based Method for Evaluating Broad-coverage Parsers. *Natural Language Engineering*, 4(2), 97-114.

Marcus, M. P., B. Santorini, and M. A. Marcinkiewics, 1993. Building a large annotated corpus of English: The Penn Treebank. *Computational Linguistics*, 19.

Merlo, P., M. W. Crocker, and C. Berthouzoz. 1997. Attaching multiple prepositional phrases: Generalized backed-off estimation. *Proceedings of the 2nd Conference on Empirical Methods in Natural Language Processing (EMNLP-97)*, pp. 149–155.

Olteanu, M. and D. Moldovan, 2005. PP-attachment Disambiguation Using Large Context. *Proceedings of the conference on Human Language Technology and Empirical Methods in Natural Language Processing*, pp. 273-280.

Ratnaparkhi, A. 1998. Statistical Models for Unsupervised Prepositional Phrase Attachment. *Proceedings of the 36th conference on Association for Computational Linguistics*, pp. 1079–1085.

Roh, Y.-H., K.-Y. Lee, and Y.-G. Kim, 2009. Incorporating Statistical Information of Lexical Dependency into a Rule-Based Parser. *Proceedings of the 23th Pacific Asia Conference on Language, Information and Computation*, pp. 493–500.

Sagae, K. and A. Lavie, 2003. Combining Rule-based and Data-driven Techniques for Grammatical Relation Extraction in Spoken Language. *Proceedings of the Eighth International Workshop in Parsing Technologies.*

Stetina, J. and M. Nagao. 1997. Corpus Based PP Attachment Ambiguity Resolution with a Semantic Dictionary. *Proceedings of the Fifth Workshop on Very Large Corpora*, pp. 66–80.

Volk, M. 2002. Combining unsupervised and supervised methods for PP attachment disambiguation. *Proceedings of the 19th International Conference on Computational Linguistics (COLING 2002)*, pp. 1–7.

Fully-Automatic Marker-based Chunking in 11 European Languages and Counts of the Number of Analogies between Chunks ⋆

Kota Takeya and Yves Lepage

IPS, Waseda University
Kitakyushu, Fukuoka 808-0135, Japan
{kota-takeya@toki, yves.lepage@aoni}.waseda.jp

Abstract. Analogy has been proposed as a possible principle for example-based machine translation. For such a framework to work properly, the training data should contain a large number of analogies between sentences. Consequently, such a framework can only work properly with short and repetitive sentences. To handle longer and more varied sentences, cutting the sentences into chunks could be a solution if the number of analogies between chunks is confirmed to be large. This paper thus reports counts of number of analogies using different numbers of chunk markers in 11 European languages. These experiments confirm that the number of analogies between chunks is very large: several tens of thousands of analogies between chunks extracted from sentences among which only very few analogies, if not none, were found.

Keywords: Analogy, Marker Hypothesis, Marker-based Chunking, Branching Entropy

1 Introduction

The example-based approach (Nagao, 1984) contrasts with the statistical approach (Brown *et al.*, 1990; Brown *et al.*, 1993) to machine translation in that it uses a bilingual corpus of aligned sentences as its main knowledge *at run time*. We aim at building an EBMT system based on proportional analogies.

A translation method based on proportional analogies has been proposed by Lepage and Denoual (2005b). The following procedure gives the basic outline of the method to perform the translation of an input chunk. Let us suppose that we have a corpus of aligned chunks in two languages, German and French. Let x = "ein großes programm und" be a source chunk to be translated into one or more target chunks $\widehat{x}$. Let the bilingual corpus consists of four chunks with their translations:

ernste programme	$\leftrightarrow$	programmes sérieux
ein ernstes programm	$\leftrightarrow$	un programme sérieux
große programme und	$\leftrightarrow$	gros programmes et
das ernste programm	$\leftrightarrow$	le programme sérieux

The method forms all possible analogies with all possible triples of chunks from the parallel corpus. Among them:

$$\text{ernste programme : ein ernstes programm :: große programme und : ein großes programm und} = x$$

⋆ This paper is a part of the outcome of research performed under a Waseda University Grant for Special Research Project (project number: 2010A-906).

Taking into account the knowledge in the bilingual corpus, analogical equation can be formed in the target language:

$$\text{programmes sérieux} \;:\; \text{un programme sérieux} \;::\; \text{gros programmes et} \;:\; \widehat{x}$$

Its solution is a candidate translation of the source chunk: $\widehat{x}$ = "un gros programme et"

For such an EBMT system to work well, the more numerous the proportional analogies, the better the translation outputs are expected to be. The method can work on small sentences like the ones in the BTEC corpus (Lepage and Denoual, 2005a), but cannot handle long sentences like the ones in the Europarl corpus (Koehn, 2005). For long sentences, translating chunk by chunk could be a solution. We have inspected the quality of translation of chunks obtained by marker-based chunking in English and French in both directions in (Takeya and Lepage, 2011a; Takeya and Lepage, 2011b). Our results have shown that more than three quarters of the chunks can be translated by the one-step analogy-based translation method, and that a little bit less than half of the chunks has at least one translation that matches exactly with one of the references. As the number of analogies is the crucial point, this paper inspects ways of counting sentences into chunks using different markers and examines the number of proportional analogies between them in 11 European languages.

The rest of the paper is organized as follows. Section 2 describes the basic notion of marker-based chunking used in the reported experiments. Section 3 explains the notion of proportional analogy. Section 4 presents the data for the experiments which are sample sentences from the Europarl corpus in 11 European languages and the experimental protocol. Section 5 describes the results of the experiments and analyzes them. A conclusion is given in Section 6.

2 Marker-based Chunking

In order to be able to apply the previous proposed method to various languages, we want to segment in a fully automatic and universal way sentences in different languages into sub-sentential units like chunks.

2.1 The Marker Hypothesis

We use the marker hypothesis for this. This hypothesis was first laid by Green (1979).

> The marker hypothesis states that all natural languages contain a small number of elements that signal the presence of particular syntactic constructions.

We perform chunking based on this notion and use a method called marker-based chunking (Gough and Way, 2004; Stroppa and Way, 2006; Van Den Bosch *et al.*, 2007). We define a chunk as a sequence of words delimited by markers. Markers should be words such as determiners (the), conjunctions (and, but, or), prepositions (in, from, to), possessive and personal pronouns (mine, you). A chunk can be created at each occurrence of a marker word. In addition, a further constraint requires that each chunk contains at least one non-marker word. Without non-marker words, a chunk would become meaningless as it would not contain any meaningful word.

As result examples, the following English, French and German sentences were processed by marker-based chunking using 50 markers. The underlined words are markers.

- [it <u>is</u>] [impossible <u>to</u>] [see why] [<u>the</u> resale right should] [<u>be</u> imposed <u>on</u>] [artists against their will] [<u>as</u> a form <u>of</u>] [copyright <u>.</u>]
- [on ne voit pas pourquoi] [<u>le</u> droit <u>de</u>] [suite doit être imposé comme une forme <u>du</u>] [droit <u>d'</u>] [auteur aux artistes , <u>et</u>] [ce contre leur volonté <u>.</u>]
- [es <u>ist</u>] [nicht einzusehen <u>,</u>] [warum] [<u>das</u> folgerecht als ausformung des urheberrechts] [<u>den</u> künstlern gegen ihren willen aufgezwungen werden soll <u>.</u>]

2.2 Determining Markers by Informativity

Gough and Way (2004) use marker-based chunking as a preprocessing step in SMT to improve the quality of translation tables and get improved results when combining their chunks with GIZA++/Moses translation table. They define a list of markers by hand and always cut left for European languages.

In contrast with their approach, we choose to automatically compute the list of markers. Frequency cannot do it: in the Europarl corpus "European" is a frequent word, but cannot be considered as a marker. We rely on some results from information theory and from our experimental results. In addition, to decide whether to cut to the left or the right of a marker, we compare the values of its branching entropy on both of its sides.

To determine which words are markers, we proceed as follows. If a language would be a perfect code, the length of each word would be a function of its number of occurrences, because, according to information theory, its emission length would be proportional to its self-information. The self-information of a word that appears $C(w)$ times in a corpus of N words is:

$$-\log \frac{C(w)}{N}$$

In an ideal code, thus:

$$l(w) = -\log \frac{C(w)}{N}$$

with $l(w)$ the length of the word, $C(w)$ its number of occurrences and N the total number of words in the text. Consequently, a word in a corpus of N words can be said to be informative if its length is much greater than its self-information in this text:

$$l(w) > -\log \frac{C(w)}{N}$$

Consequently again, words with the smallest values for the following function can be said to be informative.

$$-\log \frac{C(w)}{N} \;\; / \;\; l(w) \tag{1}$$

Conversely, markers, that is words that are not informative, should be the words with the largest values for the previous function. However, our experiments with this formula were deceptive. Rather, considering the absolute number of occurrences instead of the frequency delivers words that meet more the human intuition about linguistic markers. To summarize, the list of markers we use is the list of words with the smallest values for the following function:

$$-\log C(w) \;\; / \;\; l(w) \tag{2}$$

Table 1 shows markers obtained in accordance with the two proposed formulae. Those obtained with the latter formula (2) are true markers, on the contrary to those obtained with the former formula (1).

Figure 1(a) and 1(b) visualize the better efficiency of formula (2) over formula formula (1) to isolate words that correspond to the intuitive notion of a marker.

2.3 Left or Right Cutting

Following the famous intuition by Harris (1955) about branching entropy, Tanaka-Ishii (2005) and Jin and Tanaka-Ishii (2006) have shown how Japanese and Chinese can be segmented into words by formalizing the uncertainty using branching entropy at some point of a text.

The entropy of a random variable X with m outcomes x_i is defined as its mathematical expectation and is a measure of its overall uncertainty:

Table 1: Words ranked according to two different formulae. Formula (1) on the left, (2) on the right.

Rank	$-\log \frac{C(w)}{N}$ / $l(w)$		$-\log C(w)$ / $l(w)$	
	Word	Value	Word	Value
1	z	21.81	,	-19.00
2	/	21.08	.	-18.57
3	$	20.08	a	-17.37
4	q	19.94	i	-16.84
5	x	19.70	-	-15.15
6	1	19.40	s	-15.01
7	u	19.40	)	-14.37
8	w	19.15	(	-14.36
9	r	19.15	:	-13.74
10	&	19.15	'	-13.10
11	o	18.94	;	-13.09
12	[	18.59	?	-12.12
13	h	18.59	1	-11.54
14	j	18.54	!	-11.30
15	n	18.35	2	-10.93
16	+	18.27	%	-10.89
17	f	17.97	5	-10.61
18	y	17.97	3	-10.61
19	d	17.09	4	-10.30
20	k	17.09	6	-9.97
⋮		⋮		⋮

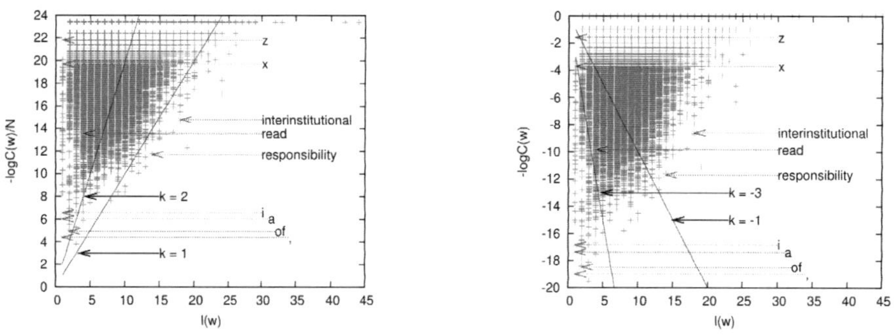

(a) $-\log \frac{C(w)}{N}$ against $l(w)$ for all words w (formula (1)). The lines stand for different values of $-\log \frac{C(w)}{N}$ / $l(w)$. Words that correspond to the intuitive notion of a marker cannot be separated from other words using these lines.

(b) $-\log C(w)$ against $l(w)$ for all words w (formula (2)). Words that correspond to the intuitive notion of a marker are clustered at the bottom left part of the triangle of dots and can thus be easily isolated using lines that stand for different values of $-\log C(w)$ / $l(w)$.

Figure 1: Distribution of words using two different formulae.

$$H(X) = -\sum_{i=1}^{m} p(x_i) \log p(x_i)$$

with $p(x_i)$ the probability of the outcome x_i.

The branching entropy at some position in a text is the entropy of the right context knowing the left context. Tanaka-Ishii (2005) computes it as the entropy of the characters that may follow a given left context of n characters.

$$H(X|X_n = x_n) = -\sum_{x} p(x|x_n) \log p(x|x_n)$$

with x being all the different characters that follow the string x_n in a given text.

We determine on which side of a marker to cut, left or right, by comparing the branching entropy on its left and the branching entropy on its right. In opposition to Tanaka-Ishii (2005), we compute branching entropies in words not in characters. If the branching entropy on the left is greater than the one on the right, it means that there is more uncertainty on the left context of the marker, i.e., the connection of the marker to its left context is weaker. In other words, the marker is more tightly connected to its right context so that it should be grouped as a chunk with its right context, rather than its left context.

Table 2 shows examples of which side to cut for different markers. In English, "(" is separated on the left while ")" is separated on the right, which is a felicitous results. On the whole, except for few mismatches, the segmentation that we obtained seems roughly acceptable.

Table 2: List of markers used for English.

Rank	$-\log C(w) \ / \ l(w)$		
	Word	Value	Cut
1	,	-19.00	right
2	.	-18.57	right
3	a	-17.37	left
4	i	-16.84	left
5	-	-15.15	left
6	s	-15.01	right
7	)	-14.37	right
8	(	-14.36	left
9	:	-13.74	right
10	'	-13.10	left
11	;	-13.09	right
12	?	-12.12	right
13	1	-11.54	left
14	!	-11.30	right
15	2	-10.93	left
16	%	-10.89	right
17	5	-10.61	left
18	3	-10.61	left
19	4	-10.30	left
20	6	-9.97	left
⋮		⋮	

3 Proportional Analogy

Proportional analogy is a general relationship between four objects, A, B, C and D, that states that 'A is to B as C is to D'. Its standard notation is $A : B :: C : D$. The following are proportional analogies between words (3), chunks (4) and sentences (5):

$$\text{possible} : \text{impossible} :: \text{partiality} : \text{impartiality} \quad (3)$$

$$\text{the book} : \text{an expensive book} :: \text{the first trip} : \text{an expensive first trip} \quad (4)$$

$$\text{I like music.} : \text{Do you go to lives?} :: \text{I like jazz music.} : \text{Do you go to jazz lives?} \quad (5)$$

A formalization has been proposed in (Lepage, 2004). This formalization reduces to the counting of number of symbol occurrences and the computation of edit distances. Precisely:

$$A : B :: C : D \Rightarrow \begin{cases} |A|_a - |B|_a = |C|_a - |D|_a, \ \forall a \\ \delta(A, B) = \delta(C, D) \end{cases}$$

where $|A|_a$ stands for the number of occurrences of character a in string A and $\delta(A, B)$ stands for the edit distance between strings A and B with only insertion and deletion as edit operations. As B and C may be exchanged in an analogy, the constraint on edit distance has also to be verified for $A : C :: B : D$, i.e., $\delta(A, C) = \delta(B, D)$. There is no need to verify the first constraint as, trivially, $|A|_a - |B|_a = |C|_a - |D|_a \Leftrightarrow |A|_a - |C|_a = |B|_a - |D|_a$.

4 Experimental Setting

4.1 Experimental Protocol

We present experiments similar to the ones reported for Japanese in (Lepage *et al.*, 2009), but on 11 European languages. Another similar experiment also has been done in (Takeya *et al.*, 2011). Here, we examine several sampling sizes and different numbers of markers. Our sampling sizes range from 10 to 100,000 sentences, and the number of markers ranges from 10 to 300 markers.

4.2 Experimental Data

We use the Europarl corpus (Koehn, 2005) in our experiments because our ultimate goal is to apply the analogy-based EBMT method to this kind of data. The Europarl corpus is a collection of proceedings of the European Parliament. Since the corpus is not exactly aligned, we aligned nearly 400,000 sentences across 11 languages properly. Our corpus comprises of about 10 million words for each of 11 official languages of the European Union: Danish (da), German (de), Greek (el), English (en), Spanish (es), Finnish (fi), French (fr), Italian (it), Dutch (nl), Portuguese (pt) and Swedish (sv). Precise statistics are given in Table 3.

Table 3: Statistics of 11 European parallel aligned corpora.

	da	de	el	en	es	fi	fr	it	nl	pt	sv
Sentences						384,237					
Words	10.4M	10.5M	10.0M	10.9M	11.5M	7.9M	12.1M	10.9M	11.0M	11.3M	9.9M
Voc.	162.2k	177.1k	156.3k	70.9k	104.9k	315.9k	90.4k	103.8k	132.2k	107.5k	165.8k

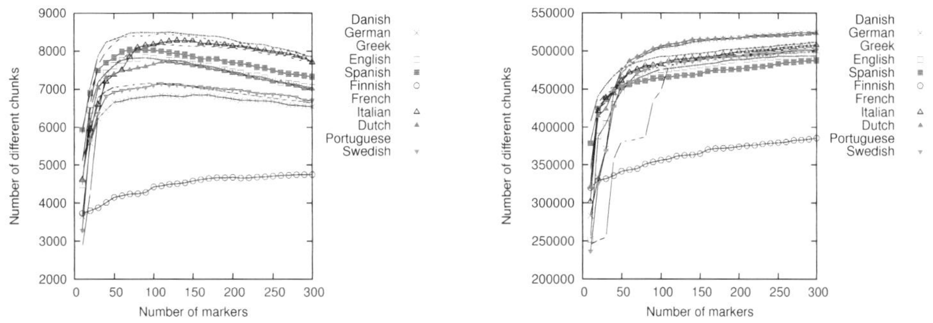

(a) Number of different chunks against number of markers used for 1,000 sentences in 11 different languages. On the contrary to Figure 2(b), in most languages, the number of different chunks obtained does not always increase.

(b) Number of different chunks against number of markers used for 100,000 sentences in 11 different languages. As expected, the more the markers, the more the number of different chunks obtained.

Figure 2: Number of different chunks against number of markers used.

5 Experimental Results

5.1 Number of different chunks obtained from different markers

By varying the number of markers, we measure how different markers affect the number of different chunks obtained. By doing so, it is possible to determine which markers are the most productive ones. Increasing the number of markers should increase the number of different chunks generated.

Figure 2(a) shows the number of different chunks obtained using different numbers of markers on 1,000 sentences in each different language. This graph shows that when the number of markers increases, the number of chunks may decrease in most languages.

Figure 2(b) shows the number of different chunks obtained using different numbers of markers on 100,000 sentences. After 20 markers, the increase slows down for every language except for Finnish. The low number of different chunks for Finnish may be explained by the morphological richness of this language, and its relative lack in prepositions.

5.2 Number of analogies between sentences

Figure 3 plots the number of proportional analogies between sentences for different numbers of sentences. Until 25,000 sentences, no analogies are found. After 50,000 sentences, the increase looks at least polynomial. The minimal number of proportional analogies is 159 for Greek for 100,000 sentences and the maximal number of proportional analogies is 698 for Danish. These numbers show clearly that an EBMT system using proportional analogies between sentences will not be able to translate any sentence.

5.3 Number of analogies between chunks

In comparison with Figure 3, Figure 4 plots the number of proportional analogies between chunks extracted from 10 to 2,500 sentences using different numbers of markers. Among Figures 4(a) to 4(d), the most productive one is 4(b). In Figure 4(b), chunks obtained from 100 sentences form very few analogies. After some 2,500 sentences, the number of proportional analogies found increases to more than 5,000 to 550,000 analogies with much variation. The minimal number of proportional analogies is 4,777 for Finnish. The maximum number of proportional analogies is 548,928 for Spanish. It is important to note that in contrast to Figure 3 not only the abscissae scale is different, but also the ordinates scale, which is different by three orders of magnitude. The curves on Figures 4 grow in fact more than thousand times faster than the ones on Figure 3.

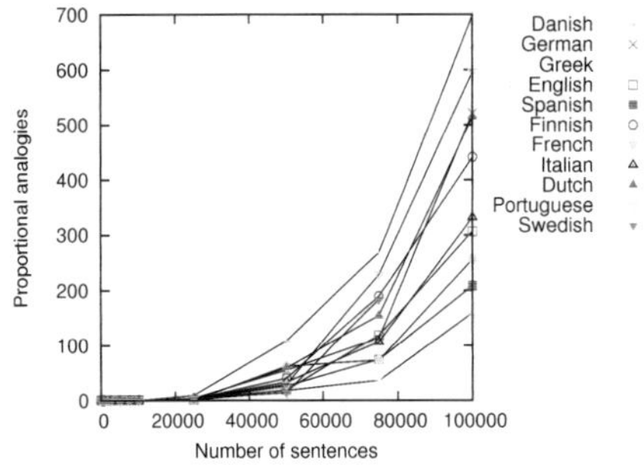

Figure 3: Number of proportional analogies between sentences obtained with an increasing number of sentences.

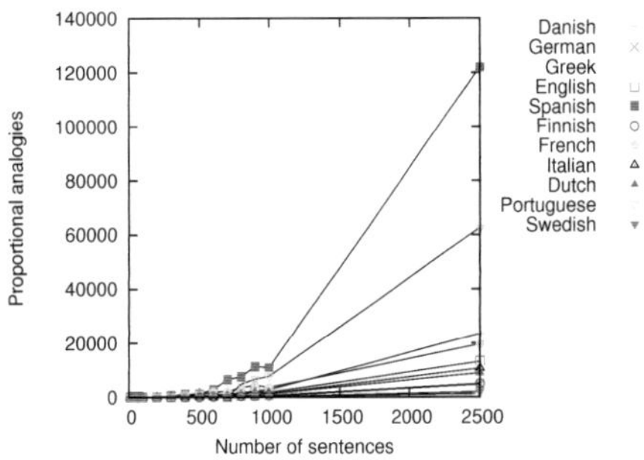

(a) Number of proportional analogies between chunks extracted from an increasing number of sentences using 10 markers.

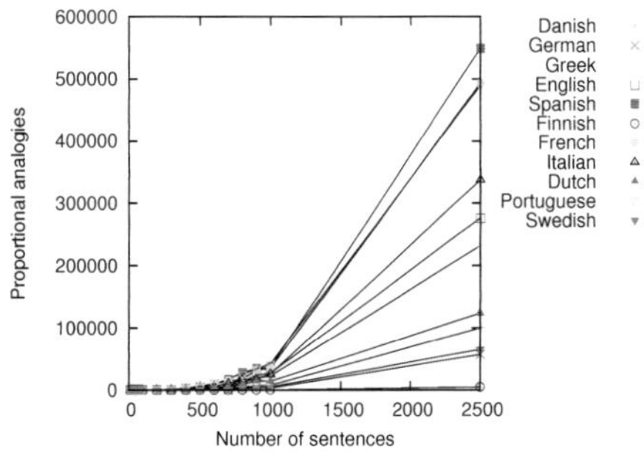

(b) Number of proportional analogies between chunks extracted from an increasing number of sentences using 100 markers.

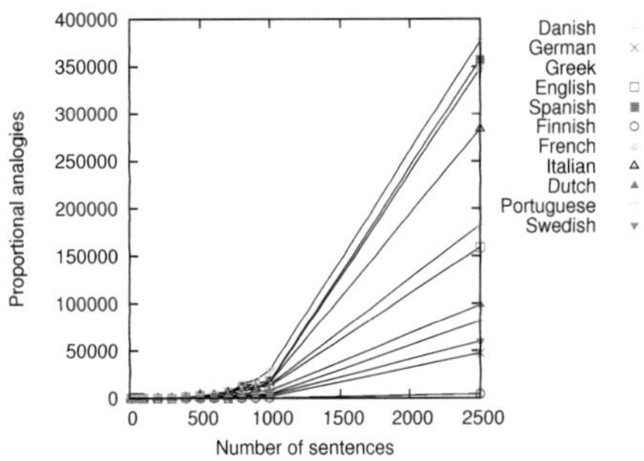

(c) Number of proportional analogies between chunks extracted from an increasing number of sentences using 200 markers.

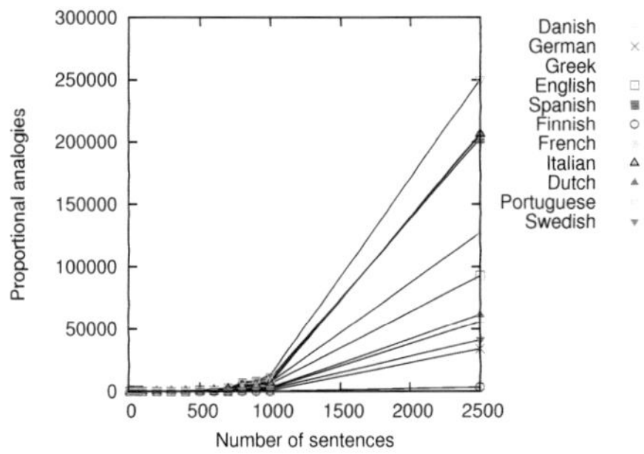

(d) Number of proportional analogies between chunks extracted from an increasing number of sentences using 300 markers.

Figure 4: Number of proportional analogies between chunks extracted from 10 to 2,500 sentences using different numbers of markers. Caution: the ordinate axis scales vary

6 Conclusion

The experiments reported in this paper are conclusive for our goal of building an EBMT system based on proportional analogies: as expected, the number of proportional analogies between chunks is by far much higher than between sentences. Beyond expectation, this number is ways much higher. We obtained more than several tens of thousands of analogies between chunks extracted from only 2,500 sentences in each language in average.

In our goal of building an EBMT sytem, future research should address the following questions.

- Propose a method to align chunks. A natural way to do so is to use lexical weights as proposed by (Koehn *et al.*, 2003; Koehn, 2010).
- Design an algorithm to reorder the chunks after translation. This is tantamount to design a reordering model of chunks.

References

Brown, P.F., J. Cocke, S.A.D. Pietra, V.J.D. Pietra, F. Jelinek, J.D. Lafferty, R.L. Mercer, and P.S. Roossin. 1990. A statistical approach to machine translation. *Computational linguistics*, 16(2), 79–85.

Brown, P.F., V.J.D. Pietra, S.A.D. Pietra, and R.L. Mercer. 1993. The mathematics of statistical machine translation: Parameter estimation. *Computational linguistics*, 19(2), 263–311.

Gough, N. and A. Way. 2004. Robust large-scale EBMT with marker-based segmentation. In *Proceedings of the 10th International Conference on Theoretical and Methodological Issues in Machine Translation (TMI-04)*, pp. 95–104.

Green, T.R.G. 1979. The necessity of syntax markers: Two experiments with artificial languages. *Journal of Verbal Learning and Verbal Behavior*, 18(4), 481–496.

Harris, Z.S. 1955. From phoneme to morpheme. *Language*, 31(2), 190–222.

Jin, Z. and K. Tanaka-Ishii. 2006. Unsupervised segmentation of Chinese text by use of branching entropy. In *Proceedings of the COLING/ACL on Main conference poster sessions*, pp. 428–435.

Koehn, P. 2005. Europarl: A parallel corpus for statistical machine translation. In *Proceedings of MT Summit X*, pp. 79–86, Phuket, Thailand.

Koehn, P. 2010. *Statistical Machine Translation*. Cambridge University Press.

Koehn, P., F.J. Och, and D. Marcu. 2003. Statistical phrase-based translation. In *Proceedings of the Human Language Technology and North American Association for Computational Linguistics Conference (HLT/NAACL)*, pp. 127–133, Edmonton, Alberta.

Lepage, Y. 2004. Analogy and formal languages. *Electronic notes in theoretical computer science*, 53, 180–191.

Lepage, Y. and E. Denoual. 2005a. ALEPH: an EBMT system based on the preservation of proportional analogies between sentences across languages. In *Proceedings of the International Workshop on Spoken Language Translation (IWSLT 2005)*, pp. 47–54.

Lepage, Y. and E. Denoual. 2005b. Purest ever example-based machine translation: Detailed presentation and assessment. *Machine Translation*, 19(3), 251–282.

Lepage, Y., J. Migeot, and E. Guillerm. 2009. A Measure of the Number of True Analogies between Chunks in Japanese. *Human Language Technology. Challenges of the Information Society*, pp. 154–164.

Nagao, M. 1984. A framework of a mechanical translation between Japanese and English by analogy principle. *Artifiical and Human Intelligence*, pp. 173–180.

Stroppa, N. and A. Way. 2006. MaTrEx: the DCU machine translation system for IWSLT 2006. In *Proceedings of the International Workshop on Spoken Language Translation*, pp. 31–36.

Takeya, K. and Y. Lepage. 2011a. Evaluation of Analogy-based Translation of Chunks obtained by Marker-based Chunking. In *Information Processing Society of Japan (IPSJ) SIG Technical Report 2011-NL-202*, pp. 1–7.

Takeya, K. and Y. Lepage. 2011b. Marker-based Chunking for Analogy-based Translation of Chunks. In *Proceedings of MT Summit XIII*, pp. 338–345.

Takeya, K., J. Sun, and Y. Lepage. 2011. The Number of Proportional Analogies between Marker-based Chunks in 11 European Languages. In *Proceedings of the 17th Annual Meeting of the Association for Natural Language Processing*, pp. 677–680, Toyohashi, Japan.

Tanaka-Ishii, K. 2005. Entropy as an indicator of context boundaries: An experiment using a web search engine. In *Proceedings of the Second International Joint Conference on Natural Language Processing*, pp. 93–105.

Van Den Bosch, A., N. Stroppa, and A. Way. 2007. A memory-based classification approach to marker-based EBMT. In *Proceedings of the METIS-II Workshop on New Approaches to Machine Translation*, pp. 63–72, Leuven, Belgium.

Extraction of Broad-Scale, High-Precision Japanese-English Parallel Translation Expressions Using Lexical Information and Rules *

Qing Ma[a], Shinya Sakagami[a], and Masaki Murata[b]

[a] Department of Applied Mathematics and Informatics, Ryukoku University,
1-5 Oei-Yokoya, Seta, Otsu 520-2194, Japan
qma@math.ryukoku.ac.jp

[b] Department of Information and Electronics, Tottori University,
4-101 Koyama-Minami, Tottori 680-8552, Japan
murata@ike.tottori-u.ac.jp

Abstract. Extraction was attempted of broad-scale, high-precision Japanese-English parallel translation expressions from large aligned parallel corpora. To acquire broad-scale parallel translation expressions, a new method was used to extract single Japanese and English word n-grams, by which as many parallel translation expressions as possible could then be extracted. To achieve high extraction precision, first, hand-crafted rules were used to prune the unnecessary words often found in expressions extracted on the basis of word n-grams, and lexical information was used to refine the parallel translation expressions. Computer experiments with aligned parallel corpora consisting of about 280,000 pairs of Japanese-English parallel sentences found that more than 125,000 pairs of parallel translation expressions could be extracted with a precision of 0.96. These figures show that the proposed methods for extracting a broad range of parallel translation expressions have reached a level high enough for practical use.

Keywords: parallel translation expression, extraction, rule, lexical information, English-writing support

1 Introduction

Non-native speakers often have problems explaining ideas or presenting achievements in written English, in part because of the large amount of time needed to determine which possible translation of an expression most suits the context. Trying to develop English-writing support tools that will enable non-native speakers to produce nearly perfect English sentences for mixed English-Japanese sentences–in which expressions without know translations are simply written in Japanese–Ma et al. (2008; 2009) have developed systems that can provide support at the word and phrase levels. That is, the given Japanese parts in the mixed English-Japanese sentences can be words or phrases. For phrase-level support in those systems, the Japanese parts are extracted from the mixed sentences and segmented into words, the candidate English equivalents of the segmented Japanese words are identified by searching through a Japanese-English dictionary, and the best equivalents of the Japanese phrases are selected from the combinations of the candidate translations of the single words. This kind of support, however, has two problems. One is the variety of the phrase patterns that the system can support is limited because the English phrases are generated only from the combinations of the candidate translations of single words. The other is the processing is time-consuming because a large number of the translations of single words results in an enormous number of combinations.

* This work was supported by a Grant-in-Aid for Scientific Research (KAKENHI (C) 19500133) from the Ministry of Education, Culture, Sports, Science and Technology, Japan.

We think that an effective way to solve these problems would be to use an approach based on translation patterns: to first construct a dictionary of the Japanese-English translation patterns and use that dictionary to provide English-writing support. We therefore tried to extract broad-scale, high-precision Japanese-English parallel translation expressions from large aligned parallel corpora first.[1] To acquire broad-scale parallel translation expressions, we used a new method to extract single Japanese and English word n-grams, by which we could then extract as many parallel translation expressions as possible. To achieve high extraction precision, we first used hand-crafted rules to prune the unnecessary words often found in expressions extracted on the basis of word n-grams, and we further used lexical information from a Japanese-English dictionary to refine these parallel translation expressions. Computer experiments with aligned parallel corpora consisting of about 280,000 pairs of Japanese-English parallel sentences found that more than 125,000 pairs of parallel translation expressions could be extracted with a precision of 0.96. These figures show that the proposed methods for extracting a broad range of parallel translation expressions have reached a level high enough for practical use.

2 System Overview

The inputs to the system developed by Ma et al. (2008; 2009) are mixed English-Japanese sentences that contain Japanese words or (noun and verb) phrases. The Japanese parts are first identified and extracted. For the word-level support, stemming is performed to provide the base forms of the words. The phrase-level support, on the other hand, starts with word segmentation. Words are stemmed and segmented using the Japanese morphological analysis tool Chasen. The candidate English equivalents of the single Japanese words are then identified by searching through the Japanese-English dictionary Eijiro. Queries for word-level support are then constructed by using the equivalent candidates and their contexts, and queries for phrase-level support are constructed by using the combinations of the candidate equivalent of the single words.[2] All queries constructed in this way are searched for in high-quality corpora using an originally developed, flexibly searchable system and searched for in huge amounts of Web data using Google Web APIs to obtain their hits. Finally, the N-best English equivalent candidates with which the queries are constructed that have the largest N numbers of hits are selected as the answers for the systems.

One problem, however, is that the system can support only an extremely limited variety of the phrase patterns. The only noun phrases that can be supported are compound nouns and noun phrases composed of adjectives and nouns, and the only verb phrases that can be supported are those composed of nouns and verbs. Gerund phrases such as "走っている犬" [(1) *hashitteiru inu*, (2) *running dog*, (3) *a running dog*][3], for example, cannot be supported. Neither can translations to different patterns, such as noun phrases to infinitive phrases, be supported. Another problem is that the processing for phrase-level support is time-consuming because the number of combinations of the translations of single words is enormous.

We think that an effective way to solve these problems would be to take an approach based on translation patterns: to first construct a dictionary of the Japanese-English translation patterns and then use that dictionary to provide English-writing support. We therefore tried first to extract broad-scale, high-precision parallel translation expressions of Japanese-English from large aligned parallel corpora.

[1] Related work is discussed in Sec. 3.1.

[2] Acquiring candidate equivalents in phrase-level support is more complicated. See Ma et al. (2009) for details.

[3] The non-English examples are also rendered in (1) *alphabetized form*, (2) *English glosses*, and (3) *English translation* (or grammar explanations if there are no proper translations) complying with the PACLIC 25 Paper Submission Guidelines. The English translations, however, will be skipped if they appear in the pairs of the parallel translation expressions.

3 Extraction of Parallel Translation Expressions

3.1 Related work

The earlier studies most closely related to our work were done by Sainoo et al. (2003) and Kitamura and Matsumoto (1996; 2005). The principal techniques used in those studies were used as our baseline in this study and are described in Sec. 3.2.1. In the study of Sainoo et al., the research object was limited to a small corpus of 8,500 Japanese-English parallel sentences, which were examples from a number of bilingual dictionaries, and only a couple dozen parallel translation expressions were extracted. The first study of Kitamura and Matsumoto (1996), on the other hand, used Japanese-English parallel corpora of three distinct domains: a computer manual, a scientific journal, and business correspondence letters. Each had about 10,000 parallel sentences, and lots of stock phrases would have been used because of the natures of the domains. Pairs therefore can be expected to be easier to extract from these corpora than the copora that cover diverse fields. From each corpus, however, no more than 3,300 pairs were extracted with precisions of 0.87, 0.92, and 0.80. The extraction scale was extremely small, and the extraction precisions were low. In addition, the recall computed on the basis of the definition given in Sec. 4.1.3 was less than or equal to 0.29, a very low figure. Furthermore, single Japanese and English word n-grams were extracted and pairs of the parallel translation expressions were acquired through a repetition processing, which fed back the interim results. However, the whole processing is time-consuming and the extraction is therefore not easy to scale up. In Kimura and Matsumoto's second study (2005) they confirmed the interim results manually, used more linguistic resources than they did in their earlier study, and introduced a method for halving the extraction time by dividing a corpus into quarters. Their method is still hard to scale up, however, because the repetition processing is costly and the results can be manually confirmed only in small-scale extraction.

Among other interesting studies on the extraction of Japanese-English parallel translation expressions are those done by Yamamoto and Matsumoto (2000) and Sato and Saito (2002-1; 2002-2). The methods proposed in those studies, however, like those proposed in the earlier studies mentioned above, have low precisions and recalls and also cannot be scaled up. These methods are thus not practical for use in the extraction of large-scale parallel translation expressions. In a study by Sato and Saito (2002-1), for example, even though the test corpus used for extraction consisted of only about 3,000 parallel sentences, whereas the training corpus consisted of 30,287 parallel sentences, more than ten times the number in the test corpus, the extraction precision was still less than or equal to 0.65. Also, in the study by Yamamoto and Matsumoto (2000), the extraction recall was extremely low: only 461 pairs of parallel translation expressions were extracted with a precision of 0.9 from 13,000 pairs of parallel sentences (meaning the recall was 0.03 based on our definition).

In contrast to the approaches used in these earlier studies, our approaches are practically oriented and intended to be used for extracting broad-scale, high-precision parallel translation expressions useful in English-writing support for all kinds of phrases. Since none of methods proposed by Sato and Saito (2002-1; 2002-2) or by Yamamoto and Matsumoto (2000), the repetition processing used by Kitamura and Matsumoto (1996), or the manually confirmation conducted by Kitamura and Matsumoto (2005) are suitable for this, we instead adapted the methods proposed by Sainoo et al. (2003) and part of the methods proposed by Kitamura and Matsumoto (1996) as the baseline method. To acquire broad-scale parallel translation expressions, we improved the baseline method for extracting single Japanese and English word n-grams so that as many parallel translation expressions as possible can be extracted. To achieve high extraction precision, we first used hand-crafted rules to prune the unnecessary words often found in expressions extracted on the basis of word n-grams, and we further used the lexical information from a Japanese-English dictionary to refine the parallel translation expressions. In addition, we used very large corpora covering a much wider range of areas and extracted a broad range of parallel translation expressions.

3.2 Methods of extraction

3.2.1 The baseline method Pairs are extracted with the baseline method of parallel translation expressions by (1) extracting the single Japanese and English word n-grams from parallel corpora, and (2) acquiring the parallel translation expressions by computing the similarity between the Japanese and English word n-grams extracted in step (1).

In step (1) each Japanese and English word sequence with an arbitrary length less than or equal to n words (referred to as "word n-gram" in this paper) that appears at least twice in both the Japanese and English sides of the parallel corpora is extracted. Because this can result in many fragmented expressions that do not make sense being extracted, we used inhibition treatment to inhibit the generation of these kinds of expressions. Suppose there are two sentences in a corpus:

s1: a b c d e f

s2: g b c d h

where a, b, $\cdots$, h are words and sequences (b c d), (b c), and (c d) are the word n-grams appearing at least twice in both the Japanese and English sides of the parallel corpora. Only (b c d) is extracted, and (b c) and (c d) are not extracted because they are the parts of (b c d).

In step (2) the similarity between Japanese and English word n-grams is calculated using the *Dice coefficient* (Kay and Röschesen, 1993) below.

$$sim(x_j, x_e) = \frac{2f(x_j, x_e)}{f(x_j) + f(x_e)}, \tag{1}$$

where x_j and x_e are respectively the Japanese and English word n-grams, $f(x_j)$ and $f(x_e)$ are respectively the appearance frequencies of x_j and x_e in the parallel corpora, and $f(x_j, x_e)$ is the frequency of x_j and x_e co-occurring in the same pairs of Japanese-English sentences. That is, the similarity between the Japanese and English word n-grams in each pair extracted in step (1) is computed, and a pair is considered a pair of parallel translation expressions if the similarity is larger than a threshold value.

3.2.2 The improved method for n-gram extraction To acquire as many parallel translation expressions as possible, we improved the method for extracting single Japanese and English word n-grams, step (1) of the baseline method described in Sec. 3.2.1.

By examining the experimental results with the baseline method, we found that a number of parallel translation expressions that could be extracted when the maximum n-gram lengths was set to a small value could not be extracted when the maximum n-gram lengths was set to the larger one. The main reasons can be considered to be as follows. In the baseline method we used inhibition treatment to remove the fragmented expressions. Thus, if the expressions that can originally be extracted when the maximum n-gram length is short, are included in the longer ones that can be extracted when the maximum n-gram length is longer, then the short ones are removed. The parallel translation expression {J: 湾岸諸国と [(1) *wagan shokoku to*, (2) *the gulf states with*], E: with the gulf states}, for example, could not be acquired when the maximum n-gram lengths was set to six because the longer English expression "E: with the gulf states is" was extracted.

To resolve this problem, we do not extract word sequences with an arbitrary length until n-gram in a lump as done in the baseline method. Instead, we extract the word sequences from 1-gram to 2-gram, from 1-gram to 3-gram, $\cdots$, from 1-gram to n-grams in independent steps. When 3-grams are extracted from the sentence "Natural language processing is a field of computer science", for example, the word sequences from 1-gram to 2-gram, i.e.,

1-grams: Nature / language / processing / is / a / field / of / computer /science

2-grams: Natural language / language processing / processing is / is a / a field / field of / of computer / computer science and the word sequences from 1-gram to 3-gram, i.e.,

1-grams: Nature / language / processing / is / a / field / of / computer /science
2-grams: Natural language / language processing / processing is / is a / a field / field of / of computer / computer science,
3-grams: Natural language processing / language processing is / processing is a / is a field / a field of / field of computer / of computer science

are extracted in each independent step.[4] We also perform the inhibition treatment on them and acquire the parallel translation expressions in these independent steps. We finally assemble the parallel translation expressions obtained in these steps and remove the overlapping ones.

Parallel translation expressions are therefore acquired with the improved method by (1) initially setting the n-gram length to two; (2) extracting the single Japanese and English word sequences from 1-gram to the n-gram from parallel corpora, performing the inhibition treatment on them, and acquiring the parallel translation expressions by computing the similarity between the Japanese and English n-grams extracted; (3) incrementing the n-gram length with 1 and repeating steps (2) and (3) until the maximum n-gram length set beforehand is reached; and finally (4) assembling the parallel translation expressions obtained by steps (2) and (3), and removing the overlapping ones.

3.2.3 The hand-crafted rules By examining the experimental results with the baseline method, we found that ungrammatical Japanese expressions starting with words such as "こと" [(1) *koto*, (2)(3) *thing*] and "いる" [(1) *iru*, (2)(3) a progressive form] and ending with the words such as "この" [(1) *kono*, (2)(3) *this*] and " いろいろな" [(1) *iroiro-na*, (2)(3) *various*] were extracted. Similarly, ungrammatical English expressions starting with possessive forms and ending with articles and auxiliary verb, for example, were extracted. We therefore manually created the following rules and used them to suppress the extraction of ungrammatical single Japanese and English word n-grams.

Rule1
Expressions are eliminated if they end with the words in the list.
List

Japanese

adnominal

e.g., この [(1) *kono*, (2)(3) *this*], あの [(1) *ano*, (2)(3) *that*], いろいろな [(1) *iroiro-na*, (2)(3) *various*]

prefix

e.g., もと [(1) *moto*, (2)(3) *the former*], アンチ [(1) *anchi*, (2)(3) *anti-*], 超 [(1) *chou*, (2)(3) *super*], 反 [(1) *han*, (2)(3) *anti-*], 新 [(1) *shin*, (2)(3) *new*]

adverb

e.g., たいそう [(1) *taisou*, (2)(3) *very*], いつも [(1) *itsumo*, (2)(3) *always*], 人一倍 [(1) *hotoichibai*, (2)(3) *more than others*]

conjunctive noun

e.g., 兼 [(1) *ken*, (2)(3) *and*], 対 [(1) *tai*, (2)(3) *versus*]

English

article (e.g., a, the), preposition (e.g., about, at, by, in, out, of), auxiliary verb (can, may, will, must, shall), to, 4W1H (what, where, who, which, how)

Rule2
Expressions are eliminated if they start with the words in the list.
List

[4] In actual n-gram extraction, the article "a" was not counted as a word in making N-grams. For details see Sec. 4.1.2.

Japanese

non-independent verb

e.g., しまう [(1) *shimau*, (2)(3) *have*], 願う [(1) *negau*, (2)(3) *wish*]

verb suffix

e.g., する [(1) *suru*, (2)(3) *do*], られる [(1)*rareru*, (2)(3) a passive, させる [(1) *saseru*, (2)(3) *make*], いる [(1) *iru*, (2)(3) a progressive form]

adjective suffix

e.g., ったらしい [(1) *ttarashii*, (2)(3) *new*], っぽい [(1) *ppoi*, (2)(3) *-ish*]

non-independent adjective

e.g., づらい [(1) *durai*, (2)(3) *difficult*], がたい [*gatai*, (2)(3) *difficult*], よい [(1) *yoi*, (2)(3) *can/may*]

non-independent noun

e.g., こと [(1) *koto*, (2)(3) *thing*], ため [(1) *tame*, (2)(3) *for*]

non-independent noun-verb

e.g., ごらん [(1) *goran*, (2)(3) *try*], ちょうだい [(1) *choudai*, (2)(3) *please*]

noun suffix

e.g., 化 [(1) *ka*, (2)(3) *-lization*], ぎみ [(1) *gimi*, (2)(3) *tend to*]

particle

e.g., は [(1) *ha*], から [(1) *kara*], を [(1) *wo*]

auxiliary verb

e.g., らしい [(1) *rashii*, (2)(3) *seem*], た [(1) *ta*, (2)(3) a past form]

English

possessive form (e.g., 's)

3.2.4 The lexical information To further improve the extraction precision, we used the lexical information to refine the parallel translation expressions extracted with the methods described in the previous sections. Each pair of parallel translation expressions is refined as follows. (1) Independent words are extracted from the Japanese side, and their English translation candidates are obtained from a Japanese-English dictionary.[5] However, the word sequences (i.e., word n-grams) with arbitrary lengths that include both independent and function words are regarded as single words, and their English translation candidates are searched for through the dictionary. (2) The translation candidates obtained in the first step and the English words of the English side are compared. For the translation candidates that match the English words, their original Japanese words and the matching English words are classified into the "matching list". Those that do not match, on the other hand, are classified into the "non-matching list". Also, the words for which translations cannot be found in the dictionary are not classified into either list. (3) The numbers of words in the two lists are compared. If the "matching list" has more words than the "non-matching list", the pair of parallel translation expressions then passes. Otherwise, the pair is eliminated. Furthermore, if the passing pairs are in many-to-many relationships, which means a Japanese expression has multiple English translations and vice versa, then the pair with the largest number of words in the "matching list" is finally selected.

We use the parallel translation expression {J: 湾岸戦争の勝利 [(1) *wagansensou no shouri*, (2) *the gulf war of victory*], E: victory in the gulf war} as an example to explain the refinement procedure described above. In step (1), we first extract the independent words "湾岸" [(1) *wangan*, (2)(3) *gulf coast*], "戦争" [(1) *sensou*, (2)(3) *war*], and "勝利" [(1) *shouri*, (2)(3) *victory*] from the

[5] The nominal verbs, which have been segmented by the morphologic analysis, are connected again as single words for dictionary searching.

Japanese side. However, although the words in pair {J: 湾岸戦争 [(1) *wangansensou*, (2)*gulf war*], E: gulf war} are in correct parallel translation, the single words "湾岸" [*gulf coast*] and "gulf" are not. This means that even a pair in perfectly correct parallel translation might be judged to be incorrect by using the lexical information if only the independent words are used. Thus, we also make n-grams with arbitrary lengths and regard them as single words for dictionary searching. As a result, we obtain the following eight expressions[6]: "湾岸" [*gulf coast*], "戦争" [*war*], "勝利" [*victory*], "湾岸戦争" [*gulf war*], "戦争の" [*of war*], "戦争の勝利" [*victory of war*], and "湾岸戦争の勝利" [*victory in the gulf war*]. We then obtain their English translation candidates by searching the dictionary. In step (2), we first check the English translation candidates of the independent words and the English expressions. As a result, "戦争" and "war" and "勝利" and "victory" are matched and classified into the "matching list", while "湾岸" and "gulf" are not matched and are classified into the "non-matching list". We then check the English translation candidates of the n-gram words and the English expression. Since the English translation candidates of "湾岸戦争" match "gulf war", we compare them with the words in the "non-matching list". Since these words partially match the words "湾岸" and "gulf", which are in the "non-matching list", they are moved to the "matching list". In this way, "matching list" has six words and and the "non-matching list" has none. Since the "matching list" has more words than the "non-matching list", the parallel translation expression passes. Furthermore, if this parallel translation expression and the other passing parallel translation expressions are in many-to-many relationships, the one with the largest number of words in the "matching list" is selected.

4 Experiments

4.1 Experimental setup

4.1.1 Data and tools The aligned Japanese-English parallel corpora that we used in the experiments consisted of the NICT corpus (Uchimoto et al., 2004), the JENNAD corpus, and the aligned Reuters corpus (Utiyama and Isahara, 2003). The NICT corpus is composed of sentence-aligned Mainichi newspaper articles (Japanese) and their translations done by professional translators and has about 40,000 pairs of parallel sentences. The JENNAD corpus is composed of automatically sentence-aligned Yomiuri newspaper articles (Japanese) and Daily Yomiuri newspaper articles (English) and has about 180,000 pairs of parallel sentences. The aligned Reuters corpus is composed of automatically sentence-aligned Reuters Japanese and English news articles and has about 70,000 pairs of parallel sentences. After the overlapping sentences were excluded, the corpora had 278,323 pairs of parallel sentences.

Eijiro was used for the Japanese-English dictionary, and Chasen and TreeTagger were used for Japanese and English morphologic analysis.

4.1.2 Extraction requirement On the basis of a preliminary examination, we found that few pairs are in correct parallel translation if either the Japanese side or English side has an n-gram longer than six or if the difference between the number of words in Japanese and English sides is larger than three. On the basis of these observations, the maximum n-gram length for extraction was set to six (however, to see the extraction results with shorter values, the experiment with a maximum n-gram of three was also performed for the baseline method.) Also, the pairs in which the difference between the number of words in Japanese and English sides is larger than three were removed from the parallel expression candidates before their similarities were computed. Single Japanese and English n-grams were extracted if they appeared at least twice on both the Japanese and English sides of the corpora. The parallel translation expression candidates were acquired on the condition that the Japanese and English n-grams co-occurred at least twice in the same pairs

[6] To reduce the processing time for making n-grams, we used the rules described in Sec. 3.2.3 to exclude expressions such as "の勝利" [(1) *no shouri*, (2) *of victory*, (3) *victory of*].

of Japanese-English sentences and their similarities were greater than or equal to 0.5. In handling English expressions, we did not distinguish between person, tense, or singular or plural forms. We also did not distiguish between capital and lower-case letters. Furthermore, we did not count the articles "a", "an", and "the" as single words when making n-gram, i.e., we regarded the word sequence "the structure reform of the labor market" as a 5-gram, not a 7-gram.

4.1.3 Evaluation methods Extraction precisions, recalls, and F-measures were used for evaluation. The precisions were obtained by manually evaluating 500 pairs selected at regular intervals from all extracted parallel translation expressions. The recalls were used to estimate how many correct expressions have been extracted relative to the size of the corpora used for extraction and were defined as follows.

$$Recall = \frac{N_{ex} \times Precision}{N_{all}},$$

where N_{ex} is the number of the extracted pairs of parallel translation expressions and N_{all} is the total number of the pairs of parallel sentences in the corpora used for extraction. Since we could not know the exact number of correct parallel translation expressions existing in the parallel corpora, we thus used the size of the corpora (i.e., the figure N_{all}), instead.[7]

4.2 Results

The extraction results are listed in Table 1, where the *Baseline (3-gram)* and *Baseline (6-gram)* are the baseline methods with the maximum n-gram lengths of three and six, respectively, the *Improved ex. (6-gram)* is the improved method with the maximum n-gram length of 6 for n-gram extraction, the *Rule* is the method applying the hand-crafted rules to the expressions when extracting n-gram using the *Improved ex. (6-gram)*, and the *Lexicon* is the method using lexical information to further refine the expressions that have already been extracted using the *Rule*.

Table 1: Number of extracted pairs of parallel translation expressions, precisions, recalls, and F-measures.

Methods	Number	Precision	Recall	F-measure
Baseline (3-gram)	258,994	0.09	0.08	0.08
Baseline (6-gram)	190,895	0.14	0.09	0.11
Improved ex. (6-gram)	808,556	0.18	0.52	0.27
Rule	481.396	0.35	0.61	0.44
Lexicon	**125,165**	**0.96**	**0.43**	**0.59**

From the table we first see that both the precision and recall of the baseline method were extremely low and the different values for the maximum n-gram length did not affect the performance much. We then see that the *Improved ex. (6-gram)* dramatically increased the number of extracted expressions, while achieving higher precision than the baseline methods. As a result, the recall was tremendously improved, and the F-measure was also largely improved. By examining the results obtained by the baseline methods and the *Improved ex. (6-gram)*, on the other hand, we found lots of parallel translation expressions, as shown in the below examples, that could be extracted using the *Improved ex. (6-gram)* but not the baseline methods. That is, the *Improved ex. (6-gram)* extracted more numerous phrases with a larger variety of patterns such as past-participle phrases with the form "V された N" [(1) *V sareta N*, (2)(3) *Ved N*] and infinitive phrases with the form "N を V するため" [(1) *N wo Vsuru tame*, (2) *N to V*, (3) *to V N*], than the baseline methods.

Examples extracted by *Improved ex. (6-gram)*

J1: 暗殺されたラビン首相

[(1) *ansatsu sareta rabin shushou*, (2) *assassinated rabin prime minister*]

E1: prime minister rabin who was assassinated

[7] As a matter of course, the recall defined in this way can be a value larger than 1 in theory, and the F-measures cannot be therefore used in a strict sense.

J2: 不均衡を縮小するため
[(1) *fukinkou wo shukushou suru tame*, (2) *imbalance reduce to*]
E2: to reduce imbalance
J3: 拉致疑惑問題
[(1) *rachigiwaku mondai*, (2)*kidnapping issue*]
E3: the kidnapping issue
J4: 揶揄された
[(1) *yayu sareta*, (2) *ridiculed*]
E4: have been ridiculed

From the table we further see that the *Rule* almost doubled the extraction precision of the *Improved ex. (6-gram)*. Thus, although the number of extracted expressions largely reduced, the recall and F-measure were still largely better than those of the *Improved ex. (6-gram)*. Furthermore, although the number of extracted expressions largely reduced, by examining the results we could also find some parallel translation expressions that could only be extracted by using the *Rule*. The parallel translation expression {J: 寄与する必要がある [(1) *kiyo suru hitsuyou ga aru*, (2) *contribute need*], E: need to contribute}, for example, has different numbers of Japanese words (five words) and English words (three words). To extract such an expression, we first need to extract all the English word sequences between 1-gram and 5-gram, as well as all those of the Japanese, and then compute their similarities. However, since the 4-gram "need to contribute <u>to</u>" existed in the corpora, the 3-gram "need to contribute" was removed by the inhibition treatment in the baseline methods and the *Improved ex. (6-gram)*. This parallel expression therefore could not be extracted in these methods. In the *Rule*, however, since the 4-gram "need to contribute <u>to</u>" ended with the word "to" and was removed by the rules, the word sequence "need to contribute" was therefore not inhibited. Thus, this parallel translation expression could be extracted by the *Rule*.

Finally, from Table 1 we see that the *Lexicon* dramatically improved the extraction precision and had a precision of 0.96, thus reaching a level high enough for practical use. Although its recall was lower than that of the *Rule*, its F-measure is much higher than that of the *Rule* and is the highest among the all methods. One reason for the lower recall with the *Lexicon* can be considered to be as follows. As mentioned in Sec. 4.1.1, the NICT corpus, a part of the parallel corpora we used, for example, is composed of Mainichi newspaper articles (Japanese) and their translations done by professional translators. This means that a number of parallel sentences of the corpora are in free translation relationships. Thus, the English words used are usually different to the translations of the Japanese words obtained from the Japanese-English dictionary, and the expressions in correct parallel translations might be judged as incorrect and removed from the final extraction results. Specifically, the parallel translation expression {J: 邱政雄財政部長 [(1) *chiu masao zaiseibuchou*, (2) *chiu paul finance minister*], E: finance minister paul chiu}, for example, could be extracted with the *Rule* and should be regarded as a correct one. Since the *Lexicon*, however, has no translations of "邱" [(1) *chiu*], "政雄" [(1) *masao*], or "部長" [(1) *buchou*] that matched "chiu", "paul", or "minister", these were classified into the "non-matching list". Also, since there were no translations for the n-grams such as "邱政雄" [(1) *chiu masao*, (2) *chiu paul*, (3) *paul chiu*] and "財政部長" [(1) *zaiseibuchou*, (2)(3) *finance minister*], the words in the "non-matching list" could not be moved to the "matching list". Thus, the parallel translation expression was judged as incorrect and removed from the final extraction results.

5 Conclusion

We presented practically oriented approaches for extracting a broad range of parallel translation expressions for use in English-writing support. Our study differs from the earlier related studies in two ways. One is that we used very large corpora covering a much wider range of areas so that we could extract a broader range of parallel translation expressions. The other is that we used a new n-gram extraction method for acquiring as many parallel translation expressions as possible, and adopted hand-crafted rules and lexical information for refining the extracted expressions. Computer experiments with aligned parallel corpora consisting of about 280,000 pairs of Japanese-English parallel sentences found that more than 125,000 pairs of parallel translation expressions could be extracted with a precision of 0.96. We think that these figures show that the proposed methods for extracting a broad range of parallel translation expressions have reached a level high enough for practical use, and to our knowledge, ours are the first practically oriented approaches for extracting a wide range of Japanese-English parallel translation expressions.

We plan to construct a dictionary of Japanese-English translation patterns using the parallel translation expressions acquired in this study and build it into an English-writing support system.

References

Kay, M. and M. Röschesen. 1993. *Text-translation alignment.* Computational Linguistics, 19(1), pp. 121–142.

Kitamura, M. and Y. Matsumoto. 1996. *Automatic extraction of word sequence correspondences in parallel corpora.* Proceedings of the 4th Workshop on Very Large Corpora, pp. 79–87.

Kitamura, M. and Y. Matsumoto. 2005. *Practical translation pattern acquisition from combined language resources.* The First International Joint Conference on Natural Language Processing, Revised Selected Papers, Lecture Notes in Artificial Intelligence 3248, pp. 244–253.

Ma, Q., K. Nakao, M. Murata and H. Isahara. 2008. *Selection of Japanese-English equivalents by integrating high-quality corpora and huge amounts of web data.* Proceedings of the Sixth International Conference on Language Resources and Evaluation (LREC2008).

Ma, Q., R. Mori and M. Murata. 2009. *Development of English-writting support systems.* Proceedings of the 11th Conference of the Pacific Association for Computational Linguistics (Pacling2009), pp. 171–176.

Sainoo, D., J. Murakami, M. Tokuhisa and S. Ikehara. 2003. *Toward automatic extraction of Japanese/English expression pattern-pairs.* IPSJ SIG Technical Reports, 2003-NL-153, pp. 113–118 (in Japanese).

Sato, K. and H. Saito. 2002-1. *Extracting word sequence correspondences with support vector machines.* Proceedings of the 20th International Conference on Computational Linguistics (COLING2002), pp. 870–876.

Sato, K. and H. Saito. 2002-2. *Extracting bilingual word pairs with maximum entropy modeling.* Proceedings of Sixth World Multiconference on Systemics, Cybernetics and Informatics (SCI2002). Vol. 3, pp. 412–417.

Uchimoto, K., Y. Zhang, K. Sudo, M. Murata, S. Sekine and H. Isahara. 2004. *Multilingual aligned parallel treebank corpus reflecting contextual information and its applications.* Proceedings of the Workshop on Multilingual Lingustic Resources (MLR2004), pp. 63–70.

Utiyama, M. and H. Isahara. 2003. *Reliable measures for aligning Japanese-English news articles and sentences.* Proceedings of the 41st Annual Meeting of the Association for Computational Linguistics (ACL2003), pp. 72–79.

Yamamoto, K. and Y. Matsumoto. 2000. *Acquisition of phrase-level bilingual correspondence using dependency Structure.* Proceedings of the 18th International Conference on Computational Linguistics (COLING2000), pp. 933–939.

Analyzing the characteristics of academic paper categories by using an index of representativeness *

Takafumi Suzuki[a], Kiyoko Uchiyama[b], Ryota Tomisaka[c], and Akiko Aizawa[b]

[a]Faculty of Sociology, Toyo University,
5-28-20, Hakusan, Bunkyo-ku, Tokyo 112-8606, Japan
takafumi_s@toyo.jp
[b]Digital Content and Media Sciences Research Division, National Institute of Informatics
2-1-2, Hitotsubashi, Chiyoda-ku, Tokyo 101-8430, Japan
{kiyoko, aizawa}@nii.ac.jp
[c]Graduate School of Information Science and Technology, The University of Tokyo
7-3-1, Hongo, Bunkyo-ku, Tokyo 112-0023, Japan
ryota.tomisaka@gmail.com

Abstract. This study proposes an index of representativeness for analyzing the characteristics of academic paper categories. Many textual indices have been proposed in the field of computational stylistics, but all of the previous indices are limited in that they (a) focus only on the styles of the texts; (b) return an absolute value for every text, and (c) are based on the number of tokens. In this study, we propose an index of representativeness that does not have the weaknesses of the previous indices. Our index is based on the h-index that was originally proposed in the field of scientometrics. We redefine it here for textual data. We show the effectiveness of our index for analyzing the characteristics that differ between four genres and three subfields in Japanese academic papers.

Keywords: academic papers, h-index, lexical indicators

1 Introduction

Many textual indices have been proposed in the field of computational stylistics. The number of tokens, i.e., the frequency of words in a document, is the simplest. Some indices use information related to words that appear only one or two times in the text, while others take the entire frequency spectrum into account (Kageura, 2000; Tweedie and Baayen, 1998). Textual indices have been studied for various applications such as authorship analysis, genre detection, and chronological text mining (Argamon *et al.*, 2007; Koppel *et al.*, 2009; Stamatatos, 2009), but they have three flaws in common: (a) they shed light only on the styles of text; (b) they return an absolute value, meaning that they do not consider the relative values for different keyword sets or the relative position of a document in the document set; and (c) they are based on the number of tokens.

Our problem is the use of textual indices to analyze the characteristics of the categories of academic papers. Since a wide variety of texts are available, these types of the 'characterization' problems, as well as the 'classification' problems, are currently increasing in importance. To deal with the characterization problems, we aim at deriving a meaningful level of knowledge

* This study was supported by Grant-in-Aid for Scientific Research 21800087 for Young Scientists (Start-up) and 23700288 for Young Scientists (B), from the Ministry of Education, Culture, Sports, Sciences and Technology, Japan, and Grant for joint research from National Institute of Informatics. This study used the text data provided by the Information Processing Society of Japan (IPSJ). Earlier version of this study was presented at 16th Annual Meeting of the Association for Natural Language Processing (NLP2010). We would like to thank all of them for helping us conducting and improving this research.

from the textual characteristics using the summarized indices given to the categories (Kageura and Abekawa, 2009; Suzuki, 2009). Our categories are stylistic (genre) as well as content-dependent (subfield); thus, our index must be capable of analyzing both of them. The categories we deal with are similar to each other but different from the conventional ones used in genre detection or topic classification. Thus, it is desirable for our index to be able to deal with the relative position of a document in a document set. Token number-based indices have a common problem in that they are affected by several frequent words. This means we should create indices that do not directly use a token number that will also require less computational effort.

Against this background, we propose an index of representativeness that overcomes the drawbacks of the previously used indices. Our index is based on the h-index that was originally proposed in the field of scientometrics (Hirsch, 2005). After transforming this index for textual data, we use it for measuring how well a document represents the entire document set regarding several perspectives determined by keyword lists. It can analyze stylistic categories as well as content-dependent ones; our index uses content words (keyword lists); that means it can be used for analyzing content-dependent categories. Furthermore, it is based on the rank-type information, instead of the token-number information; that means it can be used for analyzing genre-based categories, because the rank-type information is usually considered to represent styles (Tweedie and Baayen, 1998). Our index captures both stylistic and content-dependent characteristics (Suzuki and Kageura, 2007) based on this information. In addition, it can use different keyword lists and takes into consideration the relative position of a document in a document set; and it also uses the ranks of the types, i.e., the ranked frequencies of different words (keywords) appearing in a document. We assessed the effectiveness of our index in analyzing the different characteristics of four genres and three subfields in Japanese academic papers.

The rest of this paper is organized as follows. We first explain the original h-index and its characteristics in Section 2. In Section 3, we explain the proposed method, including the redefinition of the index for textual data. We explain the experimental setup in Section 4 and discuss the results in Section 5. We review the related work in Section 6 and conclude with final remarks in Section 7.

2 h-index

The h-index was first proposed in the field of scientometrics by (Hirsch, 2005) and is defined as follows.

> A scientist has index h if h of his or her X papers each have at least h citations and the other $(X - h)$ papers each have $\leq h$ citations.

For example, a scientist whose h is 30 has published 30 papers, each of which has at least 30 citations.

This index has many advantages over other indices. Other possible indices and their limitations are as follows: (a) the total number of papers is not a measure of the importance or impact of papers; (b) the total number of citations can be inflated by a small number of highly cited papers; (c) the citations per paper rewards low productivity papers while it penalizes high productivity papers; (d) the number of significant papers is arbitrary as to the 'significance' criteria; and (e) the number of citations for each of the q most-cited papers is not a single number and is more complicated to obtain and compare. The h-index avoids all the drawbacks of these indices, yet it can measure the broad impact of scientists' productivity. That is why it is one of the most frequently used indices for evaluating the scientific research. It was pointed out that the h-index can be defined and used for any data that follows a power law (Egghe and Rousseau, 2006b). Here, we shall redefine it for textual data. There are many modifications and sophistications associated with this index for better interpreting the phenomena in scientometrics (Egghe and Rousseau, 2006a; Sidiropoulos *et al.*, 2007), but most of these modifications and sophistications do not directly lead to better interpreting the textual data from our point of view, thus we added our own modifications to this index.

3 Proposed method

First, we briefly describe our method and our redefinition of the h-index. After that, we explain the keyword lists used in the experiment.

3.1 Overview

We analyze the characteristics of categories according to the following process.

(i.) Given a target category (a set of documents),

(ii.) extract a set of words using the keyword lists,[1]

(iii.) collect the document frequencies ($DF(w, d)$) of (ii) in (i),

(iv.) using (iii), calculate the t/b ratio (see below) for each document in a category.

(v.) The category index is the median and the iqr value of (iv).

3.1.1 Redefinition of h-index for textual data Our basic idea is to deal with the scientometric data and textual data from the integrated viewpoint of quantitative informatics. Although making a reference to a paper and using a word in a paper seems to be a different activity, many previous studies have indicated that the mathematical and quantitative characteristics shown in these two phenomena were very similar to each other.[2] Accordingly, we can define the relations between these two types of data as follows.

- researchers: documents,
- number of publications: number of word types included in the document,
- number of citations: number of documents including the word types, i.e., document frequencies ($DF(w, d)$).

The redefined h-index for the textual data is basically as follows.

> A document has an index h if h of its X word types each have $DF(w, d) \geq h$ and the other $(X - h)$ word types each have $DF(w, d) \leq h$.

This index, based on the information about the *ranks* of the *types* instead of the *number* of *tokens*, reflects how general words (words with high $DF(w, d)$) are used in the texts. It is an index of the 'representativeness' of the text in a document set. A high h-value means that general words are frequently used in the texts, whereas a low h-value means that general words are infrequently used in the texts. This index is superior to indices (a) - (e) mentioned in Section 2 because it succeeds the characteristics of the original h-index.

3.1.2 Scaling The number of types and $DF(w, d)$ are quite different in scale from the number of publications and the number of citations; thus, we shall use the following scaling.[3]

$$DF'(w, d) = \lfloor DF(w, d) \times \alpha \times \frac{V_N(d)}{max_{w \in \omega}(DF(w, d))} \rfloor$$

[1] In this paper, we used keyword lists for extracting a set of words, but part-of-speech tags or automatic term extraction can also be used according to the purposes and target data of the researches.

[2] We will investigate the reason for this in future. See also (Egghe, 2009; Kageura, 2000).

[3] The number of publications of an author will be at most 10^1 (yearly) to scale and the number of citations of a paper will be at most 10^{10} (yearly) to scale, but the number of types and DF will have larger differences in many cases.

Table 1: Basic data of our corpora

	IPSJ			author		
		$V_N(d)$			$V_N(d)$	
	doc	median	iqr	doc	median	iqr
JNL	2452	91	31.00	2753	220	80.00
MAG	1194	75	41.00	1212	201	100.25
SIG	6751	63	29.00	7333	152	76.00
TRANS	933	96	31.00	1035	214	75.50
CS	2113	65	33.00	2328	141	120.25
IE	2856	61	24.00	3108	155	66.00
FR	1782	66	30.00	1897	162	77.00

where $max_{w \in \omega}(DF(w,d))$ represents the maximum $DF(w,d)$ value of the keyword w in keyword lists ω for every document, and $V_N(d)$ represents the number of types, i.e., the number of different keywords appearing in the document.

The scaling factors adjust the difference in scale between $V_N(d)$ and $DF(w,d)$. In particular, the α parameter determines the best ratio between $V_N(d)$ and $DF(w,d)$ for every used dataset; a higher (lower) α means that a larger (smaller) number of types are included in h. We select the α that gives the highest inter-quartile range (iqr), from 0.1 to 3.0 incremented by 0.1, because large variances between documents are desirable for our purposes. Moreover, by observing the stability of the results after changing α, we can confirm the reliability of the results.[4] The final definition of our h-index for textual data is as follows. We call it h' in what follows.

> A document has index h' if h' of its X word types each have $DF'(w,d) \geq h'$ and the other $(X - h')$ word types each have $DF'(w,d) \leq h'$ each.

3.1.3 Three indices based on the h'-index We shall examine the following three kinds of h'-indices.

Top h'-index This index is exactly the same as mentioned above. We name it the top h'-index simply to distinguish it from the bottom h'-index. This index reflects how general words (ones with high $DF(w,d)$) are used in text.

Bottom h'-index This index substitutes $DF''(w,d)$ for $DF'(w,d)$ when calculating h'.

$$DF''(w,d) = \lfloor DF^*(w,d) \times \alpha \times \frac{V_N(d)}{max_{w \in \omega}(DF^*(w,d))} \rfloor$$

where

$$DF^*(w,d) = max_{w \in \omega}(DF(w,d)) + 1 - DF(w,d)$$

This is a simple substitution to change high $DF(w,d)$ values to low $DF(w,d)$ values, and vice versa. This index, as opposed to the top h' index, is a measure of how special words (ones with low $DF(w,d)$) are used in texts.

[4] It can be used as a sort of significant test.

t/b ratio The third index is the ratio between the top h' and the bottom h':

$$t/b\ ratio = \frac{top\ h'}{bottom\ h' + 1}$$

This index calculates the ratio of the top h'-index to the bottom h'-index. A high t/b ratio means that general words (high $DF(w,d)$) are more frequently used (in the level of types) than special words (low $DF(w,d)$), and a low t/b ratio means that special words are more frequently used. The top h' and bottom h' heavily depend on the number of word types. Due to this, we shall use the t/b ratio for analyzing the characteristics of the genres and subfields. The value of this index is also independent of the number of documents used in the experiments. Their variances of this index should be smaller along with the increasing number of documents, but it has no effects on our interpretation of the results.

3.2 Keyword lists

One of the privileges of our index is the calculability for different keyword lists. It is not necessary to use several keyword lists for our methods, but by selecting two different (or opposite) types of keywords, we will strengthen our discussion of the results. In this study, we used keyword lists that included (a) general and (b) specific keywords in the field of information sciences, and then we can effectively analyze the characteristics of four genres and three subfields in Japanese academic papers.

More precisely, we extracted keywords from the data by using two keyword lists: (a) the IPSJ handbook index list (Joho Syori Gakkai, 1995) and (b) the author index list. List (a) is an index that includes 5,958 basic, low-expertise terms used in information sciences. List (b) is an index list that includes 16,935 terms that authors themselves added to their papers. While (a) includes basic conceptual keywords used in information sciences, it also (b) includes high expertise keywords based on the authors' selection. List (b) also includes numbers, mathematical expressions, and symbols. Both of them include high frequency words as well as low frequency words, and include terminology words as well as rather general words. After we applied morphological analysis to the data and keyword lists, we extracted the keywords by matching. Note that we used a Japanese morphological analysis system called MeCab[5] for this purpose.

We use these two types of keywords for calculating the h'-index in order to shed light on the different characteristics of the genres and subfields; i.e., the t/b ratio using IPSJ keywords should show the representativeness for basic, low-expertise keywords, and the t/b ratio using the author keywords should show the representativeness of special, high-expertise keywords. In so doing, we can obtain meaningful knowledge for understanding the characteristics of the four genres and three subfields.[6]

4 Experimental setup

The experiments used the text data provided by the Information Processing Society of Japan (IPSJ). This data consists of four kinds of published material, i.e., journals (JNL), magazines (MAG), technical reports for special interest groups (SIG), and transactions (TRANS). The JNL consists of standard journal papers, while the SIG consists of the reports from 39 special interest groups. The TRANS is a new journal with fewer topics compared to the JNL.[7] The most signif-

[5] mecab.sourceforge.net

[6] When we incidentally calculated our index by using the keyword lists, that index separates English texts from Japanese ones quite well.

[7] In fact, JNL and TRANS are not clearly distinguished from each other in terms of the communicative purpose, audience and form. We distinguish between them in this paper because it is in the original distributed data, and we thought it is better to distinguish them for further use in our findings and discussion. It should be noted that our main findings and discussion remain true even if we merge the two categories.

Table 2: h'-index using IPSJ/author keywords

IPSJ	top median	top iqr	bottom median	bottom iqr	t/b ratio median	t/b ratio iqr
JNL	31	11.00	52	25.00	0.574	0.117
MAG	30	10.00	49	24.00	0.591	0.122
SIG	29	11.00	49	25.00	0.567	0.122
TRANS	40	11.00	73	30.00	0.531	0.097
author	**top median**	**top iqr**	**bottom median**	**bottom iqr**	**t/b ratio median**	**t/b ratio iqr**
JNL	95	17.00	202	57.00	0.469	0.065
MAG	85	20.00	201	70.00	0.412	0.051
SIG	80	11.00	167	37.00	0.472	0.067
TRANS	95	17.00	196	55.25	0.481	0.063

icant difference is that of the MAG from the others. The MAG consists of book reports, event reports, and introductory essays, while the other genres basically consist of research papers that include original research findings. Thus, the MAG should be well represented by ordinary, i.e., low-expertise, keywords, and not by professional, i.e., high-expertise, keywords.

The 39 groups of SIGs are classified into three large groups, i.e., Computer Sciences (CS), Information Environment (IE), and Frontier (FR). The CS deals with the basic and theoretical issues in the information sciences. Its papers are related to algorithms, programming, and operating systems. They include many symbols and mathematical expressions and use a lot of professional keywords. The IE deals with conventional applications such as information systems, human-computer interaction, and computer graphics. The FR includes new and various applications such as game informatics, music and computers, and computers and humanities. These papers deal with many new concepts and have many new keywords that are not likely to be of the professional sort.

We used texts including more than the median number of word types, i.e., 72 types for IPSJ keywords experiments and 172 types for author keywords experiments, in order to exclude noisy data with corrupted characters and characters in other languages.[8] Table 1 lists the number of documents[9] and the median and iqr of $V_N(d)$ for each category.

5 Results and discussion

Section 5.1 discusses the results for the four genres and three subfields, and Section 5.2 discusses the results from the empirical examination of the characteristics of the indices.

5.1 Experimental results

5.1.1 Results for JNL, MAG, SIG, and TRANS genres We calculated the h'-indices for each text. Table 2 lists the median and iqr values of the top h', bottom h', and t/b ratio for the JNL, MAG, SIG, and TRANS categories. As will be shown in Section 5.2.2., $\alpha = 1.9$ had the highest iqr (0.120) regarding the t/b ratio for the IPSJ keywords, whereas $\alpha = 1.8$ (iqr, 0.072) had the highest iqr (0.120) for the author keywords. Thus we selected these α values to create Table 2.

[8] After trying other various types of criteria, we decided to do this because it was the best way to exclude noisy data from our corpora. For applying our index to other data, this process is not needed. In the future, we will develop the methods to automatically exclude these types of noisy data.

[9] More precisely, the 'doc' value represents the number of documents including at least one (IPSJ/author) keyword. According to this, the 'doc' values are different between experiments using IPSJ and those using author keywords in Table1, but the experiments themselves were basically conducted using the same document set.

The upper right column of Table 2 shows that MAG has a much higher t/b ratio than the other three genres for the IPSJ keywords, while the lower right column shows that it has a much lower t/b ratio for the author keywords. A Wilcoxson rank sum test showed a significant difference between MAG and the other genres regarding the t/b ratio ($p < .01$).

These results clearly reflect the special characteristics of the MAG genre. MAG consists of book reports, event reports, and introductory essays; thus, its documents should indeed be represented by low-expertise keywords, rather than by high-eaxpertise keywords. These results clearly shed light on the microscopic differences between MAG and the other genres.

Table 3: h'-index using IPSJ/author keywords

	top		bottom		t/b ratio	
IPSJ	median	iqr	median	iqr	median	iqr
CS	27	12.50	46	28.00	0.569	0.133
IE	30	11.00	51	25.00	0.569	0.118
FR	30	11.00	51	25.00	0.561	0.112
	top		bottom		t/b ratio	
author	median	iqr	median	iqr	median	iqr
CS	82	9.00	162	30.25	0.497	0.058
IE	80	12.00	166	35.00	0.470	0.066
FR	80	13.00	172	40.00	0.457	0.060

5.1.2 Results for CS, IE, and FR subfields We calculated the h'-index for every text. Table 3 lists the median and iqr values of the top h', bottom h', and t/b ratio for the CS, IE, and FR subfields. The same parameter (α) values as mentioned above were selected.

The right column in Table 3 shows that the t/b ratio of FR is lower than that of the other two categories (CS/IE) for both the IPSJ keywords (upper columns) and author keywords (lower columns). It also shows that the t/b ratio of CS is higher than that of the other two categories for the author keywords. A Wilcoxson rank sum test revealed the significant differences regarding the t/b ratio between FR and the others and CS and the others for the author keywords ($p < .01$).

These results reflect the characteristics of the CS and FR subfields. The CS includes theoretical studies; thus, it is reasonable to say that it is represented by high-expertise keywords. FR deals with the frontier of information sciences, and it includes many new topics. Thus, it is reasonable to say that it is 'not' represented by high-expertise keywords.

The results using IPSJ keywords are not stable as will be shown in Section 5.2.2., however, the results are consistent with the characteristics of the three subfields, CS and IE include standard and traditional subfields, thus they are represented by low-expertise, but standard keywords in information sciences, but FR includes many new topics, thus they are not represented by these types of standard keywords either. In other words, FR includes various topics, thus it is not represented by any type of keywords lists.

5.2 Characteristics of the indices

5.2.1 Dependency of the t/b ratio on the number of types In order to confirm the dependency of these indices on the number of types, we calculated the Spearman rank coefficient. The ρs between the top, bottom h'-index, the t/b ratio, and the number of types are respectively 0.086, 0.076, and -0.019 for the IPSJ keywords and 0.881, 0.997, and -0.643 for the author keywords. These results show that the t/b ratio decreased the number of type dependencies relative to those of the top and bottom h'-indices. These results indicate that there is almost no correlation between the t/b ratio and the number of types especially for the IPSJ keywords.

5.2.2 Stability of the results for changing α Figure 1 shows the relation between α and the median of the t/b ratio. The figures show that the ranks of the four genres and three subfields are stable, except in the experiment on the three subfields using the IPSJ keywords. The stability of these results can be used for testing the reliability of the results.

6 Related work

There are many studies on textual indices. They were systematically surveyed by (Tweedie and Baayen, 1998). Textual indices have been used for judging the readability of texts (Tuldava, 1993) and detecting the authors or genres of text (Kenny, 1982; Jin and Murakami, 2003).

Lexical frequency profiles were first proposed in (Laufer and Nation, 1995), and in studies in (Laufer and Nation, 1999; Hu and Nation, 2000; Laufer, 2005; Meara, 2004; Meara, 2005; Meara, 2006; Muncie, 2002; Edwards and Collins, 2010). Although it was produced for different purposes and used mainly in English, their discussion will be useful for the scholars that are interested in the character of textual indices.

While most textual indices focus only on the styles of the text and return absolute, token based values, our index using the ranks of the frequencies of the 'types' of text enable us to analyze the microscopic differences between content-dependent categories as well as the differences between stylistic categories.

The h-index was first proposed by (Hirsch, 2005), and there have been many studies that have investigated the mathematical characteristics and empirical usefulness of this and related indices (Antonakis and Lalive, 2008; Costas and Bordons, 2007; Egghe *et al.*, 2009; Egghe and Rousseau, 2006a). Our study is the first to redefine this index for textual data.

Hisamitsu *et al.* (2000) deals with the concept of 'representativeness', but it defines the representativeness for keyword extraction. Our study defines this concept for documents.

7 Conclusion

This study proposed an index of the representativeness for analyzing the characteristics of the genres and subfields of Japanese academic papers. We conducted an experiment that showed our 'representativeness' index was very useful for analyzing the microscopic differences between the characteristics of the four genres and three subfields.

Our index was in fact slightly dependent on the number of types. Within the scope of our paper, however, major changes for our interpretation were not required. We shall investigate the effects systematically in the future.

Our resources and findings will be useful for academic mining (Ichise *et al.*, 2007), which is a growing area of artificial intelligence research, and our method for analyzing the microscopic differences in the categories such as the genres and subfields will be useful for adapting techniques from one text domain to another text domain (domain adaptation). In the future, we will systematically enumerate such categories and provide a clearer perspective on the problem.

References

Antonakis, John and Rafael Lalive. 2008. Quantifying scholarly impact: IQp versus the Hirsch h. *Journal of the American Society for Information Science and Technology*, 59(6), 956–969.

Argamon, Shlomo, Casey Whitelaw, Paul Chase, Sobhan Raj Hota, Navendu Garg, and Shlomo Levitan. 2007. Stylistic text classification using functional lexical features. *Journal of the American Society for Information Science and Technology*, 58(6), 802–822.

Costas, Rodrigo and María Bordons. 2007. The h-index: Advantages, limitations and its relation with other bibliometric indicators at the micro level. *Journal of Informetrics*, 1(3), 193–203.

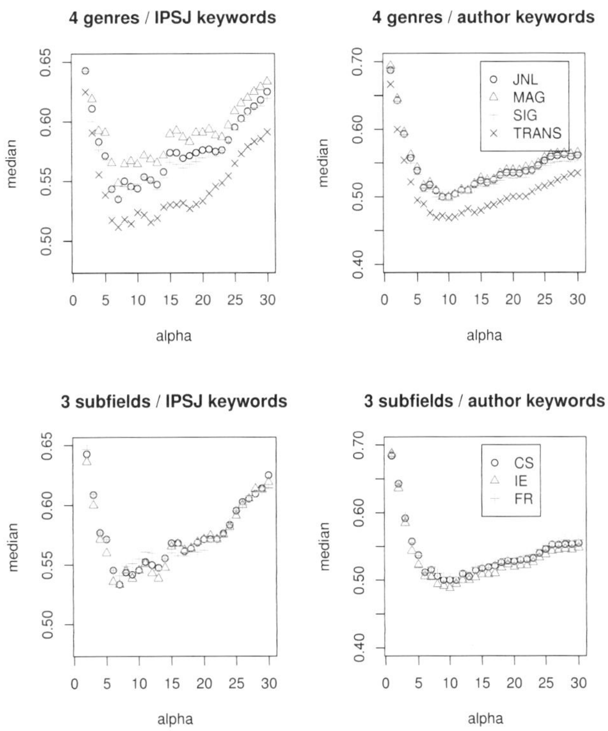

Figure 1: Relation between α and median of t/b ratio

Edwards, Roderick and Laura Collins. 2010. Lexical frequency profiles and Zipf's law. *Language Learning*.

Egghe, Leo. 2009. Performance and its relation with productivity in lotkaian systems. *Scientometrics*, 81(2), 567–585.

Egghe, Leo, Liming Liang, and Ronald Rousseau. 2009. A relation between h-index and impact factor in the power-law model. *Journal of the American Society for Information Science and Technology*, 60(11), 2362–2365.

Egghe, Leo and R. Rousseau. 2006a. Theory and practise of the *g*-index. *Scientometrics*, 69(1), 131–152.

Egghe, Leo and Ronald Rousseau. 2006b. An informetric model for the Hirsch-index. *Scientometrics*, 69(1), 121–129.

Hirsch, Jorge E. 2005. An index to quantify an individual's scientific research output. In *Proceedings of the National Academy of Science of the United States of America*, volume 102, pp. 16569–16572.

Hisamitsu, Toru, Yoshiki Niwa, Shingo Nishioka, Hirofumi Sakurai, Osamu Imaichi, Makoto Iwayama, and Akihiko Takano. 2000. Extracting terms by a combination of term freqency and a measure of term representativeness. *Terminology*, 6(2), 211–232.

Hu, Marcella Hsueh-chao and Paul Nation. 2000. Unknown vocabulary density and reading comprehension. *Reading in a Foreign Language*, 13(1), 403–430.

Ichise, Ryutaro, Setsu Fujita, Taichi Muraki, and Hideaki Takeda. 2007. Research mining using the relationships among authors, topics and papers. In *IV07: 11th International Conference Information Visualization*, pp. 425–430.

Jin, Mingzhe and Masakatsu Murakami. 2003. Bunsyo no tokei bunseki to wa. In Syunichi Amari, K Takeuchi, A Takemura, and Yukito Iba, eds., *Gengo to Shinri no Tokei: Kotoba to Kodo no Kakuritsu Moderu ni yoru Bunseki*, pp. 3–57. Iwanami Syoten, Tokyo.

Joho Syori Gakkai, ed. 1995. *Sinban Joho Syori Handobuku*. Ohmsha, Tokyo.

Kageura, Kyo. 2000. *Keiryou Johogaku*. Maruzen, Tokyo.

Kageura, Kyo and Takeshi Abekawa. 2009. Nlp meets library science: providing a set of enhanced language reference tools for online translators. In *Proceedings of A-LIEP2009: Asia-Pacific Conference on Library & Information Education and Practice*, pp. 538–547.

Kenny, Anthony. 1982. *The Computation of Style: An Introduction to Statistics for Students of Literature and Humanities*. Pergamon Press, Oxford.

Koppel, Moshe, Jonathan Schler, and Shlomo Argamon. 2009. Computational methods in authorship attribution. *Journal of the American Society for Information Science and Technology*, 60.

Laufer, Batia. 2005. Lexical frequency profiles: from monte carlo to the real world, a response to Meara (2005). *Applied Linguistics*, 26(4), 582–588.

Laufer, Batia and Paul Nation. 1999. A vocabulary-size test of controlled productive ability. *Language Testing*, 16(1), 33–51.

Laufer, Betia and Paul Nation. 1995. Vocabulary size and use: lexical richness in L2 written production. *Applied Linguistics*, 16(3), 307–322.

Meara, Paul. 2004. Modelling vocabulary loss. *Applied Linguistics*, 25(2), 137–155.

Meara, Paul. 2005. Lexical frequency profiles: a monte carlo analysis. *Applied Linguistics*, 26(1), 32–47.

Meara, Paul. 2006. Emergent properties of multilingual lexicons. *Applied Linguistics*, 27(4), 620–644.

Muncie, James. 2002. Process writing and vocabulary development: comparing Lexical Frequency Profiles across drafts. *System*, 30, 225–235.

Sidiropoulos, Antonis, Dimitrios Katsaros, and Yannis. 2007. Generalized hirsch *h*-index for disclosing latent facts in citation networks. *Scientometrics*, 72, 253–280.

Stamatatos, Efstathios. 2009. A survey of modern authorship attribution methods. *Journal of the American Society for Information Science and Technology*, 60(3), 538–556.

Suzuki, Takafumi. 2009. Extracting speaker-specific functional expressions from political speeches using random forests in order to investigate speakers' political styles. *Journal of the American Society for Information Science and Technology*, 60(8), 1596–1606.

Suzuki, Takafumi and Kyo Kageura. 2007. Exploring the microscopic characteristics of Japanese prime ministers' Diet addresses by measuring the quantity and diversity of nouns. In *PACLIC21: Proceedings of the 21th Pacific Asia Conference on Language, Information and Computation*, pp. 459–470.

Tuldava, Juhan. 1993. The statistical structure of a text and its readability. In *Quantitative Text Analysis*, pp. 215–227. Wissenschaftlicher Verlag Trier, Trier.

Tweedie, Fiona J. and R. Harald Baayen. 1998. How variable may a constant be? Measures of lexical richness in perspective. *Computers and the Humanities*, 32, 323–352.

Exploring Emotional Words for Chinese Document Chief Emotion Analysis*

Yunong Wu, Kenji Kita, Fuji Ren, Kazuyuki Matsumoto and Xin Kang

Faculty of Engineering,
University of Tokushima,
Minami-josanjima, Tokushima, 771-0206, Japan

wuyunong@iss.tokushima-u.ac.jp
{kita, ren, matumoto, kangxin}@is.tokushima-u.ac.jp

Abstract. In this study, we develop a document emotion analysis model by making use of the function of emotional words annotation. Eight basic emotion categories have been selected, including Expect, Joy, Love, Surprise, Anxiety, Sorrow, Anger and Hate, for both the word and the document level emotion analysis. We introduce two parameters, term relevance and term frequency, to evaluate the relations between the word emotions and the document emotions. Promising experimental results reveal the effectiveness of our document emotion analysis model under different emotion situations.

Keywords: emotional words annotation, document emotion analysis, term relevance, term frequency.

* This work was supported in part by a grant from the Grant-in-Aid for Scientific Research (B) numbered 21300036 and Young Scientists (B) numbered 23700252 from the Japan Society for the Promotion of Science, and Grant-in-Aid for Challenging Exploratory Research numbered 21650030 from the Ministry of Education, Science, Sports and Culture.

1 Introduction

Document emotion analysis has become a popular subject in natural language processing studies, which however has been reported to be a challenging problem since people's inner emotions are not easy to be represented exactly only through semantic labels given by machines.

Generally speaking, emotion analysis can be divided into two quite different levels: the coarse emotion analysis and the fine-grained emotion analysis. For the former study, researchers have conducted much work on dividing the documents into three classes according to their polarities: the positive documents, the negative documents, and the neutral documents. While for the latter study, researchers often concentrate on extracting some significant types of emotions, such as Expect, Joy, Love, Surprise, Anxiety, Sorrow, Anger and Hate. And this extracting process covers different textual levels, including words, sentences, paragraphs as well as documents.

In this paper we are focusing on two important parts of the fine-grained emotion analysis: emotional words annotation and document emotion analysis. Totally eight emotion categories are selected, namely, Expect, Joy, Love, Surprise, Anxiety, Sorrow, Anger and Hate.

Under the subject of emotional words annotation, most studies are concentrating on exploring a variety of emotion lexicons. Such studies include (Hu and Liu, 2004; Tokuhisa et al., 2008), in which machine learning techniques are also utilized. However, at most of the time, using emotion lexicons could not be a good idea for analyzing the emotions in the real-world texts, since the emotion lexicons are static while in the real-world the word emotions could always change in different contexts. When a certain number of the matched words are found with different emotion tags according to the emotion lexicon, this method often fails. As reported in (Fragopanagos and Taylor, 2005), emotion analysis could suffer from insufficient or misleading emotion features if context is not taken into account.

Therefore, we explore an automatic document emotion analysis model, which takes the dynamically annotated emotional words as features and explores the statistic parameters extracted from the Ren-CECps[1] (Quan and Ren, 2010) to help correctly predict the document emotions from previously generated word emotions.

We regard Conditional Random Fields (CRFs) (Lafferty et al., 2001) as the appropriate algorithm for capturing the contextual information in a sentence. For the document emotion analysis, we use the function of emotional words annotation and extract the term relevance parameter and the term frequency parameter which help to correctly accumulate the document emotions from the word emotions within this document.

Experimental result reveals that the term relevance parameter makes contribution to the document emotion, and demonstrates the effectiveness of our document emotion analysis model, which can deal with the document under different emotion situations.

The rest of this paper is organized as follows: Section 2 describes the related work. Section 3 demonstrates the emotional words annotation. Section 4 illustrates document emotion analysis. Finally Section 5 concludes this paper.

2 Related Work

Affective information processing is quite a challenging problem for artificial intelligence (Ren, 2009). Especially lots of researches have been focusing on emotion analysis on emotion polarities classification or some specific fine-grained emotions from reviews (Pang et al., 2002; Turney, 2002), feedbacks (Gamon, 2004) and blogs (Yang et al., 2007).

Most emotion classification experiments were carried out by exploring machine learning

[1] Ren-CECps is a Chinese emotion corpus which can be found at http://a1-www.is.tokushima-u.ac.jp/member/ren/Ren-CECps1.0/DocumentforRen-CECps1.0.html

methods such as Support Vector Machine (SVM) (Matsumoto et al., 2005; Chesley et al., 2006) or Conditional Random Fields (CRFs) (Zhao et al., 2008). The emotion classification experiment implemented by (Chen et al., 2007) compared the two methods and proved that the CRFs classifiers performs better.

To tag emotions from words to sentences, (Das and Bandyopadhyay, 2009) made an experiment, by using CRFs on the Bengali corpus. In his study, emotion tags are pre-assigned based on a Bengali SentiWordNet which is translated from English SentiWordNet. However, since the tagging procedure was based on an immovable word list without considering the contextual information, their result is bound to suffer from the curse of emotion lexicon with either high coverage/low precision or low coverage/high precision (Ng et al., 2006).

Recent research on document emotion analysis includes (Pang and Lee, 2002), which proposed a textual categorization based approach to recognize the positive and negative polarities of documents. Also, (Yang et al., 2007) tried to match the word emotions to the document emotions. (Alm et al., 2005) conducted a text based emotion predication experiment by employing machine learning method. These methods are either semi-automatic or automatic but depending on inflexible emotion lexicons.

In this paper, we build an automatic document emotion analysis model, with dynamically extracted emotional keywords as features to predict the document emotions. We use Ren-CECps as our data set, which is a well developed Chinese emotion corpus with emotional words as well as modification components manually tagged out considering the context.

3 Emotional Words Annotation

Emotional words are the keywords that express emotions and affect the emotions of sentences and documents. Research conducted by (Kang et al., 2010) has proved that annotating emotions of words with high precision helps emotion analysis of sentences and documents.

In general, part-of-speeches are considered as the emotional component which can supply additional information. Therefore, POS could be a favorable feature for emotional words annotation. On the other hand, since the word emotions are expressed not only by the word itself but also through the context in a sentence, we also consider three types of modification relationships in the sentence for emotional words annotation.

Our study on emotional words annotation is based on the Ren-CECps, which is a Chinese emotional corpus consisting of 1,487 Chinese blog documents with totally 35,096 sentences. Not only the large text segment such as documents, paragraphs and sentences, but also the most basic lingual units such as the words and phrases are annotated with eight basic emotion tags: Expect, Joy, Love, Surprise, Anxiety, Sorrow, Anger and Hate. Although most emotional words in Ren-CECps are tagged with more than one emotions, we regard the emotions with the highest emotion intensities[2] as the chief emotions, and will assign each emotional word a chief emotion tag.

3.1 Feature Selection

Words

We employ the words string as the feature, since the identities of words themselves are important emotion carriers, which are regarded as the basic element in emotion analysis generally.

POS (part-of-speech) Tags

It has been observed that the POS tag can convey additional information for emotion analysis. (Chesley et al., 2006) has proved the importance of verbs and adjectives through the experiment on polarity determination. In this study, we adopt all the POS tags as features for emotional words annotation.

[2] Emotional intensities (from 0.1 to 1.0) of each emotional words are given in Ren-CECps.

Degree Words
Word emotion could be influenced by the existence of degree word. For example:
"这个问题很幼稚。(This is a very naive question.)"

In the example above, with the emotional word "幼稚(naive)" modified by the degree word "很(very)" in the sentence, the intensity of sentence emotion has been increased apparently. We check each word whether it is modified by the degree word or not, and use these degree modifications as a feature.

Negative Words
With very high frequency, negative words such as "不(no)", "不会(cannot)", are made use of reversing the word meaning and shifting emotion type in the Chinese document. In the following sentence, "我不善长写诗赋词。(I am not good at writing the poems.)". As the emotional word "善长(good at)" is modified by the negative word "不(not)", the sentence emotion express a opposite emotion to the word emotion. Therefore, the appearance of the negative modifications would be considered as a feature.

Conjunctions
Simple sub-sentences can be assembled into a complex sentence with the conjunction. The occurrences of conjunctions are often accompanied with apparent emotion variations in the sentence. For example,
"虽然有些累，但我会坚持下去。(Although I felt a little tired, I will keep it up.)"

The conjunction "虽然...但(although)" is employed in the sentence, so the sentence can express much stronger emotion. As a consequence, we judge whether each word is under a conjunction modification or not, and employ this conjunction modification as a feature.

3.2 CRF Based Emotional Words Annotation

Conditional Random Fields (CRF) has been employed for recognizing the emotional words and their emotion categories. To better understand the function of the context information in emotional words annotation, we experiment on three levels of language modes: 1-gram, 2-gram and 3-gram. As depicted through expression 3.1 to expression 3.5, these N-gram models are built on each emotion features described previously to represent the context of emotional words.

Fw = {1-gram(Word)} ∪ {2-gram(Word)} ∪ {3-gram (Word)}	(3.1)
Fpos = {1-gram(POS)} ∪ {2-gram(POS)} ∪ {3-gram (POS)}	(3.2)
Fdm = {1-gram(D-mod)} ∪ {2-gram(D-mod)} ∪ {3-gram (D-mod)}	(3.3)
Fnm = {1-gram(N-mod)} ∪ {2-gram(N-mod)} ∪ {3-gram (N-mod)}	(3.4)
Fcm = {1-gram(C-mod)} ∪ {2-gram(C-mod)} ∪ {3-gram (C-mod)}	(3.5)

where "D-mod", "N-mod", "C-mod" represent the modification relations between words and degree words, negative words, conjunctions respectively, while Fw, Fpos, Fdm, Fnm and Fcm correspond to the word string features, the POS features, the degree words modification features, the negative words modification features and conjunctions modification features separately. After we filtered out some extremely short sentences, and sentences which only contain punctuations, there are 31,070 sentences left for the emotional words annotation experiments. 24,856 sentences are randomly selected for training, and the rest 6,214 sentences for testing.

3.3 Result and Discussion

Table 3.1 gives the precision, recall and F-score of emotional words annotation. We can find that the three emotions Love, Sorrow and Anxiety, get the best F-scores 60.77%, 44.13%, 44.10%, while Surprise, Hate and Anger emotions get the worst three F-scores 26.11%, 33.02%, 26.01%. For one reason, when a person is in the passive state, he may express multiple negative emotions at the same time, such as Anger and Hate, which makes it difficult even for human to annotate. For the emotion of Surprise, we think that the lack of training data directly lead to the such low recall, since the number of words conveyed Surprise is only 1.96% of whole emotional words.

Table 3.1: Precision, recall and F-score of emotional words annotation

Emotion	Precision	Recall	F-score
No_emo	0.941841	0.987083	0.963931
Joy	0.610493	0.330892	0.429170
Hate	0.553704	0.235248	0.330204
Love	0.673164	0.553813	0.607684
Sorrow	0.586558	0.353374	0.441261
Anxiety	0.531632	0.376790	0.441014
Surprise	0.543210	0.171875	0.261128
Anger	0.551724	0.170213	0.260163
Expect	0.631902	0.314504	0.419980
Av.	0.624914	0.388199	0.461615

4 Document Emotion Analysis

We propose a new method for document emotion analysis by employing the function of automatic emotional words annotation, which has been introduced in Section 3. Two parameters, term relevance tr and term frequency tf, are constructed for evaluating the relation between the word emotion (which is automatically extracted from the document) and the document emotion. Normalization is conducted so that the emotion values could be comparable among documents of different lengths.

We use 211 blog documents collected from the Internet for document emotion analysis. All these articles belong to four blog users in different emotional situations. Each document is previously segmented into words and phrases. Human experts annotated each document with at least one emotion tag from the emotion tag list (Expect, Joy, Love, Surprise, Anxiety, Sorrow, Anger and Hate), while the word emotions are not annotated.

4.1 Document Emotion Assumption

Just as the documents are composed of the words, intuitively, we assume that the document emotions are determined by the word emotions contained in the documents.

There are some reasons for this assumption: First, the document are more likely to convey the same emotion as the emotion of words. Second, although there exists some words that contain different emotions from the overall emotions of the corresponding documents, we find that the most appearance of such words follows some statistical rules. Third, the document emotions constructed by the simple accumulation of word emotions are not exact enough, since the accumulation would cause some difficulties in comparing the emotion values of documents of different lengths, while fortunately the term frequency (TF), which is a widely used parameter for document analysis, could help to normalize our document emotion values.

4.2 Document Emotion Analysis (DEA) Model

The document emotion is constructed from word emotions with two weight parameters. Our DEA model predicts the emotion of a document as an eight dimensional vector, with each element represents the possible value of corresponding emotion. Each part of the calculation processing is illustrated in detail as follows:

1) Emotion Vector of Words

we extract an emotion vector for each word in document , which is a binary-valued eight-dimensional vector with each element $\overset{1}{e_k}$ ($k=1,2\ldots,8$) representing that the kth emotion (such as Love, Hate, Sorrow, ...) is reflected from the word w_i while $\overset{0}{e_k}$ represents that the kth emotion is not reflected.

We exploit the function of emotional words annotation to recognize the emotional words in the blog documents collected from the Internet. As the documents in the test corpus are just given emotion tags in document level, we have to extract the three modification features for each sentence of test corpus before Emotional words Annotation. Our solution here is that we build three word lists by extracting degree words, negative words and conjunctions respectively from Ren-CECps. The modification words are available by means of word matching in test corpus with the three word lists.

The table 4.1 shows the portion of the eight-dimensional emotional vector of emotional words in the first document in the test corpus.

Table 4.1: Emotion word and emotion type

Emotion Words \ Emotion Types		e1	e2	e3	e4	e5	e6	e7	e8
活力 (vitality)	$e(w_1)$	0	0	1	0	0	0	0	0
幸福 (happiness)	$e(w_2)$	1	0	0	0	0	0	0	0
埋葬 (bury)	$e(w_3)$	0	0	0	1	0	0	0	0
宝贝 (baby)	$e(w_4)$	0	0	1	0	0	0	0	0
幸运 (luck)	$e(w_5)$	1	0	0	0	0	0	0	0
享受 (enjoy)	$e(w_6)$	1	0	0	0	0	0	0	0

2) Term Relevance

we construct a term relevance parameter tr_i, which reveals the relevance between the word emotion and the corresponding document emotion, for each word w_i. This is conducted by thoroughly analyzing the emotional words from the Ren-CECps emotion corpus depicted in

$$tr_i = \frac{\left|\{w_i \mid w_i \in D_j \wedge e(w_i) \sim e(D_j), j=1,\ldots,M\}\right|}{\sum_{j=1}^{M} n_{i,j}} \qquad (4.1)$$

The numerator part of equation (4.1) counts the appearance of word w_i in each document D_j with $j=1,2,\ldots M$ (Ren-CECps), where $e(w_i) \sim e(D_j)$ signifies the compatibility between the word emotions and the document emotions, say, there is at least one common emotion element shared by the word emotion vector $e(w_i)$ and the document emotion vector $e(D_j)$. Under this condition, we can use a binary variable to represent this relationship:

$$e(w_i) \sim e(D_j) = 1\{\langle e(w_i), e(D_j)\rangle > 0\} \qquad (4.2)$$

in which $e(w_i) \sim e(D_j)$ takes the value of 1 if *condition=true*, while the value of 0 if *condition=false*. $\langle a,b\rangle$ represents the inner product between two vectors a and b.

The denominator part of equation (4.1) counts the appearance of words , which is represented by $n_{i,j}$, from each document D_j . Therefore, equation (4.1) gives us an evaluation of the confidence, which we call the term relevance tr , that the emotion of word w_i is compatible with the emotion of the document which it belongs to.

The term relevance values as well as compatibility counts and appearance counts of some words in the first document in the test corpus are listed in table 4.2.

Table 4.2: Term relevance of emotional word

Emotional Word w_i	Compatibility $comp_i$	Appearance Count $count_i$	Term relevance tr_i
有害 (harmful)	5	5	1.000000
宝贝 (baby)	47	52	0.903846
活力 (vitality)	15	19	0.789474
埋葬 (bury)	10	13	0.769231
幸运 (luck)	27	41	0.658537
享受 (enjoy)	143	235	0.608511
幸福 (happiness)	323	670	0.482090
模范 (model)	0	6	0.000000

3) Term Frequency

we construct a term frequency parameter $tf_{i,j}$ for a word w_i from the document D_j as

$$tf_{i,j} = \begin{cases} \dfrac{n_{i,j}}{\sum_{w_k \in W_E} n_{k,j}} & if \;\; w_i \in W_E \\ 0 & if \;\; w_i \notin W_E \end{cases} \tag{4.3}$$

with $i = 1,2,\ldots,N$ and $j = 1,2,\ldots,M$ (Testing). Again, $n_{i,j}$ counts the appearance of word in document D_j. The term frequency here represents the proportion of the emotion values of word w_i in the emotion values of D_j . Because the document emotion is composed of the word emotions, and the number of emotional words in each document often varies, we need this term frequency to normalize the accumulation effect. Therefore, for each emotional word $w_i \in W_E$, we compute its frequencies among all the emotional words in the document D_j , and for the unemotional words $w_i \notin W_E$, we just ignore their contribution to the document emotion and assign the value of 0.

In this study, term frequency is a significant weighted parameter which measures the importance of a word in our test corpus.

For some words in the first document in the test corpus, the term frequency values as well as appearance counts and total emotional word counts are listed in table 4.3.

Table 4.3: Term frequency of emotional word

Emotional Word w_i	Appearance Count $count_i$	Total Emotional Word Count $total_j$	Term Frequency $tf_{i,j}$
活力 (vitality)	1	185	0.005405
幸福 (happiness)	1	185	0.005405
埋葬 (bury)	2	185	0.010811
宝贝 (baby)	1	185	0.005405
幸运 (luck)	1	185	0.005405
享受 (enjoy)	1	185	0.005405

4) Document Emotion Calculation

Finally, document emotion $e(D_j)$ is accumulated by word emotion $e(w_i)$ within it, weighted by term relevances tr_i and term frequencies $tf_{i,j}$ as equation (4.4) shown below:

$$e(D_j) = \sum_{w_i \in D_j} e(w_i) \cdot tf_{ij} \cdot tr_i \quad (4.4)$$

$$e(D_j) = \sum_{w_i \in D_j} e(w_i) \cdot tf_{ij} \quad (4.5)$$

4.3 Evaluation Methods

we are considering three levels of precisions for evaluating the model performance, which are depicted in equations 4.6, in which i can take the values of {1, 2, 3}.

$$precision\_(i) = \frac{Matched\ Document\ (i)}{All\ Documents} \quad (4.6)$$

In the first level of evaluation, we choose the emotion with the highest emotion value from the predicted emotion vector as the predicted document emotion. By comparing this emotion with emotions annotated by human experts, we conclude the predicted emotion is correct, if predicted emotion matches annotated emotion of the corresponding document in test corpus. We count the number of the matched documents, which i takes the value of 1, in the numerator part of equation (4.6), and count the number of documents in test corpus as *All Documents* in the denominator part.

In the second level, we refer to two emotion types with the highest values in the emotion vector as the predicted document emotion. We treat them as a correct matching if there is at least one of the two emotion types could match the annotated emotions of the corresponding document in the test corpus.

In the third level, three emotion types are under consideration as the second level.

4.4 eResults and Discussion

We use 211 documents from four blogs to test the performance of our DEA model. In order to examine the effectiveness of term relevance , we plan to carry out a comparative experiment using equation (4.5), in which term relevance is not employed. We list the three levels of precisions for the documents of each blog, and also counts the precisions of the documents from all the blogs as a whole. The detailed results are shown in the Table 4.4 and Table 4.5.

Table 4.4: Results of comparative experiment in three levels of evaluation methods

Blog ID	Num.Of Documents	Precision_1	Precision_2	Precision_3
ID1	37	0.189189	0.729730	0.837838
ID2	18	0.222222	0.777778	0.888889
ID3	73	0.068493	0.369863	0.616438
ID4	83	0.168675	0.445783	0.662651
Overall	211	0.142180	0.497630	0.696682

Compared with the three precisions of comparative experiment, experiment which utilizes term relevance gets the better performance. Therefore, we believe that term relevance makes a contribution to the document emotion analysis. Nevertheless, the value of precision_2 and precision_3 of ID 1 and ID2 for both experiments are the same, we find that they have the same number of correct predicted document emotions but not the same identities of documents.

Table 4.5: Results of adopted experiment in three evaluation methods

Blog ID	Num.Of Documents	Precision_1	Precision_2	Precision_3
ID1	37	0.270270	0.729730	0.837838
ID2	18	0.277778	0.777778	0.888889
ID3	73	0.082192	0.438356	0.657534
ID4	83	0.192771	0.46988	0.686747
Overall	211	0.175355	0.530806	0.720379

As shown in Table 4.5, the DEA model gets relatively lower precisions in the first level of evaluation for different blog documents, but achieves much better results in the second and the third level. Because most documents are conveying multiple emotions at the same time, the latter two level of precisions also confirm the promising result of our model.

The source of this test corpus also provides some insight into document emotion analysis. The blog documents used for document emotion analysis are collected from four different blog users under different emotional situations: The ID1 blog user lost his son in the earthquake and missed his child in blogs; the ID2 blog user suffered from a serious disease and wrote blogs for encouraging herself; the ID3 blog user lost her boyfriend in an accident, and wrote her beautiful memories in blogs; the ID4 blog user had been betrayed by her husband, so complained in blogs.

These documents from different emotion situations are used to test the robustness of our DEA model: Firstly, the experiment in Table 4.5 shows similar results , which proves that our DEA model can deal with different kinds of emotional situations. Secondly, through a thorough examination, we also find that the documents of the ID3 blog user get the lower emotion precision than the other blog documents. This happens when the blog user uses the positive emotional words to express negative emotions (e.g. the pleased memory of life conveyed the sadness of the current emotion). This turns to be one of the most difficult situations in our document emotion analysis: although the annotators could precisely tag the document with negative emotions, such as sorrow, it is still not easy for machines to judge the real emotions through the large amount of positive emotional words.

5 Conclusions

In this paper, we develop a document emotion analysis model by making use of the function of emotional words annotation. Two parameters, term relevance and term frequency, are introduced to evaluate the relations between the word emotions and the document emotions.

By utilizing the modification relationship in the context, we build an automatic Emotional

Words Annotation system, which could get word emotions with higher context sensitivity compared to traditional emotion lexicons.

We perform document emotion analysis by using the result of our Emotional Words Annotation. Under the relation assumption between document emotions and word emotions, we introduce term relevance and term frequency in the process. Experimental results reveal that our DEA model achieves promising performance under different emotion situations.

We notice that the incorrectly tagged word emotions through Emotional Word Annotation could influence the accuracy of document emotion analysis. One of the most important affects comes from the three word lists from which we extract the modification features for emotional word annotation, as we have mentioned in section 4.2. These word lists are totally empirical, and contain large amount of inaccuracy. The inaccurate modifications employed as the features in CRF model would finally cause the inaccurate annotated emotional words, and indirectly affect the performance of document emotion analysis.

We also find document emotion analysis become more difficult when large amount of positive emotional words are used in a blog document to express negative emotions. Although the annotators could precisely comprehend the negative emotions in the blog documents, which is still not an easy task for machines to judge such real emotions.

References

Chesley, P., B. Vincent, L. Xu, and R. Srihari. 2006. Using verbs and adjectives to automatically classify blog sentiment. *AAAI Symposium on Computational Approaches to Analysing Weblogs (AAAI-CAAW)*, pp. 27–29.

Clore, G.L., A. Ortony and M. A. Foss. 1987. *The psychological foundations of the affective lexicon. Journal of Personality and Social Psychology*, 53:751–766.

Das, D. and S. Bandyopadhyay. 2009. Word to Sentence Level Emotion Tagging for Bengali Blogs. *Proceedings of the ACL-IJCNLP 2009 Conference Short Papers*, pages 149–152, Suntec, Singapore.

Fragopanagos, N. and J.G. Taylor. 2005. Emotion Recognition in Human-Computer Interaction. Neural Networks, vol. 18, pp. 389-405.

Gamon, M. 2004. Sentiment classification on customer feedback data: noisy data, large feature vectors, and the role of linguistic analysis. *Proceedings the 20th International Conference on Computational Linguistics.*

Hu, M. and B. Liu. 2004. Mining and summarizing customer reviews. *Proceedings of the ACM SIGKDD Conference on Knowledge Discovery and Data Mining (KDD)*, pp. 168–177.

Kang, X., F. Ren and Y. Wu. 2010. Bottom Up: Exploring Word Emotions for Chinese Sentence Chief Sentiment Classification. *Proceedings of 6th International Conference on Natural Language Processing and Knowledge Engineering.*

Lafferty, J., A. McCallum and F. Pereira. 2001. Conditional random fields: Probabilistic models for segmenting and labeling sequence data. *Proceedings of International Conference on Machine Learning-01.*

Matsumoto, S., H. Takamura and M. Okumura. 2005. Sentiment Classification Using Word Sub-sequences and Dependency Sub-trees. *Proceedings of the 9th Pacific-Asia Conference on Knowledge Discovery and Data Mining.*

NG, V., S. Dasgupta and S. M. Niaz Arifin. 2006. Examining the role of linguistic knowledge sources in the automatic identification and classification of reviews. *Proceedings of the COLING/ACL 2006.*

Pang, B., L. Lee and S. Vaithyanathan. 2002. Thumbs up? Sentiment Classification using Machine Learning. *Proceedings of the Conference on Conference on Empirical Methods in Natural Language Processing.*

Quan, C. and F. Ren. 2010. *A blog emotion corpus for emotional expression analysis in Chinese.* Computer Speech and Language, Vol.24, No.1, pp.726-749

Ren, F., 2009, Affective Information Processing and Recognizing Human Emotion. *Electronic Notes in Theoretical Computer Science*, Vol.225, No.2009, pp.39-50.

Turney, P.D. 2002. Thumbs Up or Thumbs Down? Semantic Orientation Applied to Unsupervised Classification of Reviews. *Proceedings of the 40th Annual Meeting of the Association for Computational Linguistics*, Philadelphia.

Tokuhisa, R., K. Inui, and Y. Matsumoto. 2008. Emotion Classification Using Massive Examples Extracted from the Web. *Proceedings of COLING 2008*, pp. 881-888.

Yang, C., K.H-Y. Lin and H-H. Chen. 2007. Building Emotion Lexicon from Weblog Corpora. *Proceedings of the 45th Annual Meeting of the Association for Computational Linguistics.*

Yang, C., K.H.-Y. Lin and H.-H. Chen. 2007. Emotion Classification from Web Blog Corpora. *IEEE/WIC/ACM.*

Zhao, J., K. Liu and G. Wang. 2008. Adding Redundant Features for CRFs-based Sentence Sentiment Classification. *Proceedings of Empirical Methods in Natural Language Processing.*

A Construction Grammar Approach to Prepositional Phrase Attachment: Semantic Feature Analysis of V NP1 *into* NP2 Construction*

Liyin Chen[a], Siaw-Fong Chung[a], and Chao-Lin Liu[b]

[a]Department of English, National Chengchi University,
NO. 64, Sec 2, ZhiNan Rd., Wenshan District, Taipei City 11605, Taiwan
{98551505, sfchung}@nccu.edu.tw
[b]Department of Computer Science, National Chengchi University,
NO. 64, Sec 2, ZhiNan Rd., Wenshan District, Taipei City 11605, Taiwan
chaolin@nccu.edu.tw

Abstract. This paper provides a construction grammar perspective to identifying the ambiguity of prepositional phrase (PP) attachments (i.e., whether a PP is attached to the closest VP or NP1). Despite the wide discussion of these two structures (VP-attached and NP1-attached), we raise the possibility for a third parsing structure (about 11.3% from all 1845 instances analyzed), a co-attachment to both verb and noun. A co-attachment structure denotes the lack of [movement] feature in both the verb and noun surrounding a PP. This proposal is arrived when we annotate the semantic feature [-movement] to both VP and NP1, respectively, in a caused-motion construction of V NP1 *into* NP2 (e.g., *vote an individual into the presidency; shamed us into pity; define ourselves into a box*).

Keywords: construction grammar, prepositional phrase attachment, caused-motion construction.

1 Introduction

The preposition *into* describes the path of motion event which typical involves an object, or figure, moves along the path to enter a reference object, or ground (Talmy, 2000). An example of motion event is the caused-motion construction involving a verb (V) and two noun phrases (NP1 and NP2) as a direct and an indirect object, respectively. Sentence (1), extracted from the Penn Treebank Wall Street Journal (WSJ) Corpus[1] (Charniak, et al., 2000), illustrates such a V NP1 *into* NP2 construction (shown in bold with lexical categories glossed underneath). The basic semantics of the construction involves a motion event that requires the direct object (NP1) to be moved and directed to the confinement of indirect object (NP2). In this case, an unspecified number of airplanes undergo movement towards a deictic space.

(1) ***To shove*** ***even more airplanes*** ***into*** ***this space*** *is asking for trouble,*
V NP1 Prep NP2
experts say. (WSJ-V1141)

However, this type of prepositional phrases poses an ambiguity problem in parsing. Sentence (1) serves as an example for one means of parsing in which the preposition closely associates with the verb but not NP1. The second possibility of parsing is where the PP is required to be interpreted with NP1, as illustrated in bold in sentence (2).

* The authors would like to thank the anonymous reviewers for their comments on this work. This study is supported in part by National Science Council Research Grants (NSC 99-2410-H-004-206-, NSC 100-2628-H-004-137-, and NSC-100-2221-E-004-014).

[1] All the examples discussed in this paper are from the WSJ corpus unless specified.

(2) *And he soon became aware that the government was able*
to show a flow of millions of dollars in illicit funds into his account.
V NP1 Prep NP2

Here the head of NP1 (*a flow*) is to be interpreted along with *into* and NP2 (*his account*), rather than with the preceding verb (*to show*). Computational linguists have found these two structures causing parsing problems in natural language processing (NLP) and referred to this problem of determining the site of PP to be attached as the PP attachment problem (e.g., Hindle and Rooth, 1993; Volk, 2006). As illustrated in (1) and (2), this problem is conventionally formalized as a binary choice (Merlo and Ferrer, 2005), either verb-attached for (1) or noun-attached for (2). In the minimalist syntax, ternary structures like (3a) are to be transformed by deriving an explicit causative construction (3b) (Radford, 2004). The operation involves raising of the verb *roll* to join the causative verb *made* to adhere to a binary operation.

(3a) *He* ***rolled the ball down the hill.***
V NP1 Prep NP2

(3b) *He* ***made + roll the ball (roll) down the hill.***
V-causative + V NP1 trace Prep NP2
(Radford, 2004, p. 337, with gloss added)

Although the plausibility of equating the two constructions has long been questioned (e.g., Fodor, 1970), the causative structure (3b) cannot provide a direct solution to the PP attachment problem for (3a). Moreover, the binary solution to the problem has been challenged by computational linguists. For example, Merlo and Ferrer (2005) contend that such a dichotomous treatment may be a simplification. They propose to take into account of the nature of the attachment by distinguishing PP arguments from PP adjuncts. Sentence (4) is an example of two verb-attached PPs that maintain different relationships with the verb shown in the gloss.

(4) ***Put the block on the table in the morning.***
V NP1 PP argument PP adjunct
(Merlo and Ferrer, 2005, p. 342, with gloss added)

Since PP arguments carry the core message and PP adjuncts provide additional information to the core meaning, their distinction further refines NLP tasks. Although studies like Merlo and Ferrer (2005) provide novel approaches to tackle the PP attachment problem, the notion of binary sites for PP attachment has not been scrutinized. The presupposition of binary attachment sites, however, may result in a forced selection from one of the two choices and may overlook other possibilities for correct parsing. Consider the construction in bold in sentence (5) for determining the PP attachment site.

(5) *Frank* ***sneezed the tissue off the table***
V NP1 Prep NP2
(Goldberg, 1995, p. 152, with gloss added)

According to our first choice, verb-attached parsing, the verb *sneezed* is to be analyzed with NP1 *the tissue*. The grouping is semantically invalid since the verb is normally intransitive without a direct object. Yet, it is not any less awkward as the noun-attached option is considered (*the tissue off the table*). In Goldberg's (1995) seminal work on construction grammar, she discusses the basic semantics of caused-motion construction or that "the causer argument directly causes the theme argument to move along a path designated by the directional phrase: that is, 'X CAUSES Y to MOVE Z'" (p. 152). In brief, the caused-motion construction includes a directional phrase like *into* PP and entails a movement feature. However, (5) illustrates an atypical example of caused-motion construction where the construction fails to be interpreted through its components or what the PP attachment problem is based on. According to Goldberg, the semantic meaning of (5) can only be derived by taking into account of the entire construction. In other words, to address the PP attachment issue in sentences like (5), we need to take into account of a third possible structure in addition to a binary choice from verb- or noun-attachment.[2]

In this study, we take the construction grammar approach to reformalize the PP attachment problem. In addition to the conventional binary approach to determining the PP attachment sites, we suggest a third possible structure where the PP co-attaches to both verb and noun based on the construction grammar framework. We also develop a semantic analysis of the feature movement (denoted as [+movement] or [-movement]) for the verb and direct object in the V NP1 *into* NP2 construction to determine the PP attachment site. Our proposal examines the WSJ corpus data by means of manual annotation.

2 A Semantic Feature Classification

From our preliminary observations of the WSJ data, we noticed that the notion of movement is closely correlated to the verb and first noun in the V NP1 *into* NP2 construction, and the observation can be confirmed by the semantic meaning of the preposition *into*. According to Tyler and Evans (2003), the 'proto-scene', or illustration of the primary sense in spatial configuration, of *into* involves NP1 (figure) being outside NP2 (ground) and then entering the boundary of NP2. The movement feature is a distinctive feature for *into* to be distinguished from *in* as the latter expresses a locative sense. As the notion of path is encoded by the preposition, the parsing structure may reflect our proclivity to associate the notion of path with that of movement. We therefore hypothesize that the feature [±movement] can be used to determine the PP attachment site as summarized in Table 1.

Table 1: Hypotheses for determining PP-attachment sites from [±movement] specification at V and NP1.

[±movement]		Hypotheses
V	NP1	
+	-	Expected specification for verb-attached PP structure.
-	+	Expected specification for noun-attached PP structure.
-	-	Expected specification for co-attachment structure.
+	+	Undetermined.

Table 1 demonstrates the four possible outcomes after specifying [±movement] at V and NP1, each elaborated below. Constructions (in bold) in (6) and (7) exemplify verb and noun attachment, respectively, and the feature is specified in plus or minus sign for each lexical item in gloss.

(6) *They threatened* ***to crash*** ***the jet*** ***into Kuwait's royal palace.*** (WSJ-V924)
V [+] NP [-] PP

(7) *He* ***describes*** ***his launch*** ***into American society*** *In 1962,...* (WSJ-V245)
V [-] NP [+] PP

It is not difficult to see that the concept of path encoded in the PPs is more semantically coherent when interpreted with [+movement] sites such as the verb *crash* in (6) and the noun *his launch* in (7). In contrast, when the potential attachment site is [-movement] like the NP *the jet* in (6) or the verb *describe* in (7), there is no strong semantic association with the PP. However, the binary distinction of verb and noun attachment sites is not sufficient to capture the parsing of

[2] Such treatment appears to be in common with approaches that accommodate ternary branching such as Head-Driven Phrase Structure Grammar or HPSG (Pollard and Sag, 1994), or proponents like Jackendoff (2002) and Carrier and Randall (1992). In contrast to the other approaches, this study stresses the entirety of construction in which causative meaning of non-causative verbs can be derived as in the case of *sneezed* in (5). In addition, much earlier work concentrated on the analysis of ternary branching resultative constructions (e.g., Carrier & Randall, 1992; Wechsler & Noh, 2001). To the best of our knowledge, the results have not been applied to tackling the PP attachment problem.

some instances like (8). Sentence (8) exemplifies an unconventional caused-motion construction like those described by Goldberg (1995).

(8) *Watching the weekend spectacle, we return to the thought that the next U.S. President and the rest of the West's leaders should keep in mind that their primary responsibility is not* ***to baptize the Soviet Union into Western civilization.*** (WSJ-V30)

V [-] NP [-] PP

The verb *baptize* is commonly used in passive voice and is an unaccusative verb with its object as the argument. Yet, in sentence (8) we found a transitive use followed by a direction prepositional phrase. A semantic feature of movement can only be construed when the entire construction V NP1 *into* NP2 is processed simultaneously. This is the basis of our contention that in addition to previous two sites to attach PP, a co-attachment structure is required.

The last feature category [+, +] is the most complicated one among the four. Consider sentences (9) and (10). Complication arises as the intensity of [+movement] could vary and compete between the verb and noun that would result in a differential reading. For example, sentence (9) demonstrates a stronger sense of movement in the verb that results in a verb-attachment interpretation. On the contrary, sentence (10) posits a stronger feature in the noun that results in a noun-attached reading. In addition, the rate of V-NP or NP-PP occurrence may also interfere with the feature reading.

(9) *But the mess in sales isn't the only problem that* ***slowed revenue growth into single digits in the latest quarter.*** (WSJ-V1334)

V [+] NP [+] PP

(10) *Moreover, the economy shows scant evidence of* ***repeating the post-1929 slide into the Depression.*** (WSJ-V1337)

V [+] NP [+] PP

However, the determination of feature strength is subjective which requires a more objective approach such as cognitive experiments to be conclusive; therefore, we designate this category as 'undetermined'.

3 Categorization Procedures

The extracted WSJ corpus data were analyzed manually to identify the semantic category for all words in the lexical categories, V and NP1. According to Fellbaum (1990), there are 15 files or semantic domains of verbs in WordNet all of which are listed in Table 2 except for *weather.* The online WordNet Search 3.1 was used to identify the category of each verb by selecting "show all" in Display Options for each search word (Figure 1). The categorization fits our purpose of identifying the presence or absence of the semantic feature [±movement]. We based our judgment from the senses listed in the Oxford Online Dictionary (http://oxforddictionaries.com/) for *into*, except for the addition of two domains, *body* and *possession,* in Fallbaum. Table 2 summaries the semantic domains that reflect the [± movement] feature with examples. In Figure 1, the verb *induct* is used as an example to show the display of search results. While *induct* has at least five senses, the senses fall into three semantic domains, as designated in < >, namely, *social, creation* and *communication*. For each instance from the WSJ corpus, the sense of the verb was identified first by one of the authors and then matched to the WordNet search results. For example, the meaning of *induct* in sentence (11) is *introduce*, thereby assigning *communication* (sense five above) for categorization.

(11) *Typically, Mr. Grace* ***inducts his Catholic recruits into the Knights of Malta*** *and encourages their participation in charity.* (WSJ-V855)

However, if the WordNet result did not have a match with the verb under search, dictionaries (e.g., Merriam-Webster online dictionary and Collins English Dictionary) were consulted. In total, there were 30 verbs (1.6%) (mainly words with prefixes such as *reopen* and *unimpede*) consulted dictionaries for their categories.

Table 2: Semantic Categories of Verbs (Fallbaum, 1990).

[+movement]	Central Notions (with examples from WSJ)	[-movement]	Central Notions (with examples from WSJ)
Motion	Make a movement or contained motion e.g., *fall, elevate, intrude*	Cognition	Cognitive acts and states. e.g., *await, engineer, trick*
Contact	Troponyms of fasten, cover, cut and touch e.g., *chisel, nudge, pile*	Communica-tion	Verbal and non-verbal e.g., *say, cite, protest*
Change	Verbs of becoming. e.g., *substitute, accelerate, delay, empty, restructure*	Consumption	Verbs of ingesting, using, exploiting, spending and sharing e.g., *drink, wean, tax*
Creation	By mental act, artistic means or from raw material e.g., *rebuild, cast, cause*	Social	Include law, politics, economy, education family and religion. e.g., *resign, punish, hinder*
Competition	Includes sports, games and warfare. e.g., *battle, parlay, fight*	Perception	Covers the five senses. e.g., *find, witness, see*
Body	Bodily care and function words. e.g., *breathe, sweat, hypnotize, secrete, twist*	Emotion	Subject or object as the experiencer. e.g., *scare, tease, rile*
Possession	Change of possession and its preceding and resultative state. e.g., *buy, invest, spend*	Stative	Verbs of being and having. e.g., *require, defer, involve*

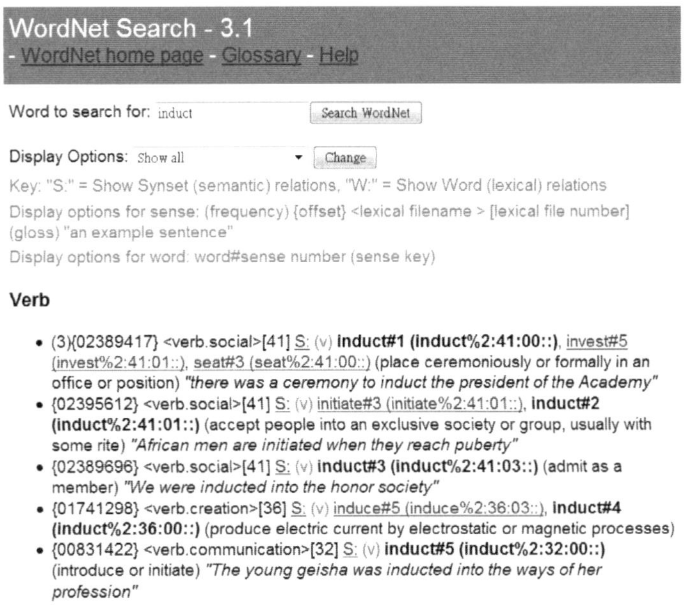

Figure 1: A screenshot of WordNet Search 3.1 search result for the verb *induct*.

The categorization of nouns in WordNet unfortunately does not focus on the notion of movement as this feature is not a primary characteristic of noun. Different criteria were used for categorizing nouns. The nouns in our constructions were grouped manually into six major categories. The [+movement] feature is found in the following three domains: movement (e.g., verb derivations like *continuation, delivery* and *expansion*), route/entry (e.g., *way, window*) and psychological/cognitive path (e.g., *insight, inquiry, research*). Most of the [+movement] nouns were easily identified as they are closely related to their morphological counterparts in the verb category (e.g., *discharge, investigation, immigration* and *investment*). The [-movement] nouns can be found under another three domains: entity (e.g., physical objects), abstraction (e.g., temporal and spatial concepts), group/person (e.g., name entities and pronouns).

4 The Corpus

The annotated Penn Treebank WSJ corpus was used for data analysis. Two sub-corpora that contain the V NP1 *into* NP2 were extracted based on the built-in annotation: verb-attached structure ((VP NP1)(*into* NP2))[3] and noun-attached structure ((VP)(NP1 *into* NP2))[4]. All the data were converted into Excel files for further processing. First, those instances without an NP (labeled as 'None' in WSJ) were excluded. Second, to provide a full coverage of verbs, only one instance per lexeme was selected for manual semantic analysis. For example, there are in total 29 instances of the V NP1 into NP2 construction for the lemma *absorb* (four for *absorb*, 22 for *absorbed*, and three for *absorbing*). Only one instance of each lexical form (*absorb, absorbed* and *absorbing*) was analyzed. In addition, instances which do not have a PP attached to either the verb or head noun in NP1 were manually eliminated. Sentence (12) exemplifies such a case as *into* is neither attached to V (*sympathizes*) nor NP1 (*a bit*), but rather to another NP (*Belushi's escape*) subsumed under NP1.

(12) *If she was as simpering in life as she is on film, one sympathizes a bit with Belushi's escape into reality-altering substances.* (WSJ-V17)

In the end, a total of 1918 types of verbs were screened, and 1845 instances were considered for further analysis along with their direct object (NP1).

5 Annotation Results

The distribution of the four types of [±movement] feature specified at V and NP1 is summarized in Table 3. Overall, over half of the PPs are attached to the verb [+, -] (51.5%). Noun-attached [+, -] and undetermined structures [+, +] fall into close range (17.4% and 19.8%, respectively). The lowest proportion is co-attachment [-, -] (11.3%) which is expected due to its atypical semantic properties.

Table 3: Distribution of four types of feature specification.

Hypothesized attachment site	[± movement]		Rate (count)
	V	NP1	
Verb-attached	+	-	51.5% (950)
Noun-attached	-	+	17.4% (321)
Co-attached	-	-	11.3% (208)
Undetermined	+	+	19.8% (366)
Total			100% (1845)

Next, we compare our annotation results with that extracted directly from the Penn Treebank which was generated from the traditional binary attachment approach. Table 4 demonstrates the feature distribution of the Penn Treebank binary attachment in percentage and counts in parentheses. A match of 65.6% for verb-attached PPs and 44.8% for noun-attached PPs can be

[3] An example of noun-attached structure: (VP (VBZ parses) (NP#1230 (NNS names)) (PP-CLR (IN into) (NP (DT every) (JJ conceivable) (NN interest) (NN group)))).

[4] An example of noun-attached structure: (VP (VB plot) (NP (DT a) (JJ peaceful) (NN course)) (PP-CLR (IN into) (NP#1080 (DT the) (NN future)))).

found across both methods. Following the feature analysis, 137 instances of noun-attached PPs are found under the verb-attached category in the Penn Treebank annotation. More than half of these instances are communication and cognitive verbs (100/137). Examples include *masterminded, consolidated, picked, implies, mandate, requested* and *protested*. For those verb-attached PPs classified under the noun category, the main verb categories are change and motion verbs (39/76), exemplified by verbs like *fermented, infusing, integrating, transforming, reached, walk, sweeping, threw* and *drops*.

Table 4: Feature analysis of the Penn Treebank computer-generated binary attachment.

Hypothesized attachment site	[± movement] V	[± movement] NP1	Penn Treebank Binary Attachment: Verb-attached PPs	Penn Treebank Binary Attachment: Noun-attached PPs
Verb-attached	+	-	60.9% (874)	18.5% (76)
Noun-attached	-	+	9.6% (137)	44.8% (184)
Co-attached	-	-	14.2% (204)	1.0% (4)
Undetermined	+	+	15.3% (219)	35.8% (147)
Total			100% (1434)	100% (411)

A further analysis of the semantic domains of all the co-attached PPs can be found in Table 5. The social, emotion, cognition and communication domains comprise of nearly 90% of the data.

Table 5: The distribution of semantic domains of verbs in [- -] category.

Verb domains	Communication	Social	Emotion	Cognition	Stative	Consumption	Perception	Total
Count	94 (45.2%)	48 (23.1%)	31 (14.9%)	16 (7.7%)	9 (4.3%)	6 (2.9%)	4 (1.9%)	208 (100%)

Both the social and communication domains consist of verbs that can only be interpreted with rhetorical force as shown bolded in (13a) and (13b), respectively.

(13a) *...**punish Iran and Iraq into an agreement** on each other's production quotas...* (WSJ-V42)

(13b) *...the courts have refused to uphold contracts in which people have voluntarily **contracted themselves into peonage or slavery**.* (WSJ-V30)

Emotion verbs are also found to have their emotional sensation evoked and passed onto NP2 as shown bolded in (14). Some of them collocate with *into* (e.g., *intimidate, scare,* and *galvanize*). This domain is almost uniformly co-occurs with human subjects (93%).

(14a) *It happened in the 1970s when the government **panicked itself into an "energy crisis,"*** (WSJ-V202)

(14a) *...**deluded ourselves into thinking** we were safe.* (WSJ-V70)

In contrast, the result for cognition verbs is rather difficult for interpretation as the category could have covered too broad a range. Verbs like *trick, sorted, plugged, instilling, reclassify, parsing,* and *categorizing,* clearly denote change at the cognitive level and are supposedly assigned to the verb-attached group. In brief, the above annotation results show that the co-attached instances for the *into* PP are more commonly associated with interpersonal functions such as communication, social and emotion.

6 Conclusion

In this study, we adopt the construction grammar framework to provide a different means to reformulate the PP attachment problem. In addition to the conventional approach that makes a binary choice between verb- and noun-attached sites, we propose a third possible parsing structure that requires a co-attachment to both the verb and noun. By exploiting the linguistic properties of caused-motion construction, we propose the use the semantic feature [movement] to parse tree structure. The co-attached structure lacks the [movement] feature at both V and NP1 because the sense of motion resides in the construction per se rather than being imposed on the attachment sites. The results indicate that 11.3% (208 instances) of the 1835 types of verbs in V NP1 *into* NP2 constructions extracted from the WSJ corpus are co-attached. It is therefore worthy of further consideration in NLP tasks involving PP-attachment.

However, there are some limitations to the feature specification approach of this study. First, more stringent criteria for feature annotation are necessary. For example, some words in communication, cognition and social interaction domains denote rhetorical forces (e.g., *entice, allure, pressure*) and their movement feature may have been overlooked. Furthermore, refinement on the undermined category [+, +] is necessary to provide more accurate figures to support our approach. Future work should also include analysis of the nouns in depth, and extend the results of this study to other prepositions and PPs in other constructions.

References

Carrier, J. and J. Randall. 1992. The argument structure and syntactic structure of resultatives. *Linguistic Inquiry,* 23(2), 173–234.

Charniak, E., D. Blaheta, N. Ge, K. Hall, J. Hale and M. Johnson. 2000. *BLLIP 1987-89 WSJ Corpus Release 1*. Linguistic Data Consortium, Philadelphia

Fellbaum, C. 1990. English verbs as a semantic net. *International Journal of Lexicography,* 3(4), 278-301.

Fodor, J. 1970. Three reasons for not deriving "kill" from "cause to die". *Linguistic Inquiry,* 1(4), 429–438.

Goldberg. A. 1995. *Constructions: A construction grammar approach to argument structure.* Chicago: The University of Chicago Press.

Hindle, D. and M. Rooth. 1993. Structural ambiguity and lexical relations. *Computational Linguistics,* 19(1), 103-120.

Jackendoff, R. 2002. Foundations of language: Brain, meaning, grammar, and evolution. Oxford: Oxford University Press.

Litkowski, K. and O. Hargraves. 2007. Sem-Eval-2007 Task 06: Word-sense disambiguation of prepositions. *Proceedings of the 4th International Workshop on Semantic Evaluations (SemEval-2007)*, pp. 24-29.

Merlo, P. and E. E. Ferrer. 2006. The notion of argument in prepositional phrase attachment. *Computational Linguistics,* 32(3), 341-377.

Radford. A. 2004. *Minimalist syntax: Exploring the structure of English.* Cambridge: Cambridge University Press.

Pollard, C. and I. A. Sag. 1994. *Head-driven phrase structure grammar.* Chicago, IL: University of Chicago Press.

Talmy, L. (2000). *Toward a cognitive semantics. Vol. II: Typology and process in concept structuring.* Cambridge, MA: The MIT Press.

Tyler, A. and V. Evans. 2003. *The semantics of English prepositions.* New York: Cambridge University Press.

Volk. M. 2006. How bad is the problem of PP-attachment? A comparison of English, German and Swedish. *Proceedings of the Third ACL-SIGSEM Workshop on Prepositions*, pp. 81-88, Trento, Italy, April 2006.

Wechsler, S. and B. Noh. 2001. On resultative predicates and clauses: Parallels between Korean and English resultatives. *Language Sciences,* 23, 391-423.

Supervised and Semi-supervised Methods based Organization Name Disambiguity

Shu Zhang[a], Jianwei Wu[b], Dequan Zheng[b], Yao Meng[a], Yingju Xia[a], and Hao Yu[a]

[a]Fujitsu Research and Development Center
Dong Si Huan Zhong Rd, Chaoyang District, Beijing and 0086, China
{zhangshu, mengyao, yjxia, yu}@cn.fujitsu.com

[b]School of Computer Science and Technology, Harbin Institute of Technology
No.92, Xidazhi Street, Harbin 150001, China
{jwwu, dqzheng}@mtlab.hit.edu.cn

Abstract. Twitter is a widespread social media, which rapidly gained worldwide popularity. Pursuing on the problem of finding related tweets to a given organization, we propose supervised and semi-supervised based methods. This is a challenging task due to the potential organization name ambiguity. The tweets and organization contain little information. The organizations in training data are different with those in test data, which leads that we could not train a classifier to a certain organization. Therefore, we induce external resources to enrich the information of organization. Supervised and semi-supervised methods are adopted in two stages to classify the tweets. This is a try to utilize both training and test data for this specific task. Our experimental results on WePS-3 are primary and encouraging, they prove the proposed techniques are effective in performing the task.

Keywords: Twitter, name ambiguity, online reputation management.

1 Introduction

Twitter is an online social networking and microblogging service, which rapidly gained worldwide popularity, with 200 million users as of 2011[1], generating over 200 million tweets and handling over 1.6 billion search queries per day[2]. How to manage this information to grasp the response of people to governmental policies, the feedback and comment of people on commercial products have received considerable attention in research community. There are some researches such as opinion mining, online reputation management, which focus on monitoring user generated media. One of the essential things of these researches is first to get the information which is related to the studied entity, such as product, company, or certain event.

This paper focuses on finding related tweets to a given organization. This is a challenging task due to the potential organization name ambiguity. For example, the name of company "*Apple*" which has a separate meaning fruit apple. The word "*Amazon*" could be used to refer river or company. Filtering spurious name matches is important to effectively detect and analyze relevant contents that people say about the organization.

To overcome the problem that the tweets and organizations contain little information, we induce external resources to enrich the information of organization. The organizations in training data are different with those in test data, which leads that we could not train a classifier to a certain organization. Therefore, supervised and semi-supervised methods are adopted in

[1] http://www.bbc.co.uk/news/business-12889048
[2] http://blog.twitter.com/2011/08/your-world-more-connected.html

two stages to classify the tweets. This is a try to utilize both training and test data for this specific task.

The remainder of the paper is organized as follows: Section 2 describes the related work on name disambiguity. Section 3 gives overview of the problem and our methods. Section 4 presents supervised method to classify tweets. Section 5 introduces semi-supervised method to classify the tweets which is a step of modifying initial classification results gotten by supervised method. Section 6 gives the experiments and results. Finally section 7 summarizes this paper.

2 Related work

In recent years, online social networks such as Twitter have attracted much interest from the research community. Twitter differs from the traditional user generated media. It allows users to generate each message with no more than 140 characters. Little context information is available. Therefore, it is a challenge for monitoring and analyzing them.

Dan *et al.* (2011) focus on identifying relevant tweets for social TV, they propose a bootstrapping algorithm which uses a small manually labeled dataset, a large dataset of unlabeled messages, and some domain knowledge to derive a classifier to filter microblogging messages which discuss television show. They extract features which contain general terms commonly associated with watching TV.

WePS-3 Online Reputation Management[3] held in 2010, aimed to identify tweets which are related to a given company. It provides standard training and test dataset that enable researchers to carry out and evaluate their methods (Amigó *et al.*, 2010). For this task, the research of (Yerva *et al.*, 2010) shows the best performance in the evaluation campaign. They adopt support vector machines (SVM) classifier with external resources, which includes Wordnet, metadata profile, category profile, Google set, and user feedback. To overcome the problem of tweets containing little context information, they create several profiles with external resources as a model for each company. Yoshida *et al.* (2010) classify organization names into "organization-like names" or "general-word-like names". They categorize each query in the first stage, and categorize each tweet in the second stage using the rules customized for each class of queries. Kalmar (2010) adopts bootstrapping method to classify the tweets. The research of (García-Cumbreras *et al.*, 2010) shows the named entities in tweets are appropriate for certain company names. Tsagkias *et al.* (2010) prove that a general classifier can be employed to predict the presence of any company in Twitter.

Perez-Tellez *et al.* (2011) propose term expansion to the ambiguous words and words which highly co-occur with it.

Our work is different from theirs: supervised and semi-supervised methods are utilized in different stages for the classification of tweets. For the task, the set of organization names in the training and test corpora are different. The model could not be trained for a certain organization. Therefore, our method aims to utilize both training data and the test data to improve the accuracy of the performance. In detail, the tweets are firstly classified by Maximum Entropy classifier trained on training data. Then Label Propagation Algorithm is utilized to classify tweets based on the test data.

3 Overview

3.1 Problem Statement

Given a set of tweets and an organization name, the task is to judge that each tweet in the set is related to the organization or not.

[3] http://nlp.uned.es/weps/

The input information per tweet contains: the tweet identifier, the entity name, the query used to retrieve the tweet, the author identifier and the tweet content. For each organization in the dataset, it gives the organization name and its homepage URL.

The output per tweet is True or False tag corresponding to related or non-related with the given organization.

Compared with the traditional classification task, this task has some challenges. One is tweets and organization name contain little information, context information is limited. The other is the set of organization names in the training and test data are different. That means no organization is present in both training data and test data, the features or model built on training data is not very suitable for the test data.

3.2 Our Method

Overcome the challenges of this task, we import external resources to get more information about the organization, such as related homepage, related Wikipedia page, and GoogleSet. We propose to combine supervised and semi-supervised methods to classify the tweets, aims to utilize the training data and at the same time dig out the proper information in the test data. The system includes the following parts:

(1) Features extraction and representation. It includes both the features from the tweets and the features of organization from external resources.

(2) Maximum entropy classifier. It is trained with the features extracted in Step (1) on the training data.

(3) Label Propagation. It includes two parts: seeds selection and graph construction. We select seeds based on the result gotten in Step (2). For one certain organization, we construct graph based on the relationship between each tweets on test data.

(4) Rule-based modification. Here, we only give one rule which processes the organization name containing more than one word, such as "Yale University". We think that "Yale University" contains more semantic information to distinguish it from other entity. The rule is if the tweet contains the full entity name (more than one word) then it is tagged as "True", treated as related with the organization.

In the following section, we give the details on how to represent and extract feature, how to build a Maximum entropy classifier and how to utilize Label Propagation algorithm to mine the test data to improve the accuracy of the performance.

4 Supervised Classifier

With the training data, we aim to train a classifier with generic features. The features should not be too general with the preference to tag tweets as True, or too narrow with the preference to tag tweets as False. Furthermore, the features should be generated automatically, with no manual labelling.

4.1 Features Extraction

The features extraction includes tweets features and organization features. In this step, we pay more attention to the organization information, which is expanded with external resources. We induce related homepage, related Wikipedia page, and GoogleSet in the following way to get the features to represent the organization.

Homepage

The URL of each organization is provided in the input. The words in homepage are more related and indicative to the organization. Therefore, these words (removed the stopwords) are chosen to represent the organization. However, some organization webpages are created by java-scripts or even flash, no text information could be extracted from them at present. Therefore, we try to get other external resources.

Wikipedia page

Aim to get higher quality information of the organization, Wikipedia disambiguation page[4] is used. For each organization name, we get some entity candidates related with it through the disambiguation page. If the wiki-webpage of the entity candidate contains the organization's homepage URL, this webpage is treated as a description of the organization, words in this webpage are extracted as features.

Metadata

Meta tags in HTML page provide high quality keywords to represent its webpage. If the webpage has metadata, they are good features to represent organization. However, only a fraction of webpages have this information available.

GoogleSet

GoogleSet provides similar words with the query words. We utilize it to enrich organization information with related words. For example, given words "Yale" and "University", associated words "Stanford", "Columbia" are returned. This kind of information is useful, it gives latent semantic category information at some extent.

Capital words

Capital words are more likely to be important words or named entity, we reinforce these words by selecting them as one type of features.

URL

URL in homepage or wiki- webpage is also a strong indictor. If the tweet contains the same URL with homepage or wiki-webpage, it is more possible to be related to the organization.

Corresponding to these types of features for organization, we extract unigrams, bigrams words, capital words and URL from tweets as features.

4.2 Representation

The representation of tweets corresponding to given organization is shown in the following:

$$Vector(T_i, O_k) = \{F_1, F_2, ..., F_n\} \quad (1)$$

Here, T_i is the tweet, O_K is the organization, F_i is one type of features described in the above section. For each F_i, the value is computed as follows.

$$Value(F_i) = \sum_m Wt_m \quad (2)$$

Wt_m is weight of feature t_m, computed by tf*idf or just given {0,1}value. t_m is the co-occurrence feature between F_i and tweet T_i. This is similar with the work of (Yerva *et al.*, 2010).

4.3 Maximum Entropy Classifier

The classifier is to classify tweets as True or False with the given feature vector. We aim to train a Maximum Entropy Classifier for this task. The principle of Maximum Entropy Model (Jaynes, 1957) is that the model should maximizes entropy, or "uncertainty" with satisfying all the constraints. This is a straightforward idea that just model what is known, and just keep uniform what is unknown. Here, we utilize all features describe above in this classification task. NLTK[5] tool is used to implement Maximum Entropy Classifier.

5 Semi-Supervised Classifier

The set of organization names in the training and test data are different, this leads to supervised classifier trained on training data is not very effective to the test data. In order to utilize or mine

[4] http://en.wikipedia.org/wiki/xxx_(disambiguation)

[5] http://www.nltk.org/

specific information for certain organization in test data, we adopt one of the classic semi-supervised methods Label Propagation to modify the classification results gotten by Maximum Entropy classifier. We aim to mine the relation among tweets related to one organization in test dataset.

The procedure of Label Propagation Algorithm (Zhu and Ghahramani, 2002) is propagating labels from the labeled vertices (served as seeds) to all the unlabeled ones through the weighed edges in a graph. Larger edge weight will make propagate easier, which means that if the similarity of two nodes is high, they tend to have the same label.

Formally, label distributions are spread across a graph $G=\{V,E,W\}$, where V is the set of n nodes, E is a set of m edges and W is an $n*n$ matrix of weights with W_{ij} as the weight of edge (i, j).

For Label Propagation Algorithm, the seeds selection and graph construction are important. Maximum Entropy classifier gives a confidence value for each tweet which is classified to True or False. Therefore, we choose N True and False tweets tagged by Maximum Entropy classifier as seeds according to its confidence value. In order to get high accuracy of seeds selection, we set N=10.

Each tweet is treated as node, the edge is constructed if two tweets have co-occurrence words, its weight is computed by Cosine similarity.

Our aim is to combine supervised and semi-supervised method to solve this task. Therefore, we select some organizations tweet set to be classified by semi-supervised classification, not all organizations. The selection process is based on the ratio of False tweets in the given organization test set tagged by Maximum Entropy classifier.

$$Ratio(O_k) = Num(False) / Num(O_k) \quad (3)$$

Here, O_K is the organization, $Num(False)$ is number of tweets tagged as False by Maximum Entropy classifier, $Num(O_K)$ is the number of tweets for the given organization. If $Ration(O_K)$ is less than the threshold, the semi-supervised classifier is applied to classify the tweets once more for organization O_K. The other organizations tweets set do not need to be classified by LP.

Here, we make use of JUNTO Label Propagation toolkit[6]. LP_ZGL (Zhu and Ghahramani, 2002), the first label propagation algorithm provided by the toolkit, is chosen in our experiment. All the parameters are set as default.

6 Experiments

6.1 Corpus and Evaluation Metric

We have conducted experiments on the WePS-3 task 2 data. The training data contain about 50 organizations. For each organization, about 400 tweets are provided with tagger {True, False}, corresponding to it is related to the organization or not. The test data also contain about 50 organizations, which are different from those in training data. There is no intersection between training data and test data. For each organization in test data, there are about 400 tweets, which are needed to be classified.

The task is to classify the tweets related or non-related to the given organization, it belongs to classification task. Therefore, we measure the performance by accuracy, precision, recall and F-measure.

6.2 Results and Analysis

The performance of classification is shown in Table.1. Here, P+ means the precision of tweets tagged as True, P- means the precision of tweets tagged as False. The Acc means the ratio of tweets tagged with correct tagger.

[6] http://code.google.com/p/junto/

Table 1: Performance of Classification

System	P+	R+	F+	P-	R-	F-	Acc
Baseline 1	1	0	0	0.57	1	0.66	0.57
Baseline 2	0.43	1	0.53	1	0	0	0.43
ME	0.64	0.45	0.44	0.63	0.81	0.66	0.71
ME+LP	0.62	0.54	0.48	0.64	0.65	0.57	0.74
ME+LP+Rule	0.63	0.57	0.49	0.65	0.64	0.58	0.75

Two Baseline systems have been induced, which tags all tweets as related (True) or non related (False). Compare our three systems, the performance is improved by adding LP algorithm and rule step by step. For the F-measure of related tweets, it improves 4%. The recall is improved 9% with a little loss of precision. The whole accuracy is also improved by 3%. It proves that combining supervised and semi-supervised methods is effective. The rule described in Section 3.2: if organization name consisting of more than one word, then the tweet contains full name is treated as related to this organization. Though only one piece of rule is used, it really improves almost all measurement value. It shows that important keywords are good features to distinguish entity.

Compared our systems with WePS participant system, our systems performance are less than the system of (Yerva *et al.*, 2010). Its accuracy value is 0.83. Its system induces manually constructed UserFeedback profile. With only homepage as features, its F-measure of related tweets is 0.3. Different from theirs, our systems are all automatically.

Figure 1 shows the influence of threshold selection for the accuracy, the threshold is described in formula (3).

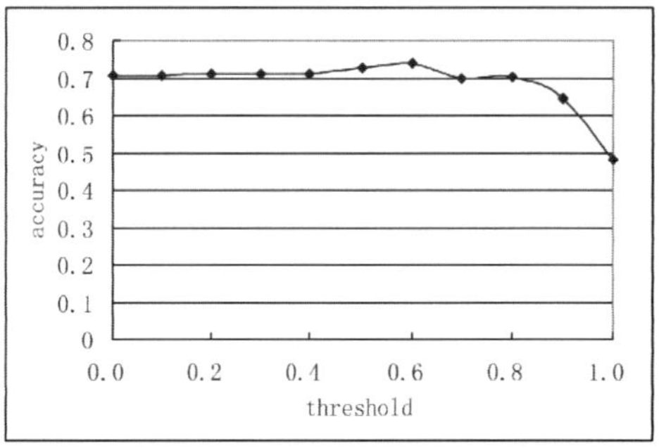

Figure 1: Influence of threshold selection for accuracy

From Figure 1, it is concluded that the performance is decreased by choosing all organizations to be classified again by LP algorithm. As we known, the performance of supervised methods is better than semi-supervised methods. The selection of organization to be classified by LP is important.

7 Conclusion

In this paper, we probe into the problem of finding related tweets to a given organization. This is a challenging task due to the potential organization name ambiguity. This task is more challenging caused by two problems: the tweets and organization contain little information, and the organizations in training data are different with those in test data. We induce external resources to enrich the information of organization. Supervised (ME) and semi-supervised (LP) methods are adopted in two stages to classify the tweets. This is a try to utilize both training and test data for this specific task. Our experimental results on WePS-3 are primary and encouraging, they prove the proposed techniques are effective in performing the task.

There is still a gap needed to be filled by further improving these techniques. For example, the performance can be improved through the semantic expansion of words using Ontology.

References

García-Cumbreras, M. A., M. García-Vega, F. Martínez-Santiago, and J. M. Peréa-Ortega. 2010. SINAI at WePS-3: Online Reputation Management. *Proceedings of the Third Web People Search Evaluation Workshop.*

Yerva, S. R., Z. Miklós, and K. Aberer. 2010. It was Easy, when Apples and Blackberries were only Fruits. *Proceedings of the Third Web People Search Evaluation Workshop.*

Tsagkias, M., and K. Balog. 2010. The University of Amsterdam at WePS3. *Proceedings of the Third Web People Search Evaluation Workshop.*

Kalmar, P.. 2010. Bootstrapping Websites for Classification of Organization Names on Twitter. *Proceedings of the Third Web People Search Evaluation Workshop.*

Yoshida, M., S. Matsushima, S. Ono, I. Sato, and H. Nakagaw. 2010. ITC-UT: Tweet Categorization by Query Categorization for On-line Reputation Management. *Proceedings of the Third Web People Search Evaluation Workshop.*

Zhu, X. J., and Z. Ghahramani. 2002. Learning from Labeled and Unlabeled Data with Label Propagation. *Technical Report CMU-CALD-02-107, Carnegie Mellon University.*

Amigó, E., J. Artiles, J. Gonzalo, D. Spina, B. Liu, and A. Corujo. 2010. WePS-3 Evaluation Campaign: Overview of the Online Reputation Management Task. *Proceedings of the Third Web People Search Evaluation Workshop.*

Jaynes, T.. 1957. Information Theory and Statistical Mechanics. *Physics Reviews*, (106), 620-630.

Perez-Tellez, F., D. Pinto, J. Cardiff, and P. Rosso. 2011. On the Difficulty of Clustering Microblog Texts for Online Reputation Management. *Proceedings of the 2nd Workshop on Computational Approaches to Subjectivity and Sentiment Analysis, ACL-HLT*, pp. 146-152.

Dan, O., J. Feng, and B. D. Davison. 2011. A Bootstrapping Approach to Identifying Relevant Tweets for Social TV. *Proceeding of fifth International AAAI Conferenc Weblogs and Social Media (ICWSM)*, pp. 462-465.

Study and Implementation of Monolingual Approach on Indonesian Question Answering for Factoid and Non-Factoid Question *

Alvin Andhika Zulen[a] and Ayu Purwarianti[b]

School of Electrical Engineering and Informatics, Bandung Institute of Technology,
Ganesha 10, Bandung 40135, West Java, Indonesia
[a] alvin.andhika@gmail.com
[b] ayu@stei.itb.ac.id

Abstract. We developed an open domain QA system that can handle factoid and non-factoid questions in Indonesian language by using monolingual approaches. EAT classification is done by identifying question word and clue words. Keyword extraction from question is done by looking at POS information of each word in question, eliminating stop words, and stemming. We use articles from Indonesian Wikipedia as corpus and Lucene framework as the base for passage retriever component, with three additional processing: query expansion, boost EAT, and boost term. For factoid questions, answer finding is done by using Named Entity Recognition. Answer scoring is done by calculating keyword occurrences and answer-keywords distance (MRR = 0.6191). For non-factoid questions, answer finding is done by identifying sentence pattern and clue words. Answer scoring is done by considering pattern priority and keyword occurrences (MRR = 0.8079).

Keywords: monolingual, open-domain, Indonesian language, factoid, non-factoid.

1 Introduction

Question Answering (QA) is a task in Natural Language Processing (NLP) that will automatically provide answers to questions posed in natural language. QA system can use a database or document collection (local or web) as the sources of the answer.

A QA system usually consists of three main components (Harabagiu *et al.*, 2000): question analyzer, passage retriever, and answer finder. Question analyzer component aims to classify the question according to the Expected Answer Type (EAT) as well as extract the keywords in question. These keywords will be used as input query in passage retriever component to get candidate documents/paragraphs that contain the answer. Answer finder component searches for candidate answers from documents/paragraphs that have been found previously. Each candidate answer will be given a score based on its compliance with the question. Some candidate answers will be selected as the best answers to the question. Each component can use various methods based on the language, question domain, question type, and available tools.

QA system for Indonesian language that has been built: handle factoid questions only (Purwarianti *et al.*, 2007; Wisudawan, 2010), handle non-factoid questions only (Yusliani, 2010), the domain of questions is limited (Mahendra *et al.*, 2008), cross lingual and use NLP tools for English (Wijono *et al.*, 2006; Wisudawan, 2010). There are also researches in NLP for Indonesian language that have been done, including parser, stemmer (Adriani *et al.*, 2007), Part-of-Speech (POS) tagger (Wicaksono and Purwarianti, 2010), and Named-Entity (NE) Tagger (Budi *et al.*, 2005).

From these studies, we obtained some things that can be explored further and improved to produce a QA system for Indonesian language using monolingual approaches with wider scope of questions that can be handled. This QA system is expected to handle factoid (Person, Organization, Location, Datetime, Quantity) and non-factoid questions (Definition, Reason, Method). Moreover, the approach to be used in this QA system is monolingual approach, with expectation to produce a QA system with better accuracy.

The rest of this paper is organized into discussion of methods that are used in each component (question analyzer, passage retriever, answer finder), experiments, and conclusions.

2 Question Analyzer

2.1 Question EAT Classification

There are several methods that commonly used in question analyzer component: question pattern matching method (Fukumoto *et al.*, 2007; Ren *et al.*, 2008; Zhang *et al.*, 2010) machine learning method (Purwarianti *et al.*, 2007), and semantic analysis method (Mahendra *et al.*, 2008). From these alternatives, this QA system uses question pattern matching method, because it doesn't need any additional tools and resources, easy to implement, and is expected to classify questions with high accuracy.

EAT classification is done by using rules which consider question words and clue words. We use clue words in the rules because question word is not enough to determine the EAT of a question. A question word can be used to ask questions with different answer types, such as "apa" (*what*) and "berapa" (*how*). Rules that we use in are listed in Table 1.

Table 1: EAT Classification Rules

EAT	Question Words	Clue Words
	Factoid	
Person	Siapa , Siapakah	-
Location	Dimana , Dimanakah	-
	Kemana , Kemanakah	-
	Darimana , Darimanakah	-
Date/Time	Kapan , Kapankah	-
	Berapa , Berapakah	tanggal, bulan, tahun, abad, jam, menit, detik
Organization	Apa , Apakah	organisasi, perusahaan, badan, institusi, lembaga, partai, komisi, sekolah, komite, universitas
Quantity	Berapa , Berapakah	-
	Non-factoid	
Definition	Apa , Apakah	definisi, yang dimaksud, pengertian, arti
Reason	Mengapa , Kenapa	-
	Apa , Apakah	penyebab, menyebabkan
Method	Bagaimana , Bagaimanakah	-
		-

2.2 Keyword Extraction

Keywords are words that can be used to describe the content of a question. Keywords can be the words in the question or other words related to the words in the question. Keywords will be used to retrieve documents and paragraphs that are estimated to contain answer to the question. In other words, wrong keywords can result in not retrieving document that contains the answer.

Keywords extraction is done by looking at POS information of each word in the question and taking words with certain POS tags as keywords (Purwarianti *et al.*, 2007). For Indonesian language, POS tagger that we used is IPOSTagger (Wicaksono and Purwarianti, 2010). POS tags that will be taken as keywords can be seen in Table 2. In the process of extracting the keywords, we also remove the stop words in the question. Stop word list that is used in this system obtained from Wibisono (2007) that has been modified by removing some of the words that should not be eliminated. Stemming process is also done to get the query in the basic word form. We use Nazief-Adriani algorithm (Adriani *et al.*, 2007) as stemming algorithm.

Table 2: Keyword POS

POS	POS Name	POS	POS Name
NN	*Common Noun*	CDO	*Ordinal Numerals*
NNP	*Proper Noun*	CDC	*Collective Numerals*
NNG	*Genitive Noun*	CDP	*Primary Numerals*
VBI	*Intransitive Verb*	JJ	*Adjective*
VBT	*Transitive Verb*	FW	*Foreign Words*

3 Passage Retriever

3.1 Corpus

Corpus in the QA system is used as a source for searching answer to the question given. The corpus must be documents in Indonesian language and should not include only a single topic/domain. There are two main alternatives of Indonesian language corpus that can be used in terms of accessing methods:

1. Offline corpus can be a collection of Indonesian articles, e.g. articles from electronic media, electronic books, and database dump of Indonesian Wikipedia articles that can be obtained at Wikimedia (2011). This corpus can be stored in text files or in databases.
2. Online corpus can be a collection of articles on the web. We must consider how to access the articles and parts of the article in using this corpus.

From these alternatives, we use offline corpus obtained from Indonesian Wikipedia, because:

- Ease of access compared to online corpus.
- More comprehensive.
- Integrated in one file, which is more efficient than storing each article in a text file.
- Java Wikipedia Library (JWPL) (Zesch *et al.*, 2011) has provided mechanisms in processing the Wikipedia dump, accessing the data that has been stored in the database, and parsing the articles in Wikipedia format into plain text format. However, there are still some weaknesses in the parser, which does not remove tags that should be removed and remove parts that should not be removed. Therefore, we made a preprocessing parser to handle the lack of JWPL parser.

3.2 Searching Technique

Searching documents and paragraphs that are considered relevant from the corpus is done through searching keywords generated from question analyzer. Searching is performed by finding documents from corpus that contain the keywords and then look for paragraphs from those documents that contain the keywords, which will be used as input to answer finder.

There are three alternatives that can be used to implement passage retriever: implementing IR systems from scratch; using search engine APIs, such as Yahoo and Google; or using IR system framework, such as Lucene and Lemur. From these alternatives, this QA system uses Lucene framework in passage retriever component, because:

- Not feasible to implement component from scratch that can handle about 150,000 documents, in terms of storage and time.
- When utilizing the search engine API, what we can do is just search for documents. Paragraph searching cannot be done. We also can't use specific document processing for Indonesian language, such as stemming and stop word elimination.

Passage retriever component is implemented by modifying Lucene framework. We applied lowercasing, symbol removal, stop word elimination, and stemming in processing of each token in the documents. We also made some modifications in passage retriever component to see the effect of these additional methods to the accuracy of the system:

1. Query expansion by adding expansions of abbreviated words, which are obtained from **Kateglo** (Lanin and Hardiyanto, 2011) and **Kamus Besar Bahasa Indonesia** (KBBI).

2. Boost paragraphs that contain the EAT of the question, with boost factor of 2.0. These paragraphs would be at a higher rank than the paragraphs that do not contain the EAT. EAT checking in paragraph is done by NE searching for factoid question and clue words searching for non-factoid question.
3. Boost term that has POS: **NN**, **NNP**, **NNG**, **VBT**, and **VBI**, with boost factor of 1.5. Verb and noun words tend to be more important as keywords than other types of words. Documents that contain these types of words will be considered more relevant.

4 Answer Finder

4.1 Factoid Question

For factoid questions, the methods that can be used include machine learning (Purwarianti *et al.*, 2007) and Named Entity Recognition (NER) (Zhang *et al.*, 2010). In machine learning methods, answer finder component uses machine learning algorithms to classify each word in the document if it is part of the answer or not. Attributes that can be used in classification such as keyword occurrences, bi-gram frequency, EAT, and POS. This method requires training data for the learning process. In NER methods, NER is used to find candidate answers by extracting NEs of the documents or paragraphs to get the candidate answers which NEs are appropriate with the EAT of the question. This method requires NE tagger tool for Indonesian language.

In this QA system, we use NER method to answer factoid question. This method was chosen because it is one of basic monolingual method to seek answers of factoid questions and has never been used in previous works. Factoid question EATs that can be handled are Person, Organization, Location, Datetime, and Quantity, which can be extracted using NE tagger.

To use this approach, we need Named Entity Tagger for Indonesian language. In this work, we implemented the NE tagger for Indonesian language by using a modified approach of Budi *et al.* (2005), with addition of feature details and NE classification rules. To extract NEs in a sentence, we identify word (token) feature, literal type feature, contextual feature, morphological feature, and POS feature. From these features, we make several rules that will classify each word in the sentence according to its NE (see example below). Sequential words with the same NE will be considered as one entity.

```
IF Token[i].Kind == "WORD" &&
   Token[i].Contextual == "Person Prefix" &&
   Token[i+1].Kind == "WORD" &&
   Token[i+1].Morphological == "TitleCase"
THEN Token[i+1].NE = "PERSON"
```

Each candidate answer for factoid questions is a NE. Steps performed on the answer finder to find candidate answers of factoid questions are:

1. Each paragraph from passage retriever component is separated into sentences.
2. Count the occurrence of keywords (stemmed and non-stemmed) in each sentence.
3. Perform NE tagging to each sentence.
4. For each sentence, take all NEs that appropriate with the EAT as candidate answers. Candidate answers that only contain keywords from question will not be included.
5. For each candidate answer, calculate the distance between the candidate answer to all the keywords from the question in sentence answer. Distance is calculated by counting the number of words between the candidate answer and the keyword.
6. Sort the candidate answers based on the number of keyword occurrences in the sentence and the distance between the candidate answers with the keywords in the sentence.

4.2 Non-Factoid Question

For non-factoid questions, the methods that can be used include pattern matching (Ren *et al.*, 2008; Fukumoto *et al.*, 2007; Yusliani, 2010; Zhang *et al.*, 2010) and semantic analysis (Niu,

2007). In pattern matching method, answer finder component uses rules that consider surface expression (sentence patterns) and linguistic clue (clue words) from the sentence. This method is the simplest monolingual method to find answers of non-factoid question and doesn't require any additional tools and resources. In semantic analysis method, questions and documents are represented in the semantic representation. Answer is obtained by uniting the representation of question with the known facts. This method requires a semantic parser for Indonesian to produce a semantic representation of Indonesian sentences. Until now, semantic parser for Indonesian has not publicly available.

In this QA system, we use pattern matching with surface expression and linguistic clue to answer non-factoid questions. Sentence answer for each category of questions has similar pattern to each other. The difference lies in the clue words that mark the answer for each question category that usually appear in the sentence answers of each question category.

We defined sentence patterns that covered all possibilities of keyword and clue word occurrences in the sentence (Table 3). List of clue words that is used can be seen in Table 4. Each pattern has a priority value. If a sentence has higher priority, the more likely it will be the answer of the question. Sentence patterns and clue words on this QA system is obtained from Yusliani (2010) with some modifications. Pattern 10-11 are additional patterns that are used to handle sentence answers that don't contain clue words.

Table 3: Answer Sentence Patterns for Non-Factoid Question

Priority	Patterns
1	All *non-stemmed* keywords + clue word + ...
1	... + clue word + all *non-stemmed* keywords
1	Sentence with all *non-stemmed* keywords. Sentence with clue word + ...
2	One or more *non-stemmed* keywords + clue word + ...
2	... + clue word + one or more *non-stemmed* keywords
2	Sentence with one or more *non-stemmed* keywords. Sentence with clue word + ...
3	One or more *stemmed* keywords + clue word + ...
3	... + clue word + one or more *stemmed* keywords
3	Sentence with one or more *stemmed* keywords. Sentence with clue word + ...
3	Sentence with all *non-stemmed* keywords.
4	Sentence with one or more *non-stemmed* keywords.
0	Others

Table 4: Clue Words in Answer Sentences for Non-Factoid Question

Category	Before Keywords	After Keywords
Definition	disebut, dikenal, dinamakan, diistilahkan	adalah, bermakna, ialah, diartikan, berarti, memiliki arti, merupakan
Reason	karena itu, oleh karena itu, oleh sebab itu, maka, itulah sebabnya, mengapa, sehingga, memungkinkan, menyebabkan, dengan demikian, mengakibatkan, penyebab,	karena, bertujuan, dikarenakan, agar disebabkan, sebab, akibat, kemudian
Method	cara, langkah, proses, untuk, prosedur, tahapan, tahap	dengan, melalui, pertama, dimulai, diawali, sebelum, setelah, kemudian

Each candidate answer for non-factoid questions is a complete paragraph. Steps performed on the answer finder to find candidate answers of non-factoid questions are:

1. Each paragraph from passage retriever component is separated into sentences.
2. Check the sentence pattern that is used in each sentence and count the occurrence of the keywords in that sentence.
3. For each paragraph, find the sentence with the highest priority and largest occurrence of keywords. This sentence is chosen as candidate answer for that paragraph.
4. Sort the candidate answers based on the priority value and the number of keyword occurrences in the sentence.

5 Experiments

5.1 Experimental Data

In this experiment, we used 169 questions obtained from respondents. Testing for this system is divided into four main scenarios with black box method: (1) *without additional searching methods **(Baseline)***; (2) *with **Query Expansion** method*; (3) *with **Boost EAT** method*; and (4) *with **Boost Term** method.*

5.2 Experiment Result

Question Analyzer

Testing on question analyzer component is done by looking at accuracy in classifying the question according to its EAT and extracting keywords from the question. Accuracy of question analyzer component in EAT classification can be seen in Table 5. Based on the test results, EAT classification by identifying question words and clue words was considered quite good.

This component also succeeds in extracting keywords from questions. It can be seen from the accuracy of passage retriever component. Keyword extraction process through the stop-words elimination, stemming, and POS tagging can produce keywords that can describe the content of the question.

Table 5: EAT Classification Accuracy

EAT	Total Questions	Accuracy
Person	21	100 %
Organization	21	100 %
Location	21	100 %
Datetime	25	100 %
Quantity	20	100 %
Definition	23	100 %
Reason	18	100 %
Method	20	100 %

Passage Retriever

Testing on passage retriever component is done by seeing whether the paragraph that contains the answers is retrieved or not. Tests conducted on all four test scenarios. The test results for each scenario can be seen in Table 6.

Table 6: Passage Retriever Accuracy

Scenario	Total Questions	Accuracy
Baseline	169	85,8%
Query expansion	169	88,76%
Boost EAT	169	88,17%
Boost term	169	85, 8%
Average	169	87,13%

Errors in this component occurred when the document/paragraph that contains the answers did not retrieved by the component. This problem happened because keywords that are used as query appear less in relevant document/paragraph or appear more in irrelevant documents / paragraphs. As a result, the answer was not in the top 30 documents or top 20 documents.

To help overcome these problems, we also modified the passage retriever components using three alternative additional processes: query expansion, boost EAT, and boost term. From the test results, boost term method has no effect to the accuracy of passage retriever component because most of keywords obtained from question are noun or verb. Query expansion and boost EAT methods are able to increase the number of relevant paragraphs that are retrieved by the component, because:

- Boost EAT method can improve the accuracy of passage retriever components because this method can promote the ranking of paragraphs that are predicted containing candidate answers (EAT of question). This helps paragraphs that have a low relevance score in baseline method, to be taken as a candidate paragraph if it contains the EAT.
- Query expansion method can add the expansion of a word in the query if the word is an acronym/ abbreviation. Words that are added can help the QA system to find relevant documents and paragraphs which do not contain the words in the query, but rather the expansion of the word.

Answer Finder

Test results for factoid questions can be seen in Table 7. The highest average MRR value was in Organization category (MRR = 0.7507) and the lowest was in Location category (MRR = 0.4951). Based on the MRR value, the performance of the component in answering factoid questions was quite good. NER method and scoring by calculate distance and keyword occurrences can be used as a good alternative method for answering factoid questions. Example of successfully answered factoid question can be seen in Figure 1.

Table 7: MRR Value for Factoid Question

EAT	Scenario 1	Scenario 2	Scenario 3	Scenario 4	Average
Person	0,6310	0,6548	0,6230	0,6310	0,63495
Organization	0,7548	0,7423	0,7548	0,7509	0,7507
Location	0,4656	0,5608	0,4884	0,4656	0,4951
Datetime	0,6244	0,7244	0,6044	0,6244	0,6444
Quantity	0,5801	0,5717	0,5496	0,5801	0,570375
Average	0,61118	0,6508	0,60404	0,6104	0,619105

======QUESTION ANALYZER======

Question : Dimana Alexander Graham Bell dilahirkan ? (*Where Alexander Graham Bell was born ?*)

EAT : LOCATION

Keywords : Alexander, Graham, Bell, dilahirkan (*born*)

======PASSAGE RETRIEVER======

1. Document : Alexander_Graham_Bell

Paragraph : Alexander Graham Bell dilahirkan di Edinburgh, Skotlandia, Britania Raya, pada 3 Maret 1847 dan meninggal di Beinn Bhreagh, Nova Scotia, Kanada, pada 2 Agustus 1922...
(*Alexander Graham Bell was born in Edinburgh, Scotland, Great Britain, on March 3, 1847 and died in Beinn Bhreagh, Nova Scotia, Canada, on August 2, 1922...*)

======ANSWER FINDER======

1. Edinburgh

Figure 1: Example of Successfully Answered Factoid Question

Test results for non-factoid questions can be seen in Table 8. The highest average MRR value was in Definition category (MRR = 0.902175) and the lowest was in Method category (MRR = 0.74375). Based on the MRR value, the performance of the component in answering non-factoid questions was quite good. Pattern matching method and scoring by calculate rule priority and keyword occurrences can be used as a good alternative method for answering non-factoid questions. We can see that answers for all non-factoid question categories have similar patterns and contain clue word in the sentences. Example of successfully answered non-factoid question can be seen in Figure 2.

Table 8: MRR Value for Non-Factoid Question

EAT	Scenario 1	Scenario 2	Scenario 3	Scenario 4	Average
Definition	0,8913	0,8913	0,9348	0,8913	0,902175

EAT	Scenario 1	Scenario 2	Scenario 3	Scenario 4	Average
Reason	0,75	0,75	0,8611	0,75	0,777775
Method	0,75	0,725	0,75	0,75	0,74375
Average	0,7971	0,7887667	0,8486333	0,7971	0,8079

======QUESTION ANALYZER======

Question : Apa yang dimaksud dengan hepatitis akut ? (*What is meant by acute hepatitis ?*)

EAT : DEFINITION

Keywords : hepatitis (*hepatitis*), akut (*acute*)

======PASSAGE RETRIEVER======

1. Document : Hepatitis

Paragraph : Hepatitis adalah peradangan pada hati karena toxin, seperti kimia atau obat ataupun agen penyebab infeksi. Hepatitis yang berlangsung kurang dari 6 bulan disebut "hepatitis akut"... (*Hepatitis is an inflammation of the liver due to toxins, such as chemicals or drugs or agents that cause infection. Hepatitis that lasts less than 6 months is called "acute hepatitis"...*)

======ANSWER FINDER======

1. Hepatitis yang berlangsung kurang dari 6 bulan disebut "hepatitis akut". (*Hepatitis that lasts less than 6 months is called "acute hepatitis"*)

Figure 2: Example of Successfully Answered Non-Factoid Question

There are still some questions (factoid and non-factoid) that can't be answered by this QA system, either the answers don't exist in the list of answers or the answers are not on 1st rank :

- Problems on the NE tagger: error in the tagging of a word/word group (Figure 3). This is due to the incompleteness of rules and attributes that are made to do the tagging. As the consequences, the answer can't be obtained, the answer is not extracted properly or appear other candidate answers that are not appropriate with the question EAT.
- The effect of the "distances" calculation in the scoring of candidate answers (Figure 4). Problems occur if the distance between candidate answer and the keywords is greater than distance between other candidates and the keywords. The ranking of the correct answer will be lower.
- The effect of the calculation of the number of keywords. Problems occur if the number of keywords in a sentence that contains the correct answer is less than in the sentence that not contains the answer. The ranking of the correct answer will be lower.
- The effect of query expansion when it is not needed can cause in retrieving other documents/paragraphs (not relevant) and the correct answer can be in lower rank.
- Documents or paragraphs are not successfully retrieved, so the correct answer can't be found (problem in passage retriever component).

=========QUESTION ANALYZER=========

Question : Siapa nama penemu telepon ? (*Who is the inventor of telephone ?*)

EAT : PERSON

Keywords : penemu (*inventor*), telepon (*telephone*)

=========ANSWER FINDER========

1. Umumnya (*Generally*)

Sentence : Umumnya penemu telepon yang lebih dikenal masyarakat adalah Alexander Graham Bell... (*Telephone inventor who is generally known to the public was Alexander Graham Bell*)

2. Alexander Graham Bell

Sentence : Lebih dari seabad dan di seluruh penjuru dunia. Alexander Graham Bell dikenal sebagai penemu telepon. (*More than a century and throughout the world, Alexander Graham Bell is known as the inventor of the telephone.*)

Figure 3: Sample Error Case for NE Problem

=========QUESTION ANALYZER=========

Question : Dimana Alexander Graham Bell meninggal ? (*Where Alexander Graham Bell was died ?*)

EAT : LOCATION

Keywords : Alexander, Graham, Bell, meninggal (*died*)

======PASSAGE RETRIEVER======

1. Document : Alexander_Graham_Bell

Paragraph : Alexander Graham Bell dilahirkan di Edinburgh, Skotlandia, Britania Raya, pada 3 Maret 1847 dan meninggal di Beinn Bhreagh, Nova Scotia, Kanada, pada 2 Agustus 1922... (*Alexander Graham Bell was born in Edinburgh, Scotland, Great Britain, on March 3, 1847 and died in Beinn Bhreagh, Nova Scotia, Canada, on August 2, 1922...*)

=========ANSWER FINDER=========

1. Edinburgh

2. Britania Raya ***(Great Britain)***

3. Beinn Bhreagh

Figure 4: Sample Error Case for Distance Calculation Problem

6 Conclusion

Conclusions obtained from this work as follows:

1. To achieve the criteria of open-domain QA system, we used database dump from Indonesian Wikipedia articles as corpus. The database dump needs to be processed before it can be used as a source of searching by the QA system.
2. EAT classification is done by using identification of questions words and clue words. Keyword extraction from the question is done by looking at POS information of each word in question, removing stop words, and stemming. From the test results, this system is able to classify all the questions according to their EAT and extract all of the keywords.
3. QA system is built using Apache Lucene framework as the base of passage retriever component. There are three additional processing on the passage retriever component to help the system in searching relevant documents and paragraphs: query expansion, boost EAT, and boost term. This component is quite good in retrieving relevant documents and paragraphs, with the accuracy obtained were 87.13%. Query expansion and boost EAT methods considered can help component to retrieve relevant documents and paragraphs.
4. Answer finding method for factoid question that is used in this system is NE Recognition. Scoring of candidate answers is done by calculating keyword occurrences in the sentences and distance between candidate answers and keywords. The average MRR value obtained was 0.61910.
5. Answer finding method for non-factoid question that is used in this system is pattern matching based on surface expression (sentence patterns) and linguistic clue (clue words). Scoring of candidate answers is done by considering rule priority and keyword occurrences in sentences. The average MRR value obtained was 0.8079.
6. From the test results, there are several questions that can't be answered by system, either the answer is not in the list of answers or the answer is not on 1st rank. The causes are deficiency in the NE tagger, documents/paragraphs that are not successfully retrieved, and the effect of scoring techniques.

References

Adriani, M., B. A. A. Nazief, J. Asian, H. E. Williams and S. M. M. Tahaghoghi. 2007. Stemming Indonesian: A Confix Stripping Approach. *ACM Transactions on Asian Language Information Processing (TALIP).*

Budi, I., S. Bressan, G. Wahyudi, Z. A. Hasibuan and B. A. A. Nazief. 2005. Named Entity Recognition for Indonesian Language: Combining Contextual, Morphological, and Part-of-Speech Features into a Knowledge Engineering Approach. *Faculty of Computer Science, Universitas Indonesia.*

Fukumoto, J. 2007. Question Answering System for Non-factoid Type Questions and Automatic Evaluation based on BE Method. *Proceedings of NTCIR-6 Workshop Meeting*, Tokyo, Japan.

Harabagiu, S. M., M. A. Pasca and S. J. Maiorano. 2000. Experiments with Open-Domain Textual Question Answering. *Proceedings of the 18th International Conference on Computational Linguistics (COLING),* Saarbruken, Germany.

Lanin, I. and R. Hardiyanto. 2011. *Kateglo on Bahtera Website.* URL: http://kateglo.bahtera.org/.

Mahendra, R., S. D. Larasati and R. Manurung. 2008. Extending an Indonesian Semantic Analysis-based Question Answering System with Linguistic and World Knowledge Axioms. *Proceedings of the 22nd Pacific Asia Conference on Language, Information, and Computation*, Cebu, Philippines.

Niu, Y. 2007. *Analysis of Semantic Classes Toward Non-Factoid Question Answering.* Ph.D. thesis, Department of Computer Science, University of Toronto, Canada.

Purwarianti, A., M. Tsuchiya and S. Nakagawa. 2007. A Machine Learning Approach for Indonesian Question Answering System. *Proceedings of the 25th IASTED International Multi-Conference: Artificial Intelligence and Applications*, Innsbruck, Austria.

Ren, H., D. Ji, Y. He, C. Teng and J. Wan. 2008. Multi-Strategy Question Answering System for NTCIR-7 C-C Task. *Proceedings of NTCIR-7 Workshop Meeting*, Tokyo, Japan.

Wibisono, Y. 2008. *Indonesian Stop Word List.* Universitas Pendidikan Indonesia. URL: http://fpmipa.upi.edu/staff/yudi/stop_words_list.txt.

Wicaksono, A. F. and Purwarianti, A. 2010. HMM Based Part-of-Speech Tagger for Bahasa Indonesia. *Proceedings of the 4th- International MALINDO Workshop (MALINDO2010)*, Jakarta, Indonesia.

Wijono, S. H., I. Budi, L. Fitria and M. Adriani. 2006. Finding Answers to Indonesian Questions from English Documents. *CLEF 2006 Workshop*, Alicante, Spain.

Wikimedia. 2011. *Indonesian Wikipedia Dump*. URL: http://dumps.wikimedia.org/idwiki/,

Wisudawan, W. F. 2010. *Analisis Pendekatan Monolingual dan Cross Language Untuk Aplikasi Tanya Jawab Otomatis Bahasa Indonesia.* Bachelor of Engineering thesis, Informatics Engineering, School of Electrical Engineering and Informatics, ITB.

Yusliani, N. 2010. *Sistem Tanya Jawab Bahasa Indonesia untuk Non Factoid Question.* Master of Engineering thesis, Informatics Engineering, School of Electrical Engineering and Informatics, ITB.

Zesch, T, R. E. D. Castilho, E. Wolf and O. Ferschke. 2011. *Java Wikipedia Library on Google Code.* Ubiquitous Knowledge Processing (UKP) Lab., Department of Computer Science, Technische Universität Darmstadt, URL: http://code.google.com/p/jwpl/.

Zhang, G., W. Zhang, Y. Bai, S. Kang and P. Wang. 2010. An Open-domain Question Answering System for NTCIR-8 C-C Task. *Proceedings of NTCIR-8 Workshop Meeting,* Tokyo, Japan.

Association for Computational Linguistics
209 N. Eighth Street
Stroudsburg, Pennsylvania 18360